KEY TO WORLD MAP PAGES

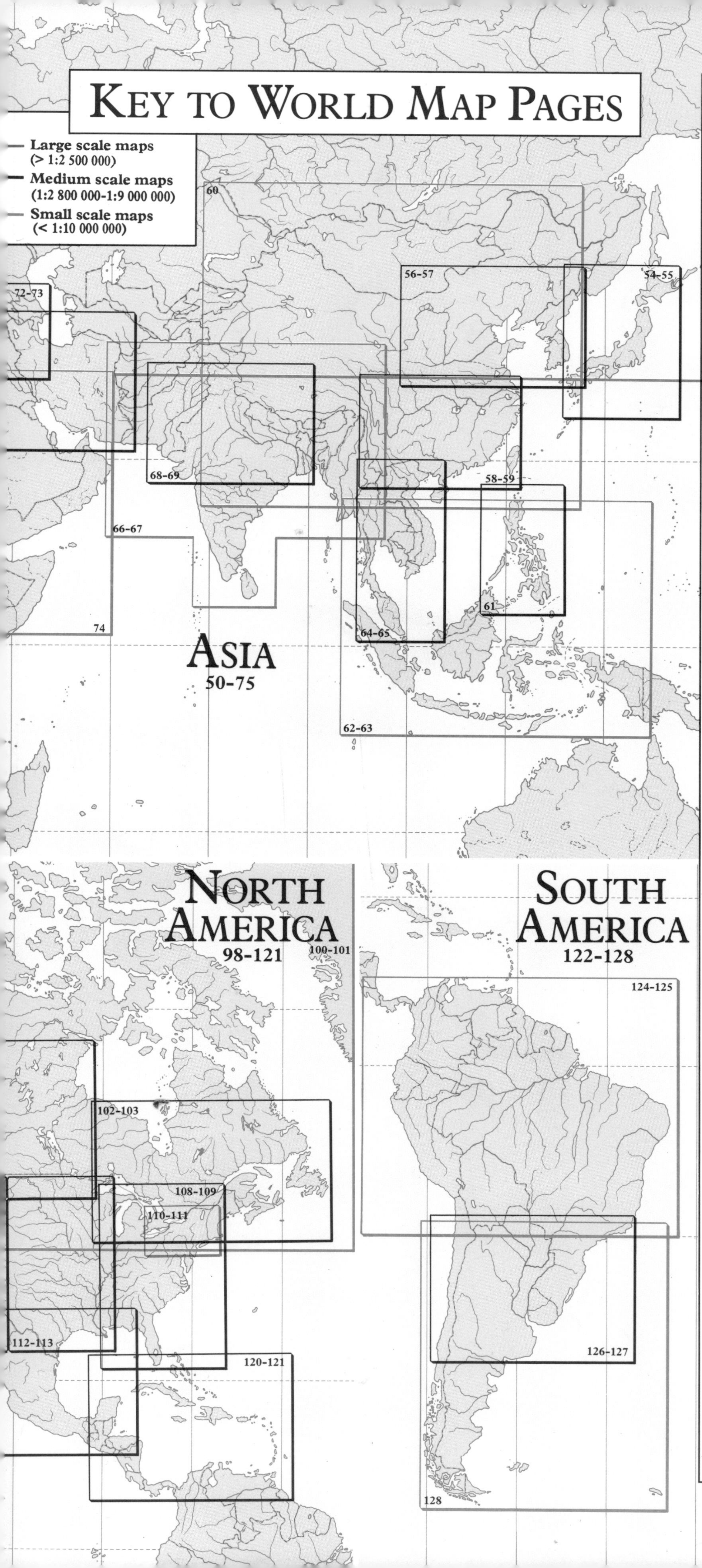

- ── Large scale maps
  (> 1:2 500 000)
- ── Medium scale maps
  (1:2 800 000–1:9 000 000)
- ── Small scale maps
  (< 1:10 000 000)

ASIA
50–75

NORTH
AMERICA
98–121   100–101

SOUTH
AMERICA
122–128

COUNTRY INDEX

Afghanistan	66	Kuwait	70–71
Albania	40	Kyrgyzstan	50
Algeria	78		
Angola	84–85	Laos	64
Argentina	126, 128	Latvia	46
Armenia	73	Lebanon	75
Australia	92–95	Lesotho	88–89
Austria	26–27	Liberia	82
Azerbaijan	73	Libya	79
		Lithuania	46
Bahamas	120–121	Luxembourg	17
Bahrain	71		
Bangladesh	67	Macedonia	40
Barbados	121	Madagascar	89
Belarus	46–47	Malawi	87
Belgium	17	Malaysia	62–63
Belize	120	Mali	78, 82–83
Benin	83	Malta	36
Bhutan	67	Mauritania	78, 82
Bolivia	124	Mauritius	77
Bosnia-		Mexico	118–119
Herzegovina	29, 40	Moldova	43
Botswana	88–89	Mongolia	60
Brazil	124–127	Morocco	78
Brunei	78	Mozambique	85, 87
Bulgaria	40–41		
Burkina Faso	82–83	Namibia	88
Burma	67	Nepal	69
Burundi	86	Netherlands	17
		New Zealand	91
Cambodia	64–65	Nicaragua	120
Cameroon	84	Niger	83
Canada	100–101	Nigeria	83
Central African		Northern Ireland	15
Republic	84	Norway	8–9
Chad	79		
Chile	124, 128	Oman	74
China	56–60		
Colombia	124	Pakistan	68
Congo	84	Panama	120
Congo, Dem. Rep.		Papua New Guinea	90
of the	84–85	Paraguay	126–127
Costa Rica	120	Peru	124
Croatia	29, 42	Philippines	61
Cuba	120–121	Poland	44–45
Cyprus	36	Portugal	34–35
Czech Republic	26–27	Puerto Rico	121
Denmark	11	Qatar	71
Djibouti	74		
Dominican		Romania	42–43
Republic	121	Russia	50–51
		Rwanda	86
Ecuador	124		
Egypt	80	Saudi Arabia	74
El Salvador	120	Scotland	14
England	12–13	Senegal	82
Equatorial Guinea	84	Sierra Leone	82
Eritrea	80–81	Singapore	65
Estonia	46	Slovak Republic	27
Ethiopia	74, 81	Slovenia	29
		Somali Republic	74
Fiji	91	South Africa	88–89
Finland	8–9	Spain	32–35, 37
France	18–21	Sri Lanka	66
French Guiana	125	Sudan	79, 81
		Surinam	124–125
Gabon	84	Swaziland	89
Gambia	82	Sweden	8–9
Georgia	73	Switzerland	25
Germany	24–25	Syria	72–73
Ghana	82–83		
Greece	38–41	Taiwan	59
Greenland	4	Tajikistan	50
Guatemala	120	Tanzania	86–87
Guinea	82	Thailand	64–65
Guinea-Bissau	82	Togo	83
Guyana	124	Trinidad and	
		Tobago	121
Haiti	121	Tunisia	78–79
Honduras	120	Turkey	72–73
Hungary	42	Turkmenistan	50
Iceland	8	Uganda	86
India	66–69	Ukraine	47
Indonesia	62–63	United Arab Emirates	71
Iran	70–71	United Kingdom	12–15
Iraq	70–71	USA	106–117
Irish Republic	15	Uruguay	126–127
Israel	75	Uzbekistan	50
Italy	28–31		
Ivory Coast	82	Venezuela	124
		Vietnam	64–65
Jamaica	120		
Japan	54–55	Wales	12–13
Jordan	75		
		Yemen	74
Kazakstan	50	Yugoslavia	40, 42
Kenya	86		
Korea, North	57	Zambia	84–85, 87
Korea, South	57	Zimbabwe	87

Map box labels: 60, 56–57, 54–55, 72–73, 68–69, 66–67, 58–59, 74, 61, 64–65, 62–63, 100–101, 124–125, 102–103, 108–109, 110–111, 112–113, 120–121, 126–127, 128

PHILIP'S

CONCISE WORLD ATLAS

PHILIP'S

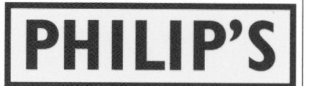

CONCISE WORLD ATLAS

ELEVENTH EDITION

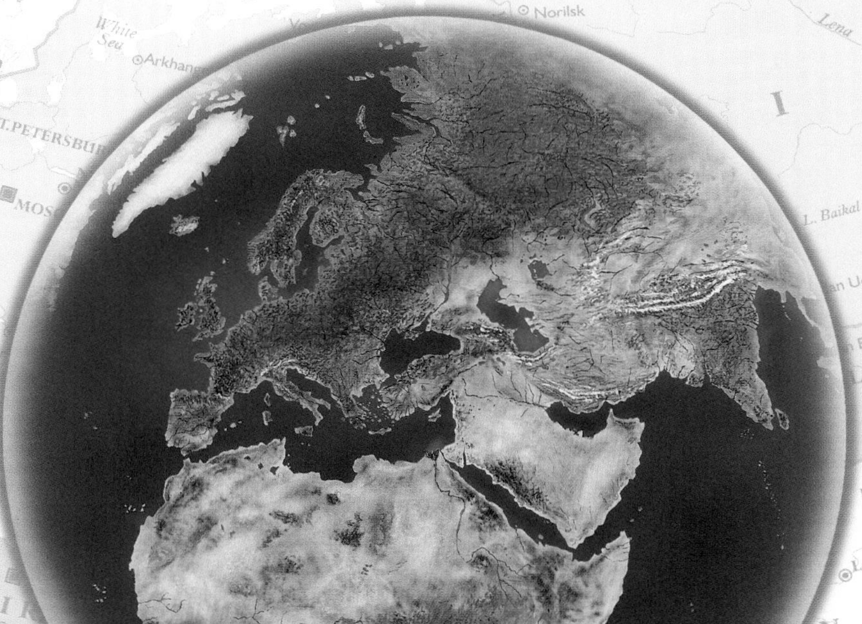

IN ASSOCIATION WITH

THE ROYAL GEOGRAPHICAL SOCIETY

WITH THE INSTITUTE OF BRITISH GEOGRAPHERS

THE EARTH IN SPACE
Cartography by Philip's

Text
Keith Lye

Illustrations
Stefan Chabluk

Star Charts
John Cox
Richard Monkhouse

PICTURE ACKNOWLEDGEMENTS
Robert Harding Picture Library /PHOTRI 13, /Bill Ross 41, /Adam Woolfitt 43
Hutchison Library /Melanie Friend 47, /John Hatt 46
Image Bank /Peter Hendrie 20, /Daniel Hummel 34, /Image Makers 8 top,
/Pete Turner 39
Images Colour Library Limited 15
Japan National Tourist Organisation 45
NASA/Galaxy Picture Library 8 bottom left
NPA Group, Edenbridge, UK 48
Panos Pictures /Howard Davies 35
Chris Rayner 19 top
Rex Features /SIPA Press /Scott Andrews 12
Science Photo Library /Martin Bond 14, /CNES, 1992 Distribution Spot
Image 27 top, /Luke Dodd 3, 6, /Earth Satellite Corporation 25 bottom,
/NASA 9 centre right, 9 top, 22, 23, 24, /David Parker 26, /Peter Ryan 27
below, /Jerry Schad 4, /Space Telescope Science Institute /NASA 9 centre left,
9 bottom right, /US Geological Survey 8 centre right
Space Telescope Science Institute /R. Williams /NASA 2
Starland Picture Library /NASA 8 centre left
Still Pictures /Francois Pierrel 28, /Heine Pedersen 31, 40
Tony Stone Images 33, /Glen Allison 38, /James Balog 16, /John Beatty 21,
/Neil Beer 30, /Kristin Finnegan 11, /Jeremy Horner 42, /Gary Norman 36,
/Frank Oberle 25 top, /Dennis Oda 17, /Nigel Press 37, /Donovan Reese 18,
19, /Hugh Sitton 32, /Richard Surman 44, /Michael Townsend 29, /World
Perspectives 10
Telegraph Colour Library /Space Frontiers 9 bottom left

Published in Great Britain in 2001
by George Philip Limited,
a division of Octopus Publishing Group Limited,
2–4 Heron Quays, London E14 4JP

Copyright © 2001 George Philip Limited

Cartography by Philip's

ISBN 0–540–08067–5

A CIP catalogue record for this book is available from the British Library.

Printed in China

Details of other Philip's titles and services can be found on our website at:
www.philips-maps.co.uk

Philip's is proud to announce that its World Atlases are
now published in association with The Royal Geographical
Society (with The Institute of British Geographers).

The Society was founded in 1830 and given a Royal
Charter in 1859 for 'the advancement of geographical
science'. It holds historical collections of national and
international importance, many of which relate to
the Society's association with and support for scientific
exploration and research from the 19th century onwards.
It was pivotal in establishing geography as a teaching and

research discipline in British universities close to
the turn of the century, and has played a key role in
geographical and environmental education ever since.

Today the Society is a leading world centre for
geographical learning – supporting education, teaching,
research and expeditions, and promoting public
understanding of the subject.

The Society welcomes those interested in geography
as members. For further information, please visit the
website at: www.rgs.org

Philip's World Maps

The reference maps which form the main body of this atlas have been prepared in accordance with the highest standards of international cartography to provide an accurate and detailed representation of the Earth. The scales and projections used have been carefully chosen to give balanced coverage of the world, while emphasizing the most densely populated and economically significant regions. A hallmark of Philip's mapping is the use of hill shading and relief colouring to create a graphic impression of landforms: this makes the maps exceptionally easy to read. However, knowledge of the key features employed in the construction and presentation of the maps will enable the reader to derive the fullest benefit from the atlas.

MAP SEQUENCE

The atlas covers the Earth continent by continent: first Europe; then its land neighbour Asia (mapped north before south, in a clockwise sequence), then Africa, Australia and Oceania, North America and South America. This is the classic arrangement adopted by most cartographers since the 16th century. For each continent, there are maps at a variety of scales. First, physical relief and political maps of the whole continent; then a series of larger-scale maps

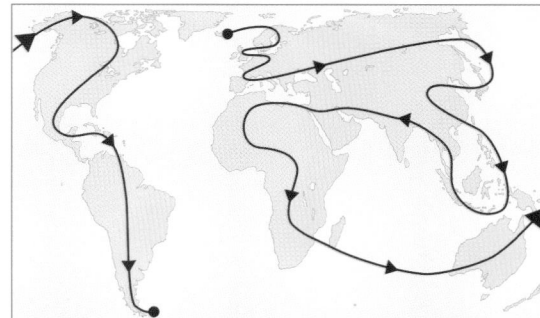

of the regions within the continent, each followed, where required, by still larger-scale maps of the most important or densely populated areas. The governing principle is that by turning the pages of the atlas, the reader moves steadily from north to south through each continent, with each map overlapping its neighbours. A key map showing this sequence, and the area covered by each map, can be found on the endpapers of the atlas.

MAP PRESENTATION

With very few exceptions (e.g. for the Arctic and Antarctic), the maps are drawn with north at the top, regardless of whether they are presented upright or sideways on the page. In the borders will be found the map title; a locator diagram showing the area covered and the page numbers for maps of adjacent areas; the scale; the projection used; the degrees of latitude and longitude; and the letters and figures used in the index for locating place names and geographical features. Physical relief maps also have a height reference panel identifying the colours used for each layer of contouring.

MAP SYMBOLS

Each map contains a vast amount of detail which can only be conveyed clearly and accurately by the use of symbols. Points and circles of varying sizes locate and identify the relative importance of towns and cities; different styles of type are employed for administrative, geographical and regional place names to aid identification. A variety of pictorial symbols denote landscape features such as glaciers, marshes and coral reefs, and man-made structures including roads, railways, airports, canals and dams. International borders are shown by red lines. Where neighbouring countries are in dispute, for example in parts of the Middle East, the maps show the *de facto* boundary between nations, regardless of the legal or historical situation. The symbols are explained on the first page of the World Maps section of the atlas.

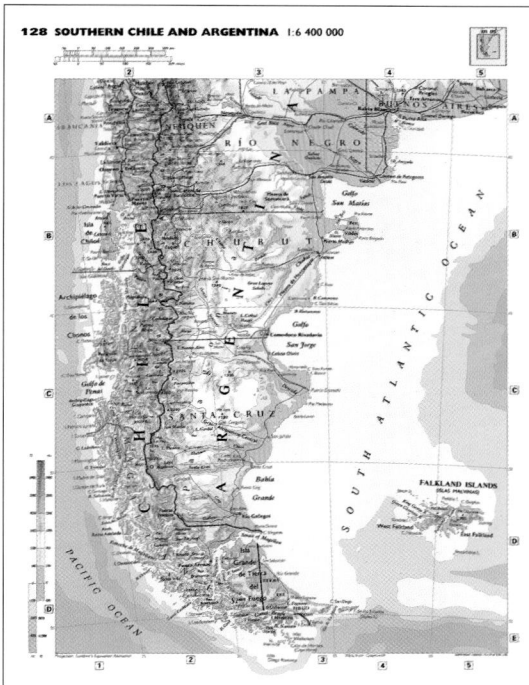

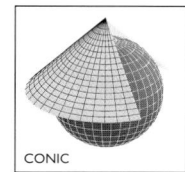  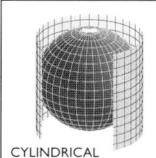

MAP SCALES

1:16 000 000
1 inch = 252 statute miles

The scale of each map is given in the numerical form known as the 'representative fraction'. The first figure is always one, signifying one unit of distance on the map; the second figure, usually in millions, is the number by which the map unit must be multiplied to give the equivalent distance on the Earth's surface. Calculations can easily be made in centimetres and kilometres, by dividing the Earth units figure by 100 000 (i.e. deleting the last five 0s). Thus 1:1 000 000 means 1 cm = 10 km. The calculation for inches and miles is more laborious, but 1 000 000 divided by 63 360 (the number of inches in a mile) shows that 1:1 000 000 means approximately 1 inch = 16 miles. The table below provides distance equivalents for scales down to 1:50 000 000.

LARGE SCALE		
1:1 000 000	1 cm = 10 km	1 inch = 16 miles
1:2 500 000	1 cm = 25 km	1 inch = 39.5 miles
1:5 000 000	1 cm = 50 km	1 inch = 79 miles
1:6 000 000	1 cm = 60 km	1 inch = 95 miles
1:8 000 000	1 cm = 80 km	1 inch = 126 miles
1:10 000 000	1 cm = 100 km	1 inch = 158 miles
1:15 000 000	1 cm = 150 km	1 inch = 237 miles
1:20 000 000	1 cm = 200 km	1 inch = 316 miles
1:50 000 000	1 cm = 500 km	1 inch = 790 miles
SMALL SCALE		

MEASURING DISTANCES

Although each map is accompanied by a scale bar, distances cannot always be measured with confidence because of the distortions involved in portraying the curved surface of the Earth on a flat page. As a general rule, the larger the map scale (i.e. the lower the number of Earth units in the representative fraction), the more accurate and reliable will be the distance measured. On small-scale maps such as those of the world and of entire continents, measurement may only

be accurate along the 'standard parallels', or central axes, and should not be attempted without considering the map projection.

MAP PROJECTIONS

CONIC	AZIMUTHAL	CYLINDRICAL

Unlike a globe, no flat map can give a true scale representation of the world in terms of area, shape and position of every region. Each of the numerous systems that have been devised for projecting the curved surface of the Earth on to a flat page involves the sacrifice of accuracy in one or more of these elements. The variations in shape and position of landmasses such as Alaska, Greenland and Australia, for example, can be quite dramatic when different projections are compared.

For this atlas, the guiding principle has been to select projections that involve the least distortion of size and distance. The projection used for each map is noted in the border. Most fall into one of three categories – conic, cylindrical or azimuthal – whose basic concepts are shown above. Each involves plotting the forms of the Earth's surface on a grid of latitude and longitude lines, which may be shown as parallels, curves or radiating spokes.

LATITUDE AND LONGITUDE

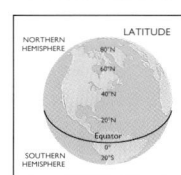 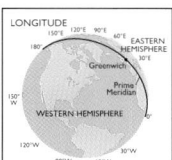 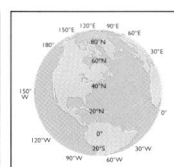

Accurate positioning of individual points on the Earth's surface is made possible by reference to the geometrical system of latitude and longitude. Latitude *parallels* are drawn west–east around the Earth and numbered by degrees north and south of the Equator, which is designated 0° of latitude. Longitude *meridians* are drawn north–south and numbered by degrees east and west of the *prime meridian*, 0° of longitude, which passes through Greenwich in England. By referring to these co-ordinates and their subdivisions of minutes (1/60th of a degree) and seconds (1/60th of a minute), any place on Earth can be located to within a few hundred yards. Latitude and longitude are indicated by blue lines on the maps; they are straight or curved according to the projection employed. Reference to these lines is the easiest way of determining the relative positions of places on different maps, and for plotting compass directions.

NAME FORMS

For ease of reference, both English and local name forms appear in the atlas. Oceans, seas and countries are shown in English throughout the atlas; country names may be abbreviated to their commonly accepted form (e.g. Germany, not The Federal Republic of Germany). Conventional English forms are also used for place names on the smaller-scale maps of the continents. However, local name forms are used on all large-scale and regional maps, with the English form given in brackets only for important cities – the large-scale map of Russia and Central Asia thus shows Moskva (Moscow). For countries which do not use a Roman script, place names have been transcribed according to the systems adopted by the British and US Geographic Names Authorities. For China, the Pin Yin system has been used, with some more widely known forms appearing in brackets, as with Beijing (Peking). Both English and local names appear in the index, the English form being cross-referenced to the local form.

Contents

World Statistics

Countries	x
Cities	xi
Climate	xii
Physical Dimensions	xiv
Regions in the News	xvi

The Earth In Space

The Universe	2–3
Star Charts and Constellations	4–7
The Solar System	8–9
The Earth: Time and Motion	10–11
The Earth from Space	12–13
The Dynamic Earth	14–15
Earthquakes and Volcanoes	16–17
Forces of Nature	18–19
Oceans and Ice	20–21
The Earth's Atmosphere	22–23
Climate and Weather	24–25
Water and Land Use	26–27
The Natural World	28–29
The Human World	30–31
Languages and Religions	32–33
International Organizations	34–35
Agriculture	36–37
Energy and Minerals	38–39
World Economies	40–41
Trade and Commerce	42–43
Travel and Communications	44–45
The World Today	46–47

World Maps

Map Symbols	**1**
The World: Political 1:71 100 000	**2–3**
Arctic Ocean 1:31 100 000	**4**
Antarctica 1:31 100 000	**5**

Europe

Europe: Physical
1:17 800 000
6

Europe: Political
1:17 800 000
7

Scandinavia
1:4 400 000
8–9

Denmark and Southern Sweden
1:2 200 000
10–11

England and Wales
1:1 800 000
12–13

Scotland
1:1 800 000
14

Ireland
1:1 800 000
15

British Isles
1:4 400 000
16

Netherlands, Belgium and Luxembourg
1:2 200 000
17

Northern France
1:2 200 000
18–19

Southern France
1:2 200 000
20–21

Middle Europe
1:4 400 000
22–23

Germany and Switzerland
1:2 200 000
24–25

Austria, Czech Republic and Slovak Republic
1:2 200 000
26–27

Northern Italy, Slovenia and Croatia
1:2 200 000
28–29

Southern Italy
1:2 200 000
30–31

Eastern Spain
1:2 200 000
32–33

Western Spain and Portugal
1:2 200 000
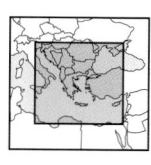
34–35

Malta, Crete, Corfu, Rhodes and Cyprus
1:900 000 / 1:1 200 000
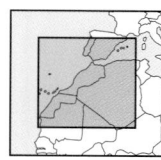
36

The Balearics, the Canaries and Madeira
1:900 000 / 1:1 800 000
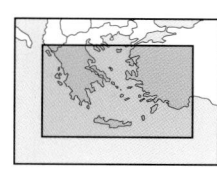
37

Southern Greece and Western Turkey
1:2 200 000
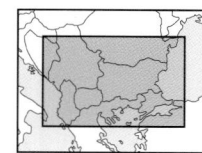
38–39

Northern Greece, Bulgaria and Yugoslavia
1:2 200 000
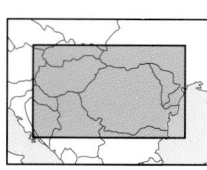
40–41

Hungary, Romania and the Lower Danube
1:2 200 000
42–43

Poland and the Southern Baltic
1:2 200 000
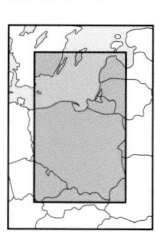
44–45

East Africa
1:7 100 000

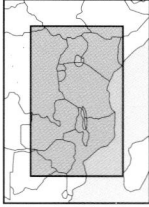

86–87

Southern Africa
1:7 100 000 / 1:7 100 000

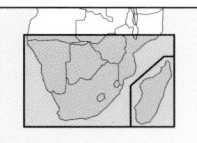

88–89

Australia and Oceania

Australia and Oceania:
 Physical and Political
1:44 400 000   90

New Zealand and Samoa, Fiji and Tonga
1:5 300 000 / 1:10 700 000

91

Western Australia
1:7 100 000

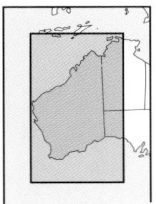

92–93

Eastern Australia
1:7 100 000

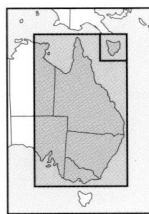

94–95

Pacific Ocean
1:48 000 000   96–97

North America

North America: Physical
1:31 100 000   98

North America: Political
1:31 100 000   99

Canada and Alaska
1:13 300 000 / 1:26 700 000

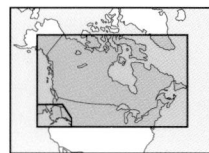

100–101

Eastern Canada
1:6 200 000

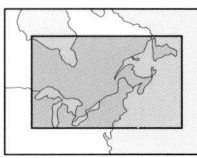

102–103

Western Canada
1:6 200 000

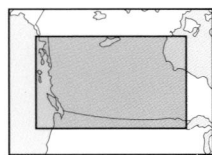

104–105

United States and Hawaii
1:10 700 000 / 1:8 900 000

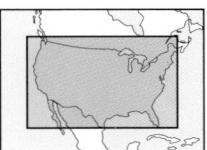

106–107

Eastern United States
1:5 300 000

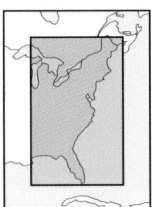

108–109

North-eastern United States
1:2 200 000

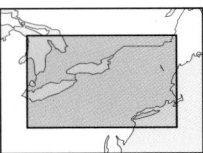

110–111

Middle United States
1:5 300 000

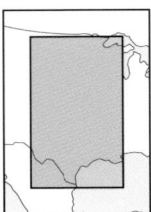

112–113

Western United States
1:5 300 000

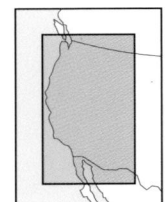

114–115

Central and Southern California
 and Western Washington
1:2 200 000

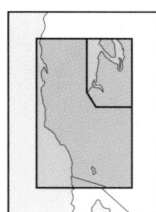

116–117

Mexico
1:7 100 000

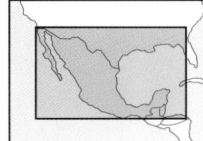

118–119

Central America and the West Indies
1:7 100 000

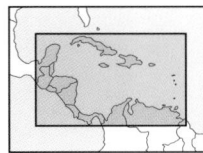

120–121

South America

South America: Physical
1:31 100 000   122

South America: Political
1:31 100 000   123

South America – North
1:14 200 000

124–125

Central South America
1:7 100 000

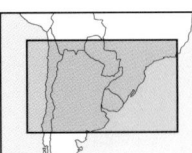

126–127

South America – South
1:14 200 000

128

Index to World Maps

129–224

World Statistics: Countries

This alphabetical list includes all the countries and territories of the world. If a territory is not completely independent, then the country it is associated with is named. The area figures give the total area of land, inland water and ice.

Units for areas and populations are thousands. The population figures are 2000 estimates. The annual income is the Gross National Product per capita in US dollars. The figures are the latest available, usually 1999 estimates.

Country/Territory	Area km² Thousands	Area miles² Thousands	Population Thousands	Capital	Annual Income US $
Afghanistan	652	252	26,511	Kabul	800
Albania	28.8	11.1	3,795	Tirana	870
Algeria	2,382	920	32,904	Algiers	1,550
American Samoa (US)	0.20	0.08	39	Pago Pago	2,600
Andorra	0.45	0.17	49	Andorra La Vella	18,000
Angola	1,247	481	13,295	Luanda	220
Anguilla (UK)	0.1	0.04	8	The Valley	6,800
Antigua & Barbuda	0.44	0.17	79	St John's	8,520
Argentina	2,767	1,068	36,238	Buenos Aires	7,600
Armenia	29.8	11.5	3,968	Yerevan	490
Aruba (Netherlands)	0.19	0.07	58	Oranjestad	22,000
Australia	7,687	2,968	18,855	Canberra	20,050
Austria	83.9	32.4	7,613	Vienna	25,970
Azerbaijan	86.6	33.4	8,324	Baku	550
Azores (Portugal)	2.2	0.87	238	Ponta Delgada	–
Bahamas	13.9	5.4	295	Nassau	20,100
Bahrain	0.68	0.26	683	Manama	7,640
Bangladesh	144	56	150,589	Dhaka	370
Barbados	0.43	0.17	265	Bridgetown	7,890
Belarus	207.6	80.1	10,697	Minsk	2,630
Belgium	30.5	11.8	9,832	Brussels	24,510
Belize	23	8.9	230	Belmopan	2,730
Benin	113	43	6,369	Porto-Novo	380
Bermuda (UK)	0.05	0.02	62	Hamilton	35,590
Bhutan	47	18.1	1,906	Thimphu	510
Bolivia	1,099	424	9,724	La Paz/Sucre	1,010
Bosnia-Herzegovina	51	20	4,601	Sarajevo	1,720
Botswana	582	225	1,822	Gaborone	3,240
Brazil	8,512	3,286	179,487	Brasília	4,420
Brunei	5.8	2.2	333	Bandar Seri Begawan	24,630
Bulgaria	111	43	9,071	Sofia	1,380
Burkina Faso	274	106	12,092	Ouagadougou	240
Burma (= Myanmar)	677	261	51,129	Rangoon	1,200
Burundi	27.8	10.7	7,358	Bujumbura	120
Cambodia	181	70	10,046	Phnom Penh	260
Cameroon	475	184	16,701	Yaoundé	580
Canada	9,976	3,852	28,488	Ottawa	19,320
Canary Is. (Spain)	7.3	2.8	1,494	Las Palmas/Santa Cruz	–
Cape Verde Is.	4	1.6	515	Praia	1,330
Cayman Is. (UK)	0.26	0.10	35	George Town	20,000
Central African Republic	623	241	4,074	Bangui	290
Chad	1,284	496	7,337	Ndjaména	200
Chile	757	292	15,272	Santiago	4,740
China	9,597	3,705	1,299,180	Beijing	780
Colombia	1,139	440	39,397	Bogotá	2,250
Comoros	2.2	0.86	670	Moroni	350
Congo	342	132	3,167	Brazzaville	670
Congo (Dem. Rep. of the)	2,345	905	49,190	Kinshasa	110
Cook Is. (NZ)	0.24	0.09	17	Avarua	900
Costa Rica	51.1	19.7	3,711	San José	2,740
Croatia	56.5	21.8	4,960	Zagreb	4,580
Cuba	111	43	11,504	Havana	1,560
Cyprus	9.3	3.6	762	Nicosia	11,960
Czech Republic	78.9	30.4	10,500	Prague	5,060
Denmark	43.1	16.6	5,153	Copenhagen	32,030
Djibouti	23.2	9	552	Djibouti	790
Dominica	0.75	0.29	87	Roseau	3,170
Dominican Republic	48.7	18.8	8,621	Santo Domingo	1,910
Ecuador	284	109	13,319	Quito	1,310
Egypt	1,001	387	64,210	Cairo	1,400
El Salvador	21	8.1	6,739	San Salvador	1,900
Equatorial Guinea	28.1	10.8	455	Malabo	1,170
Eritrea	94	36	4,523	Asmara	200
Estonia	44.7	17.3	1,647	Tallinn	3,480
Ethiopia	1,128	436	61,841	Addis Ababa	100
Faroe Is. (Denmark)	1.4	0.54	49	Tórshavn	16,000
Fiji	18.3	7.1	883	Suva	2,210
Finland	338	131	5,077	Helsinki	23,780
France	552	213	58,145	Paris	23,480
French Guiana (France)	90	34.7	130	Cayenne	6,000
French Polynesia (France)	4	1.5	268	Papeete	18,050
Gabon	268	103	1,612	Libreville	3,350
Gambia, The	11.3	4.4	1,119	Banjul	340
Georgia	69.7	26.9	5,777	Tbilisi	620
Germany	357	138	76,962	Berlin	25,350
Ghana	239	92	20,564	Accra	390
Gibraltar (UK)	0.007	0.003	32	Gibraltar Town	5,000
Greece	132	51	10,193	Athens	11,770
Greenland (Denmark)	2,176	840	60	Nuuk (Godthåb)	16,100
Grenada	0.34	0.13	83	St George's	3,450
Guadeloupe (France)	1.7	0.66	365	Basse-Terre	9,200
Guam (US)	0.55	0.21	128	Agana	19,000
Guatemala	109	42	12,222	Guatemala City	1,660
Guinea	246	95	7,830	Conakry	510
Guinea-Bissau	36.1	13.9	1,197	Bissau	160
Guyana	215	83	891	Georgetown	760
Haiti	27.8	10.7	8,003	Port-au-Prince	460
Honduras	112	43	6,846	Tegucigalpa	760
Hong Kong (China)	1.1	0.40	6,336	–	23,520
Hungary	93	35.9	10,531	Budapest	4,650
Iceland	103	40	274	Reykjavik	29,280
India	3,288	1,269	1,041,543	New Delhi	450
Indonesia	1,905	735	218,661	Jakarta	580
Iran	1,648	636	68,759	Tehran	1,760
Iraq	438	169	26,339	Baghdad	2,400
Ireland	70.3	27.1	4,086	Dublin	19,160
Israel	27	10.3	5,321	Jerusalem	17,450
Italy	301	116	57,195	Rome	19,710
Ivory Coast (Côte d'Ivoire)	322	125	17,600	Yamoussoukro	710
Jamaica	11	4.2	2,735	Kingston	2,330
Japan	378	146	128,470	Tokyo	32,230
Jordan	89.2	34.4	5,558	Amman	1,500
Kazakstan	2,717	1,049	19,006	Astana	1,230
Kenya	580	224	35,060	Nairobi	360
Kiribati	0.72	0.28	72	Tarawa	910
Korea, North	121	47	26,117	Pyŏngyang	1,000
Korea, South	99	38.2	46,403	Seoul	8,490
Kuwait	17.8	6.9	2,639	Kuwait City	22,700
Kyrgyzstan	198.5	76.6	5,403	Bishkek	300
Laos	237	91	5,463	Vientiane	280
Latvia	65	25	2,768	Riga	2,470

Country/Territory	Area km² Thousands	Area miles² Thousands	Population Thousands	Capital	Annual Income US $
Lebanon	10.4	4	3,327	Beirut	3,700
Lesotho	30.4	11.7	2,370	Maseru	550
Liberia	111	43	3,575	Monrovia	1,000
Libya	1,760	679	6,500	Tripoli	6,700
Liechtenstein	0.16	0.06	28	Vaduz	50,000
Lithuania	65.2	25.2	3,935	Vilnius	2,620
Luxembourg	2.6	1	377	Luxembourg	44,640
Macau (China)	0.02	0.006	656	Macau	16,000
Macedonia	25.7	9.9	2,157	Skopje	1,690
Madagascar	587	227	16,627	Antananarivo	250
Madeira (Portugal)	0.81	0.31	253	Funchal	–
Malawi	118	46	12,458	Lilongwe	190
Malaysia	330	127	21,983	Kuala Lumpur	3,400
Maldives	0.30	0.12	283	Malé	1,160
Mali	1,240	479	12,685	Bamako	240
Malta	0.32	0.12	366	Valletta	9,210
Marshall Is.	0.18	0.07	70	Dalap-Uliga-Darrit	1,560
Martinique (France)	1.1	0.42	362	Fort-de-France	10,700
Mauritania	1,030	412	2,702	Nouakchott	380
Mauritius	2.0	0.72	1,201	Port Louis	3,590
Mayotte (France)	0.37	0.14	141	Mamoundzou	1,430
Mexico	1,958	756	107,233	Mexico City	4,400
Micronesia, Fed. States of	0.70	0.27	110	Palikir	1,810
Moldova	33.7	13	4,707	Chişinău	370
Monaco	0.002	0.0001	30	Monaco	25,000
Mongolia	1,567	605	2,847	Ulan Bator	350
Montserrat (UK)	0.10	0.04	13	Plymouth	4,500
Morocco	447	172	31,559	Rabat	1,200
Mozambique	802	309	20,493	Maputo	230
Namibia	825	318	2,437	Windhoek	1,890
Nauru	0.02	0.008	10	Yaren District	10,000
Nepal	141	54	24,084	Katmandu	220
Netherlands	41.5	16	15,829	Amsterdam/The Hague	24,320
Netherlands Antilles (Neths)	0.99	0.38	203	Willemstad	11,500
New Caledonia (France)	18.6	7.2	195	Nouméa	11,400
New Zealand	269	104	3,662	Wellington	13,780
Nicaragua	130	50	5,261	Managua	430
Niger	1,267	489	10,752	Niamey	190
Nigeria	924	357	105,000	Abuja	310
Northern Mariana Is. (US)	0.48	0.18	50	Saipan	11,500
Norway	324	125	4,331	Oslo	32,880
Oman	212	82	2,176	Muscat	7,900
Pakistan	796	307	162,409	Islamabad	470
Palau	0.46	0.18	18	Koror	5,000
Panama	77.1	29.8	2,893	Panama City	3,070
Papua New Guinea	463	179	4,845	Port Moresby	800
Paraguay	407	157	5,538	Asunción	1,580
Peru	1,285	496	26,276	Lima	2,390
Philippines	300	116	77,473	Manila	1,020
Poland	313	121	40,366	Warsaw	3,960
Portugal	92.4	35.7	10,587	Lisbon	10,600
Puerto Rico (US)	9	3.5	3,836	San Juan	8,200
Qatar	11	4.2	499	Doha	17,100
Réunion (France)	2.5	0.97	692	Saint-Denis	4,800
Romania	238	92	24,000	Bucharest	1,520
Russia	17,075	6,592	155,096	Moscow	2,270
Rwanda	26.3	10.2	10,200	Kigali	250
St Kitts & Nevis	0.36	0.14	44	Basseterre	6,420
St Lucia	0.62	0.24	177	Castries	3,770
St Vincent & Grenadines	0.39	0.15	128	Kingstown	2,700
Samoa	2.8	1.1	171	Apia	1,020
San Marino	0.06	0.02	25	San Marino	20,000
São Tomé & Príncipe	0.96	0.37	151	São Tomé	270
Saudi Arabia	2,150	830	20,697	Riyadh	6,910
Senegal	197	76	8,716	Dakar	510
Seychelles	0.46	0.18	75	Victoria	6,540
Sierra Leone	71.7	27.7	5,437	Freetown	130
Singapore	0.62	0.24	3,000	Singapore	29,610
Slovak Republic	49	18.9	5,500	Bratislava	3,590
Slovenia	20.3	7.8	2,055	Ljubljana	9,890
Solomon Is.	28.9	11.2	429	Honiara	750
Somalia	638	246	9,736	Mogadishu	600
South Africa	1,220	471	43,666	C. Town/Pretoria/Bloem.	3,160
Spain	505	195	40,667	Madrid	14,000
Sri Lanka	65.6	25.3	19,416	Colombo	820
Sudan	2,506	967	33,625	Khartoum	330
Surinam	163	63	497	Paramaribo	1,660
Swaziland	17.4	6.7	1,121	Mbabane	1,360
Sweden	450	174	8,560	Stockholm	25,040
Switzerland	41.3	15.9	6,762	Bern	38,350
Syria	185	71	17,826	Damascus	970
Taiwan	36	13.9	22,000	Taipei	12,400
Tajikistan	143.1	55.2	7,041	Dushanbe	290
Tanzania	945	365	39,639	Dodoma	240
Thailand	513	198	63,670	Bangkok	1,960
Togo	56.8	21.9	4,861	Lomé	320
Tonga	0.75	0.29	92	Nuku'alofa	1,720
Trinidad & Tobago	5.1	2	1,484	Port of Spain	4,390
Tunisia	164	63	9,924	Tunis	2,100
Turkey	779	301	66,789	Ankara	2,900
Turkmenistan	488.1	188.5	4,585	Ashkhabad	660
Turks & Caicos Is. (UK)	0.43	0.17	12	Cockburn Town	5,000
Tuvalu	0.03	0.01	11	Fongafale	600
Uganda	236	91	26,958	Kampala	320
Ukraine	603.7	233.1	52,558	Kiev	750
United Arab Emirates	83.6	32.3	1,951	Abu Dhabi	17,870
United Kingdom	243.3	94	58,393	London	22,640
United States of America	9,373	3,619	266,096	Washington, DC	30,600
Uruguay	177	68	3,274	Montevideo	5,900
Uzbekistan	447.4	172.7	26,044	Tashkent	720
Vanuatu	12.2	4.7	206	Port-Vila	1,170
Venezuela	912	352	24,715	Caracas	3,670
Vietnam	332	127	82,427	Hanoi	370
Virgin Is. (UK)	0.15	0.06	15	Road Town	–
Virgin Is. (US)	0.34	0.13	135	Charlotte Amalie	12,500
Wallis & Futuna Is. (France)	0.20	0.08	26	Mata-Utu	–
Western Sahara	266	103	228	El Aaiún	300
Yemen	528	204	13,219	Sana	350
Yugoslavia	102.3	39.5	10,761	Belgrade	2,300
Zambia	753	291	12,267	Lusaka	320
Zimbabwe	391	151	13,123	Harare	520

World Statistics: Cities

This list shows the principal cities with more than 500,000 inhabitants (for Brazil, China and India only cities with more than 1 million inhabitants are included). The figures are taken from the most recent census or population estimate available, and as far as possible are the population of the metropolitan area, e.g. greater New York, Mexico or Paris. All the figures are in thousands. Local name forms have been used for the smaller cities (e.g. Kraków).

AFGHANISTAN
Kabul 1,565
ALGERIA
Algiers 2,168
Oran 916
ANGOLA
Luanda 2,418
ARGENTINA
Buenos Aires 11,256
Córdoba 1,208
Rosario 1,118
Mendoza 773
La Plata 642
San Miguel de Tucumán 622
Mar del Plata 512
ARMENIA
Yerevan 1,248
AUSTRALIA
Sydney 3,770
Melbourne 3,217
Brisbane 1,489
Perth 1,262
Adelaide 1,080
AUSTRIA
Vienna 1,595
AZERBAIJAN
Baku 1,720
BANGLADESH
Dhaka 6,105
Chittagong 2,041
Khulna 877
Rajshahi 517
BELARUS
Minsk 1,700
Homyel 512
BELGIUM
Brussels 948
BENIN
Cotonou 537
BOLIVIA
La Paz 1,126
Santa Cruz 767
BOSNIA-HERZEGOVINA
Sarajevo 526
BRAZIL
São Paulo 16,417
Rio de Janeiro 9,888
Salvador 2,211
Belo Horizonte 2,091
Fortaleza 1,965
Brasília 1,821
Curitiba 1,476
Recife 1,346
Pôrto Alegre 1,288
Manaus 1,157
Belém 1,144
Goiânia 1,004
BULGARIA
Sofia 1,116
BURKINA FASO
Ouagadougou 690
BURMA (MYANMAR)
Rangoon 2,513
Mandalay 533
CAMBODIA
Phnom Penh 920
CAMEROON
Douala 1,200
Yaoundé 800
CANADA
Toronto 4,344
Montréal 3,337
Vancouver 1,831
Ottawa–Hull 1,022
Edmonton 885
Calgary 831
Québec 693
Winnipeg 677
Hamilton 643
CENTRAL AFRICAN REP.
Bangui 553
CHAD
Ndjaména 530
CHILE
Santiago 5,067
CHINA
Shanghai 15,082
Beijing 12,362
Tianjin 10,687
Hong Kong (SAR)* 6,502
Chongqing 3,870
Shenyang 3,860
Wuhan 3,520
Guangzhou 3,114
Harbin 2,505
Nanjing 2,211
Xi'an 2,115
Chengdu 1,933
Dalian 1,855
Changchun 1,810
Jinan 1,660
Taiyuan 1,642
Qingdao 1,584
Fuzhou, Fujian 1,380
Zibo 1,346
Zhengzhou 1,324
Lanzhou 1,296
Anshan 1,252
Fushun 1,246
Kunming 1,242
Changsha 1,198
Hangzhou 1,185
Nanchang 1,169
Shijiazhuang 1,159
Guiyang 1,131
Ürümqi 1,130
Jilin 1,118
Tangshan 1,110
Qiqihar 1,104
Baotou 1,033
Hefei 1,000
COLOMBIA
Bogotá 6,004
Cali 1,985
Medellín 1,970
Barranquilla 1,157
Cartagena 812
CONGO
Brazzaville 937
Pointe-Noire 576
CONGO (DEM. REP.)
Kinshasa 1,655
Lubumbashi 851
Mbuji-Mayi 806
COSTA RICA
San José 1,220
CROATIA
Zagreb 931
CUBA
Havana 2,241
CZECH REPUBLIC
Prague 1,209
DENMARK
Copenhagen 1,362
DOMINICAN REPUBLIC
Santo Domingo 2,135
Santiago 691
ECUADOR
Guayaquil 1,973
Quito 1,487
EGYPT
Cairo 9,900
Alexandria 3,431
El Gîza 2,144
Shubra el Kheima 834
EL SALVADOR
San Salvador 1,522
ETHIOPIA
Addis Ababa 2,112
FINLAND
Helsinki 532
FRANCE
Paris 9,319
Lyon 1,262
Marseille 1,087
Lille 959
Bordeaux 696
Toulouse 650
Nice 516
GEORGIA
Tbilisi 1,300
GERMANY
Berlin 3,470
Hamburg 1,706
Munich 1,240
Cologne 964
Frankfurt 651
Essen 616
Dortmund 600
Stuttgart 587
Düsseldorf 571
Bremen 549
Duisburg 535
Hanover 524
GHANA
Accra 949
GREECE
Athens 3,097
GUATEMALA
Guatemala 1,167
GUINEA
Conakry 1,508
HAITI
Port-au-Prince 1,255
HONDURAS
Tegucigalpa 813
HUNGARY
Budapest 1,885
INDIA
Bombay (Mumbai) 12,572
Calcutta (Kolkata) 10,916
Delhi 7,207
Madras (Chennai) 5,361
Hyderabad 4,280
Bangalore 4,087
Ahmadabad 3,298
Pune 2,485
Kanpur 2,111
Nagpur 1,661
Lucknow 1,642
Surat 1,517
Jaipur 1,514
Coimbatore 1,136
Vadodara 1,115
Indore 1,104
Patna 1,099
Madurai 1,094
Bhopal 1,064
Vishakhapatnam 1,052
Varanasi 1,026
Ludhiana 1,012
INDONESIA
Jakarta 11,500
Surabaya 2,701
Bandung 2,368
Medan 1,910
Semarang 1,366
Palembang 1,352
Tangerang 1,198
Ujung Pandang 1,092
Bandar Lampung 832
Malang 763
Padang 721
Pakanbaru 558
Samarinda 536
Banjarmasin 535
Surakarta 516
IRAN
Tehran 6,750
Mashhad 1,964
Esfahan 1,221
Tabriz 1,166
Shiraz 1,043
Ahvaz 828
Qom 780
Bakhtaran 666
Karaj 588
IRAQ
Baghdad 3,841
Diyala 961
As Sulaymaniyah 952
Arbil 770
Al Mawsil 664
Kadhimain 521
IRELAND
Dublin 952
ISRAEL
Tel Aviv-Yafo 1,502
Jerusalem 591
ITALY
Rome 2,775
Milan 1,369
Naples 1,067
Turin 962
Palermo 698
Genoa 678
IVORY COAST
Abidjan 2,500
JAMAICA
Kingston 644
JAPAN
Tokyo–Yokohama 26,836
Osaka 10,601
Nagoya 2,152
Sapporo 1,757
Kyoto 1,464
Kobe 1,424
Fukuoka 1,285
Kawasaki 1,203
Hiroshima 1,109
Kitakyushu 1,020
Sendai 971
Chiba 857
Sakai 803
Kumamoto 650
Okayama 616
Sagamihara 571
Hamamatsu 562
Kagoshima 546
Funabashi 541
Higashiosaka 517
Hachioji 503
JORDAN
Amman 1,300
Az-Zarqâ 609
KAZAKSTAN
Almaty 1,150
Qaraghandy 573
KENYA
Nairobi 2,000
Mombasa 600
KOREA, NORTH
Pyŏngyang 2,639
Hamhung 775
Chŏngjin 754
Chinnampo 691
Sinŭiju 500
KOREA, SOUTH
Seoul 11,641
Pusan 3,814
Taegu 2,449
Inchon 2,308
Taejŏn 1,272
Kwangju 1,258
Ulsan 967
Sŏngnam 869
Puch'on 779
Suwŏn 756
Anyang 590
Chŏnju 563
Chŏngju 531
Ansan 510
P'ohang 509
KYRGYZSTAN
Bishkek 584
LATVIA
Riga 846
LEBANON
Beirut 1,900
Tripoli 500
LIBYA
Tripoli 1,083
LITHUANIA
Vilnius 580
MACEDONIA
Skopje 541
MADAGASCAR
Antananarivo 1,053
MALAYSIA
Kuala Lumpur 1,145
MALI
Bamako 800
MAURITANIA
Nouakchott 735
MEXICO
Mexico City 15,048
Guadalajara 2,847
Monterrey 2,522
Puebla 1,055
León 872
Ciudad Juárez 798
Tijuana 743
Culiacán Rosales 602
Mexicali 602
Acapulco de Juárez 592
Mérida 557
Chihuahua 530
San Luis Potosí 526
Aguascalientés 506
MOLDOVA
Chişinău 700
MONGOLIA
Ulan Bator 627
MOROCCO
Casablanca 3,079
Rabat-Salé 1,344
Fès 735
Marrakesh 621
MOZAMBIQUE
Maputo 2,000
NEPAL
Katmandu 535
NETHERLANDS
Amsterdam 1,101
Rotterdam 1,076
The Hague 694
Utrecht 548
NEW ZEALAND
Auckland 997
NICARAGUA
Managua 864
NIGERIA
Lagos 10,287
Ibadan 1,365
Ogbomosho 712
Kano 657
NORWAY
Oslo 714
PAKISTAN
Karachi 9,863
Lahore 5,085
Faisalabad 1,875
Peshawar 1,676
Gujranwala 1,663
Rawalpindi 1,290
Multan 1,257
Hyderabad 1,107
PARAGUAY
Asunción 945
PERU
Lima–Callao 6,601
Callao 638
Arequipa 620
Trujillo 509
PHILIPPINES
Manila 9,280
Quezon City 1,989
Davao 1,191
Caloocan 1,023
Cebu 662
Zamboanga 511
POLAND
Warsaw 1,638
Lódz 825
Kraków 745
Wroclaw 642
Poznań 581
PORTUGAL
Lisbon 2,561
Oporto 1,174
ROMANIA
Bucharest 2,060
RUSSIA
Moscow 9,233
Petersburg 4,883
Nizhniy Novgorod 1,425
Novosibirsk 1,400
Yekaterinburg 1,300
Samara 1,200
Omsk 1,200
Chelyabinsk 1,100
Kazan 1,100
Ufa 1,100
Volgograd 1,003
Perm 1,000
Rostov 1,000
Voronezh 908
Saratov 895
Krasnoyarsk 869
Togliatti 689
Simbirsk 678
Izhevsk 654
Krasnodar 645
Vladivostok 632
Yaroslavl 629
Khabarovsk 618
Barnaul 596
Irkutsk 585
Novokuznetsk 572
Ryazan 536
Penza 534
Orenburg 532
Tula 532
Naberezhnyye-Chelny 526
Kemerovo 503
SAUDI ARABIA
Riyadh 1,800
Jedda 1,500
Mecca 630
SENEGAL
Dakar 1,571
SIERRA LEONE
Freetown 505
SINGAPORE
Singapore 3,104
SOMALIA
Mogadishu 1,000
SOUTH AFRICA
Cape Town 2,350
East Rand 1,379
Johannesburg 1,196
Durban 1,137
Pretoria 1,080
West Rand 870
Port Elizabeth 853
Vanderbijlpark–Vereeniging 774
Soweto 597
Sasolburg 540
SPAIN
Madrid 3,029
Barcelona 1,614
Valencia 763
Sevilla 719
Zaragoza 607
Málaga 532
SRI LANKA
Colombo 1,863
SUDAN
Omdurman 1,267
Khartoum 925
Khartoum North 879
SWEDEN
Stockholm 1,744
Göteborg 775
SWITZERLAND
Zürich 1,175
Bern 942
SYRIA
Aleppo 1,591
Damascus 1,549
Homs 644
TAIWAN
Taipei 2,653
Kaohsiung 1,405
Taichung 817
Tainan 700
Panchiao 544
TAJIKISTAN
Dushanbe 524
TANZANIA
Dar-es-Salaam 1,361
THAILAND
Bangkok 5,572
TOGO
Lomé 590
TUNISIA
Tunis 1,827
TURKEY
Istanbul 7,490
Ankara 3,028
Izmir 2,333
Adana 1,472
Bursa 1,317
Konya 1,040
Gaziantep 930
Icel 908
Antalya 734
Diyarbakir 677
Kocaeli 661
Urfa 649
Kayseri 648
Manisa 641
Hatay 561
Samsun 557
Eskisehir 508
Balikesir 501
TURKMENISTAN
Ashkhabad 536
UGANDA
Kampala 773
UKRAINE
Kiev 2,630
Kharkiv 1,555
Dnipropetrovsk 1,147
Donetsk 1,088
Odesa 1,046
Zaporizhzhya 887
Lviv 802
Kryvyy Rih 720
Mariupol 510
Mykolayiv 508
UNITED KINGDOM
London 8,089
Birmingham 2,373
Manchester 2,353
Liverpool 852
Glasgow 832
Sheffield 661
Nottingham 649
Newcastle 617
Bristol 552
Leeds 529
UNITED STATES
New York 16,329
Los Angeles 12,410
Chicago 7,668
Philadelphia 4,949
Washington, DC 4,466
Detroit 4,307
Houston 3,653
Atlanta 3,331
Boston 3,240
Dallas 2,898
Minneapolis–St Paul 2,688
San Diego 2,632
St Louis 2,536
Phoenix 2,473
Baltimore 2,458
Pittsburgh 2,402
Cleveland 2,222
San Francisco 2,182
Seattle 2,180
Tampa 2,157
Miami 2,025
Newark 1,934
Denver 1,796
Portland (Or.) 1,676
Kansas City (Mo.) 1,647
Cincinnati 1,581
San Jose 1,557
Norfolk 1,529
Indianapolis 1,462
Milwaukee 1,456
Sacramento 1,441
San Antonio 1,437
Columbus (Oh.) 1,423
New Orleans 1,309
Charlotte 1,260
Buffalo 1,189
Salt Lake City 1,178
Hartford 1,151
Oklahoma 1,007
Jacksonville (Fl.) 665
Omaha 663
Memphis 614
El Paso 579
Austin 514
Nashville 505
URUGUAY
Montevideo 1,378
UZBEKISTAN
Tashkent 2,107
VENEZUELA
Caracas 2,784
Maracaibo 1,364
Valencia 1,032
Maracay 800
Barquisimeto 745
Ciudad Guayana 524
VIETNAM
Ho Chi Minh City 4,322
Hanoi 3,056
Haiphong 783
YEMEN
Sana 972
Aden 562
YUGOSLAVIA
Belgrade 1,137
ZAMBIA
Lusaka 982
ZIMBABWE
Harare 1,189
Bulawayo 622

* SAR = Special Administrative Region of China

World Statistics: Climate

Rainfall and temperature figures are provided for more than 70 cities around the world. As climate is affected by altitude, the height of each city is shown in metres beneath its name. For each location, the top row of figures shows the total rainfall or snow in millimetres, and the bottom row the average temperature in degrees Celsius; the average annual temperature and total annual rainfall are at the end of the rows. The map opposite shows the city locations.

EUROPE

CITY	JAN.	FEB.	MAR.	APR.	MAY	JUNE	JULY	AUG.	SEPT.	OCT.	NOV.	DEC.	YEAR
Athens, Greece	62	37	37	23	23	14	6	7	15	51	56	71	402
107 m	10	10	12	16	20	25	28	28	24	20	15	11	18
Berlin, Germany	46	40	33	42	49	65	73	69	48	49	46	43	603
55 m	−1	0	4	9	14	17	19	18	15	9	5	1	9
Istanbul, Turkey	109	92	72	46	38	34	34	30	58	81	103	119	816
14 m	5	6	7	11	16	20	23	23	20	16	12	8	14
Lisbon, Portugal	111	76	109	54	44	16	3	4	33	62	93	103	708
77 m	11	12	14	16	17	20	22	23	21	18	14	12	17
London, UK	54	40	37	37	46	45	57	59	49	57	64	48	593
5 m	4	5	7	9	12	16	18	17	15	11	8	5	11
Málaga, Spain	61	51	62	46	26	5	1	3	29	64	64	62	474
33 m	12	13	16	17	19	29	25	26	23	20	16	13	18
Moscow, Russia	39	38	36	37	53	58	88	71	58	45	47	54	624
156 m	−13	−10	−4	6	13	16	18	17	12	6	−1	−7	4
Odesa, Ukraine	57	62	30	21	34	34	42	37	37	13	35	71	473
64 m	−3	−1	2	9	15	20	22	22	18	12	9	1	10
Paris, France	56	46	35	42	57	54	59	64	55	50	51	50	619
75 m	3	4	8	11	15	18	20	19	17	12	7	4	12
Rome, Italy	71	62	57	51	46	37	15	21	63	99	129	93	744
17 m	8	9	11	14	18	22	25	25	22	17	13	10	16
Shannon, Ireland	94	67	56	53	61	57	77	79	86	86	96	117	929
2 m	5	5	7	9	12	14	16	16	14	11	8	6	10
Stockholm, Sweden	43	30	25	31	34	45	61	76	60	48	53	48	554
44 m	−3	−3	−1	5	10	15	18	17	12	7	3	0	7

ASIA

CITY	JAN.	FEB.	MAR.	APR.	MAY	JUNE	JULY	AUG.	SEPT.	OCT.	NOV.	DEC.	YEAR
Bahrain	8	18	13	8	<3	0	0	0	0	0	18	18	81
5 m	17	18	21	25	29	32	33	34	31	28	24	19	26
Bangkok, Thailand	8	20	36	58	198	160	160	175	305	206	66	5	1,397
2 m	26	28	29	30	29	29	28	28	28	28	26	25	28
Beirut, Lebanon	191	158	94	53	18	3	<3	<3	5	51	132	185	892
34 m	14	14	16	18	22	24	27	28	26	24	19	16	21
Bombay (Mumbai), India	3	3	3	<3	18	485	617	340	264	64	13	3	1,809
11 m	24	24	26	28	30	29	27	27	27	28	27	26	27
Calcutta, India	10	31	36	43	140	297	325	328	252	114	20	5	1,600
6 m	20	22	27	30	30	30	29	29	29	28	23	19	26
Colombo, Sri Lanka	89	69	147	231	371	224	135	109	160	348	315	147	2,365
7 m	26	26	27	28	28	27	27	27	27	27	26	26	27
Harbin, China	6	5	10	23	43	94	112	104	46	33	8	5	488
160 m	−18	−15	−5	6	13	19	22	21	14	4	−6	−16	3

ASIA (continued)

CITY	JAN.	FEB.	MAR.	APR.	MAY	JUNE	JULY	AUG.	SEPT.	OCT.	NOV.	DEC.	YEAR
Ho Chi Minh, Vietnam	15	3	13	43	221	330	315	269	335	269	114	56	1,984
9 m	26	27	29	30	29	28	28	28	27	27	27	26	28
Hong Kong, China	33	46	74	137	292	394	381	361	257	114	43	31	2,162
33 m	16	15	18	22	26	28	28	28	27	25	21	18	23
Jakarta, Indonesia	300	300	211	147	114	97	64	43	66	112	142	203	1,798
8 m	26	26	27	27	27	27	27	27	27	27	27	26	27
Kabul, Afghanistan	31	36	94	102	20	5	3	3	<3	15	20	10	338
1,815 m	−3	−1	6	13	18	22	25	24	20	14	7	3	12
Karachi, Pakistan	13	10	8	3	3	18	81	41	13	<3	3	5	196
4 m	19	20	24	28	30	31	30	29	28	28	24	20	26
Kazalinsk, Kazakstan	10	10	13	13	15	5	5	8	8	10	13	15	125
63 m	−12	−11	−3	6	18	23	25	23	16	8	−1	−7	7
New Delhi, India	23	18	13	8	13	74	180	172	117	10	3	10	640
218 m	14	17	23	28	33	34	31	30	29	26	20	15	25
Omsk, Russia	15	8	8	13	31	51	51	51	28	25	18	20	318
85 m	−22	−19	−12	−1	10	16	18	16	10	1	−11	−18	−1
Shanghai, China	48	58	84	94	94	180	147	142	130	71	51	36	1,135
7 m	4	5	9	14	20	24	28	28	23	19	12	7	16
Singapore	252	173	193	188	173	173	170	196	178	208	254	257	2,413
10 m	26	27	28	28	28	28	28	27	27	27	27	27	27
Tehran, Iran	46	38	46	36	13	3	3	3	3	8	20	31	246
1,220 m	2	5	9	16	21	26	30	29	25	18	12	6	17
Tokyo, Japan	48	74	107	135	147	165	142	152	234	208	97	56	1,565
6 m	3	4	7	13	17	21	25	26	23	17	11	6	14
Ulan Bator, Mongolia	<3	<3	3	5	10	28	76	51	23	5	5	3	208
1,325 m	−26	−21	−13	−1	6	14	16	14	8	−1	−13	−22	−3
Verkhoyansk, Russia	5	5	3	5	8	23	28	25	13	8	8	5	134
100 m	−50	−45	−32	−15	0	12	14	9	2	−15	−38	−48	−17

AFRICA

CITY	JAN.	FEB.	MAR.	APR.	MAY	JUNE	JULY	AUG.	SEPT.	OCT.	NOV.	DEC.	YEAR
Addis Ababa, Ethiopia	<3	3	25	135	213	201	206	239	102	28	<3	0	1,151
2,450 m	19	20	20	20	19	18	18	19	21	22	21	20	20
Antananarivo, Madag.	300	279	178	53	18	8	8	10	18	61	135	287	1,356
1,372 m	21	21	21	19	18	15	14	15	17	19	21	21	19
Cairo, Egypt	5	5	5	3	3	<3	0	0	<3	<3	3	5	28
116 m	13	15	18	21	25	28	28	28	26	24	20	15	22
Cape Town, S. Africa	15	8	18	48	79	84	89	66	43	31	18	10	508
17 m	21	21	20	17	14	13	12	13	14	16	18	19	17
Jo'burg, S. Africa	114	109	89	38	25	8	8	8	23	56	107	125	709
1,665 m	20	20	18	16	13	10	11	13	16	18	19	20	16

CITY	JAN.	FEB.	MAR.	APR.	MAY	JUNE	JULY	AUG.	SEPT.	OCT.	NOV.	DEC.	YEAR
AFRICA (continued)													
Khartoum, Sudan	<3	<3	<3	<3	3	8	53	71	18	5	<3	0	158
390 m	24	25	28	31	33	34	32	31	32	32	28	25	29
Kinshasa, Congo (D.R.)	135	145	196	196	158	8	3	3	31	119	221	142	1,354
325 m	26	26	27	27	26	24	23	24	25	26	26	26	25
Lagos, Nigeria	28	46	102	150	269	460	279	64	140	206	69	25	1,836
3 m	27	28	29	28	28	26	26	25	26	26	28	28	27
Lusaka, Zambia	231	191	142	18	3	<3	<3	0	<3	10	91	150	836
1,277 m	21	22	21	21	19	16	16	18	22	24	23	22	21
Monrovia, Liberia	31	56	97	216	516	973	996	373	744	772	236	130	5,138
23 m	26	26	27	27	26	25	24	25	25	25	26	26	26
Nairobi, Kenya	38	64	125	211	158	46	15	23	31	53	109	86	958
820 m	19	19	19	19	18	16	16	16	18	19	18	18	18
Timbuktu, Mali	<3	<3	3	<3	5	23	79	81	38	3	<3	<3	231
301 m	22	24	28	32	34	35	32	30	32	31	28	23	29
Tunis, Tunisia	64	51	41	36	18	8	3	8	33	51	48	61	419
66 m	10	11	13	16	19	23	26	27	25	20	16	11	18
Walvis Bay, Namibia	<3	5	8	3	3	<3	<3	3	<3	<3	<3	<3	23
7 m	19	19	19	18	17	16	15	14	14	15	17	18	18
AUSTRALIA, NEW ZEALAND AND ANTARCTICA													
Alice Springs, Aust.	43	33	28	10	15	13	8	8	8	18	31	38	252
579 m	29	28	25	20	15	12	12	14	18	23	26	28	21
Christchurch, N.Z.	56	43	48	48	66	66	69	48	46	43	48	56	638
10 m	16	16	14	12	9	6	6	7	9	12	14	16	11
Darwin, Australia	386	312	254	97	15	3	<3	3	13	51	119	239	1,491
30 m	29	29	29	29	28	26	25	26	28	29	30	29	28
Mawson, Antarctica	11	30	20	10	44	180	4	40	3	20	0	0	362
14 m	0	-5	-10	-14	-15	-16	-18	-18	-19	-13	-5	-1	-11
Perth, Australia	8	10	20	43	130	180	170	149	86	56	20	13	881
60 m	23	23	22	19	16	14	13	13	15	16	19	22	18
Sydney, Australia	89	102	127	135	127	117	117	76	73	71	73	73	1,181
42 m	22	22	21	18	15	13	12	13	15	18	19	21	17
NORTH AMERICA													
Anchorage, USA	20	18	15	10	13	18	41	66	66	56	25	23	371
40 m	-11	-8	-5	2	7	12	14	13	9	2	-5	-11	2
Chicago, USA	51	51	66	71	86	89	84	81	79	66	61	51	836
251 m	-4	-3	2	9	14	20	23	22	19	12	5	-1	10
Churchill, Canada	15	13	18	23	32	44	46	58	51	43	39	21	402
13 m	-28	-26	-20	-10	-2	6	12	11	5	-2	-12	-22	-7
Edmonton, Canada	25	19	19	22	43	77	89	78	39	17	16	25	466
676 m	-15	-10	-5	4	11	15	17	16	11	6	-4	-10	3
Honolulu, USA	104	66	79	48	25	18	23	28	36	48	64	104	643
12 m	23	18	19	20	22	24	25	26	26	24	22	19	22
Houston, USA	89	76	84	91	119	117	99	99	104	94	89	109	1,171
12 m	12	13	17	21	24	27	28	29	26	22	16	12	21

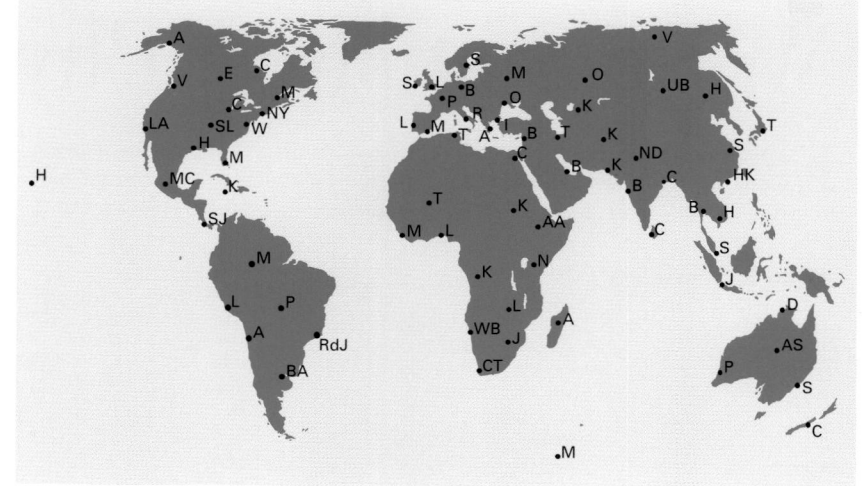

CITY	JAN.	FEB.	MAR.	APR.	MAY	JUNE	JULY	AUG.	SEPT.	OCT.	NOV.	DEC.	YEAR
NORTH AMERICA (continued)													
Kingston, Jamaica	23	15	23	31	102	89	38	91	99	180	74	36	800
34 m	25	25	25	26	26	28	28	28	27	27	26	26	26
Los Angeles, USA	79	76	71	25	10	3	<3	<3	5	15	31	66	381
95 m	13	14	14	16	17	19	21	22	21	18	16	14	17
Mexico City, Mexico	13	5	10	20	53	119	170	152	130	51	18	8	747
2,309 m	12	13	16	18	19	19	17	18	18	16	14	13	16
Miami, USA	71	53	64	81	173	178	155	160	203	234	71	51	1,516
8 m	20	20	22	23	25	27	28	28	27	25	22	21	24
Montréal, Canada	72	65	74	74	66	82	90	92	88	76	81	87	946
57 m	-10	-9	-3	-6	13	18	21	20	15	9	2	-7	6
New York City, USA	94	97	91	81	81	84	107	109	86	89	76	91	1,092
96 m	-1	-1	3	10	16	20	23	23	21	15	7	2	11
St Louis, USA	58	64	89	97	114	114	89	86	81	74	71	64	1,001
173 m	0	1	7	13	19	24	26	26	22	15	8	2	14
San José, Costa Rica	15	5	20	46	229	241	211	241	305	300	145	41	1,798
1,146 m	19	19	21	21	22	21	21	21	21	20	20	19	20
Vancouver, Canada	154	115	101	60	52	45	32	41	67	114	150	182	1,113
14 m	3	5	6	9	12	15	17	17	14	10	6	4	10
Washington, DC, USA	86	76	91	84	94	99	112	109	94	74	66	79	1,064
22 m	1	2	7	12	18	23	25	24	20	14	8	3	13
SOUTH AMERICA													
Antofagasta, Chile	0	0	0	<3	<3	3	5	3	<3	3	<3	0	13
94 m	21	21	20	18	16	15	14	14	15	16	18	19	17
Buenos Aires, Arg.	79	71	109	89	76	61	56	61	79	86	84	99	950
27 m	23	23	21	17	13	9	10	11	13	15	19	22	16
Lima, Peru	3	<3	<3	<3	5	5	8	8	8	3	3	<3	41
120 m	23	24	24	22	19	17	17	16	17	18	19	21	20
Manaus, Brazil	249	231	262	221	170	84	58	38	46	107	142	203	1,811
44 m	28	28	28	27	28	28	28	28	29	29	29	28	28
Paraná, Brazil	287	236	239	102	13	<3	3	5	28	127	231	310	1,582
260 m	23	23	23	23	21	21	21	22	24	24	24	23	23
Rio de Janeiro, Brazil	125	122	130	107	79	53	41	43	66	79	104	137	1,082
61 m	26	26	25	24	22	21	21	21	21	22	23	25	23

World Statistics: Physical Dimensions

Each topic list is divided into continents and within a continent the items are listed in order of size. The bottom part of many of the lists is selective in order to give examples from as many different countries as possible. The order of the continents is as in the atlas, Europe through to South America. The world top ten are shown in square brackets; in the case of mountains this has not been done because the world top 30 are all in Asia. The figures are rounded as appropriate.

WORLD, CONTINENTS, OCEANS

THE WORLD	km²	miles²	%
The World	509,450,000	196,672,000	–
Land	149,450,000	57,688,000	29.3
Water	360,000,000	138,984,000	70.7
Asia	44,500,000	17,177,000	29.8
Africa	30,302,000	11,697,000	20.3
North America	24,241,000	9,357,000	16.2
South America	17,793,000	6,868,000	11.9
Antarctica	14,100,000	5,443,000	9.4
Europe	9,957,000	3,843,000	6.7
Australia & Oceania	8,557,000	3,303,000	5.7
Pacific Ocean	179,679,000	69,356,000	49.9
Atlantic Ocean	92,373,000	35,657,000	25.7
Indian Ocean	73,917,000	28,532,000	20.5
Arctic Ocean	14,090,000	5,439,000	3.9

SEAS

PACIFIC	km²	miles²
South China Sea	2,974,600	1,148,500
Bering Sea	2,268,000	875,000
Sea of Okhotsk	1,528,000	590,000
East China & Yellow	1,249,000	482,000
Sea of Japan	1,008,000	389,000
Gulf of California	162,000	62,500
Bass Strait	75,000	29,000

ATLANTIC	km²	miles²
Caribbean Sea	2,766,000	1,068,000
Mediterranean Sea	2,516,000	971,000
Gulf of Mexico	1,543,000	596,000
Hudson Bay	1,232,000	476,000
North Sea	575,000	223,000
Black Sea	462,000	178,000
Baltic Sea	422,170	163,000
Gulf of St Lawrence	238,000	92,000

INDIAN	km²	miles²
Red Sea	438,000	169,000
The Gulf	239,000	92,000

MOUNTAINS

EUROPE		m	ft
Elbrus	Russia	5,642	18,510
Mont Blanc	France/Italy	4,807	15,771
Monte Rosa	Italy/Switzerland	4,634	15,203
Dom	Switzerland	4,545	14,911
Liskamm	Switzerland	4,527	14,852
Weisshorn	Switzerland	4,505	14,780
Taschorn	Switzerland	4,490	14,730
Matterhorn/Cervino	Italy/Switz.	4,478	14,691
Mont Maudit	France/Italy	4,465	14,649
Dent Blanche	Switzerland	4,356	14,291
Nadelhorn	Switzerland	4,327	14,196
Grandes Jorasses	France/Italy	4,208	13,806
Jungfrau	Switzerland	4,158	13,642
Barre des Ecrins	France	4,103	13,461
Gran Paradiso	Italy	4,061	13,323
Piz Bernina	Italy/Switzerland	4,049	13,284
Eiger	Switzerland	3,970	13,025
Monte Viso	Italy	3,841	12,602
Grossglockner	Austria	3,797	12,457
Wildspitze	Austria	3,772	12,382
Monte Disgrazia	Italy	3,678	12,066
Mulhacén	Spain	3,478	11,411
Pico de Aneto	Spain	3,404	11,168
Marmolada	Italy	3,342	10,964
Etna	Italy	3,340	10,958
Zugspitze	Germany	2,962	9,718
Musala	Bulgaria	2,925	9,596
Olympus	Greece	2,917	9,570
Triglav	Slovenia	2,863	9,393
Monte Cinto	France (Corsica)	2,710	8,891
Galdhøpiggen	Norway	2,468	8,100
Ben Nevis	UK	1,343	4,406

ASIA		m	ft
Everest	China/Nepal	8,850	29,035
K2 (Godwin Austen)	China/Kashmir	8,611	28,251
Kanchenjunga	India/Nepal	8,598	28,208
Lhotse	China/Nepal	8,516	27,939
Makalu	China/Nepal	8,481	27,824
Cho Oyu	China/Nepal	8,201	26,906
Dhaulagiri	Nepal	8,172	26,811
Manaslu	Nepal	8,156	26,758
Nanga Parbat	Kashmir	8,126	26,660
Annapurna	Nepal	8,078	26,502
Gasherbrum	China/Kashmir	8,068	26,469
Broad Peak	China/Kashmir	8,051	26,414
Xixabangma	China	8,012	26,286
Kangbachen	India/Nepal	7,902	25,925
Jannu	India/Nepal	7,902	25,925
Gayachung Kang	Nepal	7,897	25,909
Himalchuli	Nepal	7,893	25,896
Disteghil Sar	Kashmir	7,885	25,869
Nuptse	Nepal	7,879	25,849
Khunyang Chhish	Kashmir	7,852	25,761
Masherbrum	Kashmir	7,821	25,659
Nanda Devi	India	7,817	25,646
Rakaposhi	Kashmir	7,788	25,551
Batura	Kashmir	7,785	25,541
Namche Barwa	China	7,756	25,446
Kamet	India	7,756	25,446
Soltoro Kangri	Kashmir	7,742	25,400
Gurla Mandhata	China	7,728	25,354
Trivor	Pakistan	7,720	25,328
Kongur Shan	China	7,719	25,324
Tirich Mir	Pakistan	7,690	25,229
K'ula Shan	Bhutan/China	7,543	24,747
Pik Kommunizma	Tajikistan	7,495	24,590
Demavend	Iran	5,604	18,386
Ararat	Turkey	5,165	16,945
Gunong Kinabalu	Malaysia (Borneo)	4,101	13,455
Yu Shan	Taiwan	3,997	13,113
Fuji-San	Japan	3,776	12,388

AFRICA		m	ft
Kilimanjaro	Tanzania	5,895	19,340
Mt Kenya	Kenya	5,199	17,057
Ruwenzori (Margherita)	Uganda/Congo (D.R.)	5,109	16,762
Ras Dashan	Ethiopia	4,620	15,157
Meru	Tanzania	4,565	14,977
Karisimbi	Rwanda/Congo (D.R.)	4,507	14,787
Mt Elgon	Kenya/Uganda	4,321	14,176
Batu	Ethiopia	4,307	14,130
Guna	Ethiopia	4,231	13,882
Toubkal	Morocco	4,165	13,665
Irhil Mgoun	Morocco	4,071	13,356
Mt Cameroon	Cameroon	4,070	13,353
Amba Ferit	Ethiopia	3,875	13,042
Pico del Teide	Spain (Tenerife)	3,718	12,198
Thabana Ntlenyana	Lesotho	3,482	11,424
Emi Koussi	Chad	3,415	11,204
Mt aux Sources	Lesotho/S. Africa	3,282	10,768
Mt Piton	Réunion	3,069	10,069

OCEANIA		m	ft
Puncak Jaya	Indonesia	5,029	16,499
Puncak Trikora	Indonesia	4,750	15,584
Puncak Mandala	Indonesia	4,702	15,427
Mt Wilhelm	Papua NG	4,508	14,790
Mauna Kea	USA (Hawaii)	4,205	13,796
Mauna Loa	USA (Hawaii)	4,169	13,681
Mt Cook (Aoraki)	New Zealand	3,753	12,313
Mt Balbi	Solomon Is.	2,439	8,002
Orohena	Tahiti	2,241	7,352
Mt Kosciuszko	Australia	2,237	7,339

NORTH AMERICA		m	ft
Mt McKinley (Denali)	USA (Alaska)	6,194	20,321
Mt Logan	Canada	5,959	19,551
Citlaltepetl	Mexico	5,700	18,701
Mt St Elias	USA/Canada	5,489	18,008
Popocatepetl	Mexico	5,452	17,887

NORTH AMERICA (continued)		m	ft
Mt Foraker	USA (Alaska)	5,304	17,401
Ixtaccihuatl	Mexico	5,286	17,342
Lucania	Canada	5,227	17,149
Mt Steele	Canada	5,073	16,644
Mt Bona	USA (Alaska)	5,005	16,420
Mt Blackburn	USA (Alaska)	4,996	16,391
Mt Sanford	USA (Alaska)	4,940	16,207
Mt Wood	Canada	4,848	15,905
Nevado de Toluca	Mexico	4,670	15,321
Mt Fairweather	USA (Alaska)	4,663	15,298
Mt Hunter	USA (Alaska)	4,442	14,573
Mt Whitney	USA	4,418	14,495
Mt Elbert	USA	4,399	14,432
Mt Harvard	USA	4,395	14,419
Mt Rainier	USA	4,392	14,409
Blanca Peak	USA	4,372	14,344
Longs Peak	USA	4,345	14,255
Tajumulco	Guatemala	4,220	13,845
Grand Teton	USA	4,197	13,770
Mt Waddington	Canada	3,994	13,104
Mt Robson	Canada	3,954	12,972
Chirripó Grande	Costa Rica	3,837	12,589
Pico Duarte	Dominican Rep.	3,175	10,417

SOUTH AMERICA		m	ft
Aconcagua	Argentina	6,960	22,834
Bonete	Argentina	6,872	22,546
Ojos del Salado	Argentina/Chile	6,863	22,516
Pissis	Argentina	6,779	22,241
Mercedario	Argentina/Chile	6,770	22,211
Huascaran	Peru	6,768	22,204
Llullaillaco	Argentina/Chile	6,723	22,057
Nudo de Cachi	Argentina	6,720	22,047
Yerupaja	Peru	6,632	21,758
N. de Tres Cruces	Argentina/Chile	6,620	21,719
Incahuasi	Argentina/Chile	6,601	21,654
Cerro Galan	Argentina	6,600	21,654
Tupungato	Argentina/Chile	6,570	21,555
Sajama	Bolivia	6,542	21,463
Illimani	Bolivia	6,485	21,276
Coropuna	Peru	6,425	21,079
Ausangate	Peru	6,384	20,945
Cerro del Toro	Argentina	6,380	20,932
Siula Grande	Peru	6,356	20,853
Chimborazo	Ecuador	6,267	20,561
Alpamayo	Peru	5,947	19,511
Cotapaxi	Ecuador	5,896	19,344
Pico Colon	Colombia	5,800	19,029
Pico Bolivar	Venezuela	5,007	16,427

ANTARCTICA		m	ft
Vinson Massif		4,897	16,066
Mt Kirkpatrick		4,528	14,855
Mt Markham		4,349	14,268

OCEAN DEPTHS

ATLANTIC OCEAN	m	ft	
Puerto Rico (Milwaukee) Deep	9,220	30,249	[7]
Cayman Trench	7,680	25,197	[10]
Gulf of Mexico	5,203	17,070	
Mediterranean Sea	5,121	16,801	
Black Sea	2,211	7,254	
North Sea	660	2,165	
Baltic Sea	463	1,519	
Hudson Bay	258	846	

INDIAN OCEAN	m	ft
Java Trench	7,450	24,442
Red Sea	2,635	8,454
Persian Gulf	73	239

PACIFIC OCEAN	m	ft	
Mariana Trench	11,022	36,161	[1]
Tonga Trench	10,882	35,702	[2]
Japan Trench	10,554	34,626	[3]
Kuril Trench	10,542	34,587	[4]
Mindanao Trench	10,497	34,439	[5]
Kermadec Trench	10,047	32,962	[6]

PACIFIC OCEAN (continued)	m	ft	
Peru–Chile Trench	8,050	26,410	[8]
Aleutian Trench	7,822	25,662	[9]

ARCTIC OCEAN	m	ft
Molloy Deep	5,608	18,399

LAND LOWS

		m	ft
Dead Sea	Asia	−411	−1,348
Lake Assal	Africa	−156	−512
Death Valley	N. America	−86	−282
Valdés Peninsula	S. America	−40	−131
Caspian Sea	Europe	−28	−92
Lake Eyre North	Oceania	−16	−52

RIVERS

EUROPE		km	miles	
Volga	Caspian Sea	3,700	2,300	
Danube	Black Sea	2,850	1,770	
Ural	Caspian Sea	2,535	1,575	
Dnepr (Dnipro)	Black Sea	2,285	1,420	
Kama	Volga	2,030	1,260	
Don	Black Sea	1,990	1,240	
Petchora	Arctic Ocean	1,790	1,110	
Oka	Volga	1,480	920	
Belaya	Kama	1,420	880	
Dnister (Dniester)	Black Sea	1,400	870	
Vyatka	Kama	1,370	850	
Rhine	North Sea	1,320	820	
N. Dvina	Arctic Ocean	1,290	800	
Desna	Dnepr (Dnipro)	1,190	740	
Elbe	North Sea	1,145	710	
Wisla	Baltic Sea	1,090	675	
Loire	Atlantic Ocean	1,020	635	

ASIA		km	miles	
Yangtze	Pacific Ocean	6,380	3,960	[3]
Yenisey–Angara	Arctic Ocean	5,550	3,445	[5]
Huang He	Pacific Ocean	5,464	3,395	[6]
Ob–Irtysh	Arctic Ocean	5,410	3,360	[7]
Mekong	Pacific Ocean	4,500	2,795	[9]
Amur	Pacific Ocean	4,400	2,730	[10]
Lena	Arctic Ocean	4,400	2,730	
Irtysh	Ob	4,250	2,640	
Yenisey	Arctic Ocean	4,090	2,540	
Ob	Arctic Ocean	3,680	2,285	
Indus	Indian Ocean	3,100	1,925	
Brahmaputra	Indian Ocean	2,900	1,800	
Syrdarya	Aral Sea	2,860	1,775	
Salween	Indian Ocean	2,800	1,740	
Euphrates	Indian Ocean	2,700	1,675	
Vilyuy	Lena	2,650	1,645	
Kolyma	Arctic Ocean	2,600	1,615	
Amudarya	Aral Sea	2,540	1,575	
Ural	Caspian Sea	2,535	1,575	
Ganges	Indian Ocean	2,510	1,560	
Si Kiang	Pacific Ocean	2,100	1,305	
Irrawaddy	Indian Ocean	2,010	1,250	
Tarim–Yarkand	Lop Nor	2,000	1,240	
Tigris	Indian Ocean	1,900	1,180	

AFRICA		km	miles	
Nile	Mediterranean	6,670	4,140	[1]
Congo	Atlantic Ocean	4,670	2,900	[8]
Niger	Atlantic Ocean	4,180	2,595	
Zambezi	Indian Ocean	3,540	2,200	
Oubangi/Uele	Congo (D.R.)	2,250	1,400	
Kasai	Congo (D.R.)	1,950	1,210	
Shaballe	Indian Ocean	1,930	1,200	
Orange	Atlantic Ocean	1,860	1,155	
Cubango	Okavango Swamps	1,800	1,120	
Limpopo	Indian Ocean	1,600	995	
Senegal	Atlantic Ocean	1,600	995	
Volta	Atlantic Ocean	1,500	930	

AUSTRALIA		km	miles
Murray–Darling	Indian Ocean	3,750	2,330
Darling	Murray	3,070	1,905
Murray	Indian Ocean	2,575	1,600
Murrumbidgee	Murray	1,690	1,050

NORTH AMERICA		km	miles	
Mississippi–Missouri	Gulf of Mexico	6,020	3,740	[4]
Mackenzie	Arctic Ocean	4,240	2,630	
Mississippi	Gulf of Mexico	3,780	2,350	
Missouri	Mississippi	3,780	2,350	
Yukon	Pacific Ocean	3,185	1,980	
Rio Grande	Gulf of Mexico	3,030	1,880	

NORTH AMERICA (continued)		km	miles
Arkansas	Mississippi	2,340	1,450
Colorado	Pacific Ocean	2,330	1,445
Red	Mississippi	2,040	1,270
Columbia	Pacific Ocean	1,950	1,210
Saskatchewan	Lake Winnipeg	1,940	1,205
Snake	Columbia	1,670	1,040
Churchill	Hudson Bay	1,600	990
Ohio	Mississippi	1,580	980
Brazos	Gulf of Mexico	1,400	870
St Lawrence	Atlantic Ocean	1,170	730

SOUTH AMERICA		km	miles	
Amazon	Atlantic Ocean	6,450	4,010	[2]
Paraná–Plate	Atlantic Ocean	4,500	2,800	
Purus	Amazon	3,350	2,080	
Madeira	Amazon	3,200	1,990	
São Francisco	Atlantic Ocean	2,900	1,800	
Paraná	Plate	2,800	1,740	
Tocantins	Atlantic Ocean	2,750	1,710	
Paraguay	Paraná	2,550	1,580	
Orinoco	Atlantic Ocean	2,500	1,550	
Pilcomayo	Paraná	2,500	1,550	
Araguaia	Tocantins	2,250	1,400	
Juruá	Amazon	2,000	1,240	
Xingu	Amazon	1,980	1,230	
Ucayali	Amazon	1,900	1,180	
Marañón	Amazon	1,600	990	
Uruguay	Plate	1,600	990	

LAKES

EUROPE		km²	miles²
Lake Ladoga	Russia	17,700	6,800
Lake Onega	Russia	9,700	3,700
Saimaa system	Finland	8,000	3,100
Vänern	Sweden	5,500	2,100
Rybinskoye Res.	Russia	4,700	1,800

ASIA		km²	miles²	
Caspian Sea	Asia	371,800	143,550	[1]
Lake Baykal	Russia	30,500	11,780	[8]
Aral Sea	Kazakhstan/Uzbekistan	28,687	11,086	[10]
Tonlé Sap	Cambodia	20,000	7,700	
Lake Balqash	Kazakhstan	18,500	7,100	
Lake Dongting	China	12,000	4,600	
Lake Ysyk	Kyrgyzstan	6,200	2,400	
Lake Orumiyeh	Iran	5,900	2,300	
Lake Koko	China	5,700	2,200	
Lake Poyang	China	5,000	1,900	
Lake Khanka	China/Russia	4,400	1,700	
Lake Van	Turkey	3,500	1,400	

AFRICA		km²	miles²	
Lake Victoria	E. Africa	68,000	26,000	[3]
Lake Tanganyika	C. Africa	33,000	13,000	[6]
Lake Malawi/Nyasa	E. Africa	29,600	11,430	[9]
Lake Chad	C. Africa	25,000	9,700	
Lake Turkana	Ethiopia/Kenya	8,500	3,300	
Lake Volta	Ghana	8,500	3,300	
Lake Bangweulu	Zambia	8,000	3,100	
Lake Rukwa	Tanzania	7,000	2,700	
Lake Mai-Ndombe	Congo (D.R.)	6,500	2,500	
Lake Kariba	Zambia/Zimbabwe	5,300	2,000	
Lake Albert	Uganda/Congo (D.R.)	5,300	2,000	
Lake Nasser	Egypt/Sudan	5,200	2,000	
Lake Mweru	Zambia/Congo (D.R.)	4,900	1,900	
Lake Cabora Bassa	Mozambique	4,500	1,700	
Lake Kyoga	Uganda	4,400	1,700	
Lake Tana	Ethiopia	3,630	1,400	

AUSTRALIA		km²	miles²
Lake Eyre	Australia	8,900	3,400
Lake Torrens	Australia	5,800	2,200
Lake Gairdner	Australia	4,800	1,900

NORTH AMERICA		km²	miles²	
Lake Superior	Canada/USA	82,350	31,800	[2]
Lake Huron	Canada/USA	59,600	23,010	[4]
Lake Michigan	USA	58,000	22,400	[5]
Great Bear Lake	Canada	31,800	12,280	[7]
Great Slave Lake	Canada	28,500	11,000	
Lake Erie	Canada/USA	25,700	9,900	
Lake Winnipeg	Canada	24,400	9,400	
Lake Ontario	Canada/USA	19,500	7,500	
Lake Nicaragua	Nicaragua	8,200	3,200	
Lake Athabasca	Canada	8,100	3,100	
Smallwood Reservoir	Canada	6,530	2,520	
Reindeer Lake	Canada	6,400	2,500	
Nettiling Lake	Canada	5,500	2,100	
Lake Winnipegosis	Canada	5,400	2,100	

SOUTH AMERICA		km²	miles²
Lake Titicaca	Bolivia/Peru	8,300	3,200
Lake Poopo	Bolivia	2,800	1,100

ISLANDS

EUROPE		km²	miles²	
Great Britain	UK	229,880	88,700	[8]
Iceland	Atlantic Ocean	103,000	39,800	
Ireland	Ireland/UK	84,400	32,600	
Novaya Zemlya (N.)	Russia	48,200	18,600	
W. Spitzbergen	Norway	39,000	15,100	
Novaya Zemlya (S.)	Russia	33,200	12,800	
Sicily	Italy	25,500	9,800	
Sardinia	Italy	24,000	9,300	
N.E. Spitzbergen	Norway	15,000	5,600	
Corsica	France	8,700	3,400	
Crete	Greece	8,350	3,200	
Zealand	Denmark	6,850	2,600	

ASIA		km²	miles²	
Borneo	S. E. Asia	744,360	287,400	[3]
Sumatra	Indonesia	473,600	182,860	[6]
Honshu	Japan	230,500	88,980	[7]
Sulawesi (Celebes)	Indonesia	189,000	73,000	
Java	Indonesia	126,700	48,900	
Luzon	Philippines	104,700	40,400	
Mindanao	Philippines	101,500	39,200	
Hokkaido	Japan	78,400	30,300	
Sakhalin	Russia	74,060	28,600	
Sri Lanka	Indian Ocean	65,600	25,300	
Taiwan	Pacific Ocean	36,000	13,900	
Kyushu	Japan	35,700	13,800	
Hainan	China	34,000	13,100	
Timor	Indonesia	33,600	13,000	
Shikoku	Japan	18,800	7,300	
Halmahera	Indonesia	18,000	6,900	
Ceram	Indonesia	17,150	6,600	
Sumbawa	Indonesia	15,450	6,000	
Flores	Indonesia	15,200	5,900	
Samar	Philippines	13,100	5,100	
Negros	Philippines	12,700	4,900	
Bangka	Indonesia	12,000	4,600	
Palawan	Philippines	12,000	4,600	
Panay	Philippines	11,500	4,400	
Sumba	Indonesia	11,100	4,300	
Mindoro	Philippines	9,750	3,800	

AFRICA		km²	miles²	
Madagascar	Indian Ocean	587,040	226,660	[4]
Socotra	Indian Ocean	3,600	1,400	
Réunion	Indian Ocean	2,500	965	
Tenerife	Atlantic Ocean	2,350	900	
Mauritius	Indian Ocean	1,865	720	

OCEANIA		km²	miles²	
New Guinea	Indon./Papua NG	821,030	317,000	[2]
New Zealand (S.)	Pacific Ocean	150,500	58,100	
New Zealand (N.)	Pacific Ocean	114,700	44,300	
Tasmania	Australia	67,800	26,200	
New Britain	Papua NG	37,800	14,600	
New Caledonia	Pacific Ocean	19,100	7,400	
Viti Levu	Fiji	10,500	4,100	
Hawaii	Pacific Ocean	10,450	4,000	
Bougainville	Papua NG	9,600	3,700	
Guadalcanal	Solomon Is.	6,500	2,500	
Vanua Levu	Fiji	5,550	2,100	
New Ireland	Papua NG	3,200	1,200	

NORTH AMERICA		km²	miles²	
Greenland	Atlantic Ocean	2,175,600	839,800	[1]
Baffin Is.	Canada	508,000	196,100	[5]
Victoria Is.	Canada	212,200	81,900	[9]
Ellesmere Is.	Canada	212,000	81,800	[10]
Cuba	Caribbean Sea	110,860	42,800	
Newfoundland	Canada	110,680	42,700	
Hispaniola	Dom. Rep./Haiti	76,200	29,400	
Banks Is.	Canada	67,000	25,900	
Devon Is.	Canada	54,500	21,000	
Melville Is.	Canada	42,400	16,400	
Vancouver Is.	Canada	32,150	12,400	
Somerset Is.	Canada	24,300	9,400	
Jamaica	Caribbean Sea	11,400	4,400	
Puerto Rico	Atlantic Ocean	8,900	3,400	
Cape Breton Is.	Canada	4,000	1,500	

SOUTH AMERICA		km²	miles²
Tierra del Fuego	Argentina/Chile	47,000	18,100
Falkland Is. (East)	Atlantic Ocean	6,800	2,600
South Georgia	Atlantic Ocean	4,200	1,600
Galapagos (Isabela)	Pacific Ocean	2,250	870

World: Regions in the News

YUGOSLAVIA
Population 10,761,000
(Serb 62.6%, Albanian 16.5%,
Montenegrin 5%, Hungarian 3.3%,
Muslim 3.2%)
Serbia Population: 5,799,800
(Serb 87.7%, excluding the
provinces of Kosovo and
Vojvodina)
Kosovo Population: 2,084,4000
(Albanian 81.6%, Serb 9.9%)
Vojvodena Population: 1,980,800
(Serb 56.8%, Hungarian 16.9%)
Montenegro Population: 635,000
(Montenegrin 61.9%, Muslim
14.6%, Albanian 7%)

CROATIA
Population: 4,960,000
(Croat 78.1%, Serb 12.2%)

SLOVENIA
Population: 2,055,000
(Slovene 88%, Croat 3%, Serb 2%)

MACEDONIA (F. Y. R. O. M.)
Population: 2,157,000
(Macedonian 64%, Albanian 21.7%,
Turkish 5%, Romanian 3%,
Serb 2%)

BOSNIA-HERZEGOVINA
Population: 4,601,000
(Muslim 49%, Serb 31.2%,
Croat 17.2%)

FORMER YUGOSLAVIA

International boundaries
Republic boundaries
Province boundaries
Capital cities
Dayton Peace Agreement Boundary
Muslim–Croat Federation
Bosnian Serb Republic

KASHMIR

Aksai Chin – Administered by China, claimed by India
Shaksam Valley – Administered by China, claimed by India
Azad Kashmir – Administered by Pakistan, claimed by India
Northern Areas – Administered by Pakistan, claimed by India
Siachen Glacier – Administered by India, claimed by Pakistan
Jammu and Kashmir – Administered by India

FORMER YUGOSLAVIA
THE CAUCASUS
KASHMIR
THE NEAR EAST
NEW STATES IN INDIA

THREE NEW STATES IN INDIA

Chhattisgarh: Created 01/11/00
(formerly part of Madhya Pradesh)
Population: 17.6 million
Capital: Raipur

Uttaranchal: Created 09/11/00
(formerly part of Uttar Pradesh)
Population: 7.0 million
Provisional capital: Dehra Dun

Jharkhand: Created 15/11/00
(formerly part of Bihar)
Population: 26.9 million
Capital: Ranchi

THE NEAR EAST

1949 Armistice Line
1974 Cease-fire Line
Palestinian control
Joint Israeli/ Palestinian control
Efrata Main Jewish settlements in the West Bank and Gaza Strip
Halhul Main Palestinian Arab towns in the West Bank and Gaza Strip
Road corridor linking Gaza and West Bank

ISRAEL
Population: 5,321,000 (inc. East
Jerusalem and Jewish settlers in the
areas under Israeli administration.
Jewish 82%, Arab Muslim 13.8%,
Arab Christian 2.5%, Druze 1.7%)

West Bank
Population: 1,122,900 (Palestinian
Arabs 97% [of whom Arab Muslim
85%, Jewish 7%, Christian 8%])

Gaza Strip
Population: 748,400 (Arab 98%)

JORDAN
Population: 5,558,000 (Arab 99%
[of whom about 50% are Palestinian
Arab])

LEBANON
Population: 3,327,000 (Arab 93%
[of whom 83% are Lebanese Arab and
10% Palestinian Arab])

COUNTRIES AND REPUBLICS OF THE CAUCASUS REGION
RUSSIAN REPUBLICS
North Ossetia (Alania)
Population: 695,000
(Ossetian 53%, Russian 29%,
Chechen 5.2%, Armenian 1.9%)
Chechenia Population: 1,308,000
(Chechen and Ingush 70.7%,
Russian 23.1%, Armenian 1.2%)
Ingushetia (Split from Chechenia
in June 1993) Population: 250,000
GEORGIA
Population: 5,777,000
(Georgian 70.1%, Armenian 8.1%,
Russian 6.3%, Azerbaijani 5.7%,
Ossetian 3%, Greek 2%,
Abkhazian 2%)
Abkhazia Population: 537,500
(Georgian 45.7%, Abkhazian 17.8%,
Armenian 14.6%, Russian 14.3%)
Ajaria Population: 382,000
(Georgian 82.8%, Russian 7.7%,
Armenian 4%)
ARMENIA
Population: 3,968,000
(Armenian 93%, Azerbaijani 3%)
Nagorno-Karabakh
Population: 192,400 (Armenian
76.9%, Azerbaijani 21.5%)
AZERBAIJAN
Population: 8,324,000
(Azerbaijani 83%, Russian 6%,
Armenian 6%, Lezgin 2%)
Naxçivan Population: 300,400

THE CAUCASUS

International boundaries
Republic boundaries

Georgia, Armenia and Azerbaijan
achieved independence in 1991.
Abkhazia, Ajaria and South Ossetia
seek independence from Georgia.
Chechenia has been trying to break
away from Russia since 1991, but
Russia has resisted with military force.
Hostility continues between
Armenia and Azerbaijan over the
enclave of Nagorno-Karabakh.

THE EARTH
IN SPACE

THE UNIVERSE 2

STAR CHARTS AND CONSTELLATIONS 4

THE SOLAR SYSTEM 8

THE EARTH: TIME AND MOTION 10

THE EARTH FROM SPACE 12

THE DYNAMIC EARTH 14

EARTHQUAKES AND VOLCANOES 16

FORCES OF NATURE 18

OCEANS AND ICE 20

THE EARTH'S ATMOSPHERE 22

CLIMATE AND WEATHER 24

WATER AND LAND USE 26

THE NATURAL WORLD 28

THE HUMAN WORLD 30

LANGUAGES AND RELIGIONS 32

INTERNATIONAL ORGANIZATIONS 34

AGRICULTURE 36

ENERGY AND MINERALS 38

WORLD ECONOMIES 40

TRADE AND COMMERCE 42

TRAVEL AND COMMUNICATIONS 44

THE WORLD TODAY 46

The Universe

The depths of the Universe
This photograph shows some of the 1,500 or more galaxies that were recorded in the montage of photographs taken by the Hubble Space Telescope in 1995.

Just before Christmas 1995, the Hubble Space Telescope, which is in orbit about 580 km [360 miles] above the Earth, focused on a tiny area in distant space. Over a ten-day period, photographs taken by the telescope revealed unknown galaxies billions of times fainter than the human eye can see.

Because the light from these distant objects has taken so long to reach us, the photographs transmitted from the telescope and released to the media were the deepest look into space that astronomers have ever seen. The features they revealed were in existence when the Universe was less than a billion years old.

The Hubble Space Telescope is operated by the Space Telescope Science Institute in America and was launched in April 1990. The photographs it took of the Hubble Deep Field have been described by NASA as the biggest advance in astronomy since the work of the Italian scientist Galileo in the early 17th century. US scientists described these astonishing photographs as 'postcards from the edge of space and time'.

THE BIG BANG

According to research published in 2001, the Universe was created, and 'time' began, about 12,500 million (or 12.5 billion) years ago, though earlier estimates have ranged from 8 to 24 billion years. Following a colossal explosion, called the 'Big Bang', the Universe expanded in the first millionth of a second of its existence

The End of the Universe
The diagram shows two theories concerning the fate of the Universe. One theory, top, suggests that the Universe will expand indefinitely, moving into an immense dark graveyard. Another theory, bottom, suggests that the galaxies will fall back until everything is again concentrated in one point in a so-called 'Big Crunch'. This might then be followed by a new 'Big Bang'.

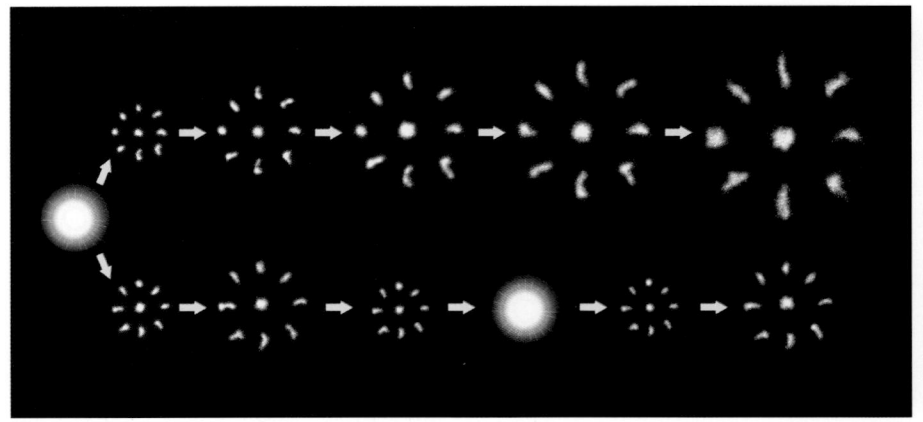

from a dimensionless point of infinite mass and density into a fireball about 30 billion km [19 million miles] across. The Universe has been expanding ever since, as demonstrated in the 1920s by Edwin Hubble, the American astronomer after whom the Hubble Space Telescope was named.

The temperature at the end of the first second was perhaps 10 billion degrees – far too hot for composite atomic nuclei to exist. As a result, the fireball consisted mainly of radiation mixed with microscopic particles of matter. Almost a million years passed before the Universe was cool enough for atoms to form.

A few billion years later, atoms in regions where matter was relatively dense began, under the influence of gravity, to move together to form proto-galaxies – masses of gas separated by empty space. The proto-galaxies were dark, because the Universe had cooled. But a few billion years later, stars began to form within the proto-galaxies as particles were drawn together. The internal pressure produced as matter condensed created the high temperatures required to cause nuclear fusion. Stars were born and later destroyed. Each generation of stars fed on the debris of extinct ones. Each generation produced larger atoms, increasing the number of different chemical elements.

THE GALAXIES

At least a billion galaxies are scattered through the Universe, though the discoveries made by the Hubble Space Telescope suggest that there may be far more than once thought, and some estimates are as high as 100 billion. The largest galaxies contain trillions of stars, while small ones contain less than a billion.

Galaxies tend to occur in groups or clusters, while some clusters appear to be grouped in vast superclusters. Our Local Cluster includes the spiral Milky Way galaxy, whose diameter is about 100,000 light-years; one light-year, the distance that light travels in one year, measures about 9,500 billion km [5,900 billion miles]. The Milky Way is a huge galaxy, shaped like a disk with a bulge at the centre. It is larger, brighter and more massive than many other known galaxies. It contains about 100 billion stars which rotate around the centre of the galaxy in the same direction as the Sun does.

One medium-sized star in the Milky Way galaxy is the Sun. After its formation, about 5 billion years ago, there was enough leftover matter around it to create the planets, asteroids,

The Home Galaxy
This schematic plan shows that our Solar System is located in one of the spiral arms of the Milky Way galaxy, a little less than 30,000 light-years from its centre. The centre of the Milky Way galaxy is not visible from Earth. Instead, it is masked by light-absorbing clouds of interstellar dust.

The Milky Way
This section of the Milky Way is dominated by Sirius, the Dog Star, top centre, in the constellation of Canis Major. Sirius is the brightest star in the sky.

moons and other bodies that together form our Solar System. The Solar System rotates around the centre of the Milky Way galaxy approximately every 225 million years.

Recent discoveries have revealed that other stars similar to our Sun have planets orbiting around them, while evidence from the Hubble Space Telescope suggests that the raw materials from which planets are formed is common in dusty disks around many stars. This provokes one of the most intriguing of all the questions that has ever faced humanity. If there are other planets in the Universe, then do living organisms exist elsewhere?

Before the time of Galileo, people thought that the Earth lay at the centre of the Universe. But we now know that our Solar System and even the Milky Way galaxy are tiny specks in the Universe as a whole. Perhaps our planet is also not unique in being the only one to support intelligent life.

Star Charts and Constellations

THE BRIGHTEST STARS

The 15 brightest stars visible from northern Europe. Magnitudes are given to the nearest tenth.

Sirius	−1.5
Arcturus	0.0
Vega	0.0
Capella	0.1
Rigel	0.1
Procyon	0.4
Betelgeuse	0.4
Altair	0.8
Aldebaran	0.8
Antares	1.0
Spica	1.0
Pollux	1.1
Fomalhaut	1.2
Deneb	1.2
Regulus	1.3

The Plough

The Plough, or Big Dipper, above glowing yellow clouds lit by city lights. It is part of a larger group called Ursa Major one of the best-known constellations of the northern hemisphere. The two bright stars to the lower right of the photograph (Merak and Dubhe) are known as the Pointers because they show the way to the Pole Star.

On a clear night, under the best conditions and far away from the glare of city lights, a person in northern Europe can look up and see about 2,500 stars. In a town, however, light pollution can reduce visibility to 200 stars or less. Over the whole celestial sphere it is possible to see about 8,500 stars with the naked eye and it is only when you look through a telescope that you begin to realize that the number of stars is countless.

SMALL AND LARGE STARS

Stars come in several sizes. Some, called neutron stars, are compact, with the same mass as the Sun but with diameters of only about 20 km [12 miles]. Larger than neutron stars are the small white dwarfs. Our Sun is a medium-sized star, but many visible stars in the night sky are giants with diameters between 10 and 100 times that of the Sun, or supergiants with diameters over 100 times that of the Sun.

Two bright stars in the constellation Orion are Betelgeuse (also known as Alpha Orionis) and Rigel (or Beta Orionis). Betelgeuse is an orange-red supergiant, whose diameter is about 400 times that of the Sun. Rigel is also a supergiant. Its diameter is about 50 times that of the Sun, but its luminosity is estimated to be over 100,000 times that of the Sun.

The stars we see in the night sky all belong to our home galaxy, the Milky Way. This name is also used for the faint, silvery band that arches across the sky. This band, a slice through our

THE CONSTELLATIONS

The constellations and their English names. Constellations visible from both hemispheres are listed.

Andromeda	Andromeda	Delphinus	Dolphin	Perseus	Perseus
Antlia	Air Pump	Dorado	Swordfish	Phoenix	Phoenix
Apus	Bird of Paradise	Draco	Dragon	Pictor	Easel
Aquarius	Water Carrier	Equuleus	Little Horse	Pisces	Fishes
Aquila	Eagle	Eridanus	River Eridanus	Piscis Austrinus	Southern Fish
Ara	Altar	Fornax	Furnace	Puppis	Ship's Stern
Aries	Ram	Gemini	Twins	Pyxis	Mariner's Compass
Auriga	Charioteer	Grus	Crane	Reticulum	Net
Boötes	Herdsman	Hercules	Hercules	Sagitta	Arrow
Caelum	Chisel	Horologium	Clock	Sagittarius	Archer
Camelopardalis	Giraffe	Hydra	Water Snake	Scorpius	Scorpion
Cancer	Crab	Hydrus	Sea Serpent	Sculptor	Sculptor
Canes Venatici	Hunting Dogs	Indus	Indian	Scutum	Shield
Canis Major	Great Dog	Lacerta	Lizard	Serpens*	Serpent
Canis Minor	Little Dog	Leo	Lion	Sextans	Sextant
Capricornus	Sea Goat	Leo Minor	Little Lion	Taurus	Bull
Carina	Ship's Keel	Lepus	Hare	Telescopium	Telescope
Cassiopeia	Cassiopeia	Libra	Scales	Triangulum	Triangle
Centaurus	Centaur	Lupus	Wolf	Triangulum Australe	
Cepheus	Cepheus	Lynx	Lynx		Southern Triangle
Cetus	Whale	Lyra	Lyre	Tucana	Toucan
Chamaeleon	Chameleon	Mensa	Table	Ursa Major	Great Bear
Circinus	Compasses	Microscopium	Microscope	Ursa Minor	Little Bear
Columba	Dove	Monoceros	Unicorn	Vela	Ship's Sails
Coma Berenices	Berenice's Hair	Musca	Fly	Virgo	Virgin
Corona Australis	Southern Crown	Norma	Level	Volans	Flying Fish
Corona Borealis	Northern Crown	Octans	Octant	Vulpecula	Fox
Corvus	Crow	Ophiuchus	Serpent Bearer		
Crater	Cup	Orion	Hunter	** In two halves: Serpens Caput, the*	
Crux	Southern Cross	Pavo	Peacock	*head, and Serpens Cauda, the tail.*	
Cygnus	Swan	Pegasus	Winged Horse		

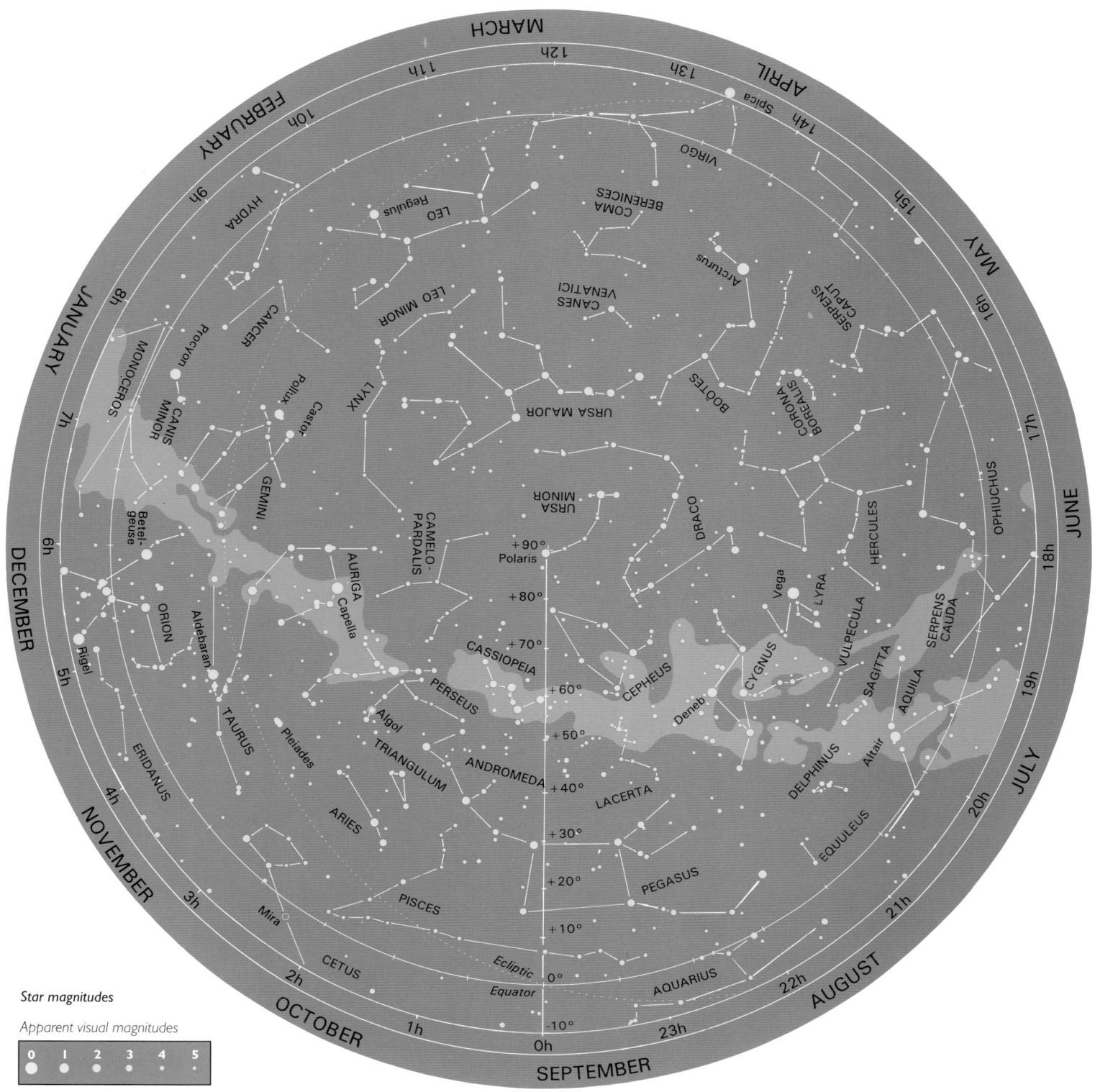

Star magnitudes

Apparent visual magnitudes

| 0 | 1 | 2 | 3 | 4 | 5 |

The Milky Way is shown in light blue on the above chart.

Star chart of the northern hemisphere

When you look into the sky, the stars seem to be on the inside of a huge dome. This gives astronomers a way of mapping them. This chart shows the sky as it would appear from the North Pole. To use the star chart above, an observer in the northern hemisphere should face south and turn the chart so that the current month appears at the bottom. The chart will then show the constellations on view at approximately 11pm Greenwich Mean Time. The map should be rotated clockwise 15° for each hour before 11pm and anticlockwise for each hour after 11pm.

galaxy, contains an enormous number of stars. The nucleus of the Milky Way galaxy cannot be seen from Earth. Lying in the direction of the constellation Sagittarius in the southern hemisphere, it is masked by clouds of dust.

THE BRIGHTNESS OF STARS

Astronomers use a scale of magnitudes to measure the brightness of stars. The brightest visible to the naked eye were originally known as first-magnitude stars, ones not so bright were second-magnitude, down to the faintest visible, which were rated as sixth-magnitude. The brighter the star, the lower the magnitude. With the advent of telescopes and the development of accurate instruments for measuring brightnesses, the magnitude scale has been refined and extended.

Very bright bodies such as Sirius, Venus and the Sun have negative magnitudes. The nearest star is Proxima Centauri, part of a multiple star system, which is 4.2 light-years away. Proxima Centauri is very faint and has a magnitude of 11.3. Alpha Centauri A, one of the two brighter members of the system, is the nearest visible star to Earth. It has a magnitude of 1.7.

These magnitudes are known as apparent magnitudes – measures of the brightnesses of the stars as they appear to us. These are the magnitudes shown on the charts on these pages. But the stars are at very different distances. The star Deneb, in the constellation Cygnus, for example, is over 1,200 light-years away. So astronomers also use absolute magnitudes – measures of how bright the stars really are. A star's absolute magnitude is the apparent magnitude it would have if it could be placed 32.6 light-years away. So Deneb, with an apparent magnitude of 1.2, has an absolute magnitude of –7.2.

The brightest star in the night sky is Sirius, the Dog Star, with a magnitude of –1.5. This medium-sized star is 8.64 light-years distant but it gives out about 20 times as much light as the Sun. After the Sun and the Moon, the brightest objects in the sky are the planets Venus, Mars and Jupiter. For example, Venus has a magnitude of up to –4. The planets have no light of their own however, and shine only because they reflect the Sun's rays. But whilst stars have fixed positions, the planets shift nightly in relation to the constellations, following a path called

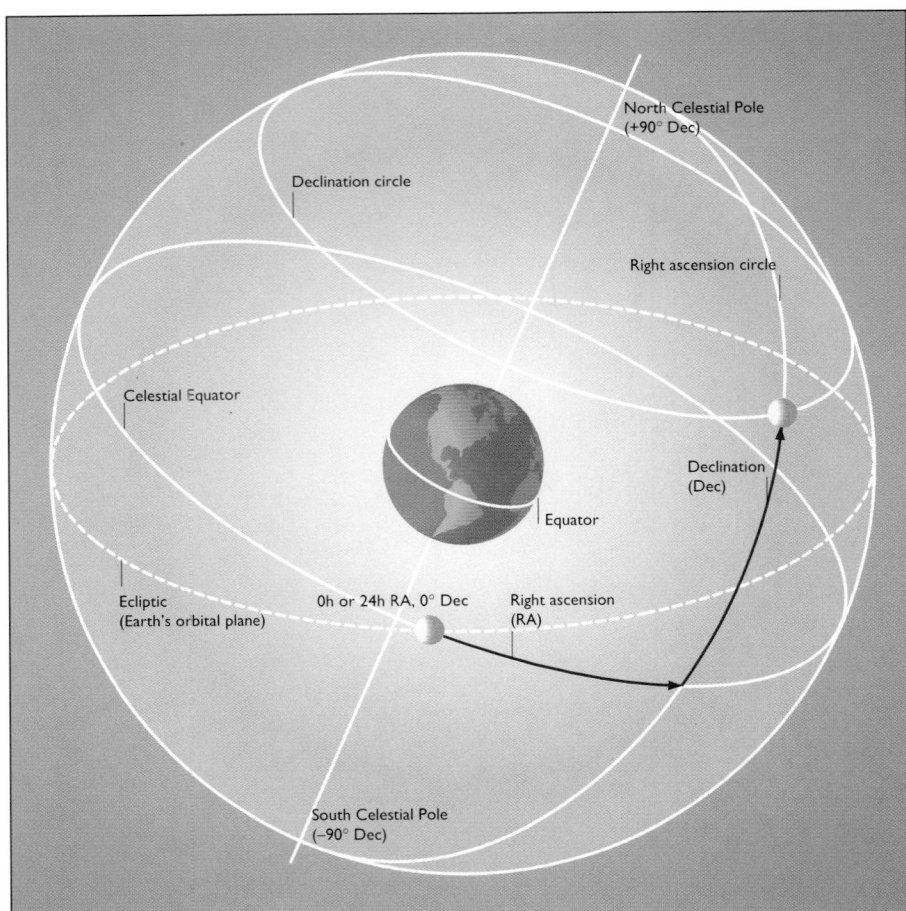

the Ecliptic (shown on the star charts). As they follow their orbits around the Sun, their distances from the Earth vary, and therefore so also do their magnitudes.

While atlas maps record the details of the Earth's surface, star charts are a guide to the heavens. An observer at the Equator can see the entire sky at some time during the year, but an observer at the poles can see only the stars in a single hemisphere. As a result, star charts of both hemispheres are produced. The northern hemisphere chart is centred on the North Celestial Pole, while the southern hemisphere chart is centred on the South Celestial Pole.

In the northern hemisphere, the North Pole is marked by the star Polaris, or North Star. Polaris lies within a degree of the point where an extension of the Earth's axis meets the sky. Polaris appears to be stationary and navigators throughout history have used it as a guide. Unfortunately, the South Pole has no convenient reference point.

Star charts of the two hemispheres are bounded by the Celestial Equator, an imaginary line in the sky directly above the terrestrial Equator. Astronomical co-ordinates, which give the location of stars, are normally stated in terms of right ascension (the equivalent of longitude) and declination (the equivalent of latitude). Because the stars appear to rotate around the Earth every 24 hours, right ascension is measured eastwards in hours and minutes. Declination is measured in degrees north or south of the Celestial Equator.

Celestial sphere

The diagram shows the imaginary surface on which astronomical positions are measured. The celestial sphere appears to rotate about the celestial poles, as though an extension of the Earth's own axis. The Earth's axis points towards the celestial poles.

The Southern Cross

The Southern Cross, or Crux, in the southern hemisphere, was classified as a constellation in the 17th century. It is as familiar to Australians and New Zealanders as the Plough (or Big Dipper) is to people in the northern hemisphere. The vertical axis of the Southern Cross points towards the South Celestial Pole.

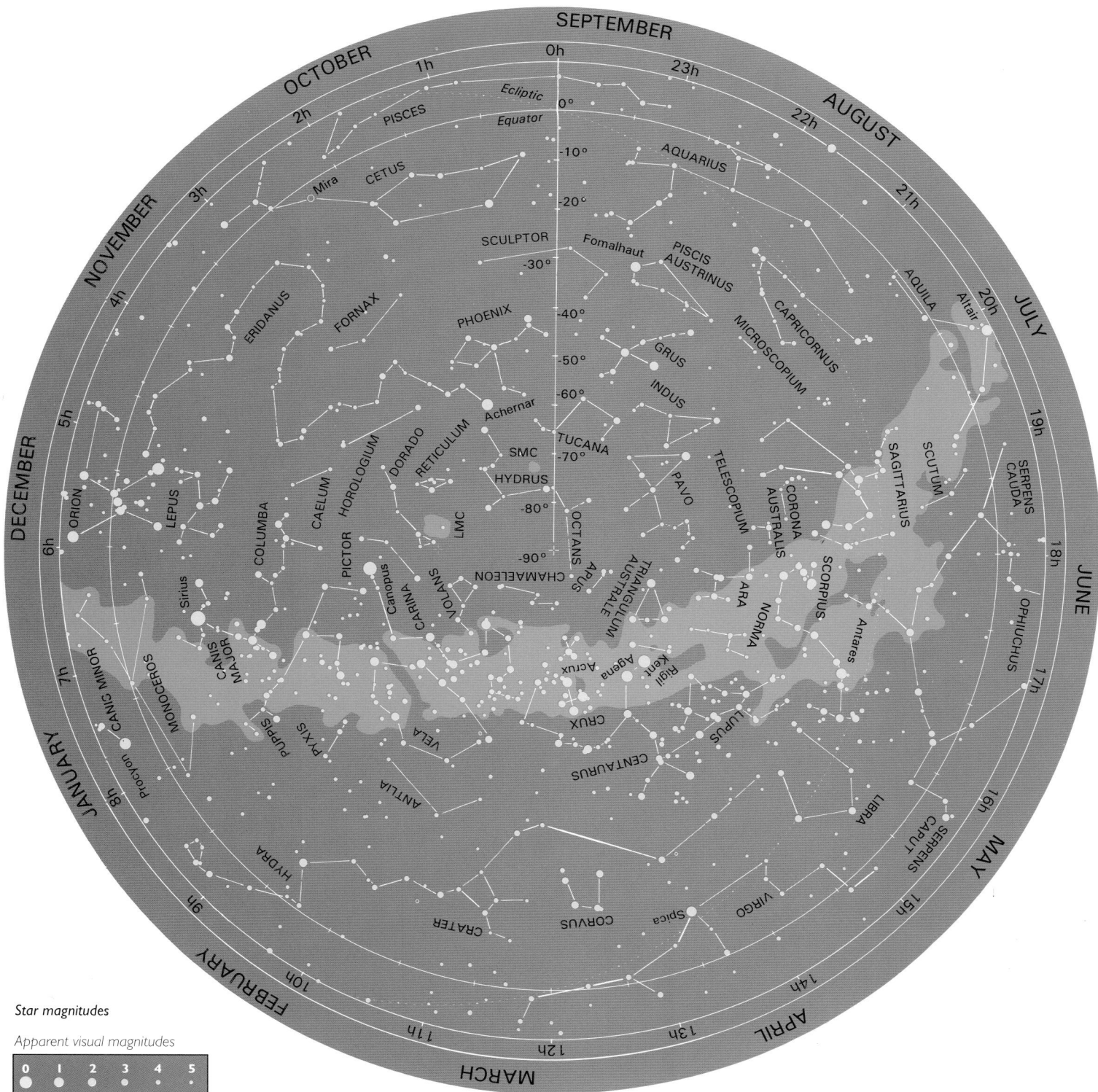

Star magnitudes

Apparent visual magnitudes

0	1	2	3	4	5

The Milky Way is shown in light blue on the above chart.

Star chart of the southern hemisphere

Many constellations in the southern hemisphere were named not by the ancients but by later astronomers. Some, including Antila (Air Pump) and Microscopium (Microscope), have modern names. The Large and Small Magellanic Clouds (LMC, SMC) are small 'satellite' galaxies of the Milky Way. To use the chart, an observer in the southern hemisphere should face north and turn the chart so that the current month appears at the bottom. The map will then show the constellations on view at approximately 11pm Greenwich Mean Time. The chart should be rotated clockwise 15° for each hour before 11pm and anticlockwise for each hour after 11pm.

CONSTELLATIONS

Every star is identifiable as a member of a constellation. The night sky contains 88 constellations, many of which were named by the ancient Greeks, Romans and other early peoples after animals and mythological characters, such as Orion and Perseus. More recently, astronomers invented names for constellations seen in the southern hemisphere, in areas not visible around the Mediterranean Sea.

Some groups of easily recognizable stars form parts of a constellation. For example, seven stars form the shape of the Plough or Big Dipper within the constellation Ursa Major. Such groups are called asterisms.

The stars in constellations lie in the same direction in space, but normally at vastly different distances. Hence, there is no real connection between them. The positions of stars seem fixed, but in fact the shapes of the constellations are changing slowly over very long periods of time. This is because the stars have their own 'proper motions', which because of the huge distances involved are imperceptible to the naked eye.

The Solar System

Although the origins of the Solar System are still a matter of debate, many scientists believe that it was formed from a cloud of gas and dust, the debris from some long-lost, exploded star. Around 5 billion years ago, material was drawn towards the hub of the rotating disk of gas and dust, where it was compressed to thermonuclear fusion temperatures. A new star, the Sun, was born, containing 99.8% of the mass of the Solar System. The remaining material was later drawn together to form the planets and the other bodies in the Solar System. Spacecraft, manned and unmanned, have greatly increased our knowledge of the Solar System since the start of the Space Age in 1957, when the Soviet Union launched the satellite Sputnik I.

THE PLANETS

Mercury is the closest planet to the Sun and the fastest moving. Space probes have revealed that its surface is covered by craters, and looks much like our Moon. Mercury is a hostile place, with no significant atmosphere and temperatures ranging between 400°C [750°F] by day and −170°C [−275°F] by night. It seems unlikely that anyone will ever want to visit this planet.

Venus is much the same size as Earth, but it is the hottest of the planets, with temperatures reaching 475°C [885°F], even at night. The reason for this scorching heat is the atmosphere, which consists mainly of carbon dioxide, a gas that traps heat thus creating a greenhouse effect. The density of the atmosphere is about 90 times that of Earth and dense clouds permanently mask the surface. Active volcanic regions discharging sulphur dioxide may account for the haze of sulphuric acid droplets in the upper atmosphere.

From planet Earth, Venus is brighter than any other star or planet and is easy to spot. It is often the first object to be seen in the evening sky and the last to be seen in the morning sky. It can even be seen in daylight.

Earth, seen from space, looks blue (because of the oceans which cover more than 70% of the planet) and white (a result of clouds in the atmosphere). The atmosphere and water make Earth the only planet known to support life. The Earth's hard outer layers, including the crust and the top of the mantle, are divided into rigid plates. Forces inside the Earth move the plates, modifying the landscape and causing earthquakes and volcanic activity. Weathering and erosion also change the surface.

Mars has many features in common with Earth, including an atmosphere with clouds and polar caps that partly melt in summer. Scientists once considered that it was the most likely planet on which other life might exist, but the two Viking space probes that went there in the 1970s found only a barren rocky surface with no trace of water. But Mars did have flowing water at one time and there are many dry channels – but these are not the fictitious 'canals'. There are also giant, dormant volcanoes.

PLANETARY DATA

Planet	Mean distance from Sun (million km)	Mass (Earth=1)	Period of orbit (Earth yrs)	Period of rotation (Earth days)	Equatorial diameter (km)	Average density (water=1)	Surface gravity (Earth=1)	Number of known satellites
Sun	—	333,000	—	25.4	1,391,000	1.41	28	—
Mercury	57.9	0.055	0.2406	58.67	4,880	5.43	0.38	0
Venus	108.2	0.815	0.6152	243.0	12,104	5.20	0.90	0
Earth	149.6	1.0	1.00	1.00	12,756	5.52	1.00	1
Mars	227.9	0.107	1.88	1.028	6,792	3.91	0.38	2
Jupiter	778.3	317.8	11.86	0.411	142,800	1.33	2.69	28
Saturn	1,426.8	95.2	29.46	0.427	120,000	0.69	1.19	30
Uranus	2,869.4	14.53	84.01	0.748	51,118	1.29	0.79	21
Neptune	4,496.3	17.14	164.8	0.710	49,528	1.64	0.98	8
Pluto	5,900.1	0.002	2447.7	6.39	2,320	2.00	0.03	1

Asteroids are small, rocky bodies. Most of them orbit the Sun between Mars and Jupiter, but some small ones can approach the Earth. The largest is Ceres, 913 km [567 miles] in diameter. There may be around a million asteroids bigger than 1 km [0.6 miles].

Jupiter, the giant planet, lies beyond Mars and the asteroid belt. Its mass is almost three times as much as all the other planets combined and, because of its size, it shines more brightly than any other planet apart from Venus and, occasionally, Mars. The four largest moons of Jupiter were discovered by Galileo. Jupiter is made up mostly of hydrogen and helium, covered by a layer of clouds. Its Great Red Spot is a high-pressure storm. Jupiter made headline news when it was struck by fragments of Comet Shoemaker–Levy 9 in July 1994. This was the greatest collision ever seen by scientists between a planet and another heavenly body. The fragments of the comet that crashed into Jupiter created huge fireballs that caused scars on the planet that remained visible for months after the event.

Saturn is structurally similar to Jupiter but it is best known for its rings. The rings measure about 270,000 km [170,000 miles] across, yet they are no more than a few hundred metres thick. Seen from Earth, the rings seem divided

into three main bands of varying brightness, but photographs sent back by the *Voyager* space probes in 1980 and 1981 showed that they are broken up into thousands of thin ringlets composed of ice particles ranging in size from a snowball to an iceberg. The origin of the rings is still a matter of debate.

Uranus was discovered in 1781 by William Herschel who first thought it was a comet. It is broadly similar to Jupiter and Saturn in composition, though its distance from the Sun makes its surface even colder. Uranus is circled by thin rings which were discovered in 1977. Unlike the rings of Saturn, the rings of Uranus are black, which explains why they cannot be seen from Earth.

Neptune, named after the mythological sea god, was discovered in 1846 as the result of mathematical predictions made by astronomers to explain irregularities in the orbit of Uranus, its near twin. Little was known about this distant

body until *Voyager 2* came close to it in 1989. Neptune has thin rings, like those of Uranus. Among its blue-green clouds is a prominent dark spot, which rotates anticlockwise every 18 hours or so.

Pluto is the smallest planet in the Solar System, even smaller than our Moon. The American astronomer Clyde Tombaugh discovered Pluto in 1930. Its orbit is odd and it sometimes comes closer to the Sun than Neptune. The nature of Pluto, a gloomy planet appropriately named after the Greek and Roman god of the underworld, is uncertain. At Pluto's distance and beyond are many small, asteroid-like bodies the first of which was found in 1992.

Comets are small icy bodies that orbit the Sun in highly elliptical orbits. When a comet swings in towards the Sun some of its ice evaporates, and the comet brightens and may become visible from Earth. The best known is Halley's Comet, which takes 76 years to orbit the Sun.

The Earth: Time and Motion

The Earth is constantly moving through space like a huge, self-sufficient spaceship. First, with the rest of the Solar System, it moves around the centre of the Milky Way galaxy. Second, it rotates around the Sun at a speed of more than 100,000 km/h [more than 60,000 mph], covering a distance of nearly 1,000 million km [600 million miles] in a little over 365 days. The Earth also spins on its axis, an imaginary line joining the North and South Poles, via the centre of the Earth, completing one turn in a day. The Earth's movements around the Sun determine our calendar, though accurate observations of

The Earth from the Moon
In 1969, Neil Armstrong and Edwin 'Buzz' Aldrin Junior were the first people to set foot on the Moon. This superb view of the Earth was taken by the crew of Apollo 11.

the stars made by astronomers help to keep our clocks in step with the rotation of the Earth around the Sun.

THE CHANGING YEAR

The Earth takes 365 days, 6 hours, 9 minutes and 9.54 seconds to complete one orbit around the Sun. We have a calendar year of 365 days, so allowance has to be made for the extra time over and above the 365 days. This is allowed for by introducing leap years of 366 days. Leap years are generally those, such as 1992 and 1996, which are divisible by four. Century years, however, are not leap years unless they are divisible by 400. Hence, 1700, 1800 and 1900 were not leap years, but the year 2000 was one. Leap years help to make the calendar conform with the solar year.

Because the Earth's axis is tilted by 23½°, the middle latitudes enjoy four distinct seasons. On 21 March, the vernal or spring equinox in the northern hemisphere, the Sun is directly overhead at the Equator and everywhere on Earth has about 12 hours of daylight and 12 hours of darkness. But as the Earth continues on its journey around the Sun, the northern hemisphere tilts more and more towards the Sun. Finally, on 21 June, the Sun is overhead at the Tropic of Cancer (latitude 23½° North). This is

The Seasons
The 23½° tilt of the Earth's axis remains constant as the Earth orbits around the Sun. As a result, first the northern and then the southern hemispheres lean towards the Sun. Annual variations in the amount of sunlight received in turn by each hemisphere are responsible for the four seasons experienced in the middle latitudes.

Tides
The daily rises and falls of the ocean's waters are caused by the gravitational pull of the Moon and the Sun. The effect is greatest on the hemisphere facing the Moon, causing a 'tidal bulge'. The diagram below shows that the Sun, Moon and Earth are in line when the spring tides occur. This causes the greatest tidal ranges. On the other hand, the neap tides occur when the pull of the Moon and the Sun are opposed. Neap tides, when tidal ranges are at their lowest, occur near the Moon's first and third quarters.

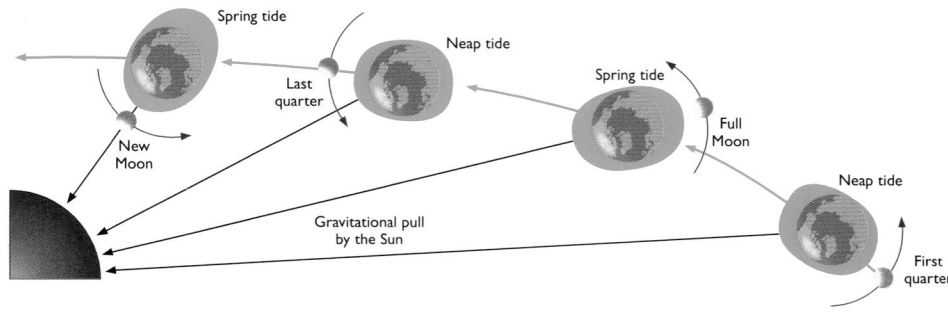

SUN DATA

DIAMETER	1.391×10^6 km
VOLUME	1.412×10^{18} km³
VOLUME (EARTH=1)	1.303×10^6
MASS	1.989×10^{30} kg
MASS (EARTH=1)	3.329×10^6
MEAN DENSITY (WATER=1)	1.409
ROTATION PERIOD	
AT EQUATOR	25.4 days
AT POLES	about 35 days
SURFACE GRAVITY	
(EARTH=1)	28
MAGNITUDE	
APPARENT	−26.9
ABSOLUTE	+4.71
TEMPERATURE	
AT SURFACE	5,400°C [5,700 K]
AT CORE	15×10^6 K

MOON DATA

DIAMETER	3,476 km
MASS (EARTH=1)	0.0123
DENSITY (WATER=1)	3.34
MEAN DISTANCE FROM EARTH	384,402 km
MAXIMUM DISTANCE (APOGEE)	406,740 km
MINIMUM DISTANCE (PERIGEE)	356,410 km
SIDERIAL ROTATION AND REVOLUTION PERIOD	27.322 days
SYNODIC MONTH (NEW MOON TO NEW MOON)	29.531 days
SURFACE GRAVITY (EARTH=1)	0.165
MAXIMUM SURFACE TEMPERATURE	+130°C [403 K]
MINIMUM SURFACE TEMPERATURE	−158°C [115 K]

Phases of the Moon

The Moon rotates more slowly than the Earth, making one complete turn on its axis in just over 27 days. This corresponds to its period of revolution around the Earth and, hence, the same hemisphere always faces us. The interval between one full Moon and the next (and also between new Moons) is about 29½ days, or one lunar month. The apparent changes in the appearance of the Moon are caused by its changing position in relation to Earth. Like the planets, the Moon produces no light of its own. It shines by reflecting the Sun's rays, varying from a slim crescent to a full circle and back again.

the summer solstice in the northern hemisphere.

The overhead Sun then moves south again until on 23 September, the autumn equinox in the northern hemisphere, the Sun is again overhead at the Equator. The overhead Sun then moves south until, on around 22 December, it is overhead at the Tropic of Capricorn. This is the winter solstice in the northern hemisphere, and the summer solstice in the southern, where the seasons are reversed.

At the poles, there are two seasons. During half of the year, one of the poles leans towards the Sun and has continuous sunlight. For the other six months, the pole leans away from the Sun and is in continuous darkness.

Regions around the Equator do not have marked seasons. Because the Sun is high in the sky throughout the year, it is always hot or warm. When people talk of seasons in the tropics, they are usually referring to other factors, such as rainy and dry periods.

DAY, NIGHT AND TIDES

As the Earth rotates on its axis every 24 hours, first one side of the planet and then the other faces the Sun and enjoys daylight, while the opposite side is in darkness.

The length of daylight varies throughout the year. The longest day in the northern hemisphere falls on the summer solstice, 21 June, while the longest day in the southern hemisphere is on 22 December. At 40° latitude, the length of daylight on the longest day is 14 hours, 30 minutes. At 60° latitude, daylight on that day lasts 18 hours, 30 minutes. On the shortest day, 22 December in the northern hemisphere and 21 June in the southern, daylight hours at 40° latitude total 9 hours and 9 minutes. At latitude 60°, daylight lasts only 5 hours, 30 minutes in the 24-hour period.

Tides are caused by the gravitational pull of the Moon and, to a lesser extent, the Sun on the waters in the world's oceans. Tides occur twice every 24 hours, 50 minutes – one complete orbit

Total eclipse of the Sun

A total eclipse is caused when the Moon passes between the Sun and the Earth. With the Sun's bright disk completely obscured, the Sun's corona, or outer atmosphere, can be viewed.

of the Moon around the Earth.

The highest tides, the spring tides, occur when the Earth, Moon and Sun are in a straight line, so that the gravitational pulls of the Moon and Sun are combined. The lowest, or neap, tides occur when the Moon, Earth and Sun form a right angle. The gravitational pull of the Moon is then opposed by the gravitational pull of the Sun. The greatest tidal ranges occur in the Bay of Fundy in North America. The greatest mean spring range is 14.5 m [47.5 ft].

The speed at which the Earth is spinning on its axis is gradually slowing down, because of the movement of tides. As a result, experts have calculated that, in about 200 million years, the day will be 25 hours long.

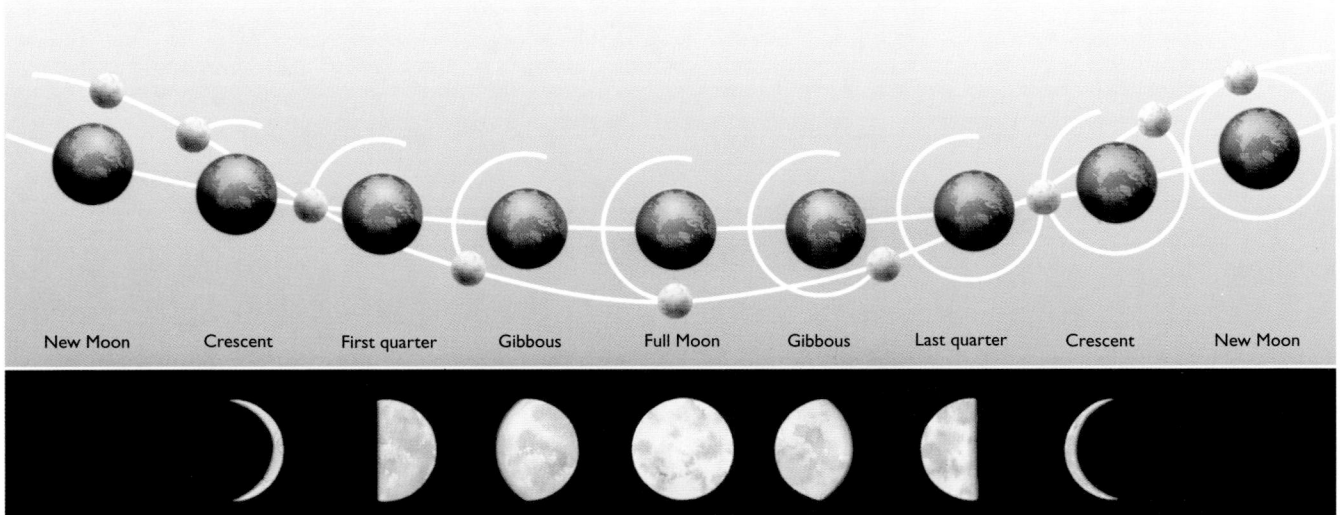

New Moon	Crescent	First quarter	Gibbous	Full Moon	Gibbous	Last quarter	Crescent	New Moon

The Earth from Space

Any last doubts about whether the Earth was round or flat were finally resolved by the appearance of the first photographs of our planet taken at the start of the Space Age. Satellite images also confirmed that map- and globe-makers had correctly worked out the shapes of the continents and the oceans.

More importantly, images of our beautiful, blue, white and brown planet from space impressed on many people that the Earth and its resources are finite. They made people realize that if we allow our planet to be damaged by such factors as overpopulation, pollution and irresponsible over-use of resources, then its future and the survival of all the living things upon it may be threatened.

VIEWS FROM ABOVE

The first aerial photographs were taken from balloons in the mid-19th century and their importance in military reconnaissance was recognized as early as the 1860s during the American Civil War.

Launch of the Space Shuttle Atlantis

Space Shuttles transport astronauts and equipment into orbit around the Earth. The American Space Shuttle Atlantis, shown below, launched the Magellan probe, which undertook a radar mapping programme of the surface of Venus in the early 1990s.

Since the end of World War II, photographs taken by aircraft have been widely used in map-making. The use of air photographs has greatly speeded up the laborious process of mapping land details and they have enabled cartographers to produce maps of the most remote parts of the world.

Aerial photographs have also proved useful because they reveal features that are not visible at ground level. For example, circles that appear on many air photographs do not correspond to visible features on the ground. Many of these mysterious shapes have turned out to be the sites of ancient settlements previously unknown to archaeologists.

IMAGES FROM SPACE

Space probes equipped with cameras and a variety of remote sensing instruments have sent back images of distant planets and moons. From these images, detailed maps have been produced, rapidly expanding our knowledge of the Solar System.

Photographs from space are also proving invaluable in the study of the Earth. One of the best known uses of space imagery is the study of the atmosphere. Polar-orbiting weather satellites that circle the Earth, together with geostationary satellites, whose motion is synchronized with the Earth's rotation, now regularly transmit images showing the changing patterns of weather systems from above. Forecasters use these images to track the development and the paths taken by hurricanes, enabling them to issue storm warnings to endangered areas, saving lives and reducing damage to property.

Remote sensing devices are now monitoring changes in temperatures over the land and sea, while photographs indicate the melting of ice sheets. Such evidence is vital in the study of global warming. Other devices reveal polluted areas, patterns of vegetation growth, and areas suffering deforestation.

In recent years, remote sensing devices have been used to monitor the damage being done to the ozone layer in the stratosphere, which prevents most of the Sun's harmful ultraviolet radiation from reaching the surface. The discovery of 'ozone holes', where the protective layer of ozone is being thinned by chlorofluorocarbons (CFCs), chemicals used in the manufacture of such things as air conditioners and refrigerators, has enabled governments to take concerted action to save our planet from imminent danger.

EARTH DATA

MAXIMUM DISTANCE FROM SUN (APHELION)
152,007,016 km

MINIMUM DISTANCE FROM SUN (PERIHELION)
147,000,830 km

LENGTH OF YEAR – SOLAR TROPICAL (EQUINOX TO EQUINOX)
365.24 days

LENGTH OF YEAR – SIDEREAL (FIXED STAR TO FIXED STAR)
365.26 days

LENGTH OF DAY – MEAN SOLAR DAY
24 hours, 03 minutes, 56 seconds

LENGTH OF DAY – MEAN SIDEREAL DAY
23 hours, 56 minutes, 4 seconds

SUPERFICIAL AREA
510,000,000 km^2

LAND SURFACE
149,000,000 km^2 (29.3%)

WATER SURFACE
361,000,000 km^2 (70.7%)

EQUATORIAL CIRCUMFERENCE
40,077 km

POLAR CIRCUMFERENCE
40,009 km

EQUATORIAL DIAMETER
12,756.8 km

POLAR DIAMETER
12,713.8 km

EQUATORIAL RADIUS
6,378.4 km

POLAR RADIUS
6,356.9 km

VOLUME OF THE EARTH
1,083,230 × 10^6 km^3

MASS OF THE EARTH
5.9 × 10^{21} tonnes

Satellite image of San Francisco Bay

Unmanned scientific satellites called ERTS (Earth Resources Technology Satellites), or Landsats, were designed to collect information about the Earth's resources. The satellites transmitted images of the land using different wavelengths of light in order to identify, in false colours, such subtle features as areas that contain minerals or areas covered with growing crops, that are not identifiable on simple photographs using the visible range of the spectrum. They were also equipped to monitor conditions in the atmosphere and oceans, and also to detect pollution levels. This Landsat image of San Francisco Bay covers an area of great interest to geologists because it lies in an earthquake zone in the path of the San Andreas fault.

The Dynamic Earth

The Earth was formed about 4.6 billion years [4,600 million years] ago from the ring of gas and dust left over after the formation of the Sun. As the Earth took shape, lighter elements, such as silicon, rose to the surface, while heavy elements, notably iron, sank towards the centre.

Gradually, the outer layers cooled to form a hard crust. The crust enclosed the dense mantle which, in turn, surrounded the even denser liquid outer and solid inner core. Around the Earth was an atmosphere, which contained abundant water

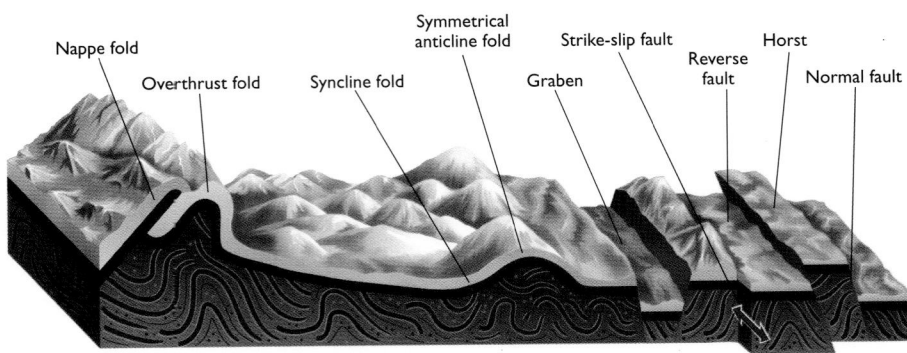

Lulworth Cove, southern England
When undisturbed by earth movements, sedimentary rock strata are generally horizontal. But lateral pressure has squeezed the Jurassic strata at Lulworth Cove into complex folds.

vapour. When the surface cooled, rainwater began to fill hollows, forming the first lakes and seas. Since that time, our planet has been subject to constant change – the result of powerful internal and external forces that still operate today.

THE HISTORY OF THE EARTH
From their study of rocks, geologists have pieced together the history of our planet and the life forms that evolved upon it. They have dated the oldest known crystals, composed of the mineral zircon, at 4.2 billion years. But the oldest rocks are younger, less than 4 billion years old. This is because older rocks have been weathered away by natural processes.

The oldest rocks that contain fossils, which are evidence of once-living organisms, are around 3.5 billion years old. But fossils are rare in rocks formed in the first 4 billion years of Earth history. This vast expanse of time is called the Precambrian. This is because it precedes the Cambrian period, at the start of which, about 590 million years ago, life was abundant in the seas.

The Cambrian is the first period in the Paleozoic (or ancient life) era. The Paleozoic era is followed by the Mesozoic (middle life) era, which witnessed the spectacular rise and fall of the dinosaurs, and the Cenozoic (recent life) era, which was dominated by the evolution of mammals. Each of the eras is divided into periods, and the periods in the Cenozoic era, covering the last 65 million years, are further divided into epochs.

THE EARTH'S CHANGING FACE
While life was gradually evolving, the face of the Earth was constantly changing. By piecing together evidence of rock structures and fossils, geologists have demonstrated that around 250 million years ago, all the world's land areas were grouped together in one huge landmass called Pangaea. Around 180 million years ago, the supercontinent Pangaea, began to break up. New oceans opened up as the continents began to move towards their present positions.

Evidence of how continents drift came from studies of the ocean floor in the 1950s and 1960s. Scientists discovered that the oceans are young features. By contrast with the continents, no part of the ocean floor is more than 200 million years old. The floors of oceans older than 200 million years have completely vanished.

Studies of long undersea ranges, called ocean ridges, revealed that the youngest rocks occur along their centres, which are the edges of huge plates – rigid blocks of the Earth's lithosphere, which is made up of the crust and the solid upper layer of the mantle. The Earth's lithosphere is split into six large and several smaller

Mountain building
Lateral pressure, which occurs when plates collide, squeezes and compresses rocks into folds. Simple symmetrical upfolds are called anticlines, while downfolds are synclines. As the pressure builds up, strata become asymmetrical and they may be tilted over to form recumbent folds. The rocks often crack under the intense pressure and the folds are sheared away and pushed forward over other rocks. These features are called overthrust folds or nappes. Plate movements also create faults along which rocks move upwards, downwards and sideways. The diagram shows a downfaulted graben, or rift valley, and an uplifted horst, or block mountain.

The Himalayas seen from Nepal
*The Himalayas are a young fold mountain range formed by a
collision between two plates. The earthquakes felt in the region
testify that the plate movements are still continuing.*

Geological time scale

*The geological time scale was
first constructed by a study of the
stratigraphic, or relative, ages of
layers of rock. But the absolute ages
of rock strata could not be fixed until
the discovery of radioactivity in the
early 20th century. Some names of
periods, such as Cambrian (Latin
for Wales), come from places where
the rocks were first studied. Others,
such as Carboniferous, refer to the
nature of the rocks formed during
the period. For example, coal seams
(containing carbon) were formed
from decayed plant matter during
the Carboniferous period.*

plates. The ocean ridges are 'constructive' plate margins, because new crustal rock is being formed there from magma that wells up from the mantle as the plates gradually move apart. By contrast, the deep ocean trenches are 'destructive' plate edges. Here, two plates are pushing against each other and one plate is descending beneath the other into the mantle where it is melted and destroyed. Geologists call these areas subduction zones.

A third type of plate edge is called a transform fault. Here two plates are moving alongside each other. The best known of these plate edges is the San Andreas fault in California, which separates the Pacific plate from the North American plate.

Slow-moving currents in the partly molten asthenosphere, which underlies the solid lithosphere, are responsible for moving the plates, a process called plate tectonics.

MOUNTAIN BUILDING

The study of plate tectonics has helped geologists to understand the mechanisms that are responsible for the creation of mountains. Many of the world's greatest ranges were created by the collision of two plates and the bending of the intervening strata into huge loops, or folds. For example, the Himalayas began to rise around 50 million years ago, when a plate supporting India collided with the huge Eurasian plate. Rocks on the floor of the intervening and long-vanished Tethys Sea were squeezed up to form the Himalayan Mountain Range.

Plate movements also create tension that cracks rocks, producing long faults along which rocks move upwards, downwards or sideways. Block mountains are formed when blocks of rock are pushed upwards along faults. Steep-sided rift valleys are formed when blocks of land sink down between faults. For example, the basin and range region of the south-western United States has both block mountains and down-faulted basins, such as Death Valley.

Pre-Cambrian	Lower	Paleozoic (Primary)		Upper		Mesozoic (Secondary)			Cenozoic (Tertiary, Quaternary)						Era
Pre-Cambrian	Cambrian	Ordovician	Silurian	Devonian	Carboniferous	Permian	Triassic	Jurassic	Cretaceous	Paleocene	Eocene	Oligocene	Miocene/Pliocene	Quaternary	System
			CALEDONIAN FOLDING		HERCYNIAN FOLDING					LARAMIDE FOLDING	ALPINE FOLDING				Orogeny
600	550	500	450	400	350	300	250	200	150	100	50				

Millions of years before present

Earthquakes and Volcanoes

On 26 January, 2001, an earthquake rocked north-west India and south-east Pakistan. Bhuj, in Gujarat state, suffered the worst damage. The death toll was estimated at 20,000, and the 'quake was felt as far away as Karachi, Delhi and Mumbai. Earlier that month, an earthquake had struck El Salvador in Central America. Around 1,200 people died, 750 of them being buried by mudslides.

THE RESTLESS EARTH

Earthquakes can occur anywhere, whenever rocks move along faults. But the most severe and most numerous earthquakes occur near the edges of the plates that make up the

San Andreas Fault, United States
Geologists call the San Andreas fault in south-western California a transform, or strike-slip, fault. Sudden movements along it cause earthquakes. In 1906, shifts of about 4.5 metres [15 ft] occurred near San Francisco, causing a massive earthquake.

Earth's lithosphere. Japan, for example, lies in a particularly unstable region above subduction zones, where plates are descending into the Earth's mantle. It lies in a zone encircling the Pacific Ocean, called the 'Pacific ring of fire'.

Plates do not move smoothly. Their edges are jagged and for most of the time they are locked together. However, pressure gradually builds up until the rocks break and the plates lurch forward, setting off vibrations ranging from slight tremors to terrifying earthquakes. The greater the pressure released, the more destructive the earthquake.

Earthquakes are also common along the ocean trenches where plates are moving apart, but they mostly occur so far from land that they do little damage. Far more destructive are the earthquakes that occur where plates are moving alongside each other. For example, the earthquakes that periodically rock south-western California are caused by movements along the San Andreas Fault.

The spot where an earthquake originates is called the focus, while the point on the Earth's surface directly above the focus is called the epicentre. Two kinds of waves, P-waves or compressional waves and S-waves or shear waves, travel from the focus to the surface where they make the ground shake. P-waves travel faster than S-waves and the time difference between their arrival at recording stations enables scientists to calculate the distance from a station to the epicentre.

Earthquakes are measured on the Richter scale, which indicates the magnitude of the shock. The most destructive earthquakes are shallow-focus, that is, the focus is within 60 km [37 miles] of the surface. A magnitude of 7.0 is a major earthquake, but earthquakes with a somewhat lower magnitude can cause tremendous damage if their epicentres are on or close to densely populated areas.

NOTABLE EARTHQUAKES (since 1900)		
Year	Location	Mag.
1906	San Francisco, USA	8.3
1906	Valparaiso, Chile	8.6
1908	Messina, Italy	7.5
1915	Avezzano, Italy	7.5
1920	Gansu, China	8.6
1923	Yokohama, Japan	8.3
1927	Nan Shan, China	8.3
1932	Gansu, China	7.6
1934	Bihar, India/Nepal	8.4
1935	Quetta, India[†]	7.5
1939	Chillan, Chile	8.3
1939	Erzincan, Turkey	7.9
1964	Anchorage, Alaska	8.4
1968	N. E. Iran	7.4
1970	N. Peru	7.7
1976	Guatemala	7.5
1976	Tangshan, China	8.2
1978	Tabas, Iran	7.7
1980	El Asnam, Algeria	7.3
1980	S. Italy	7.2
1985	Mexico City, Mexico	8.1
1988	N. W. Armenia	6.8
1990	N. Iran	7.7
1993	Maharashtra, India	6.4
1994	Los Angeles, USA	6.6
1995	Kobe, Japan	7.2
1995	Sakhalin Is., Russia	7.5
1996	Yunnan, China	7.0
1997	N. E. Iran	7.1
1998	N. Afghanistan	6.1
1998	N. E. Afghanistan	7.0
1999	Izmit, Turkey	7.4
1999	Taipei, Taiwan	7.6
2001	Gujarat, India	7.7
2001	El Salvador	6.6

[†] *now Pakistan*

Earthquakes in subduction zones
Along subduction zones, one plate is descending beneath another. The plates are locked together until the rocks break and the descending plate lurches forwards. From the point where the plate moves – the origin – seismic waves spread through the lithosphere, making the ground shake. The earthquake in Mexico City in 1985 occurred in this way.

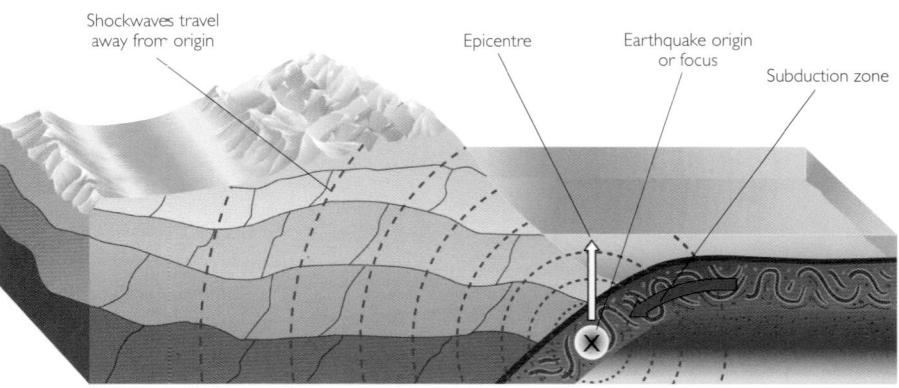

Shockwaves travel away from origin   Epicentre   Earthquake origin or focus   Subduction zone

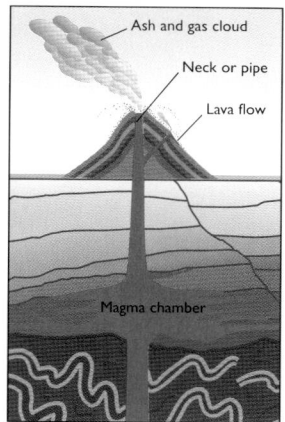

Cross-section of a volcano

Volcanoes are vents in the ground, through which magma reaches the surface. The term volcano is also used for the mountains formed from volcanic rocks. Beneath volcanoes are pockets of magma derived from the semi-molten asthenosphere in the mantle. The magma rises under pressure through the overlying rocks until it reaches the surface. There it emerges through vents as pyroclasts, ranging in size from large lumps of magma, called volcanic bombs, to fine volcanic ash and dust. In quiet eruptions, streams of liquid lava run down the side of the mountain. Side vents sometimes appear on the flanks of existing volcanoes.

Scientists have been working for years to find effective ways of forecasting earthquakes but with very limited success. Following the Kobe earthquake in 1995, many experts argued that they would be better employed developing techniques of reducing the damage caused by earthquakes, rather than pursuing an apparently vain attempt to predict them.

VOLCANIC ERUPTIONS

Most active volcanoes also occur on or near plate edges. Many undersea volcanoes along the ocean ridges are formed from magma that wells up from the asthenosphere to fill the gaps created as the plates, on the opposite sides of the ridges, move apart. Some of these volcanoes reach the surface to form islands. Iceland is a country which straddles the Mid-Atlantic Ocean Ridge. It is gradually becoming wider as magma rises to the surface through faults and vents. Other volcanoes lie alongside subduction zones. The magma that fuels them comes from the melted edges of the descending plates.

A few volcanoes lie far from plate edges. For example, Mauna Loa and Kilauea on Hawaii are situated near the centre of the huge Pacific plate. The molten magma that reaches the surface is created by a source of heat, called a 'hot spot', in the Earth's mantle.

Magma is molten rock at temperatures of about 1,100°C to 1,200°C [2,012°F to 2,192°F]. It contains gases and superheated steam. The chemical composition of magma varies. Viscous magma is rich in silica and superheated steam, while runny magma contains less silica and steam. The chemical composition of the magma affects the nature of volcanic eruptions.

Explosive volcanoes contain thick, viscous magma. When they erupt, they usually hurl clouds of ash (shattered fragments of cooled magma) into the air. By contrast, quiet volcanoes emit long streams of runny magma, or lava. However, many volcanoes are intermediate in type, sometimes erupting explosively and sometimes emitting streams of fluid lava. Explosive and intermediate volcanoes usually have a conical shape, while quiet volcanoes are flattened, resembling upturned saucers. They are often called shield volcanoes.

One dangerous type of eruption is called a *nuée ardente*, or 'glowing cloud'. It occurs when a cloud of intensely hot volcanic gases and dust particles and superheated steam are exploded from a volcano. They move rapidly downhill, burning everything in their path and choking animals and people. The blast that creates the *nuée ardente* may release the pressure inside the volcano, resulting in a tremendous explosion that hurls tall columns of ash into the air.

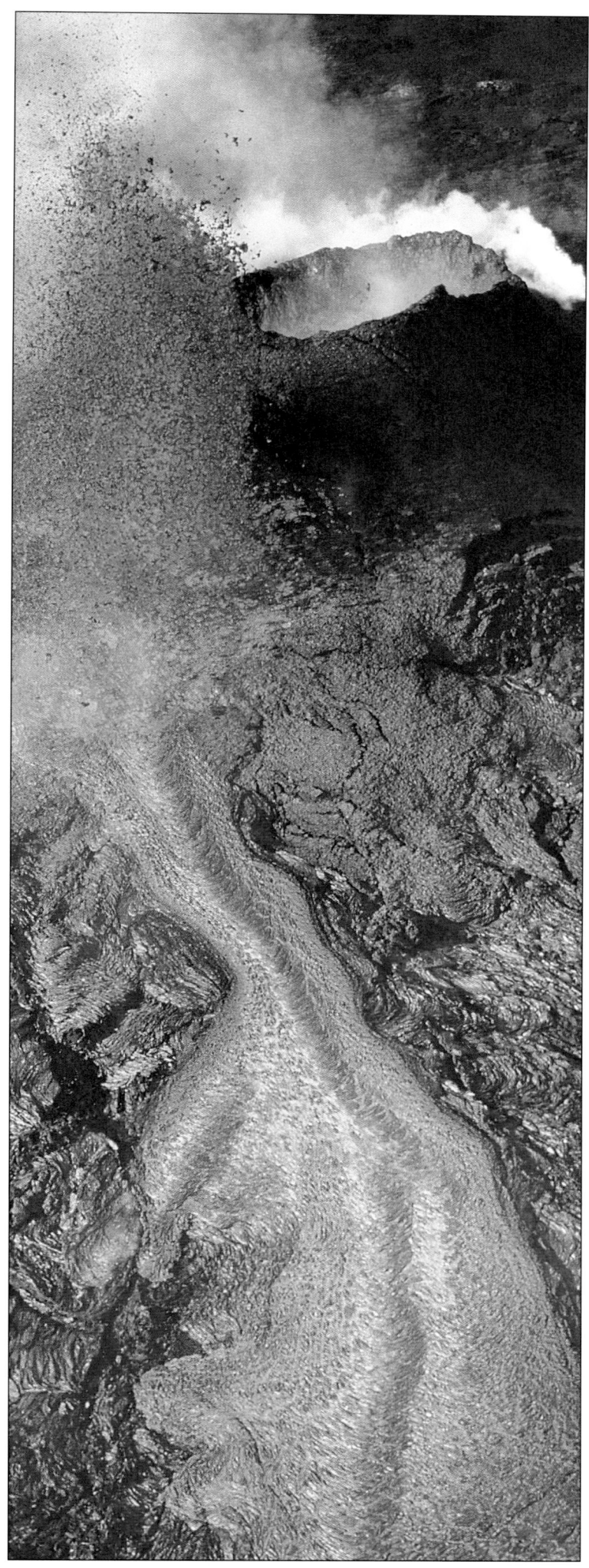

Kilauea Volcano, Hawaii

The volcanic Hawaiian islands in the North Pacific Ocean were formed as the Pacific plate moved over a 'hot spot' in the Earth's mantle. Kilauea on Hawaii emits blazing streams of liquid lava.

Forces of Nature

When the volcano Mount Pinatubo erupted in the Philippines in 1991, large areas around the mountain were covered by ash. Throughout the 1990s, rainwater mixed with the ash on sloping land, created lahars, or mudflows, which swept down river valleys burying many areas. Such incidents are not only reminders of the great forces that operate inside our planet but also of those natural forces operating on the surface, which can have dramatic effects on the land.

The chief forces acting on the surface of the Earth are weathering, running water, ice and winds. The forces of erosion seem to act slowly. One estimate suggests that an average of only 3.5 cm [1.4 in] of land is removed by natural processes every 1,000 years. This may not sound much, but over millions of years, it can reduce mountains to almost flat surfaces.

WEATHERING

Weathering occurs in all parts of the world, but the most effective type of weathering in any area depends on the climate and the nature of the rocks. For example, in cold mountain areas,

when water freezes in cracks in rocks, the ice occupies 9% more space than the water. This exerts a force which, when repeated over and over again, can split boulders apart. By contrast, in hot deserts, intense heating by day and cooling by night causes the outer layers of rocks to expand and contract until they break up and peel away like layers of an onion. These are examples of what is called mechanical weathering.

Other kinds of weathering include chemical reactions usually involving water. Rainwater containing carbon dioxide dissolved from the air or the soil is a weak acid which reacts with limestone, wearing out pits, tunnels and networks of caves in layers of limestone rock. Water also combines with some minerals, such as the feldspars in granite, to create kaolin, a white

RATES OF EROSION

	SLOW ← WEATHERING RATE → FAST		
Mineral solubility	low (e.g. quartz)	moderate (e.g. feldspar)	high (e.g. calcite)
Rainfall	low	moderate	heavy
Temperature	cold	temperate	hot
Vegetation	sparse	moderate	lush
Soil cover	bare rock	thin to moderate soil	thick soil

Weathering is the breakdown and decay of rocks in situ. It may be mechanical (physical), chemical or biological.

Rates of erosion
The chart shows that the rates at which weathering takes place depend on the chemistry and hardness of rocks, climatic factors, especially rainfall and temperature, the vegetation and the nature of the soil cover in any area. The effects of weathering are increased by human action, particularly the removal of vegetation and the exposure of soils to the rain and wind.

Grand Canyon, Arizona, at dusk
The Grand Canyon in the United States is one of the world's natural wonders. Eroded by the Colorado River and its tributaries, it is up to 1.6 km [1 mile] deep and 29 km [18 miles] wide.

clay. These are examples of chemical weathering which constantly wears away rock.

RUNNING WATER, ICE AND WIND

In moist regions, rivers are effective in shaping the land. They transport material worn away by weathering and erode the land. They wear out V-shaped valleys in upland regions, while vigorous meanders widen their middle courses. The work of rivers is at its most spectacular when earth movements lift up flat areas and rejuvenate the rivers, giving them a new erosive power capable of wearing out such features as the Grand Canyon. Rivers also have a constructive role. Some of the world's most fertile regions are deltas and flood plains composed of sediments

Glaciers

During Ice Ages, ice spreads over large areas but, during warm periods, the ice retreats. The chart shows that the volume of ice in many glaciers is decreasing, possibly as a result of global warming. Experts estimate that, between 1850 and the early 21st century, more than half of the ice in Alpine glaciers has melted.

ANNUAL FLUCTUATIONS FOR SELECTED GLACIERS

Glacier name and location	Changes in the annual mass balance†		Cumulative total
	1970–1	1990–1	1970–90
Alfotbreen, Norway	+940	+790	+12,110
Wolverine, USA	+770	−410	+2,320
Storglaciaren, Sweden	−190	+170	−120
Djankuat, Russia	−230	−310	−1,890
Grasubreen, Norway	+470	−520	−2,530
Ürümqi, China	+102	−706	−3,828
Golubin, Kyrgyzstan	−90	−722	−7,105
Hintereisferner, Austria	−600	−1,325	−9,081
Gries, Switzerland	−970	−1,480	−10,600
Careser, Italy	−650	−1,730	−11,610
Abramov, Tajikistan	−890	−420	−13,700
Sarennes, France	−1,100	−1,360	−15,020
Place, Canada	−343	−990	−15,175

† *The annual mass balance is defined as the difference between glacier accumulation and ablation (melting) averaged over the whole glacier. Balances are expressed as water equivalent in millimetres. A plus indicates an increase in the depth or length of the glacier; a minus indicates a reduction.*

Juneau Glacier, Alaska

Like huge conveyor belts, glaciers transport weathered debris from mountain regions. Rocks frozen in the ice give the glaciers teeth, enabling them to wear out typical glaciated land features.

periodically dumped there by such rivers as the Ganges, Mississippi and Nile.

Running water in the form of sea waves and currents shapes coastlines, wearing out caves, natural arches, and stacks. The sea also transports and deposits worn material to form such features as spits and bars.

Glaciers in cold mountain regions flow downhill, gradually deepening valleys and shaping dramatic landscapes. They erode steep-sided U-shaped valleys, into which rivers often plunge in large waterfalls. Other features include cirques, armchair-shaped basins bounded by knife-edged ridges called *arêtes*. When several glacial cirques erode to form radial *arêtes*, pyramidal peaks like the Matterhorn are created. Deposits of moraine, rock material dumped by the glacier, are further evidence that ice once covered large areas. The work of glaciers, like other agents of erosion, varies with the climate. In recent years, global warming has been making glaciers retreat in many areas, while several of the ice shelves in Antarctica have been breaking up.

Many land features in deserts were formed by running water at a time when the climate was much rainier than it is today. Water erosion also occurs when flash floods are caused by rare thunderstorms. But the chief agent of erosion in dry areas is wind-blown sand, which can strip the paint from cars, and undercut boulders to create mushroom-shaped rocks.

Oceans and Ice

Since the 1970s, oceanographers have found numerous hot vents on the ocean ridges. Called black smokers, the vents emit dark, mineral-rich water reaching 350°C [662°F]. Around the vents are chimney-like structures formed from minerals deposited from the hot water. The discovery of black smokers did not surprise scientists who already knew that the ridges were plate edges, where new crustal rock was being formed as molten magma welled up to the surface. But what was astonishing was that the hot water contained vast numbers of bacteria, which provided the base of a food chain that included many strange creatures, such as giant worms, eyeless shrimps and white clams. Many species were unknown to science.

Little was known about the dark world beneath the waves until about 50 years ago. But through the use of modern technology such as echo-sounders, magnetometers, research ships equipped with huge drills, submersibles that can carry scientists down to the ocean floor, and satellites, the secrets of the oceans have been gradually revealed.

The study of the ocean floor led to the discovery that the oceans are geologically young features – no more than 200 million years old. It also revealed evidence as to how oceans form and continents drift because of the action of plate tectonics.

THE BLUE PLANET

Water covers almost 71% of the Earth, which makes it look blue when viewed from space. Although the oceans are interconnected, geographers divide them into four main areas: the Pacific, Atlantic, Indian and Arctic oceans. The average depth of the oceans is 3,370 m [12,238 ft], but they are divided into several zones.

Around most continents are gently sloping continental shelves, which are flooded parts of the continents. The shelves end at the continental slope, at a depth of about 200 m [656 ft]. This slope leads steeply down to the abyss. The deepest parts of the oceans are the trenches, which reach a maximum depth of 11,033 m [36,198 ft] in the Mariana Trench in the western Pacific.

Most marine life is found in the top 200 m [656 ft], where there is sufficient sunlight for plants, called phytoplankton, to grow. Below this zone, life becomes more and more scarce, though no part of the ocean, even at the bottom of the deepest trenches, is completely without living things.

Vava'u Island, Tonga
This small coral atoll in northern Tonga consists of a central island covered by rainforest. Low coral reefs washed by the waves surround a shallow central lagoon.

Continental islands, such as the British Isles, are high parts of the continental shelves. For example, until about 7,500 years ago, when the ice sheets formed during the Ice Ages were melting, raising the sea level and filling the North Sea and the Strait of Dover, Britain was linked to mainland Europe.

By contrast, oceanic islands, such as the Hawaiian chain in the North Pacific Ocean, rise from the ocean floor. All oceanic islands are of volcanic origin, although many of them in warm parts of the oceans have sunk and are capped by layers of coral to form ring- or horseshoe-shaped atolls and coral reefs.

OCEAN WATER

The oceans contain about 97% of the world's water. Seawater contains more than 70 dissolved elements, but chloride and sodium make up 85% of the total. Sodium chloride is common salt and it makes seawater salty. The salinity of the oceans is mostly between 3.3–3.7%. Ocean water fed by icebergs or large rivers is less saline than shallow seas in the tropics, where the evaporation rate is high. Seawater is a source of salt but the water is useless for agriculture or drinking unless it is desalinated. However, land

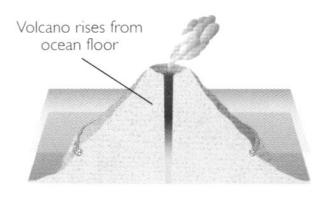

Volcano rises from ocean floor

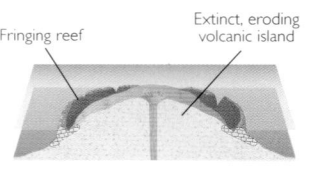

Fringing reef

Extinct, eroding volcanic island

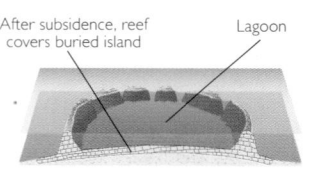

After subsidence, reef covers buried island

Lagoon

Development of an atoll
Some of the volcanoes that rise from the ocean floor reach the surface to form islands. Some of these islands subside and become submerged. As an island sinks, coral starts to grow around the rim of the volcano, building up layer upon layer of limestone deposits to form fringing reefs. Sometimes coral grows on the tip of a central cone to form an island in the middle of the atoll.

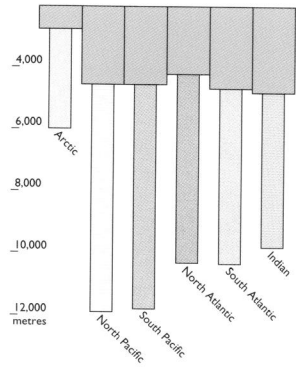

The ocean depths

The diagram shows the average depths (in dark blue) and the greatest depths in the four oceans. The North Pacific Ocean contains the world's deepest trenches, including the Mariana Trench, where the deepest manned descent was made by the bathyscaphe Trieste *in 1960. It reached a depth of 10,916 metres [35,813 ft].*

Relative sizes of the world's oceans:

PACIFIC   49%   ATLANTIC 26%
INDIAN   21%   ARCTIC   4%

Some geographers distinguish a fifth ocean, the Southern or Antarctic Ocean, but most authorities regard these waters as the southern extension of the Pacific, Atlantic and Indian oceans.

areas get a regular supply of fresh water through the hydrological cycle (see page 26).

The density of seawater depends on its salinity and temperature. Temperatures vary from –2°C [28°F], the freezing point of seawater at the poles, to around 30°C [86°F] in parts of the tropics. Density differences help to maintain the circulation of the world's oceans, especially deep-sea currents. But the main cause of currents within 350 m [1,148 ft] of the surface is the wind. Because of the Earth's rotation, currents are deflected, creating huge circular motions of surface water – clockwise in the northern hemisphere and anticlockwise in the southern hemisphere.

Ocean currents transport heat from the tropics to the polar regions and thus form part of the heat engine that drives the Earth's climates. Ocean currents have an especially marked effect on coastal climates, such as north-western Europe. In the mid-1990s, scientists warned that global warming may be weakening currents, including the warm Gulf Stream which is responsible for the mild winters experienced in north-western Europe.

ICE SHEETS, ICE CAPS AND GLACIERS

Global warming is also a threat to the world's ice sheets, ice caps and glaciers that together account for about 2% of the world's water. There are two ice sheets in the world, the largest covers most of Antarctica. With the ice reaching maximum depths of 4,800 m [15,748 ft], the Antarctic ice sheet contains about 70% of the world's fresh water, with a total volume about nine times greater than the Greenland ice sheet. Smaller bodies of ice include ice caps in northern Canada, Iceland and Scandinavia. Also throughout the world in high ranges are many valley glaciers, which help to shape dramatic mountain scenery.

Only about 11,000 years ago, during the final phase of the Pleistocene Ice Age, ice covered much of the northern hemisphere. The Ice Age, which began about 1.8 million years ago, was not a continuous period of cold. Instead, it consisted of glacial periods when the ice advanced and warmer interglacial periods when temperatures rose and the ice retreated.

Some scientists believe that we are now living in an inter-glacial period, and that glacial conditions will recur in the future. Others fear that global warming, caused mainly by pollution, may melt the world's ice, raising sea levels by up to 55 m [180 ft]. Many fertile and densely populated coastal plains, islands and cities would vanish from the map.

Weddell Sea, Antarctica

Antarctica contains two huge bays, occupied by the Ross and Weddell seas. Ice shelves extend from the ice sheet across parts of these seas. Researchers fear that warmer weather is melting Antarctica's ice sheets at a dangerous rate, after large chunks of the Larsen ice shelf and the Ronne ice shelf broke away in 1997 and 1998, respectively.

The Earth's Atmosphere

Since the discovery in 1985 of a thinning of the ozone layer, creating a so-called 'ozone hole', over Antarctica, many governments have worked to reduce the emissions of ozone-eating substances, notably the chlorofluorocarbons (CFCs) used in aerosols, refrigeration, air conditioning and dry cleaning.

Following forecasts that the ozone layer would rapidly repair itself as a result of controls on these emissions, scientists were surprised in early 1996 when a marked thinning of the ozone layer occurred over the Arctic, northern Europe, Russia and Canada. The damage, which was recorded as far south as southern Britain, was due to pollution combined with intense cold in the stratosphere. It was another sharp reminder of the dangers humanity faces when it interferes with and harms the environment.

The ozone layer in the stratosphere blocks out most of the dangerous ultraviolet B radiation in the Sun's rays. This radiation causes skin cancer and cataracts, as well as harming plants on the land and plankton in the oceans. The ozone layer is only one way in which the atmosphere protects life on Earth. The atmosphere also provides the air we breathe and the carbon dioxide required by plants. It is also a shield against meteors and it acts as a blanket to prevent heat radiated from the Earth escaping into space.

LAYERS OF AIR

The atmosphere is divided into four main layers. The troposphere at the bottom contains about 85% of the atmosphere's total mass, where most weather conditions occur. The troposphere is about 15 km [9 miles] thick over the Equator and 8 km [5 miles] thick at the poles. Temperatures decrease with height by approximately 1°C [2°F] for every 100 m [328 ft]. At the top of the troposphere is a level called the tropopause where temperatures are stable at around –55°C [–67°F]. Above the tropopause is the stratosphere, which contains the ozone layer. Here, at about 50 km [31 miles] above the Earth's surface, temperatures rise to about 0°C [32°F].

The ionosphere extends from the stratopause to about 600 km [373 miles] above the surface. Here temperatures fall up to about 80 km

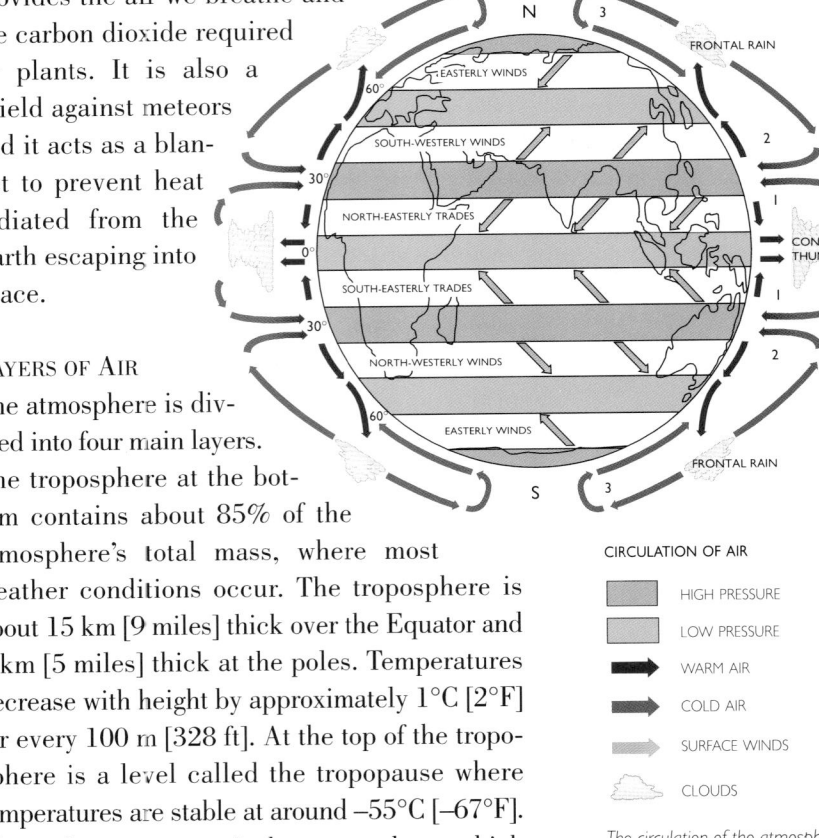

CIRCULATION OF AIR

▨	HIGH PRESSURE
▨	LOW PRESSURE
➤	WARM AIR
➤	COLD AIR
➤	SURFACE WINDS
☁	CLOUDS

The circulation of the atmosphere can be divided into three rotating but interconnected air systems, or cells. The Hadley cell (figure 1 on the above diagram) is in the tropics; the Ferrel cell (2) lies between the sub-tropics and the mid-latitudes, and the Polar cell (3) is in the high latitudes.

Moonrise seen from orbit
This photograph taken by an orbiting Shuttle shows the crescent of the Moon. Silhouetted at the horizon is a dense cloud layer. The reddish-brown band is the tropopause, which separates the blue-white stratosphere from the yellow troposphere.

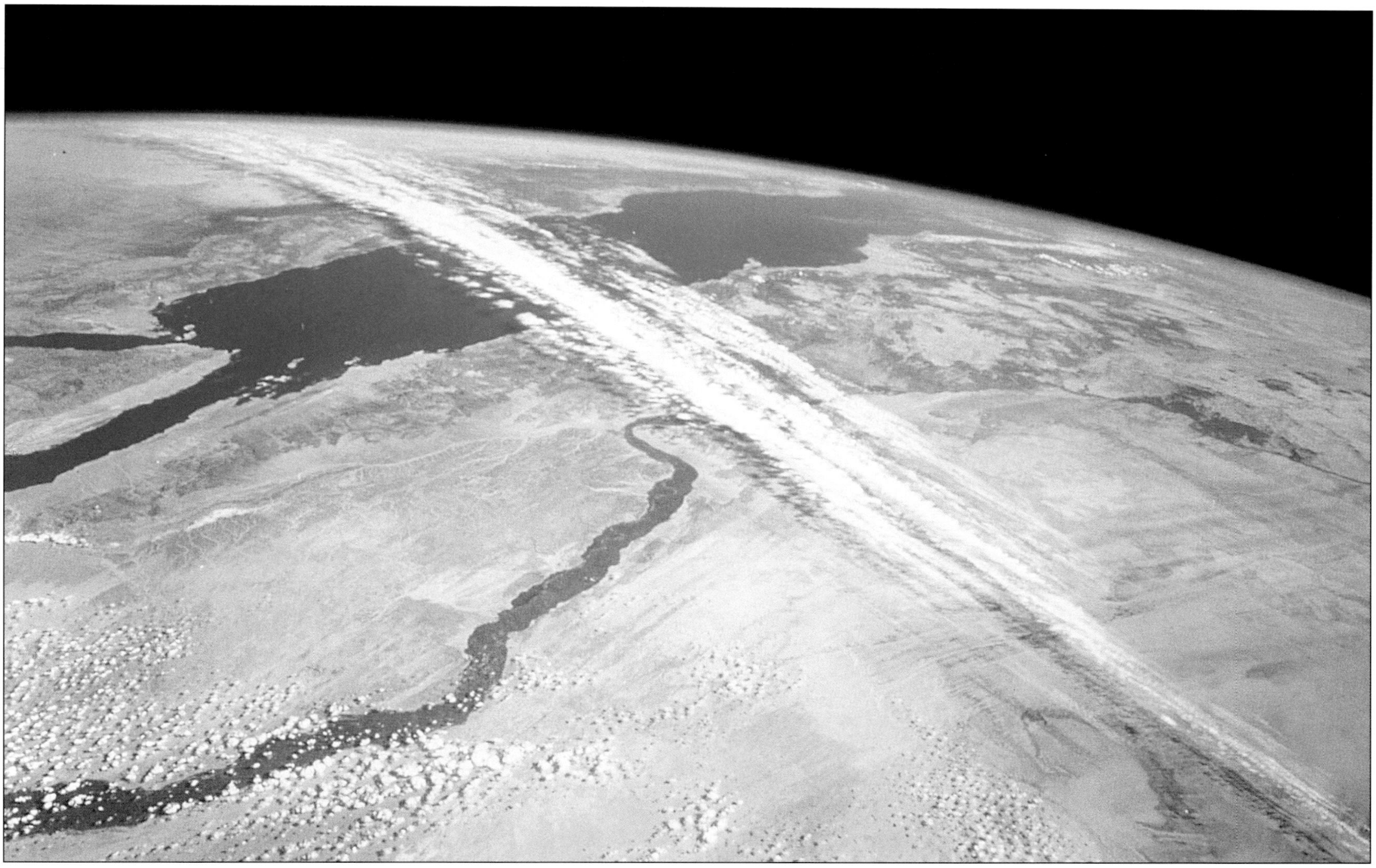

Jetstream from space

Jetstreams are strong winds that normally blow near the tropopause. Cirrus clouds mark the route of the jet stream in this photograph, which shows the Red Sea, North Africa and the Nile valley, which appears as a dark band crossing the desert.

[50 miles], but then rise. The aurorae, which occur in the ionosphere when charged particles from the Sun interact with the Earth's magnetic field, are strongest near the poles. In the exosphere, the outermost layer, the atmosphere merges into space.

CIRCULATION OF THE ATMOSPHERE

The heating of the Earth is most intense around the Equator where the Sun is high in the sky. Here warm, moist air rises in strong currents, creating a zone of low air pressure: the doldrums. The rising air eventually cools and spreads out north and south until it sinks back to the ground around latitudes 30° North and 30° South. This forms two zones of high air pressure called the horse latitudes.

From the horse latitudes, trade winds blow back across the surface towards the Equator, while westerly winds blow towards the poles. The warm westerlies finally meet the polar easterlies (cold dense air flowing from the poles). The line along which the warm and cold air streams meet is called the polar front. Depressions (or cyclones) are low air pressure frontal systems that form along the polar front.

COMPOSITION OF THE ATMOSPHERE

The air in the troposphere is made up mainly of nitrogen (78%) and oxygen (21%). Argon makes up more than 0.9% and there are also minute amounts of carbon dioxide, helium, hydrogen, krypton, methane, ozone and xenon. The atmosphere also contains water vapour, the gaseous form of water, which, when it condenses around minute specks of dust and salt, forms tiny water droplets or ice crystals. Large masses of water droplets or ice crystals form clouds.

Classification of clouds

Clouds are classified broadly into cumuliform, or 'heap' clouds, and stratiform, or 'layer' clouds. Both types occur at all levels. The highest clouds, composed of ice crystals, are cirrus, cirrostratus and cirrocumulus. Medium-height clouds include altostratus, a grey cloud that often indicates the approach of a depression, and altocumulus, a thicker and fluffier version of cirrocumulus. Low clouds include stratus, which forms dull, overcast skies; nimbostratus, a dark grey layer cloud which brings almost continuous rain and snow; cumulus, a brilliant white heap cloud; and stratocumulus, a layer cloud arranged in globular masses or rolls. Cumulonimbus, a cloud associated with thunderstorms, lightning and heavy rain, often extends from low to medium altitudes. It has a flat base, a fluffy outline and often an anvil-shaped top.

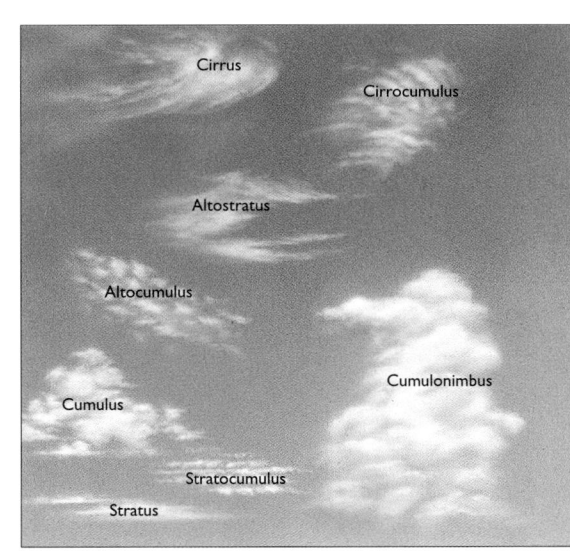

Climate and Weather

In 1992, Hurricane Andrew struck the Bahamas, Florida and Louisiana, causing record damage estimated at $30 billion. In September 1998, following heavy monsoon rains, floods submerged two-thirds of Bangladesh. The same month, in Central America, more than 7,000 people died in floods and mudslides caused by Hurricane Mitch. The economy of Honduras, already crippled by debt, was thought to have been put back by 15 to 20 years. In March 2000, the worst floods in Mozambique in 50 years devastated the country's economy.

Every year, exceptional weather conditions cause disasters around the world. Modern forecasting techniques now give people warning of advancing storms, but the toll of human deaths continues as people are powerless in the face of the awesome forces of nature.

Weather is the day-to-day condition of the atmosphere. In some places, the weather is normally stable, but in other areas, especially the middle latitudes, it is highly variable, changing with the passing of a depression. By contrast, climate is the average weather of a place, based on data obtained over a long period.

Hurricane Elena, 1995

Hurricanes form over warm oceans north and south of the Equator. Their movements are tracked by satellites, enabling forecasters to issue storm warnings as they approach land. In North America, forecasters identify them with boys' and girls' names.

CLIMATIC FACTORS

Climate depends basically on the unequal heating of the Sun between the Equator and the poles. But ocean currents and terrain also affect climate. For example, despite their northerly positions, Norway's ports remain ice-free in winter. This is because of the warming effect of the North Atlantic Drift, an extension of the Gulf Stream which flows across the Atlantic Ocean from the Gulf of Mexico.

By contrast, the cold Benguela current which flows up the coast of south-western Africa cools the coast and causes arid conditions. This is because the cold onshore winds are warmed as they pass over the land. The warm air can hold more water vapour than cold air, giving the winds a drying effect.

The terrain affects climate in several ways. Because temperatures fall with altitude, highlands are cooler than lowlands in the same

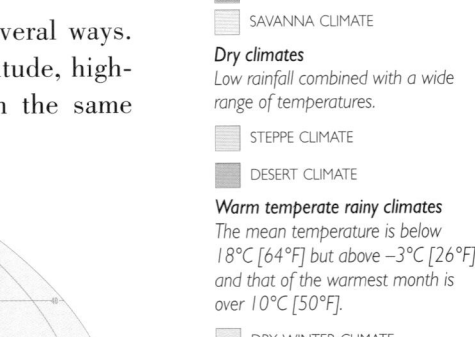

CLIMATIC REGIONS

Tropical rainy climates
All mean monthly temperatures above 18°C [64°F].

- RAINFOREST CLIMATE
- MONSOON CLIMATE
- SAVANNA CLIMATE

Dry climates
Low rainfall combined with a wide range of temperatures.

- STEPPE CLIMATE
- DESERT CLIMATE

Warm temperate rainy climates
The mean temperature is below 18°C [64°F] but above −3°C [26°F] and that of the warmest month is over 10°C [50°F].

- DRY WINTER CLIMATE
- DRY SUMMER CLIMATE
- CLIMATE WITH NO DRY SEASON

Cold temperate rainy climates
The mean temperature of the coldest month is below 3°C [37°F] but the warmest month is over 10°C [50°F].

- DRY WINTER CLIMATE
- CLIMATE WITH NO DRY SEASON

Polar climates
The temperature of the warmest month is below 10°C [50°F], giving permanently frozen subsoil.

- TUNDRA CLIMATE
- POLAR CLIMATE

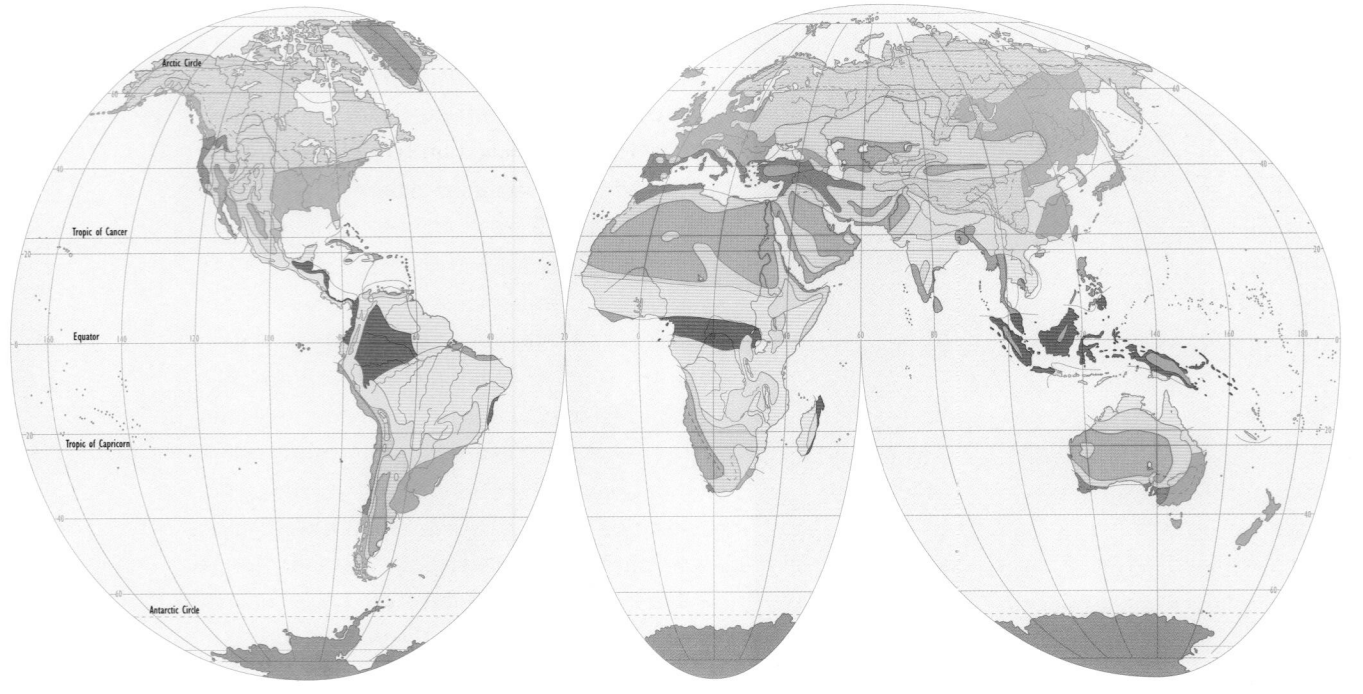

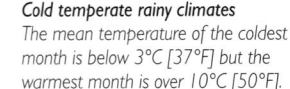

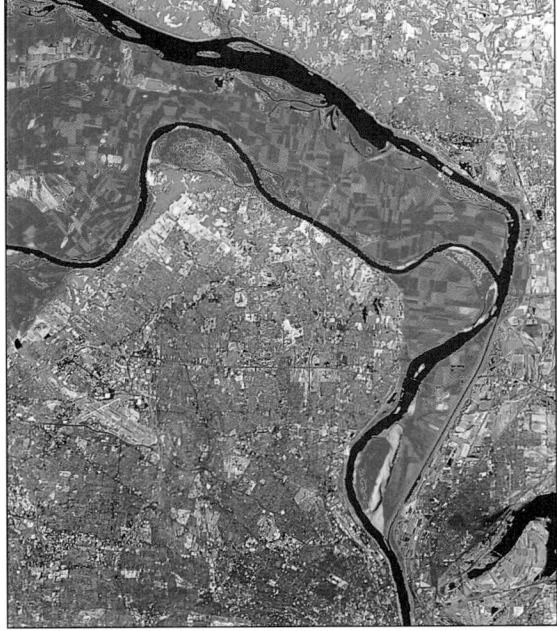

Floods in St Louis, United States
The satellite image, right, shows the extent of the floods at St Louis at the confluence of the Mississippi and the Missouri rivers in June and July 1993. The floods occurred when very heavy rainfall raised river levels by up to 14 m [46 ft]. The floods reached their greatest extent between Minneapolis in the north and a point approximately 150 km [93 miles] south of St Louis. In places, the width of the Mississippi increased to nearly 11 km [7 miles], while the Missouri reached widths of 32 km [20 miles]. In all, more than 28,000 sq km [10,800 sq miles] were inundated and hundreds of towns and cities were flooded. Damage to crops was estimated at $8 billion. The USA was hit again by flooding in early 1997, when heavy rainfall in North Dakota and Minnesota caused the Red River to flood. The flooding had a catastrophic effect on the city of Grand Forks, which was inundated for months.

Flood damage in the United States
In June and July 1993, the Mississippi River basin suffered record floods. The photograph shows a sunken church in Illinois. The flooding along the Mississippi, Missouri and other rivers caused great damage, amounting to about $12 billion. At least 48 people died in the floods.

CLIMATIC REGIONS

The two major factors that affect climate are temperature and precipitation, including rain and snow. In addition, seasonal variations and other climatic features are also taken into account. Climatic classifications vary because of the weighting given to various features. Yet most classifications are based on five main climatic types: tropical rainy climates; dry climates; warm temperate rainy climates; cold temperate rainy climates; and very cold polar climates. Some classifications also allow for the effect of altitude. The main climatic regions are subdivided according to seasonal variations and also to the kind of vegetation associated with the climatic conditions. Thus, the rainforest climate, with rain throughout the year, differs from monsoon and savanna climates, which have marked dry seasons. Similarly, parched desert climates differ from steppe climates which have enough moisture for grasses to grow.

latitude. Terrain also affects rainfall. When moist onshore winds pass over mountain ranges, they are chilled as they are forced to rise and the water vapour they contain condenses to form clouds which bring rain and snow. After the winds have crossed the mountains, the air descends and is warmed. These warm, dry winds create rain shadow (arid) regions on the lee side of the mountains.

Water and Land Use

All life on land depends on fresh water. Yet about 80 countries now face acute water shortages. The world demand for fresh water is increasing by about 2.3% a year and this demand will double every 21 years. About a billion people, mainly in developing countries, do not have access to clean drinking water and around 10 million die every year from drinking dirty water. This problem is made worse in many countries by the pollution of rivers and lakes.

In 1995, a World Bank report suggested that wars will be fought over water in the 21st century. Relations between several countries are

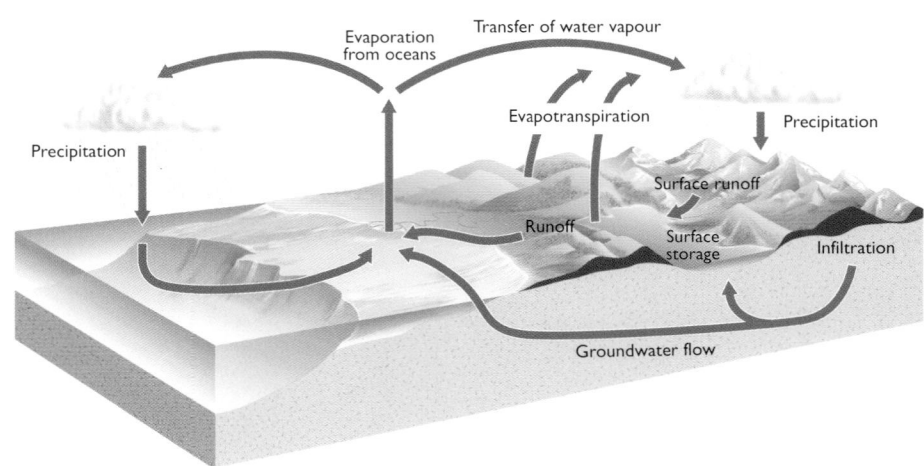

The hydrological cycle
The hydrological cycle is responsible for the continuous circulation of water around the planet. Water vapour contains and transports latent heat, or latent energy. When the water vapour condenses back into water (and falls as rain, hail or snow), the heat is released. When condensation takes place on cold nights, the cooling effect associated with nightfall is offset by the liberation of latent heat.

Hoover Dam, United States
The Hoover Dam in Arizona controls the Colorado River's flood waters. Its reservoir supplies domestic and irrigation water to the south-west, while a hydroelectric plant produces electricity.

already soured by disputes over water resources. Egypt fears that Sudan and Ethiopia will appropriate the waters of the Nile, while Syria and Iraq are concerned that Turkish dams will hold back the waters of the Euphrates.

However, experts stress that while individual countries face water crises, there is no global crisis. The chief global problems are the uneven distribution of water and its inefficient and wasteful use.

THE WORLD'S WATER SUPPLY

Of the world's total water supply, 99.4% is in the oceans or frozen in bodies of ice. Most of the rest circulates through the rocks beneath our feet as ground water. Water in rivers and lakes, in the soil and in the atmosphere together make up only 0.013% of the world's water.

The freshwater supply on land is dependent on the hydrological, or water cycle which is driven by the Sun's heat. Water is evaporated from the oceans and carried into the air as invisible water vapour. Although this vapour averages less than 2% of the total mass of the atmosphere, it is the chief component from the standpoint of weather.

When air rises, water vapour condenses into visible water droplets or ice crystals, which eventually fall to earth as rain, snow, sleet, hail or frost. Some of the precipitation that reaches the ground returns directly to the atmosphere through evaporation or transpiration via plants. Much of the rest of the water flows into the rocks to become ground water or across the surface into rivers and, eventually, back to the oceans, so completing the hydrological cycle.

WATER AND AGRICULTURE

Only about a third of the world's land area is used for growing crops, while another third

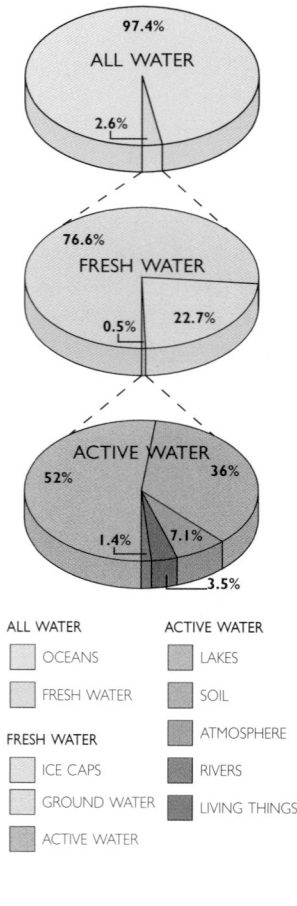

WATER DISTRIBUTION
The distribution of planetary water, by percentage.

97.4%
ALL WATER
2.6%

76.6%
FRESH WATER
0.5%   22.7%

ACTIVE WATER
52%   36%
1.4%   7.1%
3.5%

ALL WATER	ACTIVE WATER
OCEANS	LAKES
FRESH WATER	SOIL
	ATMOSPHERE
FRESH WATER	
ICE CAPS	RIVERS
GROUND WATER	LIVING THINGS
ACTIVE WATER	

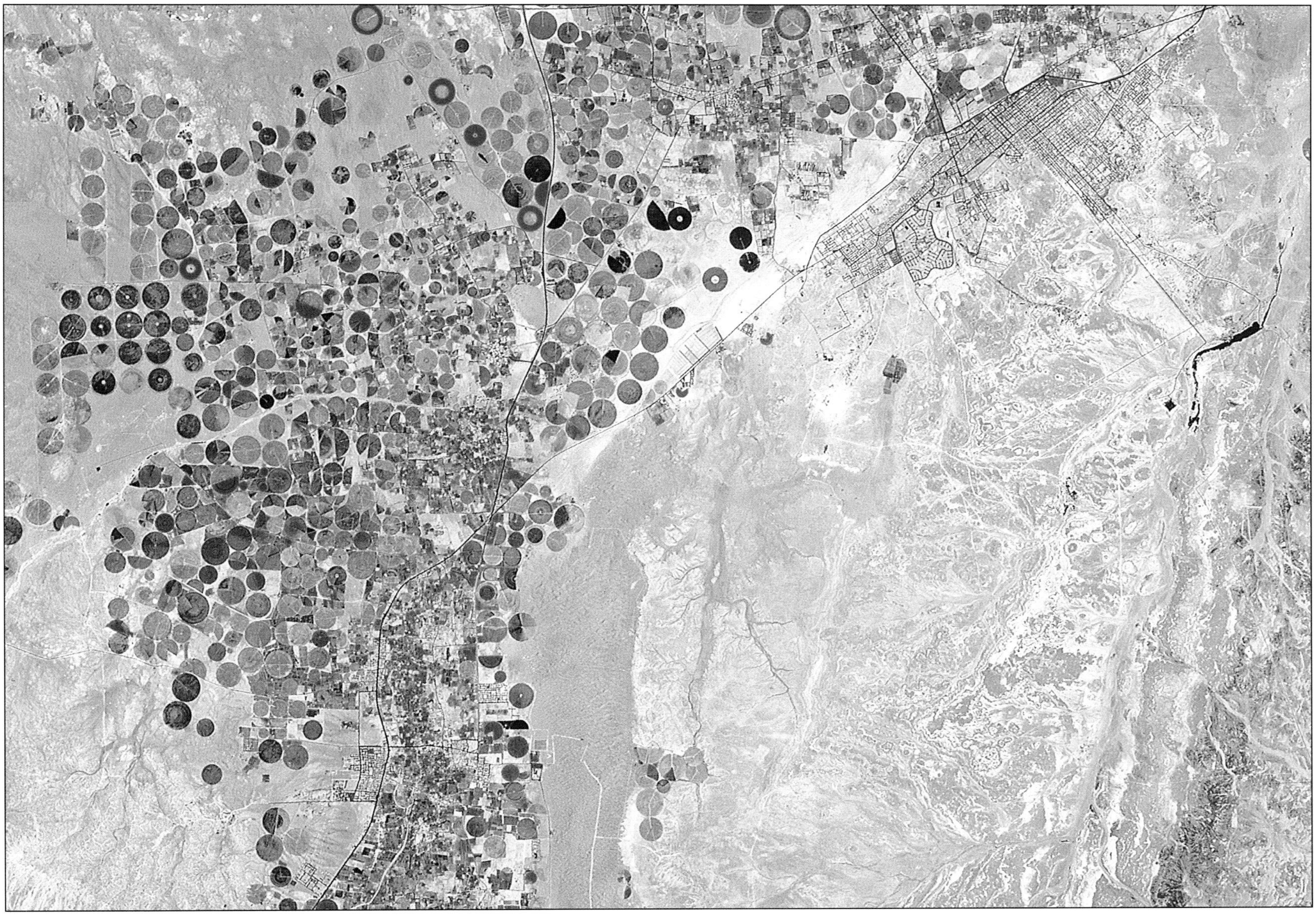

Irrigation in Saudi Arabia

Saudi Arabia is a desert country which gets its water from oases, which tap ground water supplies, and desalination plants. The sale of oil has enabled the arid countries of south-western Asia to develop their agriculture. In the above satellite image, vegetation appears brown and red.

Irrigation boom

The photograph shows a pivotal irrigation boom used to sprinkle water over a wheat field in Saudi Arabia. Irrigation in hot countries often takes place at night so that water loss through evaporation is reduced. Irrigation techniques vary from place to place. In monsoon areas with abundant water, the fields are often flooded, or the water is led to the crops along straight furrows. Sprinkler irrigation has become important since the 1940s. In other types of irrigation, the water is led through pipes which are on or under the ground. Underground pipes supply water directly to the plant roots and, as a result, water loss through evaporation is minimized.

consists of meadows and pasture. The rest of the world is unsuitable for farming, being too dry, too cold, too mountainous, or covered by dense forests. Although the demand for food increases every year, problems arise when attempts are made to increase the existing area of farmland. For example, the soils and climates of tropical forest and semi-arid regions of Africa and South America are not ideal for farming. Attempts to work such areas usually end in failure. To increase the world's food supply, scientists now concentrate on making existing farmland more productive rather than farming marginal land.

To grow crops, farmers need fertile, workable land, an equable climate, including a frost-free growing period, and an adequate supply of fresh water. In some areas, the water falls directly as rain. But many other regions depend on irrigation.

Irrigation involves water conservation through the building of dams which hold back storage reservoirs. In some areas, irrigation water comes from underground aquifers, layers of permeable and porous rocks through which ground water percolates. But in many cases, the water in the aquifers has been there for thousands of years, having accumulated at a time when the rainfall

was much greater than it is today. As a result, these aquifers are not being renewed and will, one day, dry up.

Other sources of irrigation water are desalination plants, which remove salt from seawater and pump it to farms. This is a highly expensive process and is employed in areas where water supplies are extremely low, such as the island of Malta, or in the oil-rich desert countries around the Gulf, which can afford to build huge desalination plants.

LAND USE BY CONTINENT

	Forest	Permanent pasture	Permanent crops	Arable	Non-productive
North America	32.2%	17.3%	0.3%	12.6%	37.6%
South America	51.8%	26.7%	1.5%	6.6%	13.4%
Europe	33.4%	17.5%	3.0%	26.8%	19.3%
Africa	23.2%	26.6%	0.6%	5.6%	44.0%
Asia	20.2%	25.0%	1.2%	16.0%	37.8%
Oceania	23.5%	52.2%	0.1%	5.7%	18.5%

The Natural World

In 1995, a United Nations Environment Programme report stated that 11% of all mammal species, 18% of birds and 5% of fish are now threatened with extinction. Furthermore, it predicted that half of all bird and mammal species will become extinct within 300 years, or sooner if current trends continue. This will greatly reduce the biodiversity of our planet, causing the disappearance of unique combinations of genes that could be vital in improving food yields on farms or in the production of drugs to combat diseases.

Extinctions of species have occurred throughout Earth history, but today the extinction rate is estimated to be about 10,000 times the natural average. Some scientists have even compared it with the mass extinction that wiped out the dinosaurs 65 million years ago. However, the main cause of today's high extinction rate is not some natural disaster, such as the impact of an asteroid a few kilometres across, but it is the result of human actions, most notably the destruction of natural habitats for farming and other purposes. In some densely populated areas, such as Western Europe, the natural

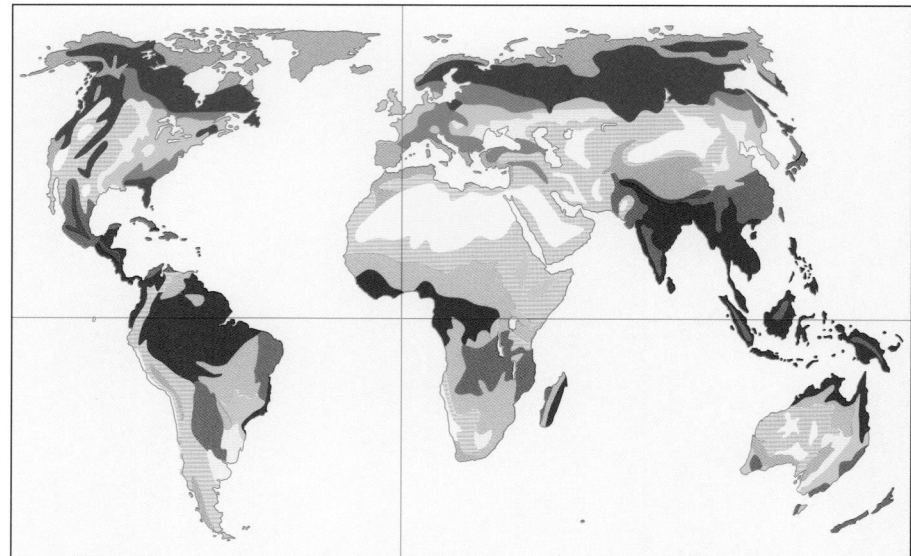

Rainforest in Rwanda

Rainforests are the most threatened of the world's biomes. Effective conservation policies must demonstrate to poor local people that they can benefit from the survival of the forests.

habitats were destroyed long ago. Today, the greatest damage is occurring in tropical rainforests, which contain more than half of the world's known species.

Modern technology has enabled people to live comfortably almost anywhere on Earth. But most plants and many animals are adapted to particular climatic conditions, and they live in association with and dependent on each other. Plant and animal communities that cover large areas are called biomes.

THE WORLD'S BIOMES

The world's biomes are defined mainly by climate and vegetation. They range from the tundra, in polar regions and high mountain regions, to the lush equatorial rainforests.

The Arctic tundra covers large areas in the polar regions of the northern hemisphere. Snow covers the land for more than half of the year and the subsoil, called permafrost, is permanently frozen. Comparatively few species can survive in this harsh, treeless environment. The main plants are hardy mosses, lichens, grasses, sedges and low shrubs. However, in summer, the tundra plays an important part in world animal geography, when its growing plants and swarms of insects provide food for migrating animals and birds that arrive from the south.

The tundra of the northern hemisphere merges in the south into a vast region of needleleaf evergreen forest, called the boreal forest or taiga. Such trees as fir, larch, pine and spruce are adapted to survive the long, bitterly cold winters of this region, but the number of plant and animal species is again small. South of the boreal forests is a zone of mixed needleleaf evergreens and broadleaf deciduous trees, which

NATURAL VEGETATION

TUNDRA & MOUNTAIN VEGETATION

NEEDLELEAF EVERGREEN FOREST

MIXED NEEDLELEAF EVERGREEN & BROADLEAF DECIDUOUS TREES

BROADLEAF DECIDUOUS WOODLAND

MID-LATITUDE GRASSLAND

EVERGREEN BROADLEAF & DECIDUOUS TREES & SHRUBS

SEMI-DESERT SCRUB

DESERT

TROPICAL GRASSLAND (SAVANNA)

TROPICAL BROADLEAF RAINFOREST & MONSOON FOREST

SUBTROPICAL BROADLEAF & NEEDLELEAF FOREST

The map shows the world's main biomes. The classification is based on the natural 'climax' vegetation of regions, a result of the climate and the terrain. But human activities have greatly modified this basic division. For example, the original deciduous forests of Western Europe and the eastern United States have largely disappeared. In recent times, human development of some semi-arid areas has turned former dry grasslands into barren desert.

Tundra in subarctic Alaska

The Denali National Park, Alaska, contains magnificent mountain scenery and tundra vegetation which flourishes during the brief summer. The park is open between 1 June and 15 September.

shed their leaves in winter. In warmer areas, this mixed forest merges into broadleaf deciduous forest, where the number and diversity of plant species is much greater.

Deciduous forests are adapted to temperate, humid regions. Evergreen broadleaf and deciduous trees grow in Mediterranean regions, with their hot, dry summers. But much of the original deciduous forest has been cut down and has given way to scrub and heathland. Grasslands occupy large areas in the middle latitudes, where the rainfall is insufficient to support forest

growth. The moister grasslands are often called prairies, while drier areas are called steppe.

The tropics also contain vast dry areas of semi-desert scrub which merges into desert, as well as large areas of savanna, which is grassland with scattered trees. Savanna regions, with their marked dry season, support a wide range of mammals.

Tropical and subtropical regions contain three types of forest biomes. The tropical rainforest, the world's richest biome measured by its plant and animal species, experiences rain and high temperatures throughout the year. Similar forests occur in monsoon regions, which have a season of very heavy rainfall. They, too, are rich in plant species, though less so than the tropical rainforest. A third type of forest is the subtropical broadleaf and needleleaf forest, found in such places as south-eastern China, south-central Africa and eastern Brazil.

NET PRIMARY PRODUCTION OF EIGHT
MAJOR BIOMES

- ▪ TROPICAL RAINFORESTS
- ▫ DECIDUOUS FORESTS
- ▫ TROPICAL GRASSLANDS
- ▪ CONIFEROUS FORESTS
- ▫ MEDITERRANEAN
- ▫ TEMPERATE GRASSLANDS
- ▫ TUNDRA
- ▫ DESERTS

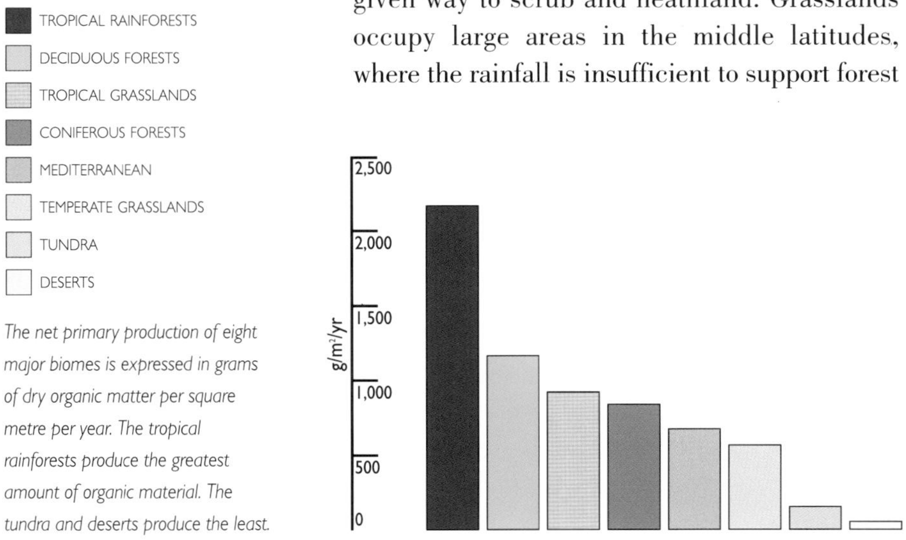

The net primary production of eight major biomes is expressed in grams of dry organic matter per square metre per year. The tropical rainforests produce the greatest amount of organic material. The tundra and deserts produce the least.

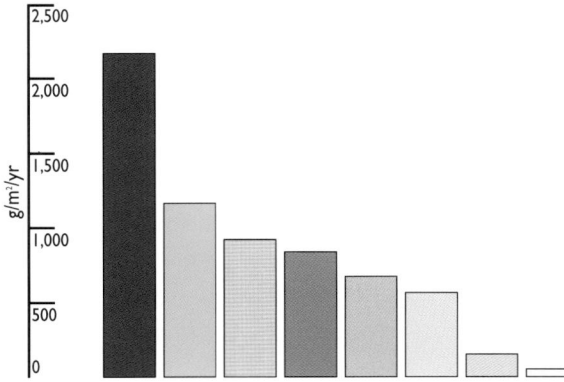

g/m³/yr — 2,500 / 2,000 / 1,500 / 1,000 / 500 / 0

The Human World

Every minute, the world's population increases by between 160 and 170. While forecasts of future growth are difficult to make, most demographers are in agreement that the world's population, which passed the 6 billion mark in October 1999, would reach 8.9 billion by 2050. It was not expected to level out until 2200, when it would peak at around 11 billion. After 2200, it is expected to level out or even decline a little. The fastest rates of increase will take place in the developing countries of Africa, Asia and Latin America – the places least able to afford the enormous costs incurred by such a rapidly expanding population.

Elevated view of Ki Lung Street, Hong Kong
Urban areas of Hong Kong, a Special Administrative Region on the southern coast of China, contain busy streets overlooked by crowded apartments.

Average world population growth rates have declined from about 2% a year in the early 1960s to 1.4% in 1998. This was partly due to a decline in fertility rates – that is, the number of births to the number of women of child-bearing age – especially in developed countries where, as income has risen, the average size of families has fallen.

Declining fertility rates were also evident in many developing countries. Even Africa shows signs of such change, though its population is expected to triple before it begins to fall. Population growth is also dependent on death rates, which are affected by such factors as famine, disease and the quality of medical care.

THE POPULATION EXPLOSION

The world's population has grown steadily throughout most of human history, though certain events triggered periods of population growth. The invention of agriculture around 10,000 years ago, led to great changes in human society. Before then, most people had obtained food by hunting animals and gathering plants. Average life expectancies were probably no more than 20 years and life was hard. However, when farmers began to produce food surpluses, people began to live settled lives. This major milestone in human history led to the development of the first cities and early civilizations.

From an estimated 8 million in 8000 BC, the world population rose to about 300 million by AD 1000. Between 1000 and 1750, the rate of world population increase was around 0.1% per year, but another period of major economic and social change – the Industrial Revolution – began in the late 18th century. The Industrial Revolution led to improvements in farm technology and increases in food production. The world population began to increase quickly as industrialization spread across Europe and into North America. By 1850, it had reached 1.2 billion. The 2 billion mark was passed in the 1920s, and then the population rapidly doubled to 4 billion by the 1970s.

POPULATION FEATURES

Population growth affects the structure of societies. In developing countries with high annual rates of population increase, the large majority of the people are young and soon to become parents themselves. For example, in Kenya, which had until recently an annual rate of population growth of around 4%, just over half

LARGEST CITIES

Within 10 years, for the first time ever, the majority of the world's population will live in urban areas. Almost all the urban growth will be in developing countries. Below is a list of cities with their estimated populations in the year 2015, in millions.

1	Tokyo	28.7
2	Mumbai (Bombay)	27.4
3	Lagos	24.1
4	Shanghai	23.2
5	Jakarta	21.5
6	São Paulo	21.0
7	Karachi	20.6
8	Beijing	19.6
9	Dhaka	19.2
10	Mexico City	19.1
11	Kolkata (Calcutta)	17.6
12	Delhi	17.5
13	New York City	17.4
14	Tianjin	17.1
15	Metro Manila	14.9
16	Cairo	14.7
17	Los Angeles	14.5
18	Seoul	13.1
19	Buenos Aires	12.5
20	Istanbul	12.1

These city populations are based on figures for urban agglomerations rather than actual city limits.

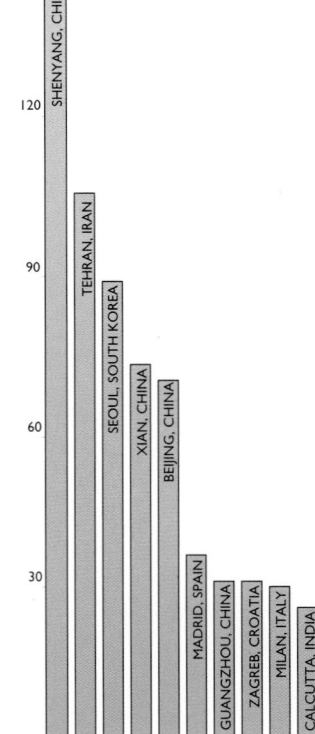

Urban air pollution
This diagram of the world's most polluted cities indicates the number of days per year when sulphur dioxide levels exceed the WHO threshhold of 150 micrograms per cubic metre.

Hong Kong's business district

By contrast with the picturesque old streets of Hong Kong, the business district of Hong Kong City, on the northern shore of Hong Kong Island, is a cluster of modern high-rise buildings. The glittering skyscrapers reflect the success of this tiny region, which has one of the strongest economies in Asia.

of the population is under 15 years of age. On the other hand, the populations of developed countries, with low population growth rates, have a fairly even spread across age groups.

Such differences are reflected in average life expectancies at birth. In rich countries, such as Australia and the United States, the average life expectancy is 77 years (74 years for men and 80 for women; women live longer, on average, than their male counterparts). As a result, an increasing proportion of the people are elderly and retired, contributing little to the economy. The reverse applies in many poor countries, where average life expectancies are below 60 years. In the early 21st century, life expectancies were falling in some southern African countries, such as Botswana, where they fell from nearly 70 to around 40 years because of the fast spread of HIV and AIDS.

Paralleling the population explosion has been a rapid growth in the number and size of cities and towns, which contained nearly half of the world's people by the 1990s. This proportion is expected to rise to nearly two-thirds by 2025.

Urbanization occurred first in areas undergoing the industrialization of their economies, but today it is also a feature of the developing world. In developing countries, people are leaving impoverished rural areas hoping to gain access to the education, health and other services available in cities. But many cities cannot provide the facilities necessitated by rapid population growth. Slums develop and pollution, crime and disease become features of everyday life.

The population explosion poses another probem for the entire world. No one knows how many people the world can support or how consumer demand will damage the fragile environments on our planet. The British economist Thomas Malthus argued in the late 18th century that overpopulation would lead to famine and war. But an increase in farm technology in the 19th and 20th centuries, combined with a green revolution, in which scientists developed high-yield crop varieties, has greatly increased food production since Malthus' time.

However, some modern scientists argue that overpopulation may become a problem in the 21st century. They argue that food shortages leading to disastrous famines will result unless population growth can be halted. Such people argue in favour of birth control programmes. China, one of the two countries with more than a billion people, has introduced a one-child family policy. Its action has slowed the growth of China's huge population.

POPULATION CHANGE 1990–2000

The population change for the years 1990–2000.

- OVER 40% POPULATION GAIN
- 30–40% POPULATION GAIN
- 20–30% POPULATION GAIN
- 10–20% POPULATION GAIN
- 0–10% POPULATION GAIN
- NO CHANGE OR LOSS

TOP 5 COUNTRIES

Kuwait	+75.0%
Namibia	+62.5%
Afghanistan	+60.1%
Mali	+55.5%
Tanzania	+54.6%

BOTTOM 5 COUNTRIES

Belgium	–0.1%
Hungary	–0.2%
Grenada	–2.4%
Germany	–3.2%
Tonga	–3.2%

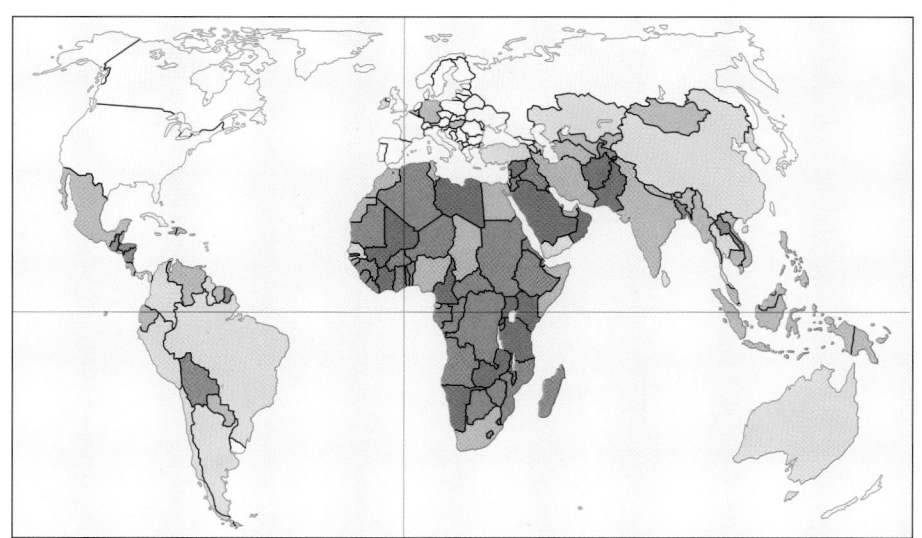

Languages and Religions

In 1995, 90-year-old Edna Guerro died in northern California. She was the last person able to speak Northern Pomo, one of about 50 Native American languages spoken in the state. Her death marked the extinction of one of the world's languages.

This event is not an isolated incident. Language experts regularly report the disappearance of languages and some of them predict that between 20 to 50% of the world's languages will no longer exist by the end of the 21st century. Improved transport and communications are partly to blame, because they bring people from various cultures into closer and closer contact. Many children no longer speak the language of their parents, preferring instead to learn the language used at their schools. The pressures on

children to speak dominant rather than minority languages are often great. In the first part of the 20th century, Native American children were punished if they spoke their native language.

The disappearance of a language represents the extinction of a way of thinking, a unique expression of the experiences and knowledge of a group of people. Language and religion together give people an identity and a sense of belonging. However, there are others who argue that the disappearance of minority languages is a step towards international understanding and economic efficiency.

THE WORLD'S LANGUAGES

Definitions of what is a language or a dialect vary and, hence, estimates of the number of languages spoken around the world range from about 3,000 to 6,000. But whatever the figure, it is clear that the number of languages far exceeds the number of countries.

Buddhist monks in Katmandu, Nepal
Hinduism is Nepal's official religion, but the Nepalese observe the festivals of both Hinduism and Buddhism. They also regard Buddhist shrines and Hindu temples as equally sacred.

RELIGIOUS ADHERENTS

Number of adherents to the world's major religions, in millions (1998).

Christian	1,980
Roman Catholic	1,300
Orthodox	240
African sects	110
Pentecostal	105
Others	225
Islam	1,300
Sunni	940
Shiite	120
Others	240
Hindu	900
Secular/Atheist/Agnostic/ Non-religious	850
Buddhist	360
Chinese Traditional	225
Indigenous/Animist	190
Sikh	23
Yoruba	20
Juche	19
Spiritism	14
Judaism	14
Baha'i	6
Jainism	4
Shinto	4

Countries with only one language tend to be small. For example, in Liechtenstein, everyone speaks German. By contrast, more than 860 languages have been identified in Papua New Guinea, whose population is only about 4.3 million people. Hence, many of its languages are spoken by only small groups of people. In fact, scientists have estimated that about a third of the world's languages are now spoken by less than 1,000 people. By contrast, more than half of the world's population speak just seven languages.

The world's languages are grouped into families. The Indo-European family consists of languages spoken between Europe and the Indian subcontinent. The growth of European empires over the last 300 years led several Indo-European languages, most notably English, French, Portuguese and Spanish, to spread throughout much of North and South America, Africa, Australia and New Zealand.

English has become the official language in many countries which together contain more than a quarter of the world's population. It is now a major international language, surpassing in importance Mandarin Chinese, a member of the Sino-Tibetan family, which is the world's leading first language. Without a knowledge of English, businessmen face many problems when conducting international trade, especially with the United States or other English-speaking countries. But proposals that English, French, Russian or some other language should become a world language seem unlikely to be acceptable to a majority of the world's peoples.

WORLD RELIGIONS

Religion is another fundamental aspect of human culture. It has inspired much of the world's finest architecture, literature, music and painting. It has also helped to shape human cultures since prehistoric times and is responsible for the codes of ethics by which most people live.

The world's major religions were all founded in Asia. Judaism, one of the first faiths to teach that there is only one god, is one of the world's oldest. Founded in south-western Asia, it influenced the more recent Christianity and Islam, two other monotheistic religions which

The Church of San Giovanni, Dolomites, Italy
Christianity has done much to shape Western civilization. Christian churches were built as places of worship, but many of them are among the finest achievements of world architecture.

now have the greatest number of followers. Hinduism, the third leading faith in terms of the numbers of followers, originated in the Indian subcontinent and most Hindus are now found in India. Another major religion, Buddhism, was founded in the subcontinent partly as a reaction to certain aspects of Hinduism. But unlike Hinduism, it has spread from India throughout much of eastern Asia.

Religion and language are powerful creative forces. They are also essential features of nationalism, which gives people a sense of belonging and pride. But nationalism is often also a cause of rivalry and tension. Cultural differences have led to racial hatred, the persecution of minorities, and to war between national groups.

MOTHER TONGUES
First-language speakers of the major languages, in millions (1999).

- MANDARIN CHINESE 885M
- SPANISH 332M
- ENGLISH 322M
- BENGALI 189M
- HINDI 182M
- PORTUGUESE 170M
- RUSSIAN 170M
- JAPANESE 125M
- GERMAN 98M
- WU CHINESE 77M

OFFICIAL LANGUAGES: % OF WORLD POPULATION

English	27.0%
Chinese	19.0%
Hindi	13.5%
Spanish	5.4%
Russian	5.2%
French	4.2%
Arabic	3.3%
Portuguese	3.0%
Malay	3.0%
Bengali	2.9%
Japanese	2.3%

Polyglot nations
The graph, right, shows countries of the world with more than 200 languages. Although it has only about 4.3 million people, Papua New Guinea holds the record for the number of languages spoken.

- Brazil (210)
- Congo (Z.) (220)
- Australia (230)
- Mexico (240)
- Cameroon (275)
- India (410)
- Nigeria (470)
- Indonesia (701)
- Papua New Guinea (862)

International Organizations

Twelve days before the surrender of Germany and four months before the final end of World War II, representatives of 50 nations met in San Francisco to create a plan to set up a peace-keeping organization, the United Nations. Since its birth on 24 October 1945, its membership has grown from 51 to 188.

Its first 50 years have been marked by failures as well as successes. While it has helped to prevent some disputes from flaring up into full-scale wars, the Blue Berets, as the UN troops are called, have been forced, because of their policy of neutrality, to stand by when atrocities are committed by rival warring groups.

THE WORK OF THE UN

The United Nations has six main organs. They include the General Assembly, where member states meet to discuss issues concerned with peace, security and development. The Security Council, containing 15 members, is concerned with maintaining world peace. The Secretariat, under the Secretary-General, helps the other organs to do their jobs effectively, while the Economic and Social Council works with specialized agencies to implement policies concerned with such matters as development, education and health. The International Court of Justice, or World Court, helps to settle disputes between member nations. The sixth organ of the UN, the Trusteeship Council, was designed to bring 11 UN trust territories to independence. Its task has now been completed.

The specialized agencies do much important

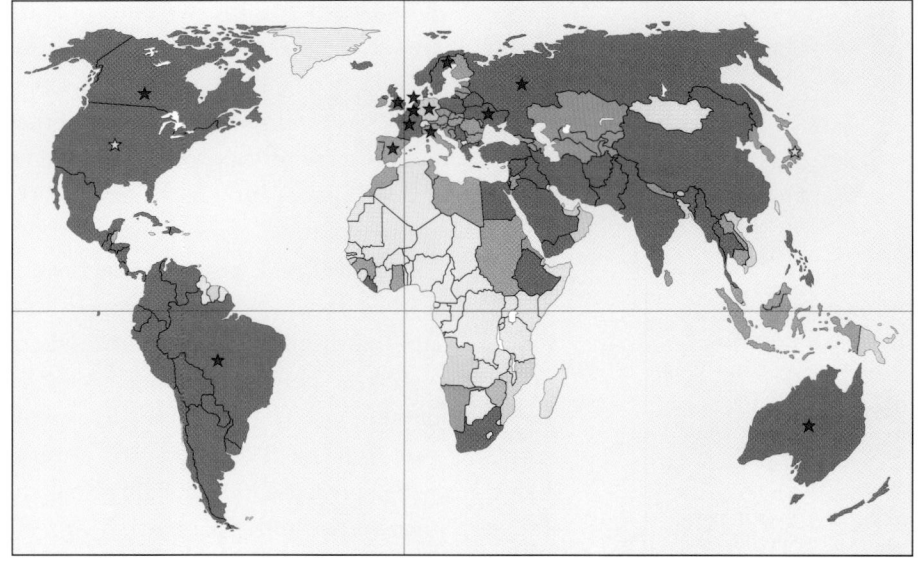

work. For example, UNICEF (United Nations International Children's Fund) has provided health care and aid for children in many parts of the world. The ILO (International Labour Organization) has improved working conditions in many areas, while the FAO (Food and Agricultural Organization) has worked to improve the production and distribution of food. Among the other agencies are organizations to help refugees, to further human rights and to control the environment. The latest agency, set up in 1995, is the WTO (World Trade Organization), which took over the work of GATT (General Agreement on Tariffs and Trade).

OTHER ORGANIZATIONS

In a world in which nations have become increasingly interdependent, many other organizations have been set up to deal with a variety of problems. Some, such as NATO (the North Atlantic Treaty Organization), are defence alliances. In the early 1990s, the end of the Cold War suggested that NATO's role might be finished, but the civil war in the former Yugoslavia showed that it still has a role in maintaining peace and security.

Other organizations encourage social and economic co-operation in various regions. Some are NGOs (non-governmental organizations), such as the Red Cross and its Muslim equivalent, the Red Crescent. Other NGOs raise funds to provide aid to countries facing major crises, such as famine.

Some major international organizations aim at economic co-operation and the removal of trade barriers. For example, the European Union has 15 members. Its economic success and the

Food aid

International organizations supply aid to people living in areas suffering from war or famine. In Bosnia-Herzegovina, the UN Protection Force supervised the movements of food aid, as did NATO on the borders of Kosovo a few years later.

MEMBERS OF THE UN
Year of joining.

- 1940s
- 1950s
- 1960s
- 1970s
- 1980s
- 1990s
- NON–MEMBERS

★ 1% – 10% CONTRIBUTION TO FUNDING

☆ OVER 10% CONTRIBUTION TO FUNDING

INTERNATIONAL AID AND GNP
Aid provided as a percentage of GNP, with total aid in brackets (1997).

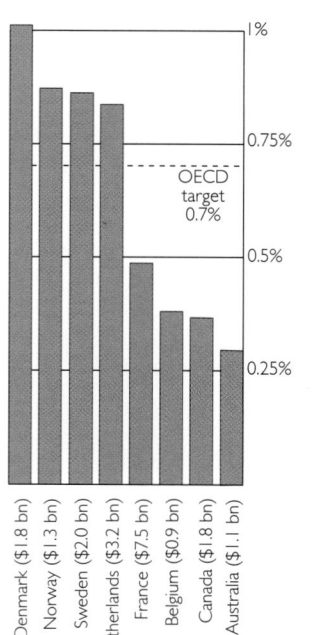

UNHCR-funded jetty, Sri Lanka
In 1994, the UN High Commission for Refugees was responsible for 23 million people. Sometimes, it has to provide transport facilities, such as this jetty, to get aid to the refugees.

adoption of a single currency, the euro, by 12 of its members, has prompted some people to support the idea of a federal Europe. But others fear that political union might lead to a loss of national sovereignty by member states.

Other groupings include ASEAN (the Association of South-east Asian Nations) which aims to reduce trade barriers between its members (Brunei, Burma [Myanmar], Cambodia, Indonesia, Laos, Malaysia, the Philippines, Singapore, Thailand and Vietnam). APEC (the Asia-Pacific Co-operation Group), founded in 1989, aims to create a free trade zone between the countries of eastern Asia, North America, Australia and New Zealand by 2020. Meanwhile, Canada, Mexico and the United States have formed NAFTA (the North American Free Trade Agreement), while other economic groupings link most of the countries in Latin America. Another grouping with a more limited but important objective is OPEC (the Organization of Oil-Exporting Countries). OPEC works to unify policies concerning trade in oil on the world markets.

Some organizations exist to discuss matters of common interest between groups of nations. The Commonwealth of Nations, for example, grew out of links created by the British Empire. In North and South America, the OAS (Organization of American States) aims to increase understanding in the Western hemisphere. The OAU (Organization of African Unity) has a similar role in Africa, while the Arab League represents the Arab nations of North Africa and the Middle East.

COUNTRIES OF THE EUROPEAN UNION

	Total land area (sq km)	Total population (2000 est.)	GNP per capita, US$ (1999)	Unemployment rate, % (1996)	Year of accession to the EU	Seats in EU parliament (1998)
Austria	83,850	7,613,000	25,970	7%	1995	21
Belgium	30,510	9,832,000	24,510	12.7%	1958	25
Denmark	43,070	5,153,000	32,030	8.7%	1973	16
Finland	338,130	5,077,000	23,780	16.3%	1995	16
France	551,500	58,145,000	23,480	12.3%	1958	87
Germany	356,910	76,962,000	25,350	10.4%	1958	99
Greece	131,990	10,193,000	11,770	10.3%	1981	25
Ireland	70,280	4,086,000	19,160	11.9%	1973	15
Italy	301,270	57,195,000	19,710	12.1%	1958	87
Luxembourg	2,590	377,000	44,640	3.3%	1958	6
Netherlands	41,526	15,829,000	24,320	6.6%	1958	31
Portugal	92,390	10,587,000	10,600	7.3%	1986	24
Spain	504,780	40,667,000	14,000	22.2%	1986	64
Sweden	449,960	8,560,000	25,040	8.1%	1995	22
United Kingdom	243,368	58,393,000	22,640	7.6%	1973	87

Agriculture

In 1999, partly because of ongoing economic turmoil in Russia, the increase in food production was less than the rise in world population, creating a small per capita fall in food production. Downward trends in world food production in the 1990s reopened an old debate – whether food production will be able to keep pace with the rapidly rising world population in the 21st century.

Some experts argue that the lower than expected production figures in the 1990s heralded a period of relative scarcity and high prices of food, which will be felt most in the poorer developing countries. Others are more optimistic. They point to the successes of the 'green revolution' which, through the use of new crop varieties produced by scientists, irrigation and the extensive use of fertilizers and pesticides,

Rice harvest, Bali, Indonesia
More than half of the world's people eat rice as their basic food. Rice grows well in tropical and subtropical regions, such as in Indonesia, India and south-eastern China.

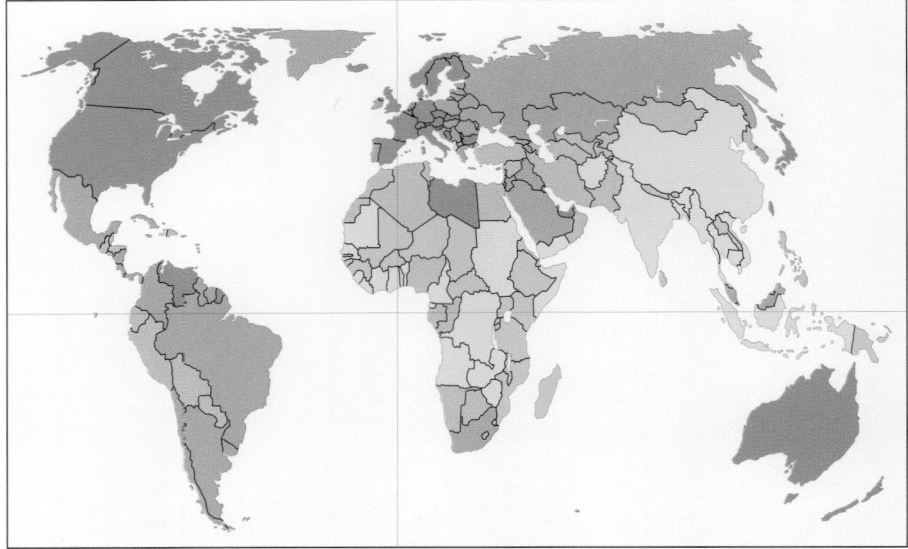

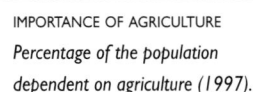
IMPORTANCE OF AGRICULTURE
Percentage of the population dependent on agriculture (1997).

OVER 75% DEPENDENT
50–75% DEPENDENT
25–50% DEPENDENT
10–25% DEPENDENT
UNDER 10% DEPENDENT

has revolutionized food production since the 1950s and 1960s.

The green revolution has led to a great expansion in the production of many crops, including such basic foods as rice, maize and wheat. In India, its effects have been spectacular. Between 1955 and 1995, grain production trebled, giving the country sufficient food reserves to prevent famine in years when droughts or floods reduce the harvest. While once India had to import food, it is now self-sufficient.

FOOD PRODUCTION

Agriculture, which supplies most of our food, together with materials to make clothes and other products, is the world's most important economic activity. But its relative importance has declined in comparison with manufacturing and service industries. As a result, the end of the 20th century marked the first time for 10,000 years when the vast majority of the people no longer had to depend for their living on growing crops and herding animals.

However, agriculture remains the dominant economic activity in many developing countries in Africa and Asia. For example, by the start of the 21st century, 80% or more of the people of Bhutan, Burundi, Nepal and Rwanda depended on farming for their living.

Many people in developing countries eke out the barest of livings by nomadic herding or shifting cultivation, combined with hunting, fishing and gathering plant foods. A large proportion of farmers live at subsistence level, producing little more than they require to provide the basic needs of their families.

The world's largest food producer and exporter is the United States, although agriculture employs

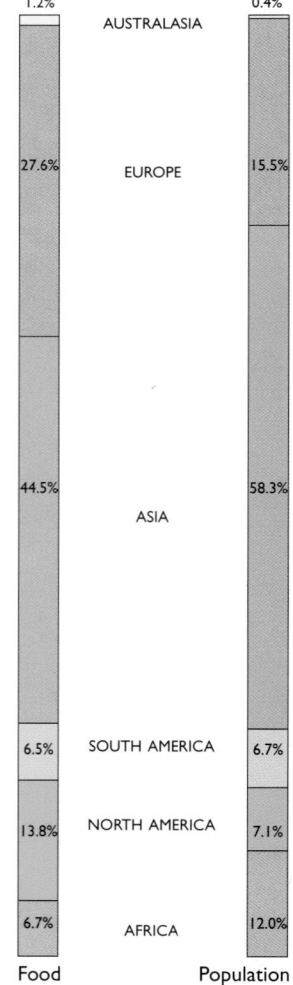

	Food	Population
AUSTRALASIA	1.2%	0.4%
EUROPE	27.6%	15.5%
ASIA	44.5%	58.3%
SOUTH AMERICA	6.5%	6.7%
NORTH AMERICA	13.8%	7.1%
AFRICA	6.7%	12.0%

A comparison of world food production and population by continent.

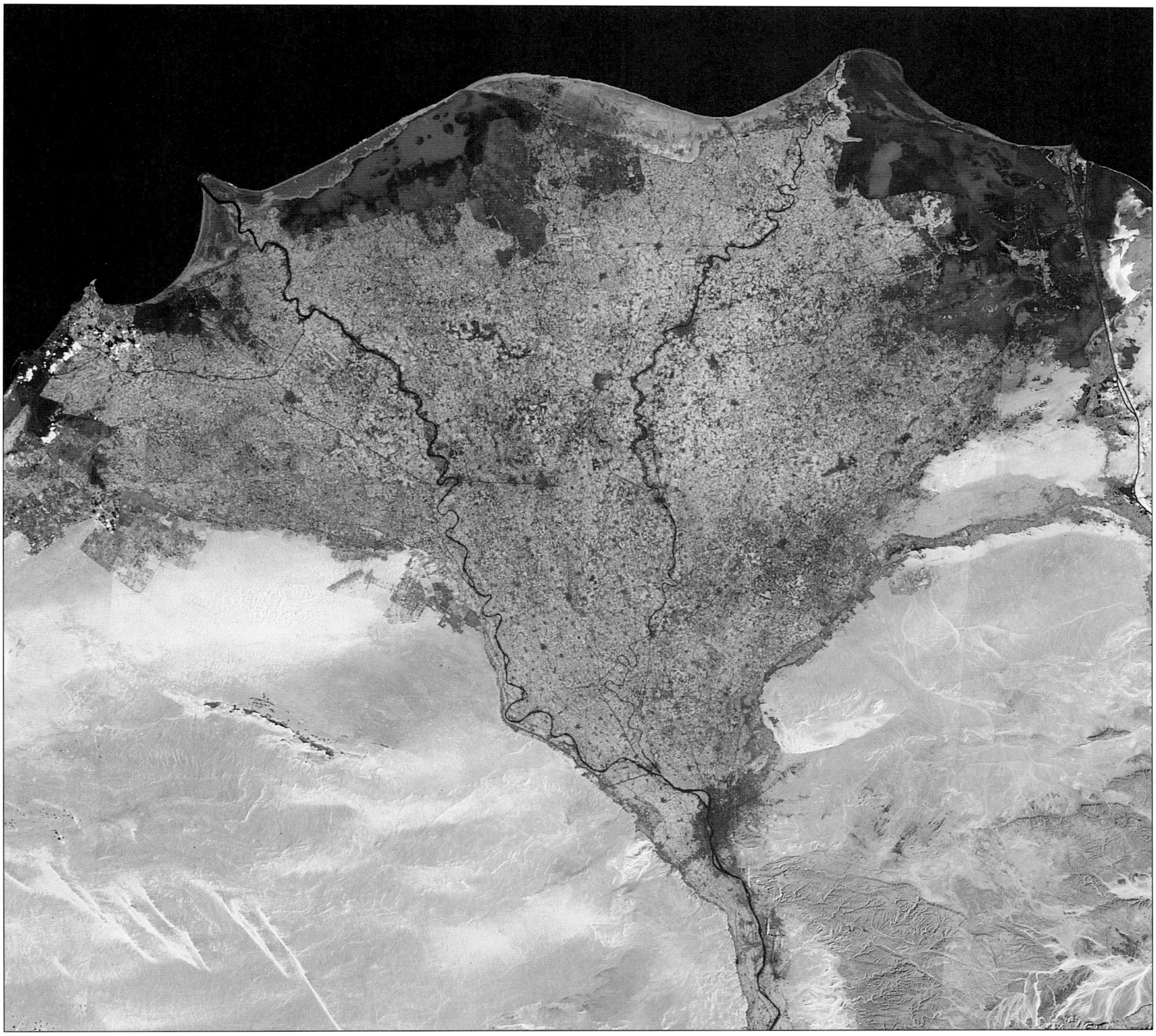

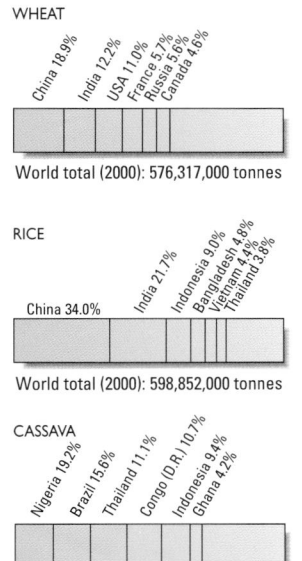

Landsat *image of the Nile delta, Egypt*

Most Egyptians live in the Nile valley and on its delta. Because much of the silt carried by the Nile now ends up on the floor of Lake Nasser, upstream of the Aswan Dam, the delta is now retreating and seawater is seeping inland. This eventuality was not foreseen when the Aswan High Dam was built in the 1960s.

around 2% of its total workforce. The high production of the United States is explained by its use of scientific methods and mechanization, which are features of agriculture throughout the developed world.

INTENSIVE OR ORGANIC FARMING

In the early 21st century, some people were beginning to question the dependence of farmers on chemical fertilizers and pesticides. Many people became concerned that the widespread use of chemicals was seriously polluting and damaging the environment.

Others objected to the intensive farming of animals to raise production and lower prices. For example, the suggestion in Britain in 1996 that BSE, or 'mad cow disease', might be passed

on to people causing CJD (Creuzfeldt-Jakob Disease) caused widespread alarm.

Such problems have led some farmers to return to organic farming, which is based on animal-welfare principles and the banning of chemical fertilizers and pesticides. The costs of organic foods are certainly higher than those produced by intensive farming, but an increasing number of consumers in the Western world are beginning to demand organic products from their retailers.

WHEAT

China 18.9% India 12.2% USA 11.0% France 5.7% Russia 5.6% Canada 4.6%

World total (2000): 576,317,000 tonnes

RICE

China 34.0% India 21.7% Indonesia 9.0% Bangladesh 4.8% Vietnam 4.4% Thailand 3.8%

World total (2000): 598,852,000 tonnes

CASSAVA

Nigeria 19.2% Brazil 15.6% Thailand 11.1% Congo (D.R.) 10.7% Indonesia 9.4% Ghana 4.2%

World total (2000): 172,737,000 tonnes

Energy and Minerals

In September 2000, Japan experienced its worst nuclear accident, when more than 400 people were exposed to harmful levels of radiation. This was the worst nuclear incident since the explosion at the Chernobyl nuclear power station, in Ukraine, in 1986. Nuclear power provides around 17% of the world's electricity and experts once thought that it would generate much of the world's energy supply. But concerns about safety and worries about the high costs make this seem unlikely. Some developed countries have already abandoned their nuclear programmes.

FOSSIL FUELS

Huge amounts of energy are needed for heating, generating electricity and for transport. In the early years of the Industrial Revolution, coal formed from organic matter buried beneath the Earth's surface, was the leading source of energy. It remains important as a raw material in the manufacture of drugs and other products and also as a fuel, despite the fact that burning coal causes air pollution and gives off carbon dioxide, an important greenhouse gas.

However, oil and natural gas, which came into wide use in the 20th century, are cheaper to produce and easier to handle than coal, while, kilogram for kilogram, they give out more heat. Oil is especially important in moving transport, supplying about 97% of the fuel required.

In 1995, proven reserves of oil were sufficient to supply the world, at current rates of production, for 43 years, while supplies of natural gas stood at about 66 years. Coal reserves are more abundant and known reserves would last 200 years at present rates of use. Although these figures must be regarded with caution, because they do not allow for future discoveries, it is clear that fossil fuel reserves will one day run out.

Wind farms in California, United States

Wind farms using giant turbines can produce electricity at a lower cost than conventional power stations. But in many areas, winds are too light or too strong for wind farms to be effective.

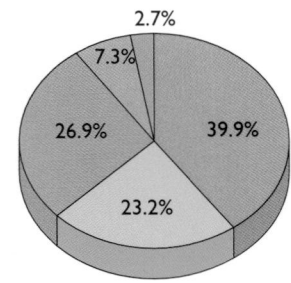

2.7%
7.3%
26.9%
39.9%
23.2%

WORLD ENERGY CONSUMPTION

- OIL
- GAS
- COAL
- NUCLEAR
- HYDRO

The diagram shows the proportion of world energy consumption in 1997 by form. Total energy consumption was 8,509.2 million tonnes of oil equivalent. Such fuels as wood, peat and animal wastes, together with renewable forms of energy, such as wind and geothermal power, are not included, although they are important in some areas.

SELECTED MINERAL PRODUCTION STATISTICS (1997)			
Bauxite		**Diamonds**	
Australia	34.9%	Australia	33.9%
Guinea	15.1%	Congo (D.R.)	18.6%
Brazil	9.8%	Botswana	17.0%
Jamaica	9.4%	Russia	16.1%
China	7.1%	S. Africa	8.5%
Gold		**Iron ore**	
S. Africa	20.5%	China	22.1%
USA	14.9%	Brazil	17.4%
Australia	13.1%	Australia	14.0%
Canada	7.0%	Ukraine	10.3%
China	6.5%	Russia	6.7%
Manganese		**Zinc**	
Ukraine	27.0%	China	16.4%
China	25.6%	Canada	14.5%
S. Africa	11.4%	Australia	14.0%
Brazil	8.0%	Peru	11.7%
Australia	7.8%	USA	8.5%

Potash mines in Utah, United States

Potash is a mineral used mainly to make fertilizers. Much of it comes from mines where deposits formed when ancient seas dried up are exploited. Potash is also extracted from salt lakes.

MINERAL DISTRIBUTION

The map shows the richest sources of the most important minerals. Major mineral locations are named. Undersea deposits, most of which are considered inaccessible, are not shown.

▽ GOLD
⬭ SILVER
◆ DIAMONDS
▽ TUNGSTEN
● IRON ORE
▪ NICKEL
⬬ CHROME
▲ MANGANESE
▢ COBALT
▲ MOLYBDENUM
▪ COPPER
▲ LEAD
● BAUXITE
▽ TIN
◆ ZINC
⬬ MERCURY

ALTERNATIVE ENERGY

Other sources of energy are therefore required. Besides nuclear energy, the main alternative to fossil fuels is water power. The costs of building dams and hydroelectric power stations is high, though hydroelectric production is comparatively cheap and it does not cause pollution. But the creation of reservoirs uproots people and, in tropical rainforests, it destroys natural habitats. Hydroelectricity is also suitable only in areas with plenty of rivers and steep slopes, such as Norway, while it is unsuitable in flat areas, such as the Netherlands.

In Brazil, alcohol made from sugar has been used to fuel cars. Initially, this government-backed policy met with great success, but it has proved to be extremely expensive. Battery-run, electric cars have also been developed in the United States, but they appear to have limited use, because of the problems involved in regular and time-consuming recharging.

Other forms of energy, which are renewable and cleaner than fossil fuels, are winds, sea waves, the rise and fall of tides, and geothermal power. These forms of energy are already used to some extent. However, their contribution in global terms seems likely to remain small in the immediate future.

MINERALS FOR INDUSTRY

In addition to energy, manufacturing industries need raw materials, including minerals, and these natural resources, like fossil fuels, are being used in such huge quantities that some experts have predicted shortages of some of them before long.

Manufacturers depend on supplies of about 80 minerals. Some, such as bauxite (aluminium ore) and iron, are abundant, but others are scarce or are found only in deposits that are uneconomical to mine. Many experts advocate a policy of recycling scrap metal, including aluminium, chromium, copper, lead, nickel and zinc. This practice would reduce pollution and conserve the energy required for extracting and refining mineral ores.

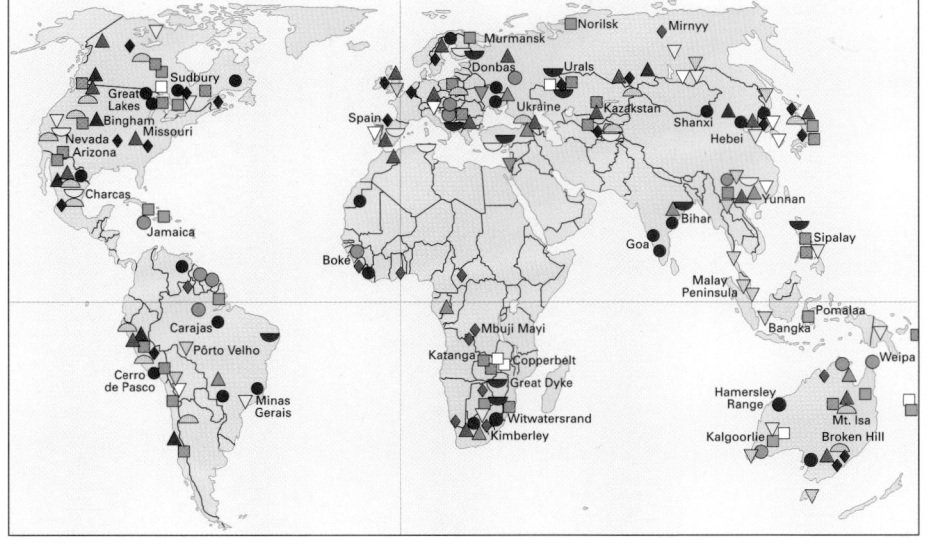

World Economies

In 1999, Tanzania had a per capita GNP (Gross National Product) of US$240, as compared with Switzerland, whose per capita GNP stood at $38,350. These figures indicate the vast gap between the economies and standards of living of the two countries.

The GNP includes the GDP (Gross Domestic Product), which consists of the total output of goods and services in a country in a given year, plus net exports – that is, the value of goods and services sold abroad less the value of foreign goods and services used in the country in the same year. The GNP divided by the population gives a country's GNP per capita. In low-income developing countries, agriculture makes a high contribution to the GNP. For example, in Tanzania, 56% of the GDP in 1995 came from

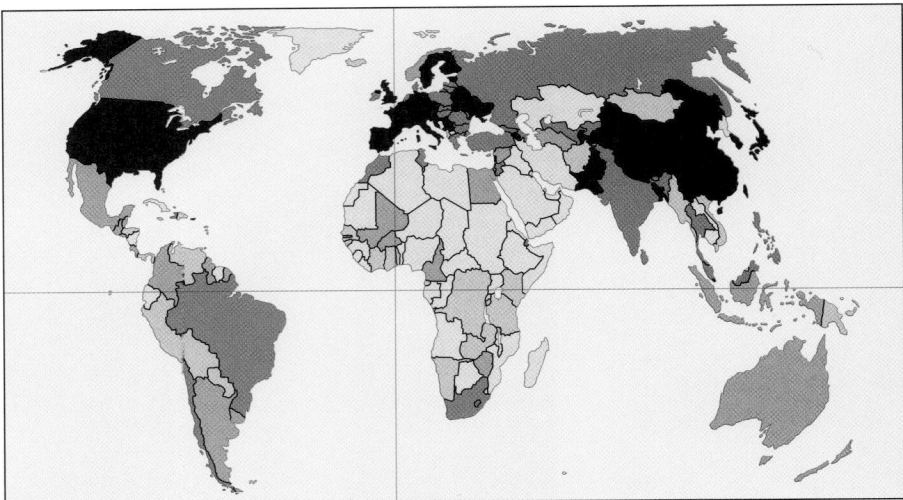

Microchip production, Taiwan

Despite its lack of resources, Taiwan is one of eastern Asia's 'tiger' economies. Its high-tech industries have helped it to achieve fast economic growth and to compete on the world market.

agriculture. On the other hand, manufacturing was small-scale and contributed only 5% of the GDP. By comparison, in high-income economies, the percentage contribution of manufacturing far exceeds that of agriculture.

INDUSTRIALIZATION

The Industrial Revolution began in Britain in the late 18th century. Before that time, most people worked on farms. But with the Industrial Revolution came factories, using machines that could manufacture goods much faster and more cheaply than those made by cottage industries which already existed.

The Industrial Revolution soon spread to several countries in mainland Europe and the United States and, by the late 19th century, it had reached Canada, Japan and Russia. At first, industrial development was based on such areas as coalfields or ironfields. But in the 20th century, the use of oil, which is easy to transport along pipelines, made it possible for industries to be set up anywhere.

Some nations, such as Switzerland, became industrialized even though they lacked natural resources. They depended instead on the specialized skills of their workers. This same pattern applies today. Some countries with rich natural resources, such as Mexico (with a per capita GNP in 1999 of $4,400), lag far behind Japan ($32,230) and Cyprus ($11,960), which lack resources and have to import many of the materials they need for their manufacturing industries.

SERVICE INDUSTRIES

Experts often refer to high-income countries as industrial economies. But manufacturing employs only one in six workers in the United

INDUSTRY AND TRADE

Manufactured goods (including machinery and transport) as a percentage of total exports.

- ▇ OVER 75%
- ▨ 50–75%
- ▨ 25–50%
- ▨ 10–25%
- ☐ UNDER 10%

Eastern Asia, including Japan (98.3%), Taiwan (92.7%) and Hong Kong (93.0%), contains countries whose exports are most dominated by manufactures. But some countries in Europe, such as Slovenia (92.5%), are also heavily dependent on manufacturing.

GROSS NATIONAL PRODUCT PER CAPITA US$ (1999 ESTIMATES)

1	Liechtenstein	50,000
2	Luxembourg	44,640
3	Switzerland	38,350
4	Bermuda	35,590
5	Norway	32,880
6	Japan	32,230
7	Denmark	32,030
8	USA	30,600
9	Singapore	29,610
10	Iceland	29,280
11	Austria	25,970
12	Germany	25,350
13	Sweden	25,040
14	Monaco	25,000
15	Belgium	24,510
16	Brunei	24,630
17	Netherlands	24,320
18	Finland	23,780
19	Hong Kong (China)	23,520
20	France	23,480

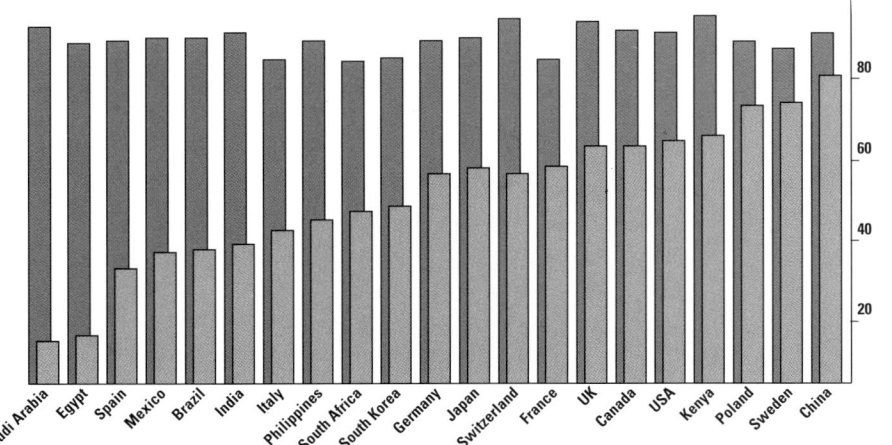

New cars awaiting transportation, Los Angeles, United States
Cars are the most important single manufactured item in world trade, followed by vehicle parts and engines. The world's leading car producers are Japan, the United States, Germany and France.

States, one in five in Britain, and one in three in Germany and Japan.

In most developed economies, the percentage of manufacturing jobs has fallen in recent years, while jobs in service industries have risen. For example, in Britain, the proportion of jobs in manufacturing fell from 37% in 1970 to 15% in 2000, while jobs in the service sector rose from just under 50% to 75%. While change in Britain was especially rapid, similar changes were taking place in most industrial economies. By the late 1990s, service industries accounted for well over half the jobs in the generally prosperous countries that made up the OECD (Organization for Economic Co-operation and Development). Instead of being called the 'industrial' economies, these countries might be better named the 'service' economies.

Service industries offer a wide range of jobs and many of them require high educational qualifications. These include finance, insurance and high-tech industries, such as computer programming, entertainment and telecommunications. Service industries also include marketing and advertising, which are essential if the cars and television sets made by manufacturers are to be sold. Another valuable service industry is tourism; in some countries, such as the Gambia, it is the major foreign exchange earner. Trade in services plays a crucial part in world economics. The share of services in world trade rose from 17% in 1980 to 22% in the 1990s.

THE WORKFORCE

Percentage of men and women between 15 and 64 years old in employment, selected countries (latest available year).

■ MEN
■ WOMEN

Trade and Commerce

The establishment of the WTO (World Trade Organization) on 1 January 1995 was the latest step in the long history of world trade. The WTO was set up by the eighth round of negotiations, popularly called the 'Uruguay round', conducted by the General Agreement on Tariffs and Trade (GATT). This treaty was signed by representatives of 125 governments in April, 1994. By the end of 2000, the WTO had 140 members.

GATT was first established in 1948. Its initial aim was to produce a charter to create a body called the International Trade Organization. This body never came into being. Instead, GATT, acting as an *ad hoc* agency, pioneered a series of agreements aimed at liberalizing world trade by reducing tariffs on imports and other obstacles to free trade.

GATT's objectives were based on the belief

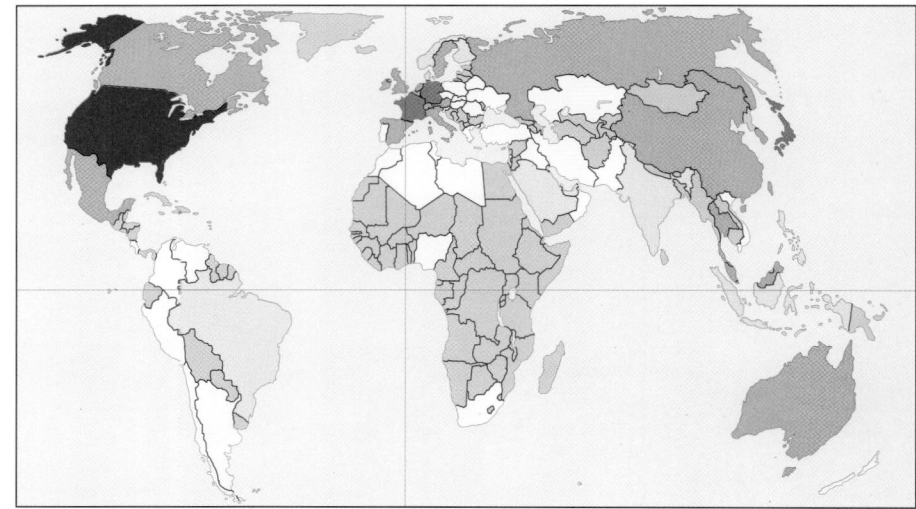

New York City Stock Exchange, United States
Stock exchanges, where stocks and shares are sold and bought, are important in channelling savings and investments to companies and governments. The world's largest stock exchange is in Tokyo, Japan.

that international trade creates wealth. Trade occurs because the world's resources are not distributed evenly between countries, and, in theory, free trade means that every country should concentrate on what it can do best and purchase from others goods and services that they can supply more cheaply. In practice, however, free trade may cause unemployment when imported goods are cheaper than those produced within the country.

Trade is sometimes an important factor in world politics, especially when trade sanctions are applied against countries whose actions incur the disapproval of the international community. For example, in the 1990s, worldwide trade sanctions were imposed on Serbia because of its involvement in the civil war in Bosnia-Herzegovina.

CHANGING TRADE PATTERNS

The early 16th century, when Europeans began to divide the world into huge empires, opened up a new era in international trade. By the 19th century, the colonial powers, who were among the first industrial powers, promoted trade with their colonies, from which they obtained unprocessed raw materials, such as food, natural fibres, minerals and timber. In return, they shipped clothes, shoes and other cheap items to the colonies.

From the late 19th century until the early 1950s, primary products dominated world trade, with oil becoming the leading item in the later part of this period. Many developing countries still depend heavily on the export of one or two primary products, such as coffee or iron ore, but overall the proportion of primary products in world trade has fallen since the 1950s. Today the most important elements in world trade are

WORLD TRADE
Percentage share of total world exports by value (1999).

- ■ OVER 10% OF WORLD TRADE
- ■ 5–10% OF WORLD TRADE
- ▨ 1–5% OF WORLD TRADE
- ▨ 0.5–1% OF WORLD TRADE
- □ 0.1–0.5% OF WORLD TRADE
- ▨ UNDER 0.1% OF WORLD TRADE

The world's leading trading nations, according to the combined value of their exports and imports, are the United States, Germany, Japan, France and the United Kingdom.

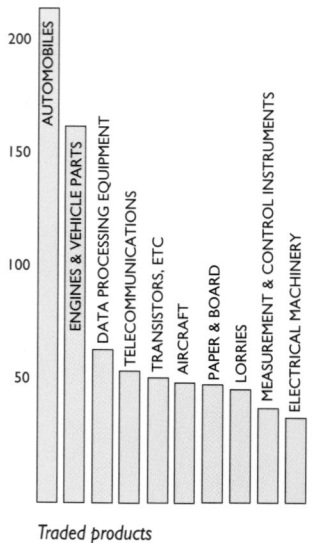

Traded products
Top ten manufactures traded by value in billions of US$ (latest available year).

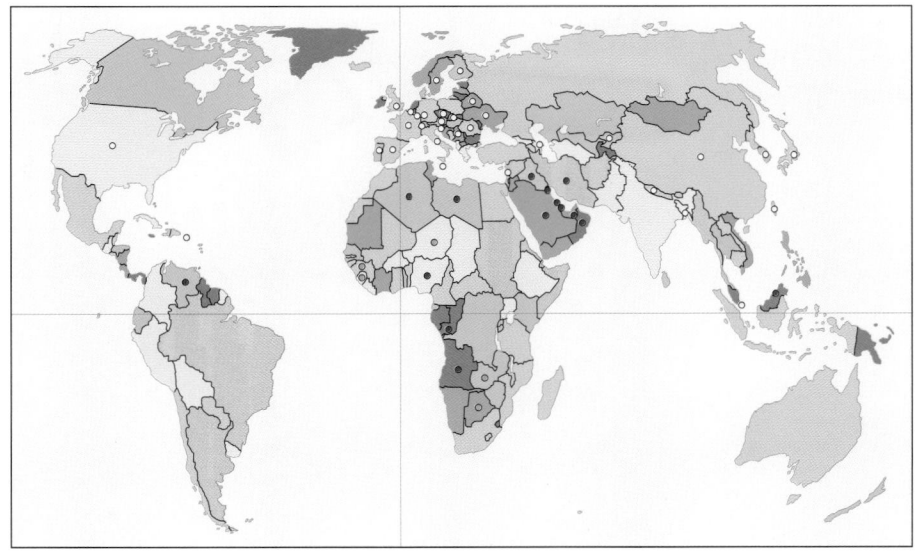

Rotterdam, Netherlands
World trade depends on transport. Rotterdam, the world's largest port, serves not only the Netherlands, but also industrial areas in parts of Germany, France and Switzerland.

DEPENDENCE ON TRADE

Value of exports as a percentage of GDP (Gross Domestic Product) 1997.

- OVER 50% GDP FROM EXPORTS
- 40–50% GDP FROM EXPORTS
- 30–40% GDP FROM EXPORTS
- 20–30% GDP FROM EXPORTS
- 10–20% GDP FROM EXPORTS
- UNDER 10% GDP FROM EXPORTS

○ MOST DEPENDENT ON INDUSTRIAL EXPORTS (OVER 75% OF TOTAL)

● MOST DEPENDENT ON FUEL EXPORTS (OVER 75% OF TOTAL)

◉ MOST DEPENDENT ON METAL & MINERAL EXPORTS (OVER 75% OF TOTAL)

manufactures and semi-manufactures, exchanged mainly between the industrialized nations.

THE WORLD'S MARKETS

Private companies conduct most of world trade, but government policies affect it. Governments which believe that certain industries are strategic, or essential for the country's future, may impose tariffs on imports, or import quotas to limit the volume of imports, if they are thought to be undercutting the domestic industries.

For example, the United States has argued that Japan has greater access to its markets than the United States has to Japan's. This might have led the United States to resort to protectionism, but instead the United States remains committed to free trade.

Other problems in international trade occur when governments give subsidies to its producers, who can then export products at low prices. Another difficulty, called 'dumping', occurs when products are sold at below the market price in order to gain a market share. One of the aims of the newly-created WTO is the phasing out of government subsidies for agricultural products, though the world's poorest countries will be exempt from many of the WTO's most severe regulations.

Governments are also concerned about the volume of imports and exports and most countries keep records of international transactions. When the total value of goods and services imported exceeds the value of goods and services exported, then the country has a deficit in its balance of payments. Large deficits can weaken a country's economy.

Travel and Communications

In the 1990s, millions of people became linked into an 'information superhighway' called the Internet. Equipped with a personal computer, an electricity supply, a telephone and a modem, people are able to communicate with others all over the world. People can now send messages by e-mail (electronic mail), they can engage in electronic discussions, contacting people with similar interests, and engage in 'chat lines', which are the latest equivalent of telephone conferences.

These new developments are likely to affect the working lives of people everywhere, enabling them to work at home whilst having many of the facilities that are available in an office. The Internet is part of an ongoing and astonishingly rapid evolution in the fields of communications and transport.

TRANSPORT

Around 200 years ago, most people never travelled far from their birthplace, but today we are much more mobile. Cars and buses now provide convenient forms of transport for many millions of people, huge ships transport massive cargoes around the world, and jet airliners, some travelling faster than the speed of sound, can transport high-value goods as well as holiday-makers to almost any part of the world.

Land transport of freight has developed greatly

Jodrell Bank Observatory, Cheshire, England
The world's first giant radio telescope began operations at Jodrell Bank in 1957. Radio telescopes can explore the Universe as far as 16 billion light-years away.

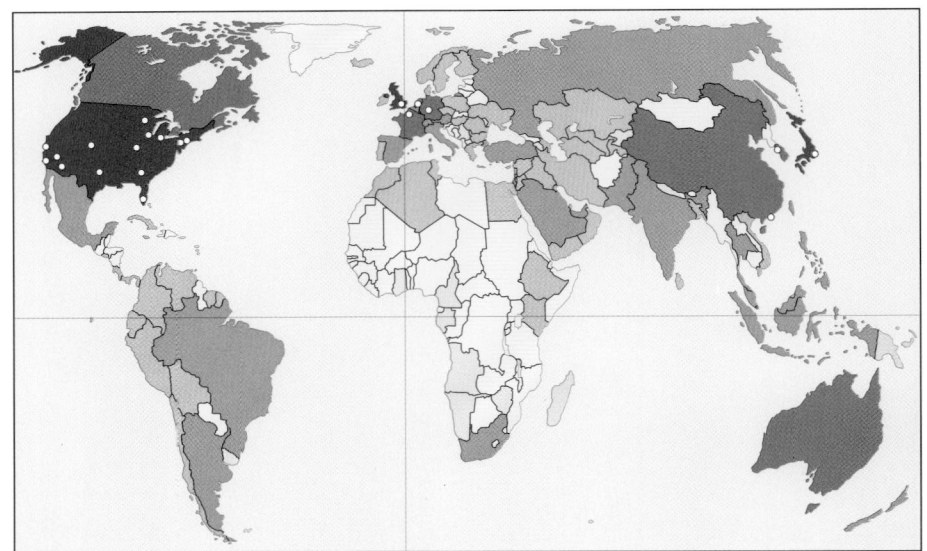

since the start of the Industrial Revolution. Canals, which became important in the 18th century, could not compete with rail transport in the 19th century. Rail transport remains important, but, during the 20th century, it suffered from competition with road transport, which is cheaper and has the advantage of carrying materials and goods from door to door.

Road transport causes pollution and the burning of fuels creates greenhouse gases that contribute to global warming. Yet privately owned cars are now the leading form of passenger traffic in developed nations, especially for journeys of less than around 400 km [250 miles]. Car owners do not have to suffer the inconvenience of waiting for public transport, such as buses, though they often have to endure traffic jams at peak travel times.

Ocean passenger traffic is now modest, but ships carry the bulk of international trade. Huge oil tankers and bulk grain carriers now ply the oceans with their cargoes, while container ships

AIR TRAVEL – PASSENGER KILOMETRES*
FLOWN *(1997).*

■	OVER 100,000 MILLION
■	50,000–100,000 MILLION
▨	10,000–50,000 MILLION
▢	1,000–10,000 MILLION
▢	500–1,000 MILLION
▢	UNDER 500 MILLION
o	MAJOR AIRPORTS (HANDLING OVER 25 MILLION PASSENGERS IN 2000)

* Passenger kilometres are the number of passengers (both international and domestic) multiplied by the distance flown by each passenger from the airport of origin.

SELECTED NEWSPAPER CIRCULATION FIGURES (1995)

France			Russia	
Le Monde		357,362	Pravda	1,373,795
Le Figaro		350,000	Ivestia	700,000
Germany			Spain	
Bild		4,500,000	El Pais	407,629
Süddeutsche Zeitung		402,866		
			United Kingdom	
Italy			The Sun	4,061,253
Corriera Della Sella		676,904	Daily Mirror	2,525,000
La Republica		655,321	Daily Express	1,270,642
La Stampa		436,047	The Times	672,802
			The Guardian	402,214
Japan				
Yomiuri Shimbun	(a.m. edition)	9,800,000	United States	
	(p.m. edition)	4,400,000	New York Times	1,724,705
Manichi Shimbun	(a.m. edition)	3,200,000	Chicago Tribune	1,110,552
	(p.m. edition)	1,900,000	Houston Chronicle	605,343

Kansai International Airport, Japan
The new airport, opened in September 1994, is built on an artificial island in Osaka Bay. The island holds the world's biggest airport terminal at nearly 2 km [1.2 miles] long.

carry mixed cargoes. Containers are boxes built to international standards that contain cargo. Containers are easy to handle, and so they reduce shipping costs, speed up deliveries and cut losses caused by breakages. Most large ports now have the facilities to handle containers.

Air transport is suitable for carrying goods that are expensive, light and compact, or perishable. However, because of the high costs of air freight, it is most suitable for carrying passengers along long-distance routes around the world. Through air travel, international tourism, with people sometimes flying considerable distances, has become a major and rapidly expanding industry.

COMMUNICATIONS

After humans first began to communicate by using the spoken word, the next great stage in the development of communications was the invention of writing around 5,500 years ago.

The invention of movable type in the mid 15th century led to the mass production of books and, in the early 17th century, the first newspapers. Newspapers now play an important part in the mass communication of information, although today radio and, even more important, television have led to a decline in the circulation of newspapers in many parts of the world.

The most recent developments have occurred in the field of electronics. Artificial communications satellites now circle the planet, relaying radio, television, telegraph and telephone signals. This enables people to watch events on the far side of the globe as they are happening. Electronic equipment is also used in many other ways, such as in navigation systems used in air, sea and space, and also in modern weaponry, as shown vividly in the television coverage of the 1991 Gulf War.

THE AGE OF COMPUTERS

One of the most remarkable applications of electronics is in the field of computers. Computers are now making a huge contribution to communications. They are able to process data at incredibly high speeds and can store vast quantities of information. For example, the work of weather forecasters has been greatly improved now that computers can process the enormous amount of data required for a single weather forecast. They also have many other applications in such fields as business, government, science and medicine.

Through the Internet, computers provide a free interchange of news and views around the world. But the dangers of misuse, such as the exchange of pornographic images, have led to calls for censorship. Censorship, however, is a blunt weapon, which can be used by authoritarian governments to suppress the free exchange of information that the new information superhighway makes possible.

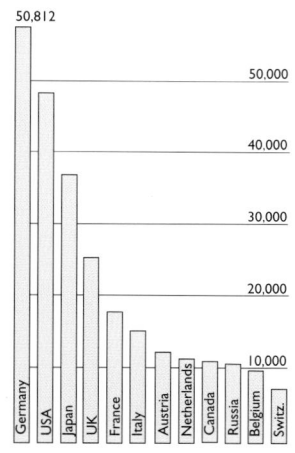

Spending on tourism
Countries spending the most on overseas tourism, US$ million (1996).

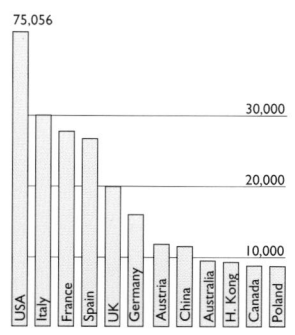

Receipts from tourism
Countries receiving the most from overseas tourism, US$ million (1996).

The World Today

The early years of the 20th century witnessed the exploration of Antarctica, the last uncharted continent. Today, less than 100 years later, tourists are able to take cruises to the icy southern continent, while almost no part of the globe is inaccessible to the determined traveller. Improved transport and images from space have made our world seem smaller.

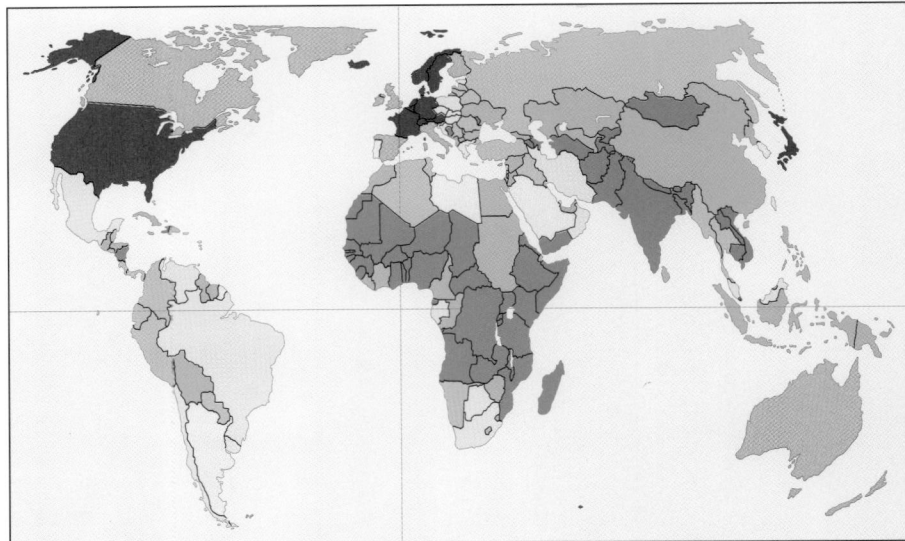

A DIVIDED WORLD

Between the end of World War II in 1945 and the late 1980s, the world was divided, politically and economically, into three main groups: the developed countries or Western democracies, with their free enterprise or mixed economies; the centrally planned or Communist countries; and the developing countries or Third World.

This division became obsolete when the former Soviet Union and its old European allies, together with the 'special economic zones' in eastern China, began the transition from centrally planned to free enterprise economies. This left the world divided into two broad camps: the prosperous developed countries and the poorer developing countries. The simplest way of distinguishing between the groups is with reference to their per capita Gross National Products (per capita GNPs).

The World Bank divides the developing countries into three main groups. At the bottom are the low-income economies, which include China, India and most of sub-Saharan Africa. In 1998, this group contained about 60% of the

world's population, but its average per capita GNP was only US$410. The other two groups are the lower-middle-income economies, with an average per capita GNP of $1,200, and the upper-middle-income economies with an average per capita GNP of $4,900. By contrast, the high-income economies, also called the developed countries, contain only 15% of the world's population but have the high (and rising) average GNP per capita of $25,730.

ECONOMIC AND SOCIAL CONTRASTS

Economic differences are coupled with other factors, such as rates of population growth. For example, in 1998, the low- and middle-income economies had a high population growth rate of 1.7%, while the growth rate in high-income economies was around 0.1%. No fewer than 18 countries in Europe experienced a natural decrease in population in 1998.

Stark contrasts exist worldwide in the quality

GROSS NATIONAL PRODUCT PER CAPITA
The value of total production divided by the population (1999).

- OVER 400% OF WORLD AVERAGE
- 200–400% OF WORLD AVERAGE
- 100–200% OF WORLD AVERAGE

[WORLD AVERAGE WEALTH PER PERSON US$6,316]

- 50–100% OF WORLD AVERAGE
- 25–50% OF WORLD AVERAGE
- 10–25% OF WORLD AVERAGE
- UNDER 10% OF WORLD AVERAGE

RICHEST COUNTRIES

Liechtenstein	$50,000
Luxembourg	$44,640
Switzerland	$38,350
Bermuda	$35,590
Norway	$32,880

POOREST COUNTRIES

Ethiopia	$100
Congo (Dem. Rep.)	$110
Burundi	$120
Sierra Leone	$130
Guinea-Bissau	$160

Porters carrying luggage for tourists, Selous Park, Tanzania
Improved and cheaper transport has led to a boom in tourism in many developing countries. Tourism provides jobs and foreign exchange, though it can undermine local cultures.

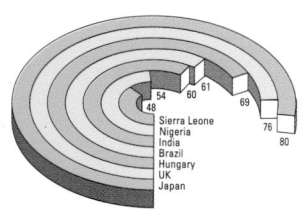

Birth control poster, China

China is the only country with more than a billion people. Central to its economic development policies is population control. Posters exhort the advantages of one-child families.

of life. Generally, the people in Western Europe and North America are better fed, healthier and have more cars and better homes than the people in low- and middle-income economies.

In 1998, the average life expectancy at birth in Africa was 50 years for men and 53 for women. By contrast, the average life expectancy in Europe was 69 for males and 72 for females. Illiteracy in low-income economies for people aged 15 and over was 39% in 1999. But for women, the percentage of those who could not read or write was 48%. Illiteracy is relatively rare for both sexes in high-income economies.

FUTURE DEVELOPMENT

In the last 50 years, despite all the aid supplied to developing countries, much of the world still suffers from poverty and economic backwardness. Some countries are even poorer now than they were a generation ago while others have become substantially richer.

The most remarkable success has been achieved in eastern Asia. Japan and the 'tiger economies' of Hong Kong, Indonesia, Malaysia, Singapore, South Korea, Thailand and Taiwan had an average annual economic growth rate of 5.5% between 1965 and 1993, while their share in the exports of manufactured goods more than doubled in the same period. In 1997, however,

an Asian market crash temporarily halted this dramatic economic expansion.

Reasons advanced to explain the success of the eastern Asian countries include low wage scales, strong family structures, low state expenditure on welfare and large investment in education for both sexes. Some of the arguments are contradictory. For example, while some argue that the success of Hong Kong is due to free enterprise, the governments of Japan and South Korea have intervened substantially in the development of their economies.

Eastern Asia's economic growth has been exceptional and probably cannot be regarded as a model for the developing world. But several factors suggest that poor countries may find progress easier in the 21st century. For example, technology is now more readily transferable between countries, while improved transport and communications make it easier for countries to take part in the world economy. But industrial development and rising living standards could lead to an increase in global pollution. Hence, any strategy for global economic expansion must also take account of environmental factors.

Years of life expectancy at birth, selected countries (1997).

The chart shows the contrasting range of average life expectancies at birth for a range of countries, including both low-income and high-income economies. Generally, improved health services are raising life expectancies. On average, women live longer than men, even in the poorer developing countries.

WESTERN CAPE, SOUTH AFRICA

WORLD MAPS

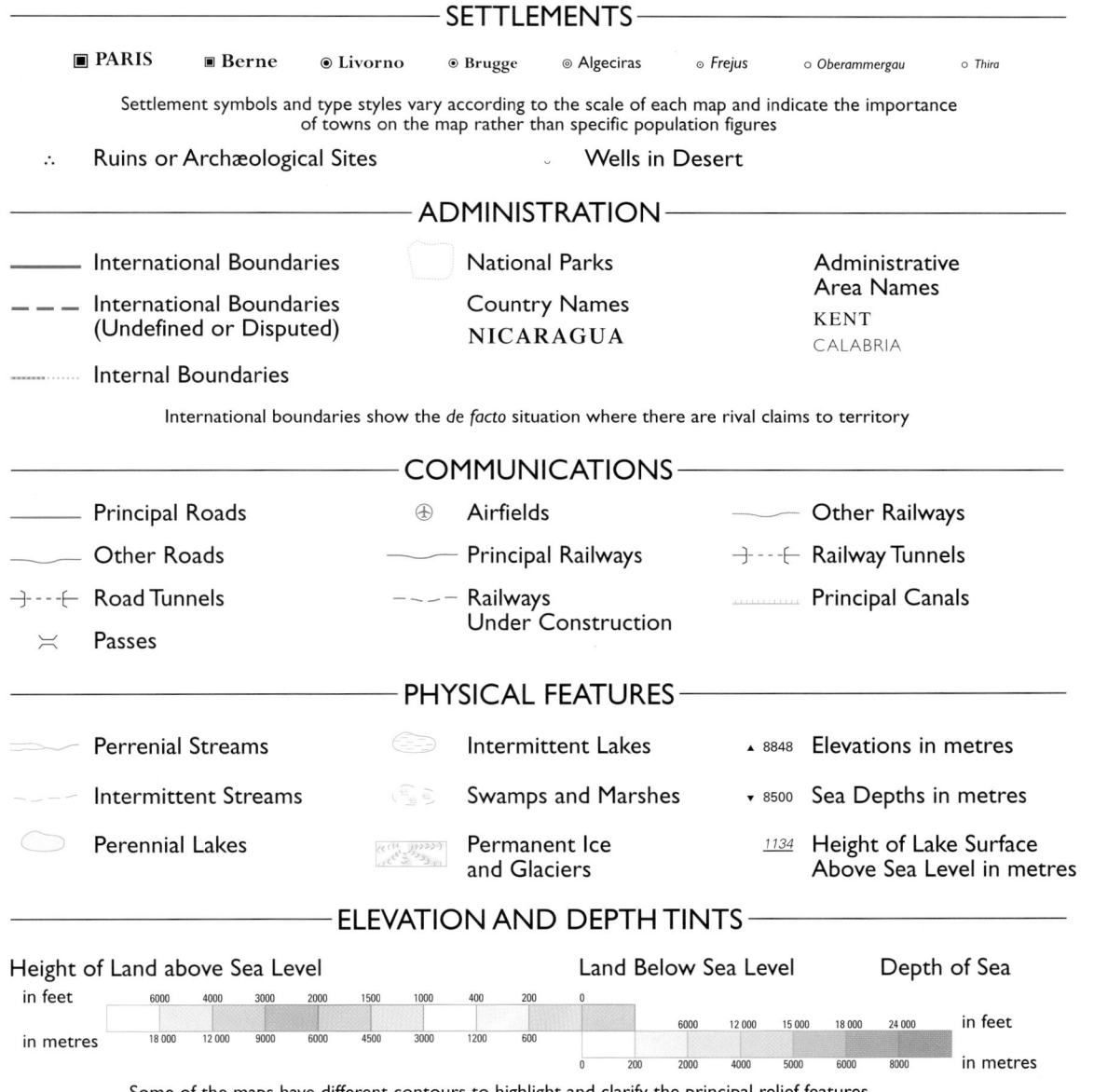

SETTLEMENTS

■ PARIS   ■ Berne   ◉ Livorno   ◎ Brugge   ◉ Algeciras   ○ *Frejus*   ○ *Oberammergau*   ○ *Thira*

Settlement symbols and type styles vary according to the scale of each map and indicate the importance
of towns on the map rather than specific population figures

∴   Ruins or Archæological Sites   ⌣   Wells in Desert

ADMINISTRATION

——— International Boundaries

– – – International Boundaries
(Undefined or Disputed)

·············· Internal Boundaries

National Parks

Country Names
NICARAGUA

Administrative
Area Names

KENT
CALABRIA

International boundaries show the *de facto* situation where there are rival claims to territory

COMMUNICATIONS

——— Principal Roads

——— Other Roads

+ - - + Road Tunnels

⌣ Passes

⊕ Airfields

——— Principal Railways

– – – Railways
Under Construction

——— Other Railways

+ - - + Railway Tunnels

············· Principal Canals

PHYSICAL FEATURES

⌐— Perrenial Streams

– – – Intermittent Streams

⬭ Perennial Lakes

⬭ Intermittent Lakes

Swamps and Marshes

Permanent Ice
and Glaciers

▲ 8848 Elevations in metres

▼ 8500 Sea Depths in metres

1134 Height of Lake Surface
Above Sea Level in metres

ELEVATION AND DEPTH TINTS

Height of Land above Sea Level   Land Below Sea Level   Depth of Sea

in feet   6000   4000   3000   2000   1500   1000   400   200   0   6000   12 000   15 000   18 000   24 000   in feet

in metres   18 000   12 000   9000   6000   4500   3000   1200   600   0   200   2000   4000   5000   6000   8000   in metres

Some of the maps have different contours to highlight and clarify the principal relief features

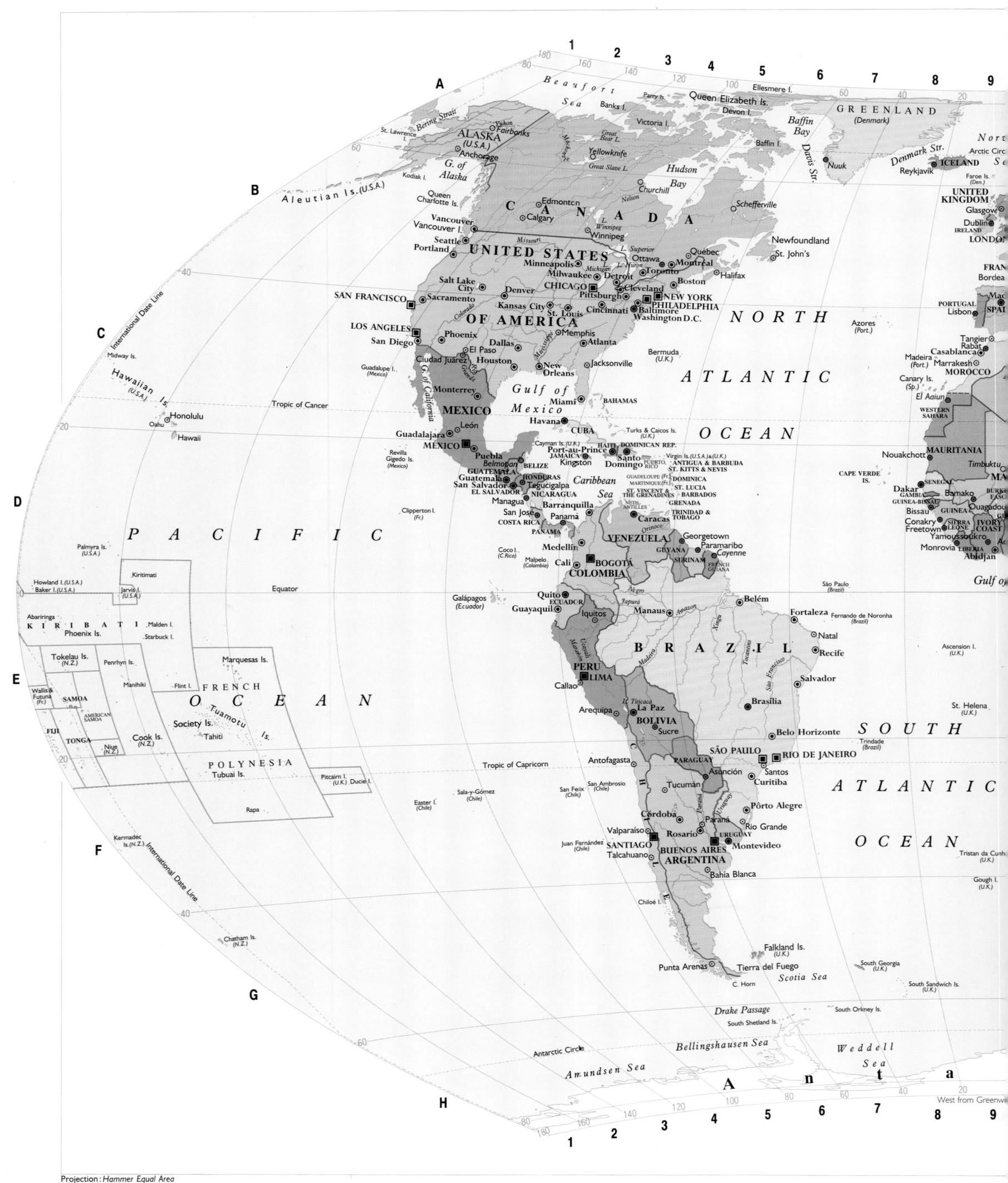

Projection: Hammer Equal Area

Hanoi ● Capital Cities

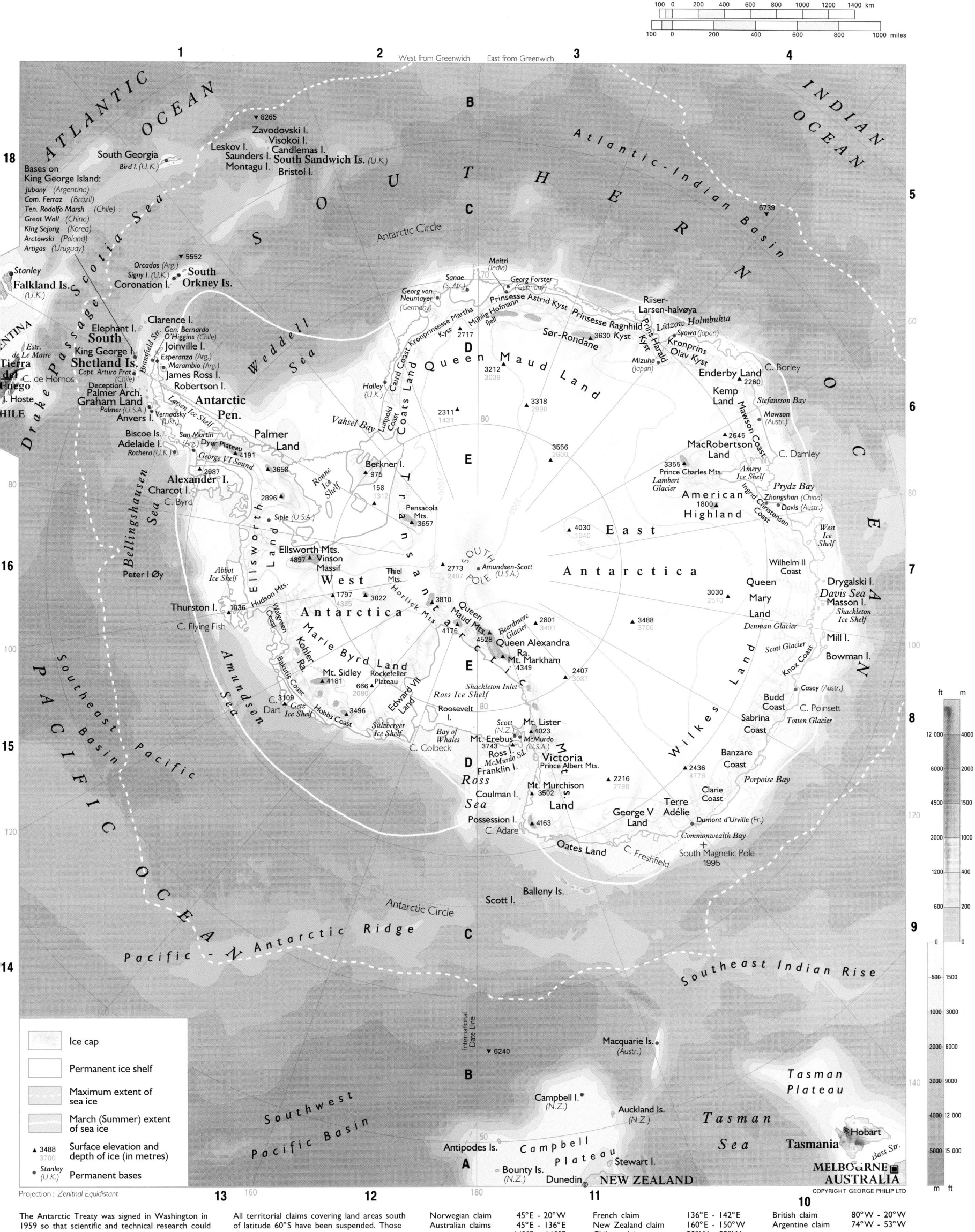

100 0 200 400 600 800 1000 1200 1400 km
100 0 200 400 600 800 1000 miles

West from Greenwich East from Greenwich

ATLANTIC OCEAN

INDIAN OCEAN

SOUTHERN

Atlantic-Indian Basin

Antarctic Circle

Scotia Sea

Weddell Sea

▼ 8265

Zavodovski I.
Leskov I. Visokoi I.
Saunders I. Candlemas I.
Montagu I. **South Sandwich Is.** (U.K.)
Bristol I.

South Georgia
Bird I. (U.K.)

Bases on King George Island:
Jubany (Argentina)
Com. Ferraz (Brazil)
Ten. Rodolfo Marsh (Chile)
Great Wall (China)
King Sejong (Korea)
Arctowski (Poland)
Artigas (Uruguay)

Stanley
Falkland Is. (U.K.)

ARGENTINA

Estr. de Le Maire
Tierra del Fuego
C. de Hornos
I. Hoste
CHILE

Drake Passage

▲ 5552
Orcadas (Arg.)
Signy I. (U.K.) **South**
Coronation I. **Orkney Is.**

Clarence I.
Elephant I. Gen. Bernardo
South O'Higgins (Chile)
King George I. Joinville I.
Shetland Is. Esperanza (Arg.)
Capt. Arturo Prat (Chile) Marambio (Arg.)
Deception I. James Ross I.
Palmer Arch. Robertson I.
Graham Land **Antarctic**
Palmer (U.S.A.) **Pen.**
Anvers I. Vernadsky (Ukr.)

Biscoe Is. San Martin (Arg.)
Adelaide I. Dyer Plateau
Rothera (U.K.) ▲ 4191
Palmer
George VI Sound **Land**
Alexander I. ▲ 3658
▲ 2987
Charcot I.
C. Byrd ▲ 2896

Siple (U.S.A.)

Abbot Ice Shelf
Ellsworth
Land
Thurston I.
▲ 1036
Hudson Mts.
C. Flying Fish
West
▲ 1797 ▲ 3022
Antarctica
Walgreen
Coast
Marie Byrd
Kohler Ra.
Bakutis Coast
▲ 3109
Dart **Land**
C. Dart Getz Ice Shelf
Hobbs Coast ▲ 3496
Mt. Sidley
▲ 4181 Rockefeller
Plateau
666 ▲
2080 Edward VII
Sulzberger **Land**
Ice Shelf
C. Colbeck
Bay of
Whales
Roosevelt I.

Maitri (India)
Sanae (S. Afr.)
Georg von Georg Forster
Neumayer (Germany)
(Germany) Prinsesse Astrid Kyst
Prinsesse Martha Mühlig Hofmann
Kyst fjell
Kronprinsesse Martha ▲ 2717
Halley (U.K.) Kyst

Queen Maud Land
▲ 3212
3039
Coats ▲ 2311
Land 1431
Luitpold ▲ 3318
Coast 2990
Berkner I.
▲ 975 ▲ 3556
158 2600
1312
Ronne Pensacola
Ice Shelf Mts.
▲ 3657
Vahsel Bay
Trans
antarctic

South Pole
Amundsen-Scott
▲ 2773 (U.S.A.)
2407
East
▲ 4030
1040 **Antarctica**

Thiel
Mts.
Queen
▲ 3810 **Maud Mts.**
4176 ▲ 4528
Ellsworth Mts. Beardmore ▲ 2801
Vinson Glacier 3491
Massif Queen Alexandra
▲ 4897 Ra.
Horlick Mts. Mt. Markham
▲ 4349
▲ 2407
3087
▲ 3030
2570

Riiser-
Larsen-halvøya
Prinsesse Ragnhild Kyst
Prins Harald Lützow Holmbukta
Kyst Syowa (Japan)
Sør-Rondane Kronprins
▲ 3630 Olav Kyst
Mizuho
(Japan)
Enderby Land
C. Borley
Kemp ▲ 2260
Land Mawson Coast
Stefansson Bay
Mawson
(Austr.)
MacRobertson ▲ 2645
Land
Amery C. Darnley
▲ 3355 Ice Shelf
Prince Charles Mts. Prydz Bay
Lambert Ingrid Zhongshan (China)
Glacier Christensen Davis (Austr.)
American Coast
1800 West
Highland Ice
Shelf
Queen
Mary
Land
Denman Glacier
Drygalski I.
Davis Sea
Masson I.
Shackleton
Ice Shelf
Mill I.
Scott Glacier
Bowman I.
Knox Coast
Wilkes Casey (Austr.)
Land C. Poinsett
Budd Totten Glacier
Coast
Sabrina
Coast
Banzare
Coast
▲ 2436
4776
Porpoise Bay
Clarie
Coast
Terre
Adélie
George V Dumont d'Urville (Fr.)
Land
Commonwealth Bay
+ South Magnetic Pole
1995

INDIAN OCEAN

▲ 6739

C

▼ 6240

▼ 6240

Ross
Sea
Scott
(N.Z.)
Ross I.
McMurdo
Mt. Erebus (U.S.A.)
▲ 3743
Franklin I. McMurdo Sd.
Mt. Lister
▲ 4023
Victoria
Prince Albert Mts.
Mt. Murchison
▲ 3502
Coulman I.
Land
Possession I.
C. Adare ▲ 4163

Shackleton Inlet
Ross Ice Shelf

Oates Land
C. Freshfield

PACIFIC OCEAN

Southeast Pacific Basin

Amundsen Sea

Bellingshausen Sea

Peter I Øy

Pacific - Antarctic Ridge

Antarctic Circle

Scott I.

Balleny Is.

Southeast Indian Rise

International Date Line

Southwest Pacific Basin

Macquarie Is.
(Austr.)

Campbell I.
(N.Z.)

Auckland Is.
(N.Z.)

Antipodes Is.

Bounty Is.
(N.Z.)

Campbell
Plateau

Stewart I.

Dunedin **NEW ZEALAND**

Tasman
Plateau

Tasman
Sea

Tasmania

Hobart

Bass Str.

MELBOURNE
AUSTRALIA
COPYRIGHT GEORGE PHILIP LTD

Legend:
Ice cap
Permanent ice shelf
Maximum extent of sea ice
March (Summer) extent of sea ice
▲ 3488 Surface elevation and
3700 depth of ice (in metres)
Stanley Permanent bases
(U.K.)

Projection : Zenithal Equidistant

ft m
12 000 4000
6000 2000
4500 1500
3000 1000
1200 400
600 200
0 0
500 1500
1000 3000
2000 6000
3000 9000
4000 12 000
5000 15 000
m ft

The Antarctic Treaty was signed in Washington in 1959 so that scientific and technical research could continue unhampered by international politics.

All territorial claims covering land areas south of latitude 60°S have been suspended. Those claims were:

Norwegian claim	45°E - 20°W
Australian claims	45°E - 136°E
	142°E - 160°E
French claim	136°E - 142°E
New Zealand claim	160°E - 150°W
Chilean claim	90°W - 53°W
British claim	80°W - 20°W
Argentine claim	74°W - 53°W

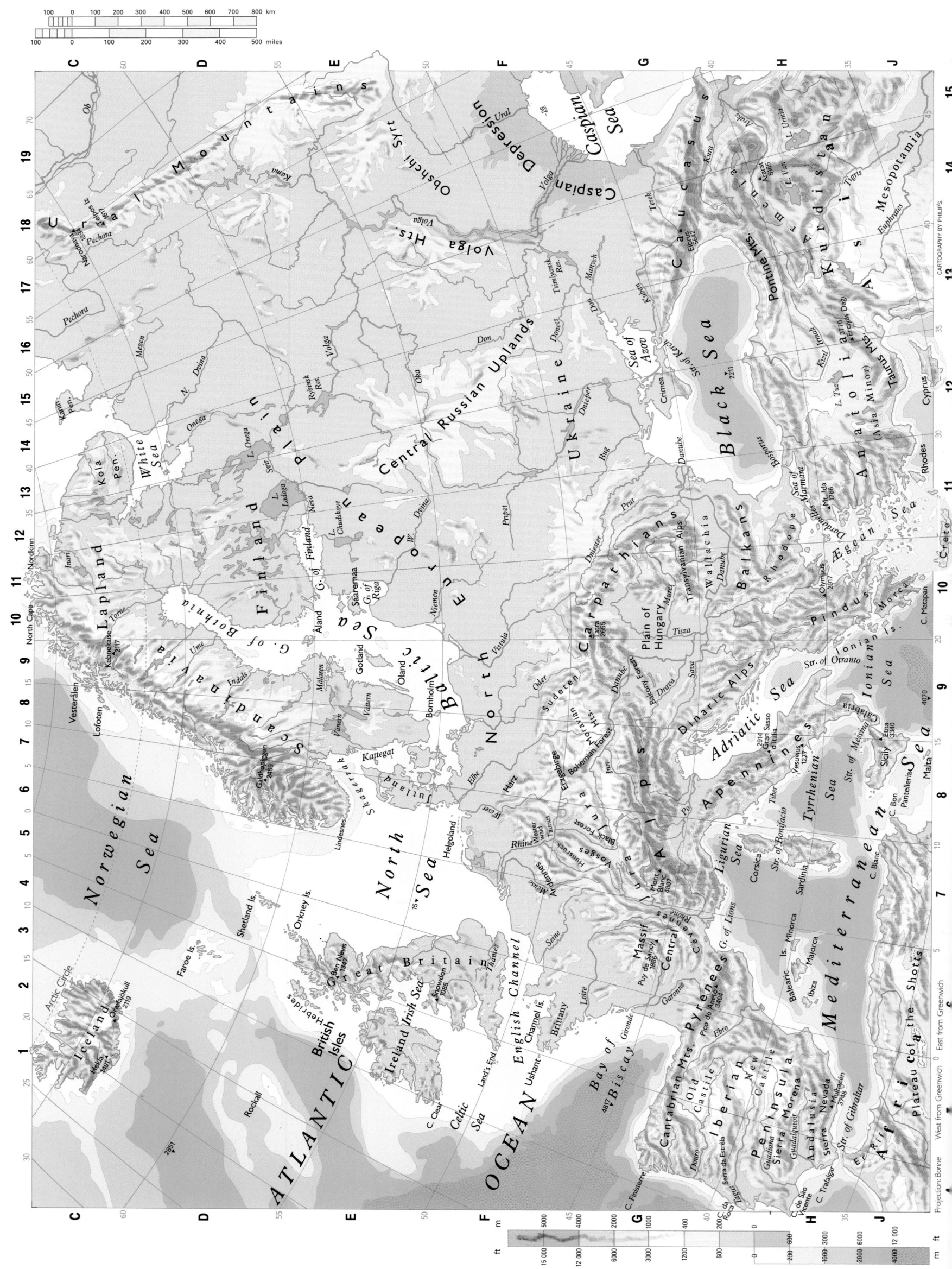

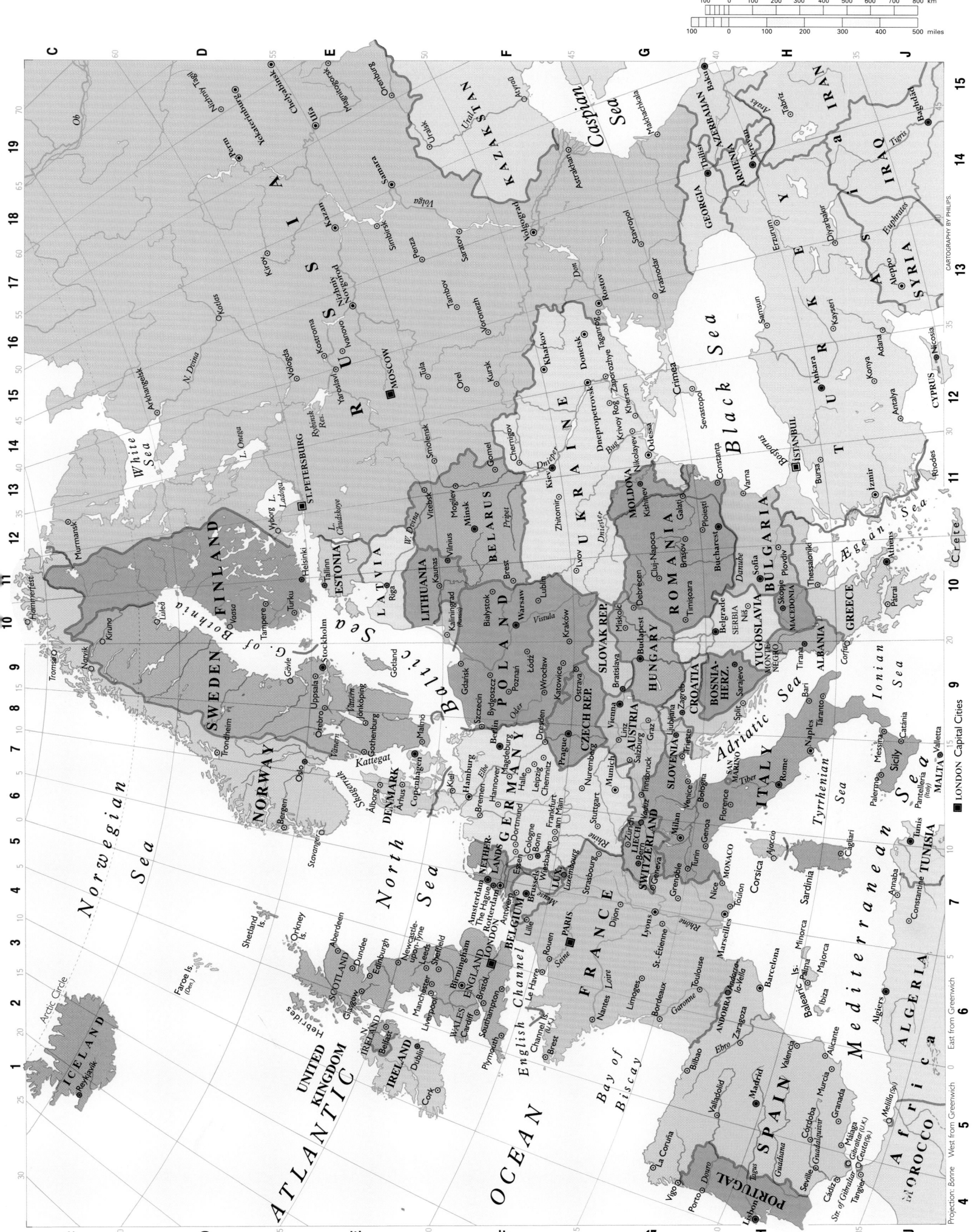

SCANDINAVIA 1:4 400 000

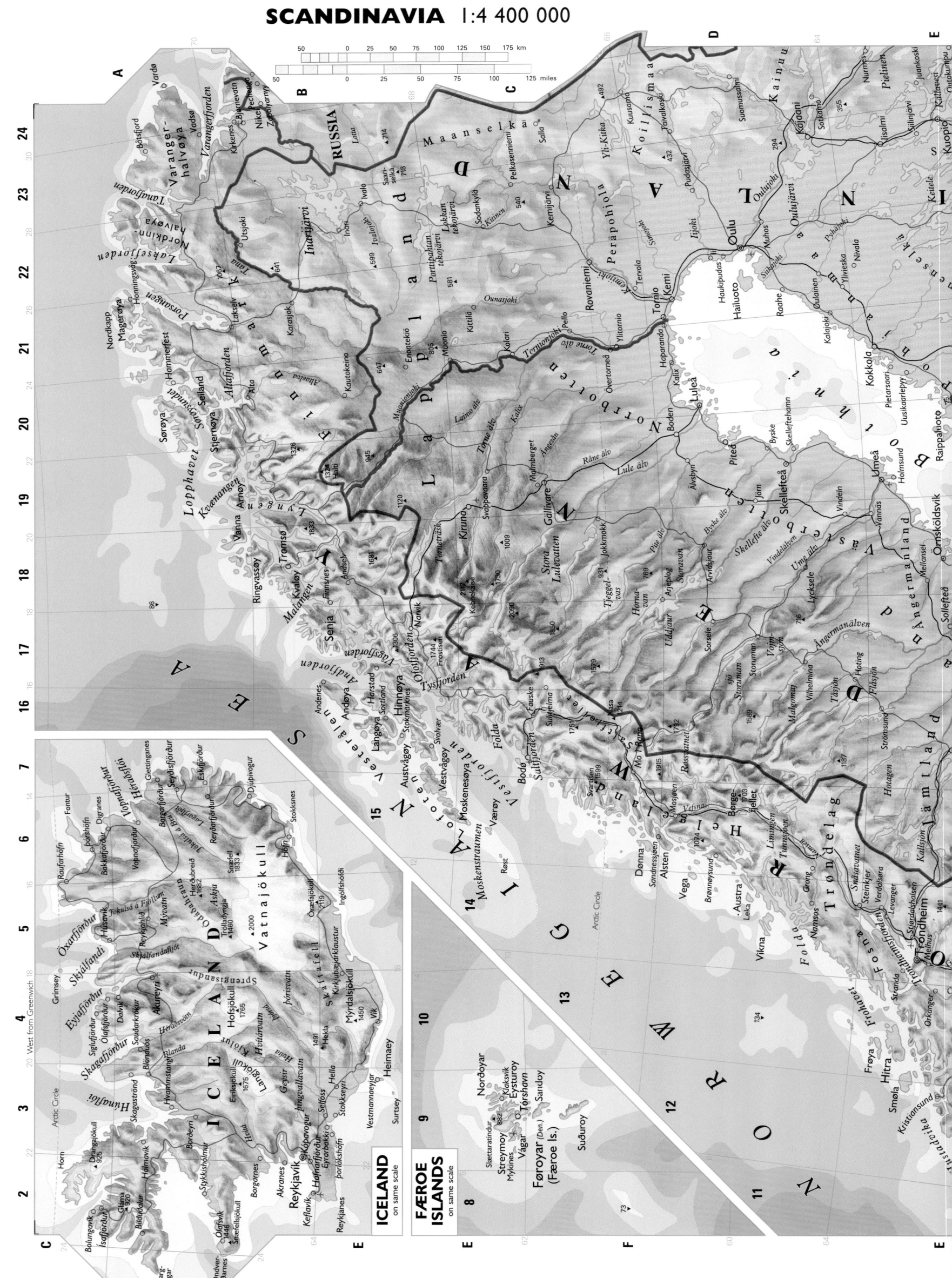

RUSSIA

ICELAND
on same scale

FÆROE ISLANDS
on same scale

Føroyar (Den.)
(Færoe Is.)

West from Greenwich

COPYRIGHT GEORGE PHILIP LTD.

Countries / Regions

F i n l a n d — Pöhjänne

E S T O N I A

L A T V I A

L I T H U A N I A

R U S S I A

B E L A R U S

S V E R I G E (Sweden)

N O R G E (Norway)

D A N M A R K (Denmark)

G E R M A N Y — Deutschland

P O L A N D — POLSKA

Svealand · Götaland · Gästrikland · Uppland · Västmanland · Södermanland · Dalarna · Härjedalen · Jämtland · Hälsingland · Värmland · Bohuslän · Dalsland · Halland · Skåne · Blekinge · Småland · Öland · Telemark · Valdres · Østerdalen · Dovrefjell · Jotunheimen · Gudbrandsdalen · Hardangervidda · Romsdalen · Rondane

Seas / Gulfs

Gulf of Finland · Gulf of Riga · Gulf of Bothnia · Ålands hav · B A L T I C S E A · Kattegat · Skagerrak · Oslofjorden · Sognefjord · Nordfjord · Kieler Bucht · Mecklenburger Bucht · Deutsche Bucht · Lille Bælt · Store Bælt · Fehmarn Belt

Selected cities and towns

Helsinki (Helsingfors) · Tampere · Turku (Åbo) · Pori · Rauma · Kotka · Kouvola · Lahti · Lappeenranta · Mikkeli · Jyväskylä · Vaasa · Seinäjoki

Tallinn · Tartu · Pärnu · Narva · Kuressaare (Ösel) · Haapsalu · Rapla · Paide

Riga · Jūrmala · Jelgava · Liepāja · Ventspils · Daugavpils · Valmiera · Cēsis · Tukums

Vilnius · Kaunas · Šiauliai · Panevėžys · Klaipėda · Marijampolė · Ukmergė · Telšiai · Plungė · Tauragė

Kaliningrad (Russia) · Chernyakhovsk · Sovetsk · Zelenogradsk · Baltiysk · Gvardeysk

STOCKHOLM · Uppsala · Västerås · Eskilstuna · Södertälje · Norrköping · Linköping · Nyköping · Gävle · Sundsvall · Härnösand · Hudiksvall · Söderhamn · Örebro · Karlstad · Falun · Borlänge · Mora · Jönköping · Växjö · Kalmar · Karlskrona · Kristianstad · Halmstad · Göteborg (Gothenburg) · Borås · Trollhättan · Lidköping · Skövde · Mariestad · Ystad · Helsingborg · Landskrona · Visby · Gotland · Bornholm · Öland · Oskarshamn · Västervik · Nässjö · Vetlanda

OSLO · Drammen · Hamar · Lillehammer · Gjøvik · Kongsvinger · Fredrikstad · Sarpsborg · Moss · Halden · Tønsberg · Sandefjord · Larvik · Skien · Porsgrunn · Kristiansand · Arendal · Grimstad · Stavanger · Bergen · Haugesund · Flekkefjord · Egersund

KØBENHAVN (Copenhagen) · Malmö · Lund · Trelleborg · Roskilde · Køge · Næstved · Slagelse · Korsør · Odense · Svendborg · Nykøbing · Ålborg · Århus · Randers · Viborg · Horsens · Vejle · Fredericia · Kolding · Esbjerg · Herning · Silkeborg · Holstebro · Skive · Thisted · Hjørring · Frederikshavn · Ribe · Haderslev · Sønderborg · Sjælland · Lolland · Falster · Langeland · Fyn · Møn

Kiel · Lübeck · Flensburg · Schleswig · Rendsburg · Neumünster · Rostock · Wismar · Stralsund · Greifswald · Cuxhaven · Helgoland · Husum · Rügen · Usedom

Gdańsk (Gdańsk) · Gdynia · Sopot · Słupsk · Koszalin · Kołobrzeg · Elbląg · Malbork · Tczew · Starogard Gdański · Bytów · Wejherowo · Rumia · Lębork

Islands: Åland (Ahvenanmaa) · Hiiumaa (Dago) · Saaremaa (Ösel) · Muhu · Ruhnu saar · Gotska Sandön · Fårö · Gotland · Öland · Bornholm · Lasø · Anholt · Læsø · Nordfriesische Inseln · Ostfriesische Inseln · Sylt · Föhr · Fehmarn

Rivers / Lakes: Mälaren · Vänern · Vättern · Hjälmaren · Ånermen · Åsnen · Daugava · Neman · Göta älv · Göta kanal · Klarälven · Österdalälven · Västerdalälven · Ljusnan · Ljungan · Indalsälven · Lågen · Glåma · Lillfjorden

Elevation scale:
m: 6000 · 4500 · 3000 · 1500 · 600 · 200 · 0
ft: 2000 · 1500 · 1000 · 500 · 200 · 150 · 0 · 150 · 300 · 600 · 1500 · 3000 · 6000
(m / ft)

Grid references: F · G · H · J · K · 9 · 12 · 13 · 14 · 15 · 16 · 17 · 18 · 19 · 20 · 21

km / miles scale bars

Gulf of Bothnia

VÄSTER- / NORRLANDS LÄN

JÄMTLANDS LÄN

Östersund

Sundsvall

HÄLSINGLAND

GÄVLEBORGS LÄN

GÄSTRIKLAND

Gävle

KOPPARBERGS LÄN

DALARNA LÄN

Falun
Borlänge

Siljan

UPPSALA LÄN

Uppsala

VÄSTMANLANDS LÄN

Västerås

STOCKHOLMS LÄN

STOCKHOLM

SÖDERMANLANDS LÄN

Eskilstuna

ÖREBRO LÄN

Örebro

NÄRKE LÄN

VÄRMLANDS LÄN

Karlstad

VASTERDALEN

Härjedalen

SÖR-TRØNDELAG

Trondheim

NORD- MØRE OG ROMSDAL

Kristiansund

Kristiansund

DOVREFJELL

Jotunheimen

OPPLAND

HEDMARK

Hamar
Lillehammer

Rondane

GUDBRANDSDALEN

Østerdalen

Glåma

AKERSHUS

OSLO

ØSTFOLD
Fredrikstad

VESTFOLD

BUSKERUD

Drammen

TELEMARK

Klarälven

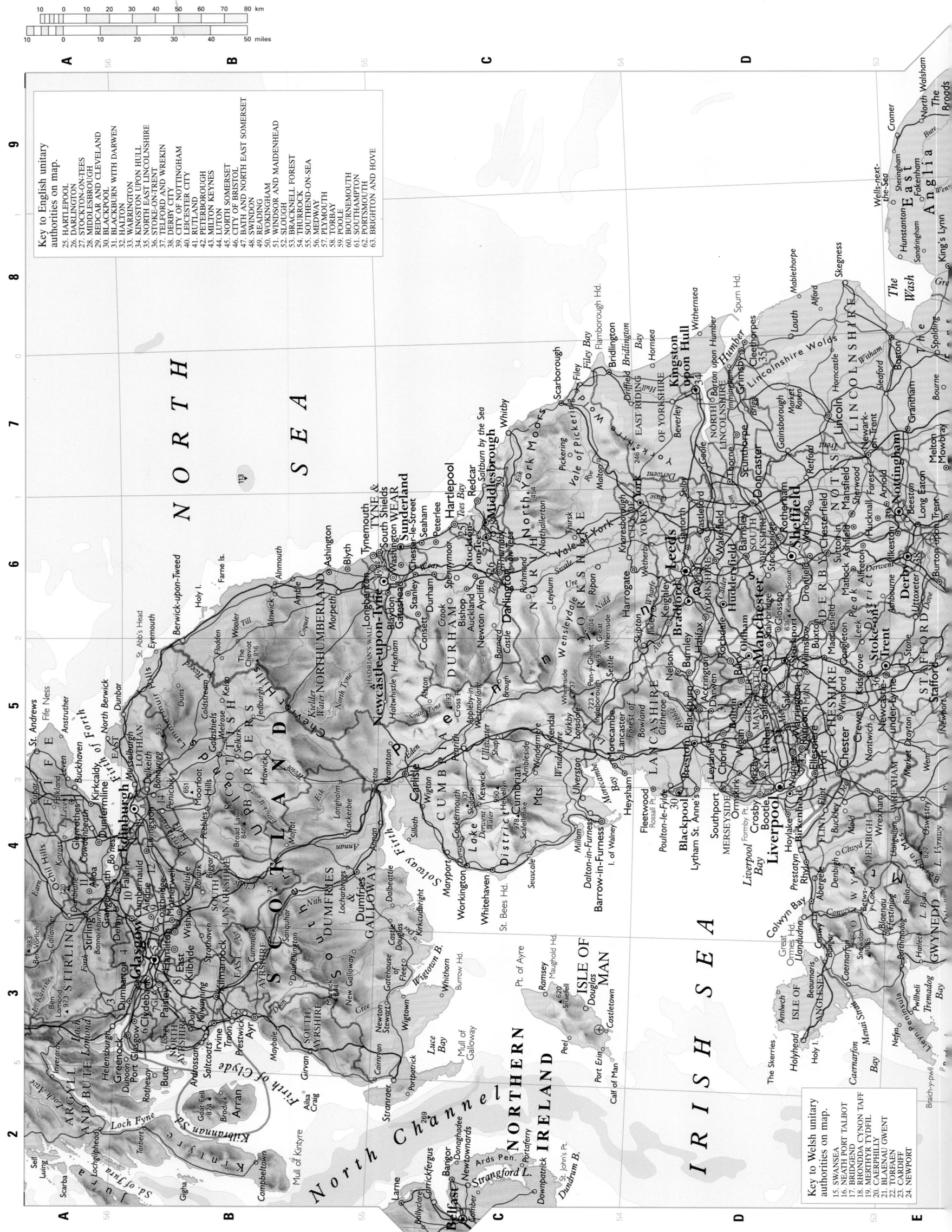

10 0 10 20 30 40 50 60 70 80 km
10 0 10 20 30 40 50 miles

Key to English unitary authorities on map.

25 HARTLEPOOL
26 DARLINGTON
27 STOCKTON-ON-TEES
28 MIDDLESBROUGH
29 REDCAR AND CLEVELAND
30 BLACKPOOL
31 BLACKBURN WITH DARWEN
32 HALTON
33 WARRINGTON
34 KINGSTON UPON HULL
35 NORTH EAST LINCOLNSHIRE
36 STOKE-ON-TRENT
37 TELFORD AND WREKIN
38 DERBY CITY
39 CITY OF NOTTINGHAM
40 LEICESTER CITY
41 RUTLAND
42 PETERBOROUGH
43 MILTON KEYNES
44 LUTON
45 NORTH SOMERSET
46 CITY OF BRISTOL
47 BATH AND NORTH EAST SOMERSET
48 SWINDON
49 READING
50 WOKINGHAM
51 WINDSOR AND MAIDENHEAD
52 SLOUGH
53 BRACKNELL FOREST
54 THURROCK
55 SOUTHEND-ON-SEA
56 MEDWAY
57 PLYMOUTH
58 TORBAY
59 POOLE
60 BOURNEMOUTH
61 SOUTHAMPTON
62 PORTSMOUTH
63 BRIGHTON AND HOVE

Key to Welsh unitary authorities on map.

15 SWANSEA
16 NEATH PORT TALBOT
17 BRIDGEND
18 RHONDDA CYNON TAFF
19 MERTHYR TYDFIL
20 CAERPHILLY
21 BLAENAU GWENT
22 TORFAEN
23 CARDIFF
24 NEWPORT

N O R T H

S E A

I R I S H

S E A

North Channel

NORTHERN
IRELAND

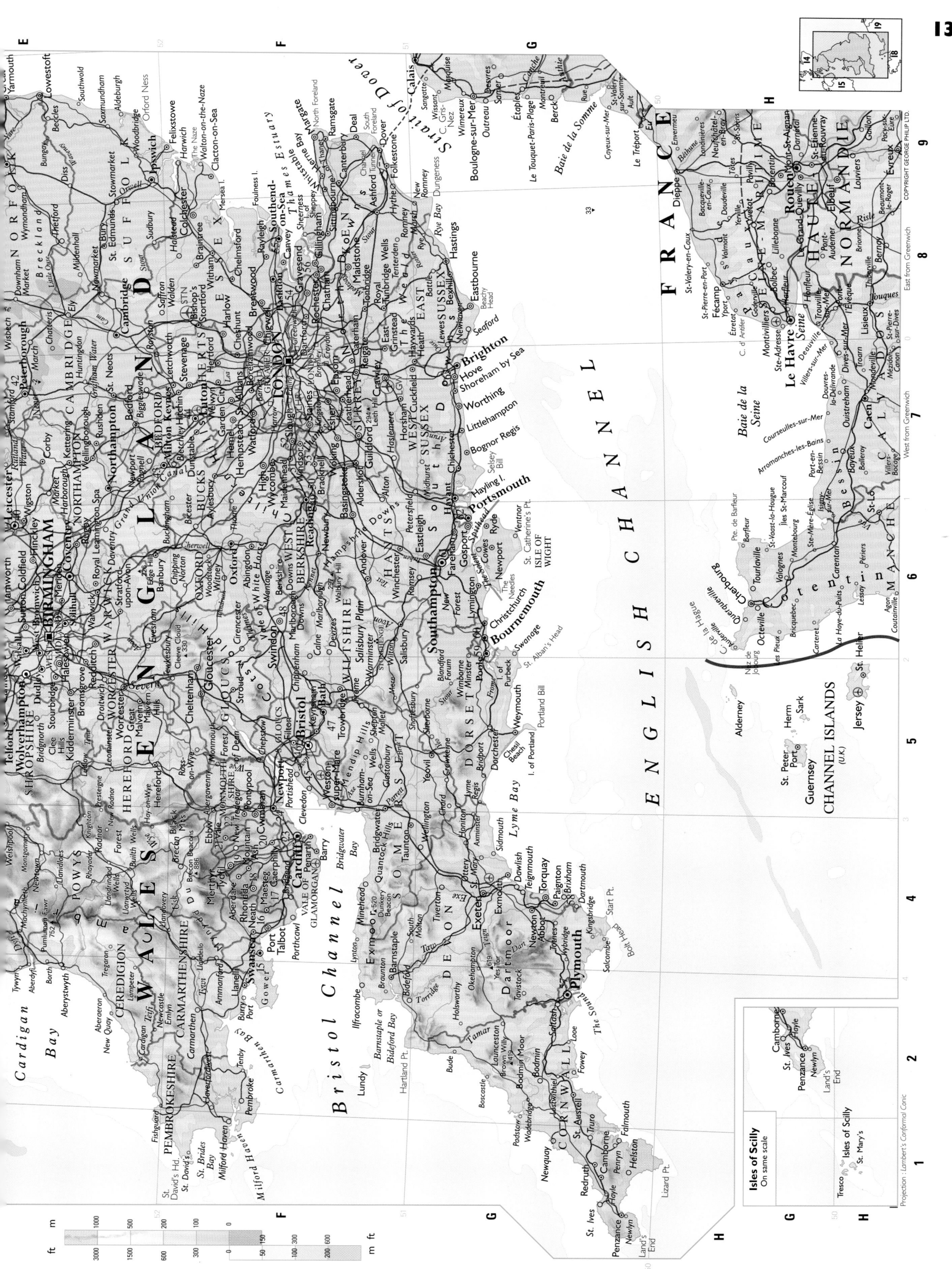

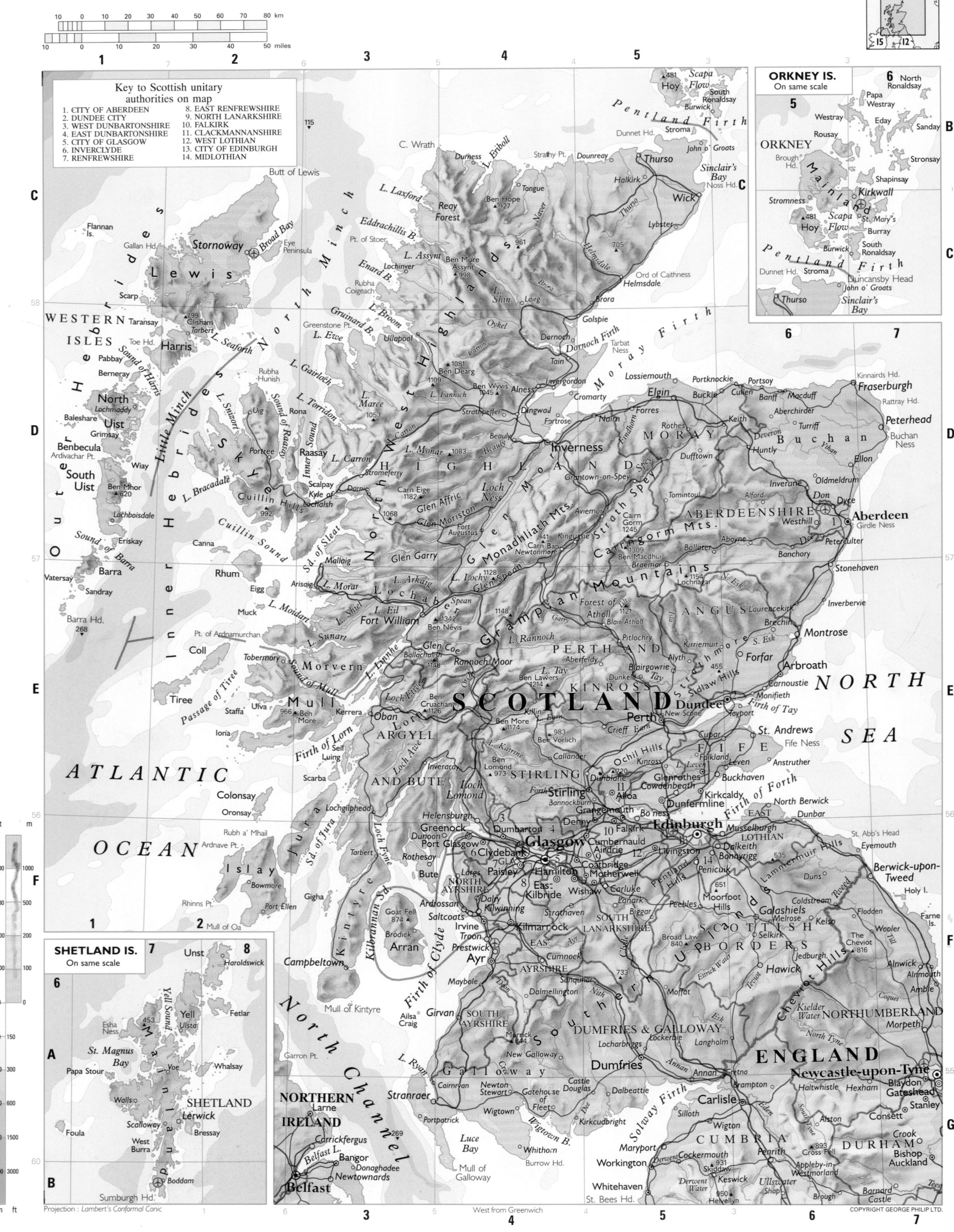

Key to Scottish unitary
authorities on map
1. CITY OF ABERDEEN   8. EAST RENFREWSHIRE
2. DUNDEE CITY   9. NORTH LANARKSHIRE
3. WEST DUNBARTONSHIRE   10. FALKIRK
4. EAST DUNBARTONSHIRE   11. CLACKMANNANSHIRE
5. CITY OF GLASGOW   12. WEST LOTHIAN
6. INVERCLYDE   13. CITY OF EDINBURGH
7. RENFREWSHIRE   14. MIDLOTHIAN

ORKNEY IS.
On same scale

SHETLAND IS.
On same scale

Projection : Lambert's Conformal Conic

West from Greenwich

COPYRIGHT GEORGE PHILIP LTD.

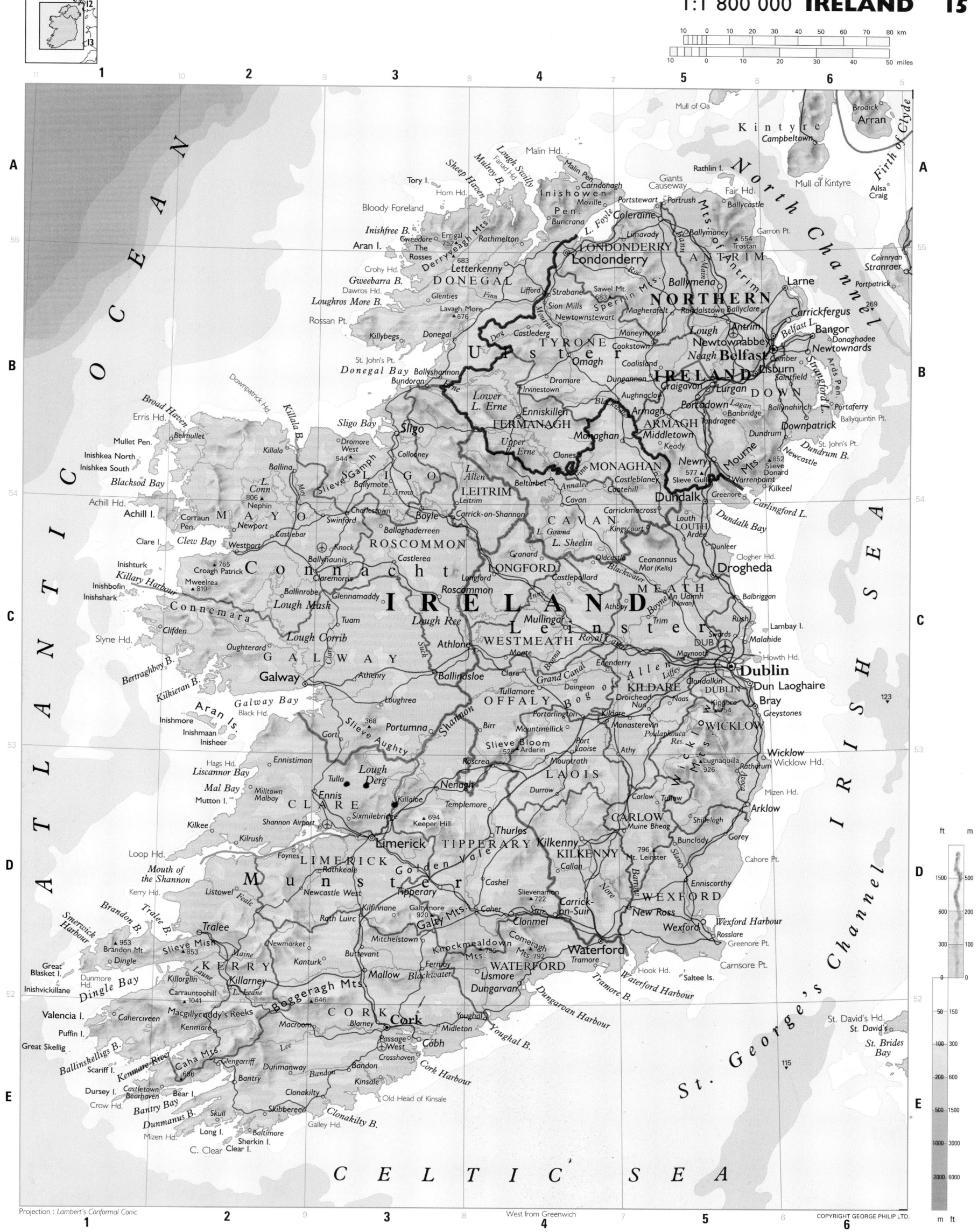

10 0 10 20 30 40 50 60 70 80 km
10 0 10 20 30 40 50 miles

A T L A N T I C   O C E A N

NORTHERN IRELAND

Ulster

IRELAND

Connacht

Leinster

Munster

Dublin

N O R T H   C H A N N E L

I R I S H   S E A

St. George's Channel

C E L T I C   S E A

Projection : Lambert's Conformal Conic

West from Greenwich

COPYRIGHT GEORGE PHILIP LTD.

50   0   25   50   75   100   125   150   175 km
50   0   25   50   75   100   125 miles

1   2   3   4   5   6   7   8   9

A

ATLANTIC OCEAN

Shetland Is.
Yell Unst Fetlar
Foula Mainland Lerwick
Askøy
Bergen
Osøyro

1224

B

316

Orkney Is.
Westray Sanday
Stronsay
Mainland Kirkwall
Hoy South Ronaldsay
Fair Isle

NORWAY
Haugesund
Kopervik Åkrahamn
Stord
Bømlo Leir
Sandnes Bryne Nærbø
Boknat
Stavanger

Pentland Firth
C. Wrath Thurso Wick
Helmsdale

Outer Hebrides
Lewis Stornoway
Harris
St. Kilda
North Uist
Benbecula
South Uist

North Minch
North West Highlands
Ullapool Lairg Golspie
789 Tain Helmsdale
Invergordon Dingwall Nairn Elgin Buckie Banff
Inverness Spey Huntly Peterhead
1182 L. Ness Aviemore Don Inverurie
Ben Nevis Grampian Mts. Aberdeen
1342 1311 Dee Ballater Stonehaven

Moray Firth
Fraserburgh

C

Skye
Rhum Eigg
Barra
Tiree Coll
Mull
Oban

Fort William
1214
Forfar Montrose
973 L. Lomond Perth Arbroath
Stirling Dundee St. Andrews
Glenrothes

SCOTLAND

NORTH SEA

Colonsay
Jura Greenock
Islay Paisley Glasgow Edinburgh
East Kilbride Hamilton Berwick-upon-Tweed
Arran Irvine Kilmarnock
Campbeltown Ayr Southern Uplands Galashiels
840 Jedburgh E16 Alnwick
Hawick Cheviot Hills

Dunfermline
Kirkcaldy
Dunbar

D

Malin Hd.
Buncrana
Aran I. Letterkenny Coleraine
Lifford Ballymena Larne
Donegal Londonderry Antrim Bangor
NORTHERN IRELAND Belfast
Omagh Lough Neagh Lisburn
Portadown Lurgan

North Channel
Firth of Clyde
Girvan Dumfries Hexham
Stranraer Annan Gateshead
Kirkcudbright Carlisle Durham
Workington Darlington
Whitehaven Cumbrian 893
Mts. 978 Stockton-on-Tees

Newcastle-upon-Tyne
South Shields
Sunderland
Hartlepool
Redcar
Middlesbrough
Scarborough

16

E

ft   m

3000 1000
1500 600
0
50 150
100 300
200 600
500 1500
1000 3000
2000 6000

m ft

Achill I.
Ballina L. Conn
Castlebar Sligo
Lough Leitrim
Westport Roscommon Cavan Clone
Lough Mask Longford Castleblaney
Connemara Athlone Lough Ree Dundalk
Galway B. Galway Ballinasloe Boyne
Aran Is. Birr Tullamore Mullingar
Ennis Lough Derg Port Laoise Liffey
Nenagh Athy Drogheda

IRELAND
Ceanannus Mor

Bundoran
Enniskillen
Lower L. Erne
Armagh Newry

Barrow-in-Furness
Douglas Lancaster
I. of Man Harrogate
York
Morecambe
Blackpool Keighley Leeds Beverley
Preston Burnley Bradford Kingston upon Hull
Blackburn Halifax Huddersfield Scunthorpe
Bolton 636 Grimsby
Manchester Oldham Doncaster Humber
Liverpool Stockport Rotherham
Warrington Sheffield Lincoln
Louth
Chesterfield Mansfield Skegness
Crewe Boston
Colwyn Bay Chester The Wash
Wrexham Derby Nottingham
Snowdon Stoke-on-Trent Trent Cromer
1085 Stafford Grantham King's Lynn
Shrewsbury Telford ENGLAND Norwich
Nuneaton Leicester Peterborough Great Yarmouth
Welshpool Corby Lowestoft
Wolverhampton Coventry Rugby Thetford
BIRMINGHAM Northampton Ely Bury St. Edmunds
Reddit: Royal Bedford Cambridge Ipswich
Worcester Leamington Spa Milton Keynes Felixstowe
Hereford Stevenage Harwich
Cheltenham Hemel Luton Harlow Colchester
Gloucester Oxford Hempstead Chelmsford
Cwmbran High Wycombe Southend-on-Sea
Newport Swindon Reading LONDON Basildon
Cardiff Bristol Newbury Slough Thames
Barry Bath Basingstoke Reigate Margate
Chatham Canterbury
Maidstone Dover
Guildford Crawley Ashford Folkestone
Winchester Hastings
Fareham Brighton Eastbourne
Salisbury Portsmouth
Havant Worthing
Southampton Isle of Wight
Bournemouth Newport
Poole Weymouth

WALES
Cardigan Bay
Aberystwyth
Cambrian Mts.
Pwllheli Bangor
Anglesey
Holyhead
Dublin
Dun Laoghaire
Bray

IRISH SEA

Galway
Limerick Tipperary Thurles
Tralee Kilrush Carrick-on-Suir
Listowel Clonmel Carlow Kilkenny
953 Mallow Waterford Wexford
Dingle Killarney Blackwater Rosslare
Carrauntoohill Dungarvan
1041 Bandon Youghal
Macgillycuddy's Reeks Cork Cóbh
Valencia I. Kinsale
Bantry
C. Clear 99

UNITED KINGDOM

Wicklow Mts.
926 Arklow

St. George's Channel

Carmarthen Brecon
886 Merthyr Tydfil Neath
Llanelli Rhondda
Swansea Port Talbot
Bristol Channel
Weston-super-Mare
Barnstaple Exmoor
Bude Taunton Yeovil
Exeter 618 Dorchester
Dartmoor Exmouth
Newquay Torbay
Truro St. Austell
Land's End Plymouth
Penzance
Isles of Scilly

NETHERLANDS
Haarle
's-Gravenhage
(Den Haag)
ROTTERDAM
Dordrecht

Den Helder

Alkm

Tex

F

CELTIC SEA

Fishguard
Haverfordwest
Milford Haven
Pembroke

English Channel

Str. of Dover Dunkerque
Boulogne-sur-Mer Calais
Le Touquet-Paris-Plage Gris-Nez
33 St-Omer Lille
Abbeville Béthune
36 Bruay-la-Buissière Lens
Valenciennes
Cambrai

BELGIUM
BRUSSEL
(Bruxelles)
Antwerpen
Brugge Mechel
Gent Aalst
Tournai
Oostende
Zeebrugge
Vlissingen
Hoek van Holland

G

Guernsey St. Peter Port Sark
Channel Is. (U.K.) St. Helier Jersey

C. de la Hague Pte. de Barfleur
Alderney Cherbourg Le Havre
St Valery C.
Valognes Trouville-sur-Mer
Cotentin Bayeux Lisieux Bolbec
Caen Seine Elbeuf

Dieppe
Fécamp Le Tréport
Pays de Caux
FRANCE
Rouen
Amiens
Picardie
St-Quentin

West from Greenwich   East from Greenwich
COPYRIGHT GEORGE PHILIP LTD.

Projection: Conical with two standard parallels

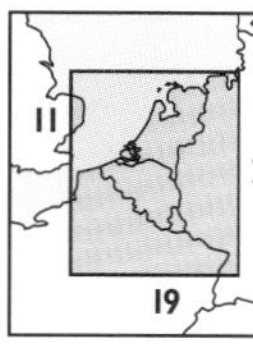

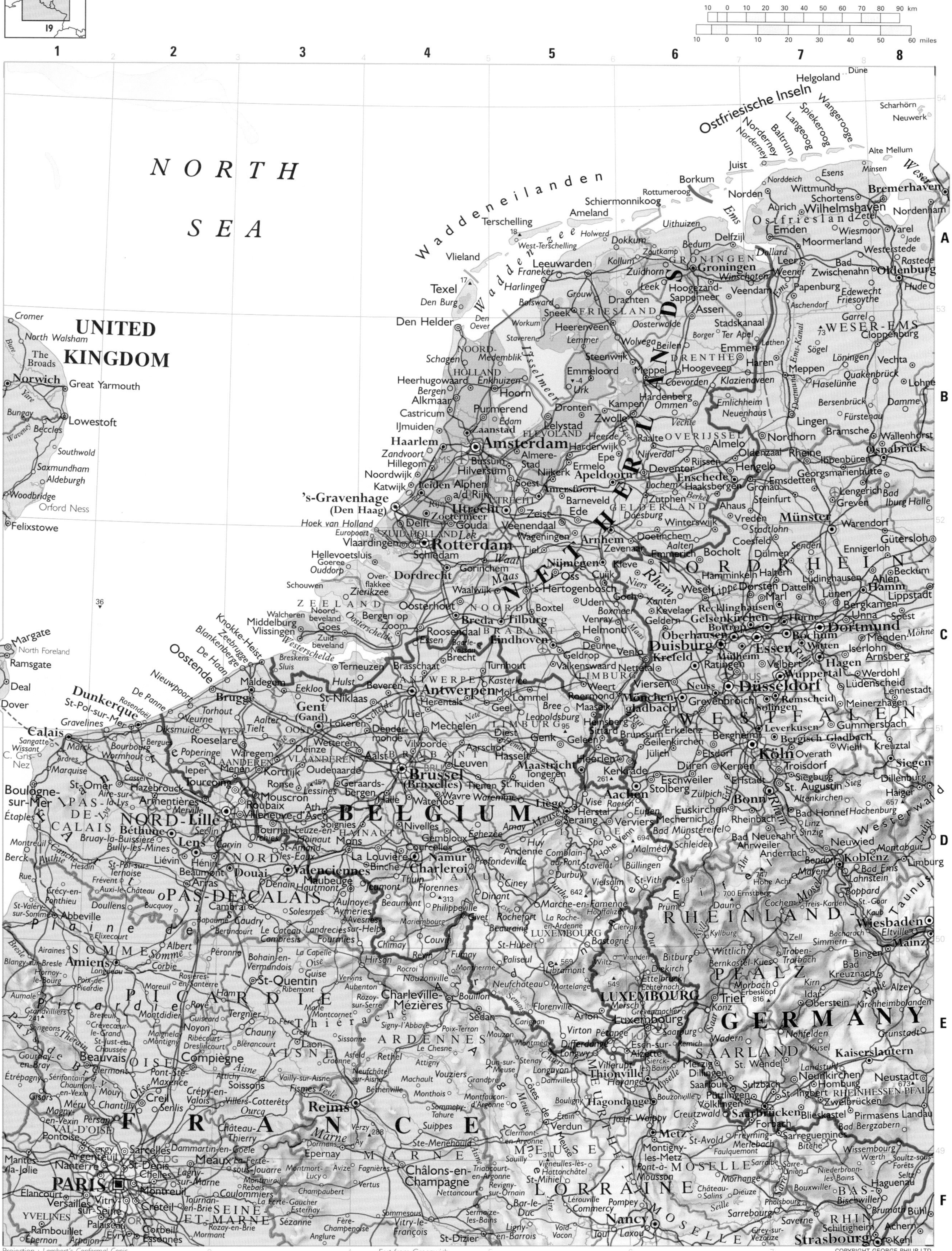

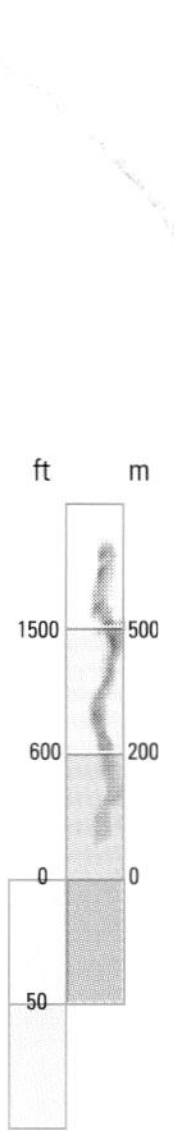

10 0 10 20 30 40 50 60 70 80 90 km
10 0 10 20 30 40 50 60 miles

NORTH SEA

UNITED KINGDOM

NETHERLANDS

BELGIUM

LUXEMBOURG

GERMANY

FRANCE

Waddeneilanden

Ostfriesische Inseln

FRIESLAND

DRENTHE

OVERIJSSEL

GELDERLAND

NOORD-HOLLAND

ZUID-HOLLAND

ZEELAND

NOORD BRABANT

LIMBURG

FLEVOLAND

NORDRHEIN

WESTFALEN

RHEINLAND-PFALZ

SAARLAND

HESSEN

VLAANDEREN

HAINAUT

NORD

PAS-DE-CALAIS

PICARDIE

SOMME

OISE

AISNE

ARDENNES

MEUSE

LORRAINE

MOSELLE

SEINE-ET-MARNE

Amsterdam · 's-Gravenhage (Den Haag) · Rotterdam · Utrecht · Haarlem · Groningen · Leeuwarden · Arnhem · Nijmegen · Eindhoven · Tilburg · Breda · Dordrecht · Zwolle · Enschede · Apeldoorn · Deventer

Antwerpen · Brussel (Bruxelles) · Gent (Gand) · Brugge · Liège · Namur · Charleroi · Mons · Oostende · Hasselt · Leuven · Mechelen · Maastricht

Luxembourg

Düsseldorf · Köln · Essen · Dortmund · Duisburg · Bonn · Münster · Wuppertal · Bochum · Aachen · Mönchengladbach · Krefeld · Koblenz · Wiesbaden · Mainz · Osnabrück · Oldenburg · Bremerhaven · Saarbrücken · Kaiserslautern · Strasbourg

Lille · Calais · Boulogne-sur-Mer · Dunkerque · Valenciennes · Amiens · Douai · Reims · Châlons-en-Champagne · Charleville-Mézières · Nancy · Metz · Thionville · Paris · Versailles · Beauvais · Compiègne · St-Quentin

Norwich · Great Yarmouth · Lowestoft · Felixstowe · Margate · Ramsgate · Dover · Deal

Helgoland · Ostfriesland · WESER-EMS

Projection: Lambert's Conformal Conic

East from Greenwich

COPYRIGHT GEORGE PHILIP LTD.

Underlined towns give their name to the administrative area in which they stand.

Projection : Lambert's Conformal Conic

West from Greenwich

DÉPARTEMENTS IN THE PARIS AREA
1. Ville de Paris
2. Seine-St-Denis
3. Val-de-Marne
4. Hauts-de-Seine

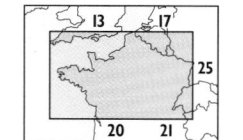

Underlined towns give their name to the
administrative area in which they stand.

COPYRIGHT GEORGE PHILIP LTD.

East from Greenwich

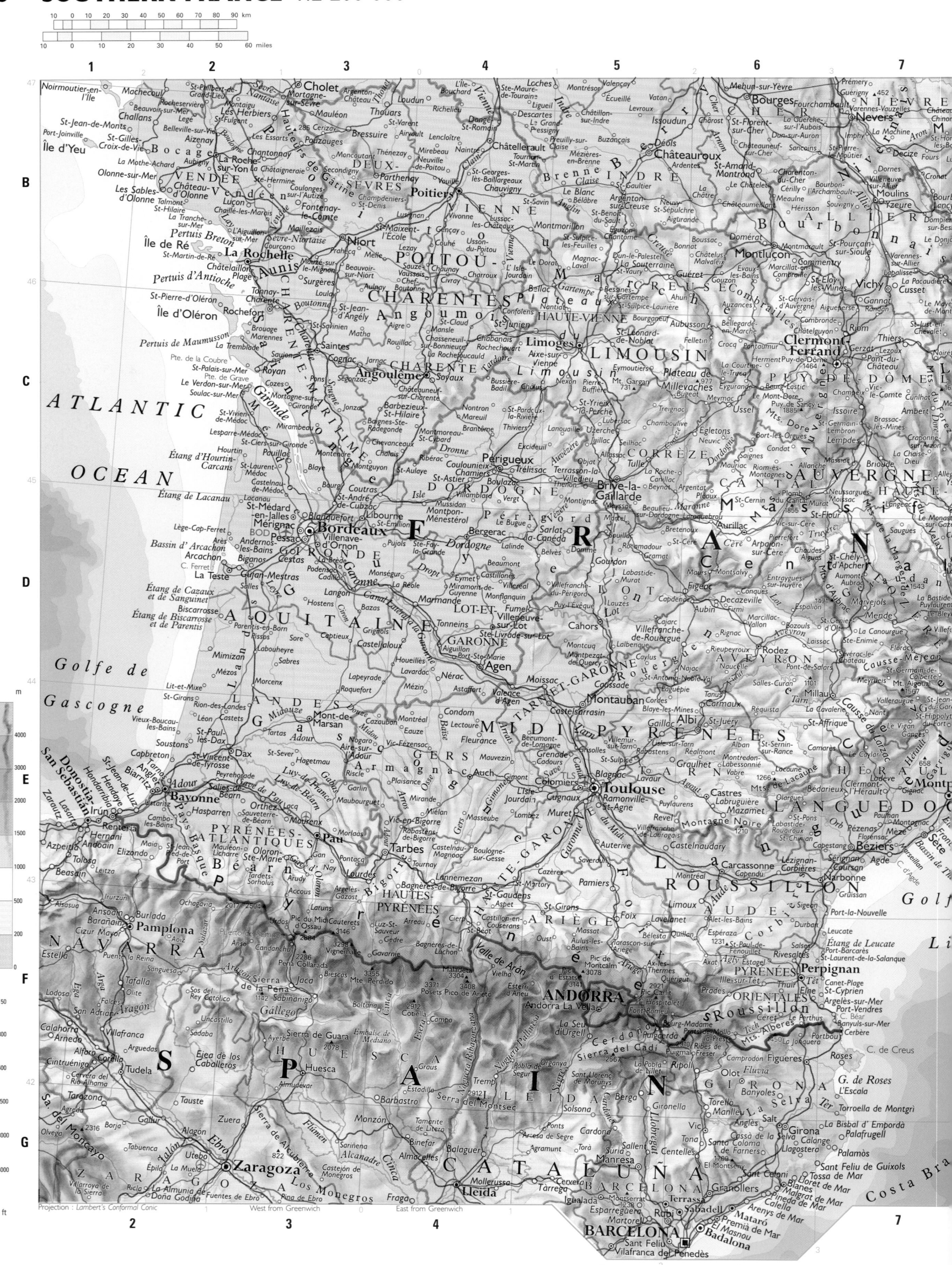

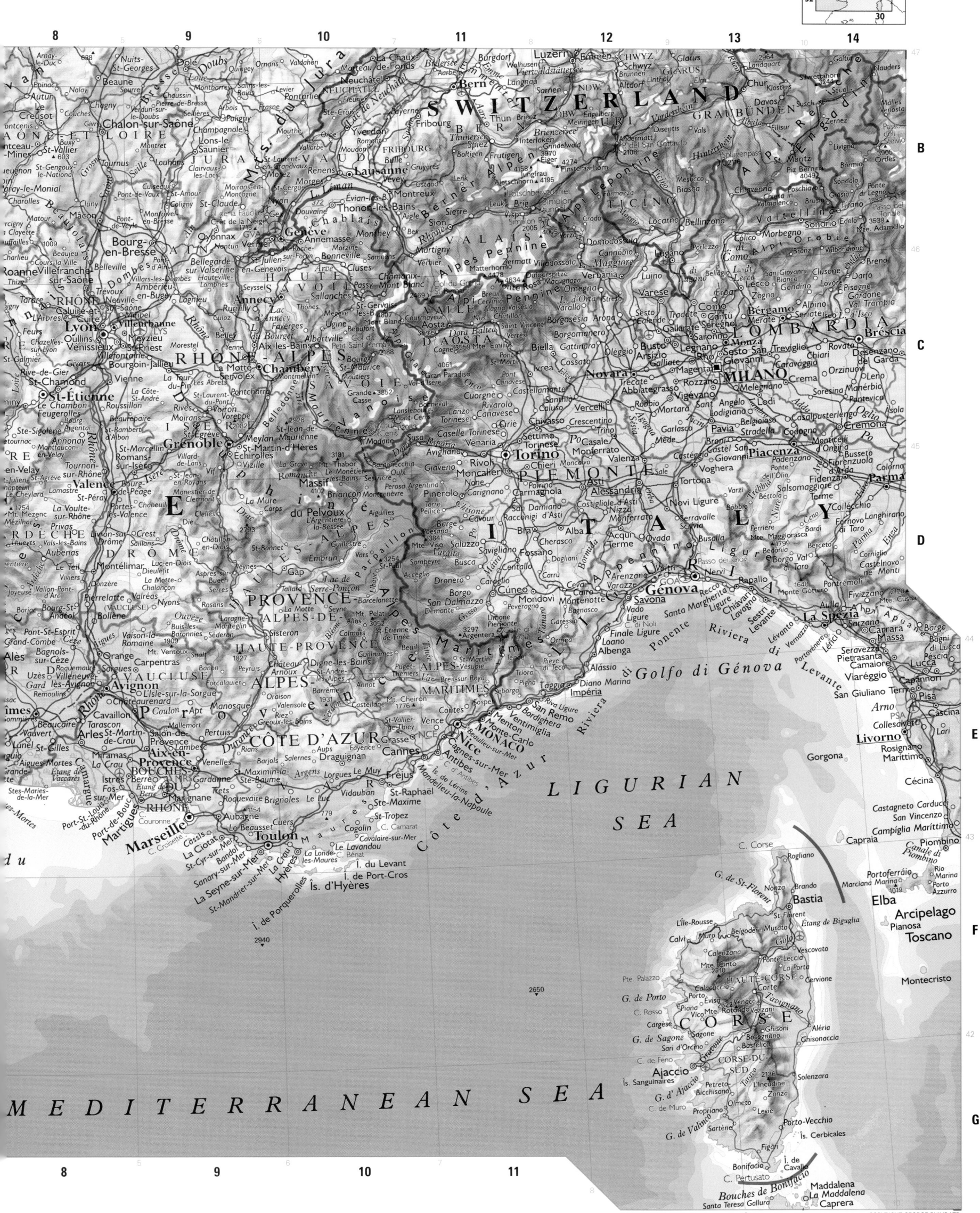

9
16
18
20
46
48
40
41

9
10
11
12
13
14
15
16
B
C
D
E
F
G
Zatoka Gdańska
Baltiysk
Kaliningrad (Russia)
Gusev
Chernyakhovsk
Gvardeysk
Bagrationovsk
Zalew Wiślany
Braniewo
Elbląg
Wejherowo
Rumia
Gdynia
Sopot
Gdańsk
Tczew
Lębork
Bytów
Malbork
Pojezierze Mazurskie
Olsztyn
Kętrzyn
Giżycko
Suwałki
Ełk
Augustów
Starogard Gdański
Kwidzyn
Iława
Ostróda
Chojnice
Świecie
Grudziądz
Chełmno
Brodnica
Działdowo
Szczytno
Bydgoszcz
Toruń
Rypin
Mława
Ostrołęka
Łomża
Białystok
Sokółka
Ciechanów
Inowrocław
Włocławek
Płock
Pułtusk
Ostrów Mazowiecka
Bielsk Podlaski
Hajnówka
Gniezno
Września
Poznań
Koło
Kutno
Legionowo
WARSZAWA (Warsaw)
Mińsk Mazowiecki
Siedlce
Biała Podlaska
Łęczyca
Łowicz
Pruszków
Otwock
Żyrardów
Skierniewice
Konin
Turek
Kalisz
Zduńska Wola
Łódź
Pabianice
Grójec
Radom
Łuków
Międzyrzec Podlaski
Ostrów Wielkopolski
Sieradz
Tomaszów Mazowiecki
Puławy
Lublin
Chełm
Włodawa
Piotrków Trybunalski
Końskie
Skarżysko-Kamienna
Starachowice
Świdnik
Kraśnik
Wrocław
Oleśnica
Wieluń
Kluczbork
Radomsko
Częstochowa
Kielce
Ostrowiec-Świętokrzyski
Sandomierz
Stalowa Wola
Zamość
Opole
Oława
Myszków
Jędrzejów
Pińczów
Tarnobrzeg
Mielec
Zawiercie
Tarnowskie Góry
Bytom
Sosnowiec
Zabrze
Gliwice
Chorzów
Katowice
Tychy
Oświęcim
Kraków
Bochnia
Tarnów
Dębica
Rzeszów
Jarosław
Przemyśl
Racibórz
Opava
Ostrava
Karviná
Havířov
Frýdek-Místek
Cieszyn
Bielsko-Biała
Żywiec
Nowy Sącz
Jasło
Krosno
Sanok
Nowy Targ
Zakopane
Dukelský Průsmyk
Šumperk
Přerov
Zlín
Považská Bystrica
Žilina
Ružomberok
Poprad
Bardejov
Prešov
Humenné
Michalovce
Košice
Martin
Nízke Tatry
Banská Bystrica
Trenčín
Prievidza
Zvolen
Slovenské Rudohorie
Lučenec
Topoľčany
Nitra
Trnava
Bratislava
Malé Karpaty
Biele Karpaty
SLOVAK REP.
Vychodné Beskydy
Západné Beskydy
Tatry
Levice
Nové Zámky
Komárno
Mosonmagyaróvár
Győr
Sopron
Tatabánya
Esztergom
Dunakeszi
Salgótarján
Vác
Gyöngyös
Eger
Miskolc
Ózd
Hatvan
Mezőkövesd
Hajdúböszörmény
Nyíregyháza
Debrecen
Sátoraljaújhely
Jászberény
BUDAPEST
Érd
Pápa
Székesfehérvár
Cegléd
Szolnok
Karcag
Veszprém
Balaton
Siófok
Dunaújváros
Nagykőrös
Kecskemét
Mezőtúr
Szombathely
Zalaegerszeg
Nagykanizsa
Kaposvár
Szekszárd
Kiskunfélegyháza
Kiskőrös
Kalocsa
Csongrád
Szentes
Békéscsaba
Gyula
Orosháza
Hódmezővásárhely
Makó
Kiskunhalas
Szeged
Baja
Pécs
Mohács
HUNGARY
Dunaj
Tisza
Duna
Drava
Sava
LITHUANIA
Vilnius
Marijampolė
Varėna
Druskininkai
Prienai
Ashmyany
Smarhon
Vileyka
Maladzyechna
Barysaw
Krupki
Shklow
Mstsislaw
Zhodzina
MINSK
Valozhyn
Cherven
Mahilyow
Krychaw
Cherykaw
Slawharad
Dzyarzhynsk
Lida
Navahrudak
Hrodzyanka
Asipovichy
Bykhaw
Hrodna
Stowbtsy
Nyasvizh
Slutsk
Babruysk
Rahachow
Zhlobin
Masty
Dzyatlava
Baranavichy
Vawkavysk
Slonim
Klyetsk
Salihorsk
Glusk
Aktsyabrski
Svyetlahorsk
Homyel
Dobrush
Lyakhavichy
Hantsavichy
Svislach
Ivatsevichy
Rechytsa
Byaroza
Tsyelyakhany
Luninyets
Pyetrikaw
Kalinkavichy
Vasilevichi
Pruzhany
Kobryn
Drahichyn
Ivanava
Pinsk
Mazyr
Khoyniki
Loyew
Zhabinka
Brest
Malaryta
Stolin
Davyd Haradok
Yelsk
BELARUS
Pripet Marshes
Pripyat
Dnyapro (Dnieper)
Nyoman
Yaselda
Horyn
Ubort
Sozh
Drut
Ptsich
Byarezina
Kamin-Kashyrskyy
Dubrovytsya
Olevsk
Ovruch
Chornobyl
Belokorovichi
Uzh
Oster
Kyyivske Vdskh.
Desna
Korosten
Malyn
Irpin
KYYIV (Kiev)
Dymer
Lyuboml
Kovel
Staryy Chartoriysk
Kostopil
Novohrad-Volynskyy
Radomyshl
Teterev
Volodymyr-Volynskyy
Novovolynsk
Rozhyshche
Kivertsi
Lutsk
Oleksandriya
Rivne
Zdolbuniv
Korets
Sluch
Zhytomyr
Korostyshev
Vasylkiv
Fastiv
Horokhiv
Chervonohrad
Dubno
Ostroh
Slavuta
Pershotravensk
Sokal
Radekhiv
Berestechko
Kremenets
Shepetivka
Polonne
Berdychiv
Bila Tserkva
Rava-Ruska
Kamyanka-Buzka
Izyaslav
Nesterov
Brody
Kozyatyn
Skvyra
Tarashcha
Yavoriv
Mostyska
Lviv (Lvov)
Zolochiv
Zbarazh
Starokonstyantyniv
Khmelnik
Horodok
Ternopil
Khmelnytskyy
Tetiyev
Lipovets
Zhashkiv
Sambir
Khodoriv
Berezhany
Skalat
Hrymayliv
Vinnytsya
Drohobych
Rogatyn
Terebovlya
Kopychyntsi
Horodok
Bar
Zhmerynka
Haysyn
Boryslav
Stryy
Truskavets
Kalush
Dnister
Buchach
Chortkiv
Skala-Podilska
Kamyanets-Podilskyy
Tulchyn
Uman
Buh
Skole
Bolekhiv
Ivano-Frankivsk
Horodenka
Zalishchyky
Mohyliv-Podilskyy
Vapnyarka
Bershad
Hayvoron
Nadvirna
Kolomyya
Khotyn
Ocnița
Balta
Uzhhorod
Volovets
Pechenizhyn
Snyatyn
Novoselytsya
Lipcani
Yampil
Chop
Mukacheve
Yaremcha
Chernivtsi
Drochia
Soroca
Ananyiv
Berehove
Khust
Yasinya
Hlyboka
Edineț
Florești
Kotovsk
Storozhynets
Rakhiv
Vynohradiv
Tyachiv
Bălți
Rîbnița
Dubăsari Vdkhr.
UKRAINE
Podilska Vysochyna
Carpathians
MOLDOVA
Basarabia
Dorohoi
Botoșani
Fălești
Cornești
Dubăsari
Rădăuți
Siret
Suceava
Orhei
Fălticeni
Pașcani
Ungheni
Chișinău
Tiraspol
Iași
Tighina
Rozdilna
Roman
Huși
Leova
Cimișlia
Dnister
Nistru
Piatra Neamț
Vaslui
Basarabeasca
Bilhorod-Dnivstrovskyy
Comrat
Artsyz
Bacău
Miercurea Ciuc
Bârlad
Ciadâr-Lunga
Tatarbunary
Onești
Cahul
Ozero Sasyk
Vulcanești
Bolhrad
Kiliya
Vylkove
Reni
Izmayil
Sulina
Tecuci
Focșani
Sărat
Galați
Brăila
Tulcea
Babadag
Lacul Razelm
Satu Mare
Sighetu Marmației
Baia Mare
Borșa
Pietrosul
Carei
Vatra Dornei
Bistrița
Someș
Oradea
Zalău
Dej
Cluj-Napoca
Reghin
Târgu Mureș
Turda
Salonta
Mureș
Crișul Negru
Crișul Alb
Munții Bihor
Abrud
Aiud
Odorheiu Secuiesc
Sfântu Gheorghe
Târnăveni
Mediaș
Sighișoara
Arad
Transilvania
Alba-Iulia
Brad
Sânnicolau Mare
Deva
Simeria
Sibiu
Făgăraș
Brașov
Săcele
Timișoara
Lugoj
Hunedoara
Carpații Meridionali
Moldoveanu
Vf. Omul
Câmpina
Râmnicu Sărat
Caransebeș
Vf. Peleaga
Petroșani
Vulcan
Parângul Mare
Câmpulung
Curtea de Argeș
Buzău
Reșița
Porta Orientalis
Târgoviște
Ploiești
Târgu-Jiu
Râmnicu Vâlcea
Ialomița
Slobozia
Bela Crkva
Portile de Fier
Pitești
Dâmbovița
Argeș
Fetești
Orșova
Drobeta-Turnu-Severin
Drăgășani
BUCUREȘTI (Bucharest)
Medgidia
Năvodari
Constanța
Craiova
Slatina
Călărași
Dobrogea
Oltenița
Roșiori-de-Vede
Silistra
Mangalia
Dunărea (Danube)
Băilești
Caracal
Olt
Alexandria
Tutrakan
Giurgiu
Ruse
Razgrad
Dobrich
Balchik
Corabia
Turnu Măgurele
Zimnicea
Vidin
Lom
Oryakhovo
Varna
Nos Kaliakra
BULGARIA
ROMANIA
Walachia
Jiu
Vedea
Subotica
Senta
Kikinda
Sombor
Bečej
Vojvodina
Tisa
Zrenjanin
Osijek
Vukovar
Novi Sad
Vršac
Petrovaradin
Vinkovci
Sremska Mitrovica
Pančevo
Zemun
Šabac
BEOGRAD (Belgrade)
Smederevo
Požarevac
Dunav
Negotin
Bor
Zaječar
Timok
Valjevo
Kragujevac
Jagodina
Čačak
Užice
Kraljevo
Višegrad
Morava
YUGOSLAVIA
Virovitica
CROATIA
Slavonski Brod
Novska
Bosanska Gradiška
Banja Luka
Brčko
Doboj
Bijeljina
Tuzla
Zvornik
Drina
BOSNIA-HERZEGOVINA
Travnik
Žepče
Zenica
Sarajevo
Cincar
Srebrenica
Han Pijesak
East from Greenwich

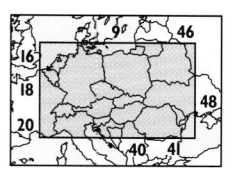

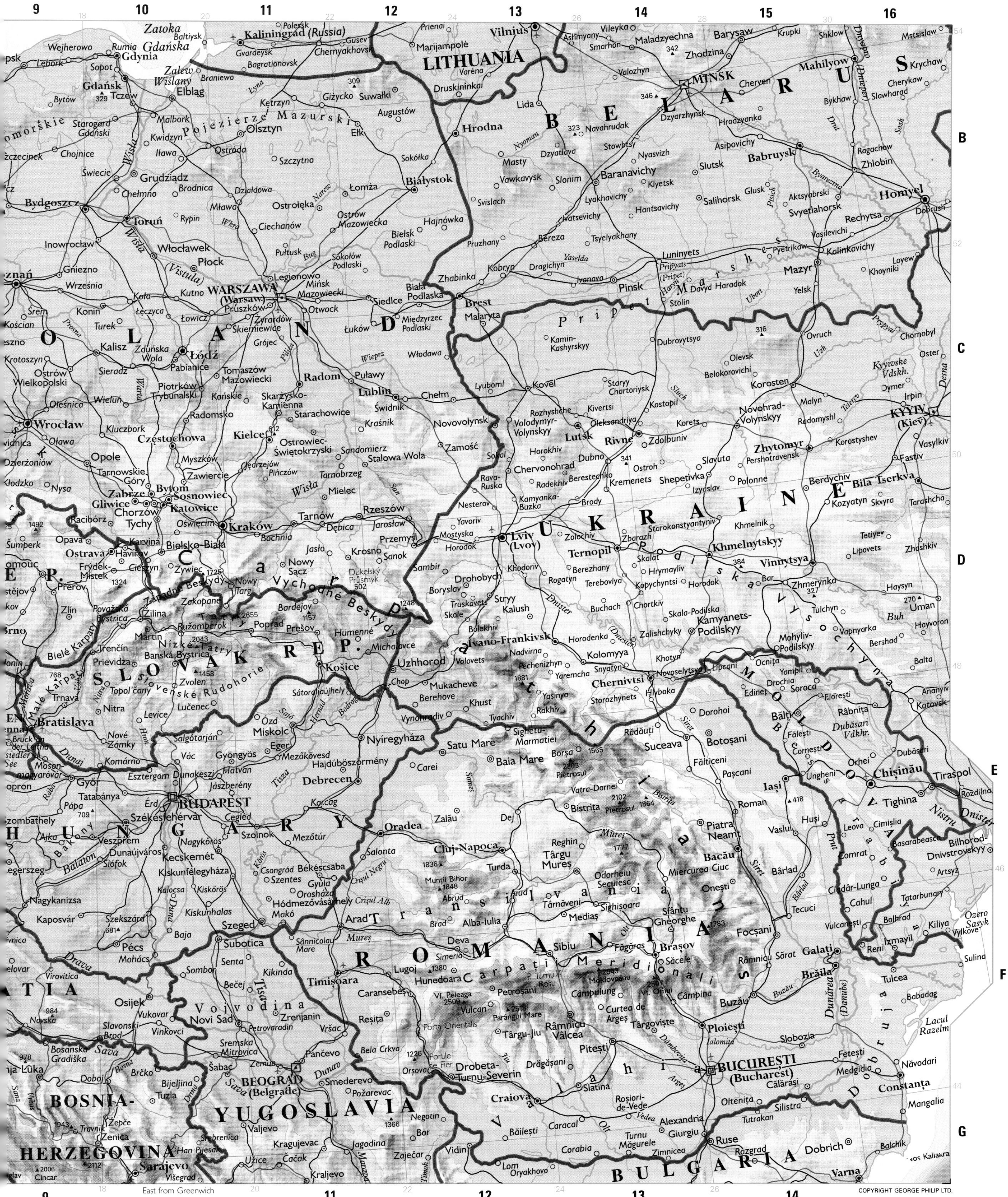

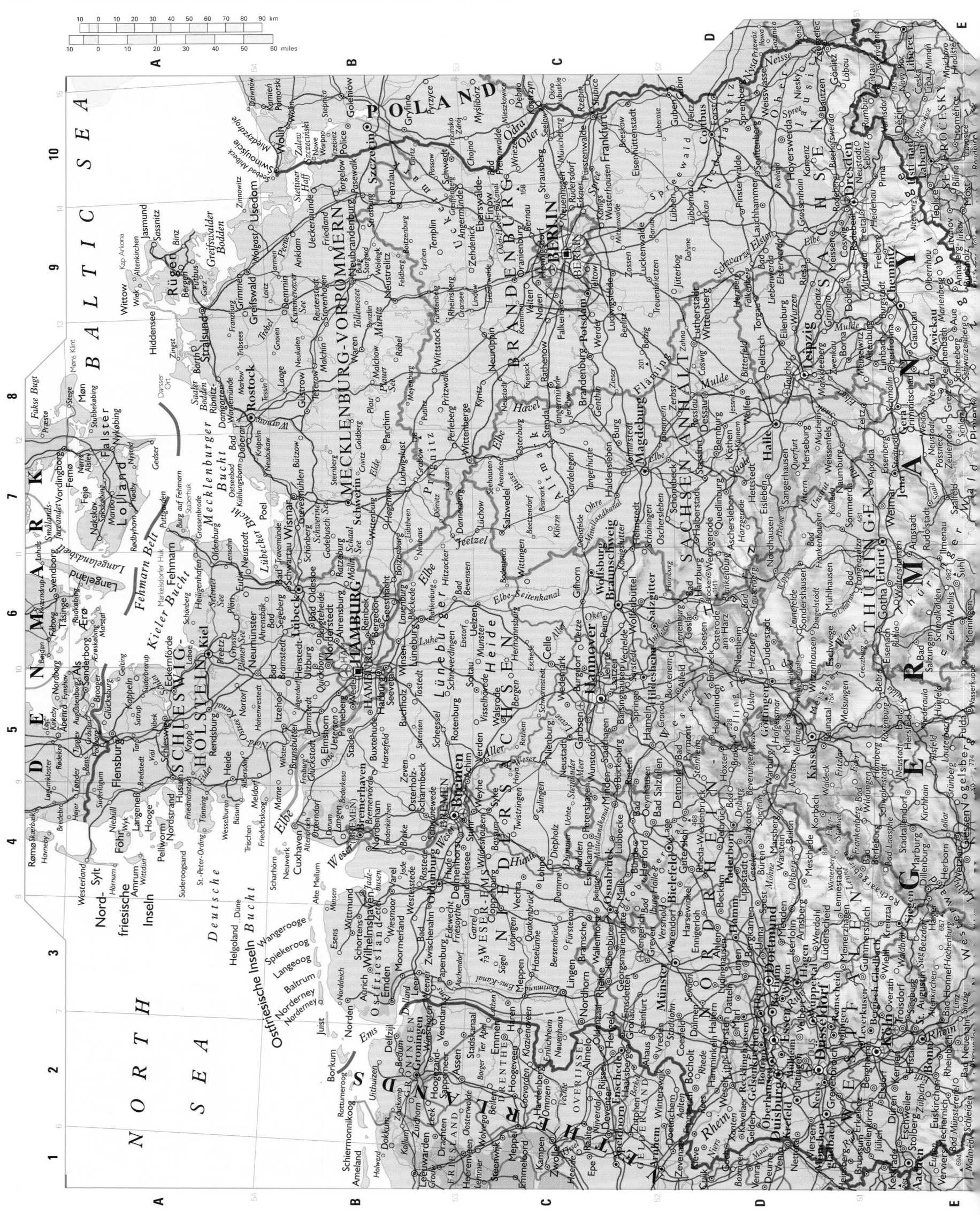

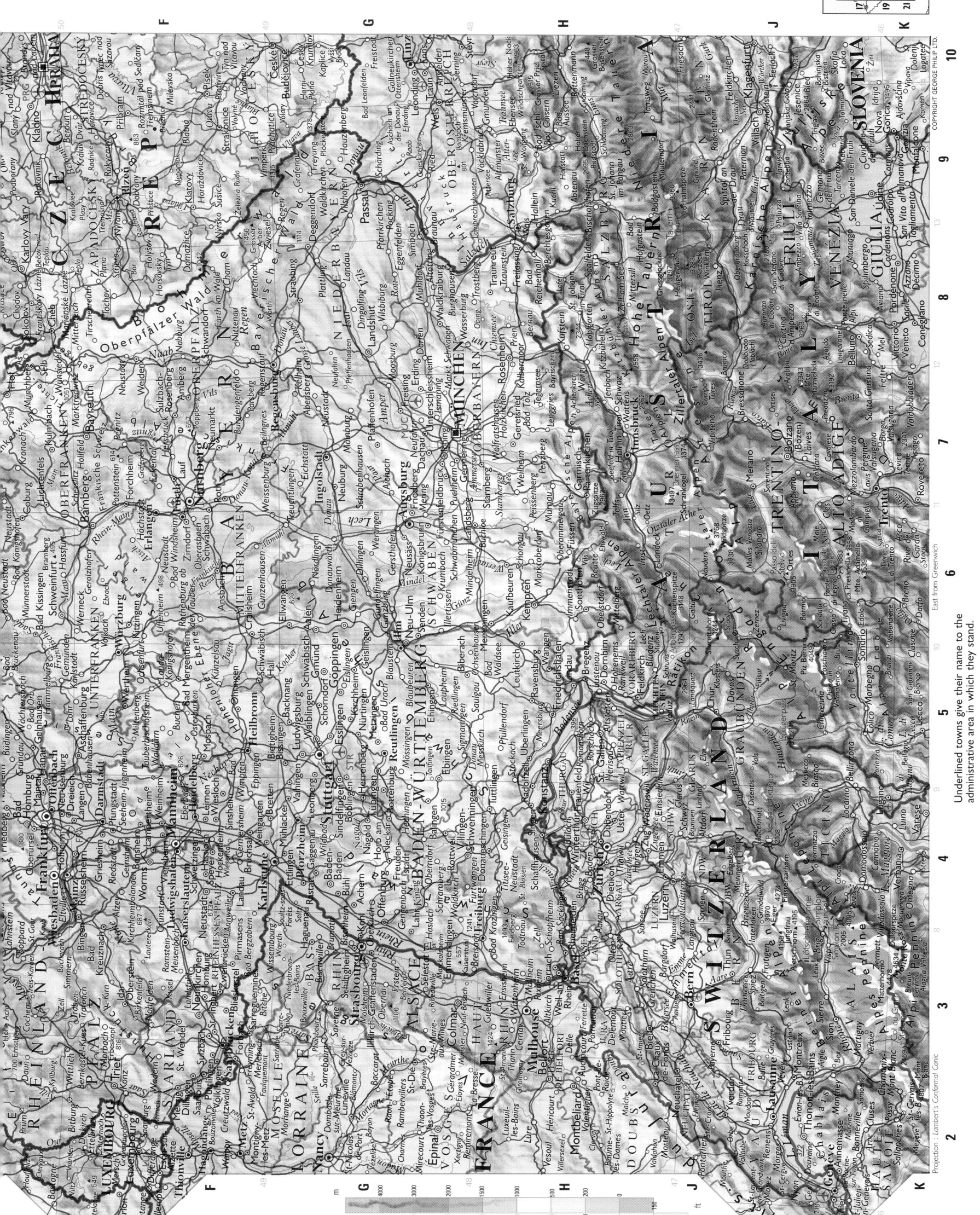

Underlined towns give their name to the administrative area in which they stand.

East from Greenwich

Projection: Lambert's Conformal Conic

COPYRIGHT GEORGE PHILIP LTD.

Underlined towns give their name to the
administrative area in which they stand.

Projection : Lambert's Conformal Conic

East from Greenwich

Underlined towns give their name to
administrative area in which they stan[d]

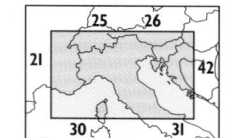

ninistrative divisions in Croatia:

rodsko-Posavska	4. Medimurska	8. Virovitičko-Podravska
oprivničko-Križevačka	6. Požeško-Slavonska	10. Zagrebačka
rapinsko-Zagorska	7. Varaždinska	

– – – – – Inter-entity boundaries as agreed
at the 1995 Dayton Peace Agreement.

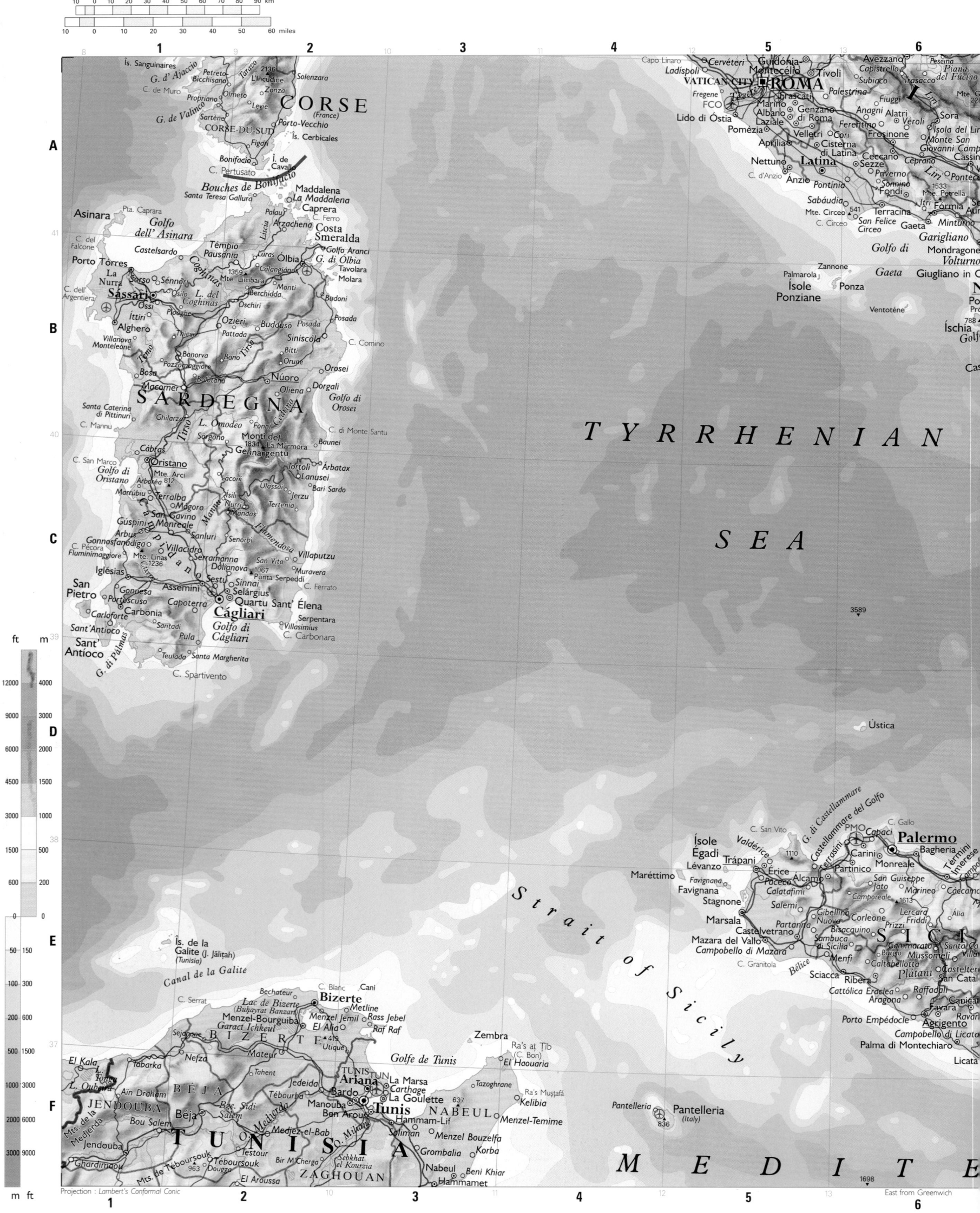

10 0 10 20 30 40 50 60 70 80 90 km
10 0 10 20 30 40 50 60 miles

CORSE
(France)
CORSE-DU-SUD

Ìs. Sanguinaires
G. d'Ajaccio
Petreto Bicchisano
L'Incudine
Zonza
Solenzara
Olmeto
Levie
Sartène
Porto-Vecchio
Ìs. Cerbicales
Figari
Bonifacio
C. Pertusato
Ì. de Cavallo
Bouches de Bonifacio
Maddalena
La Maddalena
Santa Teresa Gallura
Caprera
Palau
C. Ferro
Arzachena
Costa Smeralda
Asinara
Pta. Caprara
Golfo dell' Asinara
C. del Falcone
Castelsardo
Tempio Pausania
Luras
Golfo Aranci
Olbia
G. di Ólbia
Tavolara
Porto Torres
Sorso
Sénnori
Osilo
Calangianus
Monti
Molara
La Nurra
Berchidda
Budoni
C. dell'Argentiera
Sássari
Óschiri
L. del Coghinas
Posada
Íttiri
Ploaghe
Pattada
Buddusò
Posada
Alghero
Ozieri
Bitti
Siniscola
Villanova Monteleone
Bonorva
Bono
Orune
C. Comino
Bosa
Pozzomaggiore
Orosei
Macomer
Núoro
Oliena
Dorgali
Golfo di Orosei
Santa Caterina di Pittinuri
L. Omodeo
Fonni
Baunei
C. Mannu
Ghilarza
Sorgono
Monti del Gennargentu
C. di Monte Santu
SARDEGNA
Cábras
Oristano
Mte. Arci
Laconi
Tórtoli
Árbatax
Golfo di Oristano
Arborèa
Terralba
Mógoro
Nurri
Jerzu
Lanusei
Bari Sardo
Marrúbiu
Ísili
Mandas
Ússana
Tertenia
Gúspini
San Gavino
Monreale
Sanluri
Senorbì
C. Ferrato
Arbus
Villacidro
Gonnosfanádiga
Mte. Linas 1236
Dolianova
San Vito
Villaputzu
Fluminimaggiore
Sestu
Sínnai
Muravera
Iglésias
Decimo
Assemini
Selárgius
Punta Serpeddì
San Pietro
Gonnesa
Portoscuso
Quartu Sant' Élena
Capoterra
Villasimius
Carloforte
Carbónia
Cágliari
Serpentara
Sant'Antíoco
Santadi
Pula
Golfo di Cágliari
C. Carbonara
Sant' Antíoco
G. di Pálmas
Teulada
Santa Margherita
C. Spartivento

CORSE

TYRRHENIAN SEA

Capo Linaro
Cervéteri
Guidónia
Ladíspoli
Montecelio
Tivoli
Avezzano
Capistrello
Piana del Fucino
Pescina
VATICAN CITY
ROMA
Palestrina
Subiaco
Fregene
Marino
Genzano
Anagni
Alatri
Véroli
Sora
FCO
Albano
di Roma
Ferentino
Lido di Óstia
Laziale
Velletri
Cori
Frosinone
Isola del Liri
Monte San Giovanni Campano
Pomézia
Cisterna
Ceccano
Ceprano
Aprília
di Latina
Sezze
Pontínia
Paverno
Nettuno
Sabáudia
Sonnino
Fondi
Ítri
Formia
Anzio
Pontínia
Mte. Circeo 541
Terracina
Gaeta
Mintu
C. d'Anzio
San Felice Circeo
Gaeta
Gariglíano
C. Circeo
Golfo di
Mondragone
Volturno
Palmarola
Zannone
Giugliano in C
Ísole Ponziane
Ponza
Po.
Ventotène
Pré
Ísch
788
Golf
Ventotène
Cas

Ústica

G. di Castellammare del Golfo
C. San Vito
C. Gallo
Castellammare del Golfo
Capaci
Palermo
Ísole Égadi
Valdérice
Carini
Bagheria
1110
Términi
Lévanzo
Trápani
Erice
Monreale
Imerese
Maréttimo
Terrasini
Partinico
San Giuseppe Jato
Marineo
Favignana
Paceca
Alcamo
Cáccamo
Stagnone
Salemi
Calatafimi
Camporeale
1613
Lercara Friddi
Marsala
Gibellina
Corleone
Prizzi
Ália
Nuova
Bisacquino
SIC
Castelvetrano
Partanna
Mazara del Vallo
Sombuca di Sicilia
Santa Ca
Campobello di Mazara
Mussomeli
Villa
C. Granitola
Menfi
Caltabellotta
Castelter
Bélice
Ribera
Plátani
San Catal
Sciacca
Cattólica Eraclea
Raffadali
Aragona
Favara
Porto Empédocle
Ravan
Agrigento
Campobello di Licata
Palma di Montechiaro
Licata

Strait of Sicily

Ís. de la Galite (J. Jâlitah)
(Tunisia)
Canal de la Galite
Bechateur
C. Blanc
Cani
C. Serrat
Bizerte
Metline
Menzel-Bourguiba
Lac de Bizerte
Rass Jebel
(Buhayrat Banzart)
El Alia
Raf Raf
Sejnane
Garaet Ichkeul
Menzel Jemil
Zembra
Ra's aṭ Ṭīb
Nefza
Mateur
Utique
(C. Bon)
BIZERTE
419
El Haouaria
Tahent
Golfe de Tunis
Tazoghrane
Ra's Muṣṭafá
El Kala
Tabarka
Jedeida
TUNIS
Kelibia
I. Fona
L. Oubeira
Aïn Draham
Téborba
La Marsa
Menzel-Temime
JENDOUBA
BÉJA
Ariana
Carthage
Manouba
Bardo
La Goulette
Béja
Bée. Sidi
Tunis
NABEUL
Bou Salem
Salem
Ben Arous
Hammam-Lif
Menzel Bouzelfa
Mts. de la
Medjerda
Méjez-el-Bab
Soliman
Korba
Jendouba
963
Testour
Dougga
Grombalia
Beni Khiar
Ghardimaou
Bir M'Cherga
Sebkhat
Nabeul
Mts. de Téboursouk
el Kourzia
TUNISIA
Hammamet
Téboursouk
El Aroussa
ZAGHOUAN
S. Miliane

Pantelleria
836
Pantelleria
(Italy)

MEDITE

1698
East from Greenwich

ft m
12000 4000
9000 3000
6000 2000
4500 1500
3000 1000
1500 500
600 200
0 0
0 0
50 150
100 300
200 600
500 1500
1000 3000
2000 6000
3000 9000
m ft

Projection : Lambert's Conformal Conic

1 2 3 4 5 6

ADRIATIC SEA

IONIAN SEA

MEDITERRANEAN SEA

Underlined towns give their name to the
administrative area in which they stand.

COPYRIGHT GEORGE PHILIP LTD.

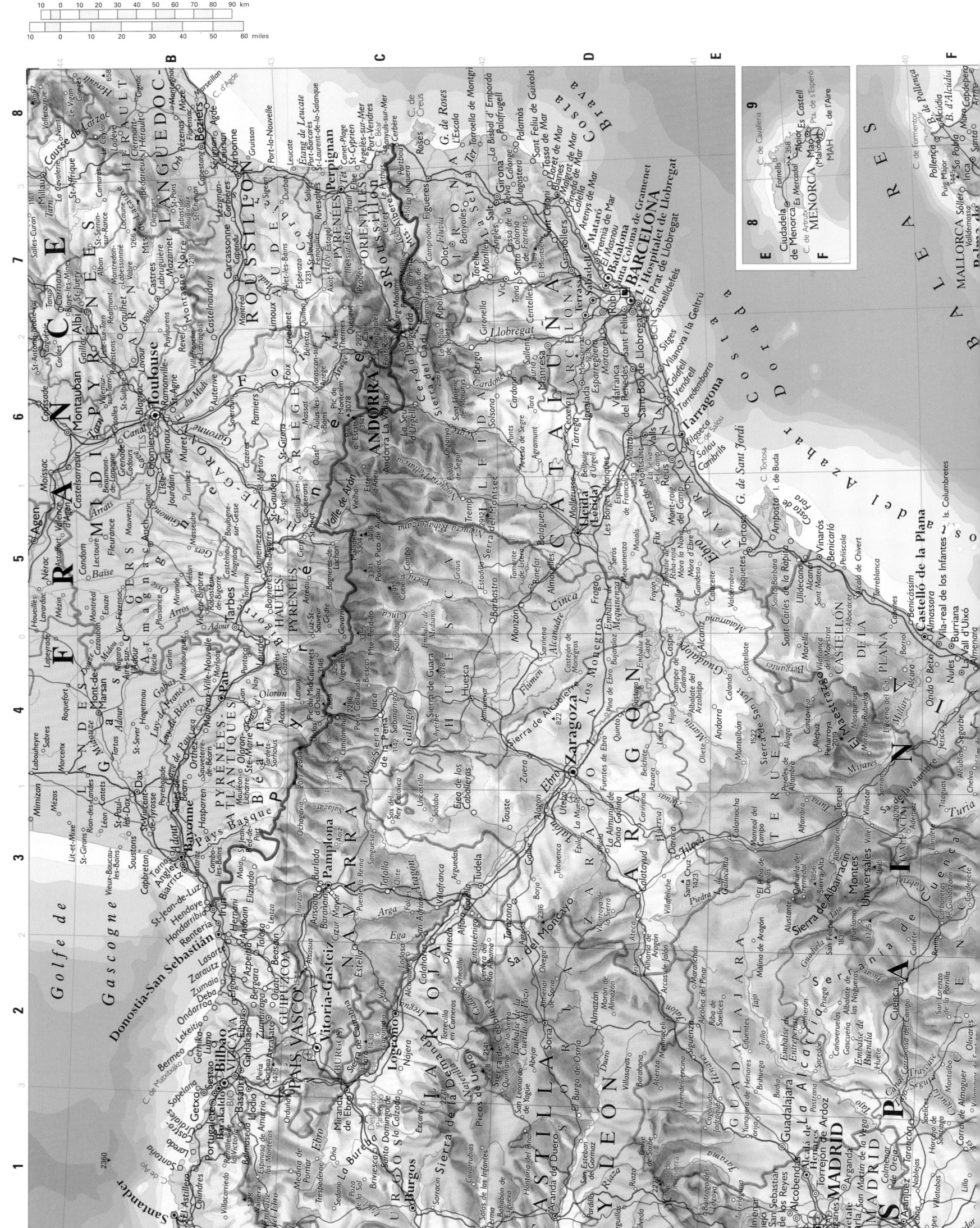

20
34
35
78

F G H J K

MEDITERRANEAN SEA

BALEARIC SEA

Golfo de Valencia

Palma
B. de Llucmajor
S'Arenal
Mogabur
Campos del Port
Santanyi
C. de Cala Figuera
C. Blanc
Porreres
Felanitx
I. des Conills
Cabrera
C. de ses Salines

Pta. Grossa
Tagomago
Santa Eulalia des Riu
Sant Joan Baptista
Sant Miquel
Sant Antoni Abat
EIVISSA (IBIZA)
San Josep
Es Vedrà
IBZ
S'Espalmador
S'Espardell
Sant Francesc de Formentera
Formentera
Pta. Rotja
C. de Barbària
Sa Conillera
475

101
2726
2850

VALENCIA
Cheste
Chiva
Buñol
Requena
Utiel
VALENCIA
Catarroja
Torrent
Paterna
Burjassot
Sueca
Cullera
Alzira
Carlet
Benifaió
Algemesí
Carcaixent
Xàtiva
Canals
Gandia
Ontinyent
Alcoi
Albaida
Muro de Alcoy
Cocentaina
Banyeres
Villena
Elda
Petrer
Novelda
Monforte del Cid
Aspe
Elche
ALICANTE
San Juan de Alicante
Villajoyosa
Benidorm
Altea
Calpe
Peñón de Ifach
Benisa
C. de la Nao
Xàbia
Denia
Oliva
Pego
Tavernes de la Valldigna
Carcaixent
El Grau
Cheste
Sierra Martés
Alberic
Pedreguer
C. de San Antonio
Teulada

Valencia
Costa Blanca

Alcázar del Rey
Quintanar
Mota del Cuervo
Pedro Muñoz
Socuéllamos
Tomelloso
Argamasilla de Alba
Manzanares
Daimiel
Membrilla
La Solana
Valdepeñas
Santa Cruz de Mudela

CASTILLA-LA MANCHA

CIUDAD REAL

Villarrobledo
La Roda
San Clemente
Minaya
Tarazona de la Mancha
Casas Ibáñez
Alborea
Chinchilla de Monte Aragón
Albacete
Almansa
Caudete
Yecla
Jumilla
Villena

ALBACETE

Alcaraz
Sierra de Alcaraz
El Bonillo
Munera
Villanueva de la Fuente
Peñas de San Pedro
Tobarra
Hellín
Liétor
Elche de la Sierra
Férez
Nerpio
Yeste
Sierra de Segura
Puebla de Don Fadrique
Huéscar
Cazorla
Quesada
Pozo Alcón
Cuevas del Almanzora

MURCIA

Murcia
Alcantarilla
Molina de Segura
Archena
Cieza
Calasparra
Caravaca de la Cruz
Cehegín
Bullas
Mula
Totana
Alhama de Murcia
Librilla
Aledo
Lorca
Puerto Lumbreras
Águilas
Mazarrón
Puerto de Mazarrón
G. de Mazarrón
C. Cope
Cartagena
La Unión
Mar Menor
C. de Palos
Los Nietos
Torre-Pacheco
San Javier
San Pedro del Pinatar
Pilar de la Horadada
Torrevieja
Guardamar del Segura
Santa Pola
Crevillente
Orihuela
Callosa de Segura
Almoradí
Dolores

ALMERIA

Almería
El Ejido
Roquetas de Mar
La Mojonera
Adra
Berja
Dalías
Vícar
Níjar
Carboneras
Mojácar
Garrucha
Vera
Cuevas del Almanzora
Huércal-Overa
Albox
Cantoria
Serón
Tíjola
Baza
Caniles
Cúllar
Orce
Galera
Castilléjar
G. de Almería
C. de Gata
Pta. del Sabinar

GRANADA

Granada
Guadix
Baza
Huéscar
Motril
Almuñécar
Salobreña
Órgiva
Lanjarón
Ugíjar
Las Alpujarras
Sierra Nevada
Mulhacén 3478
Sierra de Gádor
Sierra de los Filabres
Sa. de Baza

Linares
Úbeda
Baeza
Jaén
Mancha Real
Santisteban del Puerto

ALGERIA

ALGER (Algiers)
Cherchell
Tipasa
Blida
Médéa
Cheraga
Birkhadem
Koléa
El Affroun
Mouzaia
Boufarik
Bou Ismail
Fouka
Ain Benian
Bougara
Arba
Rouiba
El Malah
O. el Malah
Berrouaghia
Ksar el Boukhari
Ain Boucif
Birine
Ain Ousera

DJELFA

Hassi Bahbah
Guelt es Stel
1303

MEDEA
AIN DEFLA
Khemis Miliana
Miliana
El Attaf
Oued Fodda
Abadia
Ech Cheliff
Beni-Haoua
Ténès
C. Ténès
Gouraya
Damous
Sidi Akacha
Abou el Hassan
El Guelta
Bou Kadir

DAHRA
Massif de Dahra
El Marsa
C. Kramis
Mostaganem
Mazagran
Hadjadj
Sidi Ali
Kheir-Dine
RELIZANE
Djidiouia
Oued Rhiou
Ammi Moussa
Mendes
O. Mina
Massif de l'Ouarsenis
1786
1983

TISSEMSILT
Tissemsilt
Lardjem
Bordj Bounaama
Khemisti
TIARET
Tiaret
Mahdia
Frenda
Sougueur
Rahouia
Medroussa
Ghriss
Mascara
Tighennif
Bou Hanifia
Hacine
Mohammadia
MASCARA
Sig
Arzew
Golfe d'Arzew
Bethioua
Mers-el-Kébir
Oran
ORAN
Es Senia
Aïn el Turk
C. Falcon
Bou Tlélis
Misserghin
Boutlélis
Ain Temouchent
AIN TEMOUCHENT
El Amria
Hammam Bou Hadjar
Béni Saf
Ghazaouet
Nedroma
Maghnia
SIDI-BEL-ABBES
Sidi-bel-Abbès
Télagh
Sfizef
Ben Badis
Oued Taria

Cartagena
Islas Chafarinas (Sp.)
Melilla (Sp.)
Nador
Ras el Mar
C. de Trois Fourches
C. des Trois Fourches
Cap Noé
Alborán (Sp.)
Pte. Negri

East from Greenwich
West from Greenwich

G H J K

m 4000 3000 2000 1500 1000 500 200 0
ft 12000 9000 6000 4500 3000 1500 600 200 0
0 50-150 150-300 300-600 600-1500 1500-3000 3000-6000 6000-9000
m ft

Projection : Lambert's Conformal Conic

COPYRIGHT GEORGE PHILIP LTD.

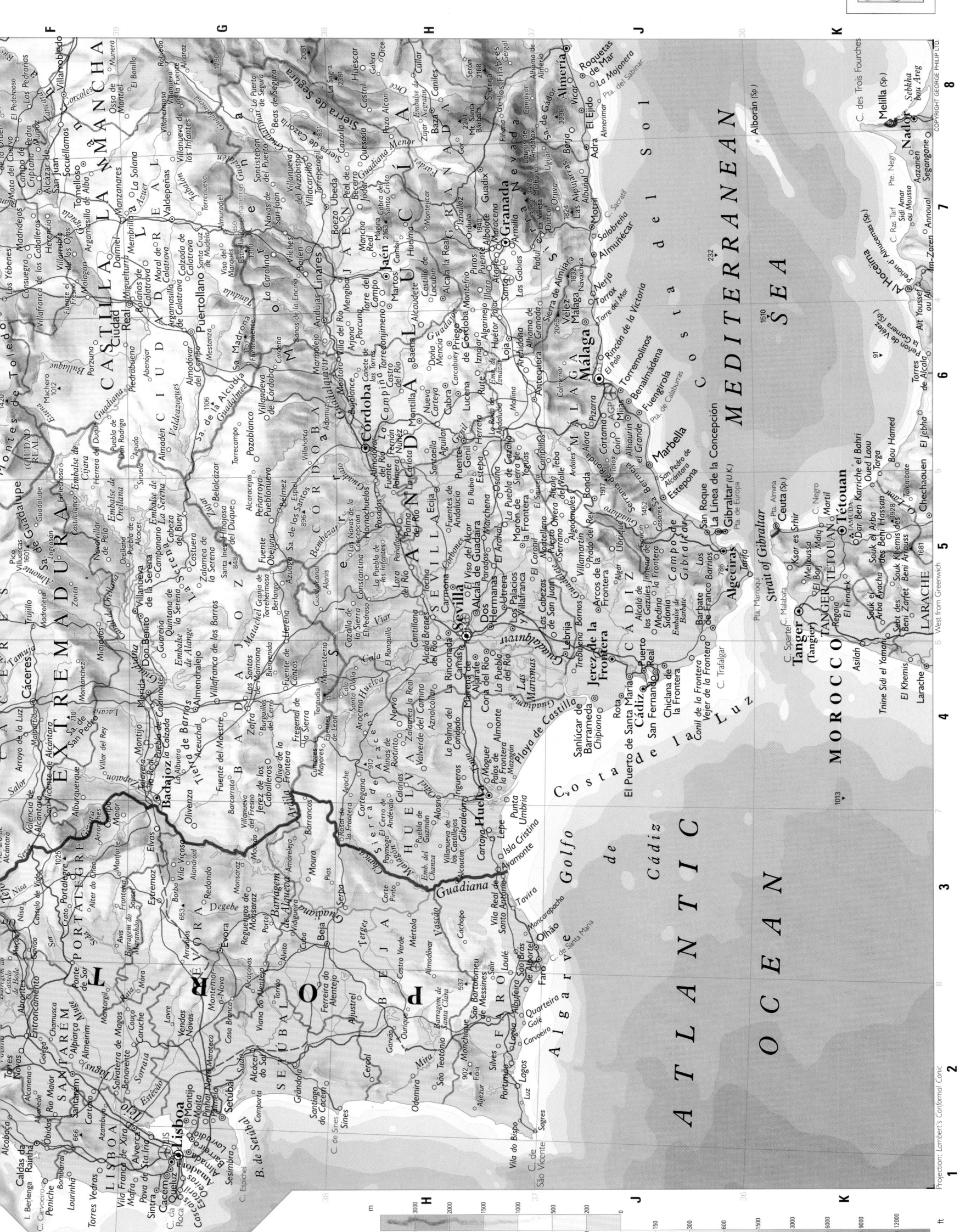

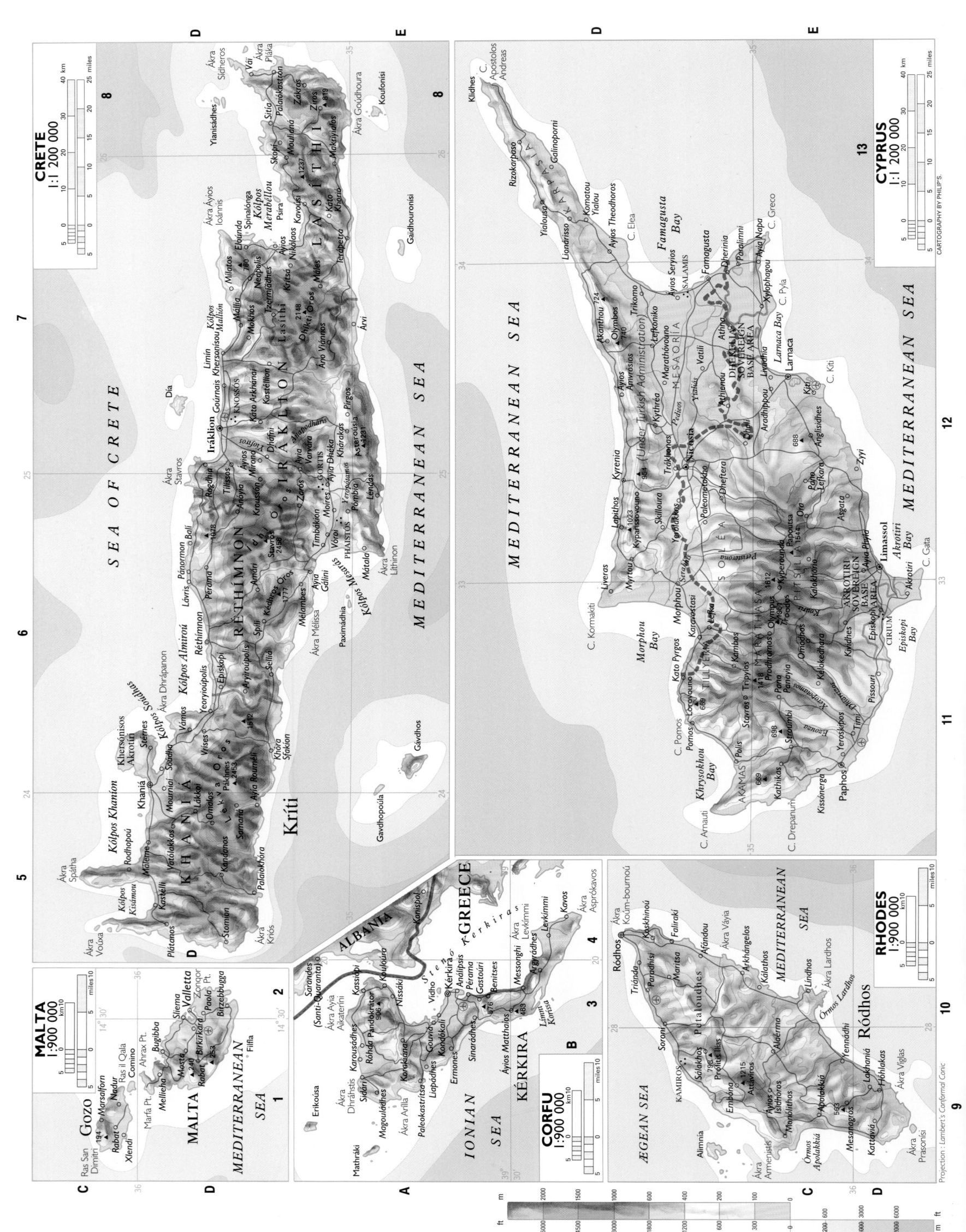

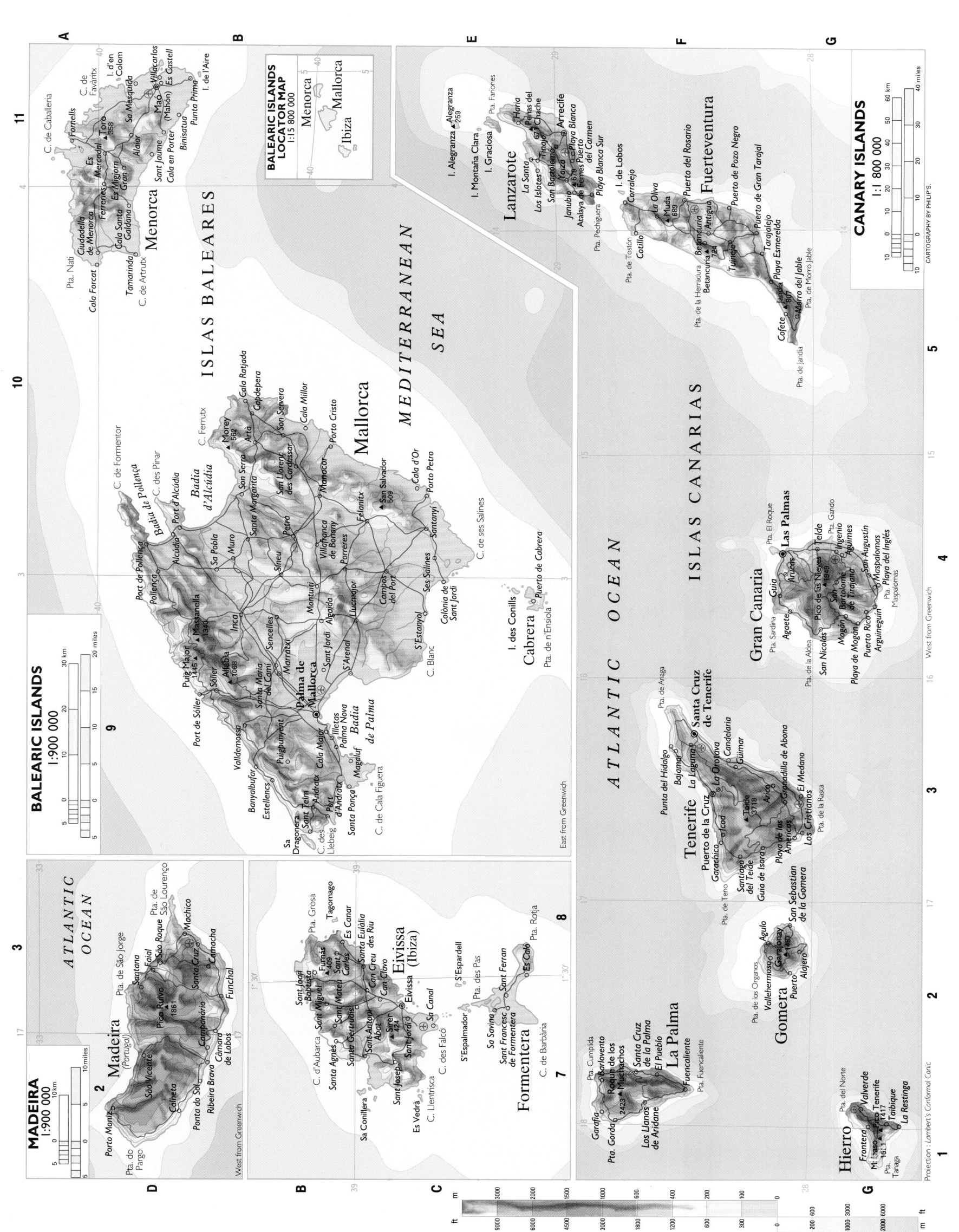

MADEIRA
1:900 000

BALEARIC ISLANDS
1:900 000

BALEARIC ISLANDS LOCATOR MAP
1:15 800 000

Menorca
Mallorca
Ibiza

CANARY ISLANDS
1:1 800 000

CARTOGRAPHY BY PHILIP'S.

Madeira
Porto Moniz
Pta. do Pargo
Calheta
Ponta do Sol
Ribeira Brava
São Vicente
Pico Ruivo 1861
Santana
Faial
S. Roque
São Jorge
Pta. de São Jorge
Pta. de São Lourenço
Machico
Caniço
Funchal
Câmara de Lobos
Campanário
Santo Cruz
Madeira (Portugal)
ATLANTIC OCEAN

Menorca
C. de Caballeria
Fornells
C. de Favàritx
I. d'en Colom
Villacarlos
Sa Mesquida
Es Mercadal
Toro 358
Alaior
Ferreries
Es Migjorn Gran
Maó (Mahón)
Sant Jaume
Cala en Porter
Punta Prima
I. de l'Aire
Ciudadella de Menorca
Cala Santa Galdana
Sant Tomàs
Binisatua
Pta. Nati
Cala Forcat
Tamarinda
C. de Artrutx

Mallorca
C. de Formentor
C. des Pinar
C. de Pollença
Port de Pollença
Pollença
Badia de Pollença
Port d'Alcúdia
Badia d'Alcúdia
Alcúdia
Massanella 1341
Puig Major 1445
Sa Pobla
Muro
Inca
Sóller
Alaró 1068
Santa Margarita
Son Serra
Artà
Morey 562
Cala Ratjada
Capdepera
Son Servera
Cala Millor
Porto Cristo
San Llorenç des Cardassar
Manacor
Sineu
Sencelles
Santa Maria del Camí
Petra
Port de Sóller
Valldemossa
Banyalbufar
Estellencs
Sa Dragonera
C. des Llebeig
Sant Elm
Port d'Andratx
Andratx
Santa Ponça
C. de Cala Figuera
Puigpunyent
Marratxí
Calvià
Cala Major
Magaluf
Palma Nova
Illetes
Palma de Mallorca
Badia de Palma
S'Arenal
Sant Jordi
Algaida
Montuïri
Llucmajor
Vilafranca de Bonany
Porreres
Campos del Port
Ses Salines
Colònia de Sant Jordi
C. Blanc
S'Estanyol
Felanitx
Santanyí
C. de ses Salines
Cala d'Or
Porto Petro
San Salvador 509
C. Ferrutx

Mallorca
ISLAS BALEARES
ISLAS BALEARS

Cabrera
I. des Conills
Pta. de n'Ensiola
C. de n'Ensiola
Puerto de Cabrera

MEDITERRANEAN SEA
East from Greenwich

Eivissa (Ibiza)
Pta. Grosa
Pta. de Sant Antoni
Portinatx
Sant Joan Baptista
Tagomago
Es Canar
Santa Eulàlia
Santa Eulària des Riu
Sant Miquel
Sant Mateu
Santa Gertrudis
Sant Carles
Sant Antoni de Portmany
Can Clavo
Can Creu
Sant Josep
Sant Jordi
Eivissa (Ibiza)
Santa Agnès
Sant Agustí
Es Vedrà
C. Llentrisca
Sa Conillera
C. des Falcó
Sa Savina
Es Pujols 409
424

Formentera
S'Espalmador
S'Espardell
Sant Ferran
Sant Francesc de Formentera
Es Caló
La Mola
Pta. des Pas
Pta. de la Gavina
Pta. Rotja
C. de Barbària
Sa Canal

Lanzarote
I. Alegranza
Alegranza 289
I. Montaña Clara
I. Graciosa
Haría
Peñas del Chache 671
La Santa
Los Islotes
San Bartolomé
Tinajo
Tiagua
Arrecife
Playa Blanca
Puerto del Carmen
Yaiza
Janubio
Atalaya de Femés
Playa Blanca Sur
Pta. Pechiguera
I. de Lobos
Pta. de Tostón

Fuerteventura
Corralejo
La Oliva
Muda 689
Cotillo
Betancuria 724
Antigua
Puerto del Rosario
Puerto de Pozo Negro
Tuineje
Tarajalejo
Puerto de Gran Tarajal
Jandía Playa Esmeralda
Pta. de la Herradura
Cofete
Morro del Jable
Pta. del Jable
Pta. de Jandía

Gran Canaria
Pta. El Roque
Pta. Gando
Arucas
Las Palmas
Telde
Gáldar
Guía
Ingenio
Agüimes
San Agustín
Agaete
Pico de las Nieves 1949
Sah
Tejeda
San Bartolomé de Tirajana
Maspalomas
Playa del Inglés
Pta. Sardina
San Nicolás
Mogán
Puerto Rico
Arguineguín
Pta. de la Aldea
Playa de Mogán

ISLAS CANARIAS
ISLAS CANARIES

Tenerife
Pta. de Anaga
Santa Cruz de Tenerife
La Laguna
Bajamar
Punta del Hidalgo
La Orotava
Puerto de la Cruz
Candelaria
Güímar
Teide 3718
Garachico
Icod
Santiago del Teide
Guía de Isora
Adeje
Arico
Granadilla de Abona
El Médano
Pta. Roja
Playa de las Américas
Los Cristianos
Pta. de la Rasca
Pta. de Teno

Gomera
Pta. de Araga
Agulo
Vallehermoso
Hermigua
San Sebastián de la Gomera
Garajonay 1487
Chipude
Alajeró
Playa de Santiago
Pta. de los Órganos

La Palma
Pta. Cumplida
Barlovento
Garafía
Pta. Gorda
Santa Cruz de la Palma
Roque de los Muchachos 2423
Los Llanos de Aridane
El Paso
Fuencaliente
Pta. Fuencaliente

Hierro
Pta. del Norte
Frontera
Valverde
Mt. Malpaso 1417
Pico de Tenerife
Taibique
La Restinga
Taraga

ATLANTIC OCEAN
West from Greenwich

Projection: Lambert's Conformal Conic

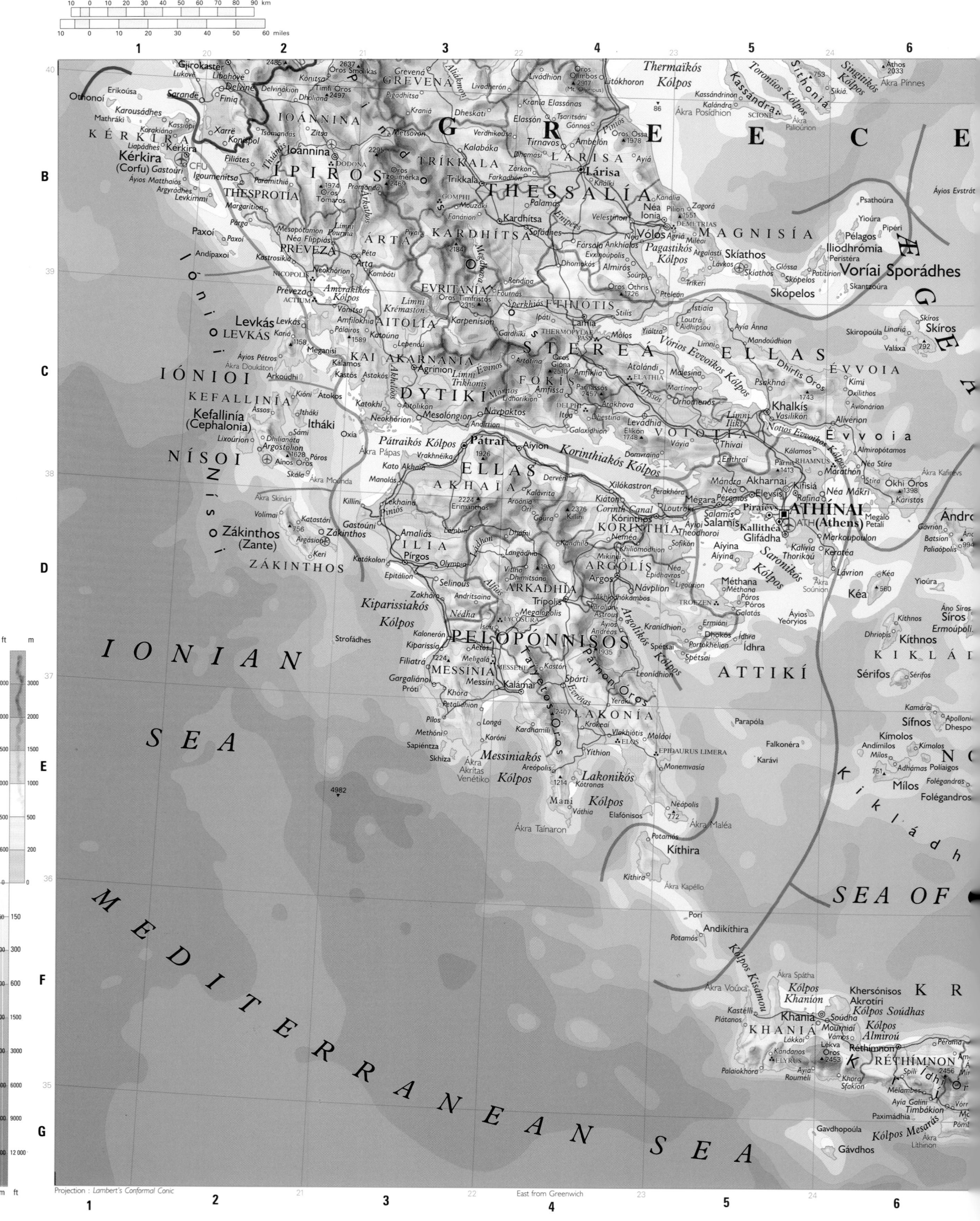

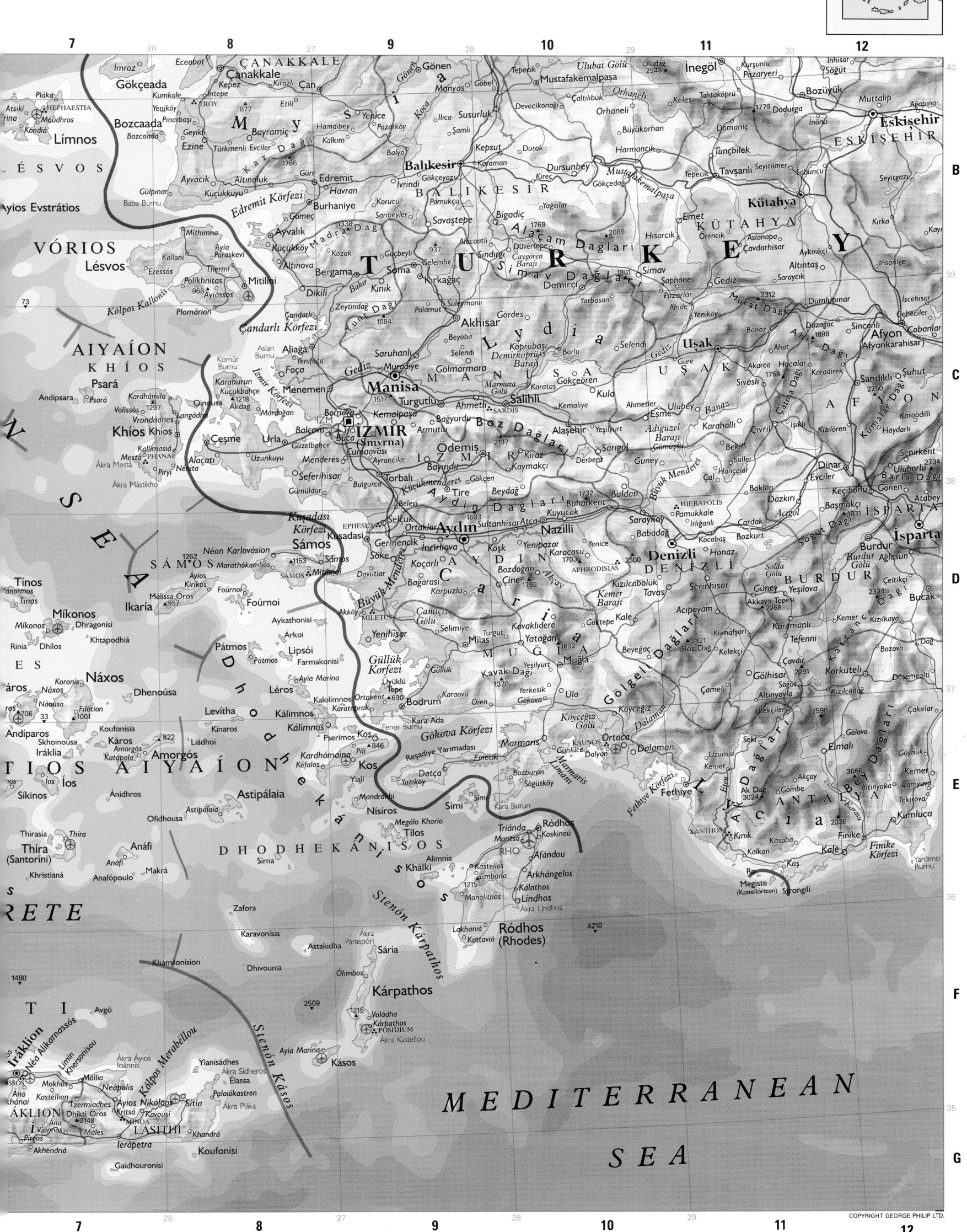

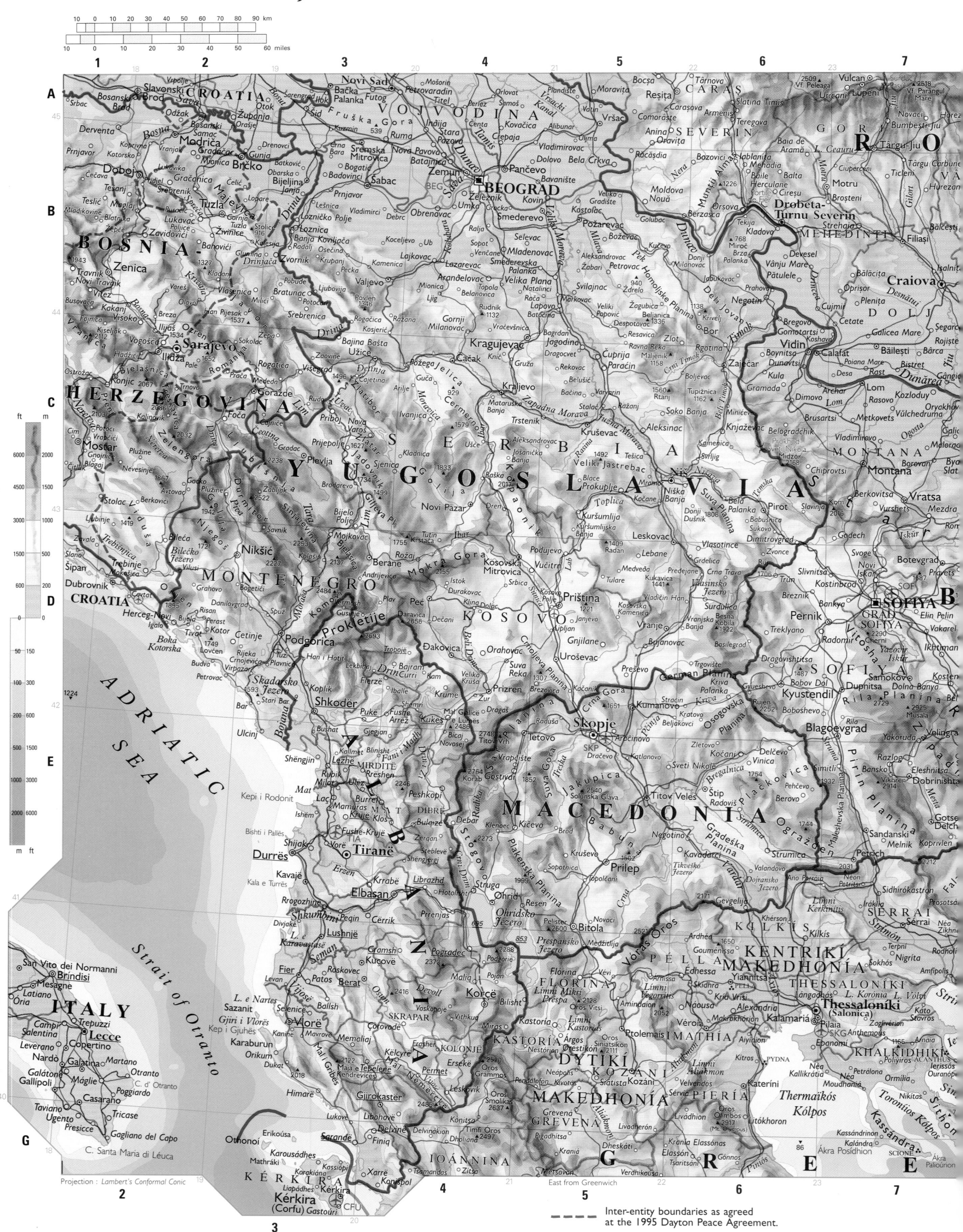

Inter-entity boundaries as agreed
at the 1995 Dayton Peace Agreement.

Underlined towns give their name to the
administrative area in which they stand.

COPYRIGHT GEORGE PHILIP LTD.

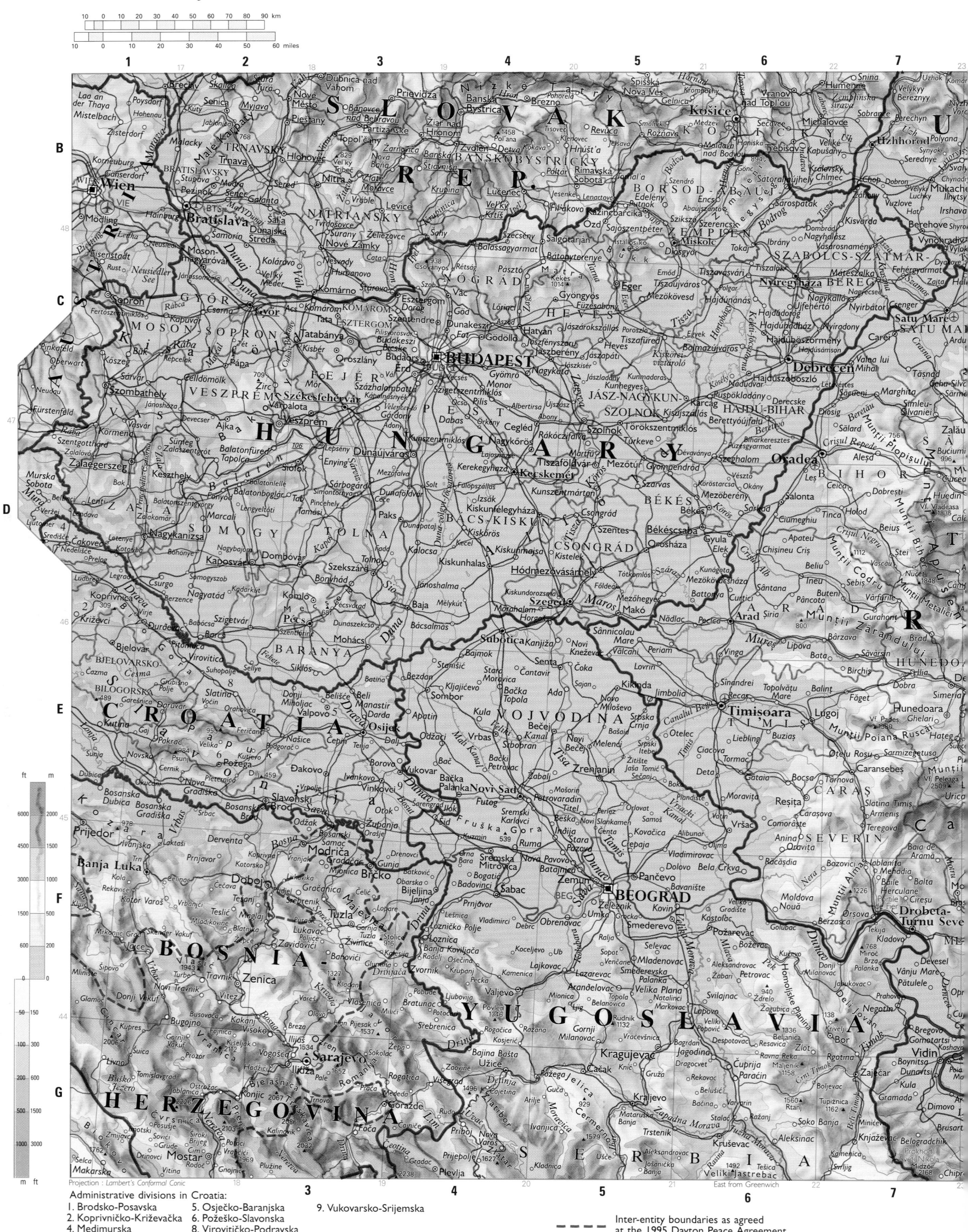

Projection : Lambert's Conformal Conic

East from Greenwich

Administrative divisions in Croatia:
1. Brodsko-Posavska
2. Koprivničko-Križevačka
4. Medimurska
5. Osiječko-Baranjska
6. Požeško-Slavonska
8. Virovitičko-Podravska
9. Vukovarsko-Srijemska

– – – – Inter-entity boundaries as agreed at the 1995 Dayton Peace Agreement.

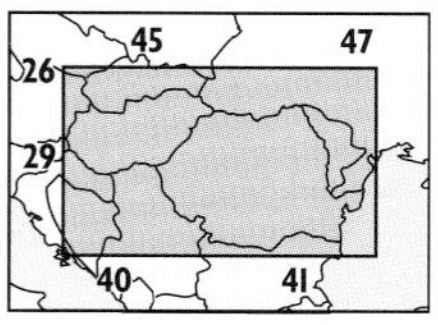

45 47
26
29
40 41

8 24 9 25 10 26 11 27 12 28 13 29 14 30

U K R A I N E

Ivano-Frankivsk
IVANO-
FRANKIVSKA
Kolomyya
VINNYTSKA

CHERNIVETSKA
Chernivtsi

M O L D O V A

Balti

Soroca
Rabnita

BOTOȘANI
Botoșani

SUCEAVA
Suceava
Gura Humorului
Câmpulung

Chișinău
(Kishinev)

IAȘI
Iași

Tiraspol

Tighina

NEAMȚ
Piatra Neamț

BISTRIȚA NĂSĂUD
Bistrița

HARGHITA

ODESKA

Cluj-
Napoca

MUREȘ
Târgu
Mureș

BACĂU
Bacău

VASLUI
Vaslui

Bârlad

Comrat

C L U J

ALBA
Alba-
Iulia

SIBIU
Sibiu

COVASNA
Sfântu
Gheorghe

VRANCEA

Focșani

GALAȚI

Cahul

Tecuci

Galați

Reni

Brașov

R O M A N I A

BRAȘOV

Brăila

TULCEA

Tulcea

PRAHOVA

BUZĂU
Buzău

BRĂILA

Petroșani

Râmnicu
Vâlcea

ARGEȘ

Târgoviște
DÂMBOVIȚA
Ploiești

IALOMIȚA
Slobozia

CONSTANȚA

Lacul Razim

VÂLCEA

Pitești

Năvodari

Constanța

Craiova

OLT

BUCUREȘTI

GIURGIU
CĂLĂRAȘI

Călărași

Medgidia

DOLJ

TELEORMAN
Alexandria

Giurgiu
Ruse

D O B R U D J A

Dobrich

B U L G A R I A

Pleven

Razgrad

BLACK SEA

COPYRIGHT GEORGE PHILIP LTD.

Underlined towns give their name to the
administrative area in which they stand.

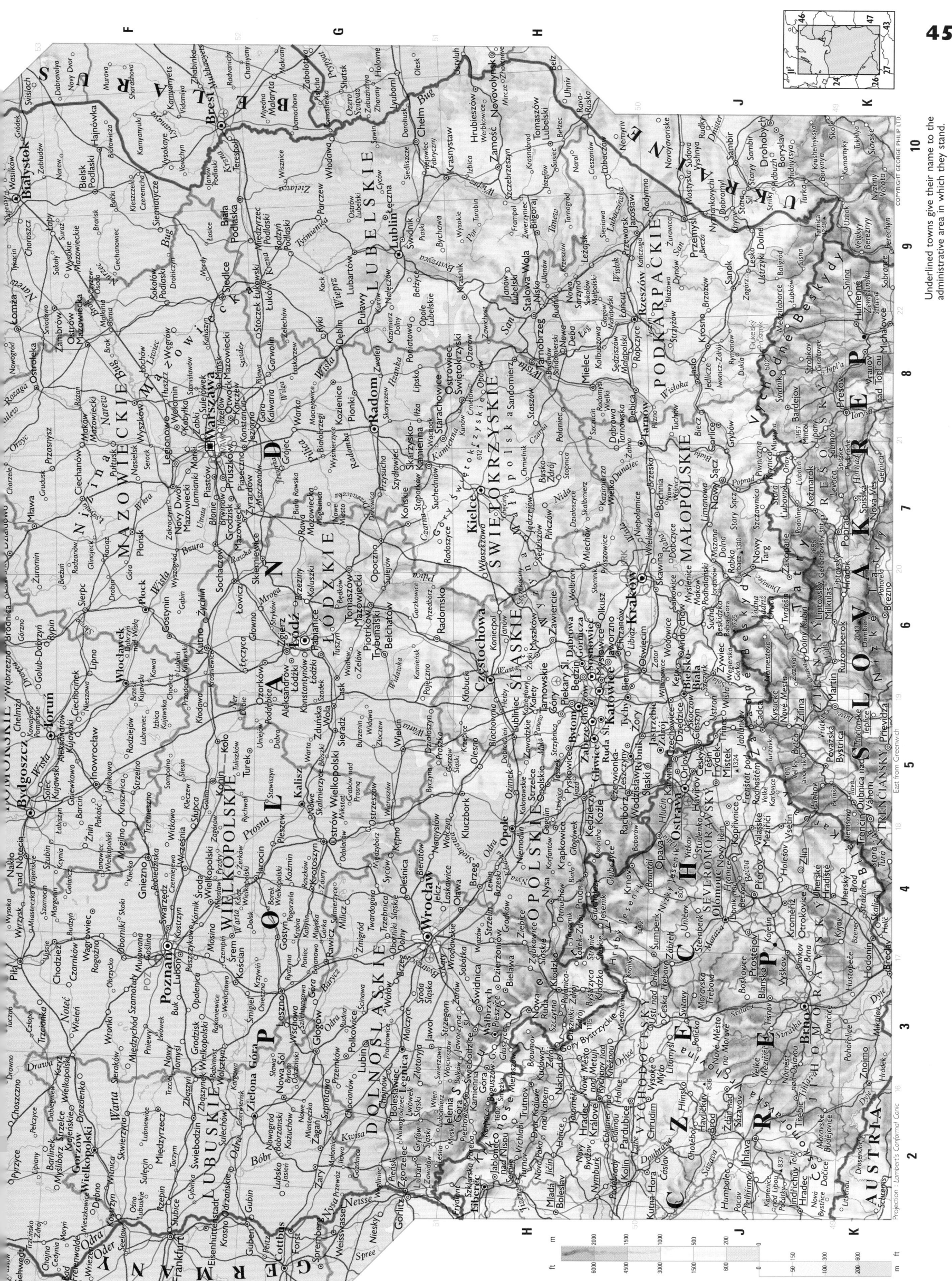

Underlined towns give their name to the
administrative area in which they stand.

COPYRIGHT GEORGE PHILIP LTD.

Projection : Lambert's Conformal Conic

East from Greenwich

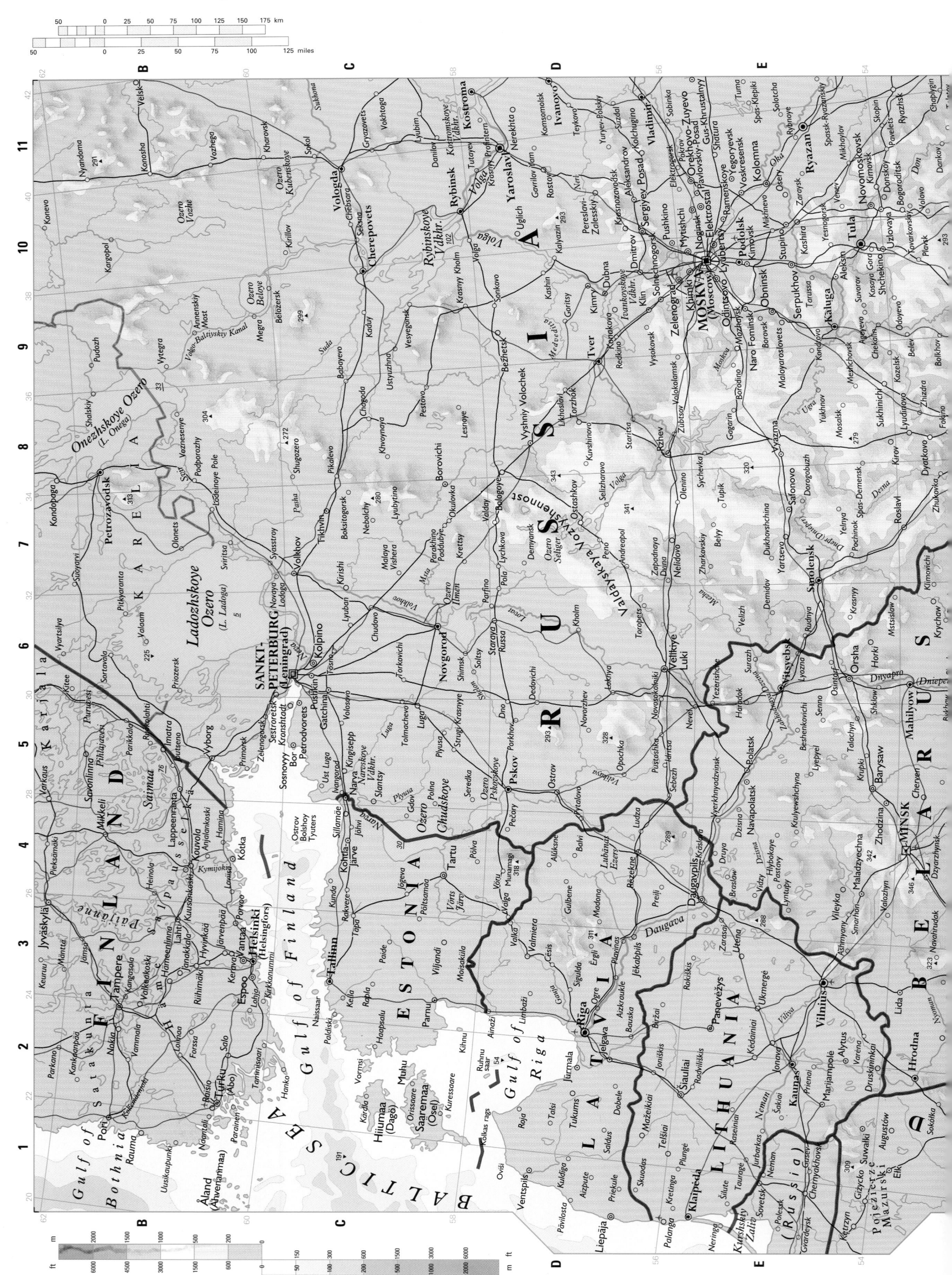

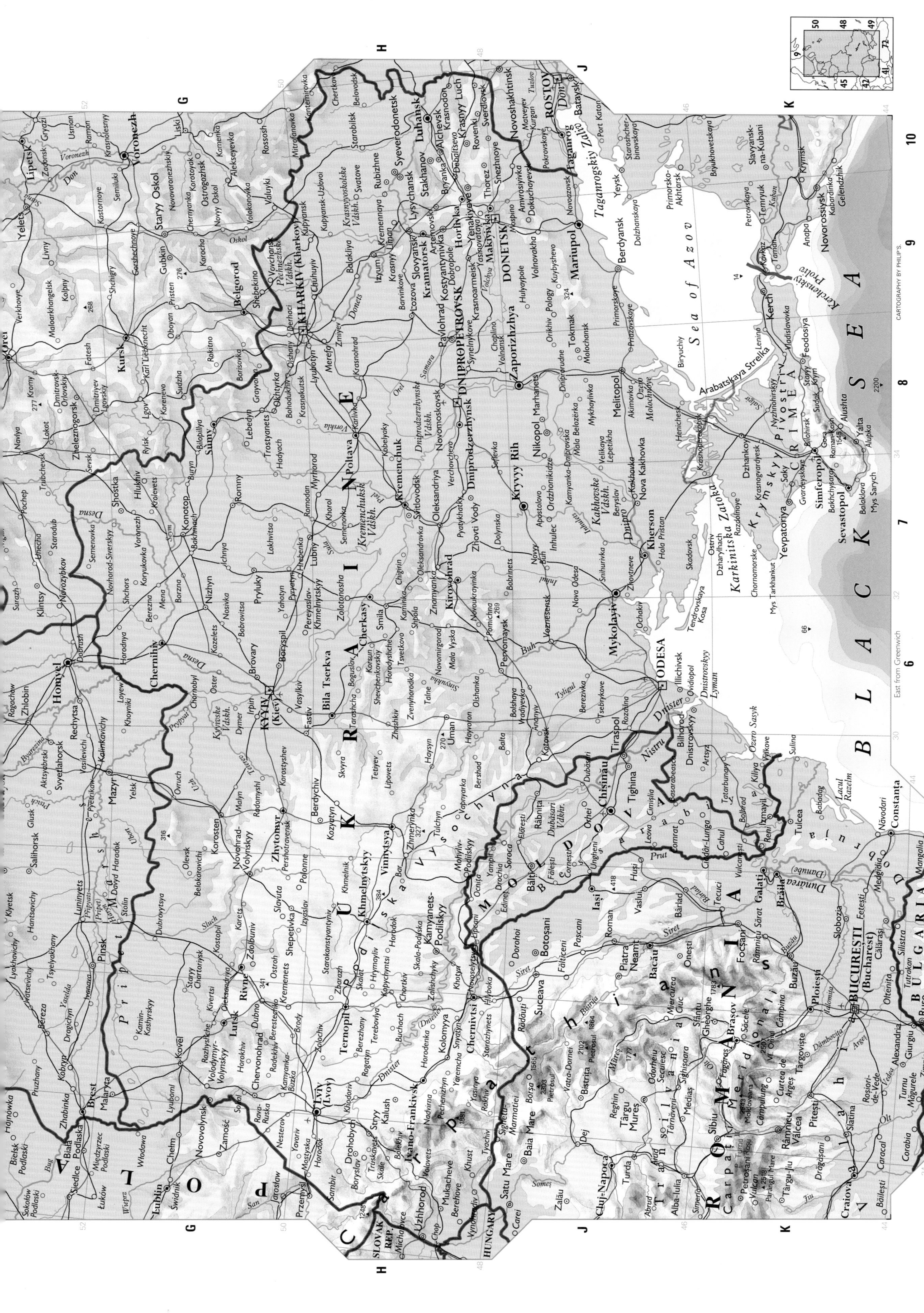

Sea of Azov

BLACK SEA

CRIMEA

UKRAINE

MOLDOVA

ROMANIA

BULGARIA

SLOVAK REP.

HUNGARY

CARPATHIANS

Transylvanian Alps

Carpathian Mountains

CARTOGRAPHY BY PHILIP'S

East from Greenwich

Projection: Conical with two standard parallels

KYIV (Kiev)
KHARKIV (Kharkov)
DNIPROPETROVSK
DONETSK
ODESA
MYKOLAYIV
ROSTOV
BUCUREŞTI (Bucharest)

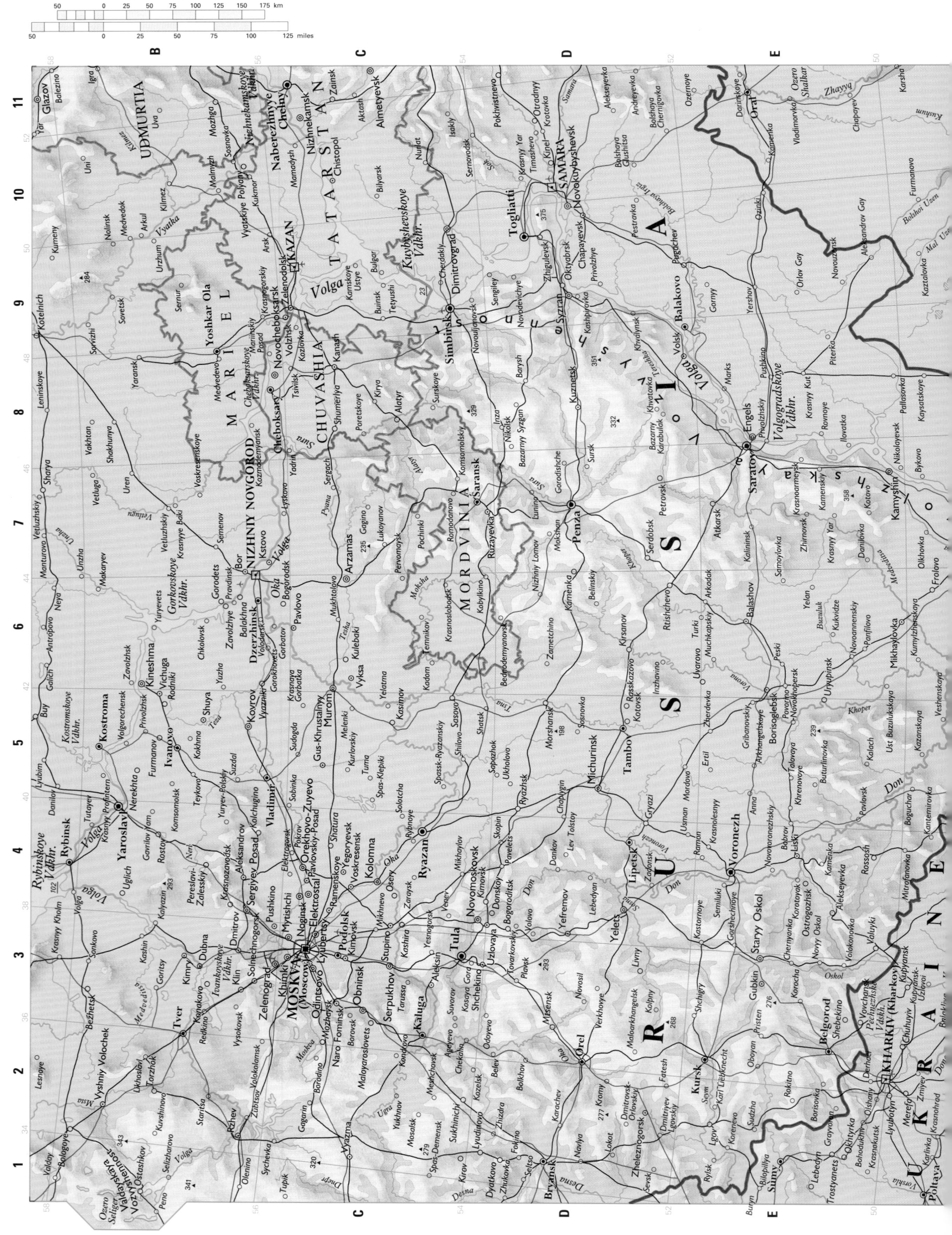

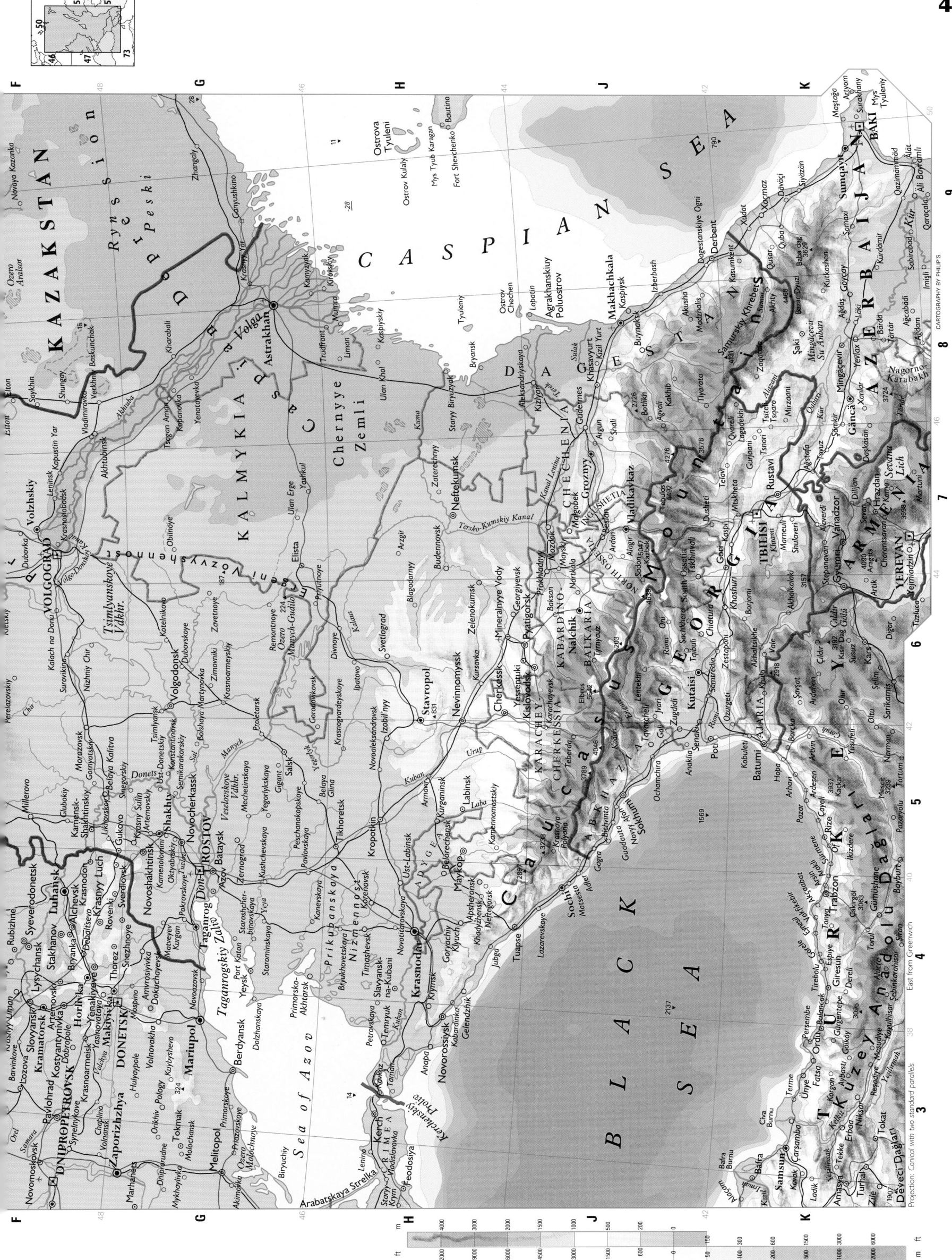

Projection: Conical with two standard parallels

East from Greenwich

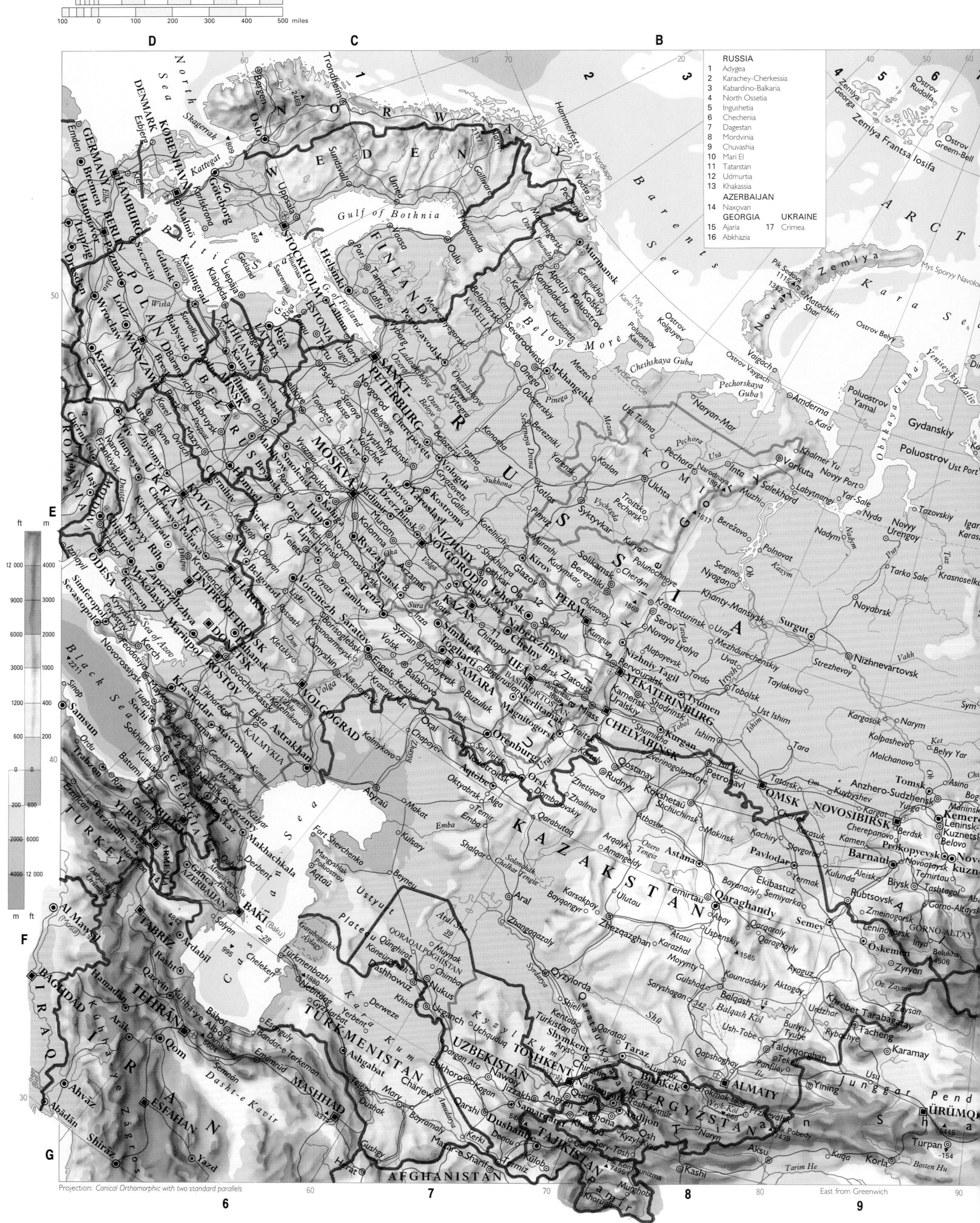

RUSSIA
1 Adygea
2 Karachey-Cherkessia
3 Kabardino-Balkaria
4 North Ossetia
5 Ingushetia
6 Chechenia
7 Dagestan
8 Mordvinia
9 Chuvashia
10 Mari El
11 Tatarstan
12 Udmurtia
13 Khakassia
AZERBAIJAN
14 Naxçivan
GEORGIA   UKRAINE
15 Ajaria   17 Crimea
16 Abkhazia

Projection: Conical Orthomorphic with two standard parallels

East from Greenwich

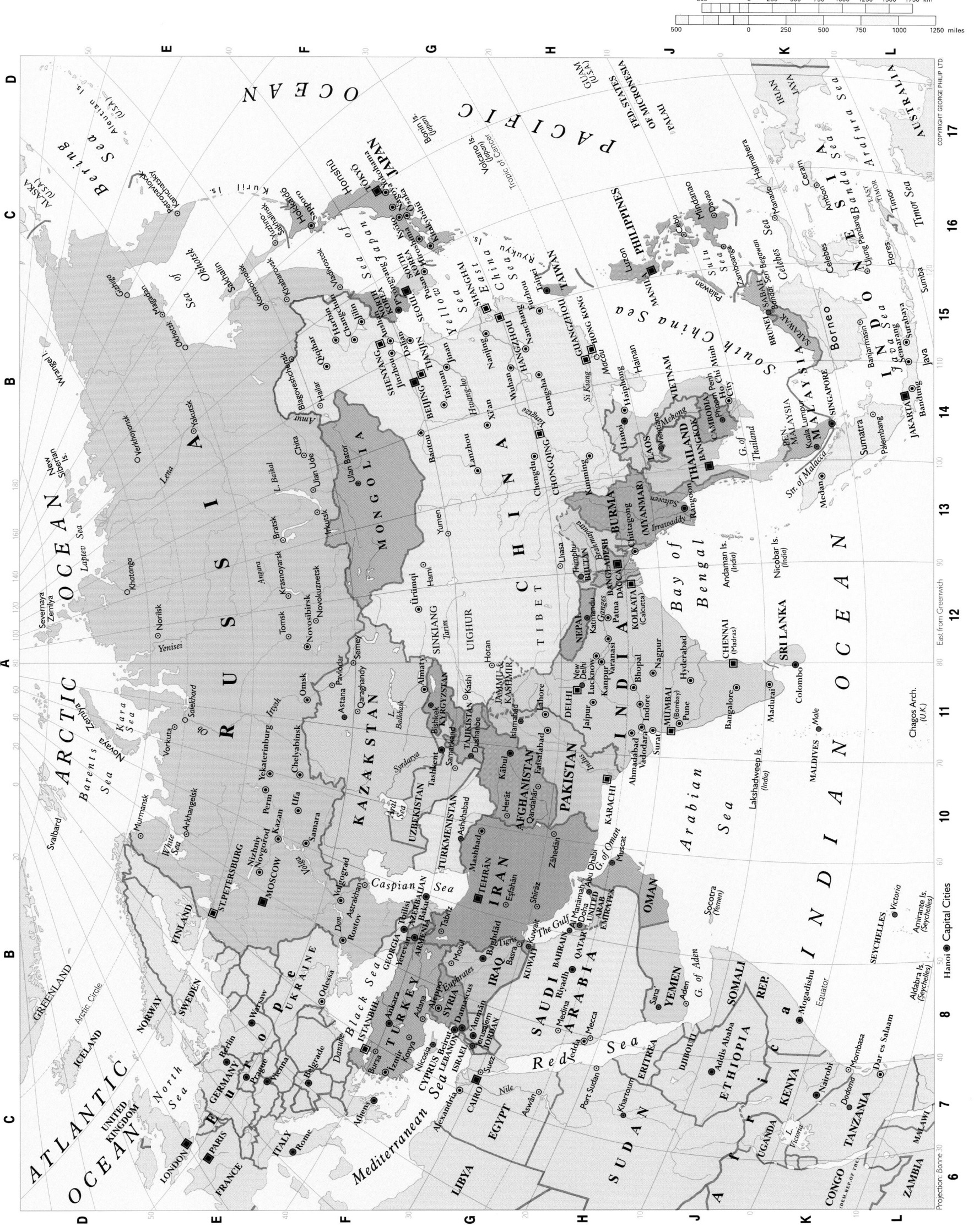

500   0   250   500   750   1000 1250 1500 1750 km

500   0   250   500   750   1000   1250 miles

COPYRIGHT GEORGE PHILIP LTD.

Projection: Bonne

Hanoi ● Capital Cities

East from Greenwich

JAPAN 1:4 400 000

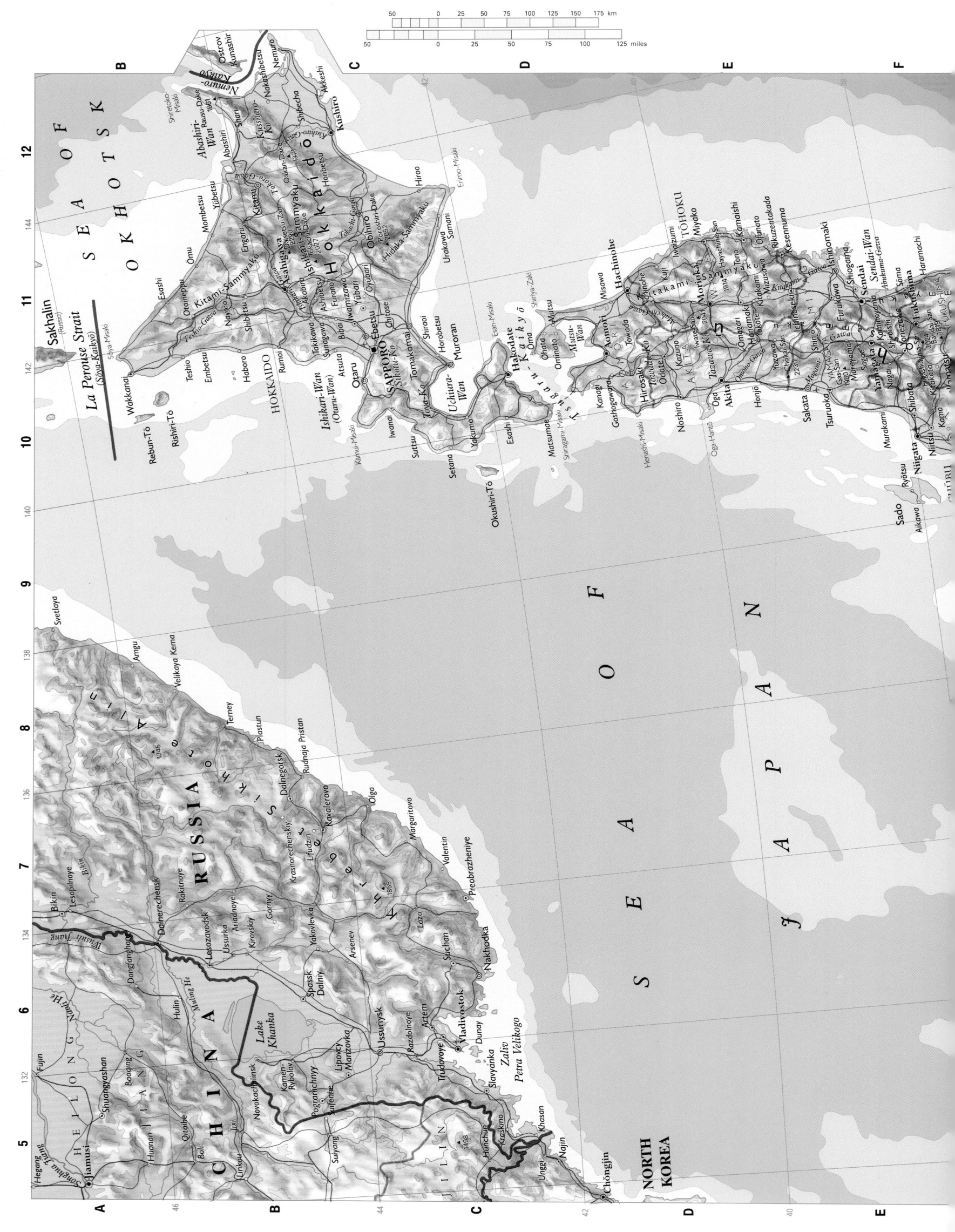

SEA OF OKHOTSK

Sakhalin (Russo)

La Perouse Strait (Sōya-Kaikyō)

HOKKAIDO

SAPPORO

HOKKAIDO

RUSSIA

CHINA

HEILONGJIANG

JILIN

Lake Khanka

Vladivostok

Zaliv Petra Velikogo

NORTH KOREA

Chōngjin

SEA OF JAPAN

TOHOKU

Hachinohe

Aomori

Akita

Sendai

Niigata

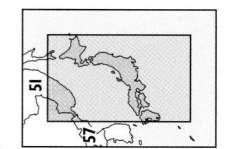

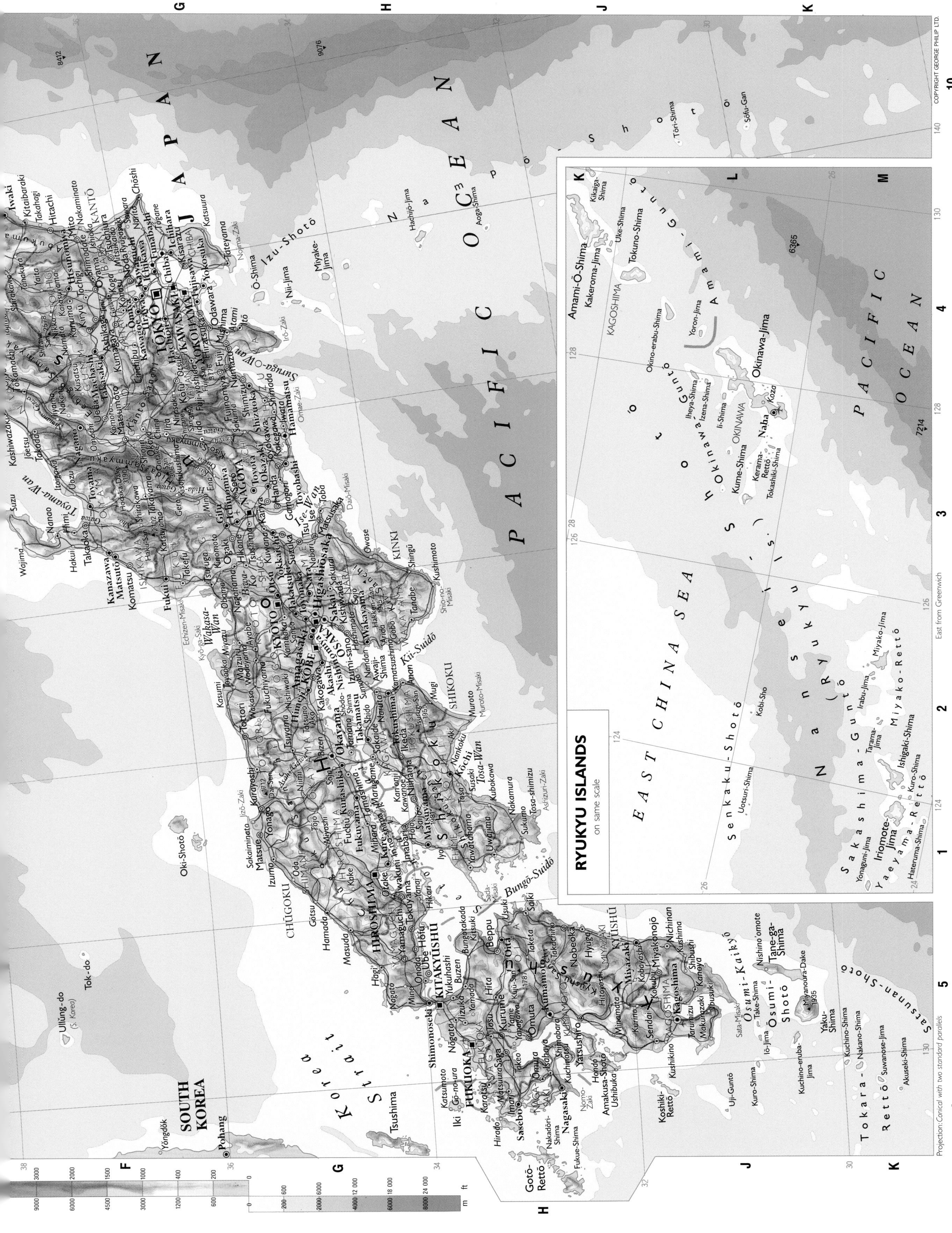

JAPAN
PACIFIC OCEAN
EAST CHINA SEA
SOUTH KOREA
Korea Strait
RYUKYU ISLANDS
on same scale
TOKYO
KYOTO
OSAKA
KOBE
NAGOYA
YOKOHAMA
KAWASAKI
HIROSHIMA
KITAKYUSHU
FUKUOKA
SHIKOKU
KYUSHU
CHUGOKU
KINKI
KANTO
Izu-Shotō
Nansei-Shotō (Ryukyu Is.)
Okinawa-Jima
Amami-Ō-Shima
Sakishima-Guntō
Senkaku-Shotō
Ōsumi-Kaikyō
Bungo-Suidō
Kii-Suidō
Tsushima
Oki-Shotō
Projection: Conical with two standard parallels
East from Greenwich
COPYRIGHT GEORGE PHILIP LTD.

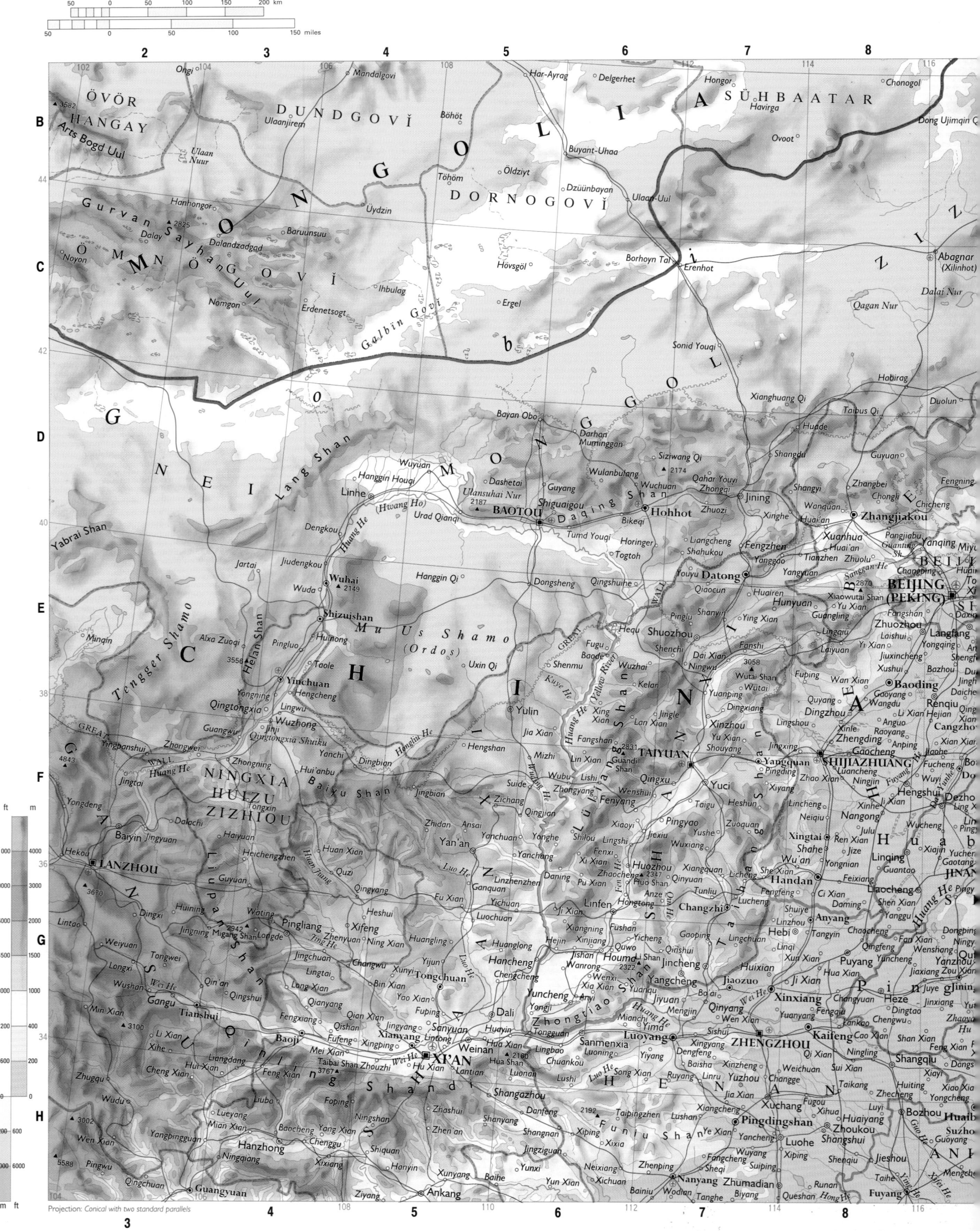

51
60
55
58
59

HARBIN
Bin Xian
Shuangcheng
Acheng
Horqin Youyi Qianqi
(Ulanhot)
Zhenlai
Baicheng
Taonan
Da'an
Maoxing
Zhaoyuan
Tuquan
Anguang
Hulingol
Hulin He
Changchunling
Qagan Nur
Qian Gorlos
Fuyu
Qian'an
Beitaolaizhao
Sanchahe
Wuchang
Tongyu
Shenjingzi
Kaoshan
Yushu
Nong'an
Dehui
Zhanyu
Beizhengzhen
Jarud Qi
Changling
Fulongquan
Jiutai
Horqin Zuoyi Zhongqi
Maolin
Huaidezhen
CHANGCHUN
JILIN
Xinkai He
Bairin Zuoqi
Kailu
Tongliao
Linxi
Bairin Youqi
Xiliao He
Shuangliao
Gongzhuling
Lishu
Siping
Yitong
Shuangyang
Fanjiatun
Xar Moron He
Jargalang
Bamiancheng
Liaoyuan
Ongniud Qi
Laoha He
Wutonghaolai
Zhangwu
Kangping
Xifeng
Dongfeng
Panshi
Huadian
Huinan
Kaiyuan
Meihekou
Hure Qi
Xiawa
Faku
Tiefa
Chifeng
Fuxin
Zhangwu
Tieling
Qingyuan
Shanchengzhen
Liuhe
Hunjiang
Heishui
Xinlitun
Xinmin
SHENYANG
FUSHUN
Beipiao
Qinghemen
Heishan
Xinbin
Tonghua
Weichang
Ningcheng
Chaoyang
Beizhen
Liaozhong
Benxi
Qingcheng
Goubangzi
Liaoyang
Daling He
Yi Xian
Panjin
ANSHAN
Anping
Tianshifu
Chengde
Lingyuan
Pingquan
Jinzhou
Jinxi
Niuzhuang
Haicheng
Lianshanguan
Kuandian
Huludao
Tianzhuangtai
Dashiqiao
Yingkou
Gaizhou
Fengcheng
Xingcheng
Liaodong
Xiuyan
Suizhong
Xiongyuecheng
Wanfu
Dandong
Donggou
Zhuanghe
Jianchangying
Qinhuangdao
Wan
Funing
Changli
Leting
Luan Xian
Tangshan
Tianjin Shi
Hangu
TIANJIN
Tanggu
Dagu
Wafangdian
Pulandian
Pikou
Jin Xian
Lüshun
DALIAN
Bo Hai
Korea Bay
Oikou
Huanghua
Miaodao Qundao
Penglai
Longkou
Daxindian
Yantai
Weihai
Huang He
Laizhou Wan
Muping
Chengshan Jiao
Wendeng
Rongcheng
Dongying
Binzhou
Laizhou
Zhaoyuan
Qixia
Shandong Bandao
Laiyang
Rushan
Nanhuang
Shidao
Haiyang
Changyi
Pingdu
Laixi
Weifang
ZIBO
Boshan
Zhoucun
Linqu
Gaomi
Jimo
Chengyang
Jiaozhou
Jiaozhou Wan
QINGDAO
Zhucheng
Laiwu
Xintai
Mengyin
Yishui
Wulian
Ju Xian
Liangcheng
Rizhao
Shijiusuo
Tangtou
Andongwei
Linyi
Gangyu
Haizhou Wan
Lianyungang
Zaozhuang
Haizhou
Lianyungang
Chenjiagang
Xinyi
Guanyun
Xiangshui
Guannan
Xuzhou
Suqian
Shuyang
Binhai
Lianshui
Funing
Sheyang
Huaiyin
Huai'an
Hongze Hu
Suzhou
Baoying
Yancheng
Liuzhuang
Bengbu
Fengyang
Gaoyou Hu
Xinghua
Dongtai
HUANG HAI
(Yellow Sea)
HEILONGJIANG
JILIN
LIAONING
Dongbei (Manchuria)
Zhangguangcai Ling
Changbai Shan
Yanshou
Shangzhi
Lalin
Yimianpo
Hengdaohezi
Mudanjiang
Linkou
Jixi
Turiy Rog
Ozero Khanka
Muling
Maqiaohe
Xiachengzi
Pogranichnyy
Hailin
Muling
Suiyang
Suifenhe
Ning'an
Shanhetun
Shulan
Golenki
Dongning
Dongjingcheng
Ussuriysk
Luozigou
Razdolnoye
Artem
Gangyao
Wulajie
Xinzhan
Emu
Jingpo Hu
Jiaohe
Huangsongdian
Chunyang
Tavrichanka
Vladivostok
Dunhua
Daxinggou
Wangqing
Shixian
Tumen
Hunchun
Mingyuegue
Yanji
Longjing
Namyang
Slavyanka
Helong
Kraskino
Posyet
Songhua Hu
Antu
Hoeamdong
Sosura
Unggi
Najin
Baishan
Fusong
Jingyu
Baihe
Hoeryong
Musan
Puryong
Pugodong
Paektu-san
Chongjin
Kyongsong
Nanam
Linjiang
Chunggang-up
Huch'ang
Hyesan
Hapsu
Kilchu
Changbai
Irhyangdong
Ondaejin
Huanren
Kasan-dong
Kapsan
Simpungdong
Musudan
Ji'an
Manp'o
Kanggye
Kimch'aek (Songjin)
Kosongni
Tanch'on
Ch'osan
Changjin
Pukch'ong
Sinch'ang
Supung Shuiku
Sinhung
Sinp'o
Hongwon
Sinuiju
Taegwan
Hamhung
Hungnam
Yongamp'o
Kusong
Kujang
Tokch'on
Tongchon-ni
Chongju
Pakch'on
Anju
Sunch'on
Yonghung
Tongjoson Man
Sonch'on
NORTH KOREA
KOREA
Sea of Japan
Kowon
Munch'on
Wonsan
Anbyon
Kojo
Sukch'on
Sunan
P'YONGYANG
Chunghwa
Kangdong
Tongyang
Koksan
Singosan
Hoeyang
Kosong
Nampo
Songnim
Sariwon
Chaeryong
Suan
Sinmak
Kumch'on
Kumhwa
Kansong
Sokch'o
Yangyang
Cho-do
Changyon
Haeju
Kaesong
Panmunjom
Ch'orwon
Chumunjin
Kangnung
Ongjin
Yonan
Paengnyong-do
Ch'unch'on
Uijongbu
Hongch'on
Samch'ok
Ullung-do
SOUL
Puch'on
Songnam
INCH'ON
Anyang
Wonju
Ansan
Suwon
Osan
Ich'on
Yoju
Chech'on
Yongju
Ulchin
Ch'onan
Ch'ongju
Andong
Yongdok
SOUTH KOREA
Sosan
Hongsong
Kongju
Yesan
Chongju
Yech'on
Uisong
Anmyon-do
Taech'on-ni
TAEJON
Sangju
Chongha
P'ohang
Nonsan
Kimch'on
Kumi
Yongch'on
Kyongju
Changgi-Ap
Kunsan
Iri
Chonju
TAEGU
Ulsan
Kimje
Kochang
Koryong
Miryang
Puan
Chongup
Namwon
Chinju
Masan
Kimhae
Tongnae
PUSAN
Chii-san
Kwangju
Ch'angwon
Chinhae
Sagwonp'o
Ch'ungmu
Sasuna
Sunch'on
Mokp'o
Yosu
Saka
Tsushima
Izuhara
Huksan-chedo
Chindo
Haenam
Korea Strait
Iki
Karatsu
Cheju-do
Cheju
Hallim
Onpyong-ni
Halla-san
Taejong
Mosulpo
Sogwipo
JAPAN
Imari
Sasebo
Kashima
Omura
Isahaya
Nagasaki
Kuchinotsu
Nakadori-Shima
Fukue-Shima
RUSSIA
1949
2020
1885
1845
2744
2541
2522
1638
1578
1915
1950
1690
1677
1108
1131
923
East from Greenwich
118
120
122
124
126
128
130
132
44
42
40
38
36
34
9
10
11
12
13
14
15
16
B
C
D
E
F
G
H
COPYRIGHT GEORGE PHILIP LTD.

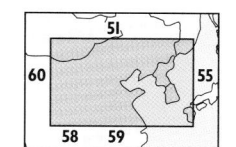

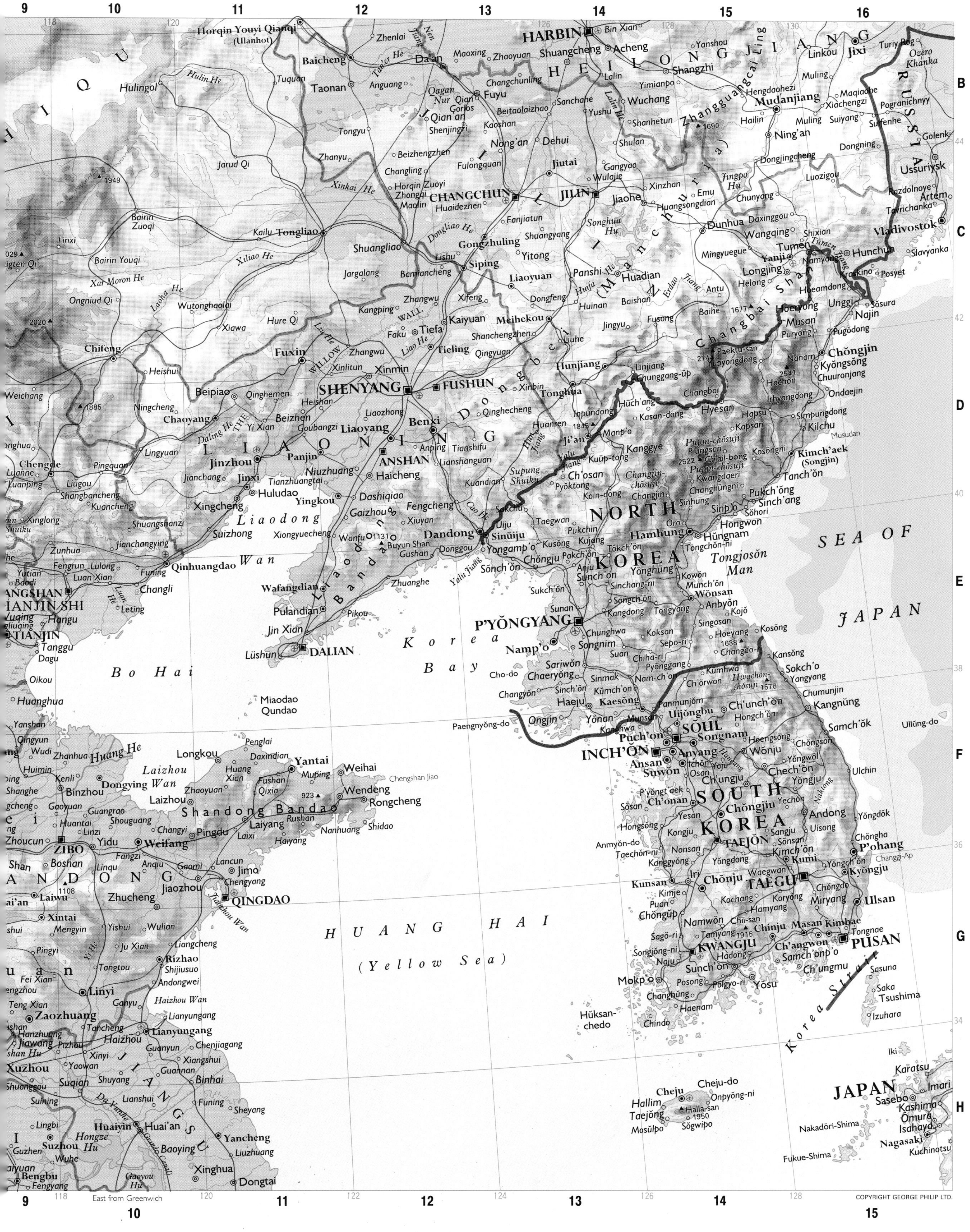

50 0 50 100 150 200 km
50 0 50 100 150 miles

ft m
12 000 4000
9000 3000
6000 2000
4500 1500
3000 1000
1200 400
600 200
0 0
200 600
2000 6000
m ft

GANSU
SHAANXI
SICHUAN
Si Chuan Pendi
CHENGDU
CHONGQING
CHONGQING SHI
GUIZHOU
GUIYANG
KUNMING
YUNNAN
GUANGXI
NANNING
LIUZHOU
KACHIN
BURMA (MYANMAR)
SHAN
THAILAND
LAOS
VIETNAM
HANOI
Haiphong
Gulf of Tonkin

Ningjing Shan
Shaluli Shan
Daxue Shan
Shan
Qionglai Shan
Daba Shan
Daliang Shan
Dalou Shan
Nu Shan
Gaoligong Shan
Wuliang Shan
Ailao Shan
Hoang Lien Son

Chang Jiang (Yangtse)
Yalong Jiang
Jinsha Jiang
Lancang Jiang (Mekong)
Nu Jiang
Wu Jiang
You Jiang
Zuo Jiang
Yu Jiang
Song Hong

Woinbogoin, Dainkog, Zogqen, Jomda, Degê, Baiyü, Baima, Sêrtar, Zamtang, Hongyuan, Aba, Songpan, Heishui
Hanzhong, Guangyuan, Mianyang, Chengdu, Chongqing, Leshan, Neijiang, Zigong, Yibin, Luzhou
Kunming, Dali, Panzhihua, Xichang, Zhaotong, Guiyang, Anshun, Zunyi, Tongren
Nanning, Liuzhou, Beihai, Qinzhou, Fangchenggang, Dongxing
Hanoi, Haiphong, Thai Nguyen, Lang Son, Lao Cai, Ha Giang, Cao Bang
Chiang Rai, Mae Sai, Keng Tung, Mong Hsu, Luang Prabang

Projection: Conical with two standard parallels

56
57
67
64
61

HENAN
ANHUI
JIANGSU
HUBEI
HUNAN
JIANGXI
ZHEJIANG
FUJIAN
GUANGDONG
TAIWAN
SHANGHAI SHI
NANJING
WUHAN
CHANGSHA
NANCHANG
HANGZHOU
SHANGHAI
GUANGZHOU
HONG KONG (XIANGGANG)
T'AIPEI
KAOHSIUNG
Dabie Shan
Jiuling Shan
Wuyi Shan
Nan Ling
Luoxiao Shan
Chang Jiang (Yangtse)
Dongting Hu
Poyang Hu
Tai Hu
Taiwan Strait
Luzon Strait
SOUTH CHINA SEA
Tropic of Cancer
East from Greenwich

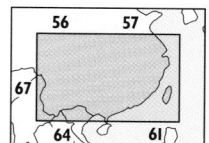

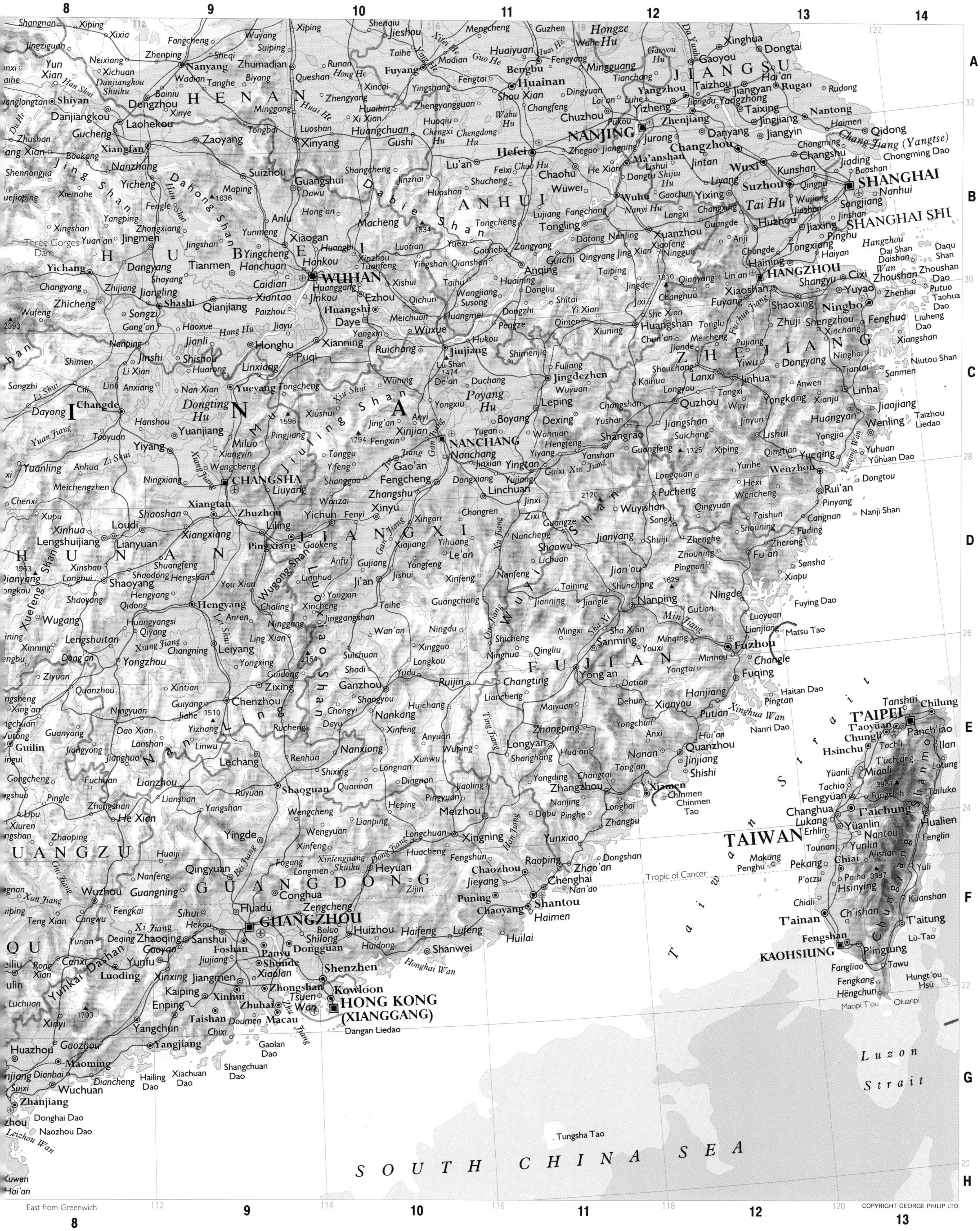

100 0 100 200 300 400 500 600 700 800 km
100 0 100 200 300 400 500 miles

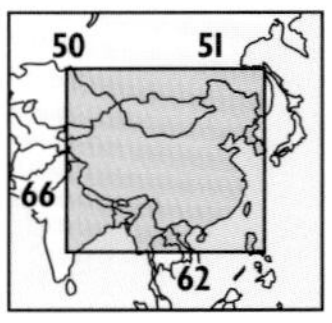

East from Greenwich

COPYRIGHT GEORGE PHILIP LTD.

Projection: Bonne

m ft
18 000
12 000
9000
6000
4500
3000
1500
1200
600
400
200
0
200 - 400
2000 6000
4000 12 000
6000 18 000

50 0 100 150 200 250 300 km
50 0 50 100 150 200 miles

1	2	3	4	5	6	7	8

A Itbayat I.
Batan I.

B *Balintang Channel*
Calayan I.
Dalupiri I. Babuyan I. Camiguin I.
Babuyan Fuga I.
Mayraira Pt. Islands
Babuyan Channel
Bacarra Bangui Claveria Santa Ana
San Nicolas Laoag Aparri Gonzaga
Batac Kabugao Gattaran Tuguegarao
Cabugao Bangued Tuao Cagayan
Vigan 2360 Mt. Cresta 1685
Santa Candon Bontoc Ilagan Palanan Pt.
C Maria San Mateo Palanan
Tagudin Roxas Santiago
Balaoan Cordillera Central
San Fernando Mt. Pulog Cordon Casiguran
Bolinao 2928 Solano
Baguio Bayombong C. San Ildefonso
Alaminos Rosario Mt. Anacuao
D Lingayen Dagupan 1852
San Carlos San Manuel
Santa Cruz Bayambang San Jose Baler Bay
Moncada Cuyapo Baler
Camiling Victoria **Luzon**
Masinloc Tarlac La Cabanatuan
Iba 2037 Paz Gapan Dingalan
Concepcion 1780 Angeles
Mt. Pinatubo San Fernando Polillo Is.
San Antonio Dinalan
Olongapo Orani **Malabon** Polillo Is.
Manila **Caloocan** Patnanongan I.
Bataan Bay **Quezon City** Jomalig I.
Cavite **MANILA**
Dasmariñas **Pasay** Santa Cruz Paracale
Tagaytay L de Bay Lucban Labo
Nasugbu San Pablo Atimonan Daet
Balayan Lipa Lucena Calauag Pandan
Lemery Batangas Lopez Catanauan Calabanga Catanduanes
Lubang Lobo Tayabas Bay Naga San Andres
Is. Verde I. Pass Boac Nabua Virac
C. Calavite Mamburao Marin- 2421 Iriga Lagonoy Gulf
Calapan duque Ligao Mayon Vol. Rapu Rapu I.
Mindoro Victoria Tablas Legazpi Tabaco
Mt. Baco Pinamalayan Donsol Sorsogon
Sablayan 2487 *SIBUYAN* Magallanes Gubat
Bongabong Romblon Bulan San Bernardino Str.
Roxas Tablas I. Ticao I. Irosin Laoang
San Jose Odiongan Aroroy Allen Mondragon
Busuanga I. Ilin I. Sibuyan I. Mandaon Catarman Gamay
Culion I. Calamian *SEA* Milagros Calbayog Arteche
Group Masbate Oras
Linapacan Str. Pandan Kalibo Placer Catbalogan Taft
Culion I. Roxas *VISAYAN* Bilinan I. Paranas Borongan
Linapacan I. Dao Pilar *SEA* Caibiran Santa General MacArthur
Cuyo Is. Tibiao 2117 Ajuy Sara Bantayan Carigara Rita Basey Guiuan
Cuyo West Pass Cuyo Bugasong Passi **Panay** Calubian Palompon Llorente
Taytay Pototan Silay Cadiz Bogo **Leyte** Tacloban Homonhon I.
Palawan San Jose **Iloilo** Sagay Tuburan Ormoc Leyte Gulf
Guimaras **Bacolod** San Carlos Danao Abuyog 10 497
Dumaran I. Jordan 2450 Camotes Is. Baybay
Hinigaran La Mandaue Camotes San Juan Dinagat I.
Honda Bay Binalbagan Carlota **Cebu** Sea Bato Maasin Dinagat
1593 Himamaylan Guihulngan Panaon I. Siargao I.
Irahuan Kabankalan Argao Bohol I. Surigao
Puerto Princesa Sipalay Bais Oslob Tagbilaran Placer Bucas Grande I.
Cagayan Is. Hinoba-an **Negros** Tanjay Dumaguete **BOHOL** Mainit Carrascal
Bayawan Siaton Siquijor I. Camiguin I. Cabadbaran Lanuza
Mt. Mantalingajan Talisayan 2012 Tandag
2085 Zamboanguita *SEA* Nasipit Tago
C. Buliluyan Dipolog Dapitan Butuan Lianga
Bugsuk I. Manukan Iligan Esperanza Marihatag
Oroquieta Bay Opol Alubijid Hinatuan
Labason Sindangan Ozamiz Cagayan de Oro Bislig
Balabac I. Liloy Iligan 2938 Malaybalay
Balabac Strait Kabasalan Pagadian Marawi City Buruan
Balambangan Bangi Siocon Tubod L. Lanao Cateel
Kudat Senoja Margosatubig **Mindanao** Baganga
Jembongan Sibuco Malabang 2815 Panabo Tagum
Langkon Kota Belud Olutanga Illana Parang Panabo
Suba Talan Bay Midsayap Mt. Apo Pantukan
Tenghilan Turtle Is. Datu Piang 2954 **Davao** Manay
Kota G. Kinabalu Pikit Digos Mati
Kinabalu 4101 Sandakan Talayan Davao San Isidro
Papar Cagayan Sulu I. Zamboanga Kalamansig Gulf
Pilas Isabela Lebak Koronadal Malita
SABAH Basilan Group Basilan I. Lamitan Palimbang 2083
MALAYSIA Pangutaran C. San Agustin
Keningau Group Samales **General**
Borneo Jolo Group Kiamba **Santos**
Melalap Jolo Tinaca Pt.
Kuamat Silam Parang Talipao Sarangani Bay
Banjaran Crocker Teluk Darvel Tapul Pata I. Sarangani Is.
Semporna Tawi-tawi Tapul *Sulu Archipelago*
Sibutu Group Group Kep. Talaud
INDONESIA

SOUTH CHINA SEA
PACIFIC OCEAN
PHILIPPINES
SULU SEA
CELEBES SEA
Mindoro Strait
Lamon Bay
Sibuyan Str.
Moro Gulf
Mindanao Trench
Sarangani

ft m
9000 3000
6000 2000
4500 1500
3000 1000
1200 600
600 200
200 600
4000 12 000
8000 24 000
m ft

59
62 63

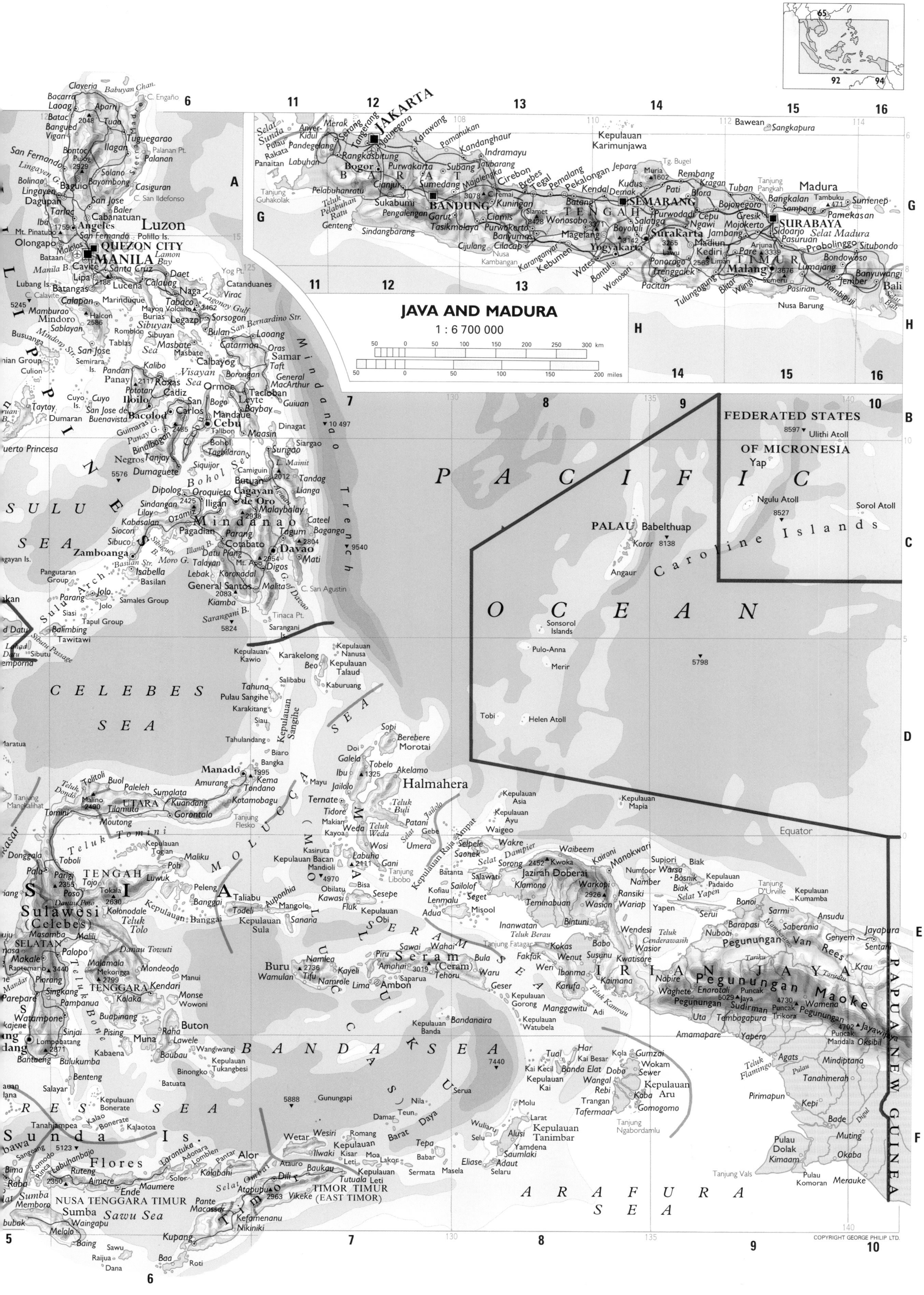

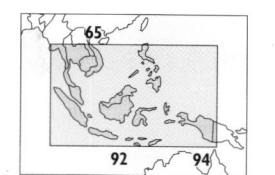

JAVA AND MADURA

1 : 6 700 000

COPYRIGHT GEORGE PHILIP LTD.

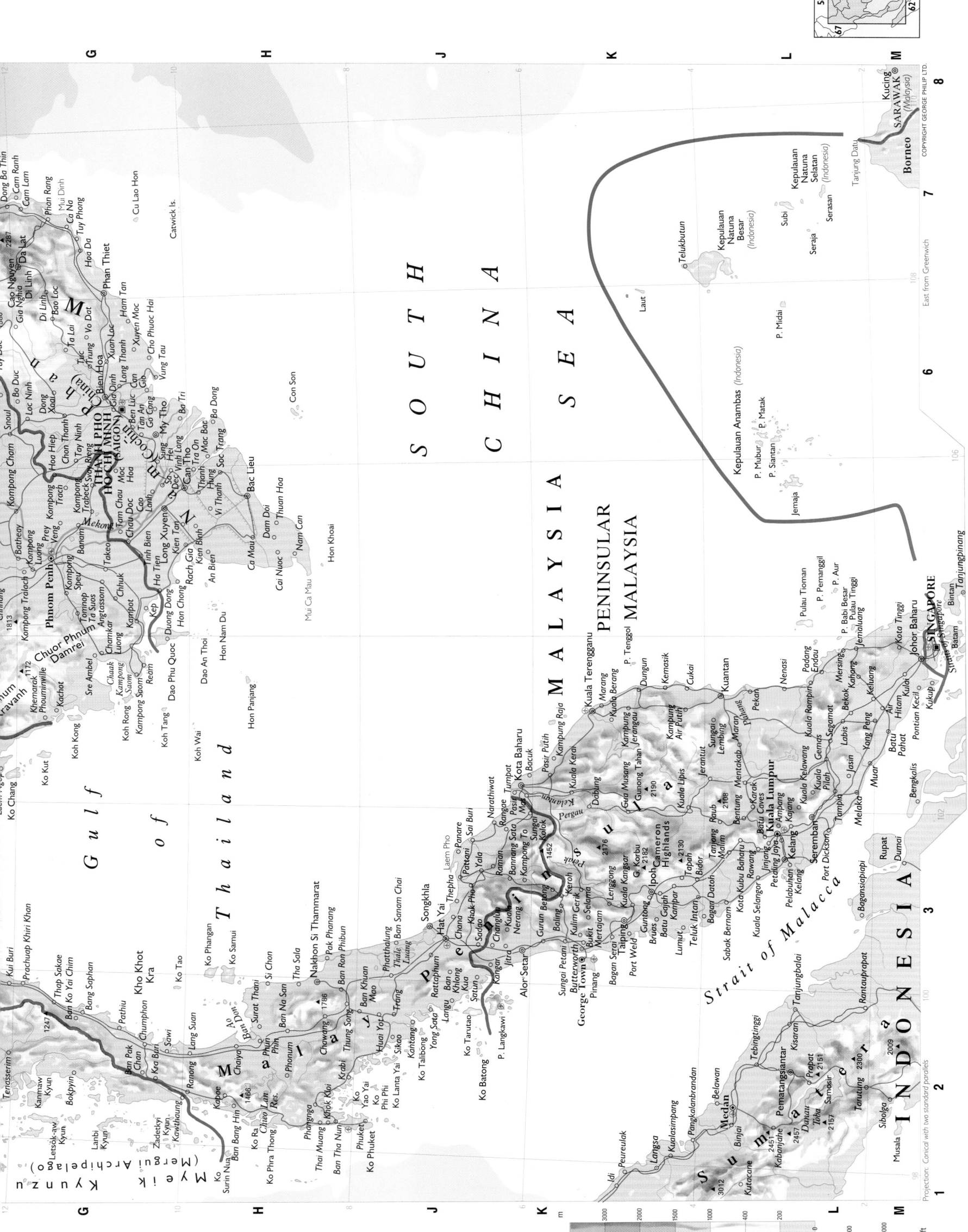

50 0   100   200   300   400 km
50 0   50   100   150   200   250 miles

ARABIAN SEA

TURKMENISTAN
AFGHANISTAN
IRAN
PAKISTAN

Tropic of Cancer

Mouths of the Indus

KARACHI

Hyderabad

Quetta

Kabul
Islamabad
RAWALPINDI
LAHORE
FAISALABAD
Amritsar
Gujranwala

DELHI
New Delhi
Jaipur
Agra
Gwalior

R A J A S T H A N
Thar Desert
PUNJAB
HARYANA
HIMACHAL PRADESH
UTTARANCH
JAMMU & KASHMIR
KASHMIR

Karakoram Range
K2
Aksai Chin

HERAT
GHOWR
ORUZGAN
GHAZNI
HELMAND
NIMRUZ
FARAH
QANDAHAR
PAKTIA
PAKTIKA
ZABOL

BALUCHISTAN
SIND
Makran Coast Range
Central Makran Range

GOA
KARNATAKA
TAMIL NADU
KERALA
ANDHRA PRADESH
MAHARASHTRA
MADHYA PRADESH
GUJARAT
Kathiawar

Ahmadabad
Vadodara (Baroda)
Surat
MUMBAI (BOMBAY)
Pune (Poona)
Nagpur
HYDERABAD

Gulf of Kachchh
Gulf of Khambhat
Rann of Kachchh

Bangalore
Mysore
Chennai (Madras)
Coimbatore
Madurai
Cochin (Kochi)
Trivandrum (Thiruvananthapuram)
C. Comorin

Palk Strait
Gulf of Mannar
Adam's Bridge

SRI LANKA
Colombo
Kandy
Galle
Dondra Head

Continuation Southwards on same scale

Projection: Conical with two standard parallels

ft   m
18 000   6000
12 000   4000
9000   3000
6000   2000
4500   1500
3000   1000
1200   400
600   200
0   0
200   600
m   ft

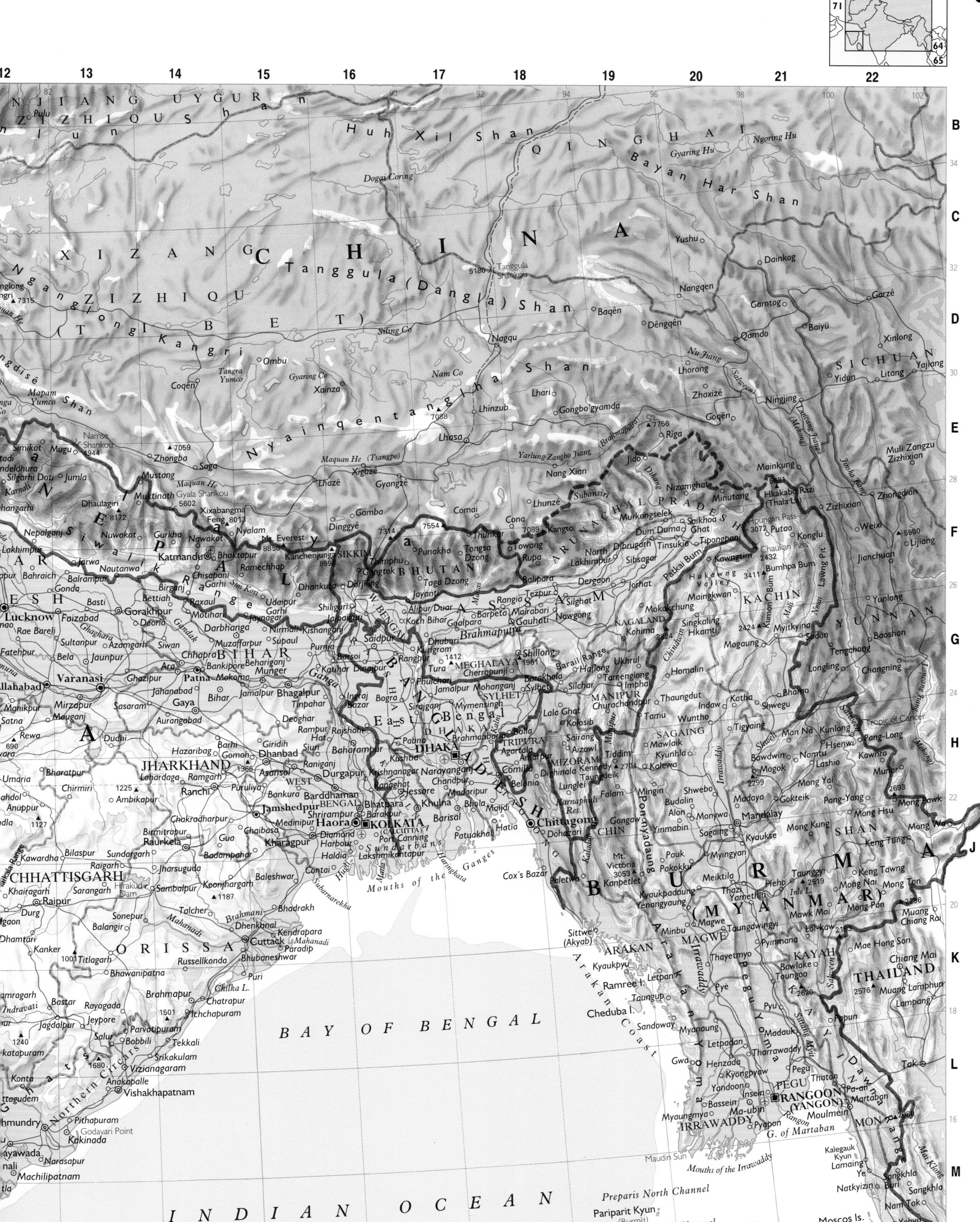

THE INDO-GANGETIC PLAIN 1:5 300 000

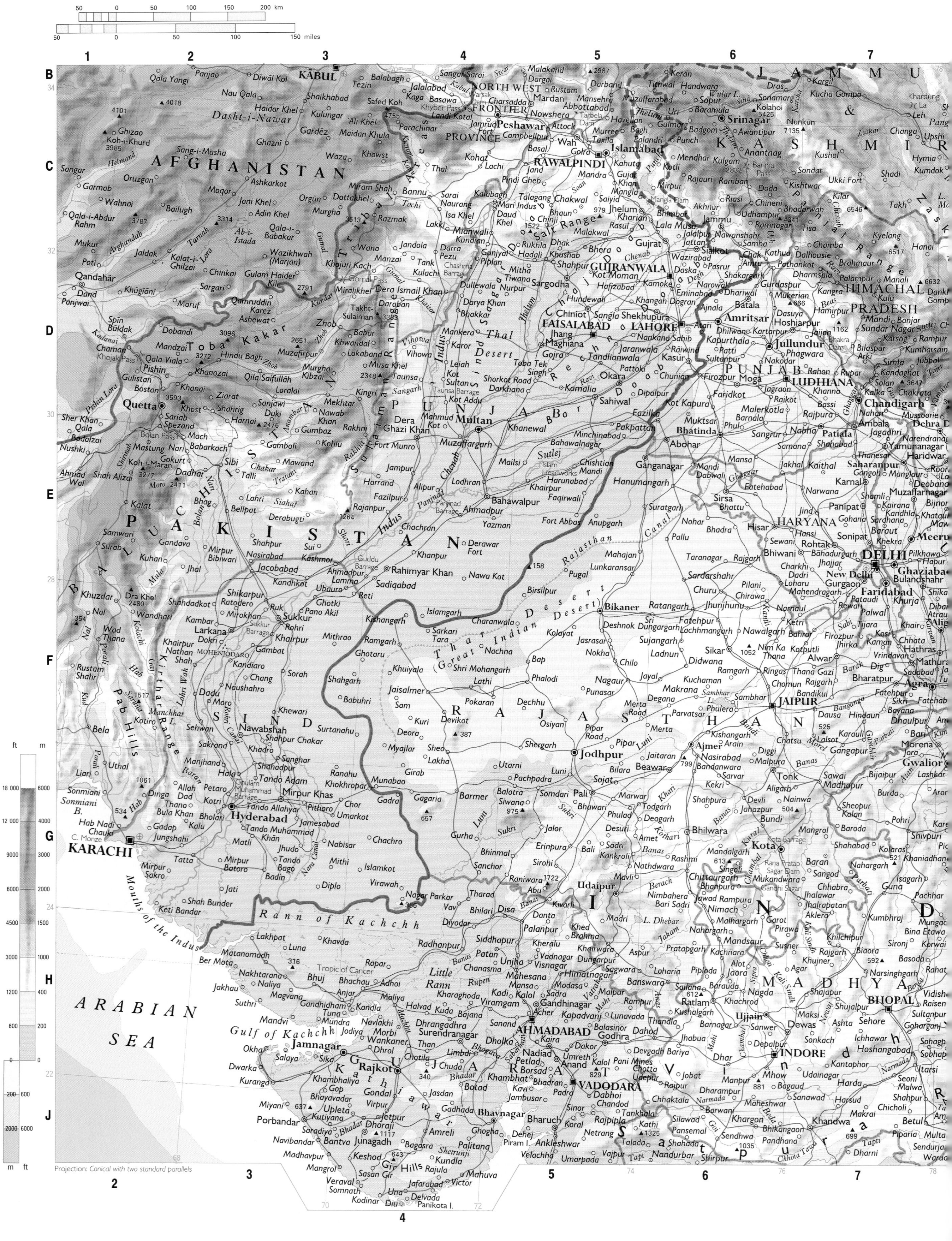

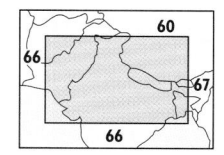

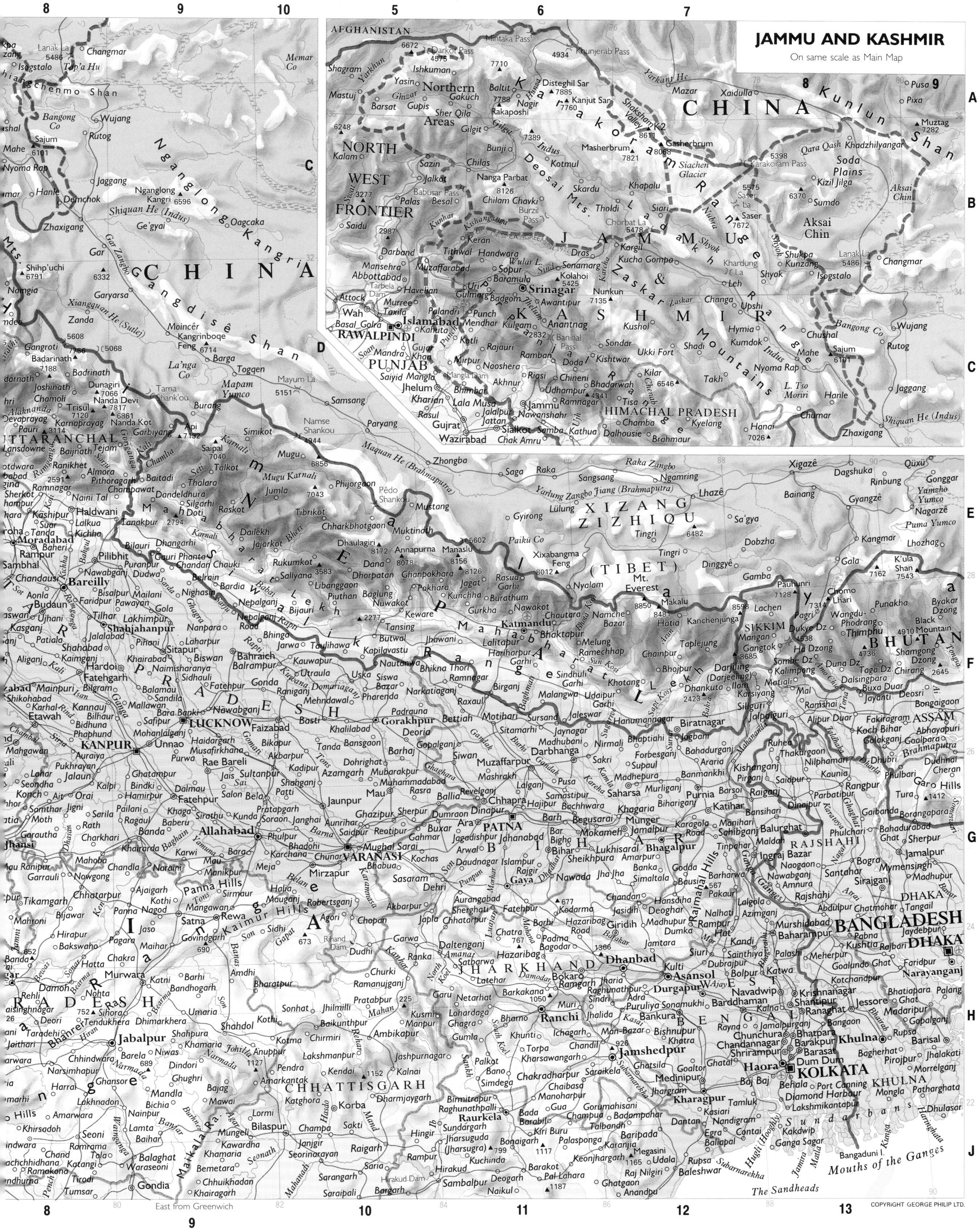

JAMMU AND KASHMIR
On same scale as Main Map

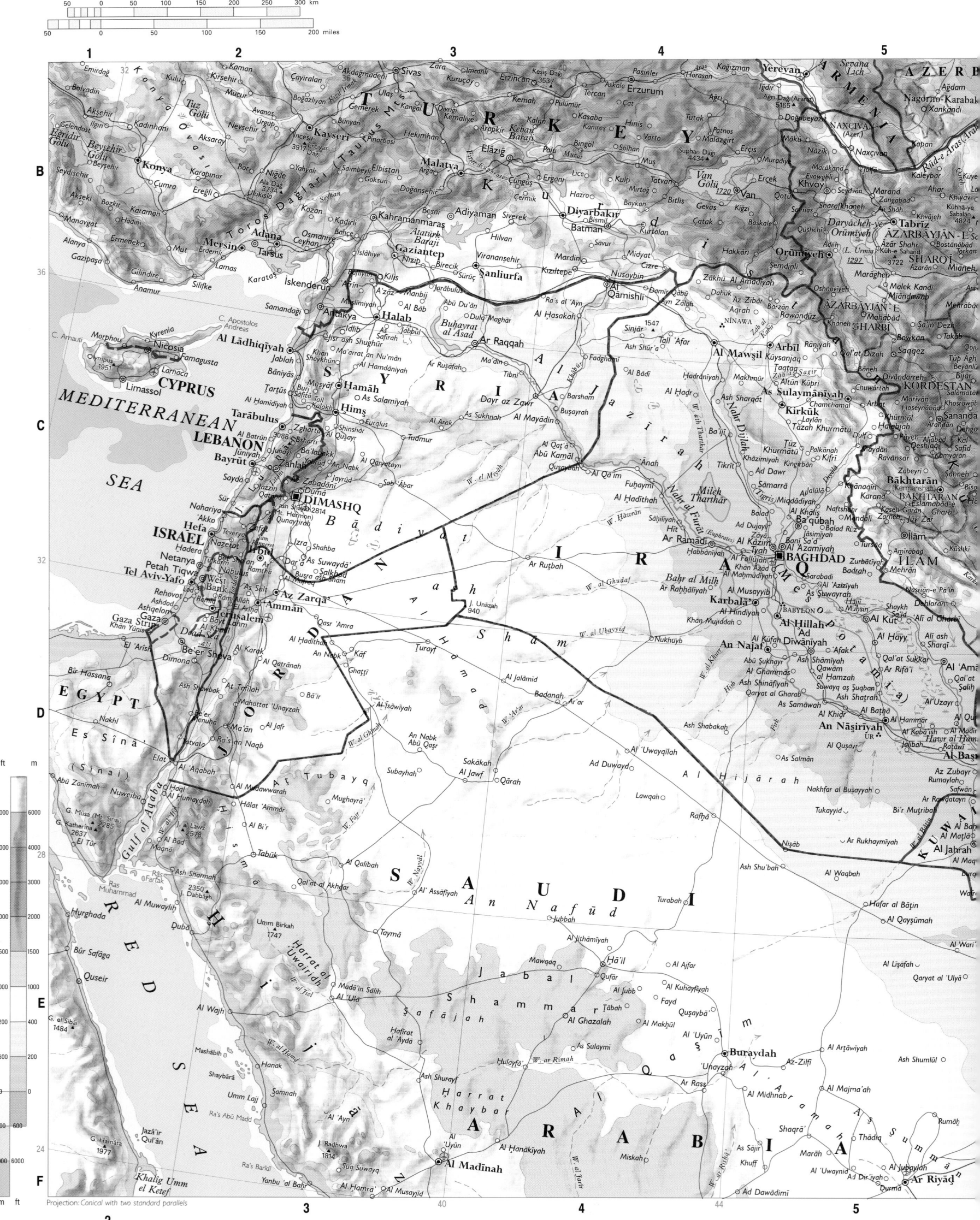

49
50
72
66
80
74

6
7
8
9
10
B
C
D
E
F
52
56
60
36
32
28
24
BAKI
Qazimämmäd
Äläť
Neftçala
Länkäran
Ästärä
Ardabīl
Tālesh
Bandar-e Anzalī
Rasht
Lāhījān
Fowman
GĪLĀN
Āstāneh
Rūd Sar
Rāmsar
Tonekābon
Now Shahr
Bābol Sar
Bābol
Āmol
Sārī
Qā'emshahr
Neka
Behshahr
MĀZANDARĀN
Reshteh-ye Kūhhā-ye Alborz
Manjil
Qazvin
Karaj
TEHRĀN
Tajrish
Rey
Eslamshahr
Damāvand
5604
Fīrūzkūh
Semnān
SEMNĀN
Garmsār
Eyvānki
Lāsjerd
MARKAZĪ
Qom
Daryācheh-ye Namak
Kāshān
Arāk
Malāyer
Nahāvand
Borūjerd
Khorramābād
Khomeyn
Golpāyegān
Natanz
Ardestān
Zavāreh
Dāmaneh
Khomeyni Shahr
Najafābād
Eşfahān
EŞFAHĀN
Nā'īn
Kūhpāyeh
Kūh-e Zard
4548
CHAHĀR MAḨALL VA BAKHTĪĀRĪ
Shahr-e Kord
Qomsheh
Varzaneh
Bāṭlāq-e Gavkhūnī
Dezfūl
Andimeshk
Shūshtar
Masjed Soleyman
Ahvāz
KHUZESTĀN
Khorramshahr
Ābādān
Bandar-e Ma'shur
Bandar-e Khomeynī
Shatt al Arab
Al Fāw
Būbiyān
Kuwayt
Mīnā' al Aḩmadī
Mīnā' Su'ud
Al Khafjī
Ra's al Mish'āb
As Saffānīyah
Manifah
Abū Ḩadrīyah
Al Jubayl
Al Qaţīf
Ad Dammām
Az Zahrān
Al Manāmah
Al Muḩarraq
BAHRAIN
Al Hufūf
Al Mubarraz
Buqayq
Al Jāfūrah
Ad Dawḩah
Al Wakrah
Dukhān
QATAR
Al Khawr
Ḩālūl
THE GULF
KOHKĪLŪYEH VA BŪYER AḨMADĪ
Yāsūj
Dehdez
Zāgros
Kūh-e Dīnār
4431
Gachsārān
Fahliān
Būshehr
BŪSHEHR
Borāzjān
Kāzerūn
Shīrāz
FĀRS
PERSEPOLIS
Marv Dasht
Daryācheh-ye Tashk
Neyrīz
Eşţahbānāt
Fasā
Jahrom
Dārāb
Lār
Kangān
Ganāveh
Bandar-e Rīg
Khārk
Kāvar
Fīrūzābād
Lāvar Meydān
Sa'ādatābād
Yazd
YAZD
Taft
Mehrīz
Ardakān
Anār
Rafsanjān
Kerman
KERMĀN
Zarand
Kūhbonān
Rāvar
Bāfq
Sīrjān
Bam
Mashīz
Bāft
Jīroft
Kūh-e Hazārān
4419
Kūh-e Jebāl Bārez
3962
Namakzār-e Shahdād
Shahdād
Dasht-e Lūt
Dasht-e Kavīr
Tabas
Ferdows
Qāyen
Bīrjand
Gonābād
KHORĀSĀN
Kavīr-e Namak
Torbat-e Ḩeydarīyeh
Torbat-e Jām
Kāshmar
Sabzevār
Neyshābūr
Mashhad
Kūh-e Bīnālūd
3314
Qūchān
Bojnūrd
Shīrvān
Kūh-e Sorkh
3020
Dāmghān
Shāhrūd
Gonbad-e Kāvūs
Gorgān
Bandar-e Torkeman
Gomishān
CASPIAN SEA
-28
995
Cheleken
Yarymadasy
Ostrov Ogurchinskiy
Türkmenbashi
Nebitdag
Khrebet Bolshoy Balkhan
1880
Gazanjyk
Gyzylarbat
Gyzyletrek
Chāt
Atrek
Kopet Dagh
Ashgabat
Tejen
Mary
Bayramaly
Yoloten
Sarakhs
Dashköpri
Chārjew
Amudarya
Kara Kum
TURKMENISTAN
AFGHANISTAN
HERĀT
Herāt
Safīd Kūh
FARĀH
Farāh
Shīndand
NĪMRŪZ
Dasht-e Mārgow
Zaranj
Zābol
Sīstān
Daryācheh-ye Sīstān
Gowd-e Zirreh
Hāmūn-i Mashkel
PAKISTAN
Zāhedān
Mīrjāveh
Khāsh
Kūh-e Taftān
4042
Dowlatābād
SĪSTĀN VA BALŪCHESTĀN
Īrānshahr
Bampūr
Hāmūn-e Jaz Mūrīān
Kūh-e Bazman
3489
Bīābān-e Kermān
Kūhhā-ye Bashākerd
Makrān
Chābahār
Gavāter
Jāsk
Rās Jiwani
HORMOZGĀN
Bandar-e Abbās
Mīnāb
Qeshm
Hormoz
Str. of Hormuz
Bandar-e Lengeh
Bandar-e Chārak
Ra's Masandam (Oman)
Ra's al Khaymah
Al Fujayrah
Dubayy
Ash Shāriqah
Ajmān
Umm al Qaywayn
Abū Ẓaby
Al 'Ayn
Gulf of Oman
Al Hajar Al Gharbī
UNITED ARAB EMIRATES
OMAN
Şuḩār
Dalmā
Şīr Banī Yās
Ruwais
Ḩabshān
Bū Ḩasā
Abū Mūsā
Sīrrī
Lāvan
Hendorābī
Qeys
Forūr
Dās
Az Zarqā'
Dank
'Ibrī
1372
East from Greenwich
COPYRIGHT GEORGE PHILIP LTD.

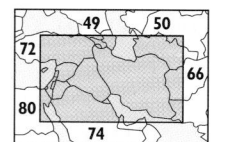

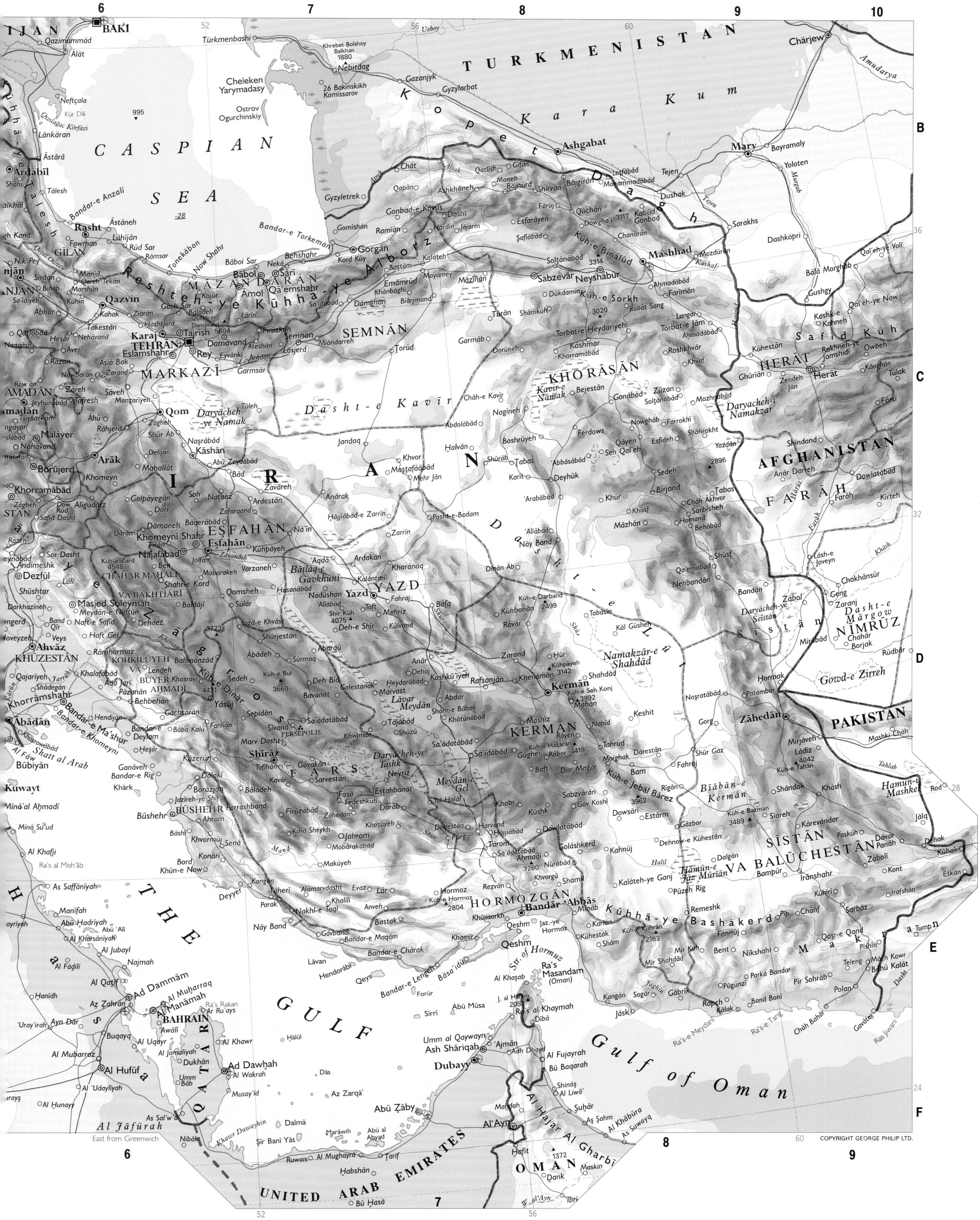

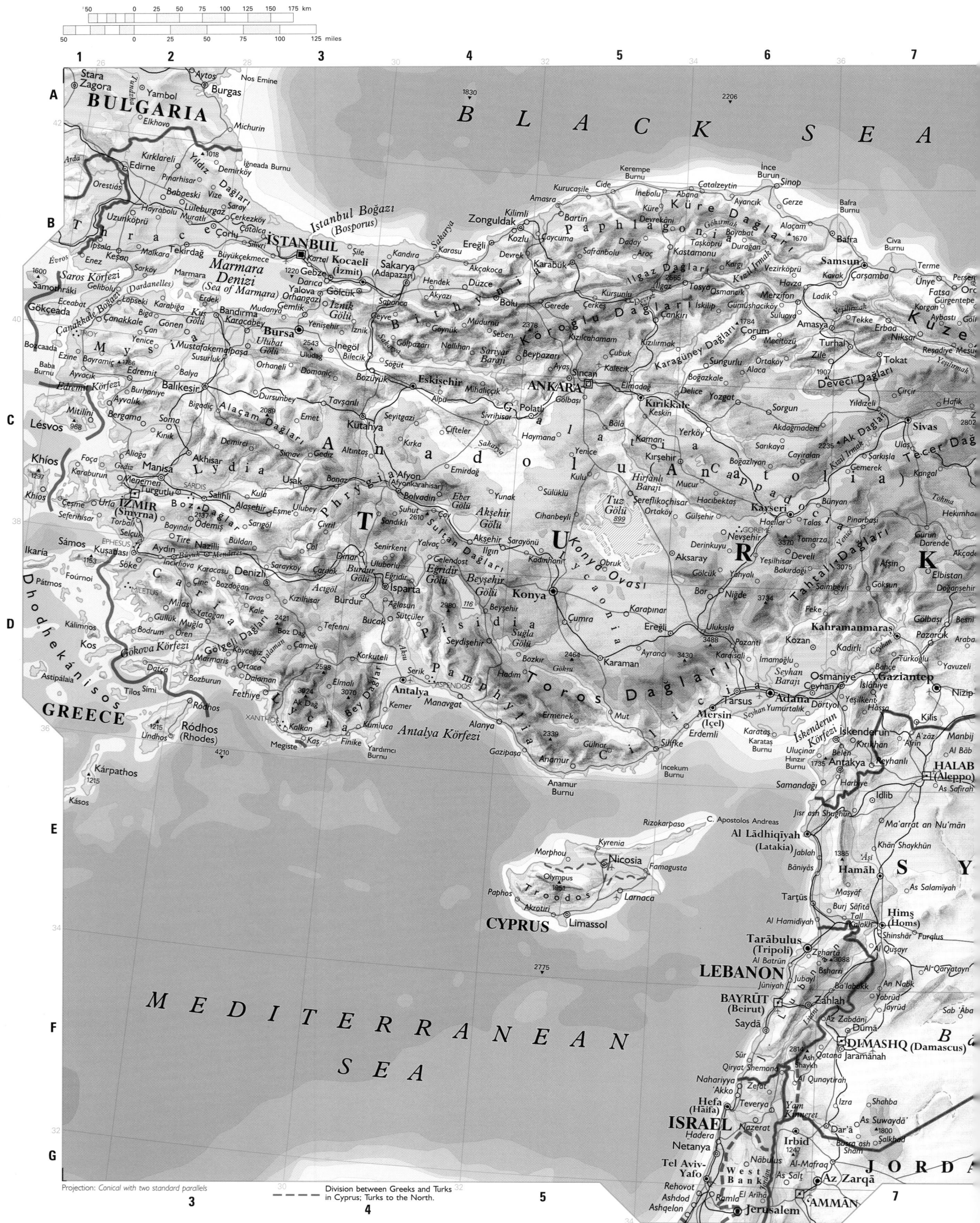

Projection: Conical with two standard parallels

– – – Division between Greeks and Turks
in Cyprus; Turks to the North.

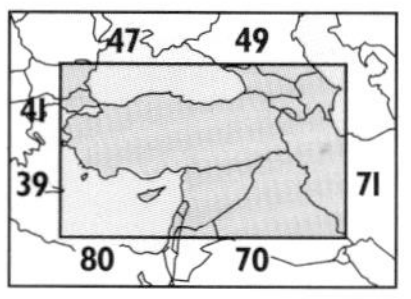

CASPIAN SEA

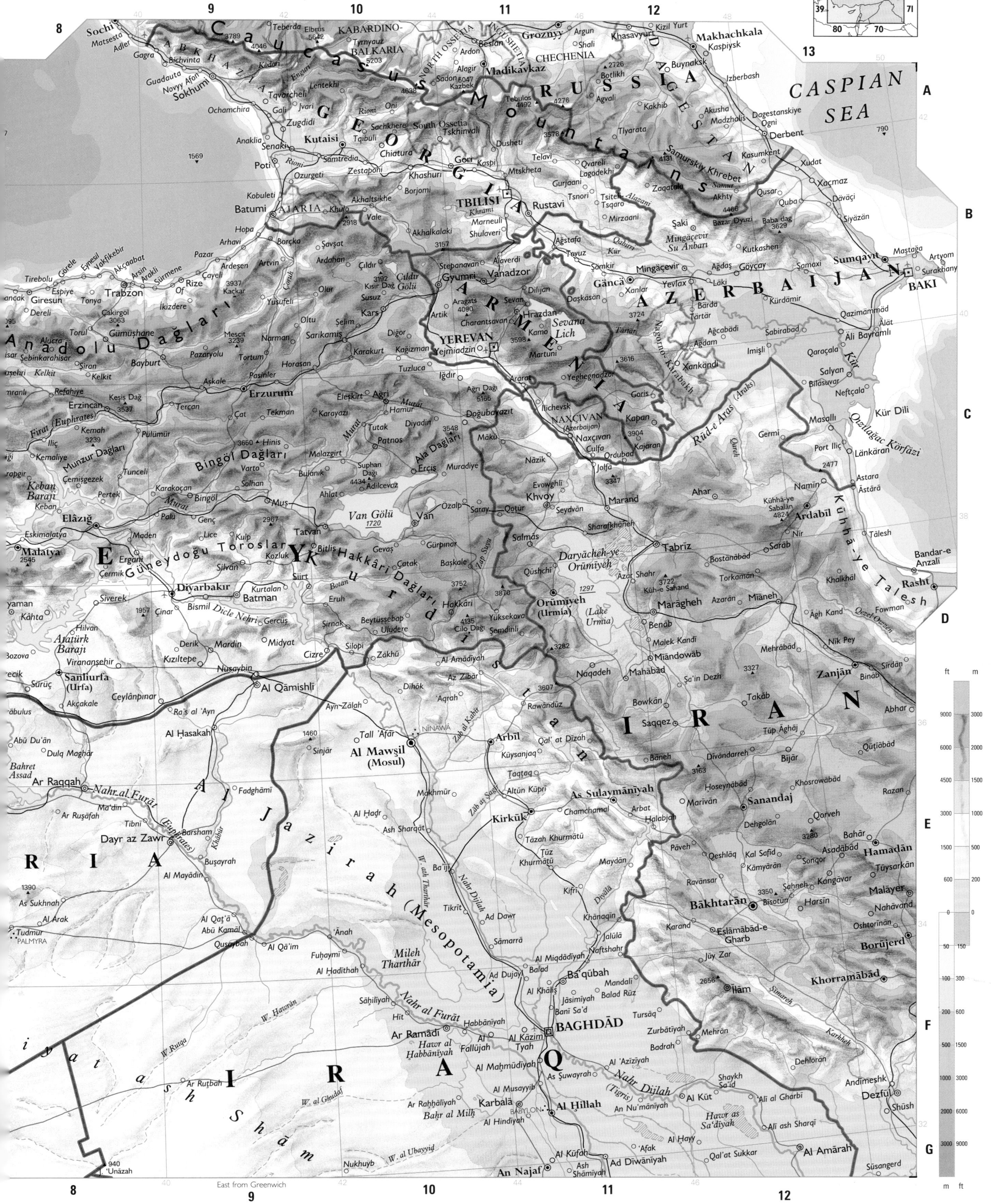

Caucasus Mountains

RUSSIA

KABARDINO-BALKARIA
NORTH OSSETIA
INGUSHETIA
CHECHENIA
DAGESTAN

GEORGIA
ABKHAZIA
AJARIA
South Ossetia

AZERBAIJAN

ARMENIA

NAXÇIVAN (Azerbaijan)

Nagorno-Karabakh

Anadolu Dağları

Güneydoğu Toroslar

Kürdistan

Bingöl Dağları

Munzur Dağları

Hakkâri Dağları

IRAN

Van Gölü 1720

Daryācheh-ye Orūmīyeh (Lake Urmia)

Kühhā-ye Talesh

Kühhā-ye Sabalān 4824

SYRIA

IRAQ

Al Jazīrah (Mesopotamia)

Bādiyat ash Shām

Nahr al Furāt (Euphrates)

Nahr Dijlah (Tigris)

Sochi
Makhachkala
Vladikavkaz
Groznyy
Tbilisi
Batumi
Kutaisi
Sokhumi
Trabzon
Erzurum
Yerevan
Gäncä
BAKI
Sumqayıt
Elâzığ
Diyarbakır
Malatya
Şanlıurfa (Urfa)
Al Mawşil (Mosul)
Arbil
Kirkūk
As Sulaymānīyah
Tabrīz
Orūmīyeh (Urmia)
Marāgheh
Zanjān
Sanandaj
Hamadān
Bākhtarān
Baghdād
Ar Ramādī
Karbalā
Al Hillah
An Najaf
Al Amārah
Dayr az Zawr
Ar Raqqah
Khorramābād
Borūjerd
Dezfūl
Ardabīl
Rasht
Bandar-e Anzalī

East from Greenwich

ft m
9000 3000
6000 2000
4500 1500
3000 1000
1500 500
600 200
0 0
50 150
100 300
200 600
500 1500
1000 3000
2000 6000
3000 9000
m ft

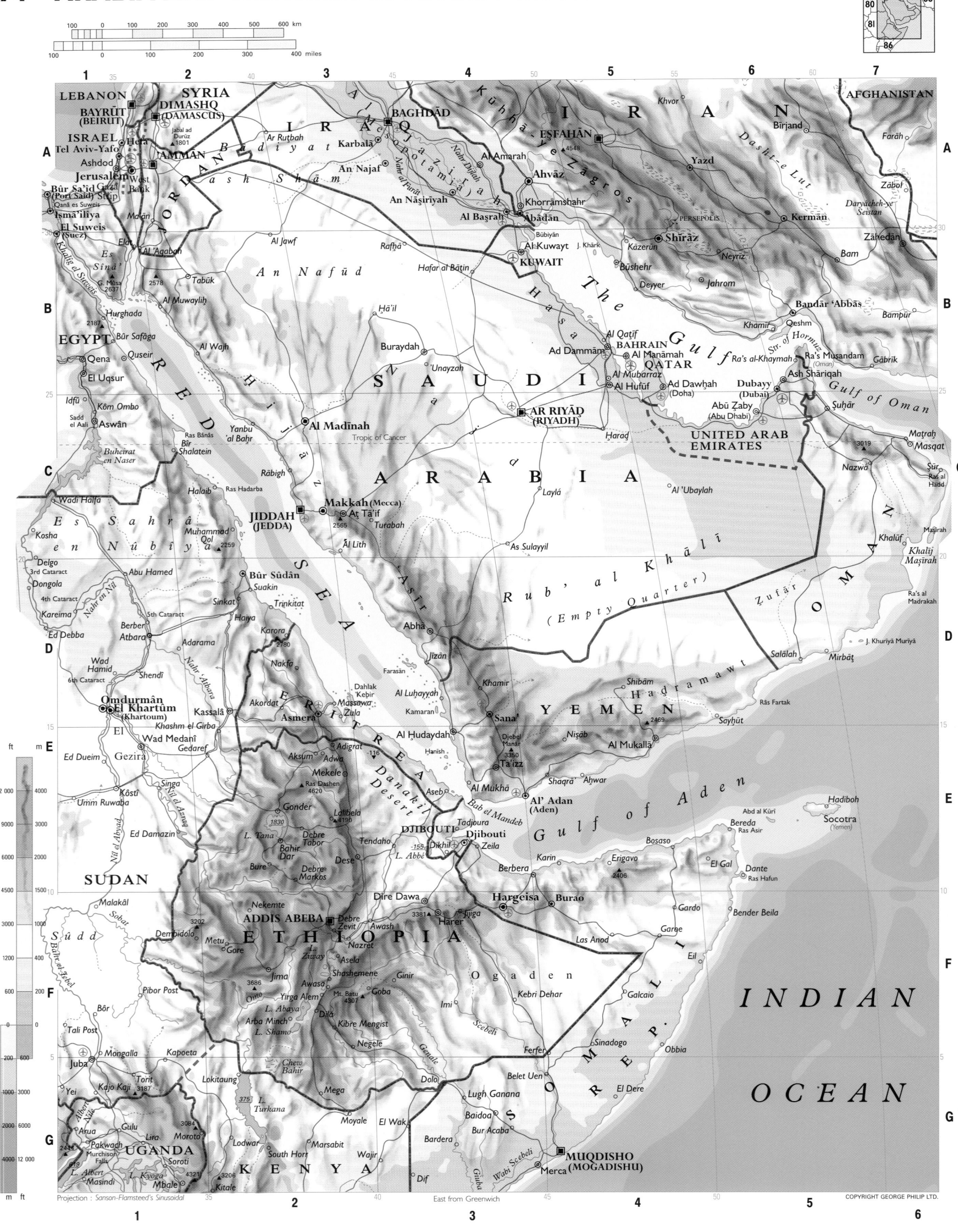

Projection: Polyconic East from Greenwich

1974 Cease Fire Lines

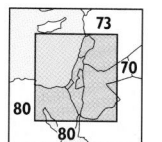

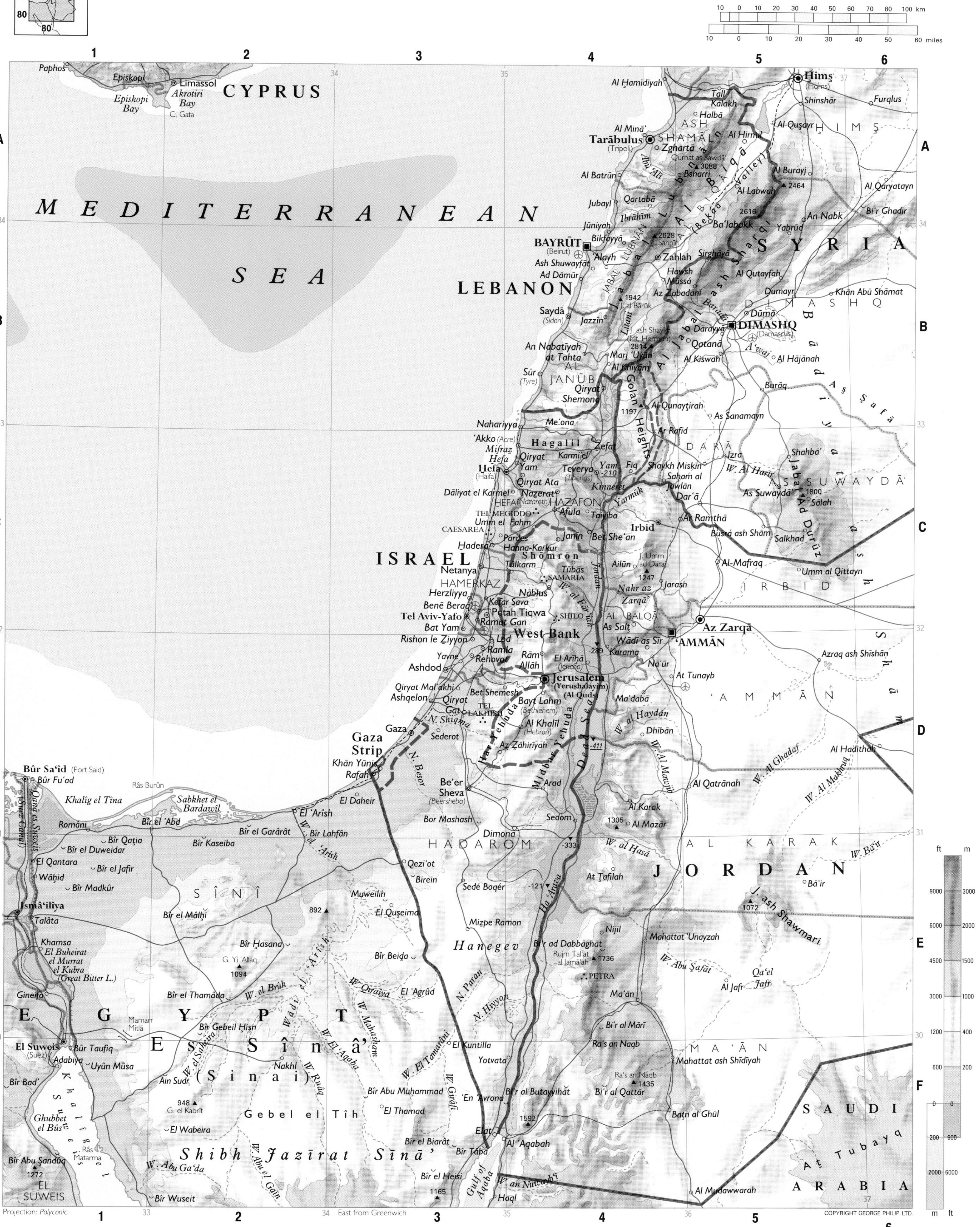

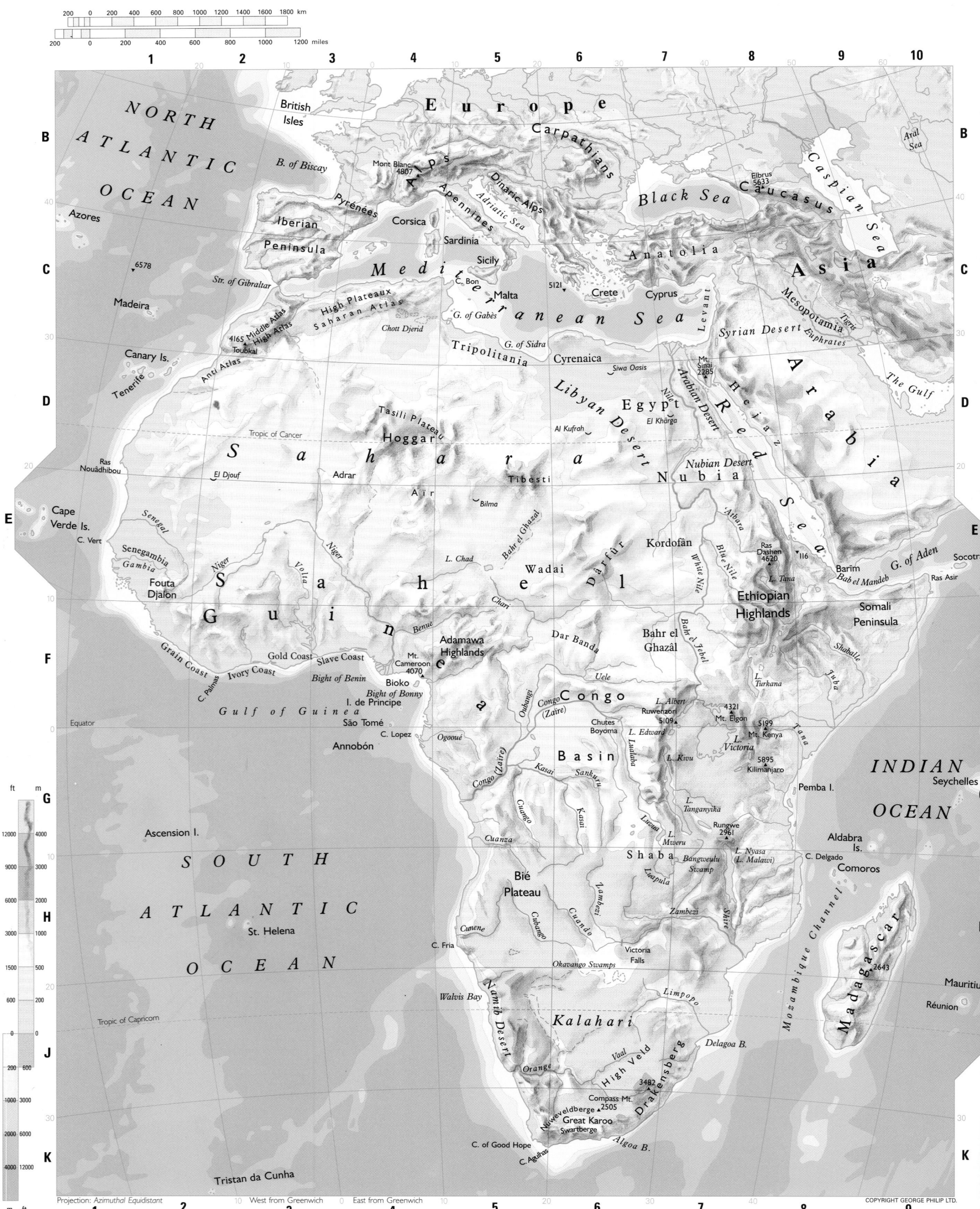

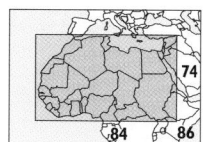

MEDITERRANEAN SEA

GREECE
TURKEY
Antalya · ADANA
CYPRUS · Antakya · **HALAB**
Al Lādhiqiyah · Nicosia
SYRIA
Tarābulus
Ródhos
Iráklion
Kríti

Bizerte · Ariana · **TUNIS** · CARTHAGE
Sicilia
MALTA
Valletta
Nabeul · Sousse
Mahdia
Sfax
Golfe de Gabès
Île de Djerba
Zarzis
Zuwārah · **Tarābulus** (Tripoli)
Az Zāwiyah · Al Khums
Gharyān · Misrātah
Mizdah
968

Him̧s
BAYRÛT (Beirut) · **DIMASHQ** (Damascus)
LEBANON
Jabal ad Durūz
1801
ISRAEL · Haifa · **AMMAN**
Tel Aviv-Yafo · Ar Ruţbah
Ashdod · **Bādiyat**
Qanā es Suweis · **JORDAN** · ash Shām
BUR Sa'id · Jerusalem · West Bank
Dumyât · Ma'ān
El Mansûra · Ismā'iliya
El Mahalla el Kubra · El 'Aqabah
Damanhûr · Al Jawf
Tanta · Es Sinā'
Zagazig · G. Mûsā · 2578 · Tabūk
EL ISKANDARIYA (Alexandria)
Marsá Matrûh · El Alamein · 2637
EL QAHIRA (Cairo)
EL GÎZA · El Suweis
Helwân · Elat · Al Muwayliḥ
El Faiyûm · Hurghada
Beni Suef · Bûr Safâga
Maghâgha · El Wajh
El Minyâ · Es Sahrâ · Esh Sharqiya
Mallawi
Manfalût · Asyût · 2187
Tahta · Bûr Safâga
Sohâg · Quseir
Girga · Qena · Al Wajh
THEBES · KARNAK
Mût · El Khârga · El Uqsur · Ras Bânâs
El Wâhât el-Dakhla · Idfû
El Wâhât el-Khârga · Kom Ombo
Sadd el Aali · Aswân
Buhairat · Bîr Shalatein
en Naser · Râbigh
ABU SIMBEL · Ras Hadarba
Wadi Halfa · Halaib

EGYPT
Sahrâ' Lîbîya
Siwa
-133 · Munkhafed el Qattâra
Al Jaghbûb
Awjilah
Zillah
1200

LIBYA
Hûn
Brach
Sabhah
Awbārī · 1082
Marzûq
Wāw al Kabīr
Al Qaţrūn
Fezzan
Ghat
Toummo
Madama
Bardai · Aozou
Pic Toussidé 3265 · Tarso Emissi 3150
Tibesti
Zouar
Emi Koussi 3415
Ma'tan as Sarra
J. Uweinat 1893

Idehan Awbārī
Chirfa
Daraj
Ghudâmis
Dehibat
Nalut
Derj

Aozou Strip
Borkou
Faya-Largeau
Dépression du Mourdi
Fada · Ennedi
Ounianga Sérir
Zagaoua
Oum Chalouba

Es Sahrâ en Nûbîya
3rd Cataract · Muhammad Qol · 2259
Kosha · **Bûr Sûdân**
Delgo · Suakin
Abu Hamed · Sinkat
Dongola · Trinkitât
Kareima · 4th Cataract
Ed Debba · Berber · Haiya
Atbara · Adarama · Karora · 2760
5th Cataract
Wad Hamid · Shendî · Nakfa
6th Cataract · **ERITREA**
Akordat

SUDAN
Malha · El Wuz
Sodiri · **El Khartûm** (Khartoum)
Omdurmân · Kassalâ
Khashm el Girba
Ed Dueim · **El Gezira** · Wâd Medanî
1954 · Umm Keddada · Gedaref
Al Junaynah · El Fâsher · El Obeid
Kutum · Umm Ruwaba · Kôstî
Zalingei · Nyâlâ · En Nahud · Er Rahad
Jebel Mara 3088 · El Odaiya · Abu Zabad
Goz Beïda · Kâdugli · Ed Damazin
1325 · Gonder · 1830
Darfûr · Kordofân
L. Tana
Bahîr Dar · Bure
Malakâl · Debre Markos
Birao · Songo · 3202
Bahr el Arab · Nekemte
ETHIOPIA
Sa'id Bundas · Bahr el Ghazâl · Dembidolo
1226 · **Bahr el Sudd** · Metu · Gore
Raga · Gogrïal · Wâw · Jima
Ghazâl · Tonj · Rumbek · 3686
Kaga Bandoro · Yalinga · Bôr
Toinya · Tali Post · L. Abaya
Amadi · Mongalla · Arba Minch · L. Shamo
CENTRAL AFRICAN REPUBLIC
Bambari · Ippy · Bakouma · Obo
Bangassou · **El Istiwâ'iya** · Juba
Sibut · Kapoeta
Bossembélé · Bomu · Yâmbió · Kajo Kaji · 3187
Banguî · Uele · Torit · Lokitaung
Zongo · Mobaye · Yei · L. Turkana
Mobayi · Ango · Chew Bahir
Bondo · Dungu · Faradje · 375

CHAD
Nguigmi · Zigey
Mao · Lac Tchad
Bosso · Bahr el Ghazal
Moussoro
Ati · Biltine
Massakory · Abéché
Ndjamena · Oum Hadjer · Mongo
Kousseri · Massenya · Am Timan
Bokoro · Abou-Deïa
Chari · Laï · Sarh
Bongor · Koumra · Ndélé
Pala · Doba
Moundou
Bétaré Oya · Bouar
Baïbokoum · Bozoum
Ngaoundéré · Paoua · Bossangoa
Banyo
CAMEROON
Maïduguri · Potiskum · Bama · Bajoga · Biu
Garoua · Guider · Maroua · Mubi · Kumo
Yola · Numan · Gashaka
Ngaoundéré
Yaoundé · Abong-Mbang · Bertoua · Batouri
Nanga-Eboko · Mbaïki · Berbérati · Carnot
Yoko · Banyo

NIGER
Fachi · Bilma
Grand Erg du Bilma
Gashua · Geidam · Maïduguri

RED SEA
SAUDI ARABIA
Al Jawf · Tabūk
Yanbu 'al Bahr
Ḩijâz

IRAQ

COPYRIGHT GEORGE PHILIP LTD.

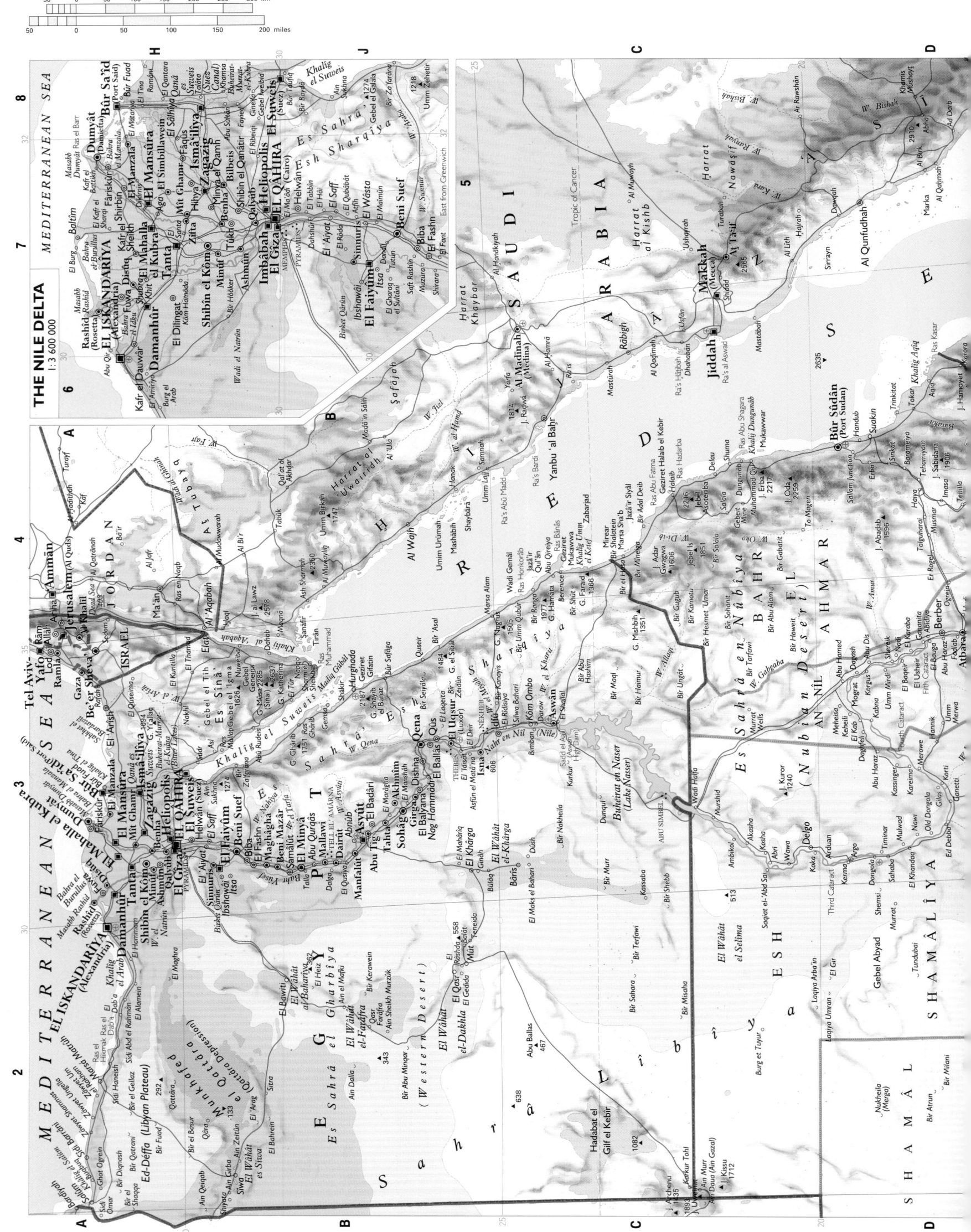

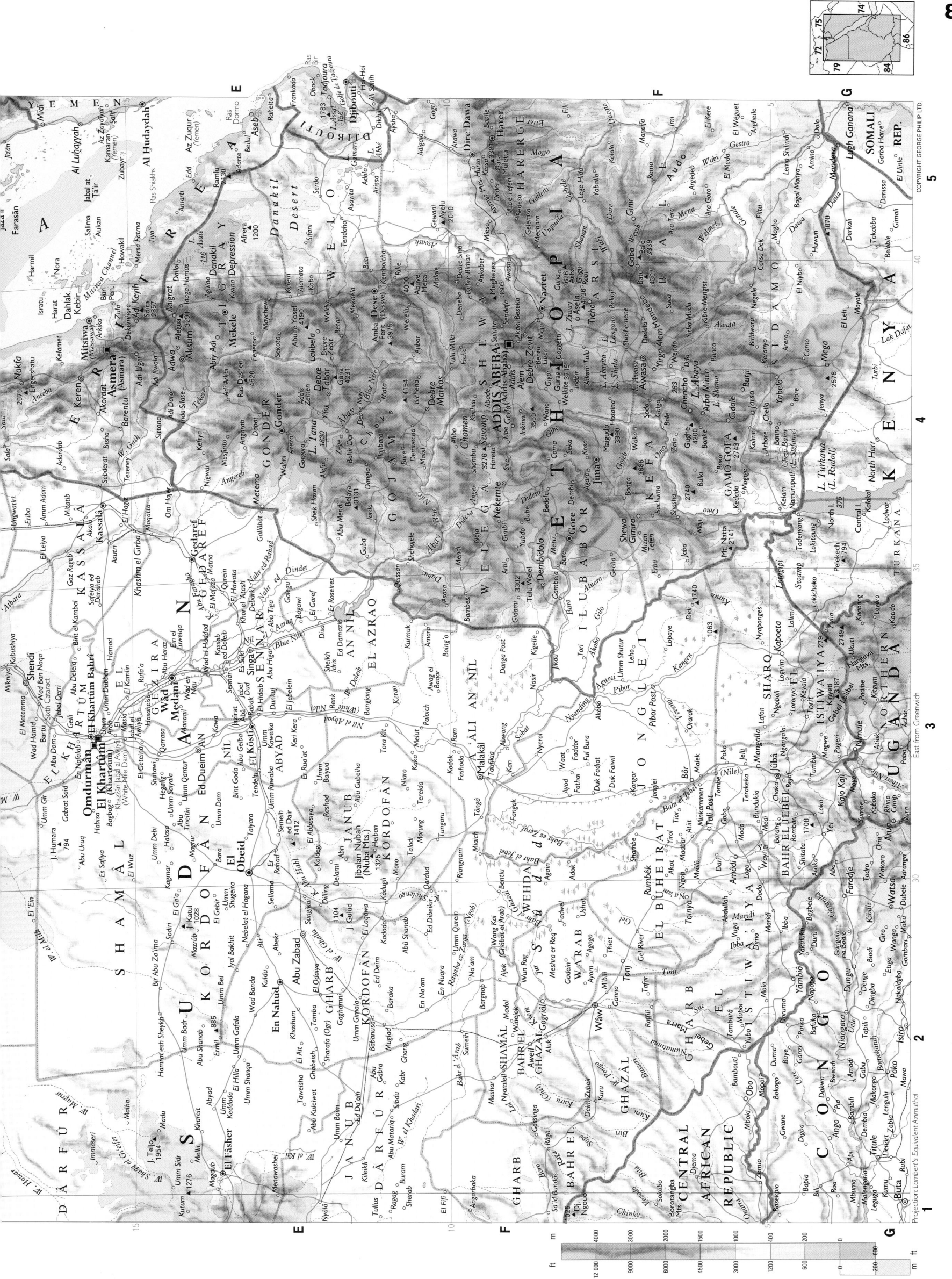

East from Greenwich

Projection: Lambert's Equivalent Azimuthal

Projection : Lambert's Equivalent Azimuthal

West from Greer

78
79
84
84

4
5
6
7
A
B
C
D
E
ALGERIA
NIGER
NIGERIA
BENIN
TOGO
GHANA
CAMEROON
CHAD
EQUATORIAL GUINEA
Adrar des Iforas
Aïr
Talak (Azbine)
Ténéré
Massif de Terazit
Monts Bagzane
Agadez (Agadès)
Tahoua
Tillabéri
Manga
Nguigmi
Niamey
Zinder
Maradi
Ouagadougou
Sokoto
Kano
Katsina
Kaduna
Zaria
Jos
Bauchi
Maiduguri
Minna
Abuja
Ilorin
Ogbomosho
Oshogbo
IBADAN
Abeokuta
LAGOS
Porto-Novo
Cotonou
Lomé
ACCRA
Tema
Kumasi
Benin City
Onitsha
Enugu
Port Harcourt
Calabar
DOUALA
Yaoundé
Makurdi
Lafia
Lokoja
Yola
Numan
Bioko
Slave Coast
Bight of Benin
Niger Delta
Bight of Bonny
GULF OF GUINEA
Lake Volta
Lac Tchad
Kainji Res.
N.E. NIGERIA
on same scale as general map
East from Greenwich

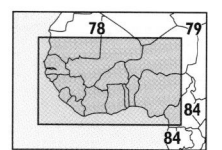

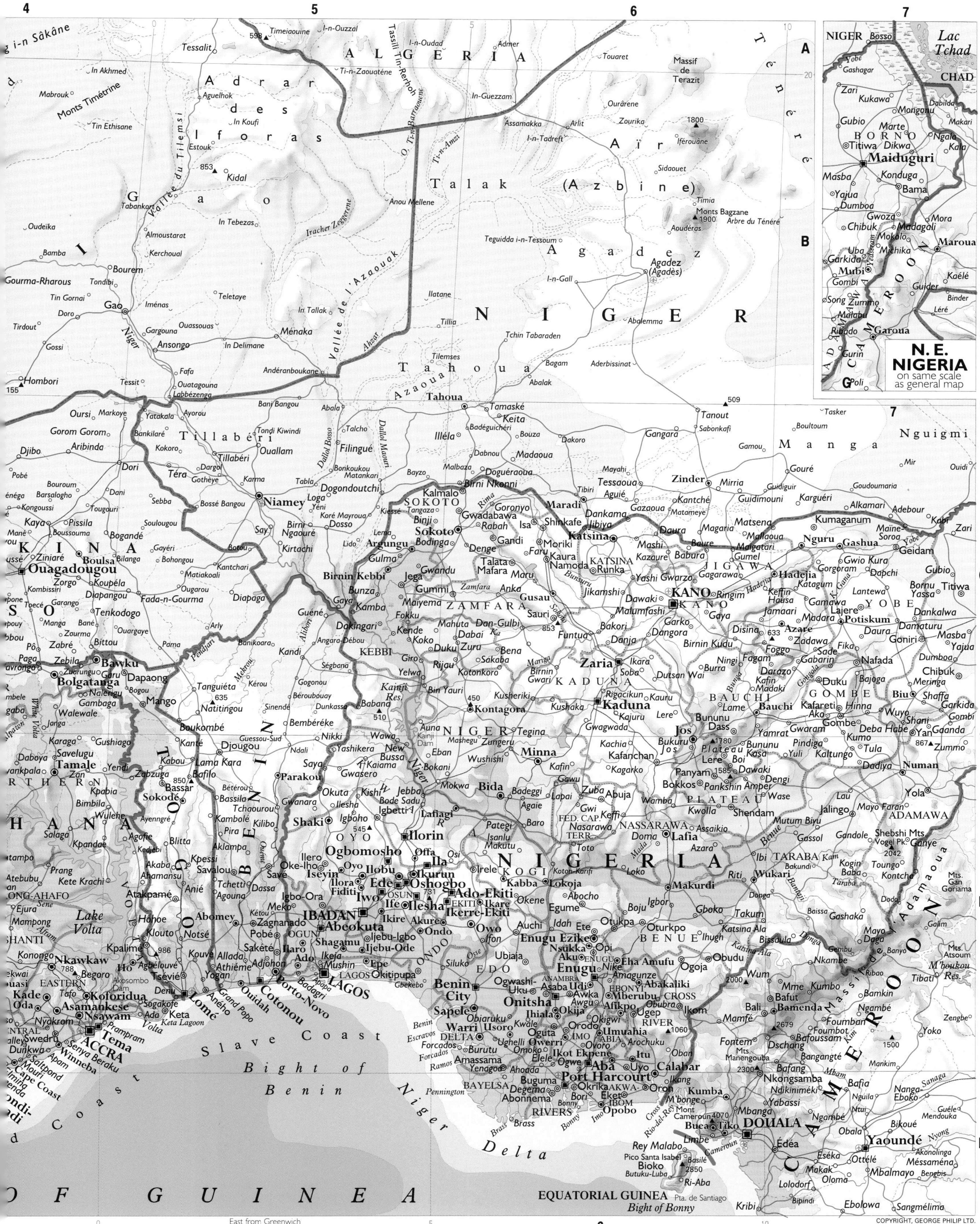

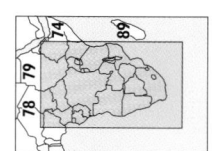

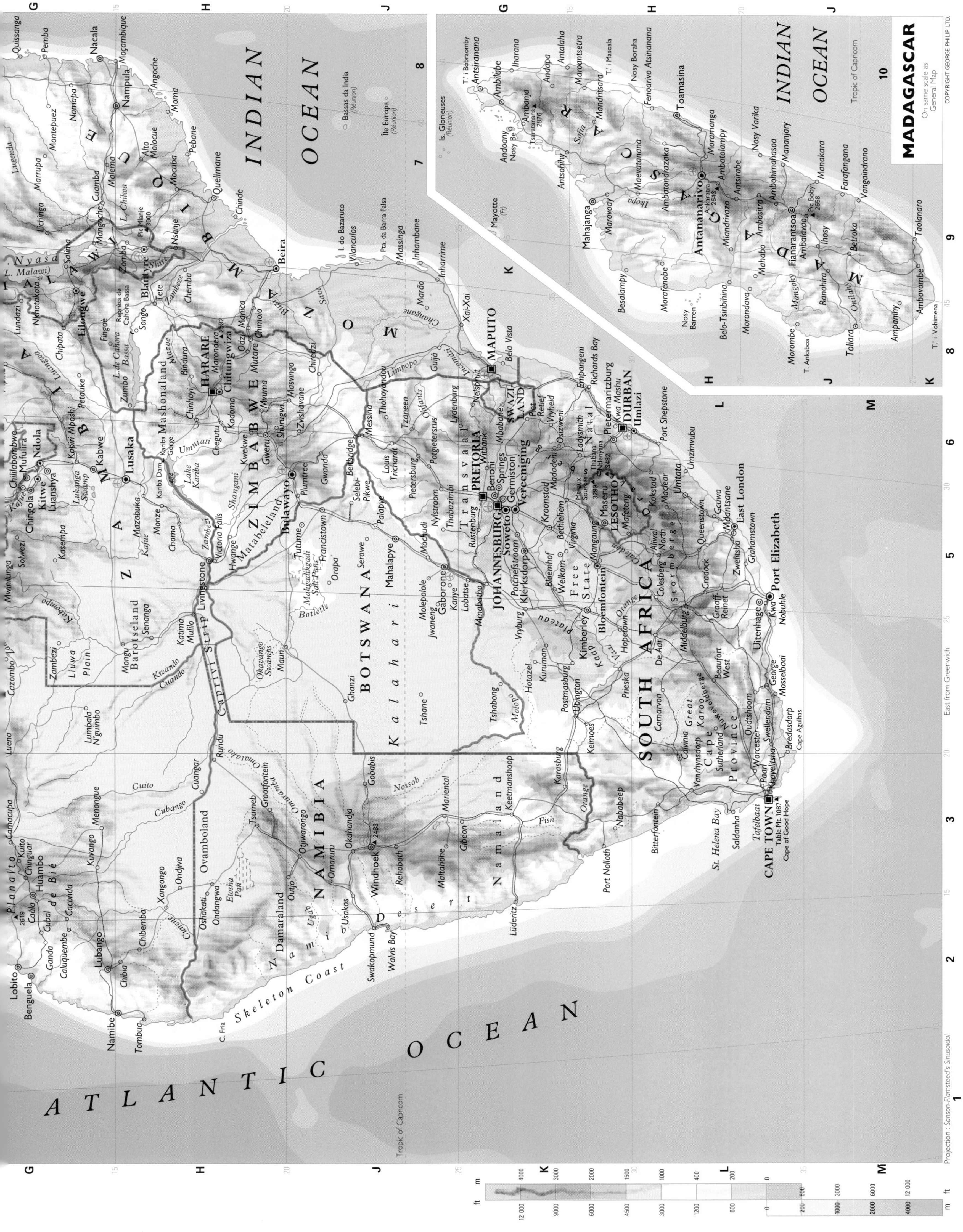

MADAGASCAR
On same scale as General Map
COPYRIGHT GEORGE PHILIP LTD.
ATLANTIC OCEAN
INDIAN OCEAN
SOUTH AFRICA
NAMIBIA
BOTSWANA
ZIMBABWE
ZAMBIA
MOZAMBIQUE
LESOTHO
SWAZILAND
CAPE TOWN
JOHANNESBURG
PRETORIA
MAPUTO
HARARE
DURBAN
Lusaka
Windhoek
Gaborone
Bulawayo
Beira
Port Elizabeth
East London
Bloemfontein
Antananarivo
Tropic of Capricorn
East from Greenwich
Projection : Sanson-Flamsteed's Sinusoidal

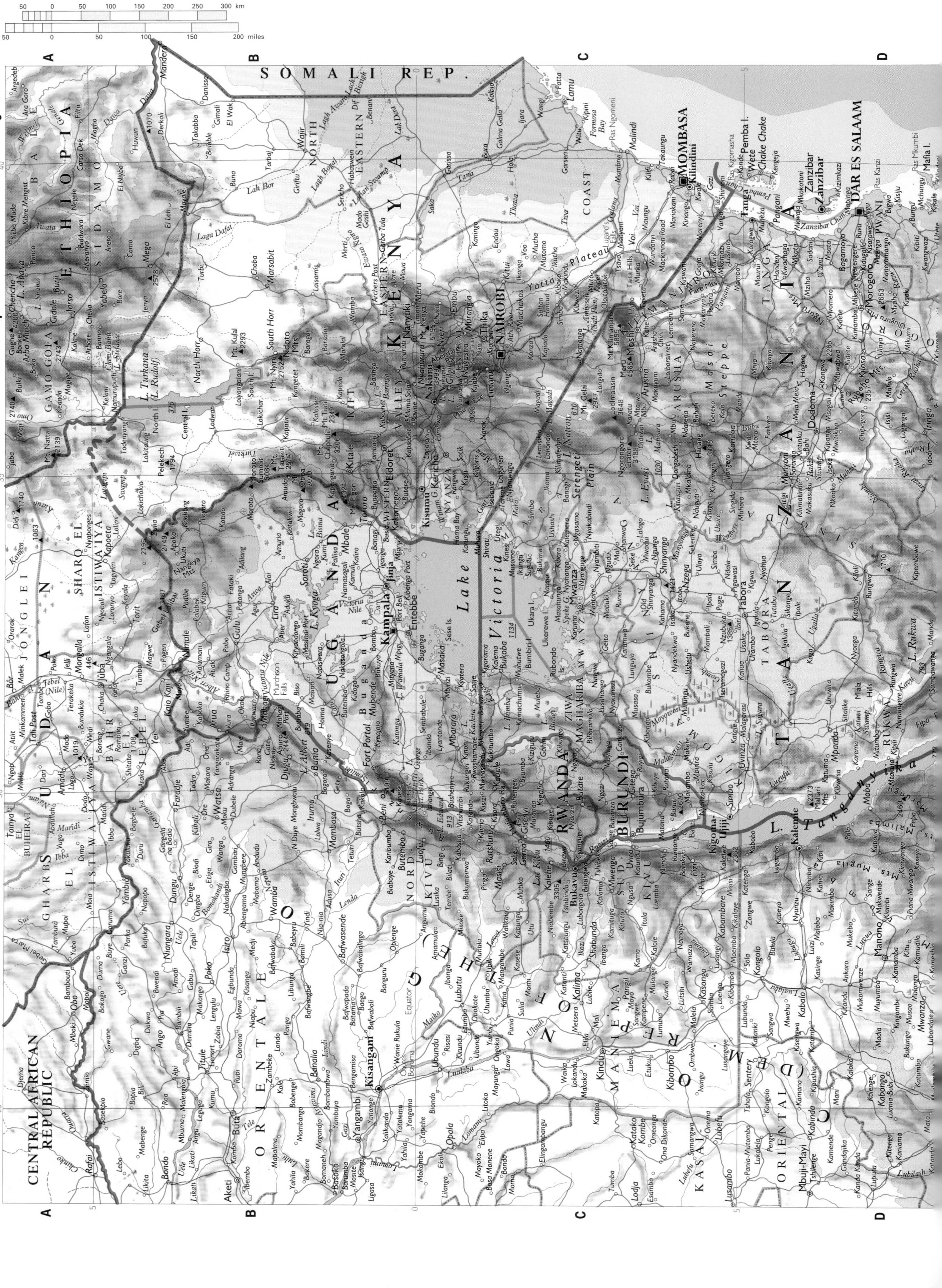

SOMALI REP.

ETHIOPIA

SUDAN

CENTRAL AFRICAN REPUBLIC

UGANDA

KENYA

NAIROBI

Kampala
Entebbe
Jinja

MOMBASA

Zanzibar

DAR ES SALAAM

TANZANIA

Lake Victoria

L. Turkana
(L. Rudolf)

L. Albert

L. Kyoga

L. Tanganyika

RWANDA
BURUNDI
Bujumbura

DEM. REP. (CONGO)

Dodoma
Tabora
Arusha
Tanga
Pemba I.
Mafia I.

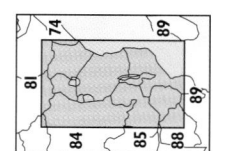

74
89
81
84
85
88
89

INDIAN OCEAN
ZAMBIA
MALAWI
MOZAMBIQUE
ZIMBABWE
BOTSWANA
NAMIBIA
ANGOLA
SOUTH AFRICA
L. Nyasa
L. Malawi
L. Kariba
Zambezi
Limpopo
Lusaka
Harare
Bulawayo
Lilongwe
Blantyre
Beira
Lubumbashi
Ndola
Kitwe
Livingstone
Victoria Falls
Francistown
Quelimane
Nampula
Moçambique
Mtwara-Mikindani
Lindi
Mbeya
Tete
Mutare
Masvingo
Gweru
Kwekwe
Kadoma
Chitungwiza
Messina
Copperbelt
Makgadikgadi Salt Pans
Projection: Lambert's Equivalent Azimuthal
East from Greenwich
COPYRIGHT GEORGE PHILIP LTD.
m
ft
6000
4000
3000
2000
1500
1000
400
200
0
18 000
12 000
9000
6000
4500
3000
1200
600
0
200–600
600–6000
2000–6000

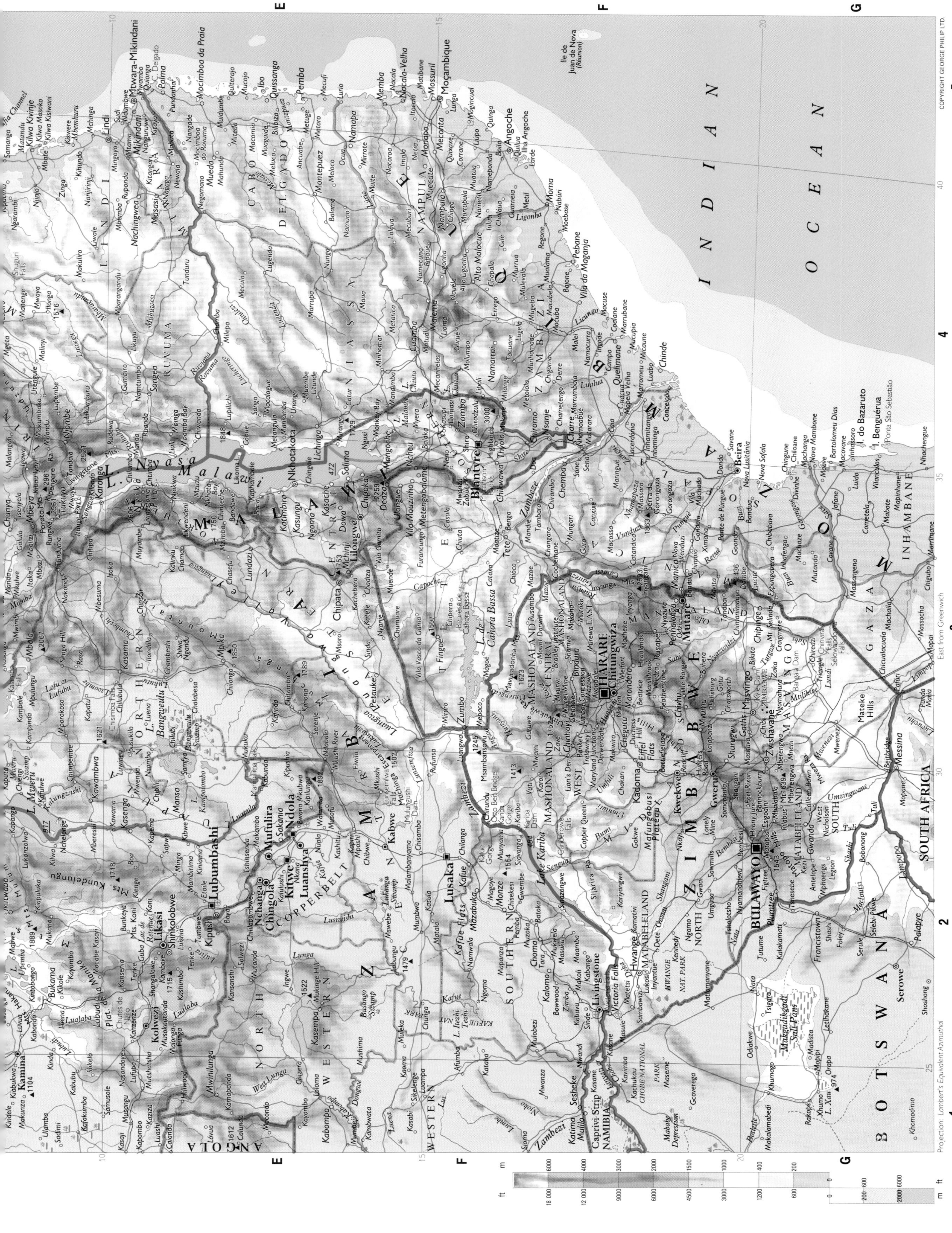

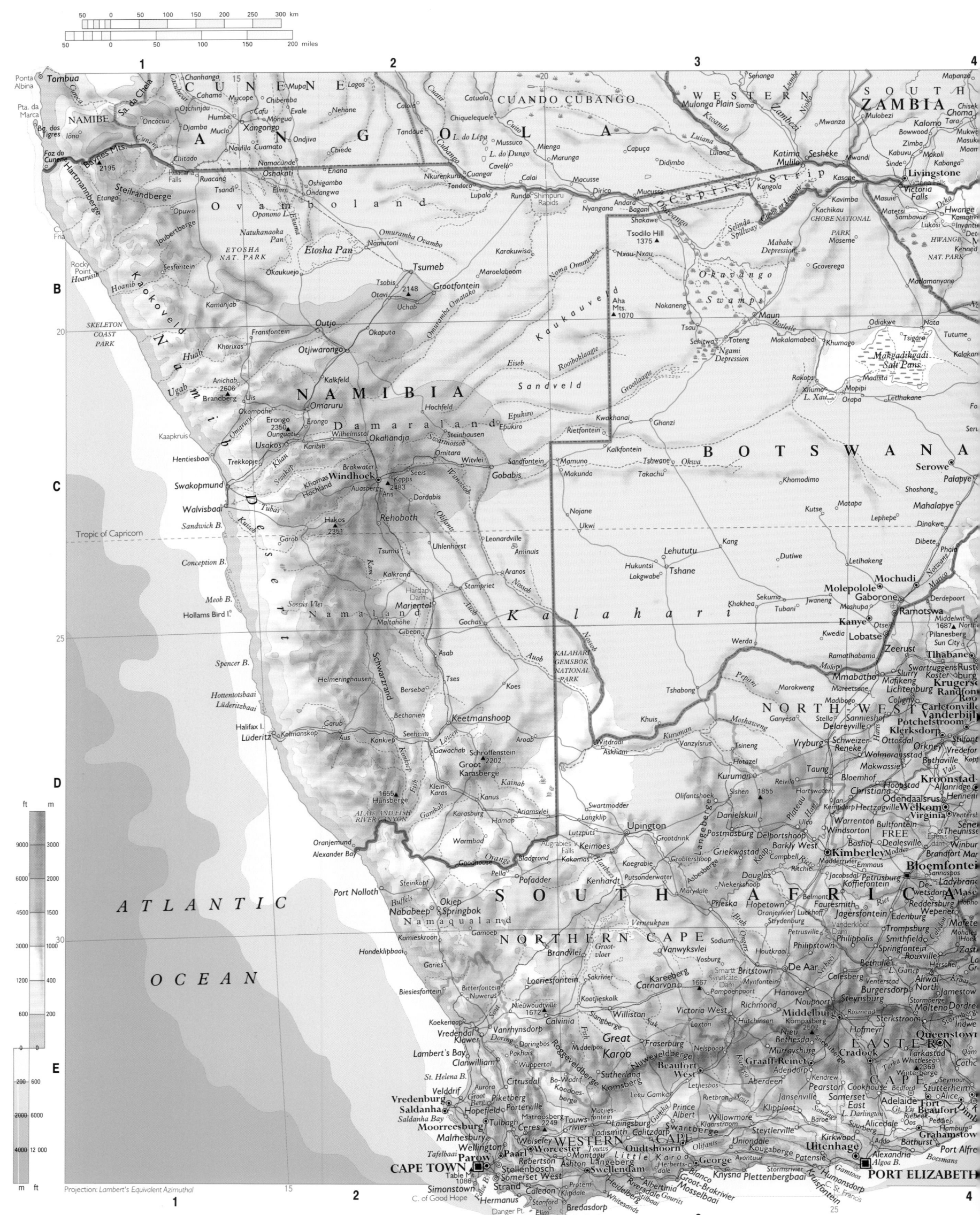

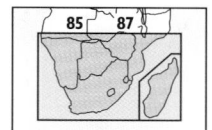

MADAGASCAR
On same scale as General Map

COPYRIGHT GEORGE PHILIP LTD.

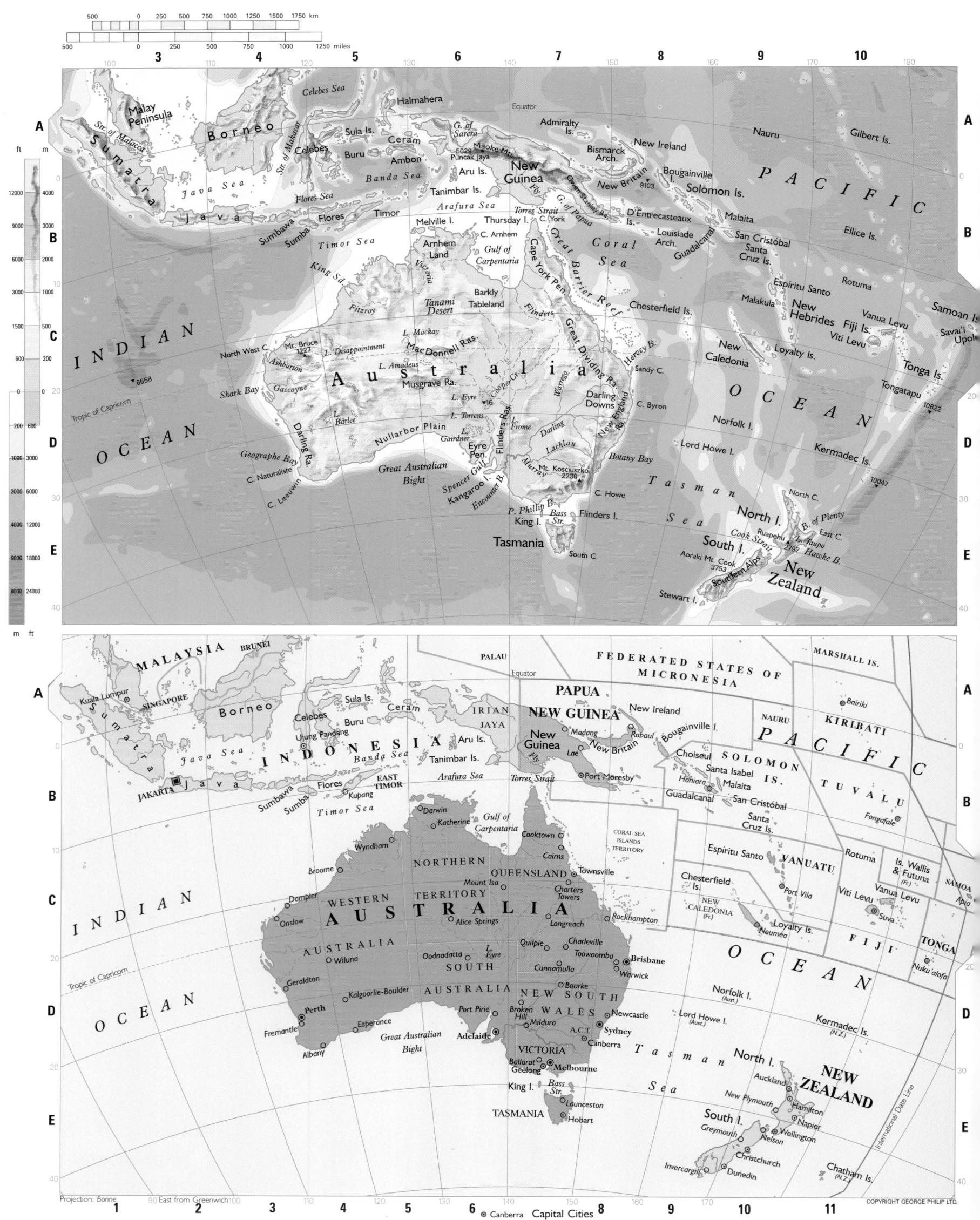

Projection: Bonne

⊙ Canberra Capital Cities

COPYRIGHT GEORGE PHILIP LTD.

96
96   96
96

50   0   50   100   150   200 km
50   0   50   100   150 miles

1   **2**   **3**   **4**   **5**   **6**   **7**

34

C. Reinga
C. Maria
van Diemen
North C.
Rangaunu B.
Houhora Heads
Doubless B.
Mongonui
Whangaroa Harb.
F
Ahipara B.
Kaitaia
Kaikohe
B. of Islands
Tauroa Pt.
Okaihau
C. Brett
Rawene
Opua
Hokianga Harbour
Hikurangi
Whangarei
Donnelly's Crossing
Whangarei Harb.
Dargaville
Bream Hd.
Waipu
Bream B.

PACIFIC

36

Little
Barrier I.
Warkworth
Great Barrier I.
Helensville
C. Rodney
C. Colville
Cuvier I.
Kaipara Harbour
Hauraki
Gulf
Takapuna
Devonport
Coromandel
Whitianga

OCEAN

North

Manukau
AUCKLAND
Papakura
Thames
Waiuku
Pukekohe
Mercer
Waihi
Mayor I.
Island
Waikato
Paeroa
Tauranga Harb.
Huntly
Te Aroha
Mount
White I.
C. Runaway
Morrinsville
Maunganui
Bay of Plenty
East C.
G
Hamilton
Tauranga
Te Puke
Whakatane
Raglan
Cambridge
Kawerau
Opotiki
Hikurangi
Te Awamutu
Rotorua
Taneatua
1753
Waipiro
Kawhia Harbour
Otorohanga
L. Rotorua
Murupara
Tolaga Bay
Te Kuiti
Kinleith
L. Tarawera
Motu
Tokoroa
Mokai
Wairakei
38
Makau
Ongarue
Taupo
Gisborne
North Taranaki
Mokau
Taumarunui
L. Taupo
Waikaremoana
Poverty Bay
Bight
Waitara
Turangi
Tarawera
Nuhaka
Waikokopu
New Plymouth
Whangamomona
Ormond
Inglewood
Ruapehu 2797
Waiouru
Mahia Pen.
Mt. Taranaki
Stratford
Ohakune
H
(Mt. Egmont)
2518
Eltham
Raetihi
Waiou
Bay
C. Egmont
Opunake
Kapuni
Taihape
View
Hawke Bay
Hawera
Waverley
Mangaweka
Napier
South Taranaki
Hunterville
Hastings
Bight
Wanganui
Marton
Waipawa
C. Kidnappers
40
Halcombe
Feilding
Waipukurau
Bulls
Danevirke
Palmerston
Foxton
Woodville
North
Shannon
Pahiatua
C. Turnagain
C. Farewell
Levin
Eketahuna
Paraparaumu
Otaki
Collingwood
Golden
Masterton
B.
D'Urville I.
Kapiti I.
Takaka
Tasman
Featherston
Carterton
Tasman
B.
Upper Hutt
Greytown
J
Mts.
Motueka
Petone
Martinborough
Karamea
Nelson
Lower Hutt
Karamea
Richmond
WELLINGTON
Bight
Havelock
Picton
Seddonville
Wakefield
Granity
Blenheim
Cook
Westport
Lyell
Murchison
Seddon
Ward
L.
Str.
Rotoroa
Inangahua
2885 Tapuaenuku
Reefton
Mt. Travers 2338
42
Blackball
Spenser
Kaikoura
Runanga
Mts.
Hanmer
Greymouth
Springs
Kaikoura
Kumara
Waiau
Hokitika
L. Brunner
South
Ross
Jacksons
Culverden
Island
Abut Hd.
Hurunui
Waikari
Waipara
Arthur's
Amberley
Rangiora
Pass
Kaiapoi
Pegasus Bay
Coleridge
New Brighton
Springfield
Christchurch
K
Whitecliffs
Methven
Riccarton
Lincoln
Lyttelton
Aoraki Mt. Cook
Staveley
Banks Pen.
3753
Akaroa
Jackson B.
Little River
Okuru
Mount
Cook
44
Mt.
Tekapo
Aspiring
Fairlie
3027
Ashburton Bight
Mt.
Temuka
Earnslaw
L. Ohau
St.
2818
Wanaka
Andrews
Milford Sd.
Arrowtown
Kurow
Waimate
Sutherland Falls
Bligh Sound
Cromwell
Tokarahi
Ngapara
George Sound
Queenstown
Naseby
Oamaru
Clyde
Maheno
Secretary I.
Alexandra
Hampden
Doubtful Sd.
Roxburgh
Dunback
Palmerston
L
Port Chalmers
Otago Harbour
Edievale
Lawrence
Fairfield
Resolution I.
Kelso
Saunders C.
Dusky Sd.
Tapanui
Milton
Breaksea Sd.
Southland
Clinton
Balclutha
Clifden
Ohai
Gore
Kaitangata
Tuatapere
Nightcaps
Mataura
Nugget Pt.
Te Waewae B.
Winton
Wyndham
Orepuki
Riverton
Invercargill
46
Bluff
Tahakopa
Owaka
South Invercargill
Foveaux Str.
Halfmoon Bay
M
Stewart I.
Southwest C.
Port Pegasus

Projection : Conical with two standard parallels
East from Greenwich
COPYRIGHT GEORGE PHILIP LTD.

TASMAN

SEA

Southern Alps

South

Island

Westland Bight

SAMOA ISLANDS
1:10 700 000

AMERICAN
SAMOA
SAMOA
Savai'i
Apia
Upolu
Pago Pago
Tutuila
West from
Greenwich
12   **13**   **14**

8   **9**   Futuna **10**   **11**
Wallis & Futuna (Fr.)
Niuafo'ou
(Tonga)
Thikombia
Labasa
Yasawa Group
Vanua Levu
Taveuni
Vanua Balavu
Lautoka
Koro
FIJI
Nandi
1323
Levuka
Ovalau
Viti Levu
Ovalau
Koro Sea
Lakeba
TONGA
Suva
Gau
(Friendly Is.)
Moala
Vava'u
Kandavu
Tofua
Vatoa
Nuku'alofa
FIJI AND TONGA
Tongatapu
ISLANDS
1:10 700 000
50   0   50   100   150   200 km
50   0   50   100   150 miles

ft   m
9000   3000
6000   2000
3000   1000
1200   400
600   200
0
200   600
2000   6000
4000   12000
6000   18000
m   ft

WESTERN AUSTRALIA
SOUTH AUSTRALIA
INDIAN OCEAN
SOUTHERN OCEAN
Great Australian Bight
Great Victoria Desert
Nullarbor Plain
Hampton Tableland
PERTH
Fremantle
Kwinana
Rockingham
Mandurah
Bunbury
Busselton
Albany
Esperance
Geraldton
Carnarvon
Kalgoorlie-Boulder
Norseman
Merredin
Northam
Katanning
Ayers Rock 868
Mt. Olga 1069
Peterman Ranges
Musgrave Ranges
Everard Ranges
Archipelago of the Recherche
Shark Bay
Dirk Hartog I.
Houtman Abrolhos
Projection: Bonne
East from Greenwich
COPYRIGHT GEORGE PHILIP LTD.

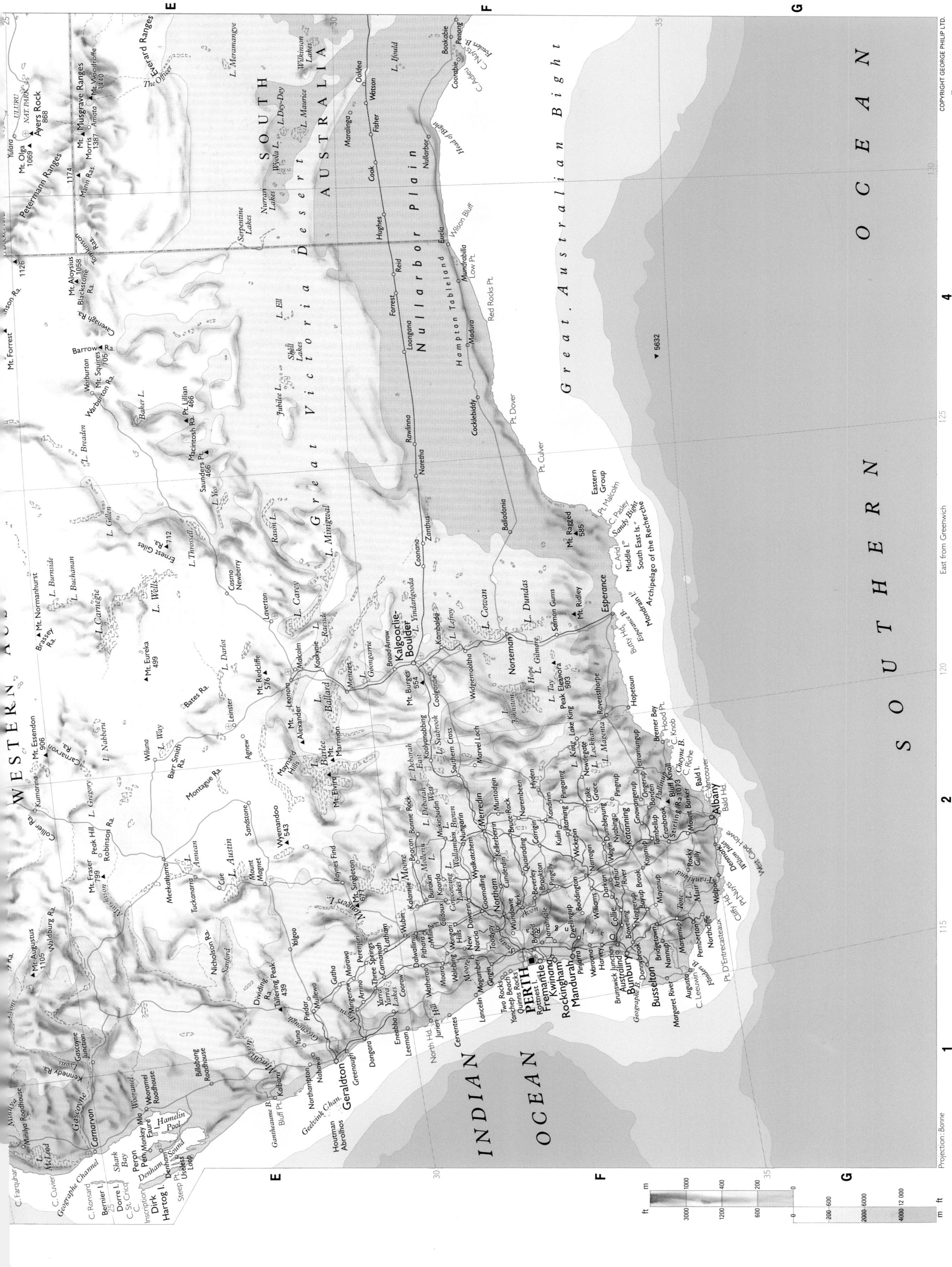

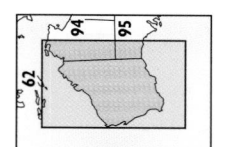

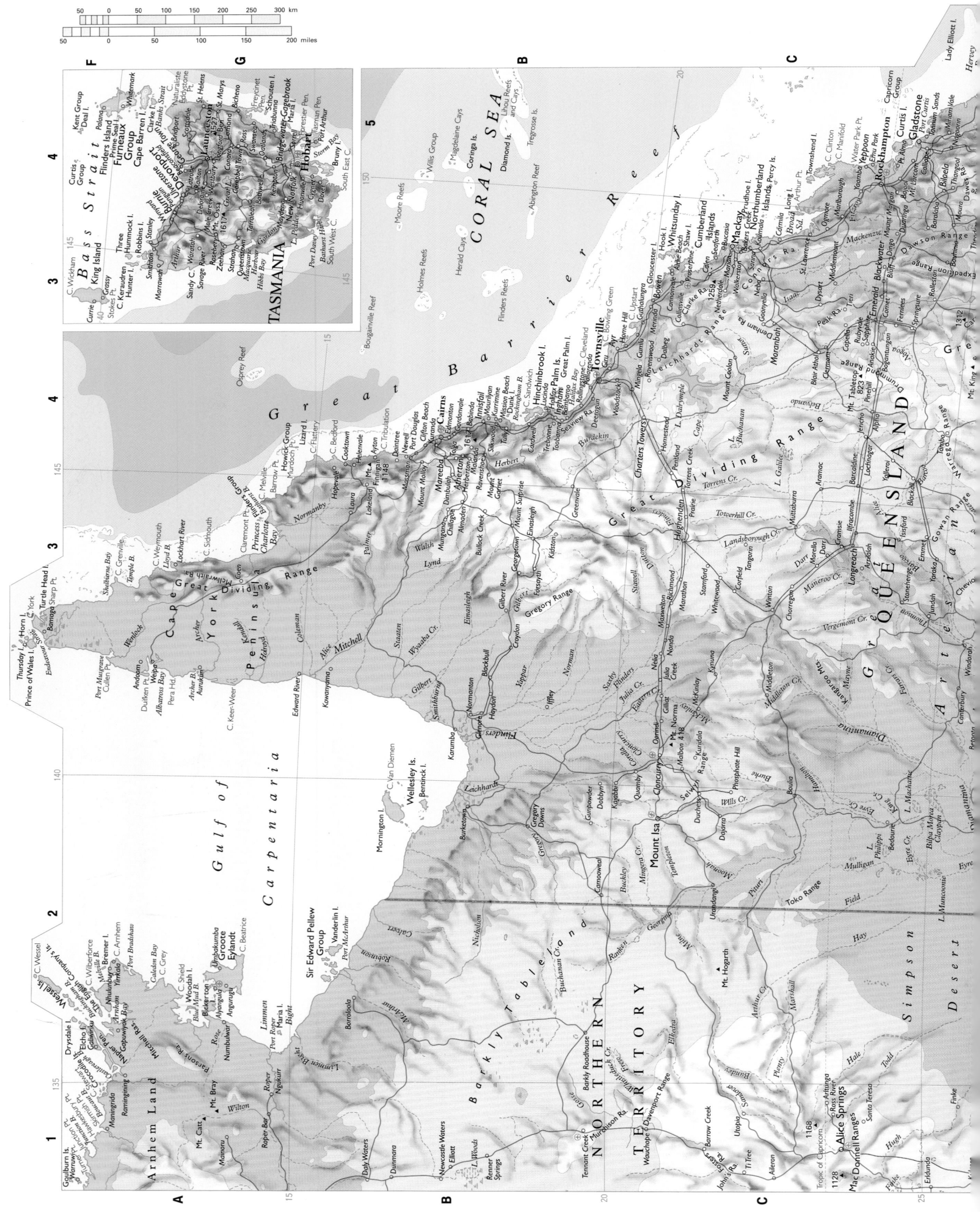

COPYRIGHT. GEORGE PHILIP LTD.

Projection: Bonne

East from Greenwich

RUSSIA

MOSKVA
Yekaterinburg
Tomsk
Novosibirsk
Astana (Aqmola)
Semey
Irkutsk
Oz. Baykal
Chita
Ob'
Lena
Okhotsk
Sea of Okhotsk
Poluostrov Kamchatka
Komandorskiye Ostrova (Russia)
Near Is. (U.S.A.)
Andrea
Be
Se

KAZAKSTAN
Aral Sea
Balqash Köl
Altai
MONGOLIA
Ulaanbaatar
Blagoveshchensk
Amur
Khabarovsk
Sakhalin
Petropavlovsk-Kamchatskiy
7822
Aleuti
Aleutian Trench

Almaty
Ürümqi
Toshkent
KYRGYZSTAN
TAJIKISTAN
CHINA
SHENYANG
Changchun
Harbin
Vladivostok
Hakodate
Sapporo
La Perouse Str.
Kurilskiye Ostrova (Russia)
Kuril Trench
10,542
Emperor Seamount Chain

BEIJING
TIANJIN
Taiyuan
Huang He
Dalian
NORTH KOREA
SÕUL
SOUTH KOREA
Sea of Japan
Sendai
Fuji-San 3776
TOKYO
Nagoya
Kyõto
Osaka JAPAN
Yokohama
Shikoku
Kyūshū
Japan Trench
10,554
Ogasawara Gunto (Japan)
South Honshu Ridge
Midway Is. (U.S.A.)
Lisianski I. (U.S.A.)

AFGHANISTAN
Kabul
Srinagar
PAKISTAN
Lahore
DELHI
Kanpur
Lhasa
Kunlun Shan
XIZANG
Lanzhou
Xi'an
CHONGQING
Nanjing
Wuhan
Chang
Chengdu
Changsha
HANGZHOU
Qingdao
Yellow Sea
Kitakyūshū
SHANGHAI
East China Sea
Himalaya
NEPAL
Mt. Everest 8850
Ganga
Brahmaputra
Kazan-Rettõ (Japan)
Minami-Tori-Shima (Japan)
Marcus
Necker
Wake I. (U.S.A.)

Hyderabad
KOLKATA (Calcutta)
DHAKA
BANGLADESH
Mandalay
BURMA
Kunming
Fuzhou
GUANGZHOU
HONG KONG
Macau
TAIWAN
Taipei
Ryūkyū-rettõ (Japan)
Hanoi
LAOS
Hainan
INDIA
Irrawaddy
Salween
Mekong

Bay of Bengal
Rangoon
THAILAND
CHENNAI (Madras)
Andaman Is. (India)
CAMBODIA
Phnom Penh
VIETNAM
Thanh Pho Ho Chi Minh
C. Engano
Luzon
Paracel Is.
MANILA
PHILIPPINES
Samar
Mindoro
Palawan
South China Sea
G. of Thailand
BANGKOK
NORTHERN MARIANAS (U.S.A.)
Saipan
GUAM (U.S.A.)
11,022
Mariana Trench
MARSHALL IS.
Bikini Atoll
Enewetak Atoll
P
A

SRI LANKA
Colombo
Nicobar Is. (India)
Kuala Lumpur
MALAYSIA
Sulu Sea
Mindanao
4101
SABAH
BRUNEI
Celebes Sea
Maluku
Mindanao Trench
10,497
Yap
Koror
PALAU
Caroline Is.
Truk
Micronesia
FEDERATED STATES OF MICRONESIA
Pohnpei
Palikir
Jaluit I.
Dalap-Uliga-Darrit
Butaritari
Howland I.
Baker
O
K

SINGAPORE
Borneo
SARAWAK
PEN. MALAYSIA
Sumatera
Palembang
Java Sea
Ujung Pandang
Sulawesi
Buru
Seram
Halmahera
Puncak Jaya 5029
IRIAN JAYA
Admiralty Is.
New Guinea
Bismarck Arch.
Rabaul
Bougainville
New Ireland
New Britain
Lae
PAPUA NEW GUINEA
NAURU
Banaba
Tarawa
Gilbert Is.
Melanesia
Micronesia
KI

INDIAN
OCEAN
Cocos Is. (Austral.)
Christmas I. (Austral.)
JAKARTA
Jawa
Surabaya
Bali
Lombok
Sumbawa
Sumba
Flores
Flores Sea
Banda Sea
7440
Timor
EAST TIMOR
Arafura Sea
Torres Strait
C. York
Port Moresby
Honiara
Guadalcanal
SOLOMON IS.
Santa Cruz Is.
9165
Fongafale
TUVALU
Phoenix Is.
Abariri
Enderb
Toke

Selat Sunda
Sunda Islands
Java Trench
Darwin
C. Arnhem
Gulf of Carpentaria
Broome
North West C.
Cairns
Townsville
Mount Isa
Coral Sea
Is. Chesterfield
7570
VANUATU
Espíritu Santo
Port Vila
NEW CALEDONIA (Fr.)
Rotuma
Is. Wallis & Futuna (Fr.)
Vanua Levu
Viti Levu
FIJI
Suva
Nuku'alofa
Is. Loyauté
Nouméa
10,822
Tongo Trench
TON
SAM
Ap

AUSTRALIA
Alice Springs
L. Eyre
Geraldton
Great Dividing Ra.
Darling
Rockhampton
Brisbane
Norfolk I. (Austral.)
Lord Howe I. (Austral.)
Kermadec I. (N.Z.)
Kermadec Trench 10,047

Perth
Great Australian Bight
Albany
Murray
Mt. Kosciuszko 2237
Sydney
Canberra
Adelaide
Melbourne
Bass Str.
Tasmania
Hobart
Lord Howe Rise
Tasman Sea
NEW ZEALAND
Auckland
Wellington
Cook Strait
Christchurch
Chath

Mid-Indian Ridge
Nouvelle Amsterdam (Fr.)
I. St. Paul (Fr.)
Aoraki Mt. Cook 3753
Dunedin
Invercargill
Bounty Is. (N.Z.)
Antipodes Is. (N.Z.)
Auckland Is. (N.Z.)
Campbell I. (N.Z.)
Macquarie Is. (Austral.)

Is. Crozet (Fr.)
Kerguelen (Fr.)
Heard I. (Austral.)

ft	m
12 000	4000
9000	3000
6000	2000
3000	1000
1500	500
600	200
0	0
200	600
1000	3000
2000	6000
4000	12 000
6000	18 000
8000	24 000

m ft

Projection: Mollweide's Homolographic   East from Greenwich

Arctic Circle
160 140

ALASKA
(U.S.A.)
Anchorage
5959
Bristol Bay
Juneau
Gulf of Alaska
S. (U.S.A.)

15

16 17 18 19 20
120 100 80 60 40 20

B

R O C K Y C A N A D A N O R T H

Prince of Wales I.
(U.S.A.) Prince Rupert
Queen Charlotte Is.
(Canada)

Edmonton
Calgary
L. Winnipeg
Regina
Winnipeg
Newfoundland

Vancouver
Vancouver I.
Victoria
Seattle
Portland
Boise
Snake
50
St. Lawrence
Québec
Montréal
Ottawa
L. Superior
L. Michigan
L. Huron
Toronto
Detroit
L. Ontario
L. Erie
Buffalo
Boston
St. John's

C

C. Mendocino
Salt Lake City
Denver
Minneapolis
CHICAGO
Pittsburgh
NEW YORK CITY
PHILADELPHIA
Baltimore
Washington D.C.

Sacramento
40
Missouri
Kansas City
St. Louis
Cincinnati

SAN FRANCISCO
6741
4418
UNITED STATES
Appalachian Mts.
A T L A N T I C

D

LOS ANGELES
San Diego
Phoenix
Oklahoma City
Memphis
Dallas
Atlanta
C. Hatteras

Guadalupe
(Mex.)
Ciudad Juárez
Houston
San Antonio
Mississippi
Jacksonville
Bermuda
(U.K.)

E

Tropic of Cancer
30
New Orleans
Gulf of Mexico
Monterrey
Miami
Florida Str.
BAHAMAS
Sargasso Sea
O C E A N

HAWAIIAN IS.
(U.S.A.)
Honolulu
Oahu
4205
Hawaii
La Habana
CUBA
West Indies

F

C. San Lucas
20
Guadalajara
MEXICO
5700
Puebla
Mérida
Canal de Yucatán
HAITI
JAMAICA
Kingston
DOMINICAN REP.
9200
PUERTO RICO
(U.S.A.)
Leeward Is.

Is. Revilla Gigedo
(Mex.)
Acapulco
7680
BELIZE
Caribbean Sea
BARBADOS

C I F I C
GUATEMALA
Guatemala
San Salvador
EL SALVADOR
HONDURAS
NICARAGUA
Managua
Barranquilla
San José
Windward Is.
Maracaibo

Palmyra Is.
(U.S.A.)
I. Clipperton
(Fr.)
10
COSTA RICA
Colón
PANAMA
Panamá
Caracas
VENEZUELA

G

Teraina
Tabuaeran
Kiritimati
I. del Coco
(Costa Rica)
Medellín
Bogotá

Jarvis I.
(U.S.A.)
Equator
I. de Malpelo
(Colombia)
Cali
COLOMBIA
0

K I B A T I
Galápagos
(Ecuador)
Quito
ECUADOR
Amazonas

Malden I.
Guayaquil
Iquitos
BRAZIL

H

Starbuck I.
C. Paliñas
10

Tongareva
Caroline I.
Is. Marquises
Trujillo

Pukapuka
Manihiki
Vostok I.
Flint I.
6369
PERU

Suwarrow Is.
Is. de la Société
Papeete
Tahiti
LIMA
Cuzco
L. Titicaca
Nevada Ancohuma
6550

J

FRENCH POLYNESIA
Is. Tuamotu
Arequipa
6866
La Paz
BOLIVIA

Cook Is.
(N.Z.)
Mururoa
Peru-
Arica

Rarotonga
Is. Tubuai
Tropic of Capricorn
Iquique
Chile
20

K

Ducie I.
Antofagasta
PARAGUAY

Pitcairn I.
(U.K.)
Sala-y-Gómez
(Chile)
San Felix
(Chile)
San Ambrosio
(Chile)
8050
Trench
San Miguel
de Tucumán
Asunción

Rapa
I. de Pascua
(Chile)
30
Córdoba
Porto
Alegre

Arch. de
Juan Fernández
(Chile)
Valparaíso
Aconcagua
6960
Rosario
URUGUAY

L

SANTIAGO
BUENOS
AIRES
Montevideo
Río de la Plata

Concepción
ARGENTINA
SOUTH

M

40
ATLANTIC

Chile Rise
6212
OCEAN

N

Pacific-Antarctic Ridge
Punta Arenas
Est. de Magallanes
Falkland Is.
(U.K.)
South Georgia
(U.K.)
Tierra del Fuego
C. de Hornos

160 140 80 60 West from Greenwich 40
COPYRIGHT GEORGE PHILIP LTD.

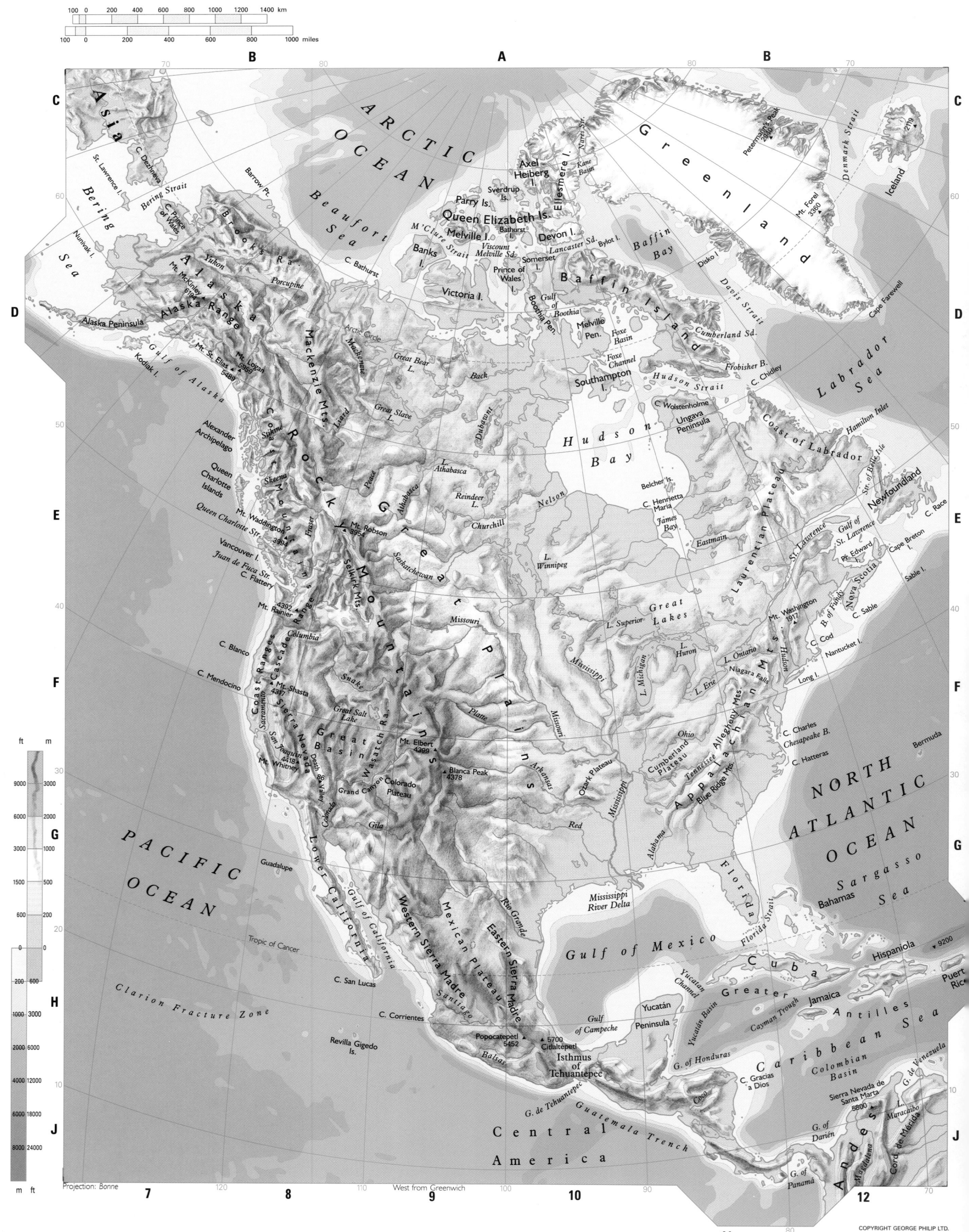

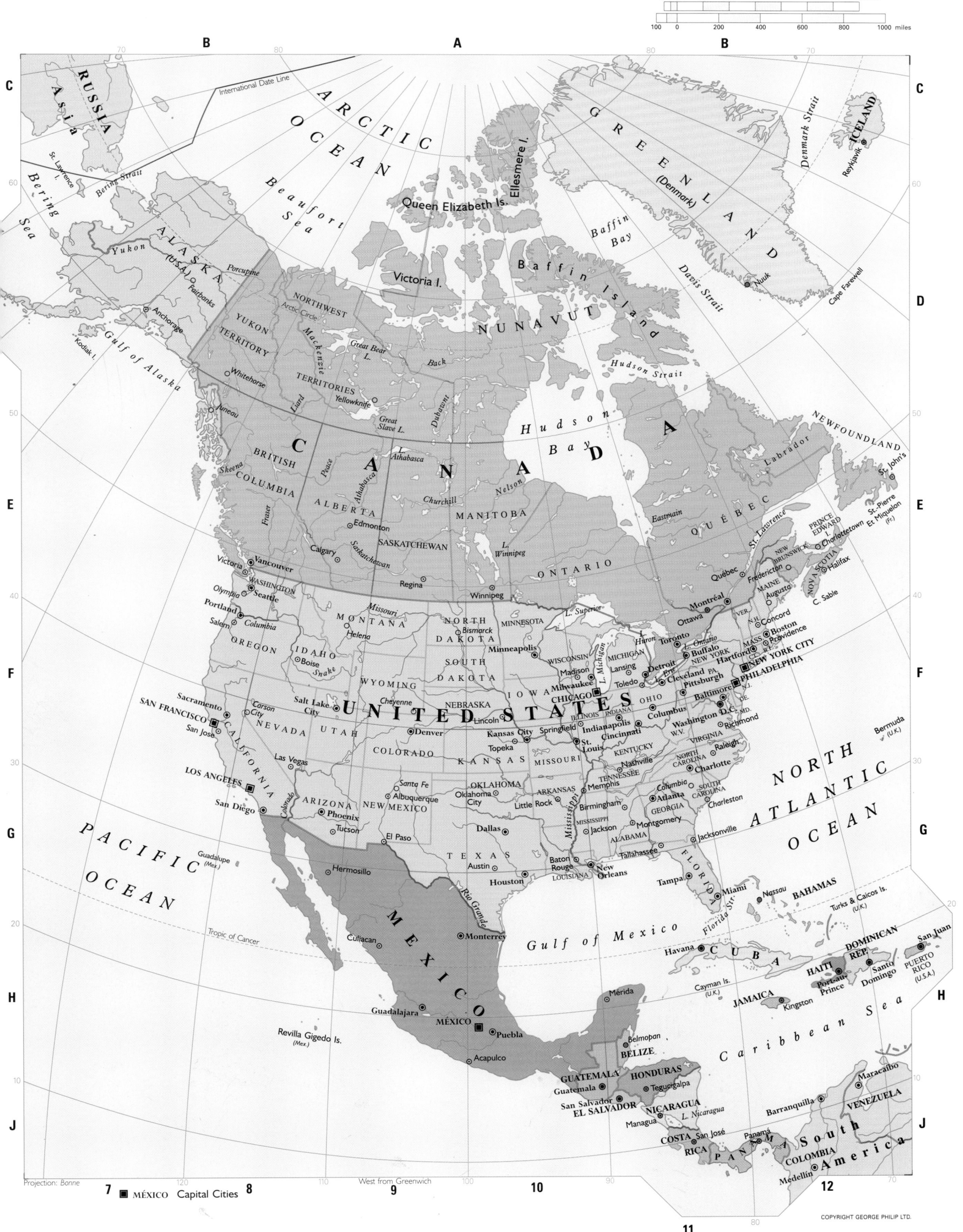

ALASKA 1:26 700 000

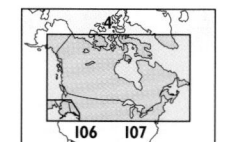

11 12 13 14 15 16

B

Devon I.
Lancaster Sound
Arctic Bay
Nanisivik
Brodeur Borden
Peninsula Pen.
Bylot I.
Eclipse
Pond Inlet
C. Adair
2136
Baffin Bay
Clyde River
C. Raper
Home B.
Qeqertarsuaq
Uummannaq
Nunavik
Upernavik
Uummannaq
Ilulissat
Qasigiannguit
Tunu
Qeqertarsuaq
Tasiilaq

G R E E N L A N D
(KALAALLIT NUNAAT)
(Denmark)

Kong Frederik VI's Kyst
2850

Fury and Hecla Str.
Igloolik
Simpson Sanirajak
Pen.
Pelly
Bay
Committee B.
Melville
Peninsula
Prince
Charles
I.
Air
Force
I.
Foxe
Basin
2591
Cumberland
Peninsula
C. Dyer
Pangnirtung
Hoare B.
Mercy C.
Cumberland Sd.
Sisimiut
Kangerlussuaq
Manitsoq
Nuuk

D a v i s   S t r a i t

Rae Isthmus
Repulse Bay
Circle
Nettilling L.
Foxe
Channel
C. Dorchester
N U N A V U T
Southampton
Salliq
Bell Pen.
Coats I.
Mansel I.
Nottingham
Ivujivik
Salluit
Kangiqsujuaq

Qeqertarsuatsiaat
Paamiut
Arsuk
Qaqortoq
Nanortalik
Uummannarsuaq

A T L A N T I C

C

Meta
Iqaluit
Hall
Peninsula
Incognita
Kimmirut
Frobisher Bay
Peninsula
Resolution I.
Cape Dorset
Amadjuak

H u d s o n   S t r a i t
C. Chidley
Quaqtaq
Akpatok I.
Kangirsuk
Ungava Bay
Kangiqsualujjuaq
1652
Hebron
Nain

L a b r a d o r
S e a
3809

Hudson
Bay
257
Ottawa Is.
Péninsule
Puvirnituq
Arnaud
L. Payne
d'Ungava
Feuilles
Koksoak
Kuujjuaq
George
Baleine
Hopedale
C. Harrison
Rigolet
Cartwright
Port Hope Simpson
Belle Isle

Sleeper Is.
Inukjuak
Str. of Belle Isle
C. Bauld
St. Anthony

King George Is.
Sanikiluaq
Baker's
Dozen
Is.
L. à l'Eau
Claire
L. Bienville
Schefferville
Smallwood
Res.
North West River
Happy Valley-
Goose Bay
Churchill
Falls
Churchill

Belcher Is.
C. Henrietta
Maria
Pte. Louis
XIV
Grande Baleine
Kuujjuarapik
Q U É B E C
Kanaaupscow
La Grande
Petitsikapau
Esker
Labrador
City
Fermont
Ashuanipi
N E W F O U N D L A N D

Peawanuck
Winisk
Chisasibi
Res. de
Caniapiscau
1135
Gagnon
Romaine
Natashquan
St-Augustin
Natashquan
Baie
Verte
Grand
Falls
Lewisporte
Gander
Bonavista

Big
Trout L.
James Bay
Akimiski I.
Wemindji
Eastmain
1190
Manicouagan
Maïcie
Havre-
St-Pierre
I. d'Anticosti
Deer
Lake
Corner Brook
Stephenville
Newfoundland
Trinity B.
Carbonear
St. John's

O N T A R I O
Attawapiskat
Fort Albany
Charlton
I.
Waskaganish
Rupert
Albanel
Res.
Manicouagan
Sept-Îles
Port-Cartier
Gulf of
St. Lawrence
Channel-Port
aux Basques
Ray
North C.
St-Pierre
et MIQUELON
(Fr)
Marystown
Placentia B.
Placentia
C. Race

D

Albany
Moosonee
Albanel
Mistassini
Chibougamau
Baie Comeau
St. Lawrence
Matane
Pén. de Gaspé
Gaspé
Cape Breton I.
Glace Bay

St. Joseph
Nakina
Kenogami
Matagami
Res. Gouin
Roberval
St-Jean
Chicoutimi
Jonquière
Rivière-du-Loup
Edmundston
Campbellton
Bathurst
Miramichi
PR. EDWARD I.
Summerside
Charlottetown
Northumberland Str.
Sydney
Port Hawkesbury
Antigonish
New Glasgow

L.
Nipigon
Geraldton
Kapuskasing
Oba
Abitibi L.
Amos
Val-d'Or
La Tuque
1190
Québec
Lévis
Grand Falls
Woodstock
Fredericton
N E W
B R U N S W I C K
Moncton
Amherst
Truro
Sable I.
(Nova Scotia)

Hearst
Cochrane
Timmins
Kirkland
Lake
Rouyn-
Noranda
New
Liskeard
Res.
Cabonga
Mont-
Laurier
Shawinigan
Trois-Rivières
Joliette
St-Hyacinthe
Thetford
Mines
N O V A   S C O T I A
Saint
John
Kentville
Dartmouth
Halifax

Thunder Bay
Marathon
Chapleau
Wawa
Sudbury
North
Bay
Parry
Sound
L. Nipissing
Pembroke
MONTRÉAL
Hull
Ottawa
Granby
Sherbrooke
M A I N E
Bangor
B. of Fundy
Digby
Bridgewater
Liverpool

Houghton
183
Marquette
Elliot
Lake
Sault Ste.
Marie
Huntsville
Outaouais
Cornwall
Burlington
Montpelier
Augusta
Lewiston
Portland
Yarmouth
C. Sable
6309

Sault Ste.
Marie
Manitoulin I.
Georgian
Bay
Barrie
Peterborough
Kingston
V E R M O N T
N E W
H A M P S H I R E
Concord
Manchester

M I C H I G A N
Manistique
Petoskey
Traverse City
Cadillac
Lake
Huron
Owen Sound
Oshawa
TORONTO
Hamilton
Belleville
L. Ontario
Syracuse
Albany
Springfield
MASS.
BOSTON
C. Cod

Escanaba
Menominee
Green
Bay
Saginaw
Flint
London
Kitchener
Niagara
Falls
Rochester
HARTFORD
CONN.
Providence
R.I.
New Haven

Wausau
WISCONSIN
Appleton
Sheboygan
MILWAUKEE
Madison
Racine
Kenosha
Rockford
Grand
Rapids
Lansing
Sarnia
Windsor
BUFFALO
NEW YORK
Elmira
Binghamton
Bridgeport
New York
Newark
N.J.

CHICAGO
Gary
South Bend
DETROIT
Toledo
CLEVELAND
Erie
Jamestown
Scranton
Allentown
Trenton
NEW YORK
INDIANA
OHIO
PENNSYLVANIA

E

West from Greenwich
COPYRIGHT GEORGE PHILIP LTD.

Projection: Lambert's Equivalent Azimuthal

101
105
112
108

6
7
8
9
A
B
C
D
LABRADOR SEA
NEWFOUNDLAND
Labrador
QUÉBEC
Newfoundland
GULF OF ST. LAWRENCE
ATLANTIC OCEAN
UNITED STATES
MAINE
NEW BRUNSWICK
NOVA SCOTIA
PRINCE EDWARD ISLAND
NEW HAMPSHIRE
Cape Breton Island
Î. d'Anticosti
Dét. de Jacques-Cartier
Dét. d'Honguedo
Cabot Strait
Str. of Belle Isle
Bay of Fundy
Northumberland Str.
ST-PIERRE ET MIQUELON (France)
Smallwood Reservoir
Rés. de Caniapiscau
Rés. Manicouagan
Mealy Mts.
Long Range Mts.
Chic-Chocs
Pén. de Gaspé
St. Lawrence
South Aulatsivik I.
Nain
Paul I.
Voisey B.
Tunungayualok I.
Nunaksaluk I.
Davis Inlet
Hopedale
Kaipokok B.
Aillik
Makkovik
Adlavik Is.
C. Harrison
Postville
Holton
Indian Harbour
Groswater B.
Rigolet
Hamilton Inlet
North River
Cartwright
Table B.
Black Tickle
Island of Ponds
Paradise River
Square Islands
Williams harbour
Charlottetown
Alexis
Port Hope Simpson
Battle Harbour
Lodge Bay
St. Lewis
Mary's Harbour
Red Bay
Belle Isle
L'Anse au Loup
L'Anse aux Meadows
Forteau
St. Anthony
Blanc-Sablon
Rivière St-Paul
St-Augustin
Hare B.
Groais I.
Bell I.
St. Barbe
Roddickton
Englee
Port au Choix
Hawke's Bay
Daniel's Harbour
Harrington Harbour
I. du Petit Mécatina
Horse Is.
C. St. John
La Scie
White B.
Baie Verte
Notre Dame B.
Fogo
Fogo I.
Musgrave Harbour
Twillingate
C. Freels
Jackson's Arm
Springdale
Lewisporte
Wesleyville
Bonavista B.
GROS MORNE NAT. PARK
Rocky Harbour
Norris Point
Trout River
Deer Lake
South Brook
Botwood
Bishop's Falls
Glenwood
Gander
Gambo
C. Bonavista
Bonavista
Catalina
B. of Islands
Pasadena
Corner Brook
Badger
Grand Falls Windsor
Buchans
Glovertown
TERRA NOVA NAT. PARK
Port Blandford
Clarenville
Trinity
Trinity B.
Old Perlican
Conception B.
Port au Port B.
Stephenville
Red Indian L.
Meelpaeg Res.
Victoria L.
Jeddore L.
Heart's Content
Carbonear
Wabana
Torbay
St. John's
Mt. Pearl
Bay Roberts
Whitless Bay
Holyrood
Avalon Peninsula
Ferryland
Trepassey
C. Race
Petit Jardin
C. St. George
St. George's B.
St. George
St. David's
South Branch
Great Codroy
St. Andrew's
C. Ray
Channel-Port aux Basques
Rose Blanche
Isle aux Morts
Burgeo
François
Granite L.
L. Grey
St. Alban's
Terrenceville
Fortune B.
Belleoram
Harbour Breton
Marystown
Grand Bank
Fortune
Burin
Argentia
Placentia
Placentia B.
St. Bride's
St. Mary's B.
C. St. Mary's
St. Lawrence
C. Pine
Miquelon
Langlade
St-Pierre
Fraser
Kogaluk
Mistastin L.
Mistinibi
L. Tudor
Harp L.
Whitegull L.
Kanairiktok
Naskaupi
Seal L.
Nipishish L.
Grand L.
Melville L.
North West River
Goose
Happy Valley-Goose Bay
Eagle
Sandwich B.
Paradise
Churchill Falls
Churchill
Twin Falls
Winokapau L.
Ossokmanuan L.
Minipi L.
Atikonak L.
Little Mecatina
Natashquan
Burnt L.
St-Paul
St-Augustin
Petit Mécatina
Olomane
Musquaro L.
Natashquan
Kegaska
Romaine
Aguanus
Nabisipi
Romaine
Magpie
L. Magpie
St-Jean
L. Manitou
Sheldrake
Havre-St-Pierre
Mingan
Caniapiscau
Baleine
George
L. le Moyne
L. Nachicapau
L. de la Hutte Sauvage
L. Chakonipau
L. Otelnuk
Wheeler
Champdoré
L. Châteauguay
Delay
Sérigny
Caniapiscau
Sable
L. Wakuach
Attikamagen L.
Schefferville
Petitsikapau L.
Menihek
Menihek Lakes
Esker
L. Néret
L. Bermen
L. Dalmas
Nitchequon
L. Nichicun
L. Naococane
Shabogamo L.
L. Opiscoteo
Labrador City
Wabush
Fermont
L. Joseph
Ashuanipi L.
Petit Lac Manicouagan
Gagnon
Moisie
Mouchalagane
L. Plétipi
Ste-Marguerite
Outardes
Manicouagan
L. Manouane
Betsiamites
L. Péribonca
Péribonca
Manouane
Rés. Pipmuacan
L. Walker
Clarke City
Moisie
Sept-Îles
Port-Cartier
Sainte-Anne
Rivière-Pentecôte
Pte. de l'Ouest
Port-Menier
Pte. du Sud-Ouest
Pte. du Sud
Pte. Heath
Godbout
Baie Trinité
Pte. des Monts
Ste-Anne-des-Monts
Mont-Louis
Grande-Vallée
Chute-aux-Outardes
Baie Comeau
Cap-Chat
PARC DE CONSERVATION DE LA GASPÉSIE
Mt. Jacques Cartier
Rivière-au-Renard
C. de Gaspé
Gaspé
Percé
Grande-Rivière
Chandler
Betsiamites
Forestville
Matane
Mont-Joli
Sayabec
Amqui
Rimouski
Les Escoumins
Alma
Chicoutimi
Saguenay
Jonquière
La Baie
Tadoussac
Bic
Trois-Pistoles
Causapscal
New Richmond
Bonaventure
Paspébiac
Miscou I.
Lamèque
Shippegan
Tracadie-Sheila
Caraquet
Chaleur Bay
Campbellton
Atholville
Matapédia
Dalhousie
Bathurst
Lac Bouchette
Petite Saguenay
St-Siméon
La Malbaie
Baie-St-Paul
PARC PROV. GRANDS JARDIN
Rivière-du-Loup
Cabano
Kedgwick
St. Quentin
Dégelis
Edmundston
St. Pascal
La Pocatière
Fort Kent
St-Jean-Port-Joli
Beaupre
Î. d'Orléans
Québec
Lévis
Montmagny
Charny
St-Pamphile
St. Leonard
Grand Falls
Mt. Carleton
Van Buren
Plaster Rock
Eagle Lake
Caribou
Presque Isle
Ashland
Perth-Andover
Neguac
Miramichi B.
Miramichi
Newcastle
Rogersville
Richibucto
Buctouche
St. Antoine
Doaktown
Hartland
Woodstock
Houlton
Patten
Chamberlain L.
Chesuncook L.
Allagash
St. John
Ste-Marie
Beauceville
St-Georges
Plessisville
Thetford Mines
Victoriaville
Asbestos
Lac-Mégantic
East Angus
Sherbrooke
Magog
Coaticook
Moosehead L.
Jackman
Greenville
Millinocket
Lincoln
Dover-Foxcroft
Bingham
Mooselookmeguntic L.
Bangor
Brewer
Skowhegan
Waterville
Ellsworth
Rumford
Augusta
Belfast
Bar Harbor
Mount Desert I.
Camden
Rockland
Berlin
St. Johnsbury
Norway
Auburn
Lewiston
Brunswick
Bath
Conway
Sebago L.
Portland
Laconia
Sanford
Saco
Biddeford
Rochester
Concord
Dover
Portsmouth
Manchester
Nashua
Haverhill
Lawrence
Gloucester
Lowell
Lynn
Newton
BOSTON
Quincy
Brockton
Woonsocket
C. Cod
Minto
Grand L.
Chipman
Fredericton
Oromocto
Fredericton Junc.
Petitcodiac
Moncton
Dieppe
Shediac
Sackville
Amherst
Springhill
Hampton
Sussex
Rothesay
Saint John
St. Stephen
St. George
Calais
Eastport
Blacks Hr.
Grand Manan I.
Machias
Chignecto B.
Parrsboro
Minas Basin
Truro
Stewiacke
Kentville
Windsor
Bridgetown
Middleton
Annapolis Royal
Digby
Enfield
Middle Sackville
Dartmouth
Halifax
Musquodoboit Harbour
Sheet Harbour
Upper Musquodoboit
KEJIMKUJIK NAT. PARK
Weymouth
L. Rossignol
Milton
Mahone Bay
Lunenburg
Bridgewater
Liverpool
St. Mary's Bay
Yarmouth
Wedgeport
Shelburne
Lockeport
Clark's Harbour
C. Sable
New Glasgow
Stellarton
Pictou
Antigonish
Mulgrave
Port Hawkesbury
Sherbrooke
Canso
Chedabucto B.
I. Madame
St. Peters
Bras d'Or L.
Port Hood
Inverness
Chéticamp
CAPE BRETON HIGHLANDS NAT. PARK
Pleasant Bay
Ingonish
St. Ann's B.
Sydney Mines
New Waterford
Glace Bay
N. Sydney
Sydney
Louisbourg
Cape North
St. Paul I.
North Cape
Tignish
Alberton
Kensington
Summerside
Borden
Charlottetown
Souris
St. Peters
East Pt.
Montague
Georgetown
Cape Tormentine
Murray Hr.
Î. Brion
Grande-Entrée
Îs. de la Madeleine (Québec)
Fatima
Cap-aux-Meules
Havre-Aubert
Sable I. (Nova Scotia)
1128
610
1135
1048
1268
572
814
381
532
820
1190
1606
55
50
45
70
65
60
West from Greenwich

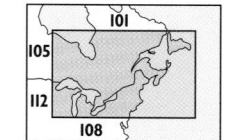

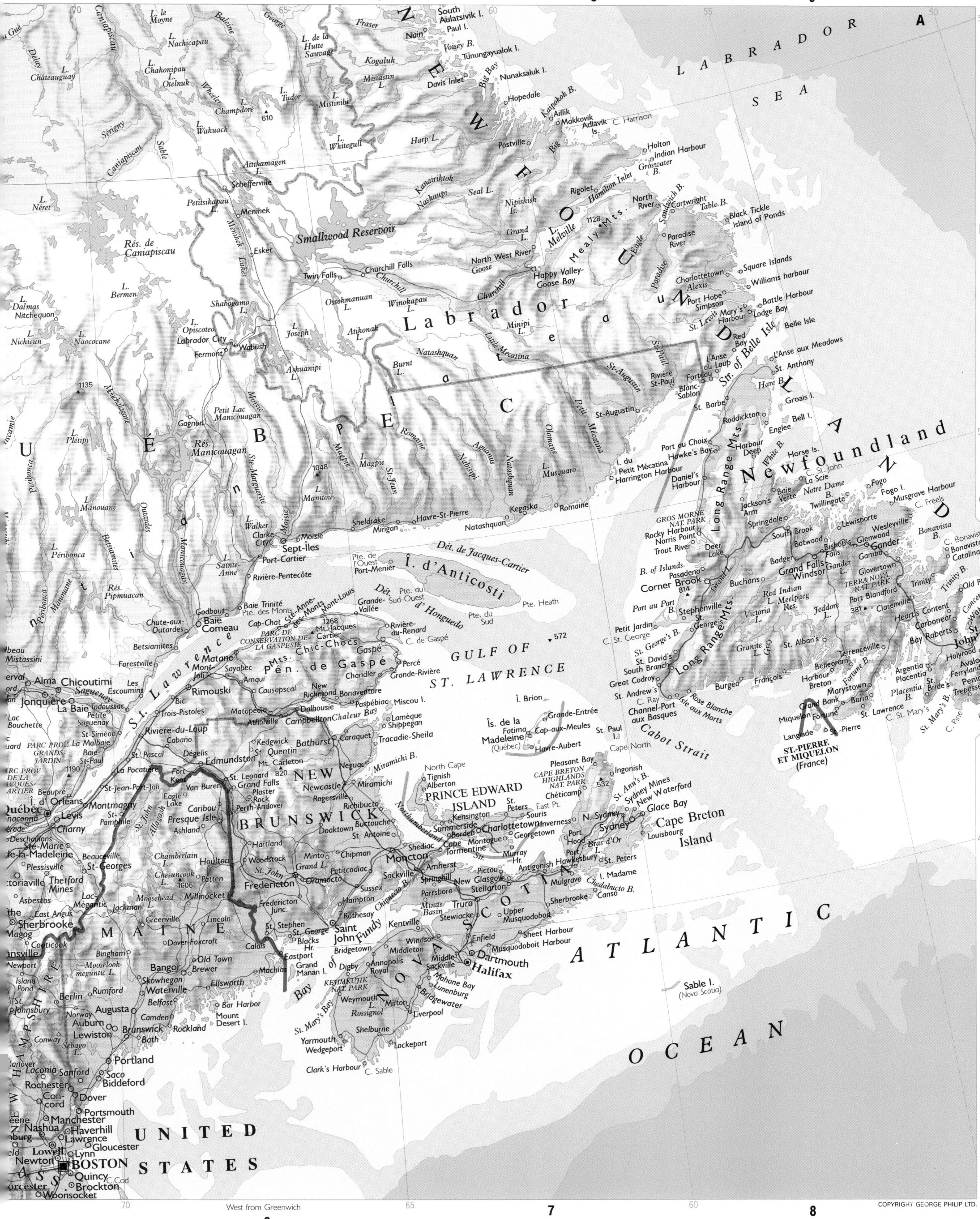

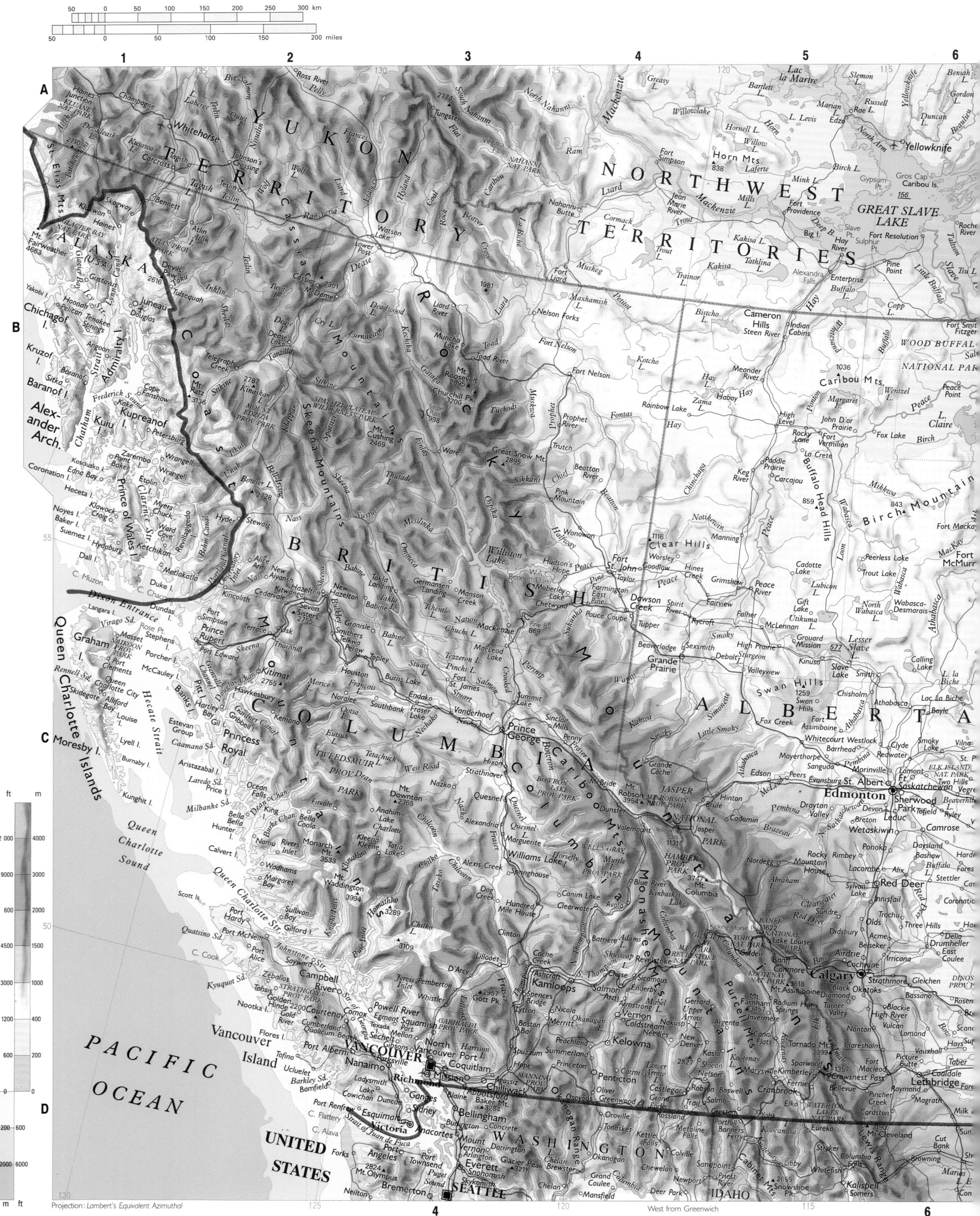

100
102
114
112

NUNAVUT
HUDSON BAY
MANITOBA
SASKATCHEWAN
ONTARIO
NORTH DAKOTA
MINNESOTA
MONTANA
LAKE WINNIPEG
Lake Winnipegosis
Lake Manitoba
Lake Athabasca
Reindeer Lake
Wollaston L.
Cedar Lake
Lake of the Woods
Lac la Ronge
Lac Seul
Southern Indian L.
Nueltin L.
Dubawnt L.
Churchill
Nelson
Saskatchewan
Winnipeg
Regina
Saskatoon
Prince Albert
Moose Jaw
Brandon
Thompson
The Pas
Flin Flon
Swift Current
North Battleford
Lloydminster
Yorkton
Weyburn
Estevan
Portage la Prairie
Selkirk
Dauphin
Kenora
Dryden
Fort Frances
Grand Forks
Minot
Williston
Duluth
Superior
Bemidji
Devils Lake
Arviat
Whale Cove
Gillam
Uranium City
Fort Chipewyan
La Ronge
Cypress Hills
Thief River Falls
International Falls
C. Churchill
C. Tatnam
Hubbart Pt.
7
8
9
10
11
A
B
C
D
60
55
50
110
105
100
95
90

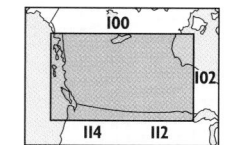

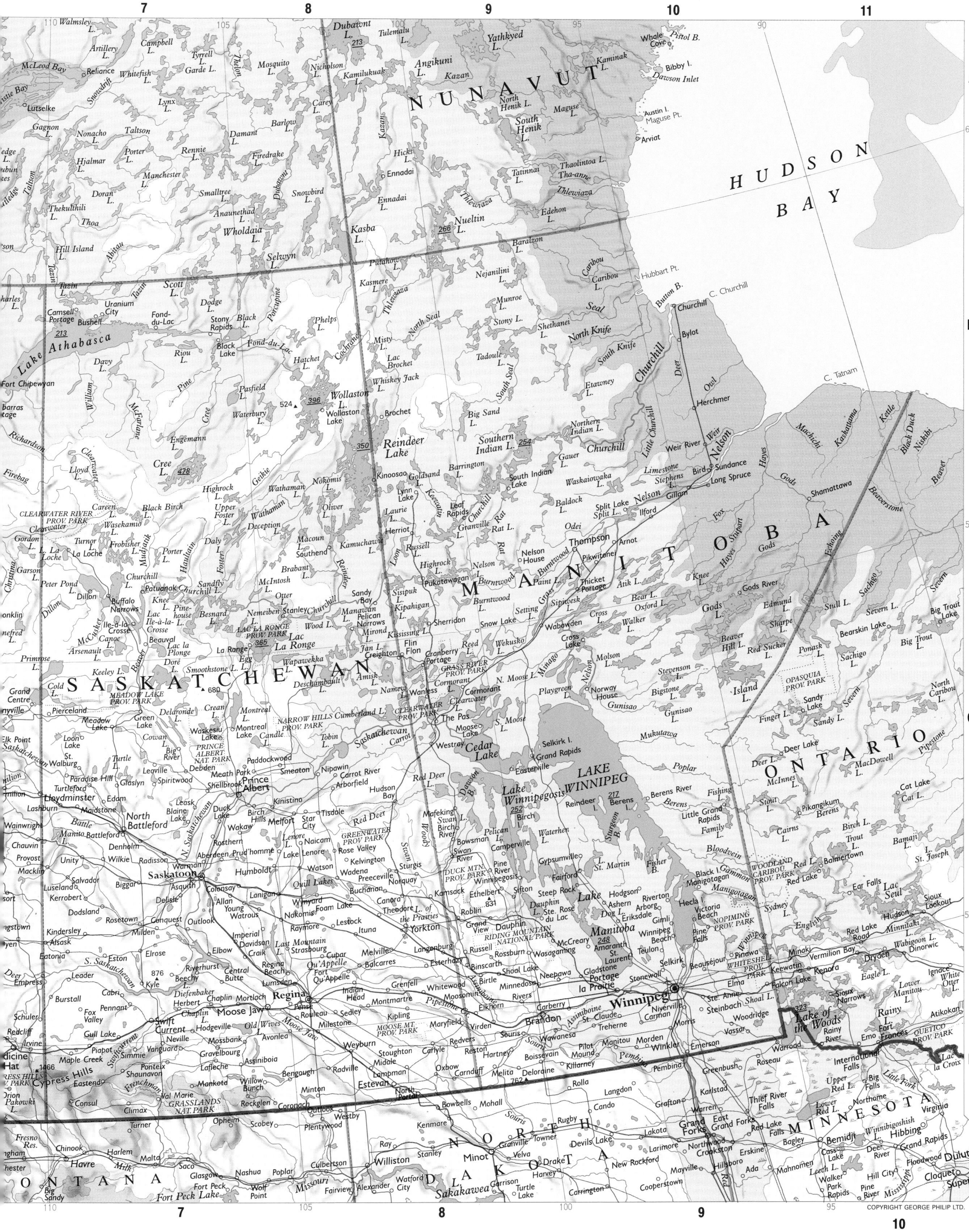

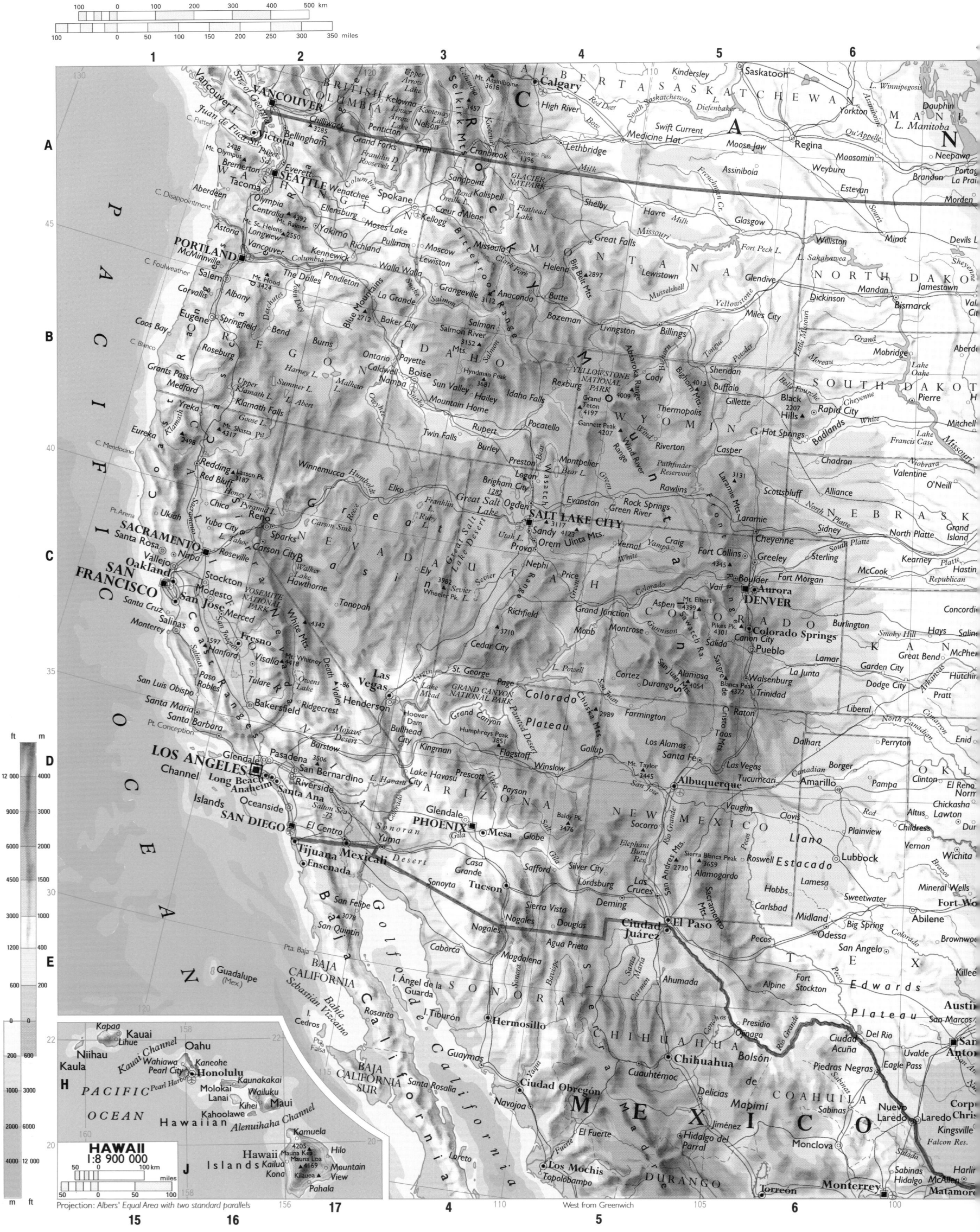

Projection: Albers' Equal Area with two standard parallels

HAWAII 1:8 900 000

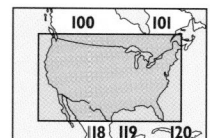

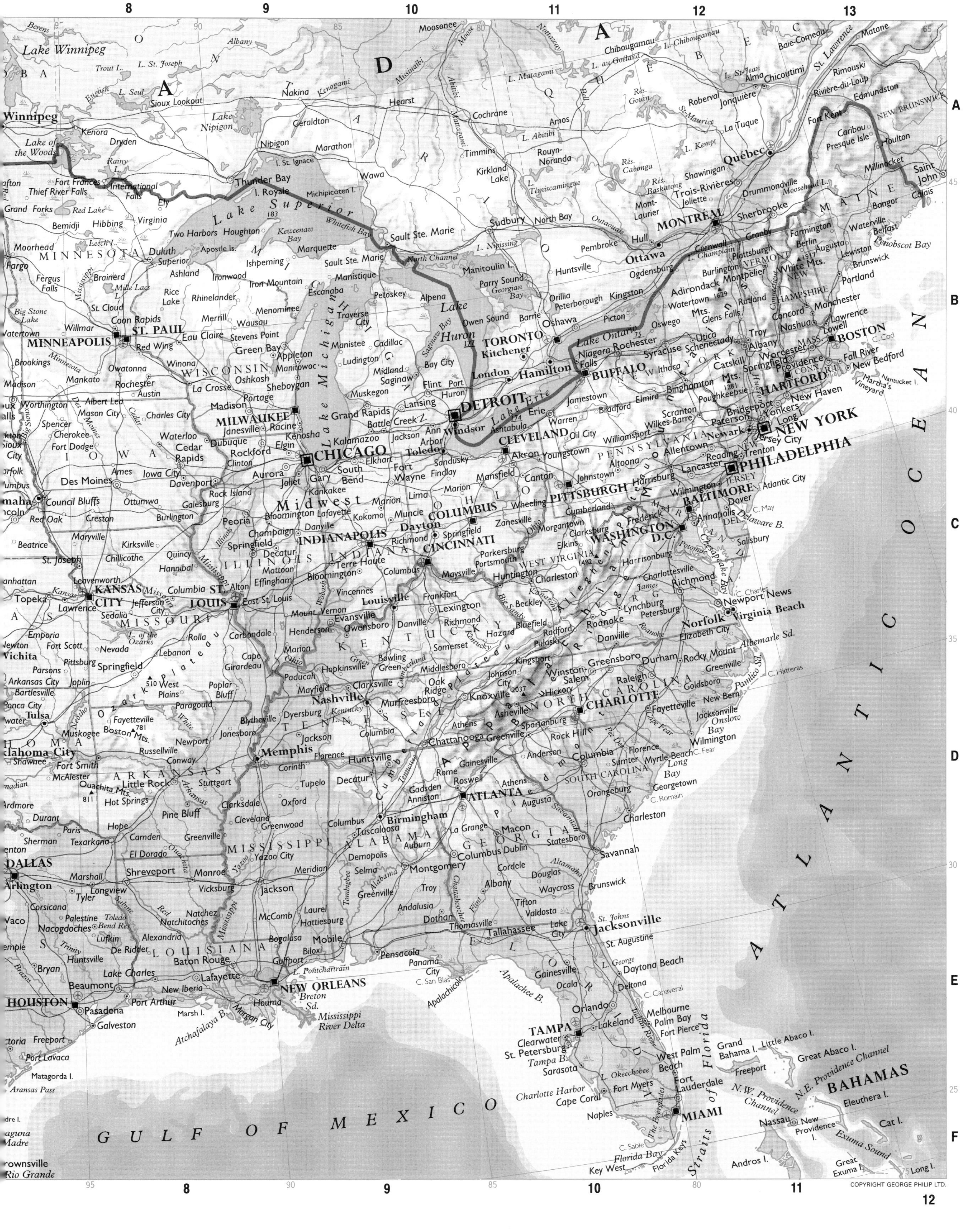

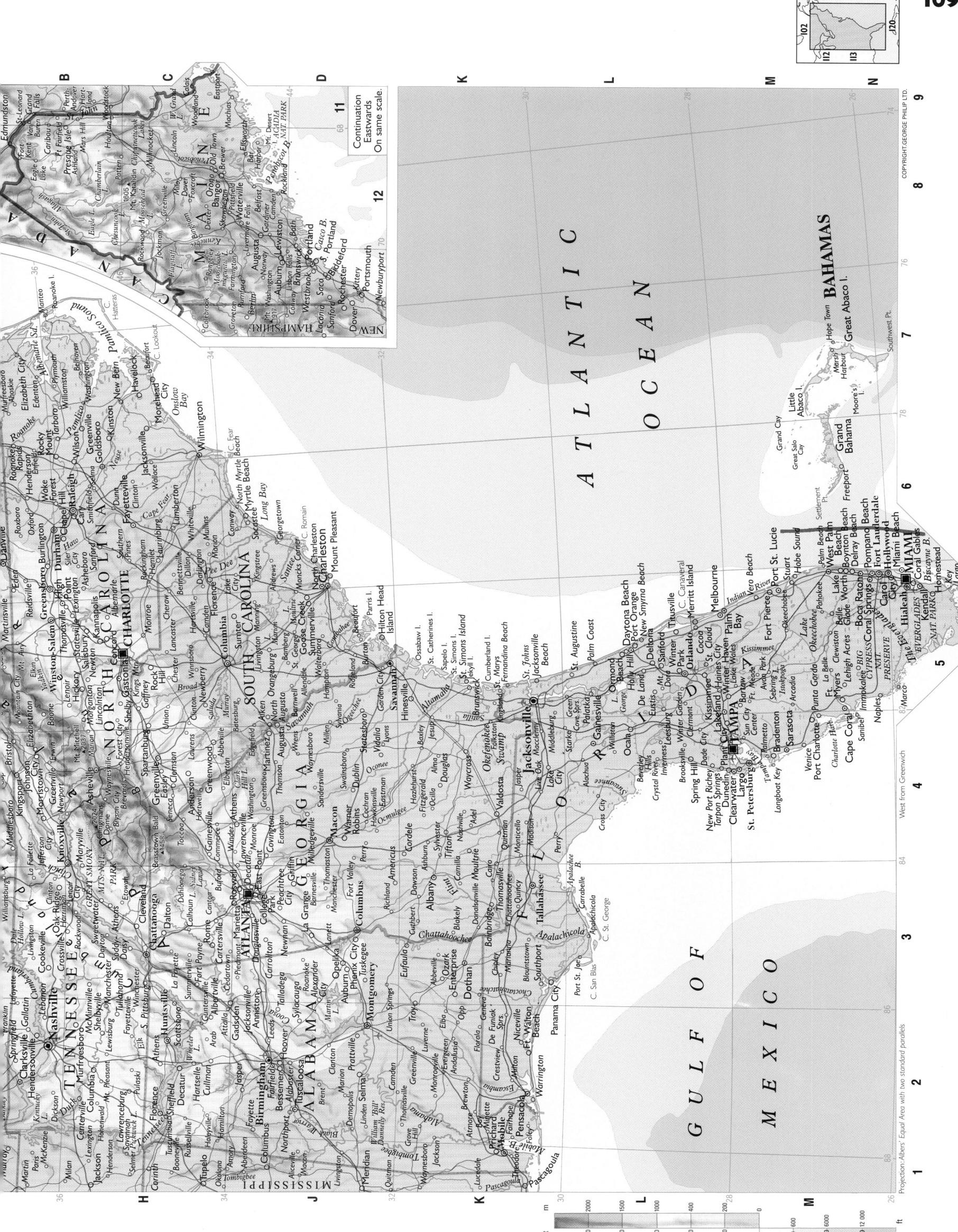

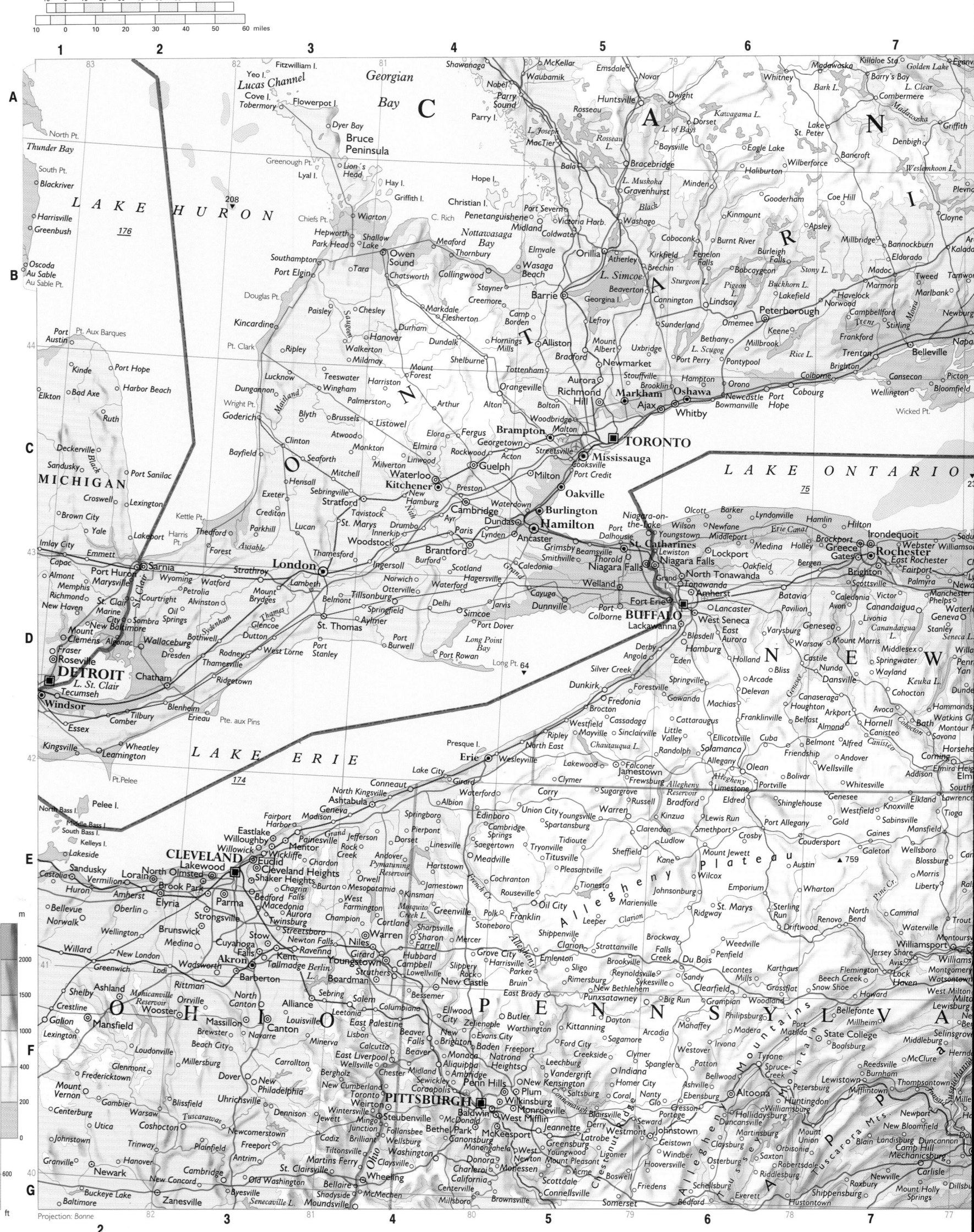

102
108
108

8
9
10
11
12
13
14
A
B
C
D
E
F
G
MONTREAL
Ottawa
QUÉBEC
L. Champlain
VERMONT
NEW HAMPSHIRE
MAINE
White Mountains
Adirondack Mountains
Green Mountains
MASSACHUSETTS
BOSTON
Worcester
Springfield
HARTFORD
CONNECTICUT
RHODE ISLAND
Providence
New Haven
Bridgeport
Stamford
Long Island Sound
Block Island Sound
Long Island
NEW YORK
NEW JERSEY
Newark
Jersey City
Trenton
PHILADELPHIA
Camden
Albany
Schenectady
Troy
Syracuse
Utica
Binghamton
Scranton
Wilkes-Barre
Allentown
Bethlehem
Reading
Lancaster
Catskill Mts.
Kittatinny Mts.
Martha´s Vineyard
ATLANTIC OCEAN
Vest from Greenwich
COPYRIGHT GEORGE PHILIP LTD.

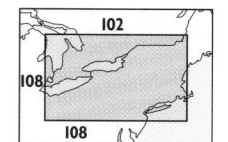

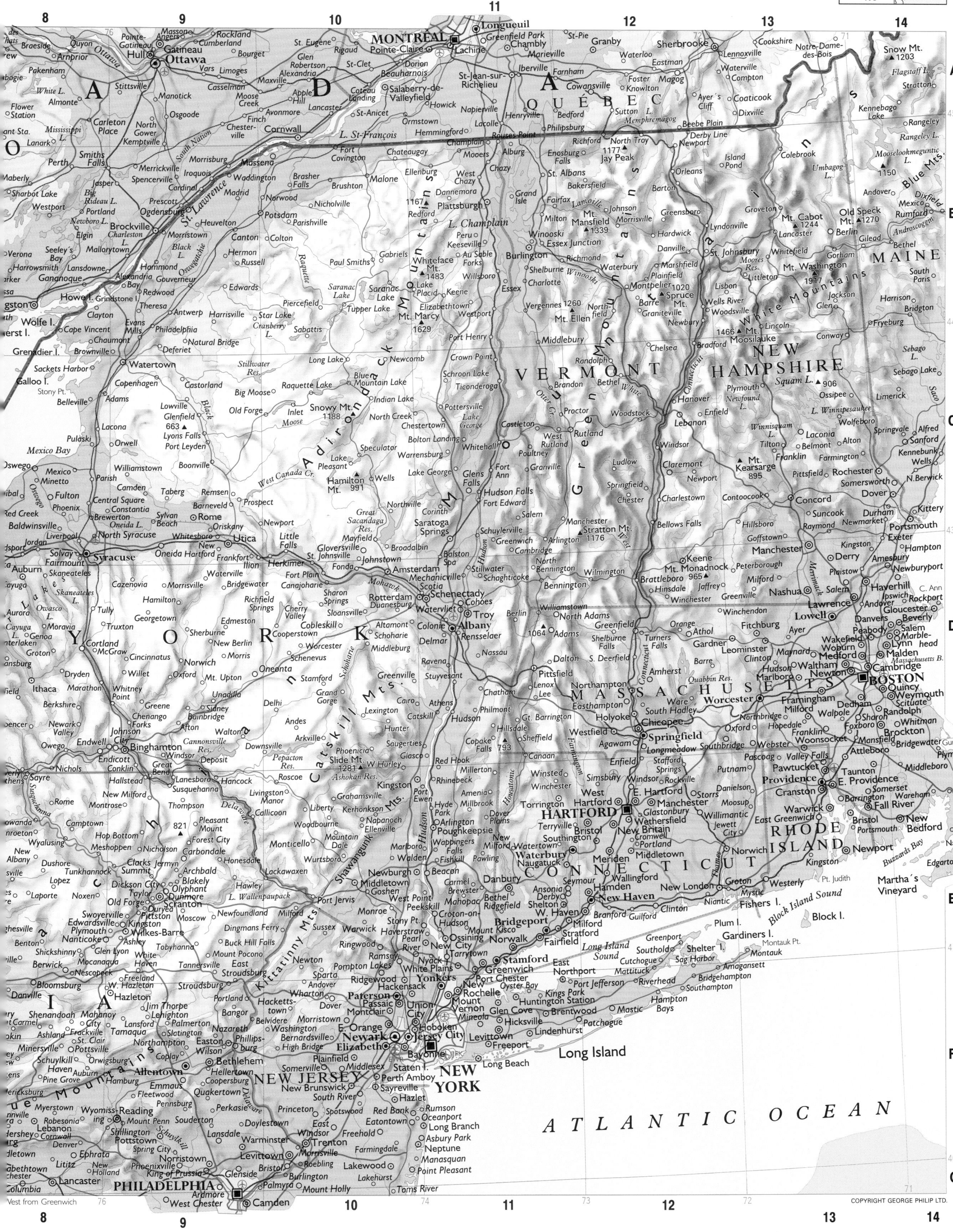

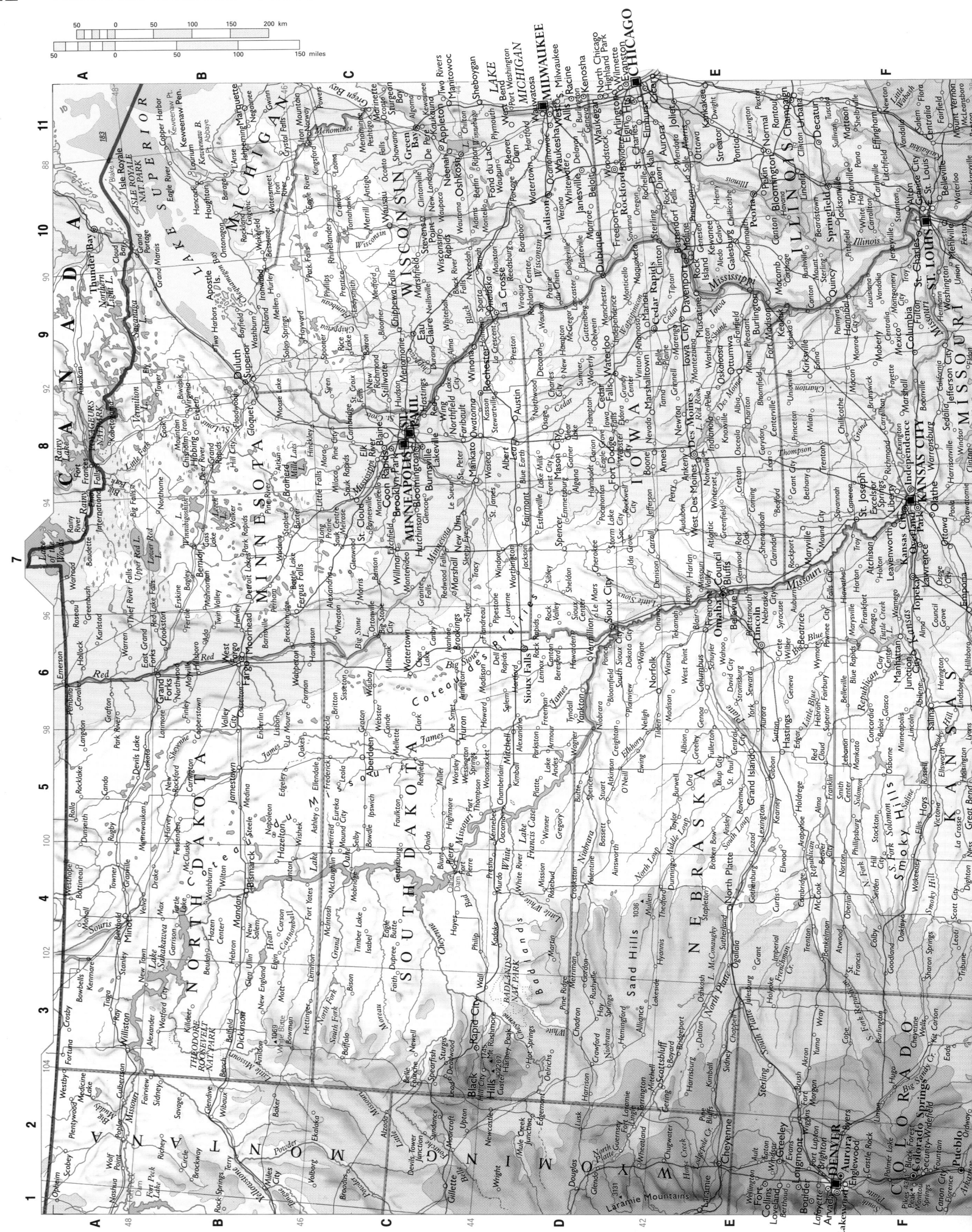

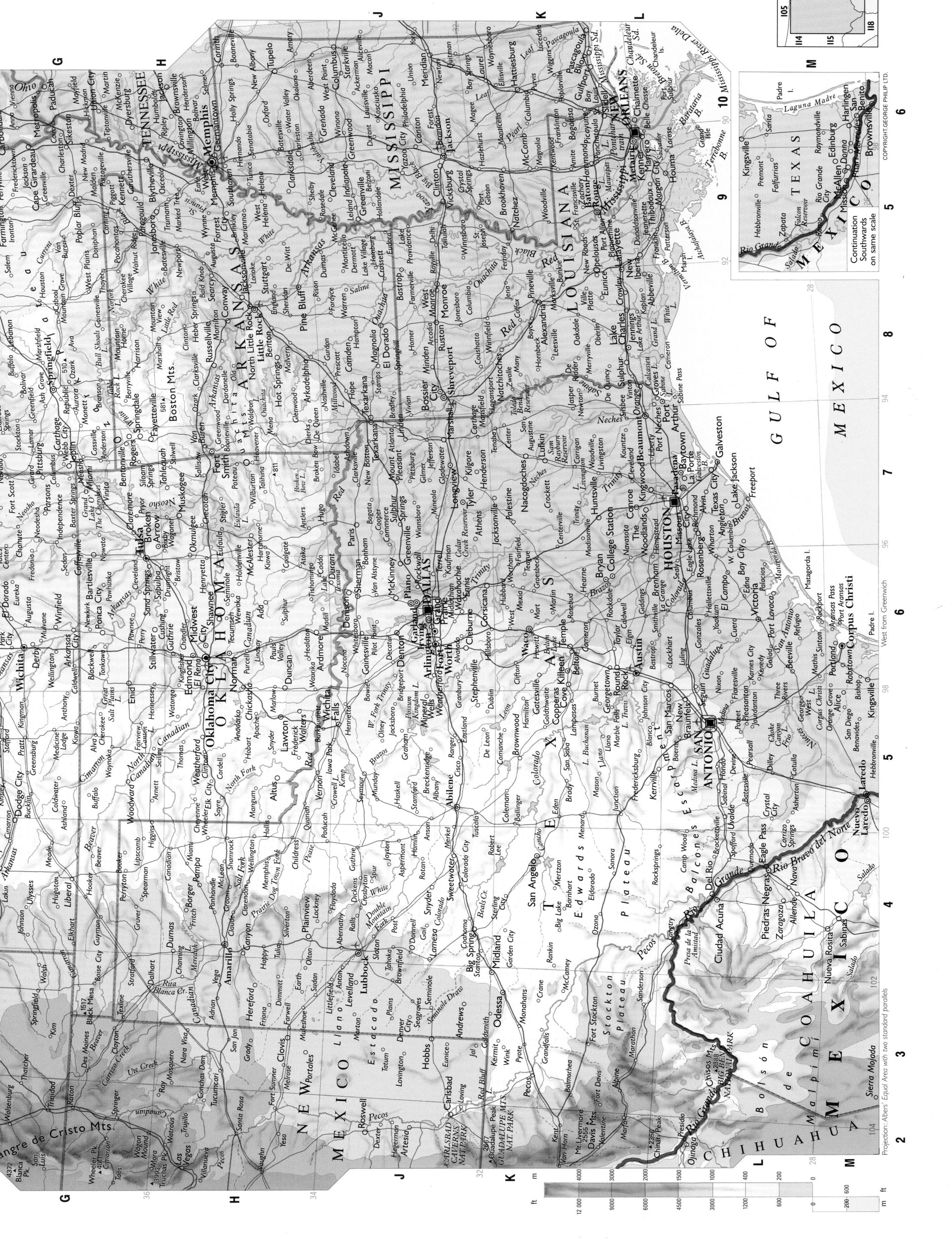

TENNESSEE

MISSISSIPPI

ARKANSAS

LOUISIANA

OKLAHOMA

NEW MEXICO

T E X A S

M E X I C O

COAHUILA

CHIHUAHUA

GULF OF MEXICO

Memphis

Little Rock

Oklahoma City

Tulsa

Dallas

Fort Worth

Arlington

Houston

San Antonio

Austin

Corpus Christi

Wichita

Lubbock

Amarillo

Odessa

Midland

New Orleans

Baton Rouge

Shreveport

Jackson

Laredo

Nuevo Laredo

Brownsville

Rio Grande

Laguna Madre

Padre I.

Edwards Plateau

Llano Estacado

Stockton Plateau

Sangre de Cristo Mts.

Boston Mts.

Ouachita Mts.

BIG BEND NAT. PARK

CARLSBAD CAVERNS NAT. PARK

GUADALUPE MTS. NAT. PARK

Projection: Albers' Equal Area with two standard parallels

West from Greenwich

Continuation Southwards on same scale

COPYRIGHT GEORGE PHILIP LTD.

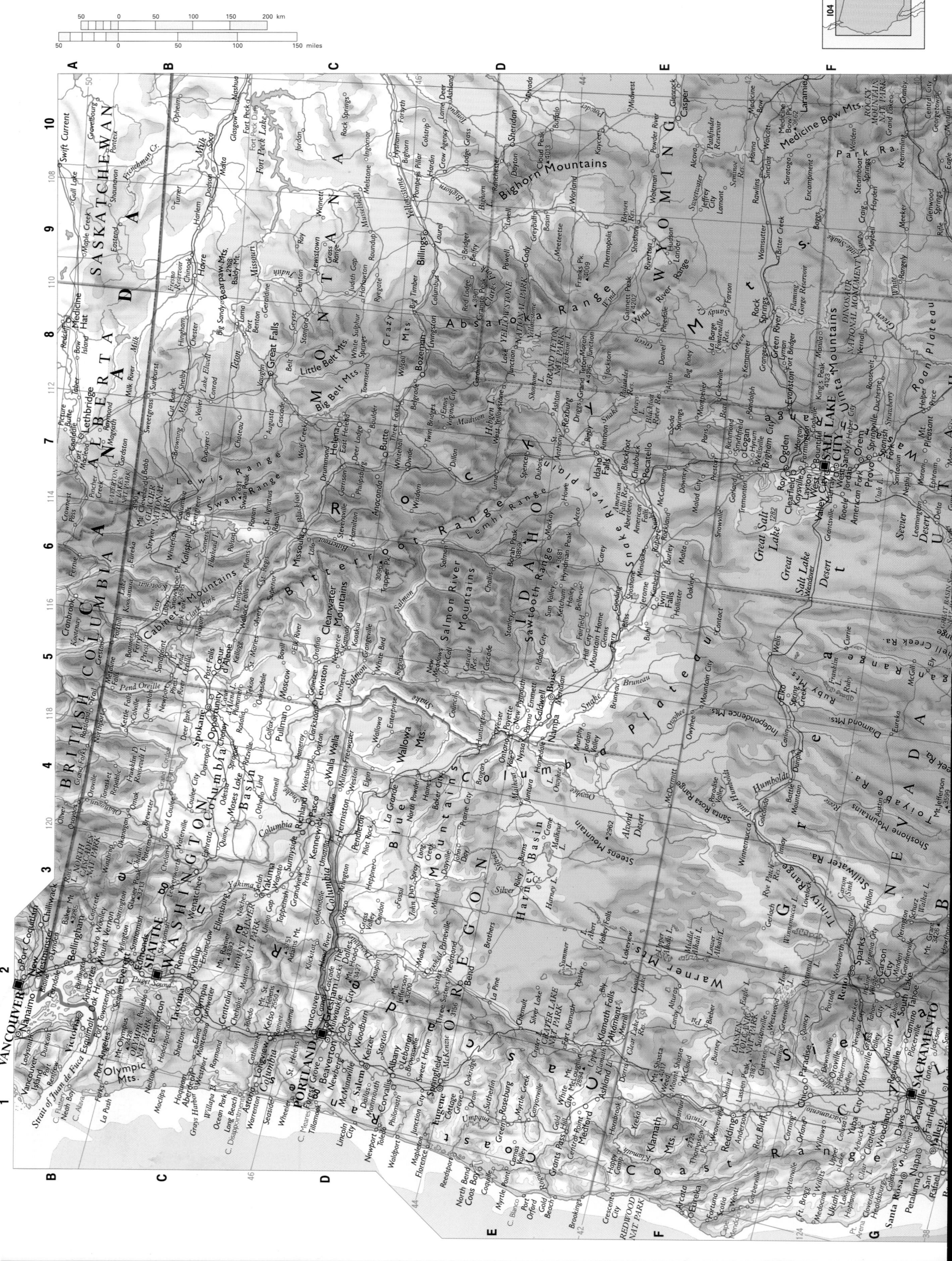

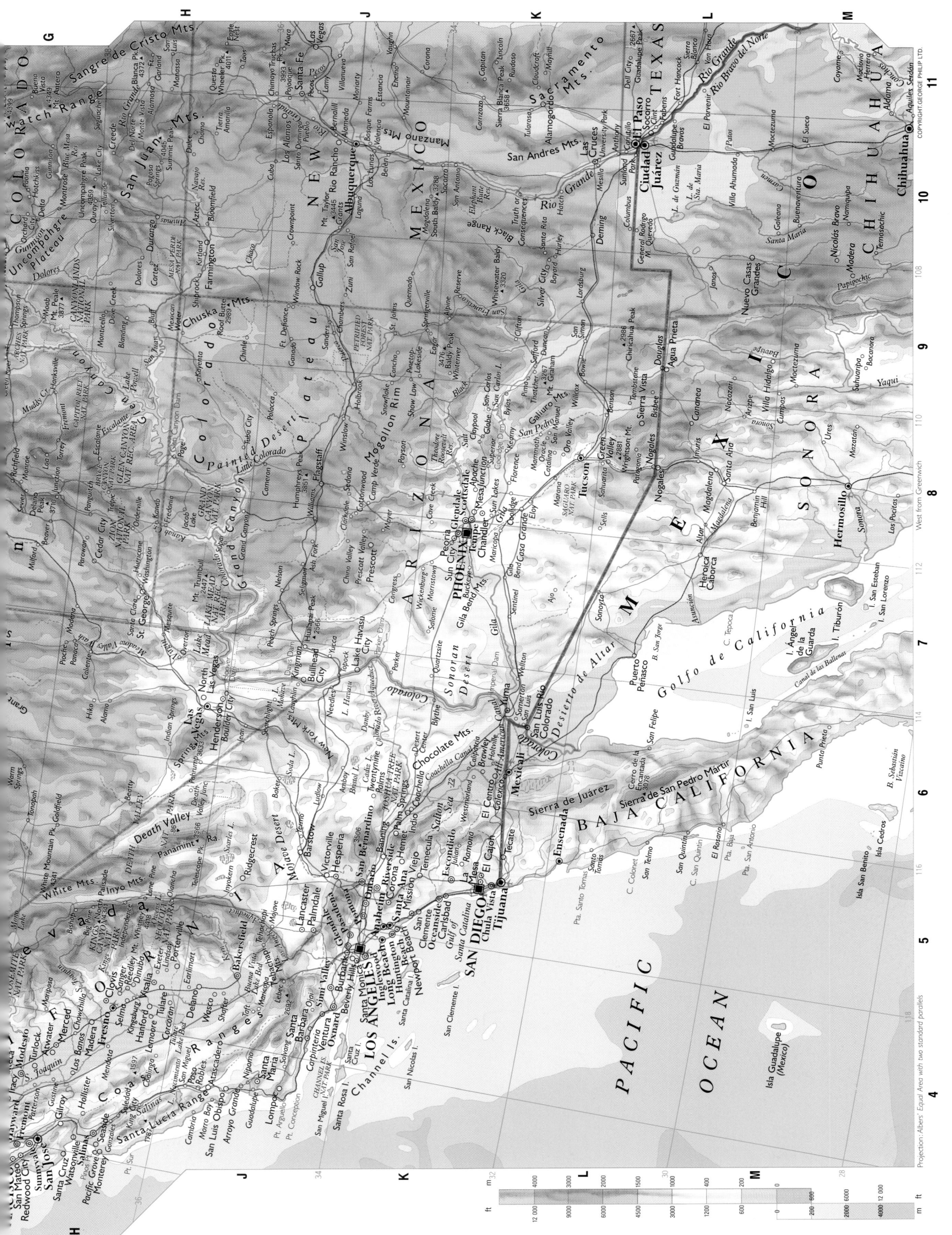

Projection: Albers' Equal Area with two standard parallels

West from Greenwich

WESTERN WASHINGTON REGION
On same scale

PACIFIC OCEAN

10 0 10 20 30 40 50 60 70 80 90 km

10 0 10 20 30 40 50 60 miles

NEVADA

ARIZONA

CALIFORNIA

BAJA CALIFORNIA

MEXICO

M o j a v e   D e s e r t

S o n o r a n   D e s e r t

Death Valley

Amargosa Range

Las Vegas

Henderson

Boulder City

Lake Mead

North Las Vegas

Overton

Kingman

Needles

Lake Havasu City

Lake Mohave

Bullhead City

Davis Dam

Hoover Dam

Mt. Tipton 2179

Colorado

Parker

Parker Dam

Blythe

Quartzsite

Signal Pk. 1439

Ehrenberg

Poston

Vidal

Barstow

Daggett

Yermo

Ludlow

Amboy

Newberry Springs

Twentynine Palms

Joshua Tree

Joshua Tree National Park

Chocolate Mts.

Coachella Canal

Salton Sea

Salton City

Indio

Coachella

Palm Desert

Palm Springs

Banning

Brawley

Imperial

El Centro

Calexico

Mexicali

Winterhaven

Yuma

Imperial Dam

Imperial Valley

Desert Hot Springs

San Bernardino

Redlands

Riverside

Moreno Valley

Perris

Hemet

San Jacinto 3293

Hesperia

Victorville

Apple Valley

Lucerne Valley

Big Bear City

Yucca Valley

Morongo Valley

Adelanto

Hi Vista

Lancaster

Palmdale

Edwards

Rosamond

Mojave

California City

Boron

Tehachapi

Bakersfield

Oildale

Delano

McFarland

Wasco

Shafter

Buena Vista L.

Maricopa

Ojai

Fillmore

Santa Paula

Ventura

Oxnard

Port Hueneme

Camarillo

Thousand Oaks

Moorpark

Simi Valley

Santa Clarita

Newhall

San Fernando

LOS ANGELES

Santa Monica

Beverly Hills

Glendale

Burbank

Pasadena

Alhambra

Monterey Park

El Monte

West Covina

Pomona

Ontario

Cucamonga

Claremont

Rancho

Fontana

Corona

Santa Ana

Anaheim

Orange

Garden Grove

Fullerton

Buena Park

Whittier

Norwalk

Downey

Inglewood

Torrance

Redondo Beach

Palos Verdes Estates

Pt. Palos Verdes

Long Beach

Huntington Beach

Newport Beach

Costa Mesa

Irvine

Laguna Beach

San Clemente

San Juan Capistrano

Mission Viejo

San Onofre

Oceanside

Carlsbad

Encinitas

Leucadia

Cardiff-by-the-Sea

Del Mar

Vista

San Marcos

Escondido

Ramona

Julian

Poway

La Mesa

El Cajon

Lemon Grove

National City

Chula Vista

Coronado

Imperial Beach

SAN DIEGO

Tijuana

Tecate

Rosarito

El Descanso

La Jolla

Fallbrook

Temecula

Elsinore

Murrieta

Sun City

Tehachapi Mts.

San Gabriel Mts.

San Bernardino Mts.

Santa Monica Mts.

San Rafael Mts.

San Jacinto Mts.

P A C I F I C   O C E A N

San Pedro Channel

Santa Catalina I.

Avalon

San Clemente I.

San Nicolas I.

Santa Barbara I.

C h a n n e l   I s l a n d s

Santa Cruz I.

Santa Rosa I.

San Miguel I.

Anacapa I.

CHANNEL ISLANDS NATIONAL PARK

Santa Barbara

Goleta

Isla Vista

Santa Barbara Channel

Gulf of Santa Catalina

Santa Maria

Lompoc

Guadalupe

Pt. Conception

Pt. Arguello

Santa Ynez

Solvang

Buellton

Los Alamos

San Luis Obispo

Arroyo Grande

Grover City

Pismo Beach

Oceano

Guadalupe

Is. los Coronados

Death Valley National Monument

Mt. Charleston 3633

Charleston Park

Mountain Pass

Kelso

Providence Mts.

MOJAVE NATIONAL RESERVE

Soda Lake

Silver Lake

Baker

Shoshone

Tecopa

Death Valley Junction

Amargosa

Telescope Pk. 3368

West from Greenwich

Projection: Bonne

m 4000 3000 2000 1500 1000 400 200 0

ft 12 000 9000 6000 4500 3000 1200 600 0

ft 2000 6000 m

ft   m

12 000   4000

9000   3000

6000   2000

4500   1500

3000   1000

1200   400

600   200

0   0

200   600

2000   6000

4000   12 000

m   ft

REFERENCE TO NUMBERS

1 Distrito Federal   5 México
2 Aguascalientes   6 Morelos
3 Guanajuato   7 Querétaro
4 Hidalgo   8 Tlaxcala

Projection: Bi-polar oblique Conical Orthomorphic   West from Greenwich

106
107
120

5
6
7
8
A
B
C
D
E
GULF OF MEXICO
Golfo de Campeche
Golfo de Tehuantepec
Golfo de Honduras
Canal de Yucatán
Tropic of Cancer
UNITED STATES
TEXAS
ARKANSAS
MISSISSIPPI
ALABAMA
GEORGIA
FLORIDA
LOUISIANA
TAMAULIPAS
VERACRUZ
PUEBLA
GUERRERO
OAXACA
CHIAPAS
TABASCO
CAMPECHE
YUCATÁN
QUINTANA ROO
GUATEMALA
BELIZE
HONDURAS
CUBA
Wichita Falls
Denison
Sherman
Paris
Hope
Camden
Texarkana
El Dorado
Greenville
Tuscaloosa
Opelika
Columbus
McRae
Denton
Greenville
Possum Kingdom Res.
Brazos
FORT WORTH
DALLAS
Marshall
Monroe
Vicksburg
Meridian
Selma
Phenix City
Montgomery
Americus
Cordele
Albany
Tifton
Ranger
Longview
Tyler
Shreveport
Tallulah
Jackson
Troy
Waycross
Abilene
Cleburne
Hillsboro
Corsicana
Toledo Bend Res.
Natchez
Laurel
Hattiesburg
Dothan
Jim Woodruff Res.
Valdosta
Brownwood
Waco
Palestine
Nacogdoches
Alexandria
McComb
Flomaton
Chattahoochee
Tallahassee
Lufkin
Sam Rayburn Reservoir
Jewett
MOBILE
Pensacola
Panama City
Lake City
Temple
Baton Rouge
Bogalusa
Biloxi
Hammond
Gulfport
Colorado
Huntsville
Bryan
Trinity
Sabine
Apalachee Bay
C. San Blas
Suwannee
Lake Charles
Lafayette
L. Pontchartrain
NEW ORLEANS
Mobile Bay
Austin
Navasota
Beaumont
Breton Sd.
HOUSTON
Port Arthur
Atchafalaya Bay
Terrebonne Bay
Mississippi River Delta
Rosenberg
Galveston
Clearwater
SAN ANTONIO
Guadalupe
Victoria
Dilley
Nueces
Alice
Corpus Christi
Laredo
Kingsville
Nuevo Laredo
Zapata
Laguna Madre
Camargo
McAllen
Harlingen
Brownsville
Reynosa
Presa M. R. Gomez
China
Matamoros
Valle Hermoso
Santa Teresa
Laguna Madre
Conchos
Mendez
San Fernando
Linares
Villagrán
Hidalgo
Santander Jiménez
Zaragoza
La Pesca
Soto la Marina
Ciudad Victoria
Sierra de Tamaulipas
Llera
Calles
Aldama
Pta. Jerez
Ocampo
Ciudad Mante
Altamira
Ciudad Madero
Tampico
Ciudad de Valles
Cárdenas
Pánuco
L. de Tamiahua
Ozuluama
Tempoal
Tantoyuca
Magozal
C. Rojo
Tamazunchale
Tuxpan
Chicontepec
Poza Rica
Papantla
Zimapán
Zacualtipán
Huichapan
Huauchinango
Nautla
Pachuca
Tulancingo
Misantla
Tula
Zumpango
Teziutlán
Jalapa Enríquez
MÉXICO
Apizaco
4282
Zempoala
Veracruz
Tlaxcala
Amecameca
PUEBLA
Citlaltépetl
5700
Coatepec
Tenango
5452
Popocatépetl
Córdoba
Alvarado
Tlacotalpan
Cuernavaca
Orizaba
San Andrés Tuxtla
1879
Paraíso
Frontera
Comalcalco
Tehuacán
Cosamaloapan
Coatzacoalcos
Villahermosa
Palizada
Balancán
Izúcar de Matamoros
Chilac
Ajalpan
Tres Valles
La Venta
Acayucan
Minatitlán
Cárdenas
Macuspana
Iguala
Chiautla
Acatlán
Huautla de Jiménez
Presa Miguel Alemán
Tenosique
San Juan Bautista Valle Nacional
Teapa
Palenque
Istmo de Tehuantepec
Jesús Carranza
Presa Netzahualcóyotl
Raudales de Malpaso
Simojovel
Ocosingo
Huajuapan de León
Asunción Nochixtlán
Chilapa
Chilpancingo
Silacayoapan
Copainalá
Chiapa de Corzo
San Cristóbal de las Casas
La Independencia
Tlaxiaco
Oaxaca
Monte Albán
Tehuantepec
Tuxtla Gutiérrez
Tierra Colorada
Tlacolula
Trinidad
Ayutla
Ometepec
Ocotlán
San Jerónimo Taviche
Ixtepec
Matías Romero
Comitán
Acapulco
Ejutla
Tehuantepec
Juchitán
Arriaga
Tonalá
Pinotepa Nacional
Miahuatlán
3139
Salina Cruz
Mar Muerto
Papagayo
Jamiltepec
Tututepec
Puerto Arista
La Concordia
Punta Maldonado
San Pedro Mixtepec
Pochutla
Pijijiapan
Mapastepec
Motozintla
Cuilco
3993
4220
Verde
Puerto Escondido
Puerto Ángel
Huixtla
Tapachula
Coatepeque
Retalhuleu
Tehuantepec
Sierra Madre
Usumacinta
Lacantún
Salinas
Ciudad del Carmen
L. de Términos
Champotón
Chenkán
Campeche
Edzná
Hopelchén
Tenabo
Bolonchenticul
Felipe Carrillo Puerto
Maxcanú
Ticul
Uxmal
Tekax
Peto
Vigía Chico
B. de la Ascensión
B. del Espíritu Santo
Mérida
Dzibilchaltún
Mayapán
Sotuta
Chichén Itzá
Valladolid
Cozumel
Isla Cozumel
Progreso
Motul
Temax
Izamal
Espita
Puerto Morelos
Dzilam de Bravo
Tizimín
El Cuyo
Río Lagartos
Pta. Yalkubul
C. Catoche
Cancún
Puerto Juárez
I. Desterrada
I. Pérez (Mexico)
Bacalar
Chetumal
B. de Chetumal
Banco Chinchorro
Corozal
Matamoros
Concepción
Orange Walk
Hondo
Ambergris Cay
Turneffe Is.
Belize City
Uaxactún
San Ignacio
Tikal
Belmopan
Benque Viejo
Dangriga
L. Petén Itzá
La Libertad
Flores
Maya Mts.
Monkey River
San Antonio
San Luis
Punta Gorda
Livingston
Puerto Barrios
Is. de la Bahía
Roatán
Puerto Castilla
Trujillo
Iriona
Tela
Balfate
Savá
Olanchito
San Pedro Sula
El Progreso
Arenal
Yoro
Sulaco
Catacamas
Juticalpa
Patuca
Sierra de los Cuchumatanes
Huehuetenango
Sebol
Cobán
L. de Izabal
Sierra de las Minas
Motagua
Gualán
Zacapa
Santa Bárbara
Santa Rosa de Copán
Copán
L. de Yojoa
Comayagua
San Marcos
Totonicapán
Sololá
Antigua
Mazatenango
Jalapa
Chiquimula
GUATEMALA
Amatitlán
La Esperanza
La Paz
Tegucigalpa
Yuscarán
Danlí
La Esperanza
Guane
La Fé
C. San Antonio
C. Corrientes
95
90
85
30
25
20
15

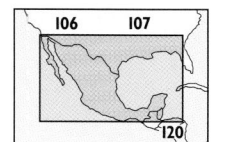

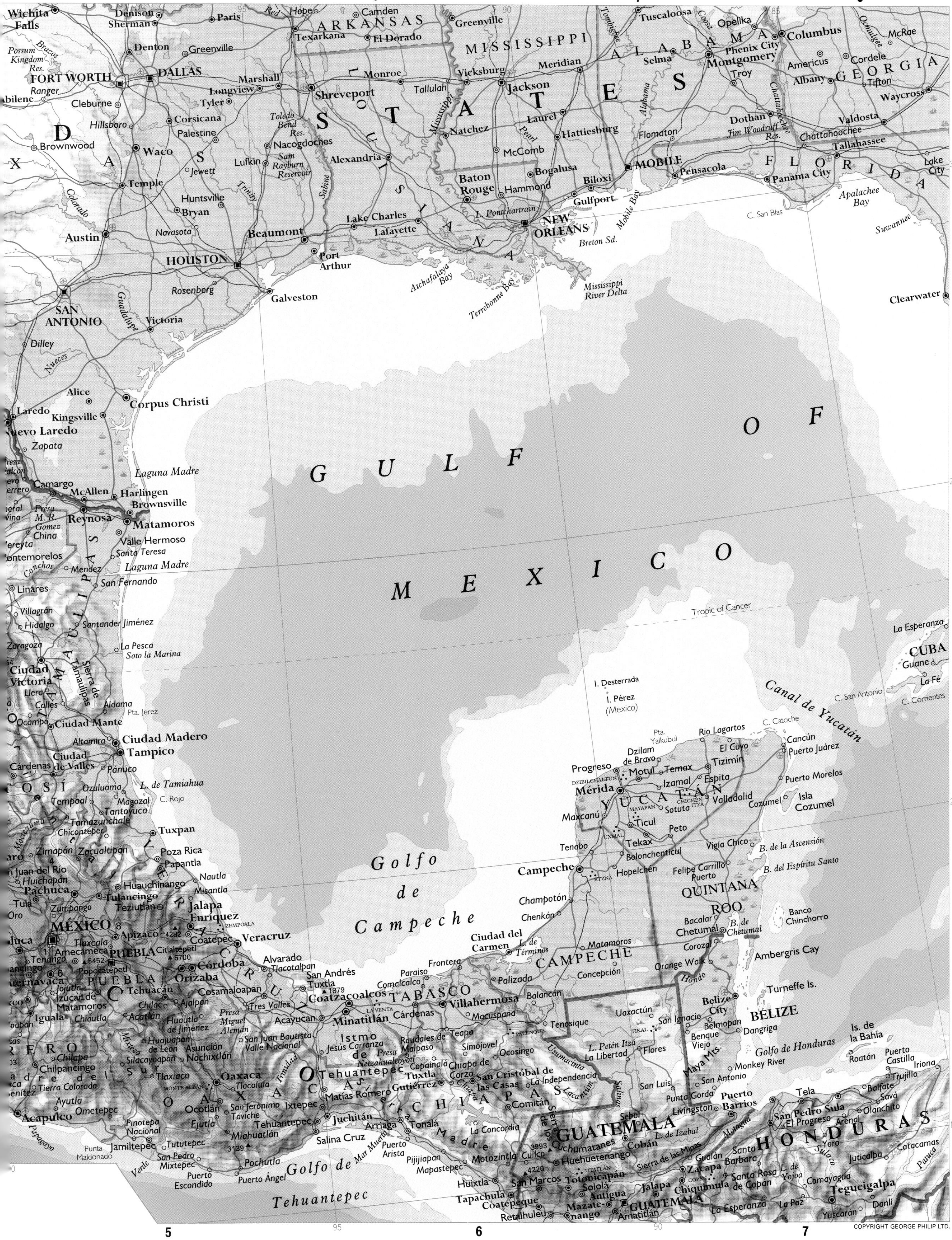

GULF OF MEXICO

PACIFIC OCEAN

U.S.A.

MEXICO

GUATEMALA

BELIZE

HONDURAS

EL SALVADOR

NICARAGUA

COSTA RICA

PANAMA

CUBA

JAMAICA

CARIBBEAN

Projection: Conical with two standard parallels

YUCATAN

QUINTANA ROO

CAMPECHE

LA HABANA (Havana)

MARIANAO

Cayman Islands (U.K.)

Swan Islands (U.S.A. & Honduras)

Cayos Miskitos (Nicaragua)

Cayos Roncador (U.S.A. & Colombia)

I. de Providencia (Colombia)

I. de San Andrés (Colombia)

Cayos de Albuquerque (Colombia)

Is. del Maiz (Nicaragua, U.S.A.)

Pedro Cays (Jamaica)

Mosquitia

Golfo del Darién

Serranía del Darién

Golfo de Panamá

Archipiélago de San Blas

Panamá Canal

Tegucigalpa

Managua

San José

San Salvador

Belmopan

Mérida

Campeche

Chetumal

Belize City

San Pedro Sula

La Ceiba

Trujillo

Puerto Cabezas

Bluefields

León

Granada

Liberia

Puntarenas

Cartago

Limón

David

Santiago

Colón

Miami

Key West

Dry Tortugas (U.S.A.)

Florida Keys

Straits of Florida

Pinar del Río

Matanzas

Cárdenas

Santa Clara

Cienfuegos

Trinidad

Sancti Spíritus

Ciego de Ávila

Camagüey

Victoria de las Tunas

Holguín

Bayamo

Manzanillo

Santiago de Cuba

Sierra Maestra

Montego Bay

Kingston

Spanish Town

ft m

12 000 — 4000

9000 — 3000

6000 — 2000

4500 — 1500

— 1000

1200 — 400

600 — 200

0

200

600

2000

4000 — 6000

— 12 000

8000 — 18 000

— 24 000

m ft

ATLANTIC OCEAN

Tropic of Cancer

AMAS

arthur's Town

The Bight
Cat I.

San Salvador I.

Conception I.

Rum Cay

Long I.

Clarence
Town

Samana Cay

Crooked I.

Albert
Town

Snug
Corner

Plana Cays

Acklins I.

Mira por vos Cay

Mayaguana I.

Cay Verde

Hogsty Reef

Little Inagua I.

Turks & Caicos
(U.K.)

Caicos Is.

Turks Is.

Lake Rosa

Great
Inagua I.

Matthew
Town

Puerto Rico Trench

Milwaukee
Deep
9200

Baracoa

Pta. de
Maisi

Î. de la
Tortue

Monte
Cristi

LA ISABELA

Santiago de los Cabelleros

Cap-
Haïtien

Puerto
Plata

San Francisco de Macorís

Nagua

Samana

Bayamón

SAN JUAN

Virgin Gorda
Virgin Is.
(U.K.)

Tortola

Anegada
Passage

Sombrero (U.K.)

Guantánamo

Paso de los
Vientos
(Windward Passage)

Jean Rabel

Port-de-
Paix

Cap-à-
Foux

Fort Liberté

Gonaïves

G. de la
Gonâve

Hinche

St-Marc

Cora

La Vega

Central

1338

Carolina

Aguadilla

Arecibo

San Juan

Carolina

Charlotte Amalie

St. Thomas

Virgin Is.
(U.S.A.)

Road Town

Anguilla (U.K.)

St.-Martin (Fr.)

St.-Barthélemy (Fr.)

HAITI

DOMINICAN
REP

Fajardo

St. Maarten
(Neth.)

Saba (Neth.)

Barbuda

Jérémie

Î. de la Gonâve

PORT-
AU-PRINCE

San Juan

L. Enriquillo

3175

Higüey

C. Engaño

Ponce

Caguas

Christiansted

St. Croix

St. Eustatius
(Neth.)

ST. KITTS
& NEVIS

ANTIGUA
& BARBUDA

Dame-
Marie

Carcasse

Massif de la Hotte

Petit
Goâve

Jacmel

2280

San Pedro
de Macorís

La Romana

B. de
Yuma

Mayaguez

Guayama

Frederiksted

Basseterre

Nevis

St. John's

Antigua

C. Carcasse

Les Cayes

Aquin

Pederñales

Barahona

Azua de
Compostela

Baní

San Cristóbal

SANTO
DOMINGO

Isla
Mona
(U.S.A.)

PUERTO
RICO
(U.S.A.)

Redonda

Montserrat
(U.K.)

Ste.-Rose

Le Moule

La Désirade

Pointe-à-Gravois

Î. à Vache

I. Beata

C. Beata

I. Saona

Guadeloupe Passage

GUADELOUPE
(Fr.)

Pointe-à-Pitre

Marie-Galante (Fr.)

Grand-Bourg

Hispaniola

Antilles

Basse-Terre
(Fr.)

Î. des Saintes

Dominica Passage

Portsmouth

DOMINICA

Roseau

vassa I.
(U.S.A.)

avila

Mayari

Moa

CARIBBEAN SEA

I. de Aves
(Venezuela)

Martinique Passage

Mt. Pelée
1397

Ste.-Marie

Le François

Rivière-Pilote

Fort-de-
France

MARTINIQUE
(Fr.)

St. Lucia Channel

Castries

Soufrière

ST. LUCIA

St. Vincent Passage

La Soufrière 1234

ST. VINCENT

Speightstown

Kingstown

Bridgetown

BARBADOS

Hillsborough

GRENADINES

St. George's

GRENADA

Lesser Antilles

Aruba
(Neth.)

Curaçao

Bonaire

NETH.
ANTILLES

Willemstad

Is. Las Aves
(Ven.)

Is. Los Roques
(Ven.)

I. Orchila
(Ven.)

I. Blanquilla (Ven.)

Is. Los Hermanos
(Ven.)

Is. Los Testigos
(Ven.)

Dragon's Mouth

Tobago

Scarborough

Pta. Gallinas

Pen. de la
Guajira

Pta.
Espada

Pen. de
Paraguaná

Punto Fijo

I. de Margarita

La Asunción

NUEVA
ESPARTA

Porlamar

Galera
Point

Port of
Spain

Trinidad

Arima

Rio Claro

SANTA
MARTA

Ríohacha

Uribia

GUAJIRA

Golfo de
Venezuela

Punta
Cardón

Puerto
Cumarebo

Cora

La Vela de Coro

FALCÓN

La Tortuga
(Ven.)

Cumaná

Carúpano

Caribe

SUCRE

Güiria

G. de Paria

San Fernando

TRINIDAD
& TOBAGO

Serpent's Mouth

ARRAN-
QUILLA

Baranoa

Soledad

ATLÁNTICO

Ciénaga

San
Rafael

Sierra Nevada de
Santa Marta
5800

Altagracia

Mene de Maurea

Tucacas

Puerto
Cabello

Maracay

Maiquetía

La Guaira

CARACAS

DISTRITO FEDERAL

Higuerote

Río Chico

Puerto
La Cruz

Barcelona

Caicara

Maturín

Caripito

MONAGAS

DELTA

MARACAIBO

La
Concepción

Villa del
Rosario

Ciudad
Ojeda

Cabimas

Mene
Grande

San Felipe

YARACUY

Valencia

CARABOBO

Valle de
Cura

ARAGUA

MIRANDA

Ocumare del Tuy

San Juan
de los Morros

Altagracia
de Orituco

Aragua de
Barcelona

Unare

Anaco

Cantaura

Tucupita

AMACURO

Fundación

Calamar

San Carlos
del Zulia

Lago de
Maracaibo

Machiques

ZULIA

TRUJILLO

LARA

BARQUISIMETO

Yaritagua de
los Morros

El Tocuyo

Villa

San Carlos

COJEDES

El Sombrero

Valle de
la Pascua

GUÁRICO

Santa María
de Ipire

El Tigre

ANZOÁTEGUI

Los Barrancos

Ciudad Guayana

Sierra Imataca

Betijoque

Valera

PORTUGUESA

Acarigua

Guanare

El Baúl

Calabozo

Pariaguán

Soledad

El Pao

Upata

MÉRIDA

Barinas

Libertad

BARINAS

Puerto de Nutrias

San Fernando
de Apure

Achaguas

APURE

Ciudad
Bolívar

Sierra

SANTANDER

Cúcuta

TÁCHIRA

Santa
Bárbara

Ciudad
Bolivia

Bruzual

VENEZUELA

Cord. de Mérida

NORTE
DE
Ocaña

BOLÍVAR

Embalse de Guri

El Callao

Tumeremo

Guasipati

West from Greenwich

COPYRIGHT GEORGE PHILIP LTD

5

6

100 0   200   400   600   800 1000 1200 1400 km
100 0   200   400   600   800   1000 miles

1   2   3   4   5   6   7

Tropic of Cancer

A

Havana   BAHAMAS   Turks & Caicos Is.   *N O R T H*
CUBA   (U.K.)

Virgin Is.
(U.K.)   *A T L A N T I C*
HAITI   DOMINICAN   San Juan
REP.   ST. KITTS   ANTIGUA &
MEXICO   JAMAICA   Port-au-   PUERTO   & NEVIS   BARBUDA
BELIZE   Kingston   Prince   RICO   Basse-Terre GUADELOUPE   *O C E A N*
(U.S.A.)   (Fr.)
GUATEMALA   HONDURAS   DOMINICA
B   Guatemala   Tegucigalpa   *C a r i b b e a n   S e a*   Fort-de-France MARTINIQUE   **B**
(Fr.)
San Salvador   Castries ST. LUCIA
EL SALVADOR   NICARAGUA   Aruba   ST. VINCENT   BARBADOS
Managua   C. de   Curaçao   Kingstown   Bridgetown
COSTA   San José   la Aguja   GRENADA   St. George's
RICA   Panamá   Barranquilla   Maracaibo   Caracas   Port of   TRINIDAD &
G. of Darién Cartagena   Barquisimeto   Valencia   Spain   TOBAGO
PANAMA   Cúcuta   Orinoco
Medellín   San Cristóbal   Ciudad Guayana
C   Gulf of Panamá   Magdalena   Bucaramanga   **VENEZUELA**   Georgetown   **C**
Cali   Bogotá   GUYANA   Paramaribo
RORAIMA   SURINAM   Cayenne
COLOMBIA   Branco   Essequibo FRENCH   C. Orange
GUIANA
AMAPÁ
Galapagos Is.   **ECUADOR**   Napo   *Amazon*   Equator
(Ecuador)   Quito   Putumayo   Marajó
Guayaquil   Japurá   Manaus   I.   Belém
D   G. of Guayaquil   Iquitos   Marañón   *Amazon*   Santarém   São Luís   Fortaleza **D**
Chiclayo   Ucayali   **AMAZONAS**   Juruá Purus Madeira Tapajós Xingu PARÁ MARANHÃO Teresina CEARÁ C. de
Trujillo   São Roque
Chimbote   ACRE   Pôrto Velho   Tocantins   PIAUÍ   Natal
PERU   RONDÔNIA   Parnaíba Campina RIO G.
Grande   DO NORTE
Callao **LIMA**   Cuzco   Madre de Dios   **B R A Z I L**   PERNAMBUCO Recife
E   L.   Mamoré   **MATO GROSSO**   TOCANTINS   ALAGOAS Maceió **E**
Titicaca   **BOLIVIA**   GOIÁS   BAHÍA SERGIPE
Arequipa La Paz   Cochabamba   Cuiabá   DIS. FED Brasília   Aracaju
Santa Cruz   Goiânia   São Francisco   Salvador
Sucre   MATO GROSSO   **MINAS GERAIS**
Iquique   DO SUL   Ribeirão   Belo   ESPÍRITO
Prêto   Horizonte   SANTO
F   Antofagasta   **PARAGUAY**   Pilcomayo   Paraná   SÃO PAULO Juiz   Vitória **F**
de Fora   R. DE J.   Campos
San Félix   Salta   PARANÁ   Campinas   Niterói
(Chile)   San Ambrosio   San Miguel   Asunción   SÃO   RIO DE
(Chile)   de Tucumán   Pilcomayo   PAULO   JANEIRO
Resistencia   Curitiba
O C E A N   A   Salado   Corrientes   *Uruguay* SANTA CATARINA
Arch. de Juan Fernández   Córdoba Santa Fe   RIO GRANDE
(Chile)   Viña del Mar   San Juan   Paraná   DO SUL
G   Valparaíso   Mendoza   Rosario   Pôrto Alegre   *S O U T H*   **G**
SANTIAGO   Talca   Buenos Aires   Pelotas
Concepción   La Plata **URUGUAY** Montevideo
Río de la Plata   *A T L A N T I C*
Valdivia   Bahía   Mar del Plata
Puerto Montt   Negro   Viedma   Blanca
Chubut   *O C E A N*
H   A   **H**
Comodoro Rivadavia
Gulf of San Jorge
Gulf of Penas
West Falkland FALKLAND IS.
(U.K.)
Magellan's Str.   Stanley
Punta Arenas   East Falkland
Tierra del Fuego   South Georgia
(U.K.)
C. Horn   West from Greenwich

■ LIMA Capital Cities

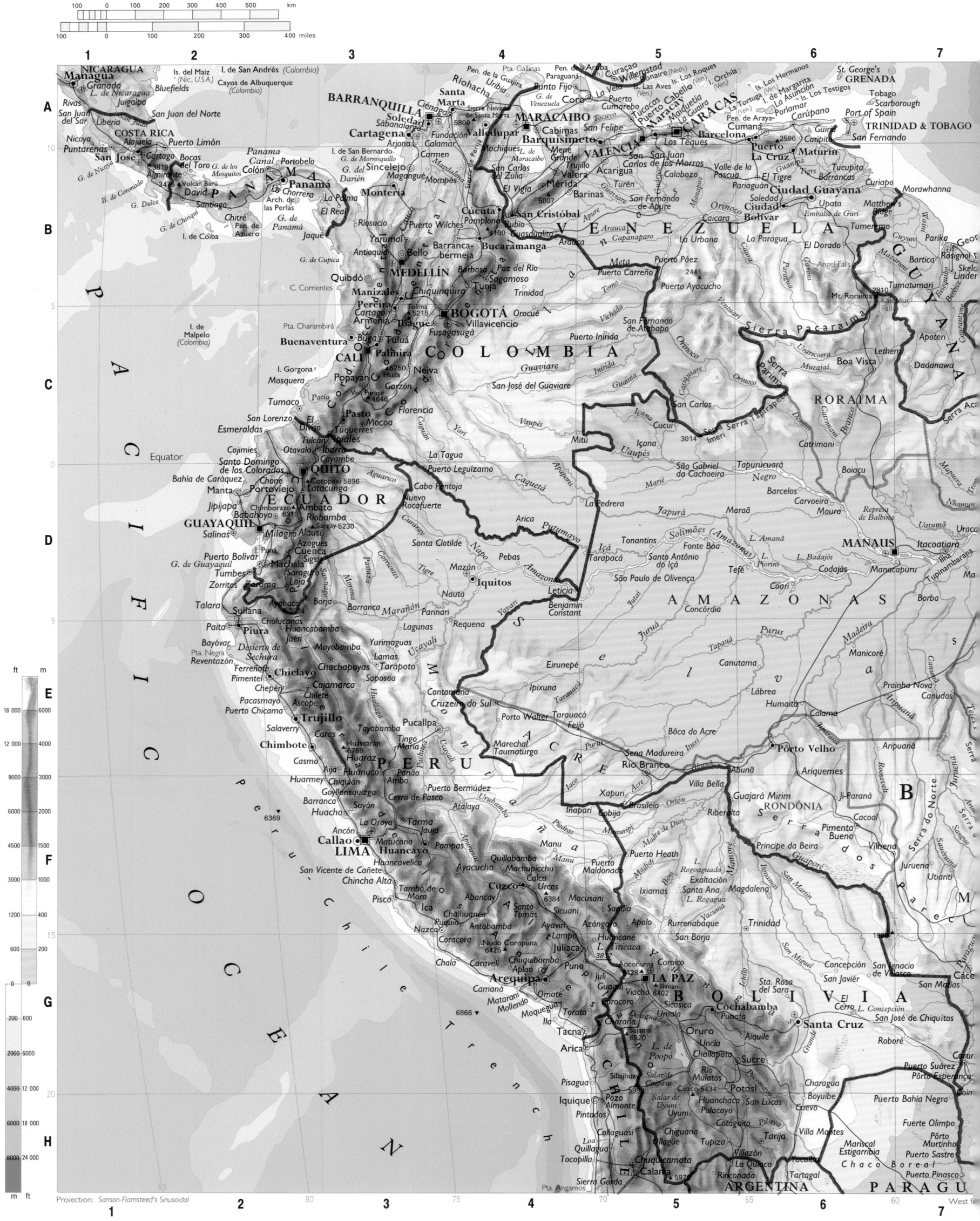

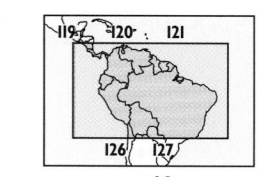

8　　**9**　　**10**　　**11**　　**12**　　**13**

A

B

A T L A N T I C

O C E A N

C

n
Nickerie
Totness　Paramaribo
Nieuw Amsterdam
w　Albina　Moengo
St-Laurent
Iracoubo　Sinnamary
Kourou
Kaw　Cayenne
Prof. Van
Blommestein-
▲1230　mer
anatop　Approuague
RINAM　St-Georges
FRENCH　Oiapoque
GUIANA　C. Orange
Serra Tumucumaque　Camopi

D

Amapá　I. de Maracá
AMAPÁ
Meriruma　Serra do　Araguari
Navio
Macapá
I. Caviana
Mazagão　I. Mexiana
Óbidos　Afuá　C. Maguarinho
Monte　Chaves
Alegre　I. Grande　I. de Soure
Prainha　de Gurupá　Vigia　Salinópolis
Juruti　Almeirim　Marajó　Curuçá　Bragança
arintins　Gurupá　Breves　**BELÉM**　Viseu
Santarém　Pôrto de Móz　Castanhal　Turiaçu
Belterra　Cametá　Abaetetuba
Aveiro　Baião　Cururupu
Brasília Legal　Tucuruí　B. de São Marcos
Altamira　**São Luís**
P A R Á
Equator
Santa Inês
Pinheiro
Rosário　Barreirinhas
Viana　Tutóia
Parnaíba
Luís Correia
Camocim

0 (Equator)

Equator

5

6059 ▼

10

Trindade
(Braz.)

15

20

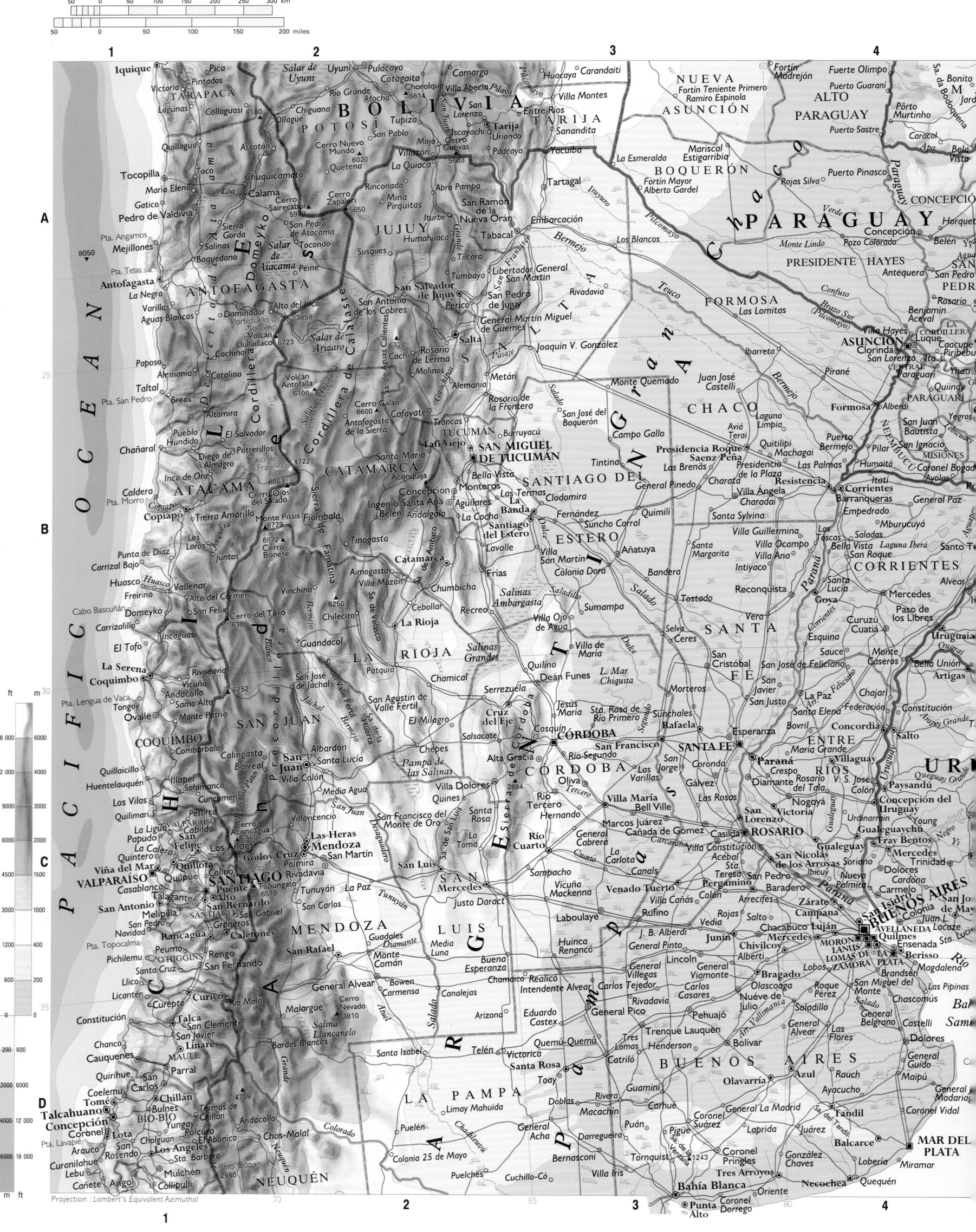

5   6   7

BELO
HORIZONTE
Nova Lima   Vitória
Sidrolândia   Olímpia   Itabirito   Itaquari
Nioaque   Três Lagoas   Andradina   Mirassol   São José   Batatais   Passos   Congonhas   Conselheiro   Pico da   Vila
                                                                                                                                                                Bandeira   Velha
                    Xavantina   Mirandópolis   Araçatuba   Catanduva   do Rio Prêto   Bebedouro   Ribeirão   Sebastião   Oliveira   Conselheiro   2880   Guaraparí
TO GROSSO   Panorama   Adamantina   São   Taquaritinga   Jaboticabal   Prêto   do Paraíso   Campo Belo   Ouro   Ponte Nova
Maracaju   Nova Alvorada   Presidente   Santo   Lins   PAULO   Mococa   Casa   Alfenas   Prêto   Carangola   Cachoeiro
de Sul   do Sul   Epitácio   Anastácio   Tupã   Araraquara   São   Branca   Vargínha   Lavras   Barbacena   Cataguases   de Itapemirim
DO SUL   Nova   Pirajuí   Garça   Bariri   São João   Três   São João
Dourados   Rio   Andradina   Presidente   Martinópolis   Marília   da Boa Vista   Pinhal   Pouso   Corações   del Rei   Ubá   Muriaé   Alegre
    Brilhante   Euclides da   Prudente   Paraguaçu   Bauru   Jaú   Rio Claro   Roços de   Alegre   São   Leopoldina   Itaperuna
Ponta Porã   Ivinhema   Cunha Paulista   Rancharia   Paulista   Araras   Caldas   Ouro Fino   Volta   Três   Cambuci
Pedro Juan Caballero   Rosana   Paranapanema   Assis   Cambará   do Rio Pardo   Piracicaba   CAMPINAS   Mogi-Mirim   Redonda   Rios   Paraíba do Sul
        Nova   Centenário do Sul   Sertanópolis   Ourinhos   Botucatu   Itu   Jundiaí   Americana   Barra   Barra do Piraí   CAMPOS
Dourados   Paranavaí   Nova   Londrina   Cornélio   Avaré   Tietê   Bragança   Cruzeiro   Nova Friburgo   Cabo de
Amambaí   Esperança   Rolândia   Procópio   Jacarèzinho   Itapetininga   SÃO PAULO   Sorocaba   Jacareí   Taubaté   Angra dos   NOVA IGUAÇ   DUQUE DE CAXIAS   São Tomé
Capitán   Umuarama   Cianorte   Maringá   Apucarana   Joaquim   São Bernardo   SANTO ANDRÉ   Reis   Petrópolis   SÃO GONÇALO   Macaé
Bado   Navirai   Mandaguari   Arapongas   Távora   Itaporanga   do Campo   Santos   NITERÓI   Cabo Frio
    Mundo Novo   Cruzeiro   Ibaiti   Itararé   Paranapiacaba   São Vicente   Guarujá   RIO DE JANEIRO   Tropic of Capricorn
Salto del Guairá   Guaíra   Goio-Erê   PARANÁ   Tibagi   Jaguariaíva   Apiaí   Juquiá   Ilha de São Sebastião
CANINDEYÚ   Porto Mendes   Ubiratã   Cândido de Abreu   Castro   Serra   Registro   Pta. de Boi
Curuguaty   Represa de   Toledo   Pitanga   BRAZIL   Prudentópolis   Ponta   Palmeira   Itanhaém
    Itaipú   Cascavel   Sa. das Araras   Guarapuava   Grossa   1889   Ilha Comprida
Hernandarias   Foz do Iguaçu   Medianeira   Iguaçu   Laranjeiras   Irati   CURITIBA   Iguape
Ciudad   Francisco   do Sul   Lapa   Antonina   Ilha do Cardoso
del Este   Beltrão   Pato Branco   União da   Palmeira   Paranaguá
PARANÁ   Bernardo   Clevelândia   Vitória   Pôrto União   Matinhos
Eldorado   de Irigoyen   Palmas   São Mateus   Rio Negro   Guaratuba
        Sa. da Fartura   do Sul   Mafra   Joinville
MISIONES   Xanxerê   1340   Caçador   São Francisco do Sul
Uruguai   Chapecó   Santa Cecília
Montevideo   Joaçaba   SANTA   Blumenau   Itajaí
Corpus   Frederico   CATARINA   Brusque
Encarnación   Westphalen   Campos   Curitibanos   Rio do Sul
Candelaria   Palmeira   Novos   São José   Ilha de Santa Catarina
    das Missões   Lajes   1808   Florianópolis
Leandro N. Alem   Erechim   Vacaria   São
Santa Rosa   Carazinho   Joaquim   Laguna
San Javier   Passo   Lagoa   Tubarão   Cabo Santa Marta Grande
Apóstoles   Fundo   Vermelha   Criciúma
Santo Ângelo   Ijuí   Cruz Alta   Araranguá
Borja   São Luís   Coxilha Grande   Bento Gonçalves   Torres
    Gonzaga   Guaporé
Santiago   RIO GRANDE   Caxias do Sul
Ibicuí   Santa Maria   Nôvo Hamburgo
Santa Cruz   Montenegro   Taquara
Alegrete   do Sul   Canoas   Osório
rio do Sul   Cachoeira do Sul   Rio Pardo   São
DO   SUL   Leopoldo   Viamão
São   PÔRTO ALEGRE
Santana do   Gabriel   Caçapava   Sa.   Encantadas
Livramento   Dom Pedrito   do Sul   Camaquã
    Sa. do Ganguçu   Tapes
Rivera Santana   Camaquã
acuarembó   Bagé   São Lourenço   Mostardas
    Pinheiro   do Sul   Canguçu
UAY   Machado   Pelotas   Lagoa dos   Patos
Fraile   Melo   São José do Norte
Muerto   Jaguarão   Rio Grande
San Gregorio   Río Branco   Mirim
Blanquillo   Vergara
Cerro   Lagoa Mangueira
Chato   Treinta y Tres
José Batlle   Lascano
y Ordóñez   Chuy
Tala   Aigua   Santa Vitória do Palmar
Iones   Minas   Castillos
iedras   Rocha
San Carlos
Maldonado
NTEVIDEO
Plata

A T L A N T I C

O C E A N

5304

West from Greenwich   COPYRIGHT GEORGE PHILIP LTD

A

B

C

D

5   6   7

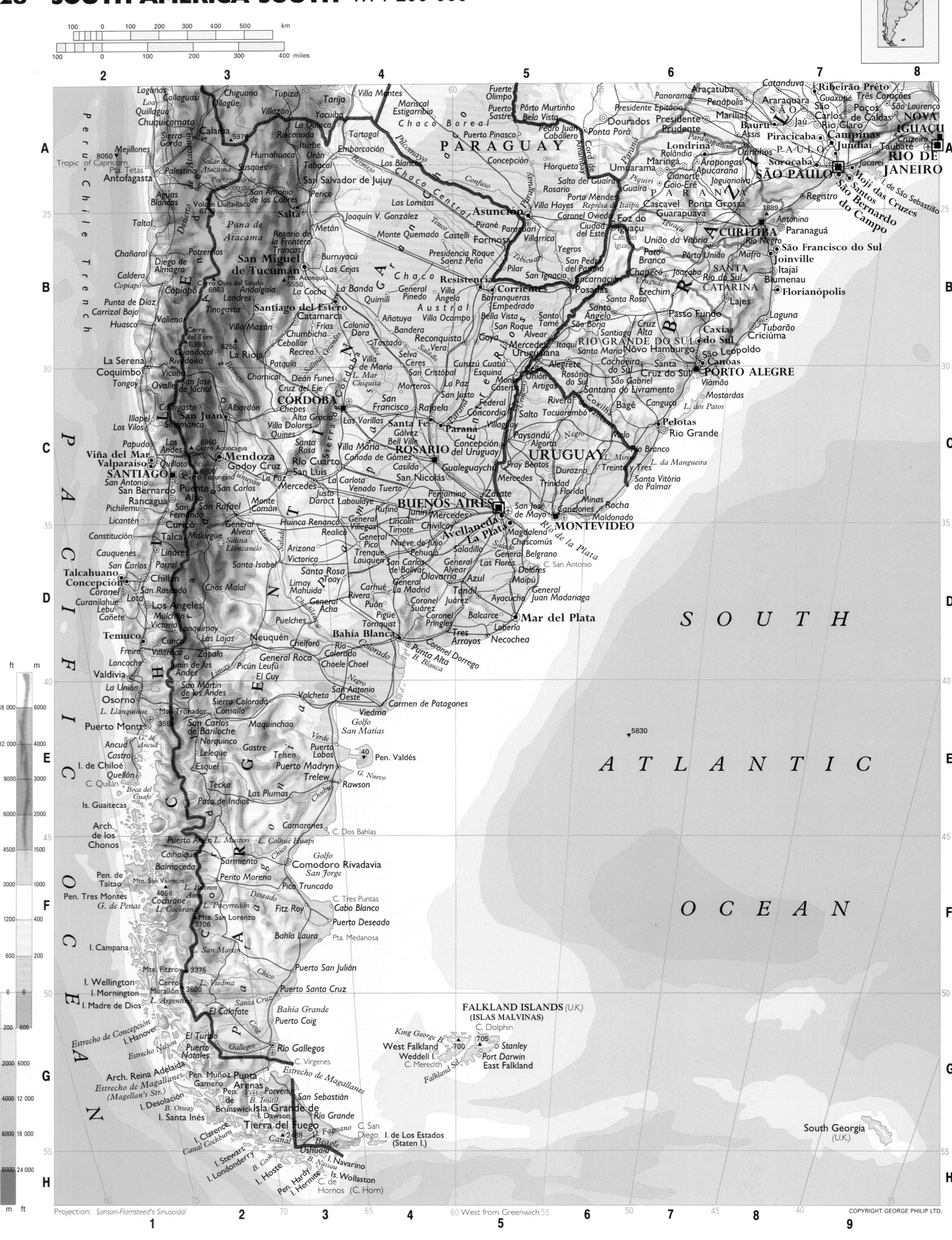

km
100   0   100   200   300   500
100   0   100   200   300   400 miles

S O U T H

A T L A N T I C

O C E A N

PARAGUAY

URUGUAY

PACIFIC OCEAN

SÃO PAULO

RIO DE JANEIRO

NOVA IGUAÇU

CURITIBA

PORTO ALEGRE

BUENOS AIRES

MONTEVIDEO

SANTIAGO

CÓRDOBA

ROSARIO

Mar del Plata

Bahía Blanca

FALKLAND ISLANDS (U.K.)
(ISLAS MALVINAS)
West Falkland
East Falkland
Stanley
Port Darwin

South Georgia
(U.K.)

Tierra del Fuego
Ushuaia
C. de Hornos (C. Horn)

Projection: Sanson-Flamsteed's Sinusoidal

COPYRIGHT GEORGE PHILIP LTD.

INDEX

The index contains the names of all the principal places and features shown on the World Maps. Each name is followed by an additional entry in italics giving the country or region within which it is located. The alphabetical order of names composed of two or more words is governed primarily by the first word and then by the second. This is an example of the rule:

Mīr Kūh, *Iran* **71**   **E8**
Mīr Shahdād, *Iran* **71**   **E8**
Mira, *Italy* **29**   **C9**
Mira por vos Cay, *Bahamas* . . **121**   **B5**
Miraj, *India* **66**   **L9**

Physical features composed of a proper name (Erie) and a description (Lake) are positioned alphabetically by the proper name. The description is positioned after the proper name and is usually abbreviated:

Erie, L., *N. Amer.* **110**   **D4**

Where a description forms part of a settlement or administrative name however, it is always written in full and put in its true alphabetic position:

Mount Morris, *U.S.A.* **110**   **D7**

Names beginning with M' and Mc are indexed as if they were spelled Mac. Names beginning St. are alphabetised under Saint, but Sankt, Sint, Sant', Santa and San are all spelt in full and are alphabetised accordingly. If the same place name occurs two or more times in the index and all are in the same country, each is followed by the name of the administrative subdivision in which it is located. The names are placed in the alphabetical order of the subdivisions. For example:

Jackson, *Ky., U.S.A.* **108**   **G4**
Jackson, *Mich., U.S.A.* **108**   **D3**
Jackson, *Minn., U.S.A.* **112**   **D7**

The number in bold type which follows each name in the index refers to the number of the map page where that feature or place will be found. This is usually the largest scale at which the place or feature appears.

The letter and figure which are in bold type immediately after the page number give the grid square on the map page, within which the feature is situated. The letter represents the latitude and the figure the longitude.

In some cases the feature itself may fall within the specified square, while the name is outside. This is usually the case only with features which are larger than a grid square.

Rivers are indexed to their mouths or confluences, and carry the symbol → after their names. A solid square ■ follows the name of a country, while an open square □ refers to a first order administrative area.

ABBREVIATIONS USED IN THE INDEX

A.C.T. – Australian Capital Territory
Afghan. – Afghanistan
Ala. – Alabama
Alta. – Alberta
Amer. – America(n)
Arch. – Archipelago
Ariz. – Arizona
Ark. – Arkansas
Atl. Oc. – Atlantic Ocean
B. – Baie, Bahía, Bay, Bucht, Bugt
B.C. – British Columbia
Bangla. – Bangladesh
Barr. – Barrage
Bos.-H. – Bosnia-Herzegovina
C. – Cabo, Cap, Cape, Coast
C.A.R. – Central African Republic
C. Prov. – Cape Province
Calif. – California
Cent. – Central
Chan. – Channel
Colo. – Colorado
Conn. – Connecticut
Cord. – Cordillera
Cr. – Creek
Czech. – Czech Republic
D.C. – District of Columbia
Del. – Delaware
Dep. – Dependency
Des. – Desert
Dist. – District
Dj. – Djebel
Domin. – Dominica
Dom. Rep. – Dominican Republic
E. – East

E. Salv. – El Salvador
Eq. Guin. – Equatorial Guinea
Fla. – Florida
Falk. Is. – Falkland Is.
G. – Golfe, Golfo, Gulf, Guba, Gebel
Ga. – Georgia
Gt. – Great, Greater
Guinea-Biss. – Guinea-Bissau
H.K. – Hong Kong
H.P. – Himachal Pradesh
Hants. – Hampshire
Harb. – Harbor, Harbour
Hd. – Head
Hts. – Heights
I.(s). – Île, Ilha, Insel, Isla, Island, Isle
Ill. – Illinois
Ind. – Indiana
Ind. Oc. – Indian Ocean
Ivory C. – Ivory Coast
J. – Jabal, Jebel, Jazira
Junc. – Junction
K. – Kap, Kapp
Kans. – Kansas
Kep. – Kepulauan
Ky. – Kentucky
L. – Lac, Lacul, Lago, Lagoa, Lake, Limni, Loch, Lough
La. – Louisiana
Liech. – Liechtenstein
Lux. – Luxembourg
Mad. P. – Madhya Pradesh
Madag. – Madagascar
Man. – Manitoba
Mass. – Massachusetts

Md. – Maryland
Me. – Maine
Medit. S. – Mediterranean Sea
Mich. – Michigan
Minn. – Minnesota
Miss. – Mississippi
Mo. – Missouri
Mont. – Montana
Mozam. – Mozambique
Mt.(e) – Mont, Monte, Monti, Montaña, Mountain
N. – Nord, Norte, North, Northern, Nouveau
N.B. – New Brunswick
N.C. – North Carolina
N. Cal. – New Caledonia
N. Dak. – North Dakota
N.H. – New Hampshire
N.I. – North Island
N.J. – New Jersey
N. Mex. – New Mexico
N.S. – Nova Scotia
N.S.W. – New South Wales
N.W.T. – North West Territory
N.Y. – New York
N.Z. – New Zealand
Nebr. – Nebraska
Neths. – Netherlands
Nev. – Nevada
Nfld. – Newfoundland
Nic. – Nicaragua
O. – Oued, Ouadi
Occ. – Occidentale
Okla. – Oklahoma
Ont. – Ontario
Or. – Orientale

Oreg. – Oregon
Os. – Ostrov
Oz. – Ozero
P. – Pass, Passo, Pasul, Pulau
P.E.I. – Prince Edward Island
Pa. – Pennsylvania
Pac. Oc. – Pacific Ocean
Papua N.G. – Papua New Guinea
Pass. – Passage
Pen. – Peninsula, Péninsule
Phil. – Philippines
Pk. – Park, Peak
Plat. – Plateau
Prov. – Province, Provincial
Pt. – Point
Pta. – Ponta, Punta
Pte. – Pointe
Qué. – Québec
Queens. – Queensland
R. – Rio, River
R.I. – Rhode Island
Ra.(s). – Range(s)
Raj. – Rajasthan
Reg. – Region
Rep. – Republic
Res. – Reserve, Reservoir
S. – San, South, Sea
Si. Arabia – Saudi Arabia
S.C. – South Carolina
S. Dak. – South Dakota
S.I. – South Island
S. Leone – Sierra Leone
Sa. – Serra, Sierra
Sask. – Saskatchewan
Scot. – Scotland
Sd. – Sound

Sev. – Severnaya
Sib. – Siberia
Sprs. – Springs
St. – Saint
Sta. – Santa, Station
Ste. – Sainte
Sto. – Santo
Str. – Strait, Stretto
Switz. – Switzerland
Tas. – Tasmania
Tenn. – Tennessee
Tex. – Texas
Tg. – Tanjung
Trin. & Tob. – Trinidad & Tobago
U.A.E. – United Arab Emirates
U.K. – United Kingdom
U.S.A. – United States of America
Ut. P. – Uttar Pradesh
Va. – Virginia
Vdkhr. – Vodokhranilishche
Vf. – Vîrful
Vic. – Victoria
Vol. – Volcano
Vt. – Vermont
W. – Wadi, West
W. Va. – West Virginia
Wash. – Washington
Wis. – Wisconsin
Wlkp. – Wielkopolski
Wyo. – Wyoming
Yorks. – Yorkshire
Yug. – Yugoslavia

A Baña

A

A Baña, *Spain* 34 C2
A Cañiza, *Spain* 34 C2
A Coruña, *Spain* 34 B2
A Estrada, *Spain* 34 C2
A Fonsagrada, *Spain* 34 B3
A Guarda, *Spain* 34 D2
A Gudiña, *Spain* 34 C3
A Rúa, *Spain* 34 C3
Aachen, *Germany* 24 E2
Aalborg = Ålborg, *Denmark* 11 G3
Aalen, *Germany* 25 G6
A'âli an Nîl □, *Sudan* 81 F3
Aalst, *Belgium* 17 D4
Aalten, *Neths.* 17 C6
Aalter, *Belgium* 17 C3
Äänekoski, *Finland* 9 E21
Aarau, *Switz.* 25 H4
Aarberg, *Switz.* 25 H3
Aare →, *Switz.* 25 H4
Aargau □, *Switz.* 25 H4
Aarhus = Århus, *Denmark* 11 H4
Aarschot, *Belgium* 17 D4
Aba, *China* 58 A3
Aba, *Dem. Rep. of the Congo* 86 B3
Aba, *Nigeria* 83 D6
Âbâ, Jazîrat, *Sudan* 81 E3
Abadab, J., *Sudan* 80 D4
Ābādān, *Iran* 71 D6
Abade, *Ethiopia* 81 F4
Ābādeh, *Iran* 71 D7
Abadin, *Spain* 34 B3
Abadla, *Algeria* 78 B5
Abaetetuba, *Brazil* 125 D9
Abagnar Qi, *China* 56 C9
Abai, *Paraguay* 127 B4
Abak, *Nigeria* 83 E6
Abakaliki, *Nigeria* 83 D6
Abakan, *Russia* 51 D10
Abala, *Niger* 83 C5
Abalak, *Niger* 83 B6
Abalemma, *Niger* 83 B6
Abana, *Turkey* 72 B6
Abancay, *Peru* 124 F4
Abano Terme, *Italy* 29 C8
Abarán, *Spain* 33 G3
Abariringa, *Kiribati* 96 H10
Abarqū, *Iran* 71 D7
Abashiri, *Japan* 54 B12
Abashiri-Wan, *Japan* 54 C12
Abaújszántó, *Hungary* 42 B6
Abava →, *Latvia* 44 A8
Ābay = Nîl el Azraq →, *Sudan* 81 D3
Abay, *Kazakstan* 50 E8
Abaya, L., *Ethiopia* 81 F4
Abaza, *Russia* 50 D9
Abbadia San Salvatore, *Italy* 29 F8
'Abbāsābād, *Iran* 71 C8
Abbay = Nîl el Azraq →, *Sudan* 81 D3
Abbaye, Pt., *U.S.A.* 108 B1
Abbé, L., *Ethiopia* 81 E5
Abbeville, *France* 19 B8
Abbeville, *Ala., U.S.A.* 109 K3
Abbeville, *La., U.S.A.* 113 L8
Abbeville, *S.C., U.S.A.* 109 H4
Abbiategrasso, *Italy* 28 C5
Abbot Ice Shelf, *Antarctica* 5 D16
Abbottabad, *Pakistan* 68 B5
Abd al Kūrī, *Ind. Oc.* 74 E5
Ābdar, *Iran* 71 D7
'Abdolābād, *Iran* 71 C8
Abdulpur, *Bangla.* 69 G13
Abéché, *Chad* 79 F10
Abejar, *Spain* 32 D2
Abekr, *Sudan* 81 E2
Abengourou, *Ivory C.* 82 D4
Abenójar, *Spain* 35 G6
Åbenrå, *Denmark* 11 J3
Abensberg, *Germany* 25 G7
Abeokuta, *Nigeria* 83 D5
Aber, *Uganda* 86 B3
Aberaeron, *U.K.* 13 E3
Aberayron = Aberaeron, *U.K.* 13 E3
Aberchirder, *U.K.* 14 D6
Abercorn = Mbala, *Zambia* 87 D3
Abercorn, *Australia* 95 D5
Aberdare, *U.K.* 13 F4
Aberdare Ra., *Kenya* 86 C4
Aberdeen, *Canada* 105 C7
Aberdeen, *S. Africa* 88 E3
Aberdeen, *U.K.* 14 D6
Aberdeen, *Ala., U.S.A.* 109 J1
Aberdeen, *Idaho, U.S.A.* 114 E7
Aberdeen, *Md., U.S.A.* 108 F7
Aberdeen, *S. Dak., U.S.A.* 112 C5
Aberdeen, *Wash., U.S.A.* 116 D3
Aberdeen, City of □, *U.K.* 14 D6
Aberdeenshire □, *U.K.* 14 D6
Aberdovey = Aberdyfi, *U.K.* 13 E3
Aberdyfi, *U.K.* 13 E3
Aberfeldy, *U.K.* 14 E5
Abergavenny, *U.K.* 13 F4
Abergele, *U.K.* 12 D4
Abernathy, *U.S.A.* 113 J4
Abert, L., *U.S.A.* 114 E3
Aberystwyth, *U.K.* 13 E3
Abhā, *Si. Arabia* 74 D3
Abhar, *Iran* 71 B6
Abhayapuri, *India* 69 F14
Abia □, *Nigeria* 83 D6
Abide, *Turkey* 39 C11
Abidiya, *Sudan* 80 D3
Abidjan, *Ivory C.* 82 D4
Abilene, *Kans., U.S.A.* 112 F6
Abilene, *Tex., U.S.A.* 113 J5
Abingdon, *U.K.* 13 F6
Abingdon, *U.S.A.* 109 G5
Abington Reef, *Australia* 94 B4
Abitau →, *Canada* 105 B7
Abitibi →, *Canada* 102 B3
Abitibi, L., *Canada* 102 C4
Abiy Adi, *Ethiopia* 81 E4
Abkhaz Republic = Abkhazia □, *Georgia* 49 J5
Abkhazia □, *Georgia* 49 J5
Abminga, *Australia* 95 D1
Abnûb, *Egypt* 80 B3
Åbo = Turku, *Finland* 9 F20
Abocho, *Nigeria* 83 D6
Abohar, *India* 68 D6
Aboisso, *Ivory C.* 82 D4
Abomey, *Benin* 83 D5
Abong-Mbang, *Cameroon* 84 D2
Abonnema, *Nigeria* 83 E6
Abony, *Hungary* 42 C5
Aboso, *Ghana* 82 D4
Abou-Deïa, *Chad* 79 F9
Aboyne, *U.K.* 14 D6
Abra Pampa, *Argentina* 126 A2
Abraham L., *Canada* 104 C5
Abrantes, *Portugal* 35 F2
Abreojos, Pta., *Mexico* 118 B2
Abri, *Esh Shamâliya, Sudan* 80 C3
Abri, *Janub Kordofân, Sudan* 81 E3
Abrud, *Romania* 42 D8
Abruzzo □, *Italy* 29 F10
Absaroka Range, *U.S.A.* 114 D9
Abtenau, *Austria* 26 D6
Abu, *India* 68 G5
Abū al Abyad, *U.A.E.* 71 E7
Abū al Khaşīb, *Iraq* 71 D6
Abū 'Alī, *Si. Arabia* 71 E6
Abū 'Alī →, *Lebanon* 75 A4
Abu Ballas, *Egypt* 80 C2
Abu Deleiq, *Sudan* 81 D3
Abu Dhabi = Abū Ẓāby, *U.A.E.* 71 E7
Abu Dis, *Sudan* 80 D3
Abu Dom, *Sudan* 81 D3
Abū Du'ān, *Syria* 70 B3
Abu el Gairi, W. →, *Egypt* 75 F2
Abu Fatma, Ras, *Sudan* 80 C4
Abu Gabra, *Sudan* 81 E2
Abu Ga'da, W. →, *Egypt* 75 F1
Abu Gelba, *Sudan* 81 E3
Abu Gubeiha, *Sudan* 81 E3
Abu Habl, Khawr →, *Sudan* 81 E3
Abū Ḩadrīyah, *Si. Arabia* 71 E6
Abu Hamed, *Sudan* 80 D3
Abu Haraz, *An Nîl el Azraq, Sudan* 80 D3
Abu Haraz, *El Gezira, Sudan* 81 E3
Abu Haraz, *Esh Shamâliya, Sudan* 80 D3
Abu Higar, *Sudan* 81 E3
Abū Kamāl, *Syria* 70 C4
Abu Kuleiwat, *Sudan* 81 E2
Abū Madd, Ra's, *Si. Arabia* 70 E3
Abu Matariq, *Sudan* 81 E2
Abu Mendi, *Ethiopia* 81 E4
Abū Mūsā, *U.A.E.* 71 E7
Abū Qaşr, *Si. Arabia* 70 D3
Abu Qir, *Egypt* 80 H7
Abu Qireiya, *Egypt* 80 C4
Abu Qurqâs, *Egypt* 80 B3
Abu Şafāt, W. →, *Jordan* 75 E5
Abu Shagara, Ras, *Sudan* 80 C4
Abu Shanab, *Sudan* 81 E2
Abu Simbel, *Egypt* 80 C3
Abū Şukhayr, *Iraq* 70 D5
Abu Sultân, *Egypt* 80 H8
Abu Tabari, *Sudan* 80 D2
Abu Tig, *Egypt* 80 B3
Abu Tiga, *Sudan* 81 E3
Abu Tineitin, *Sudan* 81 E3
Abu Uruq, *Sudan* 81 D3
Abu Zabad, *Sudan* 81 E2
Abū Ẓāby, *U.A.E.* 71 E7
Abū Zeydābād, *Iran* 71 C6
Abuja, *Nigeria* 83 D6
Abukuma-Gawa →, *Japan* 54 E10
Abukuma-Sammyaku, *Japan* 54 F10
Abunã, *Brazil* 124 E5
Abunã →, *Brazil* 124 E5
Abune Yosef, *Ethiopia* 81 E4
Aburo, *Dem. Rep. of the Congo* 86 B3
Abut Hd., *N.Z.* 91 K3
Abuye Meda, *Ethiopia* 81 E4
Abwong, *Sudan* 81 F3
Åby, *Sweden* 11 F10
Aby, Lagune, *Ivory C.* 82 D4
Abyad, *Sudan* 81 E2
Åbybro, *Denmark* 11 G3
Acadia National Park, *U.S.A.* 109 C11
Açailândia, *Brazil* 125 D9
Acajutla, *El Salv.* 120 D2
Acámbaro, *Mexico* 118 D4
Acanthus, *Greece* 40 F7
Acaponeta, *Mexico* 118 C3
Acapulco, *Mexico* 119 D5
Acarai, Serra, *Brazil* 124 C7
Acarigua, *Venezuela* 124 B5
Acatlán, *Mexico* 119 D5
Acayucan, *Mexico* 119 D6
Accéglio, *Italy* 28 D4
Accomac, *U.S.A.* 108 G8
Accous, *France* 20 E3
Accra, *Ghana* 83 D4
Accrington, *U.K.* 12 D5
Acebal, *Argentina* 126 C3
Aceh □, *Indonesia* 62 D1
Acerra, *Italy* 31 B7
Aceuchal, *Spain* 35 G4
Achalpur, *India* 66 J10
Acheng, *China* 57 B14
Achenkirch, *Austria* 26 D4
Achensee, *Austria* 26 D4
Acher, *India* 68 H5
Achern, *Germany* 25 G4
Achill Hd., *Ireland* 15 C1
Achill I., *Ireland* 15 C1
Achim, *Germany* 24 B5
Achinsk, *Russia* 51 D10
Acıgöl, *Turkey* 39 D11
Acıpayam, *Turkey* 39 D11
Acireale, *Italy* 31 E8
Ackerman, *U.S.A.* 113 J10
Acklins I., *Bahamas* 121 B5
Acme, *Canada* 104 C6
Acme, *U.S.A.* 110 F5
Aconcagua, Cerro, *Argentina* 126 C2
Aconquija, Mt., *Argentina* 126 B2
Açores, Is. dos = Azores, *Atl. Oc.* 78 A1
Acornhoek, *S. Africa* 89 C5
Acquapendente, *Italy* 29 F8
Acquasanta Terme, *Italy* 29 F10
Acquasparta, *Italy* 29 F9
Acquaviva delle Fonti, *Italy* 31 B9
Ácqui Terme, *Italy* 28 D5
Acraman, L., *Australia* 95 E2
Acre = 'Akko, *Israel* 75 C4
Acre □, *Brazil* 124 E4
Acre →, *Brazil* 124 E5
Acri, *Italy* 31 C9
Acs, *Hungary* 42 C3
Actium, *Greece* 38 C2
Acton, *Canada* 110 C4
Acuña, *Mexico* 118 B4
Ad Dammām, *Si. Arabia* 71 E6
Ad Dāmūr, *Lebanon* 75 B4
Ad Dawādimī, *Si. Arabia* 70 E5
Ad Dawḩah, *Qatar* 71 E6
Ad Dawr, *Iraq* 70 C4
Ad Dir'īyah, *Si. Arabia* 70 E5
Ad Dīwānīyah, *Iraq* 70 D5
Ad Dujayl, *Iraq* 70 C5
Ad Duwayd, *Si. Arabia* 70 D4
Ada, *Ghana* 83 D5
Ada, *Serbia, Yug.* 42 E5
Ada, *Minn., U.S.A.* 112 B6
Ada, *Okla., U.S.A.* 113 H6
Adabiya, *Egypt* 75 F1
Adair, C., *Canada* 101 A12
Adaja →, *Spain* 34 D6
Adak I., *U.S.A.* 100 C2
Adamaoua, Massif de l', *Cameroon* 83 D7
Adamawa □, *Nigeria* 83 D7
Adamawa Highlands = Adamaoua, Massif de l', *Cameroon* 83 D7
Adamello, Mte., *Italy* 28 B7
Adami Tulu, *Ethiopia* 81 F4
Adams, *Mass., U.S.A.* 111 D11
Adams, *N.Y., U.S.A.* 111 C8
Adams, *Wis., U.S.A.* 112 D10
Adam's Bridge, *Sri Lanka* 66 Q11
Adams L., *Canada* 104 C5
Adams Mt., *U.S.A.* 116 D5
Adam's Peak, *Sri Lanka* 66 R12
Adamuz, *Spain* 35 G6
Adana, *Turkey* 70 B2
Adanero, *Spain* 34 E6
Adapazarı = Sakarya, *Turkey* 72 B4
Adar Gwagwa, J., *Sudan* 80 C4
Adarama, *Sudan* 81 D3
Adare, C., *Antarctica* 5 D11
Adarte, *Eritrea* 81 E5
Adaut, *Indonesia* 63 F8
Adavale, *Australia* 95 D3
Adda →, *Italy* 28 C6
Addis Ababa = Addis Abeba, *Ethiopia* 81 F4
Addis Abeba, *Ethiopia* 81 F4
Addis Alem, *Ethiopia* 81 F4
Addis Zemen, *Ethiopia* 81 E4
Addison, *U.S.A.* 110 D7
Addo, *S. Africa* 88 E4
Adebour, *Niger* 83 C7
Ādeh, *Iran* 70 B5
Adel, *U.S.A.* 109 K4
Adelaide, *Bahamas* 120 A4
Adelaide, *S. Africa* 88 E4
Adelaide I., *Antarctica* 5 C17
Adelaide Pen., *Canada* 100 B10
Adelaide River, *Australia* 92 B5
Adelanto, *U.S.A.* 117 L9
Adele I., *Australia* 92 C3
Adélie, Terre, *Antarctica* 5 C10
Adélie Land = Adélie, Terre, *Antarctica* 5 C10
Ademuz, *Spain* 32 E3
Aden = Al 'Adan, *Yemen* 74 E4
Aden, G. of, *Asia* 74 E4
Adendorp, *S. Africa* 88 E3
Aderbissinat, *Niger* 83 B6
Adh Dhayd, *U.A.E.* 71 E7
Adhoi, *India* 68 H4
Adi, *Indonesia* 63 E8
Adi Arkai, *Ethiopia* 81 E4
Adi Daro, *Ethiopia* 81 E4
Adi Keyih, *Eritrea* 81 E4
Adi Kwala, *Eritrea* 81 E4
Adi Ugri, *Eritrea* 81 E4
Adieu, C., *Australia* 93 F5
Adieu Pt., *Australia* 92 C3
Adigala, *Ethiopia* 81 E5
Adige →, *Italy* 29 C9
Adigrat, *Ethiopia* 81 E4
Adıgüzel Barajı, *Turkey* 39 C11
Adilabad, *India* 66 K11
Adilcevaz, *Turkey* 73 C10
Adirondack Mts., *U.S.A.* 111 C10
Adıyaman, *Turkey* 73 D8
Adjohon, *Benin* 83 D5
Adjud, *Romania* 43 D12
Adjumani, *Uganda* 86 B3
Adlavik Is., *Canada* 103 A8
Adler, *Russia* 49 J4
Admer, *Algeria* 83 A6
Admiralty G., *Australia* 92 B4
Admiralty I., *U.S.A.* 104 B2
Admiralty Is., *Papua N. G.* 96 H6
Ado, *Nigeria* 83 D5
Ado-Ekiti, *Nigeria* 83 D6
Adok, *Sudan* 81 F3
Adola, *Ethiopia* 81 E5
Adonara, *Indonesia* 63 F6
Adoni, *India* 66 M10
Adony, *Hungary* 42 C3
Adour →, *France* 20 E2
Adra, *India* 69 H12
Adra, *Spain* 35 J7
Adrano, *Italy* 31 E7
Adrar, *Mauritania* 78 D3
Adrar des Iforas, *Algeria* 78 C5
Ádria, *Italy* 29 C9
Adrian, *Mich., U.S.A.* 108 E3
Adrian, *Tex., U.S.A.* 113 H3
Adriatic Sea, *Medit. S.* 6 G9
Adua, *Indonesia* 63 E7
Adwa, *Ethiopia* 81 E4
Adygea □, *Russia* 49 H5
Adzhar Republic = Ajaria □, *Georgia* 49 K6
Adzopé, *Ivory C.* 82 D4
Ægean Sea, *Medit. S.* 39 C7
Aerhtai Shan, *Mongolia* 60 B4
Ærø, *Denmark* 11 K4
Ærøskøbing, *Denmark* 11 K4
Aëtós, *Greece* 38 D3
'Afak, *Iraq* 70 C5
Afándou, *Greece* 36 C10
Afghanistan ■, *Asia* 66 C4
Afikpo, *Nigeria* 83 D6
Aflou, *Algeria* 78 B6
Afragóla, *Italy* 31 B7
Afram →, *Ghana* 83 D4
Afrera, *Ethiopia* 81 E5
Africa 76 E6
'Afrīn, *Syria* 70 B3
Afşin, *Turkey* 72 C7
Afton, *N.Y., U.S.A.* 111 D9
Afton, *Wyo., U.S.A.* 114 E8
Afuá, *Brazil* 125 D8
'Afula, *Israel* 75 C4
Afyon, *Turkey* 39 C12
Afyon □, *Turkey* 39 C12
Afyonkarahisar = Afyon, *Turkey* 39 C12
Aga, *Egypt* 80 H7
Agadès = Agadez, *Niger* 83 B6
Agadez, *Niger* 83 B6
Agadir, *Morocco* 78 B4
Agaete, *Canary Is.* 37 F4
Agaie, *Nigeria* 83 D6
Again, *Sudan* 81 F2
Ağapınar, *Turkey* 39 B12
Agar, *India* 68 H7
Agaro, *Ethiopia* 81 F4
Agartala, *India* 67 H17
Agăş, *Romania* 43 D11
Agassiz, *Canada* 104 D4
Agats, *Indonesia* 63 F9
Agawam, *U.S.A.* 111 D12
Agbélouvé, *Togo* 83 D5
Agboville, *Ivory C.* 82 D4
Ağcabädi, *Azerbaijan* 49 K8
Ağdam, *Azerbaijan* 49 L8
Ağdaş, *Azerbaijan* 49 K8
Agde, *France* 20 E7
Agde, C. d', *France* 20 E7
Agdzhabedi = Ağcabädi, *Azerbaijan* 49 K8
Agen, *France* 20 D4
Agerbæk, *Denmark* 11 J2
Agersø, *Denmark* 11 J5
Ageyevo, *Russia* 46 E9
Āgh Kand, *Iran* 71 B6
Aghireşu, *Romania* 43 D8
Aginskoye, *Russia* 51 D12
Ağlasun, *Turkey* 39 D12
Agly →, *France* 20 F7
Agnew, *Australia* 93 E3
Agnibilékrou, *Ivory C.* 82 D4
Agnita, *Romania* 43 E9
Agnone, *Italy* 29 G11
Agofie, *Ghana* 83 D5
Agogna →, *Italy* 28 C5
Agogo, *Sudan* 81 F2
Agön, *Sweden* 10 C11
Agon Coutainville, *France* 18 C5
Ágordo, *Italy* 29 B9
Agori, *India* 69 G10
Agouna, *Benin* 83 D5
Agout →, *France* 20 E5
Agra, *India* 68 F7
Agrakhanskiy Poluostrov, *Russia* 49 J8
Agramunt, *Spain* 32 D6
Agreda, *Spain* 32 D3
Ağri, *Turkey* 73 C10
Agri →, *Italy* 31 B9
Ağrı Dağı, *Turkey* 70 B5
Ağri Karakose = Ağri, *Turkey* 73 C10
Agriá, *Greece* 38 B5
Agrigento, *Italy* 30 E6
Agrínion, *Greece* 38 C3
Agrópoli, *Italy* 31 B7
Ağstafa, *Azerbaijan* 49 K7
Agua Caliente, *Baja Calif., Mexico* 117 N10
Agua Caliente, *Sinaloa, Mexico* 118 B3
Agua Caliente Springs, *U.S.A.* 117 N10
Água Clara, *Brazil* 125 H8
Agua Hechicero, *Mexico* 117 N10
Agua Prieta, *Mexico* 118 A3
Aguadilla, *Puerto Rico* 121 C6
Aguadulce, *Panama* 120 E3
Aguanga, *U.S.A.* 117 M10
Aguanish, *Canada* 103 B7
Aguanus →, *Canada* 103 B7
Aguapey →, *Argentina* 126 B4
Aguaray Guazú →, *Paraguay* 126 A4
Aguarico →, *Ecuador* 124 D3
Aguas →, *Spain* 32 D4
Aguas Blancas, *Chile* 126 A2
Aguas Calientes, Sierra de, *Argentina* 126 B2
Aguascalientes, *Mexico* 118 C4
Aguascalientes □, *Mexico* 118 C4
Agudo, *Spain* 35 G6
Águeda, *Portugal* 34 E2
Agueda →, *Spain* 34 D4
Aguelhok, *Mali* 83 B5
Aguié, *Niger* 83 C6
Aguilafuente, *Spain* 34 D6
Aguilar, *Spain* 35 H6
Aguilar de Campóo, *Spain* 34 C6
Aguilares, *Argentina* 126 B2
Aguilas, *Spain* 33 H3
Agüimes, *Canary Is.* 37 G4
Aguja, C. de la, *Colombia* 122 B3
Agulaa, *Ethiopia* 81 E4
Agulhas, C., *S. Africa* 88 E3
Agulo, *Canary Is.* 37 F2
Agung, *Indonesia* 62 F5
Agur, *Uganda* 86 B3
Agusan →, *Phil.* 61 G6
Ağva, *Turkey* 41 E13
Agvali, *Russia* 49 J8
Aha Mts., *Botswana* 88 B3
Ahaggar, *Algeria* 78 D7
Ahamansu, *Ghana* 83 D5
Ahar, *Iran* 70 B5
Ahat, *Turkey* 39 C11
Ahaus, *Germany* 24 C2
Ahipara B., *N.Z.* 91 F4
Ahir Dağı, *Turkey* 39 C12
Ahiri, *India* 66 K12
Ahlat, *Turkey* 73 C10
Ahlen, *Germany* 24 D3
Ahmad Wal, *Pakistan* 68 E1
Ahmadabad, *India* 68 H5
Aḩmadābād, *Khorāsān, Iran* 71 C9
Aḩmadābād, *Khorāsān, Iran* 71 C8
Aḩmadī, *Iran* 71 E8
Ahmadnagar, *India* 66 K9
Ahmadpur, *Pakistan* 68 E4
Ahmadpur Lamma, *Pakistan* 68 E4
Ahmar, *Ethiopia* 81 F5
Ahmedabad = Ahmadabad, *India* 68 H5
Ahmednagar = Ahmadnagar, *India* 66 K9
Ahmetbey, *Turkey* 41 E11
Ahmetler, *Turkey* 39 C11
Ahmetli, *Turkey* 39 C9
Ahoada, *Nigeria* 83 D6
Ahome, *Mexico* 118 B3
Ahoskie, *U.S.A.* 109 G7
Ahr →, *Germany* 24 E3
Ahram, *Iran* 71 D6
Ahrax Pt., *Malta* 36 D1
Ahrensbök, *Germany* 24 A6
Ahrensburg, *Germany* 24 B6
Āhū, *Iran* 71 C6
Ahuachapán, *El Salv.* 120 D2
Ahun, *France* 19 F9
Åhus, *Sweden* 11 J8
Ahvāz, *Iran* 71 D6
Ahvenanmaa = Åland, *Finland* 9 F19
Aḩwar, *Yemen* 74 E4
Ahzar →, *Mali* 83 B5
Ai →, *India* 69 F14
Ai-Ais, *Namibia* 88 D2
Aichach, *Germany* 25 G7
Aichi □, *Japan* 55 G8
Aigle, *Switz.* 25 J2
Aignay-le-Duc, *France* 19 E11
Aigoual, Mt., *France* 20 D7
Aigre, *France* 20 C4
Aigua, *Uruguay* 127 C5
Aigueperse, *France* 19 F10
Aigues →, *France* 21 D8
Aigues-Mortes, *France* 21 E8
Aigues-Mortes, G. d', *France* 21 E8
Aiguilles, *France* 21 D10
Aiguillon, *France* 20 D4
Aigurande, *France* 19 F8
Aihui, *China* 60 A7
Aija, *Peru* 124 E3
Aikawa, *Japan* 54 E9
Aiken, *U.S.A.* 109 J5
Ailao Shan, *China* 58 F3

Aileron, *Australia* 94 C1
Aillant-sur-Tholon, *France* 19 E10
Aillik, *Canada* 103 A8
Ailsa Craig, *U.K.* 14 F3
'Ailūn, *Jordan* 75 C4
Aim, *Russia* 51 D14
Aimere, *Indonesia* 63 F6
Aimogasta, *Argentina* 126 B2
Ain □, *France* 19 F12
Ain ➤, *France* 21 C9
Aïn Ben Tili, *Mauritania* 78 C4
Ain Dalla, *Egypt* 80 B2
Ain el Mafki, *Egypt* 80 B2
Ain Girba, *Egypt* 80 B2
Ain Murr, *Sudan* 80 C2
Ain Qeiqab, *Egypt* 80 B1
Aïn Sefra, *Algeria* 78 B5
Ain Sheikh Murzûk, *Egypt* 80 B2
Aïn Sudr, *Egypt* 75 F2
Ain Sukhna, *Egypt* 80 J8
Ain Zeitûn, *Egypt* 80 B2
Ainaži, *Latvia* 9 H21
Aínos Óros, *Greece* 38 C2
Ainsworth, *U.S.A.* 112 D5
Aiquile, *Bolivia* 124 G5
Aïr, *Niger* 83 B6
Air Force I., *Canada* 101 B12
Air Hitam, *Malaysia* 65 M4
Airaines, *France* 19 C8
Airdrie, *Canada* 104 C6
Airdrie, *U.K.* 14 F5
Aire ➤, *France* 19 C11
Aire ➤, *France* 12 D7
Aire, I. de l', *Spain* 37 B11
Aire-sur-la-Lys, *France* 19 B9
Aire-sur-l'Adour, *France* 20 E3
Airlie Beach, *Australia* 94 C4
Airvault, *France* 18 F6
Aisch ➤, *Germany* 25 F6
Aisne □, *France* 19 C10
Aisne ➤, *France* 19 C9
Ait, *India* 69 G8
Aitana, Sierra de, *Spain* 33 G4
Aitkin, *U.S.A.* 112 B8
Aitolía Kai Akarnanía □, *Greece* 38 C3
Aitolikón, *Greece* 38 C3
Aiud, *Romania* 43 D8
Aix-en-Provence, *France* 21 E9
Aix-la-Chapelle = Aachen,
  Germany 24 E2
Aix-les-Bains, *France* 21 C9
Aixe-sur-Vienne, *France* 20 C5
Áíyina, *Greece* 38 D5
Aíyínion, *Greece* 40 F6
Aíyion, *Greece* 38 C4
Aizawl, *India* 67 H18
Aizenay, *France* 18 F5
Aizkraukle, *Latvia* 9 H21
Aizpute, *Latvia* 9 H19
Aizuwakamatsu, *Japan* 54 F9
Ajaccio, *France* 21 G12
Ajaccio, G. d', *France* 21 G12
Ajaigarh, *India* 69 G9
Ajalpan, *Mexico* 119 D5
Ajanta Ra., *India* 66 J9
Ajari Rep. = Ajaria □, *Georgia* 49 K6
Ajaria □, *Georgia* 49 K6
Ajax, *Canada* 110 C5
Ajdābiyā, *Libya* 79 B10
Ajdovščina, *Slovenia* 29 C10
Ajibar, *Ethiopia* 81 E4
Ajka, *Hungary* 42 C2
'Ajmān, *U.A.E.* 71 E7
Ajmer, *India* 68 F6
Ajnala, *India* 68 D6
Ajo, *U.S.A.* 115 K7
Ajo, C. de, *Spain* 34 B7
Ajok, *Sudan* 81 F2
Ajuy, *Phil.* 61 F5
Ak Dağ, *Turkey* 39 E11
Ak Dağları, *Muğla, Turkey* ... 39 E11
Ak Dağları, *Sivas, Turkey* ... 72 C7
Akaba, *Togo* 83 D5
Akabira, *Japan* 54 C11
Akaki Beseka, *Ethiopia* 81 F4
Akala, *Sudan* 81 D4
Akamas □, *Cyprus* 36 D11
Akanthou, *Cyprus* 36 D12
Akarca, *Turkey* 39 C11
Akaroa, *N.Z.* 91 K4
Akasha, *Sudan* 80 C3
Akashi, *Japan* 55 G7
Akbarpur, *Bihar, India* 69 G10
Akbarpur, *Ut. P., India* 69 F10
Akçaabat, *Turkey* 73 B8
Akçadağ, *Turkey* 72 C7
Akçakale, *Turkey* 73 D8
Akçakoca, *Turkey* 72 B4
Akçaova, *Turkey* 41 E13
Akçay, *Turkey* 39 E11
Akçay ➤, *Turkey* 39 D10
Akdağ, *Turkey* 39 C8
Akdağmadeni, *Turkey* 72 C6
Akelamo, *Indonesia* 63 D7
Åkers styckebruk, *Sweden* ... 10 E11
Åkersberga, *Sweden* 10 E12
Aketi, *Dem. Rep. of the Congo* 84 D4
Akhaïa □, *Greece* 38 C3
Akhalkalaki, *Georgia* 49 K6
Akhaltsikhe, *Georgia* 49 K6
Akharnaí, *Greece* 38 C5
Akhelóös ➤, *Greece* 38 C3
Akhendriá, *Greece* 39 G7
Akhisar, *Turkey* 39 C9
Akhladhókambos, *Greece* 38 D4

Akhmîm, *Egypt* 80 B3
Akhnur, *India* 69 C6
Akhtopol, *Bulgaria* 41 D11
Akhtuba ➤, *Russia* 49 G8
Akhtubinsk, *Russia* 49 F8
Akhty, *Russia* 49 K8
Akhtyrka = Okhtyrka, *Ukraine* 47 G8
Aki, *Japan* 55 H6
Akimiski I., *Canada* 102 B3
Akimovka, *Ukraine* 47 J8
Åkirkeby, *Denmark* 11 J8
Akita, *Japan* 54 E10
Akita □, *Japan* 54 E10
Akjoujt, *Mauritania* 82 B2
Akka, *Mali* 82 B4
Akkaya Tepesi, *Turkey* 39 D11
Akkeshi, *Japan* 54 C12
'Akko, *Israel* 75 C4
Akköy, *Turkey* 39 D9
Aklampa, *Benin* 83 D5
Aklavik, *Canada* 100 B6
Aklera, *India* 68 G7
Akmenė, *Lithuania* 44 B9
Akmenrags, *Latvia* 44 B8
Akmolinsk = Astana, *Kazakstan* 50 D8
Akmonte = Almonte, *Spain* ... 35 H4
Akō, *Japan* 55 G7
Ako, *Nigeria* 83 C7
Akôbô, *Sudan* 81 F3
Akobo ➤, *Ethiopia* 81 F3
Akola, *India* 66 J10
Akonolinga, *Cameroon* 83 E7
Akor, *Mali* 82 C3
Akordat, *Eritrea* 81 D4
Akosombo Dam, *Ghana* 83 D5
Akot, *Sudan* 81 F3
Akoupé, *Ivory C.* 82 D4
Akpatok I., *Canada* 101 B13
Åkrahamn, *Norway* 9 G11
Akranes, *Iceland* 8 D2
Akreïjit, *Mauritania* 82 B3
Akrítas Venétiko, Ákra, *Greece* 38 E3
Akron, *Colo., U.S.A.* 112 E3
Akron, *Ohio, U.S.A.* 110 E3
Akrotiri, *Cyprus* 36 E11
Akrotíri, Ákra, *Greece* 41 F9
Akrotiri Bay, *Cyprus* 36 E12
Aksai Chin, *India* 69 B8
Aksaray, *Turkey* 70 B1
Aksay, *Kazakstan* 50 D6
Akşehir, *Turkey* 70 B1
Akşehir Gölü, *Turkey* 72 C4
Akstafa = Ağstafa, *Azerbaijan* 49 K7
Aksu, *China* 60 B3
Aksu ➤, *Turkey* 72 D4
Aksum, *Ethiopia* 81 E4
Aktash, *Russia* 48 C11
Aktogay, *Kazakstan* 50 E8
Aktsyabrski, *Belarus* 47 F5
Aktyubinsk = Aqtöbe,
  Kazakstan 50 D6
Aku, *Nigeria* 83 D6
Akure, *Nigeria* 83 D6
Akureyri, *Iceland* 8 D4
Akuseki-Shima, *Japan* 55 K4
Akusha, *Russia* 49 J8
Akwa-Ibom □, *Nigeria* 83 E6
Akyab = Sittwe, *Burma* 67 J18
Akyazı, *Turkey* 72 B4
Al 'Adan, *Yemen* 74 E4
Al Aḥsā = Hasa □, *Si. Arabia* . 71 E6
Al Ajfar, *Si. Arabia* 70 E4
Al Amādīyah, *Iraq* 70 B4
Al 'Amārah, *Iraq* 70 D5
Al 'Aqabah, *Jordan* 75 F4
Al Arak, *Syria* 70 C3
Al 'Aramah, *Si. Arabia* 70 E5
Al Arţāwīyah, *Si. Arabia* 70 E5
Al 'Āşimah = 'Ammān □,
  Jordan 75 D5
Al 'Assāfīyah, *Si. Arabia* 70 D3
Al 'Ayn, *Oman* 71 E7
Al 'Ayn, *Si. Arabia* 70 E3
Al 'Azamīyah, *Iraq* 70 C5
Al 'Azīzīyah, *Iraq* 70 C5
Al Bāb, *Syria* 70 B3
Al Bad', *Si. Arabia* 70 D2
Al Bādī, *Iraq* 70 C4
Al Baḥrah, *Kuwait* 70 D5
Al Baḥral Mayyit = Dead Sea,
  Asia 75 D4
Al Balqā' □, *Jordan* 75 C4
Al Bārūk, J., *Lebanon* 75 B4
Al Başrah, *Iraq* 70 D5
Al Baţḥā, *Iraq* 70 D5
Al Bayḍā, *Libya* 79 B10
Al Biqā, *Lebanon* 75 A5
Al Bi'r, *Si. Arabia* 70 D3
Al Burayj, *Syria* 75 A5
Al Faḍilī, *Si. Arabia* 71 E6
Al Fallūjah, *Iraq* 70 C4
Al Fāw, *Iraq* 71 D6
Al Fujayrah, *U.A.E.* 71 E8
Al Ghadaf, W. ➤, *Jordan* 75 D5
Al Ghammās, *Iraq* 70 D5
Al Ghazālah, *Si. Arabia* 70 E4
Al Ḥadīthah, *Iraq* 70 C4
Al Ḥadīthah, *Si. Arabia* 75 D6
Al Ḥājānah, *Syria* 75 B5
Al Hajar al Gharbi, *Oman* ... 71 E8
Al Ḥāmad, *Si. Arabia* 70 D3
Al Hamdāniyah, *Syria* 70 C3
Al Ḥamīdīyah, *Syria* 75 A4

Al Ḥammār, *Iraq* 70 D5
Al Ḥamrā', *Si. Arabia* 70 E3
Al Ḥanākīyah, *Si. Arabia* 70 E4
Al Ḥarīr, W. ➤, *Syria* 75 C4
Al Ḥasā, W. ➤, *Jordan* 75 D4
Al Ḥasakah, *Syria* 70 B4
Al Ḥaydān, W. ➤, *Jordan* ... 75 D4
Al Ḥayy, *Iraq* 70 C5
Al Ḥijarah, *Asia* 70 D4
Al Ḥillah, *Iraq* 70 C5
Al Ḥillah, *Iraq* 74 B4
Al Hindīyah, *Iraq* 70 C5
Al Hirmil, *Lebanon* 75 A5
Al Hoceïma, *Morocco* 78 A5
Al Ḥudaydah, *Yemen* 74 E3
Al Hufūf, *Si. Arabia* 71 E6
Al Ḥumayḍah, *Si. Arabia* ... 70 D2
Al Ḥunayy, *Si. Arabia* 71 E6
Al Īsāwīyah, *Si. Arabia* 70 D3
Al Jafr, *Jordan* 75 E5
Al Jāfūrah, *Si. Arabia* 71 E7
Al Jaghbūb, *Libya* 79 C10
Al Jahrah, *Kuwait* 70 D5
Al Jalāmīd, *Si. Arabia* 70 D3
Al Jamalīyah, *Qatar* 71 E6
Al Janūb □, *Lebanon* 75 B4
Al Jawf, *Libya* 79 D10
Al Jawf, *Si. Arabia* 70 D3
Al Jazirah, *Iraq* 70 C5
Al Jithāmīyah, *Si. Arabia* ... 70 E4
Al Jubayl, *Si. Arabia* 71 E6
Al Jubaylah, *Si. Arabia* 70 E5
Al Jubb, *Si. Arabia* 70 E4
Al Junaynah, *Sudan* 79 F10
Al Kabā'ish, *Iraq* 70 D5
Al Karak, *Jordan* 75 D4
Al Karak □, *Jordan* 75 E5
Al Kāzim Tyah, *Iraq* 70 C5
Al Khābūra, *Oman* 71 F8
Al Khafji, *Si. Arabia* 71 E6
Al Khalīl, *West Bank* 75 D4
Al Khāliş, *Iraq* 70 C5
Al Kharsānīyah, *Si. Arabia* .. 71 E6
Al Khaşab, *Oman* 71 E8
Al Khawr, *Qatar* 71 E6
Al Khidr, *Iraq* 70 D5
Al Khiyām, *Lebanon* 75 B4
Al Kiswah, *Syria* 75 B5
Al Kūfah, *Iraq* 70 C5
Al Kufrah, *Libya* 79 D10
Al Kuhayfiyah, *Si. Arabia* ... 70 E4
Al Kūt, *Iraq* 70 C5
Al Kuwayt, *Kuwait* 70 D5
Al Labwah, *Lebanon* 75 A5
Al Lādhiqīyah, *Syria* 70 C2
Al Līth, *Si. Arabia* 74 C3
Al Liwā', *Oman* 71 E8
Al Luḥayyah, *Yemen* 74 D3
Al Madīnah, *Iraq* 70 D5
Al Madīnah, *Si. Arabia* 70 E3
Al Mafraq, *Jordan* 75 C5
Al Maḥmūdīyah, *Iraq* 70 C5
Al Majma'ah, *Si. Arabia* 70 E5
Al Makhruq, W. ➤, *Jordan* .. 75 D6
Al Makhūl, *Si. Arabia* 70 E4
Al Manāmah, *Bahrain* 71 E6
Al Maqwa', *Kuwait* 70 D5
Al Marj, *Libya* 79 B10
Al Maţlā, *Kuwait* 70 D5
Al Mawjib, W. ➤, *Jordan* ... 75 D4
Al Mawşil, *Iraq* 70 B4
Al Mayādin, *Syria* 70 C4
Al Mazār, *Jordan* 75 D4
Al Midhnab, *Si. Arabia* 70 E5
Al Minā', *Lebanon* 75 A4
Al Miqdādīyah, *Iraq* 70 C5
Al Mubarraz, *Si. Arabia* 71 E6
Al Mudawwarah, *Jordan* 75 F5
Al Mughayrā', *U.A.E.* 71 E7
Al Muharraq, *Bahrain* 71 E6
Al Mukallā, *Yemen* 74 E4
Al Mukhā, *Yemen* 74 E3
Al Musayjīd, *Si. Arabia* 70 E3
Al Musayyib, *Iraq* 70 C5
Al Muwayh, *Si. Arabia* 80 C5
Al Muwaylih, *Si. Arabia* 70 E2
Al Owuho = Otukpa, *Nigeria* . 83 D6
Al Qā'im, *Iraq* 70 C4
Al Qalībah, *Si. Arabia* 70 D3
Al Qāmishlī, *Syria* 70 B4
Al Qaryatayn, *Syria* 75 A6
Al Qaşīm, *Si. Arabia* 70 E4
Al Qaţ'ā, *Syria* 70 C4
Al Qaţīf, *Si. Arabia* 71 E6
Al Qaţrānah, *Jordan* 75 D5
Al Qaţrūn, *Libya* 79 D9
Al Qayşūmah, *Si. Arabia* 70 D5
Al Quds = Jerusalem, *Israel* .. 75 D4
Al Qunayţirah, *Syria* 75 C4
Al Qunfudhah, *Si. Arabia* ... 80 D5
Al Qurnah, *Iraq* 70 D5
Al Quşayr, *Iraq* 70 D5
Al Quşayr, *Syria* 75 A5
Al Qutayfah, *Syria* 75 B5
Al 'Ubaylah, *Si. Arabia* 74 C5
Al 'Uḍayliyah, *Si. Arabia* 71 E6
Al 'Ulā, *Si. Arabia* 70 E3
Al 'Uqayr, *Si. Arabia* 71 E6
Al 'Uwaynid, *Si. Arabia* 70 E5
Al 'Uwayqīlah, *Si. Arabia* ... 70 D4
Al 'Uyūn, *Ḥijāz, Si. Arabia* .. 70 E3
Al 'Uyūn, *Najd, Si. Arabia* ... 70 E4
Al 'Uzayr, *Iraq* 70 D5
Al Wajh, *Si. Arabia* 70 E3
Al Wakrah, *Qatar* 71 E6

Al Waqbah, *Si. Arabia* 70 D5
Al Wari'ah, *Si. Arabia* 70 E5
Ala, *Italy* 28 C8
Ala Dağ, *Turkey* 70 B2
Ala Dağları, *Turkey* 73 C10
Alabama □, *U.S.A.* 109 J2
Alabama ➤, *U.S.A.* 109 K2
Alabaster, *U.S.A.* 109 J2
Alaca, *Turkey* 72 B6
Alacaatlı, *Turkey* 39 B10
Alaçam, *Turkey* 72 B6
Alaçam Dağları, *Turkey* 39 B10
Alaçatı, *Turkey* 39 C8
Alachua, *U.S.A.* 109 L4
Alaejos, *Spain* 34 D5
Alaérma, *Greece* 36 C9
Alagir, *Russia* 49 J7
Alagna Valsésia, *Italy* 28 C4
Alagoa Grande, *Brazil* 125 E11
Alagoas □, *Brazil* 125 E11
Alagoinhas, *Brazil* 125 F11
Alagón, *Spain* 32 D3
Alagón ➤, *Spain* 34 F4
Alaior, *Spain* 37 B11
Alajero, *Canary Is.* 37 F2
Alajuela, *Costa Rica* 120 D3
Alakamisy, *Madag.* 89 C8
Alaknanda ➤, *India* 69 D8
Alakol, Ozero, *Kazakstan* ... 60 B3
Alamarvdasht, *Iran* 71 E7
Alamata, *Ethiopia* 81 E4
Alameda, *Calif., U.S.A.* 116 H4
Alameda, *N. Mex., U.S.A.* .. 115 J10
Alaminos, *Phil.* 61 C3
Alamo, *U.S.A.* 117 J11
Alamo Crossing, *U.S.A.* 117 L13
Alamogordo, *U.S.A.* 115 K11
Alamos, *Mexico* 118 B3
Alamosa, *U.S.A.* 115 H11
Åland, *Finland* 9 F19
Alandroal, *Portugal* 35 G3
Ålands hav, *Sweden* 9 F18
Alange, Presa de, *Spain* 35 G4
Alania = North Ossetia □,
  Russia 49 J7
Alanís, *Spain* 35 G5
Alanya, *Turkey* 70 B1
Alaotra, Farihin', *Madag.* ... 89 B8
Alapayevsk, *Russia* 50 D7
Alappuzha = Alleppey, *India* . 66 Q10
Alar del Rey, *Spain* 34 C6
Alaraz, *Spain* 34 E5
Alarcón, Embalse de, *Spain* .. 32 F2
Alarobia-Vohiposa, *Madag.* .. 89 C8
Alaşehir, *Turkey* 39 C10
Alaska □, *U.S.A.* 100 B5
Alaska, G. of, *Pac. Oc.* 100 C5
Alaska Peninsula, *U.S.A.* 100 C4
Alaska Range, *U.S.A.* 100 B4
Alássio, *Italy* 28 D5
Älät, *Azerbaijan* 49 L9
Alatri, *Italy* 29 G10
Alatyr, *Russia* 48 C8
Alatyr ➤, *Russia* 48 C8
Alausí, *Ecuador* 124 D3
Alava, C., *U.S.A.* 114 B1
Alaverdi, *Armenia* 49 K7
Alavus, *Finland* 9 E20
Alava □, *Spain* 32 C2
'Alayh, *Lebanon* 75 B4
Alazani ➤, *Azerbaijan* 49 K8
Alba, *Italy* 28 D5
Alba □, *Romania* 43 D8
Alba Adriática, *Italy* 29 F10
Alba de Tormes, *Spain* 34 E5
Alba-Iulia, *Romania* 43 D8
Albac, *Romania* 42 D7
Albacete, *Spain* 33 G3
Albacete □, *Spain* 33 G3
Albæk, *Denmark* 11 G4
Ålbæk Bugt, *Denmark* 11 G4
Albaida, *Spain* 33 G4
Albalate de las Nogueras, *Spain* 32 E2
Albalate del Arzobispo, *Spain* . 32 D4
Alban, *France* 20 E6
Albanel, L., *Canada* 102 B5
Albania ■, *Europe* 40 E4
Albano Laziale, *Italy* 29 G9
Albany, *Australia* 93 G2
Albany, *Ga., U.S.A.* 109 K3
Albany, *N.Y., U.S.A.* 111 D11
Albany, *Oreg., U.S.A.* 114 D2
Albany, *Tex., U.S.A.* 113 J5
Albany ➤, *Canada* 102 B3
Albardón, *Argentina* 126 C2
Albarracín, *Spain* 32 E3
Albarracín, Sierra de, *Spain* . 32 E3
Albatera, *Spain* 33 G4
Albatross B., *Australia* 94 A3
Albegna ➤, *Italy* 29 F8
Albemarle, *U.S.A.* 109 H5
Albemarle Sd., *U.S.A.* 109 H7
Albenga, *Italy* 28 D5
Alberche ➤, *Spain* 34 F6
Alberdi, *Paraguay* 126 B4
Alberes, Mts., *France* 20 E7
Ålberga, *Sweden* 11 F10
Albert, *France* 19 C9
Albert, L., *Africa* 86 B3
Albert Edward Ra., *Australia* . 92 C4
Albert Lea, *U.S.A.* 112 D8
Albert Nile ➤, *Uganda* 86 B3
Albert Town, *Bahamas* 121 B5
Alberta □, *Canada* 104 C6

Alberti, *Argentina* 126 D3
Albertinia, *S. Africa* 88 E3
Albertirsa, *Hungary* 42 C4
Alberton, *Canada* 103 C7
Albertville = Kalemie,
  Dem. Rep. of the Congo ... 86 D2
Albertville, *France* 21 C10
Albertville, *U.S.A.* 109 H2
Albi, *France* 20 E6
Albia, *U.S.A.* 112 E8
Albina, *Surinam* 125 B8
Albina, Ponta, *Angola* 88 B1
Albino, *Italy* 28 C6
Albion, *Mich., U.S.A.* 108 D3
Albion, *Nebr., U.S.A.* 112 E6
Albion, *Pa., U.S.A.* 110 E4
Albocácer, *Spain* 32 E5
Albolote, *Spain* 35 H7
Alborán, *Medit. S.* 35 K7
Alborea, *Spain* 33 F3
Ålborg, *Denmark* 11 G3
Ålborg Bugt, *Denmark* 11 H4
Alborz, Reshteh-ye Kūhhā-ye,
  Iran 71 C7
Albox, *Spain* 33 H2
Albufeira, *Portugal* 35 H2
Albula ➤, *Switz.* 25 J5
Albuñol, *Spain* 35 J7
Albuquerque, *U.S.A.* 115 J10
Albuquerque, Cayos de,
  Caribbean 120 D3
Alburg, *U.S.A.* 111 B11
Alburno, Mte., *Italy* 31 B8
Alburquerque, *Spain* 35 F4
Alcácer do Sal, *Portugal* 35 G2
Alcáçovas, *Portugal* 35 G2
Alcalá de Chivert, *Spain* 32 E5
Alcalá de Guadaira, *Spain* ... 35 H5
Alcalá de Henares, *Spain* 34 E7
Alcalá de los Gazules, *Spain* . 35 J5
Alcalá del Júcar, *Spain* 33 F3
Alcalá del Río, *Spain* 35 H5
Alcalá del Valle, *Spain* 35 J5
Alcalá la Real, *Spain* 35 H7
Álcamo, *Italy* 30 E5
Alcanadre, *Spain* 32 C2
Alcanadre ➤, *Spain* 32 D4
Alcanar, *Spain* 32 E5
Alcanede, *Portugal* 35 F2
Alcanena, *Portugal* 35 F2
Alcañices, *Spain* 34 D4
Alcañiz, *Spain* 32 D4
Alcântara, *Brazil* 125 D10
Alcántara, Embalse de, *Spain* . 34 F4
Alcantarilla, *Spain* 33 H3
Alcaracejos, *Spain* 35 G6
Alcaraz, *Spain* 33 G2
Alcaraz, Sierra de, *Spain* 33 G2
Alcaudete, *Spain* 35 H6
Alcázar de San Juan, *Spain* .. 35 F7
Alchevsk, *Ukraine* 47 H10
Alcira = Alzira, *Spain* 33 F4
Alcobaça, *Portugal* 35 F2
Alcobendas, *Spain* 34 E7
Alcolea del Pinar, *Spain* 32 E4
Alcora, *Spain* 32 E4
Alcorcón, *Spain* 34 E7
Alcoutim, *Portugal* 35 H3
Alcova, *U.S.A.* 114 E10
Alcoy, *Spain* 33 G4
Alcubierre, Sierra de, *Spain* .. 32 D4
Alcublas, *Spain* 32 F4
Alcúdia, *Spain* 37 B10
Alcúdia, B. d', *Spain* 37 B10
Alcudia, Sierra de la, *Spain* .. 35 G6
Aldabra Is., *Seychelles* 77 G8
Aldama, *Mexico* 119 C5
Aldan, *Russia* 51 D13
Aldan ➤, *Russia* 51 C13
Aldea, Pta. de la, *Canary Is.* . 37 F4
Aldeburgh, *U.K.* 13 E9
Alder Pk., *U.S.A.* 116 K5
Alderney, *U.K.* 13 H5
Aldershot, *U.K.* 13 F7
Åled, *Sweden* 11 H6
Aledo, *U.S.A.* 112 E9
Alefa, *Ethiopia* 81 E4
Aleg, *Mauritania* 82 B2
Alegranza, *Canary Is.* 37 E6
Alegranza, I., *Canary Is.* 37 E6
Alegre, *Brazil* 127 A7
Alegrete, *Brazil* 127 B4
Aleisk, *Russia* 50 D9
Aleksandriya =
  Oleksandriya,
  Kirovohrad, Ukraine 47 H7
Aleksandriya = Oleksandriya,
  Rivne, Ukraine 47 G4
Aleksandriyskaya, *Russia* ... 49 J8
Aleksandrov, *Russia* 46 D10
Aleksandrov Gay, *Russia* 48 E9
Aleksandrovac, *Serbia, Yug.* . 40 C5
Aleksandrovka =
  Oleksandrovka, *Ukraine* ... 47 H7
Aleksandrovo, *Bulgaria* 41 C8
Aleksandrovsk-Sakhalinskiy,
  Russia 51 D15
Aleksandrów Kujawski, *Poland* 45 F5
Aleksandrów Łódzki, *Poland* . 45 G6
Alekseyevka, *Samara, Russia* . 48 D10
Alekseyevka, *Voronezh, Russia* 47 G10
Aleksin, *Russia* 46 E9
Aleksinac, *Serbia, Yug.* 40 C5
Além Paraíba, *Brazil* 127 A7

131

Alemania

Alemania, *Argentina* 126 B2
Alemania, *Chile* 126 B2
Alençon, *France* 18 D7
Alenquer, *Brazil* 125 D8
Alenuihaha Channel, *U.S.A.* .. 106 H17
Alépé, *Ivory C.* 82 D4
Aleppo = Ḩalab, *Syria* 70 B3
Aléria, *France* 21 F13
Alès, *France* 21 D8
Aleşd, *Romania* 42 C7
Alessándria, *Italy* 28 D5
Ålestrup, *Denmark* 11 H3
Ålesund, *Norway* 9 E12
Alet-les-Bains, *France* 20 F6
Aletschhorn, *Switz.* 25 J4
Aleutian Is., *Pac. Oc.* 100 C2
Aleutian Trench, *Pac. Oc.* .. 96 C10
Alexander, *U.S.A.* 112 B3
Alexander, Mt., *Australia* .. 93 E3
Alexander Arch., *U.S.A.* 100 C6
Alexander Bay, *S. Africa* ... 88 D2
Alexander City, *U.S.A.* 109 J3
Alexander I., *Antarctica* ... 5 C17
Alexandra, *N.Z.* 91 L2
Alexandra Falls, *Canada* 104 A5
Alexandria = El Iskandarîya,
  Egypt 80 H7
Alexandria, *B.C., Canada* ... 104 C4
Alexandria, *Ont., Canada* ... 102 C5
Alexandria, *Romania* 43 G10
Alexandria, *S. Africa* 88 E4
Alexandria, *U.K.* 14 F4
Alexandria, *La., U.S.A.* 113 K8
Alexandria, *Minn., U.S.A.* .. 112 C7
Alexandria, *S. Dak., U.S.A.* . 112 D6
Alexandria, *Va., U.S.A.* 108 F7
Alexandria Bay, *U.S.A.* 111 B9
Alexandroúpolis, *Greece* 41 F9
Alexis ➤, *Canada* 103 B8
Alexis Creek, *Canada* 104 C4
Alfabia, *Spain* 37 B9
Alfambra, *Spain* 32 E3
Alfândega da Fé, *Portugal* .. 34 D4
Alfaro, *Spain* 32 C3
Alfatar, *Bulgaria* 41 C11
Alfaz del Pi, *Spain* 33 G4
Alfeld, *Germany* 24 D5
Alfenas, *Brazil* 127 A6
Alfiós ➤, *Greece* 38 D3
Alföld, *Hungary* 42 D5
Alfonsine, *Italy* 29 D9
Alford, *Aberds., U.K.* 14 D6
Alford, *Lincs., U.K.* 12 D8
Alfred, *Maine, U.S.A.* 111 C14
Alfred, *N.Y., U.S.A.* 110 D7
Alfreton, *U.K.* 12 D6
Alfta, *Sweden* 10 C10
Alga, *Kazakstan* 50 E6
Algaida, *Spain* 37 B9
Algar, *Spain* 35 J5
Ålgård, *Norway* 9 G11
Algarinejo, *Spain* 35 H6
Algarve, *Portugal* 35 J2
Algeciras, *Spain* 35 J5
Algemesí, *Spain* 33 F4
Alger, *Algeria* 78 A6
Algeria ■, *Africa* 78 C6
Alghero, *Italy* 30 B1
Älghult, *Sweden* 11 G9
Algiers = Alger, *Algeria* ... 78 A6
Algoa B., *S. Africa* 88 E4
Algodonales, *Spain* 35 J5
Algodor ➤, *Spain* 34 F7
Algoma, *U.S.A.* 108 C2
Algona, *U.S.A.* 112 D7
Algonac, *U.S.A.* 110 D2
Algonquin Prov. Park, *Canada* . 102 C4
Algorta, *Uruguay* 128 C5
Alhama de Almería, *Spain* ... 35 J8
Alhama de Aragón, *Spain* 32 D3
Alhama de Granada, *Spain* ... 35 H7
Alhama de Murcia, *Spain* 33 H3
Alhambra, *U.S.A.* 117 L8
Alhaurín el Grande, *Spain* .. 35 J6
Alhucemas = Al Hoceïma,
  Morocco 78 A5
'Alī al Gharbī, *Iraq* 70 C5
'Alī ash Sharqī, *Iraq* 70 C5
Äli Bayramlı, *Azerbaijan* ... 49 L9
'Alī Khēl, *Afghan.* 68 C3
Ali Sahīh, *Djibouti* 81 E5
Alī Shāh, *Iran* 70 B5
Ália, *Italy* 30 E6
'Alīābād, *Khorāsān, Iran* ... 71 C8
'Alīābād, *Kordestān, Iran* .. 70 C5
'Alīābād, *Yazd, Iran* 71 D7
Aliaga, *Spain* 32 E4
Aliağa, *Turkey* 39 C8
Aliákmon ➤, *Greece* 40 F6
Alibo, *Ethiopia* 81 F4
Alibori ➤, *Benin* 83 C5
Alibunar, *Serbia, Yug.* 42 E5
Alicante, *Spain* 33 G4
Alicante □, *Spain* 33 G4
Alice, *S. Africa* 88 E4
Alice, *U.S.A.* 113 M5
Alice ➤, *Queens., Australia* . 94 C3
Alice ➤, *Queens., Australia* . 94 B3
Alice, Punta, *Italy* 31 C10
Alice Arm, *Canada* 104 B3
Alice Springs, *Australia* ... 94 C1
Alicedale, *S. Africa* 88 E4
Aliceville, *U.S.A.* 109 J1
Alicudi, *Italy* 31 D7
Aliganj, *India* 69 F8

Aligarh, *Raj., India* 68 G7
Aligarh, *Ut. P., India* 68 F8
Alīgūdarz, *Iran* 71 C6
Alijó, *Portugal* 34 D3
Alimnía, *Greece* 36 C9
Alingsås, *Sweden* 11 G6
Alipur, *Pakistan* 68 E4
Alipur Duar, *India* 67 F16
Aliquippa, *U.S.A.* 110 F4
Alishan, *Taiwan* 59 F13
Aliste ➤, *Spain* 34 D5
Alitus = Alytus, *Lithuania* . 9 J21
Alivérion, *Greece* 38 C6
Aliwal North, *S. Africa* 88 E4
Alix, *Canada* 104 C6
Aljezur, *Portugal* 35 H2
Aljustrel, *Portugal* 35 H2
Alkamari, *Niger* 83 C7
Alkmaar, *Neths.* 17 B4
All American Canal, *U.S.A.* . 115 K6
Allada, *Benin* 83 D5
Allagash ➤, *U.S.A.* 109 B11
Allah Dad, *Pakistan* 68 G2
Allahabad, *India* 69 G9
Allan, *Canada* 105 C7
Allanche, *France* 20 C6
Allanridge, *S. Africa* 88 D4
Allariz, *Spain* 34 C3
Allassac, *France* 20 C5
Ålleberg, *Sweden* 11 F7
Allegany, *U.S.A.* 110 D6
Allegheny ➤, *U.S.A.* 110 F5
Allegheny Mts., *U.S.A.* 108 G6
Allegheny Reservoir, *U.S.A.* . 110 E6
Allègre, *France* 20 C7
Allen, Bog of, *Ireland* 15 C5
Allen, L., *Ireland* 15 B3
Allendale, *U.S.A.* 109 J5
Allende, *Mexico* 118 B4
Allentown, *U.S.A.* 111 F9
Allentsteig, *Austria* 26 C8
Alleppey, *India* 66 Q10
Allepuz, *Spain* 32 E4
Aller ➤, *Germany* 24 C5
Alliance, *Nebr., U.S.A.* 112 D3
Alliance, *Ohio, U.S.A.* 110 F3
Allier □, *France* 19 F9
Allier ➤, *France* 19 F10
Alliford Bay, *Canada* 104 C2
Allinge, *Denmark* 11 J8
Alliston, *Canada* 102 D4
Alloa, *U.K.* 14 E5
Allones, *France* 18 D8
Allora, *Australia* 95 D5
Allos, *France* 21 D10
Alluitsup Paa, *Greenland* ... 4 C5
Alma, *Canada* 103 C5
Alma, *Ga., U.S.A.* 109 K4
Alma, *Kans., U.S.A.* 112 F6
Alma, *Mich., U.S.A.* 108 D3
Alma, *Nebr., U.S.A.* 112 E5
Alma Ata = Almaty, *Kazakstan* . 50 E8
Almacelles, *Spain* 32 D5
Almada, *Portugal* 35 G1
Almaden, *Australia* 94 B3
Almadén, *Spain* 35 G6
Almanor, L., *U.S.A.* 114 F3
Almansa, *Spain* 33 G3
Almanza, *Spain* 34 C5
Almanzor, Pico, *Spain* 34 E5
Almanzora ➤, *Spain* 33 H3
Almaş, Munţii, *Romania* 42 F7
Almassora, *Spain* 32 E4
Almaty, *Kazakstan* 50 E8
Almazán, *Spain* 32 D2
Almeirim, *Brazil* 125 D8
Almeirim, *Portugal* 35 F2
Almelo, *Neths.* 17 B6
Almenar de Soria, *Spain* 32 D2
Almenara, *Spain* 32 F4
Almenara, Sierra de la, *Spain* . 33 H3
Almendra, Embalse de, *Spain* . 34 D4
Almendralejo, *Spain* 35 G4
Almere-Stad, *Neths.* 17 B5
Almería, *Spain* 35 J8
Almería □, *Spain* 35 H8
Almería, G. de, *Spain* 33 J2
Almetyevsk, *Russia* 48 C11
Älmhult, *Sweden* 11 H8
Almirante, *Panama* 120 E3
Almiropótamos, *Greece* 38 C6
Almirós, *Greece* 38 B4
Almiroú, Kólpos, *Greece* 36 D6
Almodôvar, *Portugal* 35 H2
Almodóvar del Campo, *Spain* . 35 G6
Almodóvar del Río, *Spain* ... 35 H5
Almond, *U.S.A.* 110 D7
Almont, *U.S.A.* 110 D1
Almonte, *Canada* 111 A8
Almonte, *Spain* 35 H4
Almora, *India* 69 E8
Almoradí, *Spain* 33 G4
Almorox, *Spain* 34 E6
Almoustarat, *Mali* 83 B5
Älmsta, *Sweden* 10 E12
Almudévar, *Spain* 32 C4
Almuñécar, *Spain* 35 J7
Almunge, *Sweden* 10 E12
Almuradiel, *Spain* 35 G7
Alness, *U.K.* 14 D4
Alnmouth, *U.K.* 12 B6
Alnwick, *U.K.* 12 B6
Aloi, *Uganda* 86 B3
Alon, *Burma* 67 H19

Alor, *Indonesia* 63 F6
Alor Setar, *Malaysia* 65 J3
Álora, *Spain* 35 J6
Alosno, *Spain* 35 H3
Alot, *India* 68 H6
Aloysius, Mt., *Australia* ... 93 E4
Alpaugh, *U.S.A.* 116 K7
Alpedrinha, *Portugal* 34 E3
Alpena, *U.S.A.* 108 C4
Alpes-de-Haute-Provence □,
  France 21 D10
Alpes-Maritimes □, *France* .. 21 E11
Alpha, *Australia* 94 C4
Alphen aan den Rijn, *Neths.* . 17 B4
Alpiarça, *Portugal* 35 F2
Alpine, *Ariz., U.S.A.* 115 K9
Alpine, *Calif., U.S.A.* 117 N10
Alpine, *Tex., U.S.A.* 113 K3
Alps, *Europe* 6 F7
Alpu, *Turkey* 72 C4
Alqueta, Barragem do, *Portugal* . 35 G3
Alrø, *Denmark* 11 J4
Als, *Denmark* 11 K3
Alsace, *France* 19 D14
Alsask, *Canada* 105 C7
Alsasua, *Spain* 32 C2
Alsek ➤, *U.S.A.* 104 B1
Alsfeld, *Germany* 24 E5
Alsten, *Norway* 8 D15
Alstermo, *Sweden* 11 H9
Alston, *U.K.* 12 C5
Alta, *Norway* 8 B20
Alta, *Sierra, Spain* 32 E3
Alta Gracia, *Argentina* 126 C3
Alta Sierra, *U.S.A.* 117 K8
Altaelva ➤, *Norway* 8 B20
Altafjorden, *Norway* 8 A20
Altai = Aerhtai Shan, *Mongolia* . 60 B4
Altamaha ➤, *U.S.A.* 109 K5
Altamira, *Brazil* 125 D8
Altamira, *Chile* 126 B2
Altamira, *Mexico* 119 C5
Altamira, Cuevas de, *Spain* . 34 B6
Altamont, *U.S.A.* 111 D10
Altamura, *Italy* 31 B9
Altanbulag, *Mongolia* 60 A5
Altar, *Mexico* 118 A2
Altar, Desierto de, *Mexico* . 118 B2
Altata, *Mexico* 118 C3
Altavista, *U.S.A.* 108 G6
Altay, *China* 60 B3
Altdorf, *Switz.* 25 J4
Alte Mellum, *Germany* 24 B4
Altea, *Spain* 33 G4
Altenberg, *Germany* 24 E9
Altenbruch, *Germany* 24 B4
Altenburg, *Germany* 24 E8
Altenkirchen,
  Mecklenburg-Vorpommern,
  Germany 24 A9
Altenkirchen, *Rhld-Pfz.,*
  Germany 24 E3
Altenmarkt, *Austria* 26 D7
Alter do Chão, *Portugal* 35 F3
Altınoluk, *Turkey* 39 B8
Altınova, *Turkey* 39 B8
Altıntaş, *Turkey* 39 B12
Altınyaka, *Turkey* 39 E12
Altınyayla, *Turkey* 39 D11
Altiplano = Bolivian Plateau,
  S. Amer. 122 E4
Altkirch, *France* 19 E14
Altmark, *Germany* 24 C7
Altmühl ➤, *Germany* 25 G7
Altmunster, *Austria* 26 D6
Alto Adige = Trentino-Alto
  Adige □, *Italy* 29 B8
Alto Araguaia, *Brazil* 125 G8
Alto Cuchumatanes =
  Cuchumatanes, Sierra de los,
  Guatemala 120 C1
Alto del Carmen, *Chile* 126 B1
Alto del Inca, *Chile* 126 A2
Alto Ligonha, *Mozam.* 87 F4
Alto Molocue, *Mozam.* 87 F4
Alto Paraguai □, *Paraguay* .. 126 A4
Alto Paraná □, *Paraguay* 127 B5
Alton, *U.K.* 13 F7
Alton, *Ill., U.S.A.* 112 F9
Alton, *N.H., U.S.A.* 111 C13
Altoona, *U.S.A.* 110 F6
Altötting, *Germany* 25 G8
Altstätten, *Switz.* 25 H5
Altun Kŭprī, *Iraq* 70 C5
Altun Shan, *China* 60 C3
Alturas, *U.S.A.* 114 F3
Altus, *U.S.A.* 113 H5
Alubijid, *Phil.* 61 G6
Alucra, *Turkey* 73 B8
Aluk, *Sudan* 81 F2
Alūksne, *Latvia* 9 H22
Alunda, *Sweden* 10 D12
Alunite, *U.S.A.* 117 K12
Aluoro ➤, *Ethiopia* 81 F3
Alupka, *Ukraine* 47 K8
Alushta, *Ukraine* 47 K8
Alusi, *Indonesia* 63 F8
Alustante, *Spain* 32 E3
Alva, *U.S.A.* 113 G5
Alvaiázere, *Portugal* 34 F2
Älvängen, *Sweden* 11 G6
Alvarado, *Mexico* 119 D5
Alvarado, *U.S.A.* 113 J6
Alvaro Obregón, Presa, *Mexico* 118 B3

Älvdalen, *Sweden* 10 C8
Alvear, *Argentina* 126 B4
Alverca, *Portugal* 35 G1
Alvesta, *Sweden* 11 H8
Alvin, *U.S.A.* 113 L7
Alvinston, *Canada* 110 D3
Alvito, *Portugal* 35 G3
Alvord Desert, *U.S.A.* 114 E4
Älvros, *Sweden* 10 B8
Älvsbyn, *Sweden* 8 D19
Alwar, *India* 68 F7
Alxa Zuoqi, *China* 56 E3
Alyangula, *Australia* 94 A2
Alyata = Älät, *Azerbaijan* .. 49 L9
Alýth, *U.K.* 14 E5
Alzada, *U.S.A.* 112 C2
Alzey, *Germany* 25 F4
Alzira, *Spain* 33 F4
Am Timan, *Chad* 79 F10
Amadeus, L., *Australia* 93 D5
Amadi, *Dem. Rep. of the Congo* 86 B2
Amâdi, *Sudan* 81 F3
Amadjuak L., *Canada* 101 B12
Amadora, *Portugal* 35 G1
Amagansett, *U.S.A.* 111 F12
Amagasaki, *Japan* 55 G7
Amager, *Denmark* 11 J6
Amagunze, *Nigeria* 83 D6
Amakusa-Shotō, *Japan* 55 H5
Åmål, *Sweden* 10 E6
Amalfi, *Italy* 31 B7
Amaliás, *Greece* 38 D3
Amalner, *India* 66 J9
Amamapare, *Indonesia* 63 E9
Amambaí, *Brazil* 127 A4
Amambaí ➤, *Brazil* 127 A5
Amambay □, *Paraguay* 127 A4
Amambay, Cordillera de,
  S. Amer. 127 A4
Amami-Guntō, *Japan* 55 L4
Amami-Ō-Shima, *Japan* 55 L4
Amana, *L., Brazil* 124 D6
Amanat ➤, *India* 69 G11
Amanda Park, *U.S.A.* 116 C3
Amangeldy, *Kazakstan* 50 D7
Amantea, *Italy* 31 C9
Amapá, *Brazil* 125 C8
Amapá □, *Brazil* 125 C8
Amara, *Sudan* 81 E3
Amarante, *Brazil* 125 E10
Amarante, *Portugal* 34 D2
Amaranth, *Canada* 105 C9
Amareleja, *Portugal* 35 G3
Amargosa ➤, *U.S.A.* 117 J10
Amargosa Range, *U.S.A.* 117 J10
Amári, *Greece* 36 D6
Amarillo, *U.S.A.* 113 H4
Amarkantak, *India* 69 H9
Amârna, Tell el', *Sudan* 80 B3
Amaro, Mte., *Italy* 29 F11
Amarpur, *India* 69 G12
Amarti, *Eritrea* 81 E5
Amarwara, *India* 69 H8
Amasra, *Turkey* 72 B5
Amassama, *Nigeria* 83 D6
Amasya, *Turkey* 72 B6
Amata, *Australia* 93 E5
Amatikulu, *S. Africa* 89 D5
Amatitlán, *Guatemala* 120 D1
Amatrice, *Italy* 29 F10
Amay, *Belgium* 17 D5
Amazon = Amazonas ➤,
  S. Amer. 122 D5
Amazonas □, *Brazil* 124 E6
Amazonas □, *S. Amer.* 122 D5
Amba Ferit, *Ethiopia* 81 E4
Ambah, *India* 68 F8
Ambahakily, *Madag.* 89 C7
Ambahita, *Madag.* 89 C8
Ambala, *India* 68 D7
Ambalavao, *Madag.* 89 C8
Ambanja, *Madag.* 89 A8
Ambararata, *Madag.* 89 B8
Ambaro, Helodranon', *Madag.* . 89 A8
Ambato, *Ecuador* 124 D3
Ambato, *Madag.* 89 A8
Ambato, Sierra de, *Argentina* . 126 B2
Ambato Boeny, *Madag.* 89 B8
Ambatofinandrahana, *Madag.* . 89 C8
Ambatolampy, *Madag.* 89 B8
Ambatomainty, *Madag.* 89 B8
Ambatomanoina, *Madag.* 89 B8
Ambatondrazaka, *Madag.* 89 B8
Ambatosoratra, *Madag.* 89 B8
Ambelón, *Greece* 38 B4
Ambenja, *Madag.* 89 B8
Amberg, *Germany* 25 F7
Ambergris Cay, *Belize* 119 D7
Ambérieu-en-Bugey, *France* .. 21 C9
Amberley, *N.Z.* 91 K4
Ambert, *France* 20 C7
Ambidédi, *Mali* 82 C2
Ambikapur, *India* 69 H10
Ambikol, *Sudan* 80 C3
Amble, *U.K.* 12 B6
Ambleside, *U.K.* 12 C5

Ambo, *Peru* 124 F3
Amboahangy, *Madag.* 89 C8
Ambodifototra, *Madag.* 89 B8
Ambodilazana, *Madag.* 89 B8
Ambodiriana, *Madag.* 89 B8
Ambodiratrimo, *Madag.* 89 B8
Ambodiriana, *Madag.* 89 B8
Ambohidray, *Madag.* 89 B8
Ambohimahamasina, *Madag.* ... 89 C8
Ambohimahasoa, *Madag.* 89 C8
Ambohimanga, *Madag.* 89 C8
Ambohimitombo, *Madag.* 89 C8
Ambohitra, *Madag.* 89 A8
Amboise, *France* 18 E8
Ambon, *Indonesia* 63 E7
Ambondro, *Madag.* 89 D8
Amboseli, L., *Kenya* 86 C4
Ambositra, *Madag.* 89 C8
Ambovombe, *Madag.* 89 D8
Amboy, *U.S.A.* 117 L11
Amboyna Cay, *S. China Sea* .. 62 C4
Ambridge, *U.S.A.* 110 F4
Ambriz, *Angola* 84 F2
Amchitka I., *U.S.A.* 100 C1
Amderma, *Russia* 50 C7
Amdhi, *India* 69 H9
Ameca, *Mexico* 118 C4
Ameca ➤, *Mexico* 118 C3
Amecameca, *Mexico* 119 D5
Ameland, *Neths.* 17 A5
Amélia, *Italy* 29 F9
Amendolara, *Italy* 31 C9
Amenia, *U.S.A.* 111 E11
American Falls, *U.S.A.* 114 E7
American Falls Reservoir,
  U.S.A. 114 E7
American Fork, *U.S.A.* 114 F8
American Highland, *Antarctica* . 5 D6
American Samoa ■, *Pac. Oc.* . 91 B13
Americana, *Brazil* 127 A6
Americus, *U.S.A.* 109 K3
Amersfoort, *Neths.* 17 B5
Amersfoort, *S. Africa* 89 D4
Amery Ice Shelf, *Antarctica* . 5 C6
Ames, *U.S.A.* 112 E8
Amesbury, *U.S.A.* 111 D14
Amet, *India* 68 G5
Amfíklia, *Greece* 38 C4
Amfilokhía, *Greece* 38 C3
Amfípolis, *Greece* 40 F7
Ámfissa, *Greece* 38 C4
Amga, *Russia* 51 C14
Amga ➤, *Russia* 51 C14
Amgu, *Russia* 51 E14
Amgun ➤, *Russia* 51 D14
Amherst, *Canada* 103 C7
Amherst, *Mass., U.S.A.* 111 D12
Amherst, *N.Y., U.S.A.* 110 D6
Amherst, *Ohio, U.S.A.* 110 E2
Amherst I., *Canada* 111 B8
Amherstburg, *Canada* 102 D3
Amiata, Mte., *Italy* 29 F8
Amidon, *U.S.A.* 112 B3
Amiens, *France* 19 C9
Amindaion, *Greece* 40 F5
Åminne, *Sweden* 11 G7
Amino, *Ethiopia* 81 G5
Aminuis, *Namibia* 88 C2
Amīrābād, *Iran* 70 C5
Amirante Is., *Seychelles* ... 52 K9
Amisk L., *Canada* 105 C8
Amistad, Presa de la, *Mexico* . 118 B4
Amite, *U.S.A.* 113 K9
Amla, *India* 68 J8
Amlia I., *U.S.A.* 100 C2
Amlwch, *U.K.* 12 D3
Amm Adam, *Sudan* 81 D4
'Ammān, *Jordan* 75 D4
'Ammān □, *Jordan* 75 D5
Ammanford, *U.K.* 13 F4
Ammassalik = Tasiilaq,
  Greenland 4 C6
Ammerån ➤, *Sweden* 10 A10
Ammersee, *Germany* 25 G7
Ammon, *U.S.A.* 114 E8
Amnat Charoen, *Thailand* 64 E5
Amnura, *Bangla.* 69 G13
Amo Jiang ➤, *China* 58 F3
Åmol, *Iran* 71 B7
Amorgós, *Greece* 39 E7
Amory, *U.S.A.* 109 J1
Amos, *Canada* 102 C4
Åmot, *Norway* 9 G13
Åmotfors, *Sweden* 10 E6
Amoy = Xiamen, *China* 59 E12
Ampanavoana, *Madag.* 89 B9
Ampang, *Malaysia* 65 L3
Ampangalana, Lakandranon',
  Madag. 89 C8
Ampanihy, *Madag.* 89 C7
Amparafaravola, *Madag.* 89 B8
Amparihy, *Madag.* 89 C8
Ampasinambo, *Madag.* 89 C8
Ampasindava, Helodranon',
  Madag. 89 A8
Ampasindava, Saikanosy,
  Madag. 89 A8
Ampenan, *Indonesia* 62 F5
Amper, *Nigeria* 83 D6
Amper ➤, *Germany* 25 G7
Ampezzo, *Italy* 29 B9
Ampitsikinana, *Réunion* 89 A8
Ampombiantambo, *Madag.* 89 A8
Amposta, *Spain* 32 E5
Ampotaka, *Madag.* 89 D7
Ampoza, *Madag.* 89 C7

Amqui, *Canada* 103 C6
Amravati, *India* 66 J10
Amreli, *India* 68 J4
Amritsar, *India* 68 D6
Amroha, *India* 69 E8
Amrum, *Germany* 24 A4
Amsterdam, *Neths.* 17 B4
Amsterdam, *U.S.A.* 111 D10
Amsterdam, I. = Nouvelle-
   Amsterdam, I., *Ind. Oc.* 3 F13
Amstetten, *Austria* 26 C7
Amudarya ⇢, *Uzbekistan* 50 E6
Amundsen Gulf, *Canada* 100 A7
Amundsen Sea, *Antarctica* 5 D15
Amungen, *Sweden* 10 C9
Amuntai, *Indonesia* 62 E5
Amur ⇢, *Russia* 51 D15
Amur, W. ⇢, *Sudan* 80 D3
Amurang, *Indonesia* 63 D6
Amurrio, *Spain* 32 B1
Amursk, *Russia* 51 D14
Amusco, *Spain* 34 C6
Amvrakikós Kólpos, *Greece* ... 38 C2
Amvrosiyivka, *Ukraine* 47 J10
Amyderya = Amudarya ⇢,
   Uzbekistan 50 E6
An Bien, *Vietnam* 65 H5
An Hoa, *Vietnam* 64 E7
An Nabatīyah at Tahta,
   Lebanon 75 B4
An Nabk, *Si. Arabia* 70 D3
An Nabk, *Syria* 75 A5
An Nafūd, *Si. Arabia* 70 D4
An Najaf, *Iraq* 70 C5
An Nāşirīyah, *Iraq* 70 D5
An Nhon, *Vietnam* 64 F7
An Nîl □, *Sudan* 80 D3
An Nîl el Abyad □, *Sudan* ... 81 E3
An Nîl el Azraq □, *Sudan* ... 81 E3
An Nu'ayrīyah, *Si. Arabia* ... 71 E6
An Nu'mānīyah, *Iraq* 73 F11
An Nuwayb'ī, W. ⇢, *Si. Arabia* 75 F3
An Thoi, Dao, *Vietnam* 65 H4
An Uaimh, *Ireland* 15 C5
Anabar ⇢, *Russia* 51 B12
'Anabtā, *West Bank* 75 C4
Anaconda, *U.S.A.* 114 C7
Anacortes, *U.S.A.* 116 B4
Anacuao, Mt., *Phil.* 61 C4
Anadarko, *U.S.A.* 113 H5
Anadia, *Portugal* 34 E2
Anadolu, *Turkey* 72 C5
Anadyr, *Russia* 51 C18
Anadyr ⇢, *Russia* 51 C18
Anadyrskiy Zaliv, *Russia* ... 51 C19
Anáfi, *Greece* 39 E7
Anafópoulo, *Greece* 39 E7
Anaga, Pta. de, *Canary Is.* .. 37 F3
Anagni, *Italy* 29 G10
'Ānah, *Iraq* 70 C4
Anaheim, *U.S.A.* 117 M9
Anahim Lake, *Canada* 104 C3
Anáhuac, *Mexico* 118 B4
Anakapalle, *India* 67 L13
Anakie, *Australia* 94 C4
Anaklia, *Georgia* 49 J5
Analalava, *Madag.* 89 A8
Analavoka, *Madag.* 89 C8
Análipsis, *Greece* 36 A3
Anambar ⇢, *Pakistan* 68 D3
Anambas, Kepulauan, *Indonesia* 65 L6
Anambas Is. = Anambas,
   Kepulauan, *Indonesia* 65 L6
Anambra □, *Nigeria* 83 D6
Anamosa, *U.S.A.* 112 D9
Anamur, *Turkey* 70 B2
Anamur Burnu, *Turkey* 72 D5
Anan, *Japan* 55 H7
Anand, *India* 68 H5
Anánes, *Greece* 38 E6
Anantnag, *India* 69 C6
Ananyiv, *Ukraine* 47 J5
Anapa, *Russia* 47 K9
Anápodháris ⇢, *Greece* 36 E7
Anápolis, *Brazil* 125 G9
Anapu ⇢, *Brazil* 125 D8
Anār, *Iran* 71 D7
Anārak, *Iran* 71 C7
Anarisfjällen, *Sweden* 10 A7
Anas ⇢, *India* 68 H5
Anatolia = Anadolu, *Turkey* .. 72 C5
Anatsogno, *Madag.* 89 C7
Añatuya, *Argentina* 126 B3
Anaunethad L., *Canada* 105 A8
Anbyŏn, *N. Korea* 57 E14
Ancares, Sierra de, *Spain* ... 34 C4
Ancaster, *Canada* 110 C5
Ancenis, *France* 18 E5
Anchor Bay, *U.S.A.* 116 G3
Anchorage, *U.S.A.* 100 B5
Anci, *China* 56 E9
Ancohuma, Nevada, *Bolivia* .. 122 F14
Ancón, *Peru* 124 F3
Ancona, *Italy* 29 E10
Ancud, *Chile* 128 E2
Ancud, G. de, *Chile* 128 E2
Ancy-le-Franc, *France* 19 E11
Andacollo, *Argentina* 126 D1
Andacollo, *Chile* 126 C1
Andaingo, *Madag.* 89 B8
Andalgalá, *Argentina* 126 B2
Åndalsnes, *Norway* 9 E12
Andalucía □, *Spain* 35 H6
Andalusia = Andalucía □, *Spain* 35 H6
Andalusia, *U.S.A.* 109 K2

Andaman Is., *Ind. Oc.* 52 H13
Andaman Sea, *Ind. Oc.* 62 B1
Andamooka Opal Fields,
   Australia 95 E2
Andapa, *Madag.* 89 A8
Andara, *Namibia* 88 B3
Andelot-Blancheville, *France* . 19 D12
Andenes, *Norway* 8 B17
Andenne, *Belgium* 17 D5
Andéranboukane, *Mali* 83 B5
Andermatt, *Switz.* 25 J4
Andernach, *Germany* 24 E3
Andernos-les-Bains, *France* .. 20 D2
Anderslöv, *Sweden* 11 J7
Anderson, *Alaska, U.S.A.* 100 B5
Anderson, *Calif., U.S.A.* 114 F2
Anderson, *Ind., U.S.A.* 108 E3
Anderson, *Mo., U.S.A.* 113 G7
Anderson, *S.C., U.S.A.* 109 H4
Anderson ⇢, *Canada* 100 B1
Anderstorp, *Sweden* 11 G7
Andes, *U.S.A.* 111 D10
Andes, Cord. de los, *S. Amer.* . 122 F14
Andfjorden, *Norway* 8 B17
Andhra Pradesh □, *India* ... 66 L11
Andijon, *Uzbekistan* 50 E8
Andíkíthira, *Greece* 38 F5
Andilamena, *Madag.* 89 B8
Andīmeshk, *Iran* 71 C6
Andímilos, *Greece* 38 E6
Andíparos, *Greece* 39 D7
Andípaxoi, *Greece* 38 B2
Andírrion, *Greece* 38 C3
Andizhan = Andijon, *Uzbekistan* 50 E8
Andoain, *Spain* 32 B2
Andoany, *Madag.* 89 A8
Andong, *S. Korea* 57 F15
Andongwei, *China* 57 G10
Andoom, *Australia* 94 A3
Andorra, *Spain* 32 E4
Andorra ■, *Europe* 20 F5
Andorra La Vella, *Andorra* .. 20 F5
Andover, *U.K.* 13 F6
Andover, *Maine, U.S.A.* 111 B14
Andover, *Mass., U.S.A.* 111 D13
Andover, *N.J., U.S.A.* 111 F10
Andover, *N.Y., U.S.A.* 110 D7
Andover, *Ohio, U.S.A.* 110 E4
Andøya, *Norway* 8 B16
Andradina, *Brazil* 125 H8
Andrahary, Mt., *Madag.* 89 A8
Andraitx, *Spain* 37 B9
Andramasina, *Madag.* 89 B8
Andranopasy, *Madag.* 89 C7
Andranovory, *Madag.* 89 C7
Andratx, *Spain* 37 B9
Andreanof Is., *U.S.A.* 100 C2
Andreapol, *Russia* 46 D7
Andrews, *S.C., U.S.A.* 109 J6
Andrews, *Tex., U.S.A.* 113 J3
Andreyevka, *Russia* 48 D10
Ándria, *Italy* 31 A9
Andriamena, *Madag.* 89 B8
Andriba, *Madag.* 89 B8
Andrijevica, *Montenegro, Yug.* 40 D3
Andrítsaina, *Greece* 38 D3
Androka, *Madag.* 89 C7
Andropov = Rybinsk, *Russia* .. 46 C10
Ándros, *Greece* 38 D6
Andros I., *Bahamas* 120 B4
Andros Town, *Bahamas* 120 B4
Androscoggin ⇢, *U.S.A.* 111 C14
Andrychów, *Poland* 45 J6
Andselv, *Norway* 8 B18
Andújar, *Spain* 35 G6
Andulo, *Angola* 84 G3
Aneby, *Sweden* 11 G8
Anegada I., *U.S. Virgin Is.* ... 121 C7
Anegada Passage, *W. Indies* .. 121 C7
Aného, *Togo* 83 D5
Anenni-Noi, *Moldova* 43 D14
Aneto, Pico de, *Spain* 32 C5
Anfu, *China* 59 D10
Ang Thong, *Thailand* 64 E3
Angamos, Punta, *Chile* 126 A1
Angara ⇢, *Russia* 51 D10
Angara-Débou, *Benin* 83 C5
Angarsk, *Russia* 51 D11
Angas Hills, *Australia* 92 D4
Ånge, *Sweden* 10 B9
Ángel, Salto = Angel Falls,
   Venezuela 124 B6
Ángel de la Guarda, I., *Mexico* 118 B2
Angel Falls, *Venezuela* 124 B6
Angeles, *Phil.* 61 D4
Ängelholm, *Sweden* 11 H6
Angels Camp, *U.S.A.* 116 G6
Ängelsberg, *Sweden* 10 E10
Anger ⇢, *Ethiopia* 81 F4
Angereb ⇢, *Ethiopia* 81 E4
Ångermanälven ⇢, *Sweden* ... 10 B11
Ångermanland, *Sweden* 8 E18
Angermünde, *Germany* 24 B9
Angers, *Canada* 111 A9
Angers, *France* 18 E6
Angerville, *France* 19 D9
Ängesån ⇢, *Sweden* 8 C20
Angikuni L., *Canada* 105 A9
Anglès, *Spain* 32 D7
Anglesey, Isle of □, *U.K.* ... 12 D3

Anglet, *France* 20 E2
Angleton, *U.S.A.* 113 L7
Anglin ⇢, *France* 20 B4
Anglisidhes, *Cyprus* 36 E12
Anglure, *France* 19 D10
Angmagssalik = Tasiilaq,
   Greenland 4 C6
Ango, *Dem. Rep. of the Congo* . 86 B2
Angoche, *Mozam.* 87 F4
Angoche, I., *Mozam.* 87 F4
Angol, *Chile* 126 D1
Angola, *Ind., U.S.A.* 108 E3
Angola, *N.Y., U.S.A.* 110 D5
Angola ■, *Africa* 85 G3
Angoulême, *France* 20 C4
Angoumois, *France* 20 C4
Angra dos Reis, *Brazil* 127 A7
Angren, *Uzbekistan* 50 E8
Angtassom, *Cambodia* 65 G5
Angu, *Dem. Rep. of the Congo* . 86 B1
Anguang, *China* 57 B12
Anguilla ■, *W. Indies* 121 C7
Anguo, *China* 56 E8
Angurugu, *Australia* 94 A2
Angus □, *U.K.* 14 E6
Angwa ⇢, *Zimbabwe* 89 B5
Anhandui ⇢, *Brazil* 127 A5
Anholt, *Denmark* 11 H5
Anhua, *China* 59 C8
Anhui □, *China* 59 B11
Anhwei = Anhui □, *China* .. 59 B11
Anichab, *Namibia* 88 C1
Anídhros, *Greece* 39 E7
Anié, *Togo* 83 D5
Animas ⇢, *U.S.A.* 115 H9
Anina, *Romania* 42 E6
Aninoasa, *Romania* 43 F9
Anivorano, *Madag.* 89 B8
Anjalankoski, *Finland* 9 F22
Anjar, *India* 68 H4
Anji, *China* 59 B12
Anjou, *France* 18 E6
Anjozorobe, *Madag.* 89 B8
Anju, *N. Korea* 57 E13
Anka, *Nigeria* 83 C6
Ankaboa, Tanjona, *Madag.* ... 89 C7
Ankang, *China* 56 H5
Ankara, *Turkey* 72 C5
Ankaramena, *Madag.* 89 C8
Ankaratra, *Madag.* 85 H9
Ankarsrum, *Sweden* 11 G10
Ankavandra, *Madag.* 89 B8
Ankazoabo, *Madag.* 89 C7
Ankazobe, *Madag.* 89 B8
Ankeny, *U.S.A.* 112 E8
Ankilimalinika, *Madag.* 89 C7
Ankilizato, *Madag.* 89 C8
Ankisabe, *Madag.* 89 B8
Anklam, *Germany* 24 B9
Ankober, *Ethiopia* 81 F4
Ankoro, *Dem. Rep. of the Congo* 86 D2
Ankororoka, *Madag.* 89 D8
Anlong, *China* 58 E5
Anlu, *China* 59 B9
Anmyŏn-do, *S. Korea* 57 F14
Ånn, *Sweden* 10 A6
Ann, C., *U.S.A.* 111 D14
Ann Arbor, *U.S.A.* 108 D4
Anna, *Russia* 48 E5
Anna, *U.S.A.* 113 G10
Annaba, *Algeria* 78 A7
Annaberg-Buchholz, *Germany* . 24 E9
Annalee ⇢, *Ireland* 15 B4
Annam, *Vietnam* 64 E7
Annamitique, Chaîne, *Asia* .. 64 D6
Annan, *U.K.* 14 G5
Annan ⇢, *U.K.* 14 G5
Annapolis, *U.S.A.* 108 F7
Annapolis Royal, *Canada* 103 D6
Annapurna, *Nepal* 69 E10
Annean, L., *Australia* 93 E2
Anneberg, *Sweden* 11 G8
Annecy, *France* 21 C10
Annecy, Lac d', *France* 21 C10
Annemasse, *France* 19 F13
Annenskiy Most, *Russia* 46 B9
Anning, *China* 58 E4
Anniston, *U.S.A.* 109 J3
Annobón, *Atl. Oc.* 77 G4
Annonay, *France* 21 C8
Annot, *France* 21 E10
Annotto Bay, *Jamaica* 120 C4
Ånnsjön, *Sweden* 10 A6
Annville, *U.S.A.* 111 F8
Áno Arkhánai, *Greece* 39 F7
Áno Porróia, *Greece* 40 E7
Áno Síros, *Greece* 38 D6
Áno Viánnos, *Greece* 36 D7
Anorotsangana, *Madag.* 89 A8
Anosibe, *Madag.* 89 B8
Anou Mellene, *Mali* 83 B5
Anóyia, *Greece* 36 D6
Anping, *Hebei, China* 56 E8
Anping, *Liaoning, China* 57 D12
Anpu Gang, *China* 58 G7
Anqing, *China* 59 B11
Anren, *China* 59 D9
Ansai, *China* 56 F5
Ansbach, *Germany* 25 F6
Anseba ⇢, *Eritrea* 81 D4

Ansfelden, *Austria* 26 C7
Anshan, *China* 57 D12
Anshun, *China* 58 D5
Ansião, *Portugal* 34 F2
Ansley, *U.S.A.* 112 E5
Ansó, *Spain* 32 C4
Ansoain, *Spain* 32 C3
Anson, *U.S.A.* 113 J5
Anson B., *Australia* 92 B5
Ansongo, *Mali* 83 B5
Ansonia, *U.S.A.* 111 E11
Anstruther, *U.K.* 14 E6
Ansudu, *Indonesia* 63 E9
Antabamba, *Peru* 124 F4
Antakya, *Turkey* 70 B3
Antalaha, *Madag.* 89 A9
Antalya, *Turkey* 72 D4
Antalya □, *Turkey* 39 E12
Antalya Körfezi, *Turkey* 72 D4
Antambohobe, *Madag.* 89 C8
Antanambao-Manampotsy,
   Madag. 89 B8
Antanambe, *Madag.* 89 B8
Antananarivo, *Madag.* 89 B8
Antananarivo □, *Madag.* 89 B8
Antanifotsy, *Madag.* 89 B8
Antanimbaribe, *Madag.* 89 C7
Antanimora, *Madag.* 89 C8
Antarctic Pen., *Antarctica* ... 5 C18
Antarctica 5 E3
Antelope, *Zimbabwe* 87 G2
Antequera, *Paraguay* 126 A4
Antequera, *Spain* 35 H6
Antero, Mt., *U.S.A.* 115 G10
Antevamena, *Madag.* 89 C7
Anthemoús, *Greece* 40 F7
Anthony, *Kans., U.S.A.* 113 G5
Anthony, *N. Mex., U.S.A.* ... 115 K10
Anti Atlas, *Morocco* 78 C4
Anti-Lebanon = Ash Sharqi, Al
   Jabal, *Lebanon* 75 B5
Antibes, *France* 21 E11
Antibes, C. d', *France* 21 E11
Anticosti, Î. d', *Canada* 103 C7
Antifer, C. d', *France* 18 C7
Antigo, *U.S.A.* 112 C10
Antigonish, *Canada* 103 C7
Antigua, *Canary Is.* 37 F5
Antigua, *W. Indies* 121 C7
Antigua & Barbuda ■, *W. Indies* 121 C7
Antigua Guatemala, *Guatemala* 120 D1
Antilla, *Cuba* 120 B4
Antilles = West Indies,
   Cent. Amer. 121 D7
Antioch, *U.S.A.* 116 G5
Antioche, Pertuis d', *France* .. 20 B2
Antioquia, *Colombia* 124 B3
Antipodes Is., *Pac. Oc.* 96 M9
Antlers, *U.S.A.* 113 H7
Antoetra, *Madag.* 89 C8
Antofagasta, *Chile* 126 A1
Antofagasta □, *Chile* 126 A2
Antofagasta de la Sierra,
   Argentina 126 B2
Antofalla, *Argentina* 126 B2
Antofalla, Salar de, *Argentina* 126 B2
Anton, *U.S.A.* 113 J3
Antongila, Helodrano, *Madag.* . 89 B8
Antonibé, *Madag.* 89 B8
Antonibé, Presqu'île d', *Madag.* 89 A8
Antonina, *Brazil* 127 B6
Antrain, *France* 18 D5
Antrim, *U.K.* 15 B5
Antrim, *U.S.A.* 110 F3
Antrim □, *U.K.* 15 B5
Antrim, Mts. of, *U.K.* 15 A5
Antrim Plateau, *Australia* ... 92 C4
Antrodoco, *Italy* 29 F10
Antropovo, *Russia* 48 A6
Antsakabary, *Madag.* 89 B8
Antsalova, *Madag.* 89 B7
Antsenavolo, *Madag.* 89 C8
Antsiafabositra, *Madag.* 89 B8
Antsirabe, Antananarivo,
   Madag. 89 B8
Antsirabe, Antsiranana, *Madag.* 89 A8
Antsirabe, Mahajanga, *Madag.* 89 B8
Antsiranana, *Madag.* 89 A8
Antsiranana □, *Madag.* 89 A8
Antsohihy, *Madag.* 89 A8
Antsohimbondrona Seranana,
   Madag. 89 A8
Antu, *China* 57 C15
Antwerp = Antwerpen, *Belgium* 17 C4
Antwerp, *U.S.A.* 111 B9
Antwerpen, *Belgium* 17 C4
Antwerpen □, *Belgium* 17 C4
Anupgarh, *India* 68 E5
Anuppur, *India* 69 H9
Anuradhapura, *Sri Lanka* ... 66 Q12
Anveh, *Iran* 71 E7
Anvers = Antwerpen, *Belgium* . 17 C4
Anvers I., *Antarctica* 5 C17
Anwen, *China* 59 C13
Anxi, *Fujian, China* 59 E12
Anxi, *Gansu, China* 60 B4
Anxian, *China* 58 B5
Anxiang, *China* 59 C9
Anxious B., *Australia* 95 E1
Anyama, *Ivory C.* 82 D4
Anyang, *China* 56 F8
Anyer-Kidul, *Indonesia* 63 G11
Anyi, *Jiangxi, China* 59 C10
Anyi, *Shanxi, China* 56 G6
Anyuan, *China* 59 E10

Anyue, *China* 58 B5
Anza, *U.S.A.* 117 M10
Anze, *China* 56 F7
Anzhero-Sudzhensk, *Russia* .. 50 D9
Ánzio, *Italy* 30 A5
Aoga-Shima, *Japan* 55 H9
Aoiz, *Spain* 32 C3
Aomen = Macau □, *China* ... 59 F9
Aomori, *Japan* 54 D10
Aomori □, *Japan* 54 D10
Aonla, *India* 69 E8
Aoraki Mount Cook, *N.Z.* ... 91 K3
Aosta, *Italy* 28 C4
Aoudéras, *Niger* 83 B6
Aoukâr, *Mauritania* 82 B3
Apa ⇢, *S. Amer.* 126 A4
Apache, *U.S.A.* 113 H5
Apache Junction, *U.S.A.* 115 K8
Apalachee B., *U.S.A.* 109 L4
Apalachicola, *U.S.A.* 109 L3
Apalachicola ⇢, *U.S.A.* 109 L3
Apam, *Ghana* 83 D4
Apapa, *Nigeria* 83 D5
Apaporis ⇢, *Colombia* 124 D5
Aparri, *Phil.* 61 B4
Apateu, *Romania* 42 D6
Apatin, *Serbia, Yug.* 42 E4
Apatity, *Russia* 50 C4
Apatzingán, *Mexico* 118 D4
Apeldoorn, *Neths.* 17 B5
Apen, *Germany* 24 B3
Apennines = Appennini, *Italy* . 28 E7
Aphrodisias, *Turkey* 39 D10
Apia, *Samoa* 91 A13
Apiacás, Serra dos, *Brazil* ... 124 E7
Apies ⇢, *S. Africa* 89 D4
Apizaco, *Mexico* 119 D5
Aplao, *Peru* 124 G4
Apo, Mt., *Phil.* 63 C7
Apolakkiá, *Greece* 36 C9
Apolakkiá, Órmos, *Greece* ... 36 C9
Apolda, *Germany* 24 D7
Apollonia, *Greece* 38 E6
Apolo, *Bolivia* 124 F5
Aporé ⇢, *Brazil* 125 G8
Apostle Is., *U.S.A.* 112 B9
Apóstoles, *Argentina* 127 B4
Apostolos Andreas, C., *Cyprus* 36 D13
Apostolovo, *Ukraine* 47 J7
Apoteri, *Guyana* 124 C7
Appalachian Mts., *U.S.A.* ... 108 G6
Äppelbo, *Sweden* 10 D8
Appennini, *Italy* 28 E7
Appennino Ligure, *Italy* 28 D6
Appenzell-Ausser Rhoden □,
   Switz. 25 H5
Appenzell-Inner Rhoden □,
   Switz. 25 H5
Appiano, *Italy* 29 B8
Apple Hill, *Canada* 111 A10
Apple Valley, *U.S.A.* 117 L9
Appleby-in-Westmorland, *U.K.* 12 C5
Appleton, *U.S.A.* 108 C1
Approuague ⇢, *Fr. Guiana* .. 125 C8
Apricena, *Italy* 29 G12
Aprília, *Italy* 30 A5
Apsheronsk, *Russia* 49 H4
Apsley, *Canada* 110 B6
Apt, *France* 21 E9
Apuane, Alpi, *Italy* 28 D7
Apucarana, *Brazil* 127 A5
Apulia = Púglia □, *Italy* 31 A9
Apure ⇢, *Venezuela* 124 B5
Apurímac ⇢, *Peru* 124 F4
Apuseni, Munţii, *Romania* ... 42 D7
Āqā Jarī, *Iran* 71 D6
Aqaba = Al 'Aqabah, *Jordan* .. 75 F4
Aqaba, G. of, *Red Sea* 70 D2
'Aqabah, Khalīj al = Aqaba, G.
   of, *Red Sea* 70 D2
'Aqdā, *Iran* 71 C7
Aqiq, *Sudan* 80 D4
Aqiq, Khalīg, *Sudan* 80 D4
Aqmola = Astana, *Kazakstan* . 50 D8
'Aqrah, *Iraq* 70 B4
Aqtaū, *Kazakstan* 50 E6
Aqtöbe, *Kazakstan* 50 D6
Aquidauana, *Brazil* 125 H7
Aquiles Serdán, *Mexico* 118 B3
Aquin, *Haiti* 121 C5
Aquitaine □, *France* 20 D3
Aqviljuuaq = Pelly Bay, *Canada* 101 B11
Ar Rachidiya = Er Rachidia,
   Morocco 78 B5
Ar Rafid, *Syria* 75 C4
Ar Raḥḥālīyah, *Iraq* 70 C4
Ar Ramādī, *Iraq* 70 C4
Ar Ramthā, *Jordan* 75 C5
Ar Raqqah, *Syria* 70 C3
Ar Rass, *Si. Arabia* 70 E4
Ar Rawshān, *Si. Arabia* 80 C5
Ar Rifā'ī, *Iraq* 70 D5
Ar Riyāḍ, *Si. Arabia* 70 E5
Ar Ru'ays, *Qatar* 71 E6
Ar Rukhaymīyah, *Iraq* 70 D5
Ar Ruşāfah, *Syria* 70 C3
Ara, *India* 69 G11
Ara, *U.S.A.* 109 H2
'Arab, Bahr el ⇢, *Sudan* 81 F2
Arab, Khalīg el, *Egypt* 80 A2
'Arab, Shatt al ⇢, *Asia* 71 D6
'Araba, W. ⇢, *Egypt* 80 J8

'Arabābād, *Iran* 71 C8
Araban, *Turkey* 72 D7
Arabatskaya Strelka, *Ukraine* . 47 K8
Arabba, *Italy* 29 B8
Arabia, *Asia* 52 G8
Arabian Desert = Es Sahrâ' Esh
  Sharqîya, *Egypt* 80 B3
Arabian Gulf = Gulf, The, *Asia* 71 E6
Arabian Sea, *Ind. Oc.* 52 H10
Araç, *Turkey* 72 B5
Aracaju, *Brazil* 125 F11
Aracati, *Brazil* 125 D11
Araçatuba, *Brazil* 127 A5
Aracena, *Spain* 35 H4
Aracena, Sierra de, *Spain* ... 35 H4
Aračinovo, *Macedonia* 40 D5
Araçuaí, *Brazil* 125 G10
'Arad, *Israel* 75 D4
Arad, *Romania* 42 D6
Arad □, *Romania* 42 D6
Arādān, *Iran* 71 C7
Aradhippou, *Cyprus* 36 E12
Arafura Sea, *E. Indies* 52 K17
Aragats, *Armenia* 49 K7
Aragón □, *Spain* 32 D4
Aragón ➤, *Spain* 32 C3
Aragona, *Italy* 30 E6
Araguacema, *Brazil* 125 E9
Araguaia ➤, *Brazil* 122 D6
Araguaína, *Brazil* 125 E9
Araguari, *Brazil* 125 G9
Araguari ➤, *Brazil* 125 C9
Arain, *India* 68 F6
Arak, *Algeria* 78 C6
Arāk, *Iran* 71 C6
Araka, *Sudan* 81 G3
Arakan Coast, *Burma* 67 K19
Arakan Yoma, *Burma* 67 K19
Arákhova, *Greece* 38 C4
Arakli, *Turkey* 73 B8
Araks = Aras, Rūd-e ➤, *Asia* . 49 K9
Aral, *Kazakstan* 50 E7
Aral Sea, *Asia* 50 E7
Aral Tengizi = Aral Sea, *Asia* 50 E7
Aralsk = Aral, *Kazakstan* ... 50 E7
Aralskoye More = Aral Sea,
  Asia 50 E7
Aralsor, Ozero, *Kazakstan* ... 49 F9
Aramac, *Australia* 94 C4
Aran I., *Ireland* 15 A3
Aran Is., *Ireland* 15 C2
Aranda de Duero, *Spain* 34 D7
Arandān, *Iran* 70 C5
Arandelovac, *Serbia, Yug.* ... 40 B4
Aranjuez, *Spain* 34 E7
Aranos, *Namibia* 88 C2
Aransas Pass, *U.S.A.* 113 M6
Aranyaprathet, *Thailand* ... 64 F4
Araouane, *Mali* 82 B4
Arapahoe, *U.S.A.* 112 E5
Arapey Grande ➤, *Uruguay* . 126 C4
Arapgir, *Turkey* 70 B3
Arapiraca, *Brazil* 125 E11
Arapongas, *Brazil* 127 A5
Ar'ar, *Si. Arabia* 70 D4
Araranguá, *Brazil* 127 B6
Araraquara, *Brazil* 125 H9
Ararás, Serra das, *Brazil* ... 127 B5
Ararat, *Armenia* 73 C11
Ararat, Mt. = Ağrı Dağı, *Turkey* 70 B5
Araria, *India* 69 F12
Araripe, Chapada do, *Brazil* . 125 E11
Araruama, L. de, *Brazil* 127 A7
Aras, Rūd-e ➤, *Asia* 49 K9
Aratāne, *Mauritania* 82 B3
Arauca, *Colombia* 124 B4
Arauca ➤, *Venezuela* 124 B5
Arauco, *Chile* 126 D1
Arawa, *Ethiopia* 81 F5
Araxá, *Brazil* 125 G9
Araya, Pen. de, *Venezuela* ... 124 A6
Arba Gugu, *Ethiopia* 81 F5
Arba Minch, *Ethiopia* 81 F4
Arbat, *Iraq* 70 C5
Árbatax, *Italy* 30 C2
Arbīl, *Ethiopia* 81 F4
Arbīl, *Iraq* 70 B5
Arboga, *Sweden* 10 E9
Arbois, *France* 19 F12
Arbore, *Ethiopia* 81 F4
Arboréa, *Italy* 30 C1
Arborfield, *Canada* 105 C8
Arborg, *Canada* 105 C9
Arbre du Ténéré, *Niger* 83 B7
Arbroath, *U.K.* 14 E6
Arbuckle, *U.S.A.* 116 F4
Arbus, *Italy* 30 C1
Arc ➤, *France* 21 C10
Arc-lès-Gray, *France* 19 E12
Arcachon, *France* 20 D2
Arcachon, Bassin d', *France* . 20 D2
Arcade, *Calif., U.S.A.* 117 L8
Arcade, *N.Y., U.S.A.* 110 D6
Arcadia, *Fla., U.S.A.* 109 M5
Arcadia, *La., U.S.A.* 113 J8
Arcadia, *Pa., U.S.A.* 110 F6
Arcata, *U.S.A.* 114 F1
Arcévia, *Italy* 29 E9
Archangel = Arkhangelsk,
  Russia 50 C5
Archar, *Bulgaria* 40 C6
Archbald, *U.S.A.* 111 E9
Archena, *Spain* 33 G3
Archer ➤, *Australia* 94 A3
Archer B., *Australia* 94 A3

Archers Post, *Kenya* 86 B4
Arches National Park, *U.S.A.* . 115 G9
Archidona, *Spain* 35 H6
Arci, Mte., *Italy* 30 C1
Arcidosso, *Italy* 29 F8
Arcis-sur-Aube, *France* 19 D11
Arckaringa Cr. ➤, *Australia* . 95 D2
Arco, *Italy* 28 C7
Arco, *U.S.A.* 114 E7
Arcos = Arcos de Jalón, *Spain* . 32 D2
Arcos de Jalón, *Spain* 32 D2
Arcos de la Frontera, *Spain* . 35 J5
Arcos de Valdevez, *Portugal* . 34 D2
Arcot, *India* 66 N11
Arcozelo, *Portugal* 34 E3
Arctic Bay, *Canada* 101 A11
Arctic Ocean, *Arctic* 4 B18
Arctic Red River = Tsiigehtchic,
  Canada 100 B6
Arda ➤, *Bulgaria* 41 E10
Arda ➤, *Italy* 28 C7
Ardabīl, *Iran* 71 B6
Ardahan, *Turkey* 73 B10
Ardakān = Sepīdān, *Iran* ... 71 D7
Ardakān, *Iran* 71 C7
Ardala, *Sweden* 11 F7
Ardales, *Spain* 35 J6
Ardèche □, *France* 21 D8
Ardèche ➤, *France* 21 D8
Ardee, *Ireland* 15 C5
Arden, *Canada* 110 B8
Arden, *Denmark* 11 H3
Arden, *Calif., U.S.A.* 116 G5
Arden, *Nev., U.S.A.* 117 J11
Ardenne, *Belgium* 6 F7
Ardennes = Ardenne, *Belgium* . 6 F7
Ardennes □, *France* 19 C11
Ardentes, *France* 19 F8
Arderin, *Ireland* 15 C4
Ardeşen, *Turkey* 73 B9
Ardestān, *Iran* 71 C7
Árdhas ➤, *Greece* 41 E10
Ardhéa, *Greece* 40 F6
Ardila ➤, *Portugal* 35 G3
Ardino, *Bulgaria* 41 E9
Ardivachar Pt., *U.K.* 14 D1
Ardmore, *Okla., U.S.A.* 113 H6
Ardmore, *Pa., U.S.A.* 111 G9
Ardnamurchan, Pt. of, *U.K.* . 14 E2
Ardnave Pt., *U.K.* 14 F2
Ardon, *France* 49 J7
Ardore, *Italy* 31 D9
Ardres, *France* 19 B8
Ardrossan, *U.K.* 14 F4
Ards Pen., *U.K.* 15 B6
Arduan, *Sudan* 80 D3
Ardud, *Romania* 42 C7
Åre, *Sweden* 10 A7
Arecibo, *Puerto Rico* 121 C6
Areia Branca, *Brazil* 125 E11
Arena, Pt., *U.S.A.* 116 G3
Arenal, *Honduras* 120 C2
Arenas = Las Arenas, *Spain* . 34 B6
Arenas de San Pedro, *Spain* . 34 E5
Arendal, *Norway* 9 G13
Arendsee, *Germany* 24 C7
Arenys de Mar, *Spain* 32 D7
Arenzano, *Italy* 28 D5
Areópolis, *Greece* 38 E4
Arequipa, *Peru* 124 G4
Arero, *Ethiopia* 81 G4
Arès, *France* 20 D2
Arévalo, *Spain* 34 D6
Arezzo, *Italy* 29 E8
Arga, *Turkey* 70 B3
Arga ➤, *Spain* 32 C3
Argalastí, *Greece* 38 B5
Argamasilla de Alba, *Spain* . 35 F7
Argamasilla de Calatrava, *Spain* 35 G6
Arganda, *Spain* 34 E7
Arganil, *Portugal* 34 E2
Argedeb, *Ethiopia* 81 F5
Argelès-Gazost, *France* 20 E3
Argelès-sur-Mer, *France* ... 20 F7
Argens ➤, *France* 21 E10
Argent-sur-Sauldre, *France* . 19 E9
Argenta, *Canada* 104 C5
Argenta, *Italy* 29 D8
Argentan, *France* 18 D6
Argentário, Mte., *Italy* 29 F8
Argentat, *France* 20 C5
Argentera, *Italy* 28 D4
Argenteuil, *France* 19 D9
Argentia, *Canada* 103 C9
Argentiera, C. dell', *Italy* ... 30 B1
Argentina ■, *S. Amer.* 128 D3
Argentina Is., *Antarctica* ... 5 C17
Argentino, L., *Argentina* ... 128 G2
Argenton-Château, *France* ... 18 F6
Argenton-sur-Creuse, *France* . 19 F8
Argeş □, *Romania* 43 F9
Argeş ➤, *Romania* 43 F11
Arghandab ➤, *Afghan.* 68 D1
Argheile, *Ethiopia* 81 F5
Argo, *Sudan* 80 D3
Argolikós Kólpos, *Greece* ... 38 D4
Argolís □, *Greece* 38 D4
Argonne, *France* 19 C12
Árgos, *Greece* 38 D4
Árgos Orestikón, *Greece* ... 40 F5
Argostólion, *Greece* 38 C2
Arguedas, *Spain* 32 C3
Arguello, Pt., *U.S.A.* 117 L6
Arguineguín, *Canary Is.* ... 37 G4
Argun, *Russia* 49 J7

Argun ➤, *Russia* 51 D13
Argungu, *Nigeria* 83 C5
Argus Pk., *U.S.A.* 117 K9
Argyle, L., *Australia* 92 C4
Argyll & Bute □, *U.K.* 14 E3
Arhavi, *Turkey* 73 B9
Århus, *Denmark* 11 H4
Århus Amtskommune □,
  Denmark 11 H4
Ariadnoye, *Russia* 54 B7
Ariamsvlei, *Namibia* 88 D2
Ariano Irpino, *Italy* 31 A8
Aribinda, *Burkina Faso* 83 C4
Arica, *Chile* 124 G4
Arica, *Colombia* 124 D4
Arico, *Canary Is.* 37 F3
Arid, C., *Australia* 93 F3
Arida, *Japan* 55 G7
Ariège □, *France* 20 F5
Ariège ➤, *France* 20 E5
Arieş ➤, *Romania* 43 D8
Arihā, *Israel* 80 A4
Arilje, *Serbia, Yug.* 40 C4
Arílla, Ákra, *Greece* 36 A3
Arima, *Trin. & Tob.* 121 D7
Arinos ➤, *Brazil* 122 C5
Ario de Rosales, *Mexico* ... 118 D4
Ariogala, *Lithuania* 44 C10
Aripuanã, *Brazil* 124 E6
Aripuanã ➤, *Brazil* 122 D4
Ariquemes, *Brazil* 124 E6
Arisaig, *U.K.* 14 E3
Aristazabal I., *Canada* 104 C3
Arivonimamo, *Madag.* 89 B8
Ariza, *Spain* 32 D2
Arizaro, Salar de, *Argentina* . 126 A2
Arizona, *Argentina* 126 D2
Arizona □, *U.S.A.* 115 J8
Arizpe, *Mexico* 118 A2
Årjäng, *Sweden* 10 E6
Arjeplog, *Sweden* 8 D18
Arjona, *Colombia* 124 A3
Arjona, *Spain* 35 H6
Arjuna, *Indonesia* 63 G15
Arka, *Russia* 51 C15
Arkadak, *Russia* 48 E6
Arkadelphia, *U.S.A.* 113 H8
Arkadhía □, *Greece* 38 D4
Arkaig, L., *U.K.* 14 E3
Arkalyk = Arqalyk, *Kazakstan* . 50 D7
Arkansas □, *U.S.A.* 113 H8
Arkansas ➤, *U.S.A.* 113 J9
Arkansas City, *U.S.A.* 113 G6
Arkaroola, *Australia* 95 E2
Árkathos ➤, *Greece* 38 B3
Arkhángelos, *Greece* 36 C10
Arkhangelsk, *Russia* 50 C5
Arkhangelskoye, *Russia* ... 48 E5
Arki, *India* 68 D7
Arkiko, *Eritrea* 81 D4
Arklow, *Ireland* 15 D5
Arkona, Kap, *Germany* 24 A9
Arkösund, *Sweden* 11 F10
Arkoúdhi, *Greece* 38 C2
Arkport, *U.S.A.* 110 D7
Arktická= Artyom, *Azerbaijan* . 49 K10
Arktikcheskiy, Mys, *Russia* . 51 A10
Arkul, *Russia* 48 B10
Arkville, *U.S.A.* 111 D10
Árla, *Sweden* 10 E10
Arlanza ➤, *Spain* 34 C6
Arlanzón ➤, *Spain* 34 C6
Arlbergpass, *Austria* 26 D3
Arles, *France* 21 E8
Arlington, *S. Africa* 89 D4
Arlington, *N.Y., U.S.A.* 111 E11
Arlington, *Oreg., U.S.A.* 114 D3
Arlington, *S. Dak., U.S.A.* ... 112 C6
Arlington, *Tex., U.S.A.* 113 J6
Arlington, *Va., U.S.A.* 108 F7
Arlington, *Vt., U.S.A.* 111 C11
Arlington, *Wash., U.S.A.* ... 116 B4
Arlington Heights, *U.S.A.* ... 108 D2
Arlit, *Niger* 78 E7
Arlon, *Belgium* 17 E5
Arltunga, *Australia* 94 C1
Arly, *Burkina Faso* 83 C5
Armagh, *U.K.* 15 B5
Armagh □, *U.K.* 15 B5
Armagnac, *France* 20 E4
Armançon ➤, *France* 19 E10
Armavir, *Russia* 49 H5
Armenia, *Colombia* 124 C3
Armenia ■, *Asia* 49 K7
Armeniş, *Romania* 42 E7
Armenistís, Ákra, *Greece* ... 36 C9
Armentières, *France* 19 B9
Armilla, *Spain* 35 H7
Armour, *U.S.A.* 112 D5
Armstrong, *B.C., Canada* ... 104 C5
Armstrong, *Ont., Canada* ... 102 B2
Armutlu, Bursa, *Turkey* 41 F12
Armutlu, Izmir, *Turkey* 39 C9
Arnaía, *Greece* 40 F7
Arnarfjörður, *Iceland* 8 D2
Arnaud ➤, *Canada* 101 B12
Arnauti, C., *Cyprus* 36 D11
Arne-le-Duc, *France* 19 E11
Arnedillo, *Spain* 32 C2
Arnedo, *Spain* 32 C2
Arnett, *U.S.A.* 113 G5
Arnhem, *Neths.* 17 C5
Arnhem, C., *Australia* 94 A2
Arnhem B., *Australia* 94 A2
Arnhem Land, *Australia* ... 94 A1
Árnissa, *Greece* 40 F5
Arno ➤, *Italy* 28 E7
Arnold, *U.K.* 12 D6
Arnold, *U.S.A.* 116 G6
Arnoldstein, *Austria* 26 E6
Arnon ➤, *France* 19 E9
Arnot, *Canada* 105 B9
Arnøy, *Norway* 8 A19
Arnprior, *Canada* 102 C4
Arnsberg, *Germany* 24 D4
Arnstadt, *Germany* 24 E6
Aroab, *Namibia* 88 D2
Aroánia Óri, *Greece* 38 D4
Aroche, *Spain* 35 H4
Arochuku, *Nigeria* 83 D6
Aroland, *Germany* 24 D5
Aron, *India* 68 G6
Aron ➤, *France* 19 F10
Arona, *Italy* 28 C5
Arosa, Ría de, *Spain* 34 C2
Arpajon, *France* 19 D9
Arpajon-sur-Cère, *France* ... 20 D6
Arpaşu de Jos, *Romania* ... 43 E9
Arqalyk, *Kazakstan* 50 D7
Arrah = Ara, *India* 69 G11
Arrah, Ivory C. 82 D4
Arraiolos, *Portugal* 35 G3
Arran, *U.K.* 14 F3
Arras, *France* 19 B9
Arrasate, *Spain* 32 B2
Arrats ➤, *France* 20 D4
Arrecife, *Canary Is.* 37 F6
Arreau, *France* 20 F4
Arrée, Mts. d', *France* 18 D3
Arresø, *Denmark* 11 J6
Arriaga, Chiapas, *Mexico* ... 119 D6
Arriaga, San Luis Potosí, *Mexico* 118 C4
Arrilalah, *Australia* 94 C3
Arrino, *Australia* 93 E2
Arriondas, *Spain* 34 B5
Arromanches-les-Bains, *France* 18 C6
Arronches, *Portugal* 35 F3
Arros ➤, *France* 20 E3
Arrow, L., *Ireland* 15 B3
Arrowhead, L., *U.S.A.* 117 L9
Arrowtown, *N.Z.* 91 L2
Arroyo de la Luz, *Spain* 35 F4
Arroyo Grande, *U.S.A.* 117 K6
Ars, *Denmark* 11 H3
Ars, *Iran* 70 B5
Ars-sur-Moselle, *France* ... 19 C13
Arsenault L., *Canada* 105 B7
Arsenev, *Russia* 54 B6
Arsi □, *Ethiopia* 81 F4
Arsiero, *Italy* 29 C8
Arsin, *Turkey* 73 B8
Arsk, *Russia* 48 B9
Årsunda, *Sweden* 10 D10
Árta, *Greece* 38 B3
Artà, *Spain* 37 B10
Árta □, *Greece* 38 B3
Arteaga, *Mexico* 118 D4
Arteche, *Phil.* 61 E6
Arteijo = Arteixo, *Spain* ... 34 B2
Arteixo, *Spain* 34 B2
Artem, *Russia* 54 C6
Artem = Artyom, *Azerbaijan* . 49 K10
Artemovsk, *Russia* 51 D10
Artemovsk, *Ukraine* 47 H9
Artemovskiy, *Russia* 49 G5
Artenay, *France* 19 D8
Artern, *Germany* 24 D7
Artesa de Segre, *Spain* 32 D6
Artesia = Mosomane, *Botswana* 88 C4
Artesia, *U.S.A.* 113 J2
Arthington, *Liberia* 82 D2
Arthur, *Canada* 110 C4
Arthur ➤, *Australia* 94 G3
Arthur Cr. ➤, *Australia* ... 94 C2
Arthur Pt., *Australia* 94 C5
Arthur River, *Australia* 93 F2
Arthur's Pass, *N.Z.* 91 K3
Arthur's Town, *Bahamas* ... 121 B4
Artigas, *Uruguay* 126 C4
Artik, *Armenia* 49 K6
Artillery L., *Canada* 105 A7
Artois, *France* 19 B9
Artótína, *Greece* 38 C4
Artrutx, C. de, *Spain* 37 B10
Artsyz, *Ukraine* 47 J5
Artvin, *Turkey* 73 B9
Artyom, *Azerbaijan* 49 K10
Aru, Kepulauan, *Indonesia* . 63 F8
Aru Is. = Aru, Kepulauan,
  Indonesia 63 F8
Arua, *Uganda* 86 B3
Aruanã, *Brazil* 125 F8
Aruba ■, *W. Indies* 121 D6
Arucas, *Canary Is.* 37 F4
Arudy, *France* 20 E3
Arun ➤, *Nepal* 69 F12
Arun ➤, *U.K.* 13 G7
Arunachal Pradesh □, *India* . 67 F19
Arusha, *Tanzania* 86 C4
Arusha □, *Tanzania* 86 C4
Arusha Chini, *Tanzania* ... 86 C4
Aruwimi ➤, *Dem. Rep. of
  the Congo* 86 B1
Arvada, *Colo., U.S.A.* 112 F2
Arvada, *Wyo., U.S.A.* 114 D10
Arve ➤, *France* 19 F13

Árvi, *Greece* 36 E7
Arviat, *Canada* 105 A10
Arvidsjaur, *Sweden* 8 D18
Arvika, *Sweden* 10 E6
Arvin, *U.S.A.* 117 K8
Arwal, *India* 69 G11
Arxan, *China* 60 B6
Åryd, *Sweden* 11 H8
Aryirádhes, *Greece* 36 B3
Aryiroúpolis, *Greece* 36 D6
Arys, *Kazakstan* 50 E7
Arzachena, *Italy* 30 A2
Arzamas, *Russia* 48 C6
Arzgir, *Russia* 49 H7
Arzignano, *Italy* 29 C8
Arzúa, *Spain* 34 C2
Aš, *Czech Rep.* 26 A5
Ås, *Sweden* 10 A8
As Pontes de García Rodríguez,
  Spain 34 B3
Aş Şafā, *Syria* 75 B6
As Saffānīyah, *Si. Arabia* ... 71 E6
As Safīrah, *Syria* 70 B3
Aş Şahm, *Oman* 71 E8
As Sājir, *Si. Arabia* 70 E5
As Salamīyah, *Syria* 70 C3
As Salmān, *Iraq* 70 D5
As Salţ, *Jordan* 75 C4
As Sal'wa, *Qatar* 71 E6
As Samāwah, *Iraq* 70 D5
As Sanamayn, *Syria* 75 B5
As Sohar = Şuḩār, *Oman* ... 71 E8
As Sukhnah, *Syria* 70 C3
As Sulaymānīyah, *Iraq* 70 C5
As Sulaymī, *Si. Arabia* 70 E4
As Sulayyil, *Si. Arabia* 74 C4
As Summān, *Si. Arabia* ... 70 E5
As Suwaydā', *Syria* 75 C5
As Suwaydā' □, *Syria* 75 C5
As Suwayq, *Oman* 71 F8
Aş Şuwayrah, *Iraq* 70 C5
Åsa, *Sweden* 11 G6
Asab, *Namibia* 88 D2
Asaba, *Nigeria* 83 D6
Asad, Buḩayrat al, *Syria* ... 70 C3
Asadābād, *Iran* 73 E13
Asafo, *Ghana* 82 D4
Asahi-Gawa ➤, *Japan* 55 G6
Asahigawa, *Japan* 54 C11
Asale, L., *Ethiopia* 81 E5
Asamankese, *Ghana* 83 D4
Asan ➤, *India* 69 F8
Asansol, *India* 69 H12
Åsarna, *Sweden* 10 B8
Asayita, *Ethiopia* 81 E5
Asbe Teferi, *Ethiopia* 81 F5
Asbesberge, *S. Africa* 88 D3
Asbestos, *Canada* 103 C5
Asbury Park, *U.S.A.* 111 F10
Ascea, *Italy* 31 B8
Ascensión, *Mexico* 118 A3
Ascensión, B. de la, *Mexico* . 119 D7
Ascension I., *Atl. Oc.* 77 G2
Aschach an der Donau, *Austria* 26 C7
Aschaffenburg, *Germany* ... 25 F5
Aschendorf, *Germany* 24 B3
Aschersleben, *Germany* ... 24 D7
Asciano, *Italy* 29 E8
Áscoli Piceno, *Italy* 29 F10
Áscoli Satriano, *Italy* 31 A8
Ascope, *Peru* 124 E3
Ascotán, *Chile* 126 A2
Aseb, *Eritrea* 81 E5
Aseda, *Sweden* 11 G9
Asela, *Ethiopia* 81 F4
Åsen, *Sweden* 10 C7
Asenovgrad, *Bulgaria* 41 D8
Aserradero, *Mexico* 118 C3
Asfeld, *France* 19 C11
Asfûn el Matâ'na, *Egypt* ... 80 B3
Asgata, *Cyprus* 36 E12
Ash Fork, *U.S.A.* 115 J7
Ash Grove, *U.S.A.* 113 G8
Ash Shabakah, *Iraq* 70 D4
Ash Shamāl □, *Lebanon* ... 75 A5
Ash Shāmīyah, *Iraq* 70 D5
Ash Shāriqah, *U.A.E.* 71 E7
Ash Sharmah, *Si. Arabia* ... 70 D2
Ash Sharqāt, *Iraq* 70 C4
Ash Sharqi, Al Jabal, *Lebanon* 75 B5
Ash Shaţrah, *Iraq* 70 D5
Ash Shawbak, *Jordan* 70 D2
Ash Shawmari, J., *Jordan* ... 75 E6
Ash Shināfīyah, *Iraq* 70 D5
Ash Shu'bah, *Si. Arabia* ... 70 D5
Ash Shumlūl, *Si. Arabia* ... 70 E5
Ash Shūr'a, *Iraq* 70 C4
Ash Shurayf, *Si. Arabia* 70 E3
Ash Shuwayfāt, *Lebanon* ... 75 B4
Ashanti □, *Ghana* 83 D4
Ashau, *Vietnam* 64 D6
Ashbourne, *U.K.* 12 D6
Ashburn, *U.S.A.* 109 K4
Ashburton, *N.Z.* 91 K3
Ashburton ➤, *Australia* ... 92 D1
Ashcroft, *Canada* 104 C4
Ashdod, *Israel* 75 D3
Ashdown, *U.S.A.* 113 J7
Asheboro, *U.S.A.* 109 H6
Ashern, *Canada* 105 C9
Asherton, *U.S.A.* 113 L5
Asheville, *U.S.A.* 109 H4
Ashewat, *Pakistan* 68 D3
Asheweig ➤, *Canada* 102 B2
Ashford, *Australia* 95 D5

Ashford, U.K. 13 F8
Ashgabat, Turkmenistan 50 F6
Ashibetsu, Japan 54 C11
Ashikaga, Japan 55 F9
Ashington, U.K. 12 B6
Ashizuri-Zaki, Japan 55 H6
Ashkarkot, Afghan. 68 C2
Ashkhabad = Ashgabat,
  Turkmenistan 50 F6
Āshkhāneh, Iran 71 B8
Ashland, Kans., U.S.A. 113 G5
Ashland, Ky., U.S.A. 108 F4
Ashland, Mont., U.S.A. 114 D10
Ashland, Ohio, U.S.A. 110 F2
Ashland, Oreg., U.S.A. 114 E2
Ashland, Pa., U.S.A. 111 F8
Ashland, Va., U.S.A. 108 G7
Ashland, Wis., U.S.A. 112 B9
Ashley, N. Dak., U.S.A. 112 B5
Ashley, Pa., U.S.A. 111 E9
Ashmore Reef, Australia 92 B3
Ashmûn, Egypt 80 H7
Ashmyany, Belarus 9 J21
Ashqelon, Israel 75 D3
Ashta, India 68 H7
Ashtabula, U.S.A. 110 E4
Ashton, S. Africa 88 E3
Ashton, U.S.A. 114 D8
Ashuanipi, L., Canada 103 B6
Ashville, U.S.A. 110 F6
'Āşī →, Asia 72 D6
Asia 52 E11
Asia, Kepulauan, Indonesia .. 63 D8
Āsiā Bak, Iran 71 C6
Asiago, Italy 29 C8
Asifabad, India 66 K11
Asinara, Italy 30 A1
Asinara, G. dell', Italy 30 A1
Asino, Russia 50 D9
Asipovichy, Belarus 46 F5
'Asīr □, Si. Arabia 74 D3
Asir, Ras, Somali Rep. 74 E5
Aşkale, Turkey 73 C9
Askersund, Sweden 11 F8
Askham, S. Africa 88 D3
Askim, Norway 9 G14
Askja, Iceland 8 D5
Askøy, Norway 9 F11
Asl, Egypt 80 B3
Aslan Burnu, Turkey 39 C8
Aslanapa, Turkey 39 B11
Asmara = Asmera, Eritrea .. 81 D4
Asmera, Eritrea 81 D4
Asnæs, Denmark 11 J4
Åsnen, Sweden 11 H8
Ásola, Italy 28 C7
Asosa, Ethiopia 81 E3
Asoteriba, Jebel, Sudan 80 C4
Aspe, Spain 33 G4
Aspen, U.S.A. 115 G10
Aspendos, Turkey 72 D4
Aspermont, U.S.A. 113 J4
Aspet, France 20 E4
Aspiring, Mt., N.Z. 91 L2
Aspres-sur-Buëch, France .. 21 D9
Asprókavos, Ákra, Greece .. 36 B4
Aspromonte, Italy 31 D9
Aspur, India 68 H6
Asquith, Canada 105 C7
Assâba, Massif de l', Mauritania 82 B2
Assaikio, Nigeria 83 D6
Assal, L., Djibouti 81 E5
Assam □, India 67 G18
Assamakka, Niger 83 B6
Asse, Belgium 17 D4
Assémini, Italy 30 C1
Assen, Neths. 17 A6
Assens, Denmark 11 J3
Assini, Ivory C. 82 D4
Assiniboia, Canada 105 D7
Assiniboine →, Canada 105 D9
Assiniboine, Mt., Canada 104 C5
Assis, Brazil 127 A5
Assisi, Italy 29 E9
Ássos, Greece 38 C2
Assynt, L., U.K. 14 C3
Astaffort, France 20 D4
Astakídha, Greece 39 F8
Astakós, Greece 38 C3
Astana, Kazakhstan 50 D8
Āstāneh, Iran 71 B6
Astara, Azerbaijan 71 B6
Āstārā, Iran 73 C13
Asteroúsia, Greece 36 E7
Asti, Italy 28 D5
Astipálaia, Greece 39 E8
Astorga, Spain 34 C4
Astoria, U.S.A. 116 D3
Åstorp, Sweden 11 H6
Astrakhan, Russia 49 G9
Astudillo, Spain 34 C6
Asturias □, Spain 34 B5
Asunción, Paraguay 126 B4
Asunción Nochixtlán, Mexico .. 119 D5
Åsunden, Sweden 11 F9
Asutri, Sudan 81 D4
Aswa →, Uganda 86 B3
Aswad, Ra's al, Si. Arabia 80 C4
Aswân, Egypt 80 C3
Aswân High Dam = Sadd el
  Aali, Egypt 80 C3
Asyût, Egypt 80 B3
Asyûtī, Wadi →, Egypt 80 B3
Aszód, Hungary 42 C4

Aţ Ţafīlah, Jordan 75 E4
Aţ Ţā'if, Si. Arabia 74 C3
Aţ Ţīrāq, Si. Arabia 70 E5
Aţ Tubayq, Si. Arabia 70 D3
Atabey, Turkey 39 D12
Atacama □, Chile 126 B2
Atacama, Desierto de, Chile .. 126 A2
Atacama, Salar de, Chile 126 A2
Atakpamé, Togo 83 D5
Atalándi, Greece 38 C4
Atalaya, Peru 124 F4
Atalaya de Femes, Canary Is. .. 37 F6
Atami, Japan 55 G9
Atapupu, Indonesia 63 F6
Atâr, Mauritania 78 D3
Atarfe, Spain 35 H7
Atari, Pakistan 68 D6
Atascadero, U.S.A. 116 K6
Atasu, Kazakhstan 50 E8
Atatürk Barajı, Turkey 73 D8
Atça, Turkey 39 D10
Atchafalaya B., U.S.A. 113 L9
Atchison, U.S.A. 112 F7
Atebubu, Ghana 83 D4
Ateca, Spain 32 D3
Aterno →, Italy 29 F10
Atesine, Alpi, Italy 29 B8
Atessa, Italy 29 F11
Atfih, Egypt 80 J7
Ath, Belgium 17 D3
Athabasca, Canada 104 C6
Athabasca →, Canada 105 B6
Athabasca, L., Canada 105 B7
Athboy, Ireland 15 C5
Athenry, Ireland 15 C3
Athens = Athínai, Greece .. 38 D5
Athens, Ala., U.S.A. 109 H2
Athens, Ga., U.S.A. 109 J4
Athens, N.Y., U.S.A. 111 D11
Athens, Ohio, U.S.A. 108 F4
Athens, Pa., U.S.A. 111 E8
Athens, Tenn., U.S.A. 109 H3
Athens, Tex., U.S.A. 113 J7
Atherley, Canada 110 B5
Atherton, Australia 94 B4
Athiéme, Benin 83 D5
Athienou, Cyprus 36 D12
Athínai, Greece 38 D5
Athlone, Ireland 15 C4
Athna, Cyprus 36 D12
Athol, U.S.A. 111 D12
Atholl, Forest of, U.K. 14 E5
Atholville, Canada 103 C6
Áthos, Greece 41 F8
Athy, Ireland 15 C5
Ati, Chad 79 F9
Ati, Sudan 81 E2
Atiak, Uganda 86 B3
Atienza, Spain 32 D2
Atiit, Sudan 81 F3
Atik L., Canada 105 B9
Atikameg →, Canada 102 B3
Atikokan, Canada 102 C1
Atikonak L., Canada 103 B7
Atimonan, Phil. 61 E4
Atka, Russia 51 C16
Atka I., U.S.A. 100 C2
Atkarsk, Russia 48 E7
Atkinson, U.S.A. 112 D5
Atlanta, Ga., U.S.A. 109 J3
Atlanta, Tex., U.S.A. 113 J7
Atlantic, U.S.A. 112 E7
Atlantic City, U.S.A. 108 F8
Atlantic Ocean 2 E9
Atlas Mts. = Haut Atlas,
  Morocco 78 B4
Atlin, Canada 104 B2
Atlin, L., Canada 104 B2
Atlin Prov. Park, Canada 104 B2
Atmore, U.S.A. 109 K2
Atoka, U.S.A. 113 H6
Átokos, Greece 38 C2
Atolia, U.S.A. 117 K9
Atrai →, Bangla. 69 G13
Atrak = Atrek →, Turkmenistan 71 B8
Åtran, Sweden 11 G6
Åtran →, Sweden 11 H6
Atrauli, India 68 E8
Atrek →, Turkmenistan 71 B8
Atri, Italy 29 F10
Atsiki, Greece 39 B7
Atsoum, Mts., Cameroon .. 83 D7
Atsuta, Japan 54 C10
Attalla, U.S.A. 109 H2
Attapu, Laos 64 E6
Attáviros, Greece 36 C9
Attawapiskat, Canada 102 B3
Attawapiskat →, Canada .. 102 B3
Attawapiskat L., Canada 102 B2
Attersee, Austria 26 D6
Attica, Ind., U.S.A. 108 E2
Attica, Ohio, U.S.A. 110 E2
Attichy, France 19 C10
Attigny, France 19 C11
Attika = Attikí □, Greece 38 D5
Attikamagen L., Canada 103 B6
Attikí □, Greece 38 D5
Attleboro, U.S.A. 111 E13
Attock, Pakistan 68 C5
Attopeu = Attapu, Laos 64 E6
Attu I., U.S.A. 100 C1

Attur, India 66 P11
Atuel →, Argentina 126 D2
Åtvidaberg, Sweden 11 F10
Atwater, U.S.A. 116 H6
Atwood, Canada 110 C3
Atwood, U.S.A. 112 F4
Atyraū, Kazakhstan 50 E6
Au Sable, U.S.A. 110 B1
Au Sable →, U.S.A. 108 C4
Au Sable Forks, U.S.A. 111 B11
Au Sable Pt., U.S.A. 110 B1
Aubagne, France 21 E9
Aubarca, C. d', Spain 37 B7
Aube □, France 19 D11
Aube →, France 19 D10
Aubenas, France 21 D8
Aubenton, France 19 C11
Aubin, France 20 D6
Aubrac, Mts. d', France 20 D7
Auburn, Ala., U.S.A. 109 J3
Auburn, Calif., U.S.A. 116 G5
Auburn, Ind., U.S.A. 108 E3
Auburn, Maine, U.S.A. 109 C10
Auburn, N.Y., U.S.A. 111 D8
Auburn, Nebr., U.S.A. 112 E7
Auburn, Pa., U.S.A. 111 F8
Auburn, Wash., U.S.A. 116 C4
Auburn Ra., Australia 95 D5
Auburndale, U.S.A. 109 L5
Aubusson, France 20 C6
Auce, Latvia 44 B9
Auch, France 20 E4
Auchi, Nigeria 83 D6
Auckland, N.Z. 91 G5
Auckland Is., Pac. Oc. 96 N8
Aude □, France 20 E6
Aude →, France 20 E7
Auden, Canada 102 B2
Auderville, France 18 C5
Audierne, France 18 D2
Audincourt, France 19 E13
Audo, Ethiopia 81 F5
Audubon, U.S.A. 112 E7
Aue, Germany 24 E8
Auerbach, Germany 24 E8
Augathella, Australia 95 D4
Augrabies Falls, S. Africa .. 88 D3
Augsburg, Germany 25 G6
Augusta, Australia 93 F2
Augusta, Italy 31 E8
Augusta, Ark., U.S.A. 113 H9
Augusta, Ga., U.S.A. 109 J5
Augusta, Kans., U.S.A. 113 G6
Augusta, Maine, U.S.A. 101 D13
Augusta, Mont., U.S.A. 114 C7
Augustenborg, Denmark 11 K3
Augustów, Poland 44 E9
Augustus, Mt., Australia 93 D2
Augustus I., Australia 92 C3
Aukan, Eritrea 81 D5
Aukum, U.S.A. 116 G6
Auld, L., Australia 92 D3
Aulla, Italy 28 D6
Aulnay, France 20 B3
Aulne →, France 18 D2
Aulnoye-Aymeries, France .. 19 B10
Ault, France 18 B8
Ault, U.S.A. 112 E2
Aulus-les-Bains, France 20 F5
Aumale, France 19 C8
Aumont-Aubrac, France 20 D7
Auna, Nigeria 83 C5
Auning, Denmark 11 H4
Aunis, France 20 B3
Auponhia, Indonesia 63 E7
Auraiya, India 69 F8
Aurangabad, Bihar, India .. 69 G11
Aurangabad, Maharashtra, India 66 K9
Auray, France 18 E4
Aurich, Germany 24 B3
Aurillac, France 20 D6
Auronzo di Cadore, Italy 29 B9
Aurora, Canada 110 C5
Aurora, S. Africa 88 E2
Aurora, Colo., U.S.A. 112 F2
Aurora, Ill., U.S.A. 108 E1
Aurora, Mo., U.S.A. 113 G8
Aurora, N.Y., U.S.A. 111 D8
Aurora, Nebr., U.S.A. 112 E6
Aurora, Ohio, U.S.A. 110 E3
Aurukun, Australia 94 A3
Aus, Namibia 88 D2
Ausable →, Canada 110 C3
Auschwitz = Oświęcim, Poland 45 H6
Austerlitz = Slavkov u Brna,
  Czech Rep. 27 B9
Austin, Minn., U.S.A. 112 D8
Austin, Nev., U.S.A. 114 G5
Austin, Pa., U.S.A. 110 E6
Austin, Tex., U.S.A. 113 K6
Austin, L., Australia 93 E2
Austin I., Canada 105 A10
Austra, Norway 8 D14
Austral Is. = Tubuai Is., Pac. Oc. 97 K13
Austral Seamount Chain,
  Pac. Oc. 97 K13
Australia ■, Oceania 96 K5
Australind, Australia 93 F2
Austria ■, Europe 26 E7
Austvågøy, Norway 8 B16
Auterive, France 20 E5

Authie →, France 19 B8
Authon-du-Perche, France ... 18 D7
Autlán, Mexico 118 D4
Autun, France 19 F11
Auvergne, France 20 C7
Auvergne, Mts. d', France .. 20 C6
Auvézère →, France 20 C4
Auxerre, France 19 E10
Auxi-le-Château, France 19 B9
Auxonne, France 19 E12
Auzances, France 19 F9
Ava, U.S.A. 113 G8
Avallon, France 19 E10
Avalon, U.S.A. 117 M8
Avalon Pen., Canada 103 C9
Avanos, Turkey 70 B2
Avaré, Brazil 127 A6
Avawatz Mts., U.S.A. 117 K10
Avdan Dağı, Turkey 41 F13
Aveiro, Brazil 125 D7
Aveiro, Portugal 34 E2
Aveiro □, Portugal 34 E2
Āvej, Iran 71 C6
Avellaneda, Argentina 126 C4
Avellino, Italy 31 B7
Avenal, U.S.A. 116 K6
Aversa, Italy 31 B7
Avery, U.S.A. 114 C6
Aves, Is. las, Venezuela 121 D6
Avesnes-sur-Helpe, France .. 19 B10
Avesta, Sweden 10 D10
Aveyron □, France 20 D6
Aveyron →, France 20 D5
Avezzano, Italy 29 F10
Avgó, Greece 39 F7
Aviá Terai, Argentina 126 B3
Aviano, Italy 29 B9
Avigliana, Italy 28 C4
Avigliano, Italy 31 B8
Avignon, France 21 E8
Ávila, Spain 34 E6
Ávila □, Spain 34 E6
Ávila, Sierra de, Spain 34 E5
Ávila Beach, U.S.A. 117 K6
Avilés, Spain 34 B5
Avintes, Portugal 34 D2
Avionárion, Greece 38 C6
Avis, Portugal 35 F3
Avis, U.S.A. 110 E7
Avísio →, Italy 28 B8
Aviz = Avis, Portugal 35 F3
Avize, France 19 D11
Avlum, Denmark 11 H2
Avoca, U.S.A. 110 D7
Avoca →, Ireland 15 D5
Avola, Canada 104 C5
Avola, Italy 31 F8
Avon, U.S.A. 110 D7
Avon →, Australia 93 F2
Avon →, Bristol, U.K. 13 F5
Avon →, Dorset, U.K. 13 G6
Avon →, Warks., U.K. 13 E5
Avon Park, U.S.A. 109 M5
Avondale, Zimbabwe 87 F3
Avonlea, Canada 105 D8
Avonmore, Canada 111 A10
Avramov, Bulgaria 41 D10
Avranches, France 18 D5
Avre →, France 18 B8
Avrig, Romania 43 E9
Avrillé, France 18 E6
Avtovac, Bos.-H. 40 C2
Awag el Baqar, Sudan 81 E3
A'waj →, Syria 75 B5
Awaji-Shima, Japan 55 G7
'Awālī, Bahrain 71 E6
Awantipur, India 69 C6
Awasa, Ethiopia 81 F4
Awasa, L., Ethiopia 81 F4
Awash, Ethiopia 81 F5
Awash →, Ethiopia 81 E5
Awaso, Ghana 82 D4
Awatere →, N.Z. 91 J5
Awbārī, Libya 79 C8
Awe, L., U.K. 14 E3
Aweil, Sudan 81 F2
Awgu, Nigeria 83 D6
Awjilah, Libya 79 C10
Awka, Nigeria 83 D6
Ax-les-Thermes, France 20 F5
Axat, France 20 F6
Axe →, U.K. 13 F5
Axel Heiberg I., Canada 4 B3
Axim, Ghana 82 E4
Axintele, Romania 43 F11
Axiós →, Greece 40 F6
Axminster, U.K. 13 G4
Axvall, Sweden 11 F7
Ay, France 19 C11
Ayabaca, Peru 124 D3
Ayabe, Japan 55 G7
Ayacucho, Argentina 126 D4
Ayacucho, Peru 124 F4
Ayaguz, Kazakhstan 50 E9
Ayamé, Ivory C. 82 D4
Ayamonte, Spain 35 H3
Ayan, Russia 51 D14
Ayancık, Turkey 72 B6
Ayas, Turkey 72 B5
Ayaviri, Peru 124 F4
Aybastı, Turkey 72 B7
Aydın, Turkey 39 D9
Aydın □, Turkey 39 D9
Aydın Dağları, Turkey 39 D10

Ayelu, Ethiopia 81 E5
Ayenngré, Togo 83 D5
Ayer, U.S.A. 111 D13
Ayerbe, Spain 32 C4
Ayer's Cliff, Canada 111 A12
Ayers Rock, Australia 93 E5
Ayiá, Greece 38 B4
Ayía Aikateríni, Ákra, Greece . 36 A3
Ayía Ánna, Greece 38 C5
Ayía Dhéka, Greece 36 D6
Ayía Gálini, Greece 36 D6
Ayía Marína, Kásos, Greece . 39 F8
Ayía Marína, Léros, Greece . 39 D8
Ayía Napa, Cyprus 36 E13
Ayía Paraskeví, Greece 39 B8
Ayía Phyla, Cyprus 36 E12
Ayía Rouméli, Greece 38 F5
Ayia Varvára, Greece 36 D7
Ayiássos, Greece 39 B8
Áyioi Theódhoroi, Greece .. 38 D5
Áyion Óros □, Greece 41 F8
Áyios Amvrósios, Cyprus 36 D12
Áyios Andréas, Greece 38 D4
Áyios Evstrátios, Greece 38 B6
Áyios Ioánnis, Ákra, Greece . 36 D7
Áyios Isídhoros, Greece 36 C9
Áyios Kiríkos, Greece 39 D8
Áyios Matthaíos, Greece .. 36 B3
Áyios Mírono, Greece 39 F7
Áyios Nikólaos, Greece 36 D7
Áyios Pétros, Greece 38 C2
Áyios Seryios, Cyprus 36 D12
Áyios Theodhoros, Cyprus . 36 D13
Áyios Yeóryios, Greece 38 D5
Aykathonisi, Greece 39 D8
Aykirikçi, Turkey 39 B12
Aylesbury, U.K. 13 F7
Aylmer, Canada 110 D4
Aylmer, L., Canada 100 B8
'Ayn, Wādī al, Oman 71 F7
Ayn Dār, Si. Arabia 71 E7
Ayn Zālah, Iraq 70 B4
Ayna, Spain 33 G2
Ayod, Sudan 81 F3
Ayolas, Paraguay 126 B4
Ayom, Sudan 81 F2
Ayon, Ostrov, Russia 51 C17
Ayora, Spain 33 F3
Ayorou, Niger 83 C5
'Ayoûn el 'Atroûs, Mauritania . 82 B3
Ayr, Australia 94 B4
Ayr, Canada 110 C4
Ayr, U.K. 14 F4
Ayr →, U.K. 14 F4
Ayrancı, Turkey 72 D5
Ayrancılar, Turkey 39 C9
Ayre, Pt. of, U.K. 12 C3
Aysha, Ethiopia 81 E5
Ayton, Australia 94 B4
Aytos, Bulgaria 41 D11
Aytoska Planina, Bulgaria .. 41 D11
Ayu, Kepulauan, Indonesia . 63 D8
Ayutla, Guatemala 120 D1
Ayutla, Mexico 119 D5
Ayvacık, Turkey 72 C2
Ayvalık, Turkey 39 B8
Az Zabadānī, Syria 75 B5
Az Zāhirīyah, West Bank .. 75 D3
Az Zahrān, Si. Arabia 71 E6
Az Zarqā, Jordan 75 C5
Az Zarqā', U.A.E. 71 E7
Az Zībār, Iraq 70 B5
Az Zilfī, Si. Arabia 70 E5
Az Zubayr, Iraq 70 D5
Az Zuqur, Yemen 81 E5
Azambuja, Portugal 35 F2
Azamgarh, India 69 F10
Azángaro, Peru 124 F4
Azaouad, Mali 82 B4
Azaouak, Vallée de l', Mali .. 83 B5
Āžar Shahr, Iran 70 B5
Azara, Nigeria 83 D6
Azarān, Iran 70 B5
Azārbayjan = Azerbaijan ■,
  Asia 49 K9
Āzarbāyjān-e Gharbī □, Iran . 70 B5
Āzarbāyjān-e Sharqī □, Iran .. 70 B5
Azare, Nigeria 83 C7
Azay-le-Rideau, France 18 E7
A'zāz, Syria 70 B3
Azbine = Aïr, Niger 83 B6
Azerbaijan ■, Asia 49 K9
Azerbaijchan = Azerbaijan ■,
  Asia 49 K9
Azezo, Ethiopia 81 E4
Azimganj, India 69 G13
Aznalcóllar, Spain 35 H4
Azogues, Ecuador 124 D3
Azores, Atl. Oc. 78 A1
Azov, Russia 49 G4
Azov, Sea of, Europe 47 J9
Azovskoye More = Azov, Sea of,
  Europe 47 J9
Azpeitia, Spain 32 B2
Azraq ash Shīshān, Jordan . 75 D5
Aztec, U.S.A. 115 H10
Azúa de Compostela, Dom. Rep. 121 C5
Azuaga, Spain 35 G5
Azuara, Spain 32 D4
Azuer →, Spain 35 F7
Azuero, Pen. de, Panama .. 120 E3
Azuga, Romania 43 E10
Azul, Argentina 126 D4
Azusa, U.S.A. 117 L9
Azzano Décimo, Italy 29 C9

B

Ba Don, *Vietnam* 64 D6
Ba Dong, *Vietnam* 65 H6
Ba Ngoi = Cam Lam, *Vietnam* . 65 G7
Ba Tri, *Vietnam* 65 G6
Ba Xian = Bazhou, *China* 56 E9
Baa, *Indonesia* 63 F6
Baamonde, *Spain* 34 B3
Baarle-Nassau, *Belgium* 17 C4
Bab el Mandeb, *Red Sea* 74 E3
Baba, *Bulgaria* 40 D7
Bābā, Koh-i-, *Afghan.* 66 B5
Baba Burnu, *Turkey* 39 B8
Baba dag, *Azerbaijan* 49 K9
Bābā Kalū, *Iran* 71 D6
Babadag, *Romania* 43 F13
Babadağ, *Turkey* 39 D10
Babadayhan, *Turkmenistan* .. 50 F7
Babaeski, *Turkey* 41 E11
Babahoyo, *Ecuador* 124 D3
Babai = Sarju ➛, *India* 69 F9
Babana, *Nigeria* 83 C5
Babanusa, *Sudan* 81 E2
Babar, *Indonesia* 63 F7
Babar, *Pakistan* 68 D3
Babarkach, *Pakistan* 68 E3
Babayevo, *Russia* 46 C8
Babb, *U.S.A.* 114 B7
Babelthuap, *Pac. Oc.* 63 C8
Babenhausen, *Germany* 25 F4
Bābeni, *Romania* 43 F9
Baberu, *India* 69 G9
Babi Besar, Pulau, *Malaysia* .. 65 L4
Babia Gora, *Europe* 45 J6
Babian Jiang ➛, *China* 58 F3
Babile, *Ethiopia* 81 F5
Babimost, *Poland* 45 F2
Babinda, *Australia* 94 B4
Babine, *Canada* 104 B3
Babine ➛, *Canada* 104 B3
Babine L., *Canada* 104 C3
Babo, *Indonesia* 63 E8
Babócsa, *Hungary* 42 D2
Bābol, *Iran* 71 B7
Bābol Sar, *Iran* 71 B7
Baborów, *Poland* 45 H5
Babruysk, *Belarus* 47 F5
Babuhri, *India* 68 F3
Babuna, *Macedonia* 40 E5
Babura, *Nigeria* 83 C6
Babusar Pass, *Pakistan* 69 B5
Babushkin, *Russia* 60 A5
Babušnica, *Serbia, Yug.* 40 C6
Babuyan Chan., *Phil.* 61 B4
Babylon, *Iraq* 70 C5
Bač, *Serbia, Yug.* 42 E4
Bâc ➛, *Moldova* 43 D14
Bac Can, *Vietnam* 58 F5
Bac Giang, *Vietnam* 58 G6
Bac Lieu, *Vietnam* 65 H5
Bac Ninh, *Vietnam* 58 G6
Bac Phan, *Vietnam* 64 B5
Bac Quang, *Vietnam* 58 F5
Bacabal, *Brazil* 125 D10
Bacalar, *Mexico* 119 D7
Bacan, Kepulauan, *Indonesia* . 63 E7
Bacarra, *Phil.* 61 B4
Bacău, *Romania* 43 D11
Bacău □, *Romania* 43 D11
Baccarat, *France* 19 D13
Bacerac, *U.S.A.* 118 A3
Băcești, *Romania* 43 D12
Bach Long Vi, Dao, *Vietnam* . 64 B6
Bacharach, *Germany* 25 E3
Bachelina, *Russia* 50 D7
Bachhwara, *India* 69 G11
Bačina, *Serbia, Yug.* 40 C5
Back ➛, *Canada* 100 B9
Bačka Palanka, *Serbia, Yug.* . 42 E4
Bačka Topola, *Serbia, Yug.* ... 42 E4
Bäckebo, *Sweden* 11 H10
Bäckefors, *Sweden* 11 F6
Bäckhammar, *Sweden* 10 E8
Bački Petrovac, *Serbia, Yug.* . 42 E4
Backnang, *Germany* 25 G5
Baco, Mt., *Phil.* 61 E4
Bacolod, *Phil.* 61 F5
Bacqueville-en-Caux, *France* . 18 C8
Bács-Kiskun □, *Hungary* ... 42 D4
Bácsalmás, *Hungary* 42 D4
Bacuag = Placer, *Phil.* 61 G6
Bacuk, *Malaysia* 65 J4
Bād, *Iran* 71 C7
Bad ➛, *U.S.A.* 112 C4
Bad Aussee, *Austria* 26 D6
Bad Axe, *U.S.A.* 110 C2
Bad Bergzabern, *Germany* .. 25 F3
Bad Berleburg, *Germany* ... 24 D4
Bad Bevensen, *Germany* 24 B6
Bad Bramstedt, *Germany* ... 24 B5
Bad Brückenau, *Germany* ... 25 E5
Bad Doberan, *Germany* 24 A7
Bad Driburg, *Germany* 24 D5
Bad Ems, *Germany* 25 E3
Bad Frankenhausen, *Germany* . 24 D7
Bad Freienwalde, *Germany* .. 24 C10
Bad Goisern, *Austria* 26 D6
Bad Harzburg, *Germany* 24 D6
Bad Hersfeld, *Germany* 24 E5
Bad Hofgastein, *Austria* 26 D6
Bad Homburg, *Germany* 25 E4
Bad Honnef, *Germany* 24 E3
Bad Iburg, *Germany* 24 C4

Bad Ischl, *Austria* 26 D6
Bad Kissingen, *Germany* 25 E6
Bad Königshofen, *Germany* .. 25 E6
Bad Kreuznach, *Germany* ... 25 F3
Bad Krozingen, *Germany* ... 25 H3
Bad Laasphe, *Germany* 24 E4
Bad Lands, *U.S.A.* 112 D3
Bad Langensalza, *Germany* .. 24 D6
Bad Lauterberg, *Germany* ... 24 D6
Bad Leonfelden, *Austria* 26 C7
Bad Liebenwerda, *Germany* .. 24 D9
Bad Mergentheim, *Germany* . 25 F5
Bad Münstereifel, *Germany* .. 24 E2
Bad Nauheim, *Germany* 25 E4
Bad Neuenahr-Ahrweiler,
  Germany 24 E3
Bad Neustadt, *Germany* 25 E6
Bad Oeynhausen, *Germany* .. 24 C4
Bad Oldesloe, *Germany* 24 B6
Bad Orb, *Germany* 25 E5
Bad Pyrmont, *Germany* 24 D5
Bad Reichenhall, *Germany* .. 25 H8
Bad Säckingen, *Germany* ... 25 H3
Bad Salzuflen, *Germany* 24 C4
Bad Salzungen, *Germany* ... 24 E6
Bad Schwartau, *Germany* ... 24 B6
Bad Segeberg, *Germany* 24 B6
Bad St. Leonhard, *Austria* ... 26 E7
Bad Tölz, *Germany* 25 H7
Bad Urach, *Germany* 25 G5
Bad Vöslau, *Austria* 27 D9
Bad Waldsee, *Germany* 25 H5
Bad Wildungen, *Germany* ... 24 D5
Bad Wimpfen, *Germany* 25 F5
Bad Windsheim, *Germany* ... 25 F6
Bad Zwischenahn, *Germany* .. 24 B4
Bada Barabil, *India* 69 H11
Badagara, *India* 66 P9
Badagri, *Nigeria* 83 D5
Badajós, L., *Brazil* 124 D6
Badajoz, *Spain* 35 G4
Badajoz □, *Spain* 35 G4
Badalona, *Spain* 32 D7
Badalzai, *Afghan.* 68 E1
Badampahar, *India* 67 H15
Badanah, *Si. Arabia* 70 D4
Badarinath, *India* 69 D8
Badas, Kepulauan, *Indonesia* . 62 D3
Baddo ➛, *Pakistan* 66 F4
Bade, *Indonesia* 63 F9
Badeggi, *Nigeria* 83 D6
Badéguichéri, *Niger* 83 C6
Baden, *Austria* 27 C9
Baden, *Switz.* 25 H4
Baden, *U.S.A.* 110 F4
Baden-Baden, *Germany* 25 G4
Baden-Württemberg □,
  Germany 25 G4
Badgastein, *Austria* 26 D6
Badger, *Canada* 103 C8
Badger, *U.S.A.* 116 J7
Bādghīsāt □, *Afghan.* 66 B3
Badgom, *India* 69 B6
Badia Polésine, *Italy* 29 C8
Badin, *Pakistan* 68 G3
Badlands National Park, *U.S.A.* . 112 D3
Badogo, *Mali* 82 C3
Badoumbé, *Mali* 82 C2
Badrah, *Iraq* 70 C5
Badrinath, *India* 69 D8
Badulla, *Sri Lanka* 66 R12
Baena, *Spain* 35 H6
Baeza, *Spain* 35 H7
Bafang, *Cameroon* 83 D7
Bafatá, *Guinea-Biss.* 82 C2
Baffin B., *Canada* 101 A13
Baffin I., *Canada* 101 B12
Bafia, *Cameroon* 83 E7
Bafilo, *Togo* 83 D5
Bafing ➛, *Mali* 82 C2
Bafliyūn, *Syria* 70 B3
Bafoulabé, *Mali* 82 C2
Bafoussam, *Cameroon* 83 D7
Bāfq, *Iran* 71 D7
Bafra, *Turkey* 72 B6
Bafra Burnu, *Turkey* 72 B7
Bāft, *Iran* 71 D8
Bafut, *Cameroon* 83 D7
Bafwasende, *Dem. Rep. of
  the Congo* 86 B2
Bagam, *Niger* 83 B6
Bagamoyo, *Tanzania* 86 D4
Bagan Datoh, *Malaysia* 65 L3
Bagan Serai, *Malaysia* 65 K3
Baganga, *Phil.* 61 H7
Bagani, *Namibia* 88 B3
Bagansiapiapi, *Indonesia* ... 62 D2
Bagasra, *India* 68 J4
Bagaud, *India* 68 H6
Bagawi, *Sudan* 81 E3
Bagbag, *Sudan* 81 D3
Bagdad, *U.S.A.* 117 L11
Bagdarin, *Russia* 51 D12
Bagé, *Brazil* 127 C5
Bagenalstown = Muine Bheag,
  Ireland 15 D5
Baggs, *U.S.A.* 114 F10
Bagh, *Pakistan* 69 C5
Baghain ➛, *India* 69 G9
Baghdād, *Iraq* 70 C5
Bagheria, *Italy* 30 D6
Baghlān, *Afghan.* 66 A6
Bagley, *U.S.A.* 112 B7
Bagnara Cálabra, *Italy* 31 D8
Bagnasco, *Italy* 28 D5

Bagnères-de-Bigorre, *France* .. 20 E4
Bagnères-de-Luchon, *France* .. 20 F4
Bagni di Lucca, *Italy* 28 D7
Bagno di Romagna, *Italy* ... 29 E8
Bagnoles-de-l'Orne, *France* .. 18 D6
Bagnols-sur-Cèze, *France* ... 21 D8
Bagnorégio, *Italy* 29 F9
Bago = Pegu, *Burma* 67 L20
Bagodar, *India* 69 G11
Bagrationovsk, *Russia* 9 J19
Bagrdan, *Serbia, Yug.* 40 B5
Baguio, *Phil.* 61 C4
Bağyurdu, *Turkey* 39 C9
Bagzane, Monts, *Niger* 83 B6
Bah, *India* 69 F8
Bahabón de Esgueva, *Spain* . 34 D7
Bahadurganj, *India* 69 F12
Bahadurgarh, *India* 68 E7
Bahama, Canal Viejo de,
  W. Indies 120 B4
Bahamas ■, *N. Amer.* 121 B5
Bahār, *Iran* 73 E13
Baharampur, *India* 69 G13
Baharîya, El Wâhât al, *Egypt* . 80 B2
Bahawalnagar, *Pakistan* 68 E5
Bahawalpur, *Pakistan* 68 E4
Bahçe, *Turkey* 72 D7
Bahçecik, *Turkey* 41 F13
Baheri, *India* 69 E8
Bahgul ➛, *India* 69 F8
Bahi, *Tanzania* 86 D4
Bahi Swamp, *Tanzania* 86 D4
Bahía = Salvador, *Brazil* ... 125 F11
Bahía □, *Brazil* 125 F10
Bahía, Is. de la, *Honduras* .. 120 C2
Bahía Blanca, *Argentina* ... 126 D3
Bahía de Caráquez, *Ecuador* . 124 D2
Bahía Honda, *Cuba* 120 B3
Bahía Laura, *Argentina* 128 F3
Bahía Negra, *Paraguay* 124 H7
Bahir Dar, *Ethiopia* 81 E4
Bahmanzād, *Iran* 71 D6
Bahr el Ahmar □, *Sudan* ... 80 D4
Bahr el Ghazâl □, *Sudan* ... 81 F2
Bahr el Jabal □, *Sudan* 81 G3
Bahr Yûsef ➛, *Egypt* 80 B3
Bahraich, *India* 69 F9
Bahrain ■, *Asia* 71 E6
Bahror, *India* 68 F7
Bāhū Kalāt, *Iran* 71 E9
Bai, *Mali* 82 C4
Bai Bung, Mui = Ca Mau, Mui,
  Vietnam 65 H5
Bai Duc, *Vietnam* 64 C5
Bai Thuong, *Vietnam* 64 C5
Baia de Aramã, *Romania* ... 42 E7
Baia Mare, *Romania* 43 C8
Baia-Sprie, *Romania* 43 C8
Baião, *Brazil* 125 D9
Baïbokoum, *Chad* 79 G9
Baicheng, *China* 57 B12
Băicoi, *Romania* 43 E10
Baidoa, *Somali Rep.* 74 G3
Baie Comeau, *Canada* 103 C6
Baie-St-Paul, *Canada* 103 C5
Baie Trinité, *Canada* 103 C6
Baie Verte, *Canada* 103 C8
Baignes-Ste-Radegonde, *France* . 20 C3
Baigneux-les-Juifs, *France* .. 19 E11
Baihar, *India* 69 H9
Baihe, *China* 56 H6
Ba'iji, *Iraq* 70 C4
Baijnath, *India* 69 E8
Baikal, L. = Baykal, Oz., *Russia* . 51 D11
Baikunthpur, *India* 69 H10
Baile Atha Cliath = Dublin,
  Ireland 15 C5
Băile Govora, *Romania* 43 E9
Băile Herculane, *Romania* .. 42 F7
Băile Olănești, *Romania* ... 43 E9
Băile Tuşnad, *Romania* 43 D10
Bailén, *Spain* 35 G7
Băileşti, *Romania* 43 F8
Bailundo, *Angola* 85 G3
Bain-de-Bretagne, *France* ... 18 E5
Bainbridge, *Ga., U.S.A.* 109 K3
Bainbridge, *N.Y., U.S.A.* ... 111 D9
Baing, *Indonesia* 63 F6
Bainiu, *China* 56 H7
Baiona, *Spain* 34 C2
Ba'ir, *Jordan* 75 E5
Ba'ir □, *Jordan* 75 E5
Bais, *Phil.* 61 G5
Baisha, *China* 56 G7
Baissa, *Nigeria* 83 D7
Baitadi, *Nepal* 69 E9
Baiyin, *China* 56 F3
Baiyü, *China* 58 B2
Baiyu Shan, *China* 56 F4
Baiyuda, *Sudan* 80 D3
Baj Baj, *India* 69 H13
Baja, *Hungary* 42 D3
Baja, Pta., *Mexico* 118 B1
Baja California, *Mexico* 118 A1
Baja California □, *Mexico* .. 118 B2
Baja California Sur □, *Mexico* . 118 B2
Bajag, *India* 69 H9
Bajamar, *Canary Is.* 37 F3
Bajana, *India* 68 H4
Bājgīrān, *Iran* 71 B8
Bajimba, Mt., *Australia* 95 D5
Bajina Bašta, *Serbia, Yug.* .. 40 C3
Bajmok, *Serbia, Yug.* 42 E4
Bajo Nuevo, *Caribbean* 120 C4

Bajoga, *Nigeria* 83 C7
Bajool, *Australia* 94 C5
Bak, *Hungary* 42 D1
Bakar, *Croatia* 29 C11
Bakel, *Senegal* 82 C2
Baker, *Calif., U.S.A.* 117 K10
Baker, *Mont., U.S.A.* 112 B2
Baker, L., *Canada* 100 B10
Baker City, *U.S.A.* 114 D5
Baker I., *Pac. Oc.* 96 G10
Baker I., *U.S.A.* 104 B2
Baker L., *Australia* 93 E4
Baker Lake, *Canada* 100 B10
Baker Mt., *U.S.A.* 114 B3
Bakers Creek, *Australia* 94 C4
Baker's Dozen Is., *Canada* .. 102 A4
Bakersfield, *Calif., U.S.A.* .. 117 K8
Bakersfield, *Vt., U.S.A.* 111 B12
Bakhchysaray, *Ukraine* 47 K7
Bakhmach, *Ukraine* 47 G7
Bākhtarān, *Iran* 70 C5
Bākhtarān □, *Iran* 70 C5
Bakı, *Azerbaijan* 49 K9
Bakır ➛, *Turkey* 39 C9
Bakırdağı, *Turkey* 72 C6
Bakkafjörður, *Iceland* 8 C6
Baklan, *Turkey* 39 C11
Bako, *Ethiopia* 81 F4
Bako, *Ivory C.* 82 D3
Bakony, *Hungary* 42 C2
Bakony Forest = Bakony,
  Hungary 42 C2
Bakori, *Nigeria* 83 C6
Bakouma, *C.A.R.* 84 C4
Baksan, *Russia* 49 J6
Bakswaho, *India* 69 G8
Baku = Bakı, *Azerbaijan* ... 49 K9
Bakundi, *Nigeria* 83 D7
Bakutis Coast, *Antarctica* ... 5 D15
Baky = Bakı, *Azerbaijan* ... 49 K9
Bala, *Canada* 110 A5
Bala, *Senegal* 82 C2
Bâlâ, *Turkey* 72 C5
Bala, *U.K.* 12 E4
Bala, L., *U.K.* 12 E4
Balabac I., *Phil.* 62 C5
Balabac Str., *E. Indies* 62 C5
Balabagh, *Afghan.* 68 B4
Ba'labakk, *Lebanon* 75 B5
Balabalangan, Kepulauan,
  Indonesia 62 E5
Bălăciţa, *Romania* 43 F8
Balad, *Iraq* 70 C5
Balad Rūz, *Iraq* 70 C5
Bālādeh, *Fārs, Iran* 71 D6
Bālādeh, *Māzandaran, Iran* . 71 B6
Balaghat, *India* 66 J12
Balaghat Ra., *India* 66 K10
Balaguer, *Spain* 32 D5
Balakhna, *Russia* 48 B6
Balaklava, *Ukraine* 47 K7
Balakliya, *Ukraine* 47 H9
Balakovo, *Russia* 48 D8
Balamau, *India* 69 F9
Bālan, *Romania* 43 D10
Balancán, *Mexico* 119 D6
Balashov, *Russia* 48 E6
Balasinor, *India* 68 H5
Balasore = Baleshwar, *India* . 67 J15
Balassagyarmat, *Hungary* .. 42 B4
Balât, *Egypt* 80 B2
Balaton, *Hungary* 42 D2
Balatonboglár, *Hungary* ... 42 D2
Balatonfüred, *Hungary* 42 D2
Balatonszentgyörgy, *Hungary* . 42 D2
Balayan, *Phil.* 61 E4
Balazote, *Spain* 33 G2
Balbieriškis, *Lithuania* 44 D10
Balbigny, *France* 21 C8
Balbina, Reprêsa de, *Brazil* . 124 D7
Balboa, *Panama* 120 E4
Balbriggan, *Ireland* 15 C5
Balcarce, *Argentina* 126 D4
Balcarres, *Canada* 105 C8
Balchik, *Bulgaria* 41 C12
Balclutha, *N.Z.* 91 M2
Balcones Escarpment, *U.S.A.* . 113 L5
Bald Hd., *Australia* 93 G2
Bald I., *Australia* 93 F2
Bald Knob, *U.S.A.* 113 H9
Baldock L., *Canada* 105 B9
Baldwin, *Mich., U.S.A.* 108 D3
Baldwin, *Pa., U.S.A.* 110 F5
Baldwinsville, *U.S.A.* 111 C8
Baldy Mt., *U.S.A.* 114 B9
Baldy Peak, *U.S.A.* 115 K9
Bale, *Croatia* 29 C10
Bale, *Ethiopia* 81 F5
Bale □, *Ethiopia* 81 F5
Baleares, Is., *Spain* 37 B10
Baleine = Whale ➛, *Canada* . 103 A6
Băleni, *Romania* 43 E12
Baler, *Phil.* 61 D4
Baler Bay, *Phil.* 61 D4
Baleshare, *U.K.* 14 D1
Baleshwar, *India* 67 J15
Balezino, *Russia* 48 B11
Balfate, *Honduras* 120 C2
Bali, *Cameroon* 83 D7
Balí, *Greece* 36 D6
Bali, *India* 68 G5
Bali, *Indonesia* 62 F4

Bali □, *Indonesia* 62 F5
Bali, Selat, *Indonesia* 63 H16
Balia, *S. Leone* 82 D2
Baliapal, *India* 69 J12
Balikesir, *Turkey* 39 B9
Balikeşir □, *Turkey* 39 B9
Balıklıçeşme, *Turkey* 41 F11
Balikpapan, *Indonesia* 62 E5
Balimbing, *Phil.* 63 C5
Baling, *Malaysia* 65 K3
Balingen, *Germany* 25 G4
Balinţ, *Romania* 42 E6
Balintang Channel, *Phil.* ... 61 B4
Balkan Mts. = Stara Planina,
  Bulgaria 40 C7
Balkhash = Balqash, *Kazakstan* . 50 E8
Balkhash, Ozero = Balqash Köl,
  Kazakstan 50 E8
Balla, *Bangla.* 67 G17
Ballachulish, *U.K.* 14 E3
Balladonia, *Australia* 93 F3
Ballaghaderreen, *Ireland* ... 15 C3
Ballard, L., *Australia* 93 E3
Ballater, *U.K.* 14 D5
Ballé, *Mali* 82 B3
Ballena, Canal de, *Mexico* .. 118 B2
Balleny Is., *Antarctica* 5 C11
Balleroy, *France* 18 C6
Ballerup, *Denmark* 11 J6
Balh, *Turkey* 41 F11
Ballia, *India* 69 G11
Ballina, *Australia* 95 D5
Ballina, *Ireland* 15 B2
Ballinasloe, *Ireland* 15 C3
Ballinger, *U.S.A.* 113 K5
Ballinrobe, *Ireland* 15 C2
Ballinskelligs B., *Ireland* ... 15 E1
Ballon, *France* 18 D7
Ballsh, *Albania* 40 F3
Ballston Spa, *U.S.A.* 111 D11
Ballycastle, *U.K.* 15 A5
Ballyclare, *U.K.* 15 B5
Ballyhaunis, *Ireland* 15 C3
Ballymena, *U.K.* 15 B5
Ballymoney, *U.K.* 15 A5
Ballymote, *Ireland* 15 B3
Ballynahinch, *U.K.* 15 B6
Ballyquintin Pt., *U.K.* 15 B6
Ballyshannon, *Ireland* 15 B3
Balmaceda, *Chile* 128 F2
Balmaseda, *Spain* 32 B1
Balmazújváros, *Hungary* ... 42 C6
Balmertown, *Canada* 105 C10
Balmorhea, *U.S.A.* 113 K3
Balonne ➛, *Australia* 95 D4
Balotra, *India* 68 G5
Balqash, *Kazakstan* 50 E8
Balqash Köl, *Kazakstan* 50 E8
Balrampur, *India* 69 F10
Balş, *Romania* 43 F9
Balsas, *Mexico* 119 D5
Balsas, *Brazil* 125 E9
Balsas ➛, *Mexico* 118 D4
Bålsta, *Sweden* 10 E11
Balston Spa, *U.S.A.* 111 D11
Balta, *Ukraine* 47 H5
Baltanás, *Spain* 34 D6
Bălţi, *Moldova* 43 C12
Baltic Sea, *Europe* 9 H18
Baltîm, *Egypt* 80 H7
Baltimore, *Md., U.S.A.* 108 F7
Baltimore, *Ohio, U.S.A.* ... 110 G2
Baltit, *Pakistan* 69 A6
Baltiysk, *Russia* 9 J18
Balvi, *Latvia* 9 H22
Balya, *Turkey* 39 B9
Bam, *Iran* 71 D8
Bama, *China* 58 E6
Bama, *Nigeria* 83 C7
Bamaga, *Australia* 94 A3
Bamaji L., *Canada* 102 B1
Bamako, *Mali* 82 C3
Bamba, *Mali* 83 B4
Bambara Maoundé, *Mali* ... 82 B4
Bambari, *C.A.R.* 84 C4
Bambaya, *Guinea* 82 D2
Bamberg, *Germany* 25 F6
Bamberg, *U.S.A.* 109 J5
Bambesi, *Ethiopia* 81 F3
Bambey, *Senegal* 82 C1
Bambili, *Dem. Rep. of the Congo* . 86 B2
Bamboi, *Ghana* 82 D4
Bamenda, *Cameroon* 83 D7
Bamfield, *Canada* 104 D3
Bāmīān □, *Afghan.* 66 B5
Bamiancheng, *China* 57 C13
Bamkin, *Cameroon* 83 D7
Bampūr, *Iran* 71 E9
Ban, *Burkina Faso* 82 C4
Ban Ban, *Laos* 64 C4
Ban Bang Hin, *Thailand* ... 65 H2
Ban Chiang Klang, *Thailand* . 64 C3
Ban Chik, *Laos* 64 D4
Ban Choho, *Thailand* 64 E4
Ban Dan Lan Hoi, *Thailand* .. 64 D2
Ban Don = Surat Thani,
  Thailand 65 H2

Ban Don, *Vietnam* 64 F6
Ban Don, Ao ➤, *Thailand* 65 H2
Ban Dong, *Thailand* 64 C3
Ban Hong, *Thailand* 64 C2
Ban Kaeng, *Thailand* 64 D3
Ban Kantang, *Thailand* 65 J2
Ban Keun, *Laos* 64 C4
Ban Khai, *Thailand* 64 F3
Ban Kheun, *Laos* 64 B3
Ban Khlong Kua, *Thailand* ... 65 J3
Ban Khuan Mao, *Thailand* ... 65 J2
Ban Ko Yai Chim, *Thailand* .. 65 G2
Ban Kok, *Thailand* 64 D4
Ban Laem, *Thailand* 64 F2
Ban Lao Ngam, *Laos* 64 E6
Ban Le Kathe, *Thailand* 64 E2
Ban Mae Chedi, *Thailand* 64 C2
Ban Mae Laeng, *Thailand* 64 B2
Ban Mae Sariang, *Thailand* ... 64 C1
Ban Mê Thuôt = Buon Ma
  Thuot, *Vietnam* 64 F7
Ban Mi, *Thailand* 64 E3
Ban Muong Mo, *Laos* 64 C4
Ban Na Mo, *Laos* 64 D5
Ban Na San, *Thailand* 65 H2
Ban Na Tong, *Laos* 64 B3
Ban Nam Bac, *Laos* 64 B4
Ban Nam Ma, *Laos* 64 A3
Ban Ngang, *Laos* 64 E6
Ban Nong Bok, *Laos* 64 D5
Ban Nong Boua, *Laos* 64 E6
Ban Nong Pling, *Thailand* ... 64 E3
Ban Pak Chan, *Thailand* ... 65 G2
Ban Phai, *Thailand* 64 D4
Ban Pong, *Thailand* 64 F2
Ban Ron Phibun, *Thailand* ... 65 H2
Ban Sanam Chai, *Thailand* ... 65 J3
Ban Sangkha, *Thailand* 64 E4
Ban Tak, *Thailand* 64 D2
Ban Tako, *Thailand* 64 E4
Ban Tha Dua, *Thailand* 64 D2
Ban Tha Li, *Thailand* 64 D3
Ban Tha Nun, *Thailand* 65 H2
Ban Thahine, *Laos* 64 E5
Ban Xien Kok, *Laos* 64 B3
Ban Yen Nhan, *Vietnam* 64 B6
Banaba, *Kiribati* 96 H8
Banalia, *Dem. Rep. of the Congo* 86 B2
Banam, *Cambodia* 65 G5
Banamba, *Mali* 82 C3
Banana Is., *S. Leone* 82 D2
Bananal, I. do, *Brazil* 125 F8
Banaras = Varanasi, *India* 69 G10
Banas ➤, *Gujarat, India* 68 H4
Banas ➤, *Mad. P., India* 69 G9
Bânâs, Ras, *Egypt* 80 C4
Banaz, *Turkey* 39 C11
Banaz ➤, *Turkey* 39 C11
Banbridge, *U.K.* 15 B5
Banbury, *U.K.* 13 E6
Banchory, *U.K.* 14 D6
Banco, *Ethiopia* 81 F4
Bancroft, *Canada* 102 C4
Band, *Romania* 43 D9
Band Bonī, *Iran* 71 E8
Band Qīr, *Iran* 71 D6
Banda, *Mad. P., India* 69 G8
Banda, *Ut. P., India* 69 G9
Banda, Kepulauan, *Indonesia* .. 63 E7
Banda Aceh, *Indonesia* 62 C1
Banda Elat, *Indonesia* 63 F8
Banda Is. = Banda, Kepulauan,
  Indonesia 63 E7
Banda Sea, *Indonesia* 63 F7
Bandai-San, *Japan* 54 F10
Bandama ➤, *Ivory C.* 82 D3
Bandama Blanc ➤, *Ivory C.* .. 82 D3
Bandama Rouge ➤, *Ivory C.* .. 82 D4
Bandān, *Iran* 71 D9
Bandanaira, *Indonesia* 63 E7
Bandanwara, *India* 68 F6
Bandar = Machilipatnam, *India* 67 L12
Bandār 'Abbās, *Iran* 71 E8
Bandar-e Anzalī, *Iran* 71 B6
Bandar-e Bushehr = Būshehr,
  Iran 71 D6
Bandar-e Chārak, *Iran* 71 E7
Bandar-e Deylam, *Iran* 71 D6
Bandar-e Khomeynī, *Iran* 71 D6
Bandar-e Lengeh, *Iran* 71 E7
Bandar-e Maqām, *Iran* 71 E7
Bandar-e Ma'shur, *Iran* 71 D6
Bandar-e Rīg, *Iran* 71 D6
Bandar-e Torkeman, *Iran* 71 B7
Bandar Maharani = Muar,
  Malaysia 65 L4
Bandar Penggaram = Batu
  Pahat, *Malaysia* 65 M4
Bandar Seri Begawan, *Brunei* .. 62 C4
Bandar Sri Aman, *Malaysia* .. 62 D4
Bandawe, *Malawi* 87 E3
Bande, *Spain* 34 C3
Bandeira, Pico da, *Brazil* 127 A7
Bandera, *Argentina* 126 B3
Banderas, B. de, *Mexico* 118 C3
Bandhogarh, *India* 69 H9
Bandi ➤, *India* 68 F6
Bandiagara, *Mali* 82 C4
Bandikui, *India* 68 F7
Bandırma, *Turkey* 41 F11
Bandol, *France* 21 E9
Bandon, *Ireland* 15 E3
Bandon ➤, *Ireland* 15 E3
Bandula, *Mozam.* 87 F3
Bandundu, *Dem. Rep. of
  the Congo* 84 E3

Bandung, *Indonesia* 62 F3
Bané, *Burkina Faso* 83 C4
Băneasa, *Romania* 43 E12
Bāneh, *Iran* 70 C5
Bañeres, *Spain* 33 G4
Banes, *Cuba* 121 B4
Banff, *Canada* 104 C5
Banff, *U.K.* 14 D6
Banff Nat. Park, *Canada* 104 C5
Banfora, *Burkina Faso* 82 C4
Bang Fai ➤, *Laos* 64 D5
Bang Hieng ➤, *Laos* 64 D5
Bang Krathum, *Thailand* 64 D3
Bang Lamung, *Thailand* 64 F3
Bang Mun Nak, *Thailand* ... 64 D3
Bang Pa In, *Thailand* 64 E3
Bang Rakam, *Thailand* 64 D3
Bang Saphan, *Thailand* 65 G2
Bangaduni I., *India* 69 J13
Bangala Dam, *Zimbabwe* 87 G3
Bangalore, *India* 66 N10
Banganga ➤, *India* 68 F6
Bangangté, *Cameroon* 83 D7
Bangaon, *India* 69 H13
Bangassou, *C.A.R.* 84 D4
Banggai, *Indonesia* 63 E6
Banggai, Kepulauan, *Indonesia* 63 E6
Banggai Arch. = Banggai,
  Kepulauan, *Indonesia* 63 E6
Banggi, *Malaysia* 62 C5
Banghāzī, *Libya* 79 B10
Bangjang, *Sudan* 81 E3
Bangka, *Sulawesi, Indonesia* .. 63 D7
Bangka, *Sumatera, Indonesia* .. 62 E3
Bangka, Selat, *Indonesia* 62 E3
Bangkalan, *Indonesia* 63 G15
Bangkinang, *Indonesia* 62 D2
Bangko, *Indonesia* 62 E2
Bangkok, *Thailand* 64 F3
Bangladesh ■, *Asia* 67 H17
Bangolo, *Ivory C.* 82 D3
Bangong Co, *India* 69 B8
Bangor, *Down, U.K.* 15 B6
Bangor, *Gwynedd, U.K.* 12 D3
Bangor, *Maine, U.S.A.* 101 D13
Bangor, *Pa., U.S.A.* 111 F9
Bangued, *Phil.* 61 C4
Bangui, *C.A.R.* 84 D3
Bangui, *Phil.* 61 B4
Banguru, *Dem. Rep. of
  the Congo* 86 B2
Bangweulu, L., *Zambia* 87 E3
Bangweulu Swamp, *Zambia* .. 87 E3
Bani, *Dom. Rep.* 121 C5
Bani ➤, *Mali* 82 C4
Bani Bangou, *Niger* 83 B5
Banī Sa'd, *Iraq* 70 C5
Bania, *Ivory C.* 82 D4
Banihal Pass, *India* 69 C6
Banikoara, *Benin* 83 C5
Bāniyās, *Syria* 70 C3
Banja Luka, *Bos.-H.* 42 F2
Banjar, *India* 68 D7
Banjar ➤, *India* 69 H9
Banjarmasin, *Indonesia* 62 E4
Banjul, *Gambia* 82 C1
Banka, *India* 69 G12
Bankas, *Mali* 82 C4
Bankeryd, *Sweden* 11 G8
Banket, *Zimbabwe* 87 F3
Bankilaré, *Niger* 83 C5
Bankipore, *India* 67 G14
Banks I., *B.C., Canada* 104 C3
Banks I., *N.W.T., Canada* ... 100 A7
Banks Pen., *N.Z.* 91 K4
Banks Str., *Australia* 94 G4
Bankura, *India* 69 H12
Bankya, *Bulgaria* 40 D7
Banmankhi, *India* 69 G12
Bann ➤, *Arm., U.K.* 15 B5
Bann ➤, *L'derry., U.K.* 15 A5
Bannalec, *France* 18 E3
Bannang Sata, *Thailand* 65 J3
Banning, *U.S.A.* 117 M10
Banningville = Bandundu,
  Dem. Rep. of the Congo 84 E3
Banno, *Ethiopia* 81 G4
Bannockburn, *Canada* 110 B7
Bannockburn, *U.K.* 14 E5
Bannockburn, *Zimbabwe* 87 G2
Bannu, *Pakistan* 66 C7
Bano, *India* 69 H11
Bañolas = Banyoles, *Spain* ... 32 C7
Baños de la Encina, *Spain* ... 35 G7
Baños de Molgas, *Spain* 34 C3
Bánovce nad Bebravou,
  Slovak Rep. 27 C11
Banovići, *Bos.-H.* 42 F3
Bansgaon, *India* 69 F10
Banská Bystrica, *Slovak Rep.* .. 27 C12
Banská Štiavnica, *Slovak Rep.* . 27 C11
Bansko, *Bulgaria* 40 E7
Banskobystrický □, *Slovak Rep.* 27 C12
Banswara, *India* 68 H6
Bantaeng, *Indonesia* 63 F5
Bantaji, *Nigeria* 83 D7
Bantayan, *Phil.* 61 F5
Bantry, *Ireland* 15 E2
Bantry B., *Ireland* 15 E2
Bantul, *Indonesia* 63 G14
Bantva, *India* 68 J4
Banya, *Bulgaria* 41 D8
Banyak, Kepulauan, *Indonesia* . 62 D1
Banyalbufar, *Spain* 37 B9

Banyo, *Cameroon* 83 D7
Banyoles, *Spain* 32 C7
Banyuls-sur-Mer, *France* 20 F7
Banyumas, *Indonesia* 63 G13
Banyuwangi, *Indonesia* 63 H16
Banzare Coast, *Antarctica* 5 C9
Banzyville = Mobayi, *Dem. Rep.
  of the Congo* 84 D4
Bao Ha, *Vietnam* 58 F5
Bao Lac, *Vietnam* 64 A5
Bao Loc, *Vietnam* 65 G6
Bao'an = Shenzhen, *China* ... 59 F10
Baocheng, *China* 56 H4
Baode, *China* 56 E6
Baodi, *China* 57 E9
Baoding, *China* 56 E8
Baoji, *China* 56 G4
Baojing, *China* 58 C7
Baokang, *China* 59 B8
Baoshan, *Shanghai, China* ... 59 B13
Baoshan, *Yunnan, China* 58 E2
Baotou, *China* 56 D6
Baoxing, *China* 58 B4
Baoying, *China* 57 H10
Bap, *India* 68 F5
Bapatla, *India* 67 M12
Bapaume, *France* 19 B9
Ba'qubah, *Iraq* 70 C5
Baquedano, *Chile* 126 A2
Bar, *Montenegro, Yug.* 40 D3
Bar, *Ukraine* 47 H4
Bar Bigha, *India* 69 G11
Bar Harbor, *U.S.A.* 109 C11
Bar-le-Duc, *France* 19 D12
Bar-sur-Aube, *France* 19 D11
Bar-sur-Seine, *France* 19 D11
Bara, *India* 69 G9
Bâra, *Romania* 43 C12
Bara Banki, *India* 69 F9
Barabai, *Indonesia* 62 E5
Baraboo, *U.S.A.* 112 D10
Baracoa, *Cuba* 121 B5
Baradā ➤, *Syria* 75 B5
Baradero, *Argentina* 126 C4
Baraga, *U.S.A.* 112 B10
Bărăganul, *Romania* 43 F12
Barah ➤, *India* 68 F6
Barahona, *Dom. Rep.* 121 C5
Barahona, *Spain* 32 D2
Barail Range, *India* 67 G18
Baraka, *Indonesia* 81 E2
Baraka ➤, *Sudan* 80 D4
Barakaldo, *Spain* 32 B2
Barakar ➤, *India* 69 G12
Barakhola, *India* 67 G18
Barakot, *India* 69 J11
Barakpur, *India* 69 H13
Baralaba, *Australia* 94 C4
Baralla, *Spain* 34 C3
Baralzon L., *Canada* 105 B9
Barameiya, *Sudan* 80 D4
Baramula, *India* 69 B6
Baran, *India* 68 G7
Baran ➤, *Pakistan* 68 G3
Barañain, *Spain* 32 C3
Baranavichy, *Belarus* 47 F4
Barani, *Burkina Faso* 82 C4
Baranof, *U.S.A.* 104 B2
Baranof I., *U.S.A.* 100 C6
Baranów Sandomierski, *Poland* 45 H8
Baranya □, *Hungary* 42 E3
Baraolt, *Romania* 43 D10
Barapasi, *Indonesia* 63 E9
Barasat, *India* 69 H13
Barat Daya, Kepulauan,
  Indonesia 63 F7
Barataria B., *U.S.A.* 113 L10
Barauda, *India* 68 H6
Baraut, *India* 68 E7
Barbacena, *Brazil* 127 A7
Barbados ■, *W. Indies* 121 D8
Barban, *Croatia* 29 C11
Barbària, C. de, *Spain* 37 C7
Barbaros, *Turkey* 41 F11
Barbastro, *Spain* 32 C5
Barbate = Barbate de Franco,
  Spain 35 J5
Barbate de Franco, *Spain* 35 J5
Barberino di Mugello, *Italy* .. 29 E8
Barberton, *S. Africa* 89 D5
Barberton, *U.S.A.* 110 E3
Barbezieux-St-Hilaire, *France* . 20 C3
Barbosa, *Colombia* 124 B4
Barbourville, *U.S.A.* 109 G4
Barbuda, *W. Indies* 121 C7
Bârca, *Romania* 43 G8
Barcaldine, *Australia* 94 C4
Barcarrota, *Spain* 35 G4
Barcellona Pozzo di Gotto, *Italy* 31 D8
Barcelona, *Spain* 32 D7
Barcelona, *Venezuela* 124 A6
Barcelona □, *Spain* 32 D7
Barcelonette, *France* 21 D10
Barcelos, *Brazil* 124 D6
Barcin, *Poland* 45 F4
Barclayville, *Liberia* 82 E3
Barcoo ➤, *Australia* 94 D3
Barcs, *Hungary* 42 E2
Barczewo, *Poland* 44 E7
Bärdä, *Azerbaijan* 49 K8
Bardaï, *Chad* 79 D9
Bardas Blancas, *Argentina* ... 126 D2
Barddhaman, *India* 69 H12
Bardejov, *Slovak Rep.* 27 B14

Bardera, *Somali Rep.* 74 G3
Bardi, *Italy* 28 D6
Bardīyah, *Libya* 79 B10
Bardolino, *Italy* 28 C7
Bardonécchia, *Italy* 28 C3
Bardsey I., *U.K.* 12 E3
Bardstown, *U.S.A.* 108 G3
Barela, *India* 69 H9
Barentin, *France* 18 C7
Barenton, *France* 18 D6
Barents Sea, *Arctic* 4 B9
Barentu, *Eritrea* 81 D4
Barfleur, *France* 18 C5
Barfleur, Pte. de, *France* 18 C5
Barga, *Italy* 28 D7
Bargara, *Australia* 94 C5
Bargas, *Spain* 34 F6
Bârgăului Bistriţa, *Romania* .. 43 C9
Barge, *Italy* 28 D4
Bargnop, *Sudan* 81 F2
Bargteheide, *Germany* 24 B6
Barguzin, *Russia* 51 D11
Barh, *India* 69 G11
Barhaj, *India* 69 F10
Barharwa, *India* 69 G12
Barhi, *India* 69 G11
Bari, *India* 68 F7
Bari, *Italy* 31 A9
Bari Doab, *Pakistan* 68 D5
Bari Sadri, *India* 68 G6
Bari Sardo, *Italy* 30 C2
Barīdī, Ra's, *Si. Arabia* 70 E3
Barim, *Yemen* 76 E8
Barinas, *Venezuela* 124 B4
Baring, C., *Canada* 100 B8
Baringo, *Kenya* 86 B4
Baringo, L., *Kenya* 86 B4
Bâris, *Egypt* 80 C3
Barisal, *Bangla.* 67 H17
Barisan, Bukit, *Indonesia* 62 E2
Barito ➤, *Indonesia* 62 E4
Barjac, *France* 21 D8
Barjols, *France* 21 E10
Bark L., *Canada* 110 A7
Barka = Baraka ➤, *Sudan* .. 80 D4
Barkakana, *India* 69 H11
Barkam, *China* 58 B4
Barker, *U.S.A.* 110 C6
Barkley, L., *U.S.A.* 109 G2
Barkley Sound, *Canada* 104 D3
Barkly East, *S. Africa* 88 E4
Barkly Roadhouse, *Australia* .. 94 B2
Barkly Tableland, *Australia* ... 94 B2
Barkly West, *S. Africa* 88 D3
Barkol, Wadi ➤, *Sudan* 80 D3
Barla Dağı, *Turkey* 39 C12
Bârlad, *Romania* 43 D12
Bârlad ➤, *Romania* 43 E12
Barlee, L., *Australia* 93 E2
Barlee, Mt., *Australia* 93 D4
Barletta, *Italy* 31 A9
Barlinek, *Poland* 45 F2
Barlovento, *Canary Is.* 37 F2
Barlow L., *Canada* 105 A8
Barmedman, *Australia* 95 E4
Barmer, *India* 68 G4
Barmouth, *U.K.* 12 E3
Barmstedt, *Germany* 24 B5
Barna ➤, *India* 69 G10
Barnagar, *India* 68 H6
Barnala, *India* 68 D6
Barnard Castle, *U.K.* 12 C6
Barnaul, *Russia* 50 D9
Barnesville, *U.S.A.* 109 J3
Barnet □, *U.K.* 13 F7
Barneveld, *Neths.* 17 B5
Barneville-Cartevert, *France* .. 18 C5
Barnhart, *U.S.A.* 113 K4
Barnsley, *U.K.* 12 D6
Barnstaple, *U.K.* 13 F3
Barnstaple Bay = Bideford Bay,
  U.K. 13 F3
Barnsville, *U.S.A.* 112 B6
Barnwell, *U.S.A.* 109 J5
Baro, *Nigeria* 83 D6
Baro ➤, *Ethiopia* 81 F3
Baroda = Vadodara, *India* ... 68 H5
Baroda, *India* 68 G7
Baroe, *S. Africa* 88 E3
Baron Ra., *Australia* 92 D4
Barong, *China* 58 B2
Barotseland, *Zambia* 85 H4
Barouéli, *Mali* 82 C3
Barpeta, *India* 67 F17
Barques, Pt. Aux, *U.S.A.* 110 B2
Barquísimeto, *Venezuela* 124 A5
Barr, Ras el, *Egypt* 80 H7
Barr Smith Range, *Australia* .. 93 E3
Barra, *Brazil* 125 F10
Barra, *U.K.* 14 E1
Barra, Sd. of, *U.K.* 14 D1
Barra de Navidad, *Mexico* ... 118 D4
Barra do Corda, *Brazil* 125 E9
Barra do Piraí, *Brazil* 127 A7
Barra Falsa, Pta. da, *Mozam.* . 89 C6
Barra Hd., *U.K.* 14 E1
Barra Mansa, *Brazil* 127 A7
Barrackpur = Barakpur, *India* 69 H13
Barraigh = Barra, *U.K.* 14 E1
Barranca, *Lima, Peru* 124 F3
Barranca, *Loreto, Peru* 124 D3
Barrancabermeja, *Colombia* .. 124 B4

Barrancas, *Venezuela* 124 B6
Barrancos, *Portugal* 35 G4
Barranqueras, *Argentina* 126 B4
Barranquilla, *Colombia* 124 A4
Barraute, *Canada* 102 C4
Barre, *Mass., U.S.A.* 111 D12
Barre, *Vt., U.S.A.* 111 B12
Barreal, *Argentina* 126 C2
Barreiras, *Brazil* 125 F10
Barreirinhas, *Brazil* 125 D10
Barreiro, *Portugal* 35 G1
Barrême, *France* 21 E10
Barren, Nosy, *Madag.* 89 B7
Barretos, *Brazil* 125 H9
Barrhead, *Canada* 104 C6
Barrie, *Canada* 102 D4
Barrière, *Canada* 104 C4
Barrington, *U.S.A.* 111 E13
Barrington L., *Canada* 105 B8
Barringun, *Australia* 95 D4
Barro do Garças, *Brazil* 125 G8
Barron, *U.S.A.* 112 C9
Barrow, *U.S.A.* 100 A4
Barrow ➤, *Ireland* 15 D5
Barrow, Pt., *U.S.A.* 98 B4
Barrow Creek, *Australia* 94 C1
Barrow I., *Australia* 92 D2
Barrow-in-Furness, *U.K.* 12 C4
Barrow Pt., *Australia* 94 A3
Barrow Ra., *Australia* 93 E4
Barrow Str., *Canada* 4 B3
Barruecopardo, *Spain* 34 D4
Barruelo de Santullán, *Spain* . 34 C6
Barry, *U.K.* 13 F4
Barry's Bay, *Canada* 102 C4
Barsalogho, *Burkina Faso* 83 C4
Barsat, *Pakistan* 69 A5
Barsham, *Syria* 70 C4
Barsi, *India* 66 K9
Barsinghausen, *Germany* 24 C5
Barsoi, *India* 69 G15
Barstow, *U.S.A.* 117 L9
Barth, *Germany* 24 A8
Barthélemy, Col, *Vietnam* 64 C5
Bartica, *Guyana* 124 B7
Bartin, *Turkey* 72 B5
Bartlesville, *U.S.A.* 113 G7
Bartlett, *U.S.A.* 116 J8
Bartlett, L., *Canada* 104 A5
Bartolomeu Dias, *Mozam.* ... 87 G4
Barton upon Humber, *U.K.* .. 12 D7
Bartoszyce, *Poland* 44 D7
Bartow, *U.S.A.* 109 M5
Barú, Volcan, *Panama* 120 E3
Barumba, *Dem. Rep. of
  the Congo* 86 B1
Baruth, *Germany* 24 C9
Baruunsuu, *Mongolia* 56 C3
Barvinkove, *Ukraine* 47 H9
Barwani, *India* 68 H6
Barwice, *Poland* 44 E3
Barysaw, *Belarus* 46 E5
Barysh, *Russia* 48 D8
Barzân, *Iraq* 70 B5
Bârzava, *Romania* 42 D6
Bas-Rhin □, *France* 19 D14
Bašaid, *Serbia, Yug.* 42 E5
Bāsa'idū, *Iran* 71 E7
Basal, *Pakistan* 68 C5
Basankusa, *Dem. Rep. of
  the Congo* 84 D3
Basarabeasca, *Moldova* 43 D13
Basarabi, *Romania* 43 F13
Basauri, *Spain* 32 B2
Basawa, *Afghan.* 68 B4
Bascuñán, C., *Chile* 126 B1
Basel, *Switz.* 25 H3
Basel-Landschaft □, *Switz.* ... 25 H3
Basento ➤, *Italy* 31 B9
Bashäkerd, Kühhä-ye, *Iran* .. 71 E8
Bashaw, *Canada* 104 C6
Bāshī, *Iran* 71 D6
Bashkir Republic =
  Bashkortostan □, *Russia* ... 50 D6
Bashkortostan □, *Russia* 50 D6
Basibasy, *Madag.* 89 C7
Basilan I., *Phil.* 61 H5
Basilan Str., *Phil.* 61 H5
Basildon, *U.K.* 13 F8
Basile, *Eq. Guin.* 83 E6
Basilicata □, *Italy* 31 B9
Basim = Washim, *India* 66 J10
Basin, *U.S.A.* 114 D9
Basingstoke, *U.K.* 13 F6
Baška, *Croatia* 29 D11
Başkale, *Turkey* 73 C10
Baskatong, Rés., *Canada* 102 C4
Basle = Basel, *Switz.* 25 H3
Başmakçı, *Turkey* 39 D12
Basoda, *India* 68 H7
Basodino, *Switz.* 25 J4
Basoka, *Dem. Rep. of the Congo* 86 B1
Basque, *Pays, France* 20 E2
Basque Provinces = País
  Vasco □, *Spain* 32 C2
Basra = Al Başrah, *Iraq* 70 D5
Bass Str., *Australia* 94 F4
Bassano, *Canada* 104 C6
Bassano del Grappa, *Italy* ... 29 C8
Bassar, *Togo* 83 D5
Bassas da India, *Ind. Oc.* 85 J7
Basse-Normandie □, *France* .. 18 D6
Basse Santa-Su, *Gambia* 82 C2
Basse-Terre, *Guadeloupe* 121 C7

Bassein, *Burma* 67 L19
Basseterre, *St. Kitts & Nevis* . . . 121 C7
Bassett, *U.S.A.* 112 D5
Bassi, *India* 68 D7
Bassigny, *France* 19 E12
Bassikounou, *Mauritania* 82 B3
Bassila, *Benin* 83 D5
Bassum, *Germany* 24 C4
Båstad, *Sweden* 11 H6
Bastak, *Iran* 71 E7
Baştam, *Iran* 71 B7
Bastar, *India* 67 K12
Bastelica, *France* 21 F13
Basti, *India* 69 F10
Bastia, *France* 21 F13
Bastogne, *Belgium* 17 D5
Bastrop, *La., U.S.A.* 113 J9
Bastrop, *Tex., U.S.A.* 113 K6
Bat Yam, *Israel* 75 C3
Bata, *Eq. Guin.* 84 D1
Bata, *Romania* 42 D7
Batabanó, *Cuba* 120 B3
Batabanó, G. de, *Cuba* 120 B3
Batac, *Phil.* 61 B4
Batagai, *Russia* 51 C14
Batajnica, *Serbia, Yug.* 40 B4
Batak, *Bulgaria* 41 E8
Batala, *India* 68 D6
Batalha, *Portugal* 34 F2
Batama, *Dem. Rep. of the Congo* 86 B2
Batamay, *Russia* 51 C13
Batang, *China* 58 B2
Batang, *Indonesia* 63 G13
Batangas, *Phil.* 61 E4
Batanta, *Indonesia* 63 E8
Batatais, *Brazil* 127 A6
Batavia, *U.S.A.* 110 D6
Bataysk, *Russia* 47 J10
Batchelor, *Australia* 92 B5
Batdambang, *Cambodia* 64 F4
Bates Ra., *Australia* 93 E3
Batesburg-Leesville, *U.S.A.* . . 109 J5
Batesville, *Ark., U.S.A.* 113 H9
Batesville, *Miss., U.S.A.* 113 H10
Batesville, *Tex., U.S.A.* 113 L5
Bath, *Canada* 111 B8
Bath, *U.K.* 13 F5
Bath, *Maine, U.S.A.* 109 D11
Bath, *N.Y., U.S.A.* 110 D7
Bath & North East Somerset □,
  U.K. 13 F5
Batheay, *Cambodia* 65 G5
Bathurst = Banjul, *Gambia* . . . 82 C1
Bathurst, *Canada* 103 C6
Bathurst, *S. Africa* 88 E4
Bathurst B., *Australia* 94 A3
Bathurst Harb., *Australia* 94 G4
Bathurst I., *Australia* 92 B5
Bathurst I., *Canada* 4 B2
Bathurst Inlet, *Canada* 100 B9
Bati, *Ethiopia* 81 E5
Batie, *Burkina Faso* 82 D4
Batman, *Turkey* 70 B4
Baţn al Ghūl, *Jordan* 75 F4
Batna, *Algeria* 78 A7
Batobato = San Isidro, *Phil.* . . 61 H7
Batočina, *Serbia, Yug.* 40 B5
Batoka, *Zambia* 87 F2
Baton Rouge, *U.S.A.* 113 K9
Batong, Ko, *Thailand* 65 J2
Bátonyterenye, *Hungary* 42 C4
Batopilas, *Mexico* 118 B3
Batouri, *Cameroon* 84 D2
Båtsfjord, *Norway* 8 A23
Battambang = Batdambang,
  Cambodia 64 F4
Batticaloa, *Sri Lanka* 66 R12
Battipáglia, *Italy* 31 B7
Battle, *U.K.* 13 G8
Battle →, *Canada* 105 C7
Battle Creek, *U.S.A.* 108 D3
Battle Ground, *U.S.A.* 116 E4
Battle Harbour, *Canada* 103 B8
Battle Lake, *U.S.A.* 112 B7
Battle Mountain, *U.S.A.* 114 F5
Battlefields, *Zimbabwe* 87 F2
Battleford, *Canada* 105 C7
Battonya, *Hungary* 42 D6
Batu, *Ethiopia* 81 F4
Batu, Kepulauan, *Indonesia* . . 62 E1
Batu Caves, *Malaysia* 65 L3
Batu Gajah, *Malaysia* 65 K3
Batu Is. = Batu, Kepulauan,
  Indonesia 62 E1
Batu Pahat, *Malaysia* 65 M4
Batuata, *Indonesia* 63 F6
Batumi, *Georgia* 49 K5
Baturaja, *Indonesia* 62 E2
Baturité, *Brazil* 125 D11
Bau, *Malaysia* 62 D4
Baubau, *Indonesia* 63 F6
Bauchi, *Nigeria* 83 C6
Bauchi □, *Nigeria* 83 C7
Baud, *France* 18 E3
Baudette, *U.S.A.* 112 A7
Bauhinia, *Australia* 94 C4
Baukau, *E. Timor* 63 F7
Bauld, C., *Canada* 101 C14
Baume-les-Dames, *France* . . . 19 E13
Baunatal, *Germany* 24 D5
Baunei, *Italy* 30 B2
Baure, *Nigeria* 83 C6

Bauru, *Brazil* 127 A6
Bausi, *India* 69 G12
Bauska, *Latvia* 9 H21
Bautino, *Kazakstan* 49 H10
Bautzen, *Germany* 24 D10
Bauya, *S. Leone* 82 D2
Bavănăt, *Iran* 71 D7
Bavanište, *Serbia, Yug.* 42 F5
Bavaria = Bayern □, *Germany* . 25 G7
Båven, *Sweden* 10 E10
Bavispe →, *Mexico* 118 B3
Bawdwin, *Burma* 67 H20
Bawean, *Indonesia* 62 F4
Bawku, *Ghana* 83 C4
Bawlake, *Burma* 67 K20
Bawolung, *China* 58 C3
Baxley, *U.S.A.* 109 K4
Baxoi, *China* 58 B1
Baxter, *U.S.A.* 112 B7
Baxter Springs, *U.S.A.* 113 G7
Bay, L. de, *Phil.* 61 D4
Bay City, *Mich., U.S.A.* 108 D4
Bay City, *Tex., U.S.A.* 113 L7
Bay Minette, *U.S.A.* 109 K2
Bay Roberts, *Canada* 103 C9
Bay St. Louis, *U.S.A.* 113 K10
Bay Springs, *U.S.A.* 113 K10
Bay View, *N.Z.* 91 H6
Baya, *Dem. Rep. of the Congo* . 87 E2
Bayamo, *Cuba* 120 B4
Bayamón, *Puerto Rico* 121 C6
Bayan Har Shan, *China* 60 C4
Bayan Hot = Alxa Zuoqi, *China* 56 E3
Bayan Obo, *China* 56 D5
Bayan-Ovoo = Erdenetsogt,
  Mongolia 56 C4
Bayana, *India* 68 F7
Bayanaūyl, *Kazakstan* 50 D8
Bayandalay, *Mongolia* 56 C2
Bayanhongor, *Mongolia* 60 B5
Bayard, *N. Mex., U.S.A.* 115 K9
Bayard, *Nebr., U.S.A.* 112 E3
Bayawan, *Phil.* 61 G5
Baybay, *Phil.* 61 F6
Bayelsa □, *Nigeria* 83 E6
Bayerische Alpen, *Germany* . . 25 H7
Bayerischer Wald, *Germany* . . 25 G8
Bayern □, *Germany* 25 G7
Bayeux, *France* 18 C6
Bayfield, *Canada* 110 C3
Bayfield, *U.S.A.* 112 B9
Bayındır, *Turkey* 39 C9
Baykal, Oz., *Russia* 51 D11
Baykan, *Turkey* 70 B4
Baykonur = Bayqongyr,
  Kazakstan 50 E7
Baynes Mts., *Namibia* 88 B1
Bayombong, *Phil.* 61 C4
Bayon, *France* 19 D13
Bayona = Baiona, *Spain* 34 C2
Bayonne, *France* 20 E2
Bayonne, *U.S.A.* 111 F10
Bayovar, *Peru* 124 E2
Bayqongyr, *Kazakstan* 50 E7
Bayram-Ali = Bayramaly,
  Turkmenistan 50 F7
Bayramaly, *Turkmenistan* 50 F7
Bayramiç, *Turkey* 39 B8
Bayreuth, *Germany* 25 F7
Bayrischzell, *Germany* 25 H8
Bayrūt, *Lebanon* 75 B4
Bays, L. of, *Canada* 110 A5
Baysville, *Canada* 110 A5
Bayt Lahm, *West Bank* 75 D4
Baytown, *U.S.A.* 113 L7
Bayzo, *Niger* 83 C5
Baza, *Spain* 35 H8
Bazar Dyuzi, *Russia* 49 K8
Bazardüzü = Bazar Dyuzi,
  Russia 49 K8
Bazarny Karabulak, *Russia* . . . 48 D8
Bazarnyy Syzgan, *Russia* 48 D8
Bazas, *France* 20 D3
Bazhong, *China* 58 B6
Bazhou, *China* 56 E9
Bazmān, Kūh-e, *Iran* 71 D9
Beach, *U.S.A.* 112 B3
Beach City, *U.S.A.* 110 F3
Beachy Hd., *U.K.* 13 G8
Beacon, *Australia* 93 F2
Beacon, *U.S.A.* 111 E11
Beaconsfield, *Australia* 94 G4
Beagle, Canal, *S. Amer.* 122 J4
Beagle Bay, *Australia* 92 C3
Bealanana, *Madag.* 89 A8
Beals Cr. →, *U.S.A.* 113 J4
Beamsville, *Canada* 110 C5
Bear →, *Calif., U.S.A.* 116 G5
Bear →, *Utah, U.S.A.* 106 B4
Bear, C., *Australia* 20 F7
Bear I., *Ireland* 15 E2
Bear L., *Canada* 105 B9
Bear L., *U.S.A.* 114 F8
Beardmore, *Canada* 102 C2
Beardmore Glacier, *Antarctica* . 5 E11
Beardstown, *U.S.A.* 112 F9
Bearma →, *India* 69 G8
Bearpaw Mts., *U.S.A.* 114 B9
Bearskin Lake, *Canada* 102 B1
Beas →, *India* 68 D6
Beas de Segura, *Spain* 35 G8
Beasain, *Spain* 32 B2

Bauru, *Brazil* 127 A6
Beata, C., *Dom. Rep.* 121 C5
Beata, I., *Dom. Rep.* 121 C5
Beatrice, *U.S.A.* 112 E6
Beatrice, *Zimbabwe* 87 F3
Beatrice, C., *Australia* 94 A2
Beatton →, *Canada* 104 B4
Beatton River, *Canada* 104 B4
Beatty, *U.S.A.* 116 J10
Beaucaire, *France* 21 E8
Beauce, Plaine de la, *France* . . 19 D8
Beauceville, *Canada* 103 C5
Beaudesert, *Australia* 95 D5
Beaufort, *France* 21 C10
Beaufort, *Malaysia* 62 C5
Beaufort, *N.C., U.S.A.* 109 H7
Beaufort, *S.C., U.S.A.* 109 J5
Beaufort Sea, *Arctic* 4 B1
Beaufort West, *S. Africa* 88 E3
Beaugency, *France* 19 E8
Beauharnois, *Canada* 111 A11
Beaujeu, *France* 19 F11
Beaujolais, *France* 19 F11
Beaulieu →, *Canada* 104 A6
Beaulieu-sur-Dordogne, *France* 20 D5
Beaulieu-sur-Mer, *France* . . . 21 E11
Beauly, *U.K.* 14 D4
Beauly →, *U.K.* 14 D4
Beaumaris, *U.K.* 12 D3
Beaumont, *Belgium* 17 D4
Beaumont, *France* 20 D4
Beaumont, *U.S.A.* 113 K7
Beaumont-de-Lomagne, *France* 20 E5
Beaumont-le-Roger, *France* . . 18 C7
Beaumont-sur-Sarthe, *France* . 18 D7
Beaune, *France* 19 E11
Beaune-la-Rolande, *France* . . . 19 D9
Beaupré, *Canada* 103 C5
Beaupréau, *France* 18 E6
Beauraing, *Belgium* 17 D4
Beaurepaire, *France* 21 C9
Beauséjour, *Canada* 105 C9
Beauvais, *France* 19 C9
Beauval, *Canada* 105 B7
Beauvoir-sur-Mer, *France* 18 F4
Beauvoir-sur-Niort, *France* . . . 20 B3
Beaver, *Okla., U.S.A.* 113 G4
Beaver, *Pa., U.S.A.* 110 F4
Beaver, *Utah, U.S.A.* 115 G7
Beaver →, *B.C., Canada* . . . 104 B4
Beaver →, *Ont., Canada* . . . 102 A2
Beaver →, *Sask., Canada* . . . 105 B7
Beaver →, *U.S.A.* 113 G5
Beaver City, *U.S.A.* 112 E5
Beaver Creek, *Canada* 100 B5
Beaver Dam, *U.S.A.* 112 D10
Beaver Falls, *U.S.A.* 110 F4
Beaver Hill L., *Canada* 105 C10
Beaver I., *U.S.A.* 108 C3
Beaverhill L., *Canada* 104 C6
Beaverlodge, *Canada* 104 B5
Beaverstone →, *Canada* . . . 102 B2
Beaverton, *Canada* 110 B5
Beaverton, *U.S.A.* 116 E4
Beawar, *India* 68 F6
Bebedouro, *Brazil* 127 A6
Beboa, *Madag.* 89 B7
Bebra, *Germany* 24 E5
Beccles, *U.K.* 13 E9
Bečej, *Serbia, Yug.* 42 E5
Beceni, *Romania* 43 E11
Becerreá, *Spain* 34 C3
Béchar, *Algeria* 78 B5
Bechyně, *Czech Rep.* 26 B7
Beckley, *U.S.A.* 108 G5
Beckum, *Germany* 24 D4
Beclean, *Romania* 43 C9
Bečov nad Teplou, *Czech Rep.* . 26 A5
Bečva →, *Czech Rep.* 27 B10
Bédar, *Spain* 33 H3
Bédarieux, *France* 20 E7
Beddouza, Ras, *Morocco* 78 B4
Bedele, *Ethiopia* 81 F4
Bederkesa, *Germany* 24 B4
Bedeso, *Ethiopia* 81 F5
Bedford, *Canada* 111 A12
Bedford, *S. Africa* 88 E4
Bedford, *U.K.* 13 E7
Bedford, *Ind., U.S.A.* 108 F2
Bedford, *Iowa, U.S.A.* 112 E7
Bedford, *Ohio, U.S.A.* 110 E3
Bedford, *Pa., U.S.A.* 110 F6
Bedford, *Va., U.S.A.* 108 G6
Bedford, C., *Australia* 94 B4
Bedfordshire □, *U.K.* 13 E7
Bednja →, *Croatia* 29 B13
Bednodemyanovsk, *Russia* . . . 48 D6
Bedónia, *Italy* 28 D6
Bedourie, *Australia* 94 C2
Bedum, *Neths.* 17 A6
Będzin, *Poland* 45 H6
Beech Creek, *U.S.A.* 110 E7
Beelitz, *Germany* 24 C8
Beenleigh, *Australia* 95 D5
Be'er Menuḥa, *Israel* 70 D2
Be'er Sheva, *Israel* 75 D3
Beersheba = Be'er Sheva, *Israel* 75 D3
Beeskow, *Germany* 24 C10
Beeston, *U.K.* 12 E6
Beeville, *U.S.A.* 113 L6
Befale, *Dem. Rep. of the Congo* 84 D4
Befandriana, Mahajanga,
  Madag. 89 B8

Befandriana, *Toliara, Madag.* . 89 C7
Befasy, *Madag.* 89 C7
Befotaka, *Antsiranana, Madag.* 89 A8
Befotaka, *Fianarantsoa, Madag.* 89 C8
Bega, Canalul, *Romania* 42 E5
Bégard, *France* 18 D3
Beğendik, *Turkey* 41 F10
Begoro, *Ghana* 83 D4
Begusarai, *India* 69 G12
Behābād, *Iran* 71 C8
Behala, *India* 69 H13
Behara, *Madag.* 89 C8
Behbehān, *Iran* 71 D6
Behm Canal, *U.S.A.* 104 B2
Behshahr, *Iran* 71 B7
Bei Jiang →, *China* 59 F9
Bei'an, *China* 60 B7
Beibei, *China* 58 C6
Beihai, *China* 58 G7
Beijing, *China* 56 E9
Beijing □, *China* 56 E9
Beilen, *Neths.* 17 B6
Beiliu, *China* 59 F8
Beilngries, *Germany* 25 F7
Beilul, *Eritrea* 81 E5
Beinn na Faoghla = Benbecula,
  U.K. 14 D1
Beipan Jiang →, *China* 58 E5
Beipiao, *China* 57 D11
Beira, *Mozam.* 87 F3
Beirut = Bayrūt, *Lebanon* 75 B4
Beiseker, *Canada* 104 C6
Beitaolaizhao, *China* 57 B13
Beitbridge, *Zimbabwe* 87 G3
Beiuş, *Romania* 42 D7
Beizhen = Binzhou, *China* . . 57 F10
Beizhen, *China* 57 D11
Beizhengzhen, *China* 57 B12
Beja, *Portugal* 35 G3
Béja, *Tunisia* 79 A7
Beja □, *Portugal* 35 H3
Bejaïa, *Algeria* 78 A7
Béjar, *Spain* 34 E5
Bejestān, *Iran* 71 C8
Bekçiler, *Turkey* 39 E11
Békés, *Hungary* 42 D6
Békés □, *Hungary* 42 D6
Békéscsaba, *Hungary* 42 D6
Bekilli, *Turkey* 39 C11
Bekily, *Madag.* 89 C8
Bekisopa, *Madag.* 89 C8
Bekitro, *Madag.* 89 C8
Bekodoka, *Madag.* 89 B8
Bekoji, *Ethiopia* 81 F4
Bekok, *Malaysia* 65 L4
Bekopaka, *Madag.* 89 B7
Bekwai, *Ghana* 83 D4
Bela, *India* 69 G10
Bela, *Pakistan* 68 F2
Bela Crkva, *Serbia, Yug.* 42 F6
Bela Palanka, *Serbia, Yug.* . . . 40 C6
Bela Vista, *Brazil* 126 A4
Bela Vista, *Mozam.* 89 D5
Bélâbre, *France* 20 B5
Belalcázar, *Spain* 35 G5
Belan →, *India* 69 G9
Belanovica, *Serbia, Yug.* 40 B4
Belarus ■, *Europe* 46 F4
Belau = Palau ■, *Pac. Oc.* . . . 52 J17
Belavenona, *Madag.* 89 C8
Belaya, *Ethiopia* 81 E4
Belaya Glina, *Russia* 49 G5
Belaya Kalitva, *Russia* 49 F5
Belaya Tserkov = Bila Tserkva,
  Ukraine 47 H6
Belcești, *Romania* 43 C12
Bełchatów, *Poland* 45 G6
Belcher Is., *Canada* 102 A3
Belchite, *Spain* 32 D4
Belden, *U.S.A.* 116 E5
Belém, *Brazil* 125 D9
Belén, *Argentina* 126 B2
Belén, *Paraguay* 126 A4
Belen, *U.S.A.* 115 J10
Belene, *Bulgaria* 41 C9
Beleni, *Turkey* 72 D7
Bélesta, *France* 20 F5
Belet Uen, *Somali Rep.* 74 G4
Belev, *Russia* 46 F9
Belevi, *Turkey* 39 C9
Belfair, *U.S.A.* 116 C4
Belfast, *S. Africa* 89 D5
Belfast, *U.K.* 15 B6
Belfast, *Maine, U.S.A.* 109 C11
Belfast, *N.Y., U.S.A.* 110 D6
Belfast □, *U.K.* 15 B6
Belfield, *U.S.A.* 112 B3
Belfort, *France* 19 E13
Belfort, Territoire de □, *France* . 19 E13
Belfry, *U.S.A.* 114 D9
Belgaum, *India* 66 M9
Belgioioso, *Italy* 28 C6
Belgium ■, *Europe* 17 D4
Belgodère, *France* 21 F13
Belgorod, *Russia* 47 G9
Belgorod-Dnestrovskiy =
  Bilhorod-Dnistrovskyy,
  Ukraine 47 J6
Belgrade = Beograd,
  Serbia, Yug. 40 B4
Belgrade, *U.S.A.* 114 D8
Belhaven, *U.S.A.* 109 H7
Beli Drim →, *Europe* 40 D4

Beli Manastir, *Croatia* 42 E3
Beli Timok →, *Serbia, Yug.* . . 40 C6
Bélice →, *Italy* 30 E5
Belinskiy, *Russia* 48 D6
Beliton Is. = Belitung, *Indonesia* 62 E3
Belitung, *Indonesia* 62 E3
Beliu, *Romania* 42 D6
Belize ■, *Cent. Amer.* 119 D7
Belize City, *Belize* 119 D7
Beljakovci, *Macedonia* 40 D5
Beljanica, *Serbia, Yug.* 40 B5
Belkovskiy, Ostrov, *Russia* . . . 51 B14
Bell →, *Canada* 102 C4
Bell I., *Canada* 103 B8
Bell-Irving →, *Canada* 104 B3
Bell Peninsula, *Canada* 101 B11
Bell Ville, *Argentina* 126 C3
Bella, *Italy* 31 B8
Bella Bella, *Canada* 104 C3
Bella Coola, *Canada* 104 C3
Bella Unión, *Uruguay* 126 C4
Bella Vista, Corrientes,
  Argentina 126 B4
Bella Vista, Tucuman, Argentina 126 B2
Bellac, *France* 20 B5
Bellaire, *U.S.A.* 110 F4
Bellária, *Italy* 29 D9
Bellary, *India* 66 M10
Bellata, *Australia* 95 D4
Belle-Chasse, *U.S.A.* 113 L10
Belle Fourche, *U.S.A.* 112 C3
Belle Fourche →, *U.S.A.* 112 C3
Belle Glade, *U.S.A.* 109 M5
Belle-Île, *France* 18 E3
Belle Isle, *Canada* 103 B8
Belle Isle, Str. of, *Canada* . . . 103 B8
Belle Plaine, *U.S.A.* 112 E8
Belle Yella, *Liberia* 82 D3
Belledonne, *France* 21 C10
Bellefontaine, *U.S.A.* 108 E4
Bellefonte, *U.S.A.* 110 F7
Bellegarde, *France* 19 E9
Bellegarde-en-Marche, *France* . 20 C6
Bellegarde-sur-Valserine, *France* 19 F12
Bellême, *France* 18 D7
Belleoram, *Canada* 103 C8
Belleville, *Canada* 102 D4
Belleville, *France* 19 F11
Belleville, *Ill., U.S.A.* 112 F10
Belleville, *Kans., U.S.A.* 112 F6
Belleville, *N.Y., U.S.A.* 111 C8
Belleville-sur-Vie, *France* 18 F5
Bellevue, *Canada* 104 D6
Bellevue, *Idaho, U.S.A.* 114 E6
Bellevue, *Nebr., U.S.A.* 112 E7
Bellevue, *Ohio, U.S.A.* 110 E2
Bellevue, *Wash., U.S.A.* 116 C4
Belley, *France* 21 C9
Bellin = Kangirsuk, *Canada* . . 101 B13
Bellinge, *Denmark* 11 J4
Bellingham, *U.S.A.* 100 D7
Bellinzona, *Switz.* 25 J5
Bello, *Colombia* 124 B3
Bellows Falls, *U.S.A.* 111 C12
Bellpat, *Pakistan* 68 E3
Bellpuig d'Urgell, *Spain* 32 D6
Belluno, *Italy* 29 B9
Bellwood, *U.S.A.* 110 F6
Bélmez, *Spain* 35 G5
Belmont, *Canada* 110 D3
Belmont, *S. Africa* 88 D3
Belmont, *U.S.A.* 110 D6
Belmonte, *Brazil* 125 G11
Belmonte, *Portugal* 34 E3
Belmonte, *Spain* 33 F2
Belmopan, *Belize* 119 D7
Belmullet, *Ireland* 15 B2
Belo Horizonte, *Brazil* 125 G10
Belo-sur-Mer, *Madag.* 89 C7
Belo-Tsiribihina, *Madag.* 89 B7
Belogorsk = Bilohirsk, *Ukraine* 47 K8
Belogorsk, *Russia* 51 D13
Belogradchik, *Bulgaria* 40 C6
Belogradets, *Bulgaria* 41 C11
Beloha, *Madag.* 89 D8
Beloit, *Kans., U.S.A.* 112 F5
Beloit, *Wis., U.S.A.* 112 D10
Belokorovichi, *Ukraine* 47 G5
Belomorsk, *Russia* 50 C4
Belonia, *India* 67 H17
Belopolye = Bilopillya, *Ukraine* 47 G8
Belorechensk, *Russia* 49 H4
Belorussia = Belarus ■, *Europe* 46 F4
Beloslav, *Bulgaria* 41 C11
Belovo, *Bulgaria* 41 D8
Belovo, *Russia* 50 D9
Belovodsk, *Ukraine* 47 H10
Beloye, Ozero, *Russia* 46 B9
Beloye More, *Russia* 50 C4
Belozem, *Bulgaria* 41 D9
Belozersk, *Russia* 46 B9
Belpasso, *Italy* 31 E7
Belpre, *U.S.A.* 108 F5
Belrain, *India* 69 E9
Belt, *U.S.A.* 114 C8
Belterra, *Brazil* 125 D8
Beltinci, *Slovenia* 29 B13
Belton, *U.S.A.* 113 K6
Belton L., *U.S.A.* 113 K6
Beltsy = Bălţi, *Moldova* 43 C12
Belturbet, *Ireland* 15 B4
Belukha, *Russia* 50 E9

Beluran, *Malaysia* 62 C5
Beluša, *Slovak Rep.* 27 B11
Belušić, *Serbia, Yug.* 40 C5
Belvedere Maríttimo, *Italy* ... 31 C8
Belvès, *France* 20 D5
Belvidere, *Ill., U.S.A.* 112 D10
Belvidere, *N.J., U.S.A.* 111 F9
Belvis de la Jara, *Spain* 34 F6
Belyando ➤, *Australia* 94 C4
Belyy, *Russia* 46 E7
Belyy, Ostrov, *Russia* 50 B8
Belyy Yar, *Russia* 50 D9
Bełżec, *Poland* 45 H10
Belzig, *Germany* 24 C8
Belzoni, *U.S.A.* 113 J9
Bełżyce, *Poland* 45 G9
Bemaraha, Lembalemban' i,
  Madag. 89 B7
Bemarivo, *Madag.* 89 C7
Bemarivo ➤, *Antsiranana,*
  Madag. 89 A9
Bemarivo ➤, *Mahajanga,*
  Madag. 89 B8
Bemavo, *Madag.* 89 C8
Bembéréke, *Benin* 83 C5
Bembesi, *Zimbabwe* 87 G2
Bembesi ➤, *Zimbabwe* 87 F2
Bembézar ➤, *Spain* 35 H5
Bembibre, *Spain* 34 C4
Bemetara, *India* 69 J9
Bemidji, *U.S.A.* 112 B7
Bemolanga, *Madag.* 89 B8
Ben, *Iran* 71 C6
Benāb, *Iran* 73 D12
Benalmádena, *Spain* 35 J6
Benares = Varanasi, *India* ... 69 G10
Bénat, C., *France* 21 E10
Benavente, *Portugal* 35 G2
Benavente, *Spain* 34 C5
Benavides, *U.S.A.* 113 M5
Benavides de Órbigo, *Spain* . 34 C5
Benbecula, *U.K.* 14 D1
Bend, *U.S.A.* 114 D3
Bender Beila, *Somali Rep.* ... 74 F5
Bendery = Tighina, *Moldova* . 43 D14
Bendorf, *Germany* 24 E3
Benē Beraq, *Israel* 75 C3
Bénéna, *Mali* 82 C4
Benenitra, *Madag.* 89 C8
Benešov, *Czech Rep.* 26 B7
Benevento, *Italy* 31 A7
Benfeld, *France* 19 D14
Benga, *Mozam.* 87 F3
Bengal, Bay of, *Ind. Oc.* 67 M17
Bengbis, *Cameroon* 83 E7
Bengbu, *China* 57 H9
Benghazi = Banghāzī, *Libya* . 79 B10
Bengkalis, *Indonesia* 62 D2
Bengkulu, *Indonesia* 62 E2
Bengkulu □, *Indonesia* 62 E2
Bengough, *Canada* 105 D7
Bengtsfors, *Sweden* 10 E6
Benguela, *Angola* 85 G2
Benguérua, I., *Mozam.* 89 C6
Benha, *Egypt* 80 H7
Beni, *Dem. Rep. of the Congo* 86 B2
Beni ➤, *Bolivia* 124 F5
Beni Mazâr, *Egypt* 80 B3
Beni Mellal, *Morocco* 78 B4
Beni Suef, *Egypt* 80 J7
Beniah L., *Canada* 104 A6
Benicarló, *Spain* 32 E5
Benicássim, *Spain* 32 E5
Benicia, *U.S.A.* 116 G4
Benidorm, *Spain* 33 G4
Benin ■, *Africa* 83 D5
Benin ➤, *Nigeria* 83 D6
Benin, Bight of, *W. Afr.* 83 E5
Benin City, *Nigeria* 83 D6
Benisa, *Spain* 33 G5
Benitses, *Greece* 36 A3
Benjamin Aceval, *Paraguay* . 126 A4
Benjamin Constant, *Brazil* .. 124 D4
Benjamin Hill, *Mexico* 118 A2
Benkelman, *U.S.A.* 112 E4
Benkovac, *Croatia* 29 D12
Bennett, *Canada* 104 B2
Bennett, L., *Australia* 92 D5
Bennetta, Ostrov, *Russia* 51 B15
Bennettsville, *U.S.A.* 109 H6
Bennichchāb, *Mauritania* ... 82 B1
Bennington, *N.H., U.S.A.* ... 111 D11
Bennington, *Vt., U.S.A.* 111 D11
Bénodet, *France* 18 E2
Benoni, *S. Africa* 89 D4
Benque Viejo, *Belize* 119 D7
Bensheim, *Germany* 25 F4

Benson, *Ariz., U.S.A.* 115 L8
Benson, *Minn., U.S.A.* 112 C7
Bent, *Iran* 71 E8
Benteng, *Indonesia* 63 F6
Bentinck I., *Australia* 94 B2
Bentiu, *Sudan* 81 F2
Bento Gonçalves, *Brazil* 127 B5
Benton, *Ark., U.S.A.* 113 H8
Benton, *Calif., U.S.A.* 116 H8
Benton, *Ill., U.S.A.* 112 G10
Benton, *Pa., U.S.A.* 111 E8
Benton Harbor, *U.S.A.* 108 D2
Bentonville, *U.S.A.* 113 G7
Bentu Liben, *Ethiopia* 81 F4
Bentung, *Malaysia* 65 L3
Benue □, *Nigeria* 83 D6
Benue ➤, *Nigeria* 83 D6
Benxi, *China* 57 D12
Beo, *Indonesia* 63 D7
Beograd, *Serbia, Yug.* 40 B4
Beoumi, *Ivory C.* 82 D3
Bepan Jiang ➤, *China* 58 E6
Beppu, *Japan* 55 H5
Beqaa Valley = Al Biqā,
  Lebanon 75 A5
Ber Mota, *India* 68 H3
Berach ➤, *India* 68 G6
Beraketa, *Madag.* 89 C7
Berane, *Montenegro, Yug.* ... 40 D3
Berat, *Albania* 40 F3
Berau, Teluk, *Indonesia* 63 E8
Beravina, *Madag.* 89 B8
Berber, *Sudan* 80 D3
Berbera, *Somali Rep.* 74 E4
Berbérati, *C.A.R.* 84 D3
Berbice ➤, *Guyana* 124 B7
Berceto, *Italy* 28 D6
Berchidda, *Italy* 30 B2
Berchtesgaden, *Germany* 25 H8
Berck, *France* 19 B8
Berdichev = Berdychiv, *Ukraine* 47 H5
Berdsk, *Russia* 50 D9
Berdyansk, *Ukraine* 47 J9
Berdychiv, *Ukraine* 47 H5
Berea, *U.S.A.* 108 G3
Berebere, *Indonesia* 63 D7
Bereda, *Somali Rep.* 74 E5
Berehove, *Ukraine* 47 H2
Berekum, *Ghana* 82 D4
Berenice, *Egypt* 80 C4
Berens ➤, *Canada* 105 C9
Berens I., *Canada* 105 C9
Berens River, *Canada* 105 C9
Beresford, *U.S.A.* 112 D6
Berestechko, *Ukraine* 47 G3
Bereşti, *Romania* 43 D12
Beretău ➤, *Romania* 42 C6
Berettyó ➤, *Hungary* 42 D6
Berettyóújfalu, *Hungary* 42 C6
Berevo, *Mahajanga, Madag.* . 89 B7
Berevo, *Toliara, Madag.* 89 B7
Bereza = Byaroza, *Belarus* ... 47 F3
Berezhany, *Ukraine* 47 H3
Berezina = Byarezina ➤,
  Belarus 47 F6
Berezivka, *Ukraine* 47 J6
Berezna, *Ukraine* 47 G6
Berezniki, *Russia* 50 C5
Berezniki, *Russia* 50 D6
Berezovo, *Russia* 50 C7
Berga, *Spain* 32 C6
Berga, *Sweden* 11 G10
Bergama, *Turkey* 39 B9
Bérgamo, *Italy* 28 C6
Bergara, *Spain* 32 B2
Bergby, *Sweden* 10 D11
Bergedorf, *Germany* 24 B6
Bergeforsen, *Sweden* 10 B11
Bergen,
  Mecklenburg-Vorpommern,
  Germany 24 A9
Bergen, *Niedersachsen, Germany* 24 C5
Bergen, *Neths.* 17 B4
Bergen, *Norway* 9 F11
Bergen op Zoom, *Neths.* 17 C4
Bergerac, *France* 20 D4
Bergheim, *Germany* 24 E2
Bergholz, *U.S.A.* 110 F4
Bergisch Gladbach, *Germany* . 17 D7
Bergkamen, *Germany* 24 D3
Bergkvara, *Sweden* 11 H10
Bergshamra, *Sweden* 10 E12
Bergsjö, *Sweden* 10 C11
Bergues, *France* 19 B9
Bergviken, *Sweden* 10 C10
Bergville, *S. Africa* 89 D4
Berhala, Selat, *Indonesia* ... 62 E2
Berhampore = Baharampur,
  India 69 G13
Berhampur = Brahmapur, *India* 67 K14
Berheci ➤, *Romania* 43 E12
Bering Sea, *Pac. Oc.* 100 C1
Bering Strait, *Pac. Oc.* 100 B3
Beringovskiy, *Russia* 51 C18
Berisso, *Argentina* 126 C4
Berja, *Spain* 35 J8
Berkeley, *U.S.A.* 116 H4
Berkner I., *Antarctica* 5 D18
Berkovitsa, *Bulgaria* 40 C7
Berkshire, *U.S.A.* 111 D8
Berkshire Downs, *U.K.* 13 F6
Berlanga, *Spain* 35 G5
Berlenga, I., *Portugal* 35 F1
Berlin, *Germany* 24 C9

Berlin, *Md., U.S.A.* 108 F8
Berlin, *N.H., U.S.A.* 111 B13
Berlin, *N.Y., U.S.A.* 111 D11
Berlin, *Wis., U.S.A.* 108 D1
Berlin □, *Germany* 24 C9
Berlin L., *U.S.A.* 110 E4
Bermeja, Sierra, *Spain* 35 J5
Bermejo ➤, *Formosa, Argentina* 126 B4
Bermejo ➤, *San Juan,*
  Argentina 126 C2
Bermen, L., *Canada* 103 B6
Bermeo, *Spain* 32 B2
Bermillo de Sayago, *Spain* .. 34 D4
Bermuda ■, *Atl. Oc.* 98 F13
Bern, *Switz.* 25 J3
Bern □, *Switz.* 25 J3
Bernalda, *Italy* 31 B9
Bernalillo, *U.S.A.* 115 J10
Bernardo de Irigoyen, *Argentina* 127 B5
Bernardo O'Higgins □, *Chile* . 126 C1
Bernardsville, *U.S.A.* 111 F10
Bernasconi, *Argentina* 126 D3
Bernau, *Bayern, Germany* ... 25 H8
Bernau, *Brandenburg, Germany* 24 C9
Bernay, *France* 18 C7
Bernburg, *Germany* 24 D7
Berndorf, *Austria* 26 D9
Berne = Bern, *Switz.* 25 J3
Berne = Bern □, *Switz.* 25 J3
Berner Alpen, *Switz.* 25 J3
Berneray, *U.K.* 14 D1
Bernier I., *Australia* 93 D1
Bernina, Piz, *Switz.* 25 J5
Bernkastel-Kues, *Germany* ... 25 F3
Beroroha, *Madag.* 89 C8
Béroubouay, *Benin* 83 C5
Beroun, *Czech Rep.* 26 B7
Berounka ➤, *Czech Rep.* 26 B7
Berovo, *Macedonia* 40 E6
Berre, Étang de, *France* 21 E9
Berre-l'Étang, *France* 21 E9
Berriane, *Algeria* 78 B6
Berry, *France* 19 F8
Berry Is., *Bahamas* 120 A4
Berryessa L., *U.S.A.* 116 G4
Berryville, *U.S.A.* 113 G8
Berseba, *Namibia* 88 D2
Bersenbrück, *Germany* 24 C3
Bershad, *Ukraine* 47 H5
Berthold, *U.S.A.* 112 A4
Berthoud, *U.S.A.* 112 E2
Bertincourt, *France* 19 B9
Bertoua, *Cameroon* 84 D2
Bertraghboy B., *Ireland* 15 C2
Berwick, *U.S.A.* 111 E8
Berwick-upon-Tweed, *U.K.* ... 12 B6
Berwyn Mts., *U.K.* 12 E4
Beryslav, *Ukraine* 47 J7
Berzasca, *Romania* 42 F6
Berzence, *Hungary* 42 D2
Besal, *Pakistan* 69 B5
Besalampy, *Madag.* 89 B7
Besançon, *France* 19 E13
Besar, *Indonesia* 62 E5
Beshenkovichi, *Belarus* 46 E5
Beška, *Serbia, Yug.* 42 E5
Beslan, *Russia* 49 J7
Besna Kobila, *Serbia, Yug.* .. 40 D6
Besnard L., *Canada* 105 B7
Besni, *Turkey* 70 B3
Besor, N. ➤, *Egypt* 75 D3
Bessarabiya, *Moldova* 47 J5
Bessarabka = Basarabeasca,
  Moldova 43 D13
Bessèges, *France* 21 D8
Bessemer, *Ala., U.S.A.* 109 J2
Bessemer, *Mich., U.S.A.* 112 B9
Bessemer, *Pa., U.S.A.* 110 F4
Bessin, *France* 18 C6
Bessines-sur-Gartempe, *France* 20 B5
Beswick, *Australia* 92 B5
Bet She'an, *Israel* 75 C4
Bet Shemesh, *Israel* 75 D4
Betafo, *Madag.* 89 B8
Betancuria, *Canary Is.* 37 F5
Betanzos, *Spain* 34 B2
Bétaré Oya, *Cameroon* 84 C2
Betatao, *Madag.* 89 B8
Bétera, *Spain* 33 F4
Bétérou, *Benin* 83 D5
Bethal, *S. Africa* 89 D4
Bethanien, *Namibia* 88 D2
Bethany, *Canada* 110 B6
Bethany, *U.S.A.* 112 E7
Bethel, *Alaska, U.S.A.* 100 B3
Bethel, *Conn., U.S.A.* 111 E11
Bethel, *Maine, U.S.A.* 111 B14
Bethel, *Vt., U.S.A.* 111 C12
Bethel Park, *U.S.A.* 110 F4
Béthenville, *France* 19 C11
Bethlehem = Bayt Laḥm,
  West Bank 75 D4
Bethlehem, *S. Africa* 89 D4
Bethlehem, *U.S.A.* 111 F9
Bethulie, *S. Africa* 88 E4
Béthune, *France* 19 B9
Béthune ➤, *France* 18 C8
Betioky, *Madag.* 89 C7
Betong, *Thailand* 65 K3
Betoota, *Australia* 94 D3
Betor, *Ethiopia* 81 E4
Betroka, *Madag.* 89 C8
Betsiamites, *Canada* 103 C6
Betsiamites ➤, *Canada* 103 C6
Betsiboka ➤, *Madag.* 89 B8

Bettendorf, *U.S.A.* 112 E9
Bettiah, *India* 69 F11
Bettna, *Sweden* 11 F10
Béttola, *Italy* 28 D6
Betul, *India* 66 J10
Betung, *Malaysia* 62 D4
Betws-y-Coed, *U.K.* 12 D4
Betxi, *Spain* 32 F4
Betzdorf, *Germany* 24 E3
Beuil, *France* 21 D10
Beulah, *Mich., U.S.A.* 108 C2
Beulah, *N. Dak., U.S.A.* 112 B4
Beuvron ➤, *France* 18 E8
Beveren, *Belgium* 17 C4
Beverley, *Australia* 93 F2
Beverley, *U.K.* 12 D7
Beverley Hills, *U.S.A.* 109 L4
Beverly, *U.S.A.* 111 D14
Beverly Hills, *U.S.A.* 117 L8
Beverungen, *Germany* 24 D5
Bevoalavo, *Madag.* 89 D7
Bewas ➤, *India* 69 H8
Bex, *Switz.* 25 J3
Bexhill, *U.K.* 13 G8
Bey Dağları, *Turkey* 39 E12
Beyānlū, *Iran* 70 C5
Beyazköy, *Turkey* 41 E11
Beyçayırı, *Turkey* 41 F10
Beydağ, *Turkey* 39 C10
Beyeğaç, *Turkey* 39 D10
Beyin, *Ghana* 82 D4
Beykoz, *Turkey* 41 E13
Beyla, *Guinea* 82 D3
Beynat, *France* 20 C5
Beyneu, *Kazakhstan* 50 E6
Beyoba, *Turkey* 39 C9
Beyoğlu, *Turkey* 41 E12
Beypazarı, *Turkey* 72 B4
Beyşehir, *Turkey* 72 D4
Beyşehir Gölü, *Turkey* 70 B1
Beytüşşebap, *Turkey* 73 D10
Bezdan, *Serbia, Yug.* 42 E3
Bezhetsk, *Russia* 46 D9
Béziers, *France* 20 E7
Bezwada = Vijayawada, *India* . 67 L12
Bhabua, *India* 69 G10
Bhachau, *India* 66 H7
Bhadar ➤, *Gujarat, India* ... 68 H5
Bhadar ➤, *Gujarat, India* ... 68 J3
Bhadarwah, *India* 69 C6
Bhadohi, *India* 69 G10
Bhadra, *India* 68 E6
Bhadrakh, *India* 67 J15
Bhadran, *India* 68 H5
Bhadravati, *India* 66 N9
Bhag, *Pakistan* 68 E2
Bhagalpur, *India* 69 G12
Bhagirathi ➤, *Ut. P., India* . 69 D8
Bhagirathi ➤, *W. Bengal, India* 69 H13
Bhakkar, *Pakistan* 68 D4
Bhakra Dam, *India* 68 D7
Bhamo, *Burma* 67 G20
Bhandara, *India* 66 J11
Bhanpura, *India* 68 G6
Bhanrer Ra., *India* 69 H8
Bharat = India ■, *Asia* 66 K11
Bharatpur, *Mad. P., India* .. 69 H9
Bharatpur, *Raj., India* 68 F7
Bharno, *India* 69 H11
Bhatinda, *India* 68 D6
Bhatpara, *India* 69 H13
Bhattu, *India* 68 E6
Bhaun, *Pakistan* 68 C5
Bhaunagar = Bhavnagar, *India* 66 J8
Bhavani, *India* 66 J10
Bhavnagar, *India* 66 J8
Bhawari, *India* 68 G5
Bhayavadar, *India* 68 J4
Bhera, *Pakistan* 68 C5
Bhikangaon, *India* 68 J6
Bhilsa = Vidisha, *India* 68 H7
Bhilwara, *India* 68 G6
Bhima ➤, *India* 66 L10
Bhimbar, *Pakistan* 69 C6
Bhind, *India* 69 F8
Bhinga, *India* 69 F9
Bhinmal, *India* 68 G5
Bhiwandi, *India* 66 K8
Bhiwani, *India* 68 E7
Bhogava ➤, *India* 68 H5
Bhola, *Bangla.* 67 H17
Bholari, *Pakistan* 68 G3
Bhopal, *India* 68 H7
Bhubaneshwar, *India* 67 J14
Bhuj, *India* 66 H3
Bhusaval, *India* 66 J9
Bhutan ■, *Asia* 67 F17

Biafra, B. of = Bonny, Bight of,
  Africa 83 E6
Biak, *Indonesia* 63 E9
Biała, *Poland* 45 H4
Biała ➤, *Poland* 45 H7
Biała Piska, *Poland* 44 E9
Biała Podlaska, *Poland* 45 F10
Biała Rawska, *Poland* 45 G7
Białobrzegi, *Poland* 45 G7
Białogard, *Poland* 44 D2
Białowieża, *Poland* 45 F10
Biały Bór, *Poland* 44 E3
Białystok, *Poland* 45 E10
Biancavilla, *Italy* 31 E7
Bianco, *Italy* 31 D9
Biankouma, *Ivory C.* 82 D3
Biaora, *India* 68 H7
Bīārjmand, *Iran* 71 B7

Biaro, *Indonesia* 63 D7
Biarritz, *France* 20 E2
Biasca, *Switz.* 25 J4
Biba, *Egypt* 80 J7
Bibai, *Japan* 54 C10
Bibbiena, *Italy* 29 E8
Bibby I., *Canada* 105 A10
Bibel ➤, *Spain* 34 C3
Biberach, *Germany* 25 G5
Bibiani, *Ghana* 82 D4
Bibungwa, *Dem. Rep. of*
  the Congo 86 C2
Bic, *Canada* 103 C6
Bicaj, *Albania* 40 E4
Bicaz, *Romania* 43 D11
Bicazu Ardelean, *Romania* .. 43 D10
Bíccari, *Italy* 31 A8
Bicester, *U.K.* 13 F6
Bichena, *Ethiopia* 81 E4
Bicheno, *Australia* 94 G4
Bichia, *India* 69 H9
Bichvinta, *Georgia* 49 J5
Bickerton I., *Australia* 94 A2
Bicske, *Hungary* 42 C3
Bida, *Nigeria* 83 D6
Bidar, *India* 66 L10
Biddeford, *U.S.A.* 109 D10
Biddwara, *Ethiopia* 81 F4
Bideford, *U.K.* 13 F3
Bideford Bay, *U.K.* 13 F3
Bidhuna, *India* 69 F8
Bidor, *Malaysia* 65 K3
Bie, *Sweden* 10 E10
Bié, Planalto de, *Angola* 85 G3
Bieber, *U.S.A.* 114 F3
Biebrza ➤, *Poland* 45 E9
Biecz, *Poland* 45 J8
Biel, *Switz.* 25 H3
Bielawa, *Poland* 45 H3
Bielefeld, *Germany* 24 C4
Bielersee, *Switz.* 25 H3
Biella, *Italy* 28 C5
Bielsk Podlaski, *Poland* 45 F10
Bielsko-Biała, *Poland* 45 J6
Bien Hoa, *Vietnam* 65 G6
Bienne = Biel, *Switz.* 25 H3
Bienvenida, *Spain* 35 G4
Bienville, L., *Canada* 102 A5
Bierné, *France* 18 E6
Bierun, *Poland* 45 H6
Bierutów, *Poland* 45 G4
Biescas, *Spain* 32 C4
Biese ➤, *Germany* 24 C7
Biesiesfontein, *S. Africa* 88 E2
Bietigheim-Bissingen, *Germany* 25 G5
Bieżuń, *Poland* 45 F6
Biferno ➤, *Italy* 29 G12
Big ➤, *Canada* 103 B8
Big B. ➤, *Canada* 103 A7
Big Bear City, *U.S.A.* 117 L10
Big Bear Lake, *U.S.A.* 117 L10
Big Belt Mts., *U.S.A.* 114 C8
Big Bend, *Swaziland* 89 D5
Big Bend National Park, *U.S.A.* 113 L3
Big Black ➤, *U.S.A.* 113 K9
Big Blue ➤, *U.S.A.* 112 F6
Big Creek, *U.S.A.* 116 H7
Big Cypress National Preserve,
  U.S.A. 109 M5
Big Cypress Swamp, *U.S.A.* . 109 M5
Big Falls, *U.S.A.* 112 A8
Big Fork ➤, *U.S.A.* 112 A8
Big Horn Mts. = Bighorn Mts.,
  U.S.A. 114 D10
Big I., *Canada* 104 A5
Big Lake, *U.S.A.* 113 K4
Big Moose, *U.S.A.* 111 C10
Big Muddy Cr. ➤, *U.S.A.* ... 112 A2
Big Pine, *U.S.A.* 116 H8
Big Piney, *U.S.A.* 114 E8
Big Rapids, *U.S.A.* 108 D3
Big Rideau L., *Canada* 111 B8
Big River, *Canada* 105 C7
Big Run, *U.S.A.* 110 F6
Big Sable Pt., *U.S.A.* 108 C2
Big Salmon ➤, *Canada* 104 A2
Big Sand L., *Canada* 105 B9
Big Sandy, *U.S.A.* 114 B8
Big Sandy ➤, *U.S.A.* 108 F4
Big Sandy Cr. ➤, *U.S.A.* ... 112 F3
Big Sioux ➤, *U.S.A.* 112 D6
Big Spring, *U.S.A.* 113 J4
Big Stone City, *U.S.A.* 112 C6
Big Stone Gap, *U.S.A.* 109 G4
Big Stone L., *U.S.A.* 112 C6
Big Sur, *U.S.A.* 116 J5
Big Timber, *U.S.A.* 114 D9
Big Trout L., *Canada* 102 B2
Big Trout Lake, *Canada* 102 B2
Biga, *Turkey* 41 F11
Biğa ➤, *Turkey* 41 F11
Bigadiç, *Turkey* 39 B10
Biganos, *France* 20 D3
Biggar, *Canada* 105 C7
Biggar, *U.K.* 14 F5
Bigge I., *Australia* 92 B4
Biggenden, *Australia* 95 D5
Biggleswade, *U.K.* 13 E7
Biggs, *U.S.A.* 116 F5
Bighorn, *U.S.A.* 114 C10
Bighorn ➤, *U.S.A.* 114 C10
Bighorn L., *U.S.A.* 114 D9
Bighorn Mts., *U.S.A.* 114 D10
Bignona, *Senegal* 82 C1
Bigorre, *France* 20 E4

Bigstone L., *Canada* 105 C9
Biguglia, Étang de, *France* 21 F13
Bigwa, *Tanzania* 86 D4
Bihać, *Bos.-H.* 29 D12
Bihar, *India* 69 G11
Bihar □, *India* 69 G12
Biharamulo, *Tanzania* 86 C3
Bihariganj, *India* 69 G12
Biharkeresztes, *Hungary* 42 C6
Bihor □, *Romania* 42 D7
Bihor, Munţii, *Romania* 42 D7
Bijagós, Arquipélago dos,
  Guinea-Biss. 82 C1
Bijaipur, *India* 68 F7
Bijapur, *Karnataka, India* 66 L9
Bijapur, *Mad. P., India* 67 K12
Bījār, *Iran* 70 C5
Bijawar, *India* 69 G8
Bijeljina, *Bos.-H.* 42 F4
Bijelo Polje, *Montenegro, Yug.* . 40 C3
Bijie, *China* 58 D5
Bijnor, *India* 68 E8
Bikaner, *India* 68 E5
Bikapur, *India* 69 F10
Bikeqi, *China* 56 D6
Bikfayyā, *Lebanon* 75 B4
Bikin, *Russia* 51 E14
Bikin →, *Russia* 54 A7
Bikini Atoll, *Marshall Is.* 96 F8
Bikita, *Zimbabwe* 89 C5
Bikoué, *Cameroon* 83 E7
Bila Tserkva, *Ukraine* 47 H6
Bilanga, *Burkina Faso* 83 C4
Bilara, *India* 68 F5
Bilaspur, *Mad. P., India* 69 H10
Bilaspur, *Punjab, India* 68 D7
Biläsuvar, *Azerbaijan* 73 C13
Bilauk Taungdan, *Thailand* ... 64 F2
Bilbao, *Spain* 32 B2
Bilbeis, *Egypt* 80 H7
Bilbo = Bilbao, *Spain* 32 B2
Bilbor, *Romania* 43 C10
Bîlciureşti, *Romania* 43 F10
Bíldudalur, *Iceland* 8 D2
Bílé Karpaty, *Europe* 27 B11
Bileća, *Bos.-H.* 40 D2
Bilecik, *Turkey* 72 B4
Bilgoraj, *Poland* 45 H9
Bilgram, *India* 69 F9
Bilhaur, *India* 69 F9
Bilhorod-Dnistrovskyy, *Ukraine* . 47 J6
Bilibino, *Russia* 51 C17
Bilibiza, *Mozam.* 87 E5
Bilisht, *Albania* 40 F5
Billabalong Roadhouse,
  Australia 93 E2
Billdal, *Sweden* 11 G5
Billiluna, *Australia* 92 C4
Billings, *U.S.A.* 114 D9
Billiton Is. = Belitung, *Indonesia* 62 E3
Billsta, *Sweden* 10 A12
Billund, *Denmark* 11 J3
Bilma, *Niger* 79 E8
Bilo Gora, *Croatia* 42 E2
Biloela, *Australia* 94 C5
Bilohirsk, *Ukraine* 47 K8
Bilopillya, *Ukraine* 47 G8
Biloxi, *U.S.A.* 113 K10
Bilpa Morea Claypan, *Australia* . 94 D3
Biltine, *Chad* 79 F10
Bilyarsk, *Russia* 48 C10
Bima, *Indonesia* 63 F5
Bimban, *Egypt* 80 C3
Bimbila, *Ghana* 83 D5
Bimini Is., *Bahamas* 120 A4
Bin Xian, *Heilongjiang, China* . 57 B14
Bin Xian, *Shaanxi, China* 56 G5
Bin Yauri, *Nigeria* 83 C5
Bina-Etawah, *India* 68 G8
Bināb, *Iran* 71 B6
Binalbagan, *Phil.* 61 F5
Bīnālūd, Kūh-e, *Iran* 71 B8
Binatang = Bintangor, *Malaysia* . 62 D4
Binche, *Belgium* 17 D4
Binchuan, *China* 58 E3
Binder, *Chad* 83 D7
Bindki, *India* 69 F9
Bindslev, *Denmark* 11 G4
Bindura, *Zimbabwe* 87 F3
Binéfar, *Spain* 32 D5
Bingara, *Australia* 95 D5
Bingen, *Germany* 25 F3
Bingerville, *Ivory C.* 82 D4
Bingham, *U.S.A.* 109 C11
Binghamton, *U.S.A.* 111 D9
Bingöl, *Turkey* 70 B4
Bingöl Dağları, *Turkey* 73 C9
Bingsjö, *Sweden* 10 C9
Binh Dinh = An Nhon, *Vietnam* . 64 F7
Binh Khe, *Vietnam* 64 F7
Binh Son, *Vietnam* 64 E7
Binhai, *China* 57 G10
Binic, *France* 18 D4
Binisatua, *Spain* 37 B11
Binjai, *Indonesia* 62 D3
Binji, *Nigeria* 83 C5
Binongko, *Indonesia* 63 F6
Binscarth, *Canada* 105 C8
Bint Goda, *Sudan* 81 E3
Bintan, *Indonesia* 62 D2
Bintangor, *Malaysia* 62 D4
Bintulu, *Malaysia* 62 D4
Bintuni, *Indonesia* 63 E8
Binyang, *China* 58 F7
Binz, *Germany* 24 A9

Binzert = Bizerte, *Tunisia* 79 A7
Binzhou, *China* 57 F10
Bío Bío □, *Chile* 126 D1
Biograd na Moru, *Croatia* 29 E12
Bioko, *Eq. Guin.* 83 E6
Biokovo, *Croatia* 29 E14
Bipindi, *Cameroon* 83 E7
Bir, *India* 66 K9
Bîr, Ras, *Djibouti* 81 E5
Bîr Abu Hashim, *Egypt* 80 C3
Bîr Abu Minqar, *Egypt* 80 B2
Bîr Abu Muḥammad, *Egypt* ... 75 F3
Bi'r ad Dabbāghāt, *Jordan* 75 E4
Bi'r al Butayyiḥāt, *Jordan* 75 F4
Bi'r al Mārī, *Jordan* 75 E4
Bi'r al Qaṭṭār, *Jordan* 75 F4
Bîr 'Asal, *Egypt* 80 B3
Bîr Atrun, *Sudan* 80 D2
Bîr Beïḍa, *Egypt* 75 E3
Bîr Diqnash, *Egypt* 80 A2
Bîr el 'Abd, *Egypt* 75 D2
Bîr el Basur, *Egypt* 80 B2
Bîr el Biarât, *Egypt* 75 F3
Bîr el Duweidar, *Egypt* 75 E1
Bîr el Garârât, *Egypt* 75 D2
Bîr el Gellaz, *Egypt* 80 A2
Bîr el Heisi, *Egypt* 75 F3
Bîr el Jafir, *Egypt* 75 E1
Bîr el Mâlḥi, *Egypt* 75 E2
Bîr el Shaqqa, *Egypt* 80 A2
Bîr el Thamâda, *Egypt* 75 E2
Bîr Fuad, *Egypt* 80 A2
Bîr Gebeil Ḥişn, *Egypt* 75 E2
Bi'r Ghadīr, *Syria* 75 A6
Bîr Haimur, *Egypt* 80 C3
Bîr Ḥasana, *Egypt* 75 E2
Bîr Hööker, *Egypt* 80 H7
Bîr Kanayis, *Egypt* 80 C3
Bîr Kaseiba, *Egypt* 75 E2
Bîr Kerawein, *Egypt* 80 B2
Bîr Lahfân, *Egypt* 75 E2
Bîr Madkûr, *Egypt* 75 E1
Bîr Maql, *Egypt* 80 C3
Bîr Mîneiga, *Sudan* 80 C4
Bîr Misaha, *Egypt* 80 C2
Bîr Mogreïn, *Mauritania* 78 C2
Bîr Murr, *Egypt* 80 C3
Bi'r Muṭribah, *Kuwait* 70 D5
Bîr Nakheila, *Egypt* 80 C3
Bîr Qaţia, *Egypt* 75 E1
Bîr Qatrani, *Egypt* 80 A2
Bîr Ranga, *Egypt* 80 C4
Bîr Sahara, *Egypt* 80 C2
Bîr Seiyâla, *Egypt* 80 B3
Bîr Shalatein, *Egypt* 80 C4
Bîr Shebb, *Egypt* 80 C2
Bîr Shût, *Egypt* 80 C4
Bîr Terfawi, *Egypt* 80 C2
Bîr Umm Qubûr, *Egypt* 80 C3
Bîr Ungât, *Egypt* 80 C3
Bîr Za'fârana, *Egypt* 80 J8
Bîr Zeidûn, *Egypt* 80 B3
Biramféro, *Guinea* 82 C3
Biratnagar, *Nepal* 69 F12
Birawa, *Dem. Rep. of the Congo* 86 C2
Birch →, *Canada* 104 B6
Birch Hills, *Canada* 105 C7
Birch I., *Canada* 105 C9
Birch L., *N.W.T., Canada* 104 A5
Birch L., *Ont., Canada* 102 B1
Birch Mts., *Canada* 104 B6
Birch River, *Canada* 105 C8
Birchiş, *Romania* 42 E8
Bird, *Canada* 105 B10
Bird I. = Las Aves, Is., *W. Indies* 121 C7
Birdsville, *Australia* 94 D2
Birdum Cr. →, *Australia* 92 C5
Birecik, *Turkey* 70 B3
Birein, *Israel* 75 E3
Bireuen, *Indonesia* 62 C1
Biri →, *Sudan* 81 F2
Birifo, *Gambia* 82 C2
Birigui, *Brazil* 127 A5
Birjand, *Iran* 71 C8
Birkenfeld, *Germany* 25 F3
Birkenhead, *U.K.* 12 D4
Birkerød, *Denmark* 11 J6
Birket Qârûn, *Egypt* 80 J7
Birkfeld, *Austria* 26 D8
Bîrlad = Bârlad, *Romania* 43 D12
Birmingham, *U.K.* 13 E6
Birmingham, *U.S.A.* 109 J2
Birmitrapur, *India* 67 H14
Birni Ngaouré, *Niger* 83 C5
Birni Nkonni, *Niger* 83 C6
Birnin Gwari, *Nigeria* 83 C6
Birnin Kebbi, *Nigeria* 83 C5
Birnin Kudu, *Nigeria* 83 C6
Birobidzhan, *Russia* 51 E14
Birr, *Ireland* 15 C4
Birrie →, *Australia* 95 D4
Birsilpur, *India* 68 E5
Birsk, *Russia* 50 D6
Birštonas, *Lithuania* 44 D11
Birtle, *Canada* 105 C8
Birur, *India* 66 N9
Biryuchiy, *Ukraine* 47 J8
Biržai, *Lithuania* 9 H21
Birzebbugga, *Malta* 36 D2
Bisa, *Indonesia* 63 E7
Bisáccia, *Italy* 31 A8
Bisacquino, *Italy* 30 E6
Bisalpur, *India* 69 E8
Bisbee, *U.S.A.* 115 L9

Biscarrosse, *France* 20 D2
Biscarrosse et de Parentis, Étang
  de, *France* 20 D2
Biscay, B. of, *Atl. Oc.* 6 F5
Biscayne B., *U.S.A.* 109 N5
Biscéglie, *Italy* 31 A9
Bischheim, *France* 19 D14
Bischofshofen, *Austria* 26 D6
Bischofswerda, *Germany* 24 D10
Bischwiller, *France* 19 D14
Biscoe Bay, *Antarctica* 5 D13
Biscoe Is., *Antarctica* 5 C17
Biscostasing, *Canada* 102 C3
Biševo, *Croatia* 29 F13
Bisha, *Eritrea* 81 D4
Bishah, W. →, *Si. Arabia* 80 C5
Bishan, *China* 58 C6
Bishkek, *Kyrgyzstan* 50 E8
Bishnupur, *India* 69 H12
Bisho, *S. Africa* 89 E4
Bishop, *Calif., U.S.A.* 116 H8
Bishop, *Tex., U.S.A.* 113 M6
Bishop Auckland, *U.K.* 12 C6
Bishop's Falls, *Canada* 103 C8
Bishop's Stortford, *U.K.* 13 F8
Bisignano, *Italy* 31 C9
Bisina, L., *Uganda* 86 B3
Biskra, *Algeria* 78 B7
Biskupiec, *Poland* 44 E7
Bismarck, *U.S.A.* 112 B4
Bismarck Arch., *Papua N. G.* . 96 H7
Bismark, *Germany* 24 C7
Bismil, *Turkey* 73 D9
Biso, *Uganda* 86 B3
Bison, *U.S.A.* 112 C3
Bīsotūn, *Iran* 70 C5
Bispgården, *Sweden* 10 A10
Bissagos = Bijagós, Arquipélago
  dos, *Guinea-Biss.* 82 C1
Bissau, *Guinea-Biss.* 82 C1
Bissaula, *Nigeria* 83 D7
Bissikrima, *Guinea* 82 C2
Bissorã, *Guinea-Biss.* 82 C1
Bistcho L., *Canada* 104 B5
Bistreţ, *Romania* 43 G8
Bistrica = Ilirska-Bistrica,
  Slovenia 29 C11
Bistriţa, *Romania* 43 C9
Bistriţa →, *Romania* 43 D11
Bistriţa Năsăud □, *Romania* . 43 C9
Bistriţei, Munţii, *Romania* ... 43 C10
Biswan, *India* 69 F9
Bisztynek, *Poland* 44 D7
Bitburg, *Germany* 25 F2
Bitche, *France* 19 C14
Bithynia, *Turkey* 72 B4
Bitlis, *Turkey* 70 B4
Bitola, *Macedonia* 40 E5
Bitolj = Bitola, *Macedonia* ... 40 E5
Bitonto, *Italy* 31 A9
Bitter Creek, *U.S.A.* 114 F9
Bitter L. = Buheirat-Murrat-el-
  Kubra, *Egypt* 80 H8
Bitterfeld, *Germany* 24 D8
Bitterfontein, *S. Africa* 88 E2
Bitterroot →, *U.S.A.* 114 C6
Bitterroot Range, *U.S.A.* 114 D6
Bitterwater, *U.S.A.* 116 J6
Bitti, *Italy* 30 B2
Bittou, *Burkina Faso* 83 C4
Biu, *Nigeria* 83 C7
Bivolari, *Romania* 43 C12
Bivolu, Vf., *Romania* 43 C10
Biwa-Ko, *Japan* 55 G8
Biwabik, *U.S.A.* 112 B8
Bixad, *Romania* 43 C8
Bixby, *U.S.A.* 113 H7
Biyang, *China* 56 H7
Biysk, *Russia* 50 D9
Bizana, *S. Africa* 89 E4
Bizen, *Japan* 55 G7
Bizerte, *Tunisia* 79 A7
Bjargtangar, *Iceland* 8 D1
Bjärnum, *Sweden* 11 H7
Bjästa, *Sweden* 10 A12
Bjelasica, *Montenegro, Yug.* .. 40 D3
Bjelašnica, *Bos.-H.* 42 G3
Bjelovar, *Croatia* 29 C13
Bjerringbro, *Denmark* 11 H3
Bjørbo, *Sweden* 10 D8
Björklinge, *Sweden* 10 D11
Björneborg, *Sweden* 10 E8
Bjørnevatn, *Norway* 8 B23
Bjørnøya, *Arctic* 4 B8
Bjursås, *Sweden* 10 D9
Bjuv, *Sweden* 11 H6
Bla, *Mali* 82 C3
Blace, *Serbia, Yug.* 40 C5
Blachownia, *Poland* 45 H5
Black = Da →, *Vietnam* 58 G5
Black →, *Canada* 110 B5
Black →, *Ariz., U.S.A.* 115 K8
Black →, *Ark., U.S.A.* 113 H9
Black →, *Mich., U.S.A.* 110 D2
Black →, *N.Y., U.S.A.* 111 C8
Black →, *Wis., U.S.A.* 112 D9
Black Bay Pen., *Canada* 102 C2
Black Birch L., *Canada* 105 B7
Black Diamond, *Canada* 104 C6
Black Duck →, *Canada* 102 A2
Black Forest = Schwarzwald,
  Germany 25 G4
Black Forest, *U.S.A.* 112 F2
Black Hd., *Ireland* 15 C2
Black Hills, *U.S.A.* 112 D3

Black I., *Canada* 105 C9
Black L., *Canada* 105 B7
Black L., *Mich., U.S.A.* 108 C3
Black L., *N.Y., U.S.A.* 111 B9
Black Lake, *Canada* 105 B7
Black Mesa, *U.S.A.* 113 G3
Black Mt. = Mynydd Du, *U.K.* . 13 F4
Black Mts., *U.K.* 13 F4
Black Range, *U.S.A.* 115 K10
Black River, *Jamaica* 120 C4
Black River Falls, *U.S.A.* 112 C9
Black Sea, *Eurasia* 6 G12
Black Tickle, *Canada* 103 B8
Black Volta →, *Africa* 82 D4
Black Warrior →, *U.S.A.* 109 J2
Blackall, *Australia* 94 C4
Blackball, *N.Z.* 91 K3
Blackbull, *Australia* 94 B3
Blackburn, *U.K.* 12 D5
Blackburn with Darwen □, *U.K.* 12 D5
Blackfoot, *U.S.A.* 114 E7
Blackfoot →, *U.S.A.* 114 C7
Blackfoot River Reservoir,
  U.S.A. 114 E8
Blackpool, *U.K.* 12 D4
Blackpool □, *U.K.* 12 D4
Blackriver, *U.S.A.* 110 B1
Blacks Harbour, *Canada* 103 C6
Blacksburg, *U.S.A.* 108 G5
Blacksod B., *Ireland* 15 B1
Blackstone, *U.S.A.* 108 G7
Blackstone Ra., *Australia* 93 E4
Blackwater, *Australia* 94 C4
Blackwater →, *Meath, Ireland* . 15 C4
Blackwater →, *Waterford,
  Ireland* 15 D4
Blackwater →, *U.K.* 15 B5
Blackwater →, *U.S.A.* 113 G6
Blackwells Corner, *U.S.A.* ... 117 K7
Blacksburg, *U.S.A.* 108 G5
Bladel, *Neths.* ....
Blaenau Ffestiniog, *U.K.* 12 E4
Blaenau Gwent □, *U.K.* 13 F4
Blagaj, *Bos.-H.* 40 C1
Blagnac, *France* 20 E5
Blagodarnoye = Blagodarnyy,
  Russia 49 H6
Blagodarnyy, *Russia* 49 H6
Blagoevgrad, *Bulgaria* 40 D7
Blagoveshchensk, *Russia* 51 D13
Blain, *France* 18 E5
Blain, *U.S.A.* 110 F7
Blaine, *U.S.A.* 112 C8
Blaine, *Wash., U.S.A.* 116 B4
Blaine Lake, *Canada* 105 C7
Blair, *U.S.A.* 112 E6
Blair Athol, *Australia* 94 C4
Blair Atholl, *U.K.* 14 E5
Blairgowrie, *U.K.* 14 E5
Blairsden, *U.S.A.* 116 F6
Blairsville, *U.S.A.* 110 F5
Blaj, *Romania* 43 D8
Blake Pt., *U.S.A.* 112 A10
Blakely, *Ga., U.S.A.* 109 K3
Blakely, *Pa., U.S.A.* 111 E9
Blâmont, *France* 19 D13
Blanc, C., *Spain* 37 B9
Blanc, Mont, *Alps* 21 C10
Blanc-Sablon, *Canada* 103 B8
Blanca, B., *Argentina* 122 G4
Blanca Peak, *U.S.A.* 115 H11
Blanche, C., *Australia* 95 E1
Blanche, L., *S. Austral.,
  Australia* 95 D2
Blanche, L., *W. Austral.,
  Australia* 92 D3
Blanco, *S. Africa* 88 E3
Blanco, *U.S.A.* 113 K5
Blanco →, *Argentina* 126 C2
Blanco, C., *Costa Rica* 120 E2
Blanco, C., *U.S.A.* 114 E1
Blanda →, *Iceland* 8 D3
Blandford Forum, *U.K.* 13 G5
Blanding, *U.S.A.* 115 H9
Blanes, *Spain* 32 D7
Blangy-sur-Bresle, *France* 19 C8
Blankaholm, *Sweden* 11 G10
Blankenberge, *Belgium* 17 C3
Blankenburg, *Germany* 24 D6
Blanquefort, *France* 20 D3
Blanquilla, I., *Venezuela* 121 D7
Blanquillo, *Uruguay* 127 C4
Blansko, *Czech Rep.* 27 B9
Blantyre, *Malawi* 87 F4
Blarney, *Ireland* 15 E3
Blasdell, *U.S.A.* 110 D6
Błaszki, *Poland* 45 G5
Blatná, *Czech Rep.* 26 B6
Blato, *Croatia* 29 F13
Blaubeuren, *Germany* 25 G5
Blaustein, *Germany* 25 G5
Blåvands Huk, *Denmark* 11 J2
Blaydon, *U.K.* 12 C6
Blaye, *France* 20 D3
Blaye-les-Mines, *France* 20 D6
Blayney, *Australia* 95 E4
Błażowa, *Poland* 45 J9
Bleckede, *Germany* 24 B6
Bled, *Slovenia* 29 B11
Bleiburg, *Austria* 26 E7
Blejeşti, *Romania* 43 F10
Blekinge, *Sweden* 9 H16
Blekinge län □, *Sweden* 11 H9
Blenheim, *Canada* 110 D3
Blenheim, *N.Z.* 91 J4
Bléone →, *France* 21 D10

Blérancourt, *France* 19 C10
Bletchley, *U.K.* 13 F7
Blida, *Algeria* 78 A6
Blidö, *Sweden* 10 E12
Blidsberg, *Sweden* 11 G7
Blieskastel, *Germany* 25 F3
Bligh Sound, *N.Z.* 91 L1
Blind River, *Canada* 102 C3
Blinisht, *Albania* 40 E3
Bliss, *Idaho, U.S.A.* 114 E6
Bliss, *N.Y., U.S.A.* 110 D6
Blissfield, *U.S.A.* 110 F3
Blitar, *Indonesia* 63 H15
Blitta, *Togo* 83 D5
Block I., *U.S.A.* 111 E13
Block Island Sd., *U.S.A.* 111 E13
Blodgett Iceberg Tongue,
  Antarctica 5 C9
Bloemfontein, *S. Africa* 88 D4
Bloemhof, *S. Africa* 88 D4
Blois, *France* 18 E8
Blomskog, *Sweden* 10 E6
Blomstermåla, *Sweden* 11 H10
Blönduós, *Iceland* 8 D3
Błonie, *Poland* 45 F7
Bloodvein →, *Canada* 105 C9
Bloody Foreland, *Ireland* 15 A3
Bloomer, *U.S.A.* 112 C9
Bloomfield, *Canada* 110 C7
Bloomfield, *Iowa, U.S.A.* 112 E8
Bloomfield, *N. Mex., U.S.A.* . 115 H10
Bloomfield, *Nebr., U.S.A.* ... 112 D6
Bloomington, *Ill., U.S.A.* 112 E10
Bloomington, *Ind., U.S.A.* ... 108 F2
Bloomington, *Minn., U.S.A.* . 112 C8
Bloomsburg, *U.S.A.* 111 F8
Blora, *Indonesia* 63 G14
Blossburg, *U.S.A.* 110 E7
Blouberg, *S. Africa* 89 C4
Blountstown, *U.S.A.* 109 K3
Bludenz, *Austria* 26 D2
Blue Earth, *U.S.A.* 112 D8
Blue Mesa Reservoir, *U.S.A.* . 115 G10
Blue Mountain Lake, *U.S.A.* . 111 C10
Blue Mts., *Maine, U.S.A.* 111 B14
Blue Mts., *Oreg., U.S.A.* 114 D4
Blue Mts., *Pa., U.S.A.* 111 F8
Blue Mud B., *Australia* 94 A2
Blue Nile = Nil el Azraq →,
  Sudan 81 D3
Blue Rapids, *U.S.A.* 112 F6
Blue Ridge Mts., *U.S.A.* 109 G5
Blue River, *Canada* 104 C5
Bluefield, *U.S.A.* 108 G5
Bluefields, *Nic.* 120 D3
Bluff, *Australia* 94 C4
Bluff, *N.Z.* 91 M2
Bluff, *U.S.A.* 115 H9
Bluff Knoll, *Australia* 93 F2
Bluff Pt., *Australia* 93 E1
Bluffton, *U.S.A.* 108 E3
Blumenau, *Brazil* 127 B6
Blunt, *U.S.A.* 112 C5
Bly, *U.S.A.* 114 E3
Blyth, *Canada* 110 C3
Blyth, *U.K.* 12 B6
Blythe, *U.S.A.* 117 M12
Blytheville, *U.S.A.* 113 H10
Bo, *S. Leone* 82 D2
Bo Duc, *Vietnam* 65 G6
Bo Hai, *China* 57 E10
Bo Xian = Bozhou, *China* 56 H8
Boa Vista, *Brazil* 124 C6
Boac, *Phil.* 61 E4
Boaco, *Nic.* 120 D2
Bo'ai, *China* 56 G7
Boal, *Spain* 34 B4
Boalsburg, *U.S.A.* 110 F7
Boane, *Mozam.* 89 D5
Boardman, *U.S.A.* 110 E4
Bobai, *China* 58 F7
Bobbili, *India* 67 K13
Bóbbio, *Italy* 28 D6
Bobcaygeon, *Canada* 102 D4
Böblingen, *Germany* 25 G5
Bobo-Dioulasso, *Burkina Faso* 82 C4
Bobolice, *Poland* 44 E3
Boboshevo, *Bulgaria* 40 D7
Bobov Dol, *Bulgaria* 40 D6
Bóbr →, *Poland* 45 F2
Bobraomby, Tanjon' i, *Madag.* 89 A8
Bobrinets, *Ukraine* 47 H7
Bobrov, *Russia* 48 E5
Bobrovitsa, *Ukraine* 47 G6
Bobruysk = Babruysk, *Belarus* . 47 F5
Boby, Pic, *Madag.* 85 J9
Bôca do Acre, *Brazil* 124 E5
Boca Raton, *U.S.A.* 109 M5
Bocanda, *Ivory C.* 82 D4
Bocas del Toro, *Panama* 120 E3
Boceguillas, *Spain* 34 D7
Bochnia, *Poland* 45 J7
Bocholt, *Germany* 24 D2
Bochum, *Germany* 24 D3
Boćki, *Poland* 45 F10
Bocognano, *France* 21 F13
Bocoyna, *Mexico* 118 B3
Bocşa, *Romania* 42 E6
Boda, *Dalarna, Sweden* 10 C9
Böda, *Kalmar, Sweden* 11 G11
Bodafors, *Sweden* 11 G8
Bodaybo, *Russia* 51 D12
Boddam, *U.K.* 14 B7

Boddington, Australia 93 F2
Bode Sadu, Nigeria 83 D5
Bodega Bay, U.S.A. 116 G3
Boden, Sweden 8 D19
Bodensee, Europe 25 H5
Bodenteich, Germany 24 C6
Bodhan, India 66 K10
Bodinga, Nigeria 83 C6
Bodmin, U.K. 13 G3
Bodmin Moor, U.K. 13 G3
Bodø, Norway 8 C16
Bodrog →, Hungary 42 B6
Bodrum, Turkey 39 D9
Bódva →, Hungary 42 B5
Boën, France 21 C8
Boende, Dem. Rep. of the Congo 84 E4
Boerne, U.S.A. 113 L5
Boesmans →, S. Africa 88 E4
Boffa, Guinea 82 C2
Bogalusa, U.S.A. 113 K10
Bogan →, Australia 95 D4
Bogandé, Burkina Faso 83 C4
Bogantungan, Australia 94 C4
Bogata, U.S.A. 113 J7
Bogatić, Serbia, Yug. 40 B3
Boğazkale, Turkey 72 B6
Boğazlıyan, Turkey 72 C6
Bogen, Sweden 10 D6
Bogense, Denmark 11 J4
Bogetići, Montenegro, Yug. .. 40 D2
Boggabilla, Australia 95 D5
Boggeragh Mts., Ireland 15 D3
Boglan = Solhan, Turkey ... 70 B4
Bognor Regis, U.K. 13 G7
Bogo, Phil. 61 F6
Bogodukhov = Bohodukhiv,
   Ukraine 47 G8
Bogol Manya, Ethiopia 81 G5
Bogor, Indonesia 62 F3
Bogoroditsk, Russia 46 F10
Bogorodsk, Russia 48 B6
Bogoso, Ghana 82 D4
Bogotá, Colombia 124 C4
Bogotol, Russia 50 D9
Bogou, Togo 83 C5
Bogra, Bangla. 67 G16
Boguchany, Russia 51 D10
Boguchar, Russia 48 F5
Bogué, Mauritania 82 B2
Boguslav, Ukraine 47 H6
Boguszów-Gorce, Poland 45 H3
Bohain-en-Vermandois, France 19 C10
Bohemian Forest =
   Böhmerwald, Germany 25 F9
Bohinjska Bistrica, Slovenia . 29 B11
Böhmerwald, Germany 25 F9
Bohmte, Germany 24 C4
Bohodukhiv, Ukraine 47 G8
Bohol □, Phil. 61 G6
Bohol Sea, Phil. 63 C6
Bohongou, Burkina Faso 83 C5
Böhönye, Hungary 42 D2
Bohuslän, Sweden 11 F5
Boi, Nigeria 83 D6
Boi, I. do, Brazil 127 A6
Boiaçu, Brazil 124 D6
Boileau, C., Australia 92 C3
Boing'o, Sudan 81 F3
Boiro, Spain 34 C2
Boise, U.S.A. 114 E6
Boise City, U.S.A. 113 G3
Boissevain, Canada 105 D8
Bóite →, Italy 29 B9
Boitzenburg, Germany ... 24 B9
Boizenburg, Germany ... 24 B6
Bojador C., W. Sahara ... 78 C3
Bojana →, Albania 40 E3
Bojano, Italy 31 A7
Bojanowo, Poland 45 G3
Bøjden, Denmark 11 J4
Bojnūrd, Iran 71 B8
Bojonegoro, Indonesia .. 63 G14
Boju, Nigeria 83 D6
Boka, Serbia, Yug. 42 E5
Boka Kotorska,
   Montenegro, Yug. 40 D2
Bokala, Ivory C. 82 D4
Bokani, Nigeria 83 D6
Bokaro, India 69 H11
Boké, Guinea 82 C2
Bokhara →, Australia .. 95 D4
Bokkos, Nigeria 83 D6
Boknafjorden, Norway .. 9 G11
Bokoro, Chad 79 F9
Bokpyin, Burma 65 G2
Boksitogorsk, Russia ... 46 C7
Bol, Croatia 29 E13
Bolama, Guinea-Biss. ... 82 C1
Bolan →, Pakistan 68 E2
Bolan Pass, Pakistan ... 66 E5
Bolaños, Mexico 118 C4
Bolaños de Calatrava, Spain 35 G7
Bolayır, Turkey 41 F10
Bolbec, France 18 C7
Boldājī, Iran 71 D6
Boldeşti-Scăeni, Romania .. 43 E11
Bole, China 60 B3
Bole, Ethiopia 81 F4
Bole, Ghana 82 D4
Bolekhiv, Ukraine 47 H2
Bolesławiec, Poland ... 45 G2
Bolgatanga, Ghana 83 C4
Bolgrad = Bolhrad, Ukraine 47 K5
Bolhrad, Ukraine 47 K5
Bolinao, Phil. 61 C3

Bolintin-Vale, Romania 43 F10
Bolívar, Argentina 126 D3
Bolivar, Mo., U.S.A. 113 G8
Bolivar, N.Y., U.S.A. 110 D6
Bolivar, Tenn., U.S.A. 113 H10
Bolivia ■, S. Amer. 124 G6
Bolivian Plateau, S. Amer. .. 122 E4
Boljevac, Serbia, Yug. 40 C5
Bolkhov, Russia 46 F9
Bolków, Poland 45 H3
Bollebygd, Sweden 11 G6
Bollène, France 21 D8
Bollnäs, Sweden 10 C10
Bollon, Australia 95 D4
Bollstabruk, Sweden 10 B11
Bolmen, Sweden 11 H7
Bolobo, Dem. Rep. of the Congo 84 E3
Bologna, Italy 29 D8
Bologoye, Russia 46 D8
Bolon, Ozero, Russia ... 60 B8
Bolonchenticul, Mexico .. 119 D7
Bolótana, Italy 30 B1
Boloven, Cao Nguyen, Laos .. 64 E6
Bolpur, India 69 H12
Bolsena, Italy 29 F8
Bolsena, L. di, Italy .. 29 F8
Bolshaya Chernigovka, Russia 48 D10
Bolshaya Glushitsa, Russia .. 48 D10
Bolshaya Martynovka, Russia 49 G5
Bolshaya Vradiyevka, Ukraine 47 J6
Bolshevik, Ostrov, Russia ... 51 B11
Bolshoi Kavkas = Caucasus
   Mountains, Eurasia 49 J7
Bolshoy Anyuy →, Russia .. 51 C17
Bolshoy Begichev, Ostrov,
   Russia 51 B12
Bolshoy Lyakhovskiy, Ostrov,
   Russia 51 B15
Bolshoy Tokmak = Tokmak,
   Ukraine 47 J8
Bolshoy Tyuters, Ostrov, Russia 9 G22
Bolsward, Neths. 17 A5
Bolt Head, U.K. 13 G4
Boltaña, Spain 32 C5
Boltigen, Switz. 25 J3
Bolton, Canada 110 C5
Bolton, U.K. 12 D5
Bolton Landing, U.S.A. ... 111 C11
Bolu, Turkey 72 B4
Bolungavík, Iceland 8 C2
Boluo, China 59 F10
Bolvadin, Turkey 70 B1
Bolzano, Italy 29 B8
Bom Jesus da Lapa, Brazil .. 125 F10
Boma, Dem. Rep. of the Congo 84 F2
Bombala, Australia 95 F4
Bombarral, Portugal 35 F1
Bombay = Mumbai, India .. 66 K8
Bomboma, Dem. Rep. of
   the Congo 84 D3
Bombombwa, Dem. Rep. of
   the Congo 86 B2
Bomi Hills, Liberia 82 D2
Bomili, Dem. Rep. of the Congo 86 B2
Bømlo, Norway 9 G11
Bomokandi →, Dem. Rep. of
   the Congo 86 B2
Bomu →, C.A.R. 84 D4
Bon, C., Tunisia 76 C5
Bon Sar Pa, Vietnam .. 64 F6
Bonaigarh, India 69 J11
Bonaire, Neth. Ant. ... 121 D6
Bonanza, Nic. 120 D3
Bonaparte Arch., Australia .. 92 B3
Boñar, Spain 34 C5
Bonaventure, Canada .. 103 C6
Bonavista, Canada ... 103 C9
Bonavista, C., Canada . 103 C9
Bonavista B., Canada . 103 C9
Bondeno, Italy 29 D8
Bondo, Dem. Rep. of the Congo 86 B1
Bondoukou, Ivory C. .. 82 D4
Bondowoso, Indonesia . 63 G15
Bone, Teluk, Indonesia . 63 E6
Bonerate, Indonesia ... 63 F6
Bonerate, Kepulauan, Indonesia 63 F6
Bo'ness, U.K. 14 E5
Bonete, Cerro, Argentina . 126 B2
Bong Son = Hoai Nhon, Vietnam 64 E7
Bonga, Ethiopia 81 F4
Bongabong, Phil. 61 E4
Bongor, Chad 79 F9
Bongouanou, Ivory C. . 82 D4
Bonham, U.S.A. 113 J6
Boni, Mali 82 B4
Bonifacio, France ... 21 G13
Bonifacio, Bouches de, Medit. S. 30 A2
Bonin Is. = Ogasawara Gunto,
   Pac. Oc. 52 G18
Bonke, Ethiopia 81 F4
Bonkoukou, Niger ... 83 C5
Bonn, Germany 24 E3
Bonnat, France 19 F8
Bonne Terre, U.S.A. . 113 G9
Bonners Ferry, U.S.A. 114 B5
Bonnétable, France .. 18 D7
Bonneval, Eure-et-Loir, France 18 D8
Bonneval, Savoie, France .. 21 C11
Bonneville, France ... 19 F13
Bonnie Rock, Australia . 93 F2
Bonny, Nigeria 83 E6
Bonny, Bight of, Africa . 83 E6
Bonny →, Nigeria .. 83 E6
Bonny-sur-Loire, France . 19 E9
Bonnyrigg, U.K. 14 F5
Bonnyville, Canada .. 105 C6

Bono, Italy 30 B2
Bonoi, Indonesia 63 E9
Bonorva, Italy 30 B1
Bonsall, U.S.A. 117 M9
Bontang, Indonesia 62 D5
Bonthe, S. Leone 82 D2
Bontoc, Phil. 61 C4
Bonyeri, Ghana 82 D4
Bonyhád, Hungary 42 D3
Bonython Ra., Australia ... 92 D4
Bookabie, Australia 93 F5
Booker, U.S.A. 113 G4
Boola, Guinea 82 D3
Boonah, Australia 95 D5
Boone, Iowa, U.S.A. 112 D8
Boone, N.C., U.S.A. 109 G5
Booneville, Ark., U.S.A. . 113 H8
Booneville, Miss., U.S.A. . 109 H1
Boonville, Calif., U.S.A. . 116 F3
Boonville, Ind., U.S.A. .. 108 F2
Boonville, Mo., U.S.A. .. 112 F8
Boonville, N.Y., U.S.A. . 111 C9
Boorindal, Australia ... 95 E4
Boothia, Gulf of, Canada . 101 A11
Boothia Pen., Canada ... 100 A10
Bootle, U.K. 12 D4
Booué, Gabon 84 E2
Boppard, Germany 25 E3
Boquete, Panama 120 E3
Boquilla, Presa de la, Mexico . 118 B3
Boquillas del Carmen, Mexico 118 B4
Bor, Czech Rep. 26 B5
Bor, Russia 48 B7
Bor, Serbia, Yug. 40 B6
Bôr, Sudan 81 F3
Bor, Sweden 11 G8
Bor, Turkey 72 D6
Bor Mashash, Israel .. 75 D3
Borah Peak, U.S.A. .. 114 D7
Borang, Sudan 81 G3
Borås, Sweden 11 G6
Borāzjān, Iran 71 D6
Borba, Brazil 124 D7
Borba, Portugal 35 G3
Borborema, Planalto da, Brazil 122 D7
Borcea, Romania ... 43 F12
Borçka, Turkey 73 B9
Bord Khūn-e Now, Iran . 71 D6
Borden, Australia .. 93 F2
Borden, Canada ... 103 C7
Borden I., Canada . 4 B2
Borden Pen., Canada . 101 A11
Borders = Scottish Borders □,
   U.K. 14 F6
Borðeyri, Iceland .. 8 D3
Bordighera, Italy .. 28 E4
Bordj Fly Ste. Marie, Algeria . 78 C5
Bordj-in-Eker, Algeria . 78 D7
Bordj Omar Driss, Algeria . 78 C7
Bore, Ethiopia 81 G4
Borehamwood, U.K. . 13 F7
Borek Wielkopolski, Poland . 45 G4
Borensberg, Sweden . 11 F9
Borgå = Porvoo, Finland . 9 F21
Borgarfjörður, Iceland . 8 D7
Borgarnes, Iceland . 8 D3
Børgefjell, Norway . 8 D15
Borger, Neths. 17 B6
Borger, U.S.A. 113 H4
Borgholm, Sweden . 11 H10
Bórgia, Italy 31 D9
Borgo San Dalmazzo, Italy . 28 D4
Borgo San Lorenzo, Italy . 29 E8
Borgo Val di Taro, Italy . 28 D6
Borgo Valsugana, Italy . 29 B8
Borgomanero, Italy . 28 C5
Borgorose, Italy ... 29 F10
Borgosésia, Italy .. 28 C5
Borhoyn Tal, Mongolia . 56 C6
Bori, Nigeria 83 E6
Borikhane, Laos ... 64 C4
Borisoglebsk, Russia . 48 E6
Borisov = Barysaw, Belarus . 46 E5
Borisovka, Russia .. 47 G9
Borja, Peru 124 D3
Borja, Spain 32 D3
Borjas Blancas = Les Borges
   Blanques, Spain ... 32 D5
Borjomi, Georgia .. 49 K6
Børkop, Denmark .. 11 J3
Borkou, Chad 79 E9
Borkum, Germany . 24 B2
Borlänge, Sweden . 10 D9
Borley, C., Antarctica . 5 C5
Borlu, Turkey 39 C10
Bormida →, Italy . 28 D5
Bórmio, Italy 28 B7
Borna, Germany .. 24 D8
Borne Sulinowo, Poland . 44 E3
Borneo, E. Indies . 62 D5
Bornholm, Denmark . 11 J8
Bornholms Amtskommune □,
   Denmark 11 J8
Bornholmsgattet, Europe . 11 J8
Borno □, Nigeria . 83 C7
Bornos, Spain ... 35 J5
Bornova, Turkey . 39 C9
Bornu Yassa, Nigeria . 83 C7
Boro →, Sudan . 81 F2
Borodino, Russia . 46 E8
Borogontsy, Russia . 51 C14
Boromo, Burkina Faso . 82 C4
Boron, U.S.A. ... 117 L9
Borongan, Phil. . 61 F6

Borotangba Mts., C.A.R. 81 F2
Borotou, Ivory C. 82 D3
Borovan, Bulgaria 40 C7
Borovichi, Russia 46 C7
Borovsk, Russia 46 E9
Borrby, Sweden 11 J8
Borrego Springs, U.S.A. ... 117 M10
Borriol, Spain 32 E4
Borroloola, Australia 94 B2
Borşa, Cluj, Romania 43 D8
Borşa, Maramureş, Romania . 43 C9
Borsad, India 68 H5
Borsec, Romania 43 D10
Borsod-Abaúj-Zemplén □,
   Hungary 42 B6
Bort-les-Orgues, France .. 20 C6
Borth, U.K. 13 E3
Börtnan, Sweden 10 B7
Borūjerd, Iran 71 C6
Boryslav, Ukraine 47 H2
Boryspil, Ukraine 47 G6
Borzhomi = Borjomi, Georgia . 49 K6
Borzna, Ukraine 47 G7
Borzya, Russia 51 D12
Bosa, Italy 30 B1
Bosanska Dubica, Bos.-H. . 29 C13
Bosanska Gradiška, Bos.-H. . 42 E2
Bosanska Kostajnica, Bos.-H. . 29 C13
Bosanska Krupa, Bos.-H. .. 29 D13
Bosanski Brod, Bos.-H. ... 42 E2
Bosanski Novi, Bos.-H. .. 29 C13
Bosanski Petrovac, Bos.-H. . 29 D13
Bosanski Šamac, Bos.-H. . 42 E3
Bosansko Grahovo, Bos.-H. . 29 D13
Bosaso, Somali Rep. ... 74 E4
Boscastle, U.K. 13 G3
Bose, China 58 F6
Boshan, China 57 F9
Boshof, S. Africa ... 88 D4
Boshrūyeh, Iran 71 C8
Bosilegrad, Serbia, Yug. . 40 D6
Bosna →, Bos.-H. .. 42 E3
Bosna i Hercegovina = Bosnia-
   Herzegovina ■, Europe .. 42 G2
Bosnia-Herzegovina ■, Europe 42 G2
Bosnik, Indonesia ... 63 E9
Bosobolo, Dem. Rep. of
   the Congo 84 D3
Bosporus = İstanbul Boğazı,
   Turkey 41 E13
Bosque Farms, U.S.A. .. 115 J10
Bossangoa, C.A.R. ... 84 C3
Bossé Bangou, Niger . 83 C5
Bossier City, U.S.A. . 113 J8
Bosso, Niger 83 C7
Bosso, Dallol →, Niger . 83 C5
Bostan, Pakistan ... 68 D2
Bostānābād, Iran .. 70 B5
Bosten Hu, China .. 60 B3
Boston, U.K. 12 E7
Boston, U.S.A. ... 111 D13
Boston Bar, Canada . 104 D4
Boston Mts., U.S.A. . 113 H8
Bosut →, Croatia . 42 E3
Boswell, Canada .. 104 D5
Boswell, U.S.A. .. 110 F5
Botad, India 68 H4
Botan →, Turkey . 73 D10
Botene, Laos 64 D3
Botev, Bulgaria .. 41 D8
Botevgrad, Bulgaria . 40 D7
Bothaville, S. Africa . 88 D4
Bothnia, G. of, Europe . 8 E19
Bothwell, Australia . 94 G4
Bothwell, Canada . 110 D3
Boticas, Portugal . 34 D3
Botletle →, Botswana . 88 C3
Botlikh, Russia .. 49 J8
Botna →, Moldova . 43 D14
Botoroaga, Romania . 43 F10
Botoşani, Romania . 43 C11
Botoşani □, Romania . 43 C11
Botou, Burkina Faso . 83 C5
Botricello, Italy .. 31 D9
Botro, Ivory C. .. 82 D3
Botswana ■, Africa . 88 C3
Bottineau, U.S.A. . 112 A4
Bottnaryd, Sweden . 11 G7
Bottrop, Germany . 17 C6
Botucatu, Brazil . 127 A6
Botwood, Canada . 103 C8
Bou Djébéha, Mali . 82 B4
Boû Rjeïmât, Mauritania . 82 B1
Bouaflé, Ivory C. . 82 D3
Bouaké, Ivory C. . 82 D3
Bouar, C.A.R. ... 84 C3
Bouârfa, Morocco . 78 B5
Boucaut B., Australia . 94 A1
Bouches-du-Rhône □, France . 21 E9
Bougainville, C., Australia . 92 B4
Bougainville I., Papua N. G. . 96 H7
Bougainville Reef, Australia . 94 B4
Bougie = Bejaïa, Algeria . 78 A7
Bougouni, Mali .. 82 C3
Bouillon, Belgium . 17 E5
Boukombé, Benin . 83 C5
Boulal, Mali 82 B3
Boulazac, France . 20 C4
Boulder, Colo., U.S.A. . 112 E2
Boulder, Mont., U.S.A. . 114 C7
Boulder City, U.S.A. . 117 K12
Boulder Creek, U.S.A. . 116 H4
Boulder Dam = Hoover Dam,
   U.S.A. 117 K12

Bouli, Mauritania 82 B2
Boulia, Australia 94 C2
Bouligny, France 19 C12
Boulogne →, France 18 E5
Boulogne-sur-Gesse, France .. 20 E4
Boulogne-sur-Mer, France ... 19 B8
Bouloire, France 18 E7
Boulouli, Mali 82 B3
Boulsa, Burkina Faso 83 C4
Boultoum, Niger 83 C7
Boûmdeïd, Mauritania 82 B2
Boun Neua, Laos 64 B3
Boun Tai, Laos 64 B3
Boundary Peak, U.S.A. 116 H8
Boundiali, Ivory C. 82 D3
Bountiful, U.S.A. 114 F8
Bounty Is., Pac. Oc. 96 M9
Boura, Mali 82 C4
Bourbon-Lancy, France 19 F10
Bourbon-l'Archambault, France 19 F10
Bourbonnais, France 19 F10
Bourbonne-les-Bains, France . 19 E12
Bourbourg, France 19 B9
Bourdel L., Canada 102 A5
Bourem, Mali 83 B4
Bourg, France 20 C3
Bourg-Argental, France . 21 C8
Bourg-de-Péage, France . 21 C9
Bourg-en-Bresse, France . 19 F12
Bourg-Lastic, France .. 20 C6
Bourg-Madame, France . 20 F5
Bourg-St-Andéol, France . 21 D8
Bourg-St-Maurice, France . 21 C10
Bourganeuf, France .. 20 C5
Bourges, France 19 E9
Bourget, Canada ... 111 A9
Bourget, Lac du, France . 21 C9
Bourgneuf, B. de, France . 18 E4
Bourgneuf-en-Retz, France . 18 E5
Bourgogne, France .. 19 F11
Bourgoin-Jallieu, France . 21 C9
Bourgueil, France ... 18 E7
Bourke, Australia .. 95 E4
Bourne, U.K. 12 E7
Bournemouth, U.K. . 13 G6
Bournemouth □, U.K. . 13 G6
Bouroum, Burkina Faso . 83 C4
Bouse, U.S.A. ... 117 M13
Boussac, France .. 19 F9
Boussé, Burkina Faso . 83 C4
Boussouma, Burkina Faso . 83 C4
Boutilimit, Mauritania . 82 B2
Boutonne →, France . 20 C3
Bouvet I. = Bouvetøya,
   Antarctica 3 G10
Bouvetøya, Antarctica . 3 G10
Bouxwiller, France . 19 D14
Bouza, Niger 83 C6
Bouzonville, France . 19 C13
Bova Marina, Italy . 31 E8
Bovalino Marina, Italy . 31 D9
Bovec, Slovenia . 29 B10
Bovill, U.S.A. .. 114 C5
Bovino, Italy ... 31 A8
Bovril, Argentina . 126 C4
Bow →, Canada . 104 C6
Bow Island, Canada . 104 D6
Bowbells, U.S.A. . 112 A3
Bowdle, U.S.A. . 112 C5
Bowelling, Australia . 93 F2
Bowen, Argentina . 126 D2
Bowen, Australia . 94 C4
Bowie, Ariz., U.S.A. . 115 K9
Bowie, Tex., U.S.A. . 113 J6
Bowkān, Iran .. 70 B5
Bowland, Forest of, U.K. . 12 D5
Bowling Green, Ky., U.S.A. . 108 G2
Bowling Green, Ohio, U.S.A. . 108 E4
Bowling Green, C., Australia . 94 B4
Bowman, U.S.A. . 112 B3
Bowman I., Antarctica . 5 C8
Bowmanville, Canada . 110 C6
Bowmore, U.K. . 14 F2
Bowraville, Australia . 95 E5
Bowron →, Canada . 104 C4
Bowron Lake Prov. Park,
   Canada 104 C4
Bowser L., Canada . 104 B3
Bowsman, Canada . 105 C8
Bowwood, Zambia . 87 F2
Box Cr. →, Australia . 95 E3
Boxholm, Sweden . 11 F9
Boxmeer, Neths. . 17 C5
Boxtel, Neths. .. 17 C5
Boyabat, Turkey . 72 B6
Boyalıca, Turkey . 41 F13
Boyang, China .. 59 C11
Boyce, U.S.A. .. 113 K8
Boyd L., Canada . 102 B4
Boyle, Canada .. 104 C6
Boyle, Ireland .. 15 C3
Boyne →, Ireland . 15 C5
Boyne City, U.S.A. . 108 C3
Boynitsa, Bulgaria . 40 C6
Boynton Beach, U.S.A. . 109 M5
Boyolali, Indonesia . 63 G14
Boyoma, Chutes, Dem. Rep. of
   the Congo 86 B2
Boysen Reservoir, U.S.A. . 114 E9
Boyuibe, Bolivia . 124 G6
Boyup Brook, Australia . 93 F2
Boz Burun, Turkey . 41 F12
Boz Dağ, Turkey . 39 D11
Boz Dağları, Turkey . 39 C10

Bozburun

Bozburun, *Turkey* 39 E10
Bozcaada, *Turkey* 72 C2
Bozdoğan, *Turkey* 39 D10
Bozeman, *U.S.A.* 114 D8
Bozen = Bolzano, *Italy* 29 B8
Boževac, *Serbia, Yug.* 40 B5
Bozhou, *China* 56 H8
Bozkır, *Turkey* 72 D5
Bozkurt, *Turkey* 39 D11
Bozouls, *France* 20 D6
Bozoum, *C.A.R.* 84 C3
Bozova, *Antalya, Turkey* 39 D12
Bozova, *Sanliurfa, Turkey* 73 D8
Bozovici, *Romania* 42 F7
Bozüyük, *Turkey* 39 B12
Bra, *Italy* 28 D4
Braås, *Sweden* 11 G9
Brabant □, *Belgium* 17 D4
Brabant L., *Canada* 105 B8
Brabrand, *Denmark* 11 H4
Brač, *Croatia* 29 E13
Bracadale, L., *U.K.* 14 D2
Bracciano, *Italy* 29 F9
Bracciano, L. di, *Italy* 29 F9
Bracebridge, *Canada* 102 C4
Brach, *Libya* 79 C8
Bracieux, *France* 18 E8
Bräcke, *Sweden* 10 B9
Brackettville, *U.S.A.* 113 L4
Bracki Kanal, *Croatia* 29 E13
Bracknell, *U.K.* 13 F7
Bracknell Forest □, *U.K.* 13 F7
Brad, *Romania* 42 D7
Brádano →, *Italy* 31 B9
Bradenton, *U.S.A.* 109 M4
Bradford, *Canada* 110 B5
Bradford, *U.K.* 12 D6
Bradford, *Pa., U.S.A.* 110 E6
Bradford, *Vt., U.S.A.* 111 C12
Bradley, *Ark., U.S.A.* 113 J8
Bradley, *Calif., U.S.A.* 116 K6
Bradley Institute, *Zimbabwe* 87 F3
Brady, *U.S.A.* 113 K5
Brædstrup, *Denmark* 11 J3
Braeside, *Canada* 111 A8
Braga, *Portugal* 34 D2
Braga □, *Portugal* 34 D2
Bragadiru, *Romania* 43 G10
Bragado, *Argentina* 126 D3
Bragança, *Brazil* 125 D9
Bragança, *Portugal* 34 D4
Bragança □, *Portugal* 34 D4
Bragança Paulista, *Brazil* 127 A6
Brahmanbaria, *Bangla.* 67 H17
Brahmani →, *India* 67 J15
Brahmapur, *India* 67 K14
Brahmaputra →, *India* 69 H13
Braich-y-pwll, *U.K.* 12 E3
Brăila, *Romania* 43 E12
Brăila □, *Romania* 43 E12
Brainerd, *U.S.A.* 112 B7
Braintree, *U.K.* 13 F8
Braintree, *U.S.A.* 111 D14
Brak →, *S. Africa* 88 D3
Brake, *Germany* 24 B4
Brakel, *Germany* 24 D5
Bräkne-Hoby, *Sweden* 11 H9
Brakwater, *Namibia* 88 C2
Brålanda, *Sweden* 11 F6
Bramberg, *Germany* 25 E6
Bramdrupdam, *Denmark* 11 J3
Bramming, *Denmark* 11 J2
Brämön, *Sweden* 10 B11
Brampton, *Canada* 102 D4
Brampton, *U.K.* 12 C5
Bramsche, *Germany* 24 C3
Branco →, *Brazil* 122 D4
Brandberg, *Namibia* 88 B2
Brande, *Denmark* 11 J3
Brandenburg = Neubrandenburg, *Germany* 24 B9
Brandenburg, *Germany* 24 C8
Brandenburg □, *Germany* 24 C9
Brandfort, *S. Africa* 88 D4
Brando, *France* 21 F13
Brandon, *Canada* 105 D9
Brandon, *U.S.A.* 111 C11
Brandon B., *Ireland* 15 D1
Brandon Mt., *Ireland* 15 D1
Brandsen, *Argentina* 126 D4
Brandvlei, *S. Africa* 88 E3
Brandýs nad Labem, *Czech Rep.* 26 A7
Brănești, *Romania* 43 F11
Branford, *U.S.A.* 111 E12
Braniewo, *Poland* 44 D6
Bransfield Str., *Antarctica* 5 C18
Brańsk, *Poland* 45 F9
Branson, *U.S.A.* 113 G8
Brantford, *Canada* 102 D3
Brantôme, *France* 20 C4
Branzi, *Italy* 28 B6
Bras d'Or L., *Canada* 103 C7
Brasher Falls, *U.S.A.* 111 B10
Brasil, Planalto, *Brazil* 122 E6
Brasiléia, *Brazil* 124 F5
Brasília, *Brazil* 125 G9
Brasília Legal, *Brazil* 125 D7
Braslaw, *Belarus* 9 J22
Braslovče, *Slovenia* 29 B12
Brașov, *Romania* 43 E10
Brașov □, *Romania* 43 E10
Brass, *Nigeria* 83 E6
Brass →, *Nigeria* 83 E6
Brassac-les-Mines, *France* 20 C7
Brasschaat, *Belgium* 17 C4
Brassey, Banjaran, *Malaysia* 62 D5
Brassey Ra., *Australia* 93 E3
Brasstown Bald, *U.S.A.* 109 H4
Brastad, *Sweden* 11 F5
Brastavățu, *Romania* 43 G9
Bratan = Morozov, *Bulgaria* 41 D9
Brateș, *Romania* 43 E11
Bratislava, *Slovak Rep.* 27 C10
Bratislavský □, *Slovak Rep.* 27 C10
Bratsigovo, *Bulgaria* 41 D8
Bratsk, *Russia* 51 D11
Brattleboro, *U.S.A.* 111 D12
Bratunac, *Bos.-H.* 42 F4
Braunau, *Austria* 26 C6
Braunschweig, *Germany* 24 C6
Braunton, *U.K.* 13 F3
Bravicea, *Moldova* 43 C13
Bråviken, *Sweden* 11 F10
Bravo del Norte, Rio = Grande, Rio →, *U.S.A.* 113 N6
Brawley, *U.S.A.* 117 N11
Bray, *Ireland* 15 C5
Bray, Mt., *Australia* 94 A1
Bray-sur-Seine, *France* 19 D10
Brazeau →, *Canada* 104 C5
Brazil, *U.S.A.* 108 F2
Brazil ■, *S. Amer.* 125 F9
Brazilian Highlands = Brasil, Planalto, *Brazil* 122 E6
Brazo Sur →, *S. Amer.* 126 B4
Brazos →, *U.S.A.* 113 L7
Brazzaville, *Congo* 84 E3
Brčko, *Bos.-H.* 42 F3
Brda →, *Poland* 45 E5
Brdy, *Czech Rep.* 26 B6
Breaden, L., *Australia* 93 E4
Breaksea Sd., *N.Z.* 91 L1
Bream B., *N.Z.* 91 F5
Bream Hd., *N.Z.* 91 F5
Breas, *Chile* 126 B1
Breaza, *Romania* 43 E10
Brebes, *Indonesia* 63 G13
Brechin, *Canada* 110 B5
Brechin, *U.K.* 14 E6
Brecht, *Belgium* 17 C4
Breckenridge, *Colo., U.S.A.* 114 G10
Breckenridge, *Minn., U.S.A.* 112 B6
Breckenridge, *Tex., U.S.A.* 113 J5
Breckland, *U.K.* 13 E8
Břeclav, *Czech Rep.* 27 C9
Brecon, *U.K.* 13 F4
Brecon Beacons, *U.K.* 13 F4
Breda, *Neths.* 17 C4
Bredaryd, *Sweden* 11 G7
Bredasdorp, *S. Africa* 88 E3
Bredebro, *Denmark* 11 J2
Bredstedt, *Germany* 24 A4
Bree, *Belgium* 17 C5
Bregalnica →, *Macedonia* 40 E6
Bregenz, *Austria* 26 D2
Bregovo, *Bulgaria* 40 B6
Bréhal, *France* 18 D5
Bréhat, Î. de, *France* 18 D4
Breiðafjörður, *Iceland* 8 D2
Breil-sur-Roya, *France* 21 E11
Breisach, *Germany* 25 G3
Brejo, *Brazil* 125 D10
Bremen, *Germany* 24 B4
Bremen □, *Germany* 24 B4
Bremer Bay, *Australia* 93 F2
Bremer I., *Australia* 94 A2
Bremerhaven, *Germany* 24 B4
Bremerton, *U.S.A.* 116 C4
Bremervörde, *Germany* 24 B5
Brenes, *Spain* 35 H5
Brenham, *U.S.A.* 113 K6
Brenne, *France* 20 B5
Brennerpass, *Austria* 26 D4
Breno, *Italy* 28 C7
Brent, *U.S.A.* 109 J2
Brenta →, *Italy* 29 C9
Brentwood, *U.K.* 13 F8
Brentwood, *Calif., U.S.A.* 116 H5
Brentwood, *N.Y., U.S.A.* 111 F11
Bréscia, *Italy* 28 C7
Breskens, *Neths.* 17 C3
Breslau = Wrocław, *Poland* 45 G4
Bresle →, *France* 18 B8
Bressanone, *Italy* 29 B8
Bressay, *U.K.* 14 A7
Bresse, *France* 19 F12
Bressuire, *France* 18 F6
Brest, *Belarus* 47 F2
Brest, *France* 18 D2
Brest-Litovsk = Brest, *Belarus* 47 F2
Bretagne, *France* 18 D3
Bretçu, *Romania* 43 D11
Bretenoux, *France* 20 D5
Breteuil, *Eure, France* 18 D7
Breteuil, *Oise, France* 19 C9
Breton, *Canada* 104 C6
Breton, Pertuis, *France* 20 B2
Breton Sd., *U.S.A.* 113 L10
Brett, C., *N.Z.* 91 F5
Bretten, *Germany* 25 F4
Breuil-Cervínia, *Italy* 28 C4
Brevard, *U.S.A.* 109 H4
Breves, *Brazil* 125 D8
Brewarrina, *Australia* 95 E4
Brewer, *U.S.A.* 109 C11
Brewer, Mt., *U.S.A.* 116 J8
Brewerville, *Liberia* 82 D2
Brewster, *N.Y., U.S.A.* 111 E11
Brewster, *Ohio, U.S.A.* 110 F3
Brewster, *Wash., U.S.A.* 114 B4
Brewster, Kap = Kangikajik, *Greenland* 4 B6
Brewton, *U.S.A.* 109 K2
Breyten, *S. Africa* 89 D5
Breza, *Bos.-H.* 42 F3
Brezhnev = Naberezhnyye Chelny, *Russia* 48 C11
Brežice, *Slovenia* 29 C12
Březnice, *Czech Rep.* 26 B6
Breznik, *Bulgaria* 40 D6
Brezno, *Slovak Rep.* 27 C12
Brezoi, *Romania* 43 E9
Brezovica, *Kosovo, Yug.* 40 D5
Brezovo, *Bulgaria* 41 D9
Briançon, *France* 21 D10
Briare, *France* 19 E9
Briático, *Italy* 31 D9
Bribie I., *Australia* 95 D5
Bribri, *Costa Rica* 120 E3
Briceni, *Moldova* 43 B12
Bricquebec, *France* 18 C5
Bridgehampton, *U.S.A.* 111 F12
Bridgend, *U.K.* 13 F4
Bridgend □, *U.K.* 13 F4
Bridgeport, *Calif., U.S.A.* 116 G7
Bridgeport, *Conn., U.S.A.* 111 E11
Bridgeport, *Nebr., U.S.A.* 112 E3
Bridgeport, *Tex., U.S.A.* 113 J6
Bridger, *U.S.A.* 114 D9
Bridgeton, *U.S.A.* 108 F8
Bridgetown, *Australia* 93 F2
Bridgetown, *Barbados* 121 D8
Bridgetown, *Canada* 103 D6
Bridgewater, *Canada* 103 D7
Bridgewater, *Mass., U.S.A.* 111 E14
Bridgewater, *N.Y., U.S.A.* 111 D9
Bridgewater-Gagebrook, *Australia* 94 G4
Bridgnorth, *U.K.* 13 E5
Bridgton, *U.S.A.* 111 B14
Bridgwater, *U.K.* 13 F5
Bridgwater B., *U.K.* 13 F4
Bridlington, *U.K.* 12 C7
Bridlington B., *U.K.* 12 C7
Bridport, *Australia* 94 G4
Bridport, *U.K.* 13 G5
Briec, *France* 18 D2
Brienne-le-Château, *France* 19 D11
Brienon-sur-Armançon, *France* 19 E10
Brienz, *Switz.* 25 J4
Brienzersee, *Switz.* 25 J3
Brig, *Switz.* 25 J3
Brigg, *U.K.* 12 D7
Brigham City, *U.S.A.* 114 F7
Brighton, *Canada* 110 B7
Brighton, *U.K.* 13 G7
Brighton, *Colo., U.S.A.* 112 F2
Brighton, *N.Y., U.S.A.* 110 C7
Brignogan-Plage, *France* 18 D2
Brignoles, *France* 21 E10
Brihuega, *Spain* 32 E2
Brikama, *Gambia* 82 C1
Brilliant, *U.S.A.* 110 F4
Brilon, *Germany* 24 D4
Bríndisi, *Italy* 31 B10
Brinje, *Croatia* 29 D12
Brinkley, *U.S.A.* 113 H9
Brinnon, *U.S.A.* 116 C4
Brion, I., *Canada* 103 C7
Brionne, *France* 18 C7
Brionski, *Croatia* 29 D10
Brioude, *France* 20 C7
Briouze, *France* 18 D6
Brisbane, *Australia* 95 D5
Brisbane →, *Australia* 95 D5
Brisighella, *Italy* 29 D8
Bristol, *U.K.* 13 F5
Bristol, *Conn., U.S.A.* 111 E12
Bristol, *Pa., U.S.A.* 111 F10
Bristol, *R.I., U.S.A.* 111 E13
Bristol, *Tenn., U.S.A.* 109 G4
Bristol, City of □, *U.K.* 13 F5
Bristol B., *U.S.A.* 100 C4
Bristol Channel, *U.K.* 13 F3
Bristol I., *Antarctica* 5 B1
Bristol L., *U.S.A.* 115 J5
Bristow, *U.S.A.* 113 H6
Britain = Great Britain, *Europe* 6 E5
British Columbia □, *Canada* 104 C3
British Indian Ocean Terr. = Chagos Arch., *Ind. Oc.* 52 K11
British Isles, *Europe* 6 E5
Brits, *S. Africa* 89 D4
Britstown, *S. Africa* 88 E3
Britt, *Canada* 102 C3
Brittany = Bretagne, *France* 18 D3
Britton, *U.S.A.* 112 C6
Brive-la-Gaillarde, *France* 20 C5
Briviesca, *Spain* 34 C7
Brixen = Bressanone, *Italy* 29 B8
Brixham, *U.K.* 13 G4
Brnaze, *Croatia* 29 E13
Brno, *Czech Rep.* 27 B9
Broad →, *U.S.A.* 109 J5
Broad Arrow, *Australia* 93 F3
Broad B., *U.K.* 14 C2
Broad Haven, *Ireland* 15 B2
Broad Law, *U.K.* 14 F5
Broad Sd., *Australia* 94 C4
Broadalbin, *U.S.A.* 111 C10
Broadback →, *Canada* 102 B4
Broadhurst Ra., *Australia* 92 D3
Broads, The, *U.K.* 12 E9
Broadus, *U.S.A.* 112 C2
Broager, *Denmark* 11 K3
Broby, *Sweden* 11 H8
Broceni, *Latvia* 44 B9
Brochet, *Canada* 105 B8
Brochet, L., *Canada* 105 B8
Brocken, *Germany* 24 D6
Brockport, *U.S.A.* 110 C7
Brockton, *U.S.A.* 111 D13
Brockville, *Canada* 102 D4
Brockway, *Mont., U.S.A.* 112 B2
Brockway, *Pa., U.S.A.* 110 E6
Brocton, *U.S.A.* 110 D5
Brod, *Macedonia* 40 E5
Brodarevo, *Serbia, Yug.* 40 C3
Brodeur Pen., *Canada* 101 A11
Brodhead, Mt., *U.S.A.* 110 E7
Brodick, *U.K.* 14 F3
Brodnica, *Poland* 45 E6
Brody, *Ukraine* 47 G3
Brogan, *U.S.A.* 114 D5
Broglie, *France* 18 C7
Brok, *Poland* 45 F8
Broken Arrow, *U.S.A.* 113 G7
Broken Bow, *Nebr., U.S.A.* 112 E5
Broken Bow, *Okla., U.S.A.* 113 H7
Broken Bow Lake, *U.S.A.* 113 H7
Broken Hill = Kabwe, *Zambia* 87 E2
Brokind, *Sweden* 11 F9
Bromley □, *U.K.* 13 F8
Bromölla, *Sweden* 11 H8
Bromsgrove, *U.K.* 13 E5
Brønderslev, *Denmark* 11 G3
Brong-Ahafo □, *Ghana* 82 D4
Broni, *Italy* 28 C6
Bronkhorstspruit, *S. Africa* 89 D4
Brønnøysund, *Norway* 8 D15
Bronte, *Italy* 31 E7
Brook Park, *U.S.A.* 110 E4
Brookhaven, *U.S.A.* 113 K9
Brookings, *Oreg., U.S.A.* 114 E1
Brookings, *S. Dak., U.S.A.* 112 C6
Brooklin, *Canada* 110 C6
Brooklyn Park, *U.S.A.* 112 C8
Brooks, *Canada* 104 C6
Brooks Range, *U.S.A.* 100 B5
Brooksville, *U.S.A.* 109 L4
Brookton, *Australia* 93 F2
Brookville, *U.S.A.* 110 E5
Broom, L., *U.K.* 14 D3
Broome, *Australia* 92 C3
Broons, *France* 18 D4
Brora, *U.K.* 14 C5
Brora →, *U.K.* 14 C5
Brørup, *Denmark* 11 J2
Brösarp, *Sweden* 11 J8
Brosna →, *Ireland* 15 C4
Broșteni, *Mehedinți, Romania* 42 F7
Broșteni, *Suceava, Romania* 43 C10
Brothers, *U.S.A.* 114 E3
Brou, *France* 18 D8
Brouage, *France* 20 C2
Brough, *U.K.* 12 C5
Brough Hd., *U.K.* 14 B5
Broughton Island = Qikiqtarjuaq, *Canada* 101 B13
Broumov, *Czech Rep.* 27 A9
Brovary, *Ukraine* 47 G6
Brovst, *Denmark* 11 G3
Brown, L., *Australia* 93 F2
Brown, Pt., *Australia* 95 E1
Brown City, *U.S.A.* 110 C2
Brown Willy, *U.K.* 13 G3
Brownfield, *U.S.A.* 113 J3
Browning, *U.S.A.* 114 B7
Brownsville, *Oreg., U.S.A.* 114 D2
Brownsville, *Pa., U.S.A.* 110 F5
Brownsville, *Tenn., U.S.A.* 113 H10
Brownsville, *Tex., U.S.A.* 113 N6
Brownville, *U.S.A.* 111 C9
Brownwood, *U.S.A.* 113 K5
Browse I., *Australia* 92 B3
Bruas, *Malaysia* 65 K3
Bruay-la-Buissière, *France* 19 B9
Bruce, Mt., *Australia* 92 D2
Bruce Pen., *Canada* 110 B3
Bruce Rock, *Australia* 93 F2
Bruche →, *France* 19 D14
Bruchsal, *Germany* 25 F4
Bruck an der Leitha, *Austria* 27 C9
Bruck an der Mur, *Austria* 26 D8
Brue →, *U.K.* 13 F5
Bruges = Brugge, *Belgium* 17 C3
Brugg, *Switz.* 25 H4
Brugge, *Belgium* 17 C3
Bruin, *U.S.A.* 110 E5
Brûlé, *Canada* 104 C5
Brûlon, *France* 18 E6
Brumado, *Brazil* 125 F10
Brumath, *France* 19 D14
Brumunddal, *Norway* 9 F14
Bruneau, *U.S.A.* 114 E6
Bruneau →, *U.S.A.* 114 E6
Bruneck = Brunico, *Italy* 29 B8
Brunei = Bandar Seri Begawan, *Brunei* 62 C4
Brunei ■, *Asia* 62 D4
Brunflo, *Sweden* 10 A8
Brunico, *Italy* 29 B8
Brunna, *Sweden* 10 E11
Brunnen, *Switz.* 25 J4
Brunner, L., *N.Z.* 91 K3
Brunsbüttel, *Germany* 24 B5
Brunssum, *Neths.* 17 D5
Brunswick = Braunschweig, *Germany* 24 C6
Brunswick, *Ga., U.S.A.* 109 K5
Brunswick, *Maine, U.S.A.* 109 D11
Brunswick, *Md., U.S.A.* 108 F7
Brunswick, *Mo., U.S.A.* 112 F8
Brunswick, *Ohio, U.S.A.* 110 E3
Brunswick, Pen. de, *Chile* 128 G2
Brunswick B., *Australia* 92 C3
Brunswick Junction, *Australia* 93 F2
Bruntál, *Czech Rep.* 27 B10
Bruny I., *Australia* 94 G4
Brus Laguna, *Honduras* 120 C3
Brusartsi, *Bulgaria* 40 C7
Brush, *U.S.A.* 112 E3
Brushton, *U.S.A.* 111 B10
Brusio, *Switz.* 25 J6
Brusque, *Brazil* 127 B6
Brussel, *Belgium* 17 D4
Brussels = Brussel, *Belgium* 17 D4
Brussels, *Canada* 110 C3
Brusy, *Poland* 44 E4
Bruxelles = Brussel, *Belgium* 17 D4
Bruyères, *France* 19 D13
Bruz, *France* 18 D5
Brwinów, *Poland* 45 F7
Bryagovo, *Bulgaria* 41 E9
Bryan, *Ohio, U.S.A.* 108 E3
Bryan, *Tex., U.S.A.* 113 K6
Bryanka, *Ukraine* 47 H10
Bryansk, *Bryansk, Russia* 47 F8
Bryansk, *Dagestan, Russia* 49 H8
Bryanskoye = Bryansk, *Russia* 49 H8
Bryce Canyon National Park, *U.S.A.* 115 H7
Bryne, *Norway* 9 G11
Bryson City, *U.S.A.* 109 H4
Bryukhovetskaya, *Russia* 47 K10
Brza Palanka, *Serbia, Yug.* 40 B6
Brzeg, *Poland* 45 H4
Brzeg Dolny, *Poland* 45 G3
Brześć Kujawski, *Poland* 45 F5
Brzesko, *Poland* 45 J7
Brzeziny, *Poland* 45 G6
Brzozów, *Poland* 45 J9
Bsharri, *Lebanon* 75 A5
Bū Baqarah, *U.A.E.* 71 E8
Bu Craa, *W. Sahara* 78 C3
Bū Ḥasā, *U.A.E.* 71 F7
Bua, *Sweden* 11 G6
Bua Yai, *Thailand* 64 E4
Buapinang, *Indonesia* 63 E6
Buba, *Guinea-Biss.* 82 C2
Bubanza, *Burundi* 86 C2
Bubaque, *Guinea-Biss.* 82 C1
Bube, *Ethiopia* 81 F4
Būbiyān, *Kuwait* 71 D6
Buca, *Turkey* 39 C9
Bucak, *Turkey* 39 D12
Bucaramanga, *Colombia* 124 B4
Bucas Grande I., *Phil.* 61 G6
Bucasia, *Australia* 94 C4
Buccaneer Arch., *Australia* 92 C3
Buccino, *Italy* 31 B8
Bucecea, *Romania* 43 C11
Buchach, *Ukraine* 47 H3
Buchan, *U.K.* 14 D6
Buchan Ness, *U.K.* 14 D7
Buchanan, *Canada* 105 C8
Buchanan, *Liberia* 82 D2
Buchanan, L., *Queens., Australia* 94 C4
Buchanan, L., *W. Austral., Australia* 93 E3
Buchanan, L., *U.S.A.* 113 K5
Buchanan Cr. →, *Australia* 94 B2
Buchans, *Canada* 103 C8
Bucharest = București, *Romania* 43 F11
Buchen, *Germany* 25 F5
Buchholz, *Germany* 24 B5
Buchloe, *Germany* 25 G6
Buchon, Pt., *U.S.A.* 116 K6
Buciumi, *Romania* 42 C8
Buck Hill Falls, *U.S.A.* 111 E9
Bückeburg, *Germany* 24 C5
Buckeye, *U.S.A.* 115 K7
Buckeye Lake, *U.S.A.* 110 G2
Buckhannon, *U.S.A.* 108 F5
Buckhaven, *U.K.* 14 E5
Buckhorn L., *Canada* 110 B6
Buckie, *U.K.* 14 D6
Buckingham, *Canada* 102 C4
Buckingham, *U.K.* 13 F7
Buckingham B., *Australia* 94 A2
Buckinghamshire □, *U.K.* 13 F7
Buckle Hd., *Australia* 92 B4
Buckley, *U.K.* 12 D4
Buckley →, *Australia* 94 C2
Bucklin, *U.S.A.* 113 G5
Bucks L., *U.S.A.* 116 F5
Bucquoy, *France* 19 B9
Buctouche, *Canada* 103 C7
București, *Romania* 43 F11
Bucyrus, *U.S.A.* 108 E4
Budacu, Vf., *Romania* 43 C10
Budalin, *Burma* 67 H19
Budaörs, *Hungary* 42 C3
Budapest, *Hungary* 42 C4
Budapest □, *Hungary* 42 C4
Budaun, *India* 69 E8
Budd Coast, *Antarctica* 5 C8
Buddusò, *Italy* 30 B2
Bude, *U.K.* 13 G3
Budennovsk, *Russia* 49 H7
Budești, *Romania* 43 F11
Budge Budge = Baj Baj, *India* 69 H13
Budia, *Spain* 32 E2
Büdingen, *Germany* 25 E5
Budjala, *Dem. Rep. of the Congo* 84 D3
Budoni, *Italy* 30 B2
Búdrio, *Italy* 29 D8
Budva, *Montenegro, Yug.* 40 D2
Budzyń, *Poland* 45 F3
Buea, *Cameroon* 83 E6

Buellton, U.S.A. 117 L6
Buena Esperanza, Argentina 126 C2
Buena Park, U.S.A. 117 M9
Buena Vista, Colo., U.S.A. 115 G10
Buena Vista, Va., U.S.A. 108 G6
Buena Vista Lake Bed, U.S.A. 117 K7
Buenaventura, Colombia 124 C3
Buenaventura, Mexico 118 B3
Buendía, Embalse de, Spain 32 E2
Buenos Aires, Argentina 126 C4
Buenos Aires, Costa Rica 120 E3
Buenos Aires □, Argentina 126 D4
Buenos Aires, L., Chile 128 F2
Buffalo, Mo., U.S.A. 113 G8
Buffalo, N.Y., U.S.A. 110 D6
Buffalo, Okla., U.S.A. 113 G5
Buffalo, S. Dak., U.S.A. 112 C3
Buffalo, Wyo., U.S.A. 114 D10
Buffalo →, Canada 104 A5
Buffalo →, S. Africa 89 D5
Buffalo Head Hills, Canada 104 B5
Buffalo L., Alta., Canada 104 C6
Buffalo L., N.W.T., Canada 104 A5
Buffalo Narrows, Canada 105 B7
Buffels →, S. Africa 88 D2
Buford, U.S.A. 109 H4
Bug = Buh →, Ukraine 47 J6
Bug →, Poland 45 F8
Buga, Colombia 124 C3
Buganda, Uganda 86 C3
Buganga, Uganda 86 C3
Bugasong, Phil. 61 F5
Bugeat, France 20 C5
Bugel, Tanjung, Indonesia 63 G14
Bugibba, Malta 36 D1
Bugojno, Bos.-H. 42 F2
Bugsuk, Phil. 62 C5
Buguma, Nigeria 83 E6
Bugun Shara, Mongolia 60 B5
Buguruslan, Russia 50 D6
Buh →, Ukraine 47 J6
Buharkent, Turkey 39 D10
Buheirat-Murrat-el-Kubra, Egypt 80 H8
Buhera, Zimbabwe 89 B5
Bühl, Germany 25 G4
Buhl, U.S.A. 114 E6
Buhuşi, Romania 43 D11
Builth Wells, U.K. 13 E4
Buinsk, Russia 48 C9
Buir Nur, Mongolia 60 B6
Buis-les-Baronnies, France 21 D9
Buitrago = Buitrago del Lozoya, Spain 34 E7
Buitrago del Lozoya, Spain 34 E7
Bujalance, Spain 35 H6
Bujanovac, Serbia, Yug. 40 D5
Bujaraloz, Spain 32 D4
Buje, Croatia 29 C10
Bujumbura, Burundi 86 C2
Bük, Hungary 42 C1
Buk, Poland 45 F3
Bukachacha, Russia 51 D12
Bukama, Dem. Rep. of the Congo 87 D2
Bukavu, Dem. Rep. of the Congo 86 C2
Bukene, Tanzania 86 C3
Bukhara = Bukhoro, Uzbekistan 50 F7
Bukhoro, Uzbekistan 50 F7
Bukima, Tanzania 86 C3
Bukit Mertajam, Malaysia 65 K3
Bukittinggi, Indonesia 62 E2
Bükk, Hungary 42 B5
Bukoba, Tanzania 86 C3
Bukuru, Nigeria 83 D6
Bukuya, Uganda 86 B3
Bül, Kuh-e, Iran 71 D7
Bula, Guinea-Biss. 82 C1
Bula, Indonesia 63 E8
Bülach, Switz. 25 H4
Bulan, Phil. 61 E5
Bulancak, Turkey 73 B8
Bulandshahr, India 68 E7
Bulanık, Turkey 73 C10
Bûlâq, Egypt 80 B3
Bulawayo, Zimbabwe 87 G2
Buldan, Turkey 39 C10
Bulgar, Russia 48 C9
Bulgaria ■, Europe 41 D9
Bulgheria, Monte, Italy 31 B8
Bulgurca, Turkey 39 C9
Buli, Teluk, Indonesia 63 D7
Buliluyan, C., Phil. 61 G2
Bulki, Ethiopia 81 F4
Bulkley →, Canada 104 B3
Bull Shoals L., U.S.A. 113 G8
Bullaque →, Spain 35 G6
Bullas, Spain 33 G3
Bulle, Switz. 25 J3
Bullhead City, U.S.A. 117 K12
Büllingen, Belgium 17 D6
Bullock Creek, Australia 94 B3
Bulloo →, Australia 95 D3
Bulloo L., Australia 95 D3
Bulls, N.Z. 91 J5
Bully-les-Mines, France 19 B9
Bulnes, Chile 126 D1
Bulqizë, Albania 40 E4
Bulsar = Valsad, India 66 J8
Bultfontein, S. Africa 88 D4
Bulukumba, Indonesia 63 F6
Bulun, Russia 51 B13
Bumba, Dem. Rep. of the Congo 84 D4
Bumbeşti-Jiu, Romania 43 E8
Bumbiri I., Tanzania 86 C3
Bumbuna, S. Leone 82 D2

Bumhpa Bum, Burma 67 F20
Bumi →, Zimbabwe 87 F2
Buna, Kenya 86 B4
Bunawan, Phil. 61 G6
Bunazi, Tanzania 86 C3
Bunbury, Australia 93 F2
Bunclody, Ireland 15 D5
Buncrana, Ireland 15 A4
Bundaberg, Australia 95 C5
Bünde, Germany 24 C4
Bundey →, Australia 94 C2
Bundi, India 68 G6
Bundoran, Ireland 15 B3
Bundukia, Sudan 81 F3
Bung Kan, Thailand 64 C4
Bunga →, Nigeria 83 C6
Bungay, U.K. 13 E9
Bungil Cr. →, Australia 95 D4
Bungo-Suidō, Japan 55 H6
Bungoma, Kenya 86 B3
Bungotakada, Japan 55 H5
Bungu, Tanzania 86 D4
Bunia, Dem. Rep. of the Congo 86 B3
Bunji, Pakistan 69 B6
Bunkie, U.S.A. 113 K8
Bunnell, U.S.A. 109 L5
Buñol, Spain 33 F4
Bunsuru, Nigeria 83 C5
Buntok, Indonesia 62 E4
Bununu Dass, Nigeria 83 C6
Bununu Kasa, Nigeria 83 D6
Bünyan, Turkey 72 C6
Bunyu, Indonesia 62 D5
Bunza, Nigeria 83 C5
Buol, Indonesia 63 D6
Buon Brieng, Vietnam 64 F7
Buon Ma Thuot, Vietnam 64 F7
Buong Long, Cambodia 64 F6
Buorkhaya, Mys, Russia 51 B14
Buqayq, Si. Arabia 71 E6
Buqbuq, Egypt 80 A2
Bur Acaba, Somali Rep. 74 G3
Bûr Fuad, Egypt 80 H8
Bûr Safâga, Egypt 70 E2
Bûr Sa'îd, Egypt 80 H8
Bûr Sûdân, Sudan 80 D4
Bûr Taufiq, Egypt 80 J8
Bura, Kenya 86 C4
Burakin, Australia 93 F2
Buram, Sudan 81 E2
Burao, Somali Rep. 74 F4
Burāq, Syria 75 B5
Buraydah, Si. Arabia 70 E4
Burbank, U.S.A. 117 L8
Burda, India 68 G6
Burdekin →, Australia 94 B4
Burdur, Turkey 39 D12
Burdur □, Turkey 39 D12
Burdur Gölü, Turkey 39 D12
Burdwan = Barddhaman, India 69 H12
Bure, Gojam, Ethiopia 81 E4
Bure, Ilubabor, Ethiopia 81 F4
Bure →, U.K. 12 E9
Büren, Germany 24 D4
Bureya →, Russia 51 E13
Burford, Canada 110 C4
Burg, Germany 24 B7
Burg auf Fehmarn, Germany 24 A7
Burg el Arab, Egypt 80 H6
Burg et Tuyur, Sudan 80 C2
Burg Stargard, Germany 24 B9
Burgas, Bulgaria 41 D11
Burgas □, Bulgaria 41 D10
Burgaski Zaliv, Bulgaria 41 D11
Burgdorf, Germany 24 C6
Burgdorf, Switz. 25 H3
Burgenland □, Austria 27 D9
Burgeo, Canada 103 C8
Burgersdorp, S. Africa 88 E4
Burges, Mt., Australia 93 F3
Burghausen, Germany 25 G8
Búrgio, Italy 30 E6
Burglengenfeld, Germany 25 F8
Burgohondo, Spain 34 E6
Burgos, Spain 34 C7
Burgos □, Spain 34 C7
Burgstädt, Germany 24 E8
Burgsvik, Sweden 11 G12
Burguillos del Cerro, Spain 35 G4
Burgundy = Bourgogne, France 19 F11
Burhaniye, Turkey 39 B8
Burhanpur, India 66 J10
Burhi Gandak →, India 69 G12
Burhner →, India 69 H9
Buri Pen., Eritrea 81 D4
Burias I., Phil. 61 E5
Burica, Pta., Costa Rica 120 E3
Burien, U.S.A. 116 C4
Burigi, L., Tanzania 86 C3
Burin, Canada 103 C8
Buriram, Thailand 64 E4
Burj Sāfitā, Syria 70 C3
Burji, Ethiopia 81 F4
Burkburnett, U.S.A. 113 H5
Burke →, Australia 94 C2
Burke Chan., Canada 104 C3
Burketown, Australia 94 B2
Burkina Faso ■, Africa 82 C4
Burk's Falls, Canada 102 C4
Burlada, Spain 32 C3
Burleigh Falls, Canada 110 B6
Burley, U.S.A. 114 E7
Burlingame, U.S.A. 116 H4
Burlington, Canada 102 D4
Burlington, Colo., U.S.A. 112 F3
Burlington, Iowa, U.S.A. 112 E9

Burlington, Kans., U.S.A. 112 F7
Burlington, N.C., U.S.A. 109 G6
Burlington, N.J., U.S.A. 111 F10
Burlington, Vt., U.S.A. 111 B11
Burlington, Wash., U.S.A. 116 B4
Burlington, Wis., U.S.A. 108 D1
Burlyu-Tyube, Kazakstan 50 E8
Burma ■, Asia 67 J20
Burnaby I., Canada 104 C2
Burnet, U.S.A. 113 K5
Burney, U.S.A. 114 F3
Burnham, U.S.A. 110 F7
Burnham-on-Sea, U.K. 13 F5
Burnie, Australia 94 G4
Burnley, U.K. 12 D5
Burns, U.S.A. 114 E4
Burns Lake, Canada 104 C3
Burnside →, Canada 100 B9
Burnside, L., Australia 93 E3
Burnsville, U.S.A. 112 C8
Burnt L., Canada 103 B7
Burnt River, Canada 110 B6
Burntwood →, Canada 105 B9
Burntwood L., Canada 105 B8
Burqān, Kuwait 70 D5
Burra, Nigeria 83 C6
Burra, Australia 95 E2
Burray, U.K. 14 C6
Burrel, Albania 40 E4
Burren Junction, Australia 95 E4
Burriana, Spain 32 F4
Burro, Serranías del, Mexico 118 B4
Burrow Hd., U.K. 14 G4
Burruyacú, Argentina 126 B3
Burry Port, U.K. 13 F3
Bursa, Turkey 41 F13
Burseryd, Sweden 11 G7
Burstall, Canada 105 C7
Burton, Ohio, U.S.A. 110 E3
Burton, S.C., U.S.A. 109 J5
Burton, L., Canada 102 B4
Burton upon Trent, U.K. 12 E6
Buru, Indonesia 63 E7
Burullus, Bahra el, Egypt 80 H7
Burūn, Râs, Egypt 75 D2
Burundi ■, Africa 86 C3
Bururi, Burundi 86 C2
Burutu, Nigeria 83 D6
Burwell, U.S.A. 112 E5
Burwick, U.K. 14 C5
Bury, U.K. 12 D5
Bury St. Edmunds, U.K. 13 E8
Buryatia □, Russia 51 D11
Buryn, Ukraine 47 G7
Burzenin, Poland 45 G5
Busalla, Italy 28 D5
Buşayrah, Syria 70 C4
Busca, Italy 28 D4
Bushat, Albania 40 E3
Büshehr, Iran 71 D6
Büshehr □, Iran 71 D6
Bushell, Canada 105 B7
Bushenyi, Uganda 86 C3
Bushire = Büshehr, Iran 71 D6
Busie, Ghana 82 C4
Businga, Dem. Rep. of the Congo 84 D4
Busko-Zdrój, Poland 45 H7
Busovača, Bos.-H. 42 F2
Buşra ash Shām, Syria 75 C5
Busselton, Australia 93 F2
Busseri →, Sudan 81 F2
Busseto, Italy 28 D7
Bussière-Badil, France 20 C4
Bussolengo, Italy 28 C7
Bussum, Neths. 17 B5
Buşteni, Romania 43 E10
Busto, C., Spain 34 B4
Busto Arsízio, Italy 28 C5
Busu-Djanoa, Dem. Rep. of the Congo 84 D4
Busuanga I., Phil. 61 E3
Büsum, Germany 24 A4
Buta, Dem. Rep. of the Congo 86 B1
Butare, Rwanda 86 C2
Butaritari, Kiribati 96 G9
Bute, U.K. 14 F3
Bute Inlet, Canada 104 C4
Butembo, Uganda 86 B3
Butembo, Dem. Rep. of the Congo 86 B2
Buteni, Romania 42 D7
Butera, Italy 31 E7
Butha Qi, China 60 B7
Butiaba, Uganda 86 B3
Butler, Mo., U.S.A. 112 F7
Butler, Pa., U.S.A. 110 F5
Buton, Indonesia 63 E6
Butte, Mont., U.S.A. 114 C7
Butte, Nebr., U.S.A. 112 D5
Butte Creek →, U.S.A. 116 F5
Butterworth = Gcuwa, S. Africa 89 E4
Butterworth, Malaysia 65 K3
Buttevant, Ireland 15 D3
Buttfield, Mt., Australia 93 D4
Button B., Canada 105 B10
Buttonwillow, U.S.A. 117 K7
Butty Hd., Australia 93 F3
Butuan, Phil. 61 G6
Butung = Buton, Indonesia 63 E6
Buturlinovka, Russia 48 E5
Butzbach, Germany 25 E4
Bützow, Germany 24 B7
Buxa Duar, India 69 F16
Buxar, India 69 G10
Buxtehude, Germany 24 B5

Buxton, U.K. 12 D6
Buxy, France 19 F11
Buy, Russia 48 A5
Buynaksk, Russia 49 J8
Buyo, Ivory C. 82 D3
Buyo, L. de, Ivory C. 82 D3
Büyük Menderes →, Turkey 39 D9
Büyükçekmece, Turkey 41 E12
Büyükkarıştıran, Turkey 41 E11
Büyükkemikli Burnu, Turkey 41 F10
Büyükorhan, Turkey 39 B10
Büyükyoncalı, Turkey 41 E11
Buzançais, France 18 F8
Buzău, Romania 43 E11
Buzău □, Romania 43 E11
Buzău →, Romania 43 E12
Buzău, Pasul, Romania 43 E11
Buzen, Japan 55 H5
Buzet, Croatia 29 C10
Buzi →, Mozam. 87 F3
Buziaş, Romania 42 E6
Buzuluk, Russia 50 D6
Buzuluk →, Russia 48 E6
Buzzards B., U.S.A. 111 E14
Buzzards Bay, U.S.A. 111 E14
Bwana Mkubwe, Dem. Rep. of the Congo 87 E2
Byala, Ruse, Bulgaria 41 C9
Byala, Varna, Bulgaria 41 D11
Byala Slatina, Bulgaria 40 C7
Byarezina →, Belarus 47 F6
Byaroza, Belarus 47 F3
Bychawa, Poland 45 G9
Byczyna, Poland 45 G5
Bydgoszcz, Poland 45 E5
Byelarus = Belarus ■, Europe 46 F4
Byelorussia = Belarus ■, Europe 46 F4
Byers, U.S.A. 112 F2
Byesville, U.S.A. 110 G3
Byford, Australia 93 F2
Bykhaw, Belarus 46 F6
Bykhov = Bykhaw, Belarus 46 F6
Bykovo, Russia 48 E7
Bylas, U.S.A. 115 K8
Bylot, Canada 105 B10
Bylot I., Canada 101 A12
Byrd, C., Antarctica 5 C17
Byron Bay, Australia 95 D5
Byrranga, Gory, Russia 51 B11
Byrranga Mts. = Byrranga, Gory, Russia 51 B11
Byrum, Denmark 11 G5
Byske, Sweden 8 D19
Byske älv →, Sweden 8 D19
Bystrzyca →, Dolnoślaskie, Poland 45 G3
Bystrzyca →, Lubelskie, Poland 45 G9
Bystrzyca Kłodzka, Poland 45 H3
Bytča, Slovak Rep. 27 B11
Bytom, Poland 45 H5
Bytom Odrzański, Poland 45 G2
Bytów, Poland 44 D4
Byumba, Rwanda 86 C3
Bzenec, Czech Rep. 27 C10
Bzura →, Poland 45 F7

C

Ca →, Vietnam 64 C5
Ca Mau, Vietnam 65 H5
Ca Mau, Mui, Vietnam 65 H5
Ca Na, Vietnam 65 G7
Caacupé, Paraguay 126 B4
Caála, Angola 85 G3
Caamaño Sd., Canada 104 C3
Caazapá, Paraguay 126 B4
Caazapá □, Paraguay 127 B4
Cabadbaran, Phil. 61 G6
Cabalian = San Juan, Phil. 61 F6
Cabana, Spain 34 B2
Cabañaquinta, Spain 34 B5
Cabanatuan, Phil. 61 D4
Cabanes, Spain 32 E5
Cabano, Canada 103 C6
Čabar, Croatia 29 C11
Cabazon, U.S.A. 117 M10
Cabedelo, Brazil 125 E12
Cabeza del Buey, Spain 35 G5
Cabezón de la Sal, Spain 34 B6
Cabildo, Chile 126 C1
Cabimas, Venezuela 124 A4
Cabinda, Angola 84 F2
Cabinda □, Angola 84 F2
Cabinet Mts., U.S.A. 114 C6
Cabo Blanco, Argentina 128 F3
Cabo Frio, Brazil 127 A7
Cabo Pantoja, Peru 124 D3
Cabonga, Réservoir, Canada 102 C4
Cabool, U.S.A. 113 G8
Caboolture, Australia 95 D5
Cabora Bassa Dam = Cahora Bassa, Reprêsa de, Mozam. 87 F3
Caborca, Mexico 118 A2
Cabot, Mt., U.S.A. 111 B13
Cabot Hd., Canada 110 A3
Cabot Str., Canada 103 C8
Cabra, Spain 35 H6
Cabra del Santo Cristo, Spain 35 H7
Cábras, Italy 30 C1
Cabrera, Sierra, Spain 34 C4
Cabri, Canada 105 C7
Cabriel →, Spain 33 F3
Cabugao, Phil. 61 C4

Cacabelos, Spain 34 C4
Caçador, Brazil 127 B5
Čačak, Serbia, Yug. 40 C4
Caçapava do Sul, Brazil 127 C5
Cáccamo, Italy 30 E6
Cacém, Portugal 35 G1
Cáceres, Brazil 124 G7
Cáceres, Spain 35 F4
Cáceres □, Spain 34 F5
Cache Bay, Canada 102 C4
Cache Cr. →, U.S.A. 116 G5
Cache Creek, Canada 104 C4
Cacheu, Guinea-Biss. 82 C1
Cachi, Argentina 126 B2
Cachimbo, Serra do, Brazil 125 E7
Cachinal de la Sierra, Chile 126 A2
Cachoeira, Brazil 125 F11
Cachoeira do Sul, Brazil 127 C5
Cachoeiro de Itapemirim, Brazil 127 A7
Cachopo, Portugal 35 H3
Cacine, Guinea-Biss. 82 C1
Cacoal, Brazil 124 C4
Cacólo, Angola 84 G3
Caconda, Angola 85 G3
Čadca, Slovak Rep. 27 B11
Caddo, U.S.A. 113 H6
Cader Idris, U.K. 13 E4
Cadereyta, Mexico 118 B5
Cadí, Sierra del, Spain 32 C6
Cadibarrawirracanna, L., Australia 95 D2
Cadillac, France 20 D3
Cadillac, U.S.A. 108 C3
Cadiz, Phil. 61 F5
Cádiz, Spain 35 J4
Cadiz, Calif., U.S.A. 117 L11
Cadiz, Ohio, U.S.A. 110 F4
Cádiz □, Spain 35 J5
Cádiz, G. de, Spain 35 J3
Cadiz L., U.S.A. 115 J6
Cadney Park, Australia 95 D1
Cadomin, Canada 104 C5
Cadotte Lake, Canada 104 B5
Cadours, France 20 E5
Cadoux, Australia 93 F2
Caen, France 18 C6
Caernarfon, U.K. 12 D3
Caernarfon B., U.K. 12 D3
Caernarvon = Caernarfon, U.K. 12 D3
Caerphilly, U.K. 13 F4
Caerphilly □, U.K. 13 F4
Caesarea, Israel 75 C3
Caetité, Brazil 125 F10
Cafayate, Argentina 126 B2
Cafu, Angola 88 B2
Cagayan →, Phil. 61 B4
Cagayan de Oro, Phil. 61 G6
Cagayan Is., Phil. 61 G4
Cagayan Sulu I., Phil. 61 H3
Cagli, Italy 29 E9
Cágliari, Italy 30 C2
Cágliari, G. di, Italy 30 C2
Cagnano Varano, Italy 29 G12
Cagnes-sur-Mer, France 21 E11
Caguán →, Colombia 124 D4
Caguas, Puerto Rico 121 C6
Caha Mts., Ireland 15 E2
Cahama, Angola 88 B1
Caher, Ireland 15 D4
Cahersiveen, Ireland 15 E1
Cahora Bassa, Reprêsa de, Mozam. 87 F3
Cahore Pt., Ireland 15 D5
Cahors, France 20 D5
Cahul, Moldova 43 E13
Caì Bau, Dao, Vietnam 58 G6
Cai Nuoc, Vietnam 65 H5
Caia, Mozam. 87 F4
Caianda, Angola 87 E1
Caibarién, Cuba 120 B4
Caibiran, Phil. 61 F6
Caicara, Venezuela 124 B5
Caicó, Brazil 125 E11
Caicos Is., Turks & Caicos 121 B5
Caicos Passage, W. Indies 121 B5
Caidian, China 59 B10
Căinari, Moldova 43 E14
Caird Coast, Antarctica 5 D1
Cairn Gorm, U.K. 14 D5
Cairngorm Mts., U.K. 14 D5
Cairnryan, U.K. 14 G3
Cairns, Australia 94 B4
Cairns L., Canada 105 C10
Cairo = El Qâhira, Egypt 80 H7
Cairo, Ga., U.S.A. 109 K3
Cairo, Ill., U.S.A. 113 G10
Cairo, N.Y., U.S.A. 111 D11
Cairo Montenotte, Italy 28 D5
Caithness, Ord of, U.K. 14 C5
Cajamarca, Peru 124 E3
Cajarc, France 20 D5
Cajàzeiras, Brazil 125 E11
Čajetina, Serbia, Yug. 40 C3
Çakırgöl, Turkey 73 B8
Çakirlar, Turkey 39 E12
Čakovec, Croatia 29 B13
Çal, Turkey 39 C11
Cala, Spain 35 H4
Cala →, Spain 35 H4
Cala Cadolar, Punta de = Rojta, Pta., Spain 33 G6
Cala d'Or, Spain 37 B10
Cala en Porter, Spain 37 B11
Cala Figuera, C. de, Spain 37 B9
Cala Forcat, Spain 37 B10
Cala Major, Spain 37 B9

Cala Mezquida = Sa Mesquida,
   Spain 37 B11
Cala Millor, Spain 37 B10
Cala Ratjada, Spain 37 B10
Cala Santa Galdana, Spain .. 37 B10
Calabanga, Phil. 61 E5
Calabar, Nigeria 83 E6
Calabogie, Canada 111 A8
Calabozo, Venezuela 124 B5
Calàbria □, Italy 31 C9
Calaburras, Pta. de, Spain .. 35 J6
Calaceite, Spain 32 D5
Calacuccia, France 21 F13
Calafat, Romania 42 G7
Calafate, Argentina 128 G2
Calafell, Spain 32 D6
Calahorra, Spain 32 C3
Calais, France 19 B8
Calais, U.S.A. 109 C12
Calalaste, Cord. de, Argentina . 126 B2
Calama, Brazil 124 E6
Calama, Chile 126 A2
Calamar, Colombia 124 A4
Calamian Group, Phil. 61 F3
Calamocha, Spain 32 E3
Calamonte, Spain 35 G4
Calan, Romania 42 E7
Calañas, Spain 35 H4
Calanda, Spain 32 E4
Calang, Indonesia 62 D1
Calangiánus, Italy 30 B2
Calapan, Phil. 61 E4
Călărasi, Moldova 43 C13
Călărasi, Romania 43 F12
Călărasi □, Romania 43 F12
Calasparra, Spain 33 G3
Calatafimi, Italy 30 E5
Calatayud, Spain 32 D3
Călătele, Romania 42 D8
Calato = Kálathos, Greece ... 39 E10
Calauag, Phil. 61 E5
Calavà, C., Italy 31 D7
Calavite, C., Phil. 61 E4
Calayan, Phil. 61 B4
Calbayog, Phil. 61 E6
Calca, Peru 124 F4
Calcasieu L., U.S.A. 113 L8
Calcutta = Kolkata, India ... 69 H13
Calcutta, U.S.A. 110 F4
Caldaro, Italy 29 B8
Caldas da Rainha, Portugal .. 35 F1
Caldas de Reis, Spain 34 C2
Calder →, U.K. 12 D6
Caldera, Chile 126 B1
Caldwell, Idaho, U.S.A. 114 E5
Caldwell, Kans., U.S.A. 113 G6
Caldwell, Tex., U.S.A. 113 K6
Caledon, S. Africa 88 E2
Caledon →, S. Africa 88 E4
Caledon B., Australia 94 A2
Caledonia, Canada 110 C5
Caledonia, U.S.A. 110 D7
Calella, Spain 32 D7
Calemba, Angola 88 B2
Calen, Australia 94 C4
Calenzana, France 21 F12
Caletones, Chile 126 C1
Calexico, U.S.A. 117 N11
Calf of Man, U.K. 12 C3
Calgary, Canada 104 C6
Calheta, Madeira 37 D2
Calhoun, U.S.A. 109 H3
Cali, Colombia 124 C3
Caliente, U.S.A. 115 H6
California, Mo., U.S.A. 112 F8
California, Pa., U.S.A. 110 F5
California □, U.S.A. 116 H7
California, Baja, Mexico 118 A1
California, Baja, T.N. = Baja
   California □, Mexico 118 B2
California, Baja, T.S. = Baja
   California Sur □, Mexico .. 118 B2
California, G. de, Mexico ... 118 B2
California City, U.S.A. 117 K9
California Hot Springs, U.S.A. . 117 K8
Călimănesti, Romania 43 E9
Călimani, Muntii, Romania .. 43 C10
Calingasta, Argentina 126 C2
Calipatria, U.S.A. 117 M11
Calistoga, U.S.A. 116 G4
Calitri, Italy 31 B8
Calitzdorp, S. Africa 88 E3
Callabonna, L., Australia ... 95 D3
Callac, France 18 D3
Callan, Ireland 15 D4
Callander, U.K. 14 E4
Callao, Peru 124 F3
Calles, Mexico 119 C5
Callicoon, U.S.A. 111 E9
Calling Lake, Canada 104 B6
Calliope, Australia 94 C5
Callosa de Ensarriá, Spain .. 33 G4
Callosa de Segura, Spain ... 33 G4
Calne, U.K. 13 F6
Calola, Angola 88 B2
Calolbon = San Andres, Phil. . 61 E6
Calonge, Spain 32 D8
Caloocan, Phil. 61 D4
Calore →, Italy 31 A7
Caloundra, Australia 95 D5
Calpe, Spain 33 G5
Calpella, U.S.A. 116 F3
Calpine, U.S.A. 116 F6
Calstock, Canada 102 C3
Caltabellotta, Italy 30 E6

Caltagirone, Italy 31 E7
Caltanissetta, Italy 31 E7
Çaltılıbük, Turkey 41 G12
Caluire-et-Cuire, France 19 G11
Calulo, Angola 84 G2
Caluso, Italy 28 C4
Calvados □, France 18 C6
Calvert →, Australia 94 B2
Calvert I., Canada 104 C3
Calvert Ra., Australia 92 D3
Calvi, France 21 F12
Calviá, Spain 33 F7
Calvillo, Mexico 118 C4
Calvinia, S. Africa 88 E2
Calvo = Calvo, Mte., Italy ... 29 G12
Calvo, Mte., Italy 29 G12
Calwa, U.S.A. 116 J7
Calzada Almuradiel =
   Almuradiel, Spain 35 G7
Calzada de Calatrava, Spain .. 35 G7
Cam →, U.K. 13 E8
Cam Lam, Vietnam 65 G7
Cam Pha, Vietnam 58 G6
Cam Ranh, Vietnam 65 G7
Cam Xuyen, Vietnam 64 C6
Camabatela, Angola 84 F3
Camacha, Madeira 37 D3
Camacho, Mexico 118 C4
Camacupa, Angola 85 G3
Camaguey, Cuba 120 B4
Camaiore, Italy 28 E7
Camaná, Peru 124 G4
Camanche Reservoir, U.S.A. .. 116 G6
Camaquã, Brazil 127 C5
Camaquã →, Brazil 127 C5
Câmara de Lobos, Madeira .. 37 D3
Camarat, C., France 21 E10
Camarès, France 20 E6
Camaret-sur-Mer, France ... 18 D2
Camargo, Mexico 119 B5
Camargue, France 21 E8
Camarillo, U.S.A. 117 L7
Camariñas, Spain 34 B1
Camarón, C., Honduras 120 C2
Camarones, Argentina 128 E3
Camas, Spain 35 H4
Camas, U.S.A. 116 E4
Camas Valley, U.S.A. 114 E2
Camballin, Australia 92 C3
Cambará, Brazil 127 A5
Cambay = Khambhat, India . 68 H5
Cambay, G. of = Khambhat, G.
   of, India 66 J8
Cambil, Spain 35 H7
Cambo-les-Bains, France ... 20 E2
Cambodia ■, Asia 64 F5
Camborne, U.K. 13 G2
Cambrai, France 19 B10
Cambre, Spain 34 B2
Cambria, U.S.A. 116 K5
Cambrian Mts., U.K. 13 E4
Cambridge, Canada 102 D3
Cambridge, Jamaica 120 C4
Cambridge, N.Z. 91 G5
Cambridge, U.K. 13 E8
Cambridge, Mass., U.S.A. .. 111 D13
Cambridge, Minn., U.S.A. .. 112 C8
Cambridge, N.Y., U.S.A. ... 111 C11
Cambridge, Nebr., U.S.A. .. 112 E4
Cambridge, Ohio, U.S.A. ... 110 F3
Cambridge Bay = Ikaluktutiak,
   Canada 100 B9
Cambridge G., Australia 92 B4
Cambridge Springs, U.S.A. .. 110 E4
Cambridgeshire □, U.K. 13 E7
Cambrils, Spain 32 D6
Cambuci, Brazil 127 A7
Cambundi-Catembo, Angola . 84 G3
Camden, Ala., U.S.A. 109 K2
Camden, Ark., U.S.A. 113 J8
Camden, Maine, U.S.A. 109 C11
Camden, N.J., U.S.A. 111 G9
Camden, N.Y., U.S.A. 111 C9
Camden, S.C., U.S.A. 109 H5
Camden Sd., Australia 92 C3
Camdenton, U.S.A. 113 F8
Çameli, Turkey 39 D11
Camenca, Moldova 43 B13
Camerino, Italy 29 E10
Cameron, Ariz., U.S.A. 115 J8
Cameron, La., U.S.A. 113 L8
Cameron, Mo., U.S.A. 112 F7
Cameron, Tex., U.S.A. 113 K6
Cameron Highlands, Malaysia . 65 K3
Cameron Hills, Canada 104 B5
Cameroon ■, Africa 84 C2
Camerota, Italy 31 B8
Cameroun →, Cameroon ... 83 E6
Cameroun, Mt., Cameroon .. 83 E6
Cametá, Brazil 125 D9
Camiguin □, Phil. 61 G6
Camiguin I., Phil. 61 B4
Camiling, Phil. 61 D4
Camilla, U.S.A. 109 K3
Caminha, Portugal 34 D2
Camino, U.S.A. 116 G6
Camira Creek, Australia 95 D5
Cammal, U.S.A. 110 E7
Cammarata, Italy 30 E6
Camocim, Brazil 125 D10
Camooweal, Australia 94 B2
Camopi, Fr. Guiana 125 C8
Camotes Is., Phil. 61 F6
Camotes Sea, Phil. 61 F6
Camp Borden, Canada 110 B5

Camp Hill, U.S.A. 110 F8
Camp Nelson, U.S.A. 117 J8
Camp Pendleton, U.S.A. ... 117 M9
Camp Verde, U.S.A. 115 J8
Camp Wood, U.S.A. 113 L5
Campagna, Italy 31 B8
Campana, Argentina 126 C4
Campana, I., Chile 128 F1
Campanário, Madeira 37 D2
Campanario, Spain 35 G5
Campania □, Italy 31 B7
Campbell, S. Africa 88 D3
Campbell, Calif., U.S.A. 116 H5
Campbell, Ohio, U.S.A. 110 E4
Campbell I., Pac. Oc. 96 N8
Campbell L., Canada 105 A7
Campbell River, Canada 104 C3
Campbell Town, Australia ... 94 G4
Campbellford, Canada 110 B7
Campbellpur, Pakistan 68 C5
Campbellsville, U.S.A. 108 G3
Campbellton, Canada 103 C6
Campbeltown, U.K. 14 F3
Campeche, Mexico 119 D6
Campeche □, Mexico 119 D6
Campeche, Golfo de, Mexico . 119 D6
Campello, Spain 33 G4
Câmpeni, Romania 42 D8
Camperville, Canada 105 C8
Campi Salentina, Italy 31 B11
Câmpia Turzii, Romania 43 D8
Campidano, Italy 30 C1
Campíglia Maríttima, Italy .. 28 E7
Campillo de Altobuey, Spain . 33 F3
Campillos, Spain 35 H6
Câmpina, Romania 43 E10
Campina Grande, Brazil 125 E11
Campinas, Brazil 127 A6
Campli, Italy 29 F10
Campo, Spain 32 C5
Campo de Criptana, Spain .. 35 F7
Campo de Gibraltar, Spain .. 35 J5
Campo Grande, Brazil 125 H8
Campo Maíor, Brazil 125 D10
Campo Maior, Portugal 35 F3
Campo Mourão, Brazil 127 A5
Campo Túres, Italy 29 B8
Campobasso, Italy 31 A7
Campobello di Licata, Italy .. 30 E6
Campobello di Mazara, Italy . 30 E5
Campofelice di Roccella, Italy . 30 E6
Campomarino, Italy 29 G12
Camporeale, Italy 30 E6
Camporrobles, Spain 32 F3
Campos, Brazil 127 A7
Campos Belos, Brazil 125 F9
Campos del Puerto, Spain ... 37 B10
Campos Novos, Brazil 127 B5
Camprodón, Spain 32 C7
Camptonville, U.S.A. 116 F5
Camptown, U.S.A. 111 E8
Camrose, Canada 104 C6
Camsell Portage, Canada ... 105 B7
Çamyuva, Turkey 39 E12
Çan, Turkey 41 F11
Can Clavo, Spain 37 C7
Can Creu, Spain 37 C7
Can Gio, Vietnam 65 G6
Can Tho, Vietnam 65 G5
Canaan, U.S.A. 111 D11
Canada ■, N. Amer. 100 C10
Cañada de Gómez, Argentina . 126 C3
Canadian, U.S.A. 113 H4
Canadian →, U.S.A. 113 H7
Canajoharie, U.S.A. 111 D10
Çanakkale, Turkey 41 F10
Çanakkale □, Turkey 41 F10
Çanakkale Bogazı, Turkey ... 41 F10
Canal Flats, Canada 104 C5
Canalejas, Argentina 126 D2
Canals, Argentina 126 C3
Canals, Spain 33 G4
Canandaigua, U.S.A. 110 D7
Canandaigua L., U.S.A. 110 D7
Cananea, Mexico 118 A2
Canarias, Is., Atl. Oc. 37 F4
Canareos, Arch. de los, Cuba . 120 B3
Canary Is. = Canarias, Is.,
   Atl. Oc. 37 F4
Canaseraga, U.S.A. 110 D7
Canatlán, Mexico 118 C4
Canaveral, C., U.S.A. 109 L5
Cañaverales, Spain 32 E2
Canavieiras, Brazil 125 G11
Canby, Calif., U.S.A. 114 F3
Canby, Minn., U.S.A. 112 C6
Canby, Oreg., U.S.A. 116 E4
Cancale, France 18 D5
Canche →, France 19 B8
Cancún, Mexico 119 C7
Candanchu, Spain 32 C4
Candarlı, Turkey 39 B8
Çandarlı Körfezi, Turkey 39 C8
Candas, Spain 34 B5
Candé, France 18 E5
Candela, Italy 31 A8
Candelaria, Argentina 127 B4
Candelaria, Canary Is. 37 F3
Candeleda, Spain 34 E5
Candia = Iráklion, Greece ... 36 D7
Candia, Sea of = Crete, Sea of,
   Greece 39 E7
Candle L., Canada 105 C7

Candlemas I., Antarctica 5 B1
Cando, U.S.A. 112 A5
Candon, Phil. 61 C4
Canea = Khaniá, Greece 36 D6
Canelli, Italy 28 D5
Canelones, Uruguay 127 C4
Canet-Plage, France 20 F7
Cañete, Chile 126 D1
Cañete, Peru 124 F3
Cañete, Spain 32 E3
Cañete de las Torres, Spain .. 35 H6
Cangas, Spain 34 C2
Cangas de Narcea, Spain ... 34 B4
Cangas de Onís, Spain 34 B5
Cangnan, China 59 D13
Canguaretama, Brazil 125 E11
Canguçu, Brazil 127 C5
Canguçu, Serra do, Brazil ... 127 C5
Cangwu, China 59 F8
Cangxi, China 58 B5
Cangyuan, China 58 F2
Cangzhou, China 56 E9
Caniapiscau →, Canada ... 103 A6
Caniapiscau, Rés. de, Canada . 103 B6
Canicattì, Italy 30 E6
Canicattini Bagni, Italy 31 E8
Caniles, Spain 35 H8
Canim Lake, Canada 104 C4
Canindeyu □, Paraguay 127 A5
Canino, Italy 29 F8
Canisteo, U.S.A. 110 D7
Canisteo →, U.S.A. 110 D7
Cañitas, Mexico 118 C4
Cañizal, Spain 34 D5
Canjáyar, Spain 33 H8
Çankırı, Turkey 72 B5
Çankuzo, Burundi 86 C3
Canmore, Canada 104 C5
Canna, U.K. 14 D2
Cannanore, India 66 P9
Cannes, France 21 E11
Canning Town = Port Canning,
   India 69 H13
Cannington, Canada 110 B5
Cannóbio, Italy 28 B5
Cannock, U.K. 13 E5
Cannon Ball →, U.S.A. ... 112 B4
Cannondale Mt., Australia .. 94 D4
Cannonsville Reservoir, U.S.A. . 111 D9
Cannonvale, Australia 94 C4
Canoas, Brazil 127 B5
Canoe L., Canada 105 B7
Canon City, U.S.A. 112 F2
Canora, Canada 105 C8
Canosa di Púglia, Italy 31 A9
Canso, Canada 103 C7
Cantabria □, Spain 34 B7
Cantabria, Sierra de, Spain .. 32 C2
Cantabrian Mts. = Cantábrica,
   Cordillera, Spain 34 C5
Cantábrica, Cordillera, Spain . 34 C5
Cantal □, France 20 C6
Cantal, Plomb du, France ... 20 C6
Cantanhede, Portugal 34 E2
Cantavieja, Spain 32 E4
Cantemir, Moldova 43 D13
Cantil, U.S.A. 117 K9
Cantillana, Spain 35 H5
Canterbury, Australia 94 D3
Canterbury, U.K. 13 F9
Canterbury Bight, N.Z. 91 L3
Canterbury Plains, N.Z. 91 K3
Cantù, Italy 28 C6
Canudos, Brazil 124 E7
Canumã →, Brazil 124 D7
Canutama, Brazil 124 E6
Canutillo, U.S.A. 115 L10
Canvey, U.K. 13 F8
Canyon, U.S.A. 113 H4
Canyonlands National Park,
   U.S.A. 115 G9
Canyonville, U.S.A. 114 E2
Cao Bang, Vietnam 58 F6
Cao He →, China 57 D13
Cao Lanh, Vietnam 65 G5
Cao Xian, China 56 G8
Cáorle, Italy 29 C9
Cap-aux-Meules, Canada .. 103 C7
Cap-Chat, Canada 103 C6
Cap-de-la-Madeleine, Canada . 102 C5
Cap-Haïtien, Haiti 121 C5
Capac, U.S.A. 110 C2
Capácio, Italy 31 B8
Capanaparo →, Venezuela . 124 B5
Capánnori, Italy 28 E7
Capbreton, France 20 E2
Capdenac, France 20 D6
Capdepera, Spain 32 F8
Cape →, Australia 94 C4
Cape Barren I., Australia ... 94 G4
Cape Breton Highlands Nat.
   Park, Canada 103 C7
Cape Breton I., Canada 103 C7
Cape Charles, U.S.A. 108 G8

Cape Coast, Ghana 83 D4
Cape Coral, U.S.A. 109 M5
Cape Dorset, Canada 101 B12
Cape Fear →, U.S.A. 109 H6
Cape Girardeau, U.S.A. 113 G10
Cape May, U.S.A. 108 F8
Cape May Point, U.S.A. 108 F8
Cape Province, S. Africa 85 L3
Cape Tormentine, Canada ... 103 C7
Cape Town, S. Africa 88 E2
Cape Verde Is. ■, Atl. Oc. .. 77 E1
Cape Vincent, U.S.A. 111 B8
Cape York Peninsula, Australia . 94 A3
Capela, Brazil 125 F11
Capella, Australia 94 C4
Capendu, France 20 E6
Capestang, France 20 E7
Capim →, Brazil 125 D9
Capistrello, Italy 29 G10
Capitan, U.S.A. 115 K11
Capitol Reef National Park,
   U.S.A. 115 G8
Capitola, U.S.A. 116 J5
Capizzi, Italy 31 E7
Capoche →, Mozam. 87 F3
Capoterra, Italy 30 C1
Cappadocia, Turkey 72 C6
Capraia, Italy 28 E6
Caprara, Pta., Italy 30 A1
Caprarola, Italy 29 F9
Capreol, Canada 102 C3
Caprera, Italy 30 A2
Capri, Italy 31 B7
Capricorn Group, Australia .. 94 C5
Capricorn Ra., Australia 92 D2
Caprino Veronese, Italy 28 C7
Caprivi Strip, Namibia 88 B3
Captieux, France 20 D3
Caquetá →, Colombia 122 D4
Caracal, Romania 43 F9
Caracas, Venezuela 124 A5
Caracol, Mato Grosso do Sul,
   Brazil 126 A4
Caracol, Piauí, Brazil 125 E10
Caráglio, Italy 28 D4
Carajas, Brazil 125 E8
Carajás, Serra dos, Brazil ... 125 E8
Carangola, Brazil 127 A7
Caransebes, Romania 42 E7
Carantec, France 18 D3
Caraquet, Canada 103 C6
Caras, Peru 124 E3
Caras Severin □, Romania .. 42 E7
Carasova, Romania 42 E6
Caratasca, L., Honduras ... 120 C3
Caratinga, Brazil 125 G10
Caraúbas, Brazil 125 E11
Caravaca = Caravaca de la Cruz,
   Spain 33 G3
Caravaca de la Cruz, Spain .. 33 G3
Caravággio, Italy 28 C6
Caravela, Guinea-Biss. 82 C1
Caravelas, Brazil 125 G11
Caraveli, Peru 124 G4
Caràzinho, Brazil 127 B5
Carballino = O Carballiño, Spain . 34 C2
Carballo, Spain 34 B2
Carberry, Canada 105 D9
Carbó, Mexico 118 B2
Carbonara, C., Italy 30 C2
Carbondale, Colo., U.S.A. .. 114 G10
Carbondale, Ill., U.S.A. 113 G10
Carbondale, Pa., U.S.A. 111 E9
Carbonear, Canada 103 C9
Carboneras, Spain 33 J3
Carboneras de Guadazón,
   Spain 32 F3
Carbónia, Italy 30 C1
Carcabuey, Spain 35 H6
Carcagente = Carcaixent, Spain . 33 F4
Carcaixent, Spain 33 F4
Carcajou, Canada 104 B5
Carcar, Phil. 61 F5
Carcarana →, Argentina ... 126 C3
Carcasse, C., Haiti 121 C5
Carcassonne, France 20 E6
Carcross, Canada 104 A2
Çardak, Çanakkale, Turkey .. 41 F10
Çardak, Denizli, Turkey 39 D11
Cardamon Hills, India 66 Q10
Cardeña, Spain 35 G6
Cárdenas, Cuba 120 B3
Cárdenas, San Luis Potosí,
   Mexico 119 C5
Cárdenas, Tabasco, Mexico .. 119 D6
Cardenete, Spain 32 F3
Cardiff, U.K. 13 F4
Cardiff □, U.K. 13 F4
Cardiff-by-the-Sea, U.S.A. .. 117 M9
Cardigan, U.K. 13 E3
Cardigan B., U.K. 13 E3
Cardinal, Canada 111 B9
Cardona, Spain 32 D6
Cardona, Uruguay 126 C4
Cardoner →, Spain 32 D6
Cardoso, Ilha do, Brazil ... 127 B5
Cardston, Canada 104 D6
Cardwell, Australia 94 B4
Careen L., Canada 105 B7
Carei, Romania 42 C7
Careme = Ciremai, Indonesia . 63 G13
Carentan, France 18 C5
Carey, U.S.A. 114 E7
Carey, L., Australia 93 E3
Carey L., Canada 105 A8
Careysburg, Liberia 82 D2

Cargèse, France ... 21 F12
Carhaix-Plouguer, France 18 D3
Carhué, Argentina ... 126 D3
Caria, Turkey ... 39 D10
Cariacica, Brazil ... 125 H10
Cariati, Italy ... 31 C9
Caribbean Sea, W. Indies ... 121 D5
Cariboo Mts., Canada ... 104 C4
Caribou, U.S.A. ... 109 B12
Caribou →, Man., Canada ... 105 B10
Caribou →, N.W.T., Canada ... 104 A3
Caribou I., Canada ... 102 C2
Caribou Is., Canada ... 104 A6
Caribou L., Man., Canada ... 105 B9
Caribou L., Ont., Canada ... 102 B2
Caribou Mts., Canada ... 104 B5
Carichic, Mexico ... 118 B3
Carigara, Phil. ... 61 F6
Carignan, France ... 19 C12
Carignano, Italy ... 28 D4
Carillo, Mexico ... 118 B4
Cariñena, Spain ... 32 D3
Carinhanha, Brazil ... 125 F10
Carinhanha →, Brazil ... 125 F10
Carini, Italy ... 30 D6
Cariño, Spain ... 34 B3
Carínola, Italy ... 30 A6
Carinthia = Kärnten □, Austria ... 26 E6
Caripito, Venezuela ... 124 A6
Carlbrod = Dimitrovgrad, Serbia, Yug. ... 40 C6
Carlet, Spain ... 33 F4
Carleton, Mt., Canada ... 103 C6
Carleton Place, Canada ... 102 C4
Carletonville, S. Africa ... 88 D4
Cârlibaba, Romania ... 43 C10
Carlin, U.S.A. ... 114 F5
Carlingford L., U.K. ... 15 B5
Carlinville, U.S.A. ... 112 F10
Carlisle, U.K. ... 12 C5
Carlisle, U.S.A. ... 110 F7
Carlit, Pic, France ... 20 F5
Carloforte, Italy ... 30 C1
Carlos Casares, Argentina ... 126 D3
Carlos Tejedor, Argentina ... 126 D3
Carlow, Ireland ... 15 D5
Carlow □, Ireland ... 15 D5
Carlsbad, Calif., U.S.A. ... 117 M9
Carlsbad, N. Mex., U.S.A. ... 113 J2
Carlsbad Caverns National Park, U.S.A. ... 113 J2
Carluke, U.K. ... 14 F5
Carlyle, Canada ... 105 D8
Carmacks, Canada ... 100 B6
Carmagnola, Italy ... 28 D4
Carman, Canada ... 105 D9
Carmarthen, U.K. ... 13 F3
Carmarthen B., U.K. ... 13 F3
Carmarthenshire □, U.K. ... 13 F3
Carmaux, France ... 20 D6
Carmel, U.S.A. ... 111 E11
Carmel-by-the-Sea, U.S.A. ... 116 J5
Carmel Valley, U.S.A. ... 116 J5
Carmelo, Uruguay ... 126 C4
Carmen, Colombia ... 124 B3
Carmen, Paraguay ... 127 B4
Carmen →, Mexico ... 118 A3
Carmen, I., Mexico ... 118 B2
Carmen de Patagones, Argentina ... 128 E4
Cármenes, Spain ... 34 C5
Carmensa, Argentina ... 126 D2
Carmi, Canada ... 104 D5
Carmi, U.S.A. ... 108 F1
Carmichael, U.S.A. ... 116 G5
Carmila, Australia ... 94 C4
Carmona, Costa Rica ... 120 E2
Carmona, Spain ... 35 H5
Carn Ban, U.K. ... 14 D4
Carn Eige, U.K. ... 14 D3
Carnamah, Australia ... 93 E2
Carnarvon, Australia ... 93 D1
Carnarvon, S. Africa ... 88 E3
Carnarvon Ra., Queens., Australia ... 94 D4
Carnarvon Ra., W. Austral., Australia ... 93 E3
Carnation, U.S.A. ... 116 C5
Carndonagh, Ireland ... 15 A4
Carnduff, Canada ... 105 D8
Carnegie, U.S.A. ... 110 F4
Carnegie, L., Australia ... 93 E3
Carnic Alps = Karnische Alpen, Europe ... 26 E6
Carniche Alpi = Karnische Alpen, Europe ... 26 E6
Carnot, C.A.R. ... 84 D3
Carnot, C., Australia ... 95 E2
Carnot B., Australia ... 92 C3
Carnoustie, U.K. ... 14 E6
Carnsore Pt., Ireland ... 15 D5
Caro, U.S.A. ... 108 D4
Carol City, U.S.A. ... 109 N5
Carolina, Brazil ... 125 E9
Carolina, Puerto Rico ... 121 C6
Carolina, S. Africa ... 89 D5
Caroline I., Kiribati ... 97 H12
Caroline Is., Micronesia ... 52 J17
Caroni →, Venezuela ... 124 B6
Caronie = Nébrodi, Monti, Italy ... 31 E7
Carpathians, Europe ... 6 F10
Carpații Meridionali, Romania ... 43 E9
Carpentaria, G. of, Australia ... 94 A2
Carpentras, France ... 21 D9
Carpi, Italy ... 28 D7
Cârpineni, Moldova ... 43 D13
Carpinteria, U.S.A. ... 117 L7

Carpio, Spain ... 34 D5
Carr Boyd Ra., Australia ... 92 C4
Carrabelle, U.S.A. ... 109 L3
Carral, Spain ... 34 B2
Carranza, Presa V., Mexico ... 118 B4
Carrara, Italy ... 28 D7
Carrascal, Phil. ... 61 G6
Carrascosa del Campo, Spain ... 32 E2
Carrauntoohill, Ireland ... 15 D2
Carrick-on-Shannon, Ireland ... 15 C3
Carrick-on-Suir, Ireland ... 15 D4
Carrickfergus, U.K. ... 15 B6
Carrickmacross, Ireland ... 15 C5
Carrington, U.S.A. ... 112 B5
Carrión →, Spain ... 34 D6
Carrión de los Condes, Spain ... 34 C6
Carrizal Bajo, Chile ... 126 B1
Carrizalillo, Chile ... 126 B1
Carrizo Cr. →, U.S.A. ... 113 G3
Carrizo Springs, U.S.A. ... 113 L5
Carrizozo, U.S.A. ... 115 K11
Carroll, U.S.A. ... 112 D7
Carrollton, Ga., U.S.A. ... 109 J3
Carrollton, Ill., U.S.A. ... 112 F9
Carrollton, Ky., U.S.A. ... 108 F3
Carrollton, Mo., U.S.A. ... 112 F8
Carrollton, Ohio, U.S.A. ... 110 F3
Carron →, U.K. ... 14 D4
Carron, L., U.K. ... 14 D3
Carrot →, Canada ... 105 C8
Carrot River, Canada ... 105 C8
Carrouges, France ... 18 D6
Carrù, Italy ... 28 D4
Carruthers, Canada ... 105 C7
Carsa Dek, Ethiopia ... 81 F4
Çarşamba, Turkey ... 72 B7
Carsóli, Italy ... 29 F10
Carson, Calif., U.S.A. ... 117 M8
Carson, N. Dak., U.S.A. ... 112 B4
Carson →, U.S.A. ... 116 F8
Carson City, U.S.A. ... 116 F7
Carson Sink, U.S.A. ... 114 G4
Cartagena, Colombia ... 124 A3
Cartagena, Spain ... 33 H4
Cartago, Colombia ... 124 C3
Cartago, Costa Rica ... 120 E3
Cártama, Spain ... 35 J6
Cartaxo, Portugal ... 35 F2
Cartaya, Spain ... 35 H3
Cartersville, U.S.A. ... 109 H3
Carterton, N.Z. ... 91 J5
Carthage, Tunisia ... 30 F3
Carthage, Ill., U.S.A. ... 112 E9
Carthage, Mo., U.S.A. ... 113 G7
Carthage, N.Y., U.S.A. ... 108 D8
Carthage, Tex., U.S.A. ... 113 J7
Cartier I., Australia ... 92 B3
Cartwright, Canada ... 103 B8
Caruaru, Brazil ... 125 E11
Carúpano, Venezuela ... 124 A6
Caruthersville, U.S.A. ... 113 G10
Carvin, France ... 19 B9
Carvoeiro, Brazil ... 124 D6
Carvoeiro, C., Portugal ... 35 F1
Cary, U.S.A. ... 109 H6
Casa Branca, Portugal ... 35 G2
Casa Grande, U.S.A. ... 115 K8
Casablanca, Chile ... 126 C1
Casablanca, Morocco ... 78 B4
Casacalenda, Italy ... 29 G11
Casalbordino, Italy ... 29 F11
Casale Monferrato, Italy ... 28 C5
Casalmaggiore, Italy ... 28 D7
Casalpusterlengo, Italy ... 28 C6
Casamance →, Senegal ... 82 C1
Casarano, Italy ... 31 B11
Casares, Spain ... 35 J5
Casas Ibáñez, Spain ... 33 F3
Casasimarro, Spain ... 33 F2
Casatejada, Spain ... 34 F5
Casavieja, Spain ... 34 E6
Cascade, Idaho, U.S.A. ... 114 D5
Cascade, Mont., U.S.A. ... 114 C8
Cascade Locks, U.S.A. ... 116 E5
Cascade Ra., U.S.A. ... 116 D5
Cascade Reservoir, U.S.A. ... 114 D5
Cascais, Portugal ... 35 G1
Cascavel, Brazil ... 127 A5
Cáscina, Italy ... 28 E7
Casco B., U.S.A. ... 109 D10
Caselle Torinese, Italy ... 28 C4
Caserta, Italy ... 31 A7
Cashel, Ireland ... 15 D4
Casiguran, Phil. ... 61 C5
Casilda, Argentina ... 126 C3
Casimcea, Romania ... 43 F13
Casino, Australia ... 95 D5
Casiquiare →, Venezuela ... 124 C5
Čáslav, Czech Rep. ... 26 B8
Casma, Peru ... 124 E3
Casmalia, U.S.A. ... 117 L6
Cásola Valsénio, Italy ... 29 D8
Cásoli, Italy ... 29 F11
Caspe, Spain ... 32 D4
Casper, U.S.A. ... 114 E10
Caspian Depression, Eurasia ... 49 G9
Caspian Sea, Eurasia ... 50 E6
Cass Lake, U.S.A. ... 112 B7
Cassà de la Selva, Spain ... 32 D7
Cassadaga, U.S.A. ... 110 D5
Cassano allo Iónio, Italy ... 31 C9
Casse, Grande, France ... 21 C10
Cassel, France ... 19 B9
Casselman, Canada ... 111 A9
Casselton, U.S.A. ... 112 B6
Cassiar, Canada ... 104 B3

Cassiar Mts., Canada ... 104 B2
Cassino, Italy ... 30 A6
Cassis, France ... 21 E9
Cassville, U.S.A. ... 113 G8
Castagneto Carducci, Italy ... 28 E7
Castaic, U.S.A. ... 117 L8
Castalia, U.S.A. ... 110 E2
Castanhal, Brazil ... 125 D9
Castéggio, Italy ... 28 C6
Castejón de Monegros, Spain ... 32 D4
Castèl di Sangro, Italy ... 29 G11
Castèl San Giovanni, Italy ... 28 C6
Castèl San Pietro Terme, Italy ... 29 D8
Castelbuono, Italy ... 31 E7
Castelfidardo, Italy ... 29 E10
Castelfiorentino, Italy ... 28 E7
Castelfranco Emília, Italy ... 28 D8
Castelfranco Véneto, Italy ... 29 C8
Casteljaloux, France ... 20 D4
Castellabate, Italy ... 31 B7
Castellammare, G. di, Italy ... 30 D5
Castellammare del Golfo, Italy ... 30 D5
Castellammare di Stábia, Italy ... 31 B7
Castellamonte, Italy ... 28 C4
Castellane, France ... 21 E10
Castellaneta, Italy ... 31 B9
Castelli, Argentina ... 126 D4
Castelló de la Plana, Spain ... 32 E4
Castellón de la Plana □, Spain ... 32 E4
Castellote, Spain ... 32 E4
Castelmáuro, Italy ... 29 G11
Castelnau-de-Médoc, France ... 20 C3
Castelnau-Magnoac, France ... 20 E4
Castelnaudary, France ... 20 E5
Castelnovo ne' Monti, Italy ... 28 D7
Castelnuovo di Val di Cécina, Italy ... 28 E7
Castelo, Brazil ... 127 A7
Castelo Branco, Portugal ... 34 F3
Castelo Branco □, Portugal ... 34 F3
Castelo de Paiva, Portugal ... 34 D2
Castelo de Vide, Portugal ... 35 F3
Castelsardo, Italy ... 30 B1
Castelsarrasin, France ... 20 D5
Casteltérmini, Italy ... 30 E6
Castelvetrano, Italy ... 30 E5
Castets, France ... 20 E2
Castiglion Fiorentino, Italy ... 29 E8
Castiglione del Lago, Italy ... 29 E9
Castiglione della Pescáia, Italy ... 28 F7
Castiglione delle Stiviere, Italy ... 28 C7
Castilblanco, Spain ... 35 F5
Castile, U.S.A. ... 110 D6
Castilla, Playa de, Spain ... 35 J4
Castilla-La Mancha □, Spain ... 6 H5
Castilla y Leon □, Spain ... 34 D6
Castillo de Locubín, Spain ... 35 H7
Castillon-en-Couserans, France ... 20 F5
Castillonès, France ... 20 D4
Castillos, Uruguay ... 127 C5
Castle Dale, U.S.A. ... 114 G8
Castle Douglas, U.K. ... 14 G5
Castle Rock, Colo., U.S.A. ... 112 F2
Castle Rock, Wash., U.S.A. ... 116 D4
Castlebar, Ireland ... 15 C2
Castleblaney, Ireland ... 15 B5
Castlederg, U.K. ... 15 B4
Castleford, U.K. ... 12 D6
Castlegar, Canada ... 104 D5
Castlemaine, Australia ... 95 F3
Castlepollard, Ireland ... 15 C4
Castlerea, Ireland ... 15 C3
Castlereagh →, Australia ... 95 E4
Castlereagh B., Australia ... 94 A2
Castleton, U.S.A. ... 111 C11
Castletown, U.K. ... 12 C3
Castletown Bearhaven, Ireland ... 15 E2
Castor, Canada ... 104 C6
Castor →, Canada ... 102 B4
Castorland, U.S.A. ... 111 C9
Castres, France ... 20 E6
Castricum, Neths. ... 17 B4
Castries, St. Lucia ... 121 D7
Castro, Brazil ... 127 A6
Castro, Chile ... 128 E2
Castro Alves, Brazil ... 125 F11
Castro del Río, Spain ... 35 H6
Castro-Urdiales, Spain ... 34 B7
Castrojeriz, Spain ... 34 C6
Castropol, Spain ... 34 B4
Castroréale, Italy ... 31 D8
Castroville, U.S.A. ... 116 J5
Castrovíllari, Italy ... 31 C9
Castuera, Spain ... 35 G5
Çat, Turkey ... 73 C9
Cat Ba, Dao, Vietnam ... 64 B6
Cat I., Bahamas ... 121 B4
Cat L., Canada ... 102 B1
Cat Lake, Canada ... 102 B1
Catacamas, Honduras ... 120 D2
Cataguases, Brazil ... 127 A7
Çatak, Turkey ... 73 C10
Catalão, Brazil ... 125 G9
Catalca, Turkey ... 41 E12
Catalina, Canada ... 103 C9
Catalina, Chile ... 126 B2
Catalina, U.S.A. ... 115 K8
Catalonia = Cataluña □, Spain ... 32 D6
Cataluña □, Spain ... 34 E6
Catamarca, Argentina ... 126 B2
Catamarca □, Argentina ... 126 B2
Catanauan, Phil. ... 61 E5
Catanduanes □, Phil. ... 61 E6

Catanduva, Brazil ... 127 A6
Catánia, Italy ... 31 E8
Catánia, G. di, Italy ... 31 E8
Catanzaro, Italy ... 31 D9
Catarman, Phil. ... 61 E6
Catbalogan, Phil. ... 61 F6
Cateel, Phil. ... 61 H7
Catembe, Mozam. ... 89 D5
Caterham, U.K. ... 13 F7
Cathcart, S. Africa ... 88 E4
Cathlamet, U.S.A. ... 116 D3
Catio, Guinea-Biss. ... 82 C1
Catoche, C., Mexico ... 119 C7
Cátria, Mte., Italy ... 29 E9
Catriló, Argentina ... 126 D3
Catrimani, Brazil ... 124 C6
Catrimani →, Brazil ... 124 C6
Catskill, U.S.A. ... 111 D11
Catskill Mts., U.S.A. ... 111 D10
Catt, Mt., Australia ... 94 A1
Cattaraugus, U.S.A. ... 110 D6
Cáttolica, Italy ... 29 E9
Cáttolica Eraclea, Italy ... 30 E6
Catuala, Angola ... 88 B2
Catuane, Mozam. ... 89 D5
Catur, Mozam. ... 87 E4
Catwick Is., Vietnam ... 65 G7
Cauca →, Colombia ... 124 B4
Caucaia, Brazil ... 125 D11
Caucasus Mountains, Eurasia ... 49 J7
Caudete, Spain ... 33 G3
Caudry, France ... 19 B10
Caulnes, France ... 18 D4
Caulónia, Italy ... 31 D9
Caungula, Angola ... 84 F3
Cauquenes, Chile ... 126 D1
Caura →, Venezuela ... 124 B6
Căuresi →, Mozam. ... 87 F3
Causapscal, Canada ... 103 C6
Caussade, France ... 20 D5
Causse-Méjean, France ... 20 D7
Cauterets, France ... 20 F3
Cauvery →, India ... 66 P11
Caux, Pays de, France ... 18 C7
Cava de' Tirreni, Italy ... 31 B7
Cávado →, Portugal ... 34 D2
Cavaillon, France ... 21 E9
Cavalaire-sur-Mer, France ... 21 E10
Cavalese, Italy ... 29 B8
Cavalier, U.S.A. ... 112 A6
Cavalla = Cavally →, Africa ... 82 E3
Cavalleria, C. de, Spain ... 37 A11
Cavallo, I. de, France ... 21 G13
Cavally →, Africa ... 82 E3
Cavan, Ireland ... 15 B4
Cavan □, Ireland ... 15 C4
Cavárzere, Italy ... 29 C9
Cave Creek, U.S.A. ... 115 K7
Cavenagh Ra., Australia ... 93 E4
Caviana, I., Brazil ... 125 C8
Cavite, Phil. ... 61 D4
Cavnic, Romania ... 43 C8
Cavour, Italy ... 28 D4
Cavtat, Croatia ... 40 D7
Cawndilla L., Australia ... 95 E3
Cawnpore = Kanpur, India ... 69 F9
Caxias, Brazil ... 125 D10
Caxias do Sul, Brazil ... 127 B5
Caxito, Angola ... 84 F2
Çay, Turkey ... 72 C4
Cay Sal Bank, Bahamas ... 120 B4
Cayambe, Ecuador ... 124 C3
Çaycuma, Turkey ... 72 B5
Çayeli, Turkey ... 73 B9
Cayenne, Fr. Guiana ... 125 B8
Caygören Baraji, Turkey ... 39 B10
Çayıralan, Turkey ... 72 C6
Caylus, France ... 20 D5
Cayman Brac, Cayman Is. ... 120 C4
Cayman Is. ■, W. Indies ... 120 C3
Cayo Romano, Cuba ... 120 B4
Cayres, France ... 20 D7
Cayuga, Canada ... 110 D5
Cayuga, U.S.A. ... 111 D8
Cayuga L., U.S.A. ... 111 D8
Cazalla de la Sierra, Spain ... 35 H5
Căzănești, Romania ... 43 F12
Cazaubon, France ... 20 E3
Cazaux et de Sanguinet, Étang de, France ... 20 D2
Cazenovia, U.S.A. ... 111 D9
Cazères, France ... 20 E5
Cazin, Bos.-H. ... 29 D12
Čazma, Croatia ... 29 C13
Cazombo, Angola ... 85 G4
Cazorla, Spain ... 35 H7
Cazorla, Sierra de, Spain ... 35 G8
Cea →, Spain ... 34 C5
Ceamurlia de Jos, Romania ... 43 F13
Ceanannus Mor, Ireland ... 15 C5
Ceará = Fortaleza, Brazil ... 125 D11
Ceará □, Brazil ... 125 E11
Ceará Mirim, Brazil ... 125 E11
Ceauru, L., Romania ... 43 F8
Cebaco, I. de, Panama ... 120 E3
Cebollar, Argentina ... 126 B2
Cebollera, Sierra de, Spain ... 32 D2
Cebreros, Spain ... 34 E6
Cebu, Phil. ... 61 F5
Čečava, Bos.-H. ... 42 F2
Ceccano, Italy ... 30 A6
Cece, Hungary ... 42 D3
Cechi, Ivory C. ... 82 D4

Cecil Plains, Australia ... 95 D5
Cécina, Italy ... 28 E7
Cécina →, Italy ... 28 E7
Ceclavín, Spain ... 34 F4
Cedar →, U.S.A. ... 112 E9
Cedar City, U.S.A. ... 115 H7
Cedar Creek Reservoir, U.S.A. ... 113 J6
Cedar Falls, Iowa, U.S.A. ... 112 D8
Cedar Falls, Wash., U.S.A. ... 116 C5
Cedar Key, U.S.A. ... 109 L4
Cedar L., Canada ... 105 C9
Cedar Rapids, U.S.A. ... 112 E9
Cedartown, U.S.A. ... 109 H3
Cedarvale, Canada ... 104 B3
Cedarville, S. Africa ... 89 E4
Cedeira, Spain ... 34 B2
Cedral, Mexico ... 118 C4
Cedrino →, Italy ... 30 B2
Cedro, Brazil ... 125 E11
Cedros, I. de, Mexico ... 118 B1
Ceduna, Australia ... 95 E1
Cedynia, Poland ... 45 F1
Cée, Spain ... 34 C1
Cefalù, Italy ... 31 D7
Cega →, Spain ... 34 D6
Cegléd, Hungary ... 42 C4
Céglie Messápico, Italy ... 31 B10
Cehegín, Spain ... 33 G3
Ceheng, China ... 58 E5
Cehu-Silvaniei, Romania ... 43 C8
Ceica, Romania ... 42 D7
Ceira →, Portugal ... 34 E2
Čelákovice, Czech Rep. ... 26 A7
Celano, Italy ... 29 F10
Celanova, Spain ... 34 C3
Celaya, Mexico ... 118 C4
Celebes Sea, Indonesia ... 63 D6
Čelić, Bos.-H. ... 42 F3
Celina, U.S.A. ... 108 E3
Celinac, Bos.-H. ... 42 F2
Celje, Slovenia ... 29 B12
Celldömölk, Hungary ... 42 C2
Celle, Germany ... 24 C6
Celorico da Beira, Portugal ... 34 E3
Çeltikçi, Turkey ... 39 D12
Cemişgezek, Turkey ... 73 C8
Cenderwasih, Teluk, Indonesia ... 63 E9
Cengong, China ... 58 D7
Ceno →, Italy ... 28 D7
Centallo, Italy ... 28 D4
Centelles, Spain ... 32 D7
Center, N. Dak., U.S.A. ... 112 B4
Center, Tex., U.S.A. ... 113 K7
Centerburg, U.S.A. ... 110 F2
Centerville, Calif., U.S.A. ... 116 J7
Centerville, Iowa, U.S.A. ... 112 E8
Centerville, Pa., U.S.A. ... 110 F5
Centerville, Tenn., U.S.A. ... 109 H2
Centerville, Tex., U.S.A. ... 113 K7
Cento, Italy ... 29 D8
Central □, Ghana ... 83 D4
Central □, Kenya ... 86 C4
Central □, Malawi ... 87 E3
Central □, Zambia ... 87 E2
Central, Cordillera, Colombia ... 122 C3
Central, Cordillera, Costa Rica ... 120 D3
Central, Cordillera, Dom. Rep. ... 121 C5
Central, Cordillera, Phil. ... 61 C4
Central African Rep. ■, Africa ... 84 C4
Central America, America ... 98 H11
Central Butte, Canada ... 105 C7
Central City, Colo., U.S.A. ... 114 G11
Central City, Ky., U.S.A. ... 108 G2
Central City, Nebr., U.S.A. ... 112 E6
Central I., Kenya ... 86 B4
Central Makran Range, Pakistan ... 66 F4
Central Patricia, Canada ... 102 B1
Central Point, U.S.A. ... 114 E2
Central Russian Uplands, Europe ... 6 E13
Central Siberian Plateau, Russia ... 52 C14
Central Square, U.S.A. ... 111 C8
Centralia, Ill., U.S.A. ... 112 F10
Centralia, Mo., U.S.A. ... 112 F8
Centralia, Wash., U.S.A. ... 116 D4
Cenxi, China ... 59 F8
Ceotina →, Bos.-H. ... 40 C7
Cephalonia = Kefallinía, Greece ... 38 C2
Čepin, Croatia ... 42 E3
Ceprano, Italy ... 30 A6
Ceptura, Romania ... 43 E11
Cepu, Indonesia ... 63 G14
Ceram = Seram, Indonesia ... 63 E7
Ceram Sea = Seram Sea, Indonesia ... 63 E7
Cerbère, France ... 20 F7
Cerbicales, Is., France ... 21 G13
Cercal, Portugal ... 35 H2
Cerdaña, Spain ... 20 D5
Cère →, France ... 20 D6
Cerea, Italy ... 29 C8
Ceredigion □, U.K. ... 13 E3
Ceres, Argentina ... 126 B3
Ceres, S. Africa ... 88 E2
Ceres, U.S.A. ... 116 H6
Cerignola, Italy ... 31 A8
Cerigo = Kíthira, Greece ... 38 E5
Cérilly, France ... 19 F9
Cerisiers, France ... 19 D10
Cerizay, France ... 18 F6
Çerkeş, Turkey ... 72 B5
Çerkezköy, Turkey ... 41 E12
Cerknica, Slovenia ... 29 C11
Cerkovica, Bulgaria ... 41 C8

Cermerno, *Serbia, Yug.* **40 C4**
Çermik, *Turkey* **73 C8**
Cerna, *Romania* **43 E13**
Cerna ➤, *Romania* **43 F8**
Cernay, *France* **19 E14**
Cernik, *Croatia* **42 E2**
Cerralvo, I., *Mexico* **118 C3**
Cërrik, *Albania* **40 E3**
Cerritos, *Mexico* **118 C4**
Cerro Chato, *Uruguay* **127 C4**
Certaldo, *Italy* **28 E8**
Cervaro ➤, *Italy* **31 A8**
Cervati, Monte, *Italy* **31 B8**
Cerventes, *Australia* **93 F2**
Cervera, *Spain* **32 D6**
Cervera de Pisuerga, *Spain* ... **34 C6**
Cervera del Río Alhama, *Spain* **32 C3**
Cervéteri, *Italy* **29 F9**
Cérvia, *Italy* **29 D9**
Cervignano del Friuli, *Italy* ... **29 C10**
Cervione, *France* **21 F13**
Cervo, *Spain* **34 B3**
Cesarò, *Italy* **31 E7**
Cesena, *Italy* **29 D9**
Cesenático, *Italy* **29 D9**
Cēsis, *Latvia* **9 H21**
Česká Lípa, *Czech Rep.* **26 A7**
Česká Třebová, *Czech Rep.* ... **27 B9**
České Budějovice, *Czech Rep.* **26 C7**
České Velenice, *Czech Rep.* ... **26 C7**
Českomoravská Vrchovina,
  Czech Rep. **26 B8**
Český Brod, *Czech Rep.* **26 A7**
Český Krumlov, *Czech Rep.* ... **26 C7**
Český Těšín, *Czech Rep.* **27 B11**
Cesma ➤, *Croatia* **29 C13**
Çeşme, *Turkey* **39 C8**
Cesson-Sévigné, *France* **18 D5**
Cestas, *France* **20 D3**
Cestos ➤, *Liberia* **82 D3**
Cetate, *Romania* **42 F8**
Cetin Grad, *Croatia* **29 C12**
Cetina ➤, *Croatia* **29 E13**
Cetinje, *Montenegro, Yug.* ... **40 D2**
Cetraro, *Italy* **31 C8**
Ceuta, *N. Afr.* **78 A4**
Ceva, *Italy* **28 D5**
Cévennes, *France* **20 D7**
Ceyhan, *Turkey* **70 B2**
Ceyhan ➤, *Turkey* **72 D6**
Ceylânpınar, *Turkey* **73 D9**
Ceylon = Sri Lanka ■, *Asia* ... **66 R12**
Cèze ➤, *France* **21 D8**
Cha-am, *Thailand* **64 F2**
Cha Pa, *Vietnam* **64 A4**
Chabanais, *France* **20 C4**
Chabeuil, *France* **21 D9**
Chablais, *France* **19 F13**
Chablis, *France* **19 E10**
Chacabuco, *Argentina* **126 C3**
Chachapoyas, *Peru* **124 E3**
Chachoengsao, *Thailand* **64 F3**
Chachran, *Pakistan* **66 E7**
Chachro, *Pakistan* **68 G4**
Chaco □, *Argentina* **126 B3**
Chaco □, *Paraguay* **126 B4**
Chaco ➤, *U.S.A.* **115 H9**
Chaco Austral, *S. Amer.* **128 B4**
Chaco Boreal, *S. Amer.* **124 H6**
Chaco Central, *S. Amer.* **128 A4**
Chacon, C., *U.S.A.* **104 C2**
Chad ■, *Africa* **79 F8**
Chad, L. = Tchad, L., *Chad* ... **79 F8**
Chadan, *Russia* **51 D10**
Chadileuvú ➤, *Argentina* **126 D2**
Chadiza, *Zambia* **87 E3**
Chadron, *U.S.A.* **112 D3**
Chadyr-Lunga = Ciadâr-Lunga,
  Moldova **43 D13**
Chae Hom, *Thailand* **64 C2**
Chaem ➤, *Thailand* **64 C2**
Chaeryŏng, *N. Korea* **57 E13**
Chagai Hills = Chāh Gay,
  Afghan. **66 E3**
Chagda, *Russia* **51 D14**
Chagny, *France* **19 F11**
Chagoda, *Russia* **46 C8**
Chagos Arch., *Ind. Oc.* **52 K11**
Chagrin Falls, *U.S.A.* **110 E3**
Chāh Ākhvor, *Iran* **71 C8**
Chāh Bahar, *Iran* **71 E9**
Chāh-e Kavīr, *Iran* **71 C8**
Chāh Gay, *Afghan.* **66 E3**
Chahar Burjak, *Afghan.* **66 D3**
Chahār Mahāll va Bakhtīarī □,
  Iran **71 C6**
Chaibasa, *India* **67 H14**
Chaillé-les-Marais, *France* ... **20 B2**
Chainat, *Thailand* **64 E3**
Chaiya, *Thailand* **65 H2**
Chaj Doab, *Pakistan* **68 C5**
Chajari, *Argentina* **126 C4**
Chak Amru, *Pakistan* **68 C6**
Chaka, *Sudan* **81 G3**
Chakar ➤, *Pakistan* **68 E3**
Chakari, *Zimbabwe* **89 B4**
Chake Chake, *Tanzania* **86 D4**
Chakhānsūr, *Afghan.* **66 D3**
Chakonipau, L., *Canada* **103 A6**
Chakradharpur, *India* **69 H11**
Chakrata, *India* **68 D7**
Chakwal, *Pakistan* **68 C5**
Chala, *Peru* **124 G4**
Chalais, *France* **20 C4**

Chalchihuites, *Mexico* **118 C4**
Chalcis = Khalkís, *Greece* **38 C5**
Châlette-sur-Loing, *France* ... **19 D9**
Chaleur B., *Canada* **103 C6**
Chalfant, *U.S.A.* **116 H8**
Chalhuanca, *Peru* **124 F4**
Chalindrey, *France* **19 E12**
Chaling, *China* **59 D9**
Chalisgaon, *India* **66 J9**
Chalk River, *Canada* **102 C4**
Chalky Inlet, *N.Z.* **91 M1**
Challans, *France* **18 F5**
Challapata, *Bolivia* **124 G5**
Challis, *U.S.A.* **114 D6**
Chalmette, *U.S.A.* **113 L10**
Chalon-sur-Saône, *France* ... **19 F11**
Chalonnes-sur-Loire, *France* .. **18 E6**
Châlons-en-Champagne, *France* **19 D11**
Chälus, *France* **20 C4**
Chalyaphum, *Thailand* **64 E4**
Cham, *Germany* **25 F8**
Cham, Cu Lao, *Vietnam* **64 E7**
Chama, *U.S.A.* **115 H10**
Chamaicó, *Argentina* **126 D3**
Chaman, *Pakistan* **66 D5**
Chamba, *India* **68 C7**
Chamba, *Tanzania* **87 E4**
Chambal ➤, *India* **69 F8**
Chamberlain, *U.S.A.* **112 D5**
Chamberlain ➤, *Australia* ... **92 C4**
Chamberlain L., *U.S.A.* **109 B11**
Chambers, *U.S.A.* **115 J9**
Chambersburg, *U.S.A.* **108 F7**
Chambéry, *France* **21 C9**
Chambeshi ➤, *Zambia* **84 G6**
Chambly, *Canada* **111 A11**
Chambord, *Canada* **103 C5**
Chamboulive, *France* **20 C5**
Chamchamal, *Iraq* **70 C5**
Chamela, *Mexico* **118 D3**
Chamical, *Argentina* **126 C2**
Chamkar Luong, *Cambodia* ... **65 G4**
Chamoli, *India* **69 D8**
Chamonix-Mont Blanc, *France* **21 C10**
Chamouchouane ➤, *Canada* .. **102 C5**
Champa, *India* **69 H10**
Champagne, *Canada* **104 A1**
Champagne, *France* **19 D11**
Champagnole, *France* **19 F12**
Champaign, *U.S.A.* **108 E1**
Champassak, *Laos* **64 E5**
Champaubert, *France* **19 D10**
Champawat, *India* **69 E9**
Champdeniers-St-Denis, *France* **20 B3**
Champdoré, L., *Canada* **103 A6**
Champeix, *France* **20 C7**
Champion, *U.S.A.* **108 B4**
Champlain, *U.S.A.* **111 B11**
Champlain, L., *U.S.A.* **111 B11**
Champlitte, *France* **19 E12**
Champotón, *Mexico* **119 D6**
Champua, *India* **69 H11**
Chamusca, *Portugal* **35 F2**
Chana, *Thailand* **65 J3**
Chañaral, *Chile* **126 B1**
Chanārān, *Iran* **71 B8**
Chanasma, *India* **68 H5**
Chanco, *Chile* **126 D1**
Chand, *India* **69 J8**
Chandan, *India* **69 G12**
Chandan Chauki, *India* **69 E9**
Chandannagar, *India* **69 H13**
Chandausi, *India* **69 E8**
Chandeleur Is., *U.S.A.* **113 L10**
Chandeleur Sd., *U.S.A.* **113 L10**
Chandigarh, *India* **68 D7**
Chandil, *India* **69 H12**
Chandler, *Australia* **95 D1**
Chandler, *Canada* **103 C7**
Chandler, Ariz., *U.S.A.* **115 K8**
Chandler, Okla., *U.S.A.* **113 H6**
Chandod, *India* **68 J5**
Chandpur, *Bangla.* **67 H17**
Chandrapur, *India* **66 K11**
Chānf, *Iran* **71 E9**
Chang, *Pakistan* **68 F3**
Chang, Ko, *Thailand* **65 F4**
Ch'ang Chiang = Chang
  Jiang ➤, *China* **59 B13**
Chang Jiang ➤, *China* **59 B13**
Changa, *India* **69 C7**
Changanacheri, *India* **66 Q10**
Changane ➤, *Mozam.* **89 C5**
Changbai, *China* **57 D15**
Changbai Shan, *China* **57 D15**
Changchiak'ou = Zhangjiakou,
  China **56 D8**
Ch'angchou = Changzhou, *China* **59 B12**
Changchun, *China* **57 C13**
Changchunling, *China* **57 B13**
Changde, *China* **59 C8**
Changdo-ri, *N. Korea* **57 E14**
Changfeng, *China* **59 A11**
Changhai = Shanghai, *China* .. **59 B13**
Changhua, *China* **59 B12**
Changhua, *Taiwan* **59 E13**
Changhŭng, *S. Korea* **57 G14**
Changhŭngni, *N. Korea* **57 D15**
Changjiang, *China* **64 C7**
Changjin, *N. Korea* **57 D14**
Changjin-chŏsuji, *N. Korea* .. **57 D14**
Changle, *China* **59 E12**
Changli, *China* **57 E10**
Changling, *China* **57 B12**
Changlun, *Malaysia* **65 J3**
Changning, Hunan, *China* **59 D9**

Changning, Sichuan, *China* ... **58 C5**
Changning, Yunnan, *China* ... **58 E2**
Changping, *China* **56 D9**
Changsha, *China* **59 C9**
Changshan, *China* **59 C12**
Changshu, *China* **59 B13**
Changshun, *China* **58 D6**
Changtai, *China* **59 E11**
Changting, *China* **59 E11**
Changwu, *China* **56 G4**
Changxing, *China* **59 B12**
Changyang, *China* **59 B8**
Changyi, *China* **57 F10**
Changyŏn, *N. Korea* **57 E13**
Changyuan, *China* **56 G8**
Changzhi, *China* **56 F7**
Changzhou, *China* **59 B12**
Chanhanga, *Angola* **88 B1**
Channapatna, *India* **66 N10**
Channel Is., *U.K.* **13 H5**
Channel Is., *U.S.A.* **117 M7**
Channel Islands National Park,
  U.S.A. **117 M8**
Channel-Port aux Basques,
  Canada **103 C8**
Channel Tunnel, *Europe* **13 F9**
Channing, *U.S.A.* **113 H3**
Chantada, *Spain* **34 C3**
Chanthaburi, *Thailand* **64 F4**
Chantilly, *France* **19 C9**
Chantonnay, *France* **18 F5**
Chantrey Inlet, *Canada* **100 B10**
Chanute, *U.S.A.* **113 G7**
Chanza ➤, *Spain* **35 H3**
Chao Hu, *China* **59 B11**
Chao Phraya ➤, *Thailand* ... **64 F3**
Chao Phraya Lowlands,
  Thailand **64 E3**
Chaocheng, *China* **56 F8**
Chaohu, *China* **59 B11**
Chaoyang, Guangdong, *China* . **59 F11**
Chaoyang, Liaoning, *China* ... **57 D11**
Chaozhou, *China* **59 F11**
Chapais, *Canada* **102 C5**
Chapala, *Mozam.* **87 F4**
Chapala, L. de, *Mexico* **118 C4**
Chapayev, *Kazakstan* **48 E10**
Chapayevsk, *Russia* **48 D9**
Chapecó, *Brazil* **127 B5**
Chapel Hill, *U.S.A.* **109 H6**
Chapleau, *Canada* **102 C3**
Chaplin, *Canada* **105 C7**
Chaplin L., *Canada* **105 C7**
Chaplino, *Ukraine* **47 H9**
Chaplygin, *Russia* **46 F11**
Chappell, *U.S.A.* **112 E3**
Chapra = Chhapra, *India* **69 G11**
Chara, *Russia* **51 D12**
Charadai, *Argentina* **126 B4**
Charagua, *Bolivia* **124 G6**
Charambirá, Punta, *Colombia* . **124 C3**
Charaña, *Bolivia* **124 G5**
Charantsavan, *Armenia* **49 K7**
Charanwala, *India* **68 F5**
Charata, *Argentina* **126 B3**
Charcas, *Mexico* **118 C4**
Chard, *U.K.* **13 G5**
Chardon, *U.S.A.* **110 E3**
Chardzhou = Chärjew,
  Turkmenistan **50 F7**
Charente □, *France* **20 C4**
Charente ➤, *France* **20 C2**
Charente-Maritime □, *France* . **20 C3**
Charenton-du-Cher, *France* ... **19 F9**
Chari ➤, *Chad* **79 F8**
Chārīkār, *Afghan.* **66 B6**
Chariton ➤, *U.S.A.* **112 F8**
Chärjew, *Turkmenistan* **50 F7**
Charkhari, *India* **69 G8**
Charkhi Dadri, *India* **68 E7**
Charleroi, *Belgium* **17 D4**
Charleroi, *U.S.A.* **110 F5**
Charles, C., *U.S.A.* **108 G8**
Charles City, *U.S.A.* **112 D8**
Charles L., *Canada* **105 B6**
Charles Town, *U.S.A.* **108 F7**
Charleston, Ill., *U.S.A.* **108 F1**
Charleston, Miss., *U.S.A.* ... **113 H9**
Charleston, Mo., *U.S.A.* **113 G10**
Charleston, S.C., *U.S.A.* **109 J6**
Charleston, W. Va., *U.S.A.* .. **108 F5**
Charleston L., *Canada* **111 B9**
Charleston Peak, *U.S.A.* **117 J11**
Charlestown, *Ireland* **15 C3**
Charlestown, *S. Africa* **89 D4**
Charlestown, Ind., *U.S.A.* ... **108 F3**
Charlestown, N.H., *U.S.A.* .. **111 C12**
Charleville = Rath Luirc, *Ireland* **15 D3**
Charleville, *Australia* **95 D4**
Charleville-Mézières, *France* .. **19 C11**
Charlevoix, *U.S.A.* **108 C3**
Charlieu, *France* **19 F10**
Charlotte, Mich., *U.S.A.* **108 D3**
Charlotte, N.C., *U.S.A.* **109 H5**
Charlotte, Vt., *U.S.A.* **111 B11**
Charlotte Amalie, *U.S. Virgin Is.* **121 C7**
Charlotte Harbor, *U.S.A.* ... **109 M4**
Charlotte L., *Canada* **104 C3**
Charlottenberg, *Sweden* **10 E6**
Charlottesville, *U.S.A.* **108 F6**
Charlottetown, Nfld., *Canada* . **103 B8**
Charlottetown, P.E.I., *Canada* **103 C7**
Charlton, *U.S.A.* **112 E8**
Charlton I., *Canada* **102 B4**
Charmes, *France* **19 D13**

Charny, *Canada* **103 C5**
Charolles, *France* **19 F11**
Chârost, *France* **19 F9**
Charre, *Mozam.* **87 F4**
Charroux, *France* **20 B4**
Charsadda, *Pakistan* **68 B4**
Charters Towers, *Australia* ... **94 C4**
Chartres, *France* **18 D8**
Chascomús, *Argentina* **126 D4**
Chasefu, *Zambia* **87 E3**
Chashma Barrage, *Pakistan* .. **68 C4**
Chasseneuil-sur-Bonnieure,
  France **20 C4**
Chât, *Iran* **71 B7**
Chatal Balkan = Udvoy Balkan,
  Bulgaria **41 D10**
Château-Arnoux, *France* **21 D10**
Château-Chinon, *France* **19 E10**
Château-d'Olonne, *France* ... **20 B2**
Château-du-Loir, *France* **18 E7**
Château-Gontier, *France* **18 E6**
Château-la-Vallière, *France* .. **18 E7**
Château-Landon, *France* **19 D9**
Château-Renault, *France* **18 E7**
Château-Salins, *France* **19 D13**
Château-Thierry, *France* **19 C10**
Châteaubourg, *France* **18 D5**
Châteaubriant, *France* **18 E5**
Châteaudun, *France* **18 D8**
Châteaugay, *U.S.A.* **111 B10**
Châteaugiron, *France* **18 D5**
Châteauguay, L., *Canada* **103 A5**
Châteaulin, *France* **18 D2**
Châteaumeillant, *France* **19 F9**
Châteauneuf-du-Faou, *France* . **18 D3**
Châteauneuf-sur-Charente,
  France **20 C3**
Châteauneuf-sur-Cher, *France* **19 F9**
Châteauneuf-sur-Loire, *France* **19 E9**
Châteaurenard,
  Bouches-du-Rhône, *France* .. **21 E8**
Châteaurenard, Loiret, *France* **19 E9**
Châteauroux, *France* **19 F8**
Châteauvillain, *France* **19 D11**
Châtelaillon-Plage, *France* ... **20 B2**
Châtelguyon, *France* **20 C7**
Châtellerault, *France* **18 F7**
Châtelus-Malvaleix, *France* ... **19 F9**
Chatham = Miramichi, *Canada* **103 C6**
Chatham, *U.K.* **13 F8**
Chatham, *U.S.A.* **111 D11**
Chatham Is., *Pac. Oc.* **96 M10**
Châtillon, *Italy* **28 C4**
Châtillon-Coligny, *France* **19 E9**
Châtillon-en-Diois, *France* ... **21 D9**
Châtillon-sur-Indre, *France* .. **18 F8**
Châtillon-sur-Loire, *France* .. **19 E9**
Châtillon-sur-Seine, *France* .. **19 E11**
Chatmohar, *Bangla.* **69 G13**
Chatra, *India* **69 G11**
Chatrapur, *India* **67 K14**
Chats, L. des, *Canada* **111 A8**
Chatsu, *India* **68 F6**
Chatsworth, *Canada* **110 B4**
Chatsworth, *Zimbabwe* **87 F3**
Chattahoochee, *U.S.A.* **109 K3**
Chattahoochee ➤, *U.S.A.* ... **109 K3**
Chattanooga, *U.S.A.* **109 H3**
Chatteris, *U.K.* **13 E8**
Chaturat, *Thailand* **64 E3**
Chau Doc, *Vietnam* **65 G5**
Chaudes-Aigues, *France* **20 D7**
Chauffailles, *France* **19 F11**
Chaukan Pass, *Burma* **67 F20**
Chaumont, *France* **19 D12**
Chaumont, *U.S.A.* **111 B8**
Chaumont-en-Vexin, *France* .. **19 C8**
Chaumont-sur-Loire, *France* .. **18 E8**
Chaunay, *France* **20 B4**
Chauny, *France* **19 C10**
Chausey, Îs., *France* **18 D5**
Chaussin, *France* **19 F12**
Chautauqua L., *U.S.A.* **110 D5**
Chauvigny, *France* **18 F7**
Chauvin, *Canada* **105 C6**
Chavanges, *France* **19 D11**
Chaves, *Brazil* **125 D9**
Chaves, *Portugal* **34 D3**
Chawang, *Thailand* **65 H2**
Chazelles-sur-Lyon, *France* ... **21 C8**
Chazy, *U.S.A.* **111 B11**
Cheb, *Czech Rep.* **26 A5**
Cheboksarskoye Vdkhr., *Russia* **48 B8**
Cheboksary, *Russia* **48 B8**
Cheboygan, *U.S.A.* **108 C3**
Chebsara, *Russia* **46 C10**
Chech, Erg, *Africa* **78 D5**
Chechen, Ostrov, *Russia* **49 H8**
Chechenia □, *Russia* **49 J7**
Checheno-Ingush Republic =
  Chechenia □, *Russia* **49 J7**
Chechnya = Chechenia □,
  Russia **49 J7**
Chech'ŏn, S. Korea* **57 F15**
Chęciny, *Poland* **45 H7**
Checotah, *U.S.A.* **113 H7**
Chedabucto B., *Canada* **103 C7**
Cheduba I., *Burma* **67 K18**
Cheepie, *Australia* **95 D4**
Chef-Boutonne, *France* **20 B3**
Chegdomyn, *Russia* **51 D14**
Chegga, *Mauritania* **78 C4**
Chegutu, *Zimbabwe* **87 F3**
Chehalis, *U.S.A.* **116 D4**
Chehalis ➤, *U.S.A.* **116 D3**

Cheiron, Mt., *France* **21 E10**
Cheju do, *S. Korea* **57 H14**
Chekalin, *Russia* **46 E9**
Chekiang = Zhejiang □, *China* . **59 C13**
Chel = Kuru, Bahr el ➤, *Sudan* **81 F2**
Chela, Sa. da, *Angola* **88 B1**
Chelan, *U.S.A.* **114 C4**
Chelan, L., *U.S.A.* **114 B3**
Cheleken, *Turkmenistan* **50 F6**
Cheleken Yarymadasy,
  Turkmenistan **71 B7**
Chelforó, *Argentina* **128 D3**
Chelkar = Shalqar, *Kazakstan* . **50 E6**
Chelkar Tengiz, Solonchak,
  Kazakstan **50 E7**
Chella, *Ethiopia* **81 F4**
Chelles, *France* **19 D9**
Chełm, *Poland* **45 G10**
Chełmno, *Poland* **45 E5**
Chelmsford, *U.K.* **13 F8**
Chełmza, *Poland* **45 E5**
Chelsea, *U.S.A.* **111 C12**
Cheltenham, *U.K.* **13 F5**
Chelva, *Spain* **32 F4**
Chelyabinsk, *Russia* **50 D7**
Chelyuskin, C., *Russia* **52 B14**
Chemainus, *Canada* **116 B3**
Chemba, *Mozam.* **85 H6**
Chembar = Belinskiy, *Russia* . **48 D6**
Chemillé, *France* **18 E6**
Chemnitz, *Germany* **24 E8**
Chemult, *U.S.A.* **114 E3**
Chen, Gora, *Russia* **51 C15**
Chenab ➤, *Pakistan* **68 D4**
Chenango Forks, *U.S.A.* **111 D9**
Chencha, *Ethiopia* **81 F4**
Chenchiang = Zhenjiang, *China* **59 A12**
Cheney, *U.S.A.* **114 C5**
Chengbu, *China* **59 D8**
Chengcheng, *China* **56 G5**
Chengchou = Zhengzhou, *China* **56 G7**
Chengde, *China* **57 D9**
Chengdong Hu, *China* **59 A11**
Chengdu, *China* **58 B5**
Chenggong, *China* **58 E4**
Chenggu, *China* **56 H4**
Chenghai, *China* **59 F11**
Chengjiang, *China* **58 E4**
Chengkou, *China* **58 B7**
Ch'engmai, *China* **64 C7**
Ch'engtu = Chengdu, *China* .. **58 B5**
Chengwu, *China* **56 G8**
Chengxi Hu, *China* **59 A11**
Chengyang, *China* **57 F11**
Chenjiagang, *China* **57 G10**
Chenôve, *France* **19 E12**
Chenxi, *China* **59 C8**
Chenzhou, *China* **59 E9**
Cheo Reo, *Vietnam* **62 B3**
Cheom Ksan, *Cambodia* **64 E5**
Chepelare, *Bulgaria* **41 E8**
Chepén, *Peru* **124 E3**
Chepes, *Argentina* **126 C2**
Chepo, *Panama* **120 E4**
Chepstow, *U.K.* **13 F5**
Cheptulil, Mt., *Kenya* **86 B4**
Chequamegon B., *U.S.A.* **112 B9**
Cher □, *France* **19 E9**
Cher ➤, *France* **18 E7**
Chérади, *Italy* **31 B9**
Cherasco, *Italy* **28 D4**
Cheraw, *U.S.A.* **109 H6**
Cherbourg, *France* **18 C5**
Cherdakly, *Russia* **48 C9**
Cherdyn, *Russia* **50 C6**
Cheremkhovo, *Russia* **51 D11**
Cherepanovo, *Russia* **50 D9**
Cherepovets, *Russia* **46 C9**
Chergui, Chott ech, *Algeria* .. **78 B6**
Cherikov = Cherykaw, *Belarus* **46 F6**
Cherkasy, *Ukraine* **47 H7**
Cherkessk, *Russia* **49 H6**
Cherlak, *Russia* **50 D8**
Chernaya, *Russia* **51 B9**
Cherni, *Bulgaria* **40 D7**
Chernigov = Chernihiv, *Ukraine* **47 G6**
Chernihiv, *Ukraine* **47 G6**
Chernivtsi, *Ukraine* **47 H3**
Chernobyl = Chornobyl, *Ukraine* **47 G6**
Chernogorsk, *Russia* **51 D10**
Chernomorskoye =
  Chornomorske, *Ukraine* **47 K7**
Chernovtsy = Chernivtsi,
  Ukraine **47 H3**
Chernyakhovsk, *Russia* **9 J19**
Chernyanka, *Russia* **47 G9**
Chernysheyskiy, *Russia* **51 C12**
Chernyye Zemli, *Russia* **49 H8**
Cherokee, Iowa, *U.S.A.* **112 D7**
Cherokee, Okla., *U.S.A.* **113 G5**
Cherokee Village, *U.S.A.* **113 G9**
Cherokees, Grand Lake O' The,
  U.S.A. **113 G7**
Cherrapunji, *India* **67 G17**
Cherry Valley, Calif., *U.S.A.* . **117 M10**
Cherry Valley, N.Y., *U.S.A.* .. **111 D9**
Cherskiy, *Russia* **51 C17**
Cherskogo Khrebet, *Russia* .. **51 C15**
Chertkovo, *Russia* **47 H11**
Cherven, *Belarus* **46 F5**
Cherven-Bryag, *Bulgaria* **40 D7**
Chervonohrad, *Ukraine* **47 G3**
Cherwell ➤, *U.K.* **13 F6**

Cherykaw, Belarus 46 F6
Chesapeake, U.S.A. 108 G7
Chesapeake B., U.S.A. 108 G7
Cheshire □, U.K. 12 D5
Cheshskaya Guba, Russia 50 C5
Cheshunt, U.K. 13 F7
Chesil Beach, U.K. 13 G5
Chesley, Canada 110 B3
Cheste, Spain 33 F4
Chester, U.K. 12 D5
Chester, Calif., U.S.A. 114 F3
Chester, Ill., U.S.A. 113 G10
Chester, Mont., U.S.A. 114 B8
Chester, Pa., U.S.A. 108 F8
Chester, S.C., U.S.A. 109 H5
Chester, Vt., U.S.A. 111 C12
Chester, W. Va., U.S.A. 110 F4
Chester-le-Street, U.K. 12 C6
Chesterfield, Is., N. Cal. ... 96 J7
Chesterfield, U.K. 12 D6
Chesterfield Inlet, Canada 100 B10
Chesterton Ra., Australia 95 D4
Chestertown, U.S.A. 111 C11
Chesterville, Canada 111 A9
Chestnut Ridge, U.S.A. 110 F5
Chesuncook L., U.S.A. 109 C11
Chéticamp, Canada 103 C7
Chetrosu, Moldova 43 B12
Chetumal, Mexico 119 D7
Chetumal, B. de, Mexico 119 D7
Chetwynd, Canada 104 B4
Chevanceaux, France 20 C3
Cheviot, The, U.K. 12 B5
Cheviot Hills, U.K. 12 B5
Cheviot Ra., Australia 94 D3
Chew Bahir, Ethiopia 81 G4
Chewelah, U.S.A. 114 B5
Cheyenne, Okla., U.S.A. 113 H5
Cheyenne, Wyo., U.S.A. 112 E2
Cheyenne ➤, U.S.A. 112 C4
Cheyenne Wells, U.S.A. 112 F3
Cheyne B., Australia 93 F2
Chhabra, India 68 G7
Chhaktala, India 68 H6
Chhapra, India 69 G11
Chhata, India 68 F7
Chhatarpur, Bihar, India 69 G11
Chhatarpur, Mad. P., India ... 69 G8
Chhattisgarh □, India 69 J10
Chhep, Cambodia 64 F5
Chhindwara, Mad. P., India ... 69 H8
Chhindwara, Mad. P., India ... 69 H8
Chhlong, Cambodia 65 F5
Chhota Tawa ➤, India 68 H7
Chhoti Kali Sindh ➤, India ... 68 G6
Chhuikhadan, India 69 J9
Chhuk, Cambodia 65 G5
Chi ➤, Thailand 64 E5
Chiai, Taiwan 59 F13
Chiali, Taiwan 59 F13
Chiamboni, Somali Rep. 84 E8
Chiamussu = Jiamusi, China ... 60 B8
Chiang Dao, Thailand 64 C2
Chiang Kham, Thailand 64 C3
Chiang Khan, Thailand 64 D3
Chiang Khong, Thailand 58 G3
Chiang Mai, Thailand 64 C2
Chiang Rai, Thailand 58 H2
Chiang Saen, Thailand 58 G3
Chiapa ➤, Mexico 119 D6
Chiapa de Corzo, Mexico 119 D6
Chiapas □, Mexico 119 D6
Chiaramonte Gulfi, Italy 31 E7
Chiaravalle, Italy 29 E10
Chiaravalle Centrale, Italy ... 31 D9
Chiari, Italy 28 C6
Chiatura, Georgia 49 J6
Chiautla, Mexico 119 D5
Chiávari, Italy 28 D6
Chiavenna, Italy 28 B6
Chiba, Japan 55 G10
Chiba □, Japan 55 G10
Chibabava, Mozam. 89 C5
Chibemba, Cunene, Angola ... 85 H2
Chibemba, Huila, Angola 88 B2
Chibi, Zimbabwe 89 C5
Chibia, Angola 85 H2
Chibougamau, Canada 102 C5
Chibougamau, L., Canada 102 C5
Chibuk, Nigeria 83 C7
Chibuto, Mozam. 89 C5
Chic-Chocs, Mts., Canada 103 C6
Chicacole = Srikakulam, India . 67 K13
Chicago, U.S.A. 108 E2
Chicago Heights, U.S.A. 108 E2
Chichagof I., U.S.A. 100 C6
Chichén-Itzá, Mexico 119 C7
Chicheng, China 56 D8
Chichester, U.K. 13 G7
Chichester Ra., Australia 92 D2
Chichibu, Japan 55 F9
Ch'ich'iharh = Qiqihar, China . 51 E13
Chicholi, India 68 H8
Chickasha, U.S.A. 113 H6
Chiclana de la Frontera, Spain . 35 J4
Chiclayo, Peru 124 E3
Chico, U.S.A. 116 F5
Chico ➤, Chubut, Argentina . 128 E3
Chico ➤, Santa Cruz, Argentina 128 G3
Chicomo, Mozam. 89 C5
Chicontepec, Mexico 119 C5
Chicopee, U.S.A. 111 D12
Chicoutimi, Canada 103 C5
Chicualacuala, Mozam. 89 C5
Chidambaram, India 66 P11

Chidenguele, Mozam. 89 C5
Chidley, C., Canada 101 B13
Chiducuane, Mozam. 89 C5
Chiede, Angola 88 B2
Chiefs Pt., Canada 110 B3
Chiem Hoa, Vietnam 64 A5
Chiemsee, Germany 25 H8
Chiengi, Zambia 87 D2
Chiengmai = Chiang Mai,
  Thailand 64 C2
Chienti ➤, Italy 29 E10
Chieri, Italy 28 C4
Chiers ➤, France 19 C11
Chiesa in Valmalenco, Italy .. 28 B6
Chiese ➤, Italy 28 C7
Chieti, Italy 29 F11
Chifeng, China 57 C10
Chigirin, Ukraine 47 H7
Chignecto B., Canada 103 C7
Chiguana, Bolivia 126 A2
Chigwell, U.K. 13 F8
Chiha-ri, N. Korea 57 E14
Chihli, G. of = Bo Hai, China . 57 E10
Chihuahua, Mexico 118 B3
Chihuahua □, Mexico 118 B3
Chiili = Shieli, Kazakstan 50 E7
Chik Bollapur, India 66 N10
Chikmagalur, India 66 N9
Chikwawa, Malawi 87 F3
Chilac, Mexico 119 D5
Chilanga, Zambia 87 F2
Chilapa, Mexico 119 D5
Chilas, Pakistan 69 B6
Chilaw, Sri Lanka 66 R11
Chilcotin ➤, Canada 104 C4
Childers, Australia 95 D5
Childress, U.S.A. 113 H4
Chile ■, S. Amer. 128 D2
Chile Rise, Pac. Oc. 97 L18
Chilecito, Argentina 126 B2
Chilete, Peru 124 E3
Chilia, Braţul ➤, Romania ... 43 E14
Chililabombwe, Zambia 87 E2
Chilin = Jilin, China 57 C14
Chilka L., India 67 K14
Chilko ➤, Canada 104 C4
Chilko L., Canada 104 C4
Chillagoe, Australia 94 B3
Chillán, Chile 126 D1
Chillicothe, Ill., U.S.A. 112 E10
Chillicothe, Mo., U.S.A. 112 F8
Chillicothe, Ohio, U.S.A. 108 F4
Chilliwack, Canada 104 D4
Chilo, Italy 68 F5
Chiloane, I., Mozam. 89 C5
Chiloé, I. de, Chile 122 H3
Chilpancingo, Mexico 119 D5
Chiltern Hills, U.K. 13 F7
Chilton, U.S.A. 108 C1
Chilubi, Zambia 87 E2
Chilubula, Zambia 87 E3
Chilumba, Malawi 87 E3
Chilung, Taiwan 59 E13
Chilwa, L., Malawi 87 F4
Chimaltitán, Mexico 118 C4
Chimán, Panama 120 E4
Chimanimani, Zimbabwe 89 B5
Chimay, Belgium 17 D4
Chimayo, U.S.A. 115 H11
Chimbay, Uzbekistan 50 E6
Chimborazo, Ecuador 122 D3
Chimbote, Peru 124 E3
Chimkent = Shymkent,
  Kazakstan 50 E7
Chimoio, Mozam. 87 F3
Chimpembe, Zambia 87 D2
Chin □, Burma 67 J18
Chin Ling Shan = Qinling
  Shandi, China 56 H5
China, Mexico 119 B5
China ■, Asia 60 D6
China Lake, U.S.A. 117 K9
Chinan = Jinan, China 56 F9
Chinandega, Nic. 120 D2
Chinati Peak, U.S.A. 113 L2
Chincha Alta, Peru 122 E3
Chinchaga ➤, Canada 104 B5
Chinchilla, Australia 95 D5
Chinchilla de Monte Aragón,
  Spain 33 G3
Chinchorro, Banco, Mexico ... 119 D7
Chinchou = Jinzhou, China ... 57 D11
Chincoteague, U.S.A. 108 G8
Chinde, Mozam. 87 F4
Chindo, S. Korea 57 G14
Chindwin ➤, Burma 67 J19
Chineni, India 69 C6
Chinga, Mozam. 87 F4
Chingola, Zambia 87 E2
Chingole, Malawi 87 E3
Ch'ingtao = Qingdao, China .. 57 F11
Chinguetti, Mauritania 78 D3
Chingune, Mozam. 89 C5
Chinhae, S. Korea 57 G15
Chinhanguanine, Mozam. 89 D5
Chinhoyi, Zimbabwe 87 F3
Chini, India 68 D8
Chiniot, Pakistan 68 D5
Chínipas, Mexico 118 B3
Chinji, Pakistan 68 C5
Chinju, S. Korea 57 G15
Chinle, U.S.A. 115 H9
Chinmen, Taiwan 59 E13
Chinmen Tao, Taiwan 59 E12
Chinnampo = Namp'o, N. Korea 57 E13

Chino, Japan 55 G9
Chino, U.S.A. 117 L9
Chino Valley, U.S.A. 115 J7
Chinon, France 18 E7
Chinook, U.S.A. 114 B9
Chinsali, Zambia 87 E3
Chióggia, Italy 29 C9
Chíos = Khíos, Greece 39 C8
Chipata, Zambia 87 E3
Chiperceni, Moldova 43 C13
Chipinge, Zimbabwe 87 G3
Chipiona, Spain 35 J4
Chipley, U.S.A. 109 K3
Chipman, Canada 103 C6
Chipoka, Malawi 87 E3
Chippenham, U.K. 13 F5
Chippewa ➤, U.S.A. 112 C8
Chippewa Falls, U.S.A. 112 C9
Chipping Norton, U.K. 13 F6
Chiprovtsi, Bulgaria 40 C6
Chiputneticook Lakes, U.S.A. . 109 C11
Chiquián, Peru 124 F3
Chiquimula, Guatemala 120 D2
Chiquinquira, Colombia 124 B4
Chir ➤, Russia 49 F6
Chirala, India 66 M12
Chiramba, Mozam. 87 F3
Chirawa, India 68 E6
Chirchiq, Uzbekistan 50 E7
Chiredzi, Zimbabwe 89 C5
Chiricahua Peak, U.S.A. 115 L9
Chiriquí, G. de, Panama 120 E3
Chiriquí, L. de, Panama 120 E3
Chirivira Falls, Zimbabwe 87 G3
Chirmiri, India 67 H13
Chirnogi, Romania 43 F11
Chirpan, Bulgaria 41 D9
Chirripó Grande, Cerro,
  Costa Rica 120 E3
Chirundu, Zimbabwe 89 B4
Chisamba, Zambia 87 E2
Chisapani Garhi, Nepal 67 F14
Chisasibi, Canada 102 B4
Ch'ishan, Taiwan 59 F13
Chisholm, Canada 104 C6
Chisholm, U.S.A. 112 B8
Chishtian Mandi, Pakistan ... 68 E5
Chishui, China 58 C5
Chishui He ➤, China 58 C5
Chisimaio, Somali Rep. 77 G8
Chisimba Falls, Zambia 87 E3
Chişinău, Moldova 43 C13
Chişineu Criş, Romania 42 D6
Chisone ➤, Italy 28 D4
Chisos Mts., U.S.A. 113 L3
Chistopol, Russia 48 C10
Chita, Russia 51 D12
Chitipa, Malawi 87 D3
Chitose, Japan 54 C10
Chitral, Pakistan 66 B7
Chitré, Panama 120 E3
Chittagong, Bangla. 67 H17
Chittagong □, Bangla. 67 G17
Chittaurgarh, India 68 G6
Chittoor, India 66 N11
Chitungwiza, Zimbabwe 87 F3
Chiusi, Italy 29 E8
Chiva, Spain 33 F4
Chivasso, Italy 28 C4
Chivhu, Zimbabwe 87 F3
Chivilcoy, Argentina 126 C4
Chiwanda, Tanzania 87 E3
Chixi, China 59 G9
Chizera, Zambia 87 E2
Chkalov = Orenburg, Russia .. 50 D6
Chkolovsk, Russia 48 B6
Chloride, U.S.A. 117 K12
Chlumec nad Cidlinou,
  Czech Rep. 26 A8
Chmielnik, Poland 45 H7
Cho Bo, Vietnam 58 G5
Cho-do, N. Korea 57 E13
Cho Phuoc Hai, Vietnam 65 G6
Choba, Kenya 86 B4
Chobe National Park, Botswana 88 B4
Choch'iwŏn, S. Korea 57 F14
Chocianów, Poland 45 G2
Chociwel, Poland 44 E2
Chocolate Mts., U.S.A. 117 M11
Choctawhatchee ➤, U.S.A. .. 109 K3
Chodecz, Poland 45 F6
Chodov, Czech Rep. 26 A5
Chodziez, Poland 45 F3
Choele Choel, Argentina 128 D3
Choix, Mexico 118 B3
Chojna, Poland 45 F1
Chojnice, Poland 44 E4
Chojnów, Poland 45 G2
Chŏkai-San, Japan 54 E10
Choke, Ethiopia 81 E4
Choke Canyon L., U.S.A. 113 L5
Chokurdakh, Russia 51 B15
Cholame, U.S.A. 116 K6
Cholet, France 18 E6
Cholguan, Chile 126 D1
Choluteca, Honduras 120 D2
Choluteca ➤, Honduras 120 D2
Chom Bung, Thailand 64 F2
Chom Thong, Thailand 64 C2
Choma, Zambia 87 F2
Chomen Swamp, Ethiopia 81 F4
Chomun, India 68 F6
Chomutov, Czech Rep. 26 A6
Chon Buri, Thailand 64 F3
Chon Thanh, Vietnam 65 G6
Ch'onan, S. Korea 57 F14

Chone, Ecuador 124 D3
Chong Kai, Cambodia 64 F4
Chong Mek, Thailand 64 E5
Chongde, China 59 B13
Chŏngdo, S. Korea 57 G15
Chŏngha, S. Korea 57 F15
Chŏngjin, N. Korea 57 D15
Chŏngju, N. Korea 57 E13
Chongli, China 56 D8
Chongming, China 59 B13
Chongming Dao, China 59 B13
Chongqing, Chongqing, China . 58 C6
Chongqing, Sichuan, China ... 58 B4
Chongqing Shi □, China 58 C5
Chongren, China 59 D11
Chonguene, Mozam. 89 C5
Chŏngŭp, S. Korea 57 G14
Chongyi, China 59 E10
Chongzuo, China 58 F6
Chŏnju, S. Korea 57 G14
Chonos, Arch. de los, Chile ... 122 H3
Chop, Ukraine 47 H2
Chopim ➤, Brazil 127 B5
Chor, Pakistan 68 G3
Chorbat La, India 69 B7
Chorley, U.K. 12 D5
Chornobyl, Ukraine 47 G6
Chornomorske, Ukraine 47 K7
Chorolque, Cerro, Bolivia 126 A2
Chorregon, Australia 94 C3
Chortkiv, Ukraine 47 H3
Chorwŏn, S. Korea 57 E14
Chorzele, Poland 45 E7
Chorzów, Poland 45 H5
Chos-Malal, Argentina 126 D1
Choszczno, Poland 45 E2
Choteau, U.S.A. 114 C7
Chotěboř, Czech Rep. 26 B8
Chotila, India 68 H4
Chotta Udepur, India 68 H6
Chowchilla, U.S.A. 116 H6
Choybalsan, Mongolia 60 B6
Christchurch, N.Z. 91 K4
Christchurch, U.K. 13 G6
Christian I., Canada 110 B4
Christiana, S. Africa 88 D4
Christiansfeld, Denmark 11 J3
Christiansted, U.S. Virgin Is. . 121 C7
Christie B., Canada 105 A6
Christina ➤, Canada 105 B6
Christmas Cr. ➤, Australia .. 92 C4
Christmas I. = Kiritimati,
  Kiribati 97 G12
Christmas I., Ind. Oc. 96 J2
Christopher L., Australia 93 D4
Chrudim, Czech Rep. 26 B8
Chrzanów, Poland 45 H6
Chtimba, Malawi 87 E3
Chu = Shū, Kazakstan 50 E8
Chu ➤, Vietnam 64 C5
Chu Lai, Vietnam 64 E7
Ch'uanchou = Quanzhou, China 59 E12
Chuankou, China 56 G6
Chubbuck, U.S.A. 114 E7
Chūbu □, Japan 55 F8
Chubut ➤, Argentina 122 H4
Chuchi L., Canada 104 B4
Chuda, India 68 H4
Chudovo, Russia 46 C6
Chudskoye, Ozero, Russia 9 G22
Chūgoku □, Japan 55 G6
Chūgoku-Sanchi, Japan 55 G6
Chuguyev = Chuhuyiv, Ukraine 47 H9
Chugwater, U.S.A. 112 E2
Chuhuyiv, Ukraine 47 H9
Chukchi Sea, Russia 51 C19
Chukotskoye Nagorye, Russia . 51 C18
Chula Vista, U.S.A. 117 N9
Chulucanas, Peru 124 E2
Chulym ➤, Russia 50 D9
Chum Phae, Thailand 64 D4
Chum Saeng, Thailand 64 E3
Chumar, India 69 C8
Chumbicha, Argentina 126 B2
Chumerna, Bulgaria 41 D9
Chumikan, Russia 51 D14
Chumphon, Thailand 65 G2
Chumuare, Mozam. 87 E3
Chumunjin, S. Korea 57 F15
Chuna ➤, Russia 51 D10
Chun'an, China 59 C12
Chunchura, India 69 H13
Chunga, Zambia 87 F2
Chunggang-ŭp, N. Korea 57 D14
Chunghwa, N. Korea 57 E13
Ch'ungju, S. Korea 57 F14
Chungking = Chongqing, China 58 C6
Chungli, Taiwan 59 E13
Ch'ungmu, S. Korea 57 G15
Chungt'iaoshan = Zhongtiao
  Shan, China 56 G6
Chungyang Shanmo, Taiwan .. 59 F13
Chunian, Pakistan 68 D6
Chunya, Tanzania 87 D3
Chunyang, China 57 C15
Chuquibamba, Peru 124 G4
Chuquicamata, Chile 126 A2
Chur, Switz. 25 J5
Churachandpur, India 67 G18
Churchill, Canada 105 B10
Churchill ➤, Man., Canada .. 105 B10
Churchill ➤, Nfld., Canada .. 103 B7

Churchill, C., Canada 105 B10
Churchill Falls, Canada 103 B7
Churchill L., Canada 105 B7
Churchill Pk., Canada 104 B3
Churki, India 69 H10
Churu, India 68 E6
Churún Merú = Angel Falls,
  Venezuela 124 B6
Chushal, India 69 C8
Chuska Mts., U.S.A. 115 H9
Chusovoy, Russia 50 D6
Chute-aux-Outardes, Canada . 103 C6
Chuuronjang, N. Korea 57 D15
Chuvash Republic =
  Chuvashia □, Russia 48 C8
Chuvashia □, Russia 48 C8
Chuwārtah, Iraq 70 C5
Chuxiong, China 58 E3
Chüy = Shū ➤, Kazakstan ... 52 E10
Chuy, Uruguay 127 C5
Chuzhou, China 59 A12
Ci Xian, China 56 F8
Ciacova, Romania 42 E6
Ciadâr-Lunga, Moldova 43 D13
Ciamis, Indonesia 63 G13
Cianjur, Indonesia 63 G12
Cianorte, Brazil 127 A5
Cibola, U.S.A. 117 M12
Cicero, U.S.A. 108 E2
Cidacos ➤, Spain 32 C3
Cide, Turkey 72 B5
Ciechanów, Poland 45 F7
Ciechanowiec, Poland 45 F9
Ciechocinek, Poland 45 F5
Ciego de Avila, Cuba 120 B4
Ciénaga, Colombia 124 A4
Cienfuegos, Cuba 120 B3
Cierp, France 20 F4
Cíes, Is., Spain 34 C2
Cieszanów, Poland 45 H10
Cieszyn, Poland 45 J5
Cieza, Spain 33 G3
Çifteler, Turkey 72 C5
Cifuentes, Spain 32 E2
Cihanbeyli, Turkey 72 C5
Cihuatlán, Mexico 118 D4
Cijara, Embalse de, Spain 35 F6
Cijulang, Indonesia 63 G13
Cilacap, Indonesia 63 G13
Çıldır, Turkey 73 B10
Çıldır Gölü, Turkey 73 B10
Cili, China 59 C8
Cilibia, Romania 43 E12
Cilicia, Turkey 72 D5
Cill Chainnigh = Kilkenny,
  Ireland 15 D4
Cilo Dağı, Turkey 73 D10
Cima, U.S.A. 117 K11
Cimarron, Kans., U.S.A. 113 G4
Cimarron, N. Mex., U.S.A. ... 113 G2
Cimarron ➤, U.S.A. 113 G6
Cimişlia, Moldova 43 D13
Cimone, Mte., Italy 28 D7
Çınar, Turkey 73 D9
Çınarcık, Turkey 41 F13
Cinca ➤, Spain 32 D5
Cincar, Bos.-H. 42 G2
Cincinnati, U.S.A. 108 F3
Cincinnatus, U.S.A. 111 D9
Çine, Turkey 39 D10
Ciney, Belgium 17 D5
Cíngoli, Italy 29 E10
Cinigiano, Italy 29 F8
Cinto, Mte., France 21 F12
Cintruénigo, Spain 32 C3
Ciocile, Romania 43 F12
Ciolăneşti din Deal, Romania . 43 F10
Ciorani, Romania 43 F11
Čiovo, Croatia 29 E13
Circeo, Mte., Italy 30 A6
Çırçır, Turkey 72 C7
Circle, Alaska, U.S.A. 100 B5
Circle, Mont., U.S.A. 112 B2
Circleville, U.S.A. 108 F4
Cirebon, Indonesia 62 F3
Ciremai, Indonesia 63 G13
Cirencester, U.K. 13 F6
Cireşu, Romania 42 F7
Cirey-sur-Vezouze, France ... 19 D13
Ciriè, Italy 28 C4
Cirium, Cyprus 36 E11
Cirò, Italy 31 C10
Cirò Marina, Italy 31 C10
Ciron ➤, France 20 D3
Cisco, U.S.A. 113 J5
Cişlău, Romania 43 E11
Cisna, Poland 45 J9
Cisnădie, Romania 43 E9
Cisterna di Latina, Italy 30 A5
Cisternino, Italy 31 B10
Cistierna, Spain 34 C5
Citeli-Ckaro = Tsiteli-Tsqaro,
  Georgia 49 K8
Citlaltépetl, Mexico 119 D5
Citrus Heights, U.S.A. 116 G5
Citrusdal, S. Africa 88 E2
Città della Pieve, Italy 29 F9
Città di Castello, Italy 29 E9
Città Sant' Angelo, Italy 29 F11
Cittadella, Italy 29 C8
Cittaducale, Italy 29 F9
Cittanova, Italy 31 D9
Ciuc, Munţii, Romania 43 D11
Ciucaş, Vf., Romania 43 E10
Ciucea, Romania 42 D7
Ciuciulea, Moldova 43 C12

Ciuciuleni, *Moldova*	43	C13
Ciudad Altamirano, *Mexico*	118	D4
Ciudad Bolívar, *Venezuela*	124	B6
Ciudad Camargo, *Mexico*	118	B3
Ciudad de Valles, *Mexico*	119	C5
Ciudad del Carmen, *Mexico*	119	D6
Ciudad del Este, *Paraguay*	127	B5
Ciudad Delicias = Delicias, *Mexico*	118	B3
Ciudad Guayana, *Venezuela*	124	B6
Ciudad Guerrero, *Mexico*	118	B3
Ciudad Guzmán, *Mexico*	118	D4
Ciudad Juárez, *Mexico*	118	A3
Ciudad Madero, *Mexico*	119	C5
Ciudad Mante, *Mexico*	119	C5
Ciudad Obregón, *Mexico*	118	B3
Ciudad Real, *Spain*	35	G7
Ciudad Real □, *Spain*	35	G7
Ciudad Rodrigo, *Spain*	34	E4
Ciudad Trujillo = Santo Domingo, *Dom. Rep.*	121	C6
Ciudad Victoria, *Mexico*	119	C5
Ciudadela, *Spain*	37	B10
Ciulniţa, *Romania*	43	F12
Ciumeghiu, *Romania*	42	D6
Ciuperceni, *Romania*	42	F8
Civa Burnu, *Turkey*	72	B7
Cividale del Friuli, *Italy*	29	B10
Civita Castellana, *Italy*	29	F9
Civitanova Marche, *Italy*	29	E10
Civitavécchia, *Italy*	29	F8
Civray, *France*	20	B4
Çivril, *Turkey*	39	C11
Cixerri →, *Italy*	30	C1
Cixi, *China*	59	B13
Cizre, *Turkey*	70	B4
Cizur Mayor, *Spain*	32	C3
Clackmannanshire □, *U.K.*	14	E5
Clacton-on-Sea, *U.K.*	13	F9
Clain →, *France*	18	F7
Claire, L., *Canada*	104	B6
Clairton, *U.S.A.*	110	F5
Clairvaux-les-Lacs, *France*	19	F12
Claise →, *France*	20	B5
Clallam Bay, *U.S.A.*	116	B2
Clamecy, *France*	19	E10
Clanton, *U.S.A.*	109	J2
Clanwilliam, *S. Africa*	88	E2
Clara, *Ireland*	15	C4
Claraville, *U.S.A.*	117	K8
Clare, *U.S.A.*	108	D3
Clare □, *Ireland*	15	D3
Clare →, *Ireland*	15	C2
Clare I., *Ireland*	15	C1
Claremont, *Calif., U.S.A.*	117	L9
Claremont, *N.H., U.S.A.*	111	C12
Claremont Pt., *Australia*	94	A3
Claremore, *U.S.A.*	113	G7
Claremorris, *Ireland*	15	C3
Clarence →, *Australia*	95	D5
Clarence →, *N.Z.*	91	K4
Clarence, I., *Chile*	128	G2
Clarence I., *Antarctica*	5	C18
Clarence Str., *Australia*	92	B5
Clarence Town, *Bahamas*	121	B5
Clarendon, *Pa., U.S.A.*	110	E5
Clarendon, *Tex., U.S.A.*	113	H4
Clarenville, *Canada*	103	C9
Claresholm, *Canada*	104	D6
Clarie Coast, *Antarctica*	5	C9
Clarinda, *U.S.A.*	112	E7
Clarion, *Iowa, U.S.A.*	112	D8
Clarion, *Pa., U.S.A.*	110	E5
Clarion →, *U.S.A.*	110	E5
Clark, *U.S.A.*	112	C6
Clark, Pt., *Canada*	110	B3
Clark Fork, *U.S.A.*	114	B5
Clark Fork →, *U.S.A.*	114	B5
Clarkdale, *U.S.A.*	115	J7
Clarke City, *Canada*	103	B6
Clarke I., *Australia*	94	G4
Clarke Ra., *Australia*	94	C4
Clark's Fork →, *U.S.A.*	114	D9
Clark's Harbour, *Canada*	103	D6
Clarks Hill L., *U.S.A.*	109	J4
Clarks Summit, *U.S.A.*	111	E9
Clarksburg, *U.S.A.*	108	F5
Clarksdale, *U.S.A.*	113	H9
Clarksville, *Ark., U.S.A.*	113	H8
Clarksville, *Tenn., U.S.A.*	109	G2
Clarksville, *Tex., U.S.A.*	113	J7
Clatskanie, *U.S.A.*	116	D3
Claude, *U.S.A.*	113	H4
Claveria, *Phil.*	61	B4
Clay, *U.S.A.*	116	G5
Clay Center, *U.S.A.*	112	F6
Claypool, *U.S.A.*	115	K8
Claysburg, *U.S.A.*	110	F6
Claysville, *U.S.A.*	110	F4
Clayton, *N. Mex., U.S.A.*	113	G3
Clayton, *N.Y., U.S.A.*	111	B8
Clear, C., *Ireland*	15	E2
Clear, L., *Canada*	110	A7
Clear Hills, *Canada*	104	B5
Clear I., *Ireland*	15	E2
Clear L., *U.S.A.*	116	F4
Clear Lake, *Iowa, U.S.A.*	112	D8
Clear Lake, *S. Dak., U.S.A.*	112	C6
Clear Lake Reservoir, *U.S.A.*	114	F3
Clearfield, *Pa., U.S.A.*	110	E6
Clearfield, *Utah, U.S.A.*	114	F8
Clearlake, *U.S.A.*	114	G2
Clearlake Highlands, *U.S.A.*	116	G4
Clearwater, *Canada*	104	C4
Clearwater, *U.S.A.*	109	M4
Clearwater →, *Alta., Canada*	104	C6
Clearwater →, *Alta., Canada*	105	B6
Clearwater L., *Canada*	105	C9
Clearwater Mts., *U.S.A.*	114	C6
Clearwater Prov. Park, *Canada*	105	C8
Clearwater River Prov. Park, *Canada*	105	B7
Cleburne, *U.S.A.*	113	J6
Clee Hills, *U.K.*	13	E5
Cleethorpes, *U.K.*	12	D7
Cleeve Cloud, *U.K.*	13	F6
Clelles, *France*	21	D9
Clemson, *U.S.A.*	109	H4
Clerke Reef, *Australia*	92	C2
Clermont, *Australia*	94	C4
Clermont, *France*	19	C9
Clermont, *U.S.A.*	109	L5
Clermont-en-Argonne, *France*	19	C12
Clermont-Ferrand, *France*	20	C7
Clermont-l'Hérault, *France*	20	E7
Clerval, *France*	19	E13
Clervaux, *Lux.*	17	D6
Cles, *Italy*	28	B8
Clevedon, *U.K.*	13	F5
Cleveland, *Miss., U.S.A.*	113	J9
Cleveland, *Ohio, U.S.A.*	110	E3
Cleveland, *Okla., U.S.A.*	113	G6
Cleveland, *Tenn., U.S.A.*	109	H3
Cleveland, *Tex., U.S.A.*	113	K7
Cleveland, C., *Australia*	94	B4
Cleveland, Mt., *U.S.A.*	114	B7
Cleveland Heights, *U.S.A.*	110	E3
Clevelândia, *Brazil*	127	B5
Clew B., *Ireland*	15	C2
Clewiston, *U.S.A.*	109	M5
Clifden, *Ireland*	15	C1
Clifden, *N.Z.*	91	M1
Cliffdell, *U.S.A.*	116	D5
Cliffy Hd., *Australia*	93	G2
Clifton, *Australia*	95	D5
Clifton, *Ariz., U.S.A.*	115	K9
Clifton, *Colo., U.S.A.*	115	G9
Clifton, *Tex., U.S.A.*	113	K6
Clifton Beach, *Australia*	94	B4
Climax, *Canada*	105	D7
Clinch →, *U.S.A.*	109	H3
Clingmans Dome, *U.S.A.*	109	H4
Clint, *U.S.A.*	115	L10
Clinton, *B.C., Canada*	104	C4
Clinton, *Ont., Canada*	102	D3
Clinton, *N.Z.*	91	M2
Clinton, *Ark., U.S.A.*	113	H8
Clinton, *Conn., U.S.A.*	111	E12
Clinton, *Ill., U.S.A.*	112	E10
Clinton, *Ind., U.S.A.*	108	F2
Clinton, *Iowa, U.S.A.*	112	E9
Clinton, *Mass., U.S.A.*	111	D13
Clinton, *Miss., U.S.A.*	113	J9
Clinton, *Mo., U.S.A.*	112	F8
Clinton, *N.C., U.S.A.*	109	H6
Clinton, *Okla., U.S.A.*	113	H5
Clinton, *S.C., U.S.A.*	109	H5
Clinton, *Tenn., U.S.A.*	109	G3
Clinton, *Wash., U.S.A.*	116	C4
Clinton C., *Australia*	94	C5
Clinton Colden L., *Canada*	100	B9
Clintonville, *U.S.A.*	112	C10
Clipperton, I., *Pac. Oc.*	97	F17
Clisham, *U.K.*	14	D2
Clisson, *France*	18	E5
Clitheroe, *U.K.*	12	D5
Clo-oose, *Canada*	116	B2
Cloates, Pt., *Australia*	92	D1
Clocolan, *S. Africa*	89	D4
Clodomira, *Argentina*	126	B3
Clogher Hd., *Ireland*	15	C5
Clonakilty, *Ireland*	15	E3
Clonakilty B., *Ireland*	15	E3
Cloncurry, *Australia*	94	C3
Cloncurry →, *Australia*	94	B3
Clondalkin, *Ireland*	15	C5
Clones, *Ireland*	15	B4
Clonmel, *Ireland*	15	D4
Cloppenburg, *Germany*	24	C4
Cloquet, *U.S.A.*	112	B8
Clorinda, *Argentina*	126	B4
Cloud Bay, *Canada*	102	C2
Cloud Peak, *U.S.A.*	114	D10
Cloudcroft, *U.S.A.*	115	K11
Cloverdale, *U.S.A.*	116	G4
Clovis, *Calif., U.S.A.*	116	J7
Clovis, *N. Mex., U.S.A.*	113	H3
Cloyes-sur-le-Loir, *France*	18	E8
Cloyne, *Canada*	110	B7
Cluj □, *Romania*	43	D8
Cluj-Napoca, *Romania*	43	D8
Cluny, *France*	19	F11
Cluses, *France*	19	F13
Clusone, *Italy*	28	C6
Clutha →, *N.Z.*	91	M2
Clwyd →, *U.K.*	12	D4
Clyde, *Canada*	104	C6
Clyde, *N.Z.*	91	L2
Clyde, *U.S.A.*	110	C8
Clyde →, *U.K.*	14	F4
Clyde, Firth of, *U.K.*	14	F3
Clyde River, *Canada*	101	A13
Clydebank, *U.K.*	14	F4
Clymer, *N.Y., U.S.A.*	110	D5
Clymer, *Pa., U.S.A.*	110	D5
Ćmielów, *Poland*	45	H8
Côa →, *Portugal*	34	D3
Coachella, *U.S.A.*	117	M10
Coachella Canal, *U.S.A.*	117	N12
Coahoma, *U.S.A.*	113	J4
Coahuayana →, *Mexico*	118	D4
Coahuila □, *Mexico*	118	B4
Coal →, *Canada*	104	B3
Coalane, *Mozam.*	87	F4
Coalcomán, *Mexico*	118	D4
Coaldale, *Canada*	104	D6
Coalgate, *U.S.A.*	113	H6
Coalinga, *U.S.A.*	116	J6
Coalisland, *U.K.*	15	B5
Coalville, *U.K.*	12	E6
Coalville, *U.S.A.*	114	F8
Coari, *Brazil*	124	D6
Coast □, *Kenya*	86	C4
Coast Mts., *Canada*	104	C3
Coast Ranges, *U.S.A.*	116	G4
Coatbridge, *U.K.*	14	F4
Coatepec, *Mexico*	119	D5
Coatepeque, *Guatemala*	120	D1
Coatesville, *U.S.A.*	108	F8
Coaticook, *Canada*	103	C5
Coats I., *Canada*	101	B11
Coats Land, *Antarctica*	5	D1
Coatzacoalcos, *Mexico*	119	D6
Cobadin, *Romania*	43	F13
Cobalt, *Canada*	102	C4
Cobán, *Guatemala*	120	C1
Çobanlar, *Turkey*	39	C12
Cóbh, *Ireland*	15	E3
Cobija, *Bolivia*	124	F5
Cobleskill, *U.S.A.*	111	D10
Coboconk, *Canada*	110	B6
Cobourg, *Canada*	102	D4
Cobourg Pen., *Australia*	92	B5
Cóbué, *Mozam.*	87	E3
Coburg, *Germany*	25	E6
Coca, *Spain*	34	D6
Cocanada = Kakinada, *India*	67	L13
Cocentaina, *Spain*	33	G4
Cochabamba, *Bolivia*	124	G5
Cochem, *Germany*	25	E3
Cochemane, *Mozam.*	87	F3
Cochin, *India*	66	Q10
Cochin China = Nam-Phan, *Vietnam*	65	G6
Cochran, *U.S.A.*	109	J4
Cochrane, *Alta., Canada*	104	C6
Cochrane, *Ont., Canada*	102	C3
Cochrane, *Chile*	128	F2
Cochrane →, *Canada*	105	B8
Cochrane, L., *Chile*	128	F2
Cochranton, *U.S.A.*	110	E4
Cockburn, Canal, *Chile*	122	J3
Cockburn I., *Canada*	102	C3
Cockburn Ra., *Australia*	92	C4
Cockermouth, *U.K.*	12	C4
Cocklebiddy, *Australia*	93	F4
Coco →, *Cent. Amer.*	120	D3
Coco, I. del, *Pac. Oc.*	97	G19
Cocoa, *U.S.A.*	109	L5
Cocobeach, *Gabon*	84	D1
Cocora, *Romania*	43	F12
Cocos, B. do, *Brazil*	125	D10
Cocos Is., *Ind. Oc.*	96	J1
Cod, C., *U.S.A.*	108	D10
Codajás, *Brazil*	124	D6
Codigoro, *Italy*	29	D9
Codlea, *Romania*	43	E10
Codó, *Brazil*	125	D10
Codogno, *Italy*	28	C6
Codróipo, *Italy*	29	C10
Codru, Munţii, *Romania*	42	D7
Cody, *U.S.A.*	114	D9
Coe Hill, *Canada*	110	B7
Coelemu, *Chile*	126	D1
Coen, *Australia*	94	A3
Coesfeld, *Germany*	24	D3
Cœur d'Alene, *U.S.A.*	114	C5
Cœur d'Alene L., *U.S.A.*	114	C5
Coevorden, *Neths.*	17	B6
Cofete, *Canary Is.*	37	F5
Coffeyville, *U.S.A.*	113	G7
Coffin B., *Australia*	95	E2
Coffin Bay, *Australia*	95	E2
Coffin Bay Peninsula, *Australia*	95	E2
Cofrentes, *Spain*	33	F3
Cogalnic →, *Moldova*	43	E14
Cogealac, *Romania*	43	F13
Coghinas →, *Italy*	30	B1
Coghinas, L. del, *Italy*	30	B2
Cognac, *France*	20	C3
Cogne, *Italy*	28	C4
Cogolin, *France*	21	E10
Cogolludo, *Spain*	32	E1
Cohocton, *U.S.A.*	110	D7
Cohocton →, *U.S.A.*	110	D7
Cohoes, *U.S.A.*	111	D11
Coiba, I., *Panama*	120	E3
Coig →, *Argentina*	128	G3
Coigeach, Rubha, *U.K.*	14	C3
Coihaique, *Chile*	128	F2
Coimbatore, *India*	66	P10
Coimbra, *Brazil*	124	G7
Coimbra, *Portugal*	34	E2
Coimbra □, *Portugal*	34	E2
Coín, *Spain*	35	J6
Coipasa, Salar de, *Bolivia*	124	G5
Cojimies, *Ecuador*	124	C3
Cojocna, *Romania*	43	D8
Cojutepeque, *El Salv.*	120	D2
Čoka, *Serbia, Yug.*	42	E5
Cokeville, *U.S.A.*	114	E8
Colatina, *Brazil*	125	G10
Colbeck, C., *Antarctica*	5	D13
Colby, *U.S.A.*	112	F4
Colchester, *U.K.*	13	F8
Cold L., *Canada*	105	C7
Coldstream, *Canada*	104	C5
Coldstream, *U.K.*	14	F6
Coldwater, *Canada*	110	B5
Coldwater, *Kans., U.S.A.*	113	G5
Coldwater, *Mich., U.S.A.*	108	E3
Colebrook, *U.S.A.*	111	B13
Coleman, *U.S.A.*	113	K5
Coleman →, *Australia*	94	B3
Colenso, *S. Africa*	89	D4
Coleraine, *U.K.*	15	A5
Coleridge, L., *N.Z.*	91	K3
Coleville, *U.S.A.*	116	G7
Colfax, *Calif., U.S.A.*	116	F6
Colfax, *La., U.S.A.*	113	K8
Colfax, *Wash., U.S.A.*	114	C5
Colhué Huapi, L., *Argentina*	128	F3
Colibaşi, *Moldova*	43	E13
Colibaşi, *Romania*	43	F9
Cólico, *Italy*	28	B6
Coligny, *France*	19	F12
Coligny, *S. Africa*	89	D4
Colima, *Mexico*	118	D4
Colima □, *Mexico*	118	D4
Colima, Nevado de, *Mexico*	118	D4
Colina, *Chile*	126	C1
Colina do Norte, *Guinea-Biss.*	82	C2
Colinas, *Brazil*	125	E10
Colindres, *Spain*	34	B7
Coll, *U.K.*	14	E2
Collaguasi, *Chile*	126	A2
Collarada, Peña, *Spain*	32	C4
Collarenebri, *Australia*	95	D4
Colle di Val d'Elsa, *Italy*	28	E8
Collécchio, *Italy*	28	D7
Colleen Bawn, *Zimbabwe*	87	G2
College Park, *U.S.A.*	109	J3
College Station, *U.S.A.*	113	K6
Collesalvetti, *Italy*	28	E7
Collie, *Australia*	93	F2
Collier B., *Australia*	92	C3
Collier Ra., *Australia*	93	D2
Collina, Passo di, *Italy*	28	D7
Collingwood, *Canada*	102	D3
Collingwood, *N.Z.*	91	J4
Collins, *Canada*	102	B2
Collinsville, *Australia*	94	C4
Collipulli, *Chile*	126	D1
Collooney, *Ireland*	15	B3
Colmar, *France*	19	D14
Colmenar, *Spain*	35	J6
Colmenar de Oreja, *Spain*	34	E7
Colmenar Viejo, *Spain*	34	E7
Cologne = Köln, *Germany*	24	E2
Colom, I. d'en, *Spain*	37	B11
Colomb-Béchar = Béchar, *Algeria*	78	B5
Colombey-les-Belles, *France*	19	D12
Colombey-les-Deux-Églises, *France*	19	D11
Colombia ■, *S. Amer.*	124	C4
Colombian Basin, *S. Amer.*	98	H12
Colombo, *Sri Lanka*	66	R11
Colomiers, *France*	20	E5
Colón, *Buenos Aires, Argentina*	126	C3
Colón, *Entre Ríos, Argentina*	126	C4
Colón, *Cuba*	120	B3
Colón, *Panama*	120	E4
Colonia de Sant Jordi, *Spain*	37	B9
Colonia del Sacramento, *Uruguay*	126	C4
Colonia Dora, *Argentina*	126	B3
Colonial Beach, *U.S.A.*	108	F7
Colonie, *U.S.A.*	111	D11
Colonna, C., *Italy*	31	C10
Colonsay, *Canada*	105	C7
Colonsay, *U.K.*	14	E2
Colorado □, *U.S.A.*	115	G10
Colorado →, *Argentina*	128	D4
Colorado →, *N. Amer.*	115	L6
Colorado →, *U.S.A.*	113	L7
Colorado City, *U.S.A.*	113	J4
Colorado Plateau, *U.S.A.*	115	H8
Colorado River Aqueduct, *U.S.A.*	117	L12
Colorado Springs, *U.S.A.*	112	F2
Colorno, *Italy*	28	D7
Colotlán, *Mexico*	118	C4
Colstrip, *U.S.A.*	114	D10
Colton, *U.S.A.*	111	B10
Columbia, *Ky., U.S.A.*	108	G3
Columbia, *La., U.S.A.*	113	J8
Columbia, *Miss., U.S.A.*	113	K10
Columbia, *Mo., U.S.A.*	112	F8
Columbia, *Pa., U.S.A.*	111	F8
Columbia, *S.C., U.S.A.*	109	J5
Columbia, *Tenn., U.S.A.*	109	H2
Columbia →, *N. Amer.*	116	D2
Columbia, C., *Canada*	4	A4
Columbia, District of □, *U.S.A.*	108	F7
Columbia, Mt., *Canada*	104	C5
Columbia Basin, *U.S.A.*	114	C4
Columbia Falls, *U.S.A.*	114	B6
Columbia Mts., *Canada*	104	C5
Columbia Plateau, *U.S.A.*	114	D5
Columbiana, *U.S.A.*	110	F4
Columbretes, Is., *Spain*	32	F5
Columbus, *Ga., U.S.A.*	109	J3
Columbus, *Ind., U.S.A.*	108	F3
Columbus, *Kans., U.S.A.*	113	G7
Columbus, *Miss., U.S.A.*	109	J1
Columbus, *Mont., U.S.A.*	114	D9
Columbus, *N. Mex., U.S.A.*	115	L10
Columbus, *Nebr., U.S.A.*	112	E6
Columbus, *Ohio, U.S.A.*	108	F4
Columbus, *Tex., U.S.A.*	113	L6
Colunga, *Spain*	34	B5
Colusa, *U.S.A.*	116	F4
Colville, *U.S.A.*	114	B5
Colville →, *U.S.A.*	100	A4
Colville, C., *N.Z.*	91	G5
Colwood, *Canada*	116	B3
Coma, *Ethiopia*	81	F4
Comácchio, *Italy*	29	D9
Comalcalco, *Mexico*	119	D6
Comallo, *Argentina*	128	E2
Comana, *Romania*	43	F11
Comanche, *U.S.A.*	113	K5
Comăneşti, *Romania*	43	D11
Comarnic, *Romania*	43	E10
Comayagua, *Honduras*	120	D2
Combahee →, *U.S.A.*	109	J5
Combarbalá, *Chile*	126	C1
Combeaufontaine, *France*	19	E12
Comber, *Canada*	110	D2
Comber, *U.K.*	15	B6
Combermere, *Canada*	110	A7
Comblain-au-Pont, *Belgium*	17	D5
Combourg, *France*	18	D5
Combrailles, *France*	19	F9
Combronde, *France*	20	C7
Comeragh Mts., *Ireland*	15	D4
Comet, *Australia*	94	C4
Comilla, *Bangla.*	67	H17
Comino, *Malta*	36	C1
Comino, C., *Italy*	30	B2
Cómiso, *Italy*	31	F7
Comitán, *Mexico*	119	D6
Commentry, *France*	19	F9
Commerce, *Ga., U.S.A.*	109	H4
Commerce, *Tex., U.S.A.*	113	J7
Commercy, *France*	19	D12
Committee B., *Canada*	101	B11
Commonwealth B., *Antarctica*	5	C10
Commoron Cr. →, *Australia*	95	D5
Communism Pk. = Kommunizma, Pik, *Tajikistan*	50	F8
Como, *Italy*	28	C6
Como, Lago di, *Italy*	28	B6
Comodoro Rivadavia, *Argentina*	128	F3
Comorâşte, *Romania*	42	E6
Comorin, C., *India*	66	Q10
Comoro Is. = Comoros ■, *Ind. Oc.*	77	H8
Comoros ■, *Ind. Oc.*	77	H8
Comox, *Canada*	104	D4
Compiègne, *France*	19	C9
Comporta, *Portugal*	35	G2
Compostela, *Mexico*	118	C4
Comprida, I., *Brazil*	127	A6
Compton, *Canada*	111	A13
Compton, *U.S.A.*	117	M8
Comrat, *Moldova*	43	E13
Con Cuong, *Vietnam*	64	C5
Con Son, *Vietnam*	65	H6
Conakry, *Guinea*	82	D2
Conara, *Australia*	94	G4
Concarneau, *France*	18	E3
Conceição, *Mozam.*	87	F4
Conceição da Barra, *Brazil*	125	G11
Conceição do Araguaia, *Brazil*	125	E9
Concepción, *Argentina*	126	B2
Concepción, *Bolivia*	124	G6
Concepción, *Chile*	126	D1
Concepción, *Mexico*	119	D6
Concepción, *Paraguay*	126	A4
Concepción □, *Chile*	126	D1
Concepción →, *Mexico*	118	A2
Concepción, Est. de, *Chile*	128	G2
Concepción, L., *Bolivia*	124	G6
Concepción, Punta, *Mexico*	118	B2
Concepción del Oro, *Mexico*	118	C4
Concepción del Uruguay, *Argentina*	126	C4
Conception, Pt., *U.S.A.*	117	L6
Conception B., *Canada*	103	C9
Conception B., *Namibia*	88	C1
Conception I., *Bahamas*	121	B4
Concession, *Zimbabwe*	87	F3
Conchas Dam, *U.S.A.*	113	H2
Conches-en-Ouche, *France*	18	D7
Concho, *U.S.A.*	115	J9
Concho →, *U.S.A.*	113	K5
Conchos →, *Chihuahua, Mexico*	118	B4
Conchos →, *Tamaulipas, Mexico*	119	B5
Concord, *Calif., U.S.A.*	116	H4
Concord, *N.C., U.S.A.*	109	H5
Concord, *N.H., U.S.A.*	111	C13
Concórdia, *Argentina*	126	C4
Concórdia, *Brazil*	124	D5
Concordia, *Mexico*	118	C3
Concordia, *U.S.A.*	112	F6
Concrete, *U.S.A.*	114	B3
Condamine, *Australia*	95	D5
Condat, *France*	20	C6
Condé, *France*	18	C5
Condé-sur-Noireau, *France*	18	D6
Condeúba, *Brazil*	125	F10
Condom, *France*	20	E4
Condon, *U.S.A.*	114	D3
Conegliano, *Italy*	29	C9
Conejera, I. = Conills, I. des, *Spain*	37	B9
Conejos, *Mexico*	118	B4
Confolens, *France*	20	B4
Confuso →, *Paraguay*	126	B4
Congaz, *Moldova*	43	D13
Conghua, *China*	59	F9
Congjiang, *China*	58	E7
Congleton, *U.K.*	12	D5

Congo (Kinshasa) = Congo, Dem. Rep. of the ■, Africa .. 84 E4
Congo ■, Africa 84 E3
Congo ➤, Africa 84 F2
Congo, Dem. Rep. of the ■, Africa 84 E4
Congo Basin, Africa 84 E4
Congonhas, Brazil 127 A7
Congress, U.S.A. 115 J7
Conil = Conil de la Frontera, Spain 35 J4
Conil de la Frontera, Spain .. 35 J4
Conills, I. des, Spain 37 B9
Coniston, Canada 102 C3
Conjeeveram = Kanchipuram, India 66 N11
Conklin, Canada 105 B6
Conklin, U.S.A. 111 D9
Conn, L., Ireland 15 B2
Connacht □, Ireland 15 C2
Conneaut, U.S.A. 110 E4
Connecticut □, U.S.A. 111 E12
Connecticut ➤, U.S.A. 111 E12
Connell, U.S.A. 114 C4
Connellsville, U.S.A. 110 F5
Connemara, Ireland 15 C2
Connemaugh ➤, U.S.A. 110 F5
Connerré, France 18 D7
Connersville, U.S.A. 108 F3
Connors Ra., Australia 94 C4
Conques, France 20 D6
Conquest, Canada 105 C7
Conrad, U.S.A. 114 B8
Conroe, U.S.A. 113 K7
Consecon, Canada 110 C7
Conselheiro Lafaiete, Brazil . 127 A7
Conselve, Italy 29 C8
Consett, U.K. 12 C6
Constance = Konstanz, Germany 25 H5
Constance, L. = Bodensee, Europe 25 H5
Constanţa, Romania 43 F13
Constanţa □, Romania 43 F13
Constantia, U.S.A. 111 C8
Constantina, Spain 35 H5
Constantine, Algeria 78 A7
Constitución, Chile 126 D1
Constitución, Uruguay 126 C4
Consuegra, Spain 35 F7
Consul, Canada 105 D7
Contact, U.S.A. 114 F6
Contai, India 69 J12
Contamana, Peru 124 E4
Contarina, Italy 29 C9
Contas ➤, Brazil 125 F11
Contes, France 21 E11
Contoocook, U.S.A. 111 C13
Contra Costa, Mozam. 89 D5
Contres, France 18 E8
Contrexéville, France 19 D12
Contwoyto L., Canada 100 B8
Conversano, Italy 31 B10
Conway = Conwy, U.K. 12 D4
Conway = Conwy ➤, U.K. .. 12 D4
Conway, Ark., U.S.A. 113 H8
Conway, N.H., U.S.A. 111 C13
Conway, S.C., U.S.A. 109 J6
Conway, L., Australia 95 D2
Conwy, U.K. 12 D4
Conwy □, U.K. 12 D4
Conwy ➤, U.K. 12 D4
Coober Pedy, Australia 95 D1
Cooch Behar = Koch Bihar, India 67 F16
Cooinda, Australia 92 B5
Cook, Australia 93 F5
Cook, U.S.A. 112 B8
Cook, B., Chile 128 H3
Cook, C., Canada 104 C3
Cook, Mt. = Aoraki Mount Cook, N.Z. 91 K3
Cook Inlet, U.S.A. 100 C4
Cook Is., Pac. Oc. 97 J12
Cook Strait, N.Z. 91 J5
Cookeville, U.S.A. 109 G3
Cookhouse, S. Africa 88 E4
Cookshire, Canada 111 A13
Cookstown, U.K. 15 B5
Cooksville, Canada 110 C5
Cooktown, Australia 94 B4
Cooladdi, Australia 95 D4
Coolah, Australia 95 E4
Coolamon, Australia 95 E4
Coolgardie, Australia 93 F3
Coolidge, U.S.A. 115 K8
Coolidge Dam, U.S.A. 115 K8
Coon Rapids, U.S.A. 112 C8
Coonana, Australia 93 F3
Coondapoor, India 66 N9
Cooninie, L., Australia 95 D2
Cooper, U.S.A. 113 J7
Cooper Cr. ➤, Australia ... 95 D2
Cooperstown, N. Dak., U.S.A. 112 B5
Cooperstown, N.Y., U.S.A. . 111 D10
Coorabie, Australia 93 F5
Coorow, Australia 93 E2
Cooroy, Australia 95 D5
Coos Bay, U.S.A. 114 E1
Coosa ➤, U.S.A. 109 J2
Cootehill, Ireland 15 B4
Copahue Paso, Argentina .. 126 D1
Copainalá, Mexico 119 D6
Copake Falls, U.S.A. 111 D11
Copalnic Mănăştur, Romania . 43 C8
Copán, Honduras 120 D2
Cope, U.S.A. 112 F3
Cope, C., Spain 33 H3

Copenhagen = København, Denmark 11 J6
Copenhagen, U.S.A. 111 C9
Copertino, Italy 31 B11
Copiapó, Chile 126 B1
Copiapó ➤, Chile 126 B1
Coplay, U.S.A. 111 F9
Copp L., Canada 104 A6
Copparo, Italy 29 D8
Copper Harbor, U.S.A. 108 B2
Copper Queen, Zimbabwe . 87 F2
Copperas Cove, U.S.A. ... 113 K6
Copperbelt □, Zambia 87 E2
Coppermine = Kugluktuk, Canada 100 B8
Coppermine ➤, Canada ... 100 B8
Copperopolis, U.S.A. 116 H6
Copşa Mică, Romania 43 D9
Coquet ➤, U.K. 12 B6
Coquille, U.S.A. 114 E1
Coquimbo, Chile 126 C1
Coquimbo □, Chile 126 C1
Corabia, Romania 43 G9
Coracora, Peru 124 G4
Coraki, Australia 95 D5
Coral, U.S.A. 110 F5
Coral Gables, U.S.A. 109 N5
Coral Harbour = Salliq, Canada 101 B11
Coral Sea, Pac. Oc. 96 J7
Coral Springs, U.S.A. 109 M5
Corato, Italy 31 A9
Corbeil-Essonnes, France .. 19 D9
Corbie, France 19 C9
Corbières, France 20 F6
Corbigny, France 19 E10
Corbin, U.S.A. 108 G3
Corbones ➤, Spain 35 H5
Corby, U.K. 13 E7
Corcaigh = Cork, Ireland .. 15 E3
Corcoran, U.S.A. 116 J7
Corcubión, Spain 34 C1
Cordele, U.S.A. 109 K4
Cordell, U.S.A. 113 H5
Cordenòns, Italy 29 C9
Cordes, France 20 D5
Córdoba, Argentina 126 C3
Córdoba, Mexico 119 D5
Córdoba, Spain 35 H6
Córdoba □, Argentina 126 C3
Córdoba □, Spain 35 G6
Córdoba, Sierra de, Argentina 126 C3
Cordon, Phil. 61 C4
Cordova, U.S.A. 100 B5
Corella, Spain 32 C3
Corella ➤, Australia 94 B3
Corfield, Australia 94 C3
Corfu = Kérkira, Greece 36 A3
Corfu, Str. of, Greece 36 A4
Corgo = O Corgo, Spain ... 34 C3
Cori, Italy 30 A5
Coria, Spain 34 F4
Coria del Río, Spain 35 H4
Corigliano Cálabro, Italy ... 31 C9
Coringa Is., Australia 94 B4
Corinth = Kórinthos, Greece . 38 D4
Corinth, Miss., U.S.A. 109 H1
Corinth, N.Y., U.S.A. 111 C11
Corinth, G. of = Korinthiakós Kólpos, Greece 38 C4
Corinth Canal, Greece 38 D4
Corinto, Brazil 125 G10
Corinto, Nic. 120 D2
Cork, Ireland 15 E3
Cork □, Ireland 15 E3
Cork Harbour, Ireland 15 E3
Corlay, France 18 D3
Corleone, Italy 30 E6
Corleto Perticara, Italy 31 B9
Çorlu, Turkey 41 E11
Cormack L., Canada 104 A4
Cormòns, Italy 29 C10
Cormorant, Canada 105 C8
Cormorant L., Canada 105 C8
Corn Is. = Maíz, Is. del, Nic. . 120 D3
Cornélio Procópio, Brazil .. 127 A5
Corner Brook, Canada 103 C8
Corneşti, Moldova 43 C13
Corníglio, Italy 28 D7
Corning, Ark., U.S.A. 113 G9
Corning, Calif., U.S.A. 114 G2
Corning, Iowa, U.S.A. 112 E7
Corning, N.Y., U.S.A. 110 D7
Corno Grande, Italy 29 F10
Cornwall, Canada 102 C5
Cornwall, U.S.A. 111 F8
Cornwall □, U.K. 13 G3
Coro, Venezuela 124 A5
Coroatá, Brazil 125 D10
Corocoro, Bolivia 124 G5
Coroico, Bolivia 124 G5
Coromandel, N.Z. 91 G5
Coromandel Coast, India .. 66 N12
Corona, Calif., U.S.A. 117 M9
Corona, N. Mex., U.S.A. ... 115 J11
Coronach, Canada 105 D7
Coronado, U.S.A. 117 N9
Coronado, B. de, Costa Rica . 120 E3
Coronados, Is. los, U.S.A. .. 117 N9
Coronation, Canada 104 C6
Coronation Gulf, Canada .. 100 B8
Coronation I., Antarctica .. 5 C18
Coronation Is., Australia .. 92 B3
Coronda, Argentina 126 C3
Coronel, Chile 126 D1

Coronel Bogado, Paraguay ... 126 B4
Coronel Dorrego, Argentina . 126 D3
Coronel Oviedo, Paraguay .. 126 B4
Coronel Pringles, Argentina . 126 D3
Coronel Suárez, Argentina .. 126 D3
Coronel Vidal, Argentina ... 126 D4
Coropuna, Nevado, Peru ... 124 G4
Çorovodë, Albania 40 F4
Corozal, Belize 119 D7
Corps, France 21 D9
Corpus, Argentina 127 B4
Corpus Christi, U.S.A. 113 M6
Corpus Christi, L., U.S.A. .. 113 L6
Corral de Almaguer, Spain . 34 F7
Corralejo, Canary Is. 37 F6
Corraun Hd., Ireland 15 C2
Corréggio, Italy 28 D7
Correntes, C. das, Mozam. .. 89 C6
Corrèze □, France 20 C5
Corrèze ➤, France 20 C5
Corrib, L., Ireland 15 C2
Corridónia, Italy 29 E10
Corrientes, Argentina 126 B4
Corrientes □, Argentina ... 126 B4
Corrientes ➤, Argentina ... 126 C4
Corrientes ➤, Peru 124 D4
Corrientes, C., Colombia .. 124 B3
Corrientes, C., Cuba 120 B3
Corrientes, C., Mexico 118 C3
Corrigan, U.S.A. 113 K7
Corrigin, Australia 93 F2
Corry, U.S.A. 110 E5
Corse, France 21 G13
Corse, C., France 21 E13
Corse-du-Sud □, France ... 21 G13
Corsica = Corse, France ... 21 G13
Corsicana, U.S.A. 113 J6
Corte, France 21 F13
Corte Pinto, Portugal 35 H3
Cortegana, Spain 35 H4
Cortez, U.S.A. 115 H9
Cortina d'Ampezzo, Italy .. 29 B9
Cortland, N.Y., U.S.A. 111 D8
Cortland, Ohio, U.S.A. ... 110 E4
Cortona, Italy 29 E8
Corubal ➤, Guinea-Biss. ... 82 C2
Coruche, Portugal 35 G2
Çoruh ➤, Turkey 49 K5
Çorum, Turkey 72 B6
Corumbá, Brazil 124 G7
Corund, Romania 43 D10
Corunna = A Coruña, Spain . 34 B2
Corvallis, U.S.A. 114 D2
Corvette, L. de la, Canada .. 102 B5
Corydon, U.S.A. 112 E8
Cosalá, Mexico 118 C3
Cosamaloapan, Mexico ... 119 D5
Cosenza, Italy 31 C9
Coşereni, Romania 43 F11
Coshocton, U.S.A. 110 F3
Cosmo Newberry, Australia . 93 E3
Cosne-Cours-sur-Loire, France 19 E9
Coso Junction, U.S.A. 117 J9
Coso Pk., U.S.A. 117 J9
Cospeito, Spain 34 B3
Cosquín, Argentina 126 C3
Cossato, Italy 28 C5
Cossé-le-Vivien, France ... 18 E6
Cosson ➤, France 18 E8
Costa Blanca, Spain 33 G4
Costa Brava, Spain 32 D8
Costa del Sol, Spain 35 J6
Costa Dorada, Spain 32 D6
Costa Mesa, U.S.A. 117 M9
Costa Rica ■, Cent. Amer. . 120 E3
Costa Smeralda, Italy 30 A2
Costeşti, Romania 43 F9
Costigliole d'Asti, Italy 28 D5
Cosumnes ➤, U.S.A. 116 G5
Cotabato, Phil. 61 H6
Cotagaita, Bolivia 124 A2
Côte d'Azur, France 21 E11
Côte-d'Ivoire = Ivory Coast ■, Africa 82 D4
Côte d'Or, France 19 E11
Côte-d'Or □, France 19 E11
Coteau des Prairies, U.S.A. . 112 C6
Coteau du Missouri, U.S.A. . 112 B4
Coteau Landing, Canada .. 111 A10
Cotentin, France 18 C5
Côtes-d'Armor □, France .. 18 D4
Côtes de Meuse, France ... 19 C12
Côtes-du-Nord = Côtes-d'Armor □, France 18 D4
Cotiella, Spain 32 C5
Cotillo, Canary Is. 37 F5
Cotiujeni, Moldova 43 C13
Cotonou, Benin 83 D5
Cotopaxi, Ecuador 122 D3
Cotronei, Italy 31 C9
Cotswold Hills, U.K. 13 F5
Cottage Grove, U.S.A. 114 E2
Cottbus, Germany 24 D10
Cottonwood, U.S.A. 115 J7
Cotulla, U.S.A. 113 L5
Coubre, Pte. de la, France . 20 C2
Couçon, Portugal 35 G2
Coudersport, U.S.A. 110 E6
Couëron, France 18 E5
Couesnon ➤, France 18 D5
Couhé, France 20 B4
Couiza, France 20 F6
Coulanges-sur-Yonne, France . 19 E10

Coulee City, U.S.A. 114 C4
Coulman I., Antarctica 5 D11
Coulommiers, France 19 D10
Coulon ➤, France 21 E9
Coulonge ➤, Canada 102 C4
Coulonges-sur-l'Autize, France 20 B3
Coulounieix-Chamiers, France . 20 C4
Coulterville, U.S.A. 116 H6
Council, U.S.A. 114 D5
Council Bluffs, U.S.A. 112 E7
Council Grove, U.S.A. 112 F6
Coupeville, U.S.A. 116 B4
Courantyne ➤, S. Amer. .. 122 C5
Courcelles, Belgium 17 D4
Courçon, France 20 B3
Couronne, C., France 21 E9
Cours-la-Ville, France 19 F11
Coursan, France 20 E7
Courseulles-sur-Mer, France . 18 C6
Courtenay, Canada 104 D4
Courtenay, France 19 D10
Courtland, U.S.A. 116 G5
Courtrai = Kortrijk, Belgium . 17 D3
Courtright, Canada 110 D2
Coushatta, U.S.A. 113 J8
Coutances, France 18 C5
Coutras, France 20 C3
Coutts Crossing, Australia . 95 D5
Couvin, Belgium 17 D4
Covarrubias, Spain 34 C7
Covasna, Romania 43 E11
Covasna □, Romania 43 E10
Cove I., Canada 110 A3
Coventry, U.K. 13 E6
Covilhã, Portugal 34 E3
Covington, Ga., U.S.A. ... 109 J4
Covington, Ky., U.S.A. ... 108 F3
Covington, Okla., U.S.A. .. 113 G6
Covington, Tenn., U.S.A. .. 113 H10
Covington, Va., U.S.A. ... 108 G5
Cowan, L., Australia 93 F3
Cowan L., Canada 105 C7
Cowansville, Canada 102 C5
Coward Springs, Australia . 95 D2
Cowcowing Lakes, Australia . 93 F2
Cowdenbeath, U.K. 14 E5
Cowes, U.K. 13 G6
Cowichan L., Canada 116 B2
Cowlitz ➤, U.S.A. 116 D4
Cox, Spain 33 G4
Coxilha Grande, Brazil 127 B5
Coxim, Brazil 125 G8
Cox's Bazar, Bangla. 67 J17
Coyote Wells, U.S.A. 117 N11
Coyuca de Benítez, Mexico . 119 D4
Coyuca de Catalan, Mexico . 118 D4
Cozad, U.S.A. 112 E5
Cozes, France 20 C3
Cozumel, Mexico 119 C7
Cozumel, Isla, Mexico 119 C7
Cracow = Kraków, Poland .. 45 H6
Cracow, Australia 95 D5
Cradock, Australia 95 E2
Cradock, S. Africa 88 E4
Craig, U.S.A. 114 F10
Craigavon, U.K. 15 B5
Craigmore, Zimbabwe 87 G3
Craik, Canada 105 C7
Crailsheim, Germany 25 F6
Craiova, Romania 43 F8
Cramsie, Australia 94 C3
Cranberry L., U.S.A. 111 B10
Cranberry Portage, Canada . 105 C8
Cranbrook, Australia 93 F2
Cranbrook, Canada 104 D5
Crandon, U.S.A. 112 C10
Crane, Oreg., U.S.A. 114 E4
Crane, Tex., U.S.A. 113 K3
Cranston, U.S.A. 111 E13
Craon, France 18 E6
Craonne, France 19 C10
Crapone-sur-Arzon, France . 20 C7
Crasna, Romania 43 D12
Crasna ➤, Romania 42 C7
Crasnei, Munţii, Romania .. 43 C8
Crater L., U.S.A. 114 E2
Crater Lake National Park, U.S.A. 114 E2
Crateús, Brazil 125 E10
Crati ➤, Italy 31 C9
Crato, Brazil 125 E11
Crato, Portugal 35 F3
Craven, L., Canada 102 B4
Crawford, U.S.A. 112 D3
Crawfordsville, U.S.A. 108 E2
Crawley, U.K. 13 F7
Crazy Mts., U.S.A. 114 C8
Crean L., Canada 105 C7
Crécy-en-Ponthieu, France . 19 B8
Crediton, U.K. 13 G4
Cree ➤, Canada 105 B7
Cree L., Canada 105 B7
Creede, U.S.A. 115 H10
Creekside, U.S.A. 110 F5
Creel, Mexico 118 B3
Creemore, Canada 110 B4
Creighton, Canada 105 C8
Creighton, U.S.A. 112 D6
Creil, France 19 C9
Crema, Italy 28 C6
Cremona, Italy 28 C7
Crepaja, Serbia, Yug. 42 E5
Crépy, France 19 C10
Crépy-en-Valois, France ... 19 C9

Cres, Croatia 29 D11
Crescent City, U.S.A. 114 F1
Crescentino, Italy 28 C5
Crespo, Argentina 126 C3
Cresson, U.S.A. 110 F6
Crest, France 21 D9
Cresta, Mt., Phil. 61 C5
Crestline, Calif., U.S.A. ... 117 L9
Crestline, Ohio, U.S.A. ... 110 F2
Creston, Canada 104 D5
Creston, Calif., U.S.A. 116 K6
Creston, Iowa, U.S.A. 112 E7
Crestview, Calif., U.S.A. .. 116 H8
Crestview, Fla., U.S.A. 109 K2
Crêt de la Neige, France ... 19 F12
Crete = Kríti, Greece 36 D7
Crete, U.S.A. 112 E6
Crete, Sea of, Greece 39 E7
Créteil, France 19 D9
Creus, C. de, Spain 32 C8
Creuse □, France 19 F9
Creuse ➤, France 20 B4
Creutzwald, France 19 C13
Creuzburg, Germany 24 D6
Crèvecœur-le-Grand, France . 19 C9
Crevillente, Spain 33 G4
Crewe, U.K. 12 D5
Crewkerne, U.K. 13 G5
Criciúma, Brazil 127 B6
Cricova, Moldova 43 C13
Crieff, U.K. 14 E5
Crikvenica, Croatia 29 C11
Crimea □, Ukraine 47 K8
Crimean Pen. = Krymskyy Pivostriv, Ukraine 47 K8
Crimmitschau, Germany .. 24 E8
Cristuru Secuiesc, Romania . 43 D10
Crişul Alb ➤, Romania ... 42 D6
Crişul Negru ➤, Romania . 42 D6
Crişul Repede ➤, Romania . 42 D5
Criuleni, Moldova 43 C14
Crivitz, Germany 24 B7
Crna ➤, Macedonia 40 E5
Crna Gora = Montenegro □, Yugoslavia 40 D3
Crna Gora, Macedonia 40 D5
Crna Trava = Crna ➤, Macedonia 40 E5
Crna Trava, Serbia, Yug. ... 40 D6
Crni Drim ➤, Macedonia .. 40 E4
Crni Timok ➤, Serbia, Yug. . 40 C6
Crnoljeva Planina, Kosovo, Yug. 40 D5
Črnomelj, Slovenia 29 C12
Croagh Patrick, Ireland ... 15 C2
Croatia ■, Europe 29 C13
Crocker, Banjaran, Malaysia . 62 C5
Crockett, U.S.A. 113 K7
Crocodile = Krokodil ➤, Mozam. 89 D5
Crocodile Is., Australia ... 94 A1
Crocq, France 20 C6
Crodo, Italy 28 B5
Crohy Hd., Ireland 15 B3
Croisette, C., France 21 E9
Croisic, Pte. du, France ... 18 E4
Croix, L. La, Canada 102 C1
Croker, C., Australia 92 B5
Croker, C., Canada 110 B4
Croker I., Australia 92 B5
Cromarty, U.K. 14 D4
Cromer, U.K. 12 E9
Cromwell, N.Z. 91 L2
Cromwell, U.S.A. 111 E12
Cronat, France 19 F10
Crook, U.K. 12 C6
Crooked ➤, Canada 104 C4
Crooked ➤, U.S.A. 114 D3
Crooked I., Bahamas 121 B5
Crooked Island Passage, Bahamas 121 B5
Crookston, Minn., U.S.A. .. 112 B6
Crookston, Nebr., U.S.A. .. 112 D4
Crosby, U.K. 12 D4
Crosby, N. Dak., U.S.A. ... 112 A3
Crosby, Pa., U.S.A. 110 E6
Crosbyton, U.S.A. 113 J4
Crosía, Italy 31 C9
Cross ➤, Nigeria 83 D6
Cross City, U.S.A. 109 L4
Cross Fell, U.K. 12 C5
Cross L., Canada 105 C9
Cross Lake, Canada 105 C9
Cross River □, Nigeria 83 D6
Cross Sound, U.S.A. 100 C6
Crossett, U.S.A. 113 J9
Crosshaven, Ireland 15 E3
Crossville, U.S.A. 109 G3
Croswell, U.S.A. 110 C2
Croton-on-Hudson, U.S.A. . 111 E11
Crotone, Italy 31 C10
Crow ➤, Canada 104 B4
Crow Agency, U.S.A. 114 D10
Crow Hd., Ireland 15 E1
Crowell, U.S.A. 113 J5
Crowley, U.S.A. 113 K8
Crowley, L., U.S.A. 116 H8
Crown Point, Ind., U.S.A. . 108 E2
Crown Point, N.Y., U.S.A. . 111 C11
Crownpoint, U.S.A. 115 J9
Crows Landing, U.S.A. ... 116 H5
Crows Nest, Australia 95 D5
Crowsnest Pass, Canada .. 104 D6
Croydon, Australia 94 B3
Croydon □, U.K. 13 F7
Crozet, Is., Ind. Oc. 3 G12
Crozon, France 18 D2

Cruz, C., Cuba 120 C4
Cruz Alta, Brazil 127 B5
Cruz de Incio, Spain 34 C3
Cruz del Eje, Argentina 126 C3
Cruzeiro, Brazil 127 A7
Cruzeiro do Oeste, Brazil 127 A5
Cruzeiro do Sul, Brazil 124 E4
Cry L., Canada 104 B3
Crystal Bay, U.S.A. 116 F7
Crystal City, U.S.A. 113 L5
Crystal Falls, U.S.A. 108 B1
Crystal River, U.S.A. 109 L4
Crystal Springs, U.S.A. 113 K9
Csenger, Hungary 42 C7
Csongrád, Hungary 42 D5
Csongrád □, Hungary 42 D5
Csorna, Hungary 42 C2
Csurgo, Hungary 42 D2
Cu Lao Hon, Vietnam 65 G7
Cua Rao, Vietnam 64 C5
Cuácua →, Mozam. 87 F4
Cuamato, Angola 88 B2
Cuamba, Angola 87 E4
Cuando →, Angola 85 H4
Cuando Cubango □, Angola 88 B3
Cuangar, Angola 88 B2
Cuango = Kwango →, Dem. Rep. of the Congo 84 E3
Cuanza →, Angola 84 F2
Cuarto →, Argentina 126 C3
Cuatrociénegas, Mexico 118 B4
Cuauhtémoc, Mexico 118 B3
Cuba, Portugal 35 G3
Cuba, N. Mex., U.S.A. 115 J10
Cuba, N.Y., U.S.A. 110 D6
Cuba ■, W. Indies 120 B4
Cubango →, Africa 88 B3
Çubuk, Turkey 72 B5
Cuchumatanes, Sierra de los, Guatemala 120 C1
Cuckfield, U.K. 13 F7
Cucuí, Brazil 124 C5
Cucurpe, Mexico 118 A2
Cúcuta, Colombia 124 B4
Cudalbi, Romania 43 E12
Cuddalore, India 66 P11
Cuddapah, India 66 M11
Cuddapan, L., Australia 94 D3
Cudillero, Spain 34 B4
Cue, Australia 93 E2
Cuéllar, Spain 34 D6
Cuenca, Ecuador 124 D3
Cuenca, Spain 32 E2
Cuenca □, Spain 32 F3
Cuenca, Serranía de, Spain 32 F3
Cuerdo del Pozo, Embalse de la, Spain 32 D2
Cuernavaca, Mexico 119 D5
Cuero, U.S.A. 113 L6
Cuers, France 21 E10
Cuevas del Almanzora, Spain 33 H3
Cuevo, Bolivia 124 H6
Cugir, Romania 43 E8
Cugnaux, France 20 E5
Cuhai-Bakony →, Hungary 42 C2
Cuiabá, Brazil 125 G7
Cuiabá →, Brazil 125 G7
Cuijk, Neths. 17 C5
Cuilco, Guatemala 120 C1
Cuillin Hills, U.K. 14 D2
Cuillin Sd., U.K. 14 D2
Cuiseaux, France 19 F12
Cuito →, Angola 88 B3
Cuitzeo, L. de, Mexico 118 D4
Cujmir, Romania 42 F7
Cukai, Malaysia 65 K4
Culbertson, U.S.A. 112 A2
Culebra, Sierra de la, Spain 34 D4
Culfa, Azerbaijan 73 C11
Culgoa →, Australia 95 D4
Culiacán, Mexico 118 C3
Culiacán →, Mexico 118 C3
Culion, Phil. 61 F4
Cúllar, Spain 35 H8
Cullen, U.K. 14 D6
Cullen Pt., Australia 94 A3
Cullera, Spain 33 F4
Cullman, U.S.A. 109 H2
Culoz, France 21 C9
Culpeper, U.S.A. 108 F7
Culuene →, Brazil 125 F8
Culver, Pt., Australia 93 F3
Culverden, N.Z. 91 K4
Cumaná, Venezuela 124 A6
Cumaovası, Turkey 39 C9
Cumberland, B.C., Canada 104 D4
Cumberland, Ont., Canada 111 A9
Cumberland, U.S.A. 108 F6
Cumberland →, U.S.A. 109 G2
Cumberland, L., U.S.A. 109 G3
Cumberland I., U.S.A. 109 K5
Cumberland Is., Australia 94 C4
Cumberland L., Canada 105 C8
Cumberland Pen., Canada 101 B13
Cumberland Plateau, U.S.A. 109 H3
Cumberland Sd., Canada 101 B13
Cumbernauld, U.K. 14 F5
Cumborah, Australia 95 D4
Cumbres Mayores, Spain 35 G4
Cumbria □, U.K. 12 C5
Cumbrian Mts., U.K. 12 C5
Cumbum, India 66 M11
Cuminá →, Brazil 125 D7
Cummings Mt., U.S.A. 117 K8
Cummins, Australia 95 E2
Cumnock, U.K. 14 F4

Cumpas, Mexico 118 B3
Cumplida, Pta., Canary Is. 37 F2
Çumra, Turkey 72 D5
Cunco, Chile 128 D2
Cuncumén, Chile 126 C1
Cunderdin, Australia 93 F2
Cunene →, Angola 88 B1
Cúneo, Italy 28 D4
Çüngüş, Turkey 70 B3
Cunillera, I. = Sa Conillera, Spain 37 C7
Cunlhat, France 20 C7
Cunnamulla, Australia 95 D4
Cuorgnè, Italy 28 C4
Cupar, Canada 105 C8
Cupar, U.K. 14 E5
Cupcini, Moldova 43 B12
Cupica, G. de, Colombia 124 B3
Ćuprija, Serbia, Yug. 40 C5
Curaçao, Neth. Ant. 121 D6
Curanilahue, Chile 126 D1
Curaray →, Peru 124 D4
Cure →, France 19 E10
Curepto, Chile 126 D1
Curiapo, Venezuela 124 B6
Curicó, Chile 126 C1
Curinga, Italy 31 D9
Curitiba, Brazil 127 B6
Curitibanos, Brazil 127 B5
Currais Novos, Brazil 125 E11
Curralinho, Brazil 125 D9
Currant, U.S.A. 114 G6
Current →, U.S.A. 113 G9
Currie, Australia 94 F3
Currie, U.S.A. 114 F6
Curtea de Argeş, Romania 43 E9
Curtici, Romania 42 D6
Curtis, U.S.A. 112 E4
Curtis Group, Australia 94 F4
Curtis I., Australia 94 C5
Curuápanema →, Brazil 125 D7
Curuçá, Brazil 125 D9
Curuguaty, Paraguay 127 A4
Curup, Indonesia 62 E2
Cururupu, Brazil 125 D10
Curuzú Cuatiá, Argentina 126 B4
Curvelo, Brazil 125 G10
Cushing, U.S.A. 113 H6
Cushing, Mt., Canada 104 B3
Cusihuiriáchic, Mexico 118 B3
Cusna, Mte., Italy 28 D7
Cusset, France 19 F10
Custer, U.S.A. 112 D3
Cut Bank, U.S.A. 114 B7
Cutchogue, U.S.A. 111 E12
Cuthbert, U.S.A. 109 K3
Cutler, U.S.A. 116 J7
Cutro, Italy 31 C9
Cuttaburra →, Australia 95 D3
Cuttack, India 67 J14
Cuvier, C., Australia 93 D1
Cuvier I., N.Z. 91 G5
Cuxhaven, Germany 24 B4
Cuyahoga Falls, U.S.A. 110 E3
Cuyapo, Phil. 61 D4
Cuyo, Phil. 61 F4
Cuyo East Pass, Phil. 61 F4
Cuyo West Pass, Phil. 61 F4
Cuyuni →, Guyana 124 B7
Cuzco, Bolivia 124 H5
Cuzco, Peru 124 F4
Čvrsnica, Bos.-H. 42 G2
Cwmbran, U.K. 13 F4
Cyangugu, Rwanda 86 C2
Cybinka, Poland 45 F1
Cyclades = Kikládhes, Greece 38 E6
Cygnet, Australia 94 G4
Cynthiana, U.S.A. 108 F3
Cypress Hills, Canada 105 D7
Cypress Hills Prov. Park, Canada 105 D7
Cyprus ■, Asia 36 E12
Cyrenaica, Libya 79 C10
Czaplinek, Poland 44 E3
Czar, Canada 105 C6
Czarna, Łódzkie, Poland 45 G6
Czarna →, Świętokrzyskie, Poland 45 H8
Czarna Białostocka, Poland 45 E10
Czarna Woda, Poland 44 E5
Czarne, Poland 44 E3
Czarnków, Poland 45 F3
Czech Rep. ■, Europe 26 B8
Czechowice-Dziedzice, Poland 45 J5
Czempiń, Poland 45 F3
Czeremcha, Poland 45 F10
Czerniejewo, Poland 45 F4
Czersk, Poland 44 E4
Czerwieńsk, Poland 45 F2
Czerwionka-Leszczyny, Poland 45 H5
Częstochowa, Poland 45 H6
Człopa, Poland 45 E3
Człuchów, Poland 44 E4
Czyżew-Osada, Poland 45 F9

D

Da →, Vietnam 58 G5
Da Hinggan Ling, China 60 B7
Da Lat, Vietnam 65 G7
Da Nang, Vietnam 64 D7
Da Qaidam, China 60 C4
Da Yunhe →, China 57 G11
Da'an, China 57 B13

Dab'a, Ras el, Egypt 80 H6
Daba Shan, China 58 B7
Dabai, Nigeria 83 C6
Dabakala, Ivory C. 82 D4
Dabas, Hungary 42 C4
Dabat, Ethiopia 81 E4
Dabbagh, Jabal, Si. Arabia 70 E2
Dabhoi, India 68 H5
Dąbie, Poland 45 F5
Dabilda, Cameroon 83 C7
Dabnou, Niger 83 C6
Dabo = Pasirkuning, Indonesia 62 E2
Dabola, Guinea 82 C2
Dabou, Ivory C. 82 D4
Daboya, Ghana 83 D4
Dąbrowa Białostocka, Poland 44 E10
Dąbrowa Górnicza, Poland 45 H6
Dąbrowa Tarnowska, Poland 45 H7
Dabu, China 59 E11
Dabung, Malaysia 65 K4
Dabus →, Ethiopia 81 E4
Dacato →, Ethiopia 81 F5
Dacca = Dhaka, Bangla. 69 H14
Dacca = Dhaka □, Bangla. 69 G14
Dachau, Germany 25 G7
Dachstein, Hoher, Austria 26 D6
Dačice, Czech Rep. 26 B8
Dadanawa, Guyana 124 C7
Daday, Turkey 72 B5
Dade City, U.S.A. 109 L4
Dadhar, Pakistan 68 E2
Dadiya, Nigeria 83 D7
Dadra & Nagar Haveli □, India 66 J8
Dadri = Charkhi Dadri, India 68 E7
Dadu, Pakistan 68 F2
Dadu He →, China 58 C4
Daet, Phil. 61 D5
Dafang, China 58 D5
Dagana, Senegal 82 B1
Dagash, Sudan 80 D3
Dagestan □, Russia 49 J8
Dagestanskiye Ogni, Russia 49 J9
Daghestan Republic = Dagestan □, Russia 49 J8
Daghfeli, Sudan 80 D3
Dağlıq Qarabağ = Nagorno-Karabakh, Azerbaijan 70 B5
Dagö = Hiiumaa, Estonia 9 G20
Dagu, China 57 E9
Daguan, China 58 D4
Dagupan, Phil. 61 C4
Daguragu, Australia 92 C5
Dahab, Egypt 80 B3
Dahlak Kebir, Eritrea 81 D5
Dahlenburg, Germany 24 B6
Dahlonega, U.S.A. 109 H4
Dahme, Germany 24 D9
Dahod, India 68 H6
Dahomey = Benin ■, Africa 83 D5
Dahong Shan, China 59 B9
Dahra, Senegal 82 B1
Dahshûr, Egypt 80 J7
Dahûk, Iraq 70 B3
Dai Hao, Vietnam 64 C6
Dai-Sen, Japan 55 G6
Dai Shan, China 59 B14
Dai Xian, China 56 E7
Daicheng, China 56 E9
Daimiel, Spain 35 F7
Daingean, Ireland 15 C4
Dainkog, China 58 A1
Daintree, Australia 94 B4
Daiō-Misaki, Japan 55 G8
Dair, J. ed, Sudan 81 E3
Dairût, Egypt 80 B3
Daisetsu-Zan, Japan 54 C11
Dajarra, Australia 94 C2
Dajin Chuan →, China 58 B3
Dak Dam, Cambodia 64 F6
Dak Nhe, Vietnam 64 E6
Dak Pek, Vietnam 64 E6
Dak Song, Vietnam 65 F6
Dak Sui, Vietnam 64 E6
Dakar, Senegal 82 C1
Dakhla, W. Sahara 78 D2
Dakhla, El Wâhât el-, Egypt 80 B2
Dakingari, Nigeria 83 C5
Dakor, India 68 H5
Dakoro, Niger 83 C6
Dakota City, U.S.A. 112 D6
Đakovica, Kosovo, Yug. 40 D4
Đakovo, Croatia 42 E3
Dalaba, Guinea 82 C2
Dalachi, China 56 F3
Dalai Nur, China 56 C9
Dalälven →, Sweden 10 D10
Dalaman, Turkey 39 E10
Dalaman →, Turkey 39 E10
Dalandzadgad, Mongolia 56 C3
Dalap-Uliga-Darrit, Marshall Is. 96 G9
Dalarna, Sweden 10 D8
Dalarnas län □, Sweden 10 C8
Dālbandīn, Pakistan 66 E4
Dalbeattie, U.K. 14 G5
Dalbeg, Australia 94 C4
Dalbosjön, Sweden 11 F6
Dalby, Australia 95 D5
Dalby, Sweden 11 J7
Dale City, U.S.A. 108 F7
Dale Hollow L., U.S.A. 109 G3
Dalga, Egypt 80 B3
Dalgán, Iran 71 E8

Dalhart, U.S.A. 113 G3
Dalhousie, Canada 103 C6
Dalhousie, India 68 C6
Dali, Shaanxi, China 56 G5
Dali, Yunnan, China 58 E3
Dalian, China 57 E11
Daliang Shan, China 58 D4
Daling He →, China 57 D11
Dāliyat el Karmel, Israel 75 C4
Dalj, Croatia 42 E3
Dalkeith, U.K. 14 F5
Dallas, Oreg., U.S.A. 114 D2
Dallas, Tex., U.S.A. 113 J6
Dallol, Ethiopia 81 E5
Dalmã, U.A.E. 71 E7
Dalmacija, Croatia 29 E13
Dalmas, L., Canada 103 B5
Dalmatia = Dalmacija, Croatia 29 E13
Dalmau, India 69 F9
Dalmellington, U.K. 14 F4
Dalnegorsk, Russia 51 E14
Dalnerechensk, Russia 51 E14
Daloa, Ivory C. 82 D3
Dalou Shan, China 58 C6
Dalry, U.K. 14 F4
Dalrymple, L., Australia 94 C4
Dals Långed, Sweden 11 F6
Dalsjöfors, Sweden 11 G7
Dalsland, Sweden 11 F6
Daltenganj, India 69 H11
Dalton, Ga., U.S.A. 109 H3
Dalton, Mass., U.S.A. 111 D11
Dalton, Nebr., U.S.A. 112 E3
Dalton Iceberg Tongue, Antarctica 5 C9
Dalton-in-Furness, U.K. 12 C4
Dalupiri I., Phil. 61 B4
Dalvík, Iceland 8 D4
Dalwallinu, Australia 93 F2
Daly →, Australia 92 B5
Daly City, U.S.A. 116 H4
Daly L., Canada 105 B7
Daly River, Australia 92 B5
Daly Waters, Australia 94 B1
Dalyan, Turkey 39 E10
Dam Doi, Vietnam 65 H5
Dam Ha, Vietnam 64 B6
Daman, India 66 J8
Damanhûr, Egypt 80 H7
Damant L., Canada 105 A7
Damanzhuang, China 56 E9
Damar, Indonesia 63 F7
Damaraland, Namibia 88 C2
Damascus = Dimashq, Syria 75 B5
Damaturu, Nigeria 83 C7
Damāvand, Iran 71 C7
Damāvand, Qolleh-ye, Iran 71 C7
Damba, Angola 84 F3
Dâmbovița →, Romania 43 F10
Dâmbovița □, Romania 43 F11
Dâmbovnic →, Romania 43 F10
Dame Marie, Haiti 121 C5
Dāmghān, Iran 71 B7
Damietta = Dumyât, Egypt 80 H7
Daming, China 56 F8
Damīr Qābū, Syria 70 B4
Dammam = Ad Dammām, Si. Arabia 71 E6
Dammarie-les-Lys, France 19 D9
Dammartin-en-Goële, France 19 C9
Damme, Germany 24 C4
Damodar →, India 69 H12
Damoh, India 69 H8
Dampier, Australia 92 D2
Dampier, Selat, Indonesia 63 E8
Dampier Arch., Australia 92 D2
Damrei, Chuor Phnum, Cambodia 65 G4
Damvillers, France 19 C12
Dan-Gulbi, Nigeria 83 C6
Dan Xian, China 64 C7
Dana, Indonesia 63 F6
Dana, L., Canada 102 B4
Dana, Mt., U.S.A. 116 H7
Danakil Desert, Ethiopia 81 E5
Danané, Ivory C. 82 D3
Danao, Phil. 61 F6
Danau Poso, Indonesia 63 E6
Danba, China 58 B3
Danbury, U.S.A. 111 E11
Danby L., U.S.A. 115 J6
Dand, Afghan. 68 D1
Dandeldhura, Nepal 69 E9
Dandeli, India 66 M9
Dandîl, Egypt 80 J7
Dandong, China 57 D13
Danfeng, China 56 H6
Dangan Liedao, China 59 F10
Dangé-St-Romain, France 20 B4
Dângeni, Romania 43 C11
Danger Is. = Pukapuka, Cook Is. 97 J11
Danger Pt., S. Africa 88 E2
Dangla, Ethiopia 81 E4
Dangla Shan = Tanggula Shan, China 60 C4
Dangora, Nigeria 83 C6
Dangouadougou, Burkina Faso 82 D4
Dangrek, Phnom, Thailand 64 E5
Dangriga, Belize 119 D7
Dangshan, China 56 G9
Dangtu, China 59 B12
Dangyang, China 59 B8
Dani, Burkina Faso 83 C4
Daniel, U.S.A. 114 E8

Daniel's Harbour, Canada 103 B8
Danielskuil, S. Africa 88 D3
Danielson, U.S.A. 111 E13
Danilov, Russia 46 C11
Danilovgrad, Montenegro, Yug. 40 D3
Danilovka, Russia 48 E7
Daning, China 56 F6
Danissa, Kenya 86 B5
Danja, Nigeria 83 C6
Danjiangkou, China 59 A8
Danjiangkou Shuiku, China 59 A8
Dank, Oman 71 F8
Dankalwa, Nigeria 83 C7
Dankama, Nigeria 83 C6
Dankhar Gompa, India 66 C11
Dankov, Russia 46 F10
Danleng, China 58 B4
Danlí, Honduras 120 D2
Dannemora, U.S.A. 111 B11
Dannenberg, Germany 24 B7
Dannevirke, N.Z. 91 J6
Dannhauser, S. Africa 89 D5
Dansville, U.S.A. 110 D7
Danta, India 68 G5
Dantan, India 69 J12
Dante, Somali Rep. 74 E5
Danube = Dunărea →, Europe 43 E14
Danvers, U.S.A. 111 D14
Danville, Ill., U.S.A. 108 E2
Danville, Ky., U.S.A. 108 G3
Danville, Pa., U.S.A. 111 F8
Danville, Va., U.S.A. 109 G6
Danville, Vt., U.S.A. 111 B12
Danyang, China 59 B12
Danzhai, China 58 D6
Danzig = Gdańsk, Poland 44 D5
Dão →, Portugal 34 E2
Dao Xian, China 59 E8
Daocheng, China 58 C3
Daoukro, Ivory C. 82 D4
Dapaong, Togo 83 C5
Dapchi, Nigeria 83 C7
Dapitan, Phil. 61 G5
Daqing Shan, China 56 D6
Daqu Shan, China 59 B14
Dar Banda, Africa 76 F6
Dar el Beida = Casablanca, Morocco 78 B4
Dar es Salaam, Tanzania 86 D4
Dar Mazār, Iran 71 D8
Dar'ā, Syria 75 C5
Dar'ā □, Syria 75 C5
Dārāb, Iran 71 D7
Daraban, Pakistan 68 D4
Darabani, Romania 43 B11
Daraina, Madag. 89 A8
Daraj, Libya 79 B8
Dārān, Iran 71 C6
Daravica, Kosovo, Yug. 40 D4
Daraw, Egypt 80 C3
Dārayyā, Syria 75 B5
Darazo, Nigeria 83 C7
Darband, Pakistan 68 B5
Darband, Kūh-e, Iran 71 D8
Darbhanga, India 69 F11
D'Arcy, Canada 104 C4
Darda, Croatia 42 E3
Dardanelle, Ark., U.S.A. 113 H8
Dardanelle, Calif., U.S.A. 116 G7
Dardanelles = Çanakkale Boğazı, Turkey 41 F10
Dare →, Ethiopia 81 F5
Darende, Turkey 72 C7
Dārestān, Iran 71 D8
Darfo, Italy 28 C7
Dârfûr, Sudan 79 F10
Dargai, Pakistan 68 B4
Dargan Ata, Turkmenistan 50 E7
Dargaville, N.Z. 91 F4
Dargol, Niger 83 C5
Darhan Muminggan Lianheqi, China 56 D6
Dari, Sudan 81 F3
Darıca, Turkey 72 B3
Darién, G. del, Colombia 122 C3
Dariganga = Ovoot, Mongolia 56 B7
Darinskoye, Kazakstan 48 E10
Darjeeling = Darjiling, India 69 F13
Darjiling, India 69 F13
Darkan, Australia 93 F2
Darkhana, Pakistan 68 D5
Darkhazīneh, Iran 71 D6
Darkot Pass, Pakistan 69 A5
Darling →, Australia 95 E3
Darling Downs, Australia 95 D5
Darling Ra., Australia 93 F2
Darlington, U.K. 12 C6
Darlington, U.S.A. 109 H6
Darlington □, U.K. 12 C6
Darlington, L., S. Africa 88 E4
Darlot, L., Australia 93 E3
Darłowo, Poland 44 D3
Dărmănești, Bacău, Romania 43 D11
Dărmănești, Suceava, Romania 43 C11
Darmstadt, Germany 25 F4
Darnah, Libya 79 B10
Darnall, S. Africa 89 D5
Darney, France 19 D13
Darnley, C., Antarctica 5 C6
Darnley B., Canada 100 B7
Daroca, Spain 32 D3
Darr →, Australia 94 C3
Darra Pezu, Pakistan 68 C4
Darregueira, Argentina 126 D3
Darrington, U.S.A. 114 B3
Darsser Ort, Germany 24 A8

Dart →, U.K. 13 G4
Dart, C., Antarctica 5 D14
Dartford, U.K. 13 F8
Dartmoor, U.K. 13 G4
Dartmouth, Canada 103 D7
Dartmouth, U.K. 13 G4
Dartmouth, L., Australia 95 D4
Dartuch, C. = Artrutx, C. de, Spain 37 B10
Daruvar, Croatia 42 E2
Darvaza, Turkmenistan 50 E6
Darvel, Teluk = Lahad Datu, Teluk, Malaysia 63 D5
Darwen, U.K. 12 D5
Darwendale, Zimbabwe 89 B5
Darwha, India 66 J10
Darwin, Australia 92 B5
Darwin, U.S.A. 117 J9
Darya Khan, Pakistan 68 D4
Daryoi Amu = Amudarya →, Uzbekistan 50 E6
Dãs, U.A.E. 71 E7
Dashen, Ras, Ethiopia 81 E4
Dashetai, China 56 D5
Dashhowuz, Turkmenistan 50 E6
Dashkesan = Daşkäsän, Azerbaijan 49 K7
Dashköpri, Turkmenistan 71 B9
Dasht, Iran 71 B8
Dasht →, Pakistan 66 G2
Daska, Pakistan 68 C6
Daşkäsän, Azerbaijan 49 K7
Dassa, Benin 83 D5
Dasuya, India 68 D6
Datça, Turkey 39 E9
Datia, India 69 G8
Datian, China 59 E11
Datong, Anhui, China 59 B11
Datong, Shanxi, China 56 D7
Dattakhel, Pakistan 68 C3
Datteln, Germany 24 D3
Datu, Tanjung, Indonesia 62 D3
Datu Piang, Phil. 61 H6
Datuk, Tanjong = Datu, Tanjung, Indonesia 62 D3
Daud Khel, Pakistan 68 C4
Daudnagar, India 69 G11
Daugava →, Latvia 9 H21
Daugavpils, Latvia 9 J22
Daulpur, India 68 F7
Daun, Germany 25 E2
Dauphin, Canada 105 C8
Dauphin, U.S.A. 110 F8
Dauphin L., Canada 105 C9
Dauphiné, France 21 C9
Daura, Borno, Nigeria 83 C7
Daura, Katsina, Nigeria 83 C6
Dausa, India 68 F7
Däväçi, Azerbaijan 49 K9
Davangere, India 66 M9
Davao, Phil. 61 H6
Davao G., Phil. 61 H6
Dävar Panãh, Iran 71 E9
Davenport, Calif., U.S.A. 116 H4
Davenport, Iowa, U.S.A. 112 E9
Davenport, Wash., U.S.A. 114 C4
Davenport Ra., Australia 94 C1
Daventry, U.K. 13 E6
David, Panama 120 E3
David City, U.S.A. 112 E6
David Gorodok = Davyd Haradok, Belarus 47 F4
Davidson, Canada 105 C7
Davis, U.S.A. 116 G5
Davis Dam, U.S.A. 117 K12
Davis Inlet, Canada 103 A7
Davis Mts., U.S.A. 113 K2
Davis Sea, Antarctica 5 C7
Davis Str., N. Amer. 101 B14
Davo →, Ivory C. 82 D3
Davos, Switz. 25 J5
Davutlar, Turkey 39 D9
Davy L., Canada 105 B7
Davyd Haradok, Belarus 47 F4
Dawa →, Ethiopia 81 G5
Dawaki, Bauchi, Nigeria 83 D6
Dawaki, Kano, Nigeria 83 C6
Dawei, Burma 64 E2
Dawes Ra., Australia 94 C5
Dawlish, U.K. 13 G4
Dawna Ra., Burma 64 D2
Dawros Hd., Ireland 15 B3
Dawson, Canada 100 B6
Dawson, U.S.A. 109 K3
Dawson, I., Chile 128 G2
Dawson B., Canada 105 C8
Dawson Creek, Canada 104 B4
Dawson Inlet, Canada 105 A10
Dawson Ra., Australia 94 C4
Dawu, Hubei, China 59 B9
Dawu, Sichuan, China 58 B3
Dax, France 20 E2
Daxian, China 58 B6
Daxin, China 58 F6
Daxindian, China 57 F11
Daxinggou, China 57 C15
Daxue Shan, Sichuan, China 58 B3
Daxue Shan, Yunnan, China 58 F2
Dayao, China 58 E3
Daye, China 59 B10
Dayet en Naharat, Mali 82 B4
Dayi, China 58 B4
Dayong, China 59 C8
Dayr az Zawr, Syria 70 C4
Daysland, Canada 104 C6
Dayton, Nev., U.S.A. 116 F7

Dayton, Ohio, U.S.A. 108 F3
Dayton, Pa., U.S.A. 110 F5
Dayton, Tenn., U.S.A. 109 H3
Dayton, Wash., U.S.A. 114 C4
Dayton, Wyo., U.S.A. 114 D10
Daytona Beach, U.S.A. 109 L5
Dayu, China 59 E10
Dayville, U.S.A. 114 D4
Dazhu, China 58 B6
Dazkırı, Turkey 39 D11
Dazu, China 58 C5
De Aar, S. Africa 88 E3
De Funiak Springs, U.S.A. 109 K2
De Grey →, Australia 92 D2
De Haan, Belgium 17 C3
De Kalb, U.S.A. 112 E10
De Land, U.S.A. 109 L5
De Leon, U.S.A. 113 J5
De Panne, Belgium 17 C2
De Pere, U.S.A. 108 C1
De Queen, U.S.A. 113 H7
De Quincy, U.S.A. 113 K8
De Ridder, U.S.A. 113 K8
De Smet, U.S.A. 112 C6
De Soto, U.S.A. 112 F9
De Tour Village, U.S.A. 108 C4
De Witt, U.S.A. 113 H9
Dead Sea, Asia 75 D4
Deadwood, U.S.A. 112 C3
Deadwood L., Canada 104 B3
Deal, U.K. 13 F9
Deal I., Australia 94 F4
Dealesville, S. Africa 88 D4
De'an, China 59 C10
Dean →, Canada 104 C3
Dean, Forest of, U.K. 13 F5
Dean Chan., Canada 104 C3
Deán Funes, Argentina 126 C3
Dease →, Canada 104 B3
Dease L., Canada 104 B2
Dease Lake, Canada 104 B2
Death Valley, U.S.A. 117 J10
Death Valley Junction, U.S.A. 117 J10
Death Valley National Park, U.S.A. 117 J10
Deauville, France 18 C7
Deba, Spain 32 B2
Deba Habe, Nigeria 83 C7
Debaltsevo, Ukraine 47 H10
Debao, China 58 F6
Debar, Macedonia 40 E4
Debden, Canada 105 C7
Dębica, Poland 45 H8
Dęblin, Poland 45 G8
Dębno, Poland 45 F1
Débo, L., Mali 82 B4
Debolt, Canada 104 B5
Deborah East, L., Australia 93 F2
Deborah West, L., Australia 93 F2
Debrc, Serbia, Yug. 40 B3
Debre Birhan, Ethiopia 81 F4
Debre Markos, Ethiopia 81 E4
Debre May, Ethiopia 81 E4
Debre Sina, Ethiopia 81 F4
Debre Tabor, Ethiopia 81 E4
Debre Zevit, Ethiopia 81 F4
Debre Zeyit, Ethiopia 81 E4
Debrecen, Hungary 42 C6
Debrzno, Poland 44 E4
Dečani, Kosovo, Yug. 40 D4
Decatur, Ala., U.S.A. 109 H2
Decatur, Ga., U.S.A. 109 J3
Decatur, Ill., U.S.A. 112 F10
Decatur, Ind., U.S.A. 108 E3
Decatur, Tex., U.S.A. 113 J6
Decazeville, France 20 D6
Deccan, India 66 L11
Deception Bay, Australia 95 D5
Deception L., Canada 105 B8
Dechang, China 58 D4
Dechhu, India 68 F5
Děčín, Czech Rep. 26 A7
Decize, France 19 F10
Deckerville, U.S.A. 110 C2
Decollatura, Italy 31 C9
Decorah, U.S.A. 112 D9
Deda, Romania 43 D9
Dedéagach = Alexandroúpolis, Greece 41 F9
Deder, Ethiopia 81 F5
Dedham, U.S.A. 111 D13
Dédougou, Burkina Faso 82 C4
Dedovichi, Russia 46 D5
Dedza, Malawi 87 E3
Dee →, Aberds., U.K. 14 D6
Dee →, Dumf. & Gall., U.K. 14 G4
Dee →, Wales, U.K. 12 D4
Deep B., Canada 104 A5
Deepwater, Australia 95 D5
Deer →, Canada 105 B10
Deer L., Canada 105 C10
Deer Lake, Nfld., Canada 103 C8
Deer Lake, Ont., Canada 105 C10
Deer Lodge, U.S.A. 114 C7
Deer Park, U.S.A. 114 C5
Deer River, U.S.A. 112 B8
Deeragun, Australia 94 B4
Deerdepoort, S. Africa 88 C4
Deferiet, U.S.A. 111 B9
Defiance, U.S.A. 108 E3
Degana, India 68 F6
Dêgê, China 58 B2
Degebe →, Portugal 35 G3
Degeberga, Sweden 11 J8
Degema, Nigeria 83 E6

Degerfors, Sweden 10 E8
Degerhamn, Sweden 11 H10
Deggendorf, Germany 25 G8
Degh →, Pakistan 68 D5
Değirmendere, Turkey 41 F13
Deh Bīd, Iran 71 D7
Deh-e Shīr, Iran 71 D7
Dehaj, Iran 71 D7
Dehak, Iran 71 E9
Dehdez, Iran 71 D6
Dehej, India 68 J5
Dehestãn, Iran 71 D7
Dehgolãn, Iran 70 C5
Dehibat, Tunisia 79 B8
Dehlorãn, Iran 70 C5
Dehnow-e Kūhestãn, Iran 71 E8
Dehra Dun, India 68 D8
Dehri, India 69 G11
Dehua, China 59 E12
Dehui, China 57 B13
Deim Zubeir, Sudan 81 F2
Deinze, Belgium 17 D3
Dej, Romania 43 C8
Deje, Sweden 10 E7
Dejiang, China 58 C7
Deka →, Zimbabwe 88 B4
Dekemhare, Eritrea 81 D4
Dekese, Dem. Rep. of the Congo 84 E4
Del Mar, U.S.A. 117 N9
Del Norte, U.S.A. 115 H10
Del Rio, U.S.A. 113 L4
Delai, Sudan 80 D4
Delambre I., Australia 92 D2
Delami, Sudan 81 E3
Delano, U.S.A. 117 K7
Delano Peak, U.S.A. 115 G7
Delareyville, S. Africa 88 D4
Delaronde L., Canada 105 C7
Delavan, U.S.A. 112 D10
Delaware, U.S.A. 108 E4
Delaware □, U.S.A. 108 F8
Delaware →, U.S.A. 111 G9
Delaware B., U.S.A. 108 F8
Delay →, Canada 103 A5
Delbrück, Germany 24 D4
Delčevo, Macedonia 40 E6
Delémont, Switz. 25 H3
Delevan, U.S.A. 110 D6
Delft, Neths. 17 B4
Delfzijl, Neths. 17 A6
Delgado, C., Mozam. 87 E5
Delgerhet, Mongolia 56 B6
Delgo, Sudan 80 C3
Delhi, Canada 110 D4
Delhi, India 68 E7
Delhi, La., U.S.A. 113 J9
Delhi, N.Y., U.S.A. 111 D10
Deli Jovan, Serbia, Yug. 40 B6
Delia, Canada 104 C6
Delice, Turkey 72 C6
Delicias, Mexico 118 B3
Delījãn, Iran 71 C6
Delisle, Canada 105 C7
Delitzsch, Germany 24 D8
Dell City, U.S.A. 115 L11
Dell Rapids, U.S.A. 112 D6
Delle, France 19 E14
Delmar, U.S.A. 111 D11
Delmenhorst, Germany 24 B4
Delnice, Croatia 29 C11
Delonga, Ostrova, Russia 51 B15
Deloraine, Australia 94 G4
Deloraine, Canada 105 D8
Delphi, Greece 38 C4
Delphi, U.S.A. 108 E2
Delphos, U.S.A. 108 E3
Delportshoop, S. Africa 88 D3
Delray Beach, U.S.A. 109 M5
Delsbo, Sweden 10 C10
Delta, Colo., U.S.A. 115 G9
Delta, Utah, U.S.A. 114 G7
Delta □, Nigeria 83 D6
Delta Junction, U.S.A. 100 B5
Deltona, U.S.A. 109 L5
Delungra, Australia 95 D5
Delvada, India 68 J4
Delvinákion, Greece 38 B2
Delvinë, Albania 40 G4
Demak, Indonesia 63 G14
Demanda, Sierra de la, Spain 32 C2
Demavand = Damãvand, Iran 71 C7
Dembecha, Ethiopia 81 E4
Dembi, Ethiopia 81 F4
Dembia, Dem. Rep. of the Congo 86 B2
Dembidolo, Ethiopia 81 F3
Demchok, India 69 C8
Demer →, Belgium 17 D4
Demetrias, Greece 38 B5
Demidov, Russia 46 E6
Deming, N. Mex., U.S.A. 115 K10
Deming, Wash., U.S.A. 116 B4
Demini →, Brazil 124 D6
Demirci, Turkey 39 B10
Demirköprü Barajı, Turkey 39 C10
Demirköy, Turkey 41 E11
Demmin, Germany 24 B9
Demonte, Italy 28 D4
Demopolis, U.S.A. 109 J2
Dempo, Indonesia 62 E2
Demyansk, Russia 46 D7
Den Burg, Neths. 17 A4
Den Chai, Thailand 64 D3
Den Haag = 's-Gravenhage, Neths. 17 B4
Den Helder, Neths. 17 B4

Den Oever, Neths. 17 B5
Denain, France 19 B10
Denair, U.S.A. 116 H6
Denau, Uzbekistan 50 F7
Denbigh, Canada 110 A7
Denbigh, U.K. 12 D4
Denbighshire □, U.K. 12 D4
Dendang, Indonesia 62 E3
Dendermonde, Belgium 17 C4
Deneba, Ethiopia 81 F4
Dengchuan, China 58 E3
Denge, Nigeria 83 C6
Dengfeng, China 56 G7
Dengi, Nigeria 83 D6
Dengkou, China 56 D4
Dengzhou, China 59 A9
Denham, Australia 93 E1
Denham Ra., Australia 94 C4
Denham Sd., Australia 93 E1
Denholm, Canada 105 C7
Denia, Spain 33 G5
Denial B., Australia 95 E1
Denison, Iowa, U.S.A. 112 E7
Denison, Tex., U.S.A. 113 J6
Denison Plains, Australia 92 C4
Denizli, Turkey 39 D11
Denizli □, Turkey 39 D11
Denman Glacier, Antarctica 5 C7
Denmark, Australia 93 F2
Denmark ■, Europe 11 J3
Denmark Str., Atl. Oc. 4 C6
Dennison, U.S.A. 110 F3
Denny, U.K. 14 E5
Denpasar, Indonesia 62 F5
Denton, Mont., U.S.A. 114 C9
Denton, Tex., U.S.A. 113 J6
D'Entrecasteaux, Pt., Australia 93 F2
Denu, Ghana 83 D5
Denver, Colo., U.S.A. 112 F2
Denver, Pa., U.S.A. 111 F8
Denver City, U.S.A. 113 J3
Deoband, India 68 E7
Deogarh, India 68 G5
Deoghar, India 69 G12
Deolali, India 66 K8
Deoli = Devli, India 68 G6
Deoli, India 68 G6
Déols, France 19 F8
Deora, India 68 F4
Deori, India 69 H8
Deoria, India 69 F10
Deosai Mts., Pakistan 69 B6
Deosri, India 69 F14
Depalpur, India 68 H6
Deping, China 57 F9
Deposit, U.S.A. 111 D9
Depuch I., Australia 92 D2
Deputatskiy, Russia 51 C14
Dêqên, China 58 C2
Deqing, China 59 F8
Dera Ghazi Khan, Pakistan 68 D4
Dera Ismail Khan, Pakistan 68 D4
Derabugti, Pakistan 68 E3
Derawar Fort, Pakistan 68 E4
Derbent, Russia 49 J9
Derbent, Turkey 39 C10
Derby, Australia 92 C3
Derby, U.K. 12 E6
Derby, Conn., U.S.A. 111 E11
Derby, Kans., U.S.A. 113 G6
Derby, N.Y., U.S.A. 110 D6
Derby City □, U.K. 12 E6
Derby Line, U.S.A. 111 B12
Derbyshire □, U.K. 12 D6
Derecske, Hungary 42 C6
Dereköy, Turkey 41 E11
Dereli, Turkey 73 B8
Derg →, U.K. 15 B4
Derg, L., Ireland 15 D3
Dergachi = Derhaci, Ukraine 47 G9
Dergaon, India 67 F19
Derhaci, Ukraine 47 G9
Derik, Turkey 73 C9
Derinkuyu, Turkey 72 C6
Dermantsi, Bulgaria 41 C8
Dermott, U.S.A. 113 J9
Dêrong, China 58 C2
Derry = Londonderry, U.K. 15 B4
Derry = Londonderry □, U.K. 15 B4
Derry, N.H., U.S.A. 111 D13
Derry, Pa., U.S.A. 110 F5
Derryveagh Mts., Ireland 15 B3
Derudub, Sudan 80 D4
Derval, France 18 E5
Dervéni, Greece 38 C4
Derventa, Bos.-H. 42 F2
Derwent →, Cumb., U.K. 12 C4
Derwent →, Derby, U.K. 12 E6
Derwent →, N. Yorks., U.K. 12 D7
Derwent Water, U.K. 12 C4
Des Moines, Iowa, U.S.A. 112 E8
Des Moines, N. Mex., U.S.A. 113 G3
Des Moines →, U.S.A. 112 E9
Desa, Romania 42 G8
Desaguadero →, Argentina 126 C2
Desaguadero →, Bolivia 124 G5
Descanso, Pta., Mexico 117 N9
Descartes, France 20 B4
Deschaillons, Canada 103 C5
Deschambault L., Canada 105 C8
Deschutes →, U.S.A. 114 D3
Dese, Ethiopia 81 E4
Deseado →, Argentina 128 F3
Desenzano del Garda, Italy 28 C7
Desert Center, U.S.A. 117 M11
Desert Hot Springs, U.S.A. 117 M10
Deshnok, India 68 F5

Desna →, Ukraine 47 G6
Desnãtui →, Romania 43 G8
Desolación, I., Chile 128 G2
Despeñaperros, Paso, Spain 35 G7
Despotovac, Serbia, Yug. 40 B5
Dessau, Germany 24 D8
Dessye = Dese, Ethiopia 81 E4
Desuri, India 68 G5
Desvres, France 19 B8
Det Udom, Thailand 64 E5
Deta, Romania 42 E6
Dete, Zimbabwe 88 B4
Đetinja →, Serbia, Yug. 40 C4
Detmold, Germany 24 D4
Detour, Pt., U.S.A. 108 C2
Detroit, U.S.A. 110 D1
Detroit Lakes, U.S.A. 112 B7
Detva, Slovak Rep. 27 C12
Deurne, Neths. 17 C5
Deutsche Bucht, Germany 24 A4
Deutschlandsberg, Austria 26 E8
Deux-Sèvres □, France 18 F6
Deva, Romania 42 E7
Devakottai, India 66 Q11
Devaprayag, India 69 D8
Dévaványa, Hungary 42 C5
Deveci Dağları, Turkey 72 B7
Devecikonağı, Turkey 41 G12
Devecser, Hungary 42 C2
Develi, Turkey 72 C6
Deventer, Neths. 17 B6
Deveron →, U.K. 14 D6
Devesel, Romania 42 F7
Devgadh Bariya, India 68 H5
Devikot, India 68 F4
Devils Den, U.S.A. 116 K7
Devils Lake, U.S.A. 112 A5
Devils Paw, Canada 104 B2
Devils Tower Junction, U.S.A. 112 C2
Devin, Bulgaria 41 E8
Devine, U.S.A. 113 L5
Devizes, U.K. 13 F6
Devli, India 68 G6
Devnya, Bulgaria 41 C11
Devoll →, Albania 40 F4
Devon, Canada 104 C6
Devon □, U.K. 13 G4
Devon I., Canada 4 B3
Devonport, Australia 94 G4
Devonport, N.Z. 91 G5
Devrek, Turkey 72 B4
Devrekâni, Turkey 72 B5
Devrez →, Turkey 72 B6
Dewas, India 68 H7
Dewetsdorp, S. Africa 88 D4
Dexing, China 59 C11
Dexter, Maine, U.S.A. 109 C11
Dexter, Mo., U.S.A. 113 G10
Dexter, N. Mex., U.S.A. 113 J2
Dey-Dey, L., Australia 93 E5
Deyang, China 58 B5
Deyhūk, Iran 71 C8
Deyyer, Iran 71 E6
Dezadeash L., Canada 104 A1
Dezfūl, Iran 71 C6
Dezhneva, Mys, Russia 51 C19
Dezhou, China 56 F9
Dhadhar →, India 69 G11
Dhahaban, Si. Arabia 80 C4
Dhahiriya = Az Zāhirīyah, West Bank 75 D3
Dhahran = Az Zahrān, Si. Arabia 71 E6
Dhak, Pakistan 68 C5
Dhaka, Bangla. 69 H14
Dhaka □, Bangla. 69 G14
Dhali, Cyprus 36 D12
Dhamási, Greece 38 B4
Dhampur, India 69 E8
Dhamtari, India 67 J12
Dhanbad, India 69 H12
Dhangarhi, Nepal 67 E12
Dhankuta, Nepal 69 F12
Dhar, India 68 H6
Dharampur, India 68 H6
Dharamsala = Dharmsala, India 68 C7
Dhariwal, India 68 D6
Dharla →, Bangla. 69 G13
Dharmapuri, India 66 N11
Dharmjaygarh, India 69 H10
Dharmsala, India 68 C7
Dharni, India 68 J7
Dharwad, India 66 M9
Dhasan →, India 69 G8
Dhaulagiri, Nepal 69 E10
Dhebar, L., India 68 G6
Dheftera, Cyprus 36 D12
Dhenkanal, India 67 J14
Dhenoúsa, Greece 39 D7
Dherinia, Cyprus 36 D12
Dheskáti, Greece 38 B3
Dhespotikó, Greece 38 E6
Dhestina, Greece 38 C4
Dhiarrizos →, Cyprus 36 E11
Dhībãn, Jordan 75 D4
Dhidhimótikhon, Greece 41 E10
Dhíkti Óros, Greece 36 D7
Dhílianáta, Greece 38 C2
Dhílos, Greece 39 D7
Dhilwan, India 68 D6
Dhimarkhera, India 69 H9
Dhimitsána, Greece 38 D4
Dhírfis Óros, Greece 38 C5
Dhodhekánisos, Greece 39 E8

Dhodhekánisos □, Greece 39 E8
Dhokós, Greece 38 D5
Dholiana, Greece 38 B2
Dholka, India 68 H5
Dhomokós, Greece 38 B4
Dhoraji, India 68 J4
Dhoxáton, Greece 41 E8
Dhragonísi, Greece 39 D7
Dhráhstis, Ákra, Greece 36 A3
Dhrangadhra, India 68 H4
Dhrápanon, Ákra, Greece 36 D6
Dhriopís, Greece 38 D6
Dhrol, India 68 H4
Dhuburi, India 67 F16
Dhule, India 66 J9
Di-ib, W. →, Sudan 80 C4
Di Linh, Vietnam 65 G7
Di Linh, Cao Nguyen, Vietnam 65 G7
Día, Greece 36 D7
Diabakania, Guinea 82 C2
Diablo, Mt., U.S.A. 116 H5
Diablo Range, U.S.A. 116 J5
Diafarabé, Mali 82 C4
Diala, Mali 82 C3
Dialakoro, Mali 82 C3
Dialakoto, Senegal 82 C2
Diallassagou, Mali 82 C4
Diamante, Argentina 126 C3
Diamante, Italy 31 C8
Diamante →, Argentina 126 C2
Diamantina, Brazil 125 G10
Diamantina →, Australia 95 D2
Diamantino, Brazil 125 F7
Diamond Bar, U.S.A. 117 L9
Diamond Harbour, India 69 H13
Diamond Is., Australia 94 B5
Diamond Mts., U.S.A. 114 G6
Diamond Springs, U.S.A. 116 G6
Dian Chi, China 58 E4
Dianalund, Denmark 11 J5
Dianbai, China 59 G8
Diancheng, China 59 G8
Dianjiang, China 58 B6
Diano Marina, Italy 28 E5
Dianra, Ivory C. 82 D3
Diapaga, Burkina Faso 83 C5
Diapangou, Burkina Faso 83 C5
Diariguila, Guinea 82 C2
Dībā, Oman 71 E8
Dibai, India 68 E8
Dibaya-Lubue, Dem. Rep. of
the Congo 84 E3
Dibete, Botswana 88 C4
Dibrugarh, India 67 F19
Dickens, U.S.A. 113 J4
Dickson = Dikson, Russia 50 B9
Dickson, U.S.A. 109 G2
Dickson City, U.S.A. 111 E9
Dicle Nehri →, Turkey 73 D9
Dicomano, Italy 29 E8
Didesa, W. →, Ethiopia 81 F4
Didi, Sudan 81 F3
Didiéni, Mali 82 C3
Didsbury, Canada 104 C6
Didwana, India 68 F6
Die, France 21 D9
Diébougou, Burkina Faso 82 C4
Diecke, Guinea 82 D3
Diefenbaker, L., Canada 105 C7
Diego de Almagro, Chile 126 B1
Diego Garcia, Ind. Oc. 3 E13
Diekirch, Lux. 17 E6
Diéma, Mali 82 C3
Diembéring, Senegal 82 C1
Dien Ban, Vietnam 64 E7
Dien Bien, Vietnam 58 G4
Dien Khanh, Vietnam 65 F7
Diepholz, Germany 24 C4
Dieppe, France 18 C8
Dierks, U.S.A. 113 H8
Diest, Belgium 17 D5
Dietikon, Switz. 25 H4
Dieulefit, France 21 D9
Dieuze, France 19 D13
Dif, Somali Rep. 74 G3
Differdange, Lux. 17 E5
Dig, India 68 F7
Digba, Dem. Rep. of the Congo 86 B2
Digby, Canada 103 D6
Diggi, India 68 F6
Dighinala, Bangla. 67 H18
Dighton, U.S.A. 112 F4
Digna, Mali 82 C3
Digne-les-Bains, France 21 D10
Digoin, France 19 F11
Digor, Turkey 73 B10
Digos, Phil. 61 H6
Digranes, Iceland 8 C6
Digul →, Indonesia 63 F9
Dihang →, India 67 F19
Dijlah, Nahr →, Asia 70 D5
Dijon, France 19 E12
Dikhil, Djibouti 81 E5
Dikili, Turkey 39 B8
Dikirnis, Egypt 80 H7
Dikkil = Dikhil, Djibouti 81 E5
Dikodougou, Ivory C. 82 D3
Diksmuide, Belgium 17 C2
Dikson, Russia 50 B9
Dikwa, Nigeria 83 C7
Dila, Ethiopia 81 F4
Dili, E. Timor 63 F7
Dilijan, Armenia 49 K7
Dilizhan = Dilijan, Armenia 49 K7
Dilj, Croatia 42 E3

Dillenburg, Germany 24 E4
Dilley, U.S.A. 113 L5
Dilling, Sudan 81 E2
Dillingen, Bayern, Germany 25 G6
Dillingen, Saarland, Germany 25 F2
Dillingham, U.S.A. 100 C4
Dillon, Canada 105 B7
Dillon, Mont., U.S.A. 114 D7
Dillon, S.C., U.S.A. 109 H6
Dillon →, Canada 105 B7
Dillsburg, U.S.A. 110 F7
Dilly, Mali 82 C3
Dilolo, Dem. Rep. of the Congo 84 G4
Dimas, Mexico 118 C3
Dimashq, Syria 75 B5
Dimashq □, Syria 75 B5
Dimbaza, S. Africa 89 E4
Dimbokro, Ivory C. 82 D4
Dîmbovita = Dâmbovita →,
Romania 43 F11
Dimbulah, Australia 94 B4
Dimitrovgrad, Bulgaria 41 D9
Dimitrovgrad, Russia 48 C9
Dimitrovgrad, Serbia, Yug. 40 C6
Dimitrovo = Pernik, Bulgaria 40 D7
Dimmitt, U.S.A. 113 H3
Dimo, Sudan 81 F2
Dimona, Israel 75 D4
Dimovo, Bulgaria 40 C6
Dinagat, Phil. 61 F6
Dinajpur, Bangla. 67 G16
Dinan, France 18 D4
Dinan Āb, Iran 71 C8
Dinant, Belgium 17 D4
Dinapur, India 69 G11
Dinar, Turkey 39 C12
Dīnar, Kūh-e, Iran 71 D6
Dinara Planina, Croatia 29 D13
Dinard, France 18 D4
Dinaric Alps = Dinara Planina,
Croatia 29 D13
Dindanko, Mali 82 C3
Dinder, Nahr ed →, Sudan 81 E3
Dindigul, India 66 P11
Dindori, India 69 H9
Ding Xian = Dingzhou, China . 56 E8
Dinga, Pakistan 68 G2
Dingalan, Phil. 61 D4
Dingbian, China 56 F4
Dingelstädt, Germany 24 D6
Dingle, Ireland 15 D1
Dingle, Sweden 11 F5
Dingle B., Ireland 15 D1
Dingmans Ferry, U.S.A. 111 E10
Dingnan, China 59 E10
Dingo, Australia 94 C4
Dingolfing, Germany 25 G8
Dingtao, China 56 G8
Dinguira, Mali 82 C2
Dinguiraye, Guinea 82 C2
Dingwall, U.K. 14 D4
Dingxi, China 56 G3
Dingxiang, China 56 E7
Dingyuan, China 59 A11
Dingzhou, China 56 E8
Dinh, Mui, Vietnam 65 G7
Dinh Lap, Vietnam 58 G6
Dinokwe, Botswana 88 C4
Dinorwic, Canada 105 D10
Dinosaur National Monument,
U.S.A. 114 F9
Dinosaur Prov. Park, Canada . 104 C6
Dinuba, U.S.A. 116 J7
Diö, Sweden 11 H8
Dioïla, Mali 82 C3
Dioka, Mali 82 C2
Diongoï, Mali 82 C3
Diósgyör, Hungary 42 B5
Diosig, Romania 42 C7
Diougani, Mali 82 C4
Diouloulou, Senegal 82 C1
Dioura, Mali 82 C3
Diourbel, Senegal 82 C1
Dipalpur, Pakistan 68 D5
Diplo, Pakistan 68 G3
Dipolog, Phil. 61 G5
Dir, Pakistan 66 B7
Diré, Mali 82 B4
Dire Dawa, Ethiopia 81 F5
Diriamba, Nic. 120 D2
Dirk Hartog I., Australia 93 E1
Dirranbandi, Australia 95 D4
Disa, India 68 G5
Disa, Sudan 81 E3
Disappointment, C., U.S.A. 114 C2
Disappointment, L., Australia . 92 D3
Disentis Muster, Switz. 25 J4
Dishna, Egypt 80 B3
Disina, Nigeria 83 C6
Disko = Qeqertarsuaq,
Greenland 101 B5
Disko Bugt, Greenland 4 C5
Disna = Dzisna →, Belarus 46 E5
Diss, U.K. 13 E9
Disteghil Sar, Pakistan 69 A6
Distrito Federal □, Brazil 125 G9
Distrito Federal □, Mexico 119 D5
Disûq, Egypt 80 H7
Diu, India 68 J4
Dīvāndarreh, Iran 70 C5
Dives →, France 18 C6
Dives-sur-Mer, France 18 C6
Divichi = Däväçi, Azerbaijan . 49 K9
Divide, U.S.A. 114 D7
Dividing Ra., Australia 93 E2
Divinópolis, Brazil 125 H10

Divjake, Albania 40 F3
Divnoye, Russia 49 H6
Divo, Ivory C. 82 D3
Divriği, Turkey 73 C8
Dīwāl Kol, Afghan. 68 B2
Dixie Mt., U.S.A. 116 F6
Dixon, Calif., U.S.A. 116 G5
Dixon, Ill., U.S.A. 112 E10
Dixon Entrance, U.S.A. 100 C6
Dixville, Canada 111 A13
Diyadin, Turkey 73 C10
Diyālā □, Iraq 70 C5
Diyarbakır, Turkey 70 B4
Diyodar, India 68 G4
Djakarta = Jakarta, Indonesia . 62 F3
Djamba, Angola 88 B1
Djambala, Congo 84 E2
Djanet, Algeria 78 D7
Djawa = Jawa, Indonesia 62 F3
Djelfa, Algeria 78 B6
Djema, C.A.R. 86 A2
Djenné, Mali 82 C4
Djerba, I. de, Tunisia 79 B8
Djerid, Chott, Tunisia 78 B7
Djibo, Burkina Faso 83 C4
Djibouti, Djibouti 81 E5
Djibouti ■, Africa 81 E5
Djolu, Dem. Rep. of the Congo . 84 D4
Djougou, Benin 83 D5
Djoum, Cameroon 84 D2
Djourab, Erg du, Chad 79 E9
Djugu, Dem. Rep. of the Congo 86 B3
Djúpivogur, Iceland 8 D6
Djurås, Sweden 10 D9
Djursland, Denmark 11 H4
Dmitriya Lapteva, Proliv, Russia 51 B15
Dmitriyev Lgovskiy, Russia ... 47 F8
Dmitrov, Russia 46 D9
Dmitrovsk-Orlovskiy, Russia . 47 F8
Dnepr = Dnipro →, Ukraine 47 J7
Dneprodzerzhinsk =
Dniprodzerzhynsk, Ukraine . 47 H8
Dneprodzerzhinskoye Vdkhr. =
Dniprodzerzhynske Vdskh.,
Ukraine 47 H8
Dnepropetrovsk =
Dnipropetrovsk, Ukraine ... 47 H8
Dneprorudnoye = Dniprorudne,
Ukraine 47 J8
Dnestr = Dnister →, Europe . 47 J5
Dnestrovski = Belgorod, Russia 47 G9
Dnieper = Dnipro →, Ukraine . 47 J7
Dniester = Dnister →, Europe . 47 J6
Dnipro →, Ukraine 47 J7
Dniprodzerzhynsk, Ukraine . 47 H8
Dniprodzerzhynske Vdskh.,
Ukraine 47 H8
Dnipropetrovsk, Ukraine ... 47 H8
Dniprorudne, Ukraine 47 J8
Dnister →, Europe 47 J6
Dnistrovskyy Lyman, Ukraine . 47 J6
Dno, Russia 46 D5
Dnyapro = Dnipro →, Ukraine 47 J7
Doaktown, Canada 103 C6
Doan Hung, Vietnam 58 G5
Doany, Madag. 89 A8
Doba, Chad 79 G9
Dobandi, Pakistan 68 D2
Dobbiaco, Italy 29 B9
Dobbyn, Australia 94 B3
Dobczyce, Poland 45 J7
Dobele, Latvia 9 H20
Dobele □, Latvia 44 B10
Döbeln, Germany 24 D9
Doberai, Jazirah, Indonesia ... 63 E8
Dobiegniew, Poland 45 F2
Doblas, Argentina 126 D3
Dobo, Indonesia 63 F8
Doboj, Bos.-H. 42 F3
Dobra, Wielkopolskie, Poland . 45 G5
Dobra, Zachodnio-Pomorskie,
Poland 44 E2
Dobra, Dîmbovita, Romania ... 43 F10
Dobra, Hunedoara, Romania . 42 E7
Dobre Miasto, Poland 44 E7
Dobreşti, Romania 42 D7
Dobrich, Bulgaria 41 C11
Dobrinishta, Bulgaria 40 E7
Dobříš, Czech Rep. 26 B7
Dobrodzień, Poland 45 H5
Dobropole, Ukraine 47 H9
Dobruja, Europe 43 F13
Dobrush, Belarus 47 F6
Dobrzany, Poland 44 E2
Dobrzyń nad Wisłą, Poland . 45 F6
Doc, Mui, Vietnam 64 D6
Docker River, Australia 93 D4
Docksta, Sweden 10 A12
Doctor Arroyo, Mexico 118 C4
Doda, India 69 C6
Doda, L., Canada 102 C4
Dodecanese = Dhodhekánisos,
Greece 39 E8
Dodge City, U.S.A. 113 G5
Dodge L., Canada 105 B7
Dodgeville, U.S.A. 112 D9
Dodo, Cameroon 83 D7
Dodo, Sudan 81 F2
Dodola, Ethiopia 81 F4
Dodona, Greece 38 B2
Dodsland, Canada 105 C7
Dodson, U.S.A. 114 B9
Dodurga, Turkey 39 B11
Doesburg, Neths. 17 B6

Doetinchem, Neths. 17 C6
Dog Creek, Canada 104 C4
Dog L., Man., Canada 105 C9
Dog L., Ont., Canada 102 C2
Doğanşehir, Turkey 72 C7
Dogliani, Italy 28 D4
Dogondoutchi, Niger 83 C5
Dogran, Pakistan 68 D5
Doguéraoua, Niger 83 C6
Doha = Ad Dawḩah, Qatar ... 71 E6
Dohazari, Bangla. 67 H18
Dohrighat, India 69 F10
Doi, Indonesia 63 D7
Doi Luang, Thailand 64 C3
Doi Saket, Thailand 64 C2
Dois Irmãos, Sa., Brazil 125 E10
Dojransko Jezero, Macedonia . 40 E6
Dokkum, Neths. 17 A5
Dokri, Pakistan 68 F3
Dokuchayevsk, Ukraine 47 J9
Dol-de-Bretagne, France 18 D5
Dolac, Kosovo, Yug. 40 D4
Dolak, Pulau, Indonesia 63 F9
Dolbeau, Canada 103 C5
Dole, France 19 E12
Doleib, Wadi →, Sudan 81 E3
Dolenji Logatec, Slovenia 29 C11
Dolgellau = Dolgelley, U.K. ... 12 E4
Dolgelley = Dolgellau, U.K. ... 12 E4
Dolhasca, Romania 43 C11
Dolianova, Italy 30 C2
Dolinskaya = Dolynska, Ukraine 47 H7
Dolj □, Romania 43 F8
Dollard, Neths. 17 A7
Dolna Banya, Bulgaria 40 D7
Dolni Chiflik, Bulgaria 41 D11
Dolní Dúbník, Bulgaria 41 C8
Dolnośląskie □, Poland 45 G3
Dolný Dúbník, Slovak Rep. . 27 B12
Dolo, Ethiopia 81 G5
Dolo, Italy 29 C9
Dolomites = Dolomiti, Italy ... 29 B8
Dolomiti, Italy 29 B8
Dolores, Argentina 126 D4
Dolores, Uruguay 126 C4
Dolores, U.S.A. 115 H9
Dolores →, U.S.A. 115 G9
Dolovo, Serbia, Yug. 42 F5
Dom Pedrito, Brazil 127 C5
Doma, Nigeria 83 D6
Domaniç, Turkey 39 B11
Domariaganj →, India 69 F10
Domasi, Malawi 87 F4
Domažlice, Czech Rep. 26 B5
Dombarovskiy, Russia 50 D6
Dombås, Norway 9 E13
Dombasle-sur-Meurthe, France 19 D13
Dombes, France 21 C9
Dombóvár, Hungary 42 D3
Dombrád, Hungary 42 B6
Domel I. = Letsôk-aw Kyun,
Burma 65 G2
Domérat, France 19 F9
Domeyko, Chile 126 B1
Domeyko, Cordillera, Chile ... 126 A2
Domfront, France 18 D6
Dominador, Chile 126 A2
Dominica ■, W. Indies 121 C7
Dominica Passage, W. Indies . 121 C7
Dominican Rep. ■, W. Indies . 121 C5
Dömitz, Germany 24 B7
Domme, France 20 D5
Domneşti, Romania 43 E9
Domodóssola, Italy 28 B5
Dompaire, France 19 D13
Dompierre-sur-Besbre, France . 19 F10
Dompim, Ghana 82 D4
Domrémy-la-Pucelle, France . 19 D12
Domville, Mt., Australia 95 D5
Domvraína, Greece 38 C4
Domžale, Slovenia 29 B11
Don →, Russia 47 J10
Don →, Aberds., U.K. 14 D6
Don →, S. Yorks., U.K. 12 D7
Don, C., Australia 92 B5
Don Benito, Spain 35 G5
Dona Ana = Nhamaabué,
Mozam. 87 F4
Doña Mencía, Spain 35 H6
Donaghadee, U.K. 15 B6
Donald, Australia 95 F3
Donaldsonville, U.S.A. 113 K9
Donalsonville, U.S.A. 109 K3
Donau = Dunărea →, Europe . 17 D3
Donau →, Austria 17 D3
Donaueschingen, Germany ... 25 H4
Donauwörth, Germany 25 G6
Doncaster, U.K. 12 D6
Dondo, Mozam. 87 F3
Dondo, Teluk, Indonesia 63 D6
Dondra Head, Sri Lanka 66 S12
Donduşeni, Moldova 43 B12
Donegal, Ireland 15 B3
Donegal □, Ireland 15 B4
Donegal B., Ireland 15 B3
Donets →, Russia 49 G5
Donetsk, Ukraine 47 J9
Dong Ba Thin, Vietnam 65 F7
Dong Dang, Vietnam 58 G6
Dong Giam, Vietnam 64 C5
Dong Ha, Vietnam 64 D6

Dong Hene, Laos 64 D5
Dong Hoi, Vietnam 64 D6
Dong Jiang →, China 59 F10
Dong Khe, Vietnam 64 A6
Dong Ujimqin Qi, China 56 B9
Dong Van, Vietnam 64 A5
Dong Xoai, Vietnam 65 G6
Donga, Nigeria 83 D7
Donga →, Nigeria 83 D7
Dongara, Australia 93 E1
Dongbei, China 57 D13
Dongchuan, China 58 D4
Donges, France 18 E4
Dongfang, China 64 C7
Dongfeng, China 57 C13
Donggala, Indonesia 63 E5
Donggan, China 58 F5
Donggou, China 57 E13
Dongguan, China 59 F9
Dongguang, China 56 F9
Donghai Dao, China 59 G8
Dongjingcheng, China 57 B15
Dongkou, China 59 D8
Donglan, China 58 E6
Dongliu, China 59 B11
Dongmen, China 58 F6
Dongning, China 57 B16
Dongnyi, China 58 C3
Dongola, Sudan 80 D3
Dongping, China 56 G9
Dongshan, China 59 F11
Dongsheng, China 56 E6
Dongtai, China 57 H11
Dongting Hu, China 59 C9
Dongtou, China 59 D13
Dongxiang, China 59 C11
Dongxing, China 58 G7
Dongyang, China 59 C13
Dongzhi, China 59 B11
Doniphan, U.S.A. 113 G9
Donja Stubica, Croatia 29 C12
Donji Dušnik, Serbia, Yug. ... 40 C6
Donji Miholjac, Croatia 42 E3
Donji Milanovac, Serbia, Yug. . 40 B6
Donji Vakuf, Bos.-H. 42 F2
Dønna, Norway 8 C15
Donna, U.S.A. 113 M5
Donnaconna, Canada 103 C5
Donnelly's Crossing, N.Z. ... 91 F4
Donnybrook, Australia 93 F2
Donnybrook, S. Africa 89 D4
Donora, U.S.A. 110 F5
Donostia = Donostia-San
Sebastián, Spain 32 B3
Donostia-San Sebastián, Spain . 32 B3
Donskoy, Russia 46 F10
Donsol, Phil. 61 E5
Donzère, France 21 D8
Donzy, France 19 E10
Doon →, U.K. 14 F4
Dora, L., Australia 92 D3
Dora Báltea →, Italy 28 C5
Dora Ripária →, Italy 28 C4
Doran L., Canada 105 A7
Dorchester, U.K. 13 G5
Dorchester, C., Canada 101 B12
Dordabis, Namibia 88 C2
Dordogne □, France 20 C4
Dordogne →, France 20 C3
Dordrecht, Neths. 17 C4
Dordrecht, S. Africa 88 E4
Dore →, France 20 C7
Dore, Mts., France 20 C6
Doré L., Canada 105 C7
Doré Lake, Canada 105 C7
Dorfen, Germany 25 G8
Dorgali, Italy 30 B2
Dori, Burkina Faso 83 C4
Doring →, S. Africa 88 E2
Doringbos, S. Africa 88 E2
Dorion, Canada 111 A10
Dormaa-Ahenkro, Ghana ... 82 D4
Dormans, France 19 C10
Dormo, Ras, Eritrea 81 E5
Dornbirn, Austria 26 D2
Dornes, France 19 F10
Dorneşti, Romania 43 C11
Dornie, U.K. 14 D3
Dornoch, U.K. 14 D4
Dornoch Firth, U.K. 14 D4
Dornogovĭ □, Mongolia 56 C6
Doro, Mali 83 B4
Dorog, Hungary 42 C3
Dorogobuzh, Russia 46 E7
Dorohoi, Romania 43 C11
Döröö Nuur, Mongolia 60 B4
Dorr, Iran 71 C6
Dorre I., Australia 93 E1
Dorris, U.S.A. 114 F3
Dorset, Canada 110 A6
Dorset, U.S.A. 110 E4
Dorset □, U.K. 13 G5
Dorsten, Germany 24 D2
Dortmund, Germany 24 D3
Dortmund-Ems-Kanal →,
Germany 24 D3
Dörtyol, Turkey 72 D7
Dorum, Germany 24 B4
Doruma, Dem. Rep. of
the Congo 86 B2
Dorūneh, Iran 71 C8
Dos Bahías, C., Argentina ... 128 E3
Dos Hermanas, Spain 35 H5
Dos Palos, U.S.A. 116 J6
Döşemealtı, Turkey 39 D12

Dosso, *Niger* 83 C5
Dothan, *U.S.A.* 109 K3
Doty, *U.S.A.* 116 D3
Douai, *France* 19 B10
Douako, *Guinea* 82 D2
Douala, *Cameroon* 83 E6
Douarnenez, *France* 18 D2
Doubabougou, *Mali* 82 C3
Double Island Pt., *Australia* ... 95 D5
Double Mountain Fork ➤,
U.S.A. 113 J4
Doubrava ➤, *Czech Rep.* 26 A8
Doubs □, *France* 19 E13
Doubs ➤, *France* 19 F12
Doubtful Sd., *N.Z.* 91 L1
Doubtless B., *N.Z.* 91 F4
Doudeville, *France* 18 C7
Doué-la-Fontaine, *France* 18 E6
Douentza, *Mali* 82 C4
Douglas, *S. Africa* 88 D3
Douglas, *U.K.* 12 C3
Douglas, *Ariz., U.S.A.* 115 L9
Douglas, *Ga., U.S.A.* 109 K4
Douglas, *Wyo., U.S.A.* 112 D2
Douglas Chan., *Canada* 104 C3
Douglas Pt., *Canada* 110 B3
Douglasville, *U.S.A.* 109 J3
Doukáton, Ákra, *Greece* 38 C2
Doulevant-le-Château, *France* . 19 D11
Doullens, *France* 19 B9
Doumen, *China* 59 F9
Douna, *Mali* 82 C3
Douna, *Mali* 83 C4
Dounreay, *U.K.* 14 C5
Dourada, Serra, *Brazil* 125 F9
Dourados, *Brazil* 127 A5
Dourados ➤, *Brazil* 127 A5
Dourados, Serra dos, *Brazil* .. 127 A5
Dourdan, *France* 19 D9
Douro ➤, *Europe* 34 D2
Douvaine, *France* 19 F13
Douvres-la-Délivrande, *France* 18 C6
Douze ➤, *France* 20 E3
Dove ➤, *U.K.* 12 E6
Dove Creek, *U.S.A.* 115 H9
Dover, *Australia* 94 G4
Dover, *U.K.* 13 F9
Dover, *Del., U.S.A.* 108 F8
Dover, *N.H., U.S.A.* 111 C14
Dover, *N.J., U.S.A.* 111 F10
Dover, *Ohio, U.S.A.* 110 F3
Dover, Pt., *Australia* 93 F4
Dover, Str. of, *Europe* 13 G9
Dover-Foxcroft, *U.S.A.* 109 C11
Dover Plains, *U.S.A.* 111 E11
Dovey = Dyfi ➤, *U.K.* 13 E3
Dovrefjell, *Norway* 9 E13
Dow Rūd, *Iran* 71 C6
Dowa, *Malawi* 87 E3
Dowagiac, *U.S.A.* 108 E2
Dowerin, *Australia* 93 F2
Dowgha'i, *Iran* 71 B8
Dowlatābād, *Iran* 71 D8
Down □, *U.K.* 15 B5
Downey, *Calif., U.S.A.* 117 M8
Downey, *Idaho, U.S.A.* 114 E7
Downham Market, *U.K.* 13 E8
Downieville, *U.S.A.* 116 F6
Downpatrick, *U.K.* 15 B6
Downpatrick Hd., *Ireland* ... 15 B2
Downsville, *U.S.A.* 111 D10
Downton, Mt., *Canada* 104 C4
Dowsārī, *Iran* 71 D8
Doyle, *U.S.A.* 116 E6
Doylestown, *U.S.A.* 111 F9
Dozois, Rés., *Canada* 102 C4
Dra Khel, *Pakistan* 68 F2
Drac ➤, *France* 21 C9
Dračevo, *Macedonia* 40 E5
Drachten, *Neths.* 17 A6
Drăgănești, *Moldova* 43 C13
Drăgănești-Olt, *Romania* ... 43 F9
Drăgănești-Vlașca, *Romania* 43 F10
Dragaš, *Kosovo, Yug.* 40 D4
Drăgășani, *Romania* 43 F9
Dragichyn, *Belarus* 47 F3
Dragocvet, *Serbia, Yug.* 40 C5
Dragovishtitsa, *Bulgaria* ... 40 D6
Draguignan, *France* 21 E10
Drain, *U.S.A.* 114 E2
Drake, *U.S.A.* 112 B4
Drake Passage, *S. Ocean* ... 5 B17
Drakensberg, *S. Africa* 89 D4
Dráma, *Greece* 41 E8
Dráma □, *Greece* 41 E8
Drammen, *Norway* 9 G14
Drangajökull, *Iceland* 8 C2
Dranov, Ostrov, *Romania* ... 43 F14
Dras, *India* 69 B6
Drau = Drava ➤, *Croatia* ... 42 E3
Drava ➤, *Croatia* 42 E3
Dravograd, *Slovenia* 29 B12
Drawa ➤, *Poland* 45 F2
Drawno, *Poland* 45 E2
Drawsko Pomorskie, *Poland* . 44 E2
Drayton Valley, *Canada* 104 C6
Dreieich, *Germany* 25 E4
Dren, *Kosovo, Yug.* 40 C4
Drenthe □, *Neths.* 17 B6
Drepanum, C., *Cyprus* 36 E11
Dresden, *Canada* 110 D2
Dresden, *Germany* 24 D9
Dreux, *France* 18 D8
Drezdenko, *Poland* 45 F2
Driffield, *U.K.* 12 C7
Driftwood, *U.S.A.* 110 E6

Driggs, *U.S.A.* 114 E8
Drin ➤, *Albania* 40 D3
Drin i Zi ➤, *Albania* 40 E4
Drina ➤, *Bos.-H.* 40 B3
Drincea ➤, *Romania* 42 F7
Drinjača ➤, *Bos.-H.* 42 F4
Drissa = Vyerkhnyadzvinsk,
Belarus 46 E4
Drniš, *Croatia* 29 E13
Drøbak, *Norway* 9 G14
Drobeta-Turnu Severin,
Romania 42 F7
Drobin, *Poland* 45 F6
Drochia, *Moldova* 43 B12
Drogheda, *Ireland* 15 C5
Drogichin = Dragichyn, *Belarus* 47 F3
Drogobych = Drohobych,
Ukraine 47 H2
Drohiczyn, *Poland* 45 F9
Drohobych, *Ukraine* 47 H2
Droichead Atha = Drogheda,
Ireland 15 C5
Droichead Nua, *Ireland* 15 C5
Droitwich, *U.K.* 13 E5
Drôme □, *France* 21 D9
Drôme ➤, *France* 21 D8
Dromore, *U.K.* 15 B4
Dromore West, *Ireland* 15 B3
Dronero, *Italy* 28 D4
Dronfield, *U.K.* 12 D6
Dronne ➤, *France* 20 C3
Dronninglund, *Denmark* 11 G4
Dronten, *Neths.* 17 B5
Dropt ➤, *France* 20 D3
Drosendorf, *Austria* 26 C8
Droué, *France* 18 D8
Drumbo, *Canada* 110 C4
Drumheller, *Canada* 104 C6
Drummond, *U.S.A.* 114 C7
Drummond I., *U.S.A.* 108 C4
Drummond Pt., *Australia* ... 95 E2
Drummond Ra., *Australia* ... 94 C4
Drummondville, *Canada* ... 102 C5
Drumright, *U.S.A.* 113 H6
Druskininkai, *Lithuania* 9 J20
Drut ➤, *Belarus* 47 F6
Druya, *Belarus* 46 E4
Druzhba, *Bulgaria* 41 C12
Druzhina, *Russia* 51 C15
Drvar, *Bos.-H.* 29 D13
Drvenik, *Croatia* 29 E13
Drwęca ➤, *Poland* 45 E5
Dry Tortugas, *U.S.A.* 120 B3
Dryanovo, *Bulgaria* 41 D9
Dryden, *Canada* 105 D10
Dryden, *U.S.A.* 111 D8
Drygalski I., *Antarctica* 5 C7
Drysdale ➤, *Australia* 92 B4
Drysdale I., *Australia* 94 A2
Dschang, *Cameroon* 83 D7
Du Bois, *U.S.A.* 110 E6
Du Gué ➤, *Canada* 102 A5
Du He, *China* 59 A8
Du Quoin, *U.S.A.* 112 G10
Du'an, *China* 58 F7
Duanesburg, *U.S.A.* 111 D10
Duaringa, *Australia* 94 C4
Dubā, *Si. Arabia* 70 E2
Dubai = Dubayy, *U.A.E.* ... 71 E7
Dubāsari, *Moldova* 43 C14
Dubāsari Vdkhr., *Moldova* .. 43 C13
Dubawnt ➤, *Canada* 105 A8
Dubawnt, L., *Canada* 105 A8
Dubayy, *U.A.E.* 71 E7
Dubele, *Dem. Rep. of the Congo* 86 B2
Dübendorf, *Switz.* 25 H4
Dubica, *Croatia* 29 C13
Dublin, *Ireland* 15 C5
Dublin, *Ga., U.S.A.* 109 J4
Dublin, *Tex., U.S.A.* 113 J5
Dublin □, *Ireland* 15 C5
Dubna, *Russia* 46 D9
Dubnica nad Váhom,
Slovak Rep. 27 C11
Dubno, *Ukraine* 47 G3
Dubois, *U.S.A.* 114 D7
Dubossary = Dubāsari, *Moldova* 43 C14
Dubossary Vdkhr. = Dubāsari
Vdkhr., *Moldova* 43 C13
Dubovka, *Russia* 49 F7
Dubovskoye, *Russia* 49 G6
Dubrajpur, *India* 69 H12
Dubréka, *Guinea* 82 D2
Dubrovitsa = Dubrovytsya,
Ukraine 47 G4
Dubrovnik, *Croatia* 40 D2
Dubrovytsya, *Ukraine* 47 G4
Dubuque, *U.S.A.* 112 D9
Dubysa ➤, *Lithuania* 44 C10
Duchang, *China* 59 C11
Duchesne, *U.S.A.* 114 F8
Duchess, *Australia* 94 C2
Ducie I., *Pac. Oc.* 97 K15
Duck ➤, *U.S.A.* 109 G2
Duck Cr. ➤, *U.S.A.* 92 D2
Duck Lake, *Canada* 105 C7
Duck Mountain Prov. Park,
Canada 105 C8
Duckwall, Mt., *U.S.A.* 116 H6
Duderstadt, *Germany* 24 D6
Dudhi, *India* 67 G13
Dudinka, *Russia* 51 C9
Dudley, *U.K.* 13 E5
Dudwa, *India* 69 E9

Duékoué, *Ivory C.* 82 D3
Dueñas, *Spain* 34 D6
Duero = Douro ➤, *Europe* .. 34 D2
Dufftown, *U.K.* 14 D5
Dufourspitz, *Switz.* 25 K3
Dūghī Kalā, *Afghan.* 66 C3
Dugi Otok, *Croatia* 29 D11
Dugo Selo, *Croatia* 29 C13
Duifken Pt., *Australia* 94 A3
Duisburg, *Germany* 24 D2
Duiwelskloof, *S. Africa* 89 C5
Dujiangyan, *China* 58 B4
Duk Fadiat, *Sudan* 81 F3
Duk Faiwil, *Sudan* 81 F3
Dukat, *Albania* 40 F3
Dūkdamīn, *Iran* 71 C8
Dukelský Průsmyk, *Slovak Rep.* 27 B14
Dukhān, *Qatar* 71 E6
Dukhovshchina, *Russia* 46 E7
Duki, *Pakistan* 66 D6
Dukla, *Poland* 45 J8
Duku, *Bauchi, Nigeria* 83 C7
Duku, *Sokoto, Nigeria* 83 C5
Dulag, *Phil.* 61 F6
Dulce, *U.S.A.* 115 H10
Dulce ➤, *Argentina* 126 C3
Dulce, G., *Costa Rica* 120 E3
Dulf, *Iraq* 70 C5
Dŭlgopol, *Bulgaria* 41 C11
Dulit, Banjaran, *Malaysia* .. 62 D4
Duliu, *China* 56 E9
Dullewala, *Pakistan* 68 D4
Dullstroom, *S. Africa* 89 D5
Dülmen, *Germany* 24 D3
Dulovo, *Bulgaria* 41 C11
Dulq Maghār, *Syria* 70 B3
Duluth, *U.S.A.* 112 B8
Dum Dum, *India* 69 H13
Dum Duma, *India* 67 F19
Dūmā, *Syria* 75 B5
Dumaguete, *Phil.* 61 G5
Dumai, *Indonesia* 62 D2
Dumaran, *Phil.* 61 F3
Dumas, *Ark., U.S.A.* 113 J9
Dumas, *Tex., U.S.A.* 113 H4
Dumayr, *Syria* 75 B5
Dumbarton, *U.K.* 14 F4
Dumbleyung, *Australia* 93 F2
Dumboa, *Nigeria* 83 C7
Dumbrăveni, *Romania* 43 D9
Dumfries, *U.K.* 14 F5
Dumfries & Galloway □, *U.K.* . 14 F5
Dumitrești, *Romania* 43 E11
Dumka, *India* 69 G12
Duque de Caxias, *Brazil* ... 127 A7
Dümmer, *Germany* 24 C4
Dumoine ➤, *Canada* 102 C4
Dumoine, L., *Canada* 102 C4
Dumraon, *India* 69 G11
Dumyât, *Egypt* 80 H7
Dumyât, Masabb, *Egypt* ... 80 H7
Dún Dealgan = Dundalk,
Ireland 15 B5
Dun Laoghaire, *Ireland* 15 C5
Dun-le-Palestel, *France* 19 F8
Dun-sur-Auron, *France* 19 F9
Dun-sur-Meuse, *France* ... 19 C12
Duna = Dunărea ➤, *Europe* 43 E14
Duna ➤, *Hungary* 42 E3
Duna-völgyi-főcsatorna,
Hungary 42 D3
Dunaföldvár, *Hungary* 42 D3
Dunagiri, *India* 69 D8
Dunaj = Dunărea ➤, *Europe* 43 E14
Dunaj ➤, *Slovak Rep.* 27 D11
Dunajec ➤, *Poland* 45 H7
Dunajská Streda, *Slovak Rep.* 27 C10
Dunakeszi, *Hungary* 42 C4
Dunapataj, *Hungary* 42 D4
Dunărea ➤, *Europe* 43 E14
Dunaszekcső, *Hungary* 42 D3
Dunaújváros, *Hungary* 42 D3
Dunav = Dunărea ➤, *Europe* 43 E14
Dunavățu de Jos, *Romania* . 43 F14
Dunavtsi, *Bulgaria* 40 C6
Dunay, *Russia* 54 C6
Dunback, *N.Z.* 91 L3
Dunbar, *U.K.* 14 E6
Dunblane, *U.K.* 14 E5
Duncan, *Canada* 104 D4
Duncan, *Ariz., U.S.A.* 115 K9
Duncan, *Okla., U.S.A.* 113 H6
Duncan, L., *Canada* 102 B4
Duncan L., *Canada* 104 A6
Duncan Town, *Bahamas* ... 120 B4
Duncannon, *U.S.A.* 110 F7
Duncansby Head, *U.K.* 14 C5
Duncansville, *U.S.A.* 110 F6
Dundaga, *Latvia* 44 A9
Dundalk, *Canada* 110 B4
Dundalk, *Ireland* 15 B5
Dundalk, *U.S.A.* 108 F7
Dundalk Bay, *Ireland* 15 C5
Dundas, *Canada* 110 C5
Dundas, L., *Australia* 93 F3
Dundas, L., *Canada* 102 C2
Dundas Str., *Australia* 92 B5
Dundee, *S. Africa* 89 D5
Dundee, *U.K.* 14 E6
Dundee, *U.S.A.* 110 D8
Dundee City □, *U.K.* 14 E6
Dundgovĭ □, *Mongolia* 56 B4
Dundrum, *U.K.* 15 B6
Dundrum B., *U.K.* 15 B6
Dunedin, *N.Z.* 91 L3

Dunedin, *U.S.A.* 109 L4
Dunfermline, *U.K.* 14 E5
Dungannon, *Canada* 110 C3
Dungannon, *U.K.* 15 B5
Dungarpur, *India* 68 H5
Dungarvan, *Ireland* 15 D4
Dungarvan Harbour, *Ireland* . 15 D4
Dungeness, *U.K.* 13 G8
Dungo, L. do, *Angola* 88 B2
Dungu, *Dem. Rep. of the Congo* 86 B2
Dungun, *Malaysia* 65 K4
Dungunāb, *Sudan* 80 C4
Dungunāb, Khalij, *Sudan* .. 80 C4
Dunhua, *China* 57 C15
Dunhuang, *China* 60 B4
Dunk I., *Australia* 94 B4
Dunkassa, *Benin* 83 C5
Dunkeld, *Australia* 95 F3
Dunkeld, *U.K.* 14 E5
Dunkerque, *France* 19 A9
Dunkery Beacon, *U.K.* 13 F4
Dunkirk = Dunkerque, *France* . 19 A9
Dunkirk, *U.S.A.* 110 D5
Dunkuj, *Sudan* 81 E3
Dunkwa, *Central, Ghana* ... 82 D4
Dunkwa, *Central, Ghana* ... 83 D4
Dúnleary = Dun Laoghaire,
Ireland 15 C5
Dunleer, *Ireland* 15 C5
Dunmanus B., *Ireland* 15 E2
Dunmanway, *Ireland* 15 E2
Dunmara, *Australia* 94 B1
Dunmore, *U.S.A.* 111 E9
Dunmore Hd., *Ireland* 15 D1
Dunmore Town, *Bahamas* .. 120 A4
Dunn, *U.S.A.* 109 H6
Dunnellon, *U.S.A.* 109 L4
Dunnet Hd., *U.K.* 14 C5
Dunning, *U.S.A.* 112 E4
Dunnville, *Canada* 110 D5
Dunoon, *U.K.* 14 F4
Dunphy, *U.S.A.* 114 F5
Dunqul, *Egypt* 80 C3
Duns, *U.K.* 14 F6
Dunseith, *U.S.A.* 112 A4
Dunsmuir, *U.S.A.* 114 F2
Dunstable, *U.K.* 13 F7
Dunstan Mts., *N.Z.* 91 L2
Dunster, *Canada* 104 C5
Dunvegan L., *Canada* 105 A7
Duolun, *China* 56 C9
Duong Dong, *Vietnam* 65 G4
Dupree, *U.S.A.* 112 C4
Dupuyer, *U.S.A.* 114 B7
Durack ➤, *Australia* 92 C4
Durack Ra., *Australia* 92 C4
Durağan, *Turkey* 72 B6
Durak, *Turkey* 39 B10
Durance ➤, *France* 21 E8
Durango, *Mexico* 118 C4
Durango, *U.S.A.* 115 H10
Durango □, *Mexico* 118 C4
Durankulak, *Bulgaria* 41 C12
Durant, *Miss., U.S.A.* 113 J10
Durant, *Okla., U.S.A.* 113 J6
Duratón ➤, *Spain* 34 D6
Durazno, *Uruguay* 126 C4
Durazzo = Durrës, *Albania* . 40 E3
Durban, *France* 20 F6
Durban, *S. Africa* 89 D5
Durbuy, *Belgium* 17 D5
Dúrcal, *Spain* 35 J7
Đurđevac, *Croatia* 42 D2
Düren, *Germany* 24 E2
Durg, *India* 67 J12
Durgapur, *India* 69 H12
Durham, *Canada* 102 D3
Durham, *U.K.* 12 C6
Durham, *Calif., U.S.A.* 116 F5
Durham, *N.C., U.S.A.* 109 H6
Durham, *N.H., U.S.A.* 111 C14
Durham □, *U.K.* 12 C6
Durlești, *Moldova* 43 C13
Durma, *Si. Arabia* 70 E5
Durmitor, *Montenegro, Yug.* 40 C2
Durness, *U.K.* 14 C4
Durrës, *Albania* 40 E3
Durrow, *Ireland* 15 D4
Dursey I., *Ireland* 15 E1
Dursunbey, *Turkey* 39 B10
Durtal, *France* 18 E6
Duru, *Dem. Rep. of the Congo* 86 B2
Durusu, *Turkey* 41 E12
Durūz, Jabal ad, *Jordan* 75 C5
D'Urville, Tanjung, *Indonesia* 63 E9
D'Urville I., *N.Z.* 91 J4
Duryea, *U.S.A.* 111 E9
Dushak, *Turkmenistan* 50 F7
Dushan, *China* 58 E6
Dushanbe, *Tajikistan* 50 F7
Dushet'i, *Georgia* 49 J7
Dushore, *U.S.A.* 111 E8
Dusky Sd., *N.Z.* 91 L1
Dussejour, C., *Australia* 92 B4
Düsseldorf, *Germany* 24 D2
Dusznik-Zdrój, *Poland* 45 H3
Dutch Harbor, *U.S.A.* 100 C3
Dutlwe, *Botswana* 88 C3
Dutsan Wai, *Nigeria* 83 C6
Dutton, *Canada* 110 D3
Dutton ➤, *Australia* 94 C3

Duved, *Sweden* 10 A6
Düvertepe, *Turkey* 39 B10
Duwayhin, Khawr, *U.A.E.* ... 71 E6
Duyun, *China* 58 D6
Düzağaç, *Turkey* 39 C12
Düzce, *Turkey* 72 B4
Duzdab = Zāhedān, *Iran* ... 71 D9
Dve Mogili, *Bulgaria* 41 C9
Dvina, Severnaya ➤, *Russia* . 50 C5
Dvor, *Croatia* 29 C13
Dvůr Králové nad Labem,
Czech Rep. 26 A8
Dwarka, *India* 68 H3
Dwellingup, *Australia* 93 F2
Dwight, *Canada* 110 A5
Dwight, *U.S.A.* 108 E1
Dyatkovo, *Russia* 46 F8
Dyatlovo = Dzyatlava, *Belarus* . 46 F3
Dyce, *U.K.* 14 D6
Dyer, C., *Canada* 101 B13
Dyer Bay, *Canada* 110 A3
Dyer Plateau, *Antarctica* ... 5 D17
Dyersburg, *U.S.A.* 113 G10
Dyfi ➤, *U.K.* 13 E3
Dyje ➤, *Czech Rep.* 27 C9
Dymer, *Ukraine* 47 G6
Dynów, *Poland* 45 J9
Dysart, *Australia* 94 C4
Dzamin Üüd = Borhoyn Tal,
Mongolia 56 C6
Dzerzhinsk, *Russia* 48 B6
Dzhalinda, *Russia* 51 D13
Dzhambul = Taraz, *Kazakstan* . 50 E8
Dzhankoy, *Ukraine* 47 K8
Dzhanybek, *Kazakstan* 48 F8
Dzharylhach, Ostriv, *Ukraine* 47 J7
Dzhezkazgan = Zhezqazghan,
Kazakstan 50 E7
Dzhizak = Jizzakh, *Uzbekistan* . 50 E7
Dzhugdzur, Khrebet, *Russia* . 51 D14
Dzhvari = Jvari, *Georgia* 49 J6
Działdowo, *Poland* 45 E7
Działoszyce, *Poland* 45 H7
Działoszyn, *Poland* 45 G5
Dzibilchaltún, *Mexico* 119 C7
Dzierzgoń, *Poland* 44 E6
Dzierżoniów, *Poland* 45 H3
Dzilam de Bravo, *Mexico* ... 119 C7
Dzisna, *Belarus* 46 E5
Dzisna ➤, *Belarus* 46 E5
Dziwnów, *Poland* 44 D1
Dzungaria = Junggar Pendi,
China 60 B3
Dzuumod, *Mongolia* 60 B5
Dzyarzhynsk, *Belarus* 46 F4
Dzyatlava, *Belarus* 46 F3

E

Eabamet L., *Canada* 102 B2
Eads, *U.S.A.* 112 F3
Eagar, *U.S.A.* 115 J9
Eagle, *Alaska, U.S.A.* 100 B5
Eagle, *Colo., U.S.A.* 114 G10
Eagle ➤, *Canada* 103 B8
Eagle Butte, *U.S.A.* 112 C4
Eagle Grove, *U.S.A.* 112 D8
Eagle L., *Canada* 105 D10
Eagle L., *Calif., U.S.A.* 114 F3
Eagle L., *Maine, U.S.A.* 109 B11
Eagle Lake, *Canada* 110 A6
Eagle Lake, *Maine, U.S.A.* .. 109 B11
Eagle Lake, *Tex., U.S.A.* ... 113 L6
Eagle Mountain, *U.S.A.* ... 117 M11
Eagle Nest, *U.S.A.* 115 H11
Eagle Pass, *U.S.A.* 113 L4
Eagle Pk., *U.S.A.* 116 G7
Eagle Pt., *Australia* 92 C3
Eagle River, *Mich., U.S.A.* .. 108 B1
Eagle River, *Wis., U.S.A.* ... 112 C10
Eaglehawk, *Australia* 95 F3
Eagles Mere, *U.S.A.* 111 E8
Ealing □, *U.K.* 13 F7
Ear Falls, *Canada* 105 C10
Earle, *U.S.A.* 113 H9
Earlimart, *U.S.A.* 117 K7
Earn ➤, *U.K.* 14 E5
Earn, L., *U.K.* 14 E4
Earnslaw, Mt., *N.Z.* 91 L2
Earth, *U.S.A.* 113 H3
Easley, *U.S.A.* 109 H4
East Anglia, *U.K.* 12 E9
East Angus, *Canada* 103 C5
East Aurora, *U.S.A.* 110 D6
East Ayrshire □, *U.K.* 14 F4
East Bengal, *Bangla.* 67 H17
East Beskids = Vychodné
Beskydy, *Europe* 27 B15
East Brady, *U.S.A.* 110 F5
East, C., *N.Z.* 91 G7
East Chicago, *U.S.A.* 108 E2
East China Sea, *Asia* 60 C7
East Coulee, *Canada* 104 C6
East Dereham, *U.K.* 13 E8
East Dunbartonshire □, *U.K.* . 14 F4
East Falkland, *Falk. Is.* 128 G5
East Grand Forks, *U.S.A.* ... 112 B6
East Greenwich, *U.S.A.* 111 E13
East Grinstead, *U.K.* 13 F8
East Hartford, *U.S.A.* 111 E12
East Helena, *U.S.A.* 114 C8
East Indies, *Asia* 52 K15
East Kilbride, *U.K.* 14 F4

East Lansing, U.S.A. 108 D3
East Liverpool, U.S.A. 110 F4
East London, S. Africa 89 E4
East Lothian □, U.K. 14 F6
East Main = Eastmain, Canada 102 B4
East Northport, U.S.A. 111 F11
East Orange, U.S.A. 111 F10
East Pacific Ridge, Pac. Oc. . 97 J17
East Palestine, U.S.A. 110 F4
East Pine, Canada 104 B4
East Point, U.S.A. 109 J3
East Providence, U.S.A. 111 E13
East Pt., Canada 103 C7
East Renfrewshire □, U.K. ... 14 F4
East Retford = Retford, U.K. . 12 D7
East Riding of Yorkshire □,
  U.K. 12 D7
East Rochester, U.S.A. 110 C7
East St. Louis, U.S.A. 112 F9
East Schelde =
  Oosterschelde →, Neths. 17 C4
East Sea = Japan, Sea of, Asia . 54 E7
East Siberian Sea, Russia ... 51 B17
East Stroudsburg, U.S.A. 111 E9
East Sussex □, U.K. 13 G8
East Tawas, U.S.A. 108 C4
East Timor ■, Asia 63 F7
East Toorale, Australia 95 E4
East Walker →, U.S.A. 116 G7
East Windsor, U.S.A. 111 F10
Eastbourne, N.Z. 91 J5
Eastbourne, U.K. 13 G8
Eastend, Canada 105 D7
Easter I. = Pascua, I. de,
  Pac. Oc. 97 K17
Eastern □, Ghana 83 D4
Eastern □, Kenya 86 C4
Eastern Cape □, S. Africa 88 E4
Eastern Cr. →, Australia 94 C3
Eastern Ghats, India 66 N11
Eastern Group = Lau Group,
  Fiji 91 C9
Eastern Group, Australia 93 F3
Eastern Province □, S. Leone . 82 D2
Eastern Transvaal =
  Mpumalanga □, S. Africa .. 89 B5
Easterville, Canada 105 C9
Easthampton, U.S.A. 111 D12
Eastlake, U.S.A. 110 E3
Eastland, U.S.A. 113 J5
Eastleigh, U.K. 13 G6
Eastmain, Canada 102 B4
Eastmain →, Canada 102 B4
Eastman, Canada 111 A12
Eastman, U.S.A. 109 J4
Easton, Md., U.S.A. 108 F7
Easton, Pa., U.S.A. 111 F9
Easton, Wash., U.S.A. 116 C5
Eastpointe, U.S.A. 110 D2
Eastport, U.S.A. 109 C12
Eastsound, U.S.A. 116 B4
Eaton, U.S.A. 112 E2
Eatonia, Canada 105 C7
Eatonton, U.S.A. 109 J4
Eatontown, U.S.A. 111 F10
Eatonville, U.S.A. 116 D4
Eau Claire, U.S.A. 112 C9
Eau Claire, L. à l', Canada ... 102 A5
Eauze, France 20 E4
Eban, Nigeria 83 D5
Ebbw Vale, U.K. 13 F4
Ebeltoft, Denmark 11 H4
Ebeltoft Vig, Denmark 11 H4
Ebensburg, U.S.A. 110 F6
Ebensee, Austria 26 D6
Eber Gölü, Turkey 72 C4
Eberbach, Germany 25 F4
Eberswalde-Finow, Germany .. 24 C9
Ebetsu, Japan 54 C10
Ebian, China 58 C4
Ebingen, Germany 25 G5
Éboli, Italy 31 B8
Ebolowa, Cameroon 83 E7
Ebonyi □, Nigeria 83 D6
Ebrach, Germany 25 F6
Ébrié, Lagune, Ivory C. 82 D4
Ebro →, Spain 32 E5
Ebro, Embalse del, Spain 34 C7
Ebstorf, Germany 24 B6
Eceabat, Turkey 41 F10
Ech Cheliff, Algeria 78 A6
Echigo-Sammyaku, Japan 55 F9
Échirolles, France 21 C9
Echizen-Misaki, Japan 55 G7
Echmiadzin = Yejmiadzin,
  Armenia 49 K7
Echo Bay, N.W.T., Canada ... 100 B8
Echo Bay, Ont., Canada 102 C3
Echoing →, Canada 102 B1
Echternach, Lux. 17 E6
Ecija, Spain 35 H5
Eckental, Germany 25 F7
Eckernförde, Germany 24 A5
Eclipse Is., Australia 92 B4
Eclipse Sd., Canada 101 A11
Écommoy, France 18 E7
Écouché, France 18 D6
Ecuador ■, S. Amer. 124 D3
Écueillé, France 18 E8
Ed, Sweden 11 F5
Ed Dabbura, Sudan 80 D3
Ed Da'ein, Sudan 81 E2
Ed Dâmer, Sudan 79 F12
Ed Debba, Sudan 80 D3
Ed-Déffa, Egypt 80 A2

Ed Deim, Sudan 81 E2
Ed Dueim, Sudan 81 E3
Edam, Canada 105 C7
Edam, Neths. 17 B5
Edane, Sweden 10 E6
Eday, U.K. 14 B6
Edd, Eritrea 81 E5
Eddrachillis B., U.K. 14 C3
Eddystone Pt., Australia 94 G4
Ede, Neths. 17 B5
Ede, Nigeria 83 D5
Edéa, Cameroon 83 E7
Edebäck, Sweden 10 D7
Edehon L., Canada 105 A9
Edelény, Hungary 42 B5
Eden, N.C., U.S.A. 109 G6
Eden, N.Y., U.S.A. 110 D6
Eden, Tex., U.S.A. 113 K5
Eden →, U.K. 12 C4
Edenburg, S. Africa 88 D4
Edendale, S. Africa 89 D5
Edenderry, Ireland 15 C4
Edenton, U.S.A. 109 G7
Edenville, S. Africa 89 D4
Eder →, Germany 24 D5
Eder-Stausee, Germany 24 D4
Edewecht, Germany 24 B3
Edgar, U.S.A. 112 E6
Edgartown, U.S.A. 111 E14
Edge Hill, U.K. 13 E6
Edgefield, U.S.A. 109 J5
Edgeley, U.S.A. 112 B5
Edgemont, U.S.A. 112 D3
Edgeøya, Svalbard 4 B9
Édhessa, Greece 40 F6
Edievale, N.Z. 91 L2
Edina, Liberia 82 D2
Edina, U.S.A. 112 E8
Edinboro, U.S.A. 110 E4
Edinburgh, U.K. 14 F5
Edinburgh, City of □, U.K. ... 14 F5
Edineț, Moldova 43 B12
Edinburg, U.S.A. 113 M5
Edirne, Turkey 41 E10
Edirne □, Turkey 41 E10
Edison, U.S.A. 116 B4
Edmeston, U.S.A. 111 D9
Edmond, U.S.A. 113 H6
Edmonds, U.S.A. 116 C4
Edmonton, Australia 94 B4
Edmonton, Canada 104 C6
Edmund L., Canada 102 B1
Edmundston, Canada 103 C6
Edna, U.S.A. 113 L6
Edo □, Nigeria 83 D6
Edolo, Italy 28 B7
Edremit, Turkey 39 B9
Edremit Körfezi, Turkey 39 B8
Edsbro, Sweden 10 E12
Edsbyn, Sweden 10 C9
Edson, Canada 104 C5
Eduardo Castex, Argentina .. 126 D3
Edward, L., Africa 86 C2
Edward River, Australia 94 A3
Edward VII Land, Antarctica . 5 E13
Edwards, Calif., U.S.A. 117 L9
Edwards, N.Y., U.S.A. 111 B9
Edwards Air Force Base, U.S.A. 117 L9
Edwards Plateau, U.S.A. 113 K4
Edwardsville, U.S.A. 111 E9
Edzo, Canada 104 A5
Eeklo, Belgium 17 C3
Eferding, Austria 26 C7
Effingham, U.S.A. 108 F1
Eforie, Romania 43 F13
Ega →, Spain 32 C3
Égadi, Ísole, Italy 30 E5
Egan Range, U.S.A. 114 G6
Eganville, Canada 102 C4
Eger = Cheb, Czech Rep. 26 A5
Eger, Hungary 42 C5
Eger →, Hungary 42 C5
Egersund, Norway 9 G12
Egg L., Canada 105 B7
Eggenburg, Austria 26 C8
Eggenfelden, Germany 25 G8
Éghezée, Belgium 17 D4
Égletons, France 20 C6
Egmont, Canada 104 D4
Egmont, C., N.Z. 91 H4
Egmont, Mt. = Taranaki, Mt.,
  N.Z. 91 H5
Egra, India 69 J12
Eğridir, Turkey 72 D4
Eğridir Gölü, Turkey 70 B1
Egtved, Denmark 11 J3
Egume, Nigeria 83 D6
Éguzon-Chantôme, France ... 19 F8
Egvekinot, Russia 51 C19
Egyek, Hungary 42 C5
Egypt ■, Africa 80 B3
Eha Amufu, Nigeria 83 D6
Ehime □, Japan 55 H6
Ehingen, Germany 25 G5
Ehrenberg, U.S.A. 117 M12
Ehrwald, Austria 26 D3
Eibar, Spain 32 B2
Eichstätt, Germany 25 G7
Eidsvold, Australia 95 D5
Eidsvoll, Norway 9 F14
Eifel, Germany 25 E2
Eiffel Flats, Zimbabwe 87 F3
Eiger, Switz. 28 B5
Eigg, U.K. 14 E2
Eighty Mile Beach, Australia . 92 C3

Eil, Somali Rep. 74 F4
Eil, L., U.K. 14 E3
Eilenburg, Germany 24 D8
Ein el Luweiqa, Sudan 81 E3
Einasleigh, Australia 94 B3
Einasleigh →, Australia 94 B3
Einbeck, Germany 24 D5
Eindhoven, Neths. 17 C5
Einsiedeln, Switz. 25 H4
Eire = Ireland ■, Europe 15 C4
Eiríksjökull, Iceland 8 D3
Eirunepé, Brazil 124 E5
Eiseb →, Namibia 88 C2
Eisenach, Germany 24 E6
Eisenberg, Germany 24 E7
Eisenerz, Austria 26 D7
Eisenhüttenstadt, Germany .. 24 C10
Eisenkappel, Austria 26 E7
Eisenstadt, Austria 27 D9
Eisfeld, Germany 25 E6
Eisleben, Germany 24 D7
Eislingen, Germany 25 G5
Eivissa, Spain 37 C7
Eixe, Serra do, Spain 34 C4
Ejea de los Caballeros, Spain . 32 C3
Ejeda, Madag. 89 C7
Ejura, Ghana 83 D4
Ejutla, Mexico 119 D5
Ekalaka, U.S.A. 112 C2
Ekenässjön, Sweden 11 G9
Ekerö, Sweden 10 E11
Eket, Nigeria 83 E6
Eketahuna, N.Z. 91 J5
Ekhínos, Greece 41 E9
Ekibastuz, Kazakstan 50 D8
Ekiti □, Nigeria 83 D6
Ekoli, Dem. Rep. of the Congo . 86 C1
Ekoln, Sweden 10 E11
Ekshärad, Sweden 10 D7
Eksjö, Sweden 11 G8
Ekuma →, Namibia 88 B2
Ekwan →, Canada 102 B3
Ekwan Pt., Canada 102 B3
El Aaiún, W. Sahara 78 C3
El Abanico, Chile 126 D1
El Abbasiya, Sudan 81 E3
El 'Agrûd, Egypt 75 E3
El Ait, Sudan 81 E2
El 'Aiyat, Egypt 80 J7
El Alamein, Egypt 80 A2
El 'Aqaba, W. →, Egypt 75 E2
El 'Arag, Egypt 80 B2
El Arahal, Spain 35 H5
El Arîhâ, West Bank 75 D4
El 'Arîsh, Egypt 75 D2
El 'Arîsh, W. →, Egypt 75 D2
El Asnam = Ech Cheliff, Algeria 78 A6
El Astillero, Spain 34 B7
El Badâri, Egypt 80 B3
El Bahrein, Egypt 80 B2
El Ballâs, Egypt 80 B3
El Balyana, Egypt 80 B3
El Baqeir, Sudan 80 D3
El Barco de Ávila, Spain 34 E5
El Barco de Valdeorras = O
  Barco, Spain 34 C4
El Bauga, Sudan 80 D3
El Bawiti, Egypt 80 B2
El Bayadh, Algeria 78 B6
El Bierzo, Spain 34 C4
El Bluff, Nic. 120 D3
El Bonillo, Spain 33 G2
El Brûk, W. →, Egypt 75 E2
El Buheirat □, Sudan 81 F3
El Burgo de Osma, Spain 32 D1
El Cajon, U.S.A. 117 N10
El Campo, U.S.A. 113 L6
El Centro, U.S.A. 117 N11
El Cerro, Bolivia 124 G6
El Cerro de Andévalo, Spain . 35 H4
El Compadre, Mexico 117 N10
El Coronil, Spain 35 H5
El Cuy, Argentina 128 D3
El Cuyo, Mexico 119 C7
El Dab'a, Egypt 80 H6
El Daheir, Egypt 75 D3
El Dátil, Mexico 118 B2
El Deir, Egypt 80 B3
El Dere, Somali Rep. 74 G4
El Descanso, Mexico 117 N10
El Desemboque, Mexico 118 A2
El Dilingat, Egypt 80 H7
El Diviso, Colombia 124 C3
El Djouf, Mauritania 78 D4
El Dorado, Ark., U.S.A. 113 J8
El Dorado, Kans., U.S.A. 113 G6
El Dorado, Venezuela 124 B6
El 'Ein, Sudan 81 D2
El Ejido, Spain 35 J8
El Escorial, Spain 34 E6
El Espinar, Spain 34 D6
El Faiyûm, Egypt 80 J7
El Fâsher, Sudan 81 E2
El Fashn, Egypt 80 J7
El Ferrol = Ferrol, Spain 34 B2
El Fifi, Sudan 81 E2
El Fuerte, Mexico 118 B3
El Ga'a, Sudan 81 E2
El Gal, Somali Rep. 74 E5
El Garef, Sudan 81 E3
El Gebir, Sudan 81 E2
El Gedida, Egypt 80 B2
El Geneina = Al Junaynah,
  Sudan 79 F10
El Geteina, Sudan 81 E3
El Gezira □, Sudan 81 E3

El Gir, Sudan 80 D2
El Gîza, Egypt 80 J7
El Goléa, Algeria 78 B6
El Grau, Spain 33 G4
El Hagiz, Sudan 81 D4
El Hâi, Egypt 80 J7
El Hammam, Egypt 80 A2
El Hawata, Sudan 81 E3
El Heiz, Egypt 80 B2
El Hideib, Sudan 81 E3
El Hilla, Sudan 81 E2
El 'Idisât, Egypt 80 B3
El Iskandarîya, Egypt 80 H7
El Istiwa'iya, Sudan 79 G11
El Jadida, Morocco 78 B4
El Jardal, Honduras 120 D2
El Jebelein, Sudan 81 E3
El Kab, Sudan 80 D3
El Kala, Algeria 37 F3
El Kafr el Sharqi, Egypt 80 H7
El Kamlin, Sudan 81 D3
El Karaba, Sudan 80 D3
El Kere, Ethiopia 81 F5
El Khandaq, Sudan 80 D3
El Khârga, Egypt 80 B3
El Khartûm, Sudan 81 D3
El Khartûm □, Sudan 81 D3
El Khartûm Bahrî, Sudan 81 D3
El Kuntilla, Egypt 75 E3
El Laqâwa, Sudan 81 E2
El Laqeita, Egypt 80 B3
El Leh, Ethiopia 81 G4
El Leiya, Sudan 81 D4
El Maestrazgo, Spain 32 E4
El Mafâza, Sudan 81 E3
El Maghra, Egypt 80 A2
El Mahalla el Kubra, Egypt .. 80 H7
El Mahârîq, Egypt 80 B3
El Maîmûn, Egypt 80 J7
El Maks el Bahari, Egypt 80 C3
El Manshâh, Egypt 80 B3
El Mansûra, Egypt 80 H7
El Manzala, Egypt 80 H7
El Marâgha, Egypt 80 B3
El Masid, Sudan 81 D3
El Masnou, Spain 32 D7
El Matariya, Egypt 80 H8
El Meda, Ethiopia 81 F5
El Medano, Canary Is. 37 F3
El Metemma, Sudan 81 D3
El Milagro, Argentina 126 C2
El Minyâ, Egypt 80 B3
El Monte, U.S.A. 117 L8
El Montseny, Spain 32 D7
El Obeid, Sudan 81 E3
El Odaiya, Sudan 81 E2
El Oro, Mexico 119 D4
El Oued, Algeria 78 B7
El Palmito, Presa, Mexico 118 B3
El Paso, U.S.A. 115 L10
El Paso Robles, U.S.A. 116 K6
El Pedroso, Spain 35 H5
El Pobo de Dueñas, Spain 32 E3
El Portal, U.S.A. 116 H7
El Porvenir, Mexico 118 A3
El Prat de Llobregat, Spain .. 32 D7
El Progreso, Honduras 120 C2
El Pueblito, Mexico 118 B3
El Pueblo, Canary Is. 37 F2
El Puente del Arzobispo, Spain 34 F5
El Puerto de Santa María, Spain 35 J4
El Qâhira, Egypt 80 H7
El Qantara, Egypt 75 E1
El Qasr, Egypt 80 B2
El Quêbâbt, Egypt 80 J7
El Quseima, Egypt 75 E3
El Qusîya, Egypt 80 B3
El Râshda, Egypt 80 B3
El Real, Panama 124 B3
El Reno, U.S.A. 113 H6
El Rîdisiya, Egypt 80 C3
El Rio, U.S.A. 117 L7
El Ronquillo, Spain 35 H4
El Roque, Pta., Canary Is. 37 F4
El Rosarito, Mexico 118 B2
El Rubio, Spain 35 H5
El Saff, Egypt 80 J7
El Saheira, W. →, Egypt 75 E2
El Salto, Mexico 118 C3
El Salvador ■, Cent. Amer. .. 120 D2
El Sauce, Nic. 120 D2
El Saucejo, Spain 35 H5
El Shallal, Egypt 80 C3
El Simbillawein, Egypt 80 H7
El Sueco, Mexico 118 B3
El Suweis, Egypt 80 J8
El Tabbîn, Egypt 80 J7
El Tamarâni, W. →, Egypt ... 75 E3
El Thamad, Egypt 75 F3
El Tigre, Venezuela 124 B6
El Tîh, Gebal, Egypt 75 F2
El Tîna, Khalîg, Egypt 80 H8
El Tîna, Egypt 75 D1
El Tofo, Chile 126 B1
El Tránsito, Chile 126 B1
El Tûr, Egypt 70 D2
El Turbio, Argentina 128 G2
El Uqsur, Egypt 80 B3
El Venado, Mexico 118 C4
El Vendrell, Spain 32 D6
El Vergel, Mexico 118 B3
El Vigía, Venezuela 124 B4
El Viso del Alcor, Spain 35 H5

El Wabeira, Egypt 75 F2
El Wak, Kenya 86 B5
El Waqf, Egypt 80 B3
El Weguet, Ethiopia 81 F5
El Wuz, Sudan 81 D3
Elafónisos, Greece 38 E4
Élancourt, France 19 D8
Élassa, Greece 39 F8
Elassón, Greece 38 B4
Elat, Israel 75 F3
Eláthia, Greece 38 C4
Elâzığ, Turkey 70 B3
Elba, Italy 28 F7
Elba, U.S.A. 109 K2
Elbasan, Albania 40 E4
Elbe, U.S.A. 116 D4
Elbe →, Europe 24 B4
Elbe-Seitenkanal, Germany .. 24 C6
Elbert, Mt., U.S.A. 115 G10
Elberton, U.S.A. 109 H4
Elbeuf, France 18 C8
Elbidtan, Turkey 70 B3
Elbing = Elblag, Poland 44 D6
Elbistan, Turkey 72 C7
Elblag, Poland 44 D6
Elbow, Canada 105 C7
Elbrus, Asia 49 J6
Elburz Mts. = Alborz, Reshteh-
  ye Kühhã-ye, Iran 71 C7
Elche, Spain 33 G4
Elche de la Sierra, Spain 33 G2
Elcho I., Australia 94 A2
Elda, Spain 33 G4
Elde →, Germany 24 B7
Eldon, Mo., U.S.A. 112 F8
Eldon, Wash., U.S.A. 116 C3
Eldora, U.S.A. 112 D8
Eldorado, Argentina 127 B5
Eldorado, Canada 110 B7
Eldorado, Mexico 118 C3
Eldorado, Ill., U.S.A. 108 G1
Eldorado, Tex., U.S.A. 113 K4
Eldorado Springs, U.S.A. 113 G8
Eldoret, Kenya 86 B4
Eldred, U.S.A. 110 E6
Elea, C., Cyprus 36 D13
Eleanora, Pk., Australia 93 F3
Elefantes →, Mozam. 89 C5
Elektrogorsk, Russia 46 E10
Elektrostal, Russia 46 E10
Elele, Nigeria 83 D6
Elena, Bulgaria 41 D9
Elephant Butte Reservoir,
  U.S.A. 115 K10
Elephant I., Antarctica 5 C18
Eleshnitsa, Bulgaria 40 E7
Eleşkirt, Turkey 73 C10
Eleuthera, Bahamas 120 B4
Elevsís, Greece 38 C5
Elevtheroúpolis, Greece 41 F8
Elgin, Canada 111 B8
Elgin, U.K. 14 D5
Elgin, Ill., U.S.A. 108 D1
Elgin, N. Dak., U.S.A. 112 B4
Elgin, Oreg., U.S.A. 114 D5
Elgin, Tex., U.S.A. 113 K6
Elgoibar, Spain 32 B2
Elgon, Mt., Africa 86 B3
Eliase, Indonesia 63 F8
Elikón, Greece 38 C4
Elim, Namibia 88 B2
Elim, S. Africa 88 E2
Elin Pelin, Bulgaria 40 D7
Elista, Russia 49 G7
Elizabeth, N.J., U.S.A. 111 F10
Elizabeth, N.J., U.S.A. 111 F10
Elizabeth City, U.S.A. 109 G7
Elizabethton, U.S.A. 109 G4
Elizabethtown, Ky., U.S.A. .. 108 G3
Elizabethtown, N.Y., U.S.A. . 111 B11
Elizabethtown, Pa., U.S.A. .. 111 F8
Elizondo, Spain 32 B3
Elk, Poland 44 E9
Elk →, Canada 104 C5
Elk →, Poland 44 E9
Elk →, U.S.A. 109 H2
Elk City, U.S.A. 113 H5
Elk Creek, U.S.A. 116 F4
Elk Grove, U.S.A. 116 G5
Elk Island Nat. Park, Canada . 104 C6
Elk Lake, Canada 102 C4
Elk Point, Canada 105 C6
Elk River, Idaho, U.S.A. 114 C5
Elk River, Minn., U.S.A. 112 C8
Elkedra →, Australia 94 C2
Elkhart, Ind., U.S.A. 108 E3
Elkhart, Kans., U.S.A. 113 G4
Elkhorn, Canada 105 D8
Elkhorn →, U.S.A. 112 E6
Elkhovo, Bulgaria 41 D10
Elkin, U.S.A. 109 G5
Elkins, U.S.A. 108 F6
Elkland, U.S.A. 110 E7
Elko, Canada 104 D5
Elko, U.S.A. 114 F6
Elkton, U.S.A. 110 C1
Ell, L., Australia 93 E4
Ellef Ringnes I., Canada 4 B2
Ellen, Mt., U.S.A. 115 B12
Ellenburg, U.S.A. 111 B11
Ellendale, U.S.A. 112 B5
Ellensburg, U.S.A. 114 C3
Ellenville, U.S.A. 111 E10
Ellesmere →, Australia 91 M4
Ellesmere I., Canada 4 B4
Ellesmere Port, U.K. 12 D5

Evans Head

Ellice Is. = Tuvalu ■, Pac. Oc. 96 H9
Ellicottville, U.S.A. 110 D6
Elliot, Australia 94 B1
Elliot, S. Africa 89 E4
Elliot Lake, Canada 102 C3
Elliotdale = Xhora, S. Africa 89 E4
Ellis, U.S.A. 112 F5
Elliston, Australia 95 E1
Ellisville, U.S.A. 113 K10
Ellon, U.K. 14 D6
Ellore = Eluru, India 67 L12
Ellsworth, Kans., U.S.A. 112 F5
Ellsworth, Maine, U.S.A. 109 C11
Ellsworth Land, Antarctica 5 D16
Ellsworth Mts., Antarctica 5 D16
Ellwangen, Germany 25 G6
Ellwood City, U.S.A. 110 F4
Elm, Switz. 25 J5
Elma, Canada 105 D9
Elma, U.S.A. 116 D3
Elmadağ, Turkey 72 C5
Elmalı, Turkey 39 E11
Elmhurst, U.S.A. 108 E2
Elmina, Ghana 83 D4
Elmira, Canada 110 C4
Elmira, U.S.A. 110 D8
Elmira Heights, U.S.A. 110 D8
Elmore, U.S.A. 117 M11
Elmshorn, Germany 24 B5
Elmvale, Canada 110 B5
Elne, France 20 F6
Elora, Canada 110 C4
Elos, Greece 38 E4
Eloúnda, Greece 36 D7
Eloy, U.S.A. 115 K8
Éloyes, France 19 D13
Elrose, Canada 105 C7
Elsdorf, Germany 24 E2
Elsie, U.S.A. 116 E3
Elsinore = Helsingør, Denmark 11 H6
Elster →, Germany 24 D7
Elsterwerda, Germany 24 D9
Eltham, N.Z. 91 H5
Elton, Russia 49 F8
Elton, Ozero, Russia 49 F8
Eltville, Germany 25 E4
Eluru, India 67 L12
Elvas, Portugal 35 G3
Elven, France 18 E4
Elverum, Norway 9 F14
Elvire →, Australia 92 C4
Elvire, Mt., Australia 93 E2
Elvo →, Italy 28 C5
Elwell, L., U.S.A. 114 B8
Elwood, Ind., U.S.A. 108 E3
Elwood, Nebr., U.S.A. 112 E5
Elx = Elche, Spain 33 G4
Ely, U.K. 13 E8
Ely, Minn., U.S.A. 112 B9
Ely, Nev., U.S.A. 114 G6
Elyria, U.S.A. 110 E2
Elyrus, Greece 38 F5
Elz →, Germany 25 G3
Emådalen, Sweden 10 C8
Emāmrūd, Iran 71 B7
Emån →, Sweden 11 G10
Emba, Kazakstan 50 E6
Emba →, Kazakstan 50 E6
Embarcación, Argentina 126 A3
Embarras Portage, Canada 105 B6
Embetsu, Japan 54 B10
Embi = Emba, Kazakstan 50 E6
Embi = Emba →, Kazakstan 50 E6
Embóna, Greece 36 C9
Embrun, France 21 D10
Embu, Kenya 86 C4
Emden, Germany 24 B3
Emecik, Turkey 39 E9
Emerald, Australia 94 C4
Emerson, Canada 105 D9
Emet, Turkey 39 B11
Emi Koussi, Chad 79 E9
Emília-Romagna □, Italy 28 D8
Emilius, Mte., Italy 28 C4
Eminabad, Pakistan 68 C6
Emine, Nos, Bulgaria 41 D11
Emirdağ, Turkey 72 C4
Emlenton, U.S.A. 110 E5
Emlichheim, Germany 24 C2
Emmaboda, Sweden 11 H9
Emmaus, S. Africa 88 D4
Emmaus, U.S.A. 111 F9
Emme →, Switz. 25 H3
Emmeloord, Neths. 17 B5
Emmen, Neths. 17 B6
Emmen, Switz. 25 H4
Emmendingen, Germany 25 G3
Emmental, Switz. 25 J3
Emmerich, Germany 24 D2
Emmet, Australia 94 C3
Emmetsburg, U.S.A. 112 D7
Emmett, Idaho, U.S.A. 114 E5
Emmett, Mich., U.S.A. 110 D2
Emmonak, U.S.A. 100 B3
Emo, Canada 105 D10
Emőd, Hungary 42 C5
Emona, Bulgaria 41 D11
Empalme, Mexico 118 B2
Empangeni, S. Africa 89 D5
Empedrado, Argentina 126 B4
Emperor Seamount Chain, Pac. Oc. 96 D9
Empoli, Italy 28 E7
Emporia, Kans., U.S.A. 112 F6
Emporia, Va., U.S.A. 109 G7
Emporium, U.S.A. 110 E6
Empress, Canada 105 C7
Empty Quarter = Rub' al Khālī, Si. Arabia 74 D4
Ems →, Germany 24 B3
Emsdale, Canada 110 A5
Emsdetten, Germany 24 C3
Emu, China 57 C15
Emu Park, Australia 94 C5
'En 'Avrona, Israel 75 F4
En Nahud, Sudan 81 E2
En Nofalab, Sudan 81 D3
Ena, Japan 55 G8
Enana, Namibia 88 B2
Enånger, Sweden 10 C11
Enard B., U.K. 14 C3
Enare = Inarijärvi, Finland 8 B22
Enarotali, Indonesia 63 E9
Encampment, U.S.A. 114 F10
Encantadas, Serra, Brazil 127 C5
Encarnación, Paraguay 127 B4
Encarnación de Diaz, Mexico 118 C4
Enchi, Ghana 82 D4
Encinitas, U.S.A. 117 M9
Encino, U.S.A. 115 J11
Encs, Hungary 42 B6
Endako, Canada 104 C3
Ende, Indonesia 63 F6
Endeavour Str., Australia 94 A3
Endelave, Denmark 11 J4
Enderbury I., Kiribati 96 H10
Enderby, Canada 104 C5
Enderby I., Australia 92 D2
Enderby Land, Antarctica 5 C5
Enderlin, U.S.A. 112 B6
Endicott, U.S.A. 111 D8
Endwell, U.S.A. 111 D8
Endyalgout I., Australia 92 B5
Eneabba, Australia 93 E2
Enewetak Atoll, Marshall Is. 96 F8
Enez, Turkey 41 F10
Enfield, Canada 103 D7
Enfield, Conn., U.S.A. 111 E12
Enfield, N.H., U.S.A. 111 C12
Engadin, Switz. 25 J6
Engaño, C., Dom. Rep. 121 C6
Engaño, C., Phil. 63 A6
Engaru, Japan 54 B11
Engcobo, S. Africa 89 E4
Engelberg, Switz. 25 J4
Engels, Russia 48 E8
Engemann L., Canada 105 B7
Engershatu, Eritrea 81 D4
Enggano, Indonesia 62 F2
England, U.S.A. 113 H9
England □, U.K. 12 D7
Englee, Canada 103 B8
Englehart, Canada 102 C4
Englewood, U.S.A. 112 F2
English →, Canada 105 C10
English Bazar = Ingraj Bazar, India 69 G13
English Channel, Europe 13 G6
English River, Canada 102 C1
Engures ezers, Latvia 44 A10
Enguri →, Georgia 49 J5
Enid, U.S.A. 113 G6
Enipévs →, Greece 38 B4
Enkhuizen, Neths. 17 B5
Enköping, Sweden 10 E11
Enle, China 58 F3
Enna, Italy 31 E7
Ennadai, Canada 105 A8
Ennadai L., Canada 105 A8
Ennedi, Chad 79 E10
Enngonia, Australia 95 D4
Ennigerloh, Germany 24 D4
Ennis, Ireland 15 D3
Ennis, Mont., U.S.A. 114 D8
Ennis, Tex., U.S.A. 113 J6
Enniscorthy, Ireland 15 D5
Enniskillen, U.K. 15 B4
Ennistimon, Ireland 15 D2
Enns, Austria 26 C7
Enns →, Austria 26 C7
Enontekiö, Finland 8 B20
Enosburg Falls, U.S.A. 111 B12
Enping, China 59 F9
Enriquillo, L., Dom. Rep. 121 C5
Enschede, Neths. 17 B6
Ensenada, Argentina 126 C4
Ensenada, Mexico 118 A1
Ensenada de los Muertos, Mexico 118 C2
Enshi, China 58 B7
Ensiola, Pta. de n', Spain 37 B9
Ensisheim, France 19 E14
Entebbe, Uganda 86 B3
Enterprise, Canada 104 A5
Enterprise, Ala., U.S.A. 109 K3
Enterprise, Oreg., U.S.A. 114 D5
Entraygues-sur-Truyère, France 20 D6
Entre Ríos, Bolivia 126 A3
Entre Ríos □, Argentina 126 C4
Entrepeñas, Embalse de, Spain 32 E2
Entroncamento, Portugal 35 F2
Enugu, Nigeria 83 D6
Enugu □, Nigeria 83 D6
Enugu Ezike, Nigeria 83 D6
Enumclaw, U.S.A. 116 C5
Envermeu, France 18 C8
Enviken, Sweden 10 D9
Enying, Hungary 42 D3
Enza →, Italy 28 D7
Eólie, Ís., Italy 31 D7
Epanomí, Greece 40 F6
Epe, Neths. 17 B5
Epe, Nigeria 83 D5
Épernay, France 19 C10
Épernon, France 19 D8
Ephesus, Turkey 39 D9
Ephraim, U.S.A. 114 G8
Ephrata, Pa., U.S.A. 111 F8
Ephrata, Wash., U.S.A. 114 C4
Epidaurus Limera, Greece 38 E5
Épila, Spain 32 D3
Épinac, France 19 F11
Épinal, France 19 D13
Episkopi, Cyprus 36 E11
Episkopí, Greece 36 D6
Episkopi Bay, Cyprus 36 E11
Epitálion, Greece 38 D3
Eppan = Appiano, Italy 29 B8
Eppingen, Germany 25 F4
Epsom, U.K. 13 F7
Epukiro, Namibia 88 C2
Equatorial Guinea ■, Africa 84 D1
Er Hai, China 58 E3
Er Rachidia, Morocco 78 B5
Er Rahad, Sudan 81 E3
Er Rif, Morocco 78 A5
Er Rogel, Sudan 80 D4
Er Roseires, Sudan 81 E3
Er Rua'at, Sudan 81 E3
Eraclea, Italy 29 C9
Erāwadī Myit = Irrawaddy →, Burma 67 M19
Erāwadī Myitwanya = Irrawaddy, Mouths of the, Burma 67 M19
Erba, Italy 28 C6
Erba, Sudan 80 D4
Erba, J., Sudan 80 C4
Erbaa, Turkey 72 B7
Erbeskopf, Germany 25 F3
Erbil = Arbīl, Iraq 70 B5
Erbu, Ethiopia 81 E3
Erçek, Turkey 70 B4
Erçis, Turkey 73 C10
Erciyaş Dağı, Turkey 70 B2
Érd, Hungary 42 C3
Erdao Jiang →, China 57 C14
Erdek, Turkey 41 F11
Erdemli, Turkey 72 D6
Erdene = Ulaan-Uul, Mongolia 56 B6
Erdenetsogt, Mongolia 56 C4
Erding, Germany 25 G7
Erdre →, France 18 E5
Erebus, Mt., Antarctica 5 D11
Erechim, Brazil 127 B5
Ereğli, Konya, Turkey 70 B2
Ereğli, Zonguldak, Turkey 72 B4
Erei, Monti, Italy 31 E7
Erenhot, China 56 C7
Eresma →, Spain 34 D6
Eressós, Greece 39 B7
Erfenisdam, S. Africa 88 D4
Erftstadt, Germany 24 E2
Erft →, Germany 24 D2
Erfurt, Germany 24 E7
Erg Iguidi, Africa 78 C4
Ergani, Turkey 70 B3
Ergel, Mongolia 56 C5
Ergene →, Turkey 41 E10
Ergeni Vozvyshennost, Russia 49 G7
Ērgli, Latvia 9 H21
Erhlin, Taiwan 59 F13
Eria →, Spain 34 C5
Eriba, Sudan 81 D4
Eriboll, L., U.K. 14 C4
Érice, Italy 30 D5
Erie, U.S.A. 110 D4
Erie, L., N. Amer. 110 D4
Erie Canal, U.S.A. 110 C7
Erieau, Canada 110 D3
Erigavo, Somali Rep. 74 E4
Erikoúsa, Greece 36 A3
Eriksdale, Canada 105 C9
Erímanthos, Greece 38 D3
Erimo-misaki, Japan 54 D11
Erinpura, India 68 G5
Eriskay, U.K. 14 D1
Erithraí, Greece 38 C5
Eritrea ■, Africa 81 E4
Erjas →, Portugal 34 F3
Erkelenz, Germany 24 D2
Erkner, Germany 24 C9
Erlangen, Germany 25 F6
Erldunda, Australia 94 D1
Ermelo, Neths. 17 B5
Ermelo, S. Africa 89 D4
Ermenek, Turkey 70 B2
Ermil, Sudan 81 E2
Ermióni, Greece 38 D5
Ermones, Greece 36 A3
Ermoúpolis = Síros, Greece 38 D6
Ernakulam = Cochin, India 66 Q10
Erne →, Ireland 15 B3
Erne, Lower L., U.K. 15 B4
Erne, Upper L., U.K. 15 B4
Ernée, France 18 D6
Ernest Giles Ra., Australia 93 E3
Ernstberg, Germany 25 E2
Erode, India 66 P10
Eromanga, Australia 95 D3
Erongo, Namibia 88 C2
Erquy, France 18 D4
Erramala Hills, India 66 M11
Errer →, Ethiopia 81 F5
Errigal, Ireland 15 A3
Erris Hd., Ireland 15 B1
Ersekë, Albania 40 F4
Erskine, U.S.A. 112 B7
Erstein, France 19 D14
Ertholmene, Denmark 11 J9
Ertil, Russia 48 E5
Ertis = Irtysh →, Russia 50 C7
Eruh, Turkey 73 D10
Eruwa, Nigeria 83 D5
Ervy-le-Châtel, France 19 D10
Erwin, U.S.A. 109 G4
Eryuan, China 58 D2
Erzgebirge, Germany 24 E8
Erzin, Russia 51 D10
Erzincan, Turkey 70 B3
Erzurum, Turkey 70 B4
Es Caló, Spain 37 C8
Es Canar, Spain 37 B8
Es Mercadal, Spain 37 B11
Es Migjorn Gran, Spain 37 B11
Es Safiya, Sudan 81 D3
Es Sahrâ' Esh Sharqîya, Egypt 80 B3
Es Sînâ', Egypt 75 F3
Es Sûkî, Sudan 81 E3
Es Vedrà, Spain 37 C7
Esambo, Dem. Rep. of the Congo 86 C1
Esan-Misaki, Japan 54 D10
Esashi, Hokkaidō, Japan 54 B11
Esashi, Hokkaidō, Japan 54 D10
Esbjerg, Denmark 11 J2
Escalante, U.S.A. 115 H8
Escalante →, U.S.A. 115 H8
Escalón, Mexico 118 B4
Escambia →, U.S.A. 109 K2
Escanaba, U.S.A. 108 C2
Esch-sur-Alzette, Lux. 17 E6
Eschede, Germany 24 C6
Eschwege, Germany 24 D6
Eschweiler, Germany 24 E2
Escondido, U.S.A. 117 M9
Escravos →, Nigeria 83 D6
Escuinapa, Mexico 118 C3
Escuintla, Guatemala 120 D1
Eséka, Cameroon 83 E7
Eşen →, Turkey 39 E11
Esenguly, Turkmenistan 50 F6
Esens, Germany 24 B3
Esenyurt, Turkey 41 E12
Esera →, Spain 32 C5
Eşfahān, Iran 71 C6
Eşfahān □, Iran 71 C6
Esfarāyen, Iran 71 B8
Esfideh, Iran 71 C8
Esgueva →, Spain 34 D6
Esh Sham = Dimashq, Syria 75 B5
Esh Shamâlîya □, Sudan 80 D2
Esha Ness, U.K. 14 A7
Eshan, China 58 E4
Esher, U.K. 13 F7
Eshowe, S. Africa 89 D5
Esiama, Ghana 82 E4
Esigodini, Zimbabwe 89 C4
Esil = Ishim →, Russia 50 D8
Esino →, Italy 29 E10
Esira, Madag. 89 C8
Esk →, Cumb., U.K. 14 G5
Esk →, N. Yorks., U.K. 12 C7
Eskān, Iran 71 E9
Esker, Canada 103 B6
Eskifjörður, Iceland 8 D7
Eskilsäter, Sweden 11 F7
Eskilstuna, Sweden 10 E10
Eskimalatya, Turkey 73 C8
Eskimo Pt., Canada 100 B10
Eskişehir, Turkey 39 B12
Eskişehir □, Turkey 39 B12
Esla →, Spain 34 D4
Eslāmābād-e Gharb, Iran 70 C5
Eslāmshahr, Iran 71 C6
Eslöv, Sweden 11 J7
Eşme, Turkey 39 C10
Esmeraldas, Ecuador 124 C3
Esnagi L., Canada 102 C3
Espalion, France 20 D6
Espanola, Canada 102 C3
Espanola, U.S.A. 115 H10
Esparreguera, Spain 32 D6
Esparta, Costa Rica 120 E3
Espelkamp, Germany 24 C4
Esperance, Australia 93 F3
Esperance B., Australia 93 F3
Esperanza, Argentina 126 C3
Esperanza, Phil. 61 G6
Espéraza, France 20 F6
Espichel, C., Portugal 35 G1
Espiel, Spain 35 G5
Espigão, Serra do, Brazil 127 B5
Espinazo, Sierra del = Espinhaço, Serra do, Brazil 125 G10
Espinhaço, Serra do, Brazil 125 G10
Espinho, Portugal 34 D2
Espinilho, Serra do, Brazil 127 B5
Espinosa de los Monteros, Spain 34 B7
Espírito Santo □, Brazil 125 H10
Espíritu Santo, Vanuatu 96 J8
Espíritu Santo, B. del, Mexico 119 D7
Espíritu Santo, I., Mexico 118 C2
Espita, Mexico 119 C7
Espiye, Turkey 73 B8
Espluga de Francolí, Spain 32 D6
Espoo, Finland 9 F21
Espuña, Sierra de, Spain 33 H3
Espungabera, Mozam. 89 C5
Esquel, Argentina 128 E2
Esquimalt, Canada 104 D4
Esquina, Argentina 126 C4
Essaouira, Morocco 78 B4
Essebie, Dem. Rep. of the Congo 86 B3
Essen, Belgium 17 C4
Essen, Germany 24 D3
Essendon, Mt., Australia 93 E3
Essequibo →, Guyana 122 C5
Essex, Canada 110 D2
Essex, Calif., U.S.A. 117 L11
Essex, N.Y., U.S.A. 111 B11
Essex □, U.K. 13 F8
Essex Junction, U.S.A. 111 B11
Esslingen, Germany 25 G5
Essonne □, France 19 D9
Estaca de Bares, C. de, Spain 34 B3
Estadilla, Spain 32 C5
Estados, I. de Los, Argentina 122 J4
Estagel, France 20 F6
Eşţahbānāt, Iran 71 D7
Estância, Brazil 125 F11
Estancia, U.S.A. 115 J10
Estārm, Iran 71 D8
Estarreja, Portugal 34 E2
Estats, Pic d', Spain 32 C6
Estcourt, S. Africa 89 D4
Este, Italy 29 C8
Estelí, Nic. 120 D2
Estella, Spain 32 C2
Estellencs, Spain 37 B9
Estena →, Spain 35 F6
Estepa, Spain 35 H6
Estepona, Spain 35 J5
Esterhazy, Canada 105 C8
Esternay, France 19 D10
Esterri d'Aneu, Spain 32 C6
Estevan, Canada 105 D8
Estevan Group, Canada 104 C3
Estherville, U.S.A. 112 D7
Estissac, France 19 D10
Eston, Canada 105 C7
Estonia ■, Europe 9 G21
Estoril, Portugal 35 G1
Estouk, Mali 83 B5
Estreito, Brazil 125 E9
Estrela, Serra da, Portugal 34 E3
Estrella, Spain 35 G7
Estremoz, Portugal 35 G3
Estrondo, Serra do, Brazil 125 E9
Esztergom, Hungary 42 C3
Et Tîdra, Mauritania 82 B1
Etah, India 69 F8
Étain, France 19 C12
Étampes, France 19 D9
Etanga, Namibia 88 B1
Étaples, France 19 B8
Etawah, India 69 F8
Etawney L., Canada 105 B9
Ete, Nigeria 83 D6
Ethel, U.S.A. 116 D4
Ethelbert, Canada 105 C8
Ethiopia ■, Africa 74 F3
Ethiopian Highlands, Ethiopia 52 J7
Etili, Turkey 41 G10
Etive, L., U.K. 14 E3
Etna, Italy 31 E7
Etoile, Dem. Rep. of the Congo 87 E2
Etosha Nat. Park, Namibia 88 B2
Etosha Pan, Namibia 88 B2
Etowah, U.S.A. 109 H3
Étréchy, France 19 D9
Étrépagny, France 19 C8
Étretat, France 18 C7
Etropole, Bulgaria 41 D8
Ettelbruck, Lux. 17 E6
Ettlingen, Germany 25 G4
Ettrick Water →, U.K. 14 F6
Etuku, Dem. Rep. of the Congo 86 C2
Etulia, Moldova 43 E13
Etzatlán, Mexico 118 C4
Etzná, Mexico 119 D6
Eu, France 18 B8
Euboea = Évvoia, Greece 38 C6
Eucla, Australia 93 F4
Euclid, U.S.A. 110 E3
Eudora, U.S.A. 113 J9
Eufaula, Ala., U.S.A. 109 K3
Eufaula, Okla., U.S.A. 113 H7
Eufaula L., U.S.A. 113 H7
Eugene, U.S.A. 114 E2
Eulo, Australia 95 D4
Eunice, La., U.S.A. 113 K8
Eunice, N. Mex., U.S.A. 113 J3
Eupen, Belgium 17 D6
Euphrates = Furāt, Nahr al →, Asia 70 D5
Eure □, France 18 C8
Eure →, France 18 C8
Eure-et-Loir □, France 18 D8
Eureka, Canada 4 B3
Eureka, Calif., U.S.A. 114 F1
Eureka, Kans., U.S.A. 113 G6
Eureka, Mont., U.S.A. 114 B6
Eureka, Nev., U.S.A. 114 G5
Eureka, S. Dak., U.S.A. 112 C5
Eureka, Mt., Australia 93 E3
Europa, Île, Ind. Oc. 85 J8
Europa, Picos de, Spain 34 B6
Europa, Pta. de, Gib. 35 J5
Europe 6 E10
Europoort, Neths. 17 C4
Euskirchen, Germany 24 E2
Eustis, U.S.A. 109 L5
Eutin, Germany 24 A6
Eutsuk L., Canada 104 C3
Evale, Angola 88 B2
Evans, U.S.A. 112 E2
Evans, L., Canada 102 B4
Evans City, U.S.A. 110 F4
Evans Head, Australia 95 D5

Evans Mills, *U.S.A.* 111 B9
Evansburg, *Canada* 104 C5
Evanston, *Ill., U.S.A.* 108 E2
Evanston, *Wyo., U.S.A.* 114 F8
Evansville, *U.S.A.* 108 G2
Évaux-les-Bains, *France* 19 F9
Evaz, *Iran* 71 E7
Eveleth, *U.S.A.* 112 B8
Evensk, *Russia* 51 C16
Everard, L., *Australia* 95 E2
Everard Ranges, *Australia* 93 E5
Everest, Mt., *Nepal* 69 E12
Everett, *Pa., U.S.A.* 110 F6
Everett, *Wash., U.S.A.* 116 C4
Everglades, The, *U.S.A.* 109 N5
Everglades City, *U.S.A.* 109 N5
Everglades National Park,
  U.S.A. 109 N5
Evergreen, *Ala., U.S.A.* 109 K2
Evergreen, *Mont., U.S.A.* 114 B6
Everöd, *Sweden* 11 J8
Evertsberg, *Sweden* 10 C7
Evesham, *U.K.* 13 E6
Évian-les-Bains, *France* 19 F13
Évinos →, *Greece* 38 C3
Évisa, *France* 21 F12
Evje, *Norway* 9 G12
Évora, *Portugal* 35 G3
Évora □, *Portugal* 35 G3
Evowghlī, *Iran* 70 B5
Évreux, *France* 18 C8
Evritanía □, *Greece* 38 B3
Évron, *France* 18 D6
Évros □, *Greece* 41 E10
Évros →, *Greece* 72 B2
Evrótas →, *Greece* 38 E4
Évry, *France* 19 D9
Évvoia, *Greece* 38 C6
Évvoia □, *Greece* 38 C5
Evxinoúpolis, *Greece* 38 B4
Ewe, L., *U.K.* 14 D3
Ewing, *U.S.A.* 112 D5
Ewo, *Congo* 84 E2
Exaltación, *Bolivia* 124 F5
Excelsior Springs, *U.S.A.* 112 F7
Excideuil, *France* 20 C5
Exe →, *U.K.* 13 G4
Exeter, *Canada* 110 C3
Exeter, *U.K.* 13 G4
Exeter, *Calif., U.S.A.* 116 J7
Exeter, *N.H., U.S.A.* 111 D14
Exmoor, *U.K.* 13 F4
Exmouth, *Australia* 92 D1
Exmouth, *U.K.* 13 G4
Exmouth G., *Australia* 92 D1
Expedition Ra., *Australia* 94 C4
Extremadura □, *Spain* 35 F4
Exuma Sound, *Bahamas* 120 B4
Eyasi, L., *Tanzania* 86 C4
Eye Pen., *U.K.* 14 C2
Eyemouth, *U.K.* 14 F6
Eygurande, *France* 19 G9
Eyjafjörður, *Iceland* 8 C4
Eymet, *France* 20 D4
Eymoutiers, *France* 20 C5
Eynesil, *Turkey* 73 B8
Eyre (North), L., *Australia* ... 95 D2
Eyre (South), L., *Australia* ... 95 D2
Eyre Mts., *N.Z.* 91 L2
Eyre Pen., *Australia* 95 E2
Eysturoy, *Færoe Is.* 8 E9
Eyvānkī, *Iran* 71 C6
Ez Zeidab, *Sudan* 80 D3
Ezcaray, *Spain* 32 C1
Ežerėlis, *Lithuania* 44 D10
Ezhou, *China* 59 B10
Ezine, *Turkey* 39 B8
Ezouza →, *Cyprus* 36 E11

F

F.Y.R.O.M. = Macedonia ■,
  Europe 40 E5
Fabala, *Guinea* 82 D3
Fabens, *U.S.A.* 115 L10
Fabero, *Spain* 34 C4
Fåborg, *Denmark* 11 J4
Fabriano, *Italy* 29 E9
Făcăeni, *Romania* 43 F12
Fachi, *Niger* 79 E8
Fada, *Chad* 79 E10
Fada-n-Gourma, *Burkina Faso* 83 C5
Fadd, *Hungary* 42 D3
Faddeyevskiy, Ostrov, *Russia* . 51 B15
Faddor, *Sudan* 81 F3
Fadghāmī, *Syria* 70 C4
Fadlab, *Sudan* 80 D3
Faenza, *Italy* 29 D8
Færoe Is. = Føroyar, *Atl. Oc.* . 8 F9
Fafa, *Mali* 83 B5
Fafe, *Portugal* 34 D2
Fagam, *Nigeria* 83 C7
Făgăras, *Romania* 43 E9
Făgăras, Munţii, *Romania* 43 E9
Fägelmara, *Sweden* 11 H9
Fagerhult, *Sweden* 11 G9
Fagersta, *Sweden* 10 D9
Făget, *Romania* 42 E7
Făget, Munţii, *Romania* 43 C8
Fagnano, L., *Argentina* 128 G3
Fagnières, *France* 19 D11
Faguibine, L., *Mali* 82 B4

Fahliān, *Iran* 71 D6
Fahraj, *Kermān, Iran* 71 D8
Fahraj, *Yazd, Iran* 71 D7
Fai Tsi Long Archipelago,
  Vietnam 58 G6
Faial, *Madeira* 37 D3
Fair Haven, *U.S.A.* 108 D9
Fair Hd., *U.K.* 15 A5
Fair Oaks, *U.S.A.* 116 G5
Fairbanks, *U.S.A.* 100 B5
Fairbury, *U.S.A.* 112 E6
Fairfax, *U.S.A.* 111 B11
Fairfield, *Ala., U.S.A.* 109 J2
Fairfield, *Calif., U.S.A.* 116 G4
Fairfield, *Conn., U.S.A.* 111 E11
Fairfield, *Idaho, U.S.A.* 114 E6
Fairfield, *Ill., U.S.A.* 108 F1
Fairfield, *Iowa, U.S.A.* 112 E9
Fairfield, *Tex., U.S.A.* 113 K7
Fairford, *Canada* 105 C9
Fairhope, *U.S.A.* 109 K2
Fairlie, *N.Z.* 91 L3
Fairmead, *U.S.A.* 116 H6
Fairmont, *Minn., U.S.A.* 112 D7
Fairmont, *W. Va., U.S.A.* 108 F5
Fairmount, *Calif., U.S.A.* 117 L8
Fairmount, *N.Y., U.S.A.* 111 C8
Fairplay, *U.S.A.* 115 G11
Fairport, *U.S.A.* 110 C7
Fairport Harbor, *U.S.A.* 110 E3
Fairview, *Canada* 104 B5
Fairview, *Mont., U.S.A.* 112 B2
Fairview, *Okla., U.S.A.* 113 G5
Fairweather, Mt., *U.S.A.* 104 B1
Faisalabad, *Pakistan* 68 D5
Faith, *U.S.A.* 112 C3
Faizabad, *India* 69 F10
Fajardo, *Puerto Rico* 121 C6
Fajr, W. →, *Si. Arabia* 70 D3
Fakenham, *U.K.* 12 E8
Fåker, *Sweden* 10 A8
Fakfak, *Indonesia* 63 E8
Fakiya, *Bulgaria* 41 D11
Fakobli, *Ivory C.* 82 D3
Fakse, *Denmark* 11 J6
Fakse Bugt, *Denmark* 11 J6
Fakse Ladeplads, *Denmark* ... 11 J6
Faku, *China* 57 C12
Falaba, *S. Leone* 82 D2
Falaise, *France* 18 D6
Falaise, Mui, *Vietnam* 64 C5
Falakrón Óros, *Greece* 40 E7
Falam, *Burma* 67 H18
Falces, *Spain* 32 C3
Fălciu, *Romania* 43 D13
Falcó, C. des, *Spain* 37 C7
Falcón, Presa, *Mexico* 119 B5
Falcon Lake, *Canada* 105 D9
Falcon Reservoir, *U.S.A.* 113 M5
Falconara Marittima, *Italy* 29 E10
Falcone, C. del, *Italy* 30 B1
Falconer, *U.S.A.* 110 D5
Faléa, *Mali* 82 C2
Falémé →, *Senegal* 82 C2
Falerum, *Sweden* 11 F10
Faleshty = Făleşti, *Moldova* .. 43 C12
Făleşti, *Moldova* 43 C12
Falfurrias, *U.S.A.* 113 M5
Falher, *Canada* 104 B5
Falirakí, *Greece* 36 C10
Falkenberg, *Germany* 24 D9
Falkenberg, *Sweden* 11 H6
Falkensee, *Germany* 24 C9
Falkirk, *U.K.* 14 F5
Falkirk □, *U.K.* 14 F5
Falkland, *U.K.* 14 E5
Falkland Is. □, *Atl. Oc.* 128 G5
Falkland Sd., *Falk. Is.* 128 G5
Falkonéra, *Greece* 38 E5
Falköping, *Sweden* 11 F7
Fall River, *U.S.A.* 111 E13
Fallbrook, *U.S.A.* 117 M9
Fallon, *U.S.A.* 114 G4
Falls City, *U.S.A.* 112 E7
Falls Creek, *U.S.A.* 110 E6
Falmouth, *Jamaica* 120 C4
Falmouth, *U.K.* 13 G2
Falmouth, *U.S.A.* 111 E14
Falsa, Pta., *Mexico* 118 B1
False B., *S. Africa* 88 E2
False, C., *Honduras* 120 C3
Falso, C., *Honduras* 120 C3
Falster, *Denmark* 11 K5
Falsterbo, *Sweden* 9 J15
Fălticeni, *Romania* 43 C11
Falun, *Sweden* 10 D9
Famagusta, *Cyprus* 36 D12
Famagusta Bay, *Cyprus* 36 D13
Famalé, *Niger* 78 F6
Famatina, Sierra de, *Argentina* 126 B2
Family L., *Canada* 105 C9
Famoso, *U.S.A.* 117 K7
Fan Xian, *China* 56 G8
Fanad Hd., *Ireland* 15 A4
Fanárion, *Greece* 38 B3
Fandriana, *Madag.* 89 C8
Fang, *Thailand* 58 H2
Fang Xian, *China* 59 A8
Fangaga, *Sudan* 80 D4
Fangak, *Sudan* 81 F3
Fangchang, *China* 59 B12
Fangcheng, *China* 56 H7
Fangchenggang, *China* 58 G7
Fangliao, *Taiwan* 59 F13
Fangshan, *China* 56 E6
Fangzi, *China* 57 F10

Fani i Madh →, *Albania* 40 E4
Fanjakana, *Madag.* 89 C8
Fanjiatun, *China* 57 C13
Fannich, L., *U.K.* 14 D4
Fannūj, *Iran* 71 E8
Fano, *Italy* 29 E10
Fanshi, *China* 56 E7
Fao = Al Fāw, *Iraq* 71 D6
Faqirwali, *Pakistan* 68 E5
Fâqûs, *Egypt* 80 H7
Fara in Sabina, *Italy* 29 F9
Faradje, *Dem. Rep. of the Congo* 86 B2
Farafangana, *Madag.* 89 C8
Farâfra, El Wâhât el-, *Egypt* .. 80 B2
Farāh, *Afghan.* 66 C3
Farāh □, *Afghan.* 66 C3
Farahalana, *Madag.* 89 A9
Faraid, Gebel, *Egypt* 80 C4
Farako, *Ivory C.* 82 D4
Faramana, *Burkina Faso* 82 C4
Faranah, *Guinea* 82 C2
Farasān, Jazā'ir, *Si. Arabia* ... 74 D3
Farasan Is. = Farasān, Jazā'ir,
  Si. Arabia 74 D3
Faratsiho, *Madag.* 89 B8
Fardes →, *Spain* 35 H7
Fareham, *U.K.* 13 G6
Farewell, C., *N.Z.* 91 J4
Farewell C. = Nunap Isua,
  Greenland 101 C15
Färgelanda, *Sweden* 11 F5
Farghona, *Uzbekistan* 50 E8
Fargo, *U.S.A.* 112 B6
Fār'iah, W. al →, *West Bank* .. 75 C4
Faribault, *U.S.A.* 112 C8
Faridabad, *India* 68 E6
Faridkot, *India* 68 D6
Faridpur, *Bangla.* 69 H13
Faridpur, *India* 69 E8
Färila, *Sweden* 10 C9
Farim, *Guinea-Biss.* 82 C1
Farīmān, *Iran* 71 C8
Farina, *Australia* 95 E2
Fariones, Pta., *Canary Is.* 37 E6
Fâriskûr, *Egypt* 80 H7
Färjestaden, *Sweden* 11 H10
Farkadhón, *Greece* 38 B4
Farmakonisi, *Greece* 39 D9
Farmerville, *U.S.A.* 113 J8
Farmingdale, *U.S.A.* 111 F10
Farmington, *Canada* 104 B4
Farmington, *Calif., U.S.A.* 116 H6
Farmington, *Maine, U.S.A.* ... 109 C10
Farmington, *Mo., U.S.A.* 113 G9
Farmington, *N.H., U.S.A.* 111 C13
Farmington, *N. Mex., U.S.A.* . 115 H9
Farmington, *Utah, U.S.A.* 114 F8
Farmington →, *U.S.A.* 111 E12
Farmville, *U.S.A.* 108 G6
Farnborough, *U.K.* 13 F7
Farne Is., *U.K.* 12 B6
Farnham, *Canada* 111 A12
Farnham, Mt., *Canada* 104 C5
Faro, *Brazil* 125 D7
Faro, *Canada* 100 B6
Faro, *Portugal* 35 H3
Fårö, *Sweden* 9 H18
Faro □, *Portugal* 35 H2
Fårösund, *Sweden* 11 G13
Farquhar, C., *Australia* 93 D1
Farrars Cr. →, *Australia* 94 D3
Farrāshband, *Iran* 71 D7
Farrell, *U.S.A.* 110 E4
Farrokhī, *Iran* 71 C8
Farruch, C. = Ferrutx, C., *Spain* 37 B10
Fārs □, *Iran* 71 D7
Fársala, *Greece* 38 B4
Farsø, *Denmark* 11 H3
Farsund, *Norway* 9 G12
Fartak, Râs, *Si. Arabia* 70 D2
Fartak, Ra's, *Yemen* 74 D5
Fărţăneşti, *Romania* 43 E12
Fartura, Serra da, *Brazil* 127 B5
Faru, *Nigeria* 83 C6
Fārūj, *Iran* 71 B8
Fårup, *Denmark* 11 H3
Farvel, Kap = Nunap Isua,
  Greenland 101 C15
Farwell, *U.S.A.* 113 H3
Fasā, *Iran* 71 D7
Fasano, *Italy* 31 B10
Fashoda, *Sudan* 81 F3
Fassa, *Mali* 82 C3
Fastiv, *Ukraine* 47 G5
Fastov = Fastiv, *Ukraine* 47 G5
Fatagar, Tanjung, *Indonesia* .. 63 E8
Fatehabad, Haryana, *India* ... 68 E6
Fatehabad, *Ut. P., India* 68 F8
Fatehgarh, *India* 69 F8
Fatehpur, *Bihar, India* 69 G11
Fatehpur, *Raj., India* 68 F6
Fatehpur, *Ut. P., India* 69 G9
Fatehpur, *Ut. P., India* 69 F9
Fatehpur Sikri, *India* 68 F6
Fatesh, *Russia* 47 F8
Fathai, *Sudan* 81 F3
Fatick, *Senegal* 82 C1
Fatima, *Canada* 103 C7
Fátima, *Portugal* 35 F2
Fatsa, *Turkey* 72 B7
Faucille, Col de la, *France* 19 F13
Faulkton, *U.S.A.* 112 C5
Faulquemont, *France* 19 C13

Faure I., *Australia* 93 E1
Făurei, *Romania* 43 E12
Fauresmith, *S. Africa* 88 D4
Fauske, *Norway* 8 C16
Favara, *Italy* 30 E6
Faváritx, C. de, *Spain* 37 B11
Faverges, *France* 21 C10
Favignana, *Italy* 30 E5
Fawcett, Pt., *Australia* 92 B5
Fawn →, *Canada* 102 A2
Fawnskin, *U.S.A.* 117 L10
Faxaflói, *Iceland* 8 D2
Faxälven →, *Sweden* 10 A10
Faya-Largeau, *Chad* 79 E9
Fayd, *Si. Arabia* 70 E4
Fayence, *France* 21 E10
Fayette, *Ala., U.S.A.* 109 J2
Fayette, *Mo., U.S.A.* 112 F8
Fayetteville, *Ark., U.S.A.* 113 G7
Fayetteville, *N.C., U.S.A.* 109 H6
Fayetteville, *Tenn., U.S.A.* ... 109 H2
Fayied, *Egypt* 80 H8
Fayón, *Spain* 32 D5
Fazilka, *India* 68 D6
Fazilpur, *Pakistan* 68 E4
Fdérik, *Mauritania* 78 D3
Feale →, *Ireland* 15 D2
Fear, C., *U.S.A.* 109 J7
Feather →, *U.S.A.* 114 G3
Feather Falls, *U.S.A.* 116 F5
Featherston, *N.Z.* 91 J5
Featherstone, *Zimbabwe* 87 F3
Fécamp, *France* 18 C7
Fedala = Mohammedia,
  Morocco 78 B4
Federación, *Argentina* 126 C4
Féderal, *Argentina* 128 C5
Federal Capital Terr. □, *Nigeria* 83 D6
Federal Way, *U.S.A.* 116 C4
Fedeshkūh, *Iran* 71 D7
Fehérgyarmat, *Hungary* 42 C7
Fehmarn, *Germany* 24 A7
Fehmarn Bælt, *Europe* 11 K5
Fehmarn Belt = Fehmarn Bælt,
  Europe 11 K5
Fei Xian, *China* 57 G9
Feijó, *Brazil* 124 E4
Feilding, *N.Z.* 91 J5
Feira de Santana, *Brazil* 125 F11
Feixi, *China* 59 B11
Feixiang, *China* 56 F8
Fejér □, *Hungary* 42 C3
Fejø, *Denmark* 11 K5
Feke, *Turkey* 72 D6
Fekete →, *Hungary* 42 E3
Felanitx, *Spain* 37 B10
Feldbach, *Austria* 26 E8
Feldberg, *Baden-W., Germany* 25 H3
Feldberg,
  Mecklenburg-Vorpommern,
  Germany 24 B9
Feldkirch, *Austria* 26 D2
Feldkirchen, *Austria* 26 E7
Felipe Carrillo Puerto, *Mexico* . 119 D7
Felixburg, *Zimbabwe* 89 B5
Felixstowe, *U.K.* 13 F9
Felletin, *France* 20 C6
Felton, *U.S.A.* 116 H4
Feltre, *Italy* 29 B8
Femer Bælt = Fehmarn Bælt,
  Europe 11 K5
Femø, *Denmark* 11 K5
Femunden, *Norway* 9 E14
Fen He →, *China* 56 G6
Fene, *Spain* 34 B2
Fenelon Falls, *Canada* 110 B6
Fener Burnu, *Turkey* 39 E9
Feneroa, *Ethiopia* 81 E4
Feng Xian, *Jiangsu, China* ... 56 G9
Feng Xian, *Shaanxi, China* ... 56 H4
Fengári, *Greece* 41 F9
Fengcheng, *Jiangxi, China* ... 59 C10
Fengcheng, *Liaoning, China* .. 57 D13
Fengfeng, *China* 56 F8
Fenggang, *China* 58 D6
Fenghua, *China* 59 C13
Fenghuang, *China* 58 D7
Fengkai, *China* 59 F8
Fengkang, *Taiwan* 59 F13
Fenglin, *Taiwan* 59 F13
Fengning, *China* 56 D9
Fengqing, *China* 58 E2
Fengqiu, *China* 56 G8
Fengrun, *China* 57 E10
Fengshan, *Guangxi Zhuangzu,*
  China 58 E7
Fengshan, *Guangxi Zhuangzu,*
  China 58 E6
Fengshan, *Taiwan* 59 F13
Fengshun, *China* 59 F11
Fengtai, *Anhui, China* 59 A11
Fengtai, *Beijing, China* 56 E9
Fengxian, *China* 59 B13
Fengxin, *China* 59 C10
Fengyang, *China* 57 H9
Fengyi, *China* 58 E3
Fengyüan, *Taiwan* 59 E13
Feno, C. de, *France* 21 G12
Fenoarivo, *Fianarantsoa, Madag.* 89 C8
Fenoarivo, *Fianarantsoa, Madag.* 89 C8
Fenoarivo Afovoany, *Madag.* . 89 B8

Fenoarivo Atsinanana, *Madag.* 89 B8
Fens, The, *U.K.* 12 E7
Fensmark, *Denmark* 11 J5
Fenton, *U.S.A.* 108 D4
Fenxi, *China* 56 F6
Fenyang, *China* 56 F6
Fenyi, *China* 59 D10
Feodosiya, *Ukraine* 47 K8
Ferdows, *Iran* 71 C8
Fère-Champenoise, *France* ... 19 D10
Fère-en-Tardenois, *France* ... 19 C10
Ferentino, *Italy* 29 G10
Ferfer, *Somali Rep.* 74 F4
Fergana = Farghona, *Uzbekistan* 50 E8
Fergus, *Canada* 110 C4
Fergus Falls, *U.S.A.* 112 B6
Feričanci, *Croatia* 42 E2
Ferlach, *Austria* 26 E7
Ferland, *Canada* 102 B2
Ferlo, Vallée du, *Senegal* 82 B2
Fermanagh □, *U.K.* 15 B4
Fermo, *Italy* 29 E10
Fermont, *Canada* 103 B6
Fermoselle, *Spain* 34 D4
Fermoy, *Ireland* 15 D3
Fernán Nuñéz, *Spain* 35 H6
Fernández, *Argentina* 126 B3
Fernandina Beach, *U.S.A.* ... 109 K5
Fernando de Noronha, *Brazil* . 125 D12
Fernando Póo = Bioko,
  Eq. Guin. 83 E6
Ferndale, *U.S.A.* 116 B4
Fernie, *Canada* 104 D5
Fernlees, *Australia* 94 C4
Fernley, *U.S.A.* 114 G4
Ferozepore = Firozpur, *India* . 68 D6
Férrai, *Greece* 41 F10
Ferrandina, *Italy* 31 B9
Ferrara, *Italy* 29 D8
Ferrato, C., *Italy* 30 C2
Ferreira do Alentejo, *Portugal* . 35 G2
Ferreñafe, *Peru* 124 E3
Ferret, C., *France* 20 D2
Ferrerías, *Spain* 37 B11
Ferrette, *France* 19 E14
Ferriday, *U.S.A.* 113 K9
Ferriere, *Italy* 28 D6
Ferrières, *France* 19 D9
Ferro, Capo, *Italy* 30 A2
Ferrol, *Spain* 34 B2
Ferron, *U.S.A.* 115 G8
Ferrutx, C., *Spain* 37 B10
Ferryland, *Canada* 103 C9
Fertile, *U.S.A.* 112 B6
Fertőszentmiklós, *Hungary* ... 42 C1
Fès, *Morocco* 78 B5
Fessenden, *U.S.A.* 112 B5
Festus, *U.S.A.* 112 F9
Feté Bowé, *Senegal* 82 C2
Fetesti, *Romania* 43 F12
Fethiye, *Turkey* 39 E11
Fethiye Körfezi, *Turkey* 39 E10
Fetlar, *U.K.* 14 A8
Feuilles →, *Canada* 101 C12
Feurs, *France* 21 C8
Fez = Fès, *Morocco* 78 B5
Fezzan, *Libya* 79 C8
Fiambalá, *Argentina* 126 B2
Fianarantsoa, *Madag.* 89 C8
Fianarantsoa □, *Madag.* 89 C8
Fiche, *Ethiopia* 81 F4
Fichtelgebirge, *Germany* 25 C7
Ficksburg, *S. Africa* 89 D4
Fidenza, *Italy* 28 D7
Fiditi, *Nigeria* 83 D5
Field →, *Australia* 94 C2
Field I., *Australia* 92 B5
Fieni, *Romania* 43 E10
Fier, *Albania* 40 F3
Fierzë, *Albania* 40 D4
Fife □, *U.K.* 14 E5
Fife Ness, *U.K.* 14 E6
Fifth Cataract, *Sudan* 80 D3
Figari, *France* 21 G13
Figeac, *France* 20 D6
Figeholm, *Sweden* 11 G10
Figline Valdarno, *Italy* 29 E8
Figtree, *Zimbabwe* 87 G2
Figueira Castelo Rodrigo,
  Portugal 34 E4
Figueira da Foz, *Portugal* 34 E2
Figueiró dos Vinhos, *Portugal* . 34 F2
Figueres, *Spain* 32 C7
Figuig, *Morocco* 78 B5
Fihaonana, *Madag.* 89 B8
Fiherenana, *Madag.* 89 B8
Fiherenana →, *Madag.* 89 C7
Fiji ■, *Pac. Oc.* 91 C8
Fik, *Ethiopia* 81 F5
Filabres, Sierra de los, *Spain* . 35 H8
Filabusi, *Zimbabwe* 89 C4
Filadélfia, *Italy* 31 D9
Fil'akovo, *Slovak Rep.* 27 C12
Filey, *U.K.* 12 C7
Filey B., *U.K.* 12 C7
Filfla, *Malta* 36 D1
Filiaşi, *Romania* 43 F8
Filiátes, *Greece* 38 B3
Filiatrá, *Greece* 38 D3
Filicudi, *Italy* 31 D7
Filingué, *Niger* 83 C5
Filiouri →, *Greece* 41 E9
Filipstad, *Sweden* 10 E8
Filisur, *Switz.* 25 J5

Name	Page	Grid
Fillmore, *Calif., U.S.A.*	117	L8
Fillmore, *Utah, U.S.A.*	115	G7
Filótion, *Greece*	39	D7
Filottrano, *Italy*	29	E10
Filtu, *Ethiopia*	81	F5
Finale Emília, *Italy*	29	D8
Finale Lígure, *Italy*	28	D5
Fiñana, *Spain*	35	H8
Finch, *Canada*	111	A9
Findhorn →, *U.K.*	14	D5
Findlay, *U.S.A.*	108	E4
Finger L., *Canada*	102	B1
Finger Lakes, *U.S.A.*	111	D8
Fíngoè, *Mozam.*	87	E3
Finike, *Turkey*	39	E12
Finike Körfezi, *Turkey*	39	E12
Finiq, *Albania*	40	G4
Finistère □, *France*	18	D3
Finisterre = Fisterra, *Spain*	34	C1
Finisterre, C. = Fisterra, C., *Spain*	34	C1
Finke, *Australia*	94	D1
Finland ■, *Europe*	8	E22
Finland, G. of, *Europe*	9	G21
Finlay →, *Canada*	104	B3
Finley, *U.S.A.*	112	B6
Finn →, *Ireland*	15	B4
Finnerödja, *Sweden*	11	F8
Finnigan, Mt., *Australia*	94	B4
Finniss, C., *Australia*	95	E1
Finnmark, *Norway*	8	B20
Finnsnes, *Norway*	8	B18
Finspång, *Sweden*	11	F9
Finsteraarhorn, *Switz.*	25	J4
Finsterwalde, *Germany*	24	D9
Fiora →, *Italy*	29	F8
Fiorenzuola d'Arda, *Italy*	28	D6
Fiq, *Syria*	75	C4
Firebag →, *Canada*	105	B6
Firebaugh, *U.S.A.*	116	J6
Firedrake L., *Canada*	105	A8
Firenze, *Italy*	29	E8
Firenzuola, *Italy*	29	D8
Firk →, *Iraq*	70	D5
Firminy, *France*	21	C8
Fīrozabad, *India*	69	F8
Firozpur, *India*	68	D6
Firozpur-Jhirka, *India*	68	F7
Fīrūzābād, *Iran*	71	D7
Fīrūzkūh, *Iran*	71	C7
Firvale, *Canada*	104	C3
Fish →, *Namibia*	88	D2
Fish →, *S. Africa*	88	E3
Fish River Canyon, *Namibia*	88	D2
Fisher, *Australia*	93	F5
Fisher B., *Canada*	105	C9
Fishers I., *U.S.A.*	111	E13
Fishguard, *U.K.*	13	E3
Fishing L., *Canada*	105	C9
Fishkill, *U.S.A.*	111	E11
Fismes, *France*	19	C10
Fisterra, *Spain*	34	C1
Fisterra, C., *Spain*	34	C1
Fitchburg, *U.S.A.*	111	D13
Fitz Roy, *Argentina*	128	F3
Fitzgerald, *Canada*	104	B6
Fitzgerald, *U.S.A.*	109	K4
Fitzmaurice →, *Australia*	92	B5
Fitzroy →, *Queens., Australia*	94	C5
Fitzroy →, *W. Austral., Australia*	92	C3
Fitzroy, Mte., *Argentina*	128	F2
Fitzroy Crossing, *Australia*	92	C4
Fitzwilliam I., *Canada*	110	A3
Fiuggi, *Italy*	29	G10
Fiume = Rijeka, *Croatia*	29	C11
Five Points, *U.S.A.*	116	J6
Fivizzano, *Italy*	28	D7
Fizi, *Dem. Rep. of the Congo*	86	C2
Fjällbacka, *Sweden*	11	F5
Fjärdhundra, *Sweden*	10	E10
Fjellerup, *Denmark*	11	H4
Fjerritslev, *Denmark*	11	G3
Fjugesta, *Sweden*	10	E8
Flagstaff, *U.S.A.*	115	J8
Flagstaff L., *U.S.A.*	109	C10
Flaherty I., *Canada*	102	A4
Flåm, *Norway*	9	F12
Flambeau →, *U.S.A.*	112	C9
Flamborough Hd., *U.K.*	12	C7
Fläming, *Germany*	24	C8
Flaming Gorge Reservoir, *U.S.A.*	114	F9
Flamingo, Teluk, *Indonesia*	63	F9
Flanders = Flandre, *Europe*	19	B9
Flandre, *Europe*	19	B9
Flandre Occidentale = West-Vlaanderen □, *Belgium*	17	D2
Flandre Orientale = Oost-Vlaanderen □, *Belgium*	17	C3
Flandreau, *U.S.A.*	112	C6
Flanigan, *U.S.A.*	116	E7
Flannan Is., *U.K.*	14	C1
Flåsjön, *Sweden*	8	D16
Flat →, *Canada*	104	A3
Flathead L., *U.S.A.*	114	C7
Flattery, C., *Australia*	94	A4
Flattery, C., *U.S.A.*	116	B2
Flatwoods, *U.S.A.*	108	F4
Fleetwood, *U.K.*	12	D4
Fleetwood, *U.S.A.*	111	F9
Flekkefjord, *Norway*	9	G12
Flemington, *U.S.A.*	110	E7
Flen, *Sweden*	10	E10
Flensburg, *Germany*	24	A5
Flers, *France*	18	D6
Flesherton, *Canada*	110	B4
Flesko, Tanjung, *Indonesia*	63	D6
Fleurance, *France*	20	E4
Fleurier, *Switz.*	25	J2
Fleurieu Pen., *Australia*	95	F2
Flevoland □, *Neths.*	17	B5
Flin Flon, *Canada*	105	C8
Flinders →, *Australia*	94	B3
Flinders B., *Australia*	93	F2
Flinders Group, *Australia*	94	A3
Flinders I., *S. Austral., Australia*	95	E1
Flinders I., *Tas., Australia*	94	G4
Flinders Reefs, *Australia*	94	B4
Flint, *U.K.*	12	D4
Flint, *U.S.A.*	108	D4
Flint →, *U.S.A.*	109	K3
Flint I., *Kiribati*	97	J12
Flintshire □, *U.K.*	12	D4
Fliseryd, *Sweden*	11	G10
Flix, *Spain*	32	D5
Flixecourt, *France*	19	B9
Floby, *Sweden*	11	F7
Floda, *Sweden*	11	G6
Flodden, *U.K.*	12	B5
Flogny-la-Chapelle, *France*	19	E10
Floodwood, *U.S.A.*	112	B8
Flora, *U.S.A.*	108	F1
Florala, *U.S.A.*	109	K2
Florence = Firenze, *Italy*	29	E8
Florence, *Ala., U.S.A.*	109	H2
Florence, *Ariz., U.S.A.*	115	K8
Florence, *Colo., U.S.A.*	112	F2
Florence, *Oreg., U.S.A.*	114	E1
Florence, *S.C., U.S.A.*	109	H6
Florence, L., *Australia*	95	D2
Florencia, *Colombia*	124	C3
Florennes, *Belgium*	17	D4
Florensac, *France*	20	E7
Florenville, *Belgium*	17	E5
Flores, *Guatemala*	120	C2
Flores, *Indonesia*	63	F6
Flores I., *Canada*	104	D3
Flores Sea, *Indonesia*	63	F6
Floreşti, *Moldova*	43	C13
Floresville, *U.S.A.*	113	L5
Floriano, *Brazil*	125	E10
Florianópolis, *Brazil*	127	B6
Florida, *Cuba*	120	B4
Florida, *Uruguay*	127	C4
Florida □, *U.S.A.*	109	L5
Florida, Straits of, *U.S.A.*	120	B4
Florida B., *U.S.A.*	120	B3
Florida Keys, *U.S.A.*	109	N5
Florídia, *Italy*	31	E8
Flórina, *Greece*	40	F5
Flórina □, *Greece*	40	F5
Florø, *Norway*	9	F11
Flower Station, *Canada*	111	A8
Flowerpot I., *Canada*	110	A3
Floydada, *U.S.A.*	113	J4
Fluk, *Indonesia*	63	E7
Flúmen →, *Spain*	32	D4
Flumendosa →, *Italy*	30	C2
Fluminimaggiore, *Italy*	30	C1
Flushing = Vlissingen, *Neths.*	17	C3
Fluviá →, *Spain*	32	C8
Flying Fish, C., *Antarctica*	5	D15
Foam Lake, *Canada*	105	C8
Foča, *Bos.-H.*	40	C2
Foça, *Turkey*	39	C8
Focşani, *Romania*	43	E12
Fodécontéa, *Guinea*	82	C2
Fogang, *China*	59	F9
Fóggia, *Italy*	31	A8
Foggo, *Nigeria*	83	C6
Foglia →, *Italy*	29	E9
Fogo, *Canada*	103	C9
Fogo I., *Canada*	103	C9
Fohnsdorf, *Austria*	26	D7
Föhr, *Germany*	24	A4
Foia, *Portugal*	35	H2
Foix, *France*	20	E5
Fojnica, *Bos.-H.*	42	G2
Fokino, *Russia*	46	F8
Fokís □, *Greece*	38	C4
Fokku, *Nigeria*	83	C5
Folda, *Nord-Trøndelag, Norway*	8	D14
Folda, *Nordland, Norway*	8	C16
Földeák, *Hungary*	42	D5
Folégandros, *Greece*	38	E6
Foley, *Botswana*	88	C4
Foley, *U.S.A.*	109	K2
Foleyet, *Canada*	102	C3
Folgefonni, *Norway*	9	F12
Foligno, *Italy*	29	F9
Folkestone, *U.K.*	13	F9
Folkston, *U.S.A.*	109	K5
Follansbee, *U.S.A.*	110	F4
Follónica, *Italy*	28	F7
Follónica, G. di, *Italy*	28	F7
Folsom L., *U.S.A.*	116	G5
Fond-du-Lac, *Canada*	105	B7
Fond du Lac, *U.S.A.*	112	D10
Fond-du-Lac →, *Canada*	105	B7
Fonda, *U.S.A.*	111	D10
Fonfría, *Spain*	34	D4
Fonni, *Italy*	30	B2
Fonsagrada = A Fonsagrada, *Spain*	34	B3
Fonseca, G. de, *Cent. Amer.*	120	D2
Font-Romeu, *France*	20	F5
Fontaine-Française, *France*	19	E12
Fontainebleau, *France*	19	D9
Fontana, *U.S.A.*	117	L9
Fontas →, *Canada*	104	B4
Fonte Boa, *Brazil*	124	D5
Fontem, *Cameroon*	83	D6
Fontenay-le-Comte, *France*	20	B3
Fontenelle Reservoir, *U.S.A.*	114	E8
Fontur, *Iceland*	8	C6
Fonyód, *Hungary*	42	D2
Foochow = Fuzhou, *China*	59	D12
Foping, *China*	56	H5
Forbach, *France*	19	C13
Forbesganj, *India*	69	F12
Forcados, *Nigeria*	83	D6
Forcados →, *Nigeria*	83	D6
Forcalquier, *France*	21	E9
Forchheim, *Germany*	25	F7
Ford City, *Calif., U.S.A.*	117	K7
Ford City, *Pa., U.S.A.*	110	F5
Førde, *Norway*	9	F11
Ford's Bridge, *Australia*	95	D4
Fordyce, *U.S.A.*	113	J8
Forécariah, *Guinea*	82	D2
Forel, Mt., *Greenland*	4	C6
Foremost, *Canada*	104	D6
Forest, *Canada*	110	C3
Forest, *U.S.A.*	113	J10
Forest City, *Iowa, U.S.A.*	112	D8
Forest City, *N.C., U.S.A.*	109	H5
Forest City, *Pa., U.S.A.*	111	E9
Forest Grove, *U.S.A.*	116	E3
Forestburg, *Canada*	104	C6
Foresthill, *U.S.A.*	116	F6
Forestier Pen., *Australia*	94	G4
Forestville, *Canada*	103	C6
Forestville, *Calif., U.S.A.*	116	G4
Forestville, *N.Y., U.S.A.*	110	D5
Forez, Mts. du, *France*	20	C7
Forfar, *U.K.*	14	E6
Forks, *U.S.A.*	116	C2
Forksville, *U.S.A.*	111	E8
Forlì, *Italy*	29	D9
Forman, *U.S.A.*	112	B6
Formazza, *Italy*	28	B5
Formby Pt., *U.K.*	12	D4
Formentera, *Spain*	37	C7
Formentor, C. de, *Spain*	37	B10
Former Yugoslav Republic of Macedonia = Macedonia ■, *Europe*	40	E5
Fórmia, *Italy*	30	A6
Formígine, *Italy*	28	D7
Formosa = Taiwan ■, *Asia*	59	F13
Formosa, *Argentina*	126	B4
Formosa, *Brazil*	125	G9
Formosa □, *Argentina*	126	B4
Formosa, Serra, *Brazil*	125	F8
Formosa Bay, *Kenya*	86	C5
Formosa Strait = Taiwan Strait, *Asia*	59	E12
Fornells, *Spain*	37	A11
Fornos de Algodres, *Portugal*	34	E3
Fornovo di Taro, *Italy*	28	D7
Føroyar, *Atl. Oc.*	8	F9
Forres, *U.K.*	14	D5
Forrest, *Australia*	93	F4
Forrest, Mt., *Australia*	93	D4
Forrest City, *U.S.A.*	113	H9
Fors, *Sweden*	10	D10
Forsayth, *Australia*	94	B3
Forshaga, *Sweden*	10	E7
Förslöv, *Sweden*	11	H6
Forsmo, *Sweden*	10	A11
Forssa, *Finland*	9	F20
Forst, *Germany*	24	D10
Forsvik, *Sweden*	11	F8
Forsyth, *U.S.A.*	114	C10
Fort Albany, *Canada*	102	B3
Fort Ann, *U.S.A.*	111	C11
Fort Assiniboine, *Canada*	104	C6
Fort Augustus, *U.K.*	14	D4
Fort Beaufort, *S. Africa*	88	E4
Fort Benton, *U.S.A.*	114	C8
Fort Bragg, *U.S.A.*	114	G2
Fort Bridger, *U.S.A.*	114	F8
Fort Chipewyan, *Canada*	105	B6
Fort Collins, *U.S.A.*	112	E2
Fort-Coulonge, *Canada*	102	C4
Fort Covington, *U.S.A.*	111	B10
Fort Davis, *U.S.A.*	113	K3
Fort-de-France, *Martinique*	121	D7
Fort Defiance, *U.S.A.*	115	J9
Fort Dodge, *U.S.A.*	112	D7
Fort Edward, *U.S.A.*	111	C11
Fort Erie, *Canada*	110	D6
Fort Fairfield, *U.S.A.*	109	B12
Fort Frances, *Canada*	105	D10
Fort Garland, *U.S.A.*	115	H11
Fort George = Chisasibi, *Canada*	102	B4
Fort Good-Hope, *Canada*	100	B7
Fort Hancock, *U.S.A.*	115	L11
Fort Hope, *Canada*	102	B2
Fort Irwin, *U.S.A.*	117	K10
Fort Kent, *U.S.A.*	109	B11
Fort Klamath, *U.S.A.*	114	E3
Fort Laramie, *U.S.A.*	112	D2
Fort Lauderdale, *U.S.A.*	109	M5
Fort Liard, *Canada*	104	A4
Fort Liberté, *Haiti*	121	C5
Fort Lupton, *U.S.A.*	112	E2
Fort Mackay, *Canada*	104	B6
Fort Macleod, *Canada*	104	D6
Fort McMurray, *Canada*	104	B6
Fort McPherson, *Canada*	100	B6
Fort Madison, *U.S.A.*	112	E9
Fort Meade, *U.S.A.*	109	M5
Fort Morgan, *U.S.A.*	112	E3
Fort Myers, *U.S.A.*	109	M5
Fort Nelson, *Canada*	104	B4
Fort Nelson →, *Canada*	104	B4
Fort Norman = Tulita, *Canada*	100	B7
Fort Payne, *U.S.A.*	109	H3
Fort Peck, *U.S.A.*	114	B10
Fort Peck Dam, *U.S.A.*	114	C10
Fort Peck L., *U.S.A.*	114	C10
Fort Pierce, *U.S.A.*	109	M5
Fort Pierre, *U.S.A.*	112	C4
Fort Pierre Bordes = Ti-n-Zaouatene, *Algeria*	83	B5
Fort Plain, *U.S.A.*	111	D10
Fort Portal, *Uganda*	86	B3
Fort Providence, *Canada*	104	A5
Fort Qu'Appelle, *Canada*	105	C8
Fort Resolution, *Canada*	104	A6
Fort Rixon, *Zimbabwe*	87	G2
Fort Ross, *U.S.A.*	116	G3
Fort Rupert = Waskaganish, *Canada*	102	B4
Fort St. James, *Canada*	104	C4
Fort St. John, *Canada*	104	B4
Fort Saskatchewan, *Canada*	104	C6
Fort Scott, *U.S.A.*	113	G7
Fort Severn, *Canada*	102	A2
Fort Shevchenko, *Kazakstan*	49	H10
Fort Simpson, *Canada*	104	A4
Fort Smith, *Canada*	104	B6
Fort Smith, *U.S.A.*	113	H7
Fort Stockton, *U.S.A.*	113	K3
Fort Sumner, *U.S.A.*	113	H2
Fort Thompson, *U.S.A.*	112	C5
Fort Valley, *U.S.A.*	109	J4
Fort Vermilion, *Canada*	104	B5
Fort Walton Beach, *U.S.A.*	109	K2
Fort Wayne, *U.S.A.*	108	E3
Fort William, *U.K.*	14	E3
Fort Worth, *U.S.A.*	113	J6
Fort Yates, *U.S.A.*	112	B4
Fort Yukon, *U.S.A.*	100	B5
Fortaleza, *Brazil*	125	D11
Forteau, *Canada*	103	B8
Fortescue →, *Australia*	92	D2
Forth →, *U.K.*	14	E5
Forth, Firth of, *U.K.*	14	E6
Fortore →, *Italy*	29	G12
Fortrose, *U.K.*	14	D4
Fortuna, *Spain*	33	G3
Fortuna, *Calif., U.S.A.*	114	F1
Fortuna, *N. Dak., U.S.A.*	112	A3
Fortune, *Canada*	103	C8
Fortune B., *Canada*	103	C8
Forūr, *Iran*	71	E7
Fos-sur-Mer, *France*	21	E8
Foshan, *China*	59	F9
Fosna, *Norway*	8	E14
Fosnavåg, *Norway*	9	E11
Foso, *Ghana*	83	D4
Fossano, *Italy*	28	D4
Fossil, *U.S.A.*	114	D3
Fossombrone, *Italy*	29	E9
Foster, *Canada*	111	A12
Foster →, *Canada*	105	B7
Fosters Ra., *Australia*	94	C1
Fostoria, *U.S.A.*	108	E4
Fotadrevo, *Madag.*	89	C8
Fougamou, *Gabon*	84	E2
Fougères, *France*	18	D5
Foul Pt., *Sri Lanka*	66	Q12
Foula, *U.K.*	14	A6
Foulalaba, *Mali*	82	C3
Foulness I., *U.K.*	13	F8
Foulpointe, *Madag.*	89	B8
Foulweather, C., *U.S.A.*	106	B2
Foumban, *Cameroon*	83	D7
Foumbot, *Cameroon*	83	D7
Foundiougne, *Senegal*	82	C1
Fountain, *U.S.A.*	112	F2
Fountain Springs, *U.S.A.*	117	K8
Fourchambault, *France*	19	E10
Fouriesburg, *S. Africa*	88	D4
Fourmies, *France*	19	B11
Fournás, *Greece*	38	B3
Foúrnoi, *Greece*	39	D8
Fours, *France*	19	F10
Fourth Cataract, *Sudan*	80	D3
Fouta Djalon, *Guinea*	82	C2
Foux, Cap-à-, *Haiti*	121	C5
Foveaux Str., *N.Z.*	91	M2
Fowey, *U.K.*	13	G3
Fowler, *Calif., U.S.A.*	116	J7
Fowler, *Colo., U.S.A.*	112	F3
Fowlers B., *Australia*	93	F5
Fowman, *Iran*	71	B6
Fox →, *Canada*	105	B10
Fox Creek, *Canada*	104	C5
Fox Lake, *Canada*	104	B6
Fox Valley, *Canada*	105	C7
Foxboro, *U.S.A.*	111	D13
Foxe Basin, *Canada*	101	B12
Foxe Chan., *Canada*	101	B11
Foxe Pen., *Canada*	101	B12
Foxen, *Sweden*	10	E5
Foxton, *N.Z.*	91	J5
Foyle, Lough, *U.K.*	15	A4
Foynes, *Ireland*	15	D2
Foz, *Spain*	34	B3
Foz do Cunene, *Angola*	88	B1
Foz do Iguaçu, *Brazil*	127	B5
Fraga, *Spain*	32	D5
Fraile Muerto, *Uruguay*	127	C5
Framingham, *U.S.A.*	111	D13
Frampol, *Poland*	45	H9
Franca, *Brazil*	125	H9
Francavilla al Mare, *Italy*	29	F11
Francavilla Fontana, *Italy*	31	B10
France ■, *Europe*	7	F6
Frances →, *Canada*	104	A3
Frances L., *Canada*	104	A3
Franceville, *Gabon*	84	E2
Franche-Comté, *France*	19	F12
Francis Case, L., *U.S.A.*	112	D5
Francisco Beltrão, *Brazil*	127	B5
Francisco I. Madero, *Coahuila, Mexico*	118	B4
Francisco I. Madero, *Durango, Mexico*	118	C4
Francistown, *Botswana*	89	C4
Francofonte, *Italy*	31	E7
François, *Canada*	103	C8
François L., *Canada*	104	C3
Franeker, *Neths.*	17	A5
Frankado, *Djibouti*	81	E5
Frankenberg, *Germany*	24	D4
Frankenwald, *Germany*	25	E7
Frankford, *Canada*	110	B7
Frankfort, *S. Africa*	89	D4
Frankfort, *Ind., U.S.A.*	108	E2
Frankfort, *Kans., U.S.A.*	112	F6
Frankfort, *Ky., U.S.A.*	108	F3
Frankfort, *N.Y., U.S.A.*	111	C9
Frankfurt, *Brandenburg, Germany*	24	C10
Frankfurt, *Hessen, Germany*	25	E4
Fränkische Alb, *Germany*	25	F7
Fränkische Rezat →, *Germany*	25	F7
Fränkische Saale →, *Germany*	25	E5
Fränkische Schweiz, *Germany*	25	F7
Frankland →, *Australia*	93	G2
Franklin, *Ky., U.S.A.*	109	G2
Franklin, *La., U.S.A.*	113	L9
Franklin, *Mass., U.S.A.*	111	D13
Franklin, *N.H., U.S.A.*	111	C13
Franklin, *Nebr., U.S.A.*	112	E5
Franklin, *Pa., U.S.A.*	110	E5
Franklin, *Va., U.S.A.*	109	G7
Franklin, *W. Va., U.S.A.*	108	F6
Franklin B., *Canada*	100	B7
Franklin D. Roosevelt L., *U.S.A.*	114	B4
Franklin I., *Antarctica*	5	D11
Franklin L., *U.S.A.*	114	F6
Franklin Mts., *Canada*	100	B7
Franklin Str., *Canada*	100	A10
Franklinton, *U.S.A.*	113	K9
Franklinville, *U.S.A.*	110	D6
Franks Pk., *U.S.A.*	114	D9
Frånö, *Sweden*	10	B11
Fransfontein, *Namibia*	88	C2
Fränsta, *Sweden*	10	B10
Frantsa Iosifa, Zemlya, *Russia*	50	A6
Franz, *Canada*	102	C3
Franz Josef Land = Frantsa Iosifa, Zemlya, *Russia*	50	A6
Franzburg, *Germany*	24	A8
Frascati, *Italy*	29	G9
Fraser, *U.S.A.*	110	D2
Fraser →, *B.C., Canada*	104	D4
Fraser →, *Nfld., Canada*	103	A7
Fraser, Mt., *Australia*	93	E2
Fraser I., *Australia*	95	D5
Fraser Lake, *Canada*	104	C4
Fraserburg, *S. Africa*	88	E3
Fraserburgh, *U.K.*	14	D6
Fraserdale, *Canada*	102	C3
Frashër, *Albania*	40	F4
Frasne, *France*	19	F13
Frăteşti, *Romania*	43	G10
Frauenfeld, *Switz.*	25	H4
Fray Bentos, *Uruguay*	126	C4
Frechilla, *Spain*	34	C6
Fredericia, *Denmark*	11	J3
Frederick, *Md., U.S.A.*	108	F7
Frederick, *Okla., U.S.A.*	113	H5
Frederick, *S. Dak., U.S.A.*	112	C5
Fredericksburg, *Pa., U.S.A.*	111	F8
Fredericksburg, *Tex., U.S.A.*	113	K5
Fredericksburg, *Va., U.S.A.*	108	F7
Fredericktown, *Mo., U.S.A.*	113	G9
Fredericktown, *Ohio, U.S.A.*	110	F2
Frederico I. Madero, Presa, *Mexico*	118	B3
Frederico Westphalen, *Brazil*	127	B5
Fredericton, *Canada*	103	C6
Fredericton Junction, *Canada*	103	C6
Frederiksborg Amtskommune □, *Denmark*	11	J6
Frederikshåb = Paamiut, *Greenland*	4	C5
Frederikshavn, *Denmark*	11	G4
Frederikssund, *Denmark*	11	J6
Frederiksted, *U.S. Virgin Is.*	121	C7
Frederiksværk, *Denmark*	11	J6
Fredonia, *Ariz., U.S.A.*	115	H7
Fredonia, *Kans., U.S.A.*	113	G7
Fredonia, *N.Y., U.S.A.*	110	D5
Fredriksberg, *Sweden*	10	D8
Fredrikstad, *Norway*	9	G14
Free State □, *S. Africa*	88	D4
Freehold, *U.S.A.*	111	F10
Freel Peak, *U.S.A.*	116	G7
Freeland, *U.S.A.*	111	E9
Freels, C., *Canada*	103	C9
Freeman, *Calif., U.S.A.*	117	K9
Freeman, *S. Dak., U.S.A.*	112	D6
Freeport, *Bahamas*	120	A4
Freeport, *Ill., U.S.A.*	112	D10

Freeport, N.Y., U.S.A. ... 111 F11
Freeport, Ohio, U.S.A. ... 110 F3
Freeport, Pa., U.S.A. ... 110 F5
Freeport, Tex., U.S.A. ... 113 L7
Freetown, S. Leone ... 82 D2
Frégate, L., Canada ... 102 B5
Fregenal de la Sierra, Spain ... 35 G4
Fregene, Italy ... 29 G9
Fréhel, C., France ... 18 D4
Freiberg, Germany ... 24 E9
Freibourg = Fribourg, Switz. ... 25 J3
Freiburg, Baden-W., Germany . 25 H3
Freiburg, Niedersachsen, Germany ... 24 B5
Freilassing, Germany ... 25 H8
Freire, Chile ... 128 D2
Freirina, Chile ... 126 B1
Freising, Germany ... 25 G7
Freistadt, Austria ... 26 C7
Freital, Germany ... 24 D9
Fréjus, France ... 21 E10
Fremantle, Australia ... 93 F2
Fremont, Calif., U.S.A. ... 116 H4
Fremont, Mich., U.S.A. ... 108 D3
Fremont, Nebr., U.S.A. ... 112 E6
Fremont, Ohio, U.S.A. ... 108 E4
Fremont →, U.S.A. ... 115 G8
French Camp, U.S.A. ... 116 H5
French Creek →, U.S.A. ... 110 E5
French Guiana ■, S. Amer. ... 125 C8
French Polynesia ■, Pac. Oc. .. 97 K13
Frenchman Cr. →, N. Amer. ... 114 B10
Frenchman Cr. →, U.S.A. ... 112 E4
Frenštát pod Radhoštěm, Czech Rep. ... 27 B11
Fresco, Ivory C. ... 82 D3
Fresco →, Brazil ... 125 E8
Freshfield, C., Antarctica ... 5 C10
Fresnay-sur-Sarthe, France ... 18 D7
Fresnillo, Mexico ... 118 C4
Fresno, U.S.A. ... 116 J7
Fresno Alhandiga, Spain ... 34 E5
Fresno Reservoir, U.S.A. ... 114 B9
Freudenstadt, Germany ... 25 G4
Frévent, France ... 19 B9
Frew →, Australia ... 94 C2
Frewsburg, U.S.A. ... 110 D5
Freycinet Pen., Australia ... 94 G4
Freyming-Merlebach, France .. 19 C13
Freyung, Germany ... 25 G9
Fria, Guinea ... 82 C2
Fria, C., Namibia ... 88 B1
Friant, U.S.A. ... 116 J7
Frías, Argentina ... 126 B2
Fribourg, Switz. ... 25 J3
Fribourg □, Switz. ... 25 J3
Fridafors, Sweden ... 11 H8
Friday Harbor, U.S.A. ... 116 B3
Friedberg, Bayern, Germany .. 25 G6
Friedberg, Hessen, Germany .. 25 E4
Friedens, U.S.A. ... 110 F6
Friedland, Germany ... 24 B9
Friedrichshafen, Germany ... 25 H5
Friedrichskoog, Germany ... 24 A4
Friedrichstadt, Germany ... 24 A5
Friendly Is. = Tonga ■, Pac. Oc. 91 D11
Friendship, U.S.A. ... 110 D6
Friesach, Austria ... 26 E7
Friesack, Germany ... 24 C8
Friesland □, Neths. ... 17 A5
Friesoythe, Germany ... 24 B3
Friggesund, Sweden ... 10 C10
Frillesås, Sweden ... 11 G6
Frinnaryd, Sweden ... 11 G8
Frio →, U.S.A. ... 113 L5
Frio, C., Brazil ... 122 F6
Friol, Spain ... 34 B3
Friona, U.S.A. ... 113 H3
Fristad, Sweden ... 11 G6
Fritch, U.S.A. ... 113 H4
Fritsla, Sweden ... 11 G6
Fritzlar, Germany ... 24 D5
Friuli-Venézia Giúlia □, Italy .. 29 B9
Frobisher B., Canada ... 101 B13
Frobisher Bay = Iqaluit, Canada 101 B13
Frobisher L., Canada ... 105 B7
Frohavet, Norway ... 8 E13
Frohnleiten, Austria ... 26 D8
Frolovo, Russia ... 48 F6
Frombork, Poland ... 44 D6
Frome, U.K. ... 13 F5
Frome →, U.K. ... 13 G5
Frómista, Spain ... 34 C6
Front Range, U.S.A. ... 106 C5
Front Royal, U.S.A. ... 108 F6
Fronteira, Portugal ... 35 F3
Frontera, Canary Is. ... 37 G2
Frontera, Mexico ... 119 D6
Fronteras, Mexico ... 118 A3
Frontignan, France ... 20 E7
Frosinone, Italy ... 30 A6
Frostburg, U.S.A. ... 108 F6
Frostisen, Norway ... 8 B17
Frouard, France ... 19 D13
Frövi, Sweden ... 10 E9
Frøya, Norway ... 8 E13
Frumoasa, Romania ... 43 D10
Frunze = Bishkek, Kyrgyzstan .. 50 E8
Fruška Gora, Serbia, Yug. ... 42 E4
Frutal, Brazil ... 125 H9
Frutigen, Switz. ... 25 J3
Frýdek-Místek, Czech Rep. ... 27 B11
Frýdlant, Czech Rep. ... 26 A8
Fryeburg, U.S.A. ... 111 B14
Fryvaldov = Jeseník, Czech Rep. 27 A10
Fthiótis □, Greece ... 38 C4

Fu Jiang →, China ... 58 C6
Fu Xian = Wafangdian, China . 57 E11
Fu Xian, China ... 56 G5
Fu'an, China ... 59 D12
Fubian, China ... 58 B4
Fucécchio, Italy ... 28 E7
Fucheng, China ... 56 F9
Fuchou = Fuzhou, China ... 59 D12
Fuchū, Japan ... 55 G6
Fuchuan, China ... 59 E8
Fuchun Jiang →, China ... 59 B13
Fúcino, Piana del, Italy ... 29 F10
Fuding, China ... 59 D13
Fuencaliente, Canary Is. ... 37 F2
Fuencaliente, Spain ... 35 G6
Fuencaliente, Pta., Canary Is. .. 37 F2
Fuengirola, Spain ... 35 J6
Fuenlabrada, Spain ... 34 E7
Fuensalida, Spain ... 34 E6
Fuente-Alamo, Spain ... 33 G3
Fuente-Álamo de Murcia, Spain 33 H3
Fuente de Cantos, Spain ... 35 G4
Fuente del Maestre, Spain ... 35 G4
Fuente el Fresno, Spain ... 35 F7
Fuente Obejuna, Spain ... 35 G5
Fuente Palmera, Spain ... 35 H5
Fuentes de Andalucía, Spain .. 35 H5
Fuentes de Ebro, Spain ... 32 D4
Fuentes de León, Spain ... 35 G4
Fuentes de Oñoro, Spain ... 34 E4
Fuentesaúco, Spain ... 34 D5
Fuerte →, Mexico ... 118 B3
Fuerte Olimpo, Paraguay ... 126 A4
Fuerteventura, Canary Is. ... 37 F6
Fufeng, China ... 56 G5
Fuga I., Phil. ... 61 B4
Fugong, China ... 58 D2
Fugou, China ... 56 G8
Fugu, China ... 56 E6
Fuhai, China ... 60 B3
Fuḥaymī, Iraq ... 70 C4
Fuji, Japan ... 55 G9
Fuji-San, Japan ... 55 G9
Fuji-Yoshida, Japan ... 55 G9
Fujian □, China ... 59 E12
Fujinomiya, Japan ... 55 G9
Fujisawa, Japan ... 55 G9
Fujiyama, Mt. = Fuji-San, Japan 55 G9
Fukien = Fujian □, China ... 59 E12
Fukuchiyama, Japan ... 55 G7
Fukue-Shima, Japan ... 55 H4
Fukui, Japan ... 55 F8
Fukui □, Japan ... 55 G8
Fukuoka, Japan ... 55 H5
Fukuoka □, Japan ... 55 H5
Fukushima, Japan ... 54 F10
Fukushima □, Japan ... 54 F10
Fukuyama, Japan ... 55 G6
Fulacunda, Guinea-Biss. ... 82 C1
Fulda, U.S.A. ... 24 E5
Fulda →, Germany ... 24 D5
Fulford Harbour, Canada ... 116 B3
Fuliang, China ... 59 C11
Fullerton, Calif., U.S.A. ... 117 M9
Fullerton, Nebr., U.S.A. ... 112 E6
Fulongquan, China ... 57 B13
Fülöpszállás, Hungary ... 42 D4
Fulton, Mo., U.S.A. ... 112 F9
Fulton, N.Y., U.S.A. ... 111 C8
Fulufjället, Sweden ... 10 C6
Fuluälven →, Sweden ... 10 C7
Fumay, France ... 19 C11
Fumel, France ... 20 D4
Fumin, China ... 58 E4
Funabashi, Japan ... 55 G10
Funäsdalen, Sweden ... 10 B6
Funchal, Madeira ... 37 D3
Fundación, Colombia ... 124 A4
Fundão, Portugal ... 34 E3
Fundu Moldovei, Romania ... 43 C10
Fundulea, Romania ... 43 F11
Fundy, B. of, Canada ... 103 D6
Funhalouro, Mozam. ... 89 C5
Funing, Hebei, China ... 57 E10
Funing, Jiangsu, China ... 57 H10
Funing, Yunnan, China ... 58 F5
Funiu Shan, China ... 56 H7
Funsi, Ghana ... 82 C4
Funtua, Nigeria ... 83 C6
Fuping, Hebei, China ... 56 E8
Fuping, Shaanxi, China ... 56 G5
Fuqing, China ... 59 E12
Fuquan, China ... 58 D6
Furano, Japan ... 54 C11
Furāt, Nahr al →, Asia ... 70 D5
Fürg, Iran ... 71 D7
Furmanov, Russia ... 48 B5
Furmanovo, Kazakstan ... 48 F9
Furnás, Spain ... 37 B8
Furnas, Reprêsa de, Brazil ... 127 A6
Furneaux Group, Australia ... 94 G4
Furqlus, Syria ... 75 A6
Fürstenau, Germany ... 24 C3
Fürstenberg, Germany ... 24 B9
Fürstenfeld, Austria ... 26 D9
Fürstenfeldbruck, Germany ... 25 G7
Fürstenwalde, Germany ... 24 C10
Furth im Wald, Germany ... 25 F8
Fürth, Germany ... 25 F6
Furtwangen, Germany ... 25 G4
Furudal, Sweden ... 10 C9
Furukawa, Japan ... 54 E10
Furulund, Sweden ... 11 J7
Fury and Hecla Str., Canada .. 101 B11
Fusagasuga, Colombia ... 124 C4

Fuscaldo, Italy ... 31 C9
Fushan, Shandong, China ... 57 F11
Fushan, Shanxi, China ... 56 G6
Fushë Arrëz, Albania ... 40 D4
Fushë-Krujë, Albania ... 40 E3
Fushun, Liaoning, China ... 57 D12
Fushun, Sichuan, China ... 58 C5
Fusong, China ... 57 C14
Füssen, Germany ... 25 H6
Fusui, China ... 58 F6
Futog, Yugoslavia ... 42 E4
Futuna, Wall. & F. Is. ... 91 B8
Fuwa, Egypt ... 80 H7
Fuxian Hu, China ... 58 E4
Fuxin, China ... 57 C11
Fuyang, Anhui, China ... 56 H8
Fuyang, Zhejiang, China ... 59 B12
Fuyang He →, China ... 56 E9
Fuying Dao, China ... 59 D13
Fuyu, China ... 57 B13
Fuyuan, China ... 58 E5
Füzesgyarmat, Hungary ... 42 C6
Fuzhou, China ... 59 D12
Fylde, U.K. ... 12 D5
Fyn, Denmark ... 11 J4
Fyne, L., U.K. ... 14 F3
Fyns Amtskommune □, Denmark ... 11 J4
Fynshav, Denmark ... 11 K3

G

Ga, Ghana ... 82 D4
Gaanda, Nigeria ... 83 C7
Gabarin, Nigeria ... 83 C7
Gabas →, France ... 20 E3
Gabela, Angola ... 84 G2
Gabès, Tunisia ... 79 B8
Gabès, G. de, Tunisia ... 79 B8
Gabgaba, W. →, Egypt ... 80 C3
Gabon ■, Africa ... 84 E2
Gaborone, Botswana ... 88 C4
Gabriels, U.S.A. ... 111 B10
Gábrik, Iran ... 71 E8
Gabrovo, Bulgaria ... 41 D9
Gacé, France ... 18 D7
Gāch Sār, Iran ... 71 B6
Gachsārān, Iran ... 71 D6
Gacko, Bos.-H. ... 40 C2
Gadag, India ... 66 M9
Gadamai, Sudan ... 81 D4
Gadap, Pakistan ... 68 G2
Gadarwara, India ... 69 H8
Gadebusch, Germany ... 24 B7
Gadein, Sudan ... 81 F2
Gadhada, India ... 68 J4
Gádor, Sierra de, Spain ... 35 J8
Gadra, Pakistan ... 68 G4
Gadsden, U.S.A. ... 109 H3
Gadwal, India ... 66 L10
Gadyach = Hadyach, Ukraine .. 47 G8
Găeşti, Romania ... 43 F10
Gaeta, Italy ... 30 A6
Gaeta, G. di, Italy ... 30 A6
Gaffney, U.S.A. ... 109 H5
Gafsa, Tunisia ... 78 B7
Gagarawa, Nigeria ... 83 C6
Gagaria, India ... 68 G4
Gagarin, Russia ... 46 E8
Gaggenau, Germany ... 25 G4
Gaghamni, Sudan ... 81 E2
Gagino, Russia ... 48 C7
Gagliano del Capo, Italy ... 31 C11
Gagnef, Sweden ... 10 D9
Gagnoa, Ivory C. ... 82 D3
Gagnon, Canada ... 103 B6
Gagnon, L., Canada ... 105 A6
Gagra, Georgia ... 49 J5
Gahini, Rwanda ... 86 C3
Gahmar, India ... 69 G10
Gai Xian = Gaizhou, China ... 57 D12
Gaïdhouronísi, Greece ... 36 E7
Gail, U.S.A. ... 113 J4
Gail →, Austria ... 26 E6
Gaillac, France ... 20 E5
Gaillimh = Galway, Ireland ... 15 C2
Gaillon, France ... 18 C8
Gaines, U.S.A. ... 110 E7
Gainesville, Fla., U.S.A. ... 109 L4
Gainesville, Ga., U.S.A. ... 109 H4
Gainesville, Mo., U.S.A. ... 113 G8
Gainesville, Tex., U.S.A. ... 113 J6
Gainsborough, U.K. ... 12 D7
Gairdner, L., Australia ... 95 E2
Gairloch, L., U.K. ... 14 D3
Gaizhou, China ... 57 D12
Gaj, Croatia ... 42 E2
Gaj →, Pakistan ... 68 F2
Gakuch, Pakistan ... 69 A5
Galala, Gebel el, Egypt ... 80 J8
Galán, Cerro, Argentina ... 126 B2
Galana →, Kenya ... 86 C5
Galanta, Slovak Rep. ... 27 C10
Galapagar, Spain ... 34 E7
Galápagos, Pac. Oc. ... 122 D1
Galashiels, U.K. ... 14 F6
Galatás, Greece ... 38 D5
Galați, Romania ... 43 E13
Galați □, Romania ... 43 E12
Galatia, Turkey ... 72 C5
Galatina, Italy ... 31 B11
Galátone, Italy ... 31 B11
Galax, U.S.A. ... 109 G5
Galaxídhion, Greece ... 38 C4

Galcaio, Somali Rep. ... 74 F4
Galdhøpiggen, Norway ... 9 F12
Galeana, Chihuahua, Mexico .. 118 A3
Galeana, Nuevo León, Mexico . 118 C5
Galegu, Sudan ... 81 E4
Galela, Indonesia ... 63 D7
Galena, U.S.A. ... 100 B4
Galera, Spain ... 33 H2
Galera Pt., Trin. & Tob. ... 121 D7
Galesburg, U.S.A. ... 112 E9
Galeton, U.S.A. ... 110 E7
Galga, Ethiopia ... 81 F4
Galgate, Italy ... 31 E7
Galgóong, Romania ... 43 G8
Galich, Russia ... 48 A6
Galiche, Bulgaria ... 40 C7
Galicia □, Spain ... 34 C3
Galilee = Gelilou, Turkey ... 41 F10
Galilee, L., Australia ... 94 C4
Galilee, Sea of = Yam Kinneret, Israel ... 75 C4
Galim, Cameroon ... 83 D7
Galinoporni, Cyprus ... 36 D13
Galion, U.S.A. ... 110 F2
Galiuro Mts., U.S.A. ... 115 K8
Galiwinku, Australia ... 94 A2
Gallabat, Sudan ... 81 E4
Gallan Hd., U.K. ... 14 C1
Gallarate, Italy ... 28 C5
Gallatin, U.S.A. ... 109 G2
Gállego →, Spain ... 32 D4
Gallegos →, Argentina ... 128 G3
Galletti →, Ethiopia ... 81 F5
Galley Hd., Ireland ... 15 E3
Gallinas, Pta., Colombia ... 124 A4
Gallipoli = Gelibolu, Turkey ... 41 F10
Gallípoli, Italy ... 31 B10
Gallipolis, U.S.A. ... 108 F4
Gällivare, Sweden ... 8 C19
Gallneukirchen, Austria ... 26 C7
Gällö, Sweden ... 10 B9
Gallo, C., Italy ... 30 D6
Galloocanta, L. de, Spain ... 32 E3
Galloo I., U.S.A. ... 111 C8
Galloway, U.K. ... 14 F4
Galloway, Mull of, U.K. ... 14 G4
Gallup, U.S.A. ... 115 J9
Gallur, Spain ... 32 D3
Galoya, Sri Lanka ... 66 Q12
Galt, U.S.A. ... 116 G5
Galten, Denmark ... 11 H3
Galtür, Austria ... 26 E3
Galty Mts., Ireland ... 15 D3
Galtymore, Ireland ... 15 D3
Galva, U.S.A. ... 112 E9
Galve de Sorbe, Spain ... 32 D1
Galveston, U.S.A. ... 113 L7
Galveston B., U.S.A. ... 113 L7
Gálvez, Argentina ... 126 C3
Galway, U.S.A. ... 111 C10
Galway □, Ireland ... 15 C2
Galway B., Ireland ... 15 C2
Gam →, Vietnam ... 64 B5
Gamagōri, Japan ... 55 G8
Gamari, L., Ethiopia ... 81 E5
Gamawa, Nigeria ... 83 C7
Gamay, Phil. ... 61 E6
Gambaga, Ghana ... 83 C4
Gambat, Pakistan ... 68 F3
Gambela, Ethiopia ... 81 F3
Gambhir →, India ... 68 F6
Gambia ■, W. Afr. ... 82 C1
Gambia →, W. Afr. ... 82 C1
Gambier, U.S.A. ... 110 F2
Gambier, C., Australia ... 92 B5
Gambier Is., Australia ... 95 F2
Gambo, Canada ... 103 C9
Gamboli, Pakistan ... 68 E3
Gamboma, Congo ... 84 E3
Gamka →, S. Africa ... 88 E3
Gamkab →, Namibia ... 88 D2
Gamla Uppsala, Sweden ... 10 E11
Gamlakarleby = Kokkola, Finland ... 8 E20
Gamleby, Sweden ... 11 G10
Gammon →, Canada ... 105 C9
Gamo-Gofa □, Ethiopia ... 81 F4
Gamou, Niger ... 83 C6
Gamtoos →, S. Africa ... 88 E4
Gan, France ... 20 E3
Gan Goriama, Mts., Cameroon . 83 D7
Gan Jiang →, China ... 59 C11
Ganado, U.S.A. ... 115 J9
Gananita, Sudan ... 80 D3
Gananoque, Canada ... 102 D4
Ganāveh, Iran ... 71 D6
Gäncä, Azerbaijan ... 49 K8
Gancheng, China ... 64 C7
Gand = Gent, Belgium ... 17 C3
Ganda, Angola ... 85 G2
Gandajika, Dem. Rep. of the Congo ... 84 F4
Gandak →, India ... 69 G11
Gandava, Pakistan ... 68 E2
Gander, Canada ... 103 C9
Gander L., Canada ... 103 C9
Ganderkesee, Germany ... 24 B4
Ganderowe Falls, Zimbabwe .. 87 F2
Gandesa, Spain ... 32 D5
Gandhi Sagar, India ... 68 G6
Gandhinagar, India ... 68 H5
Gandi, Nigeria ... 83 C6
Gandía, Spain ... 33 G4
Gandino, Italy ... 28 C6
Gando, Pta., Canary Is. ... 37 G4

Gandole, Nigeria ... 83 D7
Gâneb, Mauritania ... 82 B2
Ganedidalem = Gani, Indonesia 63 D7
Ganetti, Sudan ... 80 D3
Ganga →, India ... 69 H14
Ganga Sagar, India ... 69 J13
Gangafani, Mali ... 82 C4
Gangan →, India ... 69 E8
Ganganagar, India ... 68 E5
Gangapur, India ... 68 F7
Gangara, Niger ... 83 C6
Gangaw, Burma ... 67 H19
Gangdisê Shan, China ... 67 D12
Ganges = Ganga →, India ... 69 H14
Ganges, Canada ... 104 D4
Ganges, France ... 20 E7
Ganges, Mouths of the, India .. 69 J14
Gånghester, Sweden ... 11 G7
Gangi, Italy ... 31 E7
Gângiova, Romania ... 43 G8
Gangoh, India ... 68 E7
Gangroti, India ... 69 D8
Gangtok, India ... 67 F16
Gangu, China ... 56 G3
Gangyao, China ... 57 B14
Ganj, India ... 69 F8
Ganluc, China ... 58 C4
Gannat, France ... 19 F10
Gannett Peak, U.S.A. ... 114 E9
Ganquan, China ... 56 F5
Gänserdorf, Austria ... 27 C9
Ganshui, China ... 58 C6
Gansu □, China ... 56 G3
Ganta, Liberia ... 82 D3
Gantheaume B., Australia ... 93 E1
Gantsevichi = Hantsavichy, Belarus ... 47 F4
Ganye, Nigeria ... 83 D7
Ganyem = Genyem, Indonesia . 63 E10
Ganyu, China ... 57 G10
Ganyushkino, Kazakstan ... 49 G9
Ganzhou, China ... 59 E10
Gao, Mali ... 83 B4
Gao Xian, China ... 58 C5
Gao'an, China ... 59 C10
Gaochun, China ... 59 B12
Gaohe, China ... 59 F9
Gaohebu, China ... 59 B11
Gaokeng, China ... 59 D9
Gaolan Dao, China ... 59 G9
Gaoligong Shan, China ... 58 E2
Gaoming, China ... 57 F10
Gaoping, China ... 56 G7
Gaotang, China ... 56 F9
Gaoua, Burkina Faso ... 82 C4
Gaoual, Guinea ... 82 C2
Gaoxiong = Kaohsiung, Taiwan 59 F13
Gaoyang, China ... 56 E8
Gaoyao, China ... 59 F9
Gaoyou, China ... 59 A12
Gaoyou Hu, China ... 57 H10
Gaoyuan, China ... 57 F9
Gaozhou, China ... 59 G8
Gap, France ... 21 D10
Gapan, Phil. ... 61 D4
Gapat →, India ... 69 G10
Gapuwiyak, Australia ... 94 A2
Gar, China ... 60 C2
Garabogazköl Aylagy, Turkmenistan ... 50 E6
Garachico, Canary Is. ... 37 F3
Garachiné, Panama ... 120 E4
Garafia, Canary Is. ... 37 F2
Garah, Australia ... 95 D4
Garajonay, Canary Is. ... 37 F2
Garang, India ... 83 D6
Garanhuns, Brazil ... 125 E11
Garautha, India ... 69 G8
Garawe, Liberia ... 82 E3
Garba Tula, Kenya ... 86 B4
Garberville, U.S.A. ... 114 F2
Garbiyang, India ... 69 D9
Garbsen, Germany ... 24 C4
Gard □, France ... 21 D8
Gard →, France ... 21 E8
Gardanne, France ... 21 E9
Gårdby, Sweden ... 11 H10
Garde L., Canada ... 105 A7
Gardelegen, Germany ... 24 C7
Garden City, Ga., U.S.A. ... 109 J5
Garden City, Kans., U.S.A. ... 113 G4
Garden City, Tex., U.S.A. ... 113 K4
Garden Grove, U.S.A. ... 117 M9
Gardēz, Afghan. ... 68 C3
Gardhíki, Greece ... 38 C3
Gardiner, Maine, U.S.A. ... 109 C11
Gardiners I., U.S.A. ... 111 E12
Gardner, U.S.A. ... 111 D13
Gardner Canal, Canada ... 104 C3
Gardnerville, U.S.A. ... 116 G7
Gardno, Jezioro, Poland ... 44 A5
Gardo, Somali Rep. ... 74 F4
Gardone Val Trómpia, Italy ... 28 C7
Gárdony, Hungary ... 42 C3
Garešnica, Croatia ... 29 C13
Garéssio, Italy ... 28 D5
Garey, U.S.A. ... 117 L6
Garfield, U.S.A. ... 114 C5
Garforth, U.K. ... 12 D6

Gargždai, *Lithuania* 44 C8
Gariep, *L., S. Africa* 88 E4
Garies, *S. Africa* 88 E2
Garigliano ➤, *Italy* 30 A6
Garissa, *Kenya* 86 C4
Garkida, *Nigeria* 83 C7
Garko, *Nigeria* 83 C6
Garland, *Tex., U.S.A.* 113 J6
Garland, *Utah, U.S.A.* 114 F7
Garlasco, *Italy* 28 C5
Garliava, *Lithuania* 44 D10
Garlin, *France* 20 E3
Garm, *Tajikistan* 50 F8
Garmāb, *Iran* 71 C8
Garmisch-Partenkirchen,
   Germany 25 H7
Garmo, Qullai = Kommunizma,
   Pik, *Tajikistan* 50 F8
Garmsār, *Iran* 71 C7
Garner, *U.S.A.* 112 D8
Garnett, *U.S.A.* 112 F7
Garo Hills, *India* 69 G14
Garoe, *Somali Rep.* 74 F4
Garonne ➤, *France* 20 C3
Garonne, Canal Latéral à la,
   France 20 D4
Garot, *India* 68 G6
Garoua, *Cameroon* 83 D7
Garpenberg, *Sweden* 10 D10
Garphyttan, *Sweden* 10 E8
Garrauli, *India* 69 G8
Garrel, *Germany* 24 C4
Garrigue = Garrigues, *France* .. 20 E7
Garrigues, *France* 20 E7
Garrison, *Mont., U.S.A.* 114 C7
Garrison, *N. Dak., U.S.A.* 112 B4
Garrison Res. = Sakakawea, L.,
   U.S.A. 112 B4
Garron Pt., *U.K.* 15 A6
Garrovillas, *Spain* 35 F4
Garrucha, *Spain* 33 H3
Garry ➤, *U.K.* 14 E5
Garry, *L., Canada* 100 B9
Garsen, *Kenya* 86 C5
Gärsnäs, *Sweden* 11 J8
Garson L., *Canada* 105 B6
Gartempe ➤, *France* 20 B4
Gartz, *Germany* 24 B10
Garu, *Ghana* 83 C4
Garu, *India* 69 H11
Garub, *Namibia* 88 D2
Garut, *Indonesia* 63 G12
Garvão, *Portugal* 35 H2
Garvie Mts., *N.Z.* 91 L2
Garwa = Garoua, *Cameroon* .. 83 D7
Garwa, *India* 69 G10
Garwolin, *Poland* 45 G8
Gary, *U.S.A.* 108 E2
Garz, *Germany* 24 A9
Garzê, *China* 58 B3
Garzón, *Colombia* 124 C3
Gas-San, *Japan* 54 E10
Gasan Kuli = Esenguly,
   Turkmenistan 50 F6
Gascogne, *France* 20 E4
Gascogne, G. de, *Europe* 20 E2
Gascony = Gascogne, *France* .. 20 E4
Gascoyne ➤, *Australia* 93 D1
Gascoyne Junction, *Australia* .. 93 E2
Gascueña, *Spain* 32 E2
Gash, Wadi ➤, *Ethiopia* 81 D4
Gashagar, *Nigeria* 83 C7
Gashaka, *Nigeria* 83 D7
Gasherbrum, *Pakistan* 69 B7
Gashua, *Nigeria* 83 C7
Gaspé, *Canada* 103 C7
Gaspé, C. de, *Canada* 103 C7
Gaspé, Pén. de, *Canada* 103 C6
Gaspésie, Parc de Conservation
   de la, *Canada* 103 C6
Gassan, *Burkina Faso* 82 C4
Gassol, *Nigeria* 83 D7
Gasteiz = Vitoria-Gasteiz, *Spain* . 32 C2
Gastonia, *U.S.A.* 109 H5
Gastoúni, *Greece* 38 D3
Gastoúri, *Greece* 38 B1
Gastre, *Argentina* 128 E3
Gästrikland, *Sweden* 10 D10
Gata, C., *Cyprus* 36 E12
Gata, C. de, *Spain* 33 J2
Gata, Sierra de, *Spain* 34 E4
Gataga ➤, *Canada* 104 B3
Gătaia, *Romania* 42 E6
Gatchina, *Russia* 46 C6
Gatehouse of Fleet, *U.K.* 14 G4
Gates, *U.S.A.* 110 C7
Gateshead, *U.K.* 12 C6
Gatesville, *U.S.A.* 113 K6
Gaths, *Zimbabwe* 87 G3
Gatico, *Chile* 126 A1
Gâtinais, *France* 19 D9
Gâtine, Hauteurs de, *France* .. 20 B3
Gatineau, *Canada* 111 A9
Gatineau ➤, *Canada* 102 C4
Gatineau, Parc Nat. de la,
   Canada 102 C4
Gattaran, *Phil.* 61 B4
Gattinara, *Italy* 28 C5
Gatton, *Australia* 95 D5
Gatun, L., *Panama* 120 E4
Gatyana, *S. Africa* 89 E4
Gau, *Fiji* 91 D8
Gaucín, *Spain* 35 J5
Gauer L., *Canada* 105 B9
Gauhati, *India* 67 F17

Gauja ➤, *Latvia* 9 H21
Gaula ➤, *Norway* 8 E14
Gauri Phanta, *India* 69 E9
Gausta, *Norway* 9 G13
Gauteng □, *S. Africa* 89 D4
Gāv Koshī, *Iran* 71 D8
Gāvakān, *Iran* 71 D7
Gavarnie, *France* 20 F3
Gāvāter, *Iran* 71 E9
Gāvbandī, *Iran* 71 E7
Gavdhopoúla, *Greece* 36 E6
Gávdhos, *Greece* 36 E6
Gavi, *Italy* 28 D5
Gavião, *Portugal* 35 F3
Gävle, *Sweden* 10 D11
Gävleborgs län □, *Sweden* ... 10 C10
Gävlebukten, *Sweden* 10 D11
Gavorrano, *Italy* 28 F7
Gavray, *France* 18 D5
Gavrilov Yam, *Russia* 46 D10
Gávrion, *Greece* 38 D6
Gawachab, *Namibia* 88 D2
Gawilgarh Hills, *India* 66 J10
Gawu, *Nigeria* 83 D6
Gaxun Nur, *China* 60 B5
Gaya, *India* 69 G11
Gaya, *Niger* 83 C5
Gaya, *Nigeria* 83 C6
Gayéri, *Burkina Faso* 83 C5
Gaylord, *U.S.A.* 108 C3
Gayndah, *Australia* 95 D5
Gaysin = Haysyn, *Ukraine* ... 47 H5
Gayvoron = Hayvoron, *Ukraine* 47 H5
Gaza, *Gaza Strip* 75 D3
Gaza □, *Mozam.* 89 C5
Gaza Strip □, *Asia* 75 D3
Gazanjyk, *Turkmenistan* 71 B7
Gazaoua, *Niger* 83 C6
Gāzbor, *Iran* 71 D8
Gazi, *Dem. Rep. of the Congo* . 86 B1
Gaziantep, *Turkey* 70 B3
Gazipaşa, *Turkey* 72 D5
Gbarnga, *Liberia* 82 D3
Gbekebo, *Nigeria* 83 D5
Gboko, *Nigeria* 83 D6
Gbongan, *Nigeria* 83 D5
Gcoverega, *Botswana* 88 B3
Gcuwa, *S. Africa* 89 E4
Gdańsk, *Poland* 44 D5
Gdańska, Zatoka, *Poland* 44 D6
Gdov, *Russia* 9 G22
Gdynia, *Poland* 44 D5
Geba ➤, *Guinea-Biss.* 82 C1
Gebe, *Indonesia* 63 D7
Gebeciler, *Turkey* 39 C12
Gebeit Mine, *Sudan* 80 C4
Gebel Abyad, *Sudan* 80 D2
Gebel Iweibid, *Egypt* 80 H8
Gebze, *Turkey* 41 F13
Gecha, *Ethiopia* 81 F4
Gedaref, *Sudan* 81 E4
Gedaref □, *Sudan* 81 E4
Gediz, *Turkey* 39 B11
Gediz ➤, *Turkey* 39 C8
Gedo, *Ethiopia* 81 F4
Gèdre, *France* 20 F4
Gedser, *Denmark* 11 K5
Geel, *Belgium* 17 C4
Geelong, *Australia* 95 F3
Geelvink Chan., *Australia* 93 E1
Geesthacht, *Germany* 24 B6
Geidam, *Nigeria* 83 C7
Geikie ➤, *Canada* 105 B8
Geilenkirchen, *Germany* 24 E2
Geili, *Sudan* 81 D3
Geisingen, *Germany* 25 H4
Geislingen, *Germany* 25 G5
Geistown, *U.S.A.* 110 F6
Geita, *Tanzania* 86 C3
Geju, *China* 58 F4
Gel ➤, *Sudan* 81 F2
Gel, *Meydān-e, Iran* 71 D7
Gel River, *Sudan* 81 F2
Gela, *Italy* 31 E7
Gela, G. di, *Italy* 31 F7
Gelahun, *Liberia* 82 D2
Gelderland □, *Neths.* 17 B6
Geldern, *Germany* 24 D2
Geldrop, *Neths.* 17 C5
Geleen, *Neths.* 17 D5
Gelehun, *S. Leone* 82 D2
Gelembe, *Turkey* 39 B9
Gelemso, *Ethiopia* 81 F5
Gelendost, *Turkey* 72 C4
Gelendzhik, *Russia* 47 K10
Gelibolu, *Turkey* 41 F10
Gelibolu Yarımadası, *Turkey* .. 41 F10
Gelidonya Burnu, *Turkey* 72 D4
Gelnhausen, *Germany* 25 E5
Gelnica, *Slovak Rep.* 27 C13
Gelsenkirchen, *Germany* 24 D3
Gelting, *Germany* 24 A5
Gemas, *Malaysia* 65 L4
Gembloux, *Belgium* 17 D4
Gembu, *Nigeria* 83 D7
Gemena, *Dem. Rep. of
   the Congo* 84 D3
Gemerek, *Turkey* 70 B3
Gemla, *Sweden* 11 H8
Gemlik, *Turkey* 41 F13
Gemlik Körfezi, *Turkey* 41 F12
Gemona del Friuli, *Italy* 29 B10

Gemsa, *Egypt* 80 B3
Gemünden, *Germany* 25 E5
Genale ➤, *Ethiopia* 81 F4
Genç, *Turkey* 73 C9
Gençay, *France* 20 B4
Geneina, Gebel, *Egypt* 80 B3
General Acha, *Argentina* 126 D3
General Alvear, *Buenos Aires,
   Argentina* 126 D4
General Alvear, *Mendoza,
   Argentina* 126 D2
General Artigas, *Paraguay* ... 126 B4
General Belgrano, *Argentina* .. 126 D4
General Cabrera, *Argentina* .. 126 C3
General Cepeda, *Mexico* 118 B4
General Guido, *Argentina* ... 126 D4
General Juan Madariaga,
   Argentina 126 D4
General La Madrid, *Argentina* . 126 D3
General MacArthur, *Phil.* 61 F6
General Martín Miguel de
   Güemes, *Argentina* 126 A3
General Paz, *Argentina* 126 B4
General Pico, *Argentina* 126 D3
General Pinedo, *Argentina* ... 126 B3
General Pinto, *Argentina* 126 C3
General Roca, *Argentina* 128 D3
General Santos, *Phil.* 61 H6
General Toshevo, *Bulgaria* ... 41 C12
General Trevino, *Mexico* 119 B5
General Trías, *Mexico* 118 B3
General Viamonte, *Argentina* . 126 D3
General Villegas, *Argentina* .. 126 D3
Genesee, *Idaho, U.S.A.* 114 C5
Genesee, *Pa., U.S.A.* 110 E7
Genesee ➤, *U.S.A.* 110 C7
Geneseo, *Ill., U.S.A.* 112 E9
Geneseo, *N.Y., U.S.A.* 110 D7
Geneva = Genève, *Switz.* 25 J2
Geneva, *Ala., U.S.A.* 109 K3
Geneva, *N.Y., U.S.A.* 110 D8
Geneva, *Nebr., U.S.A.* 112 E6
Geneva, *Ohio, U.S.A.* 110 E4
Geneva, L. = Léman, L., *Europe* 19 F13
Geneva, L., *U.S.A.* 108 D1
Genève, *Switz.* 25 J2
Gengenbach, *Germany* 25 G4
Gengma, *China* 58 F2
Genichesk = Henichesk, *Ukraine* 47 J8
Genil ➤, *Spain* 35 H5
Genk, *Belgium* 17 D5
Genlis, *France* 19 E12
Gennargentu, Mti. del, *Italy* .. 30 B2
Gennes, *France* 18 E6
Genoa = Génova, *Italy* 28 D5
Genoa, *N.Y., U.S.A.* 111 D8
Genoa, *Nebr., U.S.A.* 112 E6
Genoa, *Nev., U.S.A.* 116 F7
Génova, *Italy* 28 D5
Génova, G. di, *Italy* 28 E6
Genriyetty, Ostrov, *Russia* ... 51 B16
Gent = Ghent, *Belgium* 17 C3
Genteng, *Indonesia* 63 G12
Genthin, *Germany* 24 C8
Genyem, *Indonesia* 63 E10
Genzano di Lucánia, *Italy* 31 B9
Genzano di Roma, *Italy* 29 G9
Geoagiu, *Romania* 43 E8
Geographe B., *Australia* 93 F2
Geographe Chan., *Australia* .. 93 D1
Geokchay = Göyçay, *Azerbaijan* 49 K8
Georga, Zemlya, *Russia* 50 A5
George, *S. Africa* 88 E3
George ➤, *Canada* 103 A6
George, L., *Australia* 92 D3
George, L., *Uganda* 86 B3
George, L., *Fla., U.S.A.* 109 L5
George, L., *N.Y., U.S.A.* 111 C11
George Gill Ra., *Australia* 92 D5
George River =
   Kangiqsualujjuaq, *Canada* . 101 C13
George Sound, *N.Z.* 91 L1
George Town, *Australia* 94 G4
George Town, *Bahamas* 120 B4
George Town, *Cayman Is.* ... 120 C3
George Town, *Malaysia* 65 K3
George V Land, *Antarctica* .. 5 C10
George VI Sound, *Antarctica* . 5 D17
George West, *U.S.A.* 113 L5
Georgetown, *Australia* 94 B3
Georgetown, *Ont., Canada* .. 102 D4
Georgetown, *P.E.I., Canada* .. 103 C7
Georgetown, *Gambia* 82 C2
Georgetown, *Guyana* 124 B7
Georgetown, *Calif., U.S.A.* .. 116 G6
Georgetown, *Colo., U.S.A.* .. 114 G11
Georgetown, *Ky., U.S.A.* 108 F3
Georgetown, *N.Y., U.S.A.* ... 111 D9
Georgetown, *Ohio, U.S.A.* .. 108 F4
Georgetown, *S.C., U.S.A.* ... 109 J6
Georgetown, *Tex., U.S.A.* ... 113 K6
Georgia □, *U.S.A.* 109 K5
Georgia ■, *Asia* 49 J6
Georgia, Str. of, *Canada* 104 D4
Georgian B., *Canada* 102 C3
Georgina ➤, *Australia* 94 C2
Georgina I., *Canada* 110 B5
Georgiu-Dezh = Liski, *Russia* . 47 G10
Georgiyevsk, *Russia* 49 H6
Georgsmarienhütte, *Germany* . 24 C4
Gera, *Germany* 24 E8
Geraardsbergen, *Belgium* 17 D3
Geral, Serra, *Brazil* 127 B6
Geral de Goiás, Serra, *Brazil* . 125 F9
Geraldine, *U.S.A.* 114 C8
Geraldton, *Australia* 93 E1

Geraldton, *Canada* 102 C2
Gérardmer, *France* 19 D13
Gerçüş, *Turkey* 73 D9
Gerede, *Turkey* 72 B5
Gerês, Sierra do, *Portugal* ... 34 D2
Gereshk, *Afghan.* 66 D4
Geretsried, *Germany* 25 H7
Gérgal, *Spain* 33 H2
Gerik, *Malaysia* 65 K3
Gering, *U.S.A.* 112 E3
Gerlach, *U.S.A.* 114 F4
Gerlachovský štít, *Slovak Rep.* 27 B13
German Planina, *Macedonia* .. 40 D6
Germansen Landing, *Canada* . 104 B4
Germantown, *U.S.A.* 113 M10
Germany ■, *Europe* 24 E6
Germencik, *Turkey* 39 D9
Germering, *Germany* 25 G7
Germersheim, *Germany* 25 F4
Germī, *Iran* 71 B6
Germiston, *S. Africa* 89 D4
Gernika-Lumo, *Spain* 32 B2
Gernsheim, *Germany* 25 F4
Gero, *Japan* 55 G8
Gerolzhofen, *Germany* 25 F6
Gerona = Girona, *Spain* 32 D7
Gerrard, *Canada* 104 C5
Gers □, *France* 20 E4
Gers ➤, *France* 20 D4
Gersfeld, *Germany* 24 E5
Gersthofen, *Germany* 25 G6
Gerzat, *France* 20 C7
Gerze, *Turkey* 72 B6
Geseke, *Germany* 24 D4
Geser, *Indonesia* 63 E8
Gesso ➤, *Italy* 28 D4
Gestro, Wabi ➤, *Ethiopia* ... 81 G5
Getafe, *Spain* 34 E7
Getinge, *Sweden* 11 H6
Gettysburg, *Pa., U.S.A.* 108 F7
Gettysburg, *S. Dak., U.S.A.* .. 112 C5
Getxo, *Spain* 32 B2
Getz Ice Shelf, *Antarctica* ... 5 D14
Gevaş, *Turkey* 73 C10
Gévaudan, *France* 20 D7
Gevgelija, *Macedonia* 40 E6
Gévora ➤, *Spain* 35 G4
Gewani, *Ethiopia* 81 E5
Gex, *France* 19 F13
Geyikli, *Turkey* 39 B8
Geyser, *U.S.A.* 114 C8
Geyserville, *U.S.A.* 116 G4
Geyve, *Turkey* 72 B4
Ghâbat el Arab = Wang Kai,
   Sudan 81 F2
Ghabeish, *Sudan* 81 E2
Ghaggar ➤, *India* 68 E6
Ghaghara ➤, *India* 69 G11
Ghaghat ➤, *Bangla.* 69 G13
Ghagra, *India* 69 H11
Ghagra ➤, *India* 69 F9
Ghalla, Wadi el ➤, *Sudan* ... 81 E2
Ghana ■, *W. Afr.* 83 D4
Ghansor, *India* 69 H9
Ghanzi, *Botswana* 88 C3
Gharb el Istiwa'iya □, *Sudan* . 81 G3
Gharb Kordofân, *Sudan* 81 E2
Gharbîya, Es Sahrâ el, *Egypt* . 80 B2
Ghardaïa, *Algeria* 78 B6
Ghārib, G., *Egypt* 80 B3
Gharig, *Sudan* 81 E2
Gharyān, *Libya* 79 B8
Ghat, *Libya* 79 D8
Ghatal, *India* 69 H12
Ghatampur, *India* 69 F9
Ghatsila, *India* 69 H12
Ghaṭṭī, *Si. Arabia* 70 D3
Ghawdex = Gozo, *Malta* 36 C1
Ghazal, Bahr el ➤, *Chad* 79 F9
Ghazâl, Bahr el ➤, *Sudan* ... 81 F3
Ghaziabad, *India* 68 E7
Ghazipur, *India* 69 G10
Ghazni, *Afghan.* 66 C6
Ghaznī □, *Afghan.* 66 C6
Ghedi, *Italy* 28 C7
Ghelari, *Romania* 42 E7
Ghent = Gent, *Belgium* 17 C3
Gheorghe Gheorghiu-Dej =
   Onești, *Romania* 43 D11
Gheorgheni, *Romania* 43 D10
Gherla, *Romania* 43 C8
Ghidigeni, *Romania* 43 D12
Ghilarza, *Italy* 30 B1
Ghimeş-Făget, *Romania* 43 D11
Ghīnah, Wadī al ➤, *Si. Arabia* 70 D3
Ghisonaccia, *France* 21 F13
Ghisoni, *France* 21 F13
Ghizao, *Afghan.* 68 C1
Ghizar □, *Pakistan* 69 A5
Ghot Ogrein, *Egypt* 80 A2
Ghotaru, *India* 68 F4
Ghotki, *Pakistan* 68 E3
Ghowr □, *Afghan.* 66 C4
Ghudaf, W. al ➤, *Iraq* 70 C4
Ghudāmis, *Libya* 77 C7
Ghughri, *India* 69 H9
Ghugus, *India* 66 K11
Ghulam Mohammad Barrage,
   Pakistan 68 G3
Ghūrīān, *Afghan.* 66 B2
Gia Dinh, *Vietnam* 65 G6
Gia Lai = Plei Ku, *Vietnam* .. 64 F7
Gia Nghia, *Vietnam* 65 G6
Gia Ngoc, *Vietnam* 64 E7
Gia Vuc, *Vietnam* 64 E7
Giannutri, *Italy* 28 F8

Giant Forest, *U.S.A.* 116 J8
Giant Mts. = Krkonoše,
   Czech Rep. 26 A8
Giants Causeway, *U.K.* 15 A5
Giarabub = Al Jaghbūb, *Libya* . 79 C10
Giarre, *Italy* 31 E8
Giaveno, *Italy* 28 C4
Gibara, *Cuba* 120 B4
Gibb River, *Australia* 92 C4
Gibbon, *U.S.A.* 112 E5
Gibe ➤, *Ethiopia* 81 F4
Gibellina Nuova, *Italy* 30 E5
Gibeon, *Namibia* 88 D2
Gibraléon, *Spain* 35 H4
Gibraltar □, *Europe* 35 J5
Gibraltar, Str. of, *Medit. S.* .. 35 K5
Gibson Desert, *Australia* 92 D4
Gibsons, *Canada* 104 D4
Gibsonville, *U.S.A.* 116 F6
Giddings, *U.S.A.* 113 K6
Gidole, *Ethiopia* 81 F4
Giebnegáisi = Kebnekaise,
   Sweden 8 C18
Gien, *France* 19 E9
Giengen, *Germany* 25 G6
Giessen, *Germany* 24 E4
Gīfān, *Iran* 71 B8
Gifatin, Geziret, *Egypt* 80 B3
Gifhorn, *Germany* 24 C6
Gift Lake, *Canada* 104 B5
Gifu, *Japan* 55 G8
Gifu □, *Japan* 55 G8
Gigant, *Russia* 49 G5
Giganta, Sa. de la, *Mexico* ... 118 B2
Gigen, *Bulgaria* 41 C8
Gigha, *U.K.* 14 F3
Gíglio, *Italy* 28 F7
Gignac, *France* 20 E7
Gigüela ➤, *Spain* 35 F7
Gijón, *Spain* 34 B5
Gila ➤, *U.S.A.* 115 K6
Gila Bend, *U.S.A.* 115 K7
Gila Bend Mts., *U.S.A.* 115 K7
Gīlān □, *Iran* 71 B6
Gilău, *Romania* 43 D8
Gilbert ➤, *Australia* 94 B3
Gilbert Is., *Kiribati* 96 G9
Gilbert River, *Australia* 94 B3
Gilead, *U.S.A.* 111 B14
Gilf el Kebîr, Hadabat el, *Egypt* 80 C2
Gilford I., *Canada* 104 C3
Gilgil, *Kenya* 86 C4
Gilgit, *India* 69 B6
Gilgit ➤, *Pakistan* 69 B6
Giljeva Planina, *Serbia, Yug.* . 40 C3
Gillam, *Canada* 105 B10
Gilleleje, *Denmark* 11 H6
Gillen, L., *Australia* 93 E3
Gillette, *U.S.A.* 112 C2
Gilliat, *Australia* 94 C3
Gillingham, *U.K.* 13 F8
Gilmer, *U.S.A.* 113 J7
Gilmore, L., *Australia* 93 F3
Gilo ➤, *Ethiopia* 81 F3
Gilort ➤, *Romania* 43 F8
Gilroy, *U.S.A.* 116 H5
Gimbi, *Ethiopia* 81 F4
Gimli, *Canada* 105 C9
Gimo, *Sweden* 10 D12
Gimone ➤, *France* 20 E5
Gimont, *France* 20 E4
Gin Gin, *Australia* 95 D5
Ginâh, *Egypt* 80 B3
Gineifa, *Egypt* 80 H8
Gingin, *Australia* 93 F2
Gingindlovu, *S. Africa* 89 D5
Ginir, *Ethiopia* 81 F5
Ginosa, *Italy* 31 B9
Ginzo de Limia = Xinzo de
   Limia, *Spain* 34 C3
Gióia, G. di, *Italy* 31 D8
Gióia del Colle, *Italy* 31 B9
Gióia Táuro, *Italy* 31 D8
Gioiosa Iónica, *Italy* 31 D9
Gioiosa Marea, *Italy* 31 D7
Gióna, Óros, *Greece* 38 C4
Giovi, Passo dei, *Italy* 28 D5
Giovinazzo, *Italy* 31 A9
Gir Hills, *India* 68 J4
Girab, *India* 68 F4
Girâfi, W. ➤, *Egypt* 75 F3
Giraltovce, *Slovak Rep.* 27 B14
Girard, *Kans., U.S.A.* 113 G7
Girard, *Ohio, U.S.A.* 110 E4
Girard, *Pa., U.S.A.* 110 E4
Girdle Ness, *U.K.* 14 D6
Giresun, *Turkey* 73 B8
Girga, *Egypt* 80 B3
Giri ➤, *India* 68 D7
Giridih, *India* 69 G12
Girifalco, *Italy* 31 D9
Girne = Kyrenia, *Cyprus* 36 D12
Giro, *Nigeria* 83 C5
Giromagny, *France* 19 E13
Girona, *Spain* 32 D7
Girona □, *Spain* 32 C7
Gironde □, *France* 20 D3
Gironde ➤, *France* 20 C2
Gironella, *Spain* 32 C6
Giru, *Australia* 94 B4
Girvan, *U.K.* 14 F4
Gisborne, *N.Z.* 91 H7
Gisenyi, *Rwanda* 86 C2
Gislaved, *Sweden* 11 G7
Gisors, *France* 19 C8

Gitega, *Burundi* 86 C2
Giuba →, *Somali Rep.* 74 G3
Giugliano in Campania, *Italy* .. 31 B7
Giulianova, *Italy* 29 F10
Giurgeni, *Romania* 43 F12
Giurgiu, *Romania* 43 G10
Giurgiu □, *Romania* 43 F10
Giurgiuleşti, *Moldova* 43 E13
Give, *Denmark* 11 J3
Givet, *France* 19 B11
Givors, *France* 21 C8
Givry, *France* 19 F11
Giyon, *Ethiopia* 81 F4
Giza = El Gîza, *Egypt* 80 J7
Gizhiga, *Russia* 51 C17
Gizhiginskaya Guba, *Russia* .. 51 C16
Gizycko, *Poland* 44 D8
Gizzeria, *Italy* 31 D9
Gjalicë e Lumës, Mal., *Albania* 40 D4
Gjegjan, *Albania* 40 E4
Gjirokastër, *Albania* 40 F4
Gjoa Haven, *Canada* 100 B10
Gjøvik, *Norway* 9 F14
Gjuhës, Kep i, *Albania* 40 F3
Glace Bay, *Canada* 103 C8
Glacier Bay National Park and
  Preserve, *U.S.A.* 104 B1
Glacier National Park, *Canada* . 104 C5
Glacier National Park, *U.S.A.* . 114 B7
Glacier Peak, *U.S.A.* 114 B3
Gladewater, *U.S.A.* 113 J7
Gladstone, *Australia* 94 C5
Gladstone, *Canada* 105 C9
Gladstone, *U.S.A.* 108 C2
Gladwin, *U.S.A.* 108 D3
Glafsfjorden, *Sweden* 10 E6
Głagów Małapolski, *Poland* ... 45 H8
Gláma = Glomma →, *Norway* . 9 G14
Gláma, *Iceland* 8 D2
Glamis, *U.S.A.* 117 N11
Glamoč, *Bos.-H.* 29 D13
Glamsbjerg, *Denmark* 11 J4
Glarus, *Switz.* 25 H5
Glarus □, *Switz.* 25 J5
Glasco, *Kans., U.S.A.* 112 F6
Glasco, *N.Y., U.S.A.* 111 D11
Glasgow, *U.K.* 14 F4
Glasgow, *Ky., U.S.A.* 108 G3
Glasgow, *Mont., U.S.A.* 114 B10
Glasgow, City of □, *U.K.* 14 F4
Glaslyn, *Canada* 105 C7
Glastonbury, *U.K.* 13 F5
Glastonbury, *U.S.A.* 111 E12
Glauchau, *Germany* 24 E8
Glava, *Sweden* 10 E6
Glavice, *Croatia* 29 E13
Glazov, *Russia* 48 A11
Gleichen, *Canada* 104 C6
Gleisdorf, *Austria* 26 D8
Gleiwitz = Gliwice, *Poland* ... 45 H5
Glen, *U.S.A.* 111 B13
Glen Affric, *U.K.* 14 D3
Glen Canyon, *U.S.A.* 115 H8
Glen Canyon Dam, *U.S.A.* ... 115 H8
Glen Canyon National
  Recreation Area, *U.S.A.* ... 115 H8
Glen Coe, *U.K.* 14 E3
Glen Cove, *U.S.A.* 111 F11
Glen Garry, *U.K.* 14 D3
Glen Innes, *Australia* 95 D5
Glen Lyon, *U.S.A.* 111 E8
Glen Mor, *U.K.* 14 D4
Glen Moriston, *U.K.* 14 D4
Glen Robertson, *Canada* ... 111 A10
Glen Spean, *U.K.* 14 E4
Glen Ullin, *U.S.A.* 112 B4
Glénan, Îs. de, *France* 18 E3
Glencoe, *Canada* 110 D3
Glencoe, *S. Africa* 89 D5
Glencoe, *U.S.A.* 112 C7
Glendale, *Ariz., U.S.A.* 115 K7
Glendale, *Calif., U.S.A.* 117 L8
Glendale, *Zimbabwe* 87 F3
Glendive, *U.S.A.* 112 B2
Glendo, *U.S.A.* 112 D2
Glenfield, *U.S.A.* 111 C9
Glengarriff, *Ireland* 15 E2
Glenmont, *U.S.A.* 110 F2
Glenmorgan, *Australia* 95 D4
Glenn, *U.S.A.* 116 F4
Glennallen, *U.S.A.* 100 B5
Glennamaddy, *Ireland* 15 C3
Glenns Ferry, *U.S.A.* 114 E6
Glenore, *Australia* 94 B3
Glenreagh, *Australia* 95 E5
Glenrock, *U.S.A.* 114 E11
Glenrothes, *U.K.* 14 E5
Glens Falls, *U.S.A.* 111 C11
Glenside, *U.S.A.* 111 F9
Glenties, *Ireland* 15 B3
Glenville, *U.S.A.* 108 F5
Glenwood, *Canada* 103 C9
Glenwood, *Ark., U.S.A.* 113 H8
Glenwood, *Iowa, U.S.A.* 112 E7
Glenwood, *Minn., U.S.A.* ... 112 C7
Glenwood, *Wash., U.S.A.* ... 116 D5
Glenwood Springs, *U.S.A.* .. 114 G10
Glettinganes, *Iceland* 8 D7
Glifádha, *Greece* 38 D5
Glimåkra, *Sweden* 11 H8
Glina, *Croatia* 29 C13
Glinojeck, *Poland* 45 F7
Gliwice, *Poland* 45 H5
Globe, *U.S.A.* 115 K8
Glodeanu Siliştea, *Romania* .. 43 F11
Glodeni, *Moldova* 43 C12

Glödnitz, *Austria* 26 E7
Gloggnitz, *Austria* 26 D8
Głogów, *Poland* 45 G3
Głogówek, *Poland* 45 H4
Glomma →, *Norway* 9 G14
Glorieuses, Is., *Ind. Oc.* 89 A8
Glóssa, *Greece* 38 B5
Glossop, *U.K.* 12 D6
Gloucester, *U.K.* 13 F5
Gloucester, *U.S.A.* 111 D14
Gloucester I., *Australia* 94 C4
Gloucester Point, *U.S.A.* 108 G7
Gloucestershire □, *U.K.* 13 F5
Gloversville, *U.S.A.* 111 C10
Glovertown, *Canada* 103 C9
Głowno, *Poland* 45 G6
Głubczyce, *Poland* 45 H4
Glubokiy, *Russia* 49 F5
Glubokoye = Hlybokaye,
  Belarus 46 E4
Głuchołazy, *Poland* 45 H4
Glücksburg, *Germany* 24 A5
Glückstadt, *Germany* 24 B5
Glukhov = Hlukhiv, *Ukraine* .. 47 G7
Glusk, *Belarus* 47 F5
Głuszyca, *Poland* 45 H3
Glyngøre, *Denmark* 11 H2
Gmünd, *Kärnten, Austria* 26 E6
Gmünd, *Niederösterreich,
  Austria* 26 C8
Gmunden, *Austria* 26 D6
Gnarp, *Sweden* 10 B11
Gnesta, *Sweden* 10 E11
Gniew, *Poland* 44 E5
Gniewkowo, *Poland* 45 F5
Gniezno, *Poland* 45 F4
Gnjilane, *Kosovo, Yug.* 40 D5
Gnoien, *Germany* 24 B8
Gnosjö, *Sweden* 11 G7
Gnowangerup, *Australia* 93 F2
Go Cong, *Vietnam* 65 G6
Gō-no-ura, *Japan* 55 H4
Goa, *India* 66 M8
Goa □, *India* 66 M8
Goalpara, *India* 67 F17
Goaltor, *India* 69 H12
Goalundo Ghat, *Bangla.* 69 H13
Goaso, *Ghana* 82 D4
Goat Fell, *U.K.* 14 F3
Goba, *Ethiopia* 81 F4
Goba, *Mozam.* 89 D5
Gobabis, *Namibia* 88 C2
Göbel, *Turkey* 41 F12
Gobi, *Asia* 56 C6
Gobō, *Japan* 55 H7
Gobo, *Sudan* 81 F3
Göçbeyli, *Turkey* 39 B9
Goch, *Germany* 24 D2
Gochas, *Namibia* 88 C2
Godavari →, *India* 67 L13
Godavari Pt., *India* 67 L13
Godbout, *Canada* 103 C6
Godda, *India* 69 G12
Godech, *Bulgaria* 40 C7
Goderich, *Canada* 102 D3
Goderville, *France* 18 C7
Godfrey Ra., *Australia* 93 D2
Godhavn = Qeqertarsuaq,
  Greenland 4 C5
Godhra, *India* 68 H5
Gödöllő, *Hungary* 42 C4
Godoy Cruz, *Argentina* 126 C2
Gods →, *Canada* 102 A1
Gods L., *Canada* 102 B1
Gods River, *Canada* 105 C10
Godthåb = Nuuk, *Greenland* . 101 B14
Godwin Austen = K2, *Pakistan* 69 B7
Goeie Hoop, Kaap die = Good
  Hope, C. of, *S. Africa* 88 E2
Goéland, L. au, *Canada* 102 C4
Goeree, *Neths.* 17 C3
Goes, *Neths.* 17 C3
Goffstown, *U.S.A.* 111 C13
Gogama, *Canada* 102 C3
Gogebic, L., *U.S.A.* 112 B10
Goggetti, *Ethiopia* 81 F4
Gogolin, *Poland* 45 H5
Gogonou, *Benin* 83 C5
Gogra = Ghaghara →, *India* . 69 G11
Gogriâl, *Sudan* 81 F2
Gogti, *Ethiopia* 81 E5
Gohana, *India* 68 E7
Goharganj, *India* 68 H7
Goi →, *India* 68 H6
Goiânia, *Brazil* 125 G9
Goiás, *Brazil* 125 G8
Goiás □, *Brazil* 125 F9
Goio-Erê, *Brazil* 127 A5
Góis, *Portugal* 34 E2
Gojam □, *Ethiopia* 81 E4
Gojeb, Wabi →, *Ethiopia* 81 F4
Gojō, *Japan* 55 G7
Gojra, *Pakistan* 68 D5
Gökçeada, *Turkey* 41 F9
Gökçedağ, *Turkey* 39 B10
Gökçen, *Turkey* 39 C9
Gökçeören, *Turkey* 39 C10
Gökçeyazı, *Turkey* 39 B9
Gökırmak →, *Turkey* 72 B6
Gökova, *Turkey* 39 D10
Gökova Körfezi, *Turkey* 39 E9
Göksu →, *Turkey* 72 D6
Göksun, *Turkey* 72 C7
Gokteik, *Burma* 67 H20
Göktepe, *Turkey* 39 D10
Gokurt, *Pakistan* 68 E2

Gokwe, *Zimbabwe* 89 B4
Gola, *India* 69 E9
Golakganj, *India* 69 F13
Golan Heights = Hagolan, *Syria* 75 C4
Gołańcz, *Poland* 45 F4
Goläshkerd, *Iran* 71 E8
Golaya Pristen = Hola Pristan,
  Ukraine 47 J7
Gölbaşı, *Adiyaman, Turkey* ... 72 D7
Gölbaşı, *Ankara, Turkey* 72 C5
Golchikha, *Russia* 4 B12
Golconda, *U.S.A.* 114 F5
Gölcük, *Kocaeli, Turkey* 41 F13
Gölcük, *Niğde, Turkey* 72 C6
Gold, *U.S.A.* 110 E7
Gold Beach, *U.S.A.* 114 E1
Gold Coast, *W. Afr.* 83 E4
Gold Hill, *U.S.A.* 114 E2
Gold River, *Canada* 104 D3
Gołdap, *Poland* 44 D9
Goldberg, *Germany* 24 B8
Golden, *Canada* 104 C5
Golden B., *N.Z.* 91 J4
Golden Gate, *U.S.A.* 114 H2
Golden Hinde, *Canada* 104 D3
Golden Lake, *Canada* 110 A7
Golden Vale, *Ireland* 15 D3
Goldendale, *U.S.A.* 114 D3
Goldfield, *U.S.A.* 115 H5
Goldsand L., *Canada* 105 B8
Goldsboro, *U.S.A.* 109 H7
Goldsmith, *U.S.A.* 113 K3
Goldsworthy, *Australia* 92 D2
Goldthwaite, *U.S.A.* 113 K5
Golegã, *Portugal* 35 F2
Goleniów, *Poland* 44 E1
Golestānak, *Iran* 71 D7
Goleta, *U.S.A.* 117 L7
Golfito, *Costa Rica* 120 E3
Golfo Aranci, *Italy* 30 B2
Gölgeli Dağları, *Turkey* 39 D10
Gölhisar, *Turkey* 39 D11
Goliad, *U.S.A.* 113 L6
Golija, *Montenegro, Yug.* 40 C2
Golija, *Serbia, Yug.* 40 C4
Golina, *Poland* 45 F5
Gölköy, *Turkey* 72 B7
Golo →, *France* 21 F13
Gölova, *Turkey* 39 E12
Golpāyegān, *Iran* 71 C6
Gölpazarı, *Turkey* 72 B4
Golra, *Pakistan* 68 C5
Golspie, *U.K.* 14 D5
Golub-Dobrzyń, *Poland* 45 E6
Golubac, *Serbia, Yug.* 40 B5
Golyam Perelik, *Bulgaria* 41 E8
Golyama Kamchiya →, *Bulgaria* 41 C11
Goma, *Dem. Rep. of the Congo* 86 C2
Gomal Pass, *Pakistan* 68 D3
Gomati →, *India* 69 G10
Gombari, *Dem. Rep. of
  the Congo* 86 B2
Gombe, *Nigeria* 83 C7
Gombe, *Tanzania* 86 C3
Gombe →, *Tanzania* 86 C3
Gombe □, *Nigeria* 83 C7
Gombe →, *Tanzania* 86 C3
Gombi, *Nigeria* 83 C7
Gomel = Homyel, *Belarus* 47 F6
Gomera, *Canary Is.* 37 F2
Gómez Palacio, *Mexico* 118 B4
Gomīshān, *Iran* 71 B7
Gommern, *Germany* 24 C7
Gomogomo, *Indonesia* 63 F8
Gomoh, *India* 67 H15
Gomotartsi, *Bulgaria* 40 B6
Gompa = Ganta, *Liberia* 82 D3
Gomphi, *Greece* 38 B3
Gonābād, *Iran* 71 C8
Gonaïves, *Haiti* 121 C5
Gonâve, G. de la, *Haiti* 121 C5
Gonâve, I. de la, *Haiti* 121 C5
Gonbad-e Kāvūs, *Iran* 71 B7
Gönc, *Hungary* 42 B6
Gonda, *India* 69 F9
Gondal, *India* 68 J4
Gonder, *Ethiopia* 81 E4
Gonder □, *Ethiopia* 81 E4
Gondia, *India* 66 J12
Gondola, *Mozam.* 87 F3
Gondomar, *Portugal* 34 D2
Gondrecourt-le-Château, *France* 19 D12
Gönen, *Balıkesir, Turkey* 41 F11
Gönen, *Isparta, Turkey* 39 D12
Gönen →, *Turkey* 41 F11
Gong Xian, *China* 58 C5
Gong'an, *China* 59 B9
Gongcheng, *China* 59 E8
Gongga Shan, *China* 58 C3
Gongguan, *China* 58 G7
Gonghe, *China* 60 C5
Gongolgon, *Australia* 95 E4
Gongshan, *China* 58 D2
Gongzhuling, *China* 57 C13
Goniadz, *Poland* 44 E9
Goniri, *Nigeria* 83 C7
Gonjo, *China* 58 B2
Gonnesa, *Italy* 30 C1
Gónnos, *Greece* 38 B4
Gonnosfanádiga, *Italy* 30 C1
Gonzaga, *Phil.* 61 B5
Gonzales, *Calif., U.S.A.* 116 J5
Gonzales, *Tex., U.S.A.* 113 L6

González Chaves, *Argentina* .. 126 D3
Good Hope, C. of, *S. Africa* .. 88 E2
Gooderham, *Canada* 110 B6
Goodhouse, *S. Africa* 88 D2
Gooding, *U.S.A.* 114 E6
Goodland, *U.S.A.* 112 F4
Goodlow, *Canada* 104 B4
Goodooga, *Australia* 95 D4
Goodsprings, *U.S.A.* 117 K11
Goole, *U.K.* 12 D7
Goomalling, *Australia* 93 F2
Goomeri, *Australia* 95 D5
Goonda, *Mozam.* 87 F3
Goondiwindi, *Australia* 95 D5
Goongarrie, L., *Australia* 93 F3
Goonyella, *Australia* 94 C4
Goose →, *Canada* 103 B7
Goose Creek, *U.S.A.* 109 J5
Goose L., *U.S.A.* 114 F3
Gop, *India* 66 H6
Gopalganj, *India* 69 F11
Göppingen, *Germany* 25 G5
Gor, *Spain* 35 H8
Góra, *Dolnośląskie, Poland* .. 45 G3
Góra, *Mazowieckie, Poland* .. 45 F7
Góra Kalwaria, *Poland* 45 G8
Gorakhpur, *India* 69 F10
Goražde, *Bos.-H.* 42 G3
Gorbatov, *Russia* 48 B6
Gorbea, Peña, *Spain* 32 B2
Gorda, *U.S.A.* 116 K5
Gorda, Pta., *Canary Is.* 37 F2
Gorda, Pta., *Nic.* 120 D3
Gordan B., *Australia* 92 B5
Gordes, *Turkey* 39 C10
Gordon, *U.S.A.* 112 D3
Gordon →, *Australia* 94 G4
Gordon L., *Alta., Canada* 105 B6
Gordon L., *N.W.T., Canada* .. 104 A6
Gordonvale, *Australia* 94 B4
Gore, *Ethiopia* 81 F4
Gore, *N.Z.* 91 M2
Gore Bay, *Canada* 102 C3
Görele, *Turkey* 73 B8
Goreme, *Turkey* 72 C6
Gorey, *Ireland* 15 D5
Gorg, *Iran* 71 D8
Gorgān, *Iran* 71 B7
Gorgona, *Italy* 28 E6
Gorgona, I., *Colombia* 124 C3
Gorgora, *Ethiopia* 81 E4
Gorgoram, *Nigeria* 83 C7
Gorham, *U.S.A.* 111 B13
Gori, *Georgia* 49 J7
Goriganga →, *India* 69 E9
Gorinchem, *Neths.* 17 C4
Goris, *Armenia* 73 C12
Goritsy, *Russia* 46 D9
Gorízia, *Italy* 29 C10
Gorj □, *Romania* 43 E8
Gorki = Horki, *Belarus* 46 E6
Gorki = Nizhniy Novgorod,
  Russia 48 B7
Gorkiy = Nizhniy Novgorod,
  Russia 48 B7
Gorkovskoye Vdkhr., *Russia* .. 48 B6
Gorlice, *Poland* 45 J8
Görlitz, *Germany* 24 D10
Gorlovka = Horlivka, *Ukraine* . 47 H10
Gorman, *U.S.A.* 117 L8
Gorna Oryakhovitsa, *Bulgaria* . 41 C9
Gornja Radgona, *Slovenia* .. 29 B13
Gornja Tuzla, *Bos.-H.* 42 F3
Gornji Grad, *Slovenia* 29 B11
Gornji Milanovac, *Serbia, Yug.* 40 B4
Gornji Vakuf, *Bos.-H.* 42 G2
Gorno Ablanovo, *Bulgaria* ... 41 C9
Gorno-Altay □, *Russia* 50 D9
Gorno-Altaysk, *Russia* 50 D9
Gornyatskiy, *Russia* 49 F5
Gornyy, *Saratov, Russia* 48 E9
Gornyy, *Sib., Russia* 54 B6
Gorodenka = Horodenka,
  Ukraine 47 H3
Gorodets, *Russia* 48 B6
Gorodishche = Horodyshche,
  Ukraine 47 H6
Gorodishche, *Russia* 48 D7
Gorodnya = Horodnya, *Ukraine* 47 G6
Gorodok = Haradok, *Belarus* . 46 E6
Gorodok = Horodok, *Ukraine* . 47 H2
Gorodovikovsk, *Russia* 49 G5
Gorokhov = Horokhiv, *Ukraine* 47 G3
Gorokhovets, *Russia* 48 B6
Gorom Gorom, *Burkina Faso* . 83 C4
Goromonzi, *Zimbabwe* 87 F3
Gorong, Kepulauan, *Indonesia* 63 E8
Gorongose →, *Mozam.* 89 C5
Gorongoza, *Mozam.* 87 F3
Gorongoza, Sa. da, *Mozam.* .. 87 F3
Goronyo, *Nigeria* 83 C6
Górowo Iławeckie, *Poland* ... 44 D7
Gorron, *France* 18 D6
Gort, *Ireland* 15 C3
Gortis, *Greece* 36 D6
Góry Bystrzyckie, *Poland* 45 H3
Goryachiy Klyuch, *Russia* 49 H4
Gorzów Śląski, *Poland* 45 G5
Gorzów Wielkopolski, *Poland* . 45 F2

Goshen, *Ind., U.S.A.* 108 E3
Goshen, *N.Y., U.S.A.* 111 E10
Goshogawara, *Japan* 54 D10
Goslar, *Germany* 24 D6
Gospič, *Croatia* 29 D12
Gosport, *U.K.* 13 G6
Gossas, *Senegal* 82 C1
Gosse →, *Australia* 94 B1
Gossi, *Mali* 83 B4
Gossinga, *Sudan* 81 F2
Gostivar, *Macedonia* 40 E4
Gostyń, *Poland* 45 G4
Gostynin, *Poland* 45 F6
Göta älv →, *Sweden* 11 G5
Göta kanal, *Sweden* 11 F9
Götaland, *Sweden* 11 G8
Göteborg, *Sweden* 11 G5
Götene, *Sweden* 11 F7
Goteşti, *Moldova* 43 D13
Gotha, *Germany* 24 E6
Gothenburg = Göteborg,
  Sweden 11 G5
Gothenburg, *U.S.A.* 112 E4
Gothèye, *Niger* 83 C5
Gotland, *Sweden* 11 G12
Gotlands län □, *Sweden* 11 G12
Gotō-Rettō, *Japan* 55 H4
Gotse Delchev, *Bulgaria* 40 E7
Gotska Sandön, *Sweden* 9 G18
Götsu, *Japan* 55 G6
Gott Pk., *Canada* 104 C4
Góttero, Monte, *Italy* 28 D6
Göttingen, *Germany* 24 D5
Gottwald = Zmiyev, *Ukraine* . 47 H9
Gottwaldov = Zlín, *Czech Rep.* 27 B10
Goubangzi, *China* 57 D11
Gouda, *Neths.* 17 B4
Goúdhoura, Ákra, *Greece* 36 E8
Goudiry, *Senegal* 82 C2
Goudoumaria, *Niger* 83 C7
Gouéké, *Guinea* 82 D3
Gough I., *Atl. Oc.* 2 G9
Gouin, Rés., *Canada* 102 C5
Gouitafla, *Ivory C.* 82 D3
Goulburn Is., *Australia* 94 A1
Goulia, *Ivory C.* 82 C3
Goulimine, *Morocco* 78 C3
Goumbou, *Mali* 82 B3
Gouménissa, *Greece* 40 F6
Goúra, *Greece* 38 D4
Gourbassi, *Mali* 82 C2
Gourdon, *France* 20 D5
Gouré, *Niger* 83 C7
Gourin, *France* 18 D3
Gourits →, *S. Africa* 88 E3
Gourma-Rharous, *Mali* 83 B4
Goúrnais, *Greece* 36 D7
Gournay-en-Bray, *France* 19 C8
Goursi, *Burkina Faso* 82 C4
Gouverneur, *U.S.A.* 111 B9
Gouviá, *Greece* 36 A3
Gouzon, *France* 19 F9
Governador Valadares, *Brazil* 125 G10
Governor's Harbour, *Bahamas* 120 A4
Govindgarh, *India* 69 G9
Gowan Ra., *Australia* 94 D4
Gowanda, *U.S.A.* 110 D6
Gower, *U.K.* 13 F3
Gowna, L., *Ireland* 15 C4
Goya, *Argentina* 126 B4
Göyçay, *Azerbaijan* 49 K8
Goyder Lagoon, *Australia* 95 D2
Goyllarisquisga, *Peru* 124 F3
Göynük, *Antalya, Turkey* 39 E12
Göynük, *Bolu, Turkey* 72 B4
Goz Beïda, *Chad* 79 F10
Goz Regeb, *Sudan* 81 D4
Gozdnica, *Poland* 45 G2
Gozo, *Malta* 36 C1
Graaff-Reinet, *S. Africa* 88 E3
Grabo, *Ivory C.* 82 D3
Grabow, *Germany* 24 B7
Grabów nad Prosną, *Poland* .. 45 G4
Gračac, *Croatia* 29 D12
Gračanica, *Bos.-H.* 42 F3
Graçay, *France* 19 E8
Gracias a Dios, C., *Honduras* . 120 D3
Graciosa, I., *Canary Is.* 37 E6
Grad Sofiya □, *Bulgaria* 40 D7
Gradac, *Montenegro, Yug.* ... 40 C3
Gradačac, *Bos.-H.* 42 F3
Gradeška Planina, *Macedonia* . 40 E6
Gradets, *Bulgaria* 41 D10
Gradište, *Slovenia* 29 B13
Grădiştea de Munte, *Romania* . 43 E8
Grado, *Italy* 29 C10
Grado, *Spain* 34 B4
Grady, *U.S.A.* 113 H4
Graeca, Lacul, *Romania* 43 F10
Grafenau, *Germany* 25 G9
Gräfenberg, *Germany* 25 F7
Grafham Water, *U.K.* 13 E7
Grafton, *Australia* 95 D5
Grafton, *N. Dak., U.S.A.* 112 A6
Grafton, *U.S.A.* 108 F5
Graham, *Canada* 102 C1
Graham, *U.S.A.* 113 J5
Graham, Mt., *U.S.A.* 115 K9
Graham Bell, Ostrov = Greem-
  Bell, Ostrov, *Russia* 50 A7
Graham I., *Canada* 104 C2
Graham Land, *Antarctica* 5 C17
Grahamstown, *S. Africa* 88 E4
Grahamsville, *U.S.A.* 111 E10
Grahovo, *Montenegro, Yug.* .. 40 D2

Graie, Alpi, *Europe* 21 C11
Grain Coast, *W. Afr.* 82 E3
Grajaú, *Brazil* 125 E9
Grajaú →, *Brazil* 125 D10
Grajewo, *Poland* 44 E9
Gramada, *Bulgaria* 40 C6
Gramat, *France* 20 D5
Grammichele, *Italy* 31 E7
Grámmos, Óros, *Greece* 40 F4
Grampian, *U.S.A.* 110 F6
Grampian Highlands =
  Grampian Mts., *U.K.* 14 E5
Grampian Mts., *U.K.* 14 E5
Gramsh, *Albania* 40 F4
Gran Canaria, *Canary Is.* 37 G4
Gran Chaco, *S. Amer.* 126 B3
Gran Paradiso, *Italy* 28 C4
Gran Sasso d'Itália, *Italy* 29 F10
Granada, *Nic.* 120 D2
Granada, *Spain* 35 H7
Granada, *U.S.A.* 113 F3
Granada □, *Spain* 35 H7
Granadilla de Abona, *Canary Is.* 37 F3
Granard, *Ireland* 15 C4
Granbury, *U.S.A.* 113 J6
Granby, *Canada* 102 C5
Granby, *U.S.A.* 114 F11
Grand →, *Canada* 110 D5
Grand →, *Mo., U.S.A.* 112 F8
Grand →, *S. Dak., U.S.A.* 112 C4
Grand Bahama, *Bahamas* 120 A4
Grand Bank, *Canada* 103 C8
Grand Bassam, *Ivory C.* 82 D4
Grand Béréby, *Ivory C.* 82 E3
Grand-Bourg, *Guadeloupe* 121 C7
Grand Canal = Yun Ho →,
  China 57 E9
Grand Canyon, *U.S.A.* 115 H7
Grand Canyon National Park,
  U.S.A. 115 H7
Grand Cayman, *Cayman Is.* ... 120 C3
Grand Centre, *Canada* 105 C6
Grand Cess, *Liberia* 82 E3
Grand Coulee, *U.S.A.* 114 C4
Grand Coulee Dam, *U.S.A.* ... 114 C4
Grand Erg Occidental, *Algeria* . 78 B6
Grand Erg Oriental, *Algeria* .. 78 B7
Grand Falls, *Canada* 103 C6
Grand Falls-Windsor, *Canada* . 103 C8
Grand Forks, *Canada* 104 D5
Grand Forks, *U.S.A.* 112 B6
Grand Gorge, *U.S.A.* 111 D10
Grand Haven, *U.S.A.* 108 D2
Grand I., *Mich., U.S.A.* 108 B2
Grand I., *N.Y., U.S.A.* 110 D6
Grand Island, *U.S.A.* 112 E5
Grand Isle, *La., U.S.A.* 113 L9
Grand Isle, *Vt., U.S.A.* 111 B11
Grand Junction, *U.S.A.* 115 G9
Grand L., *N.B., Canada* 103 C6
Grand L., *Nfld., Canada* 103 C8
Grand L., *Nfld., Canada* 103 B7
Grand L., *U.S.A.* 113 L8
Grand Lahou, *Ivory C.* 82 D3
Grand Lake, *U.S.A.* 114 F11
Grand-Lieu, L. de, *France* 18 E5
Grand Manan I., *Canada* 103 D6
Grand Marais, *Canada* 112 B9
Grand Marais, *U.S.A.* 108 B3
Grand-Mère, *Canada* 102 C5
Grand Popo, *Benin* 83 D5
Grand Portage, *U.S.A.* 112 B10
Grand Prairie, *U.S.A.* 113 J6
Grand Rapids, *Canada* 105 C9
Grand Rapids, *Mich., U.S.A.* . 108 D2
Grand Rapids, *Minn., U.S.A.* . 112 B8
Grand St-Bernard, Col du,
  Europe 25 K3
Grampian, *U.S.A.* 114 E8
Grand Teton National Park,
  U.S.A. 114 D8
Grand Union Canal, *U.K.* 13 E7
Grand View, *Canada* 105 C9
Grandas de Salime, *Spain* 34 B4
Grande →, *Jujuy, Argentina* .. 126 A2
Grande →, *Mendoza, Argentina* 126 D2
Grande →, *Bolivia* 124 G6
Grande →, *Bahia, Brazil* 125 F10
Grande →, *Minas Gerais, Brazil* 125 H8
Grande, B., *Argentina* 128 G3
Grande, Rio →, *U.S.A.* 113 N6
Grande Baleine, R. de la →,
  Canada 102 A4
Grande Cache, *Canada* 104 C5
Grande-Entrée, *Canada* 103 C7
Grande Prairie, *Canada* 104 B5
Grande-Rivière, *Canada* 103 C7
Grande-Vallée, *Canada* 103 C6
Grandfalls, *U.S.A.* 113 K3
Grândola, *Portugal* 35 G2
Grandpré, *France* 19 C11
Grandview, *U.S.A.* 114 C4
Grandvilliers, *France* 19 C8
Graneros, *Chile* 126 C1
Grangemouth, *U.K.* 14 E5
Granger, *U.S.A.* 114 F9
Grängesberg, *Sweden* 10 D9
Grangeville, *U.S.A.* 114 D5
Granisle, *Canada* 104 C3
Granite City, *U.S.A.* 112 F9
Granite Falls, *U.S.A.* 112 C7
Granite L., *Canada* 103 C8
Granite Mt., *U.S.A.* 117 M10
Granite Pk., *U.S.A.* 114 D9
Graniteville, *U.S.A.* 111 B12
Granitola, C., *Italy* 30 E5

Granity, *N.Z.* 91 J3
Granja, *Brazil* 125 D10
Granja de Moreruela, *Spain* .. 34 D5
Granja de Torrehermosa, *Spain* . 35 G5
Gränna, *Sweden* 11 F8
Granollers, *Spain* 32 D7
Gransee, *Germany* 24 B9
Grant, *U.S.A.* 112 E4
Grant, Mt., *U.S.A.* 114 G4
Grant City, *U.S.A.* 112 E7
Grant I., *Australia* 92 B5
Grant Range, *U.S.A.* 115 G6
Grantham, *U.K.* 12 E7
Grantown-on-Spey, *U.K.* 14 D5
Grants, *U.S.A.* 115 J10
Grants Pass, *U.S.A.* 114 E2
Grantsville, *U.S.A.* 114 F7
Granville, *France* 18 D5
Granville, *N. Dak., U.S.A.* ... 112 A4
Granville, *N.Y., U.S.A.* 111 C11
Granville, *Ohio, U.S.A.* 110 F2
Granville L., *Canada* 105 B8
Graskop, *S. Africa* 89 C5
Gräsö, *Sweden* 10 D12
Grass →, *Canada* 105 B9
Grass Range, *U.S.A.* 114 C9
Grass River Prov. Park, *Canada* 105 C8
Grass Valley, *Calif., U.S.A.* .. 116 F6
Grass Valley, *Oreg., U.S.A.* .. 114 D3
Grassano, *Italy* 31 B9
Grasse, *France* 21 E10
Grassflat, *U.S.A.* 110 F6
Grasslands Nat. Park, *Canada* . 105 D7
Grassy, *Australia* 94 G3
Gråsten, *Denmark* 11 K3
Grästorp, *Sweden* 11 F6
Gratkorn, *Austria* 26 D8
Graulhet, *France* 20 E5
Graus, *Spain* 32 C5
Grave, Pte. de, *France* 20 C2
Gravelbourg, *Canada* 105 D7
Gravelines, *France* 19 A9
's-Gravenhage, *Neths.* 17 B4
Gravenhurst, *Canada* 102 D4
Gravesend, *Australia* 95 D5
Gravesend, *U.K.* 13 F8
Gravina in Púglia, *Italy* 31 B9
Gravois, Pointe-à-, *Haiti* 121 C5
Gravone →, *France* 21 G12
Gray, *France* 19 E12
Grayling, *U.S.A.* 108 C3
Grays Harbor, *U.S.A.* 114 C1
Grays L., *U.S.A.* 114 E8
Grays River, *U.S.A.* 116 D3
Grayvoron, *Russia* 47 G8
Graz, *Austria* 26 D8
Grdelica, *Serbia, Yug.* 40 D6
Greasy L., *Canada* 104 A4
Great Abaco I., *Bahamas* 120 A4
Great Artesian Basin, *Australia* 94 C3
Great Australian Bight,
  Australia 93 F5
Great Bahama Bank, *Bahamas* 120 B4
Great Barrier I., *N.Z.* 91 G5
Great Barrier Reef, *Australia* . 94 B4
Great Barrington, *U.S.A.* 111 D11
Great Basin, *U.S.A.* 114 G5
Great Basin Nat. Park, *U.S.A.* 114 G6
Great Bear →, *Canada* 100 B7
Great Bear L., *Canada* 100 B7
Great Belt = Store Bælt,
  Denmark 11 J4
Great Bend, *Kans., U.S.A.* ... 112 F5
Great Bend, *Pa., U.S.A.* 111 E9
Great Blasket I., *Ireland* 15 D1
Great Britain, *Europe* 6 E5
Great Codroy, *Canada* 103 C8
Great Dividing Ra., *Australia* . 94 C4
Great Driffield = Driffield, *U.K.* 12 C7
Great Exuma I., *Bahamas* 120 B4
Great Falls, *U.S.A.* 114 C8
Great Fish = Groot Vis →,
  S. Africa 88 E4
Great Guana Cay, *Bahamas* .. 120 B4
Great Inagua I., *Bahamas* 121 B5
Great Indian Desert = Thar
  Desert, *India* 68 F5
Great Karoo, *S. Africa* 88 E3
Great Lake, *Australia* 94 G4
Great Lakes, *N. Amer.* 98 E11
Great Malvern, *U.K.* 13 E5
Great Miami →, *U.S.A.* 108 F3
Great Ormes Head, *U.K.* 12 D4
Great Ouse →, *U.K.* 12 E8
Great Palm I., *Australia* 94 B4
Great Plains, *N. Amer.* 106 A6
Great Ruaha →, *Tanzania* ... 86 D4
Great Sacandaga Res., *U.S.A.* 111 C10
Great Saint Bernard Pass =
  Grand St-Bernard, Col du,
  Europe 25 K3
Great Salt L., *U.S.A.* 114 F7
Great Salt Lake Desert, *U.S.A.* 114 F7
Great Salt Plains L., *U.S.A.* .. 113 G5
Great Sandy Desert, *Australia* 92 D3
Great Sangi = Sangihe, Pulau,
  Indonesia 63 D7
Great Scarcies →, *S. Leone* .. 82 D2
Great Skellig, *Ireland* 15 E1
Great Slave L., *Canada* 104 A5
Great Smoky Mts. Nat. Park,
  U.S.A. 109 H4
Great Snow Mt., *Canada* 104 B4
Great Stour = Stour →, *U.K.* . 13 F9
Great Victoria Desert, *Australia* 93 E4

Great Wall, *China* 56 E5
Great Whernside, *U.K.* 12 C6
Great Yarmouth, *U.K.* 13 E9
Greater Antilles, *W. Indies* .. 121 C5
Greater London □, *U.K.* 13 F7
Greater Manchester □, *U.K.* . 12 D5
Greater Sunda Is., *Indonesia* . 62 F4
Grebbestad, *Sweden* 11 F5
Grebenka = Hrebenka, *Ukraine* 47 G7
Greco, C., *Cyprus* 36 E13
Greco, Mte., *Italy* 29 G10
Gredos, Sierra de, *Spain* 34 E6
Greece, *U.S.A.* 110 C7
Greece ■, *Europe* 38 B3
Greeley, *Colo., U.S.A.* 112 E2
Greeley, *Nebr., U.S.A.* 112 E5
Greem-Bell, Ostrov, *Russia* .. 50 A7
Green, *U.S.A.* 114 E2
Green →, *Ky., U.S.A.* 108 G2
Green →, *Utah, U.S.A.* 115 G9
Green B., *U.S.A.* 108 C2
Green Bay, *U.S.A.* 108 C2
Green Cove Springs, *U.S.A.* .. 109 L5
Green Lake, *Canada* 105 C7
Green Mts., *U.S.A.* 111 C12
Green River, *Utah, U.S.A.* ... 115 G8
Green River, *Wyo., U.S.A.* ... 114 F9
Green Valley, *U.S.A.* 115 L8
Greenbank, *U.S.A.* 116 B4
Greenbush, *Mich., U.S.A.* ... 110 B1
Greenbush, *Minn., U.S.A.* ... 112 A6
Greencastle, *U.S.A.* 108 F2
Greene, *U.S.A.* 111 D9
Greenfield, *Calif., U.S.A.* 116 J5
Greenfield, *Calif., U.S.A.* 117 K8
Greenfield, *Ind., U.S.A.* 108 F3
Greenfield, *Iowa, U.S.A.* 112 E7
Greenfield, *Mass., U.S.A.* ... 111 D12
Greenfield, *Mo., U.S.A.* 113 G8
Greenfield Park, *Canada* 111 A11
Greenland ■, *N. Amer.* 4 C5
Greenland Sea, *Arctic* 4 B7
Greenock, *U.K.* 14 F4
Greenore, *Ireland* 15 B5
Greenore Pt., *Ireland* 15 D5
Greenough, *Australia* 93 E1
Greenough →, *Australia* 93 E1
Greenough Pt., *Canada* 110 B3
Greenport, *U.S.A.* 111 E12
Greensboro, *Ga., U.S.A.* 109 J4
Greensboro, *N.C., U.S.A.* ... 109 G6
Greensburg, *Ind., U.S.A.* 108 F3
Greensburg, *Kans., U.S.A.* .. 113 G5
Greensburg, *Pa., U.S.A.* 110 F5
Greenstone Pt., *U.K.* 14 D3
Greenvale, *Australia* 94 B4
Greenville, *Liberia* 82 D3
Greenville, *Ala., U.S.A.* 109 K2
Greenville, *Calif., U.S.A.* 116 E6
Greenville, *Maine, U.S.A.* ... 109 C11
Greenville, *Mich., U.S.A.* ... 108 D3
Greenville, *Miss., U.S.A.* 113 J9
Greenville, *Mo., U.S.A.* 113 G9
Greenville, *N.C., U.S.A.* 109 H7
Greenville, *N.H., U.S.A.* 111 D13
Greenville, *N.Y., U.S.A.* 111 D10
Greenville, *Ohio, U.S.A.* 108 E3
Greenville, *Pa., U.S.A.* 110 E4
Greenville, *S.C., U.S.A.* 109 H4
Greenville, *Tenn., U.S.A.* ... 109 G4
Greenville, *Tex., U.S.A.* 113 J6
Greenwater Lake Prov. Park,
  Canada 105 C8
Greenwich, *Conn., U.S.A.* ... 111 E11
Greenwich, *N.Y., U.S.A.* 111 C11
Greenwich, *Ohio, U.S.A.* ... 110 E2
Greenwich □, *U.K.* 13 F8
Greenwood, *Canada* 104 D5
Greenwood, *Ark., U.S.A.* ... 113 H7
Greenwood, *Ind., U.S.A.* ... 108 F2
Greenwood, *Miss., U.S.A.* .. 113 J9
Greenwood, *S.C., U.S.A.* ... 109 H4
Greenwood, Mt., *Australia* .. 92 B5
Gregbe, *Ivory C.* 82 D3
Gregory, *U.S.A.* 112 D5
Gregory →, *Australia* 94 B2
Gregory, L., *S. Austral.,
  Australia* 95 D2
Gregory, L., *W. Austral.,
  Australia* 93 E2
Gregory Downs, *Australia* ... 94 B2
Gregory Ra., *Queens., Australia* 94 B3
Gregory Ra., *W. Austral.,
  Australia* 92 D3
Greiffenberg, *Germany* 24 B9
Greifswald, *Germany* 24 A9
Greifswalder Bodden, *Germany* 24 A9
Grein, *Austria* 26 C7
Greiz, *Germany* 24 E8
Gremikha, *Russia* 50 C4
Grená, *Denmark* 11 H4
Grenada, *U.S.A.* 113 J10
Grenada ■, *W. Indies* 121 D7
Grenade, *France* 20 E5
Grenadier I., *U.S.A.* 111 B8
Grenadines, *St. Vincent* 121 D7
Grenchen, *Switz.* 25 H3
Grenen, *Denmark* 11 G4
Grenfell, *Canada* 105 C8
Grenoble, *France* 21 C9
Grenville, C., *Australia* 94 A3
Grenville Chan., *Canada* 104 C3
Gréoux-les-Bains, *France* 21 E9
Gresham, *U.S.A.* 116 E4

Gresik, *Indonesia* 63 G15
Gretna, *U.K.* 14 F5
Greven, *Germany* 24 C3
Grevená, *Greece* 40 F5
Grevená □, *Greece* 40 F5
Grevenbroich, *Germany* 24 D2
Grevenmacher, *Lux.* 17 E6
Grevesmühlen, *Germany* 24 B7
Grevestrand, *Denmark* 11 J6
Grey →, *Canada* 103 C8
Grey →, *N.Z.* 91 K3
Grey, C., *Australia* 94 A2
Grey Ra., *Australia* 95 D3
Greybull, *U.S.A.* 114 D9
Greymouth, *N.Z.* 91 K3
Greystones, *Ireland* 15 C5
Greytown, *S. Africa* 89 D5
Greytown, *S. Africa* 89 D5
Gribanovskiy, *Russia* 48 E5
Gribbell I., *Canada* 104 C3
Gribës, Mal i, *Albania* 40 F3
Gridley, *U.S.A.* 116 F5
Griekwastad, *S. Africa* 88 D3
Griesheim, *Germany* 25 F4
Grieskirchen, *Austria* 26 C6
Griffin, *U.S.A.* 109 J3
Griffith, *Canada* 110 A7
Griffith I., *Canada* 110 B4
Grignols, *France* 20 D3
Grigoriopol, *Moldova* 43 C14
Grimaylov = Hrymayliv, *Ukraine* 47 H4
Grimes, *U.S.A.* 116 F5
Grimma, *Germany* 24 D8
Grimmen, *Germany* 24 A9
Grimsay, *U.K.* 14 D1
Grimsby, *Canada* 110 C5
Grimsby, *U.K.* 12 D7
Grímsey, *Iceland* 8 C5
Grimshaw, *Canada* 104 B5
Grimslöv, *Sweden* 11 H8
Grimstad, *Norway* 9 G13
Grindelwald, *Switz.* 25 J4
Grindsted, *Denmark* 11 J2
Grindstone I., *Canada* 111 B8
Grindu, *Romania* 43 F11
Grinnell, *U.S.A.* 112 E8
Grintavec, *Slovenia* 29 B11
Gris-Nez, C., *France* 19 B8
Grisolles, *France* 20 E5
Grisons = Graubünden □, *Switz.* 25 J5
Grisslehamn, *Sweden* 10 D12
Grmeč Planina, *Bos.-H.* 29 D13
Groais I., *Canada* 103 B8
Grobina, *Latvia* 44 B8
Groblersdal, *S. Africa* 89 D4
Grobming, *Austria* 26 D6
Grocka, *Serbia, Yug.* 40 B4
Gródek, *Poland* 45 E10
Grodków, *Poland* 45 H4
Grodno = Hrodna, *Belarus* .. 46 F2
Grodzisk Mazowiecki, *Poland* . 45 F7
Grodzisk Wielkopolski, *Poland* 45 F3
Grodzyanka = Hrodzyanka,
  Belarus 46 F5
Groesbeck, *U.S.A.* 113 K6
Groix, *France* 18 E3
Groix, Î. de, *France* 18 E3
Grójec, *Poland* 45 G7
Gronau, *Niedersachsen,
  Germany* 24 C5
Gronau, *Nordrhein-Westfalen,
  Germany* 24 C3
Grong, *Norway* 8 D15
Grönhögen, *Sweden* 11 H10
Groningen, *Neths.* 17 A6
Groningen □, *Neths.* 17 A6
Groom, *U.S.A.* 113 H4
Groot →, *S. Africa* 88 E3
Groot Berg →, *S. Africa* 88 E2
Groot-Brakrivier, *S. Africa* .. 88 E3
Groot Karasberge, *Namibia* .. 88 D2
Groot-Kei →, *S. Africa* 89 E4
Groot Vis →, *S. Africa* 88 E4
Grootdrink, *S. Africa* 88 D3
Groote Eylandt, *Australia* ... 94 A2
Grootfontein, *Namibia* 88 B2
Grootlaagte →, *Africa* 88 C3
Grootvloer →, *S. Africa* 88 E3
Gros C., *Canada* 104 A6
Gros Morne Nat. Park, *Canada* 103 C8
Grósio, *Italy* 28 B7
Grosne →, *France* 19 F11
Grossa, Pta., *Spain* 37 B8
Grossenbrode, *Germany* 24 A7
Grossenhain, *Germany* 24 D9
Grosser Arber, *Germany* 25 F9
Grosser Plöner See, *Germany* . 24 A6
Grosseto, *Italy* 29 F8
Grossgerungs, *Austria* 26 C7
Grossglockner, *Austria* 26 D5
Groton, *Conn., U.S.A.* 111 E12
Groton, *N.Y., U.S.A.* 111 D8
Groton, *S. Dak., U.S.A.* 112 C5
Grottáglie, *Italy* 31 B10
Grottaminarda, *Italy* 31 A8
Grottammare, *Italy* 29 F10
Grouard Mission, *Canada* ... 104 B5
Grouin, Pte. du, *France* 18 D5
Groundhog →, *Canada* 102 C3
Grouw, *Neths.* 17 A5
Grove City, *U.S.A.* 110 E4
Grove Hill, *U.S.A.* 109 K2
Groveland, *U.S.A.* 116 H6
Grover City, *U.S.A.* 117 K6
Groves, *U.S.A.* 113 L8

Groveton, *U.S.A.* 111 B13
Grožnjan, *Croatia* 29 C10
Groznyy, *Russia* 49 J7
Grubišno Polje, *Croatia* 42 E2
Grudovo, *Bulgaria* 41 D11
Grudusk, *Poland* 45 E7
Grudziądz, *Poland* 44 E5
Gruinard B., *U.K.* 14 D3
Grumo Áppula, *Italy* 31 A9
Grums, *Sweden* 10 E7
Grünberg, *Germany* 24 E4
Gründau, *Germany* 25 E5
Grundy Center, *U.S.A.* 112 D8
Grünstadt, *Germany* 25 F4
Gruvberget, *Sweden* 10 C10
Gruver, *U.S.A.* 113 G4
Gruyères, *Switz.* 25 J3
Gruža, *Serbia, Yug.* 40 C4
Gryazi, *Russia* 47 F10
Gryazovets, *Russia* 46 C11
Grybów, *Poland* 45 J7
Grycksbo, *Sweden* 10 D9
Gryfice, *Poland* 44 E2
Gryfino, *Poland* 45 E1
Gryfów Śląski, *Poland* 45 G2
Grythyttan, *Sweden* 10 E8
Gstaad, *Switz.* 25 J3
Gua, *India* 67 H14
Gua Musang, *Malaysia* 65 K3
Guacanayabo, G. de, *Cuba* .. 120 B4
Guachípas →, *Argentina* 126 B2
Guadajoz →, *Spain* 35 H6
Guadalajara, *Mexico* 118 C4
Guadalajara, *Spain* 32 E1
Guadalajara □, *Spain* 32 E2
Guadalcanal, *Solomon Is.* ... 96 H8
Guadalcanal, *Spain* 35 G5
Guadalén →, *Spain* 35 G7
Guadales, *Argentina* 126 C2
Guadalete →, *Spain* 35 J4
Guadalimar →, *Spain* 35 G7
Guadalmena →, *Spain* 35 G8
Guadalmez →, *Spain* 35 G5
Guadalope →, *Spain* 32 D4
Guadalquivir →, *Spain* 35 J4
Guadalupe = Guadeloupe ■,
  W. Indies 121 C7
Guadalupe, *Mexico* 117 N10
Guadalupe, *Spain* 35 F5
Guadalupe, *U.S.A.* 117 L6
Guadalupe →, *Mexico* 117 N10
Guadalupe →, *U.S.A.* 113 L6
Guadalupe, Sierra de, *Spain* . 35 F5
Guadalupe Bravos, *Mexico* .. 118 A3
Guadalupe I., *Pac. Oc.* 98 G8
Guadalupe Mts. Nat. Park,
  U.S.A. 113 K2
Guadalupe Peak, *U.S.A.* 113 K2
Guadalupe y Calvo, *Mexico* . 118 B3
Guadarrama, Sierra de, *Spain* 34 E7
Guadauta, *Georgia* 49 J5
Guadeloupe ■, *W. Indies* ... 121 C7
Guadeloupe Passage, *W. Indies* 121 C7
Guadiamar →, *Spain* 35 J4
Guadiana →, *Portugal* 35 H3
Guadiana Menor →, *Spain* .. 35 H7
Guadiaro →, *Spain* 35 J5
Guadiato →, *Spain* 35 H5
Guadiela →, *Spain* 32 E2
Guadix, *Spain* 35 H7
Guafo, Boca del, *Chile* 128 E2
Guaíra, *Brazil* 127 A5
Guaíra □, *Paraguay* 126 B4
Guaitecas, Is., *Chile* 128 E2
Guajará-Mirim, *Brazil* 124 F5
Guajira, Pen. de la, *Colombia* 124 A4
Gualán, *Guatemala* 120 C2
Gualdo Tadino, *Italy* 29 E9
Gualeguay, *Argentina* 126 C4
Gualeguaychú, *Argentina* ... 126 C4
Gualequay →, *Argentina* ... 126 C4
Guam ■, *Pac. Oc.* 96 F6
Guaminí, *Argentina* 126 D3
Guamúchil, *Mexico* 118 B3
Guanabacoa, *Cuba* 120 B3
Guanacaste, Cordillera del,
  Costa Rica 120 D2
Guanaceví, *Mexico* 118 B3
Guanahani = San Salvador I.,
  Bahamas 121 B5
Guanajay, *Cuba* 120 B3
Guanajuato, *Mexico* 118 C4
Guanajuato □, *Mexico* 118 C4
Guandacol, *Argentina* 126 B2
Guane, *Cuba* 120 B3
Guang'an, *China* 58 B6
Guangchang, *China* 59 D11
Guangde, *China* 59 B12
Guangdong □, *China* 59 F9
Guangfeng, *China* 59 C12
Guanghua, *China* 58 B5
Guangling, *China* 56 E8
Guangnan, *China* 58 E5
Guangning, *China* 59 F9
Guangrao, *China* 57 F10
Guangshui, *China* 59 B9
Guangshun, *China* 58 D6
Guangxi Zhuangzu Zizhiqu □,
  China 58 F7
Guangyuan, *China* 58 A5
Guangze, *China* 59 D11
Guangzhou, *China* 59 F9
Guanipa →, *Venezuela* 124 B6

Guanling, China 58 E5
Guannan, China 57 G10
Guantánamo, Cuba 121 B4
Guantao, China 56 F8
Guanyang, China 59 E8
Guanyun, China 57 G10
Guápiles, Costa Rica 120 D3
Guaporé, Bolivia 127 B5
Guaporé →, Brazil 122 E4
Guaqui, Bolivia 124 G5
Guara, Sierra de, Spain 32 C4
Guarapari, Brazil 127 A7
Guarapuava, Brazil 127 B5
Guaratinguetá, Brazil 127 A6
Guaratuba, Brazil 127 B6
Guarda, Portugal 34 E3
Guarda □, Portugal 34 E3
Guardafui, C. = Asir, Ras, Somali Rep. 74 E5
Guardamar del Segura, Spain 33 G4
Guardavalle, Italy 31 D9
Guárdia Sanframondi, Italy 31 A7
Guardo, Spain 34 C6
Guareña, Spain 35 G4
Guareña →, Spain 34 D5
Guárico □, Venezuela 124 B5
Guarujá, Brazil 127 A6
Guarus, Brazil 127 A7
Guasave, Mexico 118 B3
Guasdualito, Venezuela 124 B4
Guastalla, Italy 28 D7
Guatemala, Guatemala 120 D1
Guatemala ■, Cent. Amer. 120 C1
Guaviare →, Colombia 122 C4
Guaxupé, Brazil 127 A6
Guayama, Puerto Rico 121 C6
Guayaquil, Ecuador 124 D3
Guayaquil, G. de, Ecuador 122 D2
Guaymas, Mexico 118 B2
Guba, Dem. Rep. of the Congo 87 E2
Guba, Ethiopia 81 E4
Gūbāl, Madiq, Egypt 80 B3
Gubat, Phil. 61 E6
Gúbbio, Italy 29 E9
Guben, Germany 24 D10
Gubin, Poland 45 G1
Gubio, Nigeria 83 C7
Gubkin, Russia 47 G9
Guča, Serbia, Yug. 40 C4
Gucheng, China 59 A8
Gudata = Guadauta, Georgia 49 J5
Gudbrandsdalen, Norway 9 F14
Guddu Barrage, Pakistan 66 E6
Gudenå →, Denmark 11 H4
Gudermes, Russia 49 J8
Gudhjem, Denmark 11 J8
Gudur, India 66 M11
Guebwiller, France 19 E14
Guecho = Getxo, Spain 32 B2
Guékédou, Guinea 82 D2
Guéle Mendouka, Cameroon 83 E7
Guelph, Canada 102 D3
Guémené-Penfao, France 18 E5
Guémené-sur-Scorff, France 18 D3
Guéné, Benin 83 C5
Guer, France 18 E4
Guérande, France 18 E4
Guéret, France 19 F8
Guérigny, France 19 E10
Guerneville, U.S.A. 116 G4
Guernica = Gernika-Lumo, Spain 32 B2
Guernsey, U.K. 13 H5
Guernsey, U.S.A. 112 D2
Guerrero □, Mexico 119 D5
Guessou-Sud, Benin 83 C5
Gueugnon, France 19 F11
Guéyo, Ivory C. 82 D3
Gughe, Ethiopia 81 F4
Gügher, Iran 71 D8
Guglionesi, Italy 29 G11
Guhakolak, Tanjung, Indonesia 63 G12
Gui Jiang →, China 59 F8
Guia, Canary Is. 37 F4
Guia de Isora, Canary Is. 37 F3
Guia Lopes da Laguna, Brazil 127 A4
Guiana, S. Amer. 122 C4
Guibéroua, Ivory C. 82 D3
Guichi, China 59 B11
Guider, Cameroon 83 D7
Guidiguir, Niger 83 C6
Guidimouni, Niger 83 C6
Guiding, China 58 D6
Guidong, China 59 D9
Guidónia-Montecélio, Italy 29 F9
Guiers, L. de, Senegal 82 B1
Guigang, China 58 F7
Guiglo, Ivory C. 82 D3
Guihulñgan, Phil. 61 F6
Guijá, Mozam. 89 C5
Guijuelo, Spain 34 E5
Guildford, U.K. 13 F7
Guilford, U.S.A. 111 E12
Guilin, China 59 E8
Guillaume-Delisle L., Canada 102 A4
Guillaumes, France 21 D10
Guillestre, France 21 D10
Guilvinec, France 18 E2
Güimar, Canary Is. 37 F3
Guimarães, Portugal 34 D2
Guimaras □, Phil. 61 F5
Guinda, U.S.A. 116 G4
Guinea, Africa 76 F4
Guinea ■, W. Afr. 82 C2
Guinea, Gulf of, Atl. Oc. 83 E5

Guinea-Bissau ■, Africa 82 C2
Güines, Cuba 120 B3
Guingamp, France 18 D3
Guinguinéo, Senegal 82 C1
Guipavas, France 18 D2
Guiping, China 59 F8
Guipúzcoa □, Spain 32 B2
Guir, Mali 82 B4
Guirel, Mauritania 82 B3
Güiria, Venezuela 124 A6
Guiscard, France 19 C10
Guise, France 19 C10
Guitiriz, Spain 34 B3
Guitri, Ivory C. 82 D3
Guiuan, Phil. 61 F6
Guixi, China 59 C11
Guiyang, Guizhou, China 58 D6
Guiyang, Hunan, China 59 E9
Guizhou □, China 58 D6
Gujan-Mestras, France 20 D2
Gujar Khan, Pakistan 68 C5
Gujarat □, India 68 H4
Gujiang, China 59 D10
Gujranwala, Pakistan 68 C6
Gujrat, Pakistan 68 C6
Gukovo, Russia 49 F5
Gulbarga, India 66 L10
Gulbene, Latvia 9 H22
Gulf, The, Asia 71 E6
Gulfport, U.S.A. 113 K10
Gulin, China 58 C5
Gulistan, Pakistan 68 D2
Gull Lake, Canada 105 C7
Gullbrandstorp, Sweden 11 H6
Gullspång, Sweden 11 F8
Güllük, Turkey 39 D9
Güllük Korfezi, Turkey 39 D9
Gulma, Nigeria 83 C5
Gulmarg, India 69 B6
Gülnar, Turkey 72 D5
Gülpınar, Turkey 39 B8
Gülşehir, Turkey 72 C6
Gulshad, Kazakstan 50 E8
Gulu, Uganda 86 B3
Gülübovo, Bulgaria 41 D9
Gulud, J., Sudan 81 E2
Gulwe, Tanzania 86 D4
Gulyaypole = Hulyaypole, Ukraine 47 J9
Gumal →, Pakistan 68 D4
Gumbaz, Pakistan 68 D3
Gumel, Nigeria 83 C6
Gumiel de Hizán, Spain 34 D7
Gumla, India 69 H11
Gumlu, Australia 94 B4
Gumma □, Japan 55 F9
Gummersbach, Germany 24 D3
Gummi, Nigeria 83 C6
Gümüldür, Turkey 39 C9
Gümüşçay, Turkey 41 F11
Gümüşhacıköy, Turkey 72 B6
Gümüşhane, Turkey 73 B8
Gümüşsu, Turkey 39 C11
Gumzai, Indonesia 63 F8
Guna, Ethiopia 81 F4
Guna, India 68 G7
Gundelfingen, Germany 25 G6
Güney, Burdur, Turkey 39 D11
Güney, Denizli, Turkey 39 C11
Güneydoğu Toroslar, Turkey 73 C9
Gunisao →, Canada 105 C9
Gunisao L., Canada 105 C9
Gunjyal, Pakistan 68 C4
Günlüce, Turkey 39 E10
Gunnarskog, Sweden 10 E6
Gunnbjørn Fjeld, Greenland 4 C6
Gunnebo, Sweden 11 G10
Gunnewin, Australia 95 D4
Gunnison, Colo., U.S.A. 115 G10
Gunnison, Utah, U.S.A. 114 G8
Gunnison →, U.S.A. 115 G9
Gunpowder, Australia 94 B2
Guntakal, India 66 M10
Guntersville, U.S.A. 109 H2
Guntong, Malaysia 65 K3
Guntur, India 67 L12
Gunungapi, Indonesia 63 F7
Gunungsitoli, Indonesia 62 D1
Günz →, Germany 25 G6
Gunza, Angola 84 G2
Günzburg, Germany 25 G6
Gunzenhausen, Germany 25 F6
Guo He →, China 57 H9
Guoyang, China 56 H9
Gupis, Pakistan 69 A5
Gura Humorului, Romania 43 C10
Gura-Teghii, Romania 43 E11
Gurag, Ethiopia 81 F4
Gurahonţ, Romania 42 D7
Gurdaspur, India 68 C6
Gurdon, U.S.A. 113 J8
Güre, Balıkesir, Turkey 39 B8
Güre, Uşak, Turkey 39 C11
Gurgaon, India 68 E7
Gürgentepe, Turkey 72 B7
Gurghiu, Munţii, Romania 43 D10
Gurgueia →, Brazil 125 E10
Gurha, India 68 G4
Guri, Embalse de, Venezuela 124 B6
Gurin, Nigeria 83 D7
Gurjaani, Georgia 49 K7
Gurk →, Austria 26 E7
Gurkha, Nepal 69 E11
Gurley, Australia 95 D4
Gurnet Point, U.S.A. 111 D14
Gürpınar, Ist., Turkey 41 F12

Gürpınar, Van, Turkey 73 C10
Gürsu, Turkey 41 F13
Gurué, Mozam. 87 F4
Gurun, Malaysia 65 K3
Gürün, Turkey 72 C7
Gurupá, Brazil 125 D8
Gurupá, I. Grande de, Brazil 125 D8
Gurupi, Brazil 125 F9
Gurupi →, Brazil 125 D9
Guruwe, Zimbabwe 89 B5
Guryev = Atyraū, Kazakstan 50 E6
Gus-Khrustalnyy, Russia 48 C5
Gusau, Nigeria 83 C6
Gusev, Russia 9 J20
Gushan, China 57 E12
Gushgy, Turkmenistan 50 F7
Gushi, China 59 A10
Gushiago, Ghana 83 D4
Gusinje, Montenegro, Yug. 40 D3
Gusinoozersk, Russia 51 D11
Güssing, Austria 27 D9
Gustavsberg, Sweden 10 E12
Gustavus, U.S.A. 104 B1
Gustine, U.S.A. 116 H6
Güstrow, Germany 24 B8
Gusum, Sweden 11 F10
Guta = Kolárovo, Slovak Rep. 27 D10
Gütersloh, Germany 24 D4
Gutha, Australia 93 E2
Guthalungra, Australia 94 B4
Guthrie, Okla., U.S.A. 113 H6
Guthrie, Tex., U.S.A. 113 J4
Gutian, China 59 D12
Guttenberg, U.S.A. 112 D9
Gutu, Zimbabwe 89 B5
Guyana ■, S. Amer. 124 C7
Guyane française = French Guiana ■, S. Amer. 125 C8
Guyang, China 56 D6
Guyenne, France 20 D4
Guymon, U.S.A. 113 G4
Guyra, Australia 95 E5
Guyuan, Hebei, China 56 D8
Guyuan, Ningxia Huizu, China 56 G4
Güzelbahçe, Turkey 39 C8
Guzhang, China 58 C7
Guzhen, China 57 H9
Guzmán, L. de, Mexico 118 A3
Gvardeysk, Russia 9 J19
Gvardeyskoye, Ukraine 47 K8
Gwa, Burma 67 L19
Gwaai, Zimbabwe 87 F2
Gwabegar, Australia 95 E4
Gwadabawa, Nigeria 83 C6
Gwādar, Pakistan 66 G3
Gwagwada, Nigeria 83 C6
Gwalior, India 68 F8
Gwanara, Nigeria 83 D5
Gwanda, Zimbabwe 87 G2
Gwandu, Nigeria 83 C5
Gwane, Dem. Rep. of the Congo 86 B2
Gwaram, Nigeria 83 C7
Gwarzo, Nigeria 83 C6
Gwasero, Nigeria 83 D5
Gwda →, Poland 45 E3
Gweebarra B., Ireland 15 B3
Gweedore, Ireland 15 A3
Gweru, Zimbabwe 87 F2
Gwi, Nigeria 83 D6
Gwinn, U.S.A. 108 B2
Gwio Kura, Nigeria 83 C7
Gwoza, Nigeria 83 C7
Gwydir →, Australia 95 D4
Gwynedd □, U.K. 12 E3
Gyandzha = Gäncä, Azerbaijan 49 K8
Gyaring Hu, China 60 C4
Gydanskiy Poluostrov, Russia 50 C8
Gympie, Australia 95 D5
Gyomaendrőd, Hungary 42 D5
Gyöngyös, Hungary 42 C4
Győr, Hungary 42 C2
Győr-Moson-Sopron □, Hungary 42 C2
Gypsum Pt., Canada 104 A6
Gypsumville, Canada 105 C9
Gyueshevo, Bulgaria 40 D6
Gyula, Hungary 42 D6
Gyumri, Armenia 49 K6
Gyzylarbat, Turkmenistan 50 F6
Gyzyletrek, Turkmenistan 71 B7
Gzhatsk = Gagarin, Russia 46 E8

H

Ha 'Arava →, Israel 75 E4
Ha Coi, Vietnam 58 G6
Ha Dong, Vietnam 58 G5
Ha Giang, Vietnam 58 F5
Ha Tien, Vietnam 65 G5
Ha Tinh, Vietnam 64 C5
Ha Trung, Vietnam 64 C5
Haaksbergen, Neths. 17 B6
Haapsalu, Estonia 9 G20
Haarlem, Neths. 17 B4
Haast →, N.Z. 91 K2
Haast Bluff, Australia 92 D5
Hab →, Pakistan 68 G3
Hab Nadi Chauki, Pakistan 68 G3
Habaswein, Kenya 86 B4
Habay, Canada 104 B5
Ḩabbānīyah, Iraq 70 C4
Ḩabbānīyah, Hawr al, Iraq 73 F10
Habo, Sweden 11 G8
Haboro, Japan 54 B10

Ḩabshān, U.A.E. 71 F7
Hachenburg, Germany 24 E3
Hachijō-Jima, Japan 55 H9
Hachinohe, Japan 54 D10
Hachiōji, Japan 55 G9
Hachŏn, N. Korea 57 D15
Hacıbektaş, Turkey 72 C6
Hacılar, Turkey 72 C6
Hackås, Sweden 10 B8
Hackensack, U.S.A. 111 F10
Hackettstown, U.S.A. 111 F10
Hadali, Pakistan 68 C5
Hadarba, Ras, Sudan 80 C4
Hadarom □, Israel 75 E4
Hadd, Ra's al, Oman 74 C6
Hadejia, Nigeria 83 C7
Hadejia →, Nigeria 83 C7
Hadera, Israel 75 C3
Hadera, N. →, Israel 75 C3
Haderslev, Denmark 11 J3
Hadhramaut = Ḩadramawt, Yemen 74 D4
Hadibu, Yemen 74 E5
Hadım, Turkey 72 D5
Hadong, S. Korea 57 G14
Ḩadramawt, Yemen 74 D4
Ḩadrānīyah, Iraq 70 C4
Hadrian's Wall, U.K. 12 B5
Hadsten, Denmark 11 H4
Hadsund, Denmark 11 H4
Hadyach, Ukraine 47 G8
Haeju, N. Korea 57 E13
Haenam, S. Korea 57 G14
Haenertsburg, S. Africa 89 C4
Haerhpin = Harbin, China 57 B14
Hafar al Bāṭin, Si. Arabia 70 D5
Hafik, Turkey 72 C7
Ḩafirat al 'Aydā, Si. Arabia 70 E3
Hafit, Oman 71 F7
Hafizabad, Pakistan 68 C5
Haflong, India 67 G18
Hafnarfjörður, Iceland 8 D3
Haft Gel, Iran 71 D6
Hafun, Ras, Somali Rep. 74 E5
Hagalil, Israel 75 C4
Hagby, Sweden 11 H10
Hagen, Germany 24 D3
Hagenow, Germany 24 B7
Hagerman, U.S.A. 113 J2
Hagerstown, U.S.A. 108 F7
Hagersville, Canada 110 D4
Hagetmau, France 20 E3
Hagfors, Sweden 10 D7
Hagi, Japan 55 G5
Hagolan, Syria 75 C4
Hagondange, France 19 C13
Hags Hd., Ireland 15 D2
Hague, C. de la, France 18 C5
Hague, The = 's-Gravenhage, Neths. 17 B4
Haguenau, France 19 D14
Hai Duong, Vietnam 58 G6
Hai'an, Guangdong, China 59 G8
Hai'an, Jiangsu, China 59 A13
Haicheng, Fujian, China 59 E11
Haicheng, Liaoning, China 57 D12
Haidar Khel, Afghan. 68 C3
Haidargarh, India 69 F9
Haifa = Ḥefa, Israel 75 C4
Haifeng, China 59 F10
Haiger, Germany 24 E4
Haikou, China 60 D6
Ḥā'il, Si. Arabia 70 E4
Hailar, China 60 B6
Hailey, U.S.A. 114 E6
Haileybury, Canada 102 C4
Hailin, China 57 B15
Hailing Dao, China 59 G8
Hailong, China 57 C13
Hailuoto, Finland 8 D21
Haimen, Guangdong, China 59 F11
Haimen, Jiangsu, China 59 B13
Hainan □, China 60 E5
Hainaut □, Belgium 17 D4
Hainburg, Austria 27 C9
Haines, Alaska, U.S.A. 104 B1
Haines, Oreg., U.S.A. 114 D5
Haines City, U.S.A. 109 L5
Haines Junction, Canada 104 A1
Hainfeld, Austria 26 C8
Haining, China 59 B13
Haiphong, Vietnam 58 G6
Haitan Dao, China 59 E12
Haiti ■, W. Indies 121 C5
Haiya, Sudan 80 D4
Haiyan, China 59 B13
Haiyang, China 57 F11
Haiyuan, Guangxi Zhuangzu, China 58 F6
Haiyuan, Ningxia Huizu, China 56 F3
Haizhou, China 57 G10
Haizhou Wan, China 57 G10
Hajdú-Bihar □, Hungary 42 C6
Hajdúböszörmény, Hungary 42 C6
Hajdúdorog, Hungary 42 C6
Hajdúhadház, Hungary 42 C6
Hajdúnánás, Hungary 42 C6
Hajdúsámson, Hungary 42 C6
Hajdúszoboszló, Hungary 42 C6
Hajipur, India 69 G11
Ḩājjī Muḩsin, Iraq 70 C5
Ḩājjīābād, Iran 71 D7
Ḩājjīābād-e Zarrīn, Iran 71 C7
Hajnówka, Poland 45 F10
Hakansson, Mts., Dem. Rep. of the Congo 87 D2

Hakkâri, Turkey 70 B4
Hakkâri Dağları, Turkey 73 C10
Hakken-Zan, Japan 55 G7
Hakodate, Japan 54 D10
Hakos, Namibia 88 C2
Håksberg, Sweden 10 D9
Haku-San, Japan 55 F8
Hakui, Japan 55 F8
Hala, Pakistan 66 G6
Ḩalab, Syria 70 B3
Halabjah, Iraq 80 C4
Halasa, Sudan 81 E3
Ḩālat 'Ammār, Si. Arabia 70 D3
Halbā, Lebanon 75 A5
Halberstadt, Germany 24 D7
Halcombe, N.Z. 91 J5
Halcon, Phil. 63 B6
Halden, Norway 9 G14
Haldensleben, Germany 24 C7
Haldia, India 67 H16
Haldwani, India 69 E8
Hale →, Australia 94 C2
Halesowen, U.K. 13 E5
Haleyville, U.S.A. 109 H2
Half Assini, Ghana 82 D4
Halfmoon Bay, N.Z. 91 M2
Halfway →, Canada 104 B4
Halia, India 69 G10
Haliburton, Canada 102 C4
Halifax, Australia 94 B4
Halifax, Canada 103 D7
Halifax, U.K. 12 D6
Halifax, U.S.A. 110 F8
Halifax B., Australia 94 B4
Halifax I., Namibia 88 D2
Ḩalīl →, Iran 71 E8
Halkirk, U.K. 14 C5
Hall Beach = Sanirajak, Canada 101 B11
Hall in Tirol, Austria 26 D4
Hall Pen., Canada 101 B13
Hall Pt., Australia 92 C3
Hallabro, Sweden 11 H9
Halland □, Sweden 11 H6
Halland, Sweden 9 H15
Hallands län □, Sweden 11 H6
Hallands Väderö, Sweden 11 H6
Hallandsås, Sweden 11 H7
Halle, Belgium 17 D4
Halle, Nordrhein-Westfalen, Germany 24 C4
Halle, Sachsen-Anhalt, Germany 24 D7
Hällefors, Sweden 10 E8
Hälleforsnäs, Sweden 10 E10
Hallein, Austria 26 D6
Hällekis, Sweden 11 F7
Hallen, Sweden 10 A8
Hallettsville, U.S.A. 113 L6
Hallim, S. Korea 57 H14
Hallingdalselvi →, Norway 9 F13
Hallock, U.S.A. 112 A6
Halls Creek, Australia 92 C4
Hallsberg, Sweden 10 E9
Hallstahammar, Sweden 10 E10
Hallstatt, Austria 26 D6
Hallstavik, Sweden 10 D12
Hallstead, U.S.A. 111 E9
Halmahera, Indonesia 63 D7
Halmeu, Romania 42 C8
Halmstad, Sweden 11 H6
Hals, Denmark 11 H4
Hälsingborg = Helsingborg, Sweden 11 H6
Hälsingland, Sweden 10 C10
Halstead, U.K. 13 F8
Haltern, Germany 24 D3
Halti, Finland 8 B19
Halton □, U.K. 12 D5
Haltwhistle, U.K. 12 C5
Ḩalul, Qatar 71 E7
Halvad, India 68 H4
Ḩalvān, Iran 71 C8
Ham, France 19 C10
Ham Tan, Vietnam 65 G6
Ham Yen, Vietnam 64 A5
Hamab, Namibia 88 D2
Hamad, Sudan 81 D3
Hamada, Japan 55 G6
Hamadān, Iran 71 C6
Hamadān □, Iran 71 C6
Hamāh, Syria 70 C3
Hamamatsu, Japan 55 G8
Hamar, Norway 9 F14
Hamâta, Gebel, Egypt 70 E2
Hambantota, Sri Lanka 66 R12
Hamber Prov. Park, Canada 104 C5
Hamburg, Germany 24 B5
Hamburg, Ark., U.S.A. 113 J9
Hamburg, N.Y., U.S.A. 110 D6
Hamburg, Pa., U.S.A. 111 F9
Hamburg □, Germany 24 B5
Ḩamd, W. al →, Si. Arabia 70 E3
Hamden, U.S.A. 111 E12
Hamdibey, Turkey 39 B9
Häme, Finland 9 F21
Hämeenlinna, Finland 9 F21
Hamélé, Ghana 82 C4
Hamelin Pool, Australia 93 E1
Hameln, Germany 24 C5
Hamerkaz □, Israel 75 C3
Hamersley Ra., Australia 92 D2
Hamhung, N. Korea 57 E14
Hami, China 60 B4
Hamilton, Canada 102 D4
Hamilton, N.Z. 91 G5
Hamilton, U.K. 14 F4

Hamilton, *Ala., U.S.A.* 109 H1
Hamilton, *Mont., U.S.A.* 114 C6
Hamilton, *N.Y., U.S.A.* 111 D9
Hamilton, *Ohio, U.S.A.* 108 F3
Hamilton, *Tex., U.S.A.* 113 K5
Hamilton ➤, *Australia* 94 C2
Hamilton City, *U.S.A.* 116 F4
Hamilton Inlet, *Canada* 103 B8
Hamilton Mt., *U.S.A.* 111 C10
Hamina, *Finland* 9 F22
Hamirpur, *H.P., India* 68 D7
Hamirpur, *Ut. P., India* 69 G9
Hamitabat, *Turkey* 41 E11
Hamlet, *U.S.A.* 109 H6
Hamlin = Hameln, *Germany* .. 24 C5
Hamlin, *N.Y., U.S.A.* 110 C7
Hamlin, *Tex., U.S.A.* 113 J4
Hamm, *Germany* 24 D3
Ḩammār, Hawr al, *Iraq* 70 D5
Hammarstrand, *Sweden* 10 A10
Hammelburg, *Germany* 25 E5
Hammeren, *Denmark* 11 J8
Hammerfest, *Norway* 8 A20
Hammerum, *Denmark* 11 H3
Hamminkeln, *Germany* 24 D2
Hammond, *Ind., U.S.A.* 108 E2
Hammond, *La., U.S.A.* 113 K9
Hammond, *N.Y., U.S.A.* 111 B9
Hammondsport, *U.S.A.* 110 D7
Hammonton, *U.S.A.* 108 F8
Hamneda, *Sweden* 11 H7
Hamoyet, Jebel, *Sudan* 80 D4
Hampden, *N.Z.* 91 L3
Hampshire □, *U.K.* 13 F6
Hampshire Downs, *U.K.* 13 F6
Hampton, *N.B., Canada* 103 C6
Hampton, *Ont., Canada* 110 C6
Hampton, *Ark., U.S.A.* 113 J8
Hampton, *Iowa, U.S.A.* 112 D8
Hampton, *N.H., U.S.A.* 111 D14
Hampton, *S.C., U.S.A.* 109 J5
Hampton, *Va., U.S.A.* 108 G7
Hampton Bays, *U.S.A.* 111 F12
Hampton Tableland, *Australia* . 93 F4
Hamra, *Sweden* 10 C8
Hamrat esh Sheykh, *Sudan* ... 81 E2
Hamur, *Turkey* 73 C10
Hamyang, *S. Korea* 57 G14
Han Jiang ➤, *China* 59 F11
Han Shui, *China* 58 A7
Han Shui, *China* 59 B10
Hanak, *Si. Arabia* 70 E3
Hanamaki, *Japan* 54 E10
Hanang, *Tanzania* 86 C4
Hanau, *Germany* 25 E4
Hanbogd = Ihbulag, *Mongolia* . 56 C4
Hançalar, *Turkey* 39 C11
Hâncești, *Moldova* 43 D13
Hancheng, *China* 56 G6
Hanchuan, *China* 59 B9
Hancock, *Mich., U.S.A.* 112 B10
Hancock, *N.Y., U.S.A.* 111 E9
Handa, *Japan* 55 G8
Handan, *China* 56 F8
Handeni, *Tanzania* 86 D4
Handlová, *Slovak Rep.* 27 C11
Handub, *Sudan* 80 D4
Handwara, *India* 69 B6
Hanegev, *Israel* 75 E4
Hanford, *U.S.A.* 116 J7
Hang Chat, *Thailand* 64 C2
Hang Dong, *Thailand* 64 C2
Hangang ➤, *S. Korea* 57 F14
Hangayn Nuruu, *Mongolia* ... 60 B4
Hangchou = Hangzhou, *China* . 59 B13
Hanggin Houqi, *China* 56 D4
Hanggin Qi, *China* 56 E5
Hangu, *China* 57 E9
Hangzhou, *China* 59 B13
Hangzhou Wan, *China* 59 B13
Hanhongor, *Mongolia* 56 C3
Ḩanīdh, *Si. Arabia* 71 E6
Ḩanīsh, *Yemen* 74 E3
Haniska, *Slovak Rep.* 27 C14
Hanjiang, *China* 59 E12
Hankinson, *U.S.A.* 112 B6
Hanko, *Finland* 9 G20
Hankou, *China* 59 B10
Hanksville, *U.S.A.* 115 G8
Hanle, *India* 69 C8
Hanmer Springs, *N.Z.* 91 K4
Hann ➤, *Australia* 92 C4
Hann, Mt., *Australia* 92 C4
Hanna, *Canada* 104 C6
Hanna, *U.S.A.* 114 F10
Hannah B., *Canada* 102 B4
Hannibal, *Mo., U.S.A.* 112 F9
Hannibal, *N.Y., U.S.A.* 111 C8
Hannik, *Sudan* 80 D3
Hannover, *Germany* 24 C5
Hanö, *Sweden* 11 H8
Hanöbukten, *Sweden* 11 J8
Hanoi, *Vietnam* 58 G5
Hanover = Hannover, *Germany* . 24 C5
Hanover, *Canada* 102 D3
Hanover, *S. Africa* 88 E3
Hanover, *N.H., U.S.A.* 111 C12
Hanover, *Ohio, U.S.A.* 110 F2
Hanover, *Pa., U.S.A.* 108 F7
Hanover, I., *Chile* 128 G2
Hansdiha, *India* 69 G12
Hanshou, *China* 59 C8
Hansi, *India* 68 E6
Hanstholm, *Denmark* 11 G2
Hantsavichy, *Belarus* 47 F4
Hanumangarh, *India* 68 E6

Hanyin, *China* 58 A7
Hanyuan, *China* 58 C4
Hanzhong, *China* 56 H4
Hanzhuang, *China* 57 G9
Haora, *India* 69 H13
Haoxue, *China* 59 B9
Haparanda, *Sweden* 8 D21
Happy, *U.S.A.* 113 H4
Happy Camp, *U.S.A.* 114 F2
Happy Valley-Goose Bay,
  Canada 103 B7
Hapsu, *N. Korea* 57 D15
Hapur, *India* 68 E7
Ḩaql, *Si. Arabia* 75 F3
Har, *Indonesia* 63 F8
Har Hu, *China* 60 C4
Har Us Nuur, *Mongolia* 60 B4
Har Yehuda, *Israel* 75 D3
Ḩaraḍ, *Si. Arabia* 74 C4
Haradok, *Belarus* 46 E6
Häradsbäck, *Sweden* 11 H8
Haranomachi, *Japan* 54 F10
Harare, *Zimbabwe* 87 F3
Harat, *Eritrea* 81 D4
Harbin, *China* 57 B14
Harbiye, *Turkey* 72 D7
Harbo, *Sweden* 10 D11
Harboør, *Denmark* 11 H2
Harbor Beach, *U.S.A.* 110 C2
Harbour Breton, *Canada* 103 C8
Harbour Deep, *Canada* 103 B8
Harburg, *Germany* 24 B5
Hårby, *Denmark* 11 J4
Harda, *India* 68 H7
Hardangerfjorden, *Norway* ... 9 F12
Hardangervidda, *Norway* 9 F12
Hardap Dam, *Namibia* 88 C2
Hardenberg, *Neths.* 17 B6
Harderwijk, *Neths.* 17 B5
Hardey ➤, *Australia* 92 D2
Hardin, *U.S.A.* 114 D10
Harding, *S. Africa* 89 E4
Harding Ra., *Australia* 92 C3
Hardisty, *Canada* 104 C6
Hardoi, *India* 69 F9
Hardwar = Haridwar, *India* .. 68 E8
Hardwick, *U.S.A.* 111 B12
Hardy, Pen., *Chile* 128 H3
Hare B., *Canada* 103 B8
Hareid, *Norway* 9 E12
Haren, *Germany* 24 C3
Harer, *Ethiopia* 81 F5
Harerge □, *Ethiopia* 81 F5
Hareto, *Ethiopia* 81 F4
Harfleur, *France* 18 C7
Hargeisa, *Somali Rep.* 74 F3
Harghita □, *Romania* 43 D10
Harghita, Munții, *Romania* ... 43 D10
Hargshamn, *Sweden* 10 D12
Hari ➤, *Indonesia* 62 E2
Haria, *Canary Is.* 37 E6
Haridwar, *India* 68 E8
Harim, Jabal al, *Oman* 71 E8
Haringhata ➤, *Bangla.* 67 J16
Harīrūd ➤, *Asia* 66 A2
Härjedalen, *Sweden* 10 B7
Harlan, *Iowa, U.S.A.* 112 E7
Harlan, *Ky., U.S.A.* 109 G4
Hârlău, *Romania* 43 C11
Harlech, *U.K.* 12 E3
Harlem, *U.S.A.* 114 B9
Hårlev, *Denmark* 11 J6
Harlingen, *Neths.* 17 A5
Harlingen, *U.S.A.* 113 M6
Harlow, *U.K.* 13 F8
Harlowton, *U.S.A.* 114 C9
Harmancık, *Turkey* 39 B11
Harmånger, *Sweden* 10 C11
Harmil, *Eritrea* 81 D5
Harnai, *Pakistan* 68 D2
Harney Basin, *U.S.A.* 114 E4
Harney L., *U.S.A.* 114 E4
Harney Peak, *U.S.A.* 112 D3
Härnön, *Sweden* 10 B12
Härnösand, *Sweden* 10 B11
Haro, *Spain* 32 C2
Haroldswick, *U.K.* 14 A8
Harp L., *Canada* 103 A7
Harper, *Liberia* 82 E3
Harplinge, *Sweden* 11 H6
Harr, *Mauritania* 82 B2
Harrai, *India* 69 H8
Harrand, *Pakistan* 68 E4
Ḩarrat Khaybar, *Si. Arabia* .. 80 B5
Ḩarrat Nawāṣīf, *Si. Arabia* ... 80 C5
Harricana ➤, *Canada* 102 B4
Harriman, *U.S.A.* 109 H3
Harrington Harbour, *Canada* . 103 B8
Harris, *U.K.* 14 D2
Harris L., *Australia* 95 E2
Harris Pt., *Canada* 110 C2
Harrisburg, *Ill., U.S.A.* 113 G10
Harrisburg, *Nebr., U.S.A.* ... 112 E3
Harrisburg, *Oreg., U.S.A.* ... 114 D2
Harrismith, *S. Africa* 89 D4
Harrison, *Ark., U.S.A.* 113 G8
Harrison, *Maine, U.S.A.* 111 B14
Harrison, *Nebr., U.S.A.* 112 D3
Harrison, C., *Canada* 103 B8
Harrison L., *Canada* 104 D4
Harrisonburg, *U.S.A.* 108 F6
Harrisonville, *U.S.A.* 112 F7
Harriston, *Canada* 110 C4
Harrisville, *Mich., U.S.A.* ... 110 B1

Harrisville, *N.Y., U.S.A.* 111 B9
Harrisville, *Pa., U.S.A.* 110 E5
Harrodsburg, *U.S.A.* 108 G3
Harrogate, *U.K.* 12 C6
Harrow □, *U.K.* 13 F7
Harrowsmith, *Canada* 111 B8
Harry S. Truman Reservoir,
  U.S.A. 112 F7
Harsefeld, *Germany* 24 B5
Harsewinkel, *Germany* 24 D4
Harsīn, *Iran* 70 C5
Hârşova, *Romania* 43 F12
Harstad, *Norway* 8 B17
Harsud, *India* 68 H7
Hart, *U.S.A.* 108 D2
Hartbees ➤, *S. Africa* 88 D3
Hartberg, *Austria* 26 D8
Hartford, *Conn., U.S.A.* 111 E12
Hartford, *Ky., U.S.A.* 108 G2
Hartford, *S. Dak., U.S.A.* 112 D6
Hartford, *Wis., U.S.A.* 112 D10
Hartford City, *U.S.A.* 108 E3
Hartland, *Canada* 103 C6
Hartland Pt., *U.K.* 13 F3
Hartlepool, *U.K.* 12 C6
Hartlepool □, *U.K.* 12 C6
Hartley Bay, *Canada* 104 C3
Hartmannberge, *Namibia* ... 88 B1
Hartney, *Canada* 105 D8
Hârtop, *Moldova* 43 D13
Harts ➤, *S. Africa* 88 D3
Hartselle, *U.S.A.* 109 H2
Hartshorne, *U.S.A.* 113 H7
Hartstown, *U.S.A.* 110 E4
Hartsville, *U.S.A.* 109 H5
Hartswater, *S. Africa* 88 D3
Hartwell, *U.S.A.* 109 H4
Harvand, *Iran* 71 D7
Harvey, *Australia* 93 F2
Harvey, *Ill., U.S.A.* 108 E2
Harvey, *N. Dak., U.S.A.* 112 B5
Harwich, *U.K.* 13 F9
Haryana □, *India* 68 E7
Haryn ➤, *Belarus* 47 F4
Harz, *Germany* 24 D6
Harzgerode, *Germany* 24 D7
Hasa □, *Si. Arabia* 71 E6
Hasaheisa, *Sudan* 81 E3
Ḩasanābād, *Iran* 71 C7
Hasdo ➤, *India* 69 J10
Haselünne, *Germany* 24 C3
Hashimoto, *Japan* 55 G7
Hashtjerd, *Iran* 71 C6
Haskell, *U.S.A.* 113 J5
Hasköy, *Turkey* 41 E10
Haslach, *Germany* 25 G4
Hasle, *Denmark* 11 J8
Haslemere, *U.K.* 13 F7
Haslev, *Denmark* 11 J5
Hasparren, *France* 20 E2
Hassa, *Turkey* 72 D7
Hassela, *Sweden* 10 B10
Hasselt, *Belgium* 17 D5
Hassfurt, *Germany* 25 E6
Hassi Messaoud, *Algeria* 78 B7
Hässleholm, *Sweden* 11 H7
Hassloch, *Germany* 25 F4
Hästholmen, *Sweden* 11 F8
Hastings, *N.Z.* 91 H6
Hastings, *U.K.* 13 G8
Hastings, *Mich., U.S.A.* 108 D3
Hastings, *Minn., U.S.A.* 112 C8
Hastings, *Nebr., U.S.A.* 112 E5
Hästveda, *Sweden* 11 H7
Hat Yai, *Thailand* 65 J3
Hatanbulag = Ergel, *Mongolia* . 56 C5
Hatay = Antalya, *Turkey* 72 D4
Hatch, *U.S.A.* 115 K10
Hatchet L., *Canada* 105 B8
Hateg, *Romania* 42 E7
Hateruma-Shima, *Japan* 55 M1
Hatgal, *Mongolia* 60 A5
Hathras, *India* 68 F8
Hatia, *Bangla.* 67 H17
Ḩāṭibah, Ra's, *Si. Arabia* 80 C4
Hato Mayor, *Dom. Rep.* 121 C6
Hatta, *India* 69 G8
Hatteras, *U.S.A.* 109 H8
Hattiesburg, *U.S.A.* 113 K10
Hatvan, *Hungary* 42 C4
Hau Bon = Cheo Reo, *Vietnam* . 62 B3
Hau Duc, *Vietnam* 64 E7
Haugesund, *Norway* 9 G11
Haukipudas, *Finland* 8 D21
Haultain ➤, *Canada* 105 B7
Hauraki G., *N.Z.* 91 G5
Hausruck, *Austria* 26 C6
Haut Atlas, *Morocco* 78 B4
Haut-Rhin □, *France* 19 E14
Haut-Zaïre = Orientale □,
  Dem. Rep. of the Congo 86 B2
Haute-Corse □, *France* 21 F13
Haute-Garonne □, *France* 20 E5
Haute-Loire □, *France* 20 C7
Haute-Marne □, *France* 19 D12
Haute-Normandie □, *France* . 18 C7
Haute-Saône □, *France* 19 E13
Haute-Vienne □, *France* 20 C5
Hautes-Alpes □, *France* 21 D10
Hautes Fagnes = Hohe Venn,
  Belgium 17 D6
Hautes-Pyrénées □, *France* .. 20 F4
Hauteville-Lompnès, *France* . 21 C9
Hautmont, *France* 19 B10

Hauts-de-Seine □, *France* 19 D9
Hauts Plateaux, *Algeria* 76 C4
Hauzenberg, *Germany* 25 G9
Havana = La Habana, *Cuba* .. 120 B3
Havana, *U.S.A.* 112 E9
Havant, *U.K.* 13 G7
Havârna, *Romania* 43 B11
Havasu, L., *U.S.A.* 117 L12
Havdhem, *Sweden* 11 G12
Havel ➤, *Germany* 24 C8
Havelian, *Pakistan* 68 B5
Havelock, *Canada* 102 D4
Havelock, *N.Z.* 91 J4
Havelock, *U.S.A.* 109 H7
Haverfordwest, *U.K.* 13 F3
Haverhill, *U.S.A.* 111 D13
Haverstraw, *U.S.A.* 111 E11
Håverud, *Sweden* 11 F6
Havirga, *Mongolia* 56 B7
Havířov, *Czech Rep.* 27 B11
Havlíčkův Brod, *Czech Rep.* .. 26 B8
Havneby, *Denmark* 11 J2
Havran, *Turkey* 39 B9
Havre, *U.S.A.* 114 B9
Havre-Aubert, *Canada* 103 C7
Havre-St.-Pierre, *Canada* 103 B7
Havsa, *Turkey* 41 E10
Havza, *Turkey* 72 B6
Haw ➤, *U.S.A.* 109 H6
Hawaii □, *U.S.A.* 106 H16
Hawaii I., *Pac. Oc.* 106 J17
Hawaiian Is., *Pac. Oc.* 106 H17
Hawaiian Ridge, *Pac. Oc.* ... 97 E11
Hawarden, *U.S.A.* 112 D6
Hawea, L., *N.Z.* 91 L2
Hawera, *N.Z.* 91 H5
Hawick, *U.K.* 14 F6
Hawk Junction, *Canada* 102 C3
Hawke B., *N.Z.* 91 H6
Hawkesbury, *Canada* 102 C5
Hawkesbury I., *Canada* 104 C3
Hawkesbury Pt., *Australia* ... 94 A1
Hawkinsville, *U.S.A.* 109 J4
Hawley, *Minn., U.S.A.* 112 B6
Hawley, *Pa., U.S.A.* 111 E9
Ḩawrān, W. ➤, *Iraq* 70 C4
Hawsh Mūssá, *Lebanon* 75 B4
Hawthorne, *U.S.A.* 114 G4
Hay ➤, *Australia* 94 C2
Hay ➤, *Canada* 104 A5
Hay, C., *Australia* 92 B4
Hay L., *Canada* 104 B5
Hay-on-Wye, *U.K.* 13 E4
Hay River, *Canada* 104 A5
Hay Springs, *U.S.A.* 112 D3
Haya = Tehoru, *Indonesia* ... 63 E7
Hayachine-San, *Japan* 54 E10
Hayange, *France* 19 C13
Haydarlı, *Turkey* 39 C12
Hayden, *U.S.A.* 114 F10
Haydon, *Australia* 94 B3
Hayes ➤, *Canada* 112 C4
Hayes ➤, *Canada* 102 A1
Hayes Creek, *Australia* 92 B5
Hayle, *U.K.* 13 G2
Hayling I., *U.K.* 13 G7
Haymana, *Turkey* 72 C5
Hayrabolu, *Turkey* 41 E11
Hays, *Canada* 104 C6
Hays, *U.S.A.* 112 F5
Haysyn, *Ukraine* 47 H5
Hayvoron, *Ukraine* 47 H5
Hayward, *Calif., U.S.A.* 116 H4
Hayward, *Wis., U.S.A.* 112 B9
Haywards Heath, *U.K.* 13 G7
Ḩazafon □, *Israel* 75 C4
Hazārān, Kūh-e, *Iran* 71 D8
Hazard, *U.S.A.* 108 G4
Hazaribag, *India* 69 H11
Hazaribag Road, *India* 69 G11
Hazebrouck, *France* 19 B9
Hazelton, *Canada* 104 B3
Hazelton, *U.S.A.* 112 B4
Hazen, *U.S.A.* 112 B4
Hazlehurst, *Ga., U.S.A.* 109 K4
Hazlehurst, *Miss., U.S.A.* ... 113 K9
Hazlet, *U.S.A.* 111 F10
Hazleton, *U.S.A.* 111 F9
Hazlett, L., *Australia* 92 D4
Hazro, *Turkey* 70 B4
He Xian, *Anhui, China* 59 B12
He Xian, *Guangxi Zhuangzu,
  China* 59 E8
Head of Bight, *Australia* 93 F5
Headlands, *Zimbabwe* 87 F3
Healdsburg, *U.S.A.* 116 G4
Healdton, *U.S.A.* 113 H6
Heany Junction, *Zimbabwe* .. 89 C4
Heard I., *Ind. Oc.* 3 G13
Hearne, *U.S.A.* 113 K6
Hearst, *Canada* 102 C3
Heart ➤, *U.S.A.* 112 B4
Heart's Content, *Canada* 103 C9
Heath Pt., *Canada* 103 C7
Heavener, *U.S.A.* 113 H7
Hebbronville, *U.S.A.* 113 M5
Hebei □, *China* 56 E9
Hebel, *Australia* 95 D4
Heber, *U.S.A.* 117 N11
Heber City, *U.S.A.* 114 F8
Heber Springs, *U.S.A.* 113 H9
Hebert, *Canada* 105 C7
Hebgen L., *U.S.A.* 114 D8
Hebi, *China* 56 G8
Hebrides, *U.K.* 6 D4

Hebrides, Sea of the, *U.K.* 14 D2
Hebron = Al Khalīl, *West Bank* . 75 D4
Hebron, *Canada* 101 C13
Hebron, *N. Dak., U.S.A.* 112 B3
Hebron, *Nebr., U.S.A.* 112 E6
Heby, *Sweden* 10 E10
Hecate Str., *Canada* 104 C2
Heceta I., *Canada* 104 B2
Hechi, *China* 58 E7
Hechingen, *Germany* 25 G4
Hechuan, *China* 58 B6
Hecla, *U.S.A.* 112 C5
Hecla I., *Canada* 105 C9
Hédé, *France* 18 D5
Hede, *Sweden* 10 B7
Hedemora, *Sweden* 10 D9
Hedensted, *Denmark* 11 J3
Hedesunda, *Sweden* 10 D10
Heerde, *Neths.* 17 B6
Heerenveen, *Neths.* 17 B5
Heerhugowaard, *Neths.* 17 B4
Heerlen, *Neths.* 17 D5
Ḩefa, *Israel* 75 C4
Ḩefa □, *Israel* 75 C4
Hefei, *China* 59 B11
Hefeng, *China* 59 C8
Hegalig, *Sudan* 81 E3
Hegang, *China* 60 B8
Heiban, *Sudan* 81 E3
Heichengzhen, *China* 56 F4
Heide, *Germany* 24 A5
Heidelberg, *Germany* 25 F4
Heidelberg, *S. Africa* 88 E3
Heidenau, *Germany* 24 E9
Heidenheim, *Germany* 25 G6
Heijing, *China* 58 E3
Heilbad Heiligenstadt, *Germany* 24 D6
Heilbron, *S. Africa* 89 D4
Heilbronn, *Germany* 25 F5
Heiligenblut, *Austria* 26 D5
Heiligenhafen, *Germany* 24 A6
Heiligenhaus □, *Germany* 60 B7
Heilongjiang □, *China* 60 B7
Heilunkiang = Heilongjiang □,
  China 60 B7
Heimaey, *Iceland* 8 E3
Heinola, *Finland* 9 F22
Heinsberg, *Germany* 24 D2
Heinze Kyun, *Burma* 64 E1
Heishan, *China* 57 D12
Heishui, *Liaoning, China* 57 C10
Heishui, *Sichuan, China* 58 A4
Hejaz = Ḩijāz □, *Si. Arabia* .. 70 E3
Hejian, *China* 56 E9
Hejiang, *China* 58 C5
Hejin, *China* 56 G6
Hekimhan, *Turkey* 70 B3
Hekla, *Iceland* 8 E4
Hekou, *Guangdong, China* ... 59 F9
Hekou, *Yunnan, China* 58 F5
Hel, *Poland* 44 D5
Helagsfjället, *Sweden* 10 B6
Helan Shan, *China* 56 E3
Helechosa, *Spain* 35 F6
Helen Atoll, *Pac. Oc.* 63 D8
Helena, *Ark., U.S.A.* 113 H9
Helena, *Mont., U.S.A.* 114 C7
Helendale, *U.S.A.* 117 L9
Helensburgh, *U.K.* 14 E4
Helensville, *N.Z.* 91 G5
Helenvale, *Australia* 94 B4
Helgasjön, *Sweden* 11 H8
Helgeland, *Norway* 8 C15
Helgoland, *Germany* 24 A3
Heligoland = Helgoland,
  Germany 24 A3
Heligoland B. = Deutsche Bucht,
  Germany 24 A4
Heliopolis, *Egypt* 80 H7
Hella, *Iceland* 8 E3
Hellertown, *U.S.A.* 111 F9
Hellespont = Çanakkale Boğazı,
  Turkey 41 F10
Hellevoetsluis, *Neths.* 17 C4
Hellín, *Spain* 33 G3
Helmand □, *Afghan.* 66 D4
Helmand ➤, *Afghan.* 66 D2
Helme ➤, *Germany* 24 D7
Helmeringhausen, *Namibia* .. 88 D2
Helmond, *Neths.* 17 C5
Helmsdale, *U.K.* 14 C5
Helmsdale ➤, *U.K.* 14 C5
Helmstedt, *Germany* 24 C7
Helong, *China* 57 C15
Helper, *U.S.A.* 114 G8
Helsingborg, *Sweden* 11 H6
Helsinge, *Denmark* 11 H6
Helsingfors = Helsinki, *Finland* 9 F21
Helsingør, *Denmark* 11 H6
Helsinki, *Finland* 9 F21
Helska, Mierzeja, *Poland* 44 D5
Helston, *U.K.* 13 G2
Helvellyn, *U.K.* 12 C4
Helwân, *Egypt* 80 J7
Hemel Hempstead, *U.K.* 13 F7
Hemet, *U.S.A.* 117 M10
Hemingford, *U.S.A.* 112 D3
Hemmingford, *Canada* 111 A11
Hempstead, *U.S.A.* 113 K6
Hemse, *Sweden* 11 G12
Hemsön, *Sweden* 10 B12
Henån, *Sweden* 11 F5
Henan □, *China* 56 H8
Henares ➤, *Spain* 34 E7
Henashi-Misaki, *Japan* 54 D9
Hendaye, *France* 20 E2
Hendek, *Turkey* 72 B4

Henderson, *Argentina* 126 D3
Henderson, *Ky., U.S.A.* 108 G2
Henderson, *N.C., U.S.A.* 109 G6
Henderson, *Nev., U.S.A.* 117 J12
Henderson, *Tenn., U.S.A.* 109 H1
Henderson, *Tex., U.S.A.* 113 J7
Hendersonville, *N.C., U.S.A.* .. 109 H4
Hendersonville, *Tenn., U.S.A.* . 109 G2
Hendījān, *Iran* 71 D6
Hendorābī, *Iran* 71 E7
Heng Jiang, *China* 58 C5
Heng Xian, *China* 58 F7
Hengcheng, *China* 56 E4
Hengchun, *Taiwan* 59 F13
Hengdaohezi, *China* 57 B15
Hengelo, *Neths.* 17 B6
Hengfeng, *China* 59 C10
Hengshan, *Hunan, China* 59 D9
Hengshan, *Shaanxi, China* 56 F5
Hengshui, *China* 56 F8
Hengyang, *China* 59 D9
Henichesk, *Ukraine* 47 J8
Hénin-Beaumont, *France* 19 B9
Henlopen, C., *U.S.A.* 108 F8
Hennan, *Sweden* 10 B9
Hennebont, *France* 18 E3
Hennenman, *S. Africa* 88 D4
Hennessey, *U.S.A.* 113 G6
Hennigsdorf, *Germany* 24 C9
Henrietta, *U.S.A.* 113 J5
Henrietta, Ostrov = Genriyetty,
   Ostrov, *Russia* 51 B16
Henrietta Maria, C., *Canada* .. 102 A3
Henry, *U.S.A.* 112 E10
Henryetta, *U.S.A.* 113 H7
Henryville, *Canada* 111 A11
Hensall, *Canada* 110 C3
Henstedt-Ulzburg, *Germany* 24 B6
Hentiesbaai, *Namibia* 88 C1
Hentiyn Nuruu, *Mongolia* 60 B5
Henzada, *Burma* 67 L19
Hephaestia, *Greece* 39 B7
Heping, *China* 59 E10
Heppner, *U.S.A.* 114 D4
Hepu, *China* 58 G7
Hepworth, *Canada* 110 B3
Heqing, *China* 58 D3
Hequ, *China* 56 E6
Héraðsflói, *Iceland* 8 D6
Héraðsvötn ➔, *Iceland* 8 D4
Herald Cays, *Australia* 94 B4
Herāt, *Afghan.* 66 B3
Herāt □, *Afghan.* 66 B3
Hérault □, *France* 20 E7
Hérault ➔, *France* 20 E7
Herbault, *France* 18 E8
Herbert ➔, *Australia* 94 B4
Herberton, *Australia* 94 B4
Herbertsdale, *S. Africa* 88 E3
Herbignac, *France* 18 E4
Herborn, *Germany* 24 E4
Herby, *Poland* 45 H5
Herceg-Novi, *Montenegro, Yug.* . 40 D2
Herchmer, *Canada* 105 B10
Herðubreið, *Iceland* 8 D5
Hereford, *U.K.* 13 E5
Hereford, *U.S.A.* 113 H3
Herefordshire □, *U.K.* 13 E5
Hereke, *Turkey* 41 F13
Herencia, *Spain* 35 F7
Herentals, *Belgium* 17 C4
Herford, *Germany* 24 C4
Héricourt, *France* 19 E13
Herington, *U.S.A.* 112 F6
Herisau, *Switz.* 25 H5
Hérisson, *France* 19 F9
Herkimer, *U.S.A.* 111 D10
Herlong, *U.S.A.* 116 E6
Herm, *U.K.* 13 H5
Hermann, *U.S.A.* 112 F9
Hermannsburg, *Australia* 92 D5
Hermannsburg, *Germany* 24 C6
Hermanus, *S. Africa* 88 E2
Herment, *France* 20 C6
Hermiston, *U.S.A.* 114 D4
Hermite, I., *Chile* 128 H3
Hermon, *U.S.A.* 111 B9
Hermon, Mt. = Shaykh, J. ash,
   Lebanon 75 B4
Hermosillo, *Mexico* 118 B2
Hernád ➔, *Hungary* 42 C6
Hernandarias, *Paraguay* 127 B5
Hernandez, *U.S.A.* 116 J6
Hernando, *Argentina* 126 C3
Hernando, *U.S.A.* 113 H10
Hernani, *Spain* 32 B3
Herndon, *U.S.A.* 110 F8
Herne, *Germany* 17 C7
Herne Bay, *U.K.* 13 F9
Herning, *Denmark* 11 H2
Heroica = Caborca, *Mexico* ... 118 A2
Heroica Nogales = Nogales,
   Mexico 118 A2
Heron Bay, *Canada* 102 C2
Herradura, Pta. de la, *Canary Is.* 37 F5
Herreid, *U.S.A.* 112 C4
Herrenberg, *Germany* 25 G4
Herrera, *Spain* 35 H6
Herrera de Alcántara, *Spain* .. 35 F3
Herrera de Pisuerga, *Spain* ... 34 C6
Herrera del Duque, *Spain* 35 F5
Herrestad, *Sweden* 11 F5
Herrin, *U.S.A.* 113 G10
Herriot, *Canada* 105 B8
Herrljunga, *Sweden* 11 F7
Hersbruck, *Germany* 25 F7

Hershey, *U.S.A.* 111 F8
Hersonissos, *Greece* 36 D7
Herstal, *Belgium* 17 D5
Hertford, *U.K.* 13 F7
Hertfordshire □, *U.K.* 13 F7
's-Hertogenbosch, *Neths.* 17 C5
Hertzogville, *S. Africa* 88 D4
Hervás, *Spain* 34 E5
Hervey B., *Australia* 94 C5
Herzberg, *Brandenburg,
   Germany* 24 D9
Herzberg, *Niedersachsen,
   Germany* 24 D6
Herzliyya, *Israel* 75 C3
Herzogenburg, *Austria* 26 C8
Hešár, *Fārs, Iran* 71 D6
Hešār, *Markazī, Iran* 71 C6
Hesdin, *France* 19 B9
Heshan, *China* 58 F7
Heshui, *China* 56 G5
Heshun, *China* 56 F7
Hesperia, *U.S.A.* 117 L9
Hesse = Hessen □, *Germany* 24 E4
Hessen □, *Germany* 24 E4
Hestra, *Sweden* 11 G7
Hetch Hetchy Aqueduct, *U.S.A.* 116 H5
Hettinger, *U.S.A.* 112 C3
Hettstedt, *Germany* 24 D7
Heuvelton, *U.S.A.* 111 B9
Heves, *Hungary* 42 C5
Heves □, *Hungary* 42 C5
Hewitt, *U.S.A.* 113 K6
Hexham, *U.K.* 12 C5
Hexi, *Yunnan, China* 58 E4
Hexi, *Zhejiang, China* 59 D12
Hexigten Qi, *China* 57 C9
Heydarābād, *Iran* 71 D7
Heysham, *U.K.* 12 C5
Heyuan, *China* 59 F10
Heze, *China* 56 G8
Hezhang, *China* 58 D5
Hi Vista, *U.S.A.* 117 L9
Hialeah, *U.S.A.* 109 N5
Hiawatha, *U.S.A.* 112 F7
Hibbing, *U.S.A.* 112 B8
Hibbs B., *Australia* 94 G4
Hibernia Reef, *Australia* 92 B3
Hickman, *U.S.A.* 113 G10
Hickory, *U.S.A.* 109 H5
Hicks L., *Canada* 105 A9
Hicksville, *U.S.A.* 111 F11
Hida, *Romania* 43 C8
Hida-Gawa ➔, *Japan* 55 G8
Hida-Sammyaku, *Japan* 55 F8
Hidaka-Sammyaku, *Japan* 54 C11
Hidalgo, *Mexico* 119 C5
Hidalgo □, *Mexico* 119 C5
Hidalgo, Presa M., *Mexico* 118 B3
Hidalgo, Pta. del, *Canary Is.* . 37 F3
Hidalgo del Parral, *Mexico* ... 118 B3
Hiddensee, *Germany* 24 A9
Hieflau, *Austria* 26 D7
Hiendelaencina, *Spain* 32 D2
Hierro, *Canary Is.* 37 G1
Higashiajima-San, *Japan* 54 F10
Higashiōsaka, *Japan* 55 G7
Higgins, *U.S.A.* 113 G4
Higgins Corner, *U.S.A.* 116 F5
High Atlas = Haut Atlas,
   Morocco 78 B4
High Bridge, *U.S.A.* 111 F10
High Level, *Canada* 104 B5
High Point, *U.S.A.* 109 H6
High Prairie, *Canada* 104 B5
High River, *Canada* 104 C6
High Tatra = Tatry, *Slovak Rep.* 27 B13
High Veld, *Africa* 76 J6
High Wycombe, *U.K.* 13 F7
Highland □, *U.K.* 14 D4
Highland Park, *U.S.A.* 108 D2
Highmore, *U.S.A.* 112 C5
Highrock L., *Man., Canada* 105 B8
Highrock L., *Sask., Canada* ... 105 B7
Higüey, *Dom. Rep.* 121 C6
Hihya, *Egypt* 80 H7
Hiiumaa, *Estonia* 9 G20
Hijar, *Spain* 32 D4
Hijāz □, *Si. Arabia* 70 E3
Hijo = Tagum, *Phil.* 61 H6
Hikari, *Japan* 55 H5
Hikmak, Ras el, *Egypt* 80 A2
Hiko, *U.S.A.* 116 H11
Hikone, *Japan* 55 G8
Hikurangi, *N.Z.* 91 F5
Hikurangi, Mt., *N.Z.* 91 H6
Hildburghausen, *Germany* 24 E6
Hildesheim, *Germany* 24 C5
Hill ➔, *Australia* 93 F2
Hill City, *Idaho, U.S.A.* 114 E6
Hill City, *Kans., U.S.A.* 112 F5
Hill City, *S. Dak., U.S.A.* ... 112 D3
Hill Island L., *Canada* 105 A7
Hillared, *Sweden* 11 G7
Hillcrest Center, *U.S.A.* 117 K8
Hillegom, *Neths.* 17 B4
Hillerød, *Denmark* 11 J6
Hillerstorp, *Sweden* 11 G7
Hillsboro, *Kans., U.S.A.* 112 F6
Hillsboro, *N. Dak., U.S.A.* .. 112 B6
Hillsboro, *N.H., U.S.A.* 111 C13
Hillsboro, *Ohio, U.S.A.* 108 F4
Hillsboro, *Oreg., U.S.A.* 116 E4
Hillsboro, *Tex., U.S.A.* 113 J6
Hillsborough, *Grenada* 121 D7
Hillsdale, *Mich., U.S.A.* 108 E3
Hillsdale, *N.Y., U.S.A.* 111 D11

Hillsport, *Canada* 102 C2
Hilo, *U.S.A.* 106 J17
Hilton, *U.S.A.* 110 C7
Hilton Head Island, *U.S.A.* .. 109 J5
Hilvan, *Turkey* 73 D8
Hilversum, *Neths.* 17 B5
Himachal Pradesh □, *India* 68 D7
Himalaya, *Asia* 69 E11
Himamaylan, *Phil.* 61 F5
Himarë, *Albania* 40 F3
Himatnagar, *India* 66 H5
Himeji, *Japan* 55 G7
Himi, *Japan* 55 F8
Himmerland, *Denmark* 11 H3
Ḥimş, *Syria* 75 A5
Ḥimş □, *Syria* 75 A6
Hinche, *Haiti* 121 C5
Hinchinbrook I., *Australia* ... 94 B4
Hinckley, *U.K.* 13 E6
Hinckley, *U.S.A.* 112 B8
Hindaun, *India* 68 F7
Hindsholm, *Denmark* 11 J4
Hindu Bagh, *Pakistan* 68 D2
Hindu Kush, *Asia* 66 B7
Hindubagh, *Pakistan* 66 D5
Hindupur, *India* 66 N10
Hines Creek, *Canada* 104 B5
Hinesville, *U.S.A.* 109 K5
Hinganghat, *India* 66 J11
Hingham, *U.S.A.* 114 B8
Hingir, *India* 69 J10
Hingoli, *India* 66 K10
Hinigaran, *Phil.* 61 F5
Hinis, *Turkey* 73 C9
Hinna = Imi, *Ethiopia* 81 F5
Hinna, *Nigeria* 83 C7
Hinnerup, *Denmark* 11 H4
Hinnøya, *Norway* 8 B16
Hinojosa del Duque, *Spain* 35 G5
Hinsdale, *U.S.A.* 111 D12
Hinterrhein ➔, *Switz.* 25 J5
Hinton, *Canada* 104 C5
Hinton, *U.S.A.* 108 G5
Hınzır Burnu, *Turkey* 72 D6
Hirado, *Japan* 55 H4
Hirakud Dam, *India* 67 J13
Hiran ➔, *India* 69 H8
Hirapur, *India* 69 G8
Hiratsuka, *Japan* 55 G9
Hirfanlı Barajı, *Turkey* 72 C5
Hiroo, *Japan* 54 C11
Hirosaki, *Japan* 54 D10
Hiroshima, *Japan* 55 G6
Hiroshima □, *Japan* 55 G6
Hirson, *France* 19 C11
Hirtshals, *Denmark* 11 G3
Hisar, *India* 68 E6
Hisarcık, *Turkey* 39 B11
Hisaria, *Bulgaria* 41 D8
Hispaniola, *W. Indies* 121 C5
Ḥīt, *Iraq* 70 C4
Hita, *Japan* 55 H5
Hitachi, *Japan* 55 F10
Hitchin, *U.K.* 13 F7
Hitoyoshi, *Japan* 55 H5
Hitra, *Norway* 8 E13
Hitzacker, *Germany* 24 B7
Hixon, *Canada* 104 C4
Ḥiyyon, N. ➔, *Israel* 75 E4
Hjalmar L., *Canada* 105 A7
Hjälmaren, *Sweden* 10 E9
Hjältevad, *Sweden* 11 G9
Hjo, *Sweden* 11 F8
Hjørring, *Denmark* 11 G3
Hjortkvarn, *Sweden* 11 F9
Hkakabo Razi, *Burma* 67 E20
Hlinsko, *Czech Rep.* 26 B8
Hlobane, *S. Africa* 89 D5
Hlohovec, *Slovak Rep.* 27 C10
Hlučín, *Czech Rep.* 27 B11
Hluhluwe, *S. Africa* 89 D5
Hlukhiv, *Ukraine* 47 G7
Hlyboka, *Ukraine* 47 H3
Hlybokaye, *Belarus* 46 E4
Hnúšt'a, *Slovak Rep.* 27 C12
Ho, *Ghana* 83 D5
Ho Chi Minh City = Thanh Pho
   Ho Chi Minh, *Vietnam* 65 G6
Ho Thuong, *Vietnam* 64 C5
Hoa Binh, *Vietnam* 58 G5
Hoa Da, *Vietnam* 65 G7
Hoa Hiep, *Vietnam* 65 G5
Hoai Nhon, *Vietnam* 64 E7
Hoang Lien Son, *Vietnam* 58 F4
Hoanib ➔, *Namibia* 88 B2
Hoare B., *Canada* 101 B13
Hoarusib ➔, *Namibia* 88 B2
Hobart, *Australia* 94 G4
Hobart, *U.S.A.* 113 H5
Hobbs, *U.S.A.* 113 J3
Hobbs Coast, *Antarctica* 5 D14
Hobe Sound, *U.S.A.* 109 M5
Hoboken, *U.S.A.* 111 F10
Hobro, *Denmark* 11 H3
Hoburgen, *Sweden* 11 H12
Hocalar, *Turkey* 39 C11
Hochfeld, *Namibia* 88 C2
Hochschwab, *Austria* 26 D8
Hockenheim, *Germany* 25 F4
Hodaka-Dake, *Japan* 55 F8
Hodgeville, *Canada* 105 C7
Hodgson, *Canada* 105 C9
Hódmezővásárhely, *Hungary* ... 42 D5

Hodna, Chott el, *Algeria* 78 A6
Hodonín, *Czech Rep.* 27 C10
Hoeamdong, *N. Korea* 57 C16
Hœdic, Î. de, *France* 18 E4
Hoek van Holland, *Neths.* 17 C4
Hoengsŏng, *S. Korea* 57 F14
Hoeryong, *N. Korea* 57 C15
Hoeyang, *N. Korea* 57 E14
Hof, *Germany* 25 E7
Hofgeismar, *Germany* 24 D5
Hofheim, *Germany* 25 E4
Hofmeyr, *S. Africa* 88 E4
Höfn, *Iceland* 8 D6
Hofors, *Sweden* 10 D10
Hofsjökull, *Iceland* 8 D4
Hōfu, *Japan* 55 G5
Hogan Group, *Australia* 95 F4
Hogarth, Mt., *Australia* 94 C2
Hoggar = Ahaggar, *Algeria* ... 78 D7
Högsäter, *Sweden* 11 F6
Högsby, *Sweden* 11 G10
Högsjö, *Sweden* 10 E9
Hogsty Reef, *Bahamas* 121 B5
Hoh ➔, *U.S.A.* 116 C2
Hohe Acht, *Germany* 25 E3
Hohe Tauern, *Austria* 26 D5
Hohe Venn, *Belgium* 17 D6
Hohenau, *Austria* 27 C9
Hohenems, *Austria* 26 D2
Hohenloher Ebene, *Germany* ... 25 F5
Hohenwald, *U.S.A.* 109 H2
Hohenwestedt, *Germany* 24 A5
Hoher Rhön = Rhön, *Germany* .. 24 E5
Hohhot, *China* 56 D6
Hóhlakas, *Greece* 36 D9
Hohoe, *Ghana* 83 D5
Hoi An, *Vietnam* 64 E7
Hoi Xuan, *Vietnam* 58 G5
Hoisington, *U.S.A.* 112 F5
Højer, *Denmark* 11 K2
Hōjō, *Japan* 55 H6
Hok, *Sweden* 11 G8
Hökensås, *Sweden* 11 G8
Hokianga Harbour, *N.Z.* 91 F4
Hokitika, *N.Z.* 91 K3
Hokkaidō □, *Japan* 54 C11
Hol-Hol, *Djibouti* 81 E5
Hola Pristan, *Ukraine* 47 J7
Holbæk, *Denmark* 11 J5
Holbrook, *U.S.A.* 115 J8
Holden, *U.S.A.* 114 G7
Holdenville, *U.S.A.* 113 H6
Holdrege, *U.S.A.* 112 E5
Holešov, *Czech Rep.* 27 B10
Holguín, *Cuba* 120 B4
Holíč, *Slovak Rep.* 27 C10
Holice, *Czech Rep.* 26 A8
Höljes, *Sweden* 10 D6
Hollabrunn, *Austria* 26 C9
Hollams Bird I., *Namibia* 88 C1
Holland, *Mich., U.S.A.* 108 D2
Holland, *N.Y., U.S.A.* 110 D6
Hollandale, *U.S.A.* 113 J9
Hollandia = Jayapura, *Indonesia* 63 E10
Holley, *U.S.A.* 110 C6
Hollfeld, *Germany* 25 F7
Hollidaysburg, *U.S.A.* 110 F6
Hollis, *U.S.A.* 113 H5
Hollister, *Calif., U.S.A.* ... 116 J5
Hollister, *Idaho, U.S.A.* 114 E6
Höllviken = Höllviksnäs, *Sweden* 11 J6
Höllviksnäs, *Sweden* 11 J6
Holly Hill, *U.S.A.* 109 L5
Holly Springs, *U.S.A.* 113 H10
Hollywood, *U.S.A.* 109 N5
Holman, *Canada* 100 A8
Hólmavík, *Iceland* 8 D3
Holmen, *U.S.A.* 112 D9
Holmes Reefs, *Australia* 94 B4
Holmsjön, *Västernorrland,
   Sweden* 10 B10
Holmsjön, *Västernorrland,
   Sweden* 10 B9
Holmsland Klit, *Denmark* 11 J2
Holmsund, *Sweden* 8 E19
Holod, *Romania* 42 D7
Holroyd ➔, *Australia* 94 A3
Holstebro, *Denmark* 11 H2
Holsworthy, *U.K.* 13 G3
Holton, *Canada* 103 B8
Holton, *U.S.A.* 112 F7
Holtville, *U.S.A.* 117 N11
Holwerd, *Neths.* 17 A5
Holy I., *Angl., U.K.* 12 D3
Holy I., *Northumb., U.K.* 12 B6
Holyhead, *U.K.* 12 D3
Holyoke, *Colo., U.S.A.* 112 E3
Holyoke, *Mass., U.S.A.* 111 D12
Holyrood, *Canada* 103 C9
Holzkirchen, *Germany* 25 H7
Holzminden, *Germany* 24 D5
Homa Bay, *Kenya* 86 C3
Homalin, *Burma* 67 G19
Homand, *Iran* 71 C8
Homathko ➔, *Canada* 104 C4
Hombori, *Mali* 83 B4
Homburg, *Germany* 25 F3
Home B., *Canada* 101 B13
Home Hill, *Australia* 94 B4
Homedale, *U.S.A.* 114 E5
Homer, *Alaska, U.S.A.* 100 C4
Homer, *La., U.S.A.* 113 J8

Homer City, *U.S.A.* 110 F5
Homestead, *Australia* 94 C4
Homestead, *U.S.A.* 109 N5
Homewood, *U.S.A.* 116 F6
Homoine, *Mozam.* 89 C6
Homoljske Planina, *Serbia, Yug.* 40 B5
Homorod, *Romania* 43 D10
Homs = Ḥimş, *Syria* 75 A5
Homyel, *Belarus* 47 F6
Hon Chong, *Vietnam* 65 G5
Hon Me, *Vietnam* 64 C5
Honan = Henan □, *China* 56 H8
Honaz, *Turkey* 39 D11
Honbetsu, *Japan* 54 C11
Honcut, *U.S.A.* 116 F5
Honda Bay, *Phil.* 61 G3
Hondarribia, *Spain* 32 B3
Hondeklipbaai, *S. Africa* 88 E2
Hondo, *Japan* 55 H5
Hondo, *U.S.A.* 113 L5
Hondo ➔, *Belize* 119 D7
Honduras ■, *Cent. Amer.* 120 D2
Honduras, G. de, *Caribbean* .. 120 C2
Hønefoss, *Norway* 9 F14
Honesdale, *U.S.A.* 111 E9
Honey L., *U.S.A.* 116 E6
Honfleur, *France* 18 C7
Høng, *Denmark* 11 J5
Hong ➔, *Vietnam* 58 F5
Hong Gai, *Vietnam* 58 G6
Hong He ➔, *China* 56 H8
Hong Hu, *China* 59 C9
Hong Kong □, *China* 59 F10
Hong'an, *China* 59 B10
Hongch'ŏn, *S. Korea* 57 F14
Honghai Wan, *China* 59 F10
Honghe, *China* 58 F4
Hongjiang, *China* 58 D7
Honglu He ➔, *China* 56 F5
Hongor, *Mongolia* 56 B7
Hongsa, *Laos* 64 C3
Hongshui He ➔, *China* 58 F7
Hongsŏng, *S. Korea* 57 F14
Hongtong, *China* 56 F6
Honguedo, Détroit d', *Canada* . 103 C7
Hongwon, *N. Korea* 57 E14
Hongya, *China* 58 C4
Hongyuan, *China* 58 A4
Hongze Hu, *China* 57 H10
Honiara, *Solomon Is.* 96 H7
Honiton, *U.K.* 13 G4
Honjō, *Japan* 54 E10
Honkorâb, Ras, *Egypt* 80 C4
Honningsvåg, *Norway* 8 A21
Hönö, *Sweden* 11 G5
Honolulu, *U.S.A.* 106 H16
Hontoria del Pinar, *Spain* 32 D1
Hood, Mt., *U.S.A.* 114 D3
Hood, Pt., *Australia* 93 F2
Hood River, *U.S.A.* 114 D3
Hoodsport, *U.S.A.* 116 C3
Hooge, *Germany* 24 A4
Hoogeveen, *Neths.* 17 B6
Hoogezand-Sappemeer, *Neths.* . 17 A6
Hooghly = Hugli ➔, *India* 69 J13
Hooghly-Chinsura = Chunchura,
   India 69 H13
Hook Hd., *Ireland* 15 D5
Hook I., *Australia* 94 C4
Hook of Holland = Hoek van
   Holland, *Neths.* 17 C4
Hooker, *U.S.A.* 113 G4
Hooker Creek, *Australia* 92 C5
Hoonah, *U.S.A.* 104 B1
Hooper Bay, *U.S.A.* 100 B3
Hoopstad, *S. Africa* 88 D4
Höör, *Sweden* 11 J7
Hoorn, *Neths.* 17 B5
Hoover, *U.S.A.* 109 J2
Hoover Dam, *U.S.A.* 117 K12
Hooversville, *U.S.A.* 110 F6
Hop Bottom, *U.S.A.* 111 E9
Hopa, *Turkey* 73 B9
Hope, *Canada* 104 D4
Hope, *Ariz., U.S.A.* 117 M13
Hope, *Ark., U.S.A.* 113 J8
Hope, *S. Austral., Australia* . 95 D2
Hope, L., *W. Austral., Australia* 93 F3
Hope I., *Canada* 110 B4
Hope Town, *Bahamas* 120 A4
Hopedale, *Canada* 103 A7
Hopedale, *U.S.A.* 111 D13
Hopefield, *S. Africa* 88 E2
Hopei = Hebei □, *China* 56 E9
Hopelchén, *Mexico* 119 D7
Hopetoun, *Australia* 93 F3
Hopetown, *S. Africa* 88 D3
Hopevale, *Australia* 94 B4
Hopewell, *U.S.A.* 108 G7
Hopfgarten, *Austria* 26 D5
Hopkins, L., *Australia* 92 D4
Hopkinsville, *U.S.A.* 109 G2
Hopland, *U.S.A.* 116 G3
Hoquiam, *U.S.A.* 116 D3
Horasan, *Turkey* 73 B10
Horaždovice, *Czech Rep.* 26 B6
Horb, *Germany* 25 G4
Hörby, *Sweden* 11 J7
Horcajo de Santiago, *Spain* ... 32 F1
Horden Hills, *Australia* 92 D5
Horezu, *Romania* 43 E8
Horgen, *Switz.* 25 H4
Horgoš, *Serbia, Yug.* 42 D4
Hořice, *Czech Rep.* 26 A8

Horinger, China 56 D6
Horki, Belarus 46 E6
Horlick Mts., Antarctica 5 E15
Horlivka, Ukraine 47 H10
Hormak, Iran 71 D9
Hormoz, Iran 71 E7
Hormoz, Jaz.-ye, Iran 71 E8
Hormozgān □, Iran 71 E8
Hormoz, Kūh-e, Iran 71 E7
Hormuz, Str. of, The Gulf 71 E8
Horn, Austria 26 C8
Horn, Iceland 8 C2
Horn, Sweden 11 G9
Horn ➤, Canada 104 A5
Horn, Cape = Hornos, C. de,
  Chile 122 J4
Horn Head, Ireland 15 A3
Horn I., Australia 94 A3
Horn Mts., Canada 104 A5
Hornachuelos, Spain 35 H5
Hornavan, Sweden 8 C17
Hornbeck, U.S.A. 113 K8
Hornbrook, U.S.A. 114 F2
Hornburg, Germany 24 C6
Horncastle, U.K. 12 D7
Horndal, Sweden 10 D10
Hornell, U.S.A. 110 D7
Hornell L., Canada 104 A5
Hornepayne, Canada 102 C3
Horní Planá, Czech Rep. 26 C7
Hornings Mills, Canada 110 B4
Hornitos, U.S.A. 116 H6
Hornos, C. de, Chile 122 J4
Hornoy-le-Bourg, France 19 C8
Hornsea, U.K. 12 D7
Hornslandet, Sweden 10 C11
Hörnum, Germany 24 A4
Horobetsu, Japan 54 C10
Horodenka, Ukraine 47 H3
Horodnya, Ukraine 47 G6
Horodok, Khmelnytskyy,
  Ukraine 47 H4
Horodok, Lviv, Ukraine 47 H2
Horodyshche, Ukraine 47 H6
Horokhiv, Ukraine 47 G3
Horovice, Czech Rep. 26 B6
Horqin Youyi Qianqi, China . 57 A12
Horqueta, Paraguay 126 A4
Horred, Sweden 11 G6
Horse Creek, U.S.A. 112 E3
Horse Is., Canada 103 B8
Horsefly L., Canada 104 C4
Horseheads, U.S.A. 110 D8
Horsens, Denmark 11 J3
Horsham, Australia 95 F3
Horsham, U.K. 13 F7
Horšovský Týn, Czech Rep. .. 26 B5
Horten, Norway 9 G14
Hortobágy ➤, Hungary 42 C6
Horton, U.S.A. 112 F7
Horton ➤, Canada 100 B7
Horwood L., Canada 102 C3
Hosaina, Ethiopia 81 F4
Hose, Gunung-Gunung,
  Malaysia 62 D4
Ḩoseynābād, Khuzestān, Iran .. 71 C6
Ḩoseynābād, Kordestān, Iran .. 70 C5
Hoshangabad, India 68 H7
Hoshiarpur, India 68 D6
Hospet, India 66 M10
Hoste, I., Chile 128 H3
Hostens, France 20 D3
Hot, Thailand 64 C2
Hot Creek Range, U.S.A. ... 114 G6
Hot Springs, Ark., U.S.A. .. 113 H8
Hot Springs, S. Dak., U.S.A. . 112 D3
Hotagen, Sweden 8 E16
Hotan, China 60 C2
Hotazel, S. Africa 88 D3
Hotchkiss, U.S.A. 115 G10
Hotham, C., Australia 92 B5
Hoting, Sweden 8 D17
Hotolisht, Albania 40 E4
Hotte, Massif de la, Haiti 121 C5
Hottentotsbaai, Namibia 88 D1
Houat, Î. de, France 18 E4
Houdan, France 19 D8
Houei Sai, Laos 58 G3
Houeillès, France 20 D4
Houffalize, Belgium 17 D5
Houghton, Mich., U.S.A. ... 112 B10
Houghton, N.Y., U.S.A. 110 D6
Houghton L., U.S.A. 108 C3
Houhora Heads, N.Z. 91 F4
Houlton, U.S.A. 109 B12
Houma, U.S.A. 113 L9
Houndé, Burkina Faso 82 C4
Hourtin, France 20 C2
Hourtin-Carcans, Étang d',
  France 20 C2
Housatonic ➤, U.S.A. 111 E11
Houston, Canada 104 C3
Houston, Mo., U.S.A. 113 G9
Houston, Tex., U.S.A. 113 L7
Hout ➤, S. Africa 89 C4
Houtkraal, S. Africa 88 E3
Houtman Abrolhos, Australia . 93 E1
Hovd, Mongolia 60 B4
Hove, U.K. 13 G7
Hoveyzeh, Iran 71 D6
Hovmantorp, Sweden 11 H9
Hövsgöl, Mongolia 56 C5
Hövsgöl Nuur, Mongolia ... 60 A5
Hovsta, Sweden 10 E9
Howakil, Eritrea 81 D5
Howar, Wadi ➤, Sudan 81 D2
Howard, Australia 95 D5

Howard, Pa., U.S.A. 110 F7
Howard, S. Dak., U.S.A. 112 C6
Howe, U.S.A. 114 E7
Howe I., Canada 111 B8
Howell, U.S.A. 108 D4
Howick, Canada 111 A11
Howick, S. Africa 89 D5
Howick Group, Australia ... 94 A4
Howitt, L., Australia 95 D2
Howland I., Pac. Oc. 96 G10
Howrah = Haora, India 69 H13
Howth Hd., Ireland 15 C5
Höxter, Germany 24 D5
Hoy, U.K. 14 C5
Hoya, Germany 24 C5
Høyanger, Norway 9 F12
Hoyerswerda, Germany 24 D10
Hoylake, U.K. 12 D4
Hoyos, Spain 34 E4
Hpa-an = Pa-an, Burma 67 L20
Hpungan Pass, Burma 67 F20
Hradec Králové, Czech Rep. .. 26 A8
Hrádek, Czech Rep. 27 C9
Hranice, Czech Rep. 27 B10
Hrazdan, Armenia 49 K7
Hrebenka, Ukraine 47 G7
Hrodna, Belarus 46 F2
Hrodzyanka, Belarus 46 F5
Hron ➤, Slovak Rep. 27 D11
Hrubieszów, Poland 45 H10
Hrubý Jeseník, Czech Rep. .. 27 A10
Hrvatska = Croatia ■, Europe . 29 C13
Hrymayliv, Ukraine 47 H4
Hsenwi, Burma 67 H20
Hsiamen = Xiamen, China .. 59 E12
Hsian = Xi'an, China 56 G5
Hsinchu, Taiwan 59 E13
Hsinhailien = Lianyungang,
  China 57 G10
Hsinying, Taiwan 59 F13
Hsopket, Burma 58 F2
Hsüchou = Xuzhou, China .. 57 G9
Hu Xian, China 56 G5
Hua Hin, Thailand 64 F2
Hua Xian, Henan, China ... 56 G8
Hua Xian, Shaanxi, China .. 56 G5
Hua'an, China 59 E11
Huab ➤, Namibia 88 B2
Huacheng, China 59 E10
Huachinera, Mexico 118 A3
Huacho, Peru 124 F3
Huade, China 56 D7
Huadian, China 57 C14
Huadu, China 59 F9
Huai He ➤, China 59 A12
Huai Yot, Thailand 65 J2
Huai'an, Hebei, China 56 D8
Huai'an, Jiangsu, China ... 57 H10
Huaibei, China 56 G9
Huaibin, China 59 A10
Huaide = Gongzhuling, China . 57 C13
Huaidezhen, China 57 C13
Huaihua, China 58 D7
Huaiji, China 59 F9
Huainan, China 59 A11
Huairen, China 56 E7
Huairou, China 56 D9
Huaiyang, China 56 H8
Huaiyin, China 57 H10
Huaiyuan, Anhui, China ... 57 H9
Huaiyuan, Guangxi Zhuangzu,
  China 58 E7
Huajianzi, China 57 D13
Huajuapan de Leon, Mexico .. 119 D5
Hualapai Peak, U.S.A. 115 J7
Hualien, Taiwan 59 E13
Huallaga ➤, Peru 124 E3
Huambo, Angola 85 G3
Huan Jiang ➤, China 56 G5
Huan Xian, China 56 F4
Huancabamba, Peru 124 E3
Huancane, Peru 124 G5
Huancavelica, Peru 124 F3
Huancayo, Peru 124 F3
Huanchaca, Bolivia 124 H5
Huang Hai = Yellow Sea, China 57 G12
Huang He ➤, China 57 F10
Huang Xian, China 57 F11
Huangchuan, China 59 A10
Huanggang, China 59 B10
Huangguoshu, China 58 E5
Huangling, China 56 G5
Huanglong, China 56 G5
Huanglongtan, China 59 A8
Huangmei, China 59 B10
Huangpi, China 59 B10
Huangping, China 59 C12
Huangshan, China 59 C12
Huangshi, China 59 B10
Huangsongdian, China 57 C14
Huangyan, China 59 C13
Huangyangsi, China 59 D8
Huanjiang, China 58 E7
Huantai, China 57 F9
Huánuco, Peru 124 E3
Huaping, China 58 D3
Huaraz, Peru 124 E3
Huarmey, Peru 124 F3
Huarong, China 59 C9
Huascarán, Peru 122 D3
Huasco, Chile 126 B1
Huasco ➤, Chile 126 B1
Huasna, U.S.A. 117 K6
Huatabampo, Mexico 118 B3

Huauchinango, Mexico 119 C5
Huautla de Jiménez, Mexico .. 119 D5
Huaxi, China 58 D6
Huay Namota, Mexico 118 C4
Huayin, China 56 G6
Huayuan, China 58 C7
Huayun, China 58 B6
Huazhou, China 59 G8
Hubbard, Ohio, U.S.A. 110 E4
Hubbard, Tex., U.S.A. 113 K6
Hubbart Pt., Canada 105 B10
Hubei □, China 59 B9
Huch'ang, N. Korea 57 D14
Hucknall, U.K. 12 D6
Huddersfield, U.K. 12 D6
Hude, Germany 24 B4
Hudi, Sudan 80 D3
Hudiksvall, Sweden 10 C11
Hudson, Canada 102 B1
Hudson, Mass., U.S.A. 111 D13
Hudson, N.Y., U.S.A. 111 D11
Hudson, Wis., U.S.A. 112 C8
Hudson, Wyo., U.S.A. 114 E9
Hudson ➤, U.S.A. 111 F10
Hudson Bay, Nunavut, Canada . 101 C11
Hudson Bay, Sask., Canada .. 105 C8
Hudson Falls, U.S.A. 111 C11
Hudson Mts., Antarctica ... 5 D16
Hudson Str., Canada 101 B13
Hudson's Hope, Canada ... 104 B4
Hue, Vietnam 64 D6
Huebra ➤, Spain 34 D4
Huedin, Romania 42 D8
Huehuetenango, Guatemala . 120 C1
Huejúcar, Mexico 118 C4
Huélamo, Spain 32 E3
Huelgoat, France 18 D3
Huelma, Spain 35 H7
Huelva, Spain 35 H4
Huelva □, Spain 35 H4
Huelva ➤, Spain 35 H5
Huentelauquén, Chile 126 C1
Huércal-Overa, Spain 33 H3
Huerta, Sa. de la, Argentina . 126 C2
Huertas, C. de las, Spain ... 33 G4
Huerva ➤, Spain 32 D4
Huesca, Spain 32 C4
Huesca □, Spain 32 C5
Huéscar, Spain 33 H2
Huetamo, Mexico 118 D4
Huete, Spain 32 E2
Hugh ➤, Australia 94 D1
Hughenden, Australia 94 C3
Hughes, Australia 93 F4
Hughesville, U.S.A. 111 E8
Hugli ➤, India 69 J13
Hugo, Colo., U.S.A. 112 F3
Hugo, Okla., U.S.A. 113 H7
Hugoton, U.S.A. 113 G4
Hui Xian = Huixian, China .. 56 G7
Hui Xian, China 56 H4
Hui'an, China 59 E12
Hui'anbu, China 56 F4
Huichang, China 59 E10
Huichapán, Mexico 119 C5
Huidong, Guangdong, China . 59 F10
Huidong, Sichuan, China .. 58 D4
Huifa He ➤, China 57 C14
Huila, Nevado del, Colombia . 124 C3
Huilai, China 59 F11
Huili, China 58 D4
Huimin, China 57 F9
Huinan, China 57 C14
Huinca Renancó, Argentina .. 126 C3
Huining, China 56 G3
Huinong, China 56 E4
Huisache, Mexico 118 C4
Huishui, China 58 D6
Huisne ➤, France 18 E7
Huiting, China 56 G9
Huitong, China 58 D7
Huixian, China 56 G7
Huixtla, Mexico 119 D6
Huize, China 58 D4
Huizhou, China 59 F10
Hukawng Valley, Burma ... 67 F20
Hukou, China 59 C11
Hukuntsi, Botswana 88 C3
Hulayfā', Si. Arabia 70 E4
Huld = Ulaanjirem, Mongolia . 56 B3
Hulin He ➤, China 57 B12
Hull = Kingston upon Hull, U.K. 12 D7
Hull, Canada 102 C4
Hull ➤, U.K. 12 D7
Hulst, Neths. 17 C4
Hultsfred, Sweden 11 G9
Hulun Nur, China 60 B6
Hulyaypole, Ukraine 47 J9
Humahuaca, Argentina ... 126 A2
Humaitá, Brazil 124 E6
Humaitá, Paraguay 126 B4
Humansdorp, S. Africa ... 88 E3
Humara, J., Sudan 81 D3
Humbe, Angola 88 B1
Humber ➤, U.K. 12 D7
Humboldt, Canada 105 C7
Humboldt, Iowa, U.S.A. ... 112 D7
Humboldt, Tenn., U.S.A. .. 113 H10
Humboldt ➤, U.S.A. 114 F4
Humboldt Gletscher, Greenland 4 B4
Hume, U.S.A. 116 J8
Humenné, Slovak Rep. ... 27 C14
Hummelsta, Sweden 10 E10
Humphreys, Mt., U.S.A. .. 116 H8
Humphreys Peak, U.S.A. .. 115 J8
Humpolec, Czech Rep. ... 26 B8

Humptulips, U.S.A. 116 C3
Hūn, Libya 79 C9
Hun Jiang ➤, China 57 D13
Húnaflói, Iceland 8 D3
Hunan □, China 59 D9
Hunchun, China 57 C16
Hundested, Denmark 11 J5
Hundewali, Pakistan 68 D5
Hundred Mile House, Canada . 104 C4
Hunedoara, Romania 42 E7
Hunedoara □, Romania ... 42 E7
Hünfeld, Germany 24 E5
Hung Yen, Vietnam 58 G6
Hungary ■, Europe 27 D12
Hungary, Plain of, Europe ... 6 F10
Hungerford, Australia 95 D3
Hüngnam, N. Korea 57 E14
Hungt'ou Hsü, Taiwan ... 59 G13
Huni Valley, Ghana 82 D4
Hunneberg, Sweden 11 F6
Hunnebostrand, Sweden .. 11 F5
Hunsberge, Namibia 88 D2
Hunsrück, Germany 25 F3
Hunstanton, U.K. 12 E8
Hunte ➤, Germany 24 B4
Hunter, U.S.A. 111 D10
Hunter I., Australia 94 G3
Hunter I., Canada 104 C3
Hunters Road, Zimbabwe .. 87 F2
Hunterville, N.Z. 91 H5
Huntingburg, U.S.A. 108 F2
Huntingdon, Canada 102 C5
Huntingdon, U.K. 13 E7
Huntingdon, U.S.A. 110 F6
Huntington, Ind., U.S.A. .. 108 E3
Huntington, Oreg., U.S.A. . 114 D5
Huntington, Utah, U.S.A. .. 114 G8
Huntington, W. Va., U.S.A. . 108 F4
Huntington Beach, U.S.A. .. 117 M9
Huntington Station, U.S.A. . 111 F11
Huntly, N.Z. 91 G5
Huntly, U.K. 14 D6
Huntsville, Canada 102 C4
Huntsville, Ala., U.S.A. ... 109 H2
Huntsville, Tex., U.S.A. .. 113 K7
Hunyani ➤, Zimbabwe ... 87 F3
Hunyuan, China 56 E7
Hunza ➤, India 69 B6
Huo Xian = Huozhou, China . 56 F6
Huochang, China 56 F6
Huong Hoa, Vietnam 64 D6
Huong Khe, Vietnam 64 C5
Huonville, Australia 94 G4
Huoqiu, China 59 A11
Huoshan, Anhui, China .. 59 A12
Huoshan, Anhui, China .. 59 B11
Huoshao Dao = Lü-Tao, Taiwan 59 F13
Huozhou, China 56 F6
Hupeh = Hubei □, China .. 59 B9
Ḩūr, Iran 71 D8
Hurbanovo, Slovak Rep. ... 27 D11
Hurd, C., Canada 110 A3
Hure Qi, China 57 C11
Hurezani, Romania 43 F8
Hurghada, Egypt 80 B3
Hurley, N. Mex., U.S.A. .. 115 K9
Hurley, Wis., U.S.A. 112 B9
Huron, Calif., U.S.A. 116 J6
Huron, Ohio, U.S.A. 110 E2
Huron, S. Dak., U.S.A. ... 112 C5
Huron, L., U.S.A. 110 B2
Hurricane, U.S.A. 115 H7
Hurso, Ethiopia 81 F5
Hurunui ➤, N.Z. 91 K4
Hurup, Denmark 11 H2
Húsavík, Iceland 8 C5
Huşi, Romania 43 D13
Huskvarna, Sweden 11 G8
Hustadvika, Norway 8 E12
Hustontown, U.S.A. 110 F6
Husum, Germany 24 A5
Husum, Sweden 10 A13
Hutchinson, Kans., U.S.A. . 113 F6
Hutchinson, Minn., U.S.A. . 112 C7
Hutte Sauvage, L. de la, Canada 103 A7
Hüttenberg, Austria 26 E7
Hutton, Mt., Australia ... 95 D4
Huwun, Ethiopia 81 G5
Huy, Belgium 17 D5
Huzhou, China 59 B13
Hvalpsund, Denmark ... 11 H3
Hvammstangi, Iceland .. 8 D3
Hvar, Croatia 29 E13
Hvarski Kanal, Croatia .. 29 E13
Hvítá ➤, Iceland 8 D3
Hwachŏn-chŏsuji, S. Korea . 57 E14
Hwang Ho = Huang He ➤,
  China 57 F10
Hwange, Zimbabwe ... 87 F2
Hwange Nat. Park, Zimbabwe . 88 B4
Hyannis, Mass., U.S.A. .. 108 E10
Hyannis, Nebr., U.S.A. ... 112 E4
Hyargas Nuur, Mongolia .. 60 B4
Hybo, Sweden 10 C10
Hyde Park, U.S.A. 111 E11
Hyden, Australia 93 F2
Hyderabad, India 66 L11
Hyderabad, Pakistan ... 68 G3
Hyères, France 21 E10
Hyères, Îs. d', France ... 21 F10
Hyesan, N. Korea 57 D15
Hyland ➤, Canada 104 B3
Hyltebruk, Sweden 11 H7
Hymia, India 69 C8

Hyndman Peak, U.S.A. 114 E6
Hyōgo □, Japan 55 G7
Hyrum, U.S.A. 114 F8
Hysham, U.S.A. 114 C10
Hythe, U.K. 13 F9
Hyūga, Japan 55 H5
Hyvinge = Hyvinkää, Finland .. 9 F21
Hyvinkää, Finland 9 F21

I

I-n-Gall, Niger 83 B6
I-n-Oudad, Algeria 83 A5
I-n-Ouzzal, Algeria 83 A5
I-n-Tadreft, Niger 83 B6
Iablaniţa, Romania 42 F7
Iaco ➤, Brazil 124 E5
Iacobeni, Romania 43 C10
Iakora, Madag. 89 C8
Ialomiţa □, Romania 43 F12
Ialomiţa ➤, Romania 43 F12
Ialoveni, Moldova 43 D13
Ialpug ➤, Moldova 43 E13
Ianca, Romania 43 E12
Iara, Romania 43 D8
Iarda, Ethiopia 81 E4
Iargara, Moldova 43 D13
Iaşi, Romania 43 C12
Iaşi □, Romania 43 C12
Íasmos, Greece 41 E9
Ib ➤, India 69 J10
Iba, Phil. 61 D3
Ibadan, Nigeria 83 D5
Ibagué, Colombia 124 C3
Iballë, Albania 40 D4
Ibănești, Botoşani, Romania ... 43 B11
Ibănești, Mureş, Romania .. 43 D9
Ibar ➤, Serbia, Yug. 40 C4
Ibaraki □, Japan 55 F10
Ibarra, Ecuador 124 C3
Ibba, Sudan 81 G2
Ibba, Bahr el ➤, Sudan ... 81 F2
Ibbenbüren, Germany ... 24 C3
Ibembo, Dem. Rep. of the Congo 86 B1
Ibera, L., Argentina 126 B4
Iberian Peninsula, Europe ... 6 H5
Iberville, Canada 102 C5
Iberville, Lac d', Canada .. 102 A5
Ibi, Nigeria 83 D6
Ibi, Spain 33 G4
Ibiá, Brazil 125 G9
Ibiapaba, Sa. da, Brazil ... 125 D10
Ibicuí ➤, Brazil 127 B4
Ibicuy, Argentina 126 C4
Ibiza = Eivissa, Spain 37 C7
Iblei, Monti, Italy 31 E7
Ibo, Mozam. 87 E5
Ibonma, Indonesia 63 E8
Ibotirama, Brazil 125 F10
Ibrāhīm ➤, Lebanon 75 A4
'Ibrī, Oman 71 F8
Ibriktepe, Turkey 41 E10
Ibshawâi, Egypt 80 J7
Ibu, Indonesia 63 D7
Ibusuki, Japan 55 J5
Ica, Peru 124 F3
Iça ➤, Brazil 124 D5
Içana, Brazil 124 C5
Içana ➤, Brazil 124 C5
İçel = Mersin, Turkey 70 B2
Iceland ■, Europe 8 D4
Ich'ang = Yichang, China .. 59 B8
Ichchapuram, India 67 K14
Ichhawar, India 68 H7
Ichihara, Japan 55 G10
Ichikawa, Japan 55 G9
Ichilo ➤, Bolivia 124 G6
Ichinohe, Japan 54 D10
Ichinomiya, Japan 55 G8
Ichinoseki, Japan 54 E10
Ichnya, Ukraine 47 G7
Icod, Canary Is. 37 F3
Ida Grove, U.S.A. 112 D7
Idabel, U.S.A. 113 J7
Idaga Hamus, Ethiopia ... 81 E4
Idah, Nigeria 83 D6
Idaho □, U.S.A. 114 D7
Idaho City, U.S.A. 114 E6
Idaho Falls, U.S.A. 114 E7
Idanha-a-Nova, Portugal .. 34 F3
Idar-Oberstein, Germany .. 25 F3
Idfû, Egypt 80 C3
Ídhi Óros, Greece 36 D6
Ídhra, Greece 38 D5
Idi, Indonesia 62 C1
Idiofa, Dem. Rep. of the Congo 84 E3
Idku, Bahra el, Egypt 80 H7
Idlib, Syria 70 C3
Idre, Sweden 10 C6
Idria, U.S.A. 116 J6
Idrija, Slovenia 29 C11
Idritsa, Russia 46 D5
Idutywa, S. Africa 89 E4
Ieper, Belgium 17 D2
Ierápetra, Greece 36 E7
Ierissós, Greece 40 F7
Ierissoú Kólpos, Greece ... 40 F7
Iernut, Romania 43 D9
Iesi, Italy 29 E10
Iésolo, Italy 29 C9
Ifach, Peñón de, Spain ... 33 G5
Ifakara, Tanzania 84 F7
'Ifāl, W. al ➤, Si. Arabia .. 70 D2

165

Ifanadiana, *Madag.* 89 C8
Ife, *Nigeria* 83 D5
Iférouâne, *Niger* 83 B6
Iffley, *Australia* 94 B3
Ifon, *Nigeria* 83 D6
Iforas, Adrar des, *Africa* 83 B5
Ifould, L., *Australia* 93 F5
Iganga, *Uganda* 86 B3
Igarapava, *Brazil* 125 H9
Igarka, *Russia* 50 C9
Igatimi, *Paraguay* 127 A4
Igbetti, *Nigeria* 83 D5
Igbo-Ora, *Nigeria* 83 D5
Igboho, *Nigeria* 83 D5
Igbor, *Nigeria* 83 D6
Iğdır, *Turkey* 73 C11
Igelfors, *Sweden* 11 F9
Iggesund, *Sweden* 10 C11
Iglésias, *Italy* 30 C1
Igloolik, *Canada* 101 B11
Igluligaarjuk, *Canada* 101 B10
Iglulik = Igloolik, *Canada* 101 B11
'Igma, Gebel el, *Egypt* 80 B3
Ignace, *Canada* 102 C1
Iğneada, *Turkey* 41 E11
Iğneada Burnu, *Turkey* 41 E12
Igoumenítsa, *Greece* 38 B2
Igra, *Russia* 48 B11
Iguaçu →, *Brazil* 127 B5
Iguaçu, Cat. del, *Brazil* 127 B5
Iguaçu Falls = Iguaçu, Cat. del, *Brazil* 127 B5
Iguala, *Mexico* 119 D5
Igualada, *Spain* 32 D6
Iguassu = Iguaçu →, *Brazil* 127 B5
Iguatu, *Brazil* 125 E11
Iharana, *Madag.* 89 A9
Ihbulag, *Mongolia* 56 C4
Iheya-Shima, *Japan* 55 L3
Ihiala, *Nigeria* 83 D6
Ihosy, *Madag.* 89 C8
Ihotry, Farihy, *Madag.* 89 C7
Ihugh, *Nigeria* 83 D6
Ii, *Finland* 8 D21
Ii-Shima, *Japan* 55 L3
Iida, *Japan* 55 G8
Iijoki →, *Finland* 8 D21
Iisalmi, *Finland* 8 E22
Iiyama, *Japan* 55 F9
Iizuka, *Japan* 55 H5
Ijebu-Igbo, *Nigeria* 83 D5
Ijebu-Ode, *Nigeria* 83 D5
IJmuiden, *Neths.* 17 B4
IJssel →, *Neths.* 17 B5
IJsselmeer, *Neths.* 17 B5
Ijuí, *Brazil* 127 B5
Ijuí →, *Brazil* 127 B4
Ikalamavony, *Madag.* 89 C8
Ikale, *Nigeria* 83 D6
Ikaluktutiak, *Canada* 100 B9
Ikang, *Nigeria* 83 E6
Ikara, *Nigeria* 83 C6
Ikare, *Nigeria* 83 D6
Ikaría, *Greece* 39 D8
Ikast, *Denmark* 11 H3
Ikeda, *Japan* 55 G6
Ikeja, *Nigeria* 83 D5
Ikela, *Dem. Rep. of the Congo* 84 E4
Ikerre-Ekiti, *Nigeria* 83 D6
Ikhtiman, *Bulgaria* 40 D7
Iki, *Japan* 55 H4
Ikimba L., *Tanzania* 86 C3
Ikire, *Nigeria* 83 D5
Ikizdere, *Turkey* 73 B9
Ikom, *Nigeria* 83 D6
Ikongo, *Madag.* 89 C8
Ikopa →, *Madag.* 89 B8
Ikot Ekpene, *Nigeria* 83 D6
Ikungu, *Tanzania* 86 C3
Ikurun, *Nigeria* 83 D5
Ila, *Nigeria* 83 D5
Ilagan, *Phil.* 61 C4
Ilaka, *Madag.* 89 B8
Ilām, *Iran* 70 C5
Ilam, *Nepal* 69 F12
Ilam □, *Iran* 70 C5
Ilan, *Taiwan* 59 E13
Ilanskiy, *Russia* 51 D10
Ilaro, *Nigeria* 83 D5
Ilatane, *Niger* 83 B5
Iława, *Poland* 44 E6
Ile →, *Kazakstan* 50 E8
Ile-à-la-Crosse, *Canada* 105 B7
Ile-à-la-Crosse, Lac, *Canada* 105 B7
Île-de-France □, *France* 19 D9
Ileanda, *Romania* 43 C8
Ilebo, *Dem. Rep. of the Congo* 84 E4
Ilek, *Russia* 50 D6
Ilero, *Nigeria* 83 D5
Ilesha, Kwara, *Nigeria* 83 D5
Ilesha, Oyo, *Nigeria* 83 D5
Ilford, *Canada* 105 B9
Ilfracombe, *Australia* 94 C3
Ilfracombe, *U.K.* 13 F3
Ilgaz, *Turkey* 72 B5
Ilgaz Dağları, *Turkey* 72 B5
Ilgın, *Turkey* 72 C4
Ilhavo, *Portugal* 34 E2
Ilhéus, *Brazil* 125 F11
Ili = Ile →, *Kazakstan* 50 E8
Ilia, *Romania* 42 E7
Ilia □, *Greece* 38 D3
Iliamna L., *U.S.A.* 100 C4
Iliç, *Turkey* 73 C8
Ilıca, *Turkey* 39 B9
Ilichevsk, *Azerbaijan* 73 C11

Iligan, *Phil.* 61 G6
Iligan Bay, *Phil.* 61 G6
Ilíkí, L., *Greece* 38 C5
Ilin I., *Phil.* 61 E4
Iliodhrómia, *Greece* 38 B5
Ilion, *U.S.A.* 111 D9
Ilirska-Bistrica, *Slovenia* 29 C11
Ilkeston, *U.K.* 12 E6
Ilkley, *U.K.* 12 D6
Illampu = Ancohuma, Nevada, *Bolivia* 122 E4
Illana B., *Phil.* 61 H5
Illapel, *Chile* 126 C1
Ille-et-Vilaine □, *France* 18 D5
Ille-sur-Têt, *France* 20 F6
Illéla, *Niger* 83 C6
Iller →, *Germany* 25 G5
Illertissen, *Germany* 25 G6
Illescas, *Spain* 34 E7
Illetas, *Spain* 37 B9
Illichivsk, *Ukraine* 47 J6
Illiers-Combray, *France* 18 D8
Illimani, Nevado, *Bolivia* 124 G5
Illinois □, *U.S.A.* 112 E10
Illinois →, *U.S.A.* 107 C8
Illium = Troy, *Turkey* 39 B8
Illizi, *Algeria* 78 C7
Illkirch-Graffenstaden, *France* 19 D14
Íllora, *Spain* 35 H7
Ilm →, *Germany* 24 D7
Ilmajoki, *Finland* 9 E20
Ilmen, Ozero, *Russia* 46 C6
Ilmenau, *Germany* 24 E6
Ilo, *Peru* 124 G4
Ilobu, *Nigeria* 83 D5
Iloilo, *Phil.* 61 F5
Ilora, *Nigeria* 83 D5
Ilorin, *Nigeria* 83 D5
Ilovatka, *Russia* 48 E7
Ilovlya, *Russia* 49 F7
Ilovlya →, *Russia* 49 F7
Iłowa, *Poland* 45 G2
Ilubabor □, *Ethiopia* 81 F4
Ilva Mică, *Romania* 43 C9
Ilwaco, *U.S.A.* 116 D2
Ilwaki, *Indonesia* 63 F7
Ilyichevsk = Illichivsk, *Ukraine* 47 J6
Iłża, *Poland* 45 G8
Itzanka →, *Poland* 45 G8
Imabari, *Japan* 55 G6
Imaloto →, *Madag.* 89 C8
Imamoğlu, *Turkey* 72 D6
Imandra, Ozero, *Russia* 50 C4
Imanombo, *Madag.* 89 C8
Imari, *Japan* 55 H4
Imasa, *Sudan* 80 D4
Imathía □, *Greece* 40 F6
Imatra, *Finland* 46 B5
Imbil, *Australia* 95 D5
Iménas, *Mali* 83 B5
imeni 26 Bakinskikh Komissarov = Neftçala, *Azerbaijan* 71 B6
imeni 26 Bakinskikh Komissarov, *Turkmenistan* 71 B7
Imeri, Serra, *Brazil* 124 C5
Imerimandroso, *Madag.* 89 B8
Imi, *Ethiopia* 81 F5
Imishly = Imişli, *Azerbaijan* 49 L9
Imişli, *Azerbaijan* 49 L9
Imlay, *U.S.A.* 114 F4
Imlay City, *U.S.A.* 110 D1
Immaseri, *Sudan* 81 D2
Immenstadt, *Germany* 25 H6
Immingham, *U.K.* 12 D7
Immokalee, *U.S.A.* 109 M5
Imo □, *Nigeria* 83 D6
Imo →, *Nigeria* 83 E6
Ímola, *Italy* 29 D8
Imotski, *Croatia* 29 E14
Imperatriz, *Brazil* 125 E9
Impéria, *Italy* 28 E5
Imperial, *Canada* 105 C7
Imperial, *Calif., U.S.A.* 117 N11
Imperial, *Nebr., U.S.A.* 112 E4
Imperial Beach, *U.S.A.* 117 N9
Imperial Dam, *U.S.A.* 117 N12
Imperial Reservoir, *U.S.A.* 117 N12
Imperial Valley, *U.S.A.* 117 N11
Imperieuse Reef, *Australia* 92 C2
Impfondo, *Congo* 84 D3
Imphal, *India* 67 G18
Imphy, *France* 19 F10
Imranlı, *Turkey* 73 C8
Imroz = Gökçeada, *Turkey* 41 F9
Imroz, *Turkey* 41 F9
Imst, *Austria* 26 D3
Imuris, *Mexico* 118 A2
Imuruan B., *Phil.* 63 B5
In Akhmed, *Mali* 83 B4
In Aleï, *Mali* 82 B4
In Delimane, *Mali* 83 B5
In Guezzam, *Algeria* 83 B6
In Koufi, *Mali* 83 B5
In Salah, *Algeria* 78 C6
In Tallak, *Mali* 83 B5
In Tebezas, *Mali* 83 B5
Ina, *Japan* 55 G8
Inangahua, *N.Z.* 91 J3
Inanwatan, *Indonesia* 63 E8
Iñapari, *Peru* 124 F5
Inari, *Finland* 8 B22
Inarijärvi, *Finland* 8 B22
Inawashiro-Ko, *Japan* 54 F10
Inca, *Spain* 37 B9
Inca de Oro, *Chile* 126 B2

Incaguasi, *Chile* 126 B1
Ince Burun, *Turkey* 72 A6
Incekum Burnu, *Turkey* 72 D5
Incesu, *Turkey* 70 B2
Inch'ŏn, *S. Korea* 57 F14
Incio = Cruz de Incio, *Spain* 34 C3
Incirliova, *Turkey* 39 D9
Incline Village, *U.S.A.* 114 G4
Incomáti →, *Mozam.* 89 D5
Inda Silase, *Ethiopia* 81 E4
Indal, *Sweden* 10 B11
Indalsälven →, *Sweden* 10 B11
Indaw, *Burma* 67 G20
Indbir, *Ethiopia* 81 F4
Independence, *Calif., U.S.A.* 116 J8
Independence, *Iowa, U.S.A.* 112 D9
Independence, *Kans., U.S.A.* 113 G7
Independence, *Ky., U.S.A.* 108 F3
Independence, *Mo., U.S.A.* 112 F7
Independence Fjord, *Greenland* 4 A6
Independence Mts., *U.S.A.* 114 F5
Independența, *Romania* 43 E12
India ■, *Asia* 66 K11
Indian →, *U.S.A.* 109 M5
Indian Cabins, *Canada* 104 B5
Indian Harbour, *Canada* 103 B8
Indian Head, *Canada* 105 C8
Indian Lake, *U.S.A.* 111 C10
Indian Ocean 52 K11
Indian Springs, *U.S.A.* 117 J11
Indiana, *U.S.A.* 110 F5
Indiana □, *U.S.A.* 108 F3
Indianapolis, *U.S.A.* 108 F2
Indianola, *Iowa, U.S.A.* 112 E8
Indianola, *Miss., U.S.A.* 113 J9
Indigirka →, *Russia* 51 B15
Indija, *Serbia, Yug.* 42 E5
Indio, *U.S.A.* 117 M10
Indo-China, *Asia* 52 H14
Indonesia ■, *Asia* 62 F5
Indore, *India* 68 H6
Indramayu, *Indonesia* 63 G13
Indravati →, *India* 67 K12
Indre □, *France* 19 F8
Indre →, *France* 18 E7
Indre-et-Loire □, *France* 18 E7
Indulkana, *Australia* 95 D1
Indus →, *Pakistan* 68 G2
Indus, Mouth of the, *Pakistan* 68 H3
Inebolu, *Turkey* 72 B5
Inecik, *Turkey* 41 F11
Inegöl, *Turkey* 41 F13
Ineu, *Romania* 42 D6
Infantes = Villanueva de los Infantes, *Spain* 35 G7
Infiernillo, Presa del, *Mexico* 118 D4
Infiesto, *Spain* 34 B5
Ingelstad, *Sweden* 11 H8
Ingenio, *Canary Is.* 37 G4
Ingenio Santa Ana, *Argentina* 126 B2
Ingersoll, *Canada* 102 D3
Ingham, *Australia* 94 B4
Ingleborough, *U.K.* 12 C5
Inglewood, *Australia* 95 D5
Inglewood, *N.Z.* 91 H5
Inglewood, *U.S.A.* 117 M8
Ingólfshöfði, *Iceland* 8 E5
Ingolstadt, *Germany* 25 G7
Ingomar, *U.S.A.* 114 C10
Ingonish, *Canada* 103 C7
Ingore, *Guinea-Biss.* 82 C1
Ingraj Bazar, *India* 69 G13
Ingrid Christensen Coast, *Antarctica* 5 C6
Ingul →, = Inhul →, *Ukraine* 47 J7
Ingulec = Inhulec, *Ukraine* 47 J7
Ingulets →, = Inhulets →, *Ukraine* 47 J7
Inguri →, = Enguri →, *Georgia* 49 J5
Ingushetia □, *Russia* 49 J7
Ingwavuma, *S. Africa* 89 D5
Inhaca, *Mozam.* 89 D5
Inhafenga, *Mozam.* 89 C5
Inhambane, *Mozam.* 89 C6
Inhambane □, *Mozam.* 89 C5
Inhaminga, *Mozam.* 87 F4
Inharrime, *Mozam.* 89 C6
Inharrime →, *Mozam.* 89 C6
Inhisar, *Turkey* 39 A12
Inhul →, *Ukraine* 47 J7
Inhulec, *Ukraine* 47 J7
Inhulets →, *Ukraine* 47 J7
Iniesta, *Spain* 33 F3
Ining = Yining, *China* 50 E9
Inírida →, *Colombia* 124 C5
Inishbofin, *Ireland* 15 C1
Inisheer, *Ireland* 15 C2
Inishfree B., *Ireland* 15 A3
Inishkea North, *Ireland* 15 B1
Inishkea South, *Ireland* 15 B1
Inishmaan, *Ireland* 15 C2
Inishmore, *Ireland* 15 C2
Inishowen Pen., *Ireland* 15 A4
Inishshark, *Ireland* 15 C1
Inishturk, *Ireland* 15 C1
Inishvickillane, *Ireland* 15 D1
Injibara, *Ethiopia* 81 E4
Injune, *Australia* 95 D4
Inklin →, *Canada* 104 B2
Inland Sea = Setonaikai, *Japan* 55 G6
Inle L., *Burma* 67 J20
Inlet, *U.S.A.* 111 C10
Inn →, *Austria* 26 C6
Innamincka, *Australia* 95 D3
Inner Hebrides, *U.K.* 14 E2

Inner Mongolia = Nei Monggol Zizhiqu □, *China* 56 D7
Inner Sound, *U.K.* 14 D3
Innerkip, *Canada* 110 C4
Innetalling I., *Canada* 102 A4
Innisfail, *Australia* 94 B4
Innisfail, *Canada* 104 C6
In'noshima, *Japan* 55 G6
Innsbruck, *Austria* 26 D4
Innviertel, *Austria* 26 C6
Inny →, *Ireland* 15 C4
Inongo, *Dem. Rep. of the Congo* 84 E3
Inönü, *Turkey* 39 B12
Inoucdjouac = Inukjuak, *Canada* 101 C12
Inowrocław, *Poland* 45 F5
Inpundong, *N. Korea* 57 D14
Inscription, C., *Australia* 93 E1
Insein, *Burma* 67 L20
Insjön, *Sweden* 10 D9
Ińsko, *Poland* 44 E2
Însurăței, *Romania* 43 F12
Inta, *Russia* 50 C6
Interlaken, *Switz.* 25 J3
Interlaken, *U.S.A.* 111 D8
International Falls, *U.S.A.* 112 A8
Intiyaco, *Argentina* 126 B3
Întorsura Buzăului, *Romania* 43 E11
Inukjuak, *Canada* 101 C12
Inútil, B., *Chile* 128 G2
Inuvik, *Canada* 100 B6
Inveraray, *U.K.* 14 E3
Inverbervie, *U.K.* 14 E6
Invercargill, *N.Z.* 91 M2
Inverclyde □, *U.K.* 14 F4
Inverell, *Australia* 95 D5
Invergordon, *U.K.* 14 D4
Inverloch, *Australia* 95 F4
Invermere, *Canada* 104 C5
Inverness, *Canada* 103 C7
Inverness, *U.K.* 14 D4
Inverness, *U.S.A.* 109 L4
Inverurie, *U.K.* 14 D6
Investigator Group, *Australia* 95 E1
Inya, *Russia* 50 D9
Inyanga, *Zimbabwe* 87 F3
Inyangani, *Zimbabwe* 87 F3
Inyantue, *Zimbabwe* 88 B4
Inyo Mts., *U.S.A.* 116 J9
Inyokern, *U.S.A.* 117 K9
Inza, *Russia* 48 D8
Inzhavino, *Russia* 48 D6
Iō-Jima, *Japan* 55 J5
Ioánnina, *Greece* 38 B2
Ioánnina □, *Greece* 38 B2
Iola, *U.S.A.* 113 G7
Ion Corvin, *Romania* 43 F12
Iona, *U.K.* 14 E2
Ionia, *U.S.A.* 108 D3
Ionian Is. = Iónioi Nísoi, *Greece* 38 C2
Ionian Sea, *Medit. S.* 6 H9
Iónioi Nísoi, *Greece* 38 C2
Iónioi Nísoi □, *Greece* 38 C2
Íos, *Greece* 39 E7
Iowa □, *U.S.A.* 112 D8
Iowa →, *U.S.A.* 112 E9
Iowa City, *U.S.A.* 112 E9
Iowa Falls, *U.S.A.* 112 D8
Iowa Park, *U.S.A.* 113 J5
Ipala, *Tanzania* 86 C3
Ipameri, *Brazil* 125 G9
Ipáti, *Greece* 38 C4
Ipatinga, *Brazil* 125 G10
Ipatovo, *Russia* 49 H6
Ipel' →, *Europe* 27 D11
Ipiales, *Colombia* 124 C3
Ipin = Yibin, *China* 58 C5
Ipixuna, *Brazil* 124 E4
Ipoh, *Malaysia* 65 K3
Ippy, *C.A.R.* 84 C4
Ipsala, *Turkey* 41 F10
Ipsárion, Óros, *Greece* 41 F8
Ipswich, *Australia* 95 D5
Ipswich, *U.K.* 13 E9
Ipswich, *Mass., U.S.A.* 111 D14
Ipswich, *S. Dak., U.S.A.* 112 C5
Ipu, *Brazil* 125 D10
Iqaluit, *Canada* 101 B13
Iquique, *Chile* 124 H4
Iquitos, *Peru* 124 D4
Irabu-Jima, *Japan* 55 M2
Iracoubo, *Fr. Guiana* 125 B8
Irafshān, *Iran* 71 E9
Irahuan, *Phil.* 61 G3
Iráklia, *Kikládhes, Greece* 39 E7
Iráklia, *Sérrai, Greece* 40 E7
Iráklion, *Greece* 36 D7
Iráklion □, *Greece* 36 D7
Irala, *Paraguay* 127 B5
Iran ■, *Asia* 71 C7
Iran, Gunung-Gunung, *Malaysia* 62 D4
Iran, Plateau of, *Asia* 52 F9
Iran Ra. = Iran, Gunung-Gunung, *Malaysia* 62 D4
Iränshahr, *Iran* 71 E9
Irapuato, *Mexico* 118 C4
Iraq ■, *Asia* 70 C5
Irati, *Brazil* 127 B5
Irbes saurums, *Latvia* 44 A9
Irbid, *Jordan* 75 C4
Irbid □, *Jordan* 75 C5
Iregua →, *Spain* 32 C2
Ireland ■, *Europe* 15 C4

Irele, *Nigeria* 83 D6
Irgiz, Bolshaya →, *Russia* 48 D9
Irhyangdong, *N. Korea* 57 D15
Iri, *S. Korea* 57 G14
Irian Jaya □, *Indonesia* 63 E9
Irié, *Guinea* 82 D3
Iriga, *Phil.* 61 E5
Iringa, *Tanzania* 86 D4
Iringa □, *Tanzania* 86 D4
Iriomote-Jima, *Japan* 55 M1
Iriona, *Honduras* 120 C2
Iriri →, *Brazil* 125 D8
Irish Republic ■, *Europe* 15 C3
Irish Sea, *U.K.* 12 D3
Irkutsk, *Russia* 51 D11
Irlğanlı, *Turkey* 39 D11
Irma, *Canada* 105 C6
Irō-Zaki, *Japan* 55 G9
Iroise, Mer d', *France* 18 D2
Iron Gate = Portile de Fier, *Europe* 42 F7
Iron Mountain, *U.S.A.* 108 C1
Iron River, *U.S.A.* 112 B10
Irondequoit, *U.S.A.* 110 C7
Ironton, *Mo., U.S.A.* 113 G9
Ironton, *Ohio, U.S.A.* 108 F4
Ironwood, *U.S.A.* 112 B9
Iroquois, *Canada* 111 B9
Iroquois Falls, *Canada* 102 C3
Irosin, *Phil.* 61 E6
Irpin, *Ukraine* 47 G6
Irrara Cr. →, *Australia* 95 D4
Irrawaddy □, *Burma* 67 L19
Irrawaddy →, *Burma* 67 M19
Irrawaddy, Mouths of the, *Burma* 67 M19
Irricana, *Canada* 104 C6
Irsina, *Italy* 31 B9
Irtysh →, *Russia* 50 C7
Irumu, *Dem. Rep. of the Congo* 86 B2
Irún, *Spain* 32 B3
Irunea = Pamplona, *Spain* 32 C3
Irurzun, *Spain* 32 C3
Irvine, *U.K.* 14 F4
Irvine, *Calif., U.S.A.* 117 M9
Irvine, *Ky., U.S.A.* 108 G4
Irvinestown, *U.K.* 15 B4
Irving, *U.S.A.* 113 J6
Irvona, *U.S.A.* 110 F6
Irwin →, *Australia* 93 E1
Is, Jebel, *Sudan* 80 C4
Is-sur-Tille, *France* 19 E12
Isa, *Nigeria* 83 C6
Isa Khel, *Pakistan* 68 C4
Isaac →, *Australia* 94 C4
Isabel, *U.S.A.* 112 C4
Isabela, *Phil.* 61 H5
Isabela, I., *Mexico* 118 C3
Isabelia, Cord., *Nic.* 120 D2
Isabella Ra., *Australia* 92 D3
Isaccea, *Romania* 43 E13
Ísafjarðardjúp, *Iceland* 8 C2
Ísafjörður, *Iceland* 8 C2
Isagarh, *India* 68 G7
Isahaya, *Japan* 55 H5
Isaka, *Tanzania* 86 C3
Isakly, *Russia* 48 C10
Işalnița, *Romania* 43 F8
Isan →, *India* 69 F9
Isana = Içana →, *Brazil* 124 C5
Isanlu Makutu, *Nigeria* 83 D6
Isar →, *Germany* 25 G8
Isarco →, *Italy* 29 B8
Isari, *Greece* 38 D3
Íscar, *Spain* 34 D6
Iscehisar, *Turkey* 39 C12
Íschia, *Italy* 30 B6
Isdell →, *Australia* 92 C3
Ise, *Japan* 55 G8
Ise-Wan, *Japan* 55 G8
Isefjord, *Denmark* 11 J5
Isel →, *Austria* 26 E5
Iseo, *Italy* 28 C7
Iseo, L. d', *Italy* 28 C7
Iseramagazi, *Tanzania* 86 C3
Isère □, *France* 21 C9
Isère →, *France* 21 D8
Iserlohn, *Germany* 24 D3
Isérnia, *Italy* 31 A7
Iseyin, *Nigeria* 83 D5
Isfahan = Eşfahān, *Iran* 71 C6
Ishëm, *Albania* 40 E3
Ishigaki-Shima, *Japan* 55 M2
Ishikari-Gawa →, *Japan* 54 C10
Ishikari-Sammyaku, *Japan* 54 C11
Ishikari-Wan, *Japan* 54 C10
Ishikawa □, *Japan* 55 F8
Ishim, *Russia* 50 D7
Ishim →, *Russia* 50 D8
Ishinomaki, *Japan* 54 E10
Ishioka, *Japan* 55 F10
Ishkuman, *Pakistan* 69 A5
Ishpeming, *U.S.A.* 108 B2
Isigny-sur-Mer, *France* 18 C5
Isıklar Dağı, *Turkey* 41 F11
Işıklı, *Turkey* 39 C11
Isil Kul, *Russia* 50 D8
Ísili, *Italy* 30 C2
Isiolo, *Kenya* 86 B4
Isiro, *Dem. Rep. of the Congo* 86 B2
Isisford, *Australia* 94 C3
İskenderun, *Turkey* 70 B3
İskenderun Körfezi, *Turkey* 72 D6
İskilip, *Turkey* 72 B6
Iskür →, *Bulgaria* 41 C8
Iskür, Yazovir, *Bulgaria* 40 D7

Iskut →, *Canada* 104 B2
Isla →, *U.K.* 14 E5
Isla Cristina, *Spain* 35 H3
Isla Vista, *U.S.A.* 117 L7
Islâhiye, *Turkey* 72 D7
Islam Headworks, *Pakistan* 68 E5
Islamabad, *Pakistan* 68 C5
Islamgarh, *Pakistan* 68 F4
Islamkot, *Pakistan* 68 G4
Islampur, *India* 69 G11
Island L., *Canada* 105 C10
Island Pond, *U.S.A.* 111 B13
Islands, B. of, *Canada* 103 C8
Islands, B. of, *N.Z.* 91 F5
Islay, *U.K.* 14 F2
Isle →, *France* 20 D3
Isle of Wight □, *U.K.* 13 G6
Isle Royale, *U.S.A.* 112 B10
Isle Royale National Park,
 U.S.A. 112 B10
Isleton, *U.S.A.* 116 G5
Ismail = Izmayil, *Ukraine* ... 47 K5
Ismâ'ilîya, *Egypt* 80 H8
Ismaning, *Germany* 25 G7
Isna, *Egypt* 80 B3
Isoanala, *Madag.* 89 C8
Isogstalo, *India* 69 B8
Ísola del Liri, *Italy* 29 G10
Ísola della Scala, *Italy* 28 C7
Ísola di Capo Rizzuto, *Italy* ... 31 D10
Isparta, *Turkey* 39 D12
Isperikh, *Bulgaria* 41 C10
Íspica, *Italy* 31 F7
Israel ■, *Asia* 75 D3
Israita, *Eritrea* 81 D4
Issia, *Ivory C.* 82 D3
Issoire, *France* 20 C7
Issoudun, *France* 19 F8
Issyk-Kul, Ozero = Ysyk-Köl,
 Kyrgyzstan 50 E8
Ist, *Croatia* 29 D11
Istállós-kő, *Hungary* 42 B5
Istanbul, *Turkey* 41 E12
Istanbul □, *Turkey* 41 E12
Istanbul Boğazı, *Turkey* 41 E13
Istiaía, *Greece* 38 C5
Istok, *Kosovo, Yug.* 40 D4
Istokpoga, L., *U.S.A.* 109 M5
Istra, *Croatia* 29 C10
Istres, *France* 21 E8
Istria = Istra, *Croatia* 29 C10
Itá, *Paraguay* 126 B4
Itaberaba, *Brazil* 125 F10
Itabira, *Brazil* 125 G10
Itabirito, *Brazil* 127 A7
Itabuna, *Brazil* 125 F11
Itacaunas →, *Brazil* 125 E9
Itacoatiara, *Brazil* 124 D7
Itaipú, Reprêsa de, *Brazil* .. 127 B5
Itaituba, *Brazil* 125 D7
Itajaí, *Brazil* 127 B6
Itajubá, *Brazil* 127 A6
Itaka, *Tanzania* 87 D3
Italy ■, *Europe* 7 G8
Itamaraju, *Brazil* 125 G11
Itampolo, *Madag.* 89 C7
Itandrano, *Madag.* 89 C8
Itapecuru-Mirim, *Brazil* 125 D10
Itaperuna, *Brazil* 127 A7
Itapetininga, *Brazil* 127 A6
Itapeva, *Brazil* 127 A6
Itapicuru →, *Bahia, Brazil* .. 125 F11
Itapicuru →, *Maranhão, Brazil* 125 D10
Itapipoca, *Brazil* 125 D11
Itapuã □, *Paraguay* 127 B4
Itaquari, *Brazil* 127 A7
Itaquí, *Brazil* 126 B4
Itararé, *Brazil* 127 A6
Itarsi, *India* 68 H7
Itatí, *Argentina* 126 B4
Itbayat, *Phil.* 61 A4
Itchen →, *U.K.* 13 G6
Itéa, *Greece* 38 C4
Itezhi Tezhi, L., *Zambia* ... 87 F2
Ithaca = Itháki, *Greece* 38 C2
Ithaca, *U.S.A.* 111 D8
Itháki, *Greece* 38 C2
Itiquira →, *Brazil* 125 G7
Itō, *Japan* 55 G9
Itoigawa, *Japan* 55 F8
Iton →, *France* 18 C8
Itonamas →, *Bolivia* 124 F6
Itri, *Italy* 30 A6
Itsa, *Egypt* 80 J7
Íttiri, *Italy* 30 B1
Ittoqqortoormiit, *Greenland* . 4 B6
Itu, *Brazil* 127 A6
Itu, *Nigeria* 83 D6
Itu Aba I., *S. China Sea* ... 62 B4
Ituiutaba, *Brazil* 125 G9
Itumbiara, *Brazil* 125 G9
Ituna, *Canada* 105 C8
Itunge Port, *Tanzania* 87 D3
Iturbe, *Argentina* 126 A2
Ituri →, *Dem. Rep. of the Congo* 86 B2
Iturup, Ostrov, *Russia* 51 E15
Ituxi →, *Brazil* 124 E6
Ituyuro →, *Argentina* 126 A3
Itzehoe, *Germany* 24 B5
Ivahona, *Madag.* 89 C8
Ivaí →, *Brazil* 127 A5
Ivalo, *Finland* 8 B22
Ivalojoki →, *Finland* 8 B22
Ivanava, *Belarus* 47 F3
Ivančice, *Czech Rep.* 27 B9

Ivăneşti, *Romania* 43 D12
Ivangorod, *Russia* 46 C5
Ivanhoe, *Calif., U.S.A.* 116 J7
Ivanhoe, *Minn., U.S.A.* 112 C6
Ivanić Grad, *Croatia* 29 C13
Ivanjica, *Serbia, Yug.* 40 C4
Ivanjska, *Bos.-H.* 42 F2
Ivankoyskoye Vdkhr., *Russia* . 46 D9
Ivano-Frankivsk, *Ukraine* ... 47 H3
Ivano-Frankovsk = Ivano-
 Frankivsk, *Ukraine* 47 H3
Ivanovo = Ivanava, *Belarus* .. 47 F3
Ivanovo, *Russia* 46 D11
Ivanščica, *Croatia* 29 B13
Ivato, *Madag.* 89 C8
Ivatsevichy, *Belarus* 47 F3
Ivaylovgrad, *Bulgaria* 41 E10
Ivinheima →, *Brazil* 127 A5
Ivinhema, *Brazil* 127 A5
Ivohibe, *Madag.* 89 C8
Ivory Coast, *W. Afr.* 82 E4
Ivory Coast ■, *Africa* 82 D4
Ivösjön, *Sweden* 11 H8
Ivrea, *Italy* 28 C4
Ivrindi, *Turkey* 39 B9
Ivujivik, *Canada* 101 B12
Ivybridge, *U.K.* 13 G4
Iwaizumi, *Japan* 54 E10
Iwaki, *Japan* 55 F10
Iwakuni, *Japan* 55 G6
Iwamizawa, *Japan* 54 C10
Iwanai, *Japan* 54 C10
Iwata, *Japan* 55 G8
Iwate □, *Japan* 54 E10
Iwate-San, *Japan* 54 E10
Iwo, *Nigeria* 83 D5
Iwonicz-Zdrój, *Poland* 45 J8
Ixiamas, *Bolivia* 124 F5
Ixopo, *S. Africa* 89 E5
Ixtepec, *Mexico* 119 D5
Ixtlán del Río, *Mexico* 118 C4
Iyal Bakhit, *Sudan* 81 E2
Iyo, *Japan* 55 H6
Izabal, L. de, *Guatemala* ... 120 C2
Izamal, *Mexico* 119 C7
Izberbash, *Russia* 49 J8
Izbica, *Poland* 45 H10
Izbica Kujawska, *Poland* 45 F5
Izbiceni, *Romania* 43 G9
Izena-Shima, *Japan* 55 L3
Izgrev, *Bulgaria* 41 C10
Izhevsk, *Russia* 50 D6
Izmayil, *Ukraine* 47 K5
Izmir, *Turkey* 39 C9
Izmir □, *Turkey* 39 C9
Izmir Körfezi, *Turkey* 39 C8
Izmit = Kocaeli, *Turkey* 41 F13
Iznájar, *Spain* 35 H6
Iznalloz, *Spain* 35 H7
Iznik, *Turkey* 72 B3
Iznik Gölü, *Turkey* 41 F13
Izobil'nyy, *Russia* 49 H5
Izola, *Slovenia* 29 C10
Izra, *Syria* 75 C5
Iztochni Rodopi, *Bulgaria* .. 41 E9
Izúcar de Matamoros, *Mexico* . 119 D5
Izu-Shotō, *Japan* 55 G10
Izumi-Sano, *Japan* 55 G7
Izumo, *Japan* 55 G6
Izyaslav, *Ukraine* 47 G4
Izyum, *Ukraine* 47 H9

J

Jaba, *Ethiopia* 81 F4
Jabal at Tā'ir, *Red Sea* 81 D5
Jabalón →, *Spain* 35 G6
Jabalpur, *India* 69 H8
Jabbūl, *Syria* 70 B3
Jabiru, *Australia* 92 B5
Jablah, *Syria* 70 C3
Jablanac, *Croatia* 29 D11
Jablanica, *Bos.-H.* 42 G2
Jablonec nad Nisou, *Czech Rep.* 26 A8
Jablonica, *Slovak Rep.* 27 C10
Jablonowo Pomorskie, *Poland* . 44 E6
Jablunkov, *Czech Rep.* 27 B11
Jaboatão, *Brazil* 125 E11
Jaboticabal, *Brazil* 127 A6
Jabukovac, *Serbia, Yug.* 40 B6
Jaca, *Spain* 32 C4
Jacareí, *Brazil* 127 A6
Jacarèzinho, *Brazil* 127 A6
Jackman, *U.S.A.* 109 C10
Jacksboro, *U.S.A.* 113 J5
Jackson, *Ala., U.S.A.* 109 K2
Jackson, *Calif., U.S.A.* 116 G6
Jackson, *Ky., U.S.A.* 108 G4
Jackson, *Mich., U.S.A.* 108 D3
Jackson, *Minn., U.S.A.* 112 D7
Jackson, *Miss., U.S.A.* 113 J9
Jackson, *Mo., U.S.A.* 113 G10
Jackson, *N.H., U.S.A.* 111 B13
Jackson, *Ohio, U.S.A.* 108 F4
Jackson, *Tenn., U.S.A.* 109 H1
Jackson, *Wyo., U.S.A.* 114 E8
Jackson, *N.Z.* 91 K3
Jackson B., *N.Z.* 91 K2
Jackson L., *U.S.A.* 114 E8
Jackson's Arm, *Canada* 103 C8
Jacksonville, *U.S.A.* 109 J3
Jacksonville, *Ark., U.S.A.* . 113 H8
Jacksonville, *Calif., U.S.A.* 116 H6
Jacksonville, *Fla., U.S.A.* . 109 K5

Jacksonville, *Ill., U.S.A.* . 112 F9
Jacksonville, *N.C., U.S.A.* . 109 H7
Jacksonville, *Tex., U.S.A.* . 113 K7
Jacksonville Beach, *U.S.A.* . 109 K5
Jacmel, *Haiti* 121 C5
Jacob Lake, *U.S.A.* 115 H7
Jacobabad, *Pakistan* 68 E3
Jacobina, *Brazil* 125 F10
Jacques Cartier, Dét. de, *Canada* 103 C7
Jacques Cartier, Mt., *Canada* 103 C6
Jacques Cartier, Parc Prov.,
 Canada 103 C5
Jacqueville, *Ivory C.* 82 D4
Jacuí →, *Brazil* 127 C5
Jacumba, *U.S.A.* 117 N10
Jacundá →, *Brazil* 125 D8
Jade, *Germany* 24 B4
Jadebusen, *Germany* 24 B4
Jadotville = Likasi, *Dem. Rep. of
 the Congo* 87 E2
Jadovnik, *Serbia, Yug.* 40 C3
Jadraque, *Spain* 32 E2
Jaén, *Peru* 124 E3
Jaén, *Spain* 35 H7
Jaén □, *Spain* 35 H7
Jafarabad, *India* 68 J4
Jaffa = Tel Aviv-Yafo, *Israel* 75 C3
Jaffna, *Sri Lanka* 66 Q12
Jaffrey, *U.S.A.* 111 D12
Jagadhri, *India* 68 D7
Jagadishpur, *India* 69 G11
Jagdalpur, *India* 67 K13
Jagersfontein, *S. Africa* ... 88 D4
Jaghīn →, *Iran* 71 E8
Jagodina, *Serbia, Yug.* 40 B5
Jagraon, *India* 66 D9
Jagst →, *Germany* 25 D5
Jagtial, *India* 66 K11
Jaguariaíva, *Brazil* 127 A6
Jaguaribe →, *Brazil* 125 D11
Jagüey Grande, *Cuba* 120 B3
Jahanabad, *India* 69 G11
Jahazpur, *India* 68 G6
Jahrom, *Iran* 71 D7
Jaijon, *India* 68 D7
Jailolo, *Indonesia* 63 D7
Jailolo, Selat, *Indonesia* .. 63 D7
Jaipur, *India* 68 F6
Jais, *India* 69 F9
Jaisalmer, *India* 68 F4
Jaisinghnagar, *India* 69 H8
Jaitaran, *India* 68 F5
Jaithari, *India* 69 H8
Jājarm, *Iran* 71 B8
Jajce, *Bos.-H.* 42 F2
Jakam →, *India* 68 H6
Jakarta, *Indonesia* 62 F3
Jakhal, *India* 68 E6
Jakhau, *India* 68 D5
Jakobstad = Pietarsaari, *Finland* 8 E20
Jakupica, *Macedonia* 40 E5
Jal, *U.S.A.* 113 J3
Jalālābād, *Afghan.* 68 B4
Jalalabad, *India* 69 F8
Jalalpur Jattan, *Pakistan* .. 68 C6
Jalama, *U.S.A.* 117 L6
Jalapa, *Guatemala* 120 D2
Jalapa Enríquez, *Mexico* 119 D5
Jalasjärvi, *Finland* 9 E20
Jalaun, *India* 69 F8
Jaldhaka →, *Bangla.* 69 F13
Jalesar, *India* 68 F8
Jaleswar, *Nepal* 69 F11
Jalgaon, *India* 66 J9
Jalībah, *Iraq* 70 D5
Jalingo, *Nigeria* 83 D7
Jalisco □, *Mexico* 118 D4
Jalkot, *Pakistan* 69 B5
Jallas →, *Spain* 34 C1
Jalna, *India* 66 K9
Jalón →, *Spain* 32 D3
Jalor, *India* 68 G5
Jalpa, *Mexico* 118 C4
Jalpaiguri, *India* 67 F16
Jalūlā, *Iraq* 70 C5
Jamaari, *Nigeria* 83 C6
Jamaica ■, *W. Indies* 120 C4
Jamalpur, *Bangla.* 67 G16
Jamalpur, *India* 69 G12
Jamalpurganj, *India* 69 H13
Jamanxim →, *Brazil* 125 D7
Jambi, *Indonesia* 62 E2
Jambi □, *Indonesia* 62 E2
Jambusar, *India* 68 H5
James →, *S. Dak., U.S.A.* ... 112 D6
James →, *Va., U.S.A.* 108 G7
James B., *Canada* 102 B3
James Ranges, *Australia* 92 D5
James Ross I., *Antarctica* .. 5 C18
Jamesabad, *Pakistan* 68 G3
Jamestown, *S. Africa* 88 E4
Jamestown, *N. Dak., U.S.A.* . 112 B5
Jamestown, *N.Y., U.S.A.* 110 D5
Jamestown, *Pa., U.S.A.* 110 E4
Jamīlābād, *Iran* 71 C6
Jamiltepec, *Mexico* 119 D5
Jamira →, *India* 69 J13
Jämjö, *Sweden* 11 H9
Jamkhandi, *India* 66 L9
Jammerbugt, *Denmark* 11 G3
Jammu, *India* 68 C6
Jammu & Kashmir □, *India* ... 69 B7
Jamnagar, *India* 68 H4
Jamni →, *India* 69 G8
Jampur, *Pakistan* 68 E4

Jamrud, *Pakistan* 68 C4
Jämsä, *Finland* 9 F21
Jamshedpur, *India* 69 H12
Jamtara, *India* 69 H12
Jämtland, *Sweden* 8 E15
Jämtlands län □, *Sweden* 10 B7
Jan L., *Canada* 105 C8
Jan Mayen, *Arctic* 4 B7
Janakkala, *Finland* 9 F21
Janaúba, *Brazil* 125 G10
Jand, *Pakistan* 68 C5
Jandaq, *Iran* 71 C7
Jandia, *Canary Is.* 37 F5
Jandia, Pta. de, *Canary Is.* 37 F5
Jandola, *Pakistan* 68 C4
Jandowae, *Australia* 95 D5
Jándula →, *Spain* 35 G6
Janesville, *U.S.A.* 112 D10
Janga, *Ghana* 83 C4
Jangamo, *Mozam.* 89 C6
Janghai, *India* 69 G10
Janikowo, *Poland* 45 F5
Janin, *West Bank* 75 C4
Janina = Ioánnina □, *Greece* . 38 B2
Janja, *Bos.-H.* 42 F4
Janjevo, *Kosovo, Yug.* 40 D5
Janjgir, *India* 69 J10
Janjina, *Croatia* 29 F14
Janjina, *Madag.* 89 C8
Janos, *Mexico* 118 A3
Jánoshalma, *Hungary* 42 D4
Jánosháza, *Hungary* 42 C2
Jánossomorja, *Hungary* 42 C2
Janów, *Poland* 45 H6
Janów Lubelski, *Poland* 45 H9
Janów Podlaski, *Poland* 45 F10
Janowiec Wielkopolski, *Poland* 45 F4
Januária, *Brazil* 125 G10
Janub Dârfûr □, *Sudan* 81 E2
Janub Kordofân □, *Sudan* 81 E3
Janubio, *Canary Is.* 37 F6
Janville, *France* 19 D8
Janzé, *France* 18 E5
Jaora, *India* 68 H6
Japan ■, *Asia* 55 G8
Japan, Sea of, *Asia* 54 E7
Japan Trench, *Pac. Oc.* 52 F18
Japen = Yapen, *Indonesia* ... 63 E9
Japla, *India* 69 G11
Japurá →, *Brazil* 122 D4
Jaquarão, *Brazil* 127 C5
Jaqué, *Panama* 120 E4
Jarābulus, *Syria* 70 B3
Jaraicejo, *Spain* 35 F5
Jaraíz de la Vera, *Spain* ... 34 E5
Jarama →, *Spain* 34 E7
Jaramānah, *Syria* 72 F7
Jarandilla, *Spain* 34 E5
Jaranwala, *Pakistan* 68 D5
Jarash, *Jordan* 75 C4
Järbo, *Sweden* 10 D10
Jardim, *Brazil* 126 A4
Jardín →, *Spain* 33 G2
Jardines de la Reina, Arch. de
 los, *Cuba* 120 B4
Jargalang, *China* 57 C12
Jargalant = Hovd, *Mongolia* . 60 B4
Jari →, *Brazil* 125 D8
Jarīr, W. al →, *Si. Arabia* . 70 E4
Järlåsa, *Sweden* 10 E11
Jarmen, *Germany* 24 B9
Järna, *Dalarnas, Sweden* 10 D8
Järna, *Stockholm, Sweden* ... 10 E11
Jarnac, *France* 20 C3
Jarny, *France* 19 C12
Jarocin, *Poland* 45 G4
Jaroměř, *Czech Rep.* 26 A8
Jarosław, *Poland* 45 H9
Järpås, *Sweden* 11 F6
Järpen, *Sweden* 10 A7
Jarrahdale, *Australia* 93 F2
Jarrahi →, *Iran* 71 D6
Jarres, Plaine des, *Laos* ... 64 C4
Jarso, *Ethiopia* 81 F4
Jartai, *China* 56 E3
Jarud Qi, *China* 57 B11
Jarvis, *Canada* 110 D4
Jarvis I., *Pac. Oc.* 97 H12
Jarvorník, *Czech Rep.* 27 A10
Järvsö, *Sweden* 10 C10
Jarwa, *India* 69 F10
Jaša Tomić, *Serbia, Yug.* ... 42 E5
Jasdan, *India* 68 H4
Jashpurnagar, *India* 69 H11
Jasidih, *India* 69 G12
Jasien, *Poland* 45 G2
Jāsimīyah, *Iraq* 70 C5
Jasin, *Malaysia* 65 L4
Jāsk, *Iran* 71 E8
Jasło, *Poland* 45 J8
Jasmund, *Germany* 24 A9
Jaso, *India* 69 G9
Jasper, *Alta., Canada* 104 C5
Jasper, *Ala., U.S.A.* 109 J2
Jasper, *Fla., U.S.A.* 109 K4
Jasper, *Ind., U.S.A.* 108 F2
Jasper, *Tex., U.S.A.* 113 K8
Jasper Nat. Park, *Canada* ... 104 C5
Jasrasar, *India* 68 F5
Jastarnia, *Poland* 44 D5
Jastrebarsko, *Croatia* 29 C12
Jastrowie, *Poland* 44 E3
Jastrzębie Zdrój, *Poland* ... 45 J5

Jászapáti, *Hungary* 42 C5
Jászárokszállás, *Hungary* ... 42 C4
Jászberény, *Hungary* 42 C4
Jászkisér, *Hungary* 42 C5
Jászladány, *Hungary* 42 C5
Jataí, *Brazil* 125 G8
Jati, *Pakistan* 68 G3
Jatibarang, *Indonesia* 63 G13
Jatinegara, *Indonesia* 63 G12
Játiva = Xàtiva, *Spain* 33 G4
Jättendal, *Sweden* 10 C11
Jaú, *Brazil* 127 A6
Jauja, *Peru* 124 F3
Jaunpur, *India* 69 G10
Java = Jawa, *Indonesia* 62 F3
Java Barat □, *Indonesia* 63 G12
Java Sea, *Indonesia* 62 E3
Java Tengah □, *Indonesia* ... 63 G14
Java Timur □, *Indonesia* 63 G15
Java Trench, *Ind. Oc.* 62 F3
Javalambre, Sa. de, *Spain* .. 32 E4
Jávea, *Spain* 33 G5
Javhlant = Ulyasutay, *Mongolia* 60 B4
Jawa, *Indonesia* 62 F3
Jawad, *India* 68 G6
Jawor, *Poland* 45 G3
Jaworzno, *Poland* 45 H6
Jaworzyna Śląska, *Poland* ... 45 H3
Jay Peak, *U.S.A.* 111 B12
Jaya, Puncak, *Indonesia* 63 E9
Jayanti, *India* 67 F16
Jayapura, *Indonesia* 63 E10
Jayawijaya, Pegunungan,
 Indonesia 63 E9
Jaynagar, *India* 67 F15
Jayrūd, *Syria* 70 C3
Jayton, *U.S.A.* 113 J4
Jāz Mūrīān, Hāmūn-e, *Iran* .. 71 E8
Jazīreh-ye Shīf, *Iran* 71 D6
Jazminal, *Mexico* 118 C4
Jazzīn, *Lebanon* 75 B4
Jean, *U.S.A.* 117 K11
Jean Marie River, *Canada* ... 104 A4
Jean Rabel, *Haiti* 121 C5
Jeanerette, *U.S.A.* 113 L9
Jeanette, Ostrov = Zhannetty,
 Ostrov, *Russia* 51 B16
Jeannette, *U.S.A.* 110 F5
Jebāl Bārez, Kūh-e, *Iran* ... 71 D8
Jebba, *Nigeria* 83 D5
Jebel, Bahr el →, *Sudan* 81 F3
Jebel Dud, *Sudan* 81 E3
Jebel Qerri, *Sudan* 81 D3
Jedburgh, *U.K.* 14 F6
Jedda = Jiddah, *Si. Arabia* . 74 C2
Jeddore L., *Canada* 103 C8
Jedlicze, *Poland* 45 J8
Jędrzejów, *Poland* 45 H7
Jedwabne, *Poland* 45 E9
Jeetzel →, *Germany* 24 B7
Jefferson, *Iowa, U.S.A.* 112 D7
Jefferson, *Ohio, U.S.A.* 110 E4
Jefferson, *Tex., U.S.A.* 113 J7
Jefferson, Mt., *Nev., U.S.A.* 114 G5
Jefferson, Mt., *Oreg., U.S.A.* 114 D3
Jefferson City, *Mo., U.S.A.* 112 F8
Jefferson City, *Tenn., U.S.A.* 109 G4
Jeffersontown, *U.S.A.* 108 F3
Jeffersonville, *U.S.A.* 108 F3
Jeffrey City, *U.S.A.* 114 E10
Jega, *Nigeria* 83 C5
Jēkabpils, *Latvia* 9 H21
Jekyll I., *U.S.A.* 109 K5
Jelcz-Laskowice, *Poland* 45 G4
Jelenia Góra, *Poland* 45 H2
Jelgava, *Latvia* 9 H20
Jelgava □, *Latvia* 44 B10
Jelica, *Serbia, Yug.* 40 C4
Jelli, *Sudan* 81 F3
Jelšava, *Slovak Rep.* 27 C13
Jemaja, *Indonesia* 65 L5
Jemaluang, *Malaysia* 65 L4
Jember, *Indonesia* 63 H15
Jembongan, *Malaysia* 62 C5
Jena, *Germany* 24 E7
Jena, *U.S.A.* 113 K8
Jenbach, *Austria* 26 D4
Jenkins, *U.S.A.* 108 G4
Jenner, *U.S.A.* 116 G3
Jennings, *U.S.A.* 113 K8
Jepara, *Indonesia* 63 G14
Jequié, *Brazil* 125 F10
Jequitinhonha, *Brazil* 125 G10
Jequitinhonha →, *Brazil* 125 G11
Jerantut, *Malaysia* 65 L4
Jérémie, *Haiti* 121 C5
Jerez, Punta, *Mexico* 119 C5
Jerez de García Salinas, *Mexico* 118 C4
Jerez de la Frontera, *Spain* . 35 J4
Jerez de los Caballeros, *Spain* 35 G4
Jericho = El Arīḥā, *West Bank* 75 D4
Jericho, *Australia* 94 C4
Jerichow, *Germany* 24 C8
Jerid, Chott = Djerid, Chott,
 Tunisia 78 B7
Jermyn, *U.S.A.* 111 E9
Jerome, *U.S.A.* 114 E6
Jerramungup, *Australia* 93 F2
Jersey, *U.K.* 13 H5
Jersey City, *U.S.A.* 111 F10
Jersey Shore, *U.S.A.* 110 E7
Jerseyville, *U.S.A.* 112 F9
Jerusalem, *Israel* 75 D4
Jervis Inlet, *Canada* 104 C4
Jerzu, *Italy* 30 C2
Jesenice, *Slovenia* 29 B11
Jeseník, *Czech Rep.* 27 A10

Jesenké

Jesenké, *Slovak Rep.* 27 C13
Jesi = Iesi, *Italy* 29 E10
Jesselton = Kota Kinabalu,
  Malaysia 62 C5
Jessnitz, *Germany* 24 D8
Jessore, *Bangla.* 67 H16
Jesup, *U.S.A.* 109 K5
Jesús Carranza, *Mexico* 119 D5
Jesús María, *Argentina* 126 C3
Jetmore, *U.S.A.* 113 F5
Jetpur, *India* 68 J4
Jeumont, *France* 19 B11
Jevnaker, *Norway* 9 F14
Jewett, *U.S.A.* 110 F3
Jewett City, *U.S.A.* 111 E13
Jeyḥūnābād, *Iran* 71 C6
Jeypore, *India* 67 K13
Jeziorak, Jezioro, *Poland* 44 E6
Jeziorany, *Poland* 44 E7
Jeziorka →, *Poland* 45 F8
Jha Jha, *India* 69 G12
Jhaarkand = Jharkhand □, *India* 69 H11
Jhabua, *India* 68 H6
Jhajjar, *India* 68 E7
Jhal, *Pakistan* 68 E2
Jhal Jhao, *Pakistan* 66 F4
Jhalawar, *India* 68 G7
Jhalida, *India* 69 H11
Jhalrapatan, *India* 68 G7
Jhang Maghiana, *Pakistan* 68 D5
Jhansi, *India* 69 G8
Jhargram, *India* 69 H12
Jharia, *India* 69 H12
Jharkhand □, *India* 69 H11
Jharsuguda, *India* 67 J14
Jhelum, *Pakistan* 68 C5
Jhelum →, *Pakistan* 68 D5
Jhilmilli, *India* 69 H10
Jhudo, *Pakistan* 68 G3
Jhunjhunu, *India* 68 E6
Ji-Paraná, *Brazil* 124 F6
Ji Xian, *Hebei, China* 56 F8
Ji Xian, *Henan, China* 56 G8
Ji Xian, *Shanxi, China* 56 F6
Jia Xian, *Henan, China* 56 H7
Jia Xian, *Shaanxi, China* 56 F6
Jiading, *China* 59 B13
Jiahe, *China* 59 E9
Jialing Jiang →, *China* 58 C6
Jiamusi, *China* 60 B8
Ji'an, *Jiangxi, China* 59 D10
Ji'an, *Jilin, China* 57 D14
Jianchang, *China* 57 D11
Jianchangying, *China* 57 D10
Jianchuan, *China* 58 D2
Jiande, *China* 59 C12
Jiang'an, *China* 58 C5
Jiangbei, *China* 58 C6
Jiangcheng, *China* 58 F3
Jiangchuan, *China* 58 E4
Jiangdi, *China* 58 D4
Jiangdu, *China* 59 A12
Jiange, *China* 58 A5
Jianghua, *China* 59 E8
Jiangjin, *China* 58 C6
Jiangkou, *China* 58 D7
Jiangle, *China* 59 D11
Jiangling, *China* 59 B9
Jiangmen, *China* 59 F9
Jiangning, *China* 59 B12
Jiangshan, *China* 59 C12
Jiangsu □, *China* 57 H11
Jiangxi □, *China* 59 D11
Jiangyan, *China* 59 A13
Jiangyin, *China* 59 B13
Jiangyong, *China* 59 E8
Jiangyou, *China* 58 B5
Jianhe, *China* 58 D7
Jianli, *China* 59 C9
Jianning, *China* 59 D11
Jian'ou, *China* 59 D12
Jianshi, *China* 58 B7
Jianshui, *China* 58 F4
Jianyang, *Fujian, China* 59 D12
Jianyang, *Sichuan, China* 58 B5
Jiao Xian = Jiaozhou, *China* .. 57 F11
Jiaohe, *Hebei, China* 56 E9
Jiaohe, *Jilin, China* 57 C14
Jiaojiang, *China* 59 C13
Jiaoling, *China* 59 E11
Jiaozhou, *China* 57 F11
Jiaozhou Wan, *China* 57 F11
Jiaozuo, *China* 56 G7
Jiashan, *China* 57 B13
Jiawang, *China* 57 G9
Jiaxiang, *China* 56 G9
Jiaxing, *China* 59 B13
Jiayi = Chiai, *Taiwan* 59 F13
Jiayu, *China* 59 C9
Jibiya, *Nigeria* 83 C6
Jibou, *Romania* 43 C8
Jibuti = Djibouti ■, *Africa* .. 81 E5
Jicarón, I., *Panama* 120 E3
Jičín, *Czech Rep.* 26 A8
Jiddah, *Si. Arabia* 74 C2
Jido, *India* 67 E19
Jieshou, *China* 56 H8
Jiexiu, *China* 56 F6
Jieyang, *China* 59 F11
Jigawa □, *Nigeria* 83 C6
Jiggalong, *Australia* 92 D3
Jigni, *India* 69 G8
Jihlava, *Czech Rep.* 26 B8
Jihlava →, *Czech Rep.* 27 C9
Jihočeský □, *Czech Rep.* 26 B7
Jihomoravský □, *Czech Rep.* ... 27 B9
Jijiga, *Ethiopia* 74 F3

Jikamshi, *Nigeria* 83 C6
Jikau, *Sudan* 81 F3
Jilin, *China* 57 C14
Jilin □, *China* 57 C14
Jiloca →, *Spain* 32 D3
Jilong = Chilung, *Taiwan* 59 E13
Jim Thorpe, *U.S.A.* 111 F9
Jima, *Ethiopia* 81 F4
Jimbolia, *Romania* 42 E5
Jimena de la Frontera, *Spain* . 35 J5
Jiménez, *Mexico* 118 B4
Jimo, *China* 57 F11
Jin Jiang →, *China* 59 C10
Jin Xian = Jinzhou, *China* 56 E8
Jin Xian, *China* 57 E11
Jinan, *China* 56 F9
Jincheng, *China* 56 G7
Jinchuan, *China* 58 B4
Jind, *India* 68 E7
Jindřichův Hradec, *Czech Rep.* 26 B8
Jing He →, *China* 56 G5
Jing Shan, *China* 59 B8
Jing Xian, *China* 59 B12
Jing'an, *China* 59 C10
Jingbian, *China* 56 F5
Jingchuan, *China* 56 G4
Jingde, *China* 59 B12
Jingdezhen, *China* 59 C11
Jingdong, *China* 58 E3
Jinggangshan, *China* 59 D10
Jinggu, *China* 58 F3
Jinghai, *China* 56 E9
Jinghong, *China* 58 G3
Jingjiang, *China* 59 A13
Jingle, *China* 56 E6
Jingmen, *China* 59 B9
Jingning, *China* 56 G3
Jingpo Hu, *China* 57 C15
Jingshan, *China* 59 B9
Jingtai, *China* 56 F3
Jingxi, *China* 58 F6
Jingxing, *China* 56 E8
Jingyang, *China* 56 G5
Jingyu, *China* 57 C14
Jingyuan, *China* 56 F3
Jingzhou, *China* 58 D7
Jingziguan, *China* 56 H6
Jinhua, *China* 59 C12
Jining, *Nei Monggol Zizhiqu,*
  China 56 D7
Jining, *Shandong, China* 56 G9
Jinja, *Uganda* 86 B3
Jinjang, *Malaysia* 65 L3
Jinji, *China* 56 F4
Jinjiang, *Fujian, China* 59 E12
Jinjiang, *Yunnan, China* 58 D3
Jinjini, *Ghana* 82 D4
Jinkou, *China* 59 B10
Jinkouhe, *China* 58 C4
Jinmen Dao, *China* 59 E12
Jinning, *China* 58 E4
Jinotega, *Nic.* 120 D2
Jinotepe, *Nic.* 120 D2
Jinping, *Guizhou, China* 58 D7
Jinping, *Yunnan, China* 58 F4
Jinsha, *China* 58 D6
Jinsha Jiang →, *China* 58 C5
Jinshan, *China* 59 B13
Jinshi, *China* 59 C8
Jintan, *China* 59 B12
Jinxi, *Jiangxi, China* 59 D11
Jinxi, *Liaoning, China* 57 D11
Jinxian, *China* 59 C11
Jinxiang, *China* 56 G9
Jinyang, *China* 58 D4
Jinyun, *China* 59 C13
Jinzhai, *China* 59 B10
Jinzhou, *Hebei, China* 56 E8
Jinzhou, *Liaoning, China* 57 D11
Jiparaná →, *Brazil* 124 E6
Jipijapa, *Ecuador* 124 D2
Jiquilpan, *Mexico* 118 D4
Jishan, *China* 56 G6
Jishou, *China* 58 C7
Jishui, *China* 59 D10
Jisr ash Shughūr, *Syria* 70 C3
Jitarning, *Australia* 93 F2
Jitra, *Malaysia* 65 J3
Jiu →, *Romania* 43 G8
Jiudengkou, *China* 56 E4
Jiujiang, *Guangdong, China* ... 59 F9
Jiujiang, *Jiangxi, China* 59 C10
Jiuling Shan, *China* 59 C10
Jiulong, *China* 58 C3
Jiutai, *China* 57 B13
Jiuxincheng, *China* 56 E8
Jiuyuhang, *China* 59 B12
Jixi, *Anhui, China* 59 B12
Jixi, *Heilongjiang, China* 57 B16
Jiyang, *China* 57 F9
Jiyuan, *China* 56 G7
Jīzān, *Si. Arabia* 74 D3
Jizera →, *Czech Rep.* 26 A7
Jizl, W. →, *Si. Arabia* 80 B4
Jizl, Wādī al, *Si. Arabia* 70 E3
Jizō-Zaki, *Japan* 55 G6
Jizzakh, *Uzbekistan* 50 E7
Joaçaba, *Brazil* 127 B5
Joal Fadiout, *Senegal* 82 C1
João Pessoa, *Brazil* 125 E12
Joaquín V. González, *Argentina* 126 B3
Jobat, *India* 68 H6
Jobourg, Nez de, *France* 18 C5
Jódar, *Spain* 35 H7
Jodhpur, *India* 68 F5

Jodiya, *India* 68 H4
Jōetsu, *Japan* 55 F9
Jœuf, *France* 19 C12
Jofane, *Mozam.* 89 C5
Jogbani, *India* 69 F12
Jogjakarta = Yogyakarta,
  Indonesia 62 F4
Johannesburg, *S. Africa* 89 D4
Johannesburg, *U.S.A.* 117 K9
Johansfors, *Sweden* 11 H9
Johilla →, *India* 69 H9
John Day, *U.S.A.* 114 D4
John Day →, *U.S.A.* 114 D3
John D'Or Prairie, *Canada* 104 B5
John H. Kerr Reservoir, *U.S.A.* 109 G6
John o' Groats, *U.K.* 14 C5
Johnnie, *U.S.A.* 117 J10
John's Ra., *Australia* 94 C1
Johnson, *Kans., U.S.A.* 113 G4
Johnson, *Vt., U.S.A.* 111 B12
Johnson City, *N.Y., U.S.A.* ... 111 D9
Johnson City, *Tenn., U.S.A.* .. 109 G4
Johnson City, *Tex., U.S.A.* ... 113 K5
Johnsonburg, *U.S.A.* 110 E6
Johnsondale, *U.S.A.* 117 K8
Johnson's Crossing, *Canada* ... 104 A2
Johnston, L., *Australia* 93 F3
Johnston Falls = Mambilima
  Falls, *Zambia* 87 E2
Johnston I., *Pac. Oc.* 97 F11
Johnstone Str., *Canada* 104 C3
Johnstown, *N.Y., U.S.A.* 111 C10
Johnstown, *Ohio, U.S.A.* 110 F2
Johnstown, *Pa., U.S.A.* 110 F6
Johor Baharu, *Malaysia* 65 M4
Jōhvi, *Estonia* 9 G22
Joigny, *France* 19 E10
Joinville, *Brazil* 127 B6
Joinville, *France* 19 D12
Joinville I., *Antarctica* 5 C18
Jojutla, *Mexico* 119 D5
Jokkmokk, *Sweden* 8 C18
Jökulsá á Bru →, *Iceland* 8 D6
Jökulsá á Fjöllum →, *Iceland* . 8 C5
Jolfá, *Āzarbājān-e Sharqī, Iran* 70 B5
Jolfá, *Eşfahan, Iran* 71 C6
Joliet, *U.S.A.* 108 E1
Joliette, *Canada* 102 C5
Jolo, *Phil.* 61 J4
Jolon, *U.S.A.* 116 K5
Jomalig I., *Phil.* 61 D5
Jombang, *Indonesia* 63 G15
Jomda, *China* 58 B2
Jonava, *Lithuania* 9 J21
Jones Sound, *Canada* 4 B3
Jonesboro, *Ark., U.S.A.* 113 H9
Jonesboro, *La., U.S.A.* 113 J8
Jong →, *S. Leone* 82 D2
Jonglei, *Sudan* 81 F3
Jonglei □, *Sudan* 81 F3
Joniškis, *Lithuania* 9 H20
Jönköping, *Sweden* 11 G8
Jönköpings län □, *Sweden* 11 G8
Jonquière, *Canada* 103 C5
Jonsered, *Sweden* 11 G6
Jonzac, *France* 20 C3
Joplin, *U.S.A.* 113 G7
Jora, *India* 68 F6
Jordan, *Mont., U.S.A.* 114 C10
Jordan, *N.Y., U.S.A.* 111 C8
Jordan ■, *Asia* 75 E5
Jordan →, *Asia* 75 D4
Jordan Valley, *U.S.A.* 114 E5
Jordanów, *Poland* 45 J6
Jorhat, *India* 67 F19
Jörn, *Sweden* 8 D19
Jorong, *Indonesia* 62 E4
Jørpeland, *Norway* 9 G11
Jorquera →, *Chile* 126 B2
Jos, *Nigeria* 83 D6
Jos Plateau, *Nigeria* 83 D6
Jošanička Banja, *Serbia, Yug.* 40 C4
José Battle y Ordóñez, *Uruguay* 127 C4
Joseni, *Romania* 43 D10
Joseph, L., *Nfld., Canada* 103 B6
Joseph, L., *Ont., Canada* 110 A5
Joseph Bonaparte G., *Australia* 92 B4
Joshinath, *India* 69 D8
Joshua Tree, *U.S.A.* 117 L10
Joshua Tree National Park,
  U.S.A. 117 M10
Josselin, *France* 18 E4
Jostedalsbreen, *Norway* 9 F12
Jotunheimen, *Norway* 9 F13
Joubertberge, *Namibia* 88 B1
Joué-lès-Tours, *France* 18 E7
Jourdanton, *U.S.A.* 113 L5
Joutseno, *Finland* 46 B5
Jovellanos, *Cuba* 120 B3
Joyeuse, *France* 21 D8
Józefów, *Lubelskie, Poland* ... 45 H10
Józefów, *Mazowieckie, Poland* . 45 F8
Ju Xian, *China* 57 F10
Juan Aldama, *Mexico* 118 C4
Juan Bautista Alberdi, *Argentina* 126 C3
Juan de Fuca Str., *Canada* 116 B3
Juan de Nova, *Ind. Oc.* 89 B7
Juan Fernández, Arch. de,
  Pac. Oc. 122 G2
Juan José Castelli, *Argentina* 126 B3
Juan L. Lacaze, *Uruguay* 126 C4
Juankoski, *Finland* 8 E23
Juárez, *Argentina* 126 D4
Juárez, *Mexico* 117 N11
Juárez, Sierra de, *Mexico* 118 A1

Juàzeiro, *Brazil* 125 E10
Juàzeiro do Norte, *Brazil* 125 E11
Juba, *Sudan* 81 G3
Jubayl, *Lebanon* 75 A4
Jubbah, *Si. Arabia* 70 D4
Jubbal, *India* 68 D7
Jubbulpore = Jabalpur, *India* . 69 H8
Jübek, *Germany* 24 A5
Jubga, *Russia* 49 H4
Jubilee L., *Australia* 93 E4
Juby, C., *Morocco* 78 C3
Júcar = Xúquer →, *Spain* 33 F4
Júcaro, *Cuba* 120 B4
Juchitán, *Mexico* 119 D5
Judaea = Har Yehuda, *Israel* .. 75 D3
Judenburg, *Austria* 26 D7
Judith →, *U.S.A.* 114 C9
Judith, Pt., *U.S.A.* 111 E13
Judith Gap, *U.S.A.* 114 C9
Juelsminde, *Denmark* 11 J4
Jugoslavia = Yugoslavia ■,
  Europe 40 C4
Juigalpa, *Nic.* 120 D2
Juillac, *France* 20 C5
Juist, *Germany* 24 B2
Juiz de Fora, *Brazil* 127 A7
Jujuy □, *Argentina* 126 A2
Julesburg, *U.S.A.* 112 E3
Juli, *Peru* 124 G5
Julia Cr. →, *Australia* 94 C3
Julia Creek, *Australia* 94 C3
Juliaca, *Peru* 124 G4
Julian, *U.S.A.* 117 M10
Julian Alps = Julijske Alpe,
  Slovenia 29 B11
Julian L., *Canada* 102 B4
Julianatop, *Surinam* 125 C7
Julianehåb = Qaqortoq,
  Greenland 101 B6
Jülich, *Germany* 24 C2
Julijske Alpe, *Slovenia* 29 B11
Julimes, *Mexico* 118 B3
Jullundur, *India* 68 D6
Julu, *China* 56 F8
Jumbo, *Zimbabwe* 87 F3
Jumbo Pk., *U.S.A.* 117 J12
Jumentos Cays, *Bahamas* 120 B4
Jumilla, *Spain* 33 G3
Jumla, *Nepal* 69 E10
Jumna = Yamuna →, *India* 69 G9
Junagadh, *India* 68 J4
Junction, *Tex., U.S.A.* 113 K5
Junction, *Utah, U.S.A.* 115 G7
Junction B., *Australia* 94 A1
Junction City, *Kans., U.S.A.* . 112 F6
Junction City, *Oreg., U.S.A.* . 114 D2
Junction Pt., *Australia* 94 A1
Jundah, *Australia* 94 C3
Jundiaí, *Brazil* 127 A6
Juneau, *U.S.A.* 104 B2
Jungfrau, *Switz.* 25 J3
Junggar Pendi, *China* 60 B3
Jungshahi, *Pakistan* 68 G2
Juniata →, *U.S.A.* 110 F7
Junín, *Argentina* 126 C3
Junín de los Andes, *Argentina* 128 D2
Jūniyah, *Lebanon* 75 B4
Junlian, *China* 58 C5
Juntas, *Chile* 126 B2
Juntura, *U.S.A.* 114 E4
Jur, Nahr el →, *Sudan* 81 F2
Jura = Jura, Mts. du, *Europe* . 19 F13
Jura = Schwäbische Alb,
  Germany 25 G5
Jura, *U.K.* 14 F3
Jura □, *France* 19 F12
Jura □, *Switz.* 25 H3
Jūra →, *Lithuania* 44 C9
Jura, Mts. du, *Europe* 19 F13
Jura, Sd. of, *U.K.* 14 F3
Jurbarkas, *Lithuania* 9 J20
Jurien, *Australia* 93 F2
Jurilovca, *Romania* 43 F13
Jūrmala, *Latvia* 9 H20
Jurong, *China* 59 B12
Juruá →, *Brazil* 122 D4
Juruena, *Brazil* 124 F7
Juruena →, *Brazil* 124 E7
Juruti, *Brazil* 125 D7
Jussey, *France* 19 E12
Justo Daract, *Argentina* 126 C2
Jutaí →, *Brazil* 124 D5
Jüterbog, *Germany* 24 D9
Juticalpa, *Honduras* 120 D2
Jutland = Jylland, *Denmark* ... 11 H3
Juventud, I. de la, *Cuba* 120 B3
Juvigny-sous-Andaine, *France* . 18 D6
Jūy Zar, *Iran* 70 C5
Jūye, *China* 56 G9
Juzennecourt, *France* 19 D11
Jvari, *Georgia* 49 J6
Jwaneng, *Botswana* 85 J4
Jyderup, *Denmark* 11 J5
Jylland, *Denmark* 11 H3
Jyväskylä, *Finland* 9 E21

K

K2, *Pakistan* 69 B7
Ka →, *Nigeria* 83 C5
Kaap Plateau, *S. Africa* 88 D3
Kaapkruis, *Namibia* 88 C1
Kaapstad = Cape Town,
  S. Africa 88 E2

Kaba, *Guinea* 82 C2
Kabaena, *Indonesia* 63 F6
Kabala, *S. Leone* 82 D2
Kabale, *Uganda* 86 C3
Kabalo, *Dem. Rep. of the Congo* 86 D2
Kabambare, *Dem. Rep. of*
  the Congo 86 C2
Kabango, *Dem. Rep. of*
  the Congo 87 D2
Kabanjahe, *Indonesia* 62 D1
Kabankalan, *Phil.* 61 G5
Kabara, *Mali* 82 B4
Kabardinka, *Russia* 47 K10
Kabardino-Balkar Republic =
  Kabardino-Balkaria □, *Russia* 49 J6
Kabardino-Balkaria □, *Russia* . 49 J6
Kabarega Falls = Murchison
  Falls, *Uganda* 86 B3
Kabasalan, *Phil.* 61 H5
Kabba, *Nigeria* 83 D6
Kabetogama, *U.S.A.* 112 A8
Kabi, *Niger* 83 C7
Kabin Buri, *Thailand* 64 F3
Kabinakagami L., *Canada* 102 C3
Kabinda, *Dem. Rep. of*
  the Congo 84 F4
Kabna, *Sudan* 80 D3
Kabompo, *Zambia* 87 E1
Kabompo →, *Zambia* 85 G4
Kabondo, *Dem. Rep. of*
  the Congo 87 D2
Kabongo, *Dem. Rep. of*
  the Congo 86 D2
Kabot, *Guinea* 82 C2
Kabou, *Togo* 83 D5
Kabr, *Sudan* 81 E2
Kabūd Gonbad, *Iran* 71 B8
Kabugao, *Phil.* 61 B3
Kābul, *Afghan.* 68 B3
Kābul □, *Afghan.* 66 B6
Kābul →, *Pakistan* 68 C5
Kabunga, *Dem. Rep. of*
  the Congo 86 C2
Kaburuang, *Indonesia* 63 D7
Kabushiya, *Sudan* 81 D3
Kabwe, *Zambia* 87 E2
Kačanik, *Kosovo, Yug.* 40 D5
Kačerginė, *Lithuania* 44 D10
Kachchh, Gulf of, *India* 68 H3
Kachchh, Rann of, *India* 68 H4
Kachchhidhana, *India* 69 J8
Kachebera, *Zambia* 87 E3
Kachia, *Nigeria* 83 D6
Kachikau, *Botswana* 88 B3
Kachin □, *Burma* 58 D1
Kachira, L., *Uganda* 86 C3
Kachiry, *Kazakstan* 50 D8
Kachisi, *Ethiopia* 81 F4
Kachnara, *India* 68 H6
Kachot, *Cambodia* 65 G4
Kaçkar, *Turkey* 73 B9
Kadan, *Czech Rep.* 26 A6
Kadan Kyun, *Burma* 64 F2
Kadanai →, *Afghan.* 68 D1
Kadarkút, *Hungary* 42 D2
Kade, *Ghana* 83 D4
Kadi, *India* 68 H5
Kadınhanı, *Turkey* 72 C5
Kadiolo, *Mali* 82 C3
Kadipur, *India* 69 F10
Kadirli, *Turkey* 70 B3
Kadiyevka = Stakhanov, *Ukraine* 47 H10
Kadoka, *U.S.A.* 112 D4
Kadom, *Russia* 48 C5
Kadoma, *Zimbabwe* 87 F2
Kādugli, *Sudan* 81 E2
Kaduna, *Nigeria* 83 C6
Kaduna □, *Nigeria* 83 C6
Kaduy, *Russia* 46 C9
Kaédi, *Mauritania* 82 B2
Kaélé, *Cameroon* 83 C7
Kaeng Khoï, *Thailand* 64 E3
Kaesŏng, *N. Korea* 57 F14
Kāf, *Si. Arabia* 70 D3
Kafan = Kapan, *Armenia* 70 B5
Kafanchan, *Nigeria* 83 D6
Kafarévs, Ákra, *Greece* 38 C6
Kaffrine, *Senegal* 82 C1
Kafin, *Nigeria* 83 D6
Kafin Madaki, *Nigeria* 83 C6
Kafinda, *Zambia* 87 E3
Kafr el Battikh, *Egypt* 80 H7
Kafr el Dauwâr, *Egypt* 80 H7
Kafr el Sheikh, *Egypt* 80 H7
Kafue, *Zambia* 87 F2
Kafue →, *Zambia* 85 H5
Kafue Flats, *Zambia* 87 F2
Kafue Nat. Park, *Zambia* 87 F2
Kafulwe, *Zambia* 87 D2
Kaga, *Afghan.* 68 B4
Kaga Bandoro, *C.A.R.* 84 C3
Kagan, *Uzbekistan* 50 F7
Kagarko, *Nigeria* 83 D6
Kagawa □, *Japan* 55 G7
Kagera = Ziwa Magharība □,
  Tanzania 86 C3
Kagera →, *Uganda* 86 C3
Kağızman, *Turkey* 70 B4
Kagoro, *Sudan* 81 F3
Kagoshima, *Japan* 55 J5
Kagoshima □, *Japan* 55 J5
Kagul = Cahul, *Moldova* 43 E13
Kahak, *Iran* 71 B6
Kahama, *Tanzania* 86 C3

Kahan, *Pakistan* 68 E3
Kahang, *Malaysia* 65 L4
Kahayan →, *Indonesia* 62 E4
Kahe, *Tanzania* 86 C4
Kahnūj, *Iran* 71 E8
Kahoka, *U.S.A.* 112 E9
Kahoolawe, *U.S.A.* 106 H16
Kahramanmaraş, *Turkey* 70 B3
Kâhta, *Turkey* 73 D8
Kahuta, *Pakistan* 68 C5
Kai, Kepulauan, *Indonesia* ... 63 F8
Kai Besar, *Indonesia* 63 F8
Kai Is. = Kai, Kepulauan,
  Indonesia 63 F8
Kai Kecil, *Indonesia* 63 F8
Kaiama, *Nigeria* 83 D5
Kaiapoi, *N.Z.* 91 K4
Kaieteur Falls, *Guyana* 124 B7
Kaifeng, *China* 56 G8
Kaihua, *China* 59 C12
Kaijiang, *China* 58 B6
Kaikohe, *N.Z.* 91 F4
Kaikoura, *N.Z.* 91 K4
Kaikoura Ra., *N.Z.* 91 J4
Kailahun, *S. Leone* 82 D2
Kaili, *China* 58 D6
Kailu, *China* 57 C11
Kailua Kona, *U.S.A.* 106 J17
Kaimana, *Indonesia* 63 E8
Kaimanawa Mts., *N.Z.* 91 H5
Kaimganj, *India* 69 F8
Kaimur Hills, *India* 69 G10
Kainab →, *Namibia* 88 D2
Kainji Dam, *Nigeria* 83 D5
Kainji Res., *Nigeria* 83 C5
Kainuu, *Finland* 8 D23
Kaipara Harbour, *N.Z.* 91 G5
Kaiping, *China* 59 F9
Kaipokok B., *Canada* 103 B8
Kaira, *India* 68 H5
Kairana, *India* 68 E7
Kaironi, *Indonesia* 63 E8
Kairouan, *Tunisia* 79 A8
Kaiserslautern, *Germany* 25 F3
Kaiserstuhl, *Germany* 25 G3
Kaitaia, *N.Z.* 91 F4
Kaitangata, *N.Z.* 91 M2
Kaithal, *India* 68 E7
Kaitu →, *Pakistan* 68 C4
Kaiyang, *China* 58 D6
Kaiyuan, *Liaoning, China* 57 C13
Kaiyuan, *Yunnan, China* 58 F4
Kajaani, *Finland* 8 D22
Kajabbi, *Australia* 94 C3
Kajana = Kajaani, *Finland* ... 8 D22
Kajang, *Malaysia* 65 L3
Kajaran, *Armenia* 73 C12
Kajiado, *Kenya* 86 C4
Kajo Kaji, *Sudan* 81 G3
Kajuru, *Nigeria* 83 C6
Kaka, *Sudan* 81 E3
Kakabeka Falls, *Canada* 102 C2
Kakadu Nat. Park, *Australia* ... 92 B5
Kakamas, *S. Africa* 88 D3
Kakamega, *Kenya* 86 B3
Kakanj, *Bos.-H.* 42 F3
Kakdwip, *India* 69 J13
Kake, *Japan* 55 G6
Kake, *U.S.A.* 104 B2
Kakegawa, *Japan* 55 G9
Kakeroma-Jima, *Japan* 55 K4
Kakhib, *Russia* 49 J8
Kakhovka, *Ukraine* 47 J7
Kakhovske Vdskh., *Ukraine* ... 47 J7
Kakinada, *India* 67 L13
Kakisa →, *Canada* 104 A5
Kakisa L., *Canada* 104 A5
Kakogawa, *Japan* 55 G7
Kakwa →, *Canada* 104 C5
Kāl Gūsheh, *Iran* 71 D8
Kal Safīd, *Iran* 70 C5
Kala, *Nigeria* 83 C7
Kalaallit Nunaat = Greenland ■,
  N. Amer. 4 C5
Kalabagh, *Pakistan* 68 C4
Kalabahi, *Indonesia* 63 F6
Kalabáka, *Greece* 38 B3
Kalabana, *Mali* 82 C3
Kalach, *Russia* 48 E5
Kalach na Donu, *Russia* 49 F6
Kaladan →, *Burma* 67 J18
Kaladar, *Canada* 102 D4
Kalahari, *Africa* 88 C3
Kalahari Gemsbok Nat. Park,
  S. Africa 88 D3
Kalajoki, *Finland* 8 D20
Kālak, *Iran* 71 E8
Kalakamati, *Botswana* 89 C4
Kalakan, *Russia* 51 D12
K'alak'unlun Shank'ou =
  Karakoram Pass, *Pakistan* .. 69 B7
Kalam, *Pakistan* 69 B5
Kalama, *Dem. Rep. of the Congo* 86 C2
Kalama, *U.S.A.* 116 E4
Kalámai, *Greece* 38 D4
Kalamariá, *Greece* 40 F6
Kalamata = Kalámai, *Greece* .. 38 D4
Kalamazoo, *U.S.A.* 108 D3
Kalamazoo →, *U.S.A.* 108 D2
Kalambo Falls, *Tanzania* 87 D3
Kálamos, *Attikí, Greece* 38 C5
Kálamos, *Iónioi Nísoi, Greece* . 38 C2
Kalan, *Turkey* 70 B3

Kalankalan, *Guinea* 82 C3
Kalannie, *Australia* 93 F2
Kalāntarī, *Iran* 71 C7
Kalao, *Indonesia* 63 F6
Kalaotoa, *Indonesia* 63 F6
Kälarne, *Sweden* 10 B10
Kalasin, *Thailand* 64 D4
Kalat, *Pakistan* 66 E5
Kalāteh, *Iran* 71 B7
Kalāteh-ye Ganj, *Iran* 71 E8
Kálathos, *Greece* 39 E10
Kalaus →, *Russia* 49 H7
Kalávrita, *Greece* 38 C4
Kalbarri, *Australia* 93 E1
Kale, *Antalya, Turkey* 39 E12
Kale, *Denizli, Turkey* 39 D10
Kalecik, *Turkey* 72 B5
Kalegauk Kyun, *Burma* 67 M20
Kalehe, *Dem. Rep. of the Congo* 86 C2
Kalema, *Tanzania* 86 C3
Kalemie, *Dem. Rep. of
  the Congo* 86 D2
Kalety, *Poland* 45 H5
Kalewa, *Burma* 67 H19
Kaleybar, *Iran* 70 B5
Kalgan = Zhangjiakou, *China* .. 56 D8
Kalgoorlie-Boulder, *Australia* . 93 F3
Kali →, *India* 69 F8
Kali Sindh →, *India* 68 G6
Kaliakra, Nos, *Bulgaria* 41 C12
Kalianda, *Indonesia* 62 F3
Kalibo, *Phil.* 61 F5
Kalima, *Dem. Rep. of the Congo* 86 C2
Kalimantan □, *Indonesia* 62 E4
Kalimantan Barat □, *Indonesia* 62 E4
Kalimantan Selatan □, *Indonesia* 62 E5
Kalimantan Tengah □,
  Indonesia 62 E4
Kalimantan Timur □, *Indonesia* 62 D5
Kálimnos, *Greece* 39 D8
Kalimpong, *India* 69 F13
Kalinin = Tver, *Russia* 46 D8
Kaliningrad, *Russia* 9 J19
Kalininsk, *Russia* 48 E7
Kalinkavichy, *Belarus* 47 F5
Kalinkovichi = Kalinkavichy,
  Belarus 47 F5
Kalinovik, *Bos.-H.* 40 C2
Kalipetrovo, *Bulgaria* 41 B11
Kaliro, *Uganda* 86 B3
Kalírrákhi, *Greece* 41 F8
Kalispell, *U.S.A.* 114 B6
Kalisz, *Poland* 45 G5
Kalisz Pomorski, *Poland* 45 E2
Kaliua, *Tanzania* 86 D3
Kalívia Thorikoú, *Greece* 38 D5
Kalix, *Sweden* 8 D20
Kalix →, *Sweden* 8 D20
Kalka, *India* 68 D7
Kalkan, *Turkey* 39 E11
Kalkarindji, *Australia* 92 C5
Kalkaska, *U.S.A.* 108 C3
Kalkfeld, *Namibia* 88 C2
Kalkfontein, *Botswana* 88 C3
Kalkım, *Turkey* 39 B9
Kalkrand, *Namibia* 88 C2
Kållandsö, *Sweden* 11 F7
Kallavesi, *Finland* 8 E22
Källby, *Sweden* 11 F7
Källered, *Sweden* 11 G6
Kallimasiá, *Greece* 39 C8
Kallinge, *Sweden* 11 H9
Kallithéa, *Greece* 38 D5
Kallmet, *Albania* 40 E3
Kalloní, *Greece* 39 B8
Kallonís, Kólpos, *Greece* 39 B8
Kallsjön, *Sweden* 8 E15
Kalmalo, *Nigeria* 83 C6
Kalmar, *Sweden* 11 H10
Kalmar län □, *Sweden* 11 G10
Kalmar sund, *Sweden* 11 H10
Kalmyk Republic = Kalmykia □,
  Russia 49 G8
Kalmykia □, *Russia* 49 G8
Kalmykovo, *Kazakhstan* 50 E6
Kalna, *India* 69 H13
Kalnai, *India* 69 H10
Kalocsa, *Hungary* 42 D4
Kalofer, *Bulgaria* 41 D8
Kalokhorio, *Cyprus* 36 E12
Kaloko, *Dem. Rep. of the Congo* 86 D2
Kalol, *Gujarat, India* 68 H5
Kalol, *Gujarat, India* 68 H5
Kalolímnos, *Greece* 39 D9
Kalomo, *Zambia* 87 F2
Kalonerón, *Greece* 38 D3
Kalpi, *India* 69 F8
Kaltern = Caldaro, *Italy* 29 B8
Kaltungo, *Nigeria* 83 D7
Kalu, *Pakistan* 68 G2
Kaluga, *Russia* 46 E9
Kalulushi, *Zambia* 87 E2
Kalundborg, *Denmark* 11 J5
Kalush, *Ukraine* 47 H3
Kałuszyn, *Poland* 45 F8
Kalutara, *Sri Lanka* 66 R12
Kalvarija, *Lithuania* 44 D10
Kalyazin, *Russia* 46 D9
Kam →, *Nigeria* 83 D7
Kama, *Dem. Rep. of the Congo* 86 C2
Kama →, *Russia* 50 D6
Kamachumu, *Tanzania* 86 C3
Kamaishi, *Japan* 54 E10
Kamalia, *Pakistan* 68 D5
Kaman, *India* 68 F6

Kaman, *Turkey* 72 C5
Kamanjab, *Namibia* 88 B2
Kamapanda, *Zambia* 87 E1
Kamaran, *Yemen* 74 D3
Kamativi, *Zimbabwe* 88 B4
Kamba, *Nigeria* 83 C5
Kambalda, *Australia* 93 F3
Kambar, *Pakistan* 68 F3
Kambia, *S. Leone* 82 D2
Kambolé, *Togo* 83 D5
Kambolé, *Zambia* 87 D3
Kambos, *Cyprus* 36 D11
Kambove, *Dem. Rep. of
  the Congo* 87 E2
Kamchatka, Poluostrov, *Russia* 51 D16
Kamchatka Pen. = Kamchatka,
  Poluostrov, *Russia* 51 D16
Kamchiya →, *Bulgaria* 41 C11
Kamen, *Russia* 50 D9
Kamen-Rybolov, *Russia* 54 B6
Kamenica, *Serbia, Yug.* 40 C6
Kamenica, *Serbia, Yug.* 40 B3
Kamenice nad Lipou,
  Czech Rep. 26 B8
Kamenjak, Rt, *Croatia* 29 D10
Kamenka = Kaminka, *Ukraine* . 47 H7
Kamenka, *Kazakhstan* 48 E10
Kamenka, *Penza, Russia* 48 D6
Kamenka, *Voronezh, Russia* ... 47 G10
Kamenka Bugskaya =
  Kamyanka-Buzka, *Ukraine* .. 47 G3
Kamenka Dneprovskaya =
  Kamyanka-Dniprovska,
  Ukraine 47 J8
Kamennomostskiy, *Russia* 49 H5
Kameno, *Bulgaria* 41 D11
Kamenolomni, *Russia* 49 G5
Kamensk-Shakhtinskiy, *Russia* 49 F5
Kamensk Uralskiy, *Russia* 50 D7
Kamenskiy, *Russia* 48 E7
Kamenskoye, *Russia* 51 C17
Kamenyak, *Bulgaria* 41 C10
Kamenz, *Germany* 24 D10
Kameoka, *Japan* 55 G7
Kamiah, *U.S.A.* 114 C5
Kamień Krajeński, *Poland* 44 E4
Kamień Pomorski, *Poland* 44 E1
Kamienna →, *Poland* 45 G8
Kamienna Góra, *Poland* 45 H3
Kamieńsk, *Poland* 45 G6
Kamieskroon, *S. Africa* 88 E2
Kamilukuak, L., *Canada* 105 A8
Kamin-Kashyrskyy, *Ukraine* ... 47 G4
Kamina, *Dem. Rep. of the Congo* 87 D2
Kaminak L., *Canada* 105 A10
Kaministiquia, *Canada* 102 C1
Kaminka, *Ukraine* 47 H7
Kaminoyama, *Japan* 54 E10
Kamiros, *Greece* 36 C9
Kamituga, *Dem. Rep. of
  the Congo* 86 C2
Kamla →, *India* 69 G12
Kamloops, *Canada* 104 C4
Kamnik, *Slovenia* 29 B11
Kamo, *Armenia* 49 K7
Kamo, *Japan* 54 F9
Kamoke, *Pakistan* 68 C6
Kamp →, *Austria* 26 C8
Kampala, *Uganda* 86 B3
Kampang Chhnang, *Cambodia* 65 F5
Kampar, *Malaysia* 65 K3
Kampar →, *Indonesia* 62 D2
Kampen, *Neths.* 17 B5
Kamphaeng Phet, *Thailand* ... 64 D2
Kampolombo, L., *Zambia* 87 E2
Kampong Saom, *Cambodia* ... 65 G4
Kampong Saom, Chaak,
  Cambodia 65 G4
Kampong To, *Thailand* 65 J3
Kampot, *Cambodia* 65 G5
Kampti, *Burkina Faso* 82 C4
Kampuchea = Cambodia ■, *Asia* 64 F5
Kampung Air Putih, *Malaysia* .. 65 K4
Kampung Jerangau, *Malaysia* .. 65 K4
Kampung Raja, *Malaysia* 65 K4
Kampungbaru = Tolitoli,
  Indonesia 63 D6
Kamrau, Teluk, *Indonesia* 63 E8
Kamsack, *Canada* 105 C8
Kamsai, *India* 82 C2
Kamskoye Ustye, *Russia* 48 C9
Kamuchawie L., *Canada* 105 B8
Kamui-Misaki, *Japan* 54 C10
Kamyanets-Podilskyy, *Ukraine* 47 H4
Kamyanka-Buzka, *Ukraine* ... 47 G3
Kamyanka-Dniprovska, *Ukraine* 47 J8
Kâmyârân, *Iran* 70 C5
Kamyshin, *Russia* 48 E7
Kamyzyak, *Russia* 49 G9
Kan, *Sudan* 81 F3

Kanazawa, *Japan* 55 F8
Kanchanaburi, *Thailand* 64 E2
Kanchenjunga, *Nepal* 69 F13
Kanchipuram, *India* 66 N11
Kandahar = Qandahār, *Afghan.* 66 D4
Kandalaksha, *Russia* 50 C4
Kandangan, *Indonesia* 62 E5
Kandanghaur, *Indonesia* 63 G13
Kandanos, *Greece* 36 D5
Kandava, *Latvia* 44 A9
Kandavu, *Fiji* 91 D8
Kandhíla, *Greece* 38 D4
Kandhkot, *Pakistan* 68 E3
Kandhla, *India* 68 E7
Kandi, *Benin* 83 C5
Kandi, *India* 69 H13
Kandiaro, *Pakistan* 68 F3
Kandıra, *Turkey* 72 B4
Kandla, *India* 68 H4
Kandreho, *Madag.* 89 B8
Kandy, *Sri Lanka* 66 R12
Kane, *U.S.A.* 110 E6
Kane Basin, *Greenland* 4 B4
Kanel, *Senegal* 82 B2
Kaneohe, *U.S.A.* 106 H16
Kanevskaya, *Russia* 49 G4
Kanfanar, *Croatia* 29 C10
Kang, *Botswana* 88 C3
Kangaba, *Mali* 82 C3
Kangal, *Turkey* 72 C7
Kangān, *Fārs, Iran* 71 E7
Kangān, *Hormozgān, Iran* ... 71 E8
Kangar, *Malaysia* 65 J3
Kangaré, *Mali* 82 C3
Kangaroo Mts., *Australia* 94 C3
Kangasala, *Finland* 9 F21
Kangāvar, *Iran* 71 C6
Kangding, *China* 58 B3
Kangdong, *N. Korea* 57 E14
Kangean, Kepulauan, *Indonesia* 62 F5
Kangean Is. = Kangean,
  Kepulauan, *Indonesia* 62 F5
Kangen →, *Sudan* 81 F3
Kanggye, *N. Korea* 57 D14
Kanggyŏng, *S. Korea* 57 F14
Kanghwa, *S. Korea* 57 F14
Kangikajik, *Greenland* 4 B6
Kangiqsliniq = Rankin Inlet,
  Canada 100 B10
Kangiqsualujjuaq, *Canada* ... 101 C13
Kangiqsujuaq, *Canada* 101 B12
Kangiqtugaapik = Clyde River,
  Canada 101 A13
Kangirsuk, *Canada* 101 B13
Kangnŭng, *S. Korea* 57 F15
Kangping, *China* 57 C12
Kangra, *India* 68 C7
Kangto, *India* 67 F18
Kanhar →, *India* 69 G10
Kani, *Ivory C.* 82 D3
Kaniama, *Dem. Rep. of
  the Congo* 86 D1
Kaniapiskau = Caniapiscau →,
  Canada 103 A6
Kaniapiskau, Rés. =
  Caniapiscau, Rés. de, *Canada* 103 B6
Kanin, Poluostrov, *Russia* 50 C5
Kanin Nos, Mys, *Russia* 50 C5
Kanin Pen. = Kanin, Poluostrov,
  Russia 50 C5
Kaninë, *Albania* 40 F3
Kanjiža, *Serbia, Yug.* 42 D5
Kanjut Sar, *Pakistan* 69 A6
Kankaanpää, *Finland* 9 F20
Kankakee, *U.S.A.* 108 E2
Kankakee →, *U.S.A.* 108 E1
Kankan, *Guinea* 82 C3
Kankendy = Xankändi,
  Azerbaijan 70 B5
Kanker, *India* 67 J12
Kankossa, *Mauritania* 82 B2
Kankroli, *India* 68 G5
Kannapolis, *U.S.A.* 109 H5
Kannauj, *India* 69 F8
Kannod, *India* 66 H10
Kano, *Nigeria* 83 C6
Kano □, *Nigeria* 83 C6
Kan'onji, *Japan* 55 G6
Kanoroba, *Ivory C.* 82 D3
Kanowit, *Malaysia* 62 D4
Kanoya, *Japan* 55 J5
Kanpetlet, *Burma* 67 J18
Kanpur, *India* 69 F9
Kansas □, *U.S.A.* 112 F6
Kansas →, *U.S.A.* 112 F7
Kansas City, *Kans., U.S.A.* ... 112 F7
Kansas City, *Mo., U.S.A.* ... 112 F7
Kansenia, *Dem. Rep. of
  the Congo* 87 E2
Kansk, *Russia* 51 D10
Kansŏng, *S. Korea* 57 E15
Kansu = Gansu □, *China* 56 G3
Kantaphor, *India* 68 H7
Kantchari, *Burkina Faso* 83 C5
Kantché, *Niger* 83 C6
Kanté, *Togo* 83 D5
Kantemirovka, *Russia* 47 H10
Kantharalak, *Thailand* 64 E5
Kanthi →, *India* 68 E6
Kantō □, *Japan* 55 F9
Kantō-Sanchi, *Japan* 55 G9
Kanturk, *Ireland* 15 D3
Kanuma, *Japan* 55 F9
Kanus, *Namibia* 88 D2

Kanye, *Botswana* 88 C4
Kanzenze, *Dem. Rep. of
  the Congo* 87 E2
Kanzi, Ras, *Tanzania* 86 D4
Kaohsiung, *Taiwan* 59 F13
Kaokoveld, *Namibia* 88 B1
Kaolack, *Senegal* 82 C1
Kaoshan, *China* 57 B13
Kapaa, *U.S.A.* 106 G15
Kapadvanj, *India* 68 H5
Kapaklı, *Turkey* 41 E11
Kapan, *Armenia* 70 B5
Kapanga, *Dem. Rep. of
  the Congo* 84 F4
Kapchagai = Qapshaghay,
  Kazakstan 50 E8
Kapela = Velika Kapela, *Croatia* 29 C12
Kapéllo, Ákra, *Greece* 38 E5
Kapema, *Dem. Rep. of
  the Congo* 87 E2
Kapfenberg, *Austria* 26 D8
Kapı Dağı, *Turkey* 41 F11
Kapiri Mposhi, *Zambia* 87 E2
Kapiskau →, *Canada* 102 B3
Kapit, *Malaysia* 62 D4
Kapiti I., *N.Z.* 91 J5
Kaplan, *U.S.A.* 113 K8
Kaplice, *Czech Rep.* 26 C7
Kapoe, *Thailand* 65 H2
Kapoeta, *Sudan* 81 G3
Kápolnásnyék, *Hungary* 42 C3
Kapos →, *Hungary* 42 D3
Kaposvár, *Hungary* 42 D2
Kapowsin, *U.S.A.* 116 D4
Kappeln, *Germany* 24 A5
Kappelshamn, *Sweden* 11 G12
Kapps, *Namibia* 88 C2
Kaprije, *Croatia* 29 E12
Kapsan, *N. Korea* 57 D15
Kapsukas = Marijampolė,
  Lithuania 9 J20
Kapuas →, *Indonesia* 62 E3
Kapuas Hulu, Pegunungan,
  Malaysia 62 D4
Kapuas Hulu Ra. = Kapuas
  Hulu, Pegunungan, *Malaysia* 62 D4
Kapulo, *Dem. Rep. of the Congo* 87 D2
Kapuni, *N.Z.* 91 H5
Kapurthala, *India* 68 D6
Kapuskasing, *Canada* 102 C3
Kapuskasing →, *Canada* 102 C3
Kapustin Yar, *Russia* 49 F7
Kaputar, *Australia* 95 E5
Kaputir, *Kenya* 86 B4
Kapuvár, *Hungary* 42 C2
Kara, *Russia* 50 C7
Kará, W. →, *Si. Arabia* 80 C5
Kara Ada, *Turkey* 39 E9
Kara Bogaz Gol, Zaliv =
  Garabogazköl Aylagy,
  Turkmenistan 50 E6
Kara Burun, *Turkey* 39 E9
Kara Kalpak Republic =
  Qoraqalpoghiston □,
  Uzbekistan 50 E6
Kara Kum, *Turkmenistan* 50 F6
Kara Sea, *Russia* 50 B7
Karaadilli, *Turkey* 39 C12
Karabiğa, *Turkey* 72 B5
Karabük, *Turkey* 41 F3
Karaburun, *Albania* 40 F3
Karaburun, *Turkey* 39 C8
Karabutak = Qarabutaq,
  Kazakhstan 50 E7
Karacabey, *Turkey* 41 F12
Karacakılavuz, *Turkey* 41 E11
Karacaköy, *Turkey* 41 E12
Karacasu, *Turkey* 39 D10
Karachala = Qaraçala,
  Azerbaijan 49 L9
Karachayevsk, *Russia* 49 J5
Karachey-Cherkessia □, *Russia* 49 J5
Karachi, *Pakistan* 68 G2
Karad, *India* 66 L9
Karadirek, *Turkey* 39 C12
Karaga, *Ghana* 83 D4
Karaganda = Qaraghandy,
  Kazakhstan 50 E8
Karagayly, *Kazakhstan* 50 E8
Karaginskiy, Ostrov, *Russia* .. 51 D17
Karagola Road, *India* 69 G12
Karagüney Dağları, *Turkey* ... 72 B6
Karahallı, *Turkey* 39 C11
Karaikal, *India* 66 P11
Karaikkudi, *India* 66 P11
Karaisalı, *Turkey* 72 D6
Karaj, *Iran* 71 C6
Karak, *Malaysia* 65 L4
Karakalpakstan =
  Qoraqalpoghiston □,
  Uzbekistan 50 E6
Karakelong, *Indonesia* 63 D7
Karakitang, *Indonesia* 63 D7
Karaklis = Vanadzor, *Armenia* . 49 K7
Karakoçan, *Turkey* 73 C9
Karakol, *Kyrgyzstan* 50 E8
Karakoram Pass, *Pakistan* ... 69 B7
Karakoram Ra., *Pakistan* 69 B7
Karakurt, *Turkey* 73 B10
Karakuwisa, *Namibia* 88 B2
Karalon, *Russia* 51 D12
Karama, *Jordan* 75 D4
Karaman, *Balıkesir, Turkey* ... 39 B9
Karaman, *Konya, Turkey* 70 B2
Karamanlı, *Turkey* 39 D11

Karamay, China 60 B3
Karambu, Indonesia 62 E5
Karamea Bight, N.Z. 91 J3
Karamnasa →, India 69 G10
Karamürsel, Turkey 41 F13
Karand, Iran 70 C5
Karangana, Mali 82 C3
Karanganyar, Indonesia 63 G13
Karanjia, India 69 J11
Karankasso, Burkina Faso 82 C4
Karaova, Turkey 39 D9
Karapınar, Turkey 72 D5
Karasburg, Namibia 88 D2
Karasino, Russia 50 C9
Karasjok, Norway 8 B21
Karasu, Turkey 72 B4
Karasu →, Turkey 39 E12
Karasuk, Russia 50 D8
Karasuyama, Japan 55 F10
Karataş, Adana, Turkey 72 D6
Karataş, Manisa, Turkey 39 C10
Karataş Burnu, Turkey 72 D6
Karatau, Khrebet = Qarataū, Kazakstan 50 E7
Karatoprak, Turkey 39 D9
Karatsu, Japan 55 H5
Karaul, Russia 50 B9
Karauli, India 68 F7
Karavastasë, L. e, Albania 40 F3
Karávi, Greece 38 E5
Karavostasi, Cyprus 36 D11
Karawang, Indonesia 63 G12
Karawanken, Europe 26 E7
Karayazı, Turkey 73 C10
Karazhal, Kazakstan 50 E8
Karbalā', Iraq 70 C5
Kårböle, Sweden 10 C9
Karcag, Hungary 42 C5
Karcha →, Pakistan 69 B7
Karchana, India 69 G9
Karczew, Poland 45 F8
Kardam, Bulgaria 41 C12
Kardeljevo = Ploče, Croatia 29 E14
Kardhámila, Greece 39 C8
Kardhamíli, Greece 38 E4
Kardhítsa, Greece 38 B3
Kardhítsa □, Greece 38 B3
Kärdla, Estonia 9 G20
Kareeberge, S. Africa 88 E3
Kareha →, India 69 G12
Kareima, Sudan 80 D3
Karelia □, Russia 50 C4
Karelian Republic = Karelia □, Russia 50 C4
Karera, India 68 G8
Kārevāndar, Iran 71 E9
Kargasok, Russia 50 D9
Kargat, Russia 50 D9
Kargı, Turkey 72 B6
Kargil, India 69 B7
Kargopol, Russia 46 B10
Kargowa, Poland 45 F2
Karguéri, Niger 83 C7
Karhal, India 69 F8
Kariá, Greece 38 C2
Kariaí, Greece 41 F8
Kariān, Iran 71 E8
Karianga, Madag. 89 C8
Kariba, Zimbabwe 87 F2
Kariba, L., Zimbabwe 87 F2
Kariba Dam, Zimbabwe 87 F2
Kariba Gorge, Zambia 87 F2
Karibib, Namibia 88 C2
Karimata, Kepulauan, Indonesia 62 E3
Karimata, Selat, Indonesia 62 E3
Karimata Is. = Karimata, Kepulauan, Indonesia 62 E3
Karimnagar, India 66 K11
Karimunjawa, Kepulauan, Indonesia 62 F4
Karin, Somali Rep. 74 E4
Káristos, Greece 38 C6
Karīt, Iran 71 C8
Kariya, Japan 55 G8
Kariyangwe, Zimbabwe 89 B4
Karjala, Finland 46 A5
Karkaralinsk = Qarqaraly, Kazakstan 50 E8
Karkheh →, Iran 70 D5
Karkinitska Zatoka, Ukraine 47 K7
Karkinitskiy Zaliv = Karkinitska Zatoka, Ukraine 47 K7
Karkur Tohl, Egypt 80 C2
Karl Liebknecht, Russia 47 G8
Karl-Marx-Stadt = Chemnitz, Germany 24 E8
Karlholmsbruk, Sweden 10 D11
Karlino, Poland 44 D2
Karlivka, Ukraine 47 H8
Karlobag, Croatia 29 D12
Karlovac, Croatia 29 C12
Karlovka = Karlivka, Ukraine 47 H8
Karlovo, Bulgaria 41 D8
Karlovy Vary, Czech Rep. 26 A5
Karlsbad = Karlovy Vary, Czech Rep. 26 A5
Karlsborg, Sweden 11 F8
Karlshamn, Sweden 11 H8
Karlskoga, Sweden 10 E8
Karlskrona, Sweden 11 H9
Karlsruhe, Germany 25 F4
Karlstad, Sweden 10 E7
Karlstad, U.S.A. 112 A6
Karlstadt, Germany 25 F5
Karma, Niger 83 C5
Karmëlava, Lithuania 44 D11

Karmi'el, Israel 75 C4
Karnak, Egypt 79 C12
Karnal, India 68 E7
Karnali →, Nepal 69 E9
Karnaphuli Res., Bangla. 67 H18
Karnaprayag, India 69 D8
Karnataka □, India 66 N10
Karnes City, U.S.A. 113 L6
Karnische Alpen, Europe 26 E6
Karnobat, Bulgaria 41 D10
Kärnten □, Austria 26 E6
Karo, Mali 82 C4
Karoi, Zimbabwe 87 F2
Karonga, Malawi 87 D3
Karor, Pakistan 68 D4
Karora, Sudan 80 D4
Karounga, Mali 82 B3
Karousádhes, Greece 38 B1
Karpacz, Poland 45 H2
Karpasia □, Cyprus 36 D13
Kárpathos, Greece 39 F9
Kárpathos, Greece 39 F9
Kárpathos, Stenón, Greece 39 F9
Karpenísion, Greece 38 C3
Karpuz Burnu = Apostolos Andreas, C., Cyprus 36 D13
Karpuzlu, Turkey 39 D9
Karratha, Australia 92 D2
Kars, Turkey 73 B10
Karsakpay, Kazakstan 50 E7
Karsha, Kazakstan 48 F10
Karshi = Qarshi, Uzbekistan 50 F7
Karsiyang, India 69 F13
Karsog, India 68 D7
Karst = Kras, Croatia 29 C10
Kartal, Turkey 41 F13
Kartál Óros, Greece 41 E9
Kartaly, Russia 50 D7
Kartapur, India 68 D6
Karthaus, U.S.A. 110 E6
Kartuzy, Poland 44 D5
Karufa, Indonesia 63 E8
Karumba, Australia 94 B3
Karumo, Tanzania 86 C3
Karumwa, Tanzania 86 C3
Kārūn →, Iran 71 D6
Karungu, Kenya 86 C3
Karup, Denmark 11 H3
Karviná, Czech Rep. 27 B11
Karwan →, India 68 F8
Karwar, India 66 M9
Karwi, India 69 G9
Kaş, Turkey 39 E11
Kasaba, Turkey 39 E11
Kasache, Malawi 87 E3
Kasai →, Dem. Rep. of the Congo 84 E3
Kasaï-Oriental □, Dem. Rep. of the Congo 86 D1
Kasaji, Dem. Rep. of the Congo 87 E1
Kasama, Zambia 87 E3
Kasan-dong, N. Korea 57 D14
Kasane, Namibia 88 B3
Kasanga, Tanzania 87 D3
Kasar, Ras, Sudan 80 D4
Kasaragod, India 66 N9
Kasba L., Canada 105 A8
Kāseh Garān, Iran 70 C5
Kasempa, Zambia 87 E2
Kasenga, Dem. Rep. of the Congo 87 E2
Kasese, Uganda 86 B3
Kasewa, Zambia 87 E2
Kasganj, India 69 F8
Kashabowie, Canada 102 C1
Kashaf, Iran 71 C9
Kāshān, Iran 71 C6
Kashechewan, Canada 102 B3
Kashgar = Kashi, China 60 C2
Kashi, China 60 C2
Kashimbo, Dem. Rep. of the Congo 87 E2
Kashin, Russia 46 D9
Kashipur, India 69 E8
Kashira, Russia 46 E10
Kashiwazaki, Japan 55 F9
Kashk-e Kohneh, Afghan. 66 B3
Kashkū'īyeh, Iran 71 D7
Kashmar, Iran 71 C8
Kashmir, Asia 69 C7
Kashmor, Pakistan 68 E3
Kashpirovka, Russia 48 D9
Kashun Noerh = Gaxun Nur, China 60 B5
Kasiari, India 69 H12
Kasimov, Russia 48 C5
Kasinge, Dem. Rep. of the Congo 86 D2
Kasiruta, Indonesia 63 E7
Kaskaskia →, U.S.A. 112 G10
Kaskattama →, Canada 105 B10
Kaskinen, Finland 9 E19
Kaslo, Canada 104 D5
Kasmere L., Canada 105 B8
Kasongo, Dem. Rep. of the Congo 86 C2
Kasongo Lunda, Dem. Rep. of the Congo 84 F3
Kásos, Greece 39 F8
Kásos, Stenón, Greece 39 F8
Kaspi, Georgia 49 K7
Kaspichan, Bulgaria 41 C11
Kaspiysk, Russia 49 J8
Kaspiyskiy, Russia 49 H8
Kassab ed Doleib, Sudan 81 E3
Kassaba, Egypt 80 C2
Kassalâ, Sudan 81 D4

Kassalâ □, Sudan 81 D4
Kassándra, Greece 40 F7
Kassándrinon, Greece 40 F7
Kassel, Germany 24 D5
Kassinger, Sudan 80 D3
Kassiópi, Greece 36 A3
Kasson, U.S.A. 112 C8
Kastamonu, Turkey 72 B5
Kastav, Croatia 29 C11
Kastélli, Greece 36 D5
Kastéllion, Greece 36 D7
Kastellórizon = Megiste, Greece 39 E11
Kastéllos, Greece 39 E9
Kastellou, Ákra, Greece 39 F9
Kasterlee, Belgium 17 C4
Kastlösa, Sweden 11 H10
Kastóri, Greece 38 D4
Kastoría, Greece 40 F5
Kastoría □, Greece 40 F5
Kastorías, Límni, Greece 40 F5
Kastornoye, Russia 47 G10
Kastós, Greece 38 C2
Kastrosikiá, Greece 38 B2
Kastsyukovichy, Belarus 46 F7
Kasulu, Tanzania 86 C3
Kasumi, Japan 55 G7
Kasumkent, Russia 49 K9
Kasungu, Malawi 87 E3
Kasur, Pakistan 68 D6
Kataba, Zambia 87 F2
Katagum, Nigeria 83 C7
Katahdin, Mt., U.S.A. 109 C11
Katako Kombe, Dem. Rep. of the Congo 86 C1
Katákolon, Greece 38 D3
Katale, Tanzania 86 C3
Katanda, Katanga, Dem. Rep. of the Congo 86 D1
Katanda, Nord-Kivu, Dem. Rep. of the Congo 86 C2
Katanga □, Dem. Rep. of the Congo 86 D2
Katangi, India 69 J11
Katanning, Australia 93 F2
Katastári, Greece 38 D2
Katavi Swamp, Tanzania 86 D3
Kateríni, Greece 40 F6
Katghora, India 69 H10
Katha, Burma 67 G20
Katherîna, Gebel, Egypt 70 D2
Katherine, Australia 92 B5
Katherine Gorge, Australia 92 B5
Kathi, India 68 J6
Kathiawar, India 68 H4
Kathikas, Cyprus 36 E11
Kathua, India 68 C6
Kati, Mali 82 C3
Katihar, India 69 G12
Katima Mulilo, Zambia 88 B3
Katimbira, Malawi 87 E3
Katingan = Mendawai →, Indonesia 62 E4
Katiola, Ivory C. 82 D3
Katlanovo, Macedonia 40 E5
Katmandu, Nepal 69 F11
Katni, India 69 H9
Káto Akhaïa, Greece 38 C3
Káto Arkhánai, Greece 36 D7
Káto Khorió, Greece 36 D7
Káto Pyrgos, Cyprus 36 D11
Káto Stavros, Greece 40 F7
Katokhí, Greece 38 C3
Katompe, Dem. Rep. of the Congo 86 D2
Katonga →, Uganda 86 B3
Katoúna, Greece 38 C3
Katowice, Poland 45 H6
Katranci Dağı, Turkey 39 D12
Katrine, L., U.K. 14 E4
Katrineholm, Sweden 11 E10
Katsepe, Madag. 89 B8
Katsina, Nigeria 83 C6
Katsina □, Nigeria 83 C6
Katsina Ala, Nigeria 83 D6
Katsina Ala →, Nigeria 83 D6
Katsumoto, Japan 55 H4
Katsuura, Japan 55 G10
Katsuyama, Japan 55 F8
Kattavía, Greece 36 D9
Kattegat, Denmark 11 H5
Katthammarsvik, Sweden 11 G12
Katul, J., Sudan 81 E2
Katumba, Dem. Rep. of the Congo 86 D2
Katungu, Kenya 86 C5
Katwa, India 69 H13
Katwijk, Neths. 17 B4
Kąty Wrocławskie, Poland 45 G3
Kauai, U.S.A. 106 H15
Kauai Channel, U.S.A. 106 H15
Kaub, Germany 25 E3
Kaufbeuren, Germany 25 H6
Kaufman, U.S.A. 113 J6
Kauhajoki, Finland 9 E20
Kaukauna, U.S.A. 108 C1
Kaukauveld, Namibia 88 C3
Kaunakakai, U.S.A. 106 H16
Kaunas, Lithuania 9 J20
Kaunia, Bangla. 69 G13
Kaunos, Turkey 39 E10
Kaura Namoda, Nigeria 83 C6
Kautokeino, Norway 8 B20
Kauwapur, India 69 F10
Kavacha, Russia 51 C17
Kavadarci, Macedonia 40 E6

Kavajë, Albania 40 E3
Kavak, Turkey 72 B7
Kavak Dağı, Turkey 39 D10
Kavaklı, Turkey 41 E11
Kavaklıdere, Turkey 39 D10
Kavalerovo, Russia 54 B7
Kavali, India 66 M12
Kavála, Greece 41 F8
Kavála □, Greece 41 E8
Kavála Kólpos, Greece 41 F8
Kavār, Iran 71 D7
Kavarna, Bulgaria 41 C12
Kavi, India 68 H5
Kavimba, Botswana 88 B3
Kavīr, Dasht-e, Iran 71 C7
Kavkaz, Russia 47 K9
Kävlinge, Sweden 11 J7
Kavos, Greece 36 B4
Kavoúsi, Greece 39 F7
Kaw, Fr. Guiana 125 C8
Kawa, Sudan 81 E3
Kawagama L., Canada 110 A6
Kawagoe, Japan 55 G9
Kawaguchi, Japan 55 G9
Kawambwa, Zambia 87 D2
Kawanoe, Japan 55 G6
Kawardha, India 69 J9
Kawasaki, Japan 55 G9
Kawasi, Indonesia 63 E7
Kawerau, N.Z. 91 H6
Kawhia Harbour, N.Z. 91 H5
Kawio, Kepulauan, Indonesia 63 D7
Kawnro, Burma 67 H21
Kawthaung, Burma 65 H2
Kawthoolei = Kayin □, Burma 67 L20
Kawthule = Kayin □, Burma 67 L20
Kaxholmen, Sweden 11 G8
Kaya, Burkina Faso 83 C4
Kayah □, Burma 67 K20
Kayalıköy Barajı, Turkey 41 E11
Kayan →, Indonesia 62 D5
Kaycee, U.S.A. 114 E10
Kayeli, Indonesia 63 E7
Kayenta, U.S.A. 115 H8
Kayes, Mali 82 C2
Kayı, Turkey 39 B12
Kayima, S. Leone 82 D2
Kayin □, Burma 67 L20
Kayoa, Indonesia 63 D7
Kayomba, Zambia 87 E1
Kaysatskoye, Russia 48 F8
Kayseri, Turkey 70 B2
Kaysville, U.S.A. 114 F8
Kaz Dağı, Turkey 39 B8
Kazachye, Russia 51 B14
Kazakstan ■, Asia 50 E7
Kazan, Russia 48 C9
Kazan →, Canada 105 A9
Kazan-Rettō, Pac. Oc. 96 E6
Kazanlŭk, Bulgaria 41 D9
Kazanskaya, Russia 48 F5
Kazatin = Kozyatyn, Ukraine 47 H5
Kazaure, Nigeria 83 C6
Kāzerūn, Iran 71 D6
Kazi Magomed = Qazimämmäd, Azerbaijan 49 K9
Kazimierz Dolny, Poland 45 G8
Kazimierza Wielka, Poland 45 H7
Kazincbarcika, Hungary 42 B5
Kazlų Rūda, Lithuania 44 D10
Kaztalovka, Kazakstan 48 F9
Kazuno, Japan 54 D10
Kazym →, Russia 50 C7
Kcynia, Poland 45 F4
Ké-Macina, Mali 82 C3
Kéa, Greece 38 D6
Keady, U.K. 15 B5
Kearney, U.S.A. 112 E5
Kearny, U.S.A. 115 K8
Kearsarge, Mt., U.S.A. 111 C13
Keban, Turkey 73 C8
Keban Barajı, Turkey 70 B3
Kebbi □, Nigeria 83 C5
Kébi, Ivory C. 82 D3
Kebnekaise, Sweden 8 C18
Kebri Dehar, Ethiopia 74 F3
Kebumen, Indonesia 63 G13
Kecel, Hungary 42 D4
Kechika →, Canada 104 B3
Keçiborlu, Turkey 39 D12
Kecskemét, Hungary 42 D4
Kedada, Ethiopia 81 F4
Kedarnath, India 69 D8
Kedgwick, Canada 103 C6
Kediri, Indonesia 62 F4
Kedjebi, Ghana 83 D5
Kédougou, Senegal 82 C2
Kędzierzyn-Koźle, Poland 45 H5
Keeler, U.S.A. 116 J9
Keeley L., Canada 105 C7
Keeling Is. = Cocos Is., Ind. Oc. 96 J1
Keelung = Chilung, Taiwan 59 E13
Keene, Canada 110 B6
Keene, Calif., U.S.A. 117 K8
Keene, N.H., U.S.A. 111 D12
Keene, N.Y., U.S.A. 111 B11
Keeper Hill, Ireland 15 D3
Keer-Weer, C., Australia 94 A3
Keeseville, U.S.A. 111 B11
Keetmanshoop, Namibia 88 D2
Keewatin, Canada 105 D10
Keewatin →, Canada 105 B8

Kefa □, Ethiopia 81 F4
Kefallinía, Greece 38 C2
Kefallinía □, Greece 38 C2
Kéfalos, Greece 39 E8
Kefamenanu, Indonesia 63 F6
Kefar Sava, Israel 75 C3
Keffi, Nigeria 83 D6
Keflavík, Iceland 8 D2
Keftya, Ethiopia 81 E4
Keg River, Canada 104 B5
Kegaska, Canada 103 B7
Keheili, Sudan 80 D3
Kehl, Germany 25 G3
Keighley, U.K. 12 D6
Keila, Estonia 9 G21
Keimoes, S. Africa 88 D3
Keita, Niger 83 C6
Keitele, Finland 8 E22
Keith, U.K. 14 D6
Kejimkujik Nat. Park, Canada 103 D6
Kejser Franz Joseph Fd., Greenland 4 B6
Kekri, India 68 G6
Kelam, Ethiopia 81 G4
Kelamet, Eritrea 81 D4
Kelan, China 56 E6
Kelang, Malaysia 65 L3
Kelantan →, Malaysia 65 J4
Këlcyrë, Albania 40 F4
Kelekçi, Turkey 39 D11
Keles, Turkey 41 G13
Keleti-főcsatorna, Hungary 42 C6
Kelheim, Germany 25 G7
Kelkit, Turkey 73 B8
Kelkit →, Turkey 72 B7
Kellerberrin, Australia 93 F2
Kellett, C., Canada 4 B1
Kelleys I., U.S.A. 110 E2
Kellogg, U.S.A. 114 C5
Kells = Ceanannus Mor, Ireland 15 C5
Kelmė, Lithuania 44 C9
Kelokedhara, Cyprus 36 E11
Kelowna, Canada 104 D5
Kelseyville, U.S.A. 116 G4
Kelso, N.Z. 91 L2
Kelso, U.K. 14 F6
Kelso, U.S.A. 116 D4
Keluang, Malaysia 65 L4
Kelvington, Canada 105 C8
Kem, Russia 50 C4
Kema, Indonesia 63 D7
Kemah, Turkey 70 B3
Kemaliye, Erzincan, Turkey 73 C8
Kemaliye, Manisa, Turkey 39 C10
Kemalpaşa, Turkey 39 C9
Kemaman, Malaysia 62 D2
Kemano, Canada 104 C3
Kemasik, Malaysia 65 K4
Kembolcha, Ethiopia 81 E4
Kemer, Antalya, Turkey 39 E12
Kemer, Burdur, Turkey 39 D12
Kemer, Muğla, Turkey 39 E11
Kemer Barajı, Turkey 39 D10
Kemerovo, Russia 50 D9
Kemi, Finland 8 D21
Kemi älv = Kemijoki →, Finland 8 D21
Kemijärvi, Finland 8 C22
Kemijoki →, Finland 8 D21
Kemmerer, U.S.A. 114 F8
Kemmuna = Comino, Malta 36 C1
Kemp, L., U.S.A. 113 J5
Kemp Land, Antarctica 5 C5
Kempt, L., Canada 102 C5
Kempten, Germany 25 H6
Kempton, Australia 94 G4
Kemptville, Canada 102 C4
Ken →, India 69 G9
Kenai, U.S.A. 100 B4
Kendai, India 69 H10
Kendal, Indonesia 63 G14
Kendal, U.K. 12 C5
Kendall, U.S.A. 109 N5
Kendall →, Australia 94 A3
Kendallville, U.S.A. 108 E3
Kendari, Indonesia 63 E6
Kendawangan, Indonesia 62 E4
Kende, Nigeria 83 C5
Kendrapara, India 67 J15
Këndrevicës, Maja e, Albania 40 F3
Kendrew, S. Africa 88 E3
Kene Thao, Laos 64 D3
Kenedy, U.S.A. 113 L6
Kenema, S. Leone 82 D2
Keng Kok, Laos 64 D5
Keng Tawng, Burma 67 J21
Keng Tung, Burma 58 G3
Kengeja, Tanzania 86 D4
Kenhardt, S. Africa 88 D3
Kéniéba, Mali 82 C2
Kenitra, Morocco 78 B4
Kenli, China 57 F10
Kenmare, Ireland 15 E2
Kenmare, U.S.A. 112 A3
Kenmare River, Ireland 15 E2
Kennebago Lake, U.S.A. 111 A14
Kennebec, U.S.A. 112 D5
Kennebec →, U.S.A. 111 D11
Kennebunk, U.S.A. 111 C14
Kennedy, Zimbabwe 88 B4
Kennedy Ra., Australia 93 D2
Kennedy Taungdeik, Burma 67 H18
Kenner, U.S.A. 113 L9
Kenneth Ra., Australia 93 D2

Kennett, *U.S.A.* 113 G9
Kennewick, *U.S.A.* 114 C4
Kenogami →, *Canada* 102 B3
Kenora, *Canada* 105 D10
Kenosha, *U.S.A.* 108 D2
Kensington, *Canada* 103 C7
Kent, *Ohio, U.S.A.* 110 E3
Kent, *Tex., U.S.A.* 113 K2
Kent, *Wash., U.S.A.* 116 C4
Kent □, *U.K.* 13 F8
Kent Group, *Australia* 94 F4
Kent Pen., *Canada* 100 B9
Kentaū, *Kazakstan* 50 E7
Kentland, *U.S.A.* 108 E2
Kenton, *U.S.A.* 108 E4
Kentucky □, *U.S.A.* 108 G3
Kentucky →, *U.S.A.* 108 F3
Kentucky L., *U.S.A.* 109 G2
Kentville, *Canada* 103 C7
Kentwood, *U.S.A.* 113 K9
Kenya ■, *Africa* 86 B4
Kenya, Mt., *Kenya* 86 C4
Keo Neua, Deo, *Vietnam* 64 C5
Keokuk, *U.S.A.* 112 E9
Keonjhargarh, *India* 69 J11
Kep, *Cambodia* 65 G5
Kep, *Vietnam* 64 B6
Kepez, *Turkey* 41 F10
Kepi, *Indonesia* 63 F9
Kępice, *Poland* 44 D3
Kępno, *Poland* 45 G4
Kepsut, *Turkey* 39 B10
Kerala □, *India* 66 P10
Kerama-Rettō, *Japan* 55 L3
Keran, *Pakistan* 69 B5
Keranyo, *Ethiopia* 81 F4
Kerao →, *Sudan* 81 E3
Keratéa, *Greece* 38 D5
Keraudren, C., *Australia* 92 C2
Kerava, *Finland* 9 F21
Kerch, *Ukraine* 47 K9
Kerchenskiy Proliv, *Black Sea* . 47 K9
Kerchoual, *Mali* 83 B5
Kerempe Burnu, *Turkey* 72 A5
Keren, *Eritrea* 81 D4
Kerewan, *Gambia* 82 C1
Kerguelen, *Ind. Oc.* 3 G13
Keri, *Greece* 38 D2
Keri Kera, *Sudan* 81 E3
Kericho, *Kenya* 86 C4
Kerinci, *Indonesia* 62 E2
Kerki, *Turkmenistan* 50 F7
Kerkinítis, Límni, *Greece* 40 E7
Kérkira, *Greece* 36 A3
Kérkira □, *Greece* 38 B1
Kerkrade, *Neths.* 17 D6
Kerma, *Sudan* 80 D3
Kermadec Is., *Pac. Oc.* 96 L10
Kermadec Trench, *Pac. Oc.* .. 96 L10
Kermān, *Iran* 71 D8
Kerman, *U.S.A.* 116 J6
Kermān □, *Iran* 71 D8
Kermān, Bīābān-e, *Iran* 71 D8
Kermen, *Bulgaria* 41 D10
Kermit, *U.S.A.* 113 K3
Kern →, *U.S.A.* 117 K7
Kernhof, *Austria* 26 D8
Kernow = Cornwall □, *U.K.* ... 13 G3
Kernville, *U.S.A.* 117 K8
Keroh, *Malaysia* 65 K3
Kérou, *Benin* 83 C5
Kérouane, *Guinea* 82 D3
Kerpen, *Germany* 24 E2
Kerrera, *U.K.* 14 E3
Kerrobert, *Canada* 105 C7
Kerrville, *U.S.A.* 113 K5
Kerry □, *Ireland* 15 D2
Kerry Hd., *Ireland* 15 D2
Kersa, *Ethiopia* 81 F5
Kerulen →, *Asia* 60 B6
Kerzaz, *Algeria* 78 C5
Kesagami →, *Canada* 102 B4
Kesagami L., *Canada* 102 B3
Keşan, *Turkey* 41 F10
Kesennuma, *Japan* 54 E10
Keshit, *Iran* 71 D8
Keşiş Dağ, *Turkey* 73 C8
Keskin, *Turkey* 72 C5
Kestell, *S. Africa* 89 D4
Kestenga, *Russia* 50 C4
Keswick, *U.K.* 12 C4
Keszthely, *Hungary* 42 D2
Ket →, *Russia* 50 D9
Keta, *Ghana* 83 D5
Keta Lagoon, *Ghana* 83 D5
Ketapang, *Indonesia* 62 E4
Ketchikan, *U.S.A.* 104 B2
Ketchum, *U.S.A.* 114 E6
Kete Krachi, *Ghana* 83 D4
Ketef, Khalîg Umm el, *Egypt* .. 70 F2
Keti Bandar, *Pakistan* 68 G2
Kétou, *Benin* 83 D5
Ketri, *India* 68 E6
Kętrzyn, *Poland* 44 D8
Kettering, *U.K.* 13 E7
Kettering, *U.S.A.* 108 F3
Kettle →, *Canada* 105 B11
Kettle Falls, *U.S.A.* 114 B4
Kettle Pt., *Canada* 110 C2
Kettleman City, *U.S.A.* 116 J7
Kęty, *Poland* 45 J6
Keuka L., *U.S.A.* 110 D7
Keuruu, *Finland* 9 E21
Kevelaer, *Germany* 24 D2
Kewanee, *U.S.A.* 112 E10

Kewaunee, *U.S.A.* 108 C2
Keweenaw B., *U.S.A.* 108 B1
Keweenaw Pen., *U.S.A.* 108 B2
Keweenaw Pt., *U.S.A.* 108 B2
Key Largo, *U.S.A.* 109 N5
Key West, *U.S.A.* 107 F10
Keyala, *Sudan* 81 G3
Keynsham, *U.K.* 13 F5
Keyser, *U.S.A.* 108 F6
Kezhma, *Russia* 51 D11
Kezi, *Zimbabwe* 89 C4
Kežmarok, *Slovak Rep.* 27 B13
Khabarovsk, *Russia* 51 E14
Khabr, *Iran* 71 D8
Khābūr →, *Syria* 70 C4
Khachmas = Xaçmaz,
  Azerbaijan 49 K9
Khachrod, *India* 68 H6
Khadari, W. el →, *Sudan* 81 E2
Khadro, *Pakistan* 68 F3
Khadyzhensk, *Russia* 49 H4
Khadzhilyangar, *India* 69 B8
Khaga, *India* 69 G9
Khagaria, *India* 69 G12
Khaipur, *Pakistan* 68 E5
Khair, *India* 68 F7
Khairabad, *India* 69 F9
Khairagarh, *India* 69 J9
Khairpur, *Pakistan* 68 F3
Khairpur Nathan Shah, *Pakistan* 68 F2
Khairwara, *India* 68 H5
Khaisor →, *Pakistan* 68 D3
Khajuri Kach, *Pakistan* 68 C3
Khakassia □, *Russia* 50 D9
Khakhea, *Botswana* 88 C3
Khalafābād, *Iran* 71 D6
Khalīlī, *Iran* 71 E7
Khalkhāl, *Iran* 71 B6
Khálki, *Dhodhekánisos, Greece* . 39 E9
Khálki, *Thessalía, Greece* ... 38 B4
Khalkidhikí □, *Greece* 40 F7
Khalkís, *Greece* 38 C5
Khalmer-Sede = Tazovskiy,
  Russia 50 C8
Khalmer Yu, *Russia* 50 C7
Khalūf, *Oman* 74 C6
Kham Keut, *Laos* 64 C5
Khamaria, *India* 69 H9
Khambhaliya, *India* 68 H3
Khambhat, *India* 68 H5
Khambhat, G. of, *India* 66 J8
Khamilonísion, *Greece* 39 F8
Khamīr, *Iran* 71 E7
Khamir, *Yemen* 74 D3
Khamsa, *Egypt* 75 E1
Khān →, *Namibia* 88 C2
Khān Abū Shāmat, *Syria* 75 B5
Khān Azād, *Iraq* 70 C5
Khān Mujiddah, *Iraq* 70 C4
Khān Shaykhūn, *Syria* 70 C3
Khān Yūnis, *Gaza Strip* 75 D3
Khanai, *Pakistan* 68 D2
Khānaqīn, *Iraq* 70 C5
Khānbāghī, *Iran* 71 B7
Khandrá, *Greece* 39 F8
Khandwa, *India* 66 J10
Khandyga, *Russia* 51 C14
Khāneh, *Iran* 70 B5
Khanewal, *Pakistan* 68 D4
Khangah Dogran, *Pakistan* .. 68 D5
Khanh Duong, *Vietnam* 64 F7
Khaniá, *Greece* 36 D6
Khaniá □, *Greece* 36 D6
Khaniadhana, *India* 68 G8
Khaníon, Kólpos, *Greece* ... 36 D5
Khanka, L., *Asia* 51 E14
Khankendy = Xankändi,
  Azerbaijan 70 B5
Khanna, *India* 68 D7
Khanozai, *Pakistan* 68 D2
Khanpur, *Pakistan* 68 E4
Khanty-Mansiysk, *Russia* ... 50 C7
Khapalu, *Pakistan* 69 B7
Khapcheranga, *Russia* 51 E12
Kharabali, *Russia* 49 G8
Kharaghoda, *India* 68 H4
Kharagpur, *India* 69 H12
Khárakas, *Greece* 36 D7
Kharan Kalat, *Pakistan* 66 E4
Kharānaq, *Iran* 71 C7
Kharda, *India* 66 K9
Khardung La, *India* 69 B7
Khârga, El Wâhât-el, *Egypt* .. 80 B3
Khargon, *India* 66 J9
Khari →, *India* 68 G6
Kharian, *Pakistan* 68 C5
Kharit, Wadi el →, *Egypt* ... 80 C3
Khārk, Jazīreh-ye, *Iran* 71 D6
Kharkiv, *Ukraine* 47 H9
Kharkov = Kharkiv, *Ukraine* .. 47 H9
Kharovsk, *Russia* 46 C11
Kharsawangarh, *India* 69 H11
Kharta, *Turkey* 72 B3
Khartoum = El Khartûm, *Sudan* 81 D3
Kharuna, *Russia* 54 C5
Khasavyurt, *Russia* 49 J8
Khāsh, *Iran* 66 E2
Khashm el Girba, *Sudan* 81 E4
Khaskovo, *Bulgaria* 41 E9
Khaskovo □, *Bulgaria* 41 E9
Khatanga, *Russia* 51 B11
Khatanga →, *Russia* 51 B11

Khatauli, *India* 68 E7
Khatra, *India* 69 H12
Khātūnābād, *Iran* 71 D7
Khatyrka, *Russia* 51 C18
Khavda, *India* 68 H3
Khaybar, Ḥarrat, *Si. Arabia* .. 70 E4
Khayelitsha, *S. Africa* 85 L3
Khāzimiyah, *Iraq* 70 C4
Khazzân Jabal al Awliyâ, *Sudan* 81 D3
Khe Bo, *Vietnam* 64 C5
Khe Long, *Vietnam* 64 B5
Khed Brahma, *India* 66 G8
Khekra, *India* 68 E7
Khemarak Phouminville,
  Cambodia 65 G4
Khemisset, *Morocco* 78 B4
Khemmarat, *Thailand* 64 D5
Khenāmān, *Iran* 71 D8
Khenchela, *Algeria* 78 A7
Khersān →, *Iran* 71 D6
Khérson, *Greece* 40 E6
Kherson, *Ukraine* 47 J7
Khersónisos Akrotíri, *Greece* . 36 D6
Kheta →, *Russia* 51 B11
Khewari, *Pakistan* 68 F3
Khilchipur, *India* 68 G7
Khiliomódhion, *Greece* 38 D4
Khilok, *Russia* 51 D12
Khimki, *Russia* 46 E9
Khíos, *Greece* 39 C8
Khíos □, *Greece* 39 C8
Khirsadoh, *India* 69 H8
Khiuma = Hiiumaa, *Estonia* .. 9 G20
Khiva, *Uzbekistan* 50 E7
Khīyāv, *Iran* 70 B5
Khlebarovo, *Bulgaria* 41 C10
Khlong Khlung, *Thailand* 64 D2
Khmelnik, *Ukraine* 47 H4
Khmelnitskiy = Khmelnytskyy,
  Ukraine 47 H4
Khmelnytskyy, *Ukraine* 47 H4
Khmer Rep. = Cambodia ■,
  Asia 64 F5
Khoai, Hon, *Vietnam* 65 H5
Khodoriv, *Ukraine* 47 H3
Khodzent = Khūjand, *Tajikistan* 50 E7
Khojak Pass, *Afghan.* 68 D2
Khok Kloi, *Thailand* 65 H2
Khok Pho, *Thailand* 65 J3
Kholm, *Russia* 46 D6
Kholmsk, *Russia* 51 E15
Khomas Hochland, *Namibia* .. 88 C2
Khombole, *Senegal* 82 C1
Khomeyn, *Iran* 71 C6
Khomeynī Shahr, *Iran* 71 C6
Khomodino, *Botswana* 88 C3
Khon Kaen, *Thailand* 64 D4
Khong →, *Cambodia* 64 F5
Khong Sedone, *Laos* 64 E5
Khonuu, *Russia* 51 C15
Khoper →, *Russia* 48 F6
Khor al 'Atash, *Sudan* 81 E3
Khóra, *Greece* 38 D3
Khóra Sfakíon, *Greece* 36 D6
Khorāsān □, *Iran* 71 C8
Khorat = Nakhon Ratchasima,
  Thailand 64 E4
Khorat, Cao Nguyen, *Thailand* . 64 E4
Khorixas, *Namibia* 88 C1
Khorol, *Ukraine* 47 H7
Khorramābād, *Khorāsān, Iran* . 71 C8
Khorramābād, *Lorestān, Iran* . 71 C6
Khorrāmshahr, *Iran* 71 D6
Khorugh, *Tajikistan* 50 F8
Khosravī, *Iran* 71 D6
Khosrowābād, *Khuzestān, Iran* 71 D6
Khosrowābād, *Kordestān, Iran* 70 C5
Khost, *Pakistan* 68 D2
Khosūyeh, *Iran* 71 D7
Khotyn, *Ukraine* 47 H4
Khouribga, *Morocco* 78 B4
Khowst, *Afghan.* 68 C3
Khoyniki, *Belarus* 47 G5
Khrami →, *Georgia* 49 K7
Khrenovoye, *Russia* 48 E5
Khrisoúpolis, *Greece* 41 F8
Khristianá, *Greece* 39 E7
Khrysokhou B., *Cyprus* 36 D11
Khtapodhiá, *Greece* 39 D7
Khu Khan, *Thailand* 64 E5
Khudzhand = Khūjand,
  Tajikistan 50 E7
Khuff, *Si. Arabia* 70 E5
Khūgīānī, *Afghan.* 68 D2
Khuis, *Botswana* 88 D3
Khuiyala, *India* 68 F4
Khūjand, *Tajikistan* 50 E7
Khujner, *India* 68 H7
Khulna, *Bangla.* 67 H16
Khulna □, *Bangla.* 67 H16
Khulo, *Georgia* 49 K6
Khumago, *Botswana* 88 C3
Khūnsorkh, *Iran* 71 E8
Khunti, *India* 69 H11
Khūr, *Iran* 71 C8
Khurai, *India* 68 G8
Khurayş, *Si. Arabia* 71 E6
Khureit, *Sudan* 81 E2
Khūrīyā Mūrīyā, Jazā'ir, *Oman* 74 D6
Khurja, *India* 68 E7
Khūrmāl, *Iraq* 70 C5
Khurr, Wādī al, *Iraq* 70 C4
Khūsf, *Iran* 71 C8
Khush, *Afghan.* 66 C3
Khushab, *Pakistan* 68 C5
Khust, *Ukraine* 47 H2

Khuzdar, *Pakistan* 68 F2
Khūzestān □, *Iran* 71 D6
Khvāf, *Iran* 71 C9
Khvājeh, *Iran* 70 B5
Khvalynsk, *Russia* 48 D9
Khvānsār, *Iran* 71 D7
Khvatovka, *Russia* 48 D8
Khvor, *Iran* 71 C7
Khvorgū, *Iran* 71 E8
Khvoy, *Iran* 70 B5
Khvoynaya, *Russia* 46 C8
Khyber Pass, *Afghan.* 68 B4
Kiabukwa, *Dem. Rep. of
  the Congo* 87 D1
Kiama, *Phil.* 61 H6
Kiambi, *Dem. Rep. of the Congo* 86 D2
Kiambu, *Kenya* 86 C4
Kiangara, *Madag.* 89 B8
Kiangsi = Jiangxi □, *China* .. 59 D11
Kiangsu = Jiangsu □, *China* .. 57 H11
Kiáton, *Greece* 38 C4
Kibæk, *Denmark* 11 H2
Kibanga Port, *Uganda* 86 B3
Kibara, *Tanzania* 86 C3
Kibare, Mts., *Dem. Rep. of
  the Congo* 86 D2
Kibombo, *Dem. Rep. of
  the Congo* 86 C2
Kibondo, *Tanzania* 86 C3
Kibre Mengist, *Ethiopia* 81 F4
Kibumbu, *Burundi* 86 C2
Kibungo, *Rwanda* 86 C3
Kibuye, *Burundi* 86 C2
Kibuye, *Rwanda* 86 C2
Kibwesa, *Tanzania* 86 D2
Kibwezi, *Kenya* 86 C4
Kicasalih, *Turkey* 41 E10
Kichha, *India* 69 E8
Kichha →, *India* 69 E8
Kicking Horse Pass, *Canada* .. 104 C5
Kidal, *Mali* 83 B5
Kidderminster, *U.K.* 13 E5
Kidete, *Tanzania* 86 D4
Kidira, *Senegal* 82 C2
Kidnappers, C., *N.Z.* 91 H6
Kidsgrove, *U.K.* 12 D5
Kidston, *Australia* 94 B3
Kidugallo, *Tanzania* 86 D4
Kiel, *Germany* 24 A6
Kiel Canal = Nord-Ostsee-
  Kanal, *Germany* 24 A5
Kielce, *Poland* 45 H7
Kielder Water, *U.K.* 12 B5
Kieler Bucht, *Germany* 24 A6
Kiembara, *Burkina Faso* 82 C4
Kien Binh, *Vietnam* 65 H5
Kien Tan, *Vietnam* 65 G5
Kienge, *Dem. Rep. of the Congo* 87 E2
Kiessé, *Niger* 83 C5
Kiev = Kyyiv, *Ukraine* 47 G6
Kifaya, *Guinea* 82 C2
Kiffa, *Mauritania* 82 B2
Kifisiá, *Greece* 38 C5
Kifissós →, *Greece* 38 C5
Kifri, *Iraq* 70 C5
Kigali, *Rwanda* 86 C3
Kigarama, *Tanzania* 86 C3
Kigelle, *Sudan* 81 F3
Kigoma □, *Tanzania* 86 D2
Kigoma-Ujiji, *Tanzania* 86 C2
Kigomasha, Ras, *Tanzania* .. 86 C4
Kığzı, *Turkey* 70 B4
Kihei, *U.S.A.* 106 H16
Kihnu, *Estonia* 9 G21
Kii-Sanchi, *Japan* 55 G8
Kii-Suidō, *Japan* 55 H7
Kikaiga-Shima, *Japan* 55 K4
Kikinda, *Serbia, Yug.* 42 E5
Kikládhes, *Greece* 38 E6
Kikládhes □, *Greece* 38 E6
Kikwit, *Dem. Rep. of the Congo* 84 E3
Kil, *Sweden* 10 E7
Kilafors, *Sweden* 10 C10
Kilar, *India* 68 C7
Kilauea Crater, *U.S.A.* 106 J17
Kilbrannan Sd., *U.K.* 14 F3
Kilchu, *N. Korea* 57 D15
Kilcoy, *Australia* 95 D5
Kildare, *Ireland* 15 C5
Kildare □, *Ireland* 15 C5
Kileikli, *Sudan* 81 E2
Kilfinnane, *Ireland* 15 D3
Kilgore, *U.S.A.* 113 J7
Kilibo, *Benin* 83 D5
Kilifi, *Kenya* 86 C4
Kilimanjaro, *Tanzania* 86 C4
Kilimanjaro □, *Tanzania* 86 C4
Kilimli, *Turkey* 72 B4
Kilindini, *Kenya* 86 C4
Kilis, *Turkey* 70 B3
Kiliya, *Ukraine* 47 K5
Kilkee, *Ireland* 15 D2
Kilkeel, *U.K.* 15 B5
Kilkenny, *Ireland* 15 D4
Kilkenny □, *Ireland* 15 D4
Kilkieran B., *Ireland* 15 C2
Kilkís, *Greece* 40 F6
Kilkís □, *Greece* 40 E6
Killala, *Ireland* 15 B2
Killala B., *Ireland* 15 B2
Killaloe, *Ireland* 15 D3
Killaloe Station, *Canada* 110 A7
Killarney, *Australia* 95 D5
Killarney, *Canada* 105 D9

Killarney, *Ireland* 15 D2
Killary Harbour, *Ireland* 15 C2
Killdeer, *U.S.A.* 112 B3
Killeberg, *Sweden* 11 H8
Killeen, *U.S.A.* 113 K6
Killin, *U.K.* 14 E4
Killíni, Ilía, *Greece* 38 D3
Killíni, Korinthía, *Greece* ... 38 D4
Killorglin, *Ireland* 15 D2
Killybegs, *Ireland* 15 B3
Kilmarnock, *U.K.* 14 F4
Kilmez, *Russia* 48 B10
Kilmez →, *Russia* 48 B10
Kilondo, *Tanzania* 87 D3
Kilosa, *Tanzania* 86 D4
Kilrush, *Ireland* 15 D2
Kilwa Kisiwani, *Tanzania* 87 D4
Kilwa Kivinje, *Tanzania* 87 D4
Kilwa Masoko, *Tanzania* 87 D4
Kilwinning, *U.K.* 14 F4
Kim, *U.S.A.* 113 G3
Kim →, *Cameroon* 83 D7
Kimaam, *Indonesia* 63 F9
Kimamba, *Tanzania* 86 D4
Kimball, *Nebr., U.S.A.* 112 E3
Kimball, *S. Dak., U.S.A.* 112 D5
Kimberley, *Australia* 92 C4
Kimberley, *Canada* 104 D5
Kimberley, *S. Africa* 88 D3
Kimberly, *U.S.A.* 114 E6
Kimch'aek, *N. Korea* 57 D15
Kimch'ŏn, *S. Korea* 57 F15
Kími, *Greece* 38 C6
Kimje, *S. Korea* 57 G14
Kimmirut, *Canada* 101 B13
Kímolos, *Greece* 38 E6
Kimovsk, *Moskva, Russia* ... 46 E9
Kimovsk, *Tula, Russia* 46 E10
Kimparana, *Mali* 82 C4
Kimpese, *Dem. Rep. of
  the Congo* 84 F2
Kimry, *Russia* 46 D9
Kimstad, *Sweden* 11 F9
Kinabalu, Gunong, *Malaysia* . 62 C5
Kínaros, *Greece* 39 E8
Kinaskan L., *Canada* 104 B2
Kinbasket L., *Canada* 104 C5
Kincardine, *Canada* 102 D3
Kincolith, *Canada* 104 B3
Kinda, *Dem. Rep. of the Congo* 87 D2
Kindberg, *Austria* 26 D8
Kinde, *U.S.A.* 110 C2
Kinder Scout, *U.K.* 12 D6
Kindersley, *Canada* 105 C7
Kindia, *Guinea* 82 D2
Kindu, *Dem. Rep. of the Congo* 86 C2
Kinel, *Russia* 48 D10
Kineshma, *Russia* 48 B6
Kinesi, *Tanzania* 86 C3
King, L., *Australia* 93 F2
King, Mt., *Australia* 94 D4
King City, *U.S.A.* 116 J5
King Cr. →, *Australia* 94 C2
King Edward →, *Australia* .. 92 B4
King Frederik VI Land = Kong
  Frederik VI Kyst, *Greenland* 4 C5
King George B., *Falk. Is.* 128 G4
King George I., *Antarctica* .. 5 C18
King George Is., *Canada* 101 C11
King I. = Kadan Kyun, *Burma* . 64 F2
King I., *Australia* 94 F3
King I., *Canada* 104 C3
King Leopold Ranges, *Australia* 92 C4
King of Prussia, *U.S.A.* 111 F9
King Sd., *Australia* 92 C3
King William I., *Canada* 100 B10
King William's Town, *S. Africa* 88 E4
Kingaok = Bathurst Inlet,
  Canada 100 B9
Kingaroy, *Australia* 95 D5
Kingfisher, *U.S.A.* 113 H6
Kingirbān, *Iraq* 70 C5
Kingisepp = Kuressaare, *Estonia* 9 G20
Kingisepp, *Russia* 46 C5
Kingman, *Ariz., U.S.A.* 117 K12
Kingman, *Kans., U.S.A.* 113 G5
Kingoonya, *Australia* 95 E2
Kingri, *Pakistan* 68 D3
Kings →, *U.S.A.* 116 J7
Kings Canyon National Park,
  U.S.A. 116 J8
King's Lynn, *U.K.* 12 E8
Kings Mountain, *U.S.A.* 109 H5
Kings Park, *U.S.A.* 111 F11
Kings Peak, *U.S.A.* 114 F8
Kingsbridge, *U.K.* 13 G4
Kingsburg, *U.S.A.* 116 J7
Kingscourt, *Ireland* 15 C5
Kingsford, *U.S.A.* 108 C1
Kingsland, *U.S.A.* 109 K5
Kingsley, *U.S.A.* 112 D7
Kingsport, *U.S.A.* 109 G4
Kingston, *Canada* 102 D4
Kingston, *Jamaica* 120 C4
Kingston, *N.Z.* 91 L2
Kingston, *N.H., U.S.A.* 111 D13
Kingston, *N.Y., U.S.A.* 111 E11
Kingston, *Pa., U.S.A.* 111 E9
Kingston, *R.I., U.S.A.* 111 E13
Kingston Pk., *U.S.A.* 117 K11
Kingston upon Hull, *U.K.* ... 12 D7
Kingston upon Hull □, *U.K.* . 12 D7
Kingston-upon-Thames □, *U.K.* 13 F7
Kingstown, *St. Vincent* 121 D7
Kingstree, *U.S.A.* 109 J6
Kingsville, *Canada* 102 D3

Kingsville, *U.S.A.* 113 M6
Kingussie, *U.K.* 14 D4
Kingwood, *U.S.A.* 113 K7
Kınık, *Antalya, Turkey* 39 E11
Kınık, *İzmir, Turkey* 39 B9
Kinistino, *Canada* 105 C7
Kinkala, *Congo* 84 E2
Kinki □, *Japan* 55 H8
Kinleith, *N.Z.* 91 H5
Kinmount, *Canada* 110 B6
Kinna, *Sweden* 11 G6
Kinnairds Hd., *U.K.* 14 D6
Kinnared, *Sweden* 11 G7
Kinnarodden, *Norway* 6 A11
Kinnarp, *Sweden* 11 F7
Kinneviken, *Sweden* 11 F7
Kinngait = Cape Dorset, *Canada* 101 B12
Kino, *Mexico* 118 B2
Kinoje →, *Canada* 102 B3
Kinomoto, *Japan* 55 G8
Kinoni, *Uganda* 86 C3
Kinoosao, *Canada* 105 B8
Kinross, *U.K.* 14 E5
Kinsale, *Ireland* 15 E3
Kinsale, Old Hd. of, *Ireland* ... 15 E3
Kinsha = Chang Jiang →, *China* 59 B13
Kinshasa, *Dem. Rep. of
  the Congo* 84 E3
Kinsley, *U.S.A.* 113 G5
Kinsman, *U.S.A.* 110 E4
Kinston, *U.S.A.* 109 H7
Kintampo, *Ghana* 83 D4
Kintore Ra., *Australia* 92 D4
Kintyre, *U.K.* 14 F3
Kintyre, Mull of, *U.K.* 14 F3
Kinushseo →, *Canada* 102 A3
Kinuso, *Canada* 104 B5
Kinyangiri, *Tanzania* 86 C3
Kinyeti, *Sudan* 81 G3
Kinzig →, *Germany* 25 G3
Kinzua, *U.S.A.* 110 E6
Kinzua Dam, *U.S.A.* 110 E6
Kióni, *Greece* 38 C2
Kiosk, *Canada* 102 C4
Kiowa, *Kans., U.S.A.* 113 G5
Kiowa, *Okla., U.S.A.* 113 H7
Kipahigan L., *Canada* 105 B8
Kipanga, *Tanzania* 86 D4
Kiparíssía, *Greece* 38 D3
Kiparissiakós Kólpos, *Greece* .. 38 D3
Kipawa, L., *Canada* 102 C4
Kipembawe, *Tanzania* 86 D3
Kipengere Ra., *Tanzania* 87 D3
Kipili, *Tanzania* 86 D3
Kipini, *Kenya* 86 C5
Kipling, *Canada* 105 C8
Kippure, *Ireland* 15 C5
Kipushi, *Dem. Rep. of the Congo* 87 E2
Kirane, *Mali* 82 B2
Kiranomena, *Madag.* 89 B8
Kiraz, *Turkey* 39 C10
Kırazlı, *Turkey* 41 F10
Kirchhain, *Germany* 24 E4
Kirchheim, *Germany* 25 G5
Kirchheimbolanden, *Germany* . 25 F3
Kirchschlag, *Austria* 27 D9
Kireç, *Turkey* 39 B10
Kirensk, *Russia* 51 D11
Kirghizia = Kyrgyzstan ■, *Asia* 50 E8
Kirghizstan = Kyrgyzstan ■,
  Asia 50 E8
Kiribati ■, *Pac. Oc.* 96 H10
Kırıkhan, *Turkey* 72 D7
Kırıkkale, *Turkey* 72 C5
Kirillov, *Russia* 46 C10
Kirin = Jilin, *China* 57 C14
Kirishi, *Russia* 46 C7
Kiritimati, *Kiribati* 97 G12
Kırka, *Turkey* 39 B12
Kırkağaç, *Turkey* 39 B9
Kirkby, *U.K.* 12 D5
Kirkby Lonsdale, *U.K.* 12 C5
Kirkcaldy, *U.K.* 14 E5
Kirkcudbright, *U.K.* 14 G4
Kirkee, *India* 66 K8
Kirkenes, *Norway* 8 B23
Kirkfield, *Canada* 110 B6
Kirkjubæjarklaustur, *Iceland* . 8 E4
Kirkkonummi, *Finland* 9 F21
Kirkland Lake, *Canada* 102 C3
Kırklareli, *Turkey* 41 E11
Kırklareli □, *Turkey* 41 E11
Kirksville, *U.S.A.* 112 E8
Kirkūk, *Iraq* 70 C5
Kirkwall, *U.K.* 14 C6
Kirkwood, *S. Africa* 88 E4
Kirn, *Germany* 25 F3
Kirov, *Kaluga, Russia* 46 E8
Kirov, *Kirov, Russia* 50 D5
Kirovabad = Gäncä, *Azerbaijan* 49 K8
Kirovakan = Vanadzor, *Armenia* 49 K7
Kirovograd = Kirovohrad,
  Ukraine 47 H7
Kirovohrad, *Ukraine* 47 H7
Kirovsk = Babadayhan,
  Turkmenistan 50 F7
Kirovskiy, *Astrakhan, Russia* . 49 H9
Kirovskiy, *Kamchatka, Russia* . 51 D16
Kirovskiy, *Primorsk, Russia* .. 54 B6
Kirriemuir, *U.K.* 14 E5
Kirsanov, *Russia* 48 D6
Kırşehir, *Turkey* 70 B2
Kirtachi, *Niger* 83 C5
Kirthar Range, *Pakistan* 68 F2
Kirtland, *U.S.A.* 115 H9
Kiruna, *Sweden* 8 C19

Kirundu, *Dem. Rep. of
  the Congo* 86 C2
Kirya, *Russia* 48 C8
Kiryū, *Japan* 55 F9
Kisa, *Sweden* 11 G9
Kisaga, *Tanzania* 86 C3
Kisalaya, *Nic.* 120 D3
Kisalföld, *Hungary* 42 C2
Kisámou, Kólpos, *Greece* 36 D5
Kisanga, *Dem. Rep. of the Congo* 86 B2
Kisangani, *Dem. Rep. of
  the Congo* 86 B2
Kisar, *Indonesia* 63 F7
Kisarawe, *Tanzania* 86 D4
Kisarazu, *Japan* 55 G9
Kisbér, *Hungary* 42 C3
Kishanganga →, *Pakistan* 69 B5
Kishanganj, *India* 69 F13
Kishangarh, *Raj., India* 68 F6
Kishangarh, *Raj., India* 68 F4
Kishi, *Nigeria* 83 D5
Kishinev = Chișinău, *Moldova* . 43 C13
Kishiwada, *Japan* 55 G7
Kishtwar, *India* 69 C6
Kisielice, *Poland* 44 E6
Kisii, *Kenya* 86 C3
Kisiju, *Tanzania* 86 D4
Kisir, *Turkey* 73 B10
Kisizi, *Uganda* 86 C2
Kiskomárom = Zalakomár,
  Hungary 42 D2
Kiskőrei-víztároló, *Hungary* ... 42 C5
Kiskőrös, *Hungary* 42 D4
Kiskundorozsma, *Hungary* 42 D5
Kiskunfélegyháza, *Hungary* 42 D4
Kiskunhalas, *Hungary* 42 D4
Kiskunmajsa, *Hungary* 42 D4
Kislovodsk, *Russia* 49 J6
Kismayu = Chisimaio,
  Somali Rep. 77 G8
Kiso-Gawa →, *Japan* 55 G8
Kiso-Sammyaku, *Japan* 55 G8
Kisofukushima, *Japan* 55 G8
Kisoro, *Uganda* 86 C2
Kissidougou, *Guinea* 82 D2
Kissimmee, *U.S.A.* 109 L5
Kissimmee →, *U.S.A.* 109 M5
Kississing L., *Canada* 105 B8
Kissónerga, *Cyprus* 36 E11
Kissu, J., *Sudan* 80 C2
Kistanje, *Croatia* 29 E12
Kisújszállás, *Hungary* 42 C5
Kisumu, *Kenya* 86 C3
Kisvárda, *Hungary* 42 B7
Kiswani, *Tanzania* 86 C4
Kiswere, *Tanzania* 87 D4
Kit Carson, *U.S.A.* 112 F3
Kita, *Mali* 82 C3
Kitaibaraki, *Japan* 55 F10
Kitakami, *Japan* 54 E10
Kitakami-Gawa →, *Japan* 54 E10
Kitakami-Sammyaku, *Japan* 54 E10
Kitakata, *Japan* 54 F9
Kitakyūshū, *Japan* 55 H5
Kitale, *Kenya* 86 B4
Kitami, *Japan* 54 C11
Kitami-Sammyaku, *Japan* 54 B11
Kitangiri, L., *Tanzania* 86 C3
Kitaya, *Tanzania* 87 E5
Kitchener, *Canada* 102 D3
Kitee, *Finland* 46 A6
Kitega = Gitega, *Burundi* 86 C2
Kitengo, *Dem. Rep. of the Congo* 86 D1
Kitgum, *Uganda* 86 B3
Kíthira, *Greece* 38 E5
Kíthnos, *Greece* 38 D6
Kiti, *Cyprus* 36 E12
Kiti, C., *Cyprus* 36 E12
Kitimat, *Canada* 104 C3
Kitinen →, *Finland* 8 C22
Kitiyab, *Sudan* 81 D3
Kítros, *Greece* 40 F6
Kitsuki, *Japan* 55 H5
Kittakittaooloo, L., *Australia* . 95 D2
Kittanning, *U.S.A.* 110 F5
Kittatinny Mts., *U.S.A.* 111 F10
Kittery, *U.S.A.* 109 D10
Kittilä, *Finland* 8 C21
Kitui, *Kenya* 86 C4
Kitwanga, *Canada* 104 B3
Kitwe, *Zambia* 87 E2
Kitzbühel, *Austria* 26 D5
Kitzbüheler Alpen, *Austria* ... 26 D5
Kitzingen, *Germany* 25 F6
Kivarli, *India* 68 G5
Kivertsi, *Ukraine* 47 G3
Kividhes, *Cyprus* 36 E11
Kivik, *Sweden* 11 J8
Kivotós, *Greece* 40 F5
Kivu, L., *Dem. Rep. of
  the Congo* 86 C2
Kiyev = Kyyiv, *Ukraine* 47 G6
Kiyevskoye Vdkhr. = Kyyivske
  Vdskh., *Ukraine* 47 G6
Kıyıköy, *Turkey* 41 E12
Kiziguru, *Rwanda* 86 C3
Kızıl Adalar, *Turkey* 41 F13
Kızıl Irmak →, *Turkey* 72 B6
Kızıl Jilga, *India* 69 B8
Kizil Yurt, *Russia* 49 J8
Kızılcabölük, *Turkey* 39 D11
Kızılcadağ, *Turkey* 39 D11
Kızılcahamam, *Turkey* 72 B5
Kızılhisar, *Turkey* 72 D3
Kızılırmak →, *Turkey* 72 B5
Kızılkaya, *Turkey* 39 D12

Kızılören, *Turkey* 39 C12
Kızıltepe, *Turkey* 70 B4
Kizimkazi, *Tanzania* 86 D4
Kizlyar, *Russia* 49 J8
Kizyl-Arvat = Gyzylarbat,
  Turkmenistan 50 F6
Kjellerup, *Denmark* 11 H3
Kjölur, *Iceland* 8 D4
Kladanj, *Bos.-H.* 42 F3
Kladnica, *Serbia, Yug.* 40 C4
Kladno, *Czech Rep.* 26 A7
Kladovo, *Serbia, Yug.* 40 B6
Klaeng, *Thailand* 64 F3
Klagenfurt, *Austria* 26 E7
Klaipėda, *Lithuania* 9 J19
Klaipėda □, *Lithuania* 44 C8
Klaksvík, *Færoe Is.* 8 E9
Klamath →, *U.S.A.* 114 F1
Klamath Falls, *U.S.A.* 114 E3
Klamath Mts., *U.S.A.* 114 F2
Klamono, *Indonesia* 63 E8
Klanjec, *Croatia* 29 B12
Klappan →, *Canada* 104 B3
Klarälven →, *Sweden* 10 E7
Klässbol, *Sweden* 10 E6
Klatovy, *Czech Rep.* 26 B6
Klawer, *S. Africa* 88 E2
Klazienaveen, *Neths.* 17 B6
Klé, *Mali* 82 C3
Kłecko, *Poland* 45 F4
Kleczew, *Poland* 45 F5
Kleena Kleene, *Canada* 104 C4
Klein-Karas, *Namibia* 88 D2
Klekovača, *Bos.-H.* 29 D13
Klenoec, *Macedonia* 40 E4
Klenovec, *Slovak Rep.* 27 C12
Klerksdorp, *S. Africa* 88 D4
Kleszczele, *Poland* 45 F10
Kletnya, *Russia* 46 F7
Kletsk = Klyetsk, *Belarus* ... 47 F4
Kletskiy, *Russia* 49 F6
Kleve, *Germany* 24 D2
Klickitat, *U.S.A.* 114 D3
Klickitat →, *U.S.A.* 116 E5
Klidhes, *Cyprus* 36 D13
Klimovich, *Belarus* 46 F6
Klimovo, *Russia* 46 D9
Klin, *Russia* 46 D9
Klinaklini →, *Canada* 104 C3
Klintehamn, *Sweden* 11 G12
Klintsy, *Russia* 47 F7
Klip →, *S. Africa* 89 D4
Klipdale, *S. Africa* 88 E2
Klippan, *Sweden* 11 H7
Klipplaat, *S. Africa* 88 E3
Klisura, *Bulgaria* 41 D8
Kljajićevo, *Serbia, Yug.* 42 E4
Ključ, *Bos.-H.* 29 D13
Kłobuck, *Poland* 45 H5
Klockestrand, *Sweden* 10 B11
Kłodawa, *Poland* 45 F5
Kłodzko, *Poland* 45 H3
Klos, *Albania* 40 E4
Klosterneuburg, *Austria* 27 C9
Klosters, *Switz.* 25 J5
Klötze, *Germany* 24 C7
Klouto, *Togo* 83 D5
Kluane L., *Canada* 100 B6
Kluane Nat. Park, *Canada* 104 A1
Kluczbork, *Poland* 45 H5
Klukwan, *U.S.A.* 104 B1
Klyuchevskaya, Gora, *Russia* . 51 D17
Knäred, *Sweden* 11 H7
Knaresborough, *U.K.* 12 C6
Knee L., *Man., Canada* 102 A1
Knee L., *Sask., Canada* 105 B7
Knezha, *Bulgaria* 41 C8
Knight Inlet, *Canada* 104 C3
Knighton, *U.K.* 13 E4
Knights Ferry, *U.S.A.* 116 H6
Knights Landing, *U.S.A.* 116 G5
Knin, *Croatia* 29 D13
Knislinge, *Sweden* 11 H8
Knittelfeld, *Austria* 26 D7
Knivsta, *Sweden* 10 E11
Knjaževac, *Serbia, Yug.* 40 C6
Knob, C., *Australia* 93 F2
Knock, *Ireland* 15 C3
Knockmealdown Mts., *Ireland* . 15 D4
Knokke-Heist, *Belgium* 17 C3
Knossós, *Greece* 36 D7
Knowlton, *Canada* 111 A12
Knox, *U.S.A.* 108 E2
Knox Coast, *Antarctica* 5 C8
Knoxville, *Iowa, U.S.A.* 112 E8
Knoxville, *Pa., U.S.A.* 110 E7
Knoxville, *Tenn., U.S.A.* 109 H4
Knysna, *S. Africa* 88 E3
Knyszyn, *Poland* 44 E9
Ko Kha, *Thailand* 64 C2
Koartac = Quaqtaq, *Canada* ... 101 B13
Koba, *Indonesia* 63 F8
Kobarid, *Slovenia* 29 B10
Kobayashi, *Japan* 55 J5
Kobdo = Hovd, *Mongolia* 60 B4
Kobe, *Indonesia* 63 E7
Kōbe, *Japan* 55 G7
Kobelyaky, *Ukraine* 47 H8
København, *Denmark* 11 J6
Københavns Amtskommune □,
  Denmark 11 J6
Kobenni, *Mauritania* 82 B3
Kōbi-Sho, *Japan* 55 M1
Koblenz, *Germany* 25 E3
Kobo, *Ethiopia* 81 E4

Kobryn, *Belarus* 47 F3
Kobuleti, *Georgia* 49 K5
Kobylin, *Poland* 45 G4
Kobyłka, *Poland* 45 F8
Kobylkino, *Russia* 48 C6
Koca →, *Turkey* 41 F11
Kocabaş, *Turkey* 39 D11
Kocaeli, *Turkey* 41 F13
Kocaeli □, *Turkey* 41 F13
Kočane, *Serbia, Yug.* 40 C5
Kočani, *Macedonia* 40 E6
Koçarlı, *Turkey* 39 D9
Koceljevo, *Serbia, Yug.* 40 B3
Kočevje, *Slovenia* 29 C11
Koch Bihar, *India* 67 F16
Kochang, *S. Korea* 57 G14
Kochas, *India* 69 G10
Kochi = Cochin, *India* 66 Q10
Kōchi, *Japan* 55 H6
Kōchi □, *Japan* 55 H6
Kochiu = Gejiu, *China* 58 F4
Kock, *Poland* 45 G9
Kodarma, *India* 69 G11
Kode, *Sweden* 11 G5
Kodiak, *U.S.A.* 100 C4
Kodiak I., *U.S.A.* 100 C4
Kodinar, *India* 68 J4
Kodok, *Sudan* 81 F3
Kodori →, *Georgia* 49 J5
Koedoesberge, *S. Africa* 88 E3
Koes, *Namibia* 88 D2
Kofçaz, *Turkey* 41 E11
Koffiefontein, *S. Africa* 88 D4
Kofiau, *Indonesia* 63 E7
Köflach, *Austria* 26 D8
Koforidua, *Ghana* 83 D4
Kōfu, *Japan* 55 G9
Koga, *Japan* 55 F9
Kogaluk →, *Canada* 103 A7
Køge, *Denmark* 11 J6
Køge Bugt, *Denmark* 11 J6
Kogi □, *Nigeria* 83 D6
Kogin Baba, *Nigeria* 83 D7
Koh-i-Khurd, *Afghan.* 68 C1
Koh-i-Maran, *Pakistan* 68 E2
Kohat, *Pakistan* 68 C4
Kohima, *India* 67 G19
Kohkīlūyeh va Būyer
  Aḥmadī □, *Iran* 71 D6
Kohler Ra., *Antarctica* 5 D15
Kohlu, *Pakistan* 68 E3
Kohtla-Järve, *Estonia* 9 G22
Koillismaa, *Finland* 8 D23
Koin-dong, *N. Korea* 57 D14
Koinare, *Bulgaria* 41 C8
Koindu, *S. Leone* 82 D2
Kojetín, *Czech Rep.* 27 B10
Kojŏ, *N. Korea* 57 E14
Kojonup, *Australia* 93 F2
Kojūr, *Iran* 71 B6
Kok, Sudan* 80 C3
Kokand = Qŭqon, *Uzbekistan* .. 50 E8
Kokas, *Indonesia* 63 E8
Kokava, *Slovak Rep.* 27 C12
Kokchetav = Kökshetaū,
  Kazakstan 50 D7
Kokemäenjoki →, *Finland* 9 F19
Kokhma, *Russia* 48 B5
Koki, *Senegal* 82 B1
Kokkola, *Finland* 8 E20
Koko, *Nigeria* 83 C5
Koko Kyunzu, *Burma* 67 M18
Kokolopozo, *Ivory C.* 82 D3
Kokomo, *U.S.A.* 108 E2
Kokoro, *Niger* 83 C5
Koksan, *N. Korea* 57 E14
Kökshetaū, *Kazakstan* 50 D7
Koksoak →, *Canada* 101 C13
Kokstad, *S. Africa* 89 E4
Kokubu, *Japan* 55 J5
Kola, *Indonesia* 63 F8
Kola Pen. = Kolskiy Poluostrov,
  Russia 50 C4
Kolachi →, *Pakistan* 68 F2
Kolahoi, *India* 69 B6
Kolahun, *Liberia* 82 D2
Kolaka, *Indonesia* 63 E6
Kolar, *India* 66 N11
Kolar Gold Fields, *India* 66 N11
Kolaras, *India* 68 G7
Kolari, *Finland* 8 C20
Kolárovo, *Slovak Rep.* 27 D10
Kolašin, *Montenegro, Yug.* ... 40 D3
Kolayat, *India* 66 F8
Kolback, *Sweden* 10 E10
Kolbäcksån →, *Sweden* 10 E10
Kolberg = Kołobrzeg, *Poland* . 44 D2
Kolbermoor, *Germany* 25 H8
Kolbuszowa, *Poland* 45 H8
Kolchugino = Leninsk-
  Kuznetskiy, *Russia* 50 D9
Kolchugino, *Russia* 46 D10
Kolda, *Senegal* 82 C2
Koldegi, *Sudan* 81 E3
Kolding, *Denmark* 11 J3
Kolepom = Dolak, Pulau,
  Indonesia 63 F9
Kolguyev, Ostrov, *Russia* 50 C5
Kolia, *Ivory C.* 82 D3
Kolind, *Denmark* 11 H4
Kolkas rags, *Latvia* 9 H20
Kollam = Quilon, *India* 66 Q10
Kölleda, *Germany* 24 D7

Kollum, *Neths.* 17 A6
Kolmanskop, *Namibia* 88 D2
Köln, *Germany* 24 E2
Kolno, *Poland* 44 E8
Koło, *Poland* 45 F5
Kołobrzeg, *Poland* 44 D2
Kolokani, *Mali* 82 C3
Koloko, *Burkina Faso* 82 C3
Kololo, *Ethiopia* 81 F5
Kolomna, *Russia* 46 E10
Kolomyya, *Ukraine* 47 H3
Kolondiéba, *Mali* 82 C3
Kolonodale, *Indonesia* 63 E6
Kolonowskie, *Poland* 45 H5
Kolosib, *India* 67 G18
Kolpashevo, *Russia* 50 D9
Kolpino, *Russia* 46 C6
Kolpny, *Russia* 47 F9
Kolskiy Poluostrov, *Russia* .. 50 C4
Kolsva, *Sweden* 10 E9
Kolubara →, *Serbia, Yug.* 40 B4
Koluszki, *Poland* 45 G6
Kolwezi, *Dem. Rep. of
  the Congo* 87 E2
Kolyma →, *Russia* 51 C17
Kolymskoye Nagorye, *Russia* .. 51 C16
Kôm Hamâda, *Egypt* 80 H7
Kôm Ombo, *Egypt* 80 C3
Komadugu Gana →, *Nigeria* 83 C7
Komandorskiye Is. =
  Komandorskiye Ostrova,
  Russia 51 D17
Komandorskiye Ostrova, *Russia* 51 D17
Komárno, *Slovak Rep.* 27 D11
Komárom, *Hungary* 42 C3
Komárom-Esztergom □,
  Hungary 42 C3
Komatipoort, *S. Africa* 89 D5
Komatou Yialou, *Cyprus* 36 D13
Komatsu, *Japan* 55 F8
Komatsushima, *Japan* 55 H7
Kombissiri, *Burkina Faso* 83 C4
Kombori, *Burkina Faso* 82 C4
Kombóti, *Greece* 38 B3
Komen, *Slovenia* 29 C10
Komenda, *Ghana* 83 D4
Komi □, *Russia* 50 C6
Komiža, *Croatia* 29 E13
Komló, *Hungary* 42 D3
Kommunarsk = Alchevsk,
  Ukraine 47 H10
Kommunizma, Pik, *Tajikistan* . 50 F8
Komodo, *Indonesia* 63 F5
Komoé →, *Ivory C.* 82 D4
Komoran, Pulau, *Indonesia* ... 63 F9
Komoro, *Japan* 55 F9
Komotini, *Greece* 41 E9
Komovi, *Montenegro, Yug.* 40 D3
Kompasberg, *S. Africa* 88 E3
Kompong Bang, *Cambodia* 65 F5
Kompong Cham, *Cambodia* 65 F5
Kompong Chhnang = Kampang
  Chhnang, *Cambodia* 65 F5
Kompong Chikreng, *Cambodia* . 64 F5
Kompong Kleang, *Cambodia* ... 64 F5
Kompong Luong, *Cambodia* 65 G5
Kompong Pranak, *Cambodia* ... 64 F5
Kompong Som = Kampong
  Saom, *Cambodia* 65 G4
Kompong Som, Chhung =
  Kampong Saom, Chaak,
  Cambodia 65 G4
Kompong Speu, *Cambodia* 65 G5
Kompong Sralao, *Cambodia* ... 64 E5
Kompong Thom, *Cambodia* 64 F5
Kompong Trabeck, *Cambodia* .. 64 F5
Kompong Trabeck, *Cambodia* .. 65 G5
Kompong Trach, *Cambodia* 65 G5
Kompong Tralach, *Cambodia* .. 65 G5
Komrat = Comrat, *Moldova* ... 43 D13
Komsberg, *S. Africa* 88 E3
Komsomolets, Ostrov, *Russia* . 51 A10
Komsomolsk, *Amur, Russia* 51 D14
Komsomolsk, *Ivanovo, Russia* . 46 D11
Komsomolskiy, *Russia* 48 C7
Kömür Burnu, *Turkey* 39 C8
Kon Tum, *Vietnam* 64 E7
Kon Tum, Plateau du, *Vietnam* 64 E7
Kona, *Mali* 82 C4
Konarhã □, *Afghan.* 66 B7
Konārī, *Iran* 71 D6
Konch, *India* 69 G8
Konde, *Tanzania* 86 C4
Kondiá, *Greece* 39 B7
Kondinin, *Australia* 93 F2
Kondoa, *Tanzania* 86 C4
Kondókali, *Greece* 36 A3
Kondópaga, *Russia* 46 A8
Kondratyevo, *Russia* 51 D10
Kondrovo, *Russia* 46 E8
Konduga, *Nigeria* 83 C7
Könevergench, *Turkmenistan* .. 50 E6
Konevo, *Russia* 46 A10
Kong = Khong →, *Cambodia* 64 F5
Kong, *Ivory C.* 82 D4
Kong, Koh, *Cambodia* 65 G4
Kong Christian IX Land,
  Greenland 4 C6
Kong Christian X Land,
  Greenland 4 B6
Kong Frederik IX Land,
  Greenland 4 C5
Kong Frederik VI Kyst,
  Greenland 4 C5

Kong Frederik VIII Land, Greenland ... 4 B6
Kong Oscar Fjord, Greenland .. 4 B6
Kongeå ➤, Denmark ... 11 J2
Kongerslev, Denmark ... 11 H4
Kongju, S. Korea ... 57 F14
Konglu, Burma ... 67 F20
Kongola, Namibia ... 88 B3
Kongolo, Kasai-Or., Dem. Rep. of the Congo ... 86 D1
Kongolo, Katanga, Dem. Rep. of the Congo ... 86 D2
Kongor, Sudan ... 81 F3
Kongoussi, Burkina Faso ... 83 C4
Kongsberg, Norway ... 9 G13
Kongsvinger, Norway ... 9 F15
Kongwa, Tanzania ... 86 D4
Koni, Dem. Rep. of the Congo . 87 E2
Koni, Mts., Dem. Rep. of the Congo ... 87 E2
Koniakari, Mali ... 82 C2
Koniecpol, Poland ... 45 H6
Königs Wusterhausen, Germany 24 C9
Königsberg = Kaliningrad, Russia ... 9 J19
Königsbrunn, Germany ... 25 G6
Königslutter, Germany ... 24 C6
Konin, Poland ... 45 F5
Konispol, Albania ... 40 G4
Kónitsa, Greece ... 38 A2
Konjic, Bos.-H. ... 42 G2
Konkiep, Namibia ... 88 D2
Konkouré ➤, Guinea ... 82 D2
Könnern, Germany ... 24 D7
Kono, S. Leone ... 82 D2
Konongo, Ghana ... 83 D4
Konosha, Russia ... 46 B11
Kōnosu, Japan ... 55 F9
Konotop, Ukraine ... 47 G7
Konsankoro, Guinea ... 82 D3
Końskie, Poland ... 45 G7
Konstancin-Jeziorna, Poland .. 45 F8
Konstantinovka = Kostyantynivka, Ukraine ... 47 H9
Konstantinovsk, Russia ... 49 G5
Konstantynów Łódźki, Poland . 45 G6
Konstanz, Germany ... 25 H5
Kont, Iran ... 71 E9
Kontagora, Nigeria ... 83 C6
Kontcha, Cameroon ... 83 D7
Konya, Turkey ... 70 B2
Konya Ovası, Turkey ... 72 C5
Konz, Germany ... 25 F2
Konza, Kenya ... 86 C4
Koocanusa, L., Canada ... 114 B6
Kookynie, Australia ... 93 E3
Koolyanobbing, Australia ... 93 F2
Koonibba, Australia ... 95 E1
Koorda, Australia ... 93 F2
Kooskia, U.S.A. ... 114 C6
Kootenay ➤, U.S.A. ... 104 D5
Kootenay L., Canada ... 104 D5
Kootenay Nat. Park, Canada ... 104 C5
Kootjieskolk, S. Africa ... 88 E3
Kopanovka, Russia ... 49 G8
Kopaonik, Yugoslavia ... 40 C4
Kópavogur, Iceland ... 8 D3
Koper, Slovenia ... 29 C10
Kopervik, Norway ... 9 G11
Kopet Dagh, Asia ... 71 B8
Kopi, Australia ... 95 E2
Köping, Sweden ... 10 E10
Köpingsvik, Sweden ... 11 H10
Kopište, Croatia ... 29 F13
Koplik, Albania ... 40 D3
Köpmanholmen, Sweden ... 10 A12
Kopparberg, Sweden ... 10 E9
Koppeh Dāgh = Kopet Dagh, Asia ... 71 B8
Koppies, S. Africa ... 89 D4
Koppom, Sweden ... 10 E6
Koprivlen, Bulgaria ... 40 E7
Koprivnica, Croatia ... 29 B13
Kopřivnice, Czech Rep. ... 27 B11
Koprivshtitsa, Bulgaria ... 41 D8
Köprübaşı, Turkey ... 39 C10
Kopychyntsi, Ukraine ... 47 H3
Korab, Macedonia ... 40 E4
Korakiána, Greece ... 36 A3
Koral, India ... 68 J5
Korarou, L., Mali ... 82 B4
Korba, India ... 69 H10
Korbach, Germany ... 24 D4
Korbu, G., Malaysia ... 65 K3
Korce = Korçë, Albania ... 40 F4
Korçë, Albania ... 40 F4
Korčula, Croatia ... 29 F13
Korčulanski Kanal, Croatia 29 E13
Kord Kūy, Iran ... 71 B7
Kord Sheykh, Iran ... 71 D7
Kordestān □, Iran ... 70 C5
Kordofân, Sudan ... 79 F11
Koré Mayroua, Niger ... 83 C5
Korea, North ■, Asia ... 57 E14
Korea, South ■, Asia ... 57 G15
Korea Bay, Korea ... 57 E13
Korea Strait, Asia ... 57 H15
Korem, Ethiopia ... 81 E4
Korenevo, Russia ... 47 G8
Korenovsk, Russia ... 49 H4
Korets, Ukraine ... 47 G4
Korfantów, Poland ... 45 H4
Korgan, Turkey ... 72 B7
Korgus, Sudan ... 80 D3
Korhogo, Ivory C. ... 82 D3
Koribundu, S. Leone ... 82 D2

Korienzé, Mali ... 82 B4
Korinthía □, Greece ... 38 D4
Korinthiakós Kólpos, Greece .. 38 C4
Kórinthos, Greece ... 38 D4
Korioumé, Mali ... 82 B4
Kóríssa, Límni, Greece ... 36 B3
Kōriyama, Japan ... 54 F10
Korkuteli, Turkey ... 39 D12
Kormakiti, C., Cyprus ... 36 D11
Körmend, Hungary ... 42 C1
Kornat, Croatia ... 29 E12
Korneshty = Cornești, Moldova 43 C13
Korneuburg, Austria ... 27 C9
Kórnik, Poland ... 45 F4
Koro, Fiji ... 91 C8
Koro, Ivory C. ... 82 D3
Koro, Mali ... 82 C4
Koro Sea, Fiji ... 91 C9
Korocha, Russia ... 47 G9
Köroğlu Dağları, Turkey ... 72 B5
Korogwe, Tanzania ... 86 D4
Koronadal, Phil. ... 61 H6
Koróni, Greece ... 38 E3
Korónia, Limni, Greece ... 40 F7
Koronís, Greece ... 39 D7
Koronowo, Poland ... 45 E4
Koror, Palau ... 63 C8
Körös ➤, Hungary ... 42 D5
Köröstarcsa, Hungary ... 42 D6
Korosten, Ukraine ... 47 G5
Korostyshev, Ukraine ... 47 G5
Korotoyak, Russia ... 47 G10
Korraraika, Helodranon' i, Madag. ... 89 B7
Korsakov, Russia ... 51 E15
Korsberga, Sweden ... 11 G9
Korshunovo, Russia ... 51 D12
Korsør, Denmark ... 11 J5
Korsun Shevchenkovskiy, Ukraine ... 47 H6
Korsze, Poland ... 44 D8
Korti, Sudan ... 80 D3
Kortrijk, Belgium ... 17 D3
Korucu, Turkey ... 39 B9
Korwai, India ... 68 G8
Koryakskoye Nagorye, Russia . 51 C18
Koryŏng, S. Korea ... 57 G15
Koryukovka, Ukraine ... 47 G7
Kos, Greece ... 39 E9
Kosa, Ethiopia ... 81 F4
Kosaya Gora, Russia ... 46 E9
Kościan, Poland ... 45 F3
Kościerzyna, Poland ... 44 D4
Kosciusko, U.S.A. ... 113 J10
Kösely ➤, Hungary ... 42 C6
Kosha, Sudan ... 80 C3
Koshava, Bulgaria ... 40 B7
K'oshih = Kashi, China ... 60 C2
Koshiki-Rettō, Japan ... 55 J4
Kosi, India ... 68 F7
Kosi ➤, India ... 69 E8
Košice, Slovak Rep. ... 27 C14
Košický □, Slovak Rep. ... 27 C14
Kosjerić, Serbia, Yug. ... 40 B3
Köşk, Turkey ... 39 D10
Koskhinoú, Greece ... 36 C10
Koslan, Russia ... 50 C5
Kosŏng, N. Korea ... 57 E15
Kosovo □, Yugoslavia ... 40 D4
Kosovo Polje, Kosovo, Yug. ... 40 D5
Kosovska Kamenica, Kosovo, Yug. ... 40 D5
Kosovska Mitrovica, Kosovo, Yug. ... 40 D4
Kossou, L. de, Ivory C. ... 82 D3
Kosta, Sweden ... 11 H9
Kostajnica, Croatia ... 29 C13
Kostanjevica, Slovenia ... 29 C12
Kostenets, Bulgaria ... 40 D7
Koster, S. Africa ... 88 D4
Kôstî, Sudan ... 81 E3
Kostinbrod, Bulgaria ... 40 D7
Kostolac, Serbia, Yug. ... 40 B5
Kostopil, Ukraine ... 47 G4
Kostroma, Russia ... 46 D11
Kostromskoye Vdkhr., Russia .. 46 D11
Kostrzyn, Lubuskie, Poland ... 45 F1
Kostrzyn, Wielkopolskie, Poland 45 F4
Kostyantynivka, Ukraine ... 47 H9
Kostyukovichi = Kastsyukovichy, Belarus ... 46 F7
Koszalin, Poland ... 44 D3
Kőszeg, Hungary ... 42 C1
Kot Addu, Pakistan ... 68 D4
Kot Kapura, India ... 68 D6
Kot Moman, Pakistan ... 68 C5
Kot Sultan, Pakistan ... 68 D4
Kota, India ... 68 G6
Kota Baharu, Malaysia ... 65 J4
Kota Barrage, India ... 68 G6
Kota Belud, Malaysia ... 62 C5
Kota Kinabalu, Malaysia ... 62 C5
Kota Kubu Baharu, Malaysia .. 65 L3
Kota Tinggi, Malaysia ... 65 M4
Kotaagung, Indonesia ... 62 F2
Kotabumi, Indonesia ... 62 E2
Kotamobagu, Indonesia ... 63 D6
Kotcho L., Canada ... 104 B4
Kotdwara, India ... 69 E8
Kotel, Bulgaria ... 41 D10
Kotelnich, Russia ... 48 A9
Kotelnikovo, Russia ... 49 G6
Kotelnyy, Ostrov, Russia ... 51 B14
Kothari ➤, India ... 68 G6
Köthen, Germany ... 24 D7

Kothi, Mad. P., India ... 69 H10
Kothi, Mad. P., India ... 69 G9
Kotiro, Pakistan ... 68 F2
Kotka, Finland ... 9 F22
Kotlas, Russia ... 50 C5
Kotlenska Planina, Bulgaria ... 41 D10
Kotli, Pakistan ... 68 C5
Kotma, India ... 69 H9
Kotmul, Pakistan ... 69 B6
Koton-Karifi, Nigeria ... 83 D6
Kotonkoro, Nigeria ... 83 C6
Kotor, Montenegro, Yug. ... 40 D2
Kotor Varoš, Bos.-H. ... 42 F2
Kotoriba, Croatia ... 29 B13
Kotovo, Russia ... 48 E7
Kotovsk, Russia ... 48 D5
Kotovsk, Ukraine ... 47 J5
Kotputli, India ... 68 F7
Kotri, Pakistan ... 68 G3
Kótronas, Greece ... 38 E4
Kotturu, India ... 66 M10
Kotuy ➤, Russia ... 51 B11
Kotzebue, U.S.A. ... 100 B3
Koudougou, Burkina Faso ... 82 C4
Koufonísi, Greece ... 36 E8
Koufonísia, Greece ... 39 E7
Kougaberge, S. Africa ... 88 E3
Kouibli, Ivory C. ... 82 D3
Kouilou ➤, Congo ... 84 E2
Koula Moutou, Gabon ... 84 E2
Koulen = Kulen, Cambodia ... 64 F5
Koulikoro, Mali ... 82 C3
Kouloúra, Greece ... 36 A3
Koúm-bournoú, Ákra, Greece .. 36 C10
Koumala, Australia ... 94 C4
Koumankou, Mali ... 82 C3
Koumbia, Burkina Faso ... 82 C4
Koumbia, Guinea ... 82 C2
Koumboum, Guinea ... 82 C2
Koumpenntoum, Senegal ... 82 C2
Koumra, Chad ... 79 G9
Koun-Fao, Ivory C. ... 82 D4
Koundara, Guinea ... 82 C2
Koundian, Guinea ... 82 C2
Koungheul, Senegal ... 82 C2
Kounradskiy, Kazakstan ... 50 E8
Kountze, U.S.A. ... 113 K7
Koupéla, Burkina Faso ... 83 C4
Kourémalé, Mali ... 82 C3
Kouris ➤, Cyprus ... 36 E11
Kourou, Fr. Guiana ... 125 B8
Kourouba, Mali ... 82 C2
Kouroukoto, Mali ... 82 C2
Kouroussa, Guinea ... 82 C2
Koussané, Mali ... 82 C2
Koussane, Senegal ... 82 C2
Kousséri, Cameroon ... 79 F8
Koutiala, Mali ... 82 C3
Kouto, Ivory C. ... 82 D3
Kouvé, Togo ... 83 D5
Kouvola, Finland ... 9 F22
Kovačica, Serbia, Yug. ... 42 E5
Kovel, Ukraine ... 47 G3
Kovin, Serbia, Yug. ... 42 F5
Kovrov, Russia ... 48 B5
Kowal, Poland ... 45 F6
Kowalewo Pomorskie, Poland . 45 E5
Kowanyama, Australia ... 94 B3
Kowloon, H.K. ... 59 F10
Kowŏn, N. Korea ... 57 E14
Köyceğiz, Turkey ... 39 E10
Köyceğiz Gölü, Turkey ... 39 E10
Koyulhisar, Turkey ... 72 B7
Koyunyeri, Turkey ... 41 F10
Koza, Japan ... 55 L3
Kozak, Turkey ... 39 B9
Kozan, Turkey ... 70 B2
Kozáni, Greece ... 40 F5
Kozáni □, Greece ... 40 F5
Kozara, Bos.-H. ... 29 D14
Kozarac, Bos.-H. ... 29 D13
Kozelets, Ukraine ... 47 G6
Kozelsk, Russia ... 46 E8
Kozhikode = Calicut, India ... 66 P9
Koziegłowy, Poland ... 45 H6
Kozienice, Poland ... 45 G8
Kozje, Slovenia ... 29 B12
Kozloduy, Bulgaria ... 40 C7
Kozlovets, Bulgaria ... 41 C9
Kozlovka, Russia ... 48 C9
Kozlu, Turkey ... 72 B4
Kozluk, Turkey ... 73 C9
Koźmin, Poland ... 45 G4
Kozmodemyansk, Russia ... 48 B8
Kożuchów, Poland ... 45 G2
Kozyatyn, Ukraine ... 47 H5
Kpabia, Ghana ... 83 D4
Kpalimé, Togo ... 83 D5
Kpandae, Ghana ... 83 D4
Kpessi, Togo ... 83 D5
Kra, Isthmus of = Kra, Kho Khot, Thailand ... 65 G2
Kra, Kho Khot, Thailand ... 65 G2
Kra Buri, Thailand ... 65 G2
Kraai ➤, S. Africa ... 88 E4
Krabi, Thailand ... 65 H2
Kracheh, Cambodia ... 64 F6
Kragan, Indonesia ... 63 G14
Kragerø, Norway ... 9 G13
Kragujevac, Serbia, Yug. ... 40 B4
Krajenka, Poland ... 45 E3
Krajina, Bos.-H. ... 29 D13

Krakatau = Rakata, Pulau, Indonesia ... 62 F3
Krakatoa = Rakata, Pulau, Indonesia ... 62 F3
Krakor, Cambodia ... 64 F5
Kraków, Poland ... 45 H6
Kralanh, Cambodia ... 64 F4
Králíky, Czech Rep. ... 27 A9
Kraljevo, Serbia, Yug. ... 40 C4
Královský Chlmec, Slovak Rep. 27 C14
Kralupy nad Vltavou, Czech Rep. ... 26 A7
Kramatorsk, Ukraine ... 47 H9
Kramfors, Sweden ... 10 B11
Kraniá, Greece ... 40 G5
Kranidhion, Greece ... 38 D5
Kranj, Slovenia ... 29 B11
Kranjska Gora, Slovenia ... 29 B10
Krankskop, S. Africa ... 89 D5
Krapina, Croatia ... 29 B12
Krapina ➤, Croatia ... 29 C12
Krapkowice, Poland ... 45 H4
Kras, Croatia ... 29 C10
Kraskino, Russia ... 51 E14
Kraslava, Latvia ... 46 E4
Kraslice, Czech Rep. ... 26 A5
Krasnaya Gorbatka, Russia ... 48 C5
Krasnaya Polyana, Russia ... 49 J5
Kraśnik, Poland ... 45 H9
Krasnoarmeisk, Ukraine ... 47 H9
Krasnoarmeysk, Russia ... 48 E7
Krasnoarmeyskiy, Russia ... 49 G6
Krasnobrod, Poland ... 45 H10
Krasnodar, Russia ... 49 H4
Krasnodon, Ukraine ... 47 H10
Krasnogorskiy, Russia ... 48 B9
Krasnograd = Krasnohrad, Ukraine ... 47 H8
Krasnogvardeyskoye, Russia ... 49 H5
Krasnogvardyeysk, Ukraine ... 47 K8
Krasnohrad, Ukraine ... 47 H8
Krasnokutsk, Ukraine ... 47 G8
Krasnolesnyy, Russia ... 47 G10
Krasnoperekopsk, Ukraine ... 47 J7
Krasnorechenskiy, Russia ... 54 B7
Krasnoselkup, Russia ... 50 C9
Krasnoslobodsk, Mordvinia, Russia ... 48 C6
Krasnoslobodsk, Volgograd, Russia ... 49 F7
Krasnoturinsk, Russia ... 50 D7
Krasnovodsk = Türkmenbashi, Turkmenistan ... 50 E6
Krasnoyarsk, Russia ... 51 D10
Krasnoye = Krasnyy, Russia ... 46 E6
Krasnozavodsk, Russia ... 46 D10
Krasny Sulin, Russia ... 47 J11
Krasnystaw, Poland ... 45 H10
Krasnyy, Russia ... 46 E6
Krasnyy Kholm, Russia ... 46 C9
Krasnyy Kut, Russia ... 48 E8
Krasnyy Liman, Ukraine ... 47 H9
Krasnyy Luch, Ukraine ... 47 H10
Krasnyy Profintern, Russia ... 46 D11
Krasnyy Yar, Astrakhan, Russia 49 G9
Krasnyy Yar, Samara, Russia .. 48 D10
Krasnyy Yar, Volgograd, Russia 48 E7
Krasnyye Baki, Russia ... 48 B7
Krasnyyoskolske Vdskh., Ukraine ... 47 H9
Kraszna ➤, Hungary ... 42 B7
Kratie = Kracheh, Cambodia ... 64 F6
Kratovo, Macedonia ... 40 D6
Krau, Indonesia ... 63 E10
Kravanh, Chuor Phnum, Cambodia ... 65 G4
Krefeld, Germany ... 24 D2
Krémaston, Límni, Greece ... 38 C3
Kremen, Croatia ... 29 D12
Kremenchug = Kremenchuk, Ukraine ... 47 H7
Kremenchuk, Ukraine ... 47 H7
Kremenchuksk Vdskh., Ukraine 47 H7
Kremenets, Ukraine ... 47 G3
Kremennaya, Ukraine ... 47 H10
Kremges = Svitlovodsk, Ukraine 47 H7
Kremmen, Germany ... 24 C9
Kremmling, U.S.A. ... 114 F10
Kremnica, Slovak Rep. ... 27 C11
Krems, Austria ... 26 C8
Kremsmünster, Austria ... 26 C7
Kretinga, Lithuania ... 9 J19
Krettsy, Russia ... 46 C7
Kreuzberg, Germany ... 25 E5
Kreuztal, Germany ... 24 E4
Kría Vrísi, Greece ... 40 F6
Kribi, Cameroon ... 83 E6
Krichem, Bulgaria ... 41 D8
Krichev = Krychaw, Belarus ... 46 F7
Krim, Slovenia ... 29 C11
Kriós, Ákra, Greece ... 36 D5
Krishna ➤, India ... 67 M12
Krishnagar, India ... 69 H13
Krishnanagar, India ... 69 H13
Kristdala, Sweden ... 11 G10
Kristiansand, Norway ... 9 G13
Kristianstad, Sweden ... 11 H8
Kristiansund, Norway ... 8 E12
Kristiinankaupunki, Finland ... 9 E19
Kristinehamn, Sweden ... 10 E8
Kristinestad = Kristiinankaupunki, Finland ... 9 E19
Kríti, Greece ... 36 D7
Kritsá, Greece ... 36 D7
Krivaja ➤, Bos.-H. ... 42 F3

Krivaja ➤, Bos.-H. ... 42 F3
Krivelj, Serbia, Yug. ... 40 B6
Krivoy Rog = Kryvyy Rih, Ukraine ... 47 J7
Križevci, Croatia ... 29 B13
Krk, Croatia ... 29 C11
Krka ➤, Slovenia ... 29 C12
Krkonoše, Czech Rep. ... 26 A8
Krnov, Czech Rep. ... 27 A10
Krobia, Poland ... 45 G3
Krokeaí, Greece ... 38 E4
Krokek, Sweden ... 11 F10
Krokodil ➤, Mozam. ... 89 D5
Krokom, Sweden ... 10 A8
Krokowa, Poland ... 44 D5
Krolevets, Ukraine ... 47 G7
Kroměříž, Czech Rep. ... 27 B10
Krompachy, Slovak Rep. ... 27 C13
Kromy, Russia ... 47 F8
Kronach, Germany ... 25 E7
Krong Kaoh Kong, Cambodia .. 62 B2
Kronobergs län □, Sweden ... 11 H8
Kronprins Olav Kyst, Antarctica 5 C5
Kronshtadt, Russia ... 46 C5
Kroonstad, S. Africa ... 88 D4
Kröpelin, Germany ... 24 A7
Kropotkin, Russia ... 49 H5
Kropp, Germany ... 24 A5
Krosna, Lithuania ... 44 D10
Krośniewice, Poland ... 45 F6
Krosno, Poland ... 45 J8
Krosno Odrzańskie, Poland ... 45 F2
Krotoszyn, Poland ... 45 G4
Krotovka, Russia ... 48 D10
Kroussón, Greece ... 36 D6
Krrabë, Albania ... 40 E3
Krško, Slovenia ... 29 C12
Krstača, Serbia, Yug. ... 40 D4
Kruger Nat. Park, S. Africa ... 89 C5
Krugersdorp, S. Africa ... 89 D4
Kruisfontein, S. Africa ... 88 E3
Krujë, Albania ... 40 E3
Krulevshchina = Krulyewshchyna, Belarus ... 46 E4
Krulyewshchyna, Belarus ... 46 E4
Krumbach, Germany ... 25 G6
Krumë, Albania ... 40 D4
Krumovgrad, Bulgaria ... 41 E9
Krung Thep = Bangkok, Thailand ... 64 F3
Krupanj, Serbia, Yug. ... 40 B3
Krupina, Slovak Rep. ... 27 C12
Krupinica ➤, Slovak Rep. ... 27 C11
Krupki, Belarus ... 46 E5
Kruševac, Serbia, Yug. ... 40 C5
Kruševo, Macedonia ... 40 E5
Kruszwica, Poland ... 45 F5
Krychaw, Belarus ... 46 F6
Krymsk, Russia ... 47 K10
Krymskiy Poluostrov = Krymskyy Pivostriv, Ukraine 47 K8
Krymskyy Pivostriv, Ukraine ... 47 K8
Krynica, Poland ... 45 J7
Krynica Morska, Poland ... 44 D6
Krynki, Poland ... 45 E10
Kryvyy Rih, Ukraine ... 47 J7
Krzepice, Poland ... 45 H5
Krzeszyce, Poland ... 45 H9
Krzna ➤, Poland ... 45 F10
Krzywiń, Poland ... 45 G3
Krzyż Wielkopolski, Poland ... 45 F2
Ksar el Kebir, Morocco ... 78 B4
Ksar es Souk = Er Rachidia, Morocco ... 78 B5
Książ Wielkopolski, Poland ... 45 F4
Kstovo, Russia ... 48 B7
Ku, W. el ➤, Sudan ... 81 F2
Kuala Belait, Malaysia ... 62 D4
Kuala Berang, Malaysia ... 65 K4
Kuala Dungun = Dungun, Malaysia ... 65 K4
Kuala Kangsar, Malaysia ... 65 K3
Kuala Kelawang, Malaysia ... 65 L4
Kuala Kerai, Malaysia ... 65 K4
Kuala Lipis, Malaysia ... 65 K4
Kuala Lumpur, Malaysia ... 65 L3
Kuala Nerang, Malaysia ... 65 J3
Kuala Pilah, Malaysia ... 65 L4
Kuala Rompin, Malaysia ... 65 L4
Kuala Selangor, Malaysia ... 65 L3
Kuala Sepetang, Malaysia ... 65 K3
Kuala Terengganu, Malaysia ... 65 K4
Kualajelai, Indonesia ... 62 E4
Kualakapuas, Indonesia ... 62 E4
Kualakurun, Indonesia ... 62 E4
Kualapembuang, Indonesia ... 62 E4
Kualasimpang, Indonesia ... 62 D1
Kuancheng, China ... 57 D10
Kuandang, Indonesia ... 63 D6
Kuandian, China ... 57 D13
Kuangchou = Guangzhou, China 59 F10
Kuanshan, Taiwan ... 59 F13
Kuantan, Malaysia ... 65 L4
Kuba = Quba, Azerbaijan ... 49 K9
Kuban ➤, Russia ... 47 K9
Kubenskoye, Ozero, Russia ... 46 C10
Kubokawa, Japan ... 55 H6
Kubrat, Bulgaria ... 41 C10
Kučevo, Serbia, Yug. ... 40 B5
Kucha Gompa, India ... 69 B7
Kuchaman, India ... 68 F6
Kuchinda, India ... 69 J11
Kuchinoerabu-Jima, Japan ... 55 J5
Kuchino-Shima, Japan ... 55 K4

Kuchinotsu, *Japan* 55 H5
Kuchl, *Austria* 26 D6
Kucing = Kuching, *Malaysia* ... 62 D4
Küçükbahçe, *Turkey* 39 C8
Küçükköy, *Turkey* 39 B8
Küçükkuyu, *Turkey* 39 B8
Küçükmenderes ➤, *Turkey* .. 39 D9
Kud ➤, *Pakistan* 68 F2
Kuda, *India* 66 H7
Kudat, *Malaysia* 62 C5
Kudirkos Naumiestis, *Lithuania* 44 D9
Kudowa-Zdrój, *Poland* 45 H3
Kudus, *Indonesia* 63 G14
Kudymkar, *Russia* 50 D6
Kueiyang = Guiyang, *China* .. 58 D6
Kufra Oasis = Al Kufrah, *Libya* 79 D10
Kufstein, *Austria* 26 D5
Kugluktuk, *Canada* 100 B8
Kugong I., *Canada* 102 A4
Kūhak, *Iran* 66 F3
Kuhan, *Pakistan* 68 E2
Kühbonän, *Iran* 71 D8
Kühestak, *Iran* 71 E8
Kuhin, *Iran* 71 B6
Kūhīrī, *Iran* 71 E9
Kuhnsdorf, *Austria* 26 E7
Kühpāyeh, *Esfahan, Iran* ... 71 C7
Kühpāyeh, *Kermān, Iran* ... 71 D8
Kührän, Küh-e, *Iran* 71 E8
Kui Buri, *Thailand* 65 F2
Kuiseb ➤, *Namibia* 88 B2
Kuito, *Angola* 85 G3
Kuiu I., *U.S.A.* 104 B2
Kujang, *N. Korea* 57 E14
Kujawsko-Pomorskie □, *Poland* 44 E5
Kuji, *Japan* 54 D10
Kujū-San, *Japan* 55 H5
Kukavica, *Serbia, Yug.* 40 D5
Kukawa, *Nigeria* 83 C7
Kukës, *Albania* 40 D4
Kukmor, *Russia* 48 B10
Kukup, *Malaysia* 65 M4
Kukvidze, *Russia* 48 E6
Kula, *Bulgaria* 40 C6
Kula, *Serbia, Yug.* 42 E4
Kula, *Turkey* 39 C10
Kulachi, *Pakistan* 68 D4
Kulai, *Malaysia* 65 M4
Kulal, Mt., *Kenya* 86 B4
Kulaly, Ostrov, *Kazakstan* .. 49 H10
Kulasekarappattinam, *India* .. 66 Q11
Kulautuva, *Lithuania* 44 D10
Kuldīga, *Latvia* 9 H19
Kuldīga □, *Latvia* 44 B8
Kuldja = Yining, *China* 50 E9
Kuldu, *Sudan* 81 E2
Kulebaki, *Russia* 48 C6
Kulen, *Cambodia* 64 F5
Kulen Vakuf, *Bos.-H.* 29 D13
Kulgam, *India* 69 C6
Kulgera, *Australia* 94 D1
Kulim, *Malaysia* 65 K3
Kulin, *Australia* 93 F2
Kullen, *Sweden* 11 H6
Kulmbach, *Germany* 25 E7
Külob, *Tajikistan* 50 F7
Kulp, *Turkey* 73 C9
Kulpawn ➤, *Ghana* 83 D4
Kulsary, *Kazakstan* 50 E6
Kulti, *India* 69 H12
Kulu, *India* 68 D7
Kulu, *Turkey* 72 C5
Kulumbura, *Australia* 92 B4
Kulunda, *Russia* 50 D8
Kulungar, *Afghan.* 68 C3
Külvand, *Iran* 71 D7
Kulyab = Külob, *Tajikistan* .. 50 F7
Kuma ➤, *Russia* 49 H8
Kumafşar, *Turkey* 39 D11
Kumaganum, *Nigeria* 83 C7
Kumagaya, *Japan* 55 F9
Kumai, *Indonesia* 62 E4
Kumalar Dağı, *Turkey* 39 C12
Kumamba, Kepulauan, *Indonesia* 63 E10
Kumamoto, *Japan* 55 H5
Kumamoto □, *Japan* 55 H5
Kumanovo, *Macedonia* 40 D5
Kumara, *N.Z.* 91 K3
Kumarina, *Australia* 93 D2
Kumasi, *Ghana* 82 D4
Kumayri = Gyumri, *Armenia* . 49 K6
Kumba, *Cameroon* 83 E6
Kumbağ, *Turkey* 41 F11
Kumbakonam, *India* 66 P11
Kumbarilla, *Australia* 95 D5
Kumbhraj, *India* 68 G7
Kumbia, *Australia* 95 D5
Kumbo, *Cameroon* 83 D7
Kŭmch'ŏn, *N. Korea* 57 E14
Kumdok, *India* 69 C8
Kume-Shima, *Japan* 55 L4
Kumeny, *Russia* 48 A9
Kumharsain, *India* 68 D7
Kŭmhwa, *S. Korea* 57 E14
Kumi, *Uganda* 86 B3
Kumkale, *Turkey* 41 G10
Kumla, *Sweden* 10 E9
Kumluca, *Turkey* 39 E12
Kummerower See, *Germany* .. 24 B8
Kumo, *Nigeria* 83 C7
Kumon Bum, *Burma* 67 F20
Kumylzhenskaya, *Russia* 48 F6
Kunágota, *Hungary* 42 D6
Kunashir, Ostrov, *Russia* 51 E15

Kunda, *Estonia* 9 G22
Kunda, *India* 69 G9
Kundar ➤, *Pakistan* 68 D3
Kundian, *Pakistan* 68 C4
Kundla, *India* 68 J4
Kunga ➤, *Bangla.* 69 J13
Kungälv, *Sweden* 11 G5
Kunghit I., *Canada* 104 C2
Kungrad = Qŭnghirot, *Uzbekistan* 50 E6
Kungsängen, *Sweden* 10 E11
Kungsbacka, *Sweden* 11 G6
Kungsgården, *Sweden* 10 D10
Kungshamn, *Sweden* 11 F5
Kungsör, *Sweden* 10 E10
Kungur, *Russia* 50 D6
Kunhar ➤, *Pakistan* 69 B5
Kunhegyes, *Hungary* 42 C5
Kuningan, *Indonesia* 63 G13
Kunlong, *Burma* 58 F2
Kunlun Shan, *Asia* 60 C3
Kunming, *China* 58 E4
Kunów, *Poland* 45 H8
Kunsan, *S. Korea* 57 G14
Kunshan, *China* 59 B13
Kunszentmárton, *Hungary* .. 42 D5
Kunszentmiklós, *Hungary* .. 42 C4
Kuntaur, *Senegal* 82 C2
Kununurra, *Australia* 92 C4
Kunwari ➤, *India* 69 F8
Kunya-Urgench = Köneürgench, *Turkmenistan* 50 E6
Künzelsau, *Germany* 25 F5
Kuopio, *Finland* 8 E22
Kupa ➤, *Croatia* 29 C13
Kupang, *Indonesia* 63 F6
Kupreanof I., *U.S.A.* 104 B2
Kupres, *Bos.-H.* 42 G2
Kupyansk, *Ukraine* 47 H9
Kupyansk-Uzlovoi, *Ukraine* . 47 H9
Kuqa, *China* 60 B3
Kür ➤, *Azerbaijan* 73 C13
Kür Dili, *Azerbaijan* 71 B6
Kura = Kür ➤, *Azerbaijan* .. 73 C13
Kuranda, *Australia* 94 B4
Kuranga, *India* 68 H3
Kurashiki, *Japan* 55 G6
Kurayoshi, *Japan* 55 G6
Kürdämir, *Azerbaijan* 49 K9
Kurdistan, *Asia* 73 D10
Kürdzhali, *Bulgaria* 41 E9
Kure, *Japan* 55 G6
Küre, *Turkey* 72 B5
Küre Dağları, *Turkey* 72 B6
Kuressaare, *Estonia* 9 G20
Kurgan, *Russia* 50 D7
Kurganinsk, *Russia* 49 H5
Kurganskaya = Kurganinsk, *Russia* 49 H5
Kuri, *India* 68 F4
Kuria Maria Is. = Khurīyā Murīyā, Jazā'ir, *Oman* .. 74 D6
Kuridala, *Australia* 94 C3
Kurigram, *Bangla.* 67 G16
Kurikka, *Finland* 9 E20
Kuril Is. = Kurilskiye Ostrova, *Russia* 51 E15
Kuril Trench, *Pac. Oc.* 52 E19
Kurilsk, *Russia* 51 E15
Kurilskiye Ostrova, *Russia* .. 51 E15
Kurino, *Japan* 55 J5
Kurinskaya Kosa = Kür Dili, *Azerbaijan* 71 B6
Kurkur, *Egypt* 80 C3
Kurlovskiy, *Russia* 48 C5
Kurmuk, *Sudan* 81 E3
Kurnool, *India* 66 M11
Kuro-Shima, *Kagoshima, Japan* 55 J4
Kuro-Shima, *Okinawa, Japan* . 55 M2
Kuror, J., *Sudan* 80 C3
Kurow, *N.Z.* 91 L3
Kurów, *Poland* 45 G9
Kurram ➤, *Pakistan* 68 C4
Kurrimine, *Australia* 94 B4
Kursavka, *Russia* 49 H6
Kurshskiy Zaliv, *Russia* 9 J19
Kursk, *Russia* 47 G9
Kuršumlija, *Serbia, Yug.* 40 C5
Kuršumlijska Banja, *Serbia, Yug.* 40 C5
Kurşunlu, *Bursa, Turkey* 41 F13
Kurşunlu, *Çankırı, Turkey* .. 72 B5
Kurtalan, *Turkey* 73 D9
Kurtbey, *Turkey* 41 E10
Kuru, *Sudan* 81 F2
Kuru, Bahr el = *Sudan* 81 F2
Kurucaşile, *Turkey* 72 B5
Kuruçay, *Turkey* 70 B3
Kuruktag, *China* 60 B3
Kuruman, *S. Africa* 88 D3
Kuruman ➤, *S. Africa* 88 D3
Kurume, *Japan* 55 H5
Kurun ➤, *Sudan* 81 F3
Kurunegala, *Sri Lanka* 66 R12
Kurya, *Russia* 50 C6
Kuş Gölü, *Turkey* 41 F11
Kuşadası, *Turkey* 72 D2
Kuşadası Körfezı, *Turkey* ... 39 D8
Kusatsu, *Japan* 55 F9
Kusawa L., *Canada* 104 A1
Kusel, *Germany* 25 F3
Kushaka, *Nigeria* 83 C6
Kushalgarh, *India* 68 H6
Kushchevskaya, *Russia* 49 G4
Kusheriki, *Nigeria* 83 C6
Kushikino, *Japan* 55 J5

Kushima, *Japan* 55 J5
Kushimoto, *Japan* 55 H7
Kushiro, *Japan* 54 C12
Kushiro-Gawa ➤, *Japan* 54 C12
Kūshk, *Iran* 71 D8
Kushka = Gushgy, *Turkmenistan* 50 F7
Kūshkī, *Iran* 70 C5
Kushol, *India* 69 C7
Kushtia, *Bangla.* 67 H16
Kushum ➤, *Kazakstan* 48 F10
Kuskokwim B., *U.S.A.* 100 C3
Kusmi, *India* 69 H10
Kussharo-Ko, *Japan* 54 C12
Kustanay = Qostanay, *Kazakstan* 50 D7
Kut, Ko, *Thailand* 65 G4
Kütahya, *Turkey* 39 B12
Kütahya □, *Turkey* 39 B11
Kutaisi, *Georgia* 49 J6
Kutaraja = Banda Aceh, *Indonesia* 62 C1
Kutch, Gulf of = Kachchh, Gulf of, *India* 68 H3
Kutch, Rann of = Kachchh, Rann of, *India* 68 H4
Kutina, *Croatia* 29 C13
Kutiyana, *India* 68 J4
Kutjevo, *Croatia* 42 E2
Kutkashen, *Azerbaijan* 49 K8
Kutná Hora, *Czech Rep.* 26 B8
Kutno, *Poland* 45 F6
Kutse, *Botswana* 88 C3
Kutu, *Dem. Rep. of the Congo* . 84 E3
Kutum, *Sudan* 81 E1
Kúty, *Slovak Rep.* 27 C10
Kuujjuaq, *Canada* 101 C13
Kuujjuarapik, *Canada* 102 A4
Kuŭp-tong, *N. Korea* 57 D14
Kuusamo, *Finland* 8 D23
Kuusankoski, *Finland* 9 F22
Kuvshinovo, *Russia* 46 D8
Kuwait = Al Kuwayt, *Kuwait* . 70 D5
Kuwait ■, *Asia* 70 D5
Kuwana, *Japan* 55 G8
Kuybyshev = Samara, *Russia* . 48 D10
Kuybyshev, *Russia* 50 D8
Kuybyshevo, *Ukraine* 47 J9
Kuybyshevskoye Vdkhr., *Russia* 48 C9
Kuye He ➤, *China* 56 E6
Kūyeh, *Iran* 70 B5
Kūysanjaq, *Iraq* 70 B5
Kuyucak, *Turkey* 39 D10
Kuyumba, *Russia* 51 C10
Kuzey Anadolu Dağları, *Turkey* 72 B7
Kuzmin, *Serbia, Yug.* 42 E4
Kuznetsk, *Russia* 48 D8
Kuzomen, *Russia* 50 C4
Kvænangen, *Norway* 8 A19
Kværndrup, *Denmark* 11 J4
Kvänum, *Sweden* 11 F7
Kvaløy, *Norway* 8 B18
Kvareli = Qvareli, *Georgia* .. 49 K7
Kvarner, *Croatia* 29 D11
Kvarnerič, *Croatia* 29 D11
Kvicksund, *Sweden* 10 E10
Kvillsfors, *Sweden* 11 G9
Kvissleby, *Sweden* 10 B11
Kwa-Nobuhle, *S. Africa* 85 L5
Kwabhaca, *S. Africa* 89 E4
Kwakhanai, *Botswana* 88 C3
Kwakoegron, *Surinam* 125 B7
Kwale, *Kenya* 86 C4
Kwale, *Nigeria* 83 D6
KwaMashu, *S. Africa* 89 D5
Kwando ➤, *Africa* 88 B3
Kwangdaeri, *N. Korea* 57 D14
Kwangju, *S. Korea* 57 G14
Kwango ➤, *Dem. Rep. of the Congo* 84 E3
Kwangsi-Chuang = Guangxi Zhuangzu Zizhiqu □, *China* . 58 F7
Kwangtung = Guangdong □, *China* 59 F9
Kwara □, *Nigeria* 83 D6
Kwatisore, *Indonesia* 63 E8
KwaZulu Natal □, *S. Africa* .. 89 D5
Kweichow = Guizhou □, *China* 58 D6
Kwekwe, *Zimbabwe* 87 F2
Kwidzyn, *Poland* 44 E5
Kwiha, *Ethiopia* 81 E4
Kwinana New Town, *Australia* . 93 F2
Kwisa ➤, *Poland* 45 G2
Kwoka, *Indonesia* 63 E8
Kwolla, *Nigeria* 83 D6
Kyabra Cr. ➤, *Australia* 95 D3
Kyaikto, *Burma* 64 D1
Kyakhta, *Russia* 51 D11
Kyancutta, *Australia* 95 E2
Kyaukpadaung, *Burma* 67 J19
Kyaukpyu, *Burma* 67 K18
Kyaukse, *Burma* 67 J20
Kybartai, *Lithuania* 44 D9
Kyburz, *U.S.A.* 116 G6
Kyelang, *India* 68 C7
Kyenjojo, *Uganda* 86 B3
Kyjov, *Czech Rep.* 27 B10
Kyle, *Canada* 105 C7
Kyle Dam, *Zimbabwe* 87 G3
Kyle of Lochalsh, *U.K.* 14 D3
Kyll ➤, *Germany* 25 F2
Kyllburg, *Germany* 25 E2
Kymijoki ➤, *Finland* 9 F22
Kynuna, *Australia* 94 C3

Kyō-ga-Saki, *Japan* 55 G7
Kyoga, L., *Uganda* 86 B3
Kyogle, *Australia* 95 D5
Kyom ➤, *Sudan* 81 F2
Kyongju, *S. Korea* 57 G15
Kyongpyaw, *Burma* 67 L19
Kyŏngsŏng, *N. Korea* 57 D15
Kyōto, *Japan* 55 G7
Kyōto □, *Japan* 55 G7
Kyparissovouno, *Cyprus* 36 D12
Kyparissía, *Cyprus* 36 E11
Kyperounda, *Cyprus* 36 E11
Kyrenia, *Cyprus* 36 D12
Kyrgyzstan ■, *Asia* 50 E8
Kyritz, *Germany* 24 C8
Kyrkhult, *Sweden* 11 H8
Kyrönjoki ➤, *Finland* 8 E19
Kystatyam, *Russia* 51 C13
Kysucké Nové Mesto, *Slovak Rep.* 27 B11
Kythréa, *Cyprus* 36 D12
Kyunhla, *Burma* 67 H19
Kyuquot Sound, *Canada* 104 D3
Kyurdamir = Kürdämir, *Azerbaijan* 49 K9
Kyūshū, *Japan* 55 H5
Kyūshū □, *Japan* 55 H5
Kyūshū-Sanchi, *Japan* 55 H5
Kyustendil, *Bulgaria* 40 D6
Kyusyur, *Russia* 51 B13
Kyyiv, *Ukraine* 47 G6
Kyyivske Vdskh., *Ukraine* ... 47 G6
Kyzyl, *Russia* 51 D10
Kyzyl Kum, *Uzbekistan* 50 E7
Kyzyl-Kyya, *Kyrgyzstan* 50 E8
Kzyl-Orda = Qyzylorda, *Kazakstan* 50 E7

L

La Albuera, *Spain* 35 G4
La Alcarria, *Spain* 32 E2
La Almarcha, *Spain* 32 F2
La Almunia de Doña Godina, *Spain* 32 D3
La Asunción, *Venezuela* 124 A6
La Baie, *Canada* 103 C5
La Banda, *Argentina* 126 B3
La Bañeza, *Spain* 34 C5
La Barca, *Mexico* 118 C4
La Barge, *U.S.A.* 114 E8
La Bastide-Puylaurent, *France* . 20 D7
La Baule-Escoubiac, *France* .. 18 E4
La Belle, *U.S.A.* 109 M5
La Biche ➤, *Canada* 104 B4
La Biche, L., *Canada* 104 C6
La Bisbal d'Empordà, *Spain* .. 32 D8
La Bomba, *Mexico* 118 A1
La Brède, *France* 20 D3
La Bresse, *France* 19 D13
La Bureba, *Spain* 34 C2
La Calera, *Chile* 126 C1
La Campiña, *Spain* 35 H6
La Canal = Sa Canal, *Spain* .. 37 C7
La Canourgue, *France* 20 D7
La Capelle, *France* 19 C10
La Carlota, *Argentina* 126 C3
La Carlota, *Phil.* 61 F5
La Carlota, *Spain* 35 H6
La Carolina, *Spain* 35 G7
La Cavalerie, *France* 20 D7
La Ceiba, *Honduras* 120 C2
La Chaise-Dieu, *France* 20 C7
La Chapelle d'Angillon, *France* . 19 E9
La Chapelle-St-Luc, *France* .. 19 D11
La Chapelle-sur-Erdre, *France* . 18 E5
La Charité-sur-Loire, *France* .. 19 E10
La Chartre-sur-le-Loir, *France* . 18 E7
La Châtaigneraie, *France* ... 20 B3
La Châtre, *France* 19 F9
La Chaux-de-Fonds, *Switz.* .. 25 H2
La Chorrera, *Panama* 120 E4
La Ciotat, *France* 21 E9
La Clayette, *France* 19 F11
La Cocha, *Argentina* 126 B2
La Concepción = Ri-Aba, *Eq. Guin.* 83 E6
La Concepción, *Panama* 120 E3
La Concordia, *Mexico* 119 D6
La Coruña = A Coruña, *Spain* . 34 B2
La Coruña □, *Spain* 34 B2
La Côte-St-André, *France* ... 21 C9
La Courtine-le-Trucq, *France* . 20 C6
La Crau, Bouches-du-Rhône, *France* 21 E8
La Crau, Var, *France* 21 E10
La Crescent, *U.S.A.* 112 D7
La Crete, *Canada* 104 B5
La Crosse, Kans., *U.S.A.* ... 112 F5
La Crosse, Wis., *U.S.A.* 112 D9
La Cruz, *Costa Rica* 120 D2
La Cruz, *Mexico* 118 C3
La Désirade, *Guadeloupe* ... 121 C7
La Escondida, *Mexico* 118 C5
La Esmeralda, *Paraguay* 126 A3
La Esperanza, *Cuba* 120 B3
La Esperanza, *Honduras* 120 D2
La Estrada = A Estrada, *Spain* . 34 C2
La Faouët, *France* 18 E3
La Fayette, *U.S.A.* 109 H3
La Fé, *Cuba* 120 B3
La Fère, *France* 19 C10
La Ferté-Bernard, *France* ... 18 D7
La Ferté-Gaucher, *France* ... 19 D10

La Ferté-Macé, *France* 18 D6
La Ferté-St-Aubin, *France* ... 19 E8
La Ferté-sous-Jouarre, *France* . 19 D10
La Ferté-Vidame, *France* ... 18 D7
La Flèche, *France* 18 E6
La Follette, *U.S.A.* 109 G3
La Fregeneda, *Spain* 34 E4
La Fuente de San Esteban, *Spain* 34 E4
La Gacilly, *France* 18 E4
La Gineta, *Spain* 33 F2
La Grand-Combe, *France* ... 21 D8
La Grande, *U.S.A.* 114 D4
La Grande ➤, *Canada* 102 B5
La Grande Deux, Rés., *Canada* 102 B4
La Grande-Motte, *France* ... 21 E8
La Grande Quatre, Rés., *Canada* 102 B5
La Grande Trois, Rés., *Canada* 102 B4
La Grange, Calif., *U.S.A.* ... 116 H6
La Grange, Ga., *U.S.A.* 109 J3
La Grange, Ky., *U.S.A.* 108 F3
La Grange, Tex., *U.S.A.* 113 L6
La Grave, *France* 21 C10
La Guaira, *Venezuela* 124 A5
La Guardia = A Guarda, *Spain* . 34 C2
La Gudiña = A Gudiña, *Spain* . 34 C3
La Guerche-de-Bretagne, *France* 18 E5
La Guerche-sur-l'Aubois, *France* 19 F9
La Habana, *Cuba* 120 B3
La Haye-du-Puits, *France* ... 18 C5
La Horra, *Spain* 34 D7
La Independencia, *Mexico* ... 119 D6
La Isabela, *Dom. Rep.* 121 C5
La Jonquera, *Spain* 32 C7
La Junta, *U.S.A.* 113 F3
La Laguna, *Canary Is.* 37 F3
La Libertad, *Guatemala* 120 C1
La Libertad, *Mexico* 118 B2
La Ligua, *Chile* 126 C1
La Línea de la Concepción, *Spain* 35 J5
La Loche, *Canada* 105 B7
La Londe-les-Maures, *France* . 21 E10
La Lora, *Spain* 34 C7
La Loupe, *France* 18 D8
La Louvière, *Belgium* 17 D4
La Machine, *France* 19 F10
La Maddalena, *Italy* 30 A2
La Malbaie, *Canada* 103 C5
La Mancha, *Spain* 33 F2
La Mariña, *Spain* 34 B3
La Martre, L., *Canada* 104 A5
La Mesa, *U.S.A.* 117 N9
La Misión, *Mexico* 118 A1
La Mothe-Achard, *France* ... 18 F5
La Motte, *France* 21 D10
La Motte-Chalançon, *France* . 21 D9
La Motte-Servolex, *France* .. 21 C9
La Moure, *U.S.A.* 112 B5
La Muela, *Spain* 32 D3
La Mure, *France* 21 D9
La Negra, *Chile* 126 A1
La Oliva, *Canary Is.* 37 F6
La Orotava, *Canary Is.* 37 F3
La Oroya, *Peru* 124 F3
La Pacaudière, *France* 19 F10
La Palma, *Panama* 120 E4
La Palma, *Spain* 37 F2
La Palma del Condado, *Spain* . 35 H4
La Paloma, *Chile* 126 C1
La Pampa □, *Argentina* 126 D2
La Paragua, *Venezuela* 124 B6
La Paz, *Entre Ríos, Argentina* . 126 C4
La Paz, *San Luis, Argentina* . 126 C2
La Paz, *Bolivia* 124 G5
La Paz, *Honduras* 120 D2
La Paz, *Mexico* 118 C2
La Paz, *Phil.* 61 D4
La Paz Centro, *Nic.* 120 D2
La Pedrera, *Colombia* 124 D5
La Pérade, *Canada* 103 C5
La Perouse Str., *Asia* 54 B11
La Pesca, *Mexico* 119 C5
La Piedad, *Mexico* 118 C4
La Pine, *U.S.A.* 114 E3
La Plata, *Argentina* 126 D4
La Pobla de Lillet, *Spain* ... 32 C6
La Pocatière, *Canada* 103 C5
La Pola de Gordón, *Spain* ... 34 C5
La Porte, *Ind., U.S.A.* 108 E2
La Porte, Tex., *U.S.A.* 113 L7
La Presanella, *Italy* 28 B7
La Puebla = Sa Pobla, *Spain* . 32 F8
La Puebla de Cazalla, *Spain* .. 35 H5
La Puebla de los Infantes, *Spain* 35 H5
La Puebla de Montalbán, *Spain* 34 F6
La Puebla del Río, *Spain* 35 H4
La Puerta de Segura, *Spain* .. 35 G8
La Purísima, *Mexico* 118 B2
La Push, *U.S.A.* 116 C2
La Quiaca, *Argentina* 126 A2
La Réole, *France* 20 D3
La Restinga, *Canary Is.* 37 G2
La Rioja, *Argentina* 126 B2
La Rioja □, *Spain* 32 C2
La Robla, *Spain* 34 C5
La Roche-Bernard, *France* ... 18 E4
La Roche-Canillac, *France* ... 20 C5
La Roche-en-Ardenne, *Belgium* 17 D5
La Roche-sur-Foron, *France* .. 19 F13
La Roche-sur-Yon, *France* ... 18 F5
La Rochefoucauld, *France* ... 20 C4
La Rochelle, *France* 20 B2
La Roda, *Spain* 33 F2

Laruns

La Roda de Andalucía, *Spain* 35 H6
La Romana, *Dom. Rep.* 121 C6
La Ronge, *Canada* 105 B7
La Rumorosa, *Mexico* 117 N10
La Sabina = Sa Savina, *Spain* 37 C7
La Sagra, *Spain* 33 H2
La Salle, *U.S.A.* 112 E10
La Sanabria, *Spain* 34 C4
La Santa, *Canary Is.* 37 E6
La Sarre, *Canada* 102 C4
La Scie, *Canada* 103 C8
La Selva, *Spain* 32 C7
La Selva Beach, *U.S.A.* 116 J5
La Selva del Camp, *Spain* 32 D6
La Serena, *Chile* 126 B1
La Serena, *Spain* 35 G5
La Seu d'Urgell, *Spain* 32 C6
La Seyne-sur-Mer, *France* 21 E9
La Sila, *Italy* 31 C9
La Solana, *Spain* 35 G7
La Soufrière, *St. Vincent* 121 D7
La Souterraine, *France* 19 F8
La Spézia, *Italy* 28 D6
La Suze-sur-Sarthe, *France* 18 E7
La Tagua, *Colombia* 124 C4
La Teste, *France* 20 D2
La Tortuga, *Venezuela* 121 D6
La Tour-du-Pin, *France* 21 C9
La Tranche-sur-Mer, *France* 18 F5
La Tremblade, *France* 20 C2
La Tuque, *Canada* 102 C5
La Unión, *Chile* 128 E2
La Unión, *El Salv.* 120 D2
La Unión, *Mexico* 118 D4
La Unión, *Spain* 33 H4
La Urbana, *Venezuela* 124 B5
La Vall d'Uixó, *Spain* 32 F4
La Vecilla de Curveño, *Spain* 34 C5
La Vega, *Dom. Rep.* 121 C5
La Vela de Coro, *Venezuela* 124 A5
La Veleta, *Spain* 35 H7
La Venta, *Mexico* 119 D6
La Ventura, *Mexico* 118 C4
La Voulte-sur-Rhône, *France* 21 D8
Laa an der Thaya, *Austria* 27 C9
Laaber, Grosse →, *Germany* 25 G8
Laage, *Germany* 24 B8
Laatzen, *Germany* 24 C5
Laba →, *Russia* 49 H4
Labasa, *Fiji* 91 C8
Labason, *Phil.* 61 G5
Labastide-Murat, *France* 20 D5
Labastide-Rouairoux, *France* 20 E6
Labbézenga, *Mali* 83 B5
Labe = Elbe →, *Europe* 24 B4
Labé, *Guinea* 82 C2
Laberge, L., *Canada* 104 A1
Labin, *Croatia* 29 C11
Labinsk, *Russia* 49 H5
Labis, *Malaysia* 65 L4
Łabiszyn, *Poland* 45 F4
Labo, *Phil.* 61 D5
Laboe, *Germany* 24 A6
Laborec →, *Slovak Rep.* 27 C14
Labouheyre, *France* 20 D3
Laboulaye, *Argentina* 126 C3
Labrador, *Canada* 103 B7
Labrador City, *Canada* 103 B6
Labrador Sea, *Atl. Oc.* 101 C14
Lábrea, *Brazil* 124 E6
Labruguière, *France* 20 E6
Labuan, *Malaysia* 62 C5
Labuan, Pulau, *Malaysia* 62 C5
Labuha, *Indonesia* 63 E7
Labuhan, *Indonesia* 63 G11
Labuhanbajo, *Indonesia* 63 F6
Labuk, Telok, *Malaysia* 62 C5
Labyrinth, L., *Australia* 95 E2
Labytnangi, *Russia* 50 C7
Laç, *Albania* 40 E3
Lac Bouchette, *Canada* 103 C5
Lac Édouard, *Canada* 102 C5
Lac La Biche, *Canada* 104 C6
Lac la Martre = Wha Ti, *Canada* 100 B8
Lac La Ronge Prov. Park, *Canada* 105 B7
Lac-Mégantic, *Canada* 103 C5
Lac Thien, *Vietnam* 64 F7
Lacanau, *France* 20 D2
Lacanau, Étang de, *France* 20 D2
Lacantúm →, *Mexico* 119 D6
Lacara →, *Spain* 35 G4
Lacaune, *France* 20 E6
Lacaune, Mts. de, *France* 20 E6
Laccadive Is. = Lakshadweep Is., *India* 52 H11
Lacepede Is., *Australia* 92 C3
Lacerdónia, *Mozam.* 87 F4
Lacey, *U.S.A.* 116 C4
Lachhmangarh, *India* 68 F6
Lachi, *Pakistan* 68 C4
Lachine, *Canada* 102 C5
Lachute, *Canada* 102 C5
Lackawanna, *U.S.A.* 110 D6
Lackawaxen, *U.S.A.* 111 E10
Lacolle, *Canada* 111 A11
Lacombe, *Canada* 104 C6
Lacona, *U.S.A.* 111 C8
Láconi, *Italy* 30 C2
Laconia, *U.S.A.* 111 C13
Lacq, *France* 20 E3
Ladakh Ra., *India* 69 C8
Lądek-Zdrój, *Poland* 45 H3
Ládhon →, *Greece* 38 D3
Ladik, *Turkey* 72 B6
Ladismith, *S. Africa* 88 E3
Ladíspoli, *Italy* 29 G9
Lādīz, *Iran* 71 D9
Ladnun, *India* 68 F6
Ladoga, L. = Ladozhskoye Ozero, *Russia* 46 B6
Ladozhskoye Ozero, *Russia* 46 B6
Lady Elliott I., *Australia* 94 C5
Lady Grey, *S. Africa* 88 E4
Ladybrand, *S. Africa* 88 D4
Ladysmith, *Canada* 104 D4
Ladysmith, *S. Africa* 89 D4
Ladysmith, *U.S.A.* 112 C9
Lae, *Papua N. G.* 96 H6
Laem Ngop, *Thailand* 65 F4
Laem Pho, *Thailand* 65 J3
Læsø, *Denmark* 11 G5
Læsø Rende, *Denmark* 11 G4
Lafayette, *Colo., U.S.A.* 112 F2
Lafayette, *Ind., U.S.A.* 108 E2
Lafayette, *La., U.S.A.* 113 K9
Lafayette, *Tenn., U.S.A.* 109 G2
Laferte →, *Canada* 104 A5
Lafia, *Nigeria* 83 D6
Lafiagi, *Nigeria* 83 D6
Lafleche, *Canada* 105 D7
Lafon, *Sudan* 81 F3
Lagan, *Sweden* 11 H7
Lagan →, *Sweden* 11 H6
Lagan →, *U.K.* 15 B6
Lagarfljót →, *Iceland* 8 D6
Lage, *Germany* 24 D4
Lågen →, *Oppland, Norway* 9 F14
Lågen →, *Vestfold, Norway* 9 G14
Lägerdorf, *Germany* 24 B5
Laghouat, *Algeria* 78 B6
Lagnieu, *France* 21 C9
Lagny-sur-Marne, *France* 19 D9
Lago, *Italy* 31 C9
Lagôa, *Portugal* 35 H2
Lagoa Vermelha, *Brazil* 127 B5
Lagoaça, *Portugal* 34 D4
Lagodekhi, *Georgia* 49 K8
Lagónegro, *Italy* 31 B8
Lagonoy G., *Phil.* 61 E5
Lagos, *Nigeria* 83 D5
Lagos, *Portugal* 35 H2
Lagos □, *Nigeria* 83 D5
Lagos de Moreno, *Mexico* 118 C4
Lagrange, *Australia* 92 C3
Lagrange B., *Australia* 92 C3
Laguardia, *Spain* 32 C2
Laguépie, *France* 20 D5
Laguna, *Brazil* 127 B6
Laguna, *U.S.A.* 115 J10
Laguna Beach, *U.S.A.* 117 M9
Laguna de Duera, *Spain* 34 D6
Laguna Limpia, *Argentina* 126 B4
Lagunas, *Chile* 126 A2
Lagunas, *Peru* 124 E3
Lahad Datu, *Malaysia* 63 C5
Lahad Datu, Teluk, *Malaysia* 63 D5
Lahan Sai, *Thailand* 64 E4
Lahanam, *Laos* 64 D5
Lahar, *India* 69 F8
Laharpur, *India* 69 F9
Lahat, *Indonesia* 62 E2
Lahewa, *Indonesia* 62 D1
Lāhījān, *Iran* 71 B6
Lahn →, *Germany* 25 E3
Lahnstein, *Germany* 25 E3
Laholm, *Sweden* 11 H7
Laholmsbukten, *Sweden* 11 H6
Lahore, *Pakistan* 68 D6
Lahr, *Germany* 25 G3
Lahri, *Pakistan* 68 E3
Lahti, *Finland* 9 F21
Lahtis = Lahti, *Finland* 9 F21
Laï, *Chad* 79 G9
Lai Chau, *Vietnam* 58 F4
Lai'an, *China* 59 A12
Laibin, *China* 58 F7
Laifeng, *China* 58 C7
L'Aigle, *France* 18 D7
Laignes, *France* 19 E11
L'Aiguillon-sur-Mer, *France* 20 B2
Laila = Laylá, *Si. Arabia* 74 C4
Laingsburg, *S. Africa* 88 E3
Lainio älv →, *Sweden* 8 C20
Lairg, *U.K.* 14 C4
Laishui, *China* 56 E8
Laissac, *France* 20 D6
Láives, *Italy* 29 B8
Laiwu, *China* 57 F9
Laixi, *China* 57 F11
Laiyang, *China* 57 F11
Laiyuan, *China* 56 E8
Laizhou, *China* 57 F10
Laizhou Wan, *China* 57 F10
Laja →, *Mexico* 118 C4
Lajere, *Nigeria* 83 C7
Lajes, *Brazil* 127 B5
Lajkovac, *Serbia, Yug.* 40 B4
Lajosmizse, *Hungary* 42 C4
Lak Sao, *Laos* 64 C5
Lakaband, *Pakistan* 68 D3
Lakamané, *Mali* 82 C3
Lake Alpine, *U.S.A.* 116 G7
Lake Andes, *U.S.A.* 112 D5
Lake Arthur, *U.S.A.* 113 K8
Lake Charles, *U.S.A.* 113 K8
Lake City, *Colo., U.S.A.* 115 G10
Lake City, *Fla., U.S.A.* 109 K4
Lake City, *Mich., U.S.A.* 108 C3
Lake City, *Minn., U.S.A.* 112 C8
Lake City, *Pa., U.S.A.* 110 D4
Lake City, *S.C., U.S.A.* 109 J6
Lake Cowichan, *Canada* 104 D4
Lake District, *U.K.* 12 C4
Lake Elsinore, *U.S.A.* 117 M9
Lake George, *U.S.A.* 111 C11
Lake Grace, *Australia* 93 F2
Lake Harbour = Kimmirut, *Canada* 101 B13
Lake Havasu City, *U.S.A.* 117 L12
Lake Hughes, *U.S.A.* 117 L8
Lake Isabella, *U.S.A.* 117 K8
Lake Jackson, *U.S.A.* 113 L7
Lake Junction, *U.S.A.* 114 D8
Lake King, *Australia* 93 F2
Lake Lenore, *Canada* 105 C8
Lake Louise, *Canada* 104 C5
Lake Mead National Recreation Area, *U.S.A.* 117 K12
Lake Mills, *U.S.A.* 112 D8
Lake Placid, *U.S.A.* 111 B11
Lake Pleasant, *U.S.A.* 111 C10
Lake Providence, *U.S.A.* 113 J9
Lake St. Peter, *Canada* 110 A6
Lake Superior Prov. Park, *Canada* 102 C3
Lake Village, *U.S.A.* 113 J9
Lake Wales, *U.S.A.* 109 M5
Lake Worth, *U.S.A.* 109 M5
Lakeba, *Fiji* 91 D9
Lakefield, *Canada* 102 D4
Lakehurst, *U.S.A.* 111 F10
Lakeland, *Australia* 94 B3
Lakeland, *U.S.A.* 109 M5
Lakeport, *Calif., U.S.A.* 116 F4
Lakeport, *Mich., U.S.A.* 110 C2
Lakeside, *Ariz., U.S.A.* 115 J9
Lakeside, *Calif., U.S.A.* 117 N10
Lakeside, *Nebr., U.S.A.* 112 D3
Lakeside, *Ohio, U.S.A.* 110 E2
Lakeview, *U.S.A.* 114 E3
Lakeville, *U.S.A.* 112 C8
Lakewood, *Colo., U.S.A.* 112 F2
Lakewood, *N.J., U.S.A.* 111 F10
Lakewood, *N.Y., U.S.A.* 110 D5
Lakewood, *Ohio, U.S.A.* 110 E3
Lakewood, *Wash., U.S.A.* 116 C4
Lakha, *India* 68 F4
Lakhaniá, *Greece* 36 D9
Lakhimpur, *India* 69 F9
Lakhnadon, *India* 69 H8
Lakhonpheng, *Laos* 64 E5
Lakhpat, *India* 68 H3
Läki, *Azerbaijan* 49 K8
Lakin, *U.S.A.* 113 G4
Lakitusaki →, *Canada* 102 B3
Lakki, *Pakistan* 68 C4
Lákkoi, *Greece* 36 D5
Lakonía □, *Greece* 38 E4
Lakonikós Kólpos, *Greece* 38 E4
Lakor, *Indonesia* 63 F7
Lakota, *Ivory C.* 82 D3
Lakota, *U.S.A.* 112 A5
Laksar, *India* 68 E8
Laksefjorden, *Norway* 8 A22
Lakselv, *Norway* 8 A21
Lakshadweep Is., *India* 52 H11
Lakshmanpur, *India* 69 H10
Lakshmikantapur, *India* 69 H13
Lala Ghat, *India* 67 G18
Lala Musa, *Pakistan* 68 C5
Lalago, *Tanzania* 86 C3
Lalapanzi, *Zimbabwe* 87 F3
Lalapaşa, *Turkey* 41 E10
Lalbenque, *France* 20 D5
L'Albufera, *Spain* 33 F4
Lalganj, *India* 69 G11
Lalgola, *India* 69 G13
Lālī, *Iran* 71 C6
Lalibela, *Ethiopia* 81 E4
Lalin, *China* 57 B14
Lalín, *Spain* 34 C2
Lalin He →, *China* 57 B13
Lalinde, *France* 20 D4
Lalitapur, *Nepal* 69 F11
Lalitpur, *India* 69 G8
Lalkua, *India* 69 E8
Lalsot, *India* 68 F7
Lam, *Vietnam* 64 B6
Lam Pao Res., *Thailand* 64 D4
Lama Kara, *Togo* 83 D5
Lamaing, *Burma* 67 M20
Lamar, *Colo., U.S.A.* 112 F3
Lamar, *Mo., U.S.A.* 113 G7
Lamas, *Peru* 124 E3
Lamastre, *France* 21 D8
Lambach, *Austria* 26 C6
Lamballe, *France* 18 D4
Lambaréné, *Gabon* 84 E2
Lambay I., *Ireland* 15 C5
Lambert Glacier, *Antarctica* 5 D6
Lambert's Bay, *S. Africa* 88 E2
Lambesc, *France* 21 E9
Lambeth, *Canada* 110 D3
Lámbia, *Greece* 38 D3
Lambomakondro, *Madag.* 89 C7
Lambro →, *Italy* 28 C6
Lame, *Nigeria* 83 C6
Lame Deer, *U.S.A.* 114 D10
Lamego, *Portugal* 34 D3
Lamèque, *Canada* 103 C7
Lamesa, *U.S.A.* 113 J4
Lamía, *Greece* 38 C4
Lamitan, *Phil.* 61 H5
Lammermuir Hills, *U.K.* 14 F6
Lammhult, *Sweden* 11 G8
Lamoille →, *U.S.A.* 111 B11
Lamon B., *Phil.* 61 D5
Lamont, *Canada* 104 C6
Lamont, *Calif., U.S.A.* 117 K8
Lamont, *Wyo., U.S.A.* 114 E10
Lamotte-Beuvron, *France* 19 E9
Lampa, *Peru* 124 G4
Lampang, *Thailand* 64 C2
Lampasas, *U.S.A.* 113 K5
Lampazos de Naranjo, *Mexico* 118 B4
Lampertheim, *Germany* 25 F4
Lampeter, *U.K.* 13 E3
Lampman, *Canada* 105 D8
Lamprechtshausen, *Austria* 26 D5
Lampung □, *Indonesia* 62 F2
Lamta, *India* 69 H9
Lamu, *Kenya* 86 C5
Lamy, *U.S.A.* 115 J11
Lan Xian, *China* 56 E6
Lan Yu = Hungt'ou Hsü, *Taiwan* 59 G13
Lanak La, *India* 69 B8
Lanak'o Shank'ou = Lanak La, *India* 69 B8
Lanao, L., *Phil.* 61 H6
Lanark, *Canada* 111 A8
Lanark, *U.K.* 14 F5
Lanbi Kyun, *Burma* 65 G2
Lancang, *China* 58 F2
Lancang Jiang →, *China* 58 G3
Lancashire □, *U.K.* 12 D5
Lancaster, *Canada* 111 A10
Lancaster, *U.K.* 12 C5
Lancaster, *Calif., U.S.A.* 117 L8
Lancaster, *Ky., U.S.A.* 108 G3
Lancaster, *N.H., U.S.A.* 111 B13
Lancaster, *N.Y., U.S.A.* 110 D6
Lancaster, *Ohio, U.S.A.* 108 F4
Lancaster, *Pa., U.S.A.* 111 F8
Lancaster, *S.C., U.S.A.* 109 H5
Lancaster, *Wis., U.S.A.* 112 D9
Lancaster Sd., *Canada* 101 A11
Lancelin, *Australia* 93 F2
Lanchow = Lanzhou, *China* 56 F2
Lanciano, *Italy* 29 F11
Lancun, *China* 57 F11
Łańcut, *Poland* 45 H9
Landau, *Bayern, Germany* 25 G8
Landau, *Rhld-Pfz., Germany* 25 F4
Landeck, *Austria* 26 D3
Lander, *U.S.A.* 114 E9
Lander →, *Australia* 92 D5
Landerneau, *France* 18 D2
Landeryd, *Sweden* 11 G7
Landes, *France* 20 D2
Landes □, *France* 20 E3
Landete, *Spain* 32 F3
Landi Kotal, *Pakistan* 68 B4
Landisburg, *U.S.A.* 110 F7
Landivisiau, *France* 18 D2
Landquart, *Switz.* 25 J5
Landrecies, *France* 19 B10
Land's End, *U.K.* 13 G2
Landsberg, *Germany* 25 G6
Landsborough Cr. →, *Australia* 94 C3
Landsbro, *Sweden* 11 G8
Landshut, *Germany* 25 G8
Landskrona, *Sweden* 11 J6
Landstuhl, *Germany* 25 F3
Landvetter, *Sweden* 11 G6
Lanesboro, *U.S.A.* 111 E9
Lanester, *France* 18 E3
Lanett, *U.S.A.* 109 J3
Lang Qua, *Vietnam* 64 A5
Lang Shan, *China* 56 D4
Lang Son, *Vietnam* 58 G6
Lang Suan, *Thailand* 65 H2
Langå, *Denmark* 11 H3
La'nga Co, *China* 67 D12
Langádhas, *Greece* 40 F7
Langadhia, *Greece* 38 D4
Långan →, *Sweden* 10 A8
Langano, L., *Ethiopia* 81 F4
Langar, *Iran* 71 C9
Langara I., *Canada* 104 C2
Långås, *Sweden* 11 H6
Langdai, *China* 58 D5
Langdon, *U.S.A.* 112 A5
Långe Jan = Ölands södra udde, *Sweden* 11 H10
Langeac, *France* 20 C7
Langeais, *France* 18 E7
Langeb Baraka →, *Sudan* 80 D4
Langeberg, *S. Africa* 88 E3
Langeberge, *S. Africa* 88 D3
Langeland, *Denmark* 11 K4
Langelands Bælt, *Denmark* 11 K4
Langen, *Hessen, Germany* 25 F4
Langen, *Niedersachsen, Germany* 24 B4
Langenburg, *Canada* 105 C8
Langeneß, *Germany* 24 A4
Langenlois, *Austria* 26 C8
Langeoog, *Germany* 24 B3
Langeskov, *Denmark* 11 J4
Länghem, *Sweden* 11 G7
Langhirano, *Italy* 28 D7
Langholm, *U.K.* 14 F5
Langjökull, *Iceland* 8 D3
Langkawi, Pulau, *Malaysia* 65 J2
Langklip, *S. Africa* 88 D3
Langkon, *Malaysia* 62 C5
Langlade, *St- P. & M.* 103 C8
Langley, *Canada* 116 A4
Langnau, *Switz.* 25 J3
Langogne, *France* 20 D7
Langon, *France* 20 D3
Langøya, *Norway* 8 B16
Langreo, *Spain* 34 B5
Langres, *France* 19 E12
Langres, Plateau de, *France* 19 E12
Langsa, *Indonesia* 62 D1
Långsele, *Sweden* 10 A11
Långshyttan, *Sweden* 10 D10
Langtry, *U.S.A.* 113 L4
Langu, *Thailand* 65 J2
Languedoc, *France* 20 E7
Languedoc-Roussillon □, *France* 20 E6
Langxi, *China* 59 B12
Langxiangzhen, *China* 56 E9
Langzhong, *China* 58 B5
Lanigan, *Canada* 105 C7
Lankao, *China* 56 G8
Länkäran, *Azerbaijan* 71 B6
Lanmeur, *France* 18 D3
Lannemezan, *France* 20 E4
Lannilis, *France* 18 D2
Lannion, *France* 18 D3
L'Annonciation, *Canada* 102 C5
Lanouaille, *France* 20 C5
Lanping, *China* 58 D2
Lansdale, *U.S.A.* 111 F9
Lansdowne, *Canada* 111 B8
Lansdowne, *India* 69 E8
Lansdowne House, *Canada* 102 B2
L'Anse, *U.S.A.* 108 B1
L'Anse au Loup, *Canada* 103 B8
L'Anse aux Meadows, *Canada* 103 B8
Lansford, *U.S.A.* 111 F9
Lanshan, *China* 59 E9
Lansing, *U.S.A.* 108 D3
Lanslebourg-Mont-Cenis, *France* 21 C10
Lanta Yai, Ko, *Thailand* 65 J2
Lantewa, *Nigeria* 83 C7
Lantian, *China* 56 G5
Lanus, *Argentina* 126 C4
Lanusei, *Italy* 30 C2
Lanuza, *Phil.* 61 G7
Lanxi, *China* 59 C12
Lanzarote, *Canary Is.* 37 F6
Lanzhou, *China* 56 F2
Lanzo Torinese, *Italy* 28 C4
Lao →, *Italy* 31 C8
Lao Bao, *Laos* 64 D6
Lao Cai, *Vietnam* 58 F4
Laoag, *Phil.* 61 B4
Laoang, *Phil.* 61 E6
Laoha He →, *China* 57 C11
Laohekou, *China* 59 A8
Laois □, *Ireland* 15 D4
Laon, *France* 19 C10
Laona, *U.S.A.* 108 C1
Laos ■, *Asia* 64 D5
Lapa, *Brazil* 127 B6
Lapai, *Nigeria* 83 D6
Lapalisse, *France* 19 F10
Lapeer, *U.S.A.* 108 D4
Lapeyrade, *France* 20 D3
Lapithos, *Cyprus* 36 D12
Lapland = Lappland, *Europe* 8 B21
Laporte, *U.S.A.* 111 E8
Lapovo, *Serbia, Yug.* 40 B5
Lappeenranta, *Finland* 9 F23
Lappland, *Europe* 8 B21
Laprida, *Argentina* 126 D3
Lapseki, *Turkey* 41 F10
Laptev Sea, *Russia* 51 B13
Lapua, *Finland* 8 E20
Lăpuş →, *Romania* 43 C8
Lapuş, Munţii, *Romania* 43 C8
Lăpuşna, *Moldova* 43 D13
Łapy, *Poland* 45 F9
Laqiya Arba'in, *Sudan* 80 C2
Laqiya Umran, *Sudan* 80 D2
L'Áquila, *Italy* 29 F10
Lār, *Āzarbājān-e Sharqī, Iran* 70 B5
Lār, *Fārs, Iran* 71 E7
Larabanga, *Ghana* 82 D4
Laragne-Montéglin, *France* 21 D9
Laramie, *U.S.A.* 112 E2
Laramie →, *U.S.A.* 114 F11
Laramie Mts., *U.S.A.* 112 E2
Laranjeiras do Sul, *Brazil* 127 B5
Larantuka, *Indonesia* 63 F6
Larat, *Indonesia* 63 F8
L'Arbresle, *France* 21 C8
Lärbro, *Sweden* 11 G12
Larde, *Mozam.* 87 F4
Larder Lake, *Canada* 102 C4
Lardhos, Ákra = Líndhos, Ákra, *Greece* 36 C10
Lardhos, Órmos, *Greece* 36 C10
Laredo, *Spain* 34 B7
Laredo, *U.S.A.* 113 M5
Laredo Sd., *Canada* 104 C3
Largentière, *France* 21 D8
L'Argentière-la-Bessée, *France* 21 D10
Largo, *U.S.A.* 109 M4
Largs, *U.K.* 14 F4
Lari, *Italy* 28 E7
Lariang, *Indonesia* 63 E5
Larimore, *U.S.A.* 112 B6
Lārīn, *Iran* 71 C7
Larino, *Italy* 29 G11
Lárisa, *Greece* 38 B4
Lárisa □, *Greece* 38 B4
Larkana, *Pakistan* 68 F3
Larnaca, *Cyprus* 36 E12
Larnaca Bay, *Cyprus* 36 E12
Larne, *U.K.* 15 B6
Larned, *U.S.A.* 112 F5
Laroquebrou, *France* 20 D6
Larose, *U.S.A.* 113 L9
Larrimah, *Australia* 92 C5
Larsen Ice Shelf, *Antarctica* 5 C17
Laruns, *France* 20 F3

Larvik, *Norway* 9 G14
Larzac, Causse du, *France* 20 E7
Las Alpujarras, *Spain* 33 J1
Las Animas, *U.S.A.* 112 F3
Las Anod, *Somali Rep.* 74 F4
Las Arenas, *Spain* 34 B6
Las Aves, Is., *W. Indies* 121 C7
Las Brenãs, *Argentina* 126 B3
Las Cabezas de San Juan, *Spain* 35 J5
Las Cejas, *Argentina* 128 B4
Las Chimeneas, *Mexico* 117 N10
Las Cruces, *U.S.A.* 115 K10
Las Flores, *Argentina* 126 D4
Las Heras, *Argentina* 126 C2
Las Lajas, *Argentina* 128 D2
Las Lomitas, *Argentina* 126 A3
Las Marismas, *Spain* 35 H4
Las Minas, *Spain* 33 G3
Las Navas de la Concepción,
  Spain 35 H5
Las Navas del Marqués, *Spain* . 34 E6
Las Palmas, *Argentina* 126 B4
Las Palmas, *Canary Is.* 37 F4
Las Palmas ➤, *Mexico* 117 N10
Las Pedroñas, *Spain* 33 F2
Las Piedras, *Uruguay* 127 C4
Las Pipinas, *Argentina* 126 D4
Las Plumas, *Argentina* 128 E3
Las Rosas, *Argentina* 126 C3
Las Rozas, *Spain* 34 E7
Las Tablas, *Panama* 120 E3
Las Termas, *Argentina* 126 B3
Las Toscas, *Argentina* 126 B4
Las Truchas, *Mexico* 118 D4
Las Varillas, *Argentina* 126 C3
Las Vegas, *N. Mex., U.S.A.* .. 115 J11
Las Vegas, *Nev., U.S.A.* 117 J11
Lasarte, *Spain* 32 B2
Lascano, *Uruguay* 127 C5
Lash-e Joveyn, *Afghan.* 66 D2
Lashburn, *Canada* 105 C7
Lashio, *Burma* 67 H20
Lashkar, *India* 68 F8
Łasin, *Poland* 44 E6
Lasíthi, *Greece* 36 D7
Lasíthi □, *Greece* 36 D7
Lãsjerd, *Iran* 71 C7
Lask, *Poland* 45 G6
Łaskarzew, *Poland* 45 G8
Laško, *Slovenia* 29 B12
Lassay-les-Châteaux, *France* .. 18 D6
Lassen Pk., *U.S.A.* 114 F3
Lassen Volcanic National Park,
  U.S.A. 114 F3
Last Mountain L., *Canada* ... 105 C7
Lastchance Cr. ➤, *U.S.A.* ... 116 E5
Lastoursville, *Gabon* 84 E2
Lastovo, *Croatia* 29 F13
Lastovski Kanal, *Croatia* 29 F14
Lat Yao, *Thailand* 64 E2
Latacunga, *Ecuador* 124 D3
Latakia = Al Lādhiqīyah, *Syria* 70 C2
Latchford, *Canada* 102 C4
Latehar, *India* 69 H11
Laterza, *Italy* 31 B9
Latham, *Australia* 93 E2
Lathen, *Germany* 24 C3
Lathi, *India* 68 F4
Lathrop Wells, *U.S.A.* 117 J10
Latiano, *Italy* 31 B10
Latina, *Italy* 30 A5
Latisana, *Italy* 29 C10
Laton, *U.S.A.* 116 J7
Latorytsya ➤, *Slovak Rep.* .. 27 C14
Latouche Treville, C., *Australia* 92 C3
Latrobe, *Australia* 94 G4
Latrobe, *U.S.A.* 110 F5
Latrónico, *Italy* 31 B9
Latvia ■, *Europe* 9 H20
Lau, *Nigeria* 83 D7
Lau Group, *Fiji* 91 C9
Lauchhammer, *Germany* 24 D9
Lauda-Königshofen, *Germany* . 25 F5
Lauenburg, *Germany* 24 B6
Lauf, *Germany* 25 F7
Laughlin, *U.S.A.* 115 J6
Laujar de Andarax, *Spain* ... 33 H2
Laukaa, *Finland* 9 E21
Launceston, *Australia* 94 G4
Launceston, *U.K.* 13 G3
Laune ➤, *Ireland* 15 D2
Launglon Bok, *Burma* 64 F1
Laupheim, *Germany* 25 G5
Laura, *Australia* 94 B3
Laureana di Borrello, *Italy* ... 31 D9
Laurel, *Miss., U.S.A.* 113 K10
Laurel, *Mont., U.S.A.* 114 D9
Laurencekirk, *U.K.* 14 E6
Laurens, *U.S.A.* 109 H4
Laurentian Plateau, *Canada* .. 103 B6
Lauria, *Italy* 31 B8
Laurie L., *Canada* 105 B8
Laurinburg, *U.S.A.* 109 H6
Laurium, *U.S.A.* 108 B1
Lausanne, *Switz.* 25 J2
Laut, *Indonesia* 65 K6
Laut, Pulau, *Indonesia* 62 E5
Laut Kecil, Kepulauan,
  Indonesia 62 E5
Lauterbach, *Germany* 24 E5
Lauterecken, *Germany* 25 F3
Lautoka, *Fiji* 91 C7
Lauzès, *France* 20 D5
Lavagh More, *Ireland* 15 B3
Lavagna, *Italy* 28 D6

Laval, *France* 18 D6
Lavalle, *Argentina* 126 B2
Lavant Station, *Canada* 111 A8
Lāvar Meydān, *Iran* 71 D7
Lávara, *Greece* 41 E10
Lavardac, *France* 20 D4
Lavaur, *France* 20 E5
Lavelanet, *France* 20 F5
Lavello, *Italy* 31 A8
Laverton, *Australia* 93 E3
Lavìs, *Italy* 28 B8
Lávkos, *Greece* 38 B5
Lavos, *Portugal* 34 E2
Lavradio, *Portugal* 35 G1
Lavras, *Brazil* 127 A7
Lavre, *Portugal* 35 G2
Lávrion, *Greece* 38 D6
Lávris, *Greece* 36 D6
Lavumisa, *Swaziland* 89 D5
Lawas, *Malaysia* 62 D5
Lawele, *Indonesia* 63 F6
Lawng Pit, *Burma* 67 G20
Lawqah, *Si. Arabia* 70 D4
Lawra, *Ghana* 82 C4
Lawrence, *N.Z.* 91 L2
Lawrence, *Kans., U.S.A.* 112 F7
Lawrence, *Mass., U.S.A.* 111 D11
Lawrenceburg, *Ind., U.S.A.* .. 108 F3
Lawrenceburg, *Tenn., U.S.A.* . 109 H2
Lawrenceville, *Ga., U.S.A.* ... 109 J4
Lawrenceville, *Pa., U.S.A.* ... 110 E7
Laws, *U.S.A.* 116 H8
Lawton, *U.S.A.* 113 H5
Lawu, *Indonesia* 63 G14
Lawz, J. al, *Si. Arabia* 80 B4
Laxá, *Sweden* 11 F8
Laxford, L., *U.K.* 14 C3
Laxou, *France* 19 D13
Lay ➤, *France* 20 B2
Laylá, *Si. Arabia* 74 C4
Laylān, *Iraq* 70 C5
Layon ➤, *France* 18 E6
Layton, *U.S.A.* 114 F7
Laytonville, *U.S.A.* 114 G2
Lazarevac, *Serbia, Yug.* 40 B4
Lazarevskoye, *Russia* 49 J4
Lazarivo, *Madag.* 89 C8
Lazdijai, *Lithuania* 44 D10
Lazio □, *Italy* 29 F9
Lazo, *Moldova* 43 C13
Lazo, *Russia* 54 C6
Le Beausset, *France* 21 E9
Le Blanc, *France* 20 B5
Le Bleymard, *France* 20 D7
Le Bourgneuf-la-Fôret, *France* . 18 D6
Le Bugue, *France* 20 D4
Le Canourgue = La Canourgue,
  France 20 D7
Le Cateau Cambrésis, *France* . 19 B10
Le Caylar, *France* 20 E7
Le Chambon-Feugerolles,
  France 21 C8
Le Châtelet, *France* 19 F9
Le Chesne, *France* 19 C11
Le Cheylard, *France* 21 D8
Le Conquet, *France* 18 D2
Le Creusot, *France* 19 F11
Le Croisic, *France* 18 E4
Le Donjon, *France* 19 F10
Le Dorat, *France* 20 B5
Le François, *Martinique* 121 D7
Le Grand-Lucé, *France* 18 E7
Le Grand-Pressigny, *France* .. 18 F7
Le Grand-Quevilly, *France* ... 18 C8
Le Havre, *France* 18 C7
Le Lavandou, *France* 21 E10
Le Lion-d'Angers, *France* ... 18 E6
Le Louroux-Béconnais, *France* 18 E6
Le Luc, *France* 21 E10
Le Lude, *France* 18 E7
Le Mans, *France* 18 E7
Le Mars, *U.S.A.* 112 D6
Le Mayet-de-Montagne, *France* 19 F10
Le Mêle-sur-Sarthe, *France* .. 18 D7
Le Monastier-sur-Gazeille,
  France 20 D7
Le Monêtier-les-Bains, *France* . 21 D10
Le Mont-Dore, *France* 20 C6
Le Mont-St-Michel, *France* .. 18 D5
Le Moule, *Guadeloupe* 121 C7
Le Muy, *France* 21 E10
Le Palais, *France* 18 E3
Le Perthus, *France* 20 F6
Le Puy-en-Velay, *France* 20 C7
Le Sueur, *U.S.A.* 112 C8
Le Teil, *France* 21 D8
Le Teilleul, *France* 18 D6
Le Theil, *France* 18 D7
Le Thillot, *France* 19 E13
Le Thuy, *Vietnam* 64 D6
Le Touquet-Paris-Plage, *France* 19 B8
Le Tréport, *France* 18 B8
Le Val-d'Ajol, *France* 19 E13
Le Verdon-sur-Mer, *France* .. 20 C2
Le Vigan, *France* 20 E7
Lea ➤, *U.K.* 13 F7
Leach, *Cambodia* 65 F4
Lead, *U.S.A.* 112 C3
Leader, *Canada* 105 C7
Leadville, *U.S.A.* 115 G10
Leaf ➤, *U.S.A.* 113 K10
Leaf Rapids, *Canada* 105 B9
Leamington, *Canada* 102 D3
Leamington, *U.S.A.* 114 G7
Leamington Spa = Royal
  Leamington Spa, *U.K.* 13 E6

Le'an, *China* 59 D10
Leandro Norte Alem, *Argentina* 127 B4
Leane, L., *Ireland* 15 D2
Learmonth, *Australia* 92 D1
Leask, *Canada* 105 C7
Leatherhead, *U.K.* 13 F7
Leavenworth, *Kans., U.S.A.* .. 112 F7
Leavenworth, *Wash., U.S.A.* . 114 C3
Łeba, *Poland* 44 D4
Łeba ➤, *Poland* 44 D4
Lebach, *Germany* 25 F2
Lebak, *Phil.* 61 H6
Lebam, *U.S.A.* 116 D3
Lebane, *Serbia, Yug.* 40 D5
Lebanon, *Ind., U.S.A.* 108 E2
Lebanon, *Kans., U.S.A.* 112 F5
Lebanon, *Ky., U.S.A.* 108 G3
Lebanon, *Mo., U.S.A.* 113 G8
Lebanon, *N.H., U.S.A.* 111 C12
Lebanon, *Oreg., U.S.A.* 114 D2
Lebanon, *Pa., U.S.A.* 111 F8
Lebanon, *Tenn., U.S.A.* 109 G2
Lebanon ■, *Asia* 75 B5
Lebec, *U.S.A.* 117 L8
Lebedyan, *Russia* 47 F10
Lebedyn, *Ukraine* 47 G8
Lebel-sur-Quévillon, *Canada* . 102 C4
Lebomboberge, *S. Africa* 89 C5
Lębork, *Poland* 44 D4
Lebrija, *Spain* 35 J4
Łebsko, Jezioro, *Poland* 44 D4
Lebu, *Chile* 126 D1
Leca da Palmeira, *Portugal* .. 34 D2
Lecce, *Italy* 31 B11
Lecco, *Italy* 28 C6
Lecco, L. di, *Italy* 28 C6
Lécera, *Spain* 32 D4
Lech, *Austria* 26 D3
Lech ➤, *Germany* 25 G6
Lechang, *China* 59 E9
Lechtaler Alpen, *Austria* 26 D3
Lecontes Mills, *U.S.A.* 110 E6
Lectoure, *France* 20 E4
Łęczna, *Poland* 45 G9
Łęczyca, *Poland* 45 F6
Ledesma, *Spain* 34 D5
Ledong, *China* 64 C7
Leduc, *Canada* 104 C6
Lee, *U.S.A.* 111 D11
Lee ➤, *Ireland* 15 E3
Lee Vining, *U.S.A.* 116 H7
Leech L., *U.S.A.* 112 B7
Leechburg, *U.S.A.* 110 F5
Leeds, *U.K.* 12 D6
Leeds, *U.S.A.* 109 J2
Leek, *Neths.* 17 A6
Leek, *U.K.* 12 D5
Leeman, *Australia* 93 E1
Leeper, *U.S.A.* 110 E5
Leer, *Germany* 24 B3
Leesburg, *U.S.A.* 109 L5
Leesville, *U.S.A.* 113 K8
Leetonia, *U.S.A.* 110 F4
Leeu Gamka, *S. Africa* 88 E3
Leeuwarden, *Neths.* 17 A5
Leeuwin, C., *Australia* 93 F2
Leeward Is., *Atl. Oc.* 121 C7
Lefka, *Cyprus* 36 D11
Lefkoniko, *Cyprus* 36 D12
Lefroy, *Canada* 110 B5
Lefroy, L., *Australia* 93 F3
Łeg ➤, *Poland* 45 H8
Leganés, *Spain* 34 E7
Legazpi, *Phil.* 61 E5
Lège-Cap-Ferret, *France* 20 D2
Lege Hida, *Ethiopia* 81 F5
Legendre I., *Australia* 92 D2
Leghorn = Livorno, *Italy* 28 E7
Legionowo, *Poland* 45 F7
Legnago, *Italy* 29 C8
Legnano, *Italy* 28 C5
Legnica, *Poland* 45 G3
Legrad, *Croatia* 29 B13
Leh, *India* 69 B7
Lehigh Acres, *U.S.A.* 109 M5
Lehighton, *U.S.A.* 111 F9
Lehliu, *Romania* 43 F11
Leho, *Sudan* 81 F3
Lehrte, *Germany* 24 C5
Lehututu, *Botswana* 88 C3
Lei Shui ➤, *China* 59 D9
Leiah, *Pakistan* 68 D4
Leibnitz, *Austria* 26 E8
Leibo, *China* 58 C4
Leicester, *U.K.* 13 E6
Leicester City □, *U.K.* 13 E6
Leicestershire □, *U.K.* 13 E6
Leichhardt ➤, *Australia* 94 B2
Leichhardt Ra., *Australia* ... 94 C4
Leiden, *Neths.* 17 B4
Leie ➤, *Belgium* 17 C3
Leifers = Láives, *Italy* 29 B8
Leimen, *Germany* 25 F4
Leine ➤, *Germany* 24 C5
Leinefelde, *Germany* 24 D6
Leinster, *Australia* 93 E3
Leinster □, *Ireland* 15 C4
Leinster, Mt., *Ireland* 15 D5
Leipalingis, *Lithuania* 44 D10
Leipzig, *Germany* 24 D8
Leiria, *Portugal* 34 F2
Leiria □, *Portugal* 34 F2
Leirvik, *Norway* 9 G11
Leishan, *China* 58 D7
Leisler, Mt., *Australia* 92 D4
Leith, *U.K.* 14 F5

Leith Hill, *U.K.* 13 F7
Leitha ➤, *Europe* 27 D10
Leitrim, *Ireland* 15 B3
Leitrim □, *Ireland* 15 B4
Leitza, *Spain* 32 B3
Leiyang, *China* 59 D9
Leizhou, *China* 59 G8
Leizhou Bandao, *China* 58 G7
Leizhou Wan, *China* 59 G8
Lek ➤, *Neths.* 17 C4
Leka, *Norway* 8 D14
Lekáni, *Greece* 41 E8
Lekbibaj, *Albania* 40 D3
Lekeitio, *Spain* 32 B2
Lekhainá, *Greece* 38 D3
Lekoui, *Burkina Faso* 82 C4
Leksand, *Sweden* 10 D9
Lékva Óros, *Greece* 36 D6
Leland, *Mich., U.S.A.* 108 C3
Leland, *Miss., U.S.A.* 113 J9
Lelång, *Sweden* 10 E6
Leleque, *Argentina* 128 E2
Lelystad, *Neths.* 17 B5
Lem, *Denmark* 11 H2
Lema, *Nigeria* 83 C5
Lema Shilindi, *Ethiopia* 81 G5
Léman, L., *Europe* 19 F13
Lemera, *Dem. Rep. of the Congo* 86 C2
Lemery, *Phil.* 61 E4
Lemhi Ra., *U.S.A.* 114 D7
Lemmer, *Neths.* 17 B5
Lemmon, *U.S.A.* 112 C3
Lemon Grove, *U.S.A.* 117 N9
Lemoore, *U.S.A.* 116 J7
Lempdes, *France* 20 C7
Lemvig, *Denmark* 11 H2
Lena ➤, *Russia* 51 B13
Lenart, *Slovenia* 29 B12
Lenartovce, *Slovak Rep.* ... 27 C13
Lencloître, *France* 18 F7
Léndas, *Greece* 36 E6
Lendava, *Slovenia* 29 B13
Lendeh, *Iran* 71 D6
Lendinara, *Italy* 29 C8
Lengerich, *Germany* 24 C3
Lenggong, *Malaysia* 65 K3
Lenggries, *Germany* 25 H7
Lengshuijiang, *China* 59 D8
Lengshuitan, *China* 59 D8
Lengua de Vaca, Pta., *Chile* . 126 C1
Lengyeltóti, *Hungary* 42 D2
Lenhovda, *Sweden* 11 G9
Lenina, Kanal ➤, *Russia* ... 49 J7
Leninabad = Khŭjand, *Tajikistan* 50 E7
Leninakan = Gyumri, *Armenia* 49 K6
Leningrad = Sankt-Peterburg,
  Russia 46 C6
Lenino, *Ukraine* 47 K8
Leninogorsk, *Kazakstan* 50 D9
Leninsk, *Russia* 49 F7
Leninsk-Kuznetskiy, *Russia* . 50 D9
Leninskoye, *Russia* 48 A8
Lenk, *Switz.* 25 J3
Lenkoran = Länkäran,
  Azerbaijan 71 B6
Lenmalu, *Indonesia* 63 E8
Lenne ➤, *Germany* 24 D3
Lennestadt, *Germany* 24 D4
Lennox, *U.S.A.* 112 D6
Lennoxville, *Canada* 111 A13
Leno, *Italy* 28 C7
Lenoir, *U.S.A.* 109 H5
Lenoir City, *U.S.A.* 109 H3
Lenore L., *Canada* 105 C8
Lenox, *U.S.A.* 111 D11
Lens, *France* 19 B9
Lensahn, *Germany* 24 A6
Lensk, *Russia* 51 C12
Lenti, *Hungary* 42 D1
Lentini, *Italy* 31 E8
Lenwood, *U.S.A.* 117 L9
Lenya, *Burma* 62 B1
Lenzen, *Germany* 24 B7
Léo, *Burkina Faso* 82 C4
Leoben, *Austria* 26 D8
Leodhas = Lewis, *U.K.* 14 C2
Leola, *U.S.A.* 112 C5
Leominster, *U.K.* 13 E5
Leominster, *U.S.A.* 111 D13
Léon, *France* 20 E2
León, *Mexico* 118 C4
León, *Nic.* 120 D2
León, *Spain* 34 C5
León, *U.S.A.* 112 E8
León □, *Spain* 34 C5
Leon ➤, *U.S.A.* 113 K6
León, Montes de, *Spain* 34 C4
Leonardtown, *U.S.A.* 108 F7
Leonardville, *Namibia* 88 C2
Leonberg, *Germany* 25 G5
Leonding, *Austria* 26 C7
Leonessa, *Italy* 29 F9
Leonforte, *Italy* 31 E7
Leonídhion, *Greece* 38 D4
Leonora, *Australia* 93 E3
Leopoldina, *Brazil* 127 A7
Leopoldsburg, *Belgium* 17 C5
Leoti, *U.S.A.* 112 F4
Leoville, *Canada* 105 C7
Lepe, *Spain* 35 H3
Lepel = Lyepyel, *Belarus* ... 46 E5
Lepenoú, *Greece* 38 C3
Leping, *China* 59 C11
Lépo, L. do, *Angola* 88 B2

Lepontine, Alpi, *Italy* 28 B5
Leppävirta, *Finland* 9 E22
Lepsény, *Hungary* 42 D3
Lequeitio = Lekeitio, *Spain* .. 32 B2
Lercara Friddi, *Italy* 30 E6
Lerdo, *Mexico* 118 B4
Léré, *Chad* 83 D7
Léré, *Mali* 82 B4
Lere, *Bauchi, Nigeria* 83 D6
Lere, *Kaduna, Nigeria* 83 C6
Leribe, *Lesotho* 89 D4
Lérici, *Italy* 28 D6
Lérida = Lleida, *Spain* 32 D5
Lerma, *Spain* 34 C7
Lérins, Îs. de, *France* 21 E11
Lerma, *Spain* 34 C7
Léros, *Greece* 39 D8
Lérouville, *France* 19 D12
Lerum, *Sweden* 11 G6
Lerwick, *U.K.* 14 A7
Leş, *Romania* 42 D6
Les Abrets, *France* 21 C9
Les Andelys, *France* 18 C8
Les Borges Blanques, *Spain* .. 32 D5
Les Cayes, *Haiti* 121 C5
Les Essarts, *France* 18 F5
Les Herbiers, *France* 18 F5
Les Minquiers, Plateau des,
  Chan. Is. 18 D4
Les Pieux, *France* 18 C5
Les Ponts-de-Cé, *France* ... 18 E6
Les Riceys, *France* 19 E11
Les Sables-d'Olonne, *France* . 20 B2
Les Vans, *France* 21 D8
Lesbos = Lésvos, *Greece* ... 39 B8
L'Escala, *Spain* 32 C8
Leshan, *China* 58 C4
Lésina, *Italy* 29 G12
Lésina, L. di, *Italy* 29 G12
Lesjöfors, *Sweden* 10 E8
Lesko, *Poland* 45 J9
Leskov I., *Antarctica* 5 B1
Leskovac, *Serbia, Yug.* 40 C5
Leskovik, *Albania* 40 F4
Leśna, *Poland* 45 G2
Lesneven, *France* 18 D2
Leśnica, *Poland* 45 H5
Lešnica, *Serbia, Yug.* 40 B3
Lesnoye, *Russia* 46 C8
Lesopilnoye, *Russia* 54 A7
Lesotho ■, *Africa* 89 D4
Lesozavodsk, *Russia* 51 E14
Lesparre-Médoc, *France* 20 C3
Lessay, *France* 18 C5
Lesse ➤, *Belgium* 17 D5
Lessebo, *Sweden* 11 H9
Lesser Antilles, *W. Indies* .. 121 D7
Lesser Slave L., *Canada* 104 B5
Lesser Sunda Is., *Indonesia* . 63 F6
Lessines, *Belgium* 17 D3
Lester, *U.S.A.* 116 C5
Lestock, *Canada* 105 C8
Lesuer I., *Australia* 92 B4
Lésvos, *Greece* 39 B8
Leszno, *Poland* 45 G3
Letaba, *S. Africa* 89 C5
Letälven, *Sweden* 10 E8
Létavértes, *Hungary* 42 C6
Letchworth, *U.K.* 13 F7
Letea, Ostrov, *Romania* 43 E14
Lethbridge, *Canada* 104 D6
Lethem, *Guyana* 124 C7
Leti, Kepulauan, *Indonesia* .. 63 F7
Leti Is. = Leti, Kepulauan,
  Indonesia 63 F7
Letiahau ➤, *Botswana* 88 C3
Leticia, *Colombia* 124 D5
Leting, *China* 57 E10
Letjiesbos, *S. Africa* 88 E3
Letlhakane, *Botswana* 88 C4
Letlhakeng, *Botswana* 88 C3
Letong, *Indonesia* 62 D3
Letpadan, *Burma* 67 L19
Letpan, *Burma* 67 K19
Letsôk-aw Kyun, *Burma* 65 G2
Letterkenny, *Ireland* 15 B4
Leu, *Romania* 43 F9
Leucadia, *U.S.A.* 117 M9
Leucate, *France* 20 F7
Leucate, Étang de, *France* .. 20 F7
Leuk, *Switz.* 25 J3
Leuşeni, *Moldova* 43 D13
Leuser, G., *Indonesia* 62 D1
Leutkirch, *Germany* 25 H6
Leuven, *Belgium* 17 D4
Leuze-en-Hainaut, *Belgium* . 17 D3
Lev Tolstoy, *Russia* 46 F10
Levádhia, *Greece* 38 C4
Levan, *Albania* 40 F3
Levanger, *Norway* 8 E14
Levant, Î. du, *France* 21 E10
Lévanto, *Italy* 28 D6
Lévanzo, *Italy* 30 D5
Levelland, *U.S.A.* 113 J3
Leven, *U.K.* 14 E6
Leven, L., *U.K.* 14 E5
Leven, Toraka, *Madag.* 89 A8
Leveque C., *Australia* 92 C3
Leverano, *Italy* 31 B10
Leverkusen, *Germany* 24 D2
Levice, *Slovak Rep.* 27 C11
Lévico Terme, *Italy* 29 C8
Levie, *France* 21 G13
Levier, *France* 19 F13
Levin, *N.Z.* 91 J5
Lévis, *Canada* 103 C5
Levis, L., *Canada* 104 A5

Levítha, Greece 39 D8
Levittown, N.Y., U.S.A. 111 F11
Levittown, Pa., U.S.A. 111 F10
Levka, Bulgaria 41 E10
Levkás, Greece 38 C2
Levkás □, Greece 38 C2
Levkímmi, Greece 36 B4
Levkímmi, Ákra, Greece 36 B4
Levkôsia = Nicosia, Cyprus ... 36 D12
Levoča, Slovak Rep. 27 B13
Levroux, France 19 F8
Levski, Bulgaria 41 C9
Levskigrad = Karlovo, Bulgaria 41 D8
Levuka, Fiji 91 C8
Lewes, U.K. 13 G8
Lewes, U.S.A. 108 F8
Lewin Brzeski, Poland 45 H4
Lewis, U.K. 14 C2
Lewis ➜, U.S.A. 116 E4
Lewis, Butt of, U.K. 14 C2
Lewis Ra., Australia 92 D4
Lewis Range, U.S.A. 114 C7
Lewis Run, U.S.A. 110 E6
Lewisburg, Pa., U.S.A. 110 F8
Lewisburg, Tenn., U.S.A. 109 H2
Lewisburg, W. Va., U.S.A. ... 108 G5
Lewisporte, Canada 103 C8
Lewiston, Idaho, U.S.A. 114 C5
Lewiston, Maine, U.S.A. 109 C11
Lewiston, N.Y., U.S.A. 110 C5
Lewistown, Mont., U.S.A. 114 C9
Lewistown, Pa., U.S.A. 110 F7
Lexington, Ill., U.S.A. 112 E10
Lexington, Ky., U.S.A. 108 F3
Lexington, Mich., U.S.A. 110 C2
Lexington, Mo., U.S.A. 112 F8
Lexington, N.C., U.S.A. 109 H5
Lexington, N.Y., U.S.A. 111 D10
Lexington, Nebr., U.S.A. 112 E5
Lexington, Ohio, U.S.A. 110 F2
Lexington, Tenn., U.S.A. 109 H1
Lexington, Va., U.S.A. 108 G6
Lexington Park, U.S.A. 108 F7
Leyburn, U.K. 12 C6
Leye, China 58 E6
Leyland, U.K. 12 D5
Leyre ➜, France 20 D2
Leyte □, Phil. 61 F6
Leyte Gulf, Phil. 61 F6
Leżajsk, Poland 45 H9
Lezay, France 20 B3
Lezhë, Albania 40 E3
Lezhi, China 58 B5
Lézignan-Corbières, France ... 20 E6
Lezoux, France 20 C7
Lgov, Russia 47 G8
Lhasa, China 60 D4
Lhazê, China 60 D3
Lhokkruet, Indonesia 62 D1
Lhokseumawe, Indonesia 62 C1
L'Hospitalet de Llobregat, Spain 32 D7
Li, Thailand 64 D2
Li Shui ➜, China 59 C9
Li Xian, Gansu, China 56 G3
Li Xian, Hebei, China 56 E8
Li Xian, Hunan, China 59 C8
Liádhoi, Greece 39 E8
Liancheng, China 59 E11
Lianga, Phil. 61 G7
Liangcheng,
  Nei Monggol Zizhiqu, China . 56 D7
Liangdang, Shandong, China .. 57 G10
Liangdang, China 56 H4
Lianghe, China 58 E2
Lianghekou, China 58 C7
Liangping, China 58 B6
Liangpran, Indonesia 62 D4
Lianhua, China 59 D9
Lianjiang, Fujian, China 59 D12
Lianjiang, Guangdong, China . 59 G8
Lianping, China 59 E10
Lianshan, China 59 E9
Lianshanguan, China 57 D12
Lianshui, China 57 H10
Lianyuan, China 59 D8
Lianyungang, China 57 G10
Lianzhou, China 59 E9
Liao He ➜, China 57 D11
Liaocheng, China 56 F8
Liaodong Bandao, China 57 E12
Liaodong Wan, China 57 D11
Liaoning □, China 57 D12
Liaoyang, China 57 D12
Liaoyuan, China 57 C13
Liaozhong, China 57 D12
Liapádhes, Greece 38 B1
Liard ➜, Canada 104 A4
Liard River, Canada 104 B3
Liari, Pakistan 68 G2
Libau = Liepāja, Latvia 9 H19
Libby, U.S.A. 114 B6
Libenge, Dem. Rep. of
  the Congo 84 D3
Liberal, U.S.A. 113 G4
Liberec, Czech Rep. 26 A8
Liberia, Costa Rica 120 D2
Liberia ■, W. Afr. 82 D3
Liberty, Mo., U.S.A. 112 F7
Liberty, N.Y., U.S.A. 111 E10
Liberty, Pa., U.S.A. 110 E7
Liberty, Tex., U.S.A. 113 K7
Libiąż, Poland 45 H6
Lîbîya, Sahrâ', Africa 79 C10
Libo, China 58 E6
Libobo, Tanjung, Indonesia .. 63 E7
Libode, S. Africa 89 E4

Libohovë, Albania 40 F4
Libourne, France 20 D3
Libramont, Belgium 17 E5
Librazhd, Albania 40 E4
Libreville, Gabon 84 D1
Libya ■, N. Afr. 79 C9
Libyan Desert = Lîbîya, Sahrâ',
  Africa 79 C10
Libyan Plateau = Ed-Déffa,
  Egypt 80 A2
Licantén, Chile 126 D1
Licata, Italy 30 E6
Lice, Turkey 73 C9
Licheng, China 56 F7
Lichfield, U.K. 13 E6
Lichinga, Mozam. 87 E4
Lichtenburg, S. Africa 88 D4
Lichtenfels, Germany 25 E7
Lichuan, Hubei, China 58 B7
Lichuan, Jiangxi, China 59 D11
Licking ➜, U.S.A. 108 F3
Licosa, Punta, Italy 31 B7
Lida, Belarus 9 K21
Liden, Sweden 10 B10
Lidhorikion, Greece 38 C4
Lidhult, Sweden 11 H7
Lidköping, Sweden 11 F7
Lido, Italy 29 C9
Lido, Niger 83 C5
Lido di Roma = Óstia, Lido di,
  Italy 29 G9
Lidzbark, Poland 45 E6
Lidzbark Warmiński, Poland .. 44 D7
Liebenwalde, Germany 24 C9
Lieberose, Germany 24 D10
Liebig, Mt., Australia 92 D5
Liebling, Romania 42 E6
Liechtenstein ■, Europe 25 H5
Liège, Belgium 17 D5
Liège □, Belgium 17 D5
Liegnitz = Legnica, Poland .. 45 G3
Lienart, Dem. Rep. of the Congo 86 B2
Lienyünchiangshih =
  Lianyungang, China 57 G10
Lienz, Austria 26 E5
Liepāja, Latvia 9 H19
Liepāja □, Latvia 44 B8
Liepājas ezers, Latvia 44 B8
Lier, Belgium 17 C4
Liernais, France 19 E11
Liești, Romania 43 E12
Liévin, France 19 B9
Lièvre ➜, Canada 102 C4
Liezen, Austria 26 D7
Liffey ➜, Ireland 15 C5
Lifford, Ireland 15 B4
Liffré, France 18 D5
Lifudzin, Russia 54 B7
Ligao, Phil. 61 E5
Lightning Ridge, Australia .. 95 D4
Lignano Sabbiadoro, Italy ... 29 C10
Ligny-en-Barrois, France 19 D12
Ligonier, U.S.A. 110 F5
Ligoúrion, Greece 38 D5
Ligueil, France 18 E7
Liguria □, Italy 28 D5
Ligurian Sea, Medit. S. 6 G7
Lihou Reefs and Cays, Australia 94 B5
Lihue, U.S.A. 106 H15
Lijiang, China 58 D3
Likasi, Dem. Rep. of the Congo 87 E2
Likenäs, Sweden 10 D8
Likhoslavl, Russia 46 D8
Likhovskoy, Russia 47 H11
Likoma I., Malawi 87 E3
Likumburu, Tanzania 87 D4
L'Île-Bouchard, France 18 E7
L'Île-Rousse, France 21 F12
Liling, China 59 D9
Lilla Edet, Sweden 11 F6
Lille, France 19 B10
Lille Bælt, Denmark 11 J3
Lillebonne, France 18 C7
Lillehammer, Norway 9 F14
Lillesand, Norway 9 G13
Lillhärdal, Sweden 10 C8
Lillian Pt., Australia 93 E4
Lillo, Spain 34 F7
Lillooet, Canada 104 C4
Lillooet ➜, Canada 104 D4
Lilongwe, Malawi 87 E3
Liloy, Phil. 63 C6
Lim ➜, Bos.-H. 40 C3
Lima, Indonesia 63 E7
Lima, Peru 124 F3
Lima, Mont., U.S.A. 114 D7
Lima, Ohio, U.S.A. 108 E3
Lima ➜, Portugal 34 D2
Liman, Indonesia 63 G14
Liman, Russia 49 H8
Limanowa, Poland 45 J7
Limassol, Cyprus 36 E12
Limavady, U.K. 15 A5
Limay ➜, Argentina 128 D3
Limay Mahuida, Argentina 126 D2
Limbach-Oberfrohna, Germany . 24 E8
Limbang, Brunei 62 D5
Limbara, Mte., Italy 30 B2
Limbaži, Latvia 9 H21
Limbdi, India 68 H4
Limbe, Cameroon 83 E6
Limburg, Germany 25 E4
Limburg □, Belgium 17 C5
Limburg □, Neths. 17 C5
Limedsforsen, Sweden 10 D7
Limeira, Brazil 127 A6

Limenária, Greece 41 F8
Limerick, Ireland 15 D3
Limerick, U.S.A. 111 C14
Limerick □, Ireland 15 D3
Limestone, U.S.A. 110 D6
Limestone ➜, Canada 105 B10
Limfjorden, Denmark 11 H3
Limia = Lima ➜, Portugal ... 34 D2
Limín Khersonísou, Greece ... 39 F7
Limingen, Norway 8 D15
Limmared, Sweden 11 G7
Limmen Bight, Australia 94 A2
Limmen Bight ➜, Australia .. 94 B2
Límni, Greece 38 C5
Límnos, Greece 39 B7
Limoges, Canada 111 A9
Limoges, France 20 C5
Limón, Costa Rica 120 E3
Limon, U.S.A. 112 F3
Limone Piemonte, Italy 28 D4
Limousin, France 20 C5
Limousin, Plateaux du, France . 20 C5
Limoux, France 20 E6
Limpopo ➜, Africa 89 D5
Limuru, Kenya 86 C4
Lin Xian, China 56 F6
Lin'an, China 59 B12
Linapacan I., Phil. 61 F3
Linapacan Str., Phil. 61 F3
Linares, Chile 126 D1
Linares, Mexico 119 C5
Linares, Spain 35 G7
Linaro, Capo, Italy 29 F8
Línas Mte., Italy 30 C1
Lincang, China 58 F3
Lincheng, China 56 F8
Linchuan, China 59 D11
Lincoln, Argentina 126 C3
Lincoln, N.Z. 91 K4
Lincoln, U.K. 12 D7
Lincoln, Calif., U.S.A. 116 G5
Lincoln, Ill., U.S.A. 112 E10
Lincoln, Kans., U.S.A. 112 F5
Lincoln, Maine, U.S.A. 109 C11
Lincoln, N.H., U.S.A. 111 B13
Lincoln, N. Mex., U.S.A. 115 K11
Lincoln, Nebr., U.S.A. 112 E6
Lincoln City, U.S.A. 114 D1
Lincoln Hav = Lincoln Sea,
  Arctic 4 A5
Lincoln Sea, Arctic 4 A5
Lincolnshire □, U.K. 12 D7
Lincolnshire Wolds, U.K. 12 D7
Lincolnton, U.S.A. 109 H5
Lind, U.S.A. 114 C4
Linda, U.S.A. 116 F5
Lindau, Germany 25 H5
Linden, Guyana 124 B7
Linden, Ala., U.S.A. 109 J2
Linden, Calif., U.S.A. 116 G5
Linden, Tex., U.S.A. 113 J7
Lindenhurst, U.S.A. 111 F11
Lindesberg, Sweden 10 E9
Lindesnes, Norway 9 H12
Líndhos, Greece 36 C10
Líndhos, Ákra, Greece 36 C10
Lindi, Tanzania 87 D4
Lindi □, Tanzania 87 D4
Lindi ➜, Dem. Rep. of
  the Congo 86 B2
Lindö, Sweden 11 F10
Lindome, Sweden 11 G6
Lindoso, Portugal 34 D2
Lindow, Germany 24 C8
Lindsay, Canada 102 D4
Lindsay, Calif., U.S.A. 116 J7
Lindsay, Okla., U.S.A. 113 H6
Lindsborg, U.S.A. 112 F6
Lindsdal, Sweden 11 H10
Linesville, U.S.A. 110 E4
Linfen, China 56 F6
Ling Xian, Hunan, China 59 D9
Ling Xian, Shandong, China .. 56 F9
Lingao, China 64 C7
Lingayen, Phil. 63 A6
Lingayen G., Phil. 61 C4
Lingbi, China 57 H9
Lingbo, Sweden 10 C10
Lingchuan, Guangxi Zhuangzu,
  China 59 E8
Lingchuan, Shanxi, China 56 G7
Lingen, Germany 24 C3
Lingga, Indonesia 62 E2
Lingga, Kepulauan, Indonesia . 62 E2
Lingga Arch. = Lingga,
  Kepulauan, Indonesia 62 E2
Linghem, Sweden 11 F9
Lingle, U.S.A. 112 D2
Lingling, China 59 D8
Lingqiu, China 56 E8
Lingshan, China 58 F7
Lingshi, China 56 F6
Lingshou, China 56 E8
Lingshui, China 64 C8
Lingtai, China 56 G4
Linguère, Senegal 82 B1
Lingui, China 59 E8
Lingwu, China 56 E4
Lingyuan, China 57 D10
Lingyun, China 58 E6
Linh, China 59 C13
Linhares, Brazil 125 G10
Linhe, China 56 D4
Linjiang, China 57 D14
Linkau, Austria 26 C7
Linkou, China 57 B16

Linli, China 59 C8
Linnhe, L., U.K. 14 E3
Linqi, China 56 G7
Linqing, China 56 F8
Linqu, China 57 F10
Linru, China 56 G7
Lins, Brazil 127 A6
Linshui, China 58 B6
Linta ➜, Madag. 89 D7
Linth ➜, Switz. 25 H5
Linthal, Switz. 25 J5
Linton, Ind., U.S.A. 108 F2
Linton, N. Dak., U.S.A. 112 B4
Lintong, China 56 G5
Linwood, Canada 110 C4
Linwu, China 59 E9
Linxi, China 57 C10
Linxia, China 60 C5
Linxiang, China 59 C9
Linyanti ➜, Africa 88 B4
Linyi, China 57 G10
Linz, Austria 26 C7
Linz, Germany 24 E3
Linzhenzhen, China 56 F5
Linzi, China 57 F10
Lion, G. du, France 20 E7
Lionárisso, Cyprus 36 D13
Lioni, Italy 31 B8
Lions, G. of = Lion, G. du,
  France 20 E7
Lion's Den, Zimbabwe 87 F3
Lion's Head, Canada 110 B3
Liozno = Lyozna, Belarus 46 E6
Lipa, Phil. 61 E4
Lipali, Mozam. 87 F4
Lípari, Italy 31 D7
Lípari, I., Italy 31 D7
Lípari, Is. = Éólie, Ís., Italy 31 D7
Lipcani, Moldova 43 B11
Lipetsk, Russia 47 F10
Lipiany, Poland 45 E1
Liping, China 58 D7
Lipkany = Lipcani, Moldova .. 43 B11
Lipljan, Kosovo, Yug. 40 D5
Lipno, Poland 45 F6
Lipova, Romania 42 D6
Lipovcy Manzovka, Russia 54 B6
Lipovets, Ukraine 47 H5
Lippe ➜, Germany 24 D2
Lippstadt, Germany 24 D4
Lipscomb, U.S.A. 113 G4
Lipsk, Poland 44 E10
Lipsko, Poland 45 G8
Lipsói, Greece 39 D8
Liptovský Hrádok, Slovak Rep. 27 B12
Liptovský Mikuláš, Slovak Rep. 27 B12
Lipu, China 59 E8
Lira, Uganda 86 B3
Liri ➜, Italy 30 A6
Liria = Lliria, Spain 33 F4
Lisala, Dem. Rep. of the Congo 84 D4
Lisboa, Portugal 35 G1
Lisboa □, Portugal 35 F1
Lisbon = Lisboa, Portugal ... 35 G1
Lisbon, N. Dak., U.S.A. 112 B6
Lisbon, N.H., U.S.A. 111 B13
Lisbon, Ohio, U.S.A. 110 F4
Lisbon Falls, U.S.A. 109 D10
Lisburn, U.K. 15 B5
Liscannor B., Ireland 15 D2
Liscia ➜, Italy 30 A2
Lishe Jiang ➜, China 58 E3
Lishi, China 56 F6
Lishu, China 57 C13
Lishui, Jiangsu, China 59 B12
Lishui, Zhejiang, China 59 C12
Lisianski I., Pac. Oc. 96 E10
Lisichansk = Lysychansk,
  Ukraine 47 H10
Lisieux, France 18 C7
Liski, Russia 47 G10
L'Isle-Jourdain, Gers, France 20 E5
L'Isle-Jourdain, Vienne, France 20 B4
L'Isle-sur-la-Sorgue, France . 21 E9
Lisle-sur-Tarn, France 20 E5
Lismore, Australia 95 D5
Lismore, Ireland 15 D4
Lista, Norway 9 G12
Lister, Mt., Antarctica 5 D11
Liston, Australia 95 D5
Listowel, Canada 102 D3
Listowel, Ireland 15 D2
Lit, Sweden 10 A8
Lit-et-Mixe, France 20 D2
Litang, Guangxi Zhuangzu,
  China 58 F7
Litang, Sichuan, China 58 B3
Litang Qu ➜, China 58 C3
Litani ➜, Lebanon 75 B4
Litchfield, Calif., U.S.A. .. 116 E6
Litchfield, Conn., U.S.A. ... 111 E11
Litchfield, Ill., U.S.A. 112 F10
Litchfield, Minn., U.S.A. ... 112 C7
Liteni, Romania 43 C11
Líthinon, Ákra, Greece 36 E6
Lithuania ■, Europe 9 J20
Litija, Slovenia 29 B11
Lititz, U.S.A. 111 F8
Litókhoron, Greece 40 F6
Litoměřice, Czech Rep. 26 A7
Litomyšl, Czech Rep. 27 B9
Litschau, Austria 26 C8
Little Abaco I., Bahamas 120 A4
Little Barrier I., N.Z. 91 G5

Little Belt Mts., U.S.A. 114 C8
Little Blue ➜, U.S.A. 112 F6
Little Buffalo ➜, Canada ... 104 A6
Little Cayman, Cayman Is. ... 120 C3
Little Churchill ➜, Canada . 105 B9
Little Colorado ➜, U.S.A. .. 115 H8
Little Current, Canada 102 C3
Little Current ➜, Canada ... 102 B3
Little Falls, Minn., U.S.A. . 112 C7
Little Falls, N.Y., U.S.A. .. 111 C10
Little Fork ➜, U.S.A. 112 A8
Little Grand Rapids, Canada . 105 C9
Little Humboldt ➜, U.S.A. .. 114 F5
Little Inagua I., Bahamas ... 121 B5
Little Karoo, S. Africa 88 E3
Little Lake, U.S.A. 117 K9
Little Laut Is. = Laut Kecil,
  Kepulauan, Indonesia 62 E5
Little Mecatina = Petit-
  Mécatina ➜, Canada 103 B8
Little Minch, U.K. 14 D2
Little Missouri ➜, U.S.A. .. 112 B3
Little Ouse ➜, U.K. 13 E9
Little Rann, India 68 H4
Little Red ➜, U.S.A. 113 H9
Little River, N.Z. 91 K4
Little Rock, U.S.A. 113 H8
Little Ruaha ➜, Tanzania ... 86 D4
Little Sable Pt., U.S.A. 108 D2
Little Scarcies ➜, S. Leone 82 D2
Little Sioux ➜, U.S.A. 112 E6
Little Smoky ➜, Canada 104 C5
Little Snake ➜, U.S.A. 114 F9
Little Valley, U.S.A. 110 D6
Little Wabash ➜, U.S.A. 108 G1
Little White ➜, U.S.A. 112 D4
Littlefield, U.S.A. 113 J3
Littlehampton, U.K. 13 G7
Littleton, U.S.A. 111 B13
Litvinov, Czech Rep. 26 A6
Liu He ➜, China 57 D11
Liu Jiang ➜, China 58 F7
Liuba, China 56 H4
Liucheng, China 58 E7
Liugou, China 57 D10
Liuhe, China 57 C13
Liuheng Dao, China 59 C14
Liujiang, China 58 E7
Liukang Tenggaja = Sabalana,
  Kepulauan, Indonesia 63 F5
Liuli, Tanzania 87 E3
Liuwa Plain, Zambia 85 G4
Liuyang, China 59 C9
Liuzhou, China 58 E7
Liuzhuang, China 57 H11
Livada, Romania 42 C8
Livadherón, Greece 40 F5
Livadhia, Cyprus 36 E12
Livada, Cyprus 38 A4
Livarot, France 18 D7
Live Oak, Calif., U.S.A. 116 F5
Live Oak, Fla., U.S.A. 109 K4
Liveras, Cyprus 36 D11
Livermore, U.S.A. 116 H5
Livermore, Mt., U.S.A. 113 K2
Livermore Falls, U.S.A. 109 C11
Liverpool, Canada 103 D7
Liverpool, U.K. 12 D4
Liverpool, U.S.A. 111 C8
Liverpool Bay, U.K. 12 D4
Livigno, Italy 28 B7
Livingston, Guatemala 120 C2
Livingston, U.K. 14 F5
Livingston, Ala., U.S.A. 109 J1
Livingston, Calif., U.S.A. .. 116 H6
Livingston, Mont., U.S.A. ... 114 D8
Livingston, S.C., U.S.A. 109 J5
Livingston, Tenn., U.S.A. ... 109 G3
Livingston, Tex., U.S.A. 113 K7
Livingston, U.S.A. 111 E10
Livingston Manor, U.S.A. 111 E10
Livingstone, Zambia 87 F2
Livingstone Mts., Tanzania .. 87 D3
Livingstonia, Malawi 87 E3
Livno, Bos.-H. 42 G2
Livny, Russia 47 F9
Livonia, Mich., U.S.A. 108 D4
Livonia, N.Y., U.S.A. 110 D7
Livorno, Italy 28 E7
Livramento, Brazil 127 C4
Livron-sur-Drôme, France 21 D8
Liwale, Tanzania 87 D4
Liwiec ➜, Poland 45 F8
Lixi, China 58 D3
Lixian, China 58 B4
Lixoúrion, Greece 38 C2
Liyang, China 59 B12
Lizard I., Australia 94 A4
Lizard Pt., U.K. 13 H2
Lizzano, Italy 31 B10
Ljig, Serbia, Yug. 40 B4
Ljubija, Bos.-H. 29 D13
Ljubinje, Bos.-H. 40 D2
Ljubljana, Slovenia 29 B11
Ljubno, Slovenia 29 B11
Ljubovija, Serbia, Yug. 40 B3
Ljugarn, Sweden 11 G12
Ljung, Sweden 11 G7
Ljungan ➜, Sweden 10 B11
Ljungaverk, Sweden 10 B10
Ljungby, Sweden 9 H15
Ljungbyholm, Sweden 11 H10
Ljungdalen, Sweden 10 B6
Ljungsbro, Sweden 11 F9
Ljungskile, Sweden 11 F5
Ljusdal, Sweden 10 C10

Ljusfallshammar, Sweden 11 F9
Ljusnan →, Sweden 10 C11
Ljusne, Sweden 10 C11
Ljutomer, Slovenia 29 B13
Llagostera, Spain 32 D7
Llancanelo, Salina, Argentina . 126 D2
Llandeilo, U.K. 13 F4
Llandovery, U.K. 13 F4
Llandrindod Wells, U.K. 13 E4
Llandudno, U.K. 12 D4
Llanelli, U.K. 13 F3
Llanes, Spain 34 B6
Llangollen, U.K. 12 E4
Llanidloes, U.K. 13 E4
Llano, U.S.A. 113 K5
Llano →, U.S.A. 113 K5
Llano Estacado, U.S.A. 113 J3
Llanos, S. Amer. 122 C3
Llanquihue, L., Chile 128 E1
Llanwrtyd Wells, U.K. 13 E4
Llebeig, C. des, Spain 37 B9
Lleida, Spain 32 D5
Lleida □, Spain 32 C6
Llentrisca, C., Spain 37 C7
Llera, Mexico 119 C5
Llerena, Spain 35 G5
Lleyn Peninsula, U.K. 12 E3
Llico, Chile 126 C1
Lliria, Spain 33 F4
Llobregat →, Spain 32 D7
Llodio, Spain 32 B2
Lloret de Mar, Spain 32 D7
Lloyd B., Australia 94 A3
Lloyd L., Canada 105 B7
Lloydminster, Canada 105 C7
Llucena del Cid, Spain 32 E4
Llucmajor, Spain 37 B9
Llullaillaco, Volcán, S. Amer. . 126 A2
Lo →, Vietnam 64 B5
Loa, U.S.A. 115 G8
Loa →, Chile 126 A1
Loaita I., S. China Sea 62 B4
Loange →, Dem. Rep. of
   the Congo 84 E4
Loano, Italy 28 D5
Lobatse, Botswana 88 D4
Löbau, Germany 24 D10
Lobenstein, Germany 24 E7
Lobería, Argentina 126 D4
Löberöd, Sweden 11 J7
Łobez, Poland 44 E2
Lobito, Angola 85 G2
Lobo →, Ivory C. 82 D3
Lobos, Argentina 126 D4
Lobos, I., Mexico 118 B2
Lobos, I. de, Canary Is. 37 F6
Łobżenica, Poland 45 E4
Loc Binh, Vietnam 64 B6
Loc Ninh, Vietnam 65 G6
Locarno, Switz. 25 J4
Loch Baghasdail =
   Lochboisdale, U.K. 14 D1
Loch Garman = Wexford,
   Ireland 15 D5
Loch Nam Madadh =
   Lochmaddy, U.K. 14 D1
Lochaber, U.K. 14 E3
Locharbriggs, U.K. 14 F5
Lochboisdale, U.K. 14 D1
Loche, L. La, Canada 105 B7
Lochem, Neths. 17 B6
Loches, France 18 E7
Lochgilphead, U.K. 14 E3
Lochinver, U.K. 14 C3
Lochmaddy, U.K. 14 D1
Lochnagar, Australia 94 C4
Lochnagar, U.K. 14 E5
Łochów, Poland 45 F8
Lochy, L., U.K. 14 E4
Lock, Australia 95 E2
Lock Haven, U.S.A. 110 E7
Lockeford, U.S.A. 116 G5
Lockeport, Canada 103 D6
Lockerbie, U.K. 14 F5
Lockhart, U.S.A. 113 L6
Lockhart, L., Australia 93 F2
Lockhart River, Australia ... 94 A3
Lockney, U.S.A. 113 H4
Lockport, U.S.A. 110 C6
Locminé, France 18 E4
Locri, Italy 31 D9
Locronan, France 18 D2
Lod, Israel 75 D3
Lodeinoye Pole, Russia 46 B7
Lodève, France 20 E7
Lodge Bay, Canada 103 B8
Lodge Grass, U.S.A. 114 D10
Lodgepole Cr. →, U.S.A. ... 112 E2
Lodhran, Pakistan 68 E4
Lodi, Italy 28 C6
Lodi, Calif., U.S.A. 116 G5
Lodi, Ohio, U.S.A. 110 E3
Lodja, Dem. Rep. of the Congo 86 C1
Lodosa, Spain 32 C2
Lödöse, Sweden 11 F6
Lodwar, Kenya 86 B4
Łódź, Poland 45 G6
Łódzkie □, Poland 45 G6
Loei, Thailand 64 D3
Loengo, Dem. Rep. of the Congo 86 C2
Loeriesfontein, S. Africa ... 88 E2
Lofa →, Liberia 83 D2
Lofer, Austria 26 D5
Lofoten, Norway 8 B15
Lofsdalen, Sweden 10 B7
Lofsen →, Sweden 10 B7

Loftahammar, Sweden 11 G10
Loga, Niger 83 C5
Logan, Iowa, U.S.A. 112 E7
Logan, Ohio, U.S.A. 108 F4
Logan, Utah, U.S.A. 114 F8
Logan, W. Va., U.S.A. 108 G5
Logan, Mt., Canada 100 B5
Logandale, U.S.A. 117 J12
Logansport, Ind., U.S.A. 108 E2
Logansport, La., U.S.A. 113 K8
Logirim, Sudan 81 G3
Logo, Sudan 81 F3
Logone →, Chad 79 F9
Logroño, Spain 32 C2
Logrosán, Spain 35 F5
Løgstør, Denmark 11 H3
Løgumkloster, Denmark 11 J2
Lohals, Denmark 11 J4
Lohardaga, India 69 H11
Loharia, India 68 H6
Loharu, India 68 E6
Lohja, Finland 9 F21
Löhne, Germany 24 C4
Lohr, Germany 25 F5
Lohri Wah →, Pakistan 68 F2
Loi-kaw, Burma 67 K20
Loimaa, Finland 9 F20
Loir →, France 18 E6
Loir-et-Cher □, France 18 E8
Loire □, France 21 C8
Loire →, France 18 E4
Loire-Atlantique □, France .. 18 E5
Loiret □, France 19 E9
Loitz, Germany 24 B9
Loja, Ecuador 124 D3
Loja, Spain 35 H6
Loji = Kawasi, Indonesia ... 63 E7
Løjt Kirkeby, Denmark 11 J3
Lojung, China 58 E7
Loka, Sudan 81 G3
Lokandu, Dem. Rep. of
   the Congo 86 C2
Lokeren, Belgium 17 C3
Lokgwabe, Botswana 88 C3
Lokhvitsa, Ukraine 47 G7
Lokichokio, Kenya 86 B3
Lokitaung, Kenya 86 B4
Lokkan tekojärvi, Finland .. 8 C22
Løkken, Denmark 11 G3
Loknya, Russia 46 D6
Loko, Nigeria 83 D6
Lokoja, Nigeria 83 D6
Lokot, Russia 47 F8
Lol →, Sudan 81 F2
Lola, Guinea 82 D3
Lola, Mt., U.S.A. 116 F6
Lolibai, Gebel, Sudan 81 G3
Lolimi, Sudan 81 G3
Loliondo, Tanzania 86 C4
Lolland, Denmark 11 K5
Lollar, Germany 24 E4
Lolo, U.S.A. 114 C6
Lolodorf, Cameroon 83 E7
Lom, Bulgaria 40 C7
Lom →, Bulgaria 40 C7
Lom Kao, Thailand 64 D3
Lom Sak, Thailand 64 D3
Loma, U.S.A. 114 C8
Loma Linda, U.S.A. 117 L9
Lomami →, Dem. Rep. of
   the Congo 86 B1
Lomas de Zamóra, Argentina . 126 C4
Lombadina, Australia 92 C3
Lombárdia □, Italy 28 C6
Lombardy = Lombárdia □, Italy 28 C6
Lombez, France 20 E4
Lomblen, Indonesia 63 F6
Lombok, Indonesia 62 F5
Lomé, Togo 83 D5
Lomela, Dem. Rep. of the Congo 84 E4
Lomela →, Dem. Rep. of
   the Congo 84 E4
Lomianki, Poland 45 F7
Lomma, Sweden 11 J7
Lommel, Belgium 17 C5
Lomond, Canada 104 C6
Lomond, L., U.K. 14 E4
Lomphat, Cambodia 64 F6
Lompobatang, Indonesia .. 63 F5
Lompoc, U.S.A. 117 L6
Łomża, Poland 45 E9
Loncoche, Chile 128 D2
Londa, India 66 M9
Londiani, Kenya 86 C4
Londinières, France 18 C8
London, Canada 102 D3
London, U.K. 13 F7
London, Ky., U.S.A. 108 G3
London, Ohio, U.S.A. 108 F4
London, Greater □, U.K. .. 13 F7
Londonderry, U.K. 15 B4
Londonderry □, U.K. 15 B4
Londonderry, C., Australia . 92 B4
Londonderry, I., Chile 128 H2
Londres, Argentina 128 B3
Londrina, Brazil 127 A5
Lone Pine, U.S.A. 116 J8
Lonely Mine, Zimbabwe .. 89 B4
Long B., U.S.A. 109 J6
Long Beach, Calif., U.S.A. . 117 M8
Long Beach, N.Y., U.S.A. . 111 F11
Long Beach, Wash., U.S.A. . 116 D2
Long Branch, U.S.A. 111 F11
Long Creek, U.S.A. 114 D4
Long Eaton, U.K. 12 E6
Long I., Australia 94 C4

Long I., Bahamas 121 B4
Long I., Canada 102 B4
Long I., Ireland 15 E2
Long I., U.S.A. 111 F11
Long Island Sd., U.S.A. 111 E12
Long L., Canada 102 C2
Long Lake, U.S.A. 111 C10
Long Point B., Canada 110 D4
Long Prairie →, U.S.A. ... 112 C7
Long Pt., Canada 110 D4
Long Range Mts., Canada .. 103 C8
Long Reef, Australia 92 B4
Long Spruce, Canada 105 B10
Long Str. = Longa, Proliv, Russia 4 C16
Long Thanh, Vietnam 65 G6
Long Xian, China 56 G4
Long Xuyen, Vietnam 65 G5
Longá, Greece 38 E3
Longa, Proliv, Russia 4 C16
Long'an, China 58 F6
Longarone, Italy 29 B9
Longbenton, U.K. 12 B6
Longboat Key, U.S.A. 109 M4
Longchang, China 58 C5
Longchi, China 58 C4
Longchuan, Guangdong, China 59 E10
Longchuan, Yunnan, China . 58 E1
Longde, China 56 G4
Longeau, France 19 E12
Longford, Australia 94 G4
Longford, Ireland 15 C4
Longford □, Ireland 15 C4
Longhai, China 59 E11
Longhua, China 57 D9
Longhui, China 59 D8
Longido, Tanzania 86 C4
Longiram, Indonesia ... 62 E5
Longkou, Jiangxi, China . 59 D10
Longkou, Shandong, China 57 F11
Longlac, Canada 102 C2
Longli, China 58 D6
Longlin, China 58 E5
Longling, China 58 E2
Longmeadow, U.S.A. .. 111 D12
Longmen, China 59 F10
Longming, China 58 F6
Longmont, U.S.A. 112 E2
Longnan, China 59 E10
Longnawan, Indonesia . 62 D4
Longobucco, Italy 31 C9
Longquan, China 59 C12
Longreach, Australia .. 94 C3
Longshan, China 58 C7
Longsheng, China 59 E8
Longué-Jumelles, France 18 E6
Longueau, France 19 C9
Longueuil, Canada ... 111 A11
Longuyon, France ... 19 C12
Longvic, France 19 E12
Longview, Tex., U.S.A. . 113 J7
Longview, Wash., U.S.A. 116 D4
Longwy, France 19 C12
Longxi, China 56 G3
Longyan, China 59 E11
Longyou, China 59 C12
Longzhou, China 58 F6
Lonigo, Italy 29 C8
Löningen, Germany .. 24 C3
Lonja →, Croatia ... 29 C13
Lonoke, U.S.A. 113 H9
Lonquimay, Chile .. 128 D2
Lons-le-Saunier, France 19 F12
Lönsboda, Sweden .. 11 H8
Looe, U.K. 13 G3
Lookout, C., Canada . 102 A3
Lookout, C., U.S.A. . 109 H7
Loolmalasin, Tanzania 86 C4
Loon →, Alta., Canada 104 B5
Loon →, Man., Canada 105 B8
Loon Lake, Canada .. 105 C7
Loongana, Australia . 93 F4
Loop Hd., Ireland .. 15 D2
Lop Buri, Thailand . 64 E3
Lop Nor = Lop Nur, China 60 B4
Lop Nur, China 60 B4
Lopare, Bos.-H. ... 42 F3
Lopatin, Russia ... 49 J8
Lopatina, Gora, Russia 51 D15
Lopaye, Sudan 81 F3
Lopez, Phil. 61 E5
Lopez, U.S.A. 111 E8
Lopez, C., Gabon .. 84 E1
Lopphavet, Norway 8 A19
Lora →, Afghan. .. 66 D4
Lora, Hámūn-i-, Pakistan 66 E4
Lora Cr. →, Australia 95 D2
Lora del Río, Spain . 35 H5
Lorain, U.S.A. 110 E2
Loralai, Pakistan .. 68 D3
Lorca, Spain 33 H3
Lord Howe I., Pac. Oc. 96 L7
Lord Howe Ridge, Pac. Oc. 96 L8
Lordsburg, U.S.A. . 115 K9
Loreto, Brazil 125 E9
Loreto, Mexico ... 118 B2
Lorgues, France ... 21 E10
Lorhosso, Burkina Faso 82 C4
Lorient, France ... 18 E3
Lőrinci, Hungary .. 42 C4
Lormi, India 69 H9
Lorn, U.K. 14 E3
Lorn, Firth of, U.K. . 14 E3
Loronyo, Sudan .. 81 G3
Lorovouno, Cyprus . 36 D11

Lörrach, Germany 25 H3
Lorraine □, France 19 D13
Los, Sweden 10 C9
Los, Îles de, Guinea 82 D2
Los Alamos, Calif., U.S.A. . 117 L6
Los Alamos, N. Mex., U.S.A. 115 J10
Los Altos, U.S.A. 116 H4
Los Andes, Chile 126 C1
Los Angeles, Chile 126 D1
Los Angeles, U.S.A. 117 M8
Los Angeles, Bahia de, Mexico 118 B2
Los Angeles Aqueduct, U.S.A. 117 K9
Los Banos, U.S.A. 116 H6
Los Barrios, Spain 35 J5
Los Blancos, Argentina ... 126 A3
Los Chiles, Costa Rica 120 D3
Los Cristianos, Canary Is. .. 37 F3
Los Corrales de Buelna, Spain 34 B6
Los Gallardos, Spain 33 H3
Los Gatos, U.S.A. 116 H5
Los Hermanos Is., Venezuela 121 D7
Los Islotes, Canary Is. 37 E6
Los Llanos de Aridane,
   Canary Is. 37 F2
Los Loros, Chile 126 B1
Los Lunas, U.S.A. 115 J10
Los Mochis, Mexico 118 B3
Los Monegros, Spain 32 D4
Los Nietos, Spain 33 H4
Los Olivos, U.S.A. 117 L6
Los Palacios, Cuba 120 B3
Los Palacios y Villafranca, Spain 35 H5
Los Reyes, Mexico 118 D4
Los Roques Is., Venezuela . 121 D6
Los Santos de Maimona, Spain 35 G4
Los Teques, Venezuela ... 124 A5
Los Testigos, Is., Venezuela . 124 A6
Los Vilos, Chile 126 C1
Los Yébenes, Spain 35 F7
Łosice, Poland 45 F9
Loskop Dam, S. Africa .. 89 D4
Løsning, Denmark 11 J3
Lossiemouth, U.K. 14 D5
Lostwithiel, U.K. 13 G3
Lot □, France 20 D5
Lot →, France 20 D4
Lot-et-Garonne □, France 20 D4
Lota, Chile 126 D1
Lotagipi Swamp, Sudan . 81 G3
Lotfābād, Iran 71 B8
Lothair, S. Africa ... 89 D5
Lotorp, Sweden 11 F9
Lötschbergtunnel, Switz. 25 J3
Löttorp, Sweden 11 G11
Lotung, Taiwan 59 E13
Loubomo, Congo ... 84 E2
Loudéac, France ... 18 D4
Loudi, China 59 D8
Loudonville, U.S.A. . 110 F2
Loudun, France ... 18 E7
Loue →, France .. 19 E12
Louga, Senegal ... 82 B1
Loughborough, U.K. . 12 E6
Loughrea, Ireland .. 15 C3
Loughros More B., Ireland 15 B3
Louhans, France ... 19 F12
Louis Trichardt, S. Africa 89 C4
Louis XIV, Pte., Canada . 102 B4
Louisa, U.S.A. 108 F4
Louisbourg, Canada . 103 C8
Louise I., Canada .. 104 C2
Louiseville, Canada . 102 C5
Louisiade Arch., Papua N. G. 96 J7
Louisiana, U.S.A. .. 112 F9
Louisiana □, U.S.A. . 113 K9
Louisville, Ky., U.S.A. 108 F3
Louisville, Miss., U.S.A. 113 J10
Louisville, Ohio, U.S.A. 110 F3
Loulay, France 20 B3
Loulé, Portugal ... 35 H3
Louny, Czech Rep. . 26 A6
Loup City, U.S.A. .. 112 E5
Loups Marins, Lacs des, Canada 102 A5
Lourdes, France ... 20 E3
Lourinhã, Portugal . 35 F1
Lousã, Portugal ... 34 E2
Louth, Ireland 15 C5
Louth, U.K. 12 D7
Louth □, Ireland .. 15 C5
Loutrá Aidhipsoú, Greece 38 C5
Loutráki, Greece .. 38 D4
Louvain = Leuven, Belgium 17 D4
Louviers, France .. 18 C8
Louwsburg, S. Africa . 89 D5
Lovat →, Russia .. 46 C6
Lovćen, Montenegro, Yug. 40 D2
Lovech, Bulgaria .. 41 C8
Lovech □, Bulgaria . 41 C8
Loveland, U.S.A. .. 112 E2
Lovell, U.S.A. 114 D9
Lovelock, U.S.A. .. 114 F4
Lóvere, Italy 28 C7
Lövestad, Sweden .. 11 J7
Loviisa, Finland .. 9 F22
Loving, U.S.A. 113 J2
Lovington, U.S.A. . 113 J3
Lovisa = Loviisa, Finland . 9 F22
Lovosice, Czech Rep. . 26 A7
Lovran, Croatia ... 29 C11
Lovrin, Romania .. 42 E5
Lövstabruk, Sweden . 10 D11
Lövstabukten, Sweden . 10 D11
Low, L., Canada ... 102 B4
Low Pt., Australia .. 93 F4

Low Tatra = Nízké Tatry,
   Slovak Rep. 27 C12
Lowa, Dem. Rep. of the Congo 86 C2
Lowa →, Dem. Rep. of
   the Congo 86 C2
Lowell, U.S.A. 111 D13
Lowellville, U.S.A. 110 E4
Löwen →, Namibia 88 D2
Lower Alkali L., U.S.A. .. 114 F3
Lower Arrow L., Canada . 104 D5
Lower Austria =
   Niederösterreich □, Austria 26 C8
Lower California = Baja
   California, Mexico 118 A1
Lower Hutt, N.Z. 91 J5
Lower Lake, U.S.A. 116 G4
Lower Manitou L., Canada 105 D10
Lower Post, Canada 104 B3
Lower Red L., U.S.A. ... 112 B7
Lower Saxony =
   Niedersachsen □, Germany 24 C4
Lower Tunguska = Tunguska,
   Nizhnyaya →, Russia .. 51 C9
Lowestoft, U.K. 13 E9
Łowicz, Poland 45 F6
Lowville, U.S.A. 111 C9
Loxton, S. Africa 88 E3
Loyalton, U.S.A. 116 F6
Loyalty Is. = Loyauté, Is., N. Cal. 96 K8
Loyang = Luoyang, China . 56 G7
Loyauté, Is., N. Cal. ... 96 K8
Loyev = Loyew, Belarus . 47 G6
Loyew, Belarus 47 G6
Loyoro, Uganda 86 B3
Lož, Slovenia 29 C11
Lozère □, France 20 D7
Loznica, Serbia, Yug. .. 40 B3
Lozova, Ukraine 47 H9
Lü Shan, China 59 C11
Lü-Tao, Taiwan 59 F13
Luachimo, Angola ... 84 F4
Luajan →, India 69 G11
Lualaba →, Dem. Rep. of
   the Congo 86 B2
Luampa, Zambia 87 F1
Lu'an, China 59 B11
Luan Chau, Vietnam . 58 G4
Luan He →, China .. 57 E10
Luan Xian, China .. 57 E10
Luancheng, Guangxi Zhuangzu,
   China 58 F7
Luancheng, Hebei, China 56 F8
Luanco, Spain 34 B5
Luanda, Angola 84 F2
Luang, Thale, Thailand . 65 J3
Luang Prabang, Laos .. 58 H4
Luangwa, Zambia ... 87 F3
Luangwa →, Zambia . 87 E3
Luangwa Valley, Zambia 87 E3
Luanne, China 57 D9
Luanping, China ... 57 D9
Luanshya, Zambia .. 87 E2
Luapula □, Zambia . 87 E2
Luapula →, Africa .. 87 D2
Luarca, Spain 34 B4
Luashi, Dem. Rep. of the Congo 87 E1
Luau, Angola 84 G4
Lubaczów, Poland .. 45 H10
Luban, Poland 45 G2
Lubana, Ozero = Lubānas Ezers,
   Latvia 9 H22
Lubānas Ezers, Latvia . 9 H22
Lubang, Phil. 61 E4
Lubang Is., Phil. ... 63 B6
Lubartów, Poland .. 45 G9
Lubawa, Poland 45 E6
Lübbecke, Germany . 24 C4
Lübben, Germany .. 24 D9
Lübbenau, Germany . 24 D9
Lubbock, U.S.A. ... 113 J4
Lübeck, Germany .. 24 B6
Lübecker Bucht, Germany 24 A6
Lubefu →, Dem. Rep. of
   the Congo 86 C1
Lubelskie □, Poland . 45 G9
Lubero = Luofu, Dem. Rep. of
   the Congo 86 C2
Lubersac, France ... 20 C5
Lubicon L., Canada . 104 B5
Lubień Kujawski, Poland 45 F6
Lubilash →, Dem. Rep. of
   the Congo 84 F4
Lubin, Poland 45 G3
Lublin, Poland ... 45 G9
Lubliniec, Poland .. 45 H5
Lubnān, Jabal, Lebanon 75 B4
Lubniewice, Poland . 45 F2
Lubny, Ukraine ... 47 G7
Lubomierz, Poland . 45 G2
Luboń, Poland ... 45 F3
Lubongola, Dem. Rep. of
   the Congo 86 C2
L'ubotín, Slovak Rep. . 27 B13
Lubraniec, Poland . 45 F5
Lubsko, Poland ... 45 G1
Lübtheen, Germany . 24 B7
Lubuagan, Phil. .. 61 C4
Lubudi, Dem. Rep. of the Congo 84 F4
Lubudi →, Dem. Rep. of
   the Congo 87 D2
Lubuklinggau, Indonesia 62 E2
Lubuksikaping, Indonesia 62 D2
Lubumbashi, Dem. Rep. of
   the Congo 87 E2

Lubunda, *Dem. Rep. of the Congo* ... 86 D2
Lubungu, *Zambia* ... 87 E2
Lubuskie □, *Poland* ... 45 F2
Lubutu, *Dem. Rep. of the Congo* ... 86 C2
Luc An Chau, *Vietnam* ... 64 A5
Luc-en-Diois, *France* ... 21 D9
Lucan, *Canada* ... 110 C3
Lucania, Mt., *Canada* ... 100 B5
Lucas Channel, *Canada* ... 110 A3
Lucban, *Phil.* ... 61 D4
Lucca, *Italy* ... 28 E7
Lucé, *France* ... 18 D8
Luce Bay, *U.K.* ... 14 G4
Lucea, *Jamaica* ... 120 C4
Lucedale, *U.S.A.* ... 109 K1
Lucena, *Phil.* ... 61 E4
Lucena, *Spain* ... 35 H6
Lučenec, *Slovak Rep.* ... 27 C12
Lucera, *Italy* ... 31 A8
Lucerne = Luzern, *Switz.* ... 25 H4
Lucerne, *U.S.A.* ... 116 F4
Lucerne Valley, *U.S.A.* ... 117 L10
Lucero, *Mexico* ... 118 A3
Luchena →, *Spain* ... 33 H3
Lucheng, *China* ... 56 F7
Lucheringo →, *Mozam.* ... 87 E4
Lüchow, *Germany* ... 24 C7
Luchuan, *China* ... 59 F8
Lucia, *U.S.A.* ... 116 J5
Lucinda, *Australia* ... 94 B4
Luckau, *Germany* ... 24 D9
Luckenwalde, *Germany* ... 24 C9
Luckhoff, *S. Africa* ... 88 D3
Lucknow, *Canada* ... 110 C3
Lucknow, *India* ... 69 F9
Luçon, *France* ... 20 B2
Lüda = Dalian, *China* ... 57 E11
Luda Kamchiya →, *Bulgaria* ... 41 C11
Ludbreg, *Croatia* ... 29 B13
Lüdenscheid, *Germany* ... 24 D3
Lüderitz, *Namibia* ... 88 D2
Lüderitzbaai, *Namibia* ... 88 D2
Ludhiana, *India* ... 68 D6
Ludian, *China* ... 58 D4
Luding Qiao, *China* ... 58 C4
Lüdinghausen, *Germany* ... 24 D3
Ludington, *U.S.A.* ... 108 D2
Ludlow, *U.K.* ... 13 E5
Ludlow, *Calif., U.S.A.* ... 117 L10
Ludlow, *Pa., U.S.A.* ... 110 E6
Ludlow, *Vt., U.S.A.* ... 111 C12
Ludus, *Romania* ... 43 D9
Ludvika, *Sweden* ... 10 D9
Ludwigsburg, *Germany* ... 25 G5
Ludwigsfelde, *Germany* ... 24 C9
Ludwigshafen, *Germany* ... 25 F4
Ludwigslust, *Germany* ... 24 B7
Ludza, *Latvia* ... 46 D4
Lueki, *Dem. Rep. of the Congo* ... 86 C2
Luena, *Dem. Rep. of the Congo* ... 87 D2
Luena, *Zambia* ... 87 E3
Lüeyang, *China* ... 56 H4
Lufeng, *Guangdong, China* ... 59 F10
Lufeng, *Yunnan, China* ... 58 E4
Lufira →, *Dem. Rep. of the Congo* ... 87 D2
Lufkin, *U.S.A.* ... 113 K7
Lufupa, *Dem. Rep. of the Congo* ... 87 E1
Luga, *Russia* ... 46 C5
Luga →, *Russia* ... 46 C5
Lugano, *Switz.* ... 25 J4
Lugano, L. di, *Switz.* ... 28 C6
Lugansk = Luhansk, *Ukraine* ... 47 H10
Lugard's Falls, *Kenya* ... 86 C4
Lugela, *Mozam.* ... 87 F4
Lugenda →, *Mozam.* ... 87 E4
Lugh Ganana, *Somali Rep.* ... 74 G3
Lugnaquilla, *Ireland* ... 15 D5
Lugo, *Italy* ... 29 D8
Lugo, *Spain* ... 34 B3
Lugo □, *Spain* ... 34 C3
Lugoj, *Romania* ... 42 E6
Lugovoy = Qulan, *Kazakstan* ... 50 E8
Luhansk, *Ukraine* ... 47 H10
Luhe, *China* ... 59 A12
Luhe →, *Germany* ... 24 B6
Luhuo, *China* ... 58 B3
Luiana, *Angola* ... 88 B3
Luimneach = Limerick, *Ireland* ... 15 D3
Luing, *U.K.* ... 14 E3
Luino, *Italy* ... 28 C5
Luís Correia, *Brazil* ... 125 D10
Luitpold Coast, *Antarctica* ... 5 D1
Luiza, *Dem. Rep. of the Congo* ... 84 F4
Luizi, *Dem. Rep. of the Congo* ... 86 D2
Luján, *Argentina* ... 126 C4
Lujiang, *China* ... 59 B11
Lukang, *Taiwan* ... 59 E13
Lukanga Swamp, *Zambia* ... 87 E2
Lukavac, *Bos.-H.* ... 42 F3
Lukenie →, *Dem. Rep. of the Congo* ... 84 E3
Lukhisaral, *India* ... 69 G12
Lŭki, *Bulgaria* ... 41 E8
Lukolela, *Dem. Rep. of the Congo* ... 86 D1
Lukosi, *Zimbabwe* ... 87 F2
Lukovë, *Albania* ... 40 G3
Lukovit, *Bulgaria* ... 41 C8
Łuków, *Poland* ... 45 G9
Lukoyanov, *Russia* ... 48 C7
Lule älv →, *Sweden* ... 8 D19
Luleå, *Sweden* ... 8 D20
Lüleburgaz, *Turkey* ... 41 E11
Luliang, *China* ... 58 E4

Luling, *U.S.A.* ... 113 L6
Lulong, *China* ... 57 E10
Lulonga →, *Dem. Rep. of the Congo* ... 84 D3
Lulua →, *Dem. Rep. of the Congo* ... 84 E4
Lumajang, *Indonesia* ... 63 H15
Lumbala N'guimbo, *Angola* ... 85 G4
Lumberton, *U.S.A.* ... 109 H6
Lumbwa, *Kenya* ... 86 C4
Lumsden, *Canada* ... 105 C8
Lumsden, *N.Z.* ... 91 L2
Lumut, *Malaysia* ... 65 K3
Lumut, Tanjung, *Indonesia* ... 62 E3
Luna, *India* ... 68 H3
Lunan, *China* ... 58 E4
Lunavada, *India* ... 68 H5
Lunca, *Romania* ... 43 C10
Lunca Corbului, *Romania* ... 43 F9
Lund, *Sweden* ... 11 J7
Lundazi, *Zambia* ... 87 E3
Lunderskov, *Denmark* ... 11 J3
Lundi →, *Zimbabwe* ... 87 G3
Lundu, *Malaysia* ... 62 D3
Lundy, *U.K.* ... 13 F3
Lune →, *U.K.* ... 12 C5
Lüneburg, *Germany* ... 24 B6
Lüneburg Heath = Lüneburger Heide, *Germany* ... 24 B6
Lüneburger Heide, *Germany* ... 24 B6
Lunel, *France* ... 21 E8
Lünen, *Germany* ... 24 D3
Lunenburg, *Canada* ... 103 D7
Lunéville, *France* ... 19 D13
Lunga →, *Zambia* ... 87 E2
Lungi Airport, *S. Leone* ... 82 D2
Lunglei, *India* ... 67 H18
Luni, *India* ... 68 G5
Luni →, *India* ... 68 G4
Luninets = Luninyets, *Belarus* ... 47 F4
Luning, *U.S.A.* ... 114 G4
Lunino, *Russia* ... 48 D7
Luninyets, *Belarus* ... 47 F4
Lunkaransar, *India* ... 68 E5
Lunsemfwa →, *Zambia* ... 87 E3
Lunsemfwa Falls, *Zambia* ... 87 E2
Luo He →, *China* ... 56 G6
Luocheng, *China* ... 58 E7
Luochuan, *China* ... 56 G5
Luoci, *China* ... 58 E4
Luodian, *China* ... 58 E6
Luoding, *China* ... 59 F8
Luofu, *Dem. Rep. of the Congo* ... 86 C2
Luohe, *China* ... 56 H8
Luojiang, *China* ... 58 B5
Luonan, *China* ... 56 G6
Luoning, *China* ... 56 G6
Luoshan, *China* ... 59 A10
Luotian, *China* ... 59 B10
Luoxiao Shan, *China* ... 59 D10
Luoyang, *China* ... 56 G7
Luoyuan, *China* ... 59 D12
Luozigou, *China* ... 57 C16
Lupanshui, *China* ... 58 D5
Lupeni, *Romania* ... 43 E8
Lupilichi, *Mozam.* ... 87 E4
Łupków, *Poland* ... 45 J9
Lupoing, *China* ... 58 E5
Luquan, *China* ... 58 E4
Luque, *Paraguay* ... 126 B4
Lúras, *Italy* ... 30 B2
Luray, *U.S.A.* ... 108 F6
Lure, *France* ... 19 E13
Lurgan, *U.K.* ... 15 B5
Lusaka, *Zambia* ... 87 F2
Lusambo, *Dem. Rep. of the Congo* ... 86 C1
Lusangaye, *Dem. Rep. of the Congo* ... 86 C2
Luseland, *Canada* ... 105 C7
Lushan, *Henan, China* ... 56 H7
Lushan, *Sichuan, China* ... 58 B4
Lushi, *China* ... 56 G6
Lushnjë, *Albania* ... 40 F3
Lushoto, *Tanzania* ... 86 C4
Lushui, *China* ... 58 E2
Lüshun, *China* ... 57 E11
Lusignan, *France* ... 20 B4
Lusigny-sur-Barse, *France* ... 19 D11
Lusk, *U.S.A.* ... 112 D2
Lussac-les-Châteaux, *France* ... 20 B4
Lustenau, *Austria* ... 26 D2
Lüt, Dasht-e, *Iran* ... 71 D8
Luta = Dalian, *China* ... 57 E11
Lutherstadt Wittenberg, *Germany* ... 24 D8
Luton, *U.K.* ... 13 F7
Luton □, *U.K.* ... 13 F7
Lutselk'e, *Canada* ... 105 A6
Lutsk, *Ukraine* ... 47 G3
Lützow Holmbukta, *Antarctica* ... 5 C4
Lutzputs, *S. Africa* ... 88 D3
Luverne, *Ala., U.S.A.* ... 109 K2
Luverne, *Minn., U.S.A.* ... 112 D6
Luvua →, *Dem. Rep. of the Congo* ... 87 D2
Luvua →, *Dem. Rep. of the Congo* ... 86 D2
Luvuvhu →, *S. Africa* ... 89 C5
Luwegu →, *Tanzania* ... 87 D4
Luwuk, *Indonesia* ... 63 E6
Luxembourg, *Lux.* ... 17 E6
Luxembourg □, *Belgium* ... 17 E5
Luxembourg ■, *Europe* ... 7 F7
Luxeuil-les-Bains, *France* ... 19 E13
Luxi, *Hunan, China* ... 59 C8
Luxi, *Yunnan, China* ... 58 E4

Luxi, *Yunnan, China* ... 58 E2
Luxor = El Uqsur, *Egypt* ... 80 B3
Luy-de-Béarn →, *France* ... 20 E3
Luy-de-France →, *France* ... 20 E3
Luyi, *China* ... 56 H8
Luz-St-Sauveur, *France* ... 20 F4
Luzern, *Switz.* ... 25 H4
Luzern □, *Switz.* ... 25 H4
Luzhai, *China* ... 58 E7
Luzhou, *China* ... 58 C5
Luziânia, *Brazil* ... 125 G9
Lužnice →, *Czech Rep.* ... 26 B7
Luzon, *Phil.* ... 61 D4
Luzy, *France* ... 19 F10
Luzzi, *Italy* ... 31 C9
Lviv, *Ukraine* ... 47 H3
Lvov = Lviv, *Ukraine* ... 47 H3
Lwówek, *Poland* ... 45 F3
Lwówek Śląski, *Poland* ... 45 G2
Lyakhavichy, *Belarus* ... 47 F4
Lyaki = Läki, *Azerbaijan* ... 49 K8
Lyal I., *Canada* ... 110 B3
Lyallpur = Faisalabad, *Pakistan* ... 68 D5
Lyaskovets, *Bulgaria* ... 41 C9
Lybster, *U.K.* ... 14 C5
Lycaonia, *Turkey* ... 72 D5
Lychen, *Germany* ... 24 B9
Lychkova, *Russia* ... 46 D7
Lycia, *Turkey* ... 39 E11
Lyckeby →, *Sweden* ... 11 H9
Lycksele, *Sweden* ... 8 D18
Lycosura, *Greece* ... 38 D4
Lydda = Lod, *Israel* ... 75 D3
Lydenburg, *S. Africa* ... 89 D5
Lydia, *Turkey* ... 39 C10
Łydynia →, *Poland* ... 45 F7
Lyell, *N.Z.* ... 91 J4
Lyell I., *Canada* ... 104 C2
Lyepyel, *Belarus* ... 46 E5
Lygnern, *Sweden* ... 11 G6
Lykens, *U.S.A.* ... 111 F8
Lyman, *U.S.A.* ... 114 F8
Lyme B., *U.K.* ... 13 G4
Lyme Regis, *U.K.* ... 13 G5
Lymington, *U.K.* ... 13 G6
Lynchburg, *U.S.A.* ... 108 G6
Lynd →, *Australia* ... 94 B3
Lynd Ra., *Australia* ... 95 D4
Lynden, *Canada* ... 110 C4
Lynden, *U.S.A.* ... 116 B4
Lyndhurst, *Australia* ... 95 E2
Lyndon →, *Australia* ... 93 D1
Lyndonville, *N.Y., U.S.A.* ... 110 C6
Lyndonville, *Vt., U.S.A.* ... 111 B12
Lyngen, *Norway* ... 8 B19
Lynher Reef, *Australia* ... 92 C3
Lynn, *U.S.A.* ... 111 D14
Lynn Lake, *Canada* ... 105 B8
Lynnwood, *U.S.A.* ... 116 C4
Lynton, *U.K.* ... 13 F4
Lyntupy, *Belarus* ... 9 J22
Lynx L., *Canada* ... 105 A7
Lyon, *France* ... 21 C8
Lyonnais, *France* ... 21 C8
Lyons = Lyon, *France* ... 21 C8
Lyons, *Ga., U.S.A.* ... 109 J4
Lyons, *Kans., U.S.A.* ... 112 F5
Lyons, *N.Y., U.S.A.* ... 110 C8
Lyons →, *Australia* ... 93 E2
Lyons Falls, *U.S.A.* ... 111 C9
Lyozna, *Belarus* ... 46 E6
Lys = Leie →, *Belgium* ... 17 C3
Lysá nad Labem, *Czech Rep.* ... 26 A7
Lysekil, *Sweden* ... 11 F5
Lyskovo, *Russia* ... 48 B7
Lystrup, *Denmark* ... 11 H4
Lysvik, *Sweden* ... 10 D7
Lysychansk, *Ukraine* ... 47 H10
Lytham St. Anne's, *U.K.* ... 12 D4
Lyttelton, *N.Z.* ... 91 K4
Lytton, *Canada* ... 104 C4
Lyuban, *Russia* ... 46 C6
Lyubertsy, *Russia* ... 46 E9
Lyubim, *Russia* ... 46 C11
Lyubimets, *Bulgaria* ... 41 E10
Lyuboml, *Ukraine* ... 47 G3
Lyubotyn, *Ukraine* ... 47 H8
Lyubytino, *Russia* ... 46 C7
Lyudinovo, *Russia* ... 46 F8

M

M.R. Gomez, Presa, *Mexico* ... 119 B5
Ma →, *Vietnam* ... 58 H5
Ma'adaba, *Jordan* ... 75 D4
Maamba, *Zambia* ... 88 B4
Ma'ān, *Jordan* ... 75 E4
Ma'ān □, *Jordan* ... 75 F5
Maanselkä, *Finland* ... 8 C23
Ma'anshan, *China* ... 59 B12
Maarianhamina, *Finland* ... 9 F18
Ma'arrat an Nu'mān, *Syria* ... 70 C3
Maas →, *Neths.* ... 17 C4
Maaseik, *Belgium* ... 17 C5
Maastricht, *Neths.* ... 17 D5
Maave, *Mozam.* ... 89 C5
Mababe Depression, *Botswana* ... 88 B3
Mabalane, *Mozam.* ... 89 C5
Mabel L., *Canada* ... 104 C5

Mabenge, *Dem. Rep. of the Congo* ... 86 B1
Maberly, *Canada* ... 111 B8
Mabian, *China* ... 58 C4
Mabil, *Ethiopia* ... 81 E4
Mablethorpe, *U.K.* ... 12 D8
Mably, *France* ... 19 F11
Maboma, *Dem. Rep. of the Congo* ... 86 B2
Mabonto, *S. Leone* ... 82 D2
Mabrouk, *Mali* ... 83 B4
Mac Bac, *Vietnam* ... 65 H6
Macachín, *Argentina* ... 126 D3
Macaé, *Brazil* ... 127 A7
Macael, *Spain* ... 33 H2
Macão = Macau □, *China* ... 59 F9
Macão, *Portugal* ... 35 F3
Macapá, *Brazil* ... 125 C8
Macarthur, *Australia* ... 94 B2
McArthur, Port, *Australia* ... 94 B2
Macau, *Brazil* ... 125 E11
Macau □, *China* ... 59 F9
McBride, *Canada* ... 104 C4
McCall, *U.S.A.* ... 114 D5
McCamey, *U.S.A.* ... 113 K3
McCammon, *U.S.A.* ... 114 E7
McCauley I., *Canada* ... 104 C2
McCleary, *U.S.A.* ... 116 C3
Macclenny, *U.S.A.* ... 109 K4
Macclesfield, *U.K.* ... 12 D5
M'Clintock Chan., *Canada* ... 100 A9
McClintock Ra., *Australia* ... 92 C4
McCloud, *U.S.A.* ... 114 F2
McCluer I., *Australia* ... 92 B5
McClure, *U.S.A.* ... 110 F7
McClure, L., *U.S.A.* ... 116 H6
M'Clure Str., *Canada* ... 4 B2
McClusky, *U.S.A.* ... 112 B4
McComb, *U.S.A.* ... 113 K9
McConaughy, L., *U.S.A.* ... 112 E4
McCook, *U.S.A.* ... 112 E4
McCreary, *Canada* ... 105 C9
McCullough Mt., *U.S.A.* ... 117 K11
McCusker →, *Canada* ... 105 B7
McDame, *Canada* ... 104 B3
McDermitt, *U.S.A.* ... 114 F5
McDonald, *U.S.A.* ... 110 F4
Macdonald, L., *Australia* ... 92 D4
McDonald Is., *Ind. Oc.* ... 3 G13
MacDonnell Ranges, *Australia* ... 92 D5
MacDowell L., *Canada* ... 102 B1
Macduff, *U.K.* ... 14 D6
Maceda, *Spain* ... 34 C3
Macedonia, *U.S.A.* ... 110 E3
Macedonia ■, *Europe* ... 40 E5
Maceió, *Brazil* ... 125 E11
Maceira, *Portugal* ... 34 F2
Macenta, *Guinea* ... 82 D3
Macerata, *Italy* ... 29 E10
McFarland, *U.S.A.* ... 117 K7
McFarlane →, *Canada* ... 105 B7
McGehee, *U.S.A.* ... 113 J9
McGill, *U.S.A.* ... 114 G6
Macgillycuddy's Reeks, *Ireland* ... 15 E2
McGraw, *U.S.A.* ... 111 D8
McGregor, *U.S.A.* ... 112 D9
McGregor Ra., *Australia* ... 95 D3
Mach, *Pakistan* ... 66 E5
Māch Kowr, *Iran* ... 71 E9
Machado = Jiparaná →, *Brazil* ... 124 E6
Machagai, *Argentina* ... 126 B3
Machakos, *Kenya* ... 86 C4
Machala, *Ecuador* ... 124 D3
Machanga, *Mozam.* ... 89 C6
Machattie, L., *Australia* ... 94 C2
Machault, *France* ... 19 C11
Machava, *Mozam.* ... 89 D5
Machece, *Mozam.* ... 87 F4
Macheke, *Zimbabwe* ... 89 B5
Macheng, *China* ... 59 B10
Machero, *Spain* ... 35 F6
Machhu →, *India* ... 68 H4
Machias, *Maine, U.S.A.* ... 109 C12
Machias, *N.Y., U.S.A.* ... 110 D6
Machichi →, *Canada* ... 105 B10
Machico, *Madeira* ... 37 D3
Machilipatnam, *India* ... 67 L12
Machiques, *Venezuela* ... 124 A4
Machupicchu, *Peru* ... 124 F4
Machynlleth, *U.K.* ... 13 E4
Macia, *Mozam.* ... 89 D5
Maciejowice, *Poland* ... 45 G8
McIlwraith Ra., *Australia* ... 94 A3
Măcin, *Romania* ... 43 E13
Macina, *Mali* ... 82 C4
McInnes L., *Canada* ... 105 C10
McIntosh, *U.S.A.* ... 112 C4
McIntosh L., *Canada* ... 105 B8
Macintosh Ra., *Australia* ... 93 E4
Macintyre →, *Australia* ... 95 D5
Macizo Galaico, *Spain* ... 34 C3
Mackay, *Australia* ... 94 C4
Mackay, *U.S.A.* ... 114 E7
MacKay →, *Canada* ... 104 B6
Mackay, L., *Australia* ... 92 D4
McKay Ra., *Australia* ... 92 D3
McKeesport, *U.S.A.* ... 110 F5
McKellar, *Canada* ... 110 A5
McKenna, *U.S.A.* ... 116 D4
Mackenzie, *Canada* ... 104 B4
McKenzie, *U.S.A.* ... 109 G1

Mackenzie →, *Australia* ... 94 C4
Mackenzie →, *Canada* ... 100 B6
McKenzie →, *U.S.A.* ... 114 D2
Mackenzie Bay, *Canada* ... 4 B1
Mackenzie City = Linden, *Guyana* ... 124 B7
Mackenzie Mts., *Canada* ... 100 B6
Mackinaw City, *U.S.A.* ... 108 C3
McKinlay, *Australia* ... 94 C3
McKinlay →, *Australia* ... 94 C3
McKinley, Mt., *U.S.A.* ... 100 B4
McKinley Sea, *Arctic* ... 4 A7
McKinney, *U.S.A.* ... 113 J6
Mackinnon Road, *Kenya* ... 86 C4
McKittrick, *U.S.A.* ... 117 K7
Macklin, *Canada* ... 105 C7
McLaughlin, *U.S.A.* ... 112 C4
Maclean, *Australia* ... 95 D5
McLean, *U.S.A.* ... 113 H4
McLeansboro, *U.S.A.* ... 112 F10
Maclear, *S. Africa* ... 89 E4
McLennan, *Canada* ... 104 B5
McLeod →, *Canada* ... 104 C5
McLeod, B., *Canada* ... 105 A7
McLeod, L., *Australia* ... 93 D1
MacLeod Lake, *Canada* ... 104 C4
McLoughlin, Mt., *U.S.A.* ... 114 E2
McMechen, *U.S.A.* ... 110 G4
McMinnville, *Oreg., U.S.A.* ... 114 D2
McMinnville, *Tenn., U.S.A.* ... 109 H3
McMurdo Sd., *Antarctica* ... 5 D11
McMurray = Fort McMurray, *Canada* ... 104 B6
McMurray, *U.S.A.* ... 116 B4
Macodoene, *Mozam.* ... 89 C6
Macomb, *U.S.A.* ... 112 E9
Macomer, *Italy* ... 30 B1
Mâcon, *France* ... 19 F11
Macon, *Ga., U.S.A.* ... 109 J4
Macon, *Miss., U.S.A.* ... 109 J1
Macon, *Mo., U.S.A.* ... 112 F8
Macossa, *Mozam.* ... 87 F3
Macoun L., *Canada* ... 105 B8
Macovane, *Mozam.* ... 89 C6
McPherson, *U.S.A.* ... 112 F6
McPherson Pk., *U.S.A.* ... 117 L7
McPherson Ra., *Australia* ... 95 D5
Macquarie →, *Australia* ... 95 E4
Macquarie Harbour, *Australia* ... 94 G4
Macquarie Is., *Pac. Oc.* ... 96 N7
MacRobertson Land, *Antarctica* ... 5 D6
Macroom, *Ireland* ... 15 E3
MacTier, *Canada* ... 110 A5
Macubela, *Mozam.* ... 87 F4
Macugnaga, *Italy* ... 28 C4
Macuiza, *Mozam.* ... 87 F3
Macusani, *Peru* ... 124 F4
Macuse, *Mozam.* ... 87 F4
Macuspana, *Mexico* ... 119 D6
Macusse, *Angola* ... 88 B3
Mada →, *Nigeria* ... 83 D6
Madadeni, *S. Africa* ... 89 D5
Madagali, *Nigeria* ... 83 C7
Madagascar ■, *Africa* ... 89 C8
Madā'in Sālih, *Si. Arabia* ... 70 E3
Madama, *Niger* ... 79 D8
Madame I., *Canada* ... 103 C7
Madan, *Bulgaria* ... 41 E8
Madaoua, *Niger* ... 83 C6
Madara, *Nigeria* ... 83 C7
Madaripur, *Bangla.* ... 67 H17
Madauk, *Burma* ... 67 L20
Madawaska, *Canada* ... 110 A7
Madawaska →, *Canada* ... 102 C4
Madaya, *Burma* ... 67 H20
Madbar, *Sudan* ... 81 F3
Maddalena, *Italy* ... 30 A2
Maddaloni, *Italy* ... 31 A7
Madeira, *Atl. Oc.* ... 37 D3
Madeira →, *Brazil* ... 125 D7
Madeleine, Îs. de la, *Canada* ... 103 C7
Maden, *Turkey* ... 73 C8
Madera, *Mexico* ... 118 B3
Madera, *Calif., U.S.A.* ... 116 J6
Madera, *Pa., U.S.A.* ... 110 F6
Madha, *India* ... 66 L9
Madhavpur, *India* ... 68 J3
Madhepura, *India* ... 69 F12
Madhubani, *India* ... 69 F12
Madhupur, *India* ... 69 G12
Madhya Pradesh □, *India* ... 68 J8
Madidi →, *Bolivia* ... 124 F5
Madikeri, *India* ... 66 N9
Madill, *U.S.A.* ... 113 H6
Madimba, *Dem. Rep. of the Congo* ... 84 E3
Ma'din, *Syria* ... 70 C3
Madina, *Mali* ... 82 C3
Madinani, *Ivory C.* ... 82 D3
Madingou, *Congo* ... 84 E2
Madirovalo, *Madag.* ... 89 B8
Madison, *Calif., U.S.A.* ... 116 G5
Madison, *Fla., U.S.A.* ... 109 K4
Madison, *Ind., U.S.A.* ... 108 F3
Madison, *Nebr., U.S.A.* ... 112 E6
Madison, *Ohio, U.S.A.* ... 110 E3
Madison, *S. Dak., U.S.A.* ... 112 D6
Madison, *Wis., U.S.A.* ... 112 D10
Madison →, *U.S.A.* ... 114 D8
Madison Heights, *U.S.A.* ... 108 G6
Madisonville, *Ky., U.S.A.* ... 108 G2
Madisonville, *Tex., U.S.A.* ... 113 K7
Madista, *Botswana* ... 88 C4
Madiun, *Indonesia* ... 62 F4
Madoc, *Canada* ... 110 B7
Madol, *Sudan* ... 81 F2

Madon →, *France* 19 **D13**
Madona, *Latvia* 9 **H22**
Madonie, *Italy* 30 **E6**
Madonna di Campíglio, *Italy* .. 28 **B7**
Madra Daği, *Turkey* 39 **B9**
Madrakah, Ra's al, *Oman* 74 **D6**
Madras = Chennai, *India* 66 **N12**
Madras = Tamil Nadu □, *India* 66 **P10**
Madras, *U.S.A.* 114 **D3**
Madre, Laguna, *U.S.A.* 113 **M6**
Madre, Sierra, *Phil.* 61 **C5**
Madre de Dios →, *Bolivia* ... 122 **E4**
Madre de Dios, I., *Chile* 122 **J3**
Madre del Sur, Sierra, *Mexico* . 119 **D5**
Madre Occidental, Sierra,
 Mexico 118 **B3**
Madre Oriental, Sierra, *Mexico* 118 **C5**
Madri, *India* 68 **G5**
Madrid, *Spain* 34 **E7**
Madrid, *U.S.A.* 111 **B9**
Madrid □, *Spain* 34 **E7**
Madridejos, *Spain* 35 **F7**
Madrigal de las Altas Torres,
 Spain 34 **D6**
Madrona, Sierra, *Spain* 35 **G6**
Madroñera, *Spain* 35 **F5**
Madu, *Sudan* 81 **E2**
Madura, *Australia* 93 **F4**
Madura, *Indonesia* 63 **G15**
Madura, Selat, *Indonesia* 63 **G15**
Madurai, *India* 66 **Q11**
Madurantakam, *India* 66 **N11**
Madzhalis, *Russia* 49 **J8**
Mae Chan, *Thailand* 64 **B2**
Mae Hong Son, *Thailand* 64 **C2**
Mae Khlong →, *Thailand* 64 **F3**
Mae Phrik, *Thailand* 64 **D2**
Mae Ramat, *Thailand* 64 **D2**
Mae Rim, *Thailand* 64 **C2**
Mae Sot, *Thailand* 64 **D2**
Mae Suai, *Thailand* 58 **H2**
Mae Tha, *Thailand* 64 **C2**
Maebashi, *Japan* 55 **F9**
Maella, *Spain* 32 **D5**
Maesteg, *U.K.* 13 **F4**
Maestra, Sierra, *Cuba* 120 **B4**
Maevatanana, *Madag.* 89 **B8**
Mafeking = Mafikeng, *S. Africa* 88 **D4**
Mafeking, *Canada* 105 **C8**
Maféré, *Ivory C.* 82 **D4**
Mafeteng, *Lesotho* 88 **D4**
Mafia I., *Tanzania* 86 **D4**
Mafikeng, *S. Africa* 88 **D4**
Mafra, *Brazil* 127 **B6**
Mafra, *Portugal* 35 **G1**
Mafungabusi Plateau, *Zimbabwe* 87 **F2**
Magadan, *Russia* 51 **D16**
Magadi, *Kenya* 86 **C4**
Magadi, L., *Kenya* 86 **C4**
Magaliesburg, *S. Africa* 89 **D4**
Magallanes, Estrecho de, *Chile* 122 **J3**
Magaluf, *Spain* 33 **F7**
Magangué, *Colombia* 124 **B4**
Magaria, *Niger* 83 **C6**
Magburaka, *S. Leone* 82 **D2**
Magdalen Is. = Madeleine, Ís. de
 la, *Canada* 103 **C7**
Magdalena, *Argentina* 126 **D4**
Magdalena, *Bolivia* 124 **F6**
Magdalena, *Mexico* 118 **A2**
Magdalena, *U.S.A.* 115 **J10**
Magdalena →, *Colombia* 122 **B3**
Magdalena →, *Mexico* 118 **A2**
Magdalena, B., *Mexico* 118 **C2**
Magdalena, Llano de la, *Mexico* 118 **C2**
Magdeburg, *Germany* 24 **C7**
Magdelaine Cays, *Australia* .. 94 **B5**
Magdub, *Sudan* 81 **E2**
Magee, *U.S.A.* 113 **K10**
Magelang, *Indonesia* 62 **F4**
Magellan's Str. = Magallanes,
 Estrecho de, *Chile* 122 **J3**
Magenta, *Italy* 28 **C5**
Magenta, *Australia* 93 **F2**
Magerøya, *Norway* 8 **A21**
Maggia →, *Switz.* 25 **J4**
Maggiorasca, Mte., *Italy* 28 **D6**
Maggiore, Lago, *Italy* 28 **C5**
Maghâgha, *Egypt* 80 **B3**
Maghama, *Mauritania* 82 **B2**
Magherafelt, *U.K.* 15 **B5**
Maghreb, *N. Afr.* 78 **B5**
Magione, *Italy* 29 **E9**
Magistralnyy, *Russia* 51 **D11**
Maglaj, *Bos.-H.* 42 **F3**
Magliano in Toscana, *Italy* ... 29 **F8**
Máglie, *Italy* 31 **B11**
Magnac-Laval, *France* 20 **B5**
Magnetic Pole (North) = North
 Magnetic Pole, *Canada* .. 4 **B2**
Magnetic Pole (South) = South
 Magnetic Pole, *Antarctica* . 5 **C9**
Magnisía □, *Greece* 38 **B5**
Magnitogorsk, *Russia* 50 **D6**
Magnolia, *Ark., U.S.A.* 113 **J8**
Magnolia, *Miss., U.S.A.* 113 **K9**
Magny-en-Vexin, *France* 19 **C8**
Magog, *Canada* 103 **C5**
Magoro, *Uganda* 86 **B3**
Magosa = Famagusta, *Cyprus* . 36 **D12**
Magouládhes, *Greece* 36 **A3**
Magoye, *Zambia* 87 **F2**
Magozal, *Mexico* 119 **C5**
Magpie, L., *Canada* 103 **B7**
Magrath, *Canada* 104 **D6**
Magre →, *Spain* 33 **F4**

Magrur, *Sudan* 81 **E3**
Magrur, Wadi →, *Sudan* 81 **D2**
Magta Lahjar, *Mauritania* ... 82 **B2**
Maguan, *China* 58 **F5**
Maguarinho, C., *Brazil* 125 **D9**
Magude, *Mozam.* 89 **D5**
Maguse L., *Canada* 105 **A9**
Maguse Pt., *Canada* 105 **A10**
Magvana, *India* 68 **H3**
Magwe, *Burma* 67 **J19**
Magwe, *Sudan* 81 **G3**
Maha Sarakham, *Thailand* ... 64 **D4**
Mahābād, *Iran* 70 **B5**
Mahabharat Lekh, *Nepal* 69 **E10**
Mahabo, *Madag.* 89 **C7**
Mahadeo Hills, *India* 69 **H8**
Mahaffey, *U.S.A.* 110 **F6**
Mahagi, *Dem. Rep. of the Congo* 86 **B3**
Mahajamba →, *Madag.* 89 **B8**
Mahajamba, Helodranon' i,
 Madag. 89 **B8**
Mahajan, *India* 68 **E5**
Mahajanga, *Madag.* 89 **B8**
Mahajanga □, *Madag.* 89 **B8**
Mahajilo →, *Madag.* 89 **B8**
Mahakam →, *Indonesia* 62 **E5**
Mahalapye, *Botswana* 88 **C4**
Mahallāt, *Iran* 71 **C6**
Māhān, *Iran* 71 **D8**
Mahan →, *India* 69 **H10**
Mahanadi →, *India* 67 **J15**
Mahananda →, *India* 69 **G12**
Mahanoro, *Madag.* 89 **B8**
Mahanoy City, *U.S.A.* 111 **F8**
Maharashtra □, *India* 66 **J9**
Mahari Mts., *Tanzania* 86 **D3**
Mahasham, W. →, *Egypt* 75 **E3**
Mahasoa, *Madag.* 89 **C8**
Mahasolo, *Madag.* 89 **B8**
Mahattat ash Shīdīyah, *Jordan* 75 **F4**
Mahattat 'Unayzah, *Jordan* .. 75 **E4**
Mahavavy →, *Madag.* 89 **B8**
Mahaxay, *Laos* 64 **D5**
Mahbubnagar, *India* 66 **L10**
Mahdah, *Oman* 71 **E7**
Mahdia, *Tunisia* 79 **A8**
Mahe, *India* 69 **C8**
Mahendragarh, *India* 68 **E7**
Mahenge, *Tanzania* 87 **D4**
Maheno, *N.Z.* 91 **L3**
Mahesana, *India* 68 **H5**
Maheshwar, *India* 68 **H6**
Mahgawan, *India* 69 **F8**
Mahia Pen., *N.Z.* 91 **H6**
Mahilyow, *Belarus* 46 **F6**
Mahmiya, *Sudan* 81 **D3**
Mahmud Kot, *Pakistan* 68 **D4**
Mahmudia, *Romania* 43 **E14**
Mahmudiye, *Turkey* 39 **B12**
Mahmutbey, *Turkey* 41 **E12**
Mahnomen, *U.S.A.* 112 **B7**
Mahoba, *India* 69 **G8**
Mahón = Maó, *Spain* 37 **B11**
Mahone Bay, *Canada* 103 **D7**
Mahopac, *U.S.A.* 111 **E11**
Mahuta, *Nigeria* 83 **C5**
Mahuva, *India* 68 **J4**
Mahya Daği, *Turkey* 41 **E11**
Mai-Ndombe, L., *Dem. Rep. of
 the Congo* 84 **E3**
Mai-Sai, *Thailand* 58 **G2**
Maia, *Portugal* 34 **D2**
Maia, *Spain* 32 **B3**
Maials, *Spain* 32 **D5**
Maîche, *France* 19 **E13**
Maicurú →, *Brazil* 125 **D8**
Máida, *Italy* 31 **D9**
Maidan Khula, *Afghan.* 68 **C3**
Maidenhead, *U.K.* 13 **F7**
Maidstone, *Canada* 105 **C7**
Maidstone, *U.K.* 13 **F8**
Maiduguri, *Nigeria* 83 **C7**
Măieruş, *Romania* 43 **E10**
Maigatari, *Nigeria* 83 **C6**
Maignelay Montigny, *France* . 19 **C9**
Maigo, *Phil.* 61 **G5**
Maigudo, *Ethiopia* 81 **F4**
Maihar, *India* 69 **G9**
Maijdi, *Bangla.* 67 **H17**
Maikala Ra., *India* 67 **J12**
Mailani, *India* 69 **E9**
Maillezais, *France* 20 **B3**
Mailsi, *Pakistan* 68 **E5**
Main →, *Germany* 25 **F4**
Main →, *U.K.* 15 **B5**
Mainburg, *Germany* 25 **G7**
Maine, *France* 18 **D6**
Maine →, *Ireland* 15 **D2**
Maine □, *U.S.A.* 109 **C11**
Maine-et-Loire □, *France* 18 **E6**
Maïne-Soroa, *Niger* 83 **C7**
Maingkwan, *Burma* 67 **F20**
Mainit, L., *Phil.* 61 **G6**
Mainland, *Orkney, U.K.* 14 **C5**
Mainland, *Shet., U.K.* 14 **A7**
Mainoru, *Australia* 94 **A1**
Mainpuri, *India* 69 **F8**
Maintirano, *Madag.* 89 **B7**
Mainz, *Germany* 25 **F4**
Maipú, *Argentina* 126 **D4**
Maiquetía, *Venezuela* 124 **A5**
Máira →, *Italy* 28 **D4**

Mairabari, *India* 67 **F18**
Maisí, *Cuba* 121 **B5**
Maisí, Pta. de, *Cuba* 121 **B5**
Maitland →, *Canada* 110 **C3**
Maiyema, *Nigeria* 83 **C5**
Maiyuan, *China* 59 **E11**
Maizuru, *Japan* 55 **G7**
Maiz, Is. del, *Nic.* 120 **D3**
Majalengka, *Indonesia* 63 **G13**
Majene, *Indonesia* 63 **E5**
Maji, *Ethiopia* 81 **F4**
Majiang, *China* 58 **D6**
Majorca = Mallorca, *Spain* .. 37 **B10**
Maka, *Senegal* 82 **C2**
Makaha, *Zimbabwe* 89 **B5**
Makak, *Cameroon* 83 **E7**
Makalamabedi, *Botswana* ... 88 **C3**
Makale, *Indonesia* 63 **E5**
Makamba, *Burundi* 86 **C2**
Makari, *Cameroon* 83 **C7**
Makarikari = Makgadikgadi Salt
 Pans, *Botswana* 88 **C4**
Makarovo, *Russia* 51 **D11**
Makarska, *Croatia* 29 **E14**
Makaryev, *Russia* 48 **B6**
Makasar = Ujung Pandang,
 Indonesia 63 **F5**
Makasar, Selat, *Indonesia* ... 63 **E5**
Makasar, Str. of = Makasar,
 Selat, *Indonesia* 63 **E5**
Makat, *Kazakstan* 50 **E6**
Makedonija = Macedonia ■,
 Europe 40 **E5**
Makeni, *S. Leone* 82 **D2**
Makeyevka = Makiyivka,
 Ukraine 47 **H9**
Makgadikgadi Salt Pans,
 Botswana 88 **C4**
Makhachkala, *Russia* 49 **J8**
Makharadze = Ozurgeti, *Georgia* 49 **K5**
Makhmūr, *Iraq* 70 **C4**
Makian, *Indonesia* 63 **D7**
Makindu, *Kenya* 86 **C4**
Makinsk, *Kazakstan* 50 **D8**
Makiyivka, *Ukraine* 47 **H9**
Makkah, *Si. Arabia* 74 **C2**
Makkovik, *Canada* 103 **A8**
Makó, *Hungary* 42 **D5**
Mako, *Senegal* 82 **C2**
Makokou, *Gabon* 84 **D2**
Makongo, *Dem. Rep. of
 the Congo* 86 **B2**
Makoro, *Dem. Rep. of the Congo* 86 **B2**
Maków Mazowiecki, *Poland* .. 45 **F8**
Maków Podhalański, *Poland* .. 45 **J6**
Makrá, *Greece* 39 **E7**
Makrai, *India* 66 **H10**
Makran Coast Range, *Pakistan* 66 **G4**
Makrana, *India* 68 **F6**
Mákri, *Greece* 41 **F9**
Makriyialos, *Greece* 36 **D7**
Mākū, *Iran* 70 **B5**
Makunda, *Botswana* 88 **C3**
Makung, *Taiwan* 59 **F12**
Makurazaki, *Japan* 55 **J5**
Makurdi, *Nigeria* 83 **D6**
Makūyeh, *Iran* 71 **D7**
Makwassie, *S. Africa* 88 **D4**
Makwiro, *Zimbabwe* 89 **B5**
Mâl, *Mauritania* 82 **B2**
Mal B., *Ireland* 15 **D2**
Mala, Pta., *Panama* 120 **E3**
Mala Belozërka, *Ukraine* 47 **J8**
Mala Kapela, *Croatia* 29 **D12**
Mała Panew →, *Poland* 45 **H4**
Mala Vyska, *Ukraine* 47 **H6**
Malabang, *Phil.* 61 **H6**
Malabar Coast, *India* 66 **P9**
Malabo = Rey Malabo,
 Eq. Guin. 83 **E6**
Malabon, *Phil.* 61 **D4**
Malabu, *Nigeria* 83 **D7**
Malacca, Str. of, *Indonesia* .. 65 **L3**
Malacky, *Slovak Rep.* 27 **C10**
Malad City, *U.S.A.* 114 **E7**
Maladeta, *Spain* 32 **C5**
Maladzyechna, *Belarus* 46 **E4**
Málaga, *Spain* 35 **J6**
Málaga □, *Spain* 35 **J6**
Malagarasi, *Tanzania* 86 **D3**
Malagarasi →, *Tanzania* 86 **D2**
Malagasy Rep. = Madagascar ■,
 Africa 89 **C8**
Malagón, *Spain* 35 **F7**
Malagón →, *Spain* 35 **H3**
Malahide, *Ireland* 15 **C5**
Malaimbandy, *Madag.* 89 **C8**
Malakâl, *Sudan* 81 **F3**
Malakand, *Pakistan* 68 **B4**
Malakwal, *Pakistan* 68 **C5**
Malamala, *Indonesia* 63 **E6**
Malanda, *Australia* 94 **B4**
Malang, *Indonesia* 63 **G15**
Malangen, *Norway* 8 **B18**
Malanje, *Angola* 84 **F3**
Mälaren, *Sweden* 10 **E11**
Malargüe, *Argentina* 126 **D2**
Malartic, *Canada* 102 **C4**
Malaryta, *Belarus* 47 **G3**
Malatya, *Turkey* 70 **B3**
Malawi ■, *Africa* 87 **E3**
Malawi, L. = Nyasa, L., *Africa* 87 **E3**
Malay Pen., *Asia* 65 **J3**
Malaya Belozërka = Mala
 Belozërka, *Ukraine* 47 **J8**

Malaya Vishera, *Russia* 46 **C7**
Malaya Viska = Mala Vyska,
 Ukraine 47 **H6**
Malaybalay, *Phil.* 61 **G6**
Malāyer, *Iran* 71 **C6**
Malaysia ■, *Asia* 65 **K4**
Malazgirt, *Turkey* 70 **B4**
Malbaza, *Niger* 83 **C6**
Malbon, *Australia* 94 **C3**
Malbooma, *Australia* 95 **E1**
Malbork, *Poland* 44 **D6**
Malcésine, *Italy* 28 **C7**
Malchin, *Germany* 24 **B8**
Malchow, *Germany* 24 **B8**
Malcolm, *Australia* 93 **E3**
Malcolm, Pt., *Australia* 93 **F3**
Malczyce, *Poland* 45 **G3**
Maldah, *India* 69 **G13**
Maldegem, *Belgium* 17 **C3**
Malden, *Mass., U.S.A.* 111 **D13**
Malden, *Mo., U.S.A.* 113 **G10**
Malden I., *Kiribati* 97 **H12**
Maldives ■, *Ind. Oc.* 52 **J11**
Maldonado, *Uruguay* 127 **C5**
Maldonado, Punta, *Mexico* .. 119 **D5**
Malé, *Italy* 28 **B7**
Malé, *Maldives* 53 **J11**
Malé Karpaty, *Slovak Rep.* .. 27 **C10**
Maléa, Ákra, *Greece* 38 **E5**
Malegaon, *India* 66 **J9**
Malei, *Mozam.* 87 **F4**
Malek, *Sudan* 81 **F3**
Malek Kandī, *Iran* 70 **B5**
Malela, *Dem. Rep. of the Congo* 86 **C2**
Malema, *Mozam.* 87 **E4**
Máleme, *Greece* 36 **D5**
Maleny, *Australia* 95 **D5**
Mälerås, *Sweden* 11 **H9**
Malerkotla, *India* 68 **D6**
Máles, *Greece* 36 **D7**
Malesherbes, *France* 19 **D9**
Malesína, *Greece* 38 **C5**
Malestroit, *France* 18 **E4**
Malfa, *Italy* 31 **D7**
Malgobek, *Russia* 49 **J7**
Malgomaj, *Sweden* 8 **D17**
Malgrat = Malgrat de Mar, *Spain* 32 **D7**
Malgrat de Mar, *Spain* 32 **D7**
Malha, *Sudan* 81 **D2**
Malhargarh, *India* 68 **G6**
Malheur →, *U.S.A.* 114 **D5**
Malheur L., *U.S.A.* 114 **E4**
Mali, *Guinea* 82 **C2**
Mali ■, *Africa* 82 **C4**
Mali →, *Burma* 67 **G20**
Mali Kanal, *Serbia, Yug.* 42 **E4**
Mali Kyun, *Burma* 64 **F2**
Malibu, *U.S.A.* 117 **L8**
Maliku, *Indonesia* 63 **E6**
Malili, *Indonesia* 63 **E6**
Målilla, *Sweden* 11 **G9**
Malimba, Mts., *Dem. Rep. of
 the Congo* 86 **D2**
Malin Hd., *Ireland* 15 **A4**
Malin Pen., *Ireland* 15 **A4**
Malindi, *Kenya* 86 **C5**
Malines = Mechelen, *Belgium* . 17 **C4**
Malino, *Indonesia* 63 **D6**
Malinyi, *Tanzania* 87 **D4**
Malipo, *China* 58 **F5**
Maliq, *Albania* 40 **F4**
Malita, *Phil.* 63 **C7**
Maliwun, *Burma* 62 **B1**
Maliya, *India* 68 **H4**
Maljenik, *Serbia, Yug.* 40 **C5**
Malkara, *Turkey* 41 **F10**
Malkinia Górna, *Poland* 45 **F9**
Malko Tŭrnovo, *Bulgaria* ... 41 **E11**
Mallaig, *U.K.* 14 **D3**
Mallaoua, *Niger* 83 **C6**
Mallawan, *India* 69 **F9**
Mallawi, *Egypt* 80 **B3**
Mallemort, *France* 21 **E9**
Málles Venosta, *Italy* 28 **B7**
Mállia, *Greece* 36 **D7**
Mallión, Kólpos, *Greece* 36 **D7**
Mallorca, *Spain* 37 **B10**
Mallorytown, *Canada* 111 **B9**
Mallow, *Ireland* 15 **D3**
Malmbäck, *Sweden* 11 **G8**
Malmberget, *Sweden* 8 **C19**
Malmédy, *Belgium* 17 **D6**
Malmesbury, *S. Africa* 88 **E2**
Malmköping, *Sweden* 10 **E10**
Malmö, *Sweden* 11 **J6**
Malmslätt, *Sweden* 11 **F9**
Malmyzh, *Russia* 48 **B10**
Malnaş, *Romania* 43 **D10**
Malo Konare, *Bulgaria* 41 **D8**
Maloarkhangelsk, *Russia* ... 47 **F9**
Malolos, *Phil.* 61 **D4**
Malombe L., *Malawi* 87 **E4**
Malomice, *Poland* 45 **G2**
Malomir, *Bulgaria* 41 **D10**
Malone, *U.S.A.* 111 **B10**
Malong, *China* 58 **E4**
Małopolskie □, *Poland* 45 **J7**
Malorad, *Bulgaria* 41 **C8**
Måløy, *Norway* 9 **F11**
Maloyaroslovets, *Russia* 46 **E9**
Malpartida, *Spain* 35 **F4**
Malpaso, *Canary Is.* 37 **G1**
Malpelo, I. de, *Colombia* 124 **C2**
Malpica de Bergantiños, *Spain* . 34 **B2**
Malpur, *India* 68 **H5**

Malpura, *India* 68 **F6**
Mals = Málles Venosta, *Italy* . 28 **B7**
Malta, *Idaho, U.S.A.* 114 **E7**
Malta, *Mont., U.S.A.* 114 **B10**
Malta ■, *Europe* 36 **D2**
Maltahöhe, *Namibia* 88 **C2**
Malton, *Canada* 110 **C5**
Malton, *U.K.* 12 **C7**
Maluku, *Indonesia* 63 **E7**
Maluku □, *Indonesia* 63 **E7**
Maluku Sea = Molucca Sea,
 Indonesia 63 **E6**
Malumfashi, *Nigeria* 83 **C6**
Malung, *Sweden* 10 **D7**
Malungsfors, *Sweden* 10 **D7**
Maluwe, *Ghana* 82 **D4**
Malvan, *India* 66 **L8**
Malvern, *U.S.A.* 113 **H8**
Malvern Hills, *U.K.* 13 **E5**
Malvinas, Is. = Falkland Is. □,
 Atl. Oc. 128 **G5**
Malý Dunaj →, *Slovak Rep.* .. 27 **D11**
Malya, *Tanzania* 86 **C3**
Malyn, *Ukraine* 47 **G5**
Malyy Lyakhovskiy, Ostrov,
 Russia 51 **B15**
Mama, *Russia* 51 **D12**
Mamadysh, *Russia* 48 **C10**
Mamanguape, *Brazil* 125 **E11**
Mamarr Mitlā, *Egypt* 75 **E1**
Mamasa, *Indonesia* 63 **E5**
Mambasa, *Dem. Rep. of
 the Congo* 86 **B2**
Mamberamo →, *Indonesia* .. 63 **E9**
Mambilima Falls, *Zambia* ... 87 **E2**
Mambirima, *Dem. Rep. of
 the Congo* 87 **E2**
Mambo, *Tanzania* 86 **C4**
Mambrui, *Kenya* 86 **C5**
Mamburao, *Phil.* 61 **E4**
Mameigwess L., *Canada* 102 **B2**
Mamers, *France* 18 **D7**
Mamfé, *Cameroon* 83 **D6**
Mammoth, *U.S.A.* 115 **K8**
Mammoth Cave National Park,
 U.S.A. 108 **G3**
Mamoré →, *Bolivia* 122 **E4**
Mamou, *Guinea* 82 **C2**
Mampatá, *Guinea-Biss.* 82 **C2**
Mampikony, *Madag.* 89 **B8**
Mampong, *Ghana* 83 **D4**
Mamry, Jezioro, *Poland* 44 **D8**
Mamuju, *Indonesia* 63 **E5**
Mamuno, *Botswana* 88 **C3**
Mamuras, *Albania* 40 **E3**
Man, *Ivory C.* 82 **D3**
Man, I. of, *U.K.* 12 **C3**
Man-Bazar, *India* 69 **H12**
Man Na, *Burma* 67 **H20**
Mana →, *Fr. Guiana* 125 **B8**
Manaar, G. of = Mannar, G. of,
 Asia 66 **Q11**
Manacapuru, *Brazil* 124 **D6**
Manacor, *Spain* 37 **B10**
Manado, *Indonesia* 63 **D6**
Managua, *Nic.* 120 **D2**
Managua, L. de, *Nic.* 120 **D2**
Manakara, *Madag.* 89 **C8**
Manali, *India* 68 **C7**
Manama = Al Manāmah,
 Bahrain 71 **E6**
Manambao →, *Madag.* 89 **B7**
Manambato, *Madag.* 89 **A8**
Manambolo →, *Madag.* 89 **B7**
Manambolosy, *Madag.* 89 **B8**
Mananara →, *Madag.* 89 **B8**
Mananjary, *Madag.* 89 **C8**
Manankoro, *Mali* 82 **C3**
Manantenina, *Madag.* 89 **C8**
Manaos = Manaus, *Brazil* ... 124 **D7**
Manapire →, *Venezuela* 124 **B5**
Manapouri, *N.Z.* 91 **L1**
Manapouri, L., *N.Z.* 91 **L1**
Manaqil, *Sudan* 81 **E3**
Manār, Jabal, *Yemen* 74 **E3**
Manaravolo, *Madag.* 89 **C8**
Manas, *China* 60 **B3**
Manas →, *India* 67 **F17**
Manaslu, *Nepal* 69 **E11**
Manasquan, *U.S.A.* 111 **F10**
Manassa, *U.S.A.* 115 **H11**
Manaung, *Burma* 67 **K18**
Manaus, *Brazil* 124 **D7**
Manavgat, *Turkey* 72 **D4**
Manawan L., *Canada* 105 **B8**
Manay, *Phil.* 61 **H7**
Manbij, *Syria* 70 **B3**
Mancha Real, *Spain* 35 **H7**
Manche □, *France* 18 **C5**
Manchegorsk, *Russia* ......
Manchester, *U.K.* 12 **D5**
Manchester, *Calif., U.S.A.* .. 116 **G3**
Manchester, *Conn., U.S.A.* .. 111 **E12**
Manchester, *Ga., U.S.A.* ... 109 **J3**
Manchester, *Iowa, U.S.A.* .. 112 **D9**
Manchester, *Ky., U.S.A.* ... 108 **G4**
Manchester, *N.H., U.S.A.* .. 111 **D13**
Manchester, *N.Y., U.S.A.* .. 110 **D7**
Manchester, *Pa., U.S.A.* ... 111 **F8**
Manchester, *Tenn., U.S.A.* . 109 **H2**
Manchester, *Vt., U.S.A.* ... 111 **C11**
Manchester, *L., Canada* 105 **A7**
Manchhar L., *Pakistan* 68 **F2**
Manchuria = Dongbei, *China* . 57 **D13**

Manchurian Plain, *China* 52 E16
Manciano, *Italy* 29 F8
Mancifa, *Ethiopia* 81 F5
Mand →, *India* 69 J10
Mand →, *Iran* 71 D7
Manda, *Ludewe, Tanzania* .. 87 E3
Manda, *Mbeya, Tanzania* 86 D3
Manda, *Mbeya, Tanzania* 87 D3
Mandabé, *Madag.* 89 C7
Mandaguari, *Brazil* 127 A5
Mandah = Töhöm, *Mongolia* .. 56 B5
Mandal, *Norway* 9 G12
Mandala, Puncak, *Indonesia* ... 63 E10
Mandalay, *Burma* 67 J20
Mandale = Mandalay, *Burma* .. 67 J20
Mandalgarh, *India* 68 G6
Mandalgovi, *Mongolia* 56 B4
Mandalī, *Iraq* 70 C5
Mandan, *U.S.A.* 112 B4
Mandaon, *Phil.* 61 E5
Mandar, Teluk, *Indonesia* 63 E5
Mándas, *Italy* 30 C2
Mandaue, *Phil.* 61 F5
Mandelieu-la-Napoule, *France* . 21 E10
Mandera, *Kenya* 86 B5
Mandi, *India* 68 D7
Mandi Dabwali, *India* 68 E6
Mandiana, *Guinea* 82 C3
Mandimba, *Mozam.* 87 E4
Mandioli, *Indonesia* 63 E7
Mandla, *India* 69 H9
Mandø, *Denmark* 11 J2
Mandorah, *Australia* 92 B5
Mandoto, *Madag.* 89 B8
Mandoúdhion, *Greece* 38 C5
Mándra, *Greece* 38 C5
Mandra, *Pakistan* 68 C5
Mandrákhi, *Greece* 39 E9
Mandrare →, *Madag.* 89 D8
Mandritsara, *Madag.* 89 B8
Mandronarivo, *Madag.* 89 C8
Mandsaur, *India* 68 G6
Mandurah, *Australia* 93 F2
Mandúria, *Italy* 31 B10
Mandvi, *India* 68 H3
Mandya, *India* 66 N10
Mandzai, *Pakistan* 68 D2
Mané, *Burkina Faso* 83 C4
Maneh, *Iran* 71 B8
Manengouba, Mts., *Cameroon* . 83 E6
Manera, *Madag.* 89 C7
Manérbio, *Italy* 28 C7
Maneroo Cr. →, *Australia* 94 C3
Manfalût, *Egypt* 80 B3
Manfredónia, *Italy* 29 G12
Manfredónia, G. di, *Italy* 29 G13
Manga, *Burkina Faso* 83 C4
Manga, *Niger* 83 C7
Mangabeiras, Chapada das,
  Brazil 125 F9
Mangalia, *Romania* 43 G13
Mangalore, *India* 66 N9
Mangan, *India* 69 F13
Mangaung, *S. Africa* 85 K5
Mangawan, *India* 69 G9
Mangaweka, *N.Z.* 91 H5
Manggar, *Indonesia* 62 E3
Manggawitu, *Indonesia* 63 E8
Mangindrano, *Madag.* 89 A8
Mangkalihat, Tanjung, *Indonesia* 63 D5
Mangla, *Pakistan* 68 C5
Mangla Dam, *Pakistan* 69 C5
Manglaur, *India* 68 E7
Mangnai, *China* 60 C4
Mango, *Togo* 83 C5
Mangoche, *Malawi* 87 E4
Mangoky →, *Madag.* 89 C7
Mangole, *Indonesia* 63 E6
Mangombe, *Dem. Rep. of
  the Congo* 86 C2
Mangonui, *N.Z.* 91 F4
Mangoro →, *Madag.* 89 B8
Mangrol, *Mad. P., India* 68 J4
Mangrol, *Raj., India* 68 G6
Mangualde, *Portugal* 34 E3
Mangueira, L. da, *Brazil* 127 C5
Mangum, *U.S.A.* 113 H5
Mangyshlak Poluostrov,
  Kazakstan 50 E6
Manhattan, *U.S.A.* 112 F6
Manhiça, *Mozam.* 89 D5
Mania →, *Madag.* 89 B8
Maniago, *Italy* 28 B9
Manica, *Mozam.* 89 B5
Manica □, *Mozam.* 89 B5
Manicaland □, *Zimbabwe* 87 F3
Manicoré, *Brazil* 124 E6
Manicouagan, *Canada* 103 C6
Manicouagan, Rés., *Canada* .. 103 B6
Maniema □, *Dem. Rep. of
  the Congo* 86 C2
Manīfah, *Si. Arabia* 71 E6
Manifold, C., *Australia* 94 C5
Maniganggo, *China* 58 B2
Manigotagan, *Canada* 105 C9
Manigotagan →, *Canada* 105 C9
Manihari, *India* 69 G12
Manihiki, *Cook Is.* 97 J11
Manika, Plateau de la,
  Dem. Rep. of the Congo .. 87 E2
Manikpur, *India* 69 G9
Manila, *Phil.* 61 D4
Manila, *U.S.A.* 114 F9
Manila B., *Phil.* 61 D4
Manimpé, *Mali* 82 C3
Maningrida, *Australia* 94 A1

Maninian, *Ivory C.* 82 C3
Manipur □, *India* 67 G19
Manipur →, *Burma* 67 H19
Manisa, *Turkey* 39 C9
Manisa □, *Turkey* 39 C9
Manistee, *U.S.A.* 108 C2
Manistee →, *U.S.A.* 108 C2
Manistique, *U.S.A.* 108 C2
Manito L., *Canada* 105 C7
Manitoba □, *Canada* 105 B9
Manitoba, L., *Canada* 105 C9
Manitou, *Canada* 105 D9
Manitou, L., *Canada* 103 B6
Manitou Is., *U.S.A.* 108 C3
Manitou Springs, *U.S.A.* 112 F2
Manitoulin I., *Canada* 102 C3
Manitouwadge, *Canada* 102 C2
Manitowoc, *U.S.A.* 108 C2
Manizales, *Colombia* 124 B3
Manja, *Madag.* 89 C7
Manjacaze, *Mozam.* 89 C5
Manjakandriana, *Madag.* 89 B8
Manjhand, *Pakistan* 68 G3
Manjil, *Iran* 71 B6
Manjimup, *Australia* 93 F2
Manjra →, *India* 66 K10
Mankato, *Kans., U.S.A.* 112 F5
Mankato, *Minn., U.S.A.* 112 C8
Mankayane, *Swaziland* 89 D5
Mankera, *Pakistan* 68 D4
Mankim, *Cameroon* 83 D7
Mankono, *Ivory C.* 82 D3
Mankota, *Canada* 105 D7
Manlay = Üydzin, *Mongolia* ... 56 B4
Manlleu, *Spain* 32 C7
Manmad, *India* 66 J9
Mann Ranges, *Australia* 93 E5
Manna, *Indonesia* 62 E2
Mannar, *Sri Lanka* 66 Q11
Mannar, G. of, *Asia* 66 Q11
Mannar I., *Sri Lanka* 66 Q11
Mannheim, *Germany* 25 F4
Manning, *Canada* 104 B5
Manning, *Oreg., U.S.A.* 116 E3
Manning, *S.C., U.S.A.* 109 J5
Manning Prov. Park, *Canada* .. 104 D4
Mannu →, *Italy* 30 C2
Mannu, C., *Italy* 30 B1
Mano, *S. Leone* 82 D2
Mano →, *Liberia* 82 D2
Mano River, *Liberia* 82 D2
Manohorpur, *India* 69 H11
Manokwari, *Indonesia* 63 E8
Manolás, *Greece* 38 C3
Manombo, *Madag.* 89 C7
Manono, *Dem. Rep. of
  the Congo* 86 D2
Manoppello, *Italy* 29 F11
Manosque, *France* 21 E9
Manotick, *Canada* 111 A9
Manouane →, *Canada* 103 C5
Manouane, L., *Canada* 103 B5
Manp'o, *N. Korea* 57 D14
Manpojin = Manp'o, *N. Korea* . 57 D14
Manpur, *Mad. P., India* 68 H6
Manpur, *Mad. P., India* 69 H10
Manresa, *Spain* 32 D6
Mansa, *Gujarat, India* 68 H5
Mansa, *Punjab, India* 68 E6
Mansa, *Zambia* 87 E2
Månsåsen, *Sweden* 10 A8
Mansehra, *Pakistan* 68 B5
Mansel I., *Canada* 101 B11
Mansfield, *U.K.* 12 D6
Mansfield, *La., U.S.A.* 113 J8
Mansfield, *Mass., U.S.A.* 111 D13
Mansfield, *Ohio, U.S.A.* 110 F2
Mansfield, *Pa., U.S.A.* 110 E7
Mansfield, Mt., *U.S.A.* 111 B12
Mansilla de las Mulas, *Spain* .. 34 C5
Mansle, *France* 20 C4
Mansoa, *Guinea-Biss.* 82 C1
Manson Creek, *Canada* 104 B4
Manta, *Ecuador* 124 D2
Mantalingajan, Mt., *Phil.* 61 G2
Mantare, *Tanzania* 86 C3
Manteca, *U.S.A.* 116 H5
Manteo, *U.S.A.* 109 H8
Mantes-la-Jolie, *France* 19 D8
Manthani, *India* 66 K11
Manton, *U.S.A.* 108 C3
Mantorp, *Sweden* 11 F9
Mántova, *Italy* 28 C7
Mänttä, *Finland* 9 E21
Mantua = Mántova, *Italy* 28 C7
Manturovo, *Russia* 48 A7
Manu, *Peru* 124 F4
Manu →, *Peru* 124 F4
Manua Is., *Amer. Samoa* 91 B14
Manuel Alves →, *Brazil* 125 F9
Manui, *Indonesia* 63 E6
Manukau, *N.Z.* 91 G5
Manuripi →, *Bolivia* 124 F5
Many, *U.S.A.* 113 K8
Manyara, L., *Tanzania* 86 C4
Manyas, *Turkey* 41 F11
Manych →, *Russia* 49 G5
Manych-Gudilo, Ozero, *Russia* . 49 G6
Manyonga →, *Tanzania* 86 C3
Manyoni, *Tanzania* 86 D3
Manzai, *Pakistan* 68 C4
Manzala, Bahra el, *Egypt* 80 H7
Manzanares, *Spain* 35 F7
Manzaneda, *Spain* 34 C3

Manzanillo, *Cuba* 120 B4
Manzanillo, *Mexico* 118 D4
Manzanillo, Pta., *Panama* 120 E4
Manzano Mts., *U.S.A.* 115 J10
Manẓarīyeh, *Iran* 71 C6
Manzhouli, *China* 60 B6
Manzini, *Swaziland* 89 D5
Mao, *Chad* 79 F9
Maó, *Spain* 37 B11
Maoke, Pegunungan, *Indonesia* 63 E9
Maolin, *China* 57 C12
Maoming, *China* 59 G8
Maopi T'ou, *China* 59 G13
Maouri, Dallol →, *Niger* 83 C5
Maoxian, *China* 58 B4
Maoxing, *China* 57 B13
Mapam Yumco, *China* 60 C3
Mapastepec, *Mexico* 119 D6
Mapia, Kepulauan, *Indonesia* .. 63 D8
Mapimí, *Mexico* 118 B4
Mapimí, Bolsón de, *Mexico* ... 118 B4
Maping, *China* 59 B9
Mapinga, *Tanzania* 86 D4
Mapinhane, *Mozam.* 89 C6
Maple Creek, *Canada* 105 D7
Maple Valley, *U.S.A.* 116 C4
Mapleton, *U.S.A.* 114 D2
Mapuera →, *Brazil* 124 D7
Mapulanguene, *Mozam.* 89 C5
Maputo, *Mozam.* 89 D5
Maputo □, *Mozam.* 89 D5
Maputo, B. de, *Mozam.* 89 D5
Maqiaohe, *China* 57 B16
Maqnā, *Si. Arabia* 70 D2
Maqueda, *Spain* 34 E6
Maquela do Zombo, *Angola* ... 84 F3
Maquinchao, *Argentina* 128 E3
Maquoketa, *U.S.A.* 112 D9
Mar, Serra do, *Brazil* 127 B6
Mar Chiquita, L., *Argentina* .. 126 C3
Mar del Plata, *Argentina* 126 D4
Mar Menor, *Spain* 33 H4
Mara, *Tanzania* 86 C3
Mara □, *Tanzania* 86 C3
Maraã, *Brazil* 124 D5
Marabá, *Brazil* 125 E9
Maracá, I. de, *Brazil* 125 C8
Maracaibo, *Venezuela* 124 A4
Maracaibo, L. de, *Venezuela* .. 122 C3
Maracaju, *Brazil* 127 A4
Maracay, *Venezuela* 124 A5
Maracena, *Spain* 35 H7
Maradi, *Niger* 83 C6
Marāgheh, *Iran* 70 B5
Marāh, *Si. Arabia* 70 E5
Marajó, I. de, *Brazil* 122 D6
Marākand, *Iran* 70 B5
Maralal, *Kenya* 86 B4
Maralinga, *Australia* 93 F5
Maramaraereğlisi, *Turkey* 41 F11
Marampa, *S. Leone* 82 D2
Maramureş □, *Romania* 43 C9
Maran, *Malaysia* 65 L4
Marana, *U.S.A.* 115 K8
Maranboy, *Australia* 92 B5
Maranchón, *Spain* 32 D2
Marand, *Iran* 70 B5
Marang, *Malaysia* 65 K4
Maranguape, *Brazil* 125 D11
Maranhão = São Luís, *Brazil* .. 125 D10
Maranhão □, *Brazil* 125 E9
Marano, L. di, *Italy* 29 C10
Maranoa →, *Australia* 95 D4
Marañón →, *Peru* 122 D3
Marão, *Mozam.* 89 C5
Maraş = Kahramanmaraş,
  Turkey 70 B3
Mărăşeşti, *Romania* 43 E12
Maratea, *Italy* 31 C8
Marateca, *Portugal* 35 G2
Marathasa □, *Cyprus* 36 E11
Marathókambos, *Greece* 39 D8
Marathon, *Australia* 94 C3
Marathon, *Canada* 102 C2
Marathón, *Greece* 38 C5
Marathon, *N.Y., U.S.A.* 111 D8
Marathon, *Tex., U.S.A.* 113 K3
Marathóvouno, *Cyprus* 36 D12
Maratua, *Indonesia* 63 D5
Maravatío, *Mexico* 118 D4
Marawi City, *Phil.* 61 G6
Marāwih, *U.A.E.* 71 E7
Marbella, *Spain* 35 J6
Marble Bar, *Australia* 92 D2
Marble Falls, *U.S.A.* 113 K5
Marblehead, *U.S.A.* 111 D14
Marburg, *Germany* 24 E4
Marcal →, *Hungary* 42 C2
Marcali, *Hungary* 42 D2
Marcaria, *Italy* 28 C7
Mărcăuți, *Moldova* 43 B12
March, *U.K.* 13 E8
Marche □, *Italy* 29 E10
Marche-en-Famenne, *Belgium* . 17 D5
Marchena, *Spain* 35 H5
Marches = Marche □, *Italy* ... 29 E10
Marciana Marina, *Italy* 28 F7
Marcianise, *Italy* 31 A7
Marcigny, *France* 19 F11
Marcillat-en-Combraille, *France* 19 F9
Marck, *France* 19 B8
Marckolsheim, *France* 19 D14
Marco, *U.S.A.* 109 N5
Marcos Juárez, *Argentina* 126 C3
Mărculeşti, *Moldova* 43 C13

Marcus I. = Minami-Tori-Shima,
  Pac. Oc. 96 E7
Marcus Necker Ridge, *Pac. Oc.* 96 F9
Marcy, Mt., *U.S.A.* 111 B11
Mardan, *Pakistan* 68 B5
Mardin, *Turkey* 70 B4
Mårdsjön, *Sweden* 10 A9
Maree, L., *U.K.* 14 D3
Mareeba, *Australia* 94 B4
Mareetsane, *S. Africa* 88 D4
Maréna, *Mali* 82 C2
Marengo, *U.S.A.* 112 E8
Marennes, *France* 20 C2
Marenyi, *Kenya* 86 C4
Marerano, *Madag.* 89 C7
Maréttimo, *Italy* 30 E5
Mareuil, *France* 20 C4
Marfa, *U.S.A.* 113 K2
Marfa Pt., *Malta* 36 D1
Marganets = Marhanets, *Ukraine* 47 J8
Margaret →, *Australia* 92 C4
Margaret Bay, *Canada* 104 C3
Margaret L., *Canada* 104 B5
Margaret River, *Australia* 93 F2
Margarita, I. de, *Venezuela* .. 122 B4
Margarítion, *Greece* 38 B2
Margaritovo, *Russia* 54 C7
Margate, *S. Africa* 89 E5
Margate, *U.K.* 13 F9
Margeride, Mts. de la, *France* . 20 D7
Margherita di Savóia, *Italy* ... 31 A9
Marghita, *Romania* 42 C7
Margonin, *Poland* 45 F4
Margosatubig, *Phil.* 61 H5
Marguerite, *Canada* 104 C4
Marhanets, *Ukraine* 47 J8
Mari El □, *Russia* 48 B8
Mari Indus, *Pakistan* 68 C4
Mari Republic = Mari El □,
  Russia 48 B8
María, Sa. de, *Spain* 33 H2
María Elena, *Chile* 126 A2
María Grande, *Argentina* 126 C4
Maria I., *N. Terr., Australia* ... 94 A2
Maria I., *Tas., Australia* 94 G4
Maria van Diemen, C., *N.Z.* .. 91 F4
Mariager, *Denmark* 11 H3
Mariager Fjord, *Denmark* 11 H4
Mariakani, *Kenya* 86 C4
Marian L., *Canada* 104 A5
Mariana Trench, *Pac. Oc.* 52 H18
Marianao, *Cuba* 120 B3
Marianna, *Ark., U.S.A.* 113 H9
Marianna, *Fla., U.S.A.* 109 K3
Mariannelund, *Sweden* 11 G9
Mariánské Lázně, *Czech Rep.* . 26 B5
Marias →, *U.S.A.* 114 C8
Mariato, Punta, *Panama* 120 E3
Mariazell, *Austria* 26 D8
Maribo, *Denmark* 11 K5
Maribor, *Slovenia* 29 B12
Marico →, *Africa* 88 C4
Maricopa, *Ariz., U.S.A.* 115 K7
Maricopa, *Calif., U.S.A.* 117 K7
Marīdī, *Sudan* 81 G2
Marīdī, Wadi →, *Sudan* 81 F2
Marié →, *Brazil* 124 D5
Marie Byrd Land, *Antarctica* .. 5 D14
Marie-Galante, *Guadeloupe* .. 121 C7
Mariecourt = Kangiqsujuaq,
  Canada 101 B12
Mariefred, *Sweden* 10 E11
Marieholm, *Sweden* 11 J7
Mariembourg, *Belgium* 17 D4
Marienbad = Mariánské Lázně,
  Czech Rep. 26 B5
Marienberg, *Germany* 24 E9
Mariental, *Namibia* 88 C2
Marienville, *U.S.A.* 110 E5
Mariestad, *Sweden* 11 F7
Marietta, *Ga., U.S.A.* 109 J3
Marietta, *Ohio, U.S.A.* 108 F5
Marieville, *Canada* 111 A11
Mariga →, *Nigeria* 83 D6
Marignane, *France* 21 E9
Marihatag, *Phil.* 61 G7
Mariinsk, *Russia* 50 D9
Mariinskiy Posad, *Russia* 48 B8
Marijampolė, *Lithuania* 9 J20
Marijampolė □, *Lithuania* 44 D10
Marília, *Brazil* 127 A6
Marín, *Spain* 34 C2
Marina, *U.S.A.* 116 J5
Marinduque, *Phil.* 63 B6
Marine City, *U.S.A.* 110 D2
Marineo, *Italy* 30 E6
Marinette, *U.S.A.* 108 C2
Maringá, *Brazil* 127 A5
Marinha Grande, *Portugal* ... 34 F2
Marino, *Italy* 29 G9
Marion, *Ala., U.S.A.* 109 J2
Marion, *Ill., U.S.A.* 113 G10
Marion, *Ind., U.S.A.* 108 E3
Marion, *Iowa, U.S.A.* 112 D9
Marion, *Kans., U.S.A.* 112 F6
Marion, *N.C., U.S.A.* 109 H5
Marion, *Ohio, U.S.A.* 108 E4
Marion, *S.C., U.S.A.* 109 H6
Marion, *Va., U.S.A.* 109 G5
Marion, L., *U.S.A.* 109 J5
Mariposa, *U.S.A.* 116 H7

Mariscal Estigarribia, *Paraguay* 126 A3
Maritime Alps = Maritimes,
  Alpes, *Europe* 21 D11
Maritimes, Alpes, *Europe* 21 D11
Maritsa = Évros →, *Greece* .. 72 C12
Maritsá, *Greece* 36 C10
Mariupol, *Ukraine* 47 J9
Marīvān, *Iran* 70 C5
Marj 'Uyūn, *Lebanon* 75 B4
Marka, *Si. Arabia* 80 D5
Markam, *China* 58 C2
Markaryd, *Sweden* 11 H7
Markazī □, *Iran* 71 C6
Markdale, *Canada* 110 B4
Marked Tree, *U.S.A.* 113 H9
Markelsdorfer Huk, *Germany* . 24 A7
Market Drayton, *U.K.* 12 E5
Market Harborough, *U.K.* 13 E7
Market Rasen, *U.K.* 12 D7
Markham, *Canada* 110 C5
Markham, Mt., *Antarctica* 5 E11
Marki, *Poland* 45 F8
Markkleeberg, *Germany* 24 D8
Markleeville, *U.S.A.* 116 G7
Markoupoulon, *Greece* 38 D5
Markovac, *Serbia, Yug.* 40 B5
Markovo, *Russia* 51 C17
Markoye, *Burkina Faso* 83 C5
Marks, *Russia* 48 E8
Marksville, *U.S.A.* 113 K8
Markt Schwaben, *Germany* ... 25 G7
Marktoberdorf, *Germany* 25 H6
Marktredwitz, *Germany* 25 E8
Marl, *Germany* 24 D3
Marla, *Australia* 95 D1
Marlbank, *Canada* 110 B7
Marlboro, *Mass., U.S.A.* 111 D13
Marlboro, *N.Y., U.S.A.* 111 E11
Marlborough, *Australia* 94 C4
Marlborough, *U.K.* 13 F6
Marlborough Downs, *U.K.* ... 13 F6
Marle, *France* 19 C10
Marlin, *U.S.A.* 113 K6
Marlow, *Germany* 24 A8
Marlow, *U.S.A.* 113 H6
Marmagao, *India* 66 M8
Marmande, *France* 20 D4
Marmara, *Turkey* 41 F11
Marmara, Sea of = Marmara
  Denizi, *Turkey* 41 F12
Marmara Denizi, *Turkey* 41 F12
Marmara Gölü, *Turkey* 39 C10
Marmaris, *Turkey* 39 E10
Marmaris Limanı, *Turkey* 39 E10
Marmion, Mt., *Australia* 93 E2
Marmion L., *Canada* 102 C1
Marmolada, Mte., *Italy* 29 B8
Marmolejo, *Spain* 35 G6
Marmora, *Canada* 102 D4
Mármora, La, *Italy* 30 C2
Marnay, *France* 19 E12
Marne, *Germany* 24 B5
Marne □, *France* 19 D11
Marne →, *France* 19 D9
Marneuli, *Georgia* 49 K7
Maroala, *Madag.* 89 B8
Maroantsetra, *Madag.* 89 B8
Maroelaboom, *Namibia* 88 B2
Marofandilia, *Madag.* 89 C7
Marolambo, *Madag.* 89 C8
Maromandia, *Madag.* 89 A8
Marondera, *Zimbabwe* 87 F3
Maroni →, *Fr. Guiana* 125 B8
Marónia, *Greece* 41 F9
Maronne →, *France* 20 C5
Maroochydore, *Australia* 95 D5
Maros →, *Hungary* 42 D5
Marosakoa, *Madag.* 89 B8
Maroseranana, *Madag.* 89 B8
Maróstica, *Italy* 29 C8
Marotandrano, *Madag.* 89 B8
Marotaolano, *Madag.* 89 A8
Maroua, *Cameroon* 83 C7
Marovato, *Madag.* 89 B8
Marovoay, *Madag.* 89 B8
Marquard, *S. Africa* 88 D4
Marquesas Is. = Marquises, Is.,
  Pac. Oc. 97 H14
Marquette, *U.S.A.* 108 B2
Marquise, *France* 19 B8
Marquises, Is., *Pac. Oc.* 97 H14
Marra, Djebel, *Sudan* 79 F10
Marra, Gebel, *Sudan* 81 F2
Marracuene, *Mozam.* 89 D5
Marradi, *Italy* 29 D8
Marrakech, *Morocco* 78 B4
Marratxí, *Spain* 32 F7
Marrawah, *Australia* 94 G3
Marree, *Australia* 95 D2
Marrero, *U.S.A.* 113 L9
Marrimane, *Mozam.* 89 C5
Marromeu, *Mozam.* 89 B6
Marroquí, Punta, *Spain* 35 K5
Marrubane, *Mozam.* 87 F4
Marrúbiu, *Italy* 30 C1
Marrupa, *Mozam.* 87 E4
Mars Hill, *U.S.A.* 109 B12
Marsá 'Alam, *Egypt* 80 B3
Marsá Matrûḥ, *Egypt* 80 A2
Marsá Sha'b, *Sudan* 80 C4
Marsabit, *Kenya* 86 B4
Marsala, *Italy* 30 E5
Marsalforn, *Malta* 36 C1
Mârşani, *Romania* 43 F9
Marsberg, *Germany* 24 D4
Marsciano, *Italy* 29 F9

Marseillan, France 20 E7
Marseille, France 21 E9
Marseilles = Marseille, France 21 E9
Marsh I., U.S.A. 113 L9
Marshall, Liberia 82 D2
Marshall, Ark., U.S.A. 113 H8
Marshall, Mich., U.S.A. 108 D3
Marshall, Minn., U.S.A. 112 C7
Marshall, Mo., U.S.A. 112 F8
Marshall, Tex., U.S.A. 113 J7
Marshall →, Australia 94 C2
Marshall Is. ■, Pac. Oc. 96 G9
Marshalltown, U.S.A. 112 D8
Marshbrook, Zimbabwe 89 B5
Marshfield, Mo., U.S.A. 113 G8
Marshfield, Vt., U.S.A. 111 B12
Marshfield, Wis., U.S.A. 112 C9
Marshūn, Iran 71 B6
Mársico Nuovo, Italy 31 B8
Märsta, Sweden 10 E11
Marstal, Denmark 11 K4
Marstrand, Sweden 11 G5
Mart, U.S.A. 113 K6
Marta →, Italy 29 F8
Martaban, Burma 67 L20
Martaban, G. of, Burma 67 L20
Martano, Italy 31 B11
Martapura, Kalimantan, Indonesia 62 E4
Martapura, Sumatera, Indonesia 62 E2
Marte, Nigeria 83 C7
Martel, France 20 D5
Martelange, Belgium 17 E5
Martellago, Italy 29 C9
Martés, Sierra, Spain 33 F4
Martfű, Hungary 42 C5
Martha's Vineyard, U.S.A. 111 E14
Martigné-Ferchaud, France 18 E5
Martigny, Switz. 25 J3
Martigues, France 21 E9
Martin, Slovak Rep. 27 B11
Martin, S. Dak., U.S.A. 112 D4
Martin, Tenn., U.S.A. 113 G10
Martín →, Spain 32 D4
Martin, L., U.S.A. 109 J3
Martina Franca, Italy 31 B10
Martinborough, N.Z. 91 J5
Martinez, Calif., U.S.A. 116 G4
Martinez, Ga., U.S.A. 109 J4
Martinique ■, W. Indies 121 D7
Martinique Passage, W. Indies 121 C7
Martínon, Greece 38 C5
Martinópolis, Brazil 127 A5
Martins Ferry, U.S.A. 110 F4
Martinsberg, Austria 26 C8
Martinsburg, Pa., U.S.A. 110 F6
Martinsburg, W. Va., U.S.A. 108 F7
Martinsicuro, Italy 29 F10
Martinsville, Ind., U.S.A. 108 F2
Martinsville, Va., U.S.A. 109 G6
Marton, N.Z. 91 J5
Martorell, Spain 32 D6
Martos, Spain 35 H7
Martuni, Armenia 49 K7
Maru, Nigeria 83 C6
Marudi, Malaysia 62 D4
Maruf, Afghan. 66 D5
Marugame, Japan 55 G6
Marunga, Angola 88 B3
Marungu, Mts., Dem. Rep. of the Congo 86 D3
Marv Dasht, Iran 71 D7
Marvast, Iran 71 D7
Marvejols, France 20 D7
Marvel Loch, Australia 93 F2
Marwar, India 68 G5
Mary, Turkmenistan 50 F7
Maryborough = Port Laoise, Ireland 15 C4
Maryborough, Australia 95 D5
Maryfield, Canada 105 D8
Maryland □, U.S.A. 108 F7
Maryland Junction, Zimbabwe 87 F3
Maryport, U.K. 12 C4
Mary's Harbour, Canada 103 B8
Marystown, Canada 103 C8
Marysville, Canada 104 C3
Marysville, Calif., U.S.A. 116 F5
Marysville, Kans., U.S.A. 112 F6
Marysville, Mich., U.S.A. 110 D2
Marysville, Ohio, U.S.A. 108 E4
Marysville, Wash., U.S.A. 116 B4
Maryville, Mo., U.S.A. 112 E7
Maryville, Tenn., U.S.A. 109 H4
Marzūq, Libya 79 C8
Masahunga, Tanzania 86 C3
Masai Steppe, Tanzania 86 C4
Masaka, Uganda 86 C3
Masalembo, Kepulauan, Indonesia 62 F4
Masalima, Kepulauan, Indonesia 62 F5
Masallı, Azerbaijan 73 C13
Masamba, Indonesia 63 E6
Masan, S. Korea 57 G15
Masandam, Ra's, Oman 71 E8
Masasi, Tanzania 87 E4
Masaya, Nic. 120 D2
Masba, Nigeria 83 C7
Máscali, Italy 31 E8
Mascara, Algeria 78 A6
Mascota, Mexico 118 C4
Masela, Indonesia 63 F7
Maseru, Lesotho 88 D4
Mashaba, Zimbabwe 87 G3
Mashābih, Si. Arabia 70 E3

Mashan, China 58 F7
Mashar, Sudan 81 F2
Mashegu, Nigeria 83 D6
Masherbrum, Pakistan 69 B7
Mashhad, Iran 71 B8
Mashi, Nigeria 83 C6
Mashīz, Iran 71 D8
Māshkel, Hāmūn-i-, Pakistan 66 E3
Mashki Chāh, Pakistan 66 E3
Mashonaland, Zimbabwe 85 H6
Mashonaland Central □, Zimbabwe 89 B5
Mashonaland East □, Zimbabwe 89 B5
Mashonaland West □, Zimbabwe 89 B4
Mashrakh, India 69 F11
Mashtaga = Maştağa, Azerbaijan 49 K10
Masindi, Uganda 86 B3
Masindi Port, Uganda 86 B3
Maşīrah, Oman 74 C6
Maşīrah, Khalīj, Oman 74 C6
Masisi, Dem. Rep. of the Congo 86 C2
Masjed Soleyman, Iran 71 D6
Mask, L., Ireland 15 C2
Maskin, Oman 71 F8
Maslen Nos, Bulgaria 41 D11
Maslinica, Croatia 29 E13
Masnou = El Masnou, Spain 32 D7
Masoala, Tanjon' i, Madag. 89 B9
Masoarivo, Madag. 89 B7
Masohi = Amahai, Indonesia 63 E7
Masomeloka, Madag. 89 C8
Mason, Nev., U.S.A. 116 G7
Mason, Tex., U.S.A. 113 K5
Mason City, U.S.A. 112 D8
Maspalomas, Canary Is. 37 G4
Maspalomas, Pta., Canary Is. 37 G4
Masqat, Oman 74 C6
Massa, Italy 28 D7
Massa Maríttima, Italy 28 E7
Massachusetts □, U.S.A. 111 D13
Massachusetts B., U.S.A. 111 D14
Massafra, Italy 31 B10
Massakory, Chad 79 F9
Massanella, Spain 37 B9
Massangena, Mozam. 89 C5
Massango, Angola 84 F3
Massat, France 20 F5
Massawa = Mitsiwa, Eritrea 81 D4
Massena, U.S.A. 111 B10
Massénya, Chad 79 F9
Masset, Canada 104 C2
Masseube, France 20 E4
Massiac, France 20 C7
Massif Central, France 20 D7
Massigui, Mali 82 C3
Massillon, U.S.A. 110 F3
Massinga, Mozam. 89 C6
Massingir, Mozam. 89 C5
Mässlingen, Sweden 10 B6
Masson, Canada 111 A9
Masson I., Antarctica 5 C7
Maştağa, Azerbaijan 49 K10
Mastanli = Momchilgrad, Bulgaria 41 E9
Masterton, N.Z. 91 J5
Mastic, U.S.A. 111 F12
Mástikho, Ákra, Greece 39 C8
Mastuj, Pakistan 69 A5
Mastung, Pakistan 66 E5
Mastūrah, Si. Arabia 80 C4
Masty, Belarus 46 F3
Masuda, Japan 55 G5
Masvingo, Zimbabwe 87 G3
Masvingo □, Zimbabwe 87 G3
Maşyāf, Syria 70 C3
Maszewo, Poland 44 E2
Mat →, Albania 40 E3
Matabeleland, Zimbabwe 85 H5
Matabeleland North □, Zimbabwe 87 F2
Matabeleland South □, Zimbabwe 87 G2
Matachel →, Spain 35 G4
Matachewan, Canada 102 C3
Matadi, Dem. Rep. of the Congo 84 F2
Matagalpa, Nic. 120 D2
Matagami, Canada 102 C4
Matagami, L., Canada 102 C4
Matagorda B., U.S.A. 113 L6
Matagorda I., U.S.A. 113 L6
Matak, Indonesia 65 L6
Mátala, Greece 36 E6
Matam, Senegal 82 B2
Matameye, Niger 83 C6
Matamoros, Campeche, Mexico 119 D6
Matamoros, Coahuila, Mexico 118 B4
Matamoros, Tamaulipas, Mexico 119 B5
Ma'ṭan as Sarra, Libya 79 D10
Matandu →, Tanzania 87 D3
Matane, Canada 103 C6
Matang, China 58 F5
Matankari, Niger 83 C5
Matanomadh, India 68 H3
Matanzas, Cuba 120 B3
Matapa, Botswana 88 C3
Matapan, C. = Taínaron, Ákra, Greece 38 E4
Matapédia, Canada 103 C6
Matara, Sri Lanka 66 S12
Mataram, Indonesia 62 F5
Matarani, Peru 124 G4
Mataranka, Australia 92 B5
Matarma, Râs, Egypt 75 E1
Mataró, Spain 32 D7
Matarraña →, Spain 32 D5

Mataruška Banja, Serbia, Yug. 40 C4
Matatiele, S. Africa 89 E4
Mataura, N.Z. 91 M2
Matehuala, Mexico 118 C4
Mateke Hills, Zimbabwe 87 G3
Matera, Italy 31 B9
Matese, Monti del, Italy 31 A7
Mátészalka, Hungary 42 C7
Matetsi, Zimbabwe 87 F2
Matfors, Sweden 10 B11
Matha, France 20 C3
Mathis, U.S.A. 113 L6
Mathráki, Greece 36 A3
Mathura, India 68 F7
Mati, Phil. 61 H7
Matiakoali, Burkina Faso 83 C5
Matiali, India 69 F13
Matías Romero, Mexico 119 D5
Matibane, Mozam. 87 E5
Matima, Botswana 88 C3
Matiri Ra., N.Z. 91 J4
Matjiesfontein, S. Africa 88 E3
Matla →, India 69 J13
Matlamanyane, Botswana 88 B4
Matli, Pakistan 68 G3
Matlock, U.K. 12 D6
Matna, Sudan 81 E4
Mato Grosso □, Brazil 125 F8
Mato Grosso, Planalto do, Brazil 122 E5
Mato Grosso do Sul □, Brazil 125 G8
Matochkin Shar, Russia 50 B6
Matopo Hills, Zimbabwe 87 G2
Matopos, Zimbabwe 87 G2
Matosinhos, Portugal 34 D2
Matour, France 19 F11
Matroosberg, S. Africa 88 E2
Maţruḩ, Oman 74 C6
Matsena, Nigeria 83 C7
Matsesta, Russia 49 J4
Matsu Tao, Taiwan 59 E13
Matsue, Japan 55 G6
Matsumae, Japan 54 D10
Matsumoto, Japan 55 F9
Matsusaka, Japan 55 G8
Matsuura, Japan 55 H4
Matsuyama, Japan 55 H6
Mattancheri, India 66 Q10
Mattawa, Canada 102 C4
Matterhorn, Switz. 25 K3
Mattersburg, Austria 27 D9
Matthew Town, Bahamas 121 B5
Matthew's Ridge, Guyana 124 B6
Mattice, Canada 102 C3
Mattituck, U.S.A. 111 F12
Mattō, Japan 55 F8
Mattoon, U.S.A. 108 F1
Matuba, Mozam. 89 C5
Matucana, Peru 124 F3
Matún = Khowst, Afghan. 68 C3
Maturín, Venezuela 124 B6
Matveyev Kurgan, Russia 47 J10
Matxitxako, C., Spain 32 B2
Mau, Mad. P., India 69 F8
Mau, Ut. P., India 69 G10
Mau, Ut. P., India 69 G9
Mau Escarpment, Kenya 86 C4
Mau Ranipur, India 69 G8
Maubeuge, France 19 B10
Maubourguet, France 20 E4
Maud, Pt., Australia 92 D1
Maudin Sun, Burma 67 M19
Maués, Brazil 124 D7
Mauganj, India 69 G12
Maughold Hd., U.K. 12 C3
Mauguio, France 20 E7
Maui, U.S.A. 106 H16
Maulamyaing = Moulmein, Burma 67 L20
Maule □, Chile 126 D1
Mauléon-Licharre, France 20 E3
Maumee, U.S.A. 108 E4
Maumee →, U.S.A. 108 E4
Maumere, Indonesia 63 F6
Maun, Botswana 88 C3
Mauna Kea, U.S.A. 106 J17
Mauna Loa, U.S.A. 106 J17
Maungmagan Kyunzu, Burma 64 E1
Maupin, U.S.A. 114 D3
Maure-de-Bretagne, France 18 E5
Maurepas, L., U.S.A. 113 K9
Maures, France 21 E10
Mauriac, France 20 C6
Maurice, L., Australia 93 E5
Mauricie, Parc Nat. de la, Canada 102 C5
Maurienne, France 21 C10
Mauritania ■, Africa 78 E3
Mauritius ■, Ind. Oc. 77 J9
Mauron, France 18 D4
Maurs, France 20 D6
Mauston, U.S.A. 112 D9
Mauterndorf, Austria 26 D6
Mauthen, Austria 26 E6
Mauvezin, France 20 E4
Mauzé-sur-le-Mignon, France 20 B3
Mavli, India 68 G5
Mavrovë, Albania 40 F3
Mavuradonha Mts., Zimbabwe 87 F3
Mawa, Dem. Rep. of the Congo 86 B2
Mawai, India 69 H9
Mawana, India 68 E7
Mawand, Pakistan 68 E3
Mawk Mai, Burma 67 J20
Mawlaik, Burma 67 H19

Mawlamyine = Moulmein, Burma 67 L20
Mawqaq, Si. Arabia 70 E4
Mawson Coast, Antarctica 5 C6
Max, U.S.A. 112 B4
Maxcanú, Mexico 119 C6
Maxesibeni, S. Africa 89 E4
Maxhamish L., Canada 104 B4
Maxixe, Mozam. 89 C6
Maxville, Canada 111 A10
Maxwell, U.S.A. 116 F4
Maxwelton, Australia 94 C3
May, C., U.S.A. 108 F8
May Pen, Jamaica 120 C4
Maya →, Russia 51 D14
Maya Mts., Belize 119 D7
Mayaguana, Bahamas 121 B5
Mayagüez, Puerto Rico 121 C6
Mayahi, Niger 83 C6
Mayals = Maials, Spain 32 D5
Mayāmey, Iran 71 B7
Mayang, China 58 D7
Mayanup, Australia 93 F2
Mayapan, Mexico 119 C7
Mayarí, Cuba 121 B4
Maybell, U.S.A. 114 F9
Maybole, U.K. 14 F4
Maychew, Ethiopia 81 E4
Maydān, Iraq 70 C5
Maydena, Australia 94 G4
Mayen, Germany 25 E3
Mayenne, France 18 D6
Mayenne □, France 18 D6
Mayenne →, France 18 D6
Mayer, U.S.A. 115 J7
Mayerthorpe, Canada 104 C5
Mayfield, Ky., U.S.A. 109 G1
Mayfield, N.Y., U.S.A. 111 C10
Mayhill, U.S.A. 115 K11
Maykop, Russia 49 H5
Maymyo, Burma 64 A1
Maynard, Mass., U.S.A. 111 D13
Maynard, Wash., U.S.A. 116 C4
Maynard Hills, Australia 93 E2
Mayne →, Australia 94 C3
Maynooth, Ireland 15 C5
Mayo, Canada 100 B6
Mayo □, Ireland 15 C2
Mayo Daga, Nigeria 83 D7
Mayo Faran, Nigeria 83 D7
Mayon Volcano, Phil. 61 E5
Mayor I., N.Z. 91 G6
Mayorga, Spain 34 C5
Mayotte ■, Ind. Oc. 85 G9
Mayraira Pt., Phil. 61 B4
Mayskiy, Russia 49 J7
Maysville, U.S.A. 108 F4
Mayu, Indonesia 63 D7
Mayville, N. Dak., U.S.A. 112 B6
Mayville, N.Y., U.S.A. 110 D5
Mayya, Russia 51 C14
Mazabuka, Zambia 87 F2
Mazagán = El Jadida, Morocco 78 B4
Mazagão, Brazil 125 D8
Mazamet, France 20 E6
Mazán, Peru 124 D4
Māzandarān □, Iran 71 B7
Mazapil, Mexico 118 C4
Mazara del Vallo, Italy 30 E5
Mazarrón, Spain 33 H3
Mazarrón, G. de, Spain 33 H3
Mazaruni →, Guyana 124 B7
Mazatán, Mexico 118 B2
Mazatenango, Guatemala 120 D1
Mazatlán, Mexico 118 C3
Mažeikiai, Lithuania 9 H20
Māzhān, Iran 71 C8
Mazīnān, Iran 71 B8
Mazoe, Mozam. 87 F3
Mazoe →, Mozam. 87 F3
Mazowe, Zimbabwe 87 F3
Mazowieckie □, Poland 45 F8
Mazrūb, Sudan 81 E2
Mazu Dao, China 59 D12
Mazurian Lakes = Mazurski, Pojezierze, Poland 44 E7
Mazurski, Pojezierze, Poland 44 E7
Mazyr, Belarus 47 F5
Mba, Senegal 82 C1
Mbabane, Swaziland 89 D5
Mbagne, Mauritania 82 B2
M'bahiakro, Ivory C. 82 D4
Mbaïki, C.A.R. 84 D3
Mbala, Zambia 87 D3
Mbalabala, Zimbabwe 89 C4
Mbale, Uganda 86 B3
Mbalmayo, Cameroon 83 E7
Mbam →, Cameroon 83 E7
Mbamba Bay, Tanzania 87 E3
Mbandaka, Dem. Rep. of the Congo 84 D3
Mbanga, Cameroon 83 E6
Mbanza Congo, Angola 84 F2
Mbanza Ngungu, Dem. Rep. of the Congo 84 F2
Mbarara, Uganda 86 C3
Mbashe →, S. Africa 89 E4
Mbenkuru →, Tanzania 87 D4
Mberengwa, Zimbabwe 87 G2
Mberengwa, Mt., Zimbabwe 87 G2
Mberubu, Nigeria 83 D6
Mbesuma, Zambia 87 E3
Mbeya, Tanzania 87 D3
Mbeya □, Tanzania 86 D3
M'bili, Sudan 81 F2

Mbinga, Tanzania 87 E4
Mbini □, Eq. Guin. 84 D2
Mboki, C.A.R. 81 F2
M'bonge, Cameroon 83 E6
Mboro, Senegal 82 B1
M'boukou Res., Cameroon 83 D7
Mboune, Senegal 82 C2
Mbour, Senegal 82 C1
Mbout, Mauritania 82 B2
Mbuji-Mayi, Dem. Rep. of the Congo 86 D1
Mbulu, Tanzania 86 C4
Mburucuyá, Argentina 126 B4
Mchinja, Tanzania 87 D4
Mchinji, Malawi 87 E3
Mdantsane, S. Africa 85 L5
Mead, L., U.S.A. 117 J12
Meade, U.S.A. 113 G4
Meadow Lake, Canada 105 C7
Meadow Lake Prov. Park, Canada 105 C7
Meadow Valley Wash →, U.S.A. 117 J12
Meadville, U.S.A. 110 E4
Meaford, Canada 102 D3
Mealhada, Portugal 34 E2
Mealy Mts., Canada 103 B8
Meander River, Canada 104 B5
Meares, C., U.S.A. 114 D2
Mearim →, Brazil 125 D10
Meath □, Ireland 15 C5
Meath Park, Canada 105 C7
Meaulne, France 19 F9
Meaux, France 19 D9
Mebechi-Gawa →, Japan 54 D10
Mecanhelas, Mozam. 87 F4
Mecca = Makkah, Si. Arabia 74 C2
Mecca, U.S.A. 117 M10
Mechanicsburg, U.S.A. 110 F7
Mechanicville, U.S.A. 111 D11
Mechara, Ethiopia 81 F5
Mechelen, Belgium 17 C4
Mecheria, Algeria 78 B5
Mechernich, Germany 24 E2
Mechetinskaya, Russia 49 G5
Mecidiye, Turkey 41 F10
Mecitözü, Turkey 72 B6
Mecklenburg-Vorpommern □, Germany 24 B8
Mecklenburger Bucht, Germany 24 A7
Meconta, Mozam. 87 E4
Mecsek, Hungary 42 D3
Meda, Portugal 34 E3
Medan, Indonesia 62 D1
Medanosa, Pta., Argentina 128 F3
Mede, Italy 28 C5
Médéa, Algeria 78 A6
Medeba, Bos.-H. 42 G4
Medellín, Colombia 124 B3
Medelpad, Sweden 10 B10
Medemblik, Neths. 17 B5
Mederdra, Mauritania 82 B1
Medford, Mass., U.S.A. 111 D13
Medford, Oreg., U.S.A. 114 E2
Medford, Wis., U.S.A. 112 C9
Medgidia, Romania 43 F13
Medi, Sudan 81 F3
Media Agua, Argentina 126 C2
Media Luna, Argentina 126 C2
Medianeira, Brazil 127 B5
Medicina, Italy 29 D8
Medicine Bow, U.S.A. 114 F10
Medicine Bow Pk., U.S.A. 114 F10
Medicine Bow Ra., U.S.A. 114 F10
Medicine Hat, Canada 105 D6
Medicine Lake, U.S.A. 114 A2
Medicine Lodge, U.S.A. 113 G5
Medina = Al Madīnah, Si. Arabia 70 E3
Medina, N. Dak., U.S.A. 112 B5
Medina, N.Y., U.S.A. 110 C6
Medina, Ohio, U.S.A. 110 E3
Medina →, U.S.A. 113 L5
Medina de Pomar, Spain 34 C7
Medina de Ríoseco, Spain 34 D5
Medina del Campo, Spain 34 D6
Medina L., U.S.A. 113 L5
Medina Sidonia, Spain 35 J5
Medinaceli, Spain 32 D2
Medinipur, India 69 H12
Mediterranean Sea, Europe 6 H7
Médoc, France 20 C3
Medulin, Croatia 29 D10
Medveda, Serbia, Yug. 40 D5
Medvedevo, Russia 48 B8
Medveditsa →, Tver, Russia 46 D9
Medveditsa →, Volgograd, Russia 48 E6
Medvedok, Russia 48 B10
Medvezhi, Ostrava, Russia 51 B17
Medvezhyegorsk, Russia 50 C4
Medway □, U.K. 13 F8
Medway →, U.K. 13 F8
Medzev, Slovak Rep. 27 C13
Medzilaborce, Slovak Rep. 27 B14
Medžitlija, Macedonia 40 F5
Meekatharra, Australia 93 E2
Meeker, U.S.A. 114 F10
Meelpaeg Res., Canada 103 C8
Meersburg, Germany 25 H5
Meerut, India 68 E7
Meeteetse, U.S.A. 114 D9
Mega, Ethiopia 81 G4
Megálo Khório, Greece 39 E9
Megálo Petalí, Greece 38 D6
Megalópolis, Greece 38 D4

Meganísi, *Greece* 38 C2
Mégara, *Greece* 38 D5
Megasini, *India* 69 J12
Megdhova →, *Greece* 38 B3
Megève, *France* 21 C10
Meghalaya □, *India* 67 G17
Meghezez, *Ethiopia* 81 F4
Mégiscane, L., *Canada* 102 C4
Megiste, *Greece* 39 E11
Megra, *Russia* 46 B9
Mehadia, *Romania* 42 F7
Meharry, Mt., *Australia* ... 92 D2
Mehedeby, *Sweden* 10 D11
Mehedinţi □, *Romania* 42 F7
Meheisa, *Sudan* 80 D3
Mehlville, *U.S.A.* 112 F4
Mehndawal, *India* 69 F10
Mehr Jān, *Iran* 71 C7
Mehrābād, *Iran* 70 B5
Mehrān, *Iran* 70 D5
Mehrīz, *Iran* 71 D7
Mehun-sur-Yèvre, *France* .. 19 E9
Mei Jiang →, *China* 59 E11
Mei Xian, *China* 56 G4
Meicheng, *China* 59 C12
Meichengzhen, *China* 59 C8
Meichuan, *China* 59 B10
Meigu, *China* 58 C4
Meiktila, *Burma* 67 J19
Meinerzhagen, *Germany* ... 24 D3
Meiningen, *Germany* 24 E6
Meira, Serra de, *Spain* 34 B3
Meiringen, *Switz.* 25 J4
Meishan, *China* 58 B4
Meissen, *Germany* 24 D9
Meissner, *Germany* 24 D5
Meitan, *China* 58 D6
Meizhou, *China* 59 E11
Meja, *India* 69 G10
Mejillones, *Chile* 126 A1
Mekdela, *Ethiopia* 81 E4
Mekele, *Ethiopia* 81 E4
Mekhtar, *Pakistan* 66 D6
Meknès, *Morocco* 78 B4
Meko, *Nigeria* 83 D5
Mekong →, *Asia* 65 H6
Mekongga, *Indonesia* 63 E6
Mekrou →, *Benin* 83 C5
Mekvari = Kür →, *Azerbaijan* . 73 C13
Mel, *Italy* 29 B9
Melagiri Hills, *India* 66 N10
Melaka, *Malaysia* 65 L4
Melalap, *Malaysia* 62 C5
Mélambes, *Greece* 36 D6
Melanesia, *Pac. Oc.* 96 H7
Melbourne, *Australia* 109 L5
Melchor Múzquiz, *Mexico* . 118 B4
Melchor Ocampo, *Mexico* ... 118 C4
Méldola, *Italy* 29 D9
Meldorf, *Germany* 24 A5
Melegnano, *Italy* 28 C6
Melenci, *Serbia, Yug.* 42 E5
Melenki, *Russia* 48 C5
Mélèzes →, *Canada* 102 A5
Melfi, *Italy* 31 B8
Melfort, *Canada* 105 C8
Melfort, *Zimbabwe* 87 F3
Melgaço, *Portugal* 34 C2
Melgar de Fernamental, *Spain* . 34 C6
Melhus, *Norway* 8 E14
Melide, *Spain* 34 C2
Meligalá, *Greece* 38 D3
Melilla, *N. Afr.* 78 A5
Melilli, *Italy* 31 E8
Melipilla, *Chile* 126 C1
Mélissa, Ákra, *Greece* 36 D6
Mélissa Óros, *Greece* 39 D8
Melita, *Canada* 105 D8
Mélito di Porto Salvo, *Italy* . 31 E8
Melitopol, *Ukraine* 47 J8
Melk, *Austria* 26 C8
Mellan Fryken, *Sweden* ... 10 E7
Mellansel, *Sweden* 8 E18
Mellbystrand, *Sweden* 11 H6
Melle, *France* 20 B3
Melle, *Germany* 24 C4
Mellen, *U.S.A.* 112 B9
Mellerud, *Sweden* 11 F6
Mellette, *U.S.A.* 112 C5
Mellid = Melide, *Spain* 34 C2
Mellieha, *Malta* 36 D1
Mellit, *Sudan* 81 E2
Mellrichstadt, *Germany* ... 24 E6
Mělník, *Czech Rep.* 26 A7
Melo, *Uruguay* 127 C5
Melolo, *Indonesia* 63 F6
Melouprey, *Cambodia* 64 F5
Melrose, *U.K.* 14 F6
Melrose, Minn., *U.S.A.* ... 112 C7
Melrose, N. Mex., *U.S.A.* . 113 H3
Melstone, *U.S.A.* 114 C10
Melsungen, *Germany* 24 D5
Melton Mowbray, *U.K.* 12 E7
Melun, *France* 19 D9
Melut, *Sudan* 81 E3
Melville, *Canada* 105 C8
Melville, C., *Australia* 94 A3
Melville, L., *Canada* 103 B8
Melville B., *Australia* 94 A2
Melville I., *Australia* 92 B5
Melville I., *Canada* 4 B2
Melville Pen., *Canada* 101 B11
Mélykút, *Hungary* 42 D4
Memaliaj, *Albania* 40 F3
Memba, *Mozam.* 87 E5

Memboro, *Indonesia* 63 F5
Membrilla, *Spain* 35 G7
Memel = Klaipėda, *Lithuania* .. 9 J19
Memel, S. *Africa* 89 D4
Memmingen, *Germany* 25 H6
Mempawah, *Indonesia* 62 D3
Memphis, *Egypt* 80 J7
Memphis, Mich., *U.S.A.* ... 110 D2
Memphis, Tenn., *U.S.A.* ... 113 H10
Memphis, Tex., *U.S.A.* 113 H4
Memphremagog, L., *U.S.A.* . 111 B12
Mena, *Ukraine* 47 G7
Mena, *U.S.A.* 113 H7
Mena →, *Ethiopia* 81 F5
Menai Strait, *U.K.* 12 D3
Ménaka, *Mali* 83 B5
Menan = Chao Phraya →,
  Thailand 64 F3
Menarandra →, *Madag.* 89 D7
Menard, *U.S.A.* 113 K5
Menawashei, *Sudan* 81 E1
Mendawai →, *Indonesia* ... 62 E4
Mende, *France* 20 D7
Mendebo, *Ethiopia* 81 F4
Menden, *Germany* 24 D3
Menderes, *Turkey* 39 C9
Mendez, *Mexico* 119 B5
Mendhar, *India* 69 C6
Mendi, *Ethiopia* 81 F4
Mendip Hills, *U.K.* 13 F5
Mendocino, *U.S.A.* 114 G2
Mendocino, C., *U.S.A.* 114 F1
Mendota, Calif., *U.S.A.* ... 116 J6
Mendota, Ill., *U.S.A.* 112 E10
Mendoza, *Argentina* 126 C2
Mendoza □, *Argentina* 126 C2
Mene Grande, *Venezuela* .. 124 B4
Menemen, *Turkey* 39 C9
Menen, *Belgium* 17 D3
Menfi, *Italy* 30 E5
Mengdingjie, *China* 58 F2
Mengeš, *Slovenia* 29 B11
Menggala, *Indonesia* 62 E3
Menghai, *China* 58 G3
Mengíbar, *Spain* 35 H7
Mengjin, *China* 56 G7
Mengla, *China* 58 G3
Menglian, *China* 58 F2
Mengshan, *China* 59 E8
Mengyin, *China* 57 G9
Mengzhe, *China* 58 F3
Mengzi, *China* 58 F4
Menihek, *Canada* 103 B6
Menihek L., *Canada* 103 B6
Menin = Menen, *Belgium* .. 17 D3
Menlo Park, *U.S.A.* 116 H4
Menominee, *U.S.A.* 108 C2
Menominee →, *U.S.A.* 108 C2
Menomonie, *U.S.A.* 112 C9
Menongue, *Angola* 85 G3
Menorca, *Spain* 37 B11
Mentakab, *Malaysia* 65 L4
Mentawai, Kepulauan, *Indonesia* 62 E11
Menton, *France* 21 E11
Mentor, *U.S.A.* 110 E3
Menzies, *Australia* 93 E3
Meob B., *Namibia* 88 B2
Me'ona, *Israel* 75 B4
Meoqui, *Mexico* 118 B3
Mepaco, *Mozam.* 87 F3
Meppel, *Neths.* 17 B6
Meppen, *Germany* 24 C3
Mequinenza, *Spain* 32 D5
Mequinenza, Embalse de, *Spain* 32 D5
Mer, *France* 18 E8
Merabéllou, Kólpos, *Greece* . 36 D7
Merak, *Indonesia* 63 F12
Meramangye, L., *Australia* . 93 E5
Meran = Merano, *Italy* 29 B8
Merano, *Italy* 29 B8
Merate, *Italy* 28 C6
Merauke, *Indonesia* 63 F10
Merca, *Somali Rep.* 74 G3
Mercato Saraceno, *Italy* ... 29 E9
Merced, *U.S.A.* 116 H6
Merced →, *U.S.A.* 116 H6
Merced Pk., *U.S.A.* 116 H7
Mercedes, Buenos Aires,
  Argentina 126 C4
Mercedes, Corrientes, *Argentina* 126 B4
Mercedes, San Luis, *Argentina* . 126 C2
Mercedes, *Uruguay* 126 C4
Mercedes, *U.S.A.* 113 M6
Merceditas, *Chile* 126 B1
Mercer, *N.Z.* 91 G5
Mercer, *U.S.A.* 110 E4
Mercer Island, *U.S.A.* 116 C4
Mercury, *U.S.A.* 117 J11
Mercy C., *Canada* 101 B13
Merdrignac, *France* 18 D4
Mere, *U.K.* 13 F5
Meredith, C., *Falk. Is.* 128 G4
Meredith, L., *U.S.A.* 113 H4
Merefa, *Ukraine* 47 H9
Merei, *Romania* 43 E11
Merga = Nukheila, *Sudan* .. 80 D2
Mergui, *Burma* 64 F2
Mergui Arch. = Myeik Kyunzu,
  Burma 65 G1
Meriç, *Turkey* 41 E10
Meriç →, *Turkey* 41 F10
Mérida, *Mexico* 119 C7
Mérida, *Spain* 35 G4
Mérida, *Venezuela* 124 B4
Mérida, Cord. de, *Venezuela* . 122 C3
Meriden, *U.K.* 13 E6

Meriden, *U.S.A.* 111 E12
Meridian, Calif., *U.S.A.* ... 116 F5
Meridian, Idaho, *U.S.A.* ... 114 E5
Meridian, Miss., *U.S.A.* ... 109 J1
Mérignac, *France* 20 D3
Merinda, *Australia* 94 C4
Mérinaghène, *Senegal* 82 B1
Meringa, *Nigeria* 83 C7
Merir, *Pac. Oc.* 63 D8
Merirumã, *Brazil* 125 C8
Merkel, *U.S.A.* 113 J5
Mermaid Reef, *Australia* .. 92 C2
Merowe, *Sudan* 80 D3
Merredin, *Australia* 93 F2
Merrick, *U.K.* 14 F4
Merrickville, *Canada* 111 B9
Merrill, Oreg., *U.S.A.* 114 E3
Merrill, Wis., *U.S.A.* 112 C10
Merrimack →, *U.S.A.* 111 D14
Merriman, *U.S.A.* 112 D4
Merritt, *Canada* 104 C4
Merritt Island, *U.S.A.* 109 L5
Merry I., *Canada* 102 A4
Merryville, *U.S.A.* 113 K8
Mersa Fatma, *Eritrea* 81 E5
Mersch, *Lux.* 17 E6
Merse →, *Italy* 29 E8
Mersea I., *U.K.* 13 F8
Merseburg, *Germany* 24 D7
Mersey →, *U.K.* 12 D4
Merseyside □, *U.K.* 12 D4
Mersin, *Turkey* 70 B2
Mersing, *Malaysia* 65 L4
Merta, *India* 68 F6
Merta Road, *India* 68 F5
Merthyr Tydfil, *U.K.* 13 F4
Merthyr Tydfil □, *U.K.* 13 F4
Mértola, *Portugal* 35 H3
Mertzon, *U.S.A.* 113 K4
Méru, *France* 19 C9
Meru, *Kenya* 86 B4
Meru, *Tanzania* 86 C4
Merville, *France* 19 B9
Méry-sur-Seine, *France* ... 19 D10
Merzifon, *Turkey* 72 B6
Merzig, *Germany* 25 F2
Mesa, *U.S.A.* 115 K8
Mesa Verde National Park,
  U.S.A. 115 H9
Mesagne, *Italy* 31 B10
Mesanagrós, *Greece* 36 C9
Mesaoría □, *Cyprus* 36 D12
Mesarás, Kólpos, *Greece* .. 36 D6
Meschede, *Germany* 24 D4
Mescit, *Turkey* 73 B9
Mesfinto, *Ethiopia* 81 E4
Mesgouez, L., *Canada* 102 B5
Meshchovsk, *Russia* 46 E8
Meshed = Mashhad, *Iran* .. 71 B8
Meshoppen, *U.S.A.* 111 E8
Meshra er Req, *Sudan* 81 F2
Mesilinka →, *Canada* 104 B4
Mesilla, *U.S.A.* 115 K10
Meslay-du-Maine, *France* .. 18 E6
Mesocco, *Switz.* 25 J5
Mesolóngion, *Greece* 38 C3
Mesopotamia = Al Jazirah, *Iraq* . 70 C4
Mesopotamia, *U.S.A.* 110 E4
Mesopótamon, *Greece* 38 B2
Mesoraca, *Italy* 31 C9
Mésou Volímais = Volímai,
  Greece 38 D2
Mesquite, *U.S.A.* 115 H6
Messaad, *Algeria* 78 B6
Messac, *France* 18 E5
Messalo →, *Mozam.* 87 E4
Méssaména, *Cameroon* ... 83 E7
Messeue, *Greece* 38 D3
Messina, *Italy* 31 D8
Messina, S. *Africa* 89 C5
Messina, Str. di, *Italy* 31 D8
Messíni, *Greece* 38 D4
Messínia □, *Greece* 38 D3
Messiniakós Kólpos, *Greece* . 38 E4
Messkirch, *Germany* 25 H5
Messonghi, *Greece* 36 B3
Mesta →, *Bulgaria* 40 E7
Mestá, Ákra, *Greece* 39 C7
Mestanza, *Spain* 35 G6
Mestre, *Italy* 29 C9
Mesudiye, *Turkey* 72 B7
Meta →, S. *Amer.* 122 C4
Meta Incógnita Peninsula,
  Canada 101 B13
Metabetchouan, *Canada* .. 103 C5
Metairie, *U.S.A.* 113 L9
Metalici, Munţii, *Romania* . 42 D7
Metaline Falls, *U.S.A.* 114 B5
Metallifere, Colline, *Italy* ... 28 E8
Metán, *Argentina* 126 B3
Metangula, *Mozam.* 87 E3
Metauro →, *Italy* 29 E10
Metema, *Ethiopia* 81 E4
Metengobalame, *Mozam.* .. 87 E3
Methána, *Greece* 38 D5
Methóni, *Greece* 38 E3
Methven, *N.Z.* 91 K3
Metil, *Mozam.* 87 F4
Metkovets, *Bulgaria* 40 C7
Metković, *Croatia* 29 E14
Metlakatla, *U.S.A.* 100 C6
Metlika, *Slovenia* 29 C12
Metropolis, *U.S.A.* 113 G10
Metu, *Ethiopia* 81 F4

Metz, *France* 19 C13
Metzingen, *Germany* 25 G5
Meulaboh, *Indonesia* 62 D1
Meung-sur-Loire, *France* .. 19 E8
Meureudu, *Indonesia* 62 C1
Meurthe →, *France* 19 D13
Meurthe-et-Moselle □, *France* . 19 D13
Meuse □, *France* 19 C12
Meuse →, *Europe* 17 D5
Meuselwitz, *Germany* 24 D8
Mexia, *U.S.A.* 113 K6
Mexiana, I., *Brazil* 125 D9
Mexicali, *Mexico* 117 N11
Mexican Plateau, *Mexico* ... 98 G9
Mexican Water, *U.S.A.* ... 115 H9
México, *Mexico* 119 D5
Mexico, Maine, *U.S.A.* ... 111 B14
Mexico, Mo., *U.S.A.* 112 F9
Mexico, N.Y., *U.S.A.* 111 C8
México □, *Mexico* 119 D5
Mexico ■, Cent. Amer. 118 C4
Mexico, G. of, Cent. Amer. ... 119 C7
Mexico B., *U.S.A.* 111 C8
Meydān-e Naftūn, *Iran* 71 D6
Meydani, Ra's-e, *Iran* 71 E8
Meyenburg, *Germany* 24 B8
Meymac, *France* 20 C6
Meymaneh, *Afghan.* 66 B4
Meyrueis, *France* 20 D7
Meyssac, *France* 20 C5
Meyzieu, *France* 21 C8
Mezdra, *Bulgaria* 40 C7
Mèze, *France* 20 E7
Mezen, *Russia* 50 C5
Mezen →, *Russia* 50 C5
Mézenc, Mt., *France* 21 D8
Mezeş, Munţii, *Romania* .. 42 C8
Mezha →, *Russia* 46 E6
Mezhdurechenskiy, *Russia* . 50 D7
Mézidon-Canon, *France* ... 18 C6
Mézières-en-Brenne, *France* . 20 B5
Mézilhac, *France* 21 D8
Mézin, *France* 20 D4
Mezőberény, *Hungary* 42 D6
Mezőfalva, *Hungary* 42 D3
Mezőhegyes, *Hungary* 42 D5
Mezőkövácsháza, *Hungary* . 42 D5
Mezőkövesd, *Hungary* 42 C5
Mézos, *France* 20 D2
Mezőtúr, *Hungary* 42 C5
Mezquital, *Mexico* 118 C4
Mezzolombardo, *Italy* 28 B8
Mfolozi →, S. *Africa* 89 D5
Mgeta, *Tanzania* 87 D4
Mglin, *Russia* 47 F7
Mhlaba Hills, *Zimbabwe* .. 87 F3
Mhow, *India* 68 H6
Miahuatlán, *Mexico* 119 D5
Miajadas, *Spain* 35 F5
Miami, Fla., *U.S.A.* 109 N5
Miami, Okla., *U.S.A.* 113 G7
Miami, Tex., *U.S.A.* 113 H4
Miami Beach, *U.S.A.* 109 N5
Mian Xian, *China* 56 H4
Mianchi, *China* 56 G6
Mīāndarreh, *Iran* 71 C7
Mīāndowāb, *Iran* 70 B5
Miandrivazo, *Madag.* 89 B8
Mīāneh, *Iran* 70 B5
Mianning, *China* 58 C4
Mianwali, *Pakistan* 68 C4
Mianyang, *China* 58 B5
Mianzhu, *China* 58 B5
Miaoli, *Taiwan* 59 E13
Miarinarivo, Antananarivo,
  Madag. 89 B8
Miarinarivo, Toamasina, *Madag.* 89 B8
Miariravaratra, *Madag.* ... 89 C8
Miass, *Russia* 50 D7
Miasteczko Krajeńskie, *Poland* 45 E4
Miastko, *Poland* 44 E3
Mica, S. *Africa* 89 C5
Micăsasa, *Romania* 43 D9
Michalovce, *Slovak Rep.* ... 27 C14
Michigan □, *U.S.A.* 108 C3
Michigan, L., *U.S.A.* 108 D2
Michigan City, *U.S.A.* 108 E2
Michika, *Nigeria* 83 C7
Michipicoten I., *Canada* ... 102 C2
Michoacan □, *Mexico* 118 D4
Michurin, *Bulgaria* 41 D11
Michurinsk, *Russia* 48 D5
Mico, Pta., *Nic.* 120 D3
Micronesia, Pac. Oc. 96 G7
Micronesia, Federated States
  of ■, Pac. Oc. 96 G7
Midai, *Indonesia* 65 L6
Midale, *Canada* 105 D8
Middelburg, *Neths.* 17 C3
Middelburg, Eastern Cape,
  S. *Africa* 88 E4
Middelburg, Mpumalanga,
  S. *Africa* 89 D4
Middelfart, *Denmark* 11 J3
Middelwit, S. *Africa* 88 C4
Middle Alkali L., *U.S.A.* 114 F3
Middle East, *Asia* 52 F7
Middle Fork Feather →, *U.S.A.* . 116 F5
Middle I., *Australia* 93 F3
Middle Sackville, *Canada* .. 103 D7
Middleburg, Fla., *U.S.A.* .. 109 K5
Middleburg, N.Y., *U.S.A.* .. 111 D10
Metu, *Ethiopia* 81 F4

Middleburg, Pa., *U.S.A.* 110 F7
Middlebury, *U.S.A.* 111 B11
Middlemount, *Australia* ... 94 C4
Middleport, N.Y., *U.S.A.* ... 110 C6
Middleport, Ohio, *U.S.A.* .. 108 F4
Middlesboro, *U.S.A.* 109 G4
Middlesbrough, *U.K.* 12 C6
Middlesbrough □, *U.K.* 12 C6
Middlesex, *Belize* 120 C2
Middlesex, N.J., *U.S.A.* ... 111 F10
Middlesex, N.Y., *U.S.A.* ... 110 D7
Middleton, *Australia* 94 C3
Middleton, *Canada* 103 D6
Middleton Cr. →, *Australia* . 94 C3
Middletown, *U.K.* 15 B5
Middletown, Calif., *U.S.A.* . 116 G4
Middletown, Conn., *U.S.A.* . 111 E12
Middletown, N.Y., *U.S.A.* . 111 E10
Middletown, Ohio, *U.S.A.* .. 108 F3
Middletown, Pa., *U.S.A.* ... 111 F8
Midhurst, *U.K.* 13 G7
Mīdī, *Yemen* 81 D5
Midi, Canal du →, *France* .. 20 E5
Midi d'Ossau, Pic du, *France* . 20 F3
Midi-Pyrénées □, *France* ... 20 E5
Midland, *Canada* 102 D4
Midland, Calif., *U.S.A.* ... 117 M12
Midland, Mich., *U.S.A.* ... 108 D3
Midland, Pa., *U.S.A.* 110 F4
Midland, Tex., *U.S.A.* 113 K3
Midlands □, *Zimbabwe* 87 F2
Midleton, *Ireland* 15 E3
Midlothian, *U.S.A.* 113 J6
Midlothian □, *U.K.* 14 F5
Midongy, Tangorombohitr' i,
  Madag. 89 C8
Midongy Atsimo, *Madag.* .. 89 C8
Midou →, *France* 20 E3
Midouze →, *France* 20 E3
Midsayap, *Phil.* 61 H6
Midu, *China* 58 E3
Midway Is., *Pac. Oc.* 96 E10
Midway Wells, *U.S.A.* 117 N11
Midwest, *U.S.A.* 114 E10
Midwest City, *U.S.A.* 113 H6
Midyat, *Turkey* 70 B4
Midžor, *Bulgaria* 40 C6
Mie □, *Japan* 55 G8
Miechów, *Poland* 45 H7
Miedwie, Jezioro, *Poland* .. 45 E1
Międzybórz, *Poland* 45 G4
Międzychód, *Poland* 45 F2
Międzylesie, *Poland* 45 H3
Międzyrzec Podlaski, *Poland* . 45 G9
Międzyrzecz, *Poland* 45 F2
Międzyzdroje, *Poland* 44 E1
Miejska Górka, *Poland* 45 G3
Miélan, *France* 20 E4
Mielec, *Poland* 45 H8
Mienga, *Angola* 88 B2
Miercurea-Ciuc, *Romania* . 43 D10
Miercurea Sibiului, *Romania* 43 E8
Mieres, *Spain* 34 B5
Mieroszów, *Poland* 45 H3
Mieso, *Ethiopia* 81 F5
Mieszkowice, *Poland* 45 F1
Mifflintown, *U.S.A.* 110 F7
Mifraz Ḥefa, *Israel* 75 C4
Migennes, *France* 19 E10
Migliarino, *Italy* 29 D8
Miguel Alemán, Presa, *Mexico* . 119 D5
Miguelturra, *Spain* 35 G7
Mihăileni, *Romania* 43 C11
Mihăileşti, *Romania* 43 F10
Mihailovca, *Moldova* 43 D13
Mihalgazi, *Turkey* 39 A12
Mihaliççik, *Turkey* 72 C4
Mihara, *Japan* 55 G6
Miheşu de Cîmpie, *Romania* 43 D9
Mijas, *Spain* 35 J6
Mikasa, *Japan* 54 C10
Mikese, *Tanzania* 86 D4
Mikha-Tskhakaya = Senaki,
  Georgia 49 J6
Mikhailovka = Mykhaylivka,
  Ukraine 47 J8
Mikhaylov, *Russia* 46 E10
Mikhaylovgrad = Montana,
  Bulgaria 40 C7
Mikhaylovka, *Russia* 48 E6
Mikhnevo, *Russia* 46 E9
Mikínai, *Greece* 38 D4
Mikkeli, *Finland* 9 F22
Mikkwa →, *Canada* 104 B6
Mikniya, *Sudan* 81 D3
Mikołajki, *Poland* 44 E8
Míkonos, *Greece* 38 D7
Mikrí Préspa, Límni, *Greece* . 40 F5
Mikrón Dhérion, *Greece* .. 41 E10
Mikstat, *Poland* 45 G4
Mikulov, *Czech Rep.* 27 C9
Mikumi, *Tanzania* 86 D4
Milaca, *U.S.A.* 112 C8
Milagro, *Ecuador* 124 D3
Milagros, *Phil.* 61 E5
Milan = Milano, *Italy* 28 C6
Milan, Mo., *U.S.A.* 112 E8
Milan, Tenn., *U.S.A.* 109 H1
Milange, *Mozam.* 87 F4
Milano, *Italy* 28 C6
Milano, *Madag.* 89 A8
Milâs, *Turkey* 39 D9
Milatos, *Greece* 36 D7
Milazzo, *Italy* 31 D8
Milbank, *U.S.A.* 112 C6
Milbanke Sd., *Canada* 104 C3
Milden, *Canada* 105 C7

Mildenhall, *U.K.* 13 E8
Mildmay, *Canada* 110 B3
Mile, *China* 58 E4
Miléai, *Greece* 38 B5
Miles, *Australia* 95 D5
Miles City, *U.S.A.* 112 B2
Mileşti, *Moldova* 43 C13
Milestone, *Canada* 105 D8
Mileto, *Italy* 31 D9
Miletto, Mte., *Italy* 31 A7
Miletus, *Turkey* 39 D9
Milevsko, *Czech Rep.* 26 B7
Milford, *Calif., U.S.A.* 116 E6
Milford, *Conn., U.S.A.* 111 E11
Milford, *Del., U.S.A.* 108 F8
Milford, *Mass., U.S.A.* 111 D13
Milford, *N.H., U.S.A.* 111 D13
Milford, *Pa., U.S.A.* 111 E10
Milford, *Utah, U.S.A.* 115 G7
Milford Haven, *U.K.* 13 F2
Milford Sd., *N.Z.* 91 L1
Milḩ, Baḩr al, *Iraq* 70 C4
Milicz, *Poland* 45 G4
Milikapiti, *Australia* 92 B5
Miling, *Australia* 93 F2
Militello in Val di Catánia, *Italy* 31 E7
Milk →, *U.S.A.* 114 B10
Milk, Wadi el →, *Sudan* 80 D3
Milk River, *Canada* 104 D6
Mill I., *Antarctica* 5 C8
Mill Valley, *U.S.A.* 116 H4
Millárs →, *Spain* 32 F4
Millau, *France* 20 D7
Millbridge, *Canada* 110 B7
Millbrook, *Canada* 110 B6
Millbrook, *U.S.A.* 111 E11
Mille Lacs, L. des, *Canada* 102 C1
Mille Lacs L., *U.S.A.* 112 B8
Milledgeville, *U.S.A.* 109 J4
Millen, *U.S.A.* 109 J5
Millennium I. = Caroline I., *Kiribati* 97 H12
Miller, *U.S.A.* 112 C5
Millerovo, *Russia* 49 F5
Millersburg, *Ohio, U.S.A.* 110 F3
Millersburg, *Pa., U.S.A.* 110 F8
Millerton, *U.S.A.* 111 E11
Millerton L., *U.S.A.* 116 J7
Millevaches, Plateau de, *France* 20 C6
Millheim, *U.S.A.* 110 F7
Millington, *U.S.A.* 113 H10
Millinocket, *U.S.A.* 109 C11
Millmerran, *Australia* 95 D5
Millom, *U.K.* 12 C4
Millsboro, *U.S.A.* 110 G5
Milltown Malbay, *Ireland* 15 D2
Millville, *N.J., U.S.A.* 108 F8
Millville, *Pa., U.S.A.* 111 E8
Millwood, *U.S.A.* 113 J8
Milna, *Croatia* 29 E13
Milne →, *Australia* 94 C2
Milo, *U.S.A.* 109 C11
Mílos, *Greece* 38 E6
Miłosław, *Poland* 45 F4
Milot, *Albania* 40 E3
Milparinka, *Australia* 95 D3
Miltenberg, *Germany* 25 F5
Milton, *N.S., Canada* 103 D7
Milton, *Ont., Canada* 110 C5
Milton, *N.Z.* 91 M2
Milton, *Calif., U.S.A.* 116 G6
Milton, *Fla., U.S.A.* 109 K2
Milton, *Pa., U.S.A.* 110 F8
Milton, *Vt., U.S.A.* 111 B11
Milton-Freewater, *U.S.A.* 114 D4
Milton Keynes, *U.K.* 13 E7
Milton Keynes □, *U.K.* 13 E7
Miluo, *China* 59 C9
Milverton, *Canada* 110 C4
Milwaukee, *U.S.A.* 108 D2
Milwaukee Deep, *Atl. Oc.* 121 C6
Milwaukie, *U.S.A.* 116 E4
Mim, *Ghana* 82 D4
Mimizan, *France* 20 D2
Mimoň, *Czech Rep.* 26 A7
Min Jiang →, *Fujian, China* 59 E12
Min Jiang →, *Sichuan, China* 58 C5
Min Xian, *China* 56 G3
Mina Pirquitas, *Argentina* 126 A2
Mīnā Suʿud, *Si. Arabia* 71 D6
Mīnāʾal Aḥmadī, *Kuwait* 71 D6
Minago →, *Canada* 105 C9
Minaki, *Canada* 105 D10
Minamata, *Japan* 55 H5
Minami-Tori-Shima, *Pac. Oc.* 96 E7
Minas, *Uruguay* 127 C4
Minas, Sierra de las, *Guatemala* 120 C2
Minas Basin, *Canada* 103 C7
Minas de Rio Tinto = Minas de Riotinto, *Spain* 35 H4
Minas de Riotinto, *Spain* 35 H4
Minas Gerais □, *Brazil* 125 G9
Minatitlán, *Mexico* 119 D6
Minbu, *Burma* 67 J19
Minchinabad, *Pakistan* 68 D5
Mincio →, *Italy* 28 C7
Minčol, *Slovak Rep.* 27 B13
Mindanao, *Phil.* 61 H6
Mindanao Sea = Bohol Sea, *Phil.* 63 C6
Mindanao Trench, *Pac. Oc.* 61 F7
Mindel →, *Germany* 25 G6
Mindelheim, *Germany* 25 G6
Minden, *Canada* 110 B6
Minden, *Germany* 24 C4
Minden, *La., U.S.A.* 113 J8

Minden, *Nev., U.S.A.* 116 G7
Mindiptana, *Indonesia* 63 F10
Mindoro, *Phil.* 61 E4
Mindoro Str., *Phil.* 61 E4
Mine, *Japan* 55 G5
Minehead, *U.K.* 13 F4
Mineola, *N.Y., U.S.A.* 111 F11
Mineola, *Tex., U.S.A.* 113 J7
Mineral King, *U.S.A.* 116 J8
Mineral Wells, *U.S.A.* 113 J5
Mineralnyye Vody, *Russia* 49 H6
Minersville, *U.S.A.* 111 F8
Minerva, *U.S.A.* 110 F3
Minervino Murge, *Italy* 31 A9
Minetto, *U.S.A.* 111 C8
Mingäçevir, *Azerbaijan* 49 K8
Mingäçevir Su Anbarı, *Azerbaijan* 49 K8
Mingan, *Canada* 103 B7
Mingechaur = Mingäçevir, *Azerbaijan* 49 K8
Mingechaurskoye Vdkhr. = Mingäçevir Su Anbarı, *Azerbaijan* 49 K8
Mingela, *Australia* 94 B4
Mingenew, *Australia* 93 E2
Mingera Cr. →, *Australia* 94 C2
Minggang, *China* 59 A10
Mingguang, *China* 59 A11
Mingin, *Burma* 67 H19
Mingir, *Moldova* 43 D13
Minglanilla, *Spain* 33 F3
Minglun, *China* 58 E7
Mingo Junction, *U.S.A.* 110 F4
Mingorria, *Spain* 34 E6
Mingshan, *China* 58 B4
Mingteke Daban = Mintaka Pass, *Pakistan* 69 A6
Mingxi, *China* 59 D11
Mingyuegue, *China* 57 C15
Minho = Miño →, *Spain* 34 D2
Minhou, *China* 59 E12
Miniçevo, *Serbia, Yug.* 42 G7
Minidoka, *U.S.A.* 114 E7
Minigwal, L., *Australia* 93 E3
Minilya →, *Australia* 93 D1
Minilya Roadhouse, *Australia* 93 D1
Minipi L., *Canada* 103 B7
Mink L., *Canada* 104 A5
Minkammen, *Sudan* 81 F3
Minna, *Nigeria* 83 D6
Minneapolis, *Kans., U.S.A.* 112 F6
Minneapolis, *Minn., U.S.A.* 112 C8
Minnedosa, *Canada* 105 C9
Minnesota □, *U.S.A.* 112 B8
Minnesota →, *U.S.A.* 112 C8
Minnewaukan, *U.S.A.* 112 A5
Minnipa, *Australia* 95 E2
Minnitaki L., *Canada* 102 C1
Mino, *Japan* 55 G8
Miño, *Spain* 34 B2
Miño →, *Spain* 34 D2
Minoa, *Greece* 39 F7
Minorca = Menorca, *Spain* 37 B11
Minot, *U.S.A.* 112 A4
Minqin, *China* 56 E2
Minqing, *China* 59 D12
Minsen, *Germany* 24 B3
Minsk, *Belarus* 46 F4
Mińsk Mazowiecki, *Poland* 45 F8
Mintabie, *Australia* 95 D1
Minto, *Canada* 103 C6
Minto, L., *Canada* 102 A5
Minton, *Canada* 105 D8
Minturn, *U.S.A.* 114 G10
Minturno, *Italy* 30 A6
Minûf, *Egypt* 80 H7
Minusinsk, *Russia* 51 D10
Minutang, *India* 67 E20
Minya el Qamh, *Egypt* 80 H7
Mionica, *Bos.-H.* 42 F3
Mionica, *Serbia, Yug.* 40 B4
Miquelon, *Canada* 102 C4
Miquelon, *St-P. & M.* 103 C8
Mir, *Niger* 83 C7
Mīr Kūh, *Iran* 71 E8
Mīr Shahdād, *Iran* 71 E8
Mira, *Italy* 29 C9
Mira, *Portugal* 34 E2
Mira →, *Portugal* 35 H2
Mira por vos Cay, *Bahamas* 121 B5
Mirabella Eclano, *Italy* 31 A7
Miraj, *India* 66 L9
Miram Shah, *Pakistan* 68 C4
Miramar, *Argentina* 126 D4
Miramar, *Mozam.* 89 C6
Miramas, *France* 21 E8
Mirambeau, *France* 20 C3
Miramichi, *Canada* 103 C6
Miramichi B., *Canada* 103 C7
Miramont-de-Guyenne, *France* 20 D4
Miranda, *Brazil* 125 H7
Miranda →, *Brazil* 124 G7
Miranda de Ebro, *Spain* 32 C2
Miranda do Corvo, *Portugal* 34 E2
Miranda do Douro, *Portugal* 34 D4
Mirande, *France* 20 E4
Mirandela, *Portugal* 34 D3
Mirándola, *Italy* 28 D8
Mirandópolis, *Brazil* 127 A5
Mirango, *Malawi* 87 E3
Mirano, *Italy* 29 C9
Miras, *Albania* 40 F4
Mirassol, *Brazil* 127 A6
Mirbāṭ, *Oman* 74 D5

Mirear, *Egypt* 80 C4
Mirebeau, *Côte-d'Or, France* 19 E12
Mirebeau, *Vienne, France* 18 F7
Mirecourt, *France* 19 D13
Mirgorod = Myrhorod, *Ukraine* 47 H7
Miri, *Malaysia* 62 D4
Miriam Vale, *Australia* 94 C5
Miribel, *France* 19 G11
Mirim, L., *S. Amer.* 127 C5
Mirnyy, *Russia* 51 C12
Miročh, *Serbia, Yug.* 40 B6
Mirokhan, *Pakistan* 68 F3
Mirond L., *Canada* 105 B8
Mirosławiec, *Poland* 44 E3
Mirpur, *Pakistan* 69 C5
Mirpur Batoro, *Pakistan* 68 G3
Mirpur Bibiwari, *Pakistan* 68 E2
Mirpur Khas, *Pakistan* 68 G3
Mirpur Sakro, *Pakistan* 68 G2
Mirria, *Niger* 83 C6
Mirsk, *Poland* 45 H2
Mirtağ, *Turkey* 70 B4
Miryang, *S. Korea* 57 G15
Mirzaani, *Georgia* 49 K8
Mirzapur, *India* 69 G10
Mirzapur-cum-Vindhyachal = Mirzapur, *India* 69 G10
Misantla, *Mexico* 119 D5
Misawa, *Japan* 54 D10
Miscou I., *Canada* 103 C7
Mish'āb, Ra's al, *Si. Arabia* 71 D6
Mishan, *China* 60 B8
Mishawaka, *U.S.A.* 108 E2
Mishbih, Gebel, *Egypt* 80 C3
Mishima, *Japan* 55 G9
Misión, *Mexico* 117 N10
Misiones □, *Argentina* 127 B5
Misiones □, *Paraguay* 126 B4
Miskah, *Si. Arabia* 70 E4
Miskitos, Cayos, *Nic.* 120 D3
Miskolc, *Hungary* 42 B5
Misool, *Indonesia* 63 E8
Mişrātah, *Libya* 79 B9
Missanabie, *Canada* 102 C3
Missinaibi →, *Canada* 102 B3
Missinaibi L., *Canada* 102 C3
Mission, *Canada* 104 D4
Mission, *S. Dak., U.S.A.* 112 D4
Mission, *Tex., U.S.A.* 113 M5
Mission Beach, *Australia* 94 B4
Mission Viejo, *U.S.A.* 117 M9
Missirah, *Senegal* 82 C1
Missisa L., *Canada* 102 B2
Mississagi →, *Canada* 102 C3
Mississauga, *Canada* 110 C5
Mississippi □, *U.S.A.* 113 J10
Mississippi →, *U.S.A.* 113 L10
Mississippi L., *Canada* 111 A8
Mississippi River Delta, *U.S.A.* 113 L9
Mississippi Sd., *U.S.A.* 113 K10
Missoula, *U.S.A.* 114 C7
Missouri □, *U.S.A.* 112 F8
Missouri →, *U.S.A.* 112 F9
Missouri City, *U.S.A.* 113 L7
Missouri Valley, *U.S.A.* 112 E7
Mist, *U.S.A.* 116 E3
Mistassibi →, *Canada* 103 B5
Mistassini, *Canada* 103 C5
Mistassini →, *Canada* 103 C5
Mistassini, L., *Canada* 102 B5
Mistastin L., *Canada* 103 A7
Mistelbach, *Austria* 27 C9
Misterbianco, *Italy* 31 E8
Mistinibi, L., *Canada* 103 A7
Mistretta, *Italy* 31 E7
Misty L., *Canada* 105 B8
Misurata = Mişrātah, *Libya* 79 B9
Mît Ghamr, *Egypt* 80 H7
Mitatib, *Sudan* 81 D4
Mitchell, *Australia* 95 D4
Mitchell, *Canada* 110 C3
Mitchell, *Nebr., U.S.A.* 112 E3
Mitchell, *Oreg., U.S.A.* 114 D3
Mitchell, *S. Dak., U.S.A.* 112 D6
Mitchell →, *Australia* 94 B3
Mitchell, Mt., *U.S.A.* 109 H4
Mitchell Ranges, *Australia* 94 A2
Mitchelstown, *Ireland* 15 D3
Mitha Tiwana, *Pakistan* 68 C5
Mithi, *Pakistan* 68 G3
Mithrao, *Pakistan* 68 F3
Mitilíni, *Greece* 39 B8
Mitilinoí, *Greece* 39 D8
Mito, *Japan* 55 F10
Mitrofanovka, *Russia* 47 H10
Mitrovica = Kosovska Mitrovica, *Kosovo, Yug.* 40 D4
Mitsinjo, *Madag.* 89 B8
Mitsiwa, *Eritrea* 81 D4
Mitsiwa Channel, *Eritrea* 81 D5
Mitsukaidō, *Japan* 55 F9
Mittelberg, *Austria* 26 D3
Mittelfranken □, *Germany* 25 F6
Mittellandkanal →, *Germany* 24 C5
Mittenwalde, *Germany* 24 C9
Mitterteich, *Germany* 25 F8
Mittimatalik = Pond Inlet, *Canada* 101 A12
Mittweida, *Germany* 24 E8
Mitú, *Colombia* 124 C4
Mitumba, *Tanzania* 86 D3

Mitumba, Mts., *Dem. Rep. of the Congo* 86 D2
Mitwaba, *Dem. Rep. of the Congo* 87 D2
Mityana, *Uganda* 86 B3
Mixteco →, *Mexico* 119 D5
Miyagi □, *Japan* 54 E10
Miyah, W. el →, *Egypt* 80 C3
Miyāh, W. el →, *Syria* 70 C3
Miyake-Jima, *Japan* 55 G9
Miyako, *Japan* 54 E10
Miyako-Jima, *Japan* 55 M2
Miyako-Rettō, *Japan* 55 M2
Miyakonojō, *Japan* 55 J5
Miyani, *India* 68 J3
Miyanoura-Dake, *Japan* 55 J5
Miyazaki, *Japan* 55 J5
Miyazaki □, *Japan* 55 H5
Miyazu, *Japan* 55 G7
Miyet, Bahr el = Dead Sea, *Asia* 75 D4
Miyi, *China* 58 D4
Miyoshi, *Japan* 55 G6
Miyun, *China* 56 D9
Miyun Shuiku, *China* 56 D9
Mizan Teferi, *Ethiopia* 81 F4
Mizdah, *Libya* 79 B8
Mizen Hd., *Cork, Ireland* 15 E2
Mizen Hd., *Wick., Ireland* 15 D5
Mizhi, *China* 56 F6
Mizil, *Romania* 43 F11
Mizoram □, *India* 67 H18
Mizpe Ramon, *Israel* 75 E3
Mizusawa, *Japan* 54 E10
Mjällby, *Sweden* 11 H8
Mjöbäck, *Sweden* 11 G6
Mjölby, *Sweden* 11 F9
Mjörn, *Sweden* 11 G6
Mjøsa, *Norway* 9 F14
Mkata, *Tanzania* 86 D4
Mkokotoni, *Tanzania* 86 D4
Mkomazi, *Tanzania* 86 C4
Mkomazi →, *S. Africa* 89 E5
Mkulwe, *Tanzania* 87 D3
Mkumbi, Ras, *Tanzania* 86 D4
Mkushi, *Zambia* 87 E2
Mkushi River, *Zambia* 87 E2
Mkuze, *S. Africa* 89 D5
Mladá Boleslav, *Czech Rep.* 26 A7
Mladenovac, *Serbia, Yug.* 40 B4
Mlala Hills, *Tanzania* 86 D3
Mlange = Mulanje, *Malawi* 87 F4
Mlanje, Pic, *Malawi* 85 H7
Mlava →, *Serbia, Yug.* 40 B5
Mława, *Poland* 45 E7
Mlinište, *Bos.-H.* 29 D13
Mljet, *Croatia* 29 F14
Mljetski Kanal, *Croatia* 29 F14
Młynary, *Poland* 44 D6
Mmabatho, *S. Africa* 88 D4
Mme, *Cameroon* 83 D7
Mnichovo Hradiště, *Czech Rep.* 26 A7
Mo i Rana, *Norway* 8 C16
Moa, *Cuba* 121 B4
Moa, *Indonesia* 63 F7
Moa →, *S. Leone* 82 D2
Moab, *U.S.A.* 115 G9
Moala, *Fiji* 91 D8
Moama, *Australia* 95 F3
Moamba, *Mozam.* 89 D5
Moapa, *U.S.A.* 117 J12
Moate, *Ireland* 15 C4
Moba, *Dem. Rep. of the Congo* 86 D2
Mobārakābād, *Iran* 71 D7
Mobaye, *C.A.R.* 84 D4
Mobayi, *Dem. Rep. of the Congo* 84 D4
Moberly Lake, *Canada* 104 B4
Moberly, *U.S.A.* 112 F8
Mobile, *U.S.A.* 109 K1
Mobile B., *U.S.A.* 109 K2
Mobridge, *U.S.A.* 112 C4
Mobutu Sese Seko, L. = Albert, L., *Africa* 86 B3
Moc Chau, *Vietnam* 64 B5
Moc Hoa, *Vietnam* 65 G5
Mocabe Kasari, *Dem. Rep. of the Congo* 87 D2
Moçambique, *Mozam.* 87 F5
Moçâmedes = Namibe, *Angola* 85 H2
Mocanaqua, *U.S.A.* 111 E8
Mochudi, *Botswana* 88 C4
Mocimboa da Praia, *Mozam.* 87 E5
Mociu, *Romania* 43 D9
Möckeln, *Sweden* 11 H8
Mockfjärd, *Sweden* 10 D8
Moclips, *U.S.A.* 116 C2
Mocoa, *Colombia* 124 C3
Mococa, *Brazil* 127 A6
Mocorito, *Mexico* 118 B3
Moctezuma, *Mexico* 118 B3
Moctezuma →, *Mexico* 119 C5
Mocúzari, Presa, *Mexico* 118 B3
Mocuba, *Mozam.* 87 F4
Modane, *France* 21 C10
Modasa, *India* 68 H5
Modder →, *S. Africa* 88 D3
Modderrivier, *S. Africa* 88 D3
Módena, *Italy* 28 D7
Modena, *U.S.A.* 115 H7
Módica, *Italy* 31 F7
Mödling, *Austria* 27 C9
Modo, *Sudan* 81 F3
Modra, *Slovak Rep.* 27 C10
Modriča, *Bos.-H.* 42 F3
Moe, *Australia* 95 F4
Moebase, *Mozam.* 87 F4
Moëlan-sur-Mer, *France* 18 E3

Moengo, *Surinam* 125 B8
Moffat, *U.K.* 14 F5
Moga, *India* 68 D6
Mogadishu = Muqdisho, *Somali Rep.* 74 G4
Mogador = Essaouira, *Morocco* 78 B4
Mogadouro, *Portugal* 34 D4
Mogalakwena →, *S. Africa* 89 C4
Mogami-Gawa →, *Japan* 54 E10
Mogán, *Canary Is.* 37 G4
Mogaung, *Burma* 67 G20
Mogente = Moixent, *Spain* 33 G4
Mogho, *Ethiopia* 81 G5
Mogi das Cruzes, *Brazil* 127 A6
Mogi-Guaçu →, *Brazil* 127 A6
Mogi-Mirim, *Brazil* 127 A6
Mogielnica, *Poland* 45 G7
Mogige, *Ethiopia* 81 F4
Mogilev = Mahilyow, *Belarus* 46 F6
Mogilev-Podolskiy = Mohyliv-Podilskyy, *Ukraine* 47 H4
Mogilno, *Poland* 45 F4
Mogincual, *Mozam.* 87 F5
Mogliano Véneto, *Italy* 29 C9
Mogocha, *Russia* 51 D12
Mogok, *Burma* 67 H20
Mogollon Rim, *U.S.A.* 115 J8
Mógoro, *Italy* 30 C1
Mograt, *Sudan* 80 D3
Moguer, *Spain* 35 H4
Mohács, *Hungary* 42 E3
Mohales Hoek, *Lesotho* 88 E4
Mohall, *U.S.A.* 112 A4
Mohammadābād, *Iran* 71 B8
Mohammedia, *Morocco* 78 B4
Mohana →, *India* 69 G11
Mohanlalganj, *India* 69 F9
Mohave, L., *U.S.A.* 117 K12
Mohawk →, *U.S.A.* 111 D11
Moheda, *Sweden* 11 G8
Mohenjodaro, *Pakistan* 68 F3
Mohicanville Reservoir, *U.S.A.* 110 F3
Möhne →, *Germany* 24 D3
Mohoro, *Tanzania* 86 D4
Mohyliv-Podilskyy, *Ukraine* 47 H4
Moia, *Sudan* 81 F2
Moidart, L., *U.K.* 14 E3
Moineşti, *Romania* 43 D11
Moira →, *Canada* 110 B7
Moirans, *France* 21 C9
Moirans-en-Montagne, *France* 19 F12
Moíres, *Greece* 36 D6
Moisaküla, *Estonia* 9 G21
Moisie, *Canada* 103 B7
Moisie →, *Canada* 103 B7
Moissac, *France* 20 D5
Moita, *Portugal* 35 G2
Moixent, *Spain* 33 G4
Möja, *Sweden* 10 E12
Mojácar, *Spain* 33 H3
Mojados, *Spain* 34 D6
Mojave, *U.S.A.* 117 K8
Mojave Desert, *U.S.A.* 117 L10
Mojiang, *China* 58 F3
Mojo, *Ethiopia* 81 F5
Mojkovac, *Montenegro, Yug.* 40 C3
Mojo, *Bolivia* 126 A2
Mojo, *Ethiopia* 81 F5
Mojokerto, *Indonesia* 63 G15
Mokai, *N.Z.* 91 H5
Mokambo, *Dem. Rep. of the Congo* 87 E2
Mokameh, *India* 69 G11
Mokau, *N.Z.* 91 H5
Mokelumne →, *U.S.A.* 116 G5
Mokelumne Hill, *U.S.A.* 116 G6
Mokhós, *Greece* 36 D7
Mokhotlong, *Lesotho* 89 D4
Mokokchung, *India* 67 F19
Mokolo, *Cameroon* 83 C7
Mokolo →, *S. Africa* 89 C4
Mokp'o, *S. Korea* 57 G14
Mokra Gora, *Yugoslavia* 40 D4
Mokronog, *Slovenia* 29 C12
Moksha →, *Russia* 48 C6
Mokshan, *Russia* 48 D7
Mokwa, *Nigeria* 83 D6
Mol, *Belgium* 17 C5
Mola di Bari, *Italy* 31 A10
Molale, *Ethiopia* 81 E4
Moláoi, *Greece* 38 E4
Molara, *Italy* 30 B2
Molat, *Croatia* 29 D11
Molchanovo, *Russia* 50 D9
Mold, *U.K.* 12 D4
Moldava nad Bodvou, *Slovak Rep.* 27 C14
Moldavia = Moldova ■, *Europe* 43 C13
Moldavia, *Romania* 43 D10
Molde, *Norway* 8 E12
Moldova ■, *Europe* 43 C13
Moldova Nouă, *Romania* 42 F6
Moldoveanu, Vf., *Romania* 43 F8
Moldoviţa, *Romania* 43 C10
Mole →, *U.K.* 13 F7
Mole Creek, *Australia* 94 G4
Molepolole, *Botswana* 88 C4
Molfetta, *Italy* 31 A9
Molina de Aragón, *Spain* 32 E3
Molina de Segura, *Spain* 33 G3
Moline, *U.S.A.* 112 E9
Molinella, *Italy* 29 D8
Molinos, *Argentina* 126 B2
Moliro, *Dem. Rep. of the Congo* 86 D3

Morvern *(header)*

Moliterno, *Italy* 31 B8
Molkom, *Sweden* 10 E7
Mölle, *Sweden* 11 H6
Molledo, *Spain* 34 B6
Mollendo, *Peru* 124 G4
Mollerin, L., *Australia* 93 F2
Mollerussa, *Spain* 32 D5
Mollina, *Spain* 35 H6
Mölln, *Germany* 24 B6
Mölltorp, *Sweden* 11 F8
Mölnlycke, *Sweden* 11 G6
Molochansk, *Ukraine* 47 J8
Molochnoye, Ozero, *Ukraine* .. 47 J8
Molodechno = Maladzyechna, *Belarus* 46 E4
Molokai, *U.S.A.* 106 H16
Molopo →, *Africa* 88 D3
Mólos, *Greece* 38 C4
Molotov = Perm, *Russia* 50 D6
Molsheim, *France* 19 D14
Molson L., *Canada* 105 C9
Molteno, *S. Africa* 88 E4
Molu, *Indonesia* 63 F8
Molucca Sea, *Indonesia* 63 E6
Moluccas = Maluku, *Indonesia* . 63 E7
Moma, *Dem. Rep. of the Congo* 86 C1
Moma, *Mozam.* 87 F4
Mombasa, *Kenya* 86 C4
Mombetsu, *Japan* 54 B11
Mombuey, *Spain* 34 C4
Momchilgrad, *Bulgaria* 41 E9
Momi, *Dem. Rep. of the Congo* 86 C2
Mompós, *Colombia* 124 B4
Møn, *Denmark* 11 K6
Mon □, *Burma* 67 L20
Mona, Canal de la, *W. Indies* . 121 C6
Mona, Isla, *Puerto Rico* 121 C6
Mona, Pta., *Costa Rica* 120 E3
Monaca, *U.S.A.* 110 F4
Monaco ■, *Europe* 21 E11
Monadhliath Mts., *U.K.* 14 D4
Monadnock, Mt., *U.S.A.* 111 D12
Monaghan, *Ireland* 15 B5
Monaghan □, *Ireland* 15 B5
Monahans, *U.S.A.* 113 K3
Monapo, *Mozam.* 87 E5
Monar, L., *U.K.* 14 D3
Monarch Mt., *Canada* 104 C3
Monashee Mts., *Canada* 104 C5
Monastir = Bitola, *Macedonia* . 40 E5
Moncada, *Phil.* 61 D4
Moncalieri, *Italy* 28 D4
Moncalvo, *Italy* 28 C5
Moncão, *Portugal* 34 C2
Moncarapacho, *Portugal* 35 H3
Moncayo, Sierra del, *Spain* . 32 D3
Mönchengladbach, *Germany* . 24 D2
Monchique, *Portugal* 35 H2
Moncks Corner, *U.S.A.* 109 J5
Monclova, *Mexico* 118 B4
Moncontour, *France* 18 D4
Moncton, *Canada* 103 C7
Mondariz, *Spain* 34 C2
Mondego →, *Portugal* 34 E2
Mondego, C., *Portugal* 34 E2
Mondeodo, *Indonesia* 63 E6
Mondeville, *France* 18 C6
Mondolfo, *Italy* 29 E10
Mondoñedo, *Spain* 34 B3
Mondovì, *Italy* 28 D4
Mondragon, *Phil.* 61 E6
Mondragone, *Italy* 30 A6
Mondrain I., *Australia* 93 F3
Monemvasía, *Greece* 38 E5
Monessen, *U.S.A.* 110 F5
Monesterio, *Spain* 35 G4
Monestier-de-Clermont, *France* 21 D9
Monett, *U.S.A.* 113 G8
Moneymore, *U.K.* 15 B5
Monfalcone, *Italy* 29 C10
Monflanquin, *France* 20 D4
Monforte, *Portugal* 35 F3
Monforte de Lemos, *Spain* 34 C3
Mong Hsu, *Burma* 58 G2
Mong Kung, *Burma* 67 J20
Mong Nai, *Burma* 67 J20
Mong Pawk, *Burma* 67 H21
Mong Ping, *Burma* 58 G2
Mong Ton, *Burma* 67 J21
Mong Wa, *Burma* 67 J22
Mong Yai, *Burma* 67 H21
Mongalla, *Sudan* 81 F3
Mongers, L., *Australia* 93 E2
Monghyr = Munger, *India* 69 G12
Mongibello = Etna, *Italy* 31 E7
Mongo, *Chad* 79 F9
Mongo →, *S. Leone* 82 D2
Mongolia ■, *Asia* 51 E10
Mongonu, *Nigeria* 83 C7
Mongu, *Zambia* 85 H4
Môngua, *Angola* 88 B2
Monifieth, *U.K.* 14 E6
Monistrol-sur-Loire, *France* . 21 C8
Monkey Bay, *Malawi* 87 E4
Monkey Mia, *Australia* 93 E1
Monkey River, *Belize* 119 D7
Mońki, *Poland* 44 E9
Monkoto, *Dem. Rep. of the Congo* 84 E4
Monkton, *Canada* 110 C3
Monmouth, *U.K.* 13 F5
Monmouth, *Ill., U.S.A.* 112 E9
Monmouth, *Oreg., U.S.A.* 114 D2
Monmouthshire □, *U.K.* 13 F5
Mono L., *U.S.A.* 116 H7

Monolith, *U.S.A.* 117 K8
Monólithos, *Greece* 36 C9
Monongahela, *U.S.A.* 110 F5
Monópoli, *Italy* 31 B10
Monor, *Hungary* 42 C4
Monóvar, *Spain* 33 G4
Monreal del Campo, *Spain* . 32 E3
Monreale, *Italy* 30 D6
Monroe, *Ga., U.S.A.* 109 J4
Monroe, *La., U.S.A.* 113 J8
Monroe, *Mich., U.S.A.* 108 E4
Monroe, *N.C., U.S.A.* 109 H5
Monroe, *N.Y., U.S.A.* 111 E10
Monroe, *Utah, U.S.A.* 115 G7
Monroe, *Wash., U.S.A.* 116 C5
Monroe, *Wis., U.S.A.* 112 D10
Monroe City, *U.S.A.* 112 F9
Monroeton, *U.S.A.* 111 E8
Monroeville, *Ala., U.S.A.* 109 K2
Monroeville, *Pa., U.S.A.* 110 F5
Monrovia, *Liberia* 82 D2
Mons, *Belgium* 17 D3
Møns Klint, *Denmark* 11 K6
Monsaraz, *Portugal* 35 G3
Monse, *Indonesia* 63 E6
Monségur, *France* 20 D4
Monsélice, *Italy* 29 C8
Mönsterås, *Sweden* 11 G10
Mont Cenis, Col du, *France* .. 21 C10
Mont-de-Marsan, *France* 20 E3
Mont-Joli, *Canada* 103 C6
Mont-Laurier, *Canada* 102 C4
Mont-Louis, *Canada* 103 C6
Mont-roig del Camp, *Spain* . 32 D5
Mont-St-Michel, Le = Le Mont-
   St-Michel, *France* 18 D5
Mont Tremblant, Parc Recr. du,
   Canada 102 C5
Montabaur, *Germany* 24 E3
Montagnac, *France* 20 E7
Montagnana, *Italy* 29 C8
Montagu, *S. Africa* 88 E3
Montague, *Canada* 103 C7
Montague, I., *Mexico* 118 A2
Montague Ra., *Australia* 93 E2
Montague Sd., *Australia* 92 B4
Montaigu, *France* 18 F5
Montalbán, *Spain* 32 E4
Montalbano Iónico, *Italy* 31 B9
Montalbo, *Spain* 32 F2
Montalcino, *Italy* 29 E8
Montalegre, *Portugal* 34 D3
Montalto, *Italy* 31 D8
Montalto di Castro, *Italy* 29 F8
Montalto Uffugo, *Italy* 31 C9
Montalvo, *U.S.A.* 117 L7
Montamarta, *Spain* 34 D5
Montana, *Bulgaria* 40 C7
Montaña, *Peru* 124 E4
Montana □, *Bulgaria* 40 C7
Montana □, *U.S.A.* 114 C9
Montaña Clara, I., *Canary Is.* . 37 E6
Montánchez, *Spain* 35 F4
Montargil, *Portugal* 35 F2
Montargis, *France* 19 E9
Montauban, *France* 20 D5
Montauk, *U.S.A.* 111 E13
Montauk Pt., *U.S.A.* 111 E13
Montbard, *France* 19 E11
Montbarrey, *France* 19 E12
Montbéliard, *France* 19 E13
Montblanc, *France* 32 D6
Montbrison, *France* 21 C8
Montcalm, Pic de, *France* 20 F5
Montceau-les-Mines, *France* .. 19 F11
Montcenis, *France* 21 B8
Montclair, *U.S.A.* 111 F10
Montcornet, *France* 19 C11
Montcuq, *France* 20 D5
Montdidier, *France* 19 C9
Monte Albán, *Mexico* 119 D5
Monte Alegre, *Brazil* 125 D8
Monte Azul, *Brazil* 125 G10
Monte Bello Is., *Australia* 92 D2
Monte-Carlo, *Monaco* 21 E11
Monte Caseros, *Argentina* .. 126 C4
Monte Comán, *Argentina* .. 126 C2
Monte Cristi, *Dom. Rep.* 121 C5
Monte Lindo →, *Paraguay* ... 126 A4
Monte Patria, *Chile* 126 C1
Monte Quemado, *Argentina* . 126 B3
Monte Redondo, *Portugal* .. 34 F2
Monte Rio, *U.S.A.* 116 G4
Monte San Giovanni Campano,
   Italy 30 A6
Monte San Savino, *Italy* 29 E8
Monte Sant' Angelo, *Italy* 29 G12
Monte Santu, C. di, *Italy* 30 B2
Monte Vista, *U.S.A.* 115 H10
Monteagudo, *Argentina* 127 B5
Montealegre del Castillo, *Spain* 33 G3
Montebello, *Canada* 102 C5
Montebello Iónico, *Italy* 31 E8
Montebelluna, *Italy* 29 C9
Montebourg, *France* 18 C5
Montecastrilli, *Italy* 29 F9
Montecatini Terme, *Italy* 28 E7
Montecito, *U.S.A.* 117 L7
Montecristo, *Italy* 28 F7
Montefalco, *Italy* 29 F9
Montefiascone, *Italy* 29 F9
Montefrío, *Spain* 35 H7
Montegiórgio, *Italy* 29 E10
Montego Bay, *Jamaica* 120 C4
Montehermoso, *Spain* 34 E4

Montejicar, *Spain* 35 H7
Montélimar, *France* 21 D8
Montella, *Italy* 31 B8
Montellano, *Spain* 35 J5
Montello, *U.S.A.* 112 D10
Montemor-o-Novo, *Portugal* . 35 G2
Montemor-o-Velho, *Portugal* . 34 E2
Montemorelos, *Mexico* 119 B5
Montendre, *France* 20 C3
Montenegro, *Brazil* 127 B5
Montenegro □, *Yugoslavia* .. 40 D3
Montenero di Bisáccia, *Italy* . 29 G11
Montepuez, *Mozam.* 87 E4
Montepuez →, *Mozam.* 87 E5
Montepulciano, *Italy* 29 E8
Montereale, *Italy* 29 F10
Montereau-Faut-Yonne, *France* 19 D9
Monterey, *U.S.A.* 116 J5
Monterey B., *U.S.A.* 116 J5
Montería, *Colombia* 124 B3
Monteros, *Argentina* 126 B2
Monterotondo, *Italy* 29 F9
Monterrey, *Mexico* 118 B4
Montes Claros, *Brazil* 125 G10
Montesano, *U.S.A.* 116 D3
Montesano sulla Marcellana,
   Italy 31 B8
Montesárchio, *Italy* 31 A7
Montescaglioso, *Italy* 31 B9
Montesilvano, *Italy* 29 F11
Montevarchi, *Italy* 29 E8
Montevideo, *Uruguay* 127 C4
Montevideo, *U.S.A.* 112 C7
Montezuma, *U.S.A.* 112 E8
Montfaucon, *France* 18 E5
Montfaucon-d'Argonne, *France* 19 C12
Montfaucon-en-Velay, *France* . 21 C8
Montfort, *France* 18 D5
Montfort-le-Gesnois, *France* .. 18 D7
Montgenèvre, *France* 21 D10
Montgomery = Sahiwal, *Pakistan* 68 D5
Montgomery, *U.K.* 13 E4
Montgomery, *Ala., U.S.A.* 109 J2
Montgomery, *Pa., U.S.A.* 110 E8
Montgomery, *W. Va., U.S.A.* . 108 F5
Montgomery City, *U.S.A.* 112 F9
Montguyon, *France* 20 C3
Monthermé, *France* 19 C11
Monthey, *Switz.* 25 J2
Monthois, *France* 19 C11
Monti, *Italy* 30 B2
Monticelli d'Ongina, *Italy* 28 C6
Monticello, *Ark., U.S.A.* 113 J9
Monticello, *Fla., U.S.A.* 109 K4
Monticello, *Ind., U.S.A.* 108 E2
Monticello, *Iowa, U.S.A.* 112 D9
Monticello, *Ky., U.S.A.* 109 G3
Monticello, *Minn., U.S.A.* 112 C8
Monticello, *Miss., U.S.A.* 113 K9
Monticello, *N.Y., U.S.A.* 111 E10
Monticello, *Utah, U.S.A.* 115 H9
Montichiari, *Italy* 28 C7
Montier-en-Der, *France* 19 D11
Montignac, *France* 20 C5
Montigny-les-Metz, *France* .. 19 C13
Montigny-sur-Aube, *France* .. 19 E11
Montijo, *Portugal* 35 G2
Montijo, *Spain* 35 G4
Montilla, *Spain* 35 H6
Montivilliers, *France* 18 C7
Montluçon, *France* 19 F9
Montmagny, *Canada* 103 C5
Montmarault, *France* 19 F9
Montmartre, *Canada* 105 C8
Montmédy, *France* 19 C12
Montmélian, *France* 21 C10
Montmirail, *France* 19 D10
Montmoreau-St-Cybard, *France* 20 C4
Montmorillon, *France* 20 B4
Montmort-Lucy, *France* 19 D10
Monto, *Australia* 94 C5
Montoire-sur-le-Loir, *France* .. 18 E7
Montório al Vomano, *Italy* 29 F10
Montoro, *Spain* 35 G6
Montour Falls, *U.S.A.* 110 D8
Montoursville, *U.S.A.* 110 E8
Montpelier, *Idaho, U.S.A.* 114 E8
Montpelier, *Vt., U.S.A.* 111 B12
Montpellier, *France* 20 E7
Montpezat-de-Quercy, *France* . 20 D5
Montpon-Ménestérol, *France* . 20 C4
Montréal, *Canada* 102 C5
Montréal, *Aude, France* 20 E6
Montréal, *Gers, France* 20 E4
Montreal L., *Canada* 102 C3
Montreal L., *Canada* 105 C7
Montreal Lake, *Canada* 105 C7
Montredon-Labessonnié, *France* 20 E6
Montrésor, *France* 18 E8
Montret, *France* 19 F12
Montreuil, *Pas-de-Calais, France* 19 B8
Montreuil, *Seine-St-Denis,
   France* 19 D9
Montreuil-Bellay, *France* 18 E6
Montreux, *Switz.* 25 J2
Montrevel-en-Bresse, *France* .. 19 F12
Montrichard, *France* 18 E8
Montrose, *U.K.* 14 E6
Montrose, *Colo., U.S.A.* 115 G10
Montrose, *Pa., U.S.A.* 111 E9
Monts, Pte. des, *Canada* 103 C6
Montsalvy, *France* 20 D6
Montsant, Serra de, *Spain* .. 32 D6
Montsauche-les-Settons, *France* 19 E11
Montsec, Serra del, *Spain* .. 32 C5
Montserrat, *Spain* 32 D6

Montserrat ■, *W. Indies* 121 C7
Montuenga, *Spain* 34 D6
Montuïri, *Spain* 37 B9
Monywa, *Burma* 67 H19
Monza, *Italy* 28 C6
Monze, *Zambia* 87 F2
Monze, C., *Pakistan* 68 G2
Monzón, *Spain* 32 D5
Mooers, *U.S.A.* 111 B11
Mooi →, *S. Africa* 89 D5
Mooi River, *S. Africa* 89 D4
Moonah →, *Australia* 94 C2
Moonda, L., *Australia* 94 D3
Moonie, *Australia* 95 D5
Moonie →, *Australia* 95 D4
Moora, *Australia* 93 F2
Moorcroft, *U.S.A.* 112 C2
Moore →, *Australia* 93 F2
Moore, L., *Australia* 93 E2
Moore Park, *Australia* 94 C5
Moore Reefs, *Australia* 94 B4
Moorefield, *U.S.A.* 108 F6
Moores Res., *U.S.A.* 111 B13
Moorfoot Hills, *U.K.* 14 F5
Moorhead, *U.S.A.* 112 B6
Moormerland, *Germany* 24 B3
Moorpark, *U.S.A.* 117 L8
Moorreesburg, *S. Africa* 88 E2
Moosburg, *Germany* 25 G7
Moose →, *Canada* 102 B3
Moose →, *U.S.A.* 111 C9
Moose Creek, *Canada* 111 A10
Moose Factory, *Canada* 102 B3
Moose Jaw, *Canada* 105 C7
Moose Jaw →, *Canada* 105 C7
Moose Lake, *Canada* 105 C8
Moose Lake, *U.S.A.* 112 B8
Moose Mountain Prov. Park,
   Canada 105 D8
Moosehead L., *U.S.A.* 109 C11
Mooselookmeguntic L., *U.S.A.* 109 C10
Moosilauke, Mt., *U.S.A.* 111 B13
Moosomin, *Canada* 105 C8
Moosonee, *Canada* 102 B3
Moosup, *U.S.A.* 111 E13
Mopane, *S. Africa* 89 C4
Mopeia Velha, *Mozam.* 87 F4
Mopipi, *Botswana* 88 C3
Mopoi, *C.A.R.* 86 A2
Mopti, *Mali* 82 C4
Moqatta, *Sudan* 81 E4
Moqor, *Afghan.* 68 C2
Moquegua, *Peru* 124 G4
Mór, *Hungary* 42 C3
Móra, *Portugal* 35 G2
Mora, *Spain* 35 F7
Mora, *Sweden* 10 C8
Mora, *Minn., U.S.A.* 112 C8
Mora, *N. Mex., U.S.A.* 115 J11
Mora →, *U.S.A.* 113 H2
Mora de Ebro = Mòra d'Ebre,
   Spain 32 D5
Mora de Rubielos, *Spain* 32 E4
Mòra d'Ebre, *Spain* 32 D5
Mora la Nova, *Spain* 32 D5
Morača →, *Montenegro, Yug.* . 40 D3
Moradabad, *India* 69 E8
Morafenobe, *Madag.* 89 B7
Morag, *Poland* 44 E6
Moral de Calatrava, *Spain* .. 35 G7
Moraleja, *Spain* 34 E4
Moramanga, *Madag.* 89 B8
Moran, *Kans., U.S.A.* 113 G7
Moran, *Wyo., U.S.A.* 114 E8
Moranbah, *Australia* 94 C4
Morano Cálabro, *Italy* 31 C9
Morant Cays, *Jamaica* 120 C4
Morant Pt., *Jamaica* 120 C4
Morar, *India* 68 F8
Morar, L., *U.K.* 14 E3
Moratalla, *Spain* 33 G3
Moratuwa, *Sri Lanka* 66 R11
Morava →, *Slovak Rep.* 27 D9
Morava →, *Serbia, Yug.* 40 C4
Moravia, *U.S.A.* 111 D8
Moravian Hts. = Českomoravská
   Vrchovina, *Czech Rep.* 26 B8
Moravica →, *Serbia, Yug.* 40 C4
Moraviţa, *Romania* 42 E6
Moravská Třebová, *Czech Rep.* 27 B9
Moravské Budějovice,
   Czech Rep. 26 B8
Morawa, *Australia* 93 E2
Morawhanna, *Guyana* 124 B7
Moray □, *U.K.* 14 D5
Moray Firth, *U.K.* 14 D5
Morbach, *Germany* 25 F3
Morbegno, *Italy* 28 B6
Morbi, *India* 68 H4
Morbihan □, *France* 18 E4
Mörbylånga, *Sweden* 11 H10
Morcenx, *France* 20 D3
Morcone, *Italy* 31 A7
Mordelles, *France* 18 D5
Morden, *Canada* 105 D9
Mordoğan, *Turkey* 39 C8
Mordovian Republic =
   Mordvinia □, *Russia* 48 C7
Mordovo, *Russia* 48 D5
Mordvinia □, *Russia* 48 C7
Mordy, *Poland* 45 F9
Morea, *Greece* 6 H10
Moreau →, *U.S.A.* 112 C4
Morecambe, *U.K.* 12 C5
Morecambe B., *U.K.* 12 C5
Moree, *Australia* 95 D4

Morehead, *U.S.A.* 108 F4
Morehead City, *U.S.A.* 109 H7
Morel →, *India* 68 F7
Morelia, *Mexico* 118 D4
Morella, *Australia* 94 C3
Morella, *Spain* 32 E4
Morelos, *Mexico* 118 B3
Morelos □, *Mexico* 119 D5
Morena, *India* 68 F8
Morena, Sierra, *Spain* 35 G7
Moreni, *Romania* 43 F10
Moreno Valley, *U.S.A.* 117 M10
Morestel, *France* 21 C9
Moreton I., *Australia* 95 D5
Moreuil, *France* 19 C9
Morey, *Spain* 37 B10
Morez, *France* 19 F13
Morgan, *U.S.A.* 114 F8
Morgan City, *U.S.A.* 113 L9
Morgan Hill, *U.S.A.* 116 H5
Morganfield, *U.S.A.* 108 G2
Morganton, *U.S.A.* 109 H5
Morgantown, *U.S.A.* 108 F6
Morgenzon, *S. Africa* 89 D4
Morges, *Switz.* 25 J2
Morghak, *Iran* 71 D8
Morgongåva, *Sweden* 10 E10
Morhange, *France* 19 D13
Morhar →, *India* 69 G11
Mori, *Italy* 28 C7
Moriarty, *U.S.A.* 115 J10
Moribaya, *Guinea* 82 D3
Morice →, *Canada* 104 C3
Moriki, *Nigeria* 83 C6
Morinville, *Canada* 104 C6
Morioka, *Japan* 54 E10
Moris, *Mexico* 118 B3
Morlaàs, *France* 20 E3
Morlaix, *France* 18 D3
Mörlunda, *Sweden* 11 G9
Mormanno, *Italy* 31 C8
Mormant, *France* 19 D9
Mornington, I., *Australia* 94 B2
Mornington, *Chile* 128 F1
Mornington I., *Australia* 94 B2
Mórnos →, *Greece* 38 C3
Moro, *Pakistan* 68 F2
Moro, *Sudan* 81 E3
Moro →, *Pakistan* 68 E2
Moro G., *Phil.* 61 H5
Morocco ■, *N. Afr.* 78 B4
Morogoro, *Tanzania* 86 D4
Morogoro □, *Tanzania* 86 D4
Moroleón, *Mexico* 118 C4
Morombe, *Madag.* 89 C7
Moron, *Argentina* 126 C4
Morón, *Cuba* 120 B4
Morón de Almazán, *Spain* 32 D2
Morón de la Frontera, *Spain* .. 35 H5
Morona →, *Peru* 124 D3
Morondava, *Madag.* 89 C7
Morondo, *Ivory C.* 82 D3
Morongo Valley, *U.S.A.* 117 L10
Moroni, *Comoros Is.* 77 H8
Moronou, *Ivory C.* 82 D4
Morotai, *Indonesia* 63 D7
Moroto, *Uganda* 86 B3
Moroto Summit, *Kenya* 86 B3
Morozov, *Bulgaria* 41 D9
Morozovsk, *Russia* 49 F5
Morpeth, *U.K.* 12 B6
Morphou, *Cyprus* 36 D11
Morphou Bay, *Cyprus* 36 D11
Morrilton, *U.S.A.* 113 H8
Morrinhos, *Brazil* 125 G9
Morrinsville, *N.Z.* 91 G5
Morris, *Canada* 105 D9
Morris, *Ill., U.S.A.* 112 E10
Morris, *Minn., U.S.A.* 112 C7
Morris, *N.Y., U.S.A.* 111 D9
Morris, *Pa., U.S.A.* 110 E7
Morris, Mt., *Australia* 93 E5
Morrisburg, *Canada* 111 B9
Morristown, *Ariz., U.S.A.* 115 K7
Morristown, *N.J., U.S.A.* 111 F10
Morristown, *N.Y., U.S.A.* 111 B9
Morristown, *Tenn., U.S.A.* 109 G4
Morrisville, *N.Y., U.S.A.* 111 D9
Morrisville, *Pa., U.S.A.* 111 F10
Morrisville, *Vt., U.S.A.* 111 B12
Morro, Pta., *Chile* 126 B1
Morro Bay, *U.S.A.* 116 K6
Morro del Jable, *Canary Is.* .. 37 F5
Morro Jable, Pta. de, *Canary Is.* 37 F5
Morrosquillo, G. de, *Colombia* 120 E4
Mörrum, *Sweden* 11 H8
Morrumbene, *Mozam.* 89 C6
Mörrumsån →, *Sweden* 11 H8
Mors, *Denmark* 11 H2
Morshansk, *Russia* 48 D5
Mörsil, *Sweden* 10 A7
Mortagne →, *France* 19 D13
Mortagne-au-Perche, *France* .. 18 D7
Mortagne-sur-Gironde, *France* . 20 C3
Mortagne-sur-Sèvre, *France* .. 18 F6
Mortain, *France* 18 D6
Mortara, *Italy* 28 C5
Morteau, *France* 19 E13
Morteros, *Argentina* 126 C3
Mortlach, *Canada* 105 C7
Morton, *Tex., U.S.A.* 113 J3
Morton, *Wash., U.S.A.* 116 D4
Morvan, *France* 19 E11
Morven, *Australia* 95 D4
Morvern, *U.K.* 14 E3

Moryń, Poland 45 F1
Morzine, France 19 F13
Mosalsk, Russia 46 E8
Mosbach, Germany 25 F5
Mošćenice, Croatia 29 C11
Mosciano Sant' Angelo, Italy 29 F10
Moscos Is., Burma 64 E1
Moscow = Moskva, Russia 46 E9
Moscow, Idaho, U.S.A. 114 C5
Moscow, Pa., U.S.A. 111 E9
Mosel →, Europe 19 B14
Moselle = Mosel →, Europe 19 B14
Moselle □, France 19 D13
Moses Lake, U.S.A. 114 C4
Mosgiel, N.Z. 91 L3
Moshaweng →, S. Africa 88 D3
Moshi, Tanzania 86 C4
Moshupa, Botswana 88 C4
Mosina, Poland 45 F3
Mosjøen, Norway 8 D15
Moskenesøya, Norway 8 C15
Moskenstraumen, Norway 8 C15
Moskva, Russia 46 E9
Moskva →, Russia 46 E10
Moslavačka Gora, Croatia 29 C13
Mosomane, Botswana 88 C4
Mosonmagyaróvár, Hungary 42 C2
Mošorin, Serbia, Yug. 42 E5
Mospino, Ukraine 47 J9
Mosquera, Colombia 124 C3
Mosquero, U.S.A. 113 H3
Mosqueruela, Spain 32 E4
Mosquitia, Honduras 120 C3
Mosquito Coast = Mosquitia, Honduras 120 C3
Mosquito Creek L., U.S.A. 110 E4
Mosquito L., Canada 105 A8
Mosquitos, G. de los, Panama 120 E3
Moss, Norway 9 G14
Mossbank, Canada 105 D7
Mossburn, N.Z. 91 L2
Mosselbaai, S. Africa 88 E3
Mossendjo, Congo 84 E2
Mossingen, Germany 25 G5
Mossman, Australia 94 B4
Mossoró, Brazil 125 E11
Mossuril, Mozam. 87 E5
Most, Czech Rep. 26 A6
Mosta, Malta 36 D1
Mostaganem, Algeria 78 A6
Mostar, Bos.-H. 42 G2
Mostardas, Brazil 127 C5
Mostiska = Mostyska, Ukraine 47 H2
Móstoles, Spain 34 E7
Mosty = Masty, Belarus 46 F3
Mostyska, Ukraine 47 H2
Mosul = Al Mawşil, Iraq 70 B4
Mosûlpo, S. Korea 57 H14
Mota, Ethiopia 81 E4
Mota del Cuervo, Spain 33 F2
Mota del Marqués, Spain 34 D5
Motagua →, Guatemala 120 C2
Motala, Sweden 11 F9
Motaze, Mozam. 89 C5
Motça, Romania 43 C11
Moth, India 69 G8
Motherwell, U.K. 14 F5
Motihari, India 69 F11
Motilla del Palancar, Spain 33 F3
Motnik, Slovenia 29 B11
Motovun, Croatia 29 C10
Motozintla de Mendoza, Mexico 119 D6
Motril, Spain 35 J7
Motru, Romania 42 F7
Motru →, Romania 43 F8
Mott, U.S.A. 112 B3
Móttola, Italy 31 B10
Motueka, N.Z. 91 J4
Motueka →, N.Z. 91 J4
Motul, Mexico 119 C7
Mouchalagane →, Canada 103 B6
Moúdhros, Greece 39 B7
Mouding, China 58 E3
Moudjeria, Mauritania 82 B2
Moudon, Switz. 25 J2
Mouila, Gabon 84 E2
Mouliana, Greece 36 D7
Moulins, France 19 F10
Moulmein, Burma 67 L20
Moulouya, O. →, Morocco 78 B5
Moultrie, U.S.A. 109 K4
Moultrie, L., U.S.A. 109 J5
Mound City, Mo., U.S.A. 112 E7
Mound City, S. Dak., U.S.A. 112 C4
Moúnda, Ákra, Greece 38 C2
Moundou, Chad 79 G9
Moundsville, U.S.A. 110 G4
Moung, Cambodia 64 F4
Mount Airy, U.S.A. 109 G5
Mount Albert, Canada 110 B5
Mount Barker, Australia 93 F2
Mount Brydges, Canada 110 D3
Mount Burr, Australia 95 F3
Mount Carmel, Ill., U.S.A. 108 F2
Mount Carmel, Pa., U.S.A. 111 F8
Mount Charleston, U.S.A. 117 J11
Mount Clemens, U.S.A. 110 D2
Mount Coolon, Australia 94 C4
Mount Darwin, Zimbabwe 87 F3
Mount Desert I., U.S.A. 109 C11
Mount Dora, U.S.A. 109 L5
Mount Edziza Prov. Park, Canada 104 B2
Mount Fletcher, S. Africa 89 E4
Mount Forest, Canada 102 D3
Mount Garnet, Australia 94 B4

Mount Holly, U.S.A. 111 G10
Mount Holly Springs, U.S.A. 110 F7
Mount Hope, Australia 95 E2
Mount Isa, Australia 94 C2
Mount Jewett, U.S.A. 110 E6
Mount Kisco, U.S.A. 111 E11
Mount Laguna, U.S.A. 117 N10
Mount Larcom, Australia 94 C5
Mount Magnet, Australia 93 E2
Mount Maunganui, N.Z. 91 G6
Mount Molloy, Australia 94 B4
Mount Morgan, Australia 94 C5
Mount Morris, U.S.A. 110 D7
Mount Pearl, Canada 103 C9
Mount Penn, U.S.A. 111 F9
Mount Perry, Australia 95 D5
Mount Pleasant, Iowa, U.S.A. 112 E9
Mount Pleasant, Mich., U.S.A. 108 D3
Mount Pleasant, Pa., U.S.A. 110 F5
Mount Pleasant, S.C., U.S.A. 109 J6
Mount Pleasant, Tenn., U.S.A. 109 H2
Mount Pleasant, Tex., U.S.A. 113 J7
Mount Pleasant, Utah, U.S.A. 114 G8
Mount Pocono, U.S.A. 111 E9
Mount Rainier Nat. Park, U.S.A. 116 D5
Mount Revelstoke Nat. Park, Canada 104 C5
Mount Robson Prov. Park, Canada 104 C5
Mount Selinda, Zimbabwe 89 C5
Mount Shasta, U.S.A. 114 F2
Mount Signal, U.S.A. 117 N11
Mount Sterling, Ill., U.S.A. 112 F9
Mount Sterling, Ky., U.S.A. 108 F4
Mount Surprise, Australia 94 B3
Mount Union, U.S.A. 110 F7
Mount Upton, U.S.A. 111 D9
Mount Vernon, Ill., U.S.A. 108 F1
Mount Vernon, Ind., U.S.A. 112 F10
Mount Vernon, N.Y., U.S.A. 111 F11
Mount Vernon, Ohio, U.S.A. 110 F2
Mount Vernon, Wash., U.S.A. 116 B4
Mountain Ash, U.K. 13 F4
Mountain Center, U.S.A. 117 M10
Mountain City, Nev., U.S.A. 114 F6
Mountain City, Tenn., U.S.A. 109 G5
Mountain Dale, U.S.A. 111 E10
Mountain Grove, U.S.A. 113 G8
Mountain Home, Ark., U.S.A. 113 G8
Mountain Home, Idaho, U.S.A. 114 E6
Mountain Iron, U.S.A. 112 B8
Mountain Pass, U.S.A. 117 K11
Mountain View, Ark., U.S.A. 113 H8
Mountain View, Calif., U.S.A. 116 H4
Mountain View, Hawaii, U.S.A. 106 J17
Mountainair, U.S.A. 115 J10
Mountlake Terrace, U.S.A. 116 C4
Mountmellick, Ireland 15 C4
Mountrath, Ireland 15 D4
Moura, Australia 94 C4
Moura, Brazil 124 D6
Moura, Portugal 35 G3
Mourão, Portugal 35 G3
Mourdi, Dépression du, Chad 79 E10
Mourdiah, Mali 82 C3
Mourenx, France 20 E3
Mouri, Ghana 83 D4
Mourilyan, Australia 94 B4
Mourmelon-le-Grand, France 19 C11
Mourne →, U.K. 15 B4
Mourne Mts., U.K. 15 B5
Mourniaí, Greece 36 D6
Mournies = Mourniaí, Greece 36 D6
Mouscron, Belgium 17 D3
Moussoro, Chad 79 F9
Mouthe, France 19 F13
Moutier, Switz. 25 H3
Moûtiers, France 21 C10
Moutong, Indonesia 63 D6
Mouy, France 19 C9
Mouzáki, Greece 38 B3
Mouzon, France 19 C12
Movas, Mexico 118 B3
Moville, Ireland 15 A4
Mowandjum, Australia 92 C3
Moy →, Ireland 15 B2
Moyale, Kenya 81 G4
Moyamba, S. Leone 82 D2
Moyen Atlas, Morocco 78 B4
Moyne, L. le, Canada 103 A6
Moyo, Indonesia 62 F5
Moyobamba, Peru 124 E3
Moyyero →, Russia 51 C11
Moyynty, Kazakhstan 50 E8
Mozambique = Moçambique, Mozam. 87 F5
Mozambique ■, Africa 87 F4
Mozambique Chan., Africa 89 B7
Mozdok, Russia 49 J7
Mozdūrān, Iran 71 B9
Mozhaysk, Russia 46 E9
Mozhga, Russia 48 B11
Mozhnābād, Iran 71 C9
Mozirje, Slovenia 29 B11
Mozyr = Mazyr, Belarus 47 F5
Mpanda, Tanzania 86 D3
Mpésoba, Mali 82 C3
Mphoengs, Zimbabwe 89 C4
Mpika, Zambia 87 E3
Mpulungu, Zambia 87 D3
Mpumalanga, S. Africa 89 D5
Mpumalanga □, S. Africa 89 B5
Mpwapwa, Tanzania 86 D4
Mqanduli, S. Africa 89 E4
Mqinvartsveri = Kazbek, Russia 49 J7
Mrągowo, Poland 44 E8

Mramor, Serbia, Yug. 40 C5
Mrkonjić Grad, Bos.-H. 42 F2
Mrkopalj, Croatia 29 C11
Mrocza, Poland 45 E4
Msambansovu, Zimbabwe 87 F3
M'sila →, Algeria 78 A6
Msoro, Zambia 87 E3
Msta →, Russia 46 C6
Mstislav = Mstsislaw, Belarus 46 E6
Mstsislaw, Belarus 46 E6
Mszana Dolna, Poland 45 J7
Mszczonów, Poland 45 G7
Mtama, Tanzania 87 E4
Mtamvuna →, S. Africa 89 E5
Mtilikwe →, Zimbabwe 87 G3
Mtsensk, Russia 46 F9
Mtskheta, Georgia 49 K7
Mtubatuba, S. Africa 89 D5
Mtwalume, S. Africa 89 E5
Mtwara-Mikindani, Tanzania 87 E5
Mu Gia, Deo, Vietnam 64 D5
Mu Us Shamo, China 56 E5
Muang Chiang Rai = Chiang Rai, Thailand 58 H2
Muang Khong, Laos 64 E5
Muang Lamphun, Thailand 64 C2
Muang Pak Beng, Laos 58 H3
Muar, Malaysia 65 L4
Muarabungo, Indonesia 62 E2
Muaraenim, Indonesia 62 E2
Muarajuloi, Indonesia 62 E4
Muarakaman, Indonesia 62 E5
Muaratebo, Indonesia 62 E2
Muaratembesi, Indonesia 62 E2
Muaratewe, Indonesia 62 E4
Mubarakpur, India 69 F10
Mubarraz = Al Mubarraz, Si. Arabia 71 E6
Mubende, Uganda 86 B3
Mubi, Nigeria 83 C7
Mubur, Pulau, Indonesia 65 L6
Mucajaí →, Brazil 124 C6
Muchachos, Roque de los, Canary Is. 37 G2
Mücheln, Germany 24 D7
Muchinga Mts., Zambia 87 E3
Muchkapskiy, Russia 48 E6
Muchuan, China 58 C5
Muck, U.K. 14 E2
Muckadilla, Australia 95 D4
Mucur, Turkey 72 C6
Mucuri, Brazil 125 G11
Mucusso, Angola 88 B3
Muda, Canary Is. 37 F6
Mudanjiang, China 57 B15
Mudanya, Turkey 41 F12
Muddy Cr. →, U.S.A. 115 H8
Mudjatik →, Canada 105 B7
Mudurnu, Turkey 72 B4
Muecate, Mozam. 87 E4
Mueda, Mozam. 87 E4
Mueller Ra., Australia 92 C4
Muende, Mozam. 87 E3
Muerto, Mar, Mexico 119 D6
Mufu Shan, China 59 C10
Mufulira, Zambia 87 E2
Mufumbiro Range, Africa 86 C2
Mugardos, Spain 34 B2
Muge, Portugal 35 F2
Múggia, Italy 29 C10
Mughal Sarai, India 69 G10
Mughayrā', Si. Arabia 70 D3
Mugi, Japan 55 H7
Mugia = Muxía, Spain 34 B1
Mugila, Mts., Dem. Rep. of the Congo 86 D2
Muğla, Turkey 39 D10
Muğla □, Turkey 39 D10
Muglad, Sudan 81 E2
Müglizh, Bulgaria 41 D9
Mugu, Nepal 69 E10
Muhammad, Ras, Egypt 70 E2
Muhammad Qol, Sudan 80 C4
Muhammadabad, India 69 F10
Muhesi →, Tanzania 86 D4
Mühlacker, Germany 25 G4
Mühldorf, Germany 25 G8
Mühlhausen, Germany 24 D6
Mühlig Hofmann fjell, Antarctica 5 D3
Mühlviertel, Austria 26 C7
Muhos, Finland 8 D22
Muhu, Estonia 9 G20
Muhutwe, Tanzania 86 C3
Muine Bheag, Ireland 15 D5
Muir, L., Australia 93 F2
Mujnak = Moynaq, Uzbekistan 50 E6
Mukacheve, Ukraine 47 H2
Mukachevo = Mukacheve, Ukraine 47 H2
Mukah, Malaysia 62 D4
Mukandwara, India 68 G6
Mukawwa, Geziret, Egypt 80 C4
Mukdahan, Thailand 64 D5
Mukden = Shenyang, China 57 D12
Mukerian, India 68 D6
Mukhtolovo, Russia 48 C6
Mukhtuya = Lensk, Russia 51 C12
Mukinbudin, Australia 93 F2
Mukishi, Dem. Rep. of the Congo 87 D1
Mukomuko, Indonesia 62 E2
Mukomwenze, Dem. Rep. of the Congo 86 D2
Muktsar, India 68 D6
Mukur = Moqor, Afghan. 68 C2

Mukutawa →, Canada 105 C9
Mukwela, Zambia 87 F2
Mula, Spain 33 G3
Mula →, Pakistan 68 F2
Mulange, Dem. Rep. of the Congo 86 C2
Mulanje, Malawi 87 F4
Mulchén, Chile 126 D1
Mulde →, Germany 24 D8
Mule Creek Junction, U.S.A. 112 D2
Muleba, Tanzania 86 C3
Mulejé, Mexico 118 B2
Muleshoe, U.S.A. 113 H3
Muletta, Gara, Ethiopia 81 F5
Mulgrave, Canada 103 C7
Mulhacén, Spain 35 H7
Mülheim, Germany 24 D2
Mulhouse, France 19 E14
Muli, China 58 D3
Muling, China 57 B16
Mull, U.K. 14 E3
Mull, Sound of, U.K. 14 E3
Mullaittivu, Sri Lanka 66 Q12
Mullen, U.S.A. 112 D4
Mullens, U.S.A. 108 G5
Muller, Pegunungan, Indonesia 62 D4
Mullet Pen., Ireland 15 B1
Mullewa, Australia 93 E2
Müllheim, Germany 25 H3
Mulligan →, Australia 94 D2
Mullingar, Ireland 15 C4
Mullins, U.S.A. 109 H6
Mullsjö, Sweden 11 G7
Mullumbimby, Australia 95 D5
Mulobezi, Zambia 87 F2
Mulroy B., Ireland 15 A4
Multan, Pakistan 68 D4
Mulumbe, Mts., Dem. Rep. of the Congo 87 D2
Mulungushi Dam, Zambia 87 E2
Mulvane, U.S.A. 113 G6
Mulwad, Sudan 80 D3
Mumbai, India 66 K8
Mumbwa, Zambia 87 F2
Mumra, Russia 49 H8
Mun →, Thailand 64 E5
Muna, Indonesia 63 F6
Munabao, India 68 G4
Munamagi, Estonia 9 H22
Münchberg, Germany 25 E7
Müncheberg, Germany 24 C10
München, Germany 25 G7
Munchen-Gladbach = Mönchengladbach, Germany 24 D2
Muncho Lake, Canada 104 B3
Munch'ŏn, N. Korea 57 E14
Muncie, U.S.A. 108 E3
Muncoonie, L., Australia 94 D2
Mundabbera, Australia 95 D5
Munday, U.S.A. 113 J5
Münden, Germany 24 D5
Mundiwindi, Australia 92 D3
Mundo →, Spain 33 G2
Mundo Novo, Brazil 125 F10
Mundra, India 68 H3
Mundrabilla, Australia 93 F4
Munera, Spain 33 F2
Mungallala, Australia 95 D4
Mungallala Cr. →, Australia 95 D4
Mungana, Australia 94 B3
Mungaoli, India 68 G8
Mungari, Mozam. 87 F3
Mungbere, Dem. Rep. of the Congo 86 B2
Mungeli, India 69 H9
Munger, India 69 G12
Munich = München, Germany 25 G7
Munising, U.S.A. 108 B2
Munka-Ljungby, Sweden 11 H6
Munkebo, Denmark 11 J4
Munkedal, Sweden 11 F5
Munkfors, Sweden 10 E7
Munku-Sardyk, Russia 51 D11
Münnerstadt, Germany 25 E6
Munroe L., Canada 105 B9
Munsan, S. Korea 57 F14
Munster, France 19 D14
Munster, Niedersachsen, Germany 24 C6
Münster, Nordrhein-Westfalen, Germany 24 D3
Munster □, Ireland 15 D3
Muntadgin, Australia 93 F2
Muntele Mare, Vf., Romania 43 D8
Muntok, Indonesia 62 E3
Munyama, Zambia 87 F2
Munzur Dağları, Turkey 73 C8
Muong Beng, Laos 58 F4
Muong Boum, Vietnam 58 F4
Muong Et, Laos 64 B5
Muong Hai, Laos 58 G4
Muong Hiem, Laos 64 B4
Muong Houn, Laos 58 F3
Muong Hung, Vietnam 58 G4
Muong Kau, Laos 64 E5
Muong Khao, Laos 64 C4
Muong Khoua, Laos 58 F4
Muong Liep, Laos 64 C4
Muong May, Laos 64 E6
Muong Ngeun, Laos 58 G4
Muong Ngoi, Laos 58 G4
Muong Nhie, Vietnam 58 F4
Muong Nong, Laos 64 D6
Muong Ou Tay, Laos 58 F3
Muong Oua, Laos 64 C3

Muong Peun, Laos 58 G4
Muong Phalane, Laos 64 D5
Muong Phieng, Laos 64 C3
Muong Phine, Laos 64 D6
Muong Sai, Laos 58 G3
Muong Saiapoun, Laos 64 C3
Muong Sen, Vietnam 64 C5
Muong Sing, Laos 58 G3
Muong Son, Laos 58 G4
Muong Soui, Laos 64 C4
Muong Va, Laos 58 G4
Muong Xia, Vietnam 64 B5
Muonio, Finland 8 C20
Muonionjoki →, Finland 8 C20
Muping, China 57 F11
Mupoi, Sudan 81 F2
Muqaddam, Wadi →, Sudan 80 D3
Muqdisho, Somali Rep. 74 G4
Mur →, Austria 27 E9
Mur-de-Bretagne, France 18 D4
Muradiye, Manisa, Turkey 39 C9
Muradiye, Van, Turkey 73 C10
Murakami, Japan 54 E9
Murallón, Cerro, Chile 128 F2
Muranda, Rwanda 86 C2
Murang'a, Kenya 86 C4
Murashi, Russia 50 D5
Murat, France 20 C6
Murat →, Turkey 73 C9
Murat Dağı, Turkey 39 C11
Muratlı, Turkey 41 E11
Murato, France 21 F13
Murau, Austria 26 D7
Muravera, Italy 30 C2
Murayama, Japan 54 E10
Murça, Portugal 34 D3
Murchison →, Australia 93 E1
Murchison, Mt., Antarctica 5 D11
Murchison Falls, Uganda 86 B3
Murchison Ra., Australia 94 C1
Murchison Rapids, Malawi 87 F3
Murcia, Spain 33 G3
Murcia □, Spain 33 H3
Murdo, U.S.A. 112 D4
Murdoch Pt., Australia 94 A3
Mürefte, Turkey 41 F11
Mureș □, Romania 43 D9
Mureș →, Romania 42 D5
Mureșul = Mureș →, Romania 42 D5
Muret, France 20 E5
Murewa, Zimbabwe 89 B5
Murfreesboro, N.C., U.S.A. 109 G7
Murfreesboro, Tenn., U.S.A. 109 H2
Murgab = Murghob, Tajikistan 50 F8
Murgab →, Turkmenistan 71 B9
Murgenella, Australia 92 B5
Murgeni, Romania 43 D13
Murgha Kibzai, Pakistan 68 D3
Murghob, Tajikistan 50 F8
Murgon, Australia 95 D5
Muri, India 69 H11
Muria, Indonesia 63 G14
Muriaé, Brazil 127 A7
Murias de Paredes, Spain 34 C4
Muriel Mine, Zimbabwe 87 F3
Müritz, Germany 24 B8
Murka, Kenya 86 C4
Murliganj, India 69 G12
Murmansk, Russia 50 C4
Murnau, Germany 25 H7
Muro, France 21 F12
Muro, Spain 37 B10
Muro, C. de, France 21 G12
Muro de Alcoy, Spain 33 G4
Murom, Russia 48 C6
Muroran, Japan 54 C10
Muros, Spain 34 C1
Muros y de Noya, Ría de, Spain 34 C1
Muroto, Japan 55 H7
Muroto-Misaki, Japan 55 H7
Murowana Goślina, Poland 45 F3
Murphy, U.S.A. 114 E5
Murphys, U.S.A. 116 G6
Murrat, Sudan 80 D2
Murrat Wells, Sudan 80 C3
Murray, Ky., U.S.A. 109 G1
Murray, Utah, U.S.A. 114 F8
Murray, L., U.S.A. 109 H5
Murray Harbour, Canada 103 C7
Murraysburg, S. Africa 88 E3
Murree, Pakistan 68 C5
Murrieta, U.S.A. 117 M9
Murro di Porco, Capo, Italy 31 F8
Murshid, Sudan 80 C3
Murshidabad, India 69 G13
Murska Sobota, Slovenia 29 B13
Murtle L., Canada 104 C5
Murtoa, Portugal 34 E2
Murtosa, Portugal 34 E2
Murungu, Tanzania 86 C3
Mururoa, Pac. Oc. 97 K14
Murwara, India 69 H9
Murwillumbah, Australia 95 D5
Mürz →, Austria 26 D8
Mürzzuschlag, Austria 26 D8
Muş, Turkey 70 B4
Mûsa, Gebel, Egypt 70 D2
Musa Khel, Pakistan 68 D3
Musala, Bulgaria 40 D7
Musala, Indonesia 62 D1
Musan, N. Korea 57 C15
Musangu, Dem. Rep. of the Congo 87 E1
Musasa, Tanzania 86 C3

Nastapoka ➝, *Canada* 102 A4
Nastapoka, Is., *Canada* 102 A4
Nasugbu, *Phil.* 61 D4
Näsum, *Sweden* 11 H8
Näsviken, *Sweden* 10 C10
Nata, *Botswana* 88 C4
Nata ➝, *Botswana* 88 C4
Natal, *Brazil* 125 E11
Natal, *Indonesia* 62 D1
Natal, *S. Africa* 85 K6
Natalinci, *Serbia, Yug.* 42 F5
Naṭanz, *Iran* 71 C6
Natashquan, *Canada* 103 B7
Natashquan ➝, *Canada* 103 B7
Natchez, *U.S.A.* 113 K9
Natchitoches, *U.S.A.* 113 K8
Nathdwara, *India* 68 G5
Nati, Pta., *Spain* 37 A10
Nation ➝, *Canada* 104 B4
National City, *U.S.A.* 117 N9
Natitingou, *Benin* 83 C5
Natividad, I., *Mexico* 118 B1
Natkyizin, *Burma* 64 E1
Natron, L., *Tanzania* 86 C4
Natrona Heights, *U.S.A.* 110 F5
Natrûn, W. el ➝, *Egypt* 80 H7
Nättraby, *Sweden* 11 H9
Natukanaoka Pan, *Namibia* ... 88 B2
Natuna Besar, Kepulauan,
  Indonesia 65 L7
Natuna Is. = Natuna Besar,
  Kepulauan, *Indonesia* 65 L7
Natuna Selatan, Kepulauan,
  Indonesia 65 L7
Natural Bridge, *U.S.A.* 111 B9
Naturaliste, C., *Australia* . 94 G4
Nau Qala, *Afghan.* 68 B3
Naucelle, *France* 20 D6
Nauders, *Austria* 26 E3
Nauen, *Germany* 24 C8
Naugatuck, *U.S.A.* 111 E11
Naujaat = Repulse Bay, *Canada* 101 B11
Naumburg, *Germany* 24 D7
Nā'ūr at Tunayb, *Jordan* 75 D4
Nauru ■, *Pac. Oc.* 96 H8
Naushahra = Nowshera,
  Pakistan 66 C8
Naushahro, *Pakistan* 68 F3
Naushon I., *U.S.A.* 111 E14
Nauta, *Peru* 124 D4
Nautanwa, *India* 67 F13
Nautla, *Mexico* 119 C5
Nava, *Mexico* 118 B4
Nava, *Spain* 34 B5
Nava del Rey, *Spain* 34 D5
Navadwip, *India* 69 H13
Navahermosa, *Spain* 35 F6
Navahrudak, *Belarus* 46 F3
Navajo Reservoir, *U.S.A.* ... 115 H10
Navalcarnero, *Spain* 34 E6
Navalmoral de la Mata, *Spain* 34 F5
Navalvillar de Pela, *Spain* . 35 F5
Navan = An Uaimh, *Ireland* .. 15 C5
Navapolatsk, *Belarus* 46 E5
Navarino, I., *Chile* 128 H3
Navarra □, *Spain* 32 C3
Navarre, *U.S.A.* 110 F3
Navarro ➝, *U.S.A.* 116 F3
Navas de San Juan, *Spain* ... 35 G7
Navasota, *U.S.A.* 113 K6
Navassa I., *W. Indies* 121 C5
Nävekvarn, *Sweden* 11 F10
Naver ➝, *U.K.* 14 C4
Navia, *Spain* 34 B4
Navia ➝, *Spain* 34 B4
Navia de Suarna, *Spain* 34 C3
Navibandar, *India* 68 J3
Navidad, *Chile* 126 C1
Naviraí, *Brazil* 127 A5
Navlakhi, *India* 68 H4
Navlya, *Russia* 47 F8
Năvodari, *Romania* 43 F13
Navoi = Nawoiy, *Uzbekistan* . 50 E7
Navojoa, *Mexico* 118 B3
Navolato, *Mexico* 118 C3
Návpaktos, *Greece* 38 C3
Návplion, *Greece* 38 D4
Navrongo, *Ghana* 83 C4
Navsari, *India* 66 J8
Nawa Kot, *Pakistan* 68 E4
Nawab Khan, *Pakistan* 68 D3
Nawabganj, *Ut. P., India* ... 69 F9
Nawabganj, *Ut. P., India* ... 69 E8
Nawabshah, *Pakistan* 68 F3
Nawada, *India* 69 G11
Nawakot, *Nepal* 69 F11
Nawalgarh, *India* 68 F6
Nawanshahr, *India* 69 C6
Nawar, Dasht-i-, *Afghan.* ... 68 C3
Nawi, *Sudan* 80 D3
Nawoiy, *Uzbekistan* 50 E7
Naxçıvan, *Azerbaijan* 70 B5
Naxçıvan □, *Azerbaijan* 50 F5
Náxos, *Greece* 39 D7
Nay, *France* 20 E3
Nay, Mui, *Vietnam* 62 B3
Näy Band, *Büshehr, Iran* 71 E7
Näy Band, *Khorāsān, Iran* ... 71 C8
Nayakhan, *Russia* 51 C16
Nayarit □, *Mexico* 118 C4
Nayé, *Senegal* 82 C2
Nayong, *China* 58 D5
Nayoro, *Japan* 54 B11
Nayyāl, W. ➝, *Si. Arabia* .. 70 D3
Nazaré, *Brazil* 125 F11

Nazaré, *Portugal* 35 F1
Nazareth = Nazerat, *Israel* . 75 C4
Nazareth, *U.S.A.* 111 F9
Nazas, *Mexico* 118 B4
Nazas ➝, *Mexico* 118 B4
Nazca, *Peru* 124 F4
Naze, The, *U.K.* 13 F9
Nazerat, *Israel* 75 C4
Nāzik, *Iran* 70 B5
Nazilli, *Turkey* 39 D10
Nazko, *Canada* 104 C4
Nazko ➝, *Canada* 104 C4
Nazret, *Ethiopia* 81 F4
Nazwá, *Oman* 74 C6
Nchanga, *Zambia* 87 E2
Ncheu, *Malawi* 87 E3
Ndala, *Tanzania* 86 C3
Ndalatando, *Angola* 84 F2
Ndali, *Benin* 83 D5
Ndareda, *Tanzania* 86 C4
Ndélé, *C.A.R.* 84 C4
Ndikinimeki, *Cameroon* 83 E7
N'Dioum, *Senegal* 82 B2
Ndjamena, *Chad* 79 F8
Ndola, *Zambia* 87 E2
Ndoto Mts., *Kenya* 86 B4
Nduguti, *Tanzania* 86 C3
Néa Alikarnassós, *Greece* ... 39 F7
Néa Ankhíalos, *Greece* 38 B4
Néa Epídhavros, *Greece* 38 D5
Néa Flippiás, *Greece* 38 B2
Néa Ionía, *Greece* 38 B4
Néa Kallikrátia, *Greece* 40 F7
Néa Mákri, *Greece* 38 C5
Néa Moudhaniá, *Greece* 40 F7
Néa Péramos, *Attikí, Greece* 38 C5
Néa Péramos, *Kaválla, Greece* 41 F8
Néa Víssi, *Greece* 41 E10
Néa Zíkhna, *Greece* 40 E7
Neagh, Lough, *U.K.* 15 B5
Neah Bay, *U.S.A.* 116 B2
Neale, L., *Australia* 92 D5
Neamţ □, *Romania* 43 C11
Neápolis, *Kozáni, Greece* ... 40 F5
Neápolis, *Kríti, Greece* 36 D7
Neápolis, *Lakonía, Greece* .. 38 E5
Near Is., *U.S.A.* 100 C11
Neath, *U.K.* 13 F4
Neath Port Talbot □, *U.K.* .. 13 F4
Nebbou, *Burkina Faso* 83 C4
Nebine Cr. ➝, *Australia* 95 D4
Nebitdag, *Turkmenistan* 50 F6
Nebo, *Australia* 94 C4
Nebolchy, *Russia* 46 C7
Nebraska □, *U.S.A.* 112 E5
Nebraska City, *U.S.A.* 112 E7
Nébrodi, Monti, *Italy* 31 E7
Necedah, *U.S.A.* 112 C9
Nechako ➝, *Canada* 104 C4
Neches ➝, *U.S.A.* 113 L8
Neckar ➝, *Germany* 25 F4
Necochea, *Argentina* 126 D4
Neda ➝, *Greece* 38 D3
Nedelino, *Bulgaria* 41 E9
Nedelišće, *Croatia* 29 B13
Nédha ➝, *Greece* 38 D3
Needles, *Canada* 104 D5
Needles, *U.S.A.* 117 L12
Needles, The, *U.K.* 13 G6
Neembucú □, *Paraguay* 126 B4
Neemuch = Nimach, *India* 68 G6
Neenah, *U.S.A.* 108 C1
Neepawa, *Canada* 105 C9
Neftçala, *Azerbaijan* 71 B6
Neftegorsk, *Russia* 49 H14
Neftekumsk, *Russia* 49 H7
Nefyn, *U.K.* 12 E3
Négala, *Mali* 82 C3
Negapatam = Nagappattinam,
  India 66 P11
Negaunee, *U.S.A.* 108 B2
Negele, *Ethiopia* 81 F4
Negev Desert = Hanegev, *Israel* 75 E4
Negoiul, Vf., *Romania* 43 E9
Negombo, *Sri Lanka* 66 R11
Negotin, *Serbia, Yug.* 40 B6
Negotino, *Macedonia* 40 E6
Negra, Peña, *Spain* 34 C4
Negra, Pta., *Peru* 122 D2
Negrais, C. = Maudin Sun,
  Burma 67 M19
Negreşti, *Romania* 43 D12
Negreşti-Oaş, *Romania* 43 C8
Negril, *Jamaica* 120 C4
Negro ➝, *Argentina* 122 H4
Negro ➝, *Brazil* 122 D4
Negro ➝, *Uruguay* 127 C4
Negros, *Phil.* 61 G5
Negru Vodă, *Romania* 43 G13
Neguac, *Canada* 103 C6
Nehalem ➝, *U.S.A.* 116 E3
Nehāvand, *Iran* 71 C6
Nehbandān, *Iran* 71 D9
Nehoiu, *Romania* 43 E11
Nei Monggol Zizhiqu □, *China* 56 D7
Neijiang, *China* 58 C5
Neillsville, *U.S.A.* 112 C9
Neilton, *U.S.A.* 116 C2
Neiva, *Colombia* 124 C3
Neixiang, *China* 56 H6
Nejanilini L., *Canada* 105 B9
Nejd = Najd, *Si. Arabia* 74 B3
Nejo, *Ethiopia* 81 F4
Nekā, *Iran* 71 B7

Nekemte, *Ethiopia* 81 F4
Nêkheb, *Egypt* 80 B3
Neksø, *Denmark* 11 J9
Nelas, *Portugal* 34 E3
Nelia, *Australia* 94 C3
Nelidovo, *Russia* 46 D7
Neligh, *U.S.A.* 112 D5
Nelkan, *Russia* 51 D14
Nellore, *India* 66 M11
Nelson, *Canada* 104 D5
Nelson, *N.Z.* 91 J4
Nelson, *U.K.* 12 D5
Nelson, *Ariz., U.S.A.* 115 J7
Nelson ➝, *Canada* 105 C9
Nelson, Estrecho, *Chile* 128 G2
Nelson Forks, *Canada* 104 B4
Nelson House, *Canada* 105 B9
Nelson L., *Canada* 105 B8
Nelspoort, *S. Africa* 88 E3
Nelspruit, *S. Africa* 89 D5
Néma, *Mauritania* 82 B3
Neman, *Russia* 9 J20
Neman ➝, *Lithuania* 9 J19
Neméa, *Greece* 38 D4
Nemeiben L., *Canada* 105 B7
Nemërçkë, Mal, *Albania* 40 F4
Nemira, Vf., *Romania* 43 D11
Némiscau, *Canada* 102 B4
Némiscau, L., *Canada* 102 B4
Nemours, *France* 19 D9
Nemunas = Neman ➝,
  Lithuania 9 J19
Nemuro, *Japan* 54 C12
Nemuro-Kaikyō, *Japan* 54 C12
Nen Jiang ➝, *China* 57 B13
Nenagh, *Ireland* 15 D3
Nenasi, *Malaysia* 65 L4
Nene ➝, *U.K.* 13 E8
Nénita, *Greece* 39 C8
Nenjiang, *China* 60 B7
Neno, *Malawi* 87 F3
Neodesha, *U.S.A.* 113 G7
Neokhórion,
  Aitolía kai Akarnanía, Greece 38 C3
Neokhórion, *Árta, Greece* ... 38 B2
Néon Karlovásion, *Greece* ... 39 D8
Néon Petrítsi, *Greece* 40 E7
Neosho, *U.S.A.* 113 G7
Neosho ➝, *U.S.A.* 113 H7
Nepal ■, *Asia* 69 F11
Nepalganj, *Nepal* 69 E9
Nepalganj Road, *India* 69 E9
Nephi, *U.S.A.* 114 G8
Nephin, *Ireland* 15 B2
Nepi, *Italy* 29 F9
Nepomuk, *Czech Rep.* 26 B6
Neptune, *U.S.A.* 111 F10
Nera ➝, *Italy* 29 F9
Nera ➝, *Romania* 42 F6
Nérac, *France* 20 D4
Nerang, *Australia* 95 D5
Neratovice, *Czech Rep.* 26 A7
Nerchinsk, *Russia* 51 D12
Nereju, *Romania* 43 E11
Nerekhta, *Russia* 46 D11
Néret, L., *Canada* 103 B5
Neretvanski Kanal, *Croatia* . 29 E14
Neringa, *Lithuania* 9 J19
Nerja, *Spain* 35 J7
Nerl ➝, *Russia* 46 D11
Nerpio, *Spain* 33 G2
Nerva, *Spain* 35 H4
Nervi, *Italy* 28 D6
Neryungri, *Russia* 51 D13
Nescopeck, *U.S.A.* 111 E8
Nesebŭr, *Bulgaria* 41 D11
Ness, L., *U.K.* 14 D4
Ness City, *U.S.A.* 112 F5
Nesterov, *Poland* 47 G2
Nestórion, *Greece* 40 F5
Néstos ➝, *Greece* 41 E8
Nesvady, *Slovak Rep.* 27 D11
Nesvizh = Nyasvizh, *Belarus* 47 F4
Netanya, *Israel* 75 C3
Netarhat, *India* 69 H11
Nete ➝, *Belgium* 17 C4
Netherdale, *Australia* 94 C4
Netherlands ■, *Europe* 17 C5
Netherlands Antilles ■,
  W. Indies 124 A5
Neto ➝, *Italy* 31 C10
Netrang, *India* 68 J5
Nettancourt, *France* 19 D11
Nettetal, *Germany* 24 D2
Nettilling L., *Canada* 101 B12
Nettuno, *Italy* 30 A5
Netzahualcoyotl, Presa, *Mexico* 119 D6
Neu-Isenburg, *Germany* 25 E4
Neu-Ulm, *Germany* 25 G6
Neubrandenburg, *Germany* 24 B9
Neubukow, *Germany* 24 A7
Neuburg, *Germany* 25 G7
Neuchâtel, *Switz.* 25 J2
Neuchâtel □, *Switz.* 25 J2
Neuchâtel, Lac de, *Switz.* .. 25 J2
Neudau, *Austria* 26 D9
Neuenhagen, *Germany* 24 C9
Neuf-Brisach, *France* 19 D14
Neufahrn, *Bayern, Germany* .. 25 G8
Neufahrn, *Bayern, Germany* .. 25 G7
Neufchâteau, *Belgium* 17 E5
Neufchâteau, *France* 19 D12
Neufchâtel-en-Bray, *France* . 18 C8

Neufchâtel-sur-Aisne, *France* 19 C11
Neuhaus, *Germany* 24 B6
Neuillé-Pont-Pierre, *France* 18 E7
Neuilly-St-Front, *France* ... 19 C10
Neukalen, *Germany* 24 B8
Neumarkt, *Germany* 25 F7
Neumünster, *Germany* 24 A5
Neung-sur-Beuvron, *France* .. 19 E8
Neunkirchen, *Austria* 26 D9
Neunkirchen, *Germany* 25 F3
Neuquén, *Argentina* 128 D3
Neuquén □, *Argentina* 126 D2
Neuruppin, *Germany* 24 C8
Neusäss, *Germany* 25 G6
Neuse ➝, *U.S.A.* 109 H7
Neusiedl, *Austria* 27 D9
Neusiedler See, *Austria* 27 D9
Neuss, *Germany* 24 D2
Neussargues-Moissac, *France* 20 C7
Neustadt, *Bayern, Germany* .. 25 F8
Neustadt, *Bayern, Germany* .. 25 G7
Neustadt, *Bayern, Germany* .. 25 F6
Neustadt, *Bayern, Germany* .. 25 E7
Neustadt, *Brandenburg,
  Germany* 24 C8
Neustadt, *Hessen, Germany* .. 24 E5
Neustadt, *Niedersachsen,
  Germany* 24 C5
Neustadt, *Rhld.-Pfz., Germany* 25 F4
Neustadt, *Sachsen, Germany* . 24 D10
Neustadt, *Schleswig-Holstein,
  Germany* 24 A6
Neustadt, *Thüringen, Germany* 24 E7
Neustrelitz, *Germany* 24 B9
Neuvic, *France* 20 C6
Neuville-sur-Saône, *France* . 21 C8
Neuvy-le-Roi, *France* 18 E7
Neuvy-St-Sépulchre, *France* . 19 F8
Neuvy-sur-Barangeon, *France* 19 E9
Neuwerk, *Germany* 24 B4
Neuwied, *Germany* 24 E3
Neva ➝, *Russia* 46 C6
Nevada, *Iowa, U.S.A.* 112 D8
Nevada, *Mo., U.S.A.* 113 G7
Nevada □, *U.S.A.* 114 G5
Nevada City, *U.S.A.* 116 F6
Nevado, Cerro, *Argentina* ... 126 D2
Nevel, *Russia* 46 D5
Nevers, *France* 19 F10
Nevesinje, *Bos.-H.* 40 C2
Neville, *Canada* 105 D7
Nevinnomyssk, *Russia* 49 H6
Nevis, *St. Kitts & Nevis* ... 121 C7
Nevrokop = Gotse Delchev,
  Bulgaria 40 E7
Nevşehir, *Turkey* 70 B2
New ➝, *U.S.A.* 108 F5
New Aiyansh, *Canada* 104 B3
New Albany, *Ind., U.S.A.* ... 108 F3
New Albany, *Miss., U.S.A.* .. 113 H10
New Albany, *Pa., U.S.A.* 111 E8
New Amsterdam, *Guyana* 124 B7
New Angledool, *Australia* ... 95 D4
New Baltimore, *U.S.A.* 110 D2
New Bedford, *U.S.A.* 111 E14
New Berlin, *N.Y., U.S.A.* ... 111 D9
New Berlin, *Pa., U.S.A.* 110 F8
New Bern, *U.S.A.* 109 H7
New Bethlehem, *U.S.A.* 110 F5
New Bloomfield, *U.S.A.* 110 F7
New Boston, *U.S.A.* 113 J7
New Braunfels, *U.S.A.* 113 L5
New Brighton, *N.Z.* 91 K4
New Brighton, *U.S.A.* 110 F4
New Britain, *Papua N. G.* ... 96 H7
New Britain, *U.S.A.* 111 E12
New Brunswick, *U.S.A.* 111 F10
New Brunswick □, *Canada* 103 C6
New Bussa, *Nigeria* 83 D5
New Caledonia ■, *Pac. Oc.* . 96 K8
New Castle = Castilla-La
  Mancha □, *Spain* 6 H5
New Castle, *Ind., U.S.A.* ... 108 F3
New Castle, *Pa., U.S.A.* 110 F4
New City, *U.S.A.* 111 E11
New Concord, *U.S.A.* 110 G3
New Cumberland, *U.S.A.* 110 F4
New Cuyama, *U.S.A.* 117 L7
New Delhi, *India* 68 E7
New Denver, *Canada* 104 D5
New Don Pedro Reservoir,
  U.S.A. 116 H6
New England, *U.S.A.* 112 B3
New England Ra., *Australia* . 95 E5
New Forest, *U.K.* 13 G6
New Galloway, *U.K.* 14 F4
New Glasgow, *Canada* 103 C7
New Guinea, *Oceania* 52 K17
New Hamburg, *Canada* 110 C4
New Hampshire □, *U.S.A.* 111 C13
New Hampton, *U.S.A.* 112 D8
New Hanover, *S. Africa* 89 D5
New Hartford, *U.S.A.* 111 D9
New Haven, *Conn., U.S.A.* ... 111 E12
New Haven, *Mich., U.S.A.* ... 110 D2
New Hazelton, *Canada* 104 B3
New Hebrides = Vanuatu ■,
  Pac. Oc. 96 J8
New Holland, *U.S.A.* 111 F8
New Iberia, *U.S.A.* 113 K9
New Ireland, *Papua N. G.* ... 96 H7
New Jersey □, *U.S.A.* 108 E8
New Kensington, *U.S.A.* 110 F5
New Lexington, *U.S.A.* 108 F4
New Liskeard, *Canada* 102 C4
New London, *Conn., U.S.A.* .. 111 E12

New London, *Ohio, U.S.A.* ... 110 E2
New London, *Wis., U.S.A.* ... 112 C10
New Madrid, *U.S.A.* 113 G10
New Martinsville, *U.S.A.* ... 108 F5
New Meadows, *U.S.A.* 114 D5
New Melones L., *U.S.A.* 116 H6
New Mexico □, *U.S.A.* 115 J10
New Milford, *Conn., U.S.A.* . 111 E11
New Milford, *Pa., U.S.A.* ... 111 E9
New Norcia, *Australia* 93 F2
New Norfolk, *Australia* 94 G4
New Orleans, *U.S.A.* 113 L9
New Philadelphia, *U.S.A.* ... 110 F3
New Plymouth, *N.Z.* 91 H5
New Plymouth, *U.S.A.* 114 E5
New Port Richey, *U.S.A.* 109 L4
New Providence, *Bahamas* 120 A4
New Quay, *U.K.* 13 E3
New Radnor, *U.K.* 13 E4
New Richmond, *Canada* 103 C6
New Richmond, *U.S.A.* 112 C8
New Roads, *U.S.A.* 113 K9
New Rochelle, *U.S.A.* 111 F11
New Rockford, *U.S.A.* 112 B5
New Romney, *U.K.* 13 G8
New Ross, *Ireland* 15 D5
New Salem, *U.S.A.* 112 B4
New Scone, *U.K.* 14 E5
New Siberian I. = Novaya Sibir,
  Ostrov, *Russia* 51 B16
New Siberian Is. =
  Novosibirskiye Ostrova,
  Russia 51 B15
New Smyrna Beach, *U.S.A.* ... 109 L5
New Town, *U.S.A.* 112 B3
New Tredegar, *U.K.* 13 F4
New Ulm, *U.S.A.* 112 C7
New Waterford, *Canada* 103 C7
New Westminster, *Canada* 116 A4
New York, *U.S.A.* 111 F11
New York □, *U.S.A.* 111 D9
New York Mts., *U.S.A.* 115 J6
New Zealand ■, *Oceania* 91 J6
Newaj ➝, *India* 68 G7
Newala, *Tanzania* 87 E4
Newark, *Del., U.S.A.* 108 F8
Newark, *N.J., U.S.A.* 111 F10
Newark, *N.Y., U.S.A.* 110 C7
Newark, *Ohio, U.S.A.* 110 F2
Newark-on-Trent, *U.K.* 12 D7
Newark Valley, *U.S.A.* 111 D8
Newberg, *U.S.A.* 114 D2
Newberry, *Mich., U.S.A.* 108 B3
Newberry, *S.C., U.S.A.* 109 H5
Newberry Springs, *U.S.A.* ... 117 L10
Newboro L., *Canada* 111 B8
Newbridge = Droichead Nua,
  Ireland 15 C5
Newburgh, *Canada* 110 B8
Newburgh, *U.S.A.* 111 E10
Newbury, *U.K.* 13 F6
Newbury, *N.H., U.S.A.* 111 B12
Newbury, *Vt., U.S.A.* 111 B12
Newburyport, *U.S.A.* 109 D10
Newcastle, *N.B., Canada* 103 C6
Newcastle, *Ont., Canada* 102 D4
Newcastle, *S. Africa* 89 D4
Newcastle, *U.K.* 15 B6
Newcastle, *Calif., U.S.A.* .. 116 G5
Newcastle, *Wyo., U.S.A.* 112 D2
Newcastle Emlyn, *U.K.* 13 E3
Newcastle Ra., *Australia* ... 92 C5
Newcastle-under-Lyme, *U.K.* . 12 D5
Newcastle-upon-Tyne, *U.K.* .. 12 C6
Newcastle Waters, *Australia* 94 B1
Newcastle West, *Ireland* 15 D2
Newcomb, *U.S.A.* 111 C10
Newcomerstown, *U.S.A.* 110 F3
Newdegate, *Australia* 93 F2
Newell, *Australia* 94 B4
Newell, *U.S.A.* 112 C3
Newfane, *U.S.A.* 110 C6
Newfield, *U.S.A.* 111 D8
Newfound L., *U.S.A.* 111 C13
Newfoundland, *Canada* 98 E14
Newfoundland, *U.S.A.* 111 E9
Newfoundland □, *Canada* 103 B8
Newhall, *U.S.A.* 117 L8
Newhaven, *U.K.* 13 G8
Newkirk, *U.S.A.* 113 G6
Newlyn, *U.K.* 13 G2
Newman, *Australia* 92 D2
Newman, *U.S.A.* 116 H5
Newmarket, *Canada* 110 B5
Newmarket, *Ireland* 15 D2
Newmarket, *U.K.* 13 E8
Newmarket, *U.S.A.* 111 C14
Newnan, *U.S.A.* 109 J3
Newport, *Ireland* 15 C2
Newport, *I. of W., U.K.* 13 G6
Newport, *Newport, U.K.* 13 F5
Newport, *Ark., U.S.A.* 113 H9
Newport, *Ky., U.S.A.* 108 F3
Newport, *N.H., U.S.A.* 111 C12
Newport, *N.Y., U.S.A.* 111 C9
Newport, *Oreg., U.S.A.* 114 D1
Newport, *Pa., U.S.A.* 110 F7
Newport, *R.I., U.S.A.* 111 E13
Newport, *Tenn., U.S.A.* 109 H4
Newport, *Vt., U.S.A.* 111 B12
Newport, *Wash., U.S.A.* 114 B5
Newport □, *U.K.* 13 F4
Newport Beach, *U.S.A.* 117 M9
Newport News, *U.S.A.* 108 G7
Newport Pagnell, *U.K.* 13 E7
Newquay, *U.K.* 13 G2

Newry, *U.K.* 15 B5
Newton, *Ill., U.S.A.* 112 F10
Newton, *Iowa, U.S.A.* 112 E8
Newton, *Kans., U.S.A.* 113 F6
Newton, *Mass., U.S.A.* 111 D13
Newton, *Miss., U.S.A.* 113 J10
Newton, *N.C., U.S.A.* 109 H5
Newton, *N.J., U.S.A.* 111 E10
Newton, *Tex., U.S.A.* 113 K8
Newton Abbot, *U.K.* 13 G4
Newton Aycliffe, *U.K.* 12 C6
Newton Falls, *U.S.A.* 110 E4
Newton Stewart, *U.K.* 14 G4
Newtonmore, *U.K.* 14 D4
Newtown, *U.K.* 13 E4
Newtownabbey, *U.K.* 15 B6
Newtownards, *U.K.* 15 B6
Newtownbarry = Bunclody,
 Ireland 15 D5
Newtownstewart, *U.K.* 15 B4
Newville, *U.S.A.* 110 F7
Nexon, *France* 20 C5
Neya, *Russia* 48 A6
Neyrīz, *Iran* 71 D7
Neyshābūr, *Iran* 71 B8
Nezhin = Nizhyn, *Ukraine* 47 G6
Nezperce, *U.S.A.* 114 C5
Ngabang, *Indonesia* 62 D3
Ngabordamlu, Tanjung,
 Indonesia 63 F8
N'Gage, *Angola* 84 F3
Ngala, *Nigeria* 83 C7
Ngambé, *Cameroon* 83 D7
Ngambé, *Cameroon* 83 E7
Ngami Depression, *Botswana* .. 88 C3
Ngamo, *Zimbabwe* 87 F2
Ngangala, *Sudan* 81 G3
Nganglong Kangri, *China* 67 C12
Ngao, *Thailand* 64 C2
Ngaoundéré, *Cameroon* 84 C2
Ngapara, *N.Z.* 91 L3
Ngara, *Tanzania* 86 C3
Ngawi, *Indonesia* 63 G14
Ngeoboli, *Sudan* 81 G3
Ngoma, *Malawi* 87 E3
Ngomahura, *Zimbabwe* 87 G3
Ngomba, *Tanzania* 87 D3
Ngop, *Sudan* 81 F3
Ngoring Hu, *China* 60 C4
Ngorkou, *Mali* 82 B4
Ngorongoro, *Tanzania* 86 C4
Ngozi, *Burundi* 86 C2
Ngudu, *Tanzania* 86 C3
Nguigmi, *Niger* 79 F8
Nguila, *Cameroon* 83 E7
Nguiu, *Australia* 92 B5
Ngukurr, *Australia* 94 A1
Ngulu Atoll, *Pac. Oc.* 63 C9
Ngunga, *Tanzania* 86 C3
Nguru, *Nigeria* 83 C7
Nguru Mts., *Tanzania* 86 D4
Nguyen Binh, *Vietnam* 58 F5
Nha Trang, *Vietnam* 65 F7
Nhacoongo, *Mozam.* 89 C6
Nhamaabué, *Mozam.* 87 F4
Nhamundá →, *Brazil* 125 D7
Nhangulaze, L., *Mozam.* 89 C5
Nho Quan, *Vietnam* 58 G5
Nhulunbuy, *Australia* 94 A2
Nia-nia, *Dem. Rep. of the Congo* 86 B2
Niafounké, *Mali* 82 B4
Niagara Falls, *Canada* 102 D4
Niagara Falls, *U.S.A.* 110 C6
Niagara-on-the-Lake, *Canada* . 110 C5
Niah, *Malaysia* 62 D4
Niamey, *Niger* 83 C5
Niandan-Koro, *Guinea* 82 C3
Nianforando, *Guinea* 82 D2
Niangara, *Dem. Rep. of
 the Congo* 86 B2
Niangbo, *Ivory C.* 82 D3
Niangoloko, *Burkina Faso* 82 C4
Niantic, *U.S.A.* 111 E12
Niaro, *Sudan* 81 E3
Nias, *Indonesia* 62 D1
Niassa □, *Mozam.* 87 E4
Nibāk, *Si. Arabia* 71 E7
Nibe, *Denmark* 11 H3
Nicaragua ■, *Cent. Amer.* 120 D2
Nicaragua, L. de, *Nic.* 120 D2
Nicastro, *Italy* 31 D9
Nice, *France* 21 E11
Niceville, *U.S.A.* 109 K2
Nichicun, L., *Canada* 103 B5
Nichinan, *Japan* 55 J5
Nicholás, Canal, *W. Indies* .. 120 B3
Nicholasville, *U.S.A.* 108 G3
Nichols, *U.S.A.* 111 D8
Nicholson, *Australia* 92 C4
Nicholson, *U.S.A.* 111 E9
Nicholson →, *Australia* 94 B2
Nicholson L., *Canada* 105 A8
Nicholson Ra., *Australia* 93 E2
Nicholville, *U.S.A.* 111 B10
Nicobar Is., *Ind. Oc.* 52 J13
Nicola, *Canada* 104 C4
Nicolls Town, *Bahamas* 120 A4
Nicopolis, *Greece* 38 B2
Nicosia, *Cyprus* 36 D12
Nicosia, *Italy* 31 E7
Nicótera, *Italy* 31 D8
Nicoya, *Costa Rica* 120 D2
Nicoya, G. de, *Costa Rica* ... 120 E3
Nicoya, Pen. de, *Costa Rica* . 120 E2
Nidd →, *U.K.* 12 D6

Nidda, *Germany* 25 E5
Nidda →, *Germany* 25 E4
Nidwalden □, *Switz.* 25 J4
Nidzica, *Poland* 45 E7
Nied →, *Germany* 19 C13
Niederaula, *Germany* 24 E5
Niederbayern □, *Germany* 25 G8
Niederbronn-les-Bains, *France* . 19 D14
Niedere Tauern, *Austria* 26 D7
Niederlausitz, *Germany* 24 D9
Niederösterreich □, *Austria* . 26 C8
Niedersachsen □, *Germany* 24 C4
Niekerkshoop, *S. Africa* 88 D3
Niellé, *Ivory C.* 82 C3
Niemba, *Dem. Rep. of the Congo* 86 D2
Niemen = Neman →, *Lithuania* . 9 J19
Niemodlin, *Poland* 45 H4
Nienburg, *Germany* 24 C5
Niepołomice, *Poland* 45 H7
Niers →, *Germany* 24 D1
Niesky, *Germany* 24 D10
Nieszawa, *Poland* 45 F5
Nieu Bethesda, *S. Africa* 88 E3
Nieuw Amsterdam, *Surinam* 125 B7
Nieuw Nickerie, *Surinam* 125 B7
Nieuwoudtville, *S. Africa* ... 88 E2
Nieuwpoort, *Belgium* 17 C2
Nieves, Pico de las, *Canary Is.* . 37 G4
Nièvre □, *France* 19 E10
Niga, *Mali* 82 C3
Niğde, *Turkey* 70 B2
Nigel, *S. Africa* 89 D4
Niger □, *Nigeria* 83 D6
Niger ■, *W. Afr.* 83 B7
Niger →, *W. Afr.* 83 D6
Niger Delta, *Africa* 83 E6
Nigeria ■, *W. Afr.* 83 D6
Nighasin, *India* 69 E9
Nightcaps, *N.Z.* 91 L2
Nigríta, *Greece* 40 F7
Nii-Jima, *Japan* 55 G9
Niigata, *Japan* 54 F9
Niigata □, *Japan* 55 F9
Niihama, *Japan* 55 H6
Niihau, *U.S.A.* 106 H14
Niimi, *Japan* 55 G6
Niitsu, *Japan* 54 F9
Níjar, *Spain* 33 J2
Nijil, *Jordan* 75 E4
Nijkerk, *Neths.* 17 B5
Nijmegen, *Neths.* 17 C5
Nijverdal, *Neths.* 17 B6
Nīk Pey, *Iran* 71 B6
Nike, *Nigeria* 83 D6
Nikiniki, *Indonesia* 63 F6
Nikísiani, *Greece* 41 F8
Nikítas, *Greece* 40 F7
Nikki, *Benin* 83 D5
Nikkō, *Japan* 55 F9
Nikolayev = Mykolayiv, *Ukraine* 47 J7
Nikolayevsk, *Russia* 48 E7
Nikolayevsk-na-Amur, *Russia* . 51 D15
Nikolsk, *Russia* 48 D8
Nikolskoye, *Russia* 51 D17
Nikopol, *Bulgaria* 41 C8
Nikopol, *Ukraine* 47 J8
Niksar, *Turkey* 72 B7
Nīkshahr, *Iran* 71 E9
Nikšić, *Montenegro, Yug.* 40 D2
Nîl, Nahr en →, *Africa* 80 H7
Nîl el Abyad →, *Sudan* 81 D3
Nîl el Azraq →, *Sudan* 81 D3
Nila, *Indonesia* 63 F7
Niland, *U.S.A.* 117 M11
Nile = Nîl, Nahr en →, *Africa* . 80 H7
Niles, *Mich., U.S.A.* 108 E2
Niles, *Ohio, U.S.A.* 110 E4
Nilüfer →, *Turkey* 41 F12
Nim Ka Thana, *India* 68 F6
Nimach, *India* 68 G6
Nimbahera, *India* 68 G6
Nîmes, *France* 21 E8
Nimfaíon, Ákra = Pínnes, Ákra,
 Greece 41 F8
Nimule, *Sudan* 81 G3
Nin, *Croatia* 29 D12
Nīnawā □, *Iraq* 70 B4
Nindigully, *Australia* 95 D4
Nineveh = Nīnawā, *Iraq* 70 B4
Ning Xian, *China* 56 G4
Ning'an, *China* 57 B15
Ningbo, *China* 59 C13
Ningcheng, *China* 57 D10
Ningde, *China* 59 D12
Ningdu, *China* 59 D10
Ninggang, *China* 59 D9
Ningguo, *China* 59 B12
Ninghai, *China* 59 C13
Ninghua, *China* 59 D11
Ningi, *Nigeria* 83 C6
Ningjin, *China* 56 F8
Ningjing Shan, *China* 58 C2
Ninglang, *China* 58 D3
Ningling, *China* 56 G8
Ningming, *China* 58 F6
Ningnan, *China* 58 D4
Ningpo = Ningbo, *China* 59 C13
Ningqiang, *China* 56 H4
Ningshan, *China* 56 H5
Ningsia Hui A.R. = Ningxia
 Huizu Zizhiqu □, *China* ... 56 F4
Ningwu, *China* 56 E7
Ningxia Huizu Zizhiqu □, *China* 56 F4
Ningxiang, *China* 59 C9
Ningyang, *China* 56 G9

Ningyuan, *China* 59 E8
Ninh Binh, *Vietnam* 58 G5
Ninh Giang, *Vietnam* 64 B6
Ninh Hoa, *Vietnam* 64 F7
Ninh Ma, *Vietnam* 64 F7
Ninove, *Belgium* 17 D4
Nioaque, *Brazil* 127 A4
Niobrara, *U.S.A.* 112 D6
Niobrara →, *U.S.A.* 112 D6
Niono, *Mali* 82 C3
Nionsamoridougou, *Guinea* 82 D3
Nioro du Rip, *Senegal* 82 C1
Nioro du Sahel, *Mali* 82 B3
Niort, *France* 20 B3
Nipawin, *Canada* 105 C8
Nipigon, *Canada* 102 C2
Nipigon, L., *Canada* 102 C2
Nipishish L., *Canada* 103 B7
Nipissing, L., *Canada* 102 C4
Nipomo, *U.S.A.* 117 K6
Nipton, *U.S.A.* 117 K11
Niquelândia, *Brazil* 125 F9
Nīr, *Iran* 70 B5
Nirasaki, *Japan* 55 G9
Nirmal, *India* 66 K11
Nirmali, *India* 69 F12
Niš, *Serbia, Yug.* 40 C5
Nisa, *Portugal* 35 F3
Niṣāb, *Si. Arabia* 70 D5
Niṣāb, *Yemen* 74 E4
Nišava →, *Serbia, Yug.* 40 C5
Niscemi, *Italy* 31 E7
Nishinomiya, *Japan* 55 G7
Nishino'omote, *Japan* 55 J5
Nishiwaki, *Japan* 55 G7
Nísiros, *Greece* 39 E9
Niška Banja, *Serbia, Yug.* ... 40 C6
Niskibi →, *Canada* 102 A2
Nisko, *Poland* 45 H9
Nisporeni, *Moldova* 43 C13
Nisqually →, *U.S.A.* 116 C4
Nissáki, *Greece* 36 A3
Nissan →, *Sweden* 11 H6
Nissum Bredning, *Denmark* 11 H2
Nissum Fjord, *Denmark* 11 H2
Nistru = Dnister →, *Europe* .. 47 J6
Nisutlin →, *Canada* 104 A2
Nitchequon, *Canada* 103 B5
Niterói, *Brazil* 127 A7
Nith →, *Canada* 110 C4
Nith →, *U.K.* 14 F5
Nitra, *Slovak Rep.* 27 C11
Nitra →, *Slovak Rep.* 27 C11
Nitriansky □, *Slovak Rep.* ... 27 C11
Nittedal, *Germany* 25 F8
Niuafo'ou, *Tonga* 91 B11
Niue, *Cook Is.* 97 J11
Niulan Jiang →, *China* 58 D4
Niut, *Indonesia* 62 D4
Niutou Shan, *China* 59 C13
Niuzhuang, *China* 57 D12
Nivala, *Finland* 8 E21
Nivelles, *Belgium* 17 D4
Nivernais, *France* 19 E10
Niwas, *India* 69 H9
Nixon, *U.S.A.* 113 L6
Nizamabad, *India* 66 K11
Nizamghat, *India* 67 E19
Nizhne Kolymsk, *Russia* 51 C17
Nizhnegorskiy = Nyzhnohirskyy,
 Ukraine 47 K8
Nizhnekamsk, *Russia* 48 C10
Nizhneudinsk, *Russia* 51 D10
Nizhnevartovsk, *Russia* 50 C8
Nizhniy Chir, *Russia* 49 F6
Nizhniy Lomov, *Russia* 48 D6
Nizhniy Novgorod, *Russia* 48 B7
Nizhniy Tagil, *Russia* 50 D6
Nizhyn, *Ukraine* 47 G6
Nizina Mazowiecka, *Poland* ... 45 F8
Nizip, *Turkey* 70 B3
Nízké Tatry, *Slovak Rep.* 27 C12
Nízký Jeseník, *Czech Rep.* ... 27 B10
Nizza Monferrato, *Italy* 28 D5
Njakwa, *Malawi* 87 E3
Njanji, *Zambia* 87 E3
Njazidja = Grande Comore,
 Comoros Is. [not present]
Njinjo, *Tanzania* 87 D4
Njombe, *Tanzania* 87 D3
Njombe →, *Tanzania* 86 D4
Njurundabommen, *Sweden* 10 B11
Nkambe, *Cameroon* 83 D7
Nkana, *Zambia* 87 E2
Nkandla, *S. Africa* 89 D5
Nkawkaw, *Ghana* 83 D4
Nkayi, *Zimbabwe* 87 F2
Nkhotakota, *Malawi* 87 E3
Nkongsamba, *Cameroon* 83 E6
Nkurenkuru, *Namibia* 88 B2
Nkwanta, *Ghana* 83 D4
Nmai →, *Burma* 58 F2
Noakhali = Maijdi, *Bangla.* .. 67 H17
Nobel, *Canada* 110 A4
Nobeoka, *Japan* 55 H5
Noblejas, *Spain* 34 F7
Noblesville, *U.S.A.* 108 E3
Noce →, *Italy* 28 B8
Nocera Inferiore, *Italy* 31 B7
Nocera Umbra, *Italy* 29 E9
Noci, *Italy* 31 B10
Nocona, *U.S.A.* 113 J6
Nocrich, *Romania* 43 E9
Noda, *Japan* 55 G9
Nogales, *Mexico* 118 A2
Nogales, *U.S.A.* 115 L8

Nogaro, *France* 20 E3
Nogat →, *Poland* 44 D6
Nōgata, *Japan* 55 H5
Nogent, *France* 19 D12
Nogent-le-Rotrou, *France* 18 D7
Nogent-sur-Seine, *France* 19 D10
Noggerup, *Australia* 93 F2
Noginsk, *Moskva, Russia* 46 E10
Noginsk, *Tunguska, Russia* ... 51 C10
Nogoa →, *Australia* 94 C4
Nogoyá, *Argentina* 126 C4
Nógrád □, *Hungary* 42 C4
Noguera Pallaresa →, *Spain* .. 32 D5
Noguera Ribagorzana →, *Spain* . 32 D5
Nohar, *India* 68 E6
Nohfelden, *Germany* 25 F3
Nohta, *India* 69 H8
Noia, *Spain* 34 C2
Noire, Montagne, *France* 20 E6
Noires, Mts., *France* 18 D3
Noirétable, *France* 20 C7
Noirmoutier, Î. de, *France* .. 18 F4
Noirmoutier-en-l'Île, *France* . 18 F4
Nojane, *Botswana* 88 C3
Nojima-Zaki, *Japan* 55 G9
Nok Kundi, *Pakistan* 66 E3
Nokaneng, *Botswana* 88 B3
Nokia, *Finland* 9 F20
Nokomis, *Canada* 105 C8
Nokomis L., *Canada* 105 B8
Nol, *Sweden* 11 G6
Nola, *C.A.R.* 84 D3
Nola, *Italy* 31 B7
Nolay, *France* 19 F11
Noli, C. di, *Italy* 28 D5
Nolinsk, *Russia* 48 B9
Noma Omuramba →, *Namibia* 88 B3
Nombre de Dios, *Panama* 120 E4
Nome, *U.S.A.* 100 B3
Nomo-Zaki, *Japan* 55 H4
Nonacho L., *Canada* 105 A7
Nonancourt, *France* 18 D8
Nonda, *Australia* 94 C3
None, *Italy* 28 D4
Nong Chang, *Thailand* 64 E2
Nong Het, *Laos* 64 C4
Nong Khai, *Thailand* 64 D4
Nong'an, *China* 57 B13
Nongoma, *S. Africa* 89 D5
Nonoava, *Mexico* 118 B3
Nonoava →, *Mexico* 118 B3
Nonthaburi, *Thailand* 64 F3
Nontron, *France* 20 C4
Nonza, *France* 21 F13
Noonamah, *Australia* 92 B5
Noord Brabant □, *Neths.* 17 C5
Noord Holland □, *Neths.* 17 B4
Noordbeveland, *Neths.* 17 C3
Noordoostpolder, *Neths.* 17 B5
Noordwijk, *Neths.* 17 B4
Nootka I., *Canada* 104 D3
Nopiming Prov. Park, *Canada* . 105 C9
Nora, *Eritrea* 81 D5
Nora, *Sweden* 10 E9
Noralee, *Canada* 104 C3
Noranda = Rouyn-Noranda,
 Canada 102 C4
Norberg, *Sweden* 10 D9
Nórcia, *Italy* 29 F10
Norco, *U.S.A.* 117 M9
Nord □, *France* 19 B10
Nord-Kivu □, *Dem. Rep. of
 the Congo* 86 C2
Nord-Ostsee-Kanal, *Germany* .. 24 A5
Nord-Pas-de-Calais □, *France* . 19 B9
Nordaustlandet, *Svalbard* 4 B9
Nordborg, *Denmark* 11 J3
Nordby, *Denmark* 11 J2
Norddeich, *Germany* 24 B3
Nordegg, *Canada* 104 C5
Norden, *Germany* 24 B3
Nordenham, *Germany* 24 B4
Norderney, *Germany* 24 B3
Norderstedt, *Germany* 24 B6
Nordfjord, *Norway* 9 F11
Nordfriesische Inseln, *Germany* 24 A4
Nordhausen, *Germany* 24 D6
Nordhorn, *Germany* 24 C3
Nordøyar, *Færoe Is.* 8 E9
Nordingrå, *Sweden* 10 B12
Nordjyllands Amtskommune □,
 Denmark 11 G4
Nordkapp, *Norway* 8 A21
Nordkapp, *Svalbard* 4 A9
Nordkinn = Kinnarodden,
 Norway 6 A11
Nordkinn-halvøya, *Norway* 8 A22
Nordland □, *Norway* [not present]
Nördlingen, *Germany* 25 G6
Nordrhein-Westfalen □,
 Germany 24 D3
Nordstrand, *Germany* 24 A4
Nordvik, *Russia* 51 B12
Nore →, *Ireland* 15 D4
Norfolk, *Nebr., U.S.A.* 112 D6
Norfolk, *Va., U.S.A.* 108 G7
Norfolk □, *U.K.* 13 E8
Norfolk I., *Pac. Oc.* 96 K8
Norfork L., *U.S.A.* 113 G8
Norilsk, *Russia* 51 C9
Norma, Mt., *Australia* 94 C3
Normal, *U.S.A.* 112 E10
Norman, *U.S.A.* 113 H6
Norman →, *Australia* 94 B3
Norman Wells, *Canada* 100 B7
Normanby →, *Australia* 94 A3
Normandin, *Canada* 102 C5

Normanhurst, Mt., *Australia* ... 93 E3
Normanton, *Australia* 94 B3
Normétal, *Canada* 102 C4
Norquay, *Canada* 105 C8
Norquinco, *Argentina* 128 E2
Norra Dellen, *Sweden* 10 C10
Norra Ulvön, *Sweden* 10 A12
Norrahammar, *Sweden* 11 G8
Norrbotten □, *Sweden* 8 C19
Nørre Åby, *Denmark* 11 J3
Nørre Alslev, *Denmark* 11 K5
Nørresundby, *Denmark* 11 G3
Norrhult, *Sweden* 11 G9
Norris Point, *Canada* 103 C8
Norristown, *U.S.A.* 111 F9
Norrköping, *Sweden* 11 F10
Norrland, *Sweden* 9 E16
Norrsundet, *Sweden* 10 D11
Norrtälje, *Sweden* 10 E12
Norseman, *Australia* 93 F3
Norsk, *Russia* 51 D14
Norte, Pta. del, *Canary Is.* . 37 G2
Norte, Serra do, *Brazil* 124 F7
North, C., *Canada* 103 C7
North Adams, *U.S.A.* 111 D11
North Arm, *Canada* 104 A5
North Augusta, *U.S.A.* 109 J5
North Ayrshire □, *U.K.* 14 F4
North Bass I., *U.S.A.* 110 E2
North Battleford, *Canada* 105 C7
North Bay, *Canada* 102 C4
North Belcher Is., *Canada* ... 102 A4
North Bend, *Oreg., U.S.A.* ... 114 E1
North Bend, *Pa., U.S.A.* 110 E7
North Bend, *Wash., U.S.A.* ... 116 C5
North Bennington, *U.S.A.* 111 D11
North Berwick, *U.K.* 14 E6
North Berwick, *U.S.A.* 111 C14
North C., *Canada* 103 C7
North C., *N.Z.* 91 F4
North Canadian →, *U.S.A.* 113 H7
North Canton, *U.S.A.* 110 F3
North Cape = Nordkapp,
 Norway 8 A21
North Cape = Nordkapp,
 Svalbard 4 A9
North Caribou L., *Canada* 102 B1
North Carolina □, *U.S.A.* 109 H6
North Cascades National Park,
 U.S.A. 114 B3
North Channel, *Canada* 102 C3
North Channel, *U.K.* 14 F3
North Charleston, *U.S.A.* 109 J6
North Chicago, *U.S.A.* 108 D2
North Creek, *U.S.A.* 111 C11
North Dakota □, *U.S.A.* 112 B5
North Downs, *U.K.* 13 F8
North East, *U.S.A.* 110 D5
North East Frontier Agency =
 Arunachal Pradesh □, *India* . 67 F19
North East Lincolnshire □, *U.K.* 12 D7
North Eastern □, *Kenya* 86 B5
North Esk →, *U.K.* 14 E6
North European Plain, *Europe* . 6 E10
North Foreland, *U.K.* 13 F9
North Fork, *U.S.A.* 116 H7
North Fork American →, *U.S.A.* 116 G5
North Fork Feather →, *U.S.A.* . 116 F5
North Fork Grand →, *U.S.A.* .. 112 C3
North Fork Red →, *U.S.A.* 113 H5
North Frisian Is. =
 Nordfriesische Inseln,
 Germany 24 A4
North Gower, *Canada* 111 A9
North Hd., *Australia* 93 F1
North Henik L., *Canada* 105 A9
North Highlands, *U.S.A.* 116 G5
North Horr, *Kenya* 86 B4
North I., *Kenya* 86 B4
North I., *N.Z.* 91 H5
North Kingsville, *U.S.A.* 110 E4
North Knife →, *Canada* 105 B10
North Koel →, *India* 69 G10
North Korea ■, *Asia* 57 E14
North Lakhimpur, *India* 67 F19
North Lanarkshire □, *U.K.* ... 14 F5
North Las Vegas, *U.S.A.* 117 J11
North Lincolnshire □, *U.K.* .. 12 D7
North Little Rock, *U.S.A.* ... 113 H8
North Loup →, *U.S.A.* 112 E5
North Magnetic Pole, *Canada* . 4 B2
North Minch, *U.K.* 14 C3
North Moose L., *Canada* 105 C8
North Myrtle Beach, *U.S.A.* .. 109 J6
North Nahanni →, *Canada* 104 A4
North Olmsted, *U.S.A.* 110 E3
North Ossetia □, *Russia* 49 J7
North Pagai, I. = Pagai Utara,
 Pulau, *Indonesia* 62 E2
North Palisade, *U.S.A.* 116 H8
North Platte, *U.S.A.* 112 E4
North Platte →, *U.S.A.* 112 E4
North Pole, *Arctic* .... 4 A
North Portal, *Canada* 105 D8
North Powder, *U.S.A.* 114 D5
North Pt., *U.S.A.* 110 A1
North Rhine Westphalia =
 Nordrhein-Westfalen □,
 Germany 24 D3
North River, *Canada* 103 B8
North Ronaldsay, *U.K.* 14 B6
North Saskatchewan →, *Canada* 105 C7
North Sea, *Europe* 6 D6
North Seal →, *Canada* 105 B9
North Somerset □, *U.K.* 13 F5

North Sporades = Vóriai
  Sporádhes, *Greece* 38 B5
North Sydney, *Canada* 103 C7
North Syracuse, *U.S.A.* 111 C8
North Taranaki Bight, *N.Z.* ... 91 H5
North Thompson ➤, *Canada* ... 104 C4
North Tonawanda, *U.S.A.* 110 C6
North Troy, *U.S.A.* 111 B12
North Truchas Pk., *U.S.A.* ... 115 J11
North Twin I., *Canada* 102 B4
North Tyne ➤, *U.K.* 12 B5
North Uist, *U.K.* 14 D1
North Vancouver, *Canada* ... 104 D4
North Vernon, *U.S.A.* 108 F3
North Wabasca L., *Canada* ... 104 B6
North Walsham, *U.K.* 12 E9
North-West □, *S. Africa* 88 D4
North West C., *Australia* 92 D1
North West Christmas I. Ridge,
  Pac. Oc. 97 G11
North West Frontier □, *Pakistan* 68 C4
North West Highlands, *U.K.* ... 14 D4
North West River, *Canada* ... 103 B7
North Western □, *Zambia* ... 87 E2
North Wildwood, *U.S.A.* 108 F8
North York Moors, *U.K.* 12 C7
North Yorkshire □, *U.K.* 12 C6
Northallerton, *U.K.* 12 C6
Northam, *Australia* 93 F2
Northam, *S. Africa* 88 C4
Northampton, *Australia* 93 E1
Northampton, *U.K.* 13 E7
Northampton, *Mass., U.S.A.* ... 111 D12
Northampton, *Pa., U.S.A.* ... 111 F9
Northamptonshire □, *U.K.* ... 13 E7
Northbridge, *U.S.A.* 111 D13
Northcliffe, *Australia* 93 F2
Northeast Providence Chan.,
  W. Indies 120 A4
Northeim, *Germany* 24 D6
Northern □, *Ghana* 83 D4
Northern □, *Malawi* 87 E3
Northern □, *Zambia* 87 E3
Northern Areas □, *Pakistan* ... 69 A5
Northern Cape □, *S. Africa* ... 88 D3
Northern Circars, *India* 67 L13
Northern Indian L., *Canada* ... 105 B9
Northern Ireland □, *U.K.* ... 15 B5
Northern Light L., *Canada* ... 102 C1
Northern Marianas ■, *Pac. Oc.* 96 F6
Northern Province □, *S. Leone* 82 D2
Northern Province □, *S. Africa* 89 C4
Northern Territory □, *Australia* 92 D5
Northfield, *Minn., U.S.A.* ... 112 C8
Northfield, *Vt., U.S.A.* 111 B12
Northland □, *N.Z.* 91 F4
Northome, *U.S.A.* 112 B7
Northport, *Ala., U.S.A.* 109 J2
Northport, *Wash., U.S.A.* ... 114 B5
Northumberland □, *U.K.* 12 B6
Northumberland Is., *Australia* . 94 C4
Northumberland Str., *Canada* . 103 C7
Northville, *U.S.A.* 111 C10
Northwest Providence Channel,
  W. Indies 120 A4
Northwest Territories □, *Canada* 100 B9
Northwood, *Iowa, U.S.A.* ... 112 D8
Northwood, *N. Dak., U.S.A.* ... 112 B6
Norton, *U.S.A.* 112 F5
Norton, *Zimbabwe* 87 F3
Norton Sd., *U.S.A.* 100 B3
Nortorf, *Germany* 24 A5
Norwalk, *Calif., U.S.A.* 117 M8
Norwalk, *Conn., U.S.A.* 111 E11
Norwalk, *Iowa, U.S.A.* 112 E8
Norwalk, *Ohio, U.S.A.* 110 E2
Norway, *Maine, U.S.A.* 109 C10
Norway, *Mich., U.S.A.* 108 C2
Norway ■, *Europe* 8 E14
Norway House, *Canada* 105 C9
Norwegian Sea, *Atl. Oc.* ... 4 C8
Norwich, *Canada* 110 D4
Norwich, *U.K.* 13 E9
Norwich, *Conn., U.S.A.* ... 111 E12
Norwich, *N.Y., U.S.A.* 111 D9
Norwood, *Canada* 110 B7
Norwood, *U.S.A.* 111 B10
Noshiro, *Japan* 54 D10
Nosivka, *Ukraine* 47 G6
Nosovka = Nosivka, *Ukraine* ... 47 G6
Noṣratābād, *Iran* 71 D8
Noss Hd., *U.K.* 14 C5
Nossebro, *Sweden* 11 F6
Nossob ➤, *S. Africa* 88 D3
Nossombougou, *Mali* 82 C3
Nosy Barren, *Madag.* 85 H8
Nosy Be, *Madag.* 85 G9
Nosy Boraha, *Madag.* 89 B8
Nosy Lava, *Madag.* 89 A8
Nosy Varika, *Madag.* 89 C8
Noté ➤, *Poland* 45 F2
Notikewin ➤, *Canada* 104 B5
Notio Aigaio = Notios
  Aiyaíon □ 39 E7
Notios Aiyaíon □ 39 E7
Notios Evvoïkos Kólpos, *Greece* 38 C5
Noto, *Italy* 31 F8
Noto, G. di, *Italy* 31 F8
Notodden, *Norway* 9 G13
Notre Dame B., *Canada* ... 103 C8
Notre Dame de Koartac =
  Quaqtaq, *Canada* 101 B13
Notre-Dame-des-Bois, *Canada* 111 A13
Notre Dame d'Ivugivic =
  Ivujivik, *Canada* 101 B12
Notre-Dame-du-Nord, *Canada* 102 C4

Notsé, *Togo* 83 D5
Nottawasaga B., *Canada* ... 110 B4
Nottaway ➤, *Canada* 102 B4
Nottingham, *U.K.* 12 E6
Nottingham, City of □, *U.K.* ... 12 E6
Nottingham I., *Canada* 101 B12
Nottinghamshire □, *U.K.* ... 12 D6
Nottoway ➤, *U.S.A.* 108 G7
Notwane ➤, *Botswana* ... 88 C4
Nouâdhibou, *Mauritania* ... 78 D2
Nouâdhibou, Ras, *Mauritania* 78 D2
Nouakchott, *Mauritania* ... 82 B1
Nouâmghâr, *Mauritania* ... 82 B1
Nouméa, *N. Cal.* 96 K8
Nouna, *Burkina Faso* 82 C4
Noupoort, *S. Africa* 88 E3
Nouveau Comptoir = Wemindji,
  Canada 102 B4
Nouvelle-Amsterdam, I.,
  Ind. Oc. 3 F13
Nouvelle-Calédonie = New
  Caledonia ■, *Pac. Oc.* ... 96 K8
Nouzonville, *France* 19 C11
Nová Baňa, *Slovak Rep.* ... 27 C11
Nová Bystřice, *Czech Rep.* ... 26 B8
Nova Casa Nova, *Brazil* ... 125 E10
Nova Esperança, *Brazil* ... 127 A5
Nova Friburgo, *Brazil* 127 A7
Nova Gaia = Cambundi-
  Catembo, *Angola* 84 G3
Nova Gorica, *Slovenia* 29 C10
Nova Gradiška, *Croatia* ... 42 E2
Nova Iguaçu, *Brazil* 127 A7
Nova Iorque, *Brazil* 125 E10
Nova Kakhovka, *Ukraine* ... 47 J7
Nova Lamego, *Guinea-Biss.* ... 82 C2
Nova Lima, *Brazil* 127 A7
Nova Lisboa = Huambo, *Angola* 85 G3
Nova Lusitânia, *Mozam.* ... 87 F3
Nova Mambone, *Mozam.* ... 89 C6
Nova Odesa, *Ukraine* 47 J6
Nová Paka, *Czech Rep.* ... 26 A8
Nova Pavova, *Serbia, Yug.* ... 42 F5
Nova Scotia □, *Canada* ... 103 C7
Nova Siri, *Italy* 31 B9
Nova Sofala, *Mozam.* 89 C5
Nova Varoš, *Serbia, Yug.* ... 40 C3
Nova Venécia, *Brazil* 125 G10
Nova Zagora, *Bulgaria* ... 41 D10
Novaci, *Macedonia* 40 E5
Novaci, *Romania* 43 E8
Novaféltria, *Italy* 29 E9
Novaleksandrovskaya =
  Novoaleksandrovsk, *Russia* . 49 H5
Novannenskiy = Novoannenskiy,
  Russia 48 E6
Novar, *Canada* 110 A5
Novara, *Italy* 28 C5
Novato, *U.S.A.* 116 G4
Novaya Kakhovka = Nova
  Kakhovka, *Ukraine* 47 J7
Novaya Kazanka, *Kazakstan* ... 49 F9
Novaya Ladoga, *Russia* ... 46 B7
Novaya Lyalya, *Russia* ... 50 D7
Novaya Sibir, Ostrov, *Russia* . 51 B16
Novaya Zemlya, *Russia* ... 50 B6
Nové Město, *Slovak Rep.* ... 27 C10
Nové Město na Moravě,
  Czech Rep. 26 B9
Nové Město nad Metují,
  Czech Rep. 27 A9
Nové Zámky, *Slovak Rep.* ... 27 C11
Novelda, *Spain* 33 G4
Novellara, *Italy* 28 D7
Noventa Vicentina, *Italy* ... 29 C8
Novgorod, *Russia* 46 C6
Novgorod-Severskiy =
  Novhorod-Siverskyy, *Ukraine* 47 G7
Novhorod-Siverskyy, *Ukraine* ... 47 G7
Novi Bečej, *Serbia, Yug.* ... 42 E5
Novi Iskar, *Bulgaria* 40 D7
Novi Kneževac, *Serbia, Yug.* . 42 D5
Novi Lígure, *Italy* 28 D5
Novi Pazar, *Bulgaria* 41 C11
Novi Pazar, *Serbia, Yug.* ... 40 C4
Novi Sad, *Serbia, Yug.* ... 42 E4
Novi Slankamen, *Serbia, Yug.* 42 E5
Novi Travnik, *Bos.-H.* ... 42 F2
Novi Vinodolski, *Croatia* ... 29 C11
Novigrad, *Istra, Croatia* ... 29 C11
Novigrad, *Zadar, Croatia* ... 29 D12
Novigradsko More, *Croatia* ... 29 D12
Nôvo Hamburgo, *Brazil* ... 127 B5
Novo Mesto, *Slovenia* ... 29 C12
Novo Miloševo, *Serbia, Yug.* . 42 E5
Novo Remanso, *Brazil* ... 125 E10
Novoaleksandrovsk, *Russia* . 49 H5
Novoannenskiy, *Russia* ... 48 E6
Novoataysk, *Russia* 50 D9
Novoazovsk, *Ukraine* 47 J10
Novocheboksarsk, *Russia* ... 48 B8
Novocherkassk, *Russia* ... 49 G5
Novodevichye, *Russia* ... 48 D9
Novogrudok = Navahrudak,
  Belarus 46 F3
Novohrad-Volynskyy, *Ukraine* . 47 G4
Novokachalinsk, *Russia* ... 54 B6
Novokazalinsk = Zhangaqazaly,
  Kazakstan 50 E7
Novokhopersk, *Russia* ... 48 E5
Novokuybyshevsk, *Russia* ... 48 D9
Novokuznetsk, *Russia* ... 50 D9
Novomirgorod, *Ukraine* ... 47 H6
Novomoskovsk, *Russia* ... 46 E10
Novomoskovsk, *Ukraine* ... 47 H8

Novopolotsk = Navapolatsk,
  Belarus 46 E5
Novorossiysk, *Russia* 47 K9
Novorybnoye, *Russia* 51 B11
Novorzhev, *Russia* 46 D5
Novosej, *Albania* 40 E4
Novoselytsya, *Ukraine* ... 47 H4
Novoshakhtinsk, *Russia* ... 47 J10
Novosibirsk, *Russia* 50 D9
Novosibirskiye Ostrova, *Russia* 51 B15
Novosil, *Russia* 47 F9
Novosokolniki, *Russia* ... 46 D6
Novotitarovskaya, *Russia* ... 49 H4
Novotroitsk, *Russia* 50 D6
Novoukrayinka, *Ukraine* ... 47 H6
Novouljanovsk, *Russia* ... 48 C9
Novouzensk, *Russia* 48 E9
Novovolynsk, *Ukraine* ... 47 G3
Novovoronezhskiy, *Russia* ... 47 G10
Novozybkov, *Russia* 47 F6
Novska, *Croatia* 29 C14
Novvy Urengoy, *Russia* ... 50 C8
Nový Bor, *Czech Rep.* ... 26 A7
Novy Bug = Novyy Buh, *Ukraine* 47 J7
Nový Bydžov, *Czech Rep.* ... 26 A8
Nový Jičín, *Czech Rep.* ... 27 B11
Novyy Afon, *Georgia* ... 49 J5
Novyy Buh, *Ukraine* 47 J7
Novyy Oskol, *Russia* 47 G9
Novyy Port, *Russia* 50 C8
Now Shahr, *Iran* 71 B6
Nowa Deba, *Poland* 45 H8
Nowa Ruda, *Poland* 45 H3
Nowa Sarzyna, *Poland* ... 45 H9
Nowa Sól, *Poland* 45 G2
Nowata, *U.S.A.* 113 G7
Nowbarān, *Iran* 71 C6
Nowe, *Poland* 44 E5
Nowe Miasteczko, *Poland* ... 45 G2
Nowe Miasto, *Poland* 45 G7
Nowe Miasto Lubawskie,
  Poland 44 E6
Nowe Skalmierzyce, *Poland* ... 45 G4
Nowe Warpno, *Poland* ... 44 E1
Nowghāb, *Iran* 71 C8
Nowgong, *Assam, India* ... 67 F18
Nowgong, *Mad. P., India* ... 69 G8
Nowogard, *Poland* 44 E2
Nowogród, *Poland* 45 E8
Nowogród Bobrzanski, *Poland* . 45 G2
Nowogrodziec, *Poland* ... 45 G2
Nowshera, *Pakistan* 66 C8
Nowy Dwór Gdański, *Poland* . 44 D6
Nowy Sącz, *Poland* 45 J7
Nowy Staw, *Poland* 44 D6
Nowy Targ, *Poland* 45 J7
Nowy Tomyśl, *Poland* ... 45 F3
Nowy Wiśnicz, *Poland* ... 45 J7
Noxen, *U.S.A.* 111 E8
Noxon, *U.S.A.* 114 C6
Noyabr'sk, *Russia* 50 C8
Noyant, *France* 18 E7
Noyers, *France* 19 E10
Noyon, *France* 19 C9
Noyon, *Mongolia* 56 C2
Nozay, *France* 18 E5
Nqutu, *S. Africa* 89 D5
Nsanje, *Malawi* 87 F4
Nsawam, *Ghana* 83 D4
Nsomba, *Zambia* 87 E3
Nsukka, *Nigeria* 83 D6
Ntui, *Cameroon* 83 E7
Nu Jiang ➤, *China* 58 E2
Nu Shan, *China* 58 E2
Nuba Mts. = Nubah, Jibalan,
  Sudan 81 E3
Nubah, Jibalan, *Sudan* ... 81 E3
Nubia, *Africa* 76 D7
Nubian Desert = Nûbîya, Es
  Sahrâ en, *Sudan* 80 C3
Nûbîya, Es Sahrâ en, *Sudan* ... 80 C3
Nubledo, *Spain* 34 B5
Nuboai, *Indonesia* 63 E9
Nubra ➤, *India* 69 B7
Nucet, *Romania* 42 D7
Nueces ➤, *U.S.A.* 113 M6
Nueltin L., *Canada* 105 A9
Nueva Asunción □, *Paraguay* . 126 A3
Nueva Carteya, *Spain* ... 35 H6
Nueva Gerona, *Cuba* 120 B3
Nueva Palmira, *Uruguay* ... 126 C4
Nueva Rosita, *Mexico* ... 118 B4
Nueva San Salvador, *El Salv.* . 120 D2
Nueva Tabarca, *Spain* ... 33 G4
Nuéve de Julio, *Argentina* ... 126 D3
Nuevitas, *Cuba* 120 B4
Nuevo, G., *Argentina* ... 128 E4
Nuevo Casas Grandes, *Mexico* . 118 A3
Nuevo Guerrero, *Mexico* ... 119 B5
Nuevo Laredo, *Mexico* ... 119 B5
Nuevo León □, *Mexico* ... 118 C5
Nuevo Rocafuerte, *Ecuador* . 124 D3
Nugget Pt., *N.Z.* 91 M2
Nugrus, Gebel, *Egypt* ... 80 C3
Nuhaka, *N.Z.* 91 H6
Nuits-St-Georges, *France* ... 19 E11
Nukey Bluff, *Australia* ... 95 E2
Nukheila, *Sudan* 80 D2
Nukhuyb, *Iraq* 70 C4
Nuku'alofa, *Tonga* 91 E12
Nukus, *Uzbekistan* 50 E6
Nules, *Spain* 32 F4
Nullagine, *Australia* ... 92 D3
Nullagine ➤, *Australia* ... 92 D3
Nullarbor, *Australia* ... 93 F5

Nullarbor Plain, *Australia* ... 93 F4
Numalla, L., *Australia* ... 95 D3
Numan, *Nigeria* 83 D7
Numata, *Japan* 55 F9
Numatinna ➤, *Sudan* ... 81 F2
Numazu, *Japan* 55 G9
Numbulwar, *Australia* ... 94 A2
Numfoor, *Indonesia* 63 E8
Nunaksaluk I., *Canada* ... 103 A7
Nunap Isua, *Greenland* ... 101 C15
Nunavut □, *Canada* 101 B11
Nunda, *U.S.A.* 110 D7
Nungarin, *Australia* 93 F2
Nungo, *Mozam.* 87 E4
Nungwe, *Tanzania* 86 C3
Nunivak I., *U.S.A.* 100 B3
Nunkun, *India* 69 C7
Núoro, *Italy* 30 B2
Nūrābād, *Iran* 71 E8
Nure ➤, *Italy* 28 C6
Nuremberg = Nürnberg,
  Germany 25 F7
Nuri, *Mexico* 118 B3
Nurlat, *Russia* 48 C10
Nurmes, *Finland* 8 E23
Nürnberg, *Germany* 25 F7
Nurpur, *Pakistan* 68 D4
Nurra, La, *Italy* 30 B1
Nurran, L. = Terewah, L.,
  Australia 95 D4
Nurrari Lakes, *Australia* ... 93 E5
Nurri, *Italy* 30 C2
Nürtingen, *Germany* 25 G5
Nurzec ➤, *Poland* 45 F9
Nus, *Italy* 28 C4
Nusa Barung, *Indonesia* ... 63 H15
Nusa Kambangan, *Indonesia* . 63 G13
Nusa Tenggara Barat □,
  Indonesia 62 F5
Nusa Tenggara Timur □,
  Indonesia 63 F6
Nusaybin, *Turkey* 73 D9
Nushki, *Pakistan* 68 E2
Nuuk, *Greenland* 101 B14
Nuwakot, *Nepal* 69 E10
Nuweiba', *Egypt* 70 D2
Nuwerus, *S. Africa* 88 E2
Nuweveldberge, *S. Africa* ... 88 E3
Nuyts, C., *Australia* ... 93 F5
Nuyts, Pt., *Australia* ... 93 G2
Nuyts Arch., *Australia* ... 95 E1
Nxau-Nxau, *Botswana* ... 88 B3
Nyaake, *Liberia* 82 E3
Nyabing, *Australia* 93 F2
Nyack, *U.S.A.* 111 E11
Nyagan, *Russia* 50 C7
Nyahanga, *Tanzania* ... 86 C3
Nyahua, *Tanzania* 86 D3
Nyahururu, *Kenya* 86 B4
Nyainqentanglha Shan, *China* . 60 C4
Nyakanazi, *Tanzania* ... 86 C3
Nyakrom, *Ghana* 83 D4
Nyâlâ, *Sudan* 81 E1
Nyamandhlovu, *Zimbabwe* ... 87 F2
Nyambiti, *Tanzania* 86 C3
Nyamlell, *Sudan* 81 F2
Nyamwaga, *Tanzania* ... 86 C3
Nyandekwa, *Tanzania* ... 86 C3
Nyanding ➤, *Sudan* ... 81 F3
Nyandoma, *Russia* 46 B11
Nyangana, *Namibia* 88 B3
Nyanguge, *Tanzania* ... 86 C3
Nyankpala, *Ghana* 83 D4
Nyanza, *Rwanda* 86 C2
Nyanza □, *Kenya* 86 C3
Nyanza-Lac, *Burundi* ... 86 C2
Nyaponges, *Sudan* 81 F3
Nyasa, L., *Africa* 87 E3
Nyasvizh, *Belarus* 47 F4
Nyazura, *Zimbabwe* 87 F3
Nyazwidzi ➤, *Zimbabwe* . 87 F3
Nyborg, *Denmark* 11 J4
Nybro, *Sweden* 11 H9
Nyda, *Russia* 50 C8
Nyeri, *Kenya* 86 C4
Nyerol, *Sudan* 81 F3
Nyhammar, *Sweden* 10 D8
Nyinahin, *Ghana* 82 D4
Nyíracsád, *Hungary* 42 C6
Nyírbátor, *Hungary* 42 C7
Nyíregyháza, *Hungary* ... 42 C6
Nykøbing, Storstrøm, *Denmark* 11 K5
Nykøbing, Vestsjælland,
  Denmark 11 J5
Nykøbing, Viborg, *Denmark* ... 11 H2
Nyköping, *Sweden* 11 F11
Nykroppa, *Sweden* 10 E8
Nyland, *Sweden* 10 A11
Nylstroom, *S. Africa* ... 89 C4
Nymburk, *Czech Rep.* ... 26 A8
Nynäshamn, *Sweden* ... 11 F11
Nyoma Rap, *India* 69 C8
Nyoman = Neman ➤, *Lithuania* 9 J19
Nyon, *Switz.* 25 J2
Nyong ➤, *Cameroon* ... 83 E6
Nyons, *France* 21 D9
Nyou, *Burkina Faso* 83 C4
Nýrsko, *Czech Rep.* 26 B6
Nysa, *Poland* 45 H4
Nysa ➤, *Europe* 24 C10
Nysa Kłodzka ➤, *Poland* ... 45 H4
Nysäter, *Sweden* 10 E6
Nyssa, *U.S.A.* 114 E5
Nysted, *Denmark* 11 K5
Nyunzu, *Dem. Rep. of the Congo* 86 D2

Nyurba, *Russia* 51 C12
Nyzhnohirskyy, *Ukraine* ... 47 K8
Nzébéla, *Guinea* 82 D3
Nzega, *Tanzania* 86 C3
Nzérékoré, *Guinea* 82 D3
Nzeto, *Angola* 84 F2
Nzilo, Chutes de, *Dem. Rep. of
  the Congo* 87 E2
Nzo ➤, *Ivory C.* 82 D3
Nzubuka, *Tanzania* 86 C3

O

O Barco, *Spain* 34 C4
O Carballiño, *Spain* 34 C2
O Corgo, *Spain* 34 C3
O Pino, *Spain* 34 C2
O Porriño, *Spain* 34 C2
Ô-Shima, *Japan* 55 G9
Oa, Mull of, *U.K.* 14 F2
Oacoma, *U.S.A.* 112 D5
Oahe, L., *U.S.A.* 112 C4
Oahe Dam, *U.S.A.* 112 C4
Oahu, *U.S.A.* 106 H16
Oak Harbor, *U.S.A.* 116 B4
Oak Hill, *U.S.A.* 108 G5
Oak Ridge, *U.S.A.* 109 G3
Oak View, *U.S.A.* 117 L7
Oakan-Dake, *Japan* 54 C12
Oakdale, *Calif., U.S.A.* ... 116 H6
Oakdale, *La., U.S.A.* ... 113 K8
Oakes, *U.S.A.* 112 B5
Oakesdale, *U.S.A.* 114 C5
Oakey, *Australia* 95 D5
Oakfield, *U.S.A.* 110 C6
Oakham, *U.K.* 13 E7
Oakhurst, *U.S.A.* 116 H7
Oakland, *U.S.A.* 116 H4
Oakley, *Idaho, U.S.A.* ... 114 E7
Oakley, *Kans., U.S.A.* ... 112 F4
Oakover ➤, *Australia* ... 92 D3
Oakridge, *U.S.A.* 114 E2
Oakville, *Canada* 110 C5
Oakville, *U.S.A.* 116 D4
Oamaru, *N.Z.* 91 L3
Oancea, *Romania* 43 E12
Oasis, *Calif., U.S.A.* ... 117 M10
Oasis, *Nev., U.S.A.* ... 116 H9
Oates Land, *Antarctica* ... 5 C11
Oatlands, *Australia* 94 G4
Oatman, *U.S.A.* 117 K12
Oaxaca, *Mexico* 119 D5
Oaxaca □, *Mexico* 119 D5
Ob ➤, *Russia* 50 C7
Oba, *Canada* 102 C3
Obala, *Cameroon* 83 E7
Obama, *Japan* 55 G7
Oban, *Nigeria* 83 D6
Oban, *U.K.* 14 E3
Obbia, *Somali Rep.* ... 74 F4
Obera, *Argentina* 127 B4
Oberammergau, *Germany* ... 25 H7
Oberasbach, *Germany* ... 25 F6
Oberbayern □, *Germany* ... 25 G7
Oberdrauburg, *Austria* ... 26 E5
Oberfranken □, *Germany* ... 25 F7
Oberhausen, *Germany* ... 24 D2
Oberkirch, *Germany* ... 25 G4
Oberlausitz, *Germany* ... 24 D10
Oberlin, *Kans., U.S.A.* ... 112 F4
Oberlin, *La., U.S.A.* ... 113 K8
Oberlin, *Ohio, U.S.A.* ... 110 E2
Obernai, *France* 19 D14
Oberndorf, *Germany* ... 25 G4
Oberösterreich □, *Austria* ... 26 C7
Oberpfalz □, *Germany* ... 25 F8
Oberpfälzer Wald, *Germany* ... 25 F8
Oberstdorf, *Germany* ... 25 H6
Oberursel, *Germany* ... 25 E4
Oberwart, *Austria* 27 D9
Obi, Kepulauan, *Indonesia* ... 63 E7
Obi = Obi, Kepulauan,
  Indonesia 63 E7
Obiaruku, *Nigeria* 83 D6
Óbidos, *Brazil* 125 D7
Óbidos, *Portugal* 35 F1
Obihiro, *Japan* 54 C11
Obilatu, *Indonesia* 63 E7
Obilnoye, *Russia* 49 G7
Obing, *Germany* 25 G8
Objat, *France* 20 C5
Obluchye, *Russia* 51 E14
Obninsk, *Russia* 46 E9
Obo, *C.A.R.* 86 A2
Oboa, Mt., *Uganda* ... 86 B3
Obock, *Djibouti* 81 E5
Oborniki, *Poland* 45 F3
Oborniki Śląskie, *Poland* ... 45 G3
Oboyan, *Russia* 47 G9
Obozerskaya = Obozerskiy,
  Russia 50 C5
Obozerskiy, *Russia* ... 50 C5
Obrenovac, *Serbia, Yug.* ... 40 B4
Obrovac, *Croatia* 29 D12
Obruk, *Turkey* 72 C5
Obrzycko, *Poland* 45 F3
Observatory Inlet, *Canada* ... 104 B3
Obshchi Syrt, *Russia* ... 6 E16
Obskaya Guba, *Russia* ... 50 C8
Obuasi, *Ghana* 83 D4
Obubra, *Nigeria* 83 D6
Obudu, *Nigeria* 83 D6
Obwalden □, *Switz.* ... 25 J4
Obzor, *Bulgaria* 41 D11

Ocala, *U.S.A.* 109 L4
Ocampo, *Chihuahua, Mexico* . . 118 B3
Ocampo, *Tamaulipas, Mexico* . 119 C5
Ocaña, *Spain* 34 F7
Occidental, Cordillera,
  Colombia 122 C3
Ocean City, *Md., U.S.A.* 108 F8
Ocean City, *N.J., U.S.A.* 108 F8
Ocean City, *Wash., U.S.A.* . . . 116 C2
Ocean Falls, *Canada* 104 C3
Ocean I. = Banaba, *Kiribati* . . . 96 H8
Ocean Park, *U.S.A.* 116 D2
Oceano, *U.S.A.* 117 K6
Oceanport, *U.S.A.* 111 F10
Oceanside, *U.S.A.* 117 M9
Ochagavía, *Spain* 32 C3
Ochakiv, *Ukraine* 47 J6
Ochamchira, *Georgia* 49 J5
Ochil Hills, *U.K.* 14 E5
Ochsenfurt, *Germany* 25 F6
Ochsenhausen, *Germany* 25 G5
Ocilla, *U.S.A.* 109 K4
Ockelbo, *Sweden* 10 D10
Ocmulgee ➤, *U.S.A.* 109 K4
Ocna Mureş, *Romania* 43 D8
Ocna Sibiului, *Romania* 43 E9
Ocnele Mari, *Romania* 43 E9
Ocniţa, *Moldova* 43 B12
Oconee ➤, *U.S.A.* 109 K4
Oconto, *U.S.A.* 108 C2
Oconto Falls, *U.S.A.* 108 C1
Ocosingo, *Mexico* 119 D6
Ocotal, *Nic.* 120 D2
Ocotlán, *Mexico* 118 C4
Ocotlán de Morelos, *Mexico* . . 119 D5
Ocreza ➤, *Portugal* 35 F3
Ócsa, *Hungary* 42 C4
Octeville, *France* 18 C5
Oda, *Ghana* 83 D4
Ōda, *Japan* 55 G6
Oda, J., *Sudan* 80 C4
Óðáðahraun, *Iceland* 8 D5
Ödåkra, *Sweden* 11 H6
Odate, *Japan* 54 D10
Odawara, *Japan* 55 G9
Odda, *Norway* 9 F12
Odder, *Denmark* 11 J4
Odei ➤, *Canada* 105 B9
Odemira, *Portugal* 35 H2
Ödemiş, *Turkey* 39 C9
Odendaalsrus, *S. Africa* 88 D4
Odensbacken, *Sweden* 10 E9
Odense, *Denmark* 11 J4
Odenwald, *Germany* 25 F5
Oder ➤, *Europe* 24 B10
Oder-Havel Kanal, *Germany* . . 24 C10
Oderzo, *Italy* 29 C9
Odesa, *Ukraine* 47 J6
Ödeshög, *Sweden* 11 F8
Odessa = Odesa, *Ukraine* 47 J6
Odessa, *Canada* 111 B8
Odessa, *Tex., U.S.A.* 113 K3
Odessa, *Wash., U.S.A.* 114 C4
Odiakwe, *Botswana* 88 C4
Odiel ➤, *Spain* 35 H4
Odienné, *Ivory C.* 82 D3
Odintsovo, *Russia* 46 E9
Odiongan, *Phil.* 61 E4
Odobeşti, *Romania* 43 E12
Odolanów, *Poland* 45 G4
O'Donnell, *U.S.A.* 113 J4
Odorheiu Secuiesc, *Romania* . . 43 D10
Odoyevo, *Russia* 46 F9
Odra = Oder ➤, *Europe* 24 B10
Odra ➤, *Spain* 34 C6
Odžaci, *Serbia, Yug.* 42 E4
Odžak, *Bos.-H.* 42 E3
Odzi, *Zimbabwe* 89 B5
Odzi ➤, *Zimbabwe* 89 B5
Oebisfelde, *Germany* 24 C6
Oeiras, *Brazil* 125 E10
Oeiras, *Portugal* 35 G1
Oelrichs, *U.S.A.* 112 D3
Oelsnitz, *Germany* 25 E8
Oelwein, *U.S.A.* 112 D9
Oenpelli, *Australia* 92 B5
Oetz, *Austria* 26 D3
Of, *Turkey* 73 B9
Ofanto ➤, *Italy* 31 A9
Offa, *Nigeria* 83 D5
Offaly □, *Ireland* 15 C4
Offenbach, *Germany* 25 E4
Offenburg, *Germany* 25 G3
Offida, *Italy* 29 F10
Ofidhousa, *Greece* 39 E8
Ofotfjorden, *Norway* 8 B17
Ōfunato, *Japan* 54 E10
Oga, *Japan* 54 E9
Oga-Hantō, *Japan* 54 E9
Ogaden, *Ethiopia* 74 F3
Ōgaki, *Japan* 55 G8
Ogallala, *U.S.A.* 112 E4
Ogasawara Gunto, *Pac. Oc.* . . . 52 G18
Ogbomosho, *Nigeria* 83 D5
Ogden, *U.S.A.* 114 F7
Ogdensburg, *U.S.A.* 111 B9
Ogeechee ➤, *U.S.A.* 109 K5
Ogilby, *U.S.A.* 117 N12
Oglio ➤, *Italy* 28 C7
Ogmore, *Australia* 94 C4
Ognon ➤, *France* 19 E12
Ogoki, *Nigeria* 83 D6
Ogoki, *Canada* 102 B2
Ogoki ➤, *Canada* 102 B2
Ogoki L., *Canada* 102 B2

Ogoki Res., *Canada* 102 B2
Ogooué ➤, *Gabon* 84 E1
Ogosta ➤, *Bulgaria* 40 C7
Ogowe = Ogooué ➤, *Gabon* . . 84 E1
Ogr = Sharafa, *Sudan* 81 E2
Ogražden, *Macedonia* 40 E6
Ogre, *Latvia* 9 H21
Ogrein, *Sudan* 80 D3
Ogulin, *Croatia* 29 C12
Ogun □, *Nigeria* 83 D5
Ogurchinskiy, Ostrov,
  Turkmenistan 71 B7
Oguta, *Nigeria* 83 D6
Ogwashi-Uku, *Nigeria* 83 D6
Ogwe, *Nigeria* 83 E6
Ohai, *N.Z.* 91 L2
Ohakune, *N.Z.* 91 H5
Ohata, *Japan* 54 D10
Ohau, L., *N.Z.* 91 L2
Ohio □, *U.S.A.* 110 F2
Ohio ➤, *U.S.A.* 108 G1
Ohře ➤, *Czech Rep.* 26 A7
Ohre ➤, *Germany* 24 C7
Ohrid, *Macedonia* 40 E4
Ohridsko Jezero, *Macedonia* . . 40 E4
Ohrigstad, *S. Africa* 89 C5
Öhringen, *Germany* 25 F5
Oi Qu, *China* 58 C2
Oiapoque, *Brazil* 125
Oikou, *China* 57 E9
Oil City, *U.S.A.* 110 E5
Oil Springs, *Canada* 110 D2
Oildale, *U.S.A.* 117 K7
Oinousa, *Greece* 39 C8
Oise □, *France* 19 C9
Oise ➤, *France* 19 C9
Ōita, *Japan* 55 H5
Ōita □, *Japan* 55 H5
Oiticica, *Brazil* 125 E10
Ojacaliente, *Mexico* 118 C4
Ojai, *U.S.A.* 117 L7
Ojinaga, *Mexico* 118 B4
Ojiya, *Japan* 55 F9
Ojos del Salado, Cerro,
  Argentina 126 B2
Oka ➤, *Russia* 48 B7
Okaba, *Indonesia* 63 F9
Okahandja, *Namibia* 88 C2
Okanagan L., *Canada* 104 D5
Okanogan, *U.S.A.* 114 B4
Okanogan ➤, *U.S.A.* 114 B4
Okány, *Hungary* 42 D6
Okaputa, *Namibia* 88 C2
Okara, *Pakistan* 68 D5
Okaukuejo, *Namibia* 88 B2
Okavango Swamps, *Botswana* . . 88 B3
Okaya, *Japan* 55 F9
Okayama, *Japan* 55 G6
Okayama □, *Japan* 55 G6
Okazaki, *Japan* 55 G8
Oke-Iho, *Nigeria* 83 D5
Okeechobee, *U.S.A.* 109 M5
Okeechobee, L., *U.S.A.* 109 M5
Okefenokee Swamp, *U.S.A.* . . 109 K4
Okehampton, *U.K.* 13 G4
Okene, *Nigeria* 83 D6
Oker ➤, *Germany* 24 C6
Okha, *India* 68 H3
Okha, *Russia* 51 D15
Ókhi Óros, *Greece* 38 C6
Okhotsk, *Russia* 51 D15
Okhotsk, Sea of, *Asia* 51 D15
Okhotskiy Perevoz, *Russia* 51 C14
Okhtyrka, *Ukraine* 47 G8
Oki-Shotō, *Japan* 55 F6
Okiep, *S. Africa* 88 D2
Okigwi, *Nigeria* 83 D6
Okija, *Nigeria* 83 D6
Okinawa □, *Japan* 55 L4
Okinawa-Guntō, *Japan* 55 L4
Okinawa-Jima, *Japan* 55 L4
Okino-erabu-Shima, *Japan* . . . 55 L4
Okitipupa, *Nigeria* 83 D5
Oklahoma □, *U.S.A.* 113 H6
Oklahoma City, *U.S.A.* 113 H6
Okmulgee, *U.S.A.* 113 H7
Oknitsa = Ocniţa, *Moldova* . . . 43 B12
Oko, W. ➤, *Sudan* 80 C4
Okolo, *Uganda* 86 B3
Okolona, *U.S.A.* 113 J10
Okombahe, *Namibia* 88 C2
Okonek, *Poland* 44 E3
Okotoks, *Canada* 104 C6
Okrika, *Nigeria* 83 E6
Oksibil, *Indonesia* 63 E10
Oktabrsk = Oktyabrsk,
  Kazakstan 50 E6
Oktyabrsk, *Kazakstan* 50 E6
Oktyabrsk, *Russia* 48 D9
Oktyabrskiy = Aktsyabrski,
  Belarus 47 F5
Oktyabrskiy, *Russia* 49 G5
Oktyabrskoy Revolyutsii,
  Ostrov, *Russia* 51 B10
Oktyabrskoye = Zhovtneve,
  Ukraine 47 J7
Okulovka, *Russia* 46 C7
Okuru, *N.Z.* 91 K2
Okushiri-Tō, *Japan* 54 C9
Okuta, *Nigeria* 83 D5
Okwa ➤, *Botswana* 88 C3
Ola, *U.S.A.* 113 H8
Ólafsfjörður, *Iceland* 8 C4
Ólafsvík, *Iceland* 8 D2
Olaine, *Latvia* 44 B10
Olancha, *U.S.A.* 117 J8

Olancha Pk., *U.S.A.* 117 J8
Olanchito, *Honduras* 120 C2
Öland, *Sweden* 11 H10
Ölands norra udde, *Sweden* . . . 11 G11
Ölands södra udde, *Sweden* . . . 11 H10
Olargues, *France* 20 E6
Olascoaga, *Argentina* 126 D3
Olathe, *U.S.A.* 112 F7
Olavarría, *Argentina* 126 D3
Oława, *Poland* 45 H4
Olbernhau, *Germany* 24 E9
Ólbia, *Italy* 30 B2
Ólbia, G. di, *Italy* 30 B2
Olching, *Germany* 25 G7
Olcott, *U.S.A.* 110 C6
Old Bahama Chan. = Bahama,
  Canal Viejo de, *W. Indies* . . . 120 B4
Old Baldy Pk. = San Antonio,
  Mt., *U.S.A.* 117 L9
Old Castile = Castilla y Leon □,
  Spain 34 D6
Old Crow, *Canada* 100 B6
Old Dale, *U.S.A.* 117 L11
Old Dongola, *Sudan* 80 D3
Old Forge, *N.Y., U.S.A.* 111 C10
Old Forge, *Pa., U.S.A.* 111 E9
Old Perlican, *Canada* 103 C9
Old Shinyanga, *Tanzania* 86 C3
Old Speck Mt., *U.S.A.* 111 B14
Old Town, *U.S.A.* 109 C11
Old Washington, *U.S.A.* 110 F3
Old Wives L., *Canada* 105 C7
Oldbury, *U.K.* 13 F5
Oldcastle, *Ireland* 15 C4
Oldeani, *Tanzania* 86 C4
Oldenburg, *Niedersachsen,
  Germany* 24 B4
Oldenburg, *Schleswig-Holstein,
  Germany* 24 A6
Oldenzaal, *Neths.* 17 B6
Oldham, *U.K.* 12 D5
Oldman ➤, *Canada* 104 D6
Oldmeldrum, *U.K.* 14 D6
Olds, *Canada* 104 C6
Oldziyt, *Mongolia* 56 B5
Olean, *U.S.A.* 110 D6
Olecko, *Poland* 44 D9
Oléggio, *Italy* 28 C5
Oleiros, *Portugal* 34 F3
Oleiros, *Spain* 34 B2
Olekma ➤, *Russia* 51 C13
Olekminsk, *Russia* 51 C13
Oleksandriya, *Kirovohrad,
  Ukraine* 47 H7
Oleksandriya, *Rivne, Ukraine* . . 47 G4
Oleksandrovka, *Ukraine* 47 H7
Olema, *U.S.A.* 116 G4
Olenek, *Russia* 51 C12
Olenek ➤, *Russia* 51 B13
Olenino, *Russia* 46 D7
Oléron, Î. d', *France* 20 C2
Oleśnica, *Poland* 45 G4
Olesno, *Poland* 45 H5
Olevsk, *Ukraine* 47 G4
Olga, *Russia* 51 E14
Olga, L., *Canada* 102 C4
Olga, Mt., *Australia* 93 E5
Ølgod, *Denmark* 11 J2
Olhão, *Portugal* 35 H3
Olib, *Croatia* 29 D11
Oliena, *Italy* 30 B2
Oliete, *Spain* 32 D4
Olifants ➤, *Africa* 89 C5
Olifants ➤, *Namibia* 88 C2
Olifantshoek, *S. Africa* 88 D3
Ólimbos, *Greece* 39 F9
Ólimbos, Óros, *Greece* 40 F6
Olímpia, *Brazil* 127 A6
Olinda, *Brazil* 125 E12
Olite, *Spain* 32 C3
Oliva, *Argentina* 126 C3
Oliva, *Spain* 33 G4
Oliva, Punta del, *Spain* 34 B5
Oliva de la Frontera, *Spain* . . . 35 G4
Olivares, *Spain* 32 F2
Olivehurst, *U.S.A.* 116 F5
Oliveira de Azeméis, *Portugal* . . 34 E2
Oliveira do Douro, *Portugal* . . . 34 D2
Olivenza, *Spain* 35 G3
Oliver, *Canada* 104 D5
Oliver L., *Canada* 105 B8
Olivet, *France* 19 E8
Olkhovka, *Russia* 48 F7
Olkusz, *Poland* 45 H6
Ollagüe, *Chile* 126 A2
Olmedo, *Spain* 34 D6
Olmeto, *France* 21 G12
Olney, *Ill., U.S.A.* 108 F1
Olney, *Tex., U.S.A.* 113 J5
Olofström, *Sweden* 11 H8
Oloma, *Cameroon* 83 E7
Olomane ➤, *Canada* 103 B7
Olomouc, *Czech Rep.* 27 B10
Olonets, *Russia* 46 B7
Olongapo, *Phil.* 61 D4
Olonne-sur-Mer, *France* 20 B2
Oloron, Gave d' ➤, *France* . . . 20 E2
Oloron-Ste-Marie, *France* 20 E3
Olot, *Spain* 32 C7
Olovo, *Bos.-H.* 42 F3
Oloy ➤, *Russia* 51 C16
Olsberg, *Germany* 24 D4
Olshammar, *Sweden* 11 F8
Olshanka, *Ukraine* 47 H6
Olshany, *Ukraine* 47 G8

Olsztyn, *Poland* 44 E7
Olsztynek, *Poland* 44 E7
Olt □, *Romania* 43 F9
Olt ➤, *Romania* 43 G9
Olteniţa, *Romania* 43 F11
Olton, *U.S.A.* 113 H3
Oltu, *Turkey* 73 B9
Oluanpi, *Taiwan* 59 G13
Olula del Rio, *Spain* 33 H2
Olur, *Turkey* 73 B10
Olutanga, *Phil.* 61 H5
Olvega, *Spain* 32 D2
Olvera, *Spain* 35 J5
Olymbos, *Cyprus* 36 D12
Olympia, *Greece* 38 D3
Olympia, *U.S.A.* 116 D4
Olympic Dam, *Australia* 95 E2
Olympic Mts., *U.S.A.* 116 C3
Olympic Nat. Park, *U.S.A.* 116 C3
Olympus, *Cyprus* 36 E11
Olympus, Mt. = Ólimbos, Óros,
  Greece 40 F6
Olympus, Mt. = Uludağ, *Turkey* . 41 F13
Olympus, Mt., *U.S.A.* 116 C3
Olyphant, *U.S.A.* 111 E9
Om ➤, *Russia* 50 D8
Om Hajer, *Eritrea* 81 E4
Om Koi, *Thailand* 64 D2
Ōma, *Japan* 54 D10
Ōmachi, *Japan* 55 F8
Omae-Zaki, *Japan* 55 G9
Ōmagari, *Japan* 54 E10
Omagh, *U.K.* 15 B4
Omagh □, *U.K.* 15 B4
Omaha, *U.S.A.* 112 E7
Omak, *U.S.A.* 114 B4
Omalos, *Greece* 36 D5
Oman ■, *Asia* 74 C6
Oman, G. of, *Asia* 71 E8
Omaruru, *Namibia* 88 C2
Omaruru ➤, *Namibia* 88 C1
Omate, *Peru* 124 G4
Ombai, Selat, *Indonesia* 63 F6
Omb=, *Gabon* 84 E1
Ombrone ➤, *Italy* 28 F8
Omdurmân, *Sudan* 81 D3
Omegna, *Italy* 28 C5
Omemee, *Canada* 110 B6
Omeonga, *Dem. Rep. of
  the Congo* 86 C1
Ometepe, I. de, *Nic.* 120 D2
Ometepec, *Mexico* 119 D5
Ominato, *Japan* 54 D10
Omineca ➤, *Canada* 104 B4
Omiš, *Croatia* 29 E13
Omišalj, *Croatia* 29 C11
Omitara, *Namibia* 88 C2
Ōmiya, *Japan* 55 G9
Omme Å ➤, *Denmark* 11 J2
Ommen, *Neths.* 17 B6
Ömnögovĭ □, *Mongolia* 56 C3
Omo ➤, *Ethiopia* 81 F4
Omodeo, L., *Italy* 30 B1
Omodhos, *Cyprus* 36 E11
Omoko, *Nigeria* 83 D6
Omolon ➤, *Russia* 51 C16
Omono-Gawa ➤, *Japan* 54 E10
Omsk, *Russia* 50 D8
Omsukchan, *Russia* 51 C16
Ōmu, *Japan* 54 B11
Omul, Vf., *Romania* 43 E10
Omulew ➤, *Poland* 45 E8
Omura, *Japan* 55 H4
Omuramba Omatako ➤,
  Namibia 88 B2
Omuramba Ovambo ➤,
  Namibia 88 B2
Omurtag, *Bulgaria* 41 C10
Ōmuta, *Japan* 55 H5
Oña, *Spain* 34 C7
Onaga, *U.S.A.* 112 F6
Onalaska, *U.S.A.* 112 D9
Onancock, *U.S.A.* 108 G8
Onang, *Indonesia* 63 E5
Onaping L., *Canada* 102 C3
Oñati, *Spain* 32 B2
Onavas, *Mexico* 118 B3
Onawa, *U.S.A.* 112 D6
Oncócua, *Angola* 88 B1
Onda, *Spain* 32 F4
Ondaejin, *N. Korea* 57 D15
Ondangwa, *Namibia* 88 B2
Ondarroa, *Spain* 32 B2
Ondava ➤, *Slovak Rep.* 27 C14
Ondjiva, *Angola* 88 B2
Ondo, *Nigeria* 83 D5
Ondo □, *Nigeria* 83 D6
Öndörhaan, *Mongolia* 56 B5
Öndörshil, *Mongolia* 56 B5
Öndverðarnes, *Iceland* 8 D1
One Tree, *Australia* 95 E3
Onega, *Russia* 50 C4
Onega ➤, *Russia* 6 C13
Onega, L. = Onezhskoye Ozero,
  Russia 46 B8
Oneida, *U.S.A.* 111 C9
Oneida L., *U.S.A.* 111 C9
O'Neill, *U.S.A.* 112 D5
Onekotan, Ostrov, *Russia* 51 E16
Onema, *Dem. Rep. of the Congo* 86 C1
Oneonta, *U.S.A.* 111 D9
Oneşti, *Romania* 43 D11
Onezhskoye Ozero, *Russia* . . . 46 B8
Ongarue, *N.Z.* 91 H5
Ongers ➤, *S. Africa* 88 E3
Ongerup, *Australia* 93 F2

Ongjin, *N. Korea* 57 F13
Ongkharak, *Thailand* 64 E3
Ongniud Qi, *China* 57 C10
Ongoka, *Dem. Rep. of the Congo* 86 C2
Ongole, *India* 66 M12
Ongon = Havirga, *Mongolia* . . 56 B7
Oni, *Georgia* 49 J6
Onida, *U.S.A.* 112 C4
Onilahy ➤, *Madag.* 89 C7
Onitsha, *Nigeria* 83 D6
Onoda, *Japan* 55 G5
Onpyŏng-ni, *S. Korea* 57 H14
Ons, I. de, *Spain* 34 C2
Onslow, *Australia* 92 D2
Onslow B., *U.S.A.* 109 H7
Ontake-San, *Japan* 55 G8
Ontario, *Calif., U.S.A.* 117 L9
Ontario, *Oreg., U.S.A.* 114 D5
Ontario □, *Canada* 102 B2
Ontario, L., *N. Amer.* 110 C7
Ontinyent, *Spain* 33 G4
Ontonagon, *U.S.A.* 112 B10
Ontur, *Spain* 33 G3
Onyx, *U.S.A.* 117 K8
Oodnadatta, *Australia* 95 D2
Ooldea, *Australia* 93 F5
Oombulgurri, *Australia* 92 C4
Oorindi, *Australia* 94 C3
Oost-Vlaanderen □, *Belgium* . . 17 C3
Oostende, *Belgium* 17 C2
Oosterhout, *Neths.* 17 C4
Oosterschelde ➤, *Neths.* 17 C4
Oosterwolde, *Neths.* 17 B6
Ootacamund =
  Udagamandalam, *India* 66 P10
Ootsa L., *Canada* 104 C3
Opaka, *Bulgaria* 41 C10
Opala, *Dem. Rep. of the Congo* . 86 C1
Opalenica, *Poland* 45 F3
Opan, *Bulgaria* 41 D9
Opanake, *Sri Lanka* 66 R12
Opasatika, *Canada* 102 C3
Opasquia Prov. Park, *Canada* . . 102 B1
Opatija, *Croatia* 29 C11
Opatów, *Poland* 45 H8
Opava, *Czech Rep.* 27 B10
Opelika, *U.S.A.* 109 J3
Opelousas, *U.S.A.* 113 K8
Opémisca, L., *Canada* 102 C5
Opheim, *U.S.A.* 114 B10
Ophthalmia Ra., *Australia* 92 D2
Opi, *Nigeria* 83 D6
Opinaca ➤, *Canada* 102 B4
Opinaca, Rés., *Canada* 102 B4
Opinnagau ➤, *Canada* 102 B3
Opiscoteo, L., *Canada* 103 B6
Opobo, *Nigeria* 83 E6
Opochka, *Russia* 46 D5
Opoczno, *Poland* 45 G7
Opole, *Poland* 45 H4
Opole Lubelskie, *Poland* 45 G8
Opolskie □, *Poland* 45 H5
Oponono L., *Namibia* 88 B2
Oporto = Porto, *Portugal* 34 D2
Opotiki, *N.Z.* 91 H6
Opp, *U.S.A.* 109 K2
Oppdal, *Norway* 9 E13
Óppido Mamertina, *Italy* 31 D8
Opportunity, *U.S.A.* 114 C5
Oprişor, *Romania* 42 F8
Oprtalj, *Croatia* 29 C10
Opua, *N.Z.* 91 F5
Opunake, *N.Z.* 91 H4
Opuwo, *Namibia* 88 B1
Opuzen, *Croatia* 29 E14
Ora, *Cyprus* 36 E12
Oracle, *U.S.A.* 115 K8
Oradea, *Romania* 42 C6
Öræfajökull, *Iceland* 8 D5
Orahovac, *Kosovo, Yug.* 40 D4
Orahovica, *Croatia* 42 E2
Orai, *India* 69 G8
Oraison, *France* 21 E9
Oral = Zhayyq ➤, *Kazakstan* . . 50 E6
Oral, *Kazakstan* 48 E10
Oran, *Algeria* 78 A5
Orange, *France* 21 D8
Orange, *Calif., U.S.A.* 117 M9
Orange, *Mass., U.S.A.* 111 D12
Orange, *Tex., U.S.A.* 113 K8
Orange, *Va., U.S.A.* 108 F6
Orange ➤, *S. Africa* 88 D2
Orange, C., *Brazil* 125 C8
Orange Cove, *U.S.A.* 116 J7
Orange Free State = Free
  State □, *S. Africa* 88 D4
Orange Grove, *U.S.A.* 113 M6
Orange Walk, *Belize* 119 D7
Orangeburg, *U.S.A.* 109 J5
Orangeville, *Canada* 102 D3
Orango, *Guinea-Biss.* 82 C1
Orani, *Phil.* 61 D4
Oranienburg, *Germany* 24 C9
Oranje = Orange ➤, *S. Africa* . . 88 D2
Oranje Vrystaat = Free State □,
  S. Africa 88 D4
Oranjemund, *Namibia* 88 D2
Oranjerivier, *S. Africa* 88 D3
Orapa, *Botswana* 85 J5
Orarak, *Sudan* 81 F3
Oras, *Phil.* 61 E6
Orašje, *Bos.-H.* 42 E3
Orăştie, *Romania* 43 E8
Orașul Stalin = Braşov, *Romania* 43 E10
Orava ➤, *Slovak Rep.* 27 B12

Orava, Vodna nádriž, Slovak Rep. ... 27 B12
Oravița, Romania ... 42 E6
Orb →, France ... 20 E7
Orba →, Italy ... 28 D5
Ørbæk, Denmark ... 11 J4
Orbe, Switz. ... 25 J2
Orbec, France ... 18 C7
Orbetello, Italy ... 29 F8
Órbigo →, Spain ... 34 C5
Orbisonia, U.S.A. ... 110 F7
Örbyhus, Sweden ... 10 D11
Orcas I., U.S.A. ... 116 B4
Orce, Spain ... 33 H2
Orce →, Spain ... 33 H2
Orchard City, U.S.A. ... 115 G10
Orchies, France ... 19 B10
Orchila, I., Venezuela ... 121 D6
Órcia →, Italy ... 29 F8
Orco →, Italy ... 28 C4
Orcutt, U.S.A. ... 117 L6
Ord, U.S.A. ... 112 E5
Ord →, Australia ... 92 C4
Ord, Mt., Australia ... 92 C4
Ordenes = Ordes, Spain ... 34 B2
Orderville, U.S.A. ... 115 H7
Ordes, Spain ... 34 B2
Ording = St-Peter-Ording, Germany ... 24 A4
Ordos = Mu Us Shamo, China ... 56 E5
Ordu, Turkey ... 72 B7
Ordubad, Azerbaijan ... 73 C12
Orduña, Álava, Spain ... 32 C2
Orduña, Granada, Spain ... 35 H7
Ordway, U.S.A. ... 112 F3
Ordzhonikidze = Vladikavkaz, Russia ... 49 J7
Ordzhonikidze, Ukraine ... 47 J8
Ore, Dem. Rep. of the Congo ... 86 B2
Ore Mts. = Erzgebirge, Germany ... 24 E8
Örebić, Croatia ... 29 F14
Örebro, Sweden ... 10 E9
Örebro län □, Sweden ... 10 E8
Oregon, U.S.A. ... 112 D10
Oregon □, U.S.A. ... 114 E3
Oregon City, U.S.A. ... 116 E4
Öregrund, Sweden ... 10 D12
Öregrundsgrepen, Sweden ... 10 D12
Orekhov = Orikhiv, Ukraine ... 47 J8
Orekhovo-Zuyevo, Russia ... 46 E10
Orel, Russia ... 47 F9
Orel →, Ukraine ... 47 H8
Orellana, Spain ... 35 F5
Orellana, Canal de, Spain ... 35 F5
Orellana, Embalse de, Spain ... 35 F5
Orem, U.S.A. ... 114 F8
Ören, Turkey ... 39 D9
Orenburg, Russia ... 50 D6
Örencik, Turkey ... 39 B11
Orense = Ourense, Spain ... 34 C3
Orense □, Spain ... 34 C3
Orepuki, N.Z. ... 91 M1
Orestiás, Greece ... 41 E10
Orestos Pereyra, Mexico ... 118 B3
Öresund, Europe ... 11 J6
Orford Ness, U.K. ... 13 E9
Organà = Organyà, Spain ... 32 C6
Organos, Pta. de los, Canary Is. ... 37 F2
Organyà, Spain ... 32 C6
Orgaz, Spain ... 35 F7
Orgeyev = Orhei, Moldova ... 43 C13
Orhaneli, Turkey ... 41 G12
Orhaneli →, Turkey ... 41 G12
Orhangazi, Turkey ... 41 F13
Orhei, Moldova ... 43 C13
Orhon Gol →, Mongolia ... 60 A5
Ória, Italy ... 31 B10
Orient □, Dem. Rep. of the Congo ... 86 B2
Oriente, Argentina ... 126 D3
Orihuela, Spain ... 33 G4
Orihuela del Tremedal, Spain ... 32 E3
Orikhiv, Ukraine ... 47 J8
Orikum, Albania ... 40 F3
Orillia, Canada ... 102 D4
Orinoco →, Venezuela ... 122 C4
Orion, Canada ... 105 D6
Oriskany, U.S.A. ... 111 C9
Orissa □, India ... 67 K14
Orissaare, Estonia ... 9 G20
Oristano, Italy ... 30 C1
Oristano, G. di, Italy ... 30 C1
Orizaba, Mexico ... 119 D5
Orizare, Bulgaria ... 41 D11
Orjen, Bos.-H. ... 40 D2
Orjiva, Spain ... 35 J7
Orkanger, Norway ... 8 E13
Örkelljunga, Sweden ... 11 H7
Örken, Sweden ... 11 G9
Örkény, Hungary ... 42 C4
Orkla →, Norway ... 8 E13
Orkney, S. Africa ... 88 D4
Orkney □, U.K. ... 14 B5
Orkney Is., U.K. ... 14 B6
Orland, U.S.A. ... 116 F4
Orlando, U.S.A. ... 109 L5
Orlando, C. d', Italy ... 31 D7
Orléanais, France ... 19 D5
Orléans, France ... 19 E8
Orleans, U.S.A. ... 111 B12
Orléans, I. d', Canada ... 103 C5
Orlice →, Czech Rep. ... 26 A8
Orlov, Slovak Rep. ... 27 B13
Orlov Gay, Russia ... 48 E9
Orlová, Czech Rep. ... 27 B11

Orlovat, Serbia, Yug. ... 42 E5
Ormara, Pakistan ... 66 G4
Ormea, Italy ... 28 D4
Ormília, Greece ... 40 F7
Ormoc, Phil. ... 61 F6
Ormond, N.Z. ... 91 H6
Ormond Beach, U.S.A. ... 109 L5
Ormož, Slovenia ... 29 B13
Ormskirk, U.K. ... 12 D5
Ormstown, Canada ... 111 A11
Ornans, France ... 19 E13
Orne □, France ... 18 D7
Orne →, France ... 18 C6
Orneta, Poland ... 44 D7
Örnö, Sweden ... 10 E12
Örnsköldsvik, Sweden ... 10 A12
Oro, N. Korea ... 57 D14
Oro →, Mexico ... 118 B3
Oro Grande, U.S.A. ... 117 L9
Oro Valley, U.S.A. ... 115 K8
Orobie, Alpi, Italy ... 28 B6
Orocué, Colombia ... 124 C4
Orodara, Burkina Faso ... 82 C4
Orodo, Nigeria ... 83 D6
Orofino, U.S.A. ... 114 C5
Orol Dengizi = Aral Sea, Asia ... 50 E7
Oromocto, Canada ... 103 C6
Oron, Nigeria ... 83 E6
Orono, Canada ... 110 C6
Orono, U.S.A. ... 109 C11
Oronsay, U.K. ... 14 E2
Oropesa, Spain ... 34 F5
Oroquieta, Phil. ... 61 G5
Orosei, Italy ... 30 B2
Orosei, G. di, Italy ... 30 B2
Orosháza, Hungary ... 42 D5
Oroszlány, Hungary ... 42 C3
Orotukan, Russia ... 51 C16
Oroville, Calif., U.S.A. ... 116 F5
Oroville, Wash., U.S.A. ... 114 B4
Oroville, L., U.S.A. ... 116 F5
Orrefors, Sweden ... 11 H9
Orrviken, Sweden ... 10 A8
Orrville, U.S.A. ... 110 F3
Orsa, Sweden ... 10 C8
Orsara di Púglia, Italy ... 31 A8
Orsasjön, Sweden ... 10 C8
Orsha, Belarus ... 46 E6
Orsjö, Sweden ... 11 H9
Orsk, Russia ... 50 D6
Orşova, Romania ... 42 F7
Ørsted, Denmark ... 11 H4
Örsundsbro, Sweden ... 10 E11
Orta, L. d', Italy ... 28 C5
Orta Nova, Italy ... 31 A8
Ortaca, Turkey ... 39 E10
Ortakent, Turkey ... 39 D9
Ortaklar, Turkey ... 39 D9
Ortaköy, Çorum, Turkey ... 72 B6
Ortaköy, Niğde, Turkey ... 72 C6
Orte, Italy ... 29 F9
Ortegal, C., Spain ... 34 B3
Orthez, France ... 20 E3
Ortigueira, Spain ... 34 B3
Orting, U.S.A. ... 116 C4
Ortisei, Italy ... 29 B8
Ortles, Italy ... 28 B7
Ortón →, Bolivia ... 124 F5
Ortona, Italy ... 29 F11
Ortonville, U.S.A. ... 112 C6
Orūmīyeh, Iran ... 70 B5
Orūmīyeh, Daryācheh-ye, Iran ... 70 B5
Orune, Italy ... 30 B2
Oruro, Bolivia ... 124 G5
Orust, Sweden ... 11 F5
Oruzgān □, Afghan. ... 66 C5
Orvault, France ... 18 E5
Orvieto, Italy ... 29 F9
Orwell, N.Y., U.S.A. ... 111 C9
Orwell, Ohio, U.S.A. ... 110 E4
Orwell →, U.K. ... 13 F9
Orwigsburg, U.S.A. ... 111 F8
Oryakhovo, Bulgaria ... 40 C7
Orzinuovi, Italy ... 28 C6
Orzyc →, Poland ... 45 F8
Orzysz, Poland ... 44 E8
Osa →, Poland ... 44 E5
Osa, Pen. de, Costa Rica ... 120 E3
Osage, U.S.A. ... 112 D8
Osage →, U.S.A. ... 112 F9
Osage City, U.S.A. ... 112 F7
Ōsaka, Japan ... 55 G7
Osan, S. Korea ... 57 F14
Osawatomie, U.S.A. ... 112 F7
Osborne, U.S.A. ... 112 F5
Osby, Sweden ... 11 H7
Osceola, Ark., U.S.A. ... 113 H10
Osceola, Iowa, U.S.A. ... 112 E8
Oschatz, Germany ... 24 D9
Oschersleben, Germany ... 24 C7
Óschiri, Italy ... 30 B2
Oscoda, U.S.A. ... 110 B1
Osečina, Serbia, Yug. ... 40 B3
Ösel = Saaremaa, Estonia ... 9 G20
Osery, Russia ... 46 E10
Osgode, Canada ... 111 A9
Osh, Kyrgyzstan ... 50 E8
Oshakati, Namibia ... 85 H3
Oshawa, Canada ... 102 D4
Oshigambo, Namibia ... 88 B2
Oshkosh, Nebr., U.S.A. ... 112 E3
Oshkosh, Wis., U.S.A. ... 112 C10
Oshmyany = Ashmyany, Belarus ... 9 J21
Oshnovīyeh, Iran ... 70 B5
Oshogbo, Nigeria ... 83 D5
Oshtorīnān, Iran ... 71 C6

Oshwe, Dem. Rep. of the Congo ... 84 E3
Osi, Nigeria ... 83 D6
Osieczna, Poland ... 45 G3
Osijek, Croatia ... 42 E3
Ósilo, Italy ... 30 B1
Ósimo, Italy ... 29 E10
Osintorf, Belarus ... 46 E6
Osipenko = Berdyansk, Ukraine ... 47 J9
Osipovichi = Asipovichy, Belarus ... 46 F5
Osiyan, India ... 68 F5
Osizweni, S. Africa ... 89 D5
Oskaloosa, U.S.A. ... 112 E8
Oskarshamn, Sweden ... 11 G10
Oskarström, Sweden ... 11 H6
Öskemen, Kazakstan ... 50 E9
Oskol →, Ukraine ... 47 H9
Oslo, Norway ... 9 G14
Oslob, Phil. ... 61 G5
Oslofjorden, Norway ... 9 G14
Osmanabad, India ... 66 K10
Osmancık, Turkey ... 72 B6
Osmaniye, Turkey ... 70 B3
Osmanlı, Turkey ... 41 E10
Ösmo, Sweden ... 10 F11
Osnabrück, Germany ... 24 C4
Ośno Lubuskie, Poland ... 45 F1
Osoblaha, Czech Rep. ... 27 A10
Osogovska Planina, Macedonia ... 40 D6
Osor, Italy ... 29 D11
Osorio, Brazil ... 127 B5
Osorno, Chile ... 128 E2
Osorno, Spain ... 34 C6
Osoyoos, Canada ... 104 D5
Osøyro, Norway ... 9 F11
Ospika →, Canada ... 104 B4
Osprey Reef, Australia ... 94 A4
Oss, Neths. ... 17 C5
Ossa, Mt., Australia ... 94 G4
Óssa, Óros, Greece ... 38 B4
Ossa de Montiel, Spain ... 33 G2
Ossabaw I., U.S.A. ... 109 K5
Osse →, France ... 20 D4
Osse →, Nigeria ... 83 D6
Ossi, Italy ... 30 B1
Ossining, U.S.A. ... 111 E11
Ossipee, U.S.A. ... 111 C13
Ossokmanuan L., Canada ... 103 B7
Ossora, Russia ... 51 D17
Ostashkov, Russia ... 46 D7
Östavall, Sweden ... 10 B9
Oste →, Germany ... 24 B5
Ostend = Oostende, Belgium ... 17 C2
Oster, Ukraine ... 47 G6
Osterburg, Germany ... 24 C7
Osterburg, U.S.A. ... 110 F6
Osterburken, Germany ... 25 F5
Österbybruk, Sweden ... 10 D11
Österbymo, Sweden ... 11 G9
Österdalälven, Sweden ... 10 C7
Österdalen, Norway ... 9 F14
Österfärnebo, Sweden ... 10 D10
Osterforse, Sweden ... 10 A11
Östergötlands län □, Sweden ... 11 F9
Osterholz-Scharmbeck, Germany ... 24 B4
Österild, Denmark ... 11 G2
Osterode, Germany ... 24 D6
Östersund, Sweden ... 10 A8
Östervåla, Sweden ... 10 D11
Ostfriesische Inseln, Germany ... 24 B3
Ostfriesland, Germany ... 24 B3
Östhammar, Sweden ... 10 D12
Óstia, Lido di, Italy ... 29 G9
Ostíglia, Italy ... 29 C8
Ostmark, Sweden ... 10 D6
Ostra Husby, Sweden ... 11 F10
Ostrava, Czech Rep. ... 27 B11
Ostróda, Poland ... 44 E6
Ostrogozhsk, Russia ... 47 G10
Ostroh, Ukraine ... 47 G4
Ostrołęka, Poland ... 45 E8
Ostrov, Bulgaria ... 41 C8
Ostrov, Czech Rep. ... 26 A5
Ostrov, Romania ... 43 F12
Ostrov, Russia ... 46 D5
Ostrów Lubelski, Poland ... 45 G9
Ostrów Mazowiecka, Poland ... 45 F8
Ostrów Wielkopolski, Poland ... 45 G4
Ostrowiec-Świętokrzyski, Poland ... 45 H8
Ostrožac, Bos.-H. ... 42 G2
Ostrzeszów, Poland ... 45 G4
Ostseebad Kühlungsborn, Germany ... 24 A7
Osttirol □, Austria ... 26 E5
Ostuni, Italy ... 31 B10
Osum →, Albania ... 40 F4
Osŭm →, Bulgaria ... 41 C8
Ōsumi-Kaikyō, Japan ... 55 J5
Ōsumi-Shotō, Japan ... 55 J5
Osun □, Nigeria ... 83 D5
Osuna, Spain ... 35 H5
Oswegatchie →, U.S.A. ... 111 B9
Oswego, U.S.A. ... 111 C8
Oswego →, U.S.A. ... 111 C8
Oswestry, U.K. ... 12 E4
Oświęcim, Poland ... 45 H6
Otago □, N.Z. ... 91 L2
Otago Harbour, N.Z. ... 91 L3
Ōtake, Japan ... 55 G6
Otaki, N.Z. ... 91 J5
Otaru, Japan ... 54 C10

Otaru-Wan = Ishikari-Wan, Japan ... 54 C10
Otava, Czech Rep. ... 26 B7
Otavalo, Ecuador ... 124 C3
Otavi, Namibia ... 88 B2
Otchinjau, Angola ... 88 B1
Otelec, Romania ... 42 E5
Otelnuk L., Canada ... 103 A6
Oțelu Roşu, Romania ... 42 E7
Otero de Rey = Outeiro de Rei, Spain ... 34 B3
Othello, U.S.A. ... 114 C4
Othonoí, Greece ... 38 B1
Óthris, Óros, Greece ... 38 B4
Otjiwarongo, Namibia ... 88 C2
Otmuchów, Poland ... 45 H4
Otočac, Croatia ... 29 D12
Otoineppu, Japan ... 54 B11
Otok, Croatia ... 29 E13
Otorohanga, N.Z. ... 91 H5
Otoskwin →, Canada ... 102 B2
Otra →, Norway ... 9 G13
Otradnyy, Russia ... 48 D10
Otranto, Italy ... 31 B11
Otranto, C. d', Italy ... 31 B11
Otranto, Str. of, Italy ... 31 B11
Otrokovice, Czech Rep. ... 27 B10
Otse, S. Africa ... 88 D4
Ōtsu, Japan ... 55 G7
Ōtsuki, Japan ... 55 G9
Ottawa = Outaouais →, Canada ... 102 C5
Ottawa, Canada ... 102 C4
Ottawa, Ill., U.S.A. ... 112 E10
Ottawa, Kans., U.S.A. ... 112 F7
Ottawa Is., Canada ... 101 C11
Ottélé, Cameroon ... 83 E7
Ottensheim, Austria ... 26 C7
Otter Cr. →, U.S.A. ... 111 B11
Otter L., Canada ... 105 B8
Otterndorf, Germany ... 24 B4
Otterup, Denmark ... 11 J4
Otterville, Canada ... 110 D4
Ottery St. Mary, U.K. ... 13 G4
Otto Beit Bridge, Zimbabwe ... 87 F2
Ottosdal, S. Africa ... 88 D4
Ottumwa, U.S.A. ... 112 E8
Otu, Nigeria ... 83 D5
Otukpo, Nigeria ... 83 D6
Oturkpo, Nigeria ... 83 D6
Otway, B., Chile ... 128 G2
Otwock, Poland ... 45 F8
Ötztaler Ache →, Austria ... 26 D3
Ötztaler Alpen, Austria ... 26 E3
Ou →, Laos ... 64 B4
Ou Neua, Laos ... 58 F3
Ou-Sammyaku, Japan ... 54 E10
Ouachita →, U.S.A. ... 113 K9
Ouachita, L., U.S.A. ... 113 H8
Ouachita Mts., U.S.A. ... 113 H7
Ouagadougou, Burkina Faso ... 83 C4
Ouahigouya, Burkina Faso ... 82 C4
Ouahran = Oran, Algeria ... 78 A5
Oualâta, Mauritania ... 82 B3
Ouallam, Niger ... 83 C5
Ouallene, Algeria ... 78 D6
Ouargaye, Burkina Faso ... 83 C5
Ouargla, Algeria ... 78 B7
Ouarkoye, Burkina Faso ... 82 C4
Ouarzazate, Morocco ... 78 B4
Ouassouas, Mali ... 83 B5
Ouatagouna, Mali ... 83 B5
Oubangi →, Dem. Rep. of the Congo ... 84 E3
Ouche →, France ... 19 E12
Ouddorp, Neths. ... 17 C3
Oude Rijn →, Neths. ... 17 B4
Oudeïka, Mali ... 83 B5
Oudenaarde, Belgium ... 17 D3
Oudon, France ... 18 E6
Oudtshoorn, S. Africa ... 88 E3
Ouellé, Ivory C. ... 82 D4
Ouémé →, Benin ... 83 D5
Ouessa, Burkina Faso ... 82 C4
Ouessant, Î. d', France ... 18 D1
Ouesso, Congo ... 84 D3
Ouest, Pte. de l', Canada ... 103 C7
Ouezzane, Morocco ... 78 B4
Ougarou, Burkina Faso ... 83 C5
Oughterard, Ireland ... 15 C2
Ouidah, Benin ... 83 D5
Ouidi, Niger ... 83 C7
Ouistreham, France ... 18 C6
Oujda, Morocco ... 78 B5
Oujeft, Mauritania ... 82 A2
Oulainen, Finland ... 8 D21
Ould Yenjé, Mauritania ... 82 B2
Oullins, France ... 21 C8
Oulu, Finland ... 8 D21
Oulujärvi, Finland ... 8 D22
Oulujoki →, Finland ... 8 D21
Oulx, Italy ... 28 C3
Oum Chalouba, Chad ... 79 E10
Oum Hadjer, Chad ... 79 F9
Oumé, Ivory C. ... 82 D3
Ounasjoki →, Finland ... 8 C21
Ounguati, Namibia ... 88 C2
Ounianga Sérir, Chad ... 79 E10
Our →, Lux. ... 17 E6
Ouranópolis, Greece ... 40 F7
Ourârene, Niger ... 83 B6
Ouray, U.S.A. ... 115 G10
Ourcq →, France ... 19 C10
Ourense, Spain ... 34 C3
Ouricuri, Brazil ... 125 E10
Ourinhos, Brazil ... 127 A6
Ourique, Portugal ... 35 H2

Ouro Fino, Brazil ... 127 A6
Ouro-Ndia, Mali ... 82 B4
Ouro Prêto, Brazil ... 127 A7
Ouro Sogui, Senegal ... 82 B2
Oursi, Burkina Faso ... 83 C4
Ourthe →, Belgium ... 17 D5
Ouse →, E. Susx., U.K. ... 13 G8
Ouse →, N. Yorks., U.K. ... 12 D7
Oust, France ... 20 F5
Oust →, France ... 18 E4
Outaouais →, Canada ... 102 C5
Outardes →, Canada ... 103 C6
Outeiro de Rei, Spain ... 34 B3
Outer Hebrides, U.K. ... 14 D1
Outes = Serra de Outes, Spain ... 34 C2
Outjo, Namibia ... 88 C2
Outlook, Canada ... 105 C7
Outokumpu, Finland ... 8 E23
Outreau, France ... 19 B8
Ouvèze →, France ... 21 E8
Ouzouer-le-Marché, France ... 19 E8
Ovada, Italy ... 28 D5
Ovalau, Fiji ... 91 C8
Ovalle, Chile ... 126 C1
Ovamboland, Namibia ... 88 B2
Ovar, Portugal ... 34 E2
Overath, Germany ... 24 E3
Overflakkee, Neths. ... 17 C4
Overijssel □, Neths. ... 17 B6
Overland Park, U.S.A. ... 112 F7
Overton, U.S.A. ... 117 J12
Övertorneå, Sweden ... 8 C20
Överum, Sweden ... 11 F10
Ovid, U.S.A. ... 111 D8
Ovidiopol, Ukraine ... 47 J6
Ovidiu, Romania ... 43 F13
Oviedo, Spain ... 34 B5
Oviksfjällen, Sweden ... 10 A7
Oviši, Latvia ... 9 H19
Ovoot, Mongolia ... 56 B7
Övör Hangay □, Mongolia ... 56 B2
Ovoro, Nigeria ... 83 D6
Øvre Årdal, Norway ... 9 F12
Øvre Fryken, Sweden ... 10 E7
Ovruch, Ukraine ... 47 G5
Owaka, N.Z. ... 91 M2
Owambo = Ovamboland, Namibia ... 88 B2
Owasco L., U.S.A. ... 111 D8
Owase, Japan ... 55 G8
Owatonna, U.S.A. ... 112 C8
Owbeh, Afghan. ... 66 B3
Owego, U.S.A. ... 111 D8
Owen Falls Dam, Uganda ... 86 B3
Owen Sound, Canada ... 102 D3
Owens →, U.S.A. ... 116 J9
Owens L., U.S.A. ... 117 J9
Owensboro, U.S.A. ... 108 G2
Owerri, Nigeria ... 83 D6
Owl →, Canada ... 105 B10
Owo, Nigeria ... 83 D6
Owosso, U.S.A. ... 108 D3
Owyhee, U.S.A. ... 114 F5
Owyhee →, U.S.A. ... 114 E5
Owyhee, L., U.S.A. ... 114 E5
Ox Mts. = Slieve Gamph, Ireland ... 15 B3
Oxarfjörður, Iceland ... 8 C5
Oxbow, Canada ... 105 D8
Oxelösund, Sweden ... 11 F11
Oxford, N.Z. ... 91 K4
Oxford, U.K. ... 13 F6
Oxford, Mass., U.S.A. ... 111 D13
Oxford, Miss., U.S.A. ... 113 H10
Oxford, N.C., U.S.A. ... 109 G6
Oxford, N.Y., U.S.A. ... 111 D9
Oxford, Ohio, U.S.A. ... 108 F3
Oxford L., Canada ... 105 C9
Oxfordshire □, U.K. ... 13 F6
Oxía, Greece ... 38 C3
Oxie, Sweden ... 11 J7
Oxílithos, Greece ... 38 C6
Oxnard, U.S.A. ... 117 L7
Oxsjövålen, Sweden ... 10 B7
Oxus = Amudarya →, Uzbekistan ... 50 E6
Oya, Malaysia ... 62 D4
Oyama, Japan ... 55 F9
Oyem, Gabon ... 84 D2
Oyen, Canada ... 105 C6
Oykel →, U.K. ... 14 D4
Oymyakon, Russia ... 51 C15
Oyo, Nigeria ... 83 D5
Oyo □, Nigeria ... 83 D5
Oyonnax, France ... 19 F12
Oyster Bay, U.S.A. ... 111 F11
Öyūbari, Japan ... 54 C11
Ózalp, Turkey ... 73 C10
Ozamiz, Phil. ... 61 G5
Ozark, Ala., U.S.A. ... 109 K3
Ozark, Ark., U.S.A. ... 113 H8
Ozark, Mo., U.S.A. ... 113 G8
Ozark Plateau, U.S.A. ... 113 G9
Ozarks, L. of the, U.S.A. ... 112 F8
Ozarów, Poland ... 45 H8
Ózd, Hungary ... 42 B5
Ozernoye, Russia ... 48 E10
Ozette L., U.S.A. ... 116 B2
Ozieri, Italy ... 30 B2
Ozimek, Poland ... 45 H5
Ozinki, Russia ... 48 E9
Ozona, U.S.A. ... 113 K4
Ozorków, Poland ... 45 G6
Ozren, Bos.-H. ... 42 G3
Ozuluama, Mexico ... 119 C5
Ozun, Romania ... 43 E10
Ozurgeti, Georgia ... 49 K5

P

Pa, *Burkina Faso* 82 C4
Pa-an, *Burma* 67 L20
Pa Mong Dam, *Thailand* 64 D4
Pa Sak ➤, *Thailand* 62 B2
Paamiut, *Greenland* 4 C5
Paar ➤, *Germany* 25 G7
Paarl, *S. Africa* 88 E2
Pab Hills, *Pakistan* 68 F2
Pabbay, *U.K.* 14 D1
Pabianice, *Poland* 45 G6
Pabna, *Bangla.* 67 G16
Pabo, *Uganda* 86 B3
Pacaja ➤, *Brazil* 125 D8
Pacaraima, Sa., *S. Amer.* 122 C4
Pacasmayo, *Peru* 124 E3
Paceco, *Italy* 30 E5
Pachhar, *India* 68 G7
Pachino, *Italy* 31 F8
Pachitea ➤, *Peru* 124 E4
Pachmarhi, *India* 69 H8
Pachpadra, *India* 66 G8
Pachuca, *Mexico* 119 C5
Pacific, *Canada* 104 C3
Pacific-Antarctic Ridge, *Pac. Oc.* 97 M16
Pacific Grove, *U.S.A.* 116 J5
Pacific Ocean, *Pac. Oc.* 97 G14
Pacific Rim Nat. Park, *Canada* . 116 B2
Pacifica, *U.S.A.* 116 H4
Pacitan, *Indonesia* 63 H14
Packwood, *U.S.A.* 116 D5
Pacov, *Czech Rep.* 26 B8
Pacy-sur-Eure, *France* 18 C8
Padaido, Kepulauan, *Indonesia* 63 E9
Padang, *Indonesia* 62 E2
Padang Endau, *Malaysia* 65 L4
Padangpanjang, *Indonesia* 62 E2
Padangsidempuan, *Indonesia* .. 62 D1
Padborg, *Denmark* 11 K3
Paddle Prairie, *Canada* 104 B5
Paddockwood, *Canada* 105 C7
Paderborn, *Germany* 24 D4
Padeş, Vf., *Romania* 42 E7
Padina, *Romania* 43 F12
Padma, *India* 69 G11
Pádova, *Italy* 29 C8
Padra, *India* 68 H5
Padrauna, *India* 69 F10
Padre I., *U.S.A.* 113 M6
Padrón, *Spain* 34 C2
Padstow, *U.K.* 13 G3
Padua = Pádova, *Italy* 29 C8
Paducah, *Ky., U.S.A.* 108 G1
Paducah, *Tex., U.S.A.* 113 H4
Padul, *Spain* 35 H7
Paengnyŏng-do, *S. Korea* 57 F13
Paeroa, *N.Z.* 91 G5
Paesana, *Italy* 28 D4
Pafúri, *Mozam.* 89 C5
Pag, *Croatia* 29 D12
Paga, *Ghana* 83 C4
Pagadian, *Phil.* 61 H5
Pagai Selatan, Pulau, *Indonesia* 62 E2
Pagai Utara, Pulau, *Indonesia* . 62 E2
Pagalu = Annobón, *Atl. Oc.* .. 77 G4
Pagara, *India* 69 G9
Pagastikós Kólpos, *Greece* 38 B5
Pagatan, *Indonesia* 62 E5
Page, *U.S.A.* 115 H8
Pagégiai, *Lithuania* 44 C8
Pago Pago, *Amer. Samoa* 91 B13
Pagosa Springs, *U.S.A.* 115 H10
Pagwa River, *Canada* 102 B2
Pahala, *U.S.A.* 106 J17
Pahang □, *Malaysia* 65 L4
Pahiatua, *N.Z.* 91 J5
Pahokee, *U.S.A.* 109 M5
Pahrump, *U.S.A.* 117 J11
Pahute Mesa, *U.S.A.* 116 H10
Pai, *Thailand* 64 C2
Paicines, *U.S.A.* 116 J5
Paide, *Estonia* 9 G21
Paignton, *U.K.* 13 G4
Paiho, *Taiwan* 59 F13
Päijänne, *Finland* 9 F21
Pailani, *India* 69 G9
Pailin, *Cambodia* 64 F4
Paimpol, *France* 18 D3
Painan, *Indonesia* 62 E2
Painesville, *U.S.A.* 110 E3
Paint Hills = Wemindji, *Canada* 102 B4
Paint L., *Canada* 105 B9
Painted Desert, *U.S.A.* 115 J8
Paintsville, *U.S.A.* 108 G4
País Vasco □, *Spain* 32 C2
Paisley, *Canada* 110 B3
Paisley, *U.K.* 14 F4
Paisley, *U.S.A.* 114 E3
Paita, *Peru* 124 E2
Paiva ➤, *Portugal* 34 D2
Paizhou, *China* 59 B9
Pajares, *Spain* 34 B5
Pajares, Puerto de, *Spain* 34 C5
Pajeczno, *Poland* 45 G5
Pak Lay, *Laos* 64 C3
Pak Phanang, *Thailand* 65 H3
Pak Sane, *Laos* 64 C4
Pak Song, *Laos* 64 E6
Pak Suong, *Laos* 58 H4
Pakaur, *India* 69 G12
Pakenham, *Canada* 111 A8
Pákhnes, *Greece* 36 D6
Pakhuis, *S. Africa* 88 E2
Pakistan ■, *Asia* 68 E4

Pakkading, *Laos* 64 C4
Pakokku, *Burma* 67 J19
Pakość, *Poland* 45 F5
Pakowki L., *Canada* 105 D6
Pakpattan, *Pakistan* 68 D5
Pakrac, *Croatia* 42 E2
Pakruojis, *Lithuania* 44 C10
Paks, *Hungary* 42 D3
Paktīā □, *Afghan.* 66 C6
Pakwach, *Uganda* 86 B3
Pakxe, *Laos* 64 E5
Pal Lahara, *India* 69 J11
Pala, *Chad* 79 G9
Pala, *Dem. Rep. of the Congo* . 86 D2
Pala, *U.S.A.* 117 M9
Palabek, *Uganda* 86 B3
Palacios, *U.S.A.* 113 L6
Palafrugell, *Spain* 32 D8
Palagiano, *Italy* 31 B10
Palagonía, *Italy* 31 E7
Palagruža, *Croatia* 29 F13
Palaiókastron, *Greece* 36 D8
Palaiokhóra, *Greece* 36 D5
Pálairos, *Greece* 38 C2
Palaiseau, *France* 19 D9
Palam, *India* 66 K10
Palamás, *Greece* 38 B4
Palamòs, *Spain* 32 D8
Palampur, *India* 68 C7
Palamut, *Turkey* 39 C9
Palana, *Australia* 94 F4
Palana, *Russia* 51 D16
Palanan, *Phil.* 61 C5
Palanan Pt., *Phil.* 61 C5
Palandri, *Pakistan* 69 C5
Palanga, *Lithuania* 9 J19
Palangkaraya, *Indonesia* 62 E4
Palani Hills, *India* 66 P10
Palanpur, *India* 68 G5
Palapye, *Botswana* 88 C4
Palas, *Pakistan* 69 B5
Palas de Rei, *Spain* 34 C3
Palashi, *India* 69 H13
Palasponga, *India* 69 J11
Palatka, *Russia* 51 C16
Palatka, *U.S.A.* 109 L5
Palau, *Italy* 30 A2
Palau ■, *Pac. Oc.* 52 J17
Palauk, *Burma* 64 F2
Palawan, *Phil.* 61 G3
Palayankottai, *India* 66 Q10
Palazzo, Pte., *France* 21 F12
Palazzo San Gervásio, *Italy* ... 31 B8
Palazzolo Acréide, *Italy* 31 E7
Paldiski, *Estonia* 9 G21
Pale, *Bos.-H.* 42 G3
Paleleh, *Indonesia* 63 D6
Palembang, *Indonesia* 62 E2
Palencia, *Spain* 34 C6
Palencia □, *Spain* 34 C6
Palenque, *Mexico* 119 D6
Paleokastrítsa, *Greece* 36 A3
Paleometokho, *Cyprus* 36 D12
Palermo, *Italy* 30 D6
Palermo, *U.S.A.* 114 G3
Palestina, *Chile* 128 A3
Palestine, *Asia* 75 D4
Palestine, *U.S.A.* 113 K7
Palestrina, *Italy* 29 G9
Paletwa, *Burma* 67 J18
Palghat, *India* 66 P10
Palgrave, Mt., *Australia* 92 D2
Pali, *India* 68 G5
Palikir, *Micronesia* 96 G7
Palinuro, *Italy* 31 B8
Palinuro, C., *Italy* 31 B8
Palioúrion, Ákra, *Greece* 40 G7
Palisades Reservoir, *U.S.A.* ... 114 E8
Paliseul, *Belgium* 17 E5
Palitana, *India* 68 J4
Palizada, *Mexico* 119 D6
Palk Bay, *Asia* 66 Q11
Palk Strait, *Asia* 66 Q11
Palkānah, *Iraq* 70 C5
Palkot, *India* 69 H11
Palla Road = Dinokwe,
  Botswana 88 C4
Pallanza = Verbánia, *Italy* 28 C5
Pallarenda, *Australia* 94 B4
Pallasovka, *Russia* 48 E8
Pallës, Bishti i, *Albania* 40 E3
Pallinup ➤, *Australia* 93 F2
Pallisa, *Uganda* 86 B3
Pallu, *India* 68 E6
Palm Bay, *U.S.A.* 109 L5
Palm Beach, *U.S.A.* 109 M6
Palm Coast, *U.S.A.* 109 L5
Palm Desert, *U.S.A.* 117 M10
Palm Is., *Australia* 94 B4
Palm Springs, *U.S.A.* 117 M10
Palma, *Mozam.* 87 E5
Palma, B. de, *Spain* 37 B9
Palma de Mallorca, *Spain* 37 B9
Palma del Río, *Spain* 35 H5
Palma di Montechiaro, *Italy* .. 30 E6
Palma Soriano, *Cuba* 120 B4
Palmares, *Brazil* 125 E11
Palmarola, *Italy* 30 B5
Palmas, *Brazil* 127 B5
Palmas, C., *Liberia* 82 E3
Pálmas, G. di, *Italy* 30 D1
Palmdale, *U.S.A.* 117 L8
Palmeira das Missões, *Brazil* .. 127 B5
Palmeira dos Índios, *Brazil* ... 125 E11
Palmela, *Portugal* 35 G2
Palmer ➤, *Australia* 94 B3
Palmer Arch., *Antarctica* 5 C17
Palmer Lake, *U.S.A.* 112 F2
Palmer Land, *Antarctica* 5 D18
Palmerston, *Canada* 110 C4
Palmerston, *N.Z.* 91 L3
Palmerston North, *N.Z.* 91 J5
Palmerton, *U.S.A.* 111 F9
Palmetto, *U.S.A.* 109 M4
Palmi, *Italy* 31 D8
Palmira, *Argentina* 126 C2
Palmira, *Colombia* 124 C3
Palmyra = Tudmur, *Syria* 70 C3
Palmyra, *Mo., U.S.A.* 112 F9
Palmyra, *N.J., U.S.A.* 111 F9
Palmyra, *N.Y., U.S.A.* 110 C7
Palmyra, *Pa., U.S.A.* 111 F8
Palmyra Is., *Pac. Oc.* 97 G11
Palo Alto, *U.S.A.* 116 H4
Palo Verde, *U.S.A.* 117 M12
Paloich, *Sudan* 81 E3
Palompon, *Phil.* 61 F6
Palopo, *Indonesia* 63 E6
Palos, C. de, *Spain* 33 H4
Palos de la Frontera, *Spain* ... 35 H4
Palos Verdes, *U.S.A.* 117 M8
Palos Verdes, Pt., *U.S.A.* 117 M8
Pålsboda, *Sweden* 10 E9
Palu, *Indonesia* 63 E5
Palu, *Turkey* 70 B3
Paluke, *Liberia* 82 D3
Paluzza, *Italy* 29 B10
Palwal, *India* 68 E7
Pama, *Burkina Faso* 83 C5
Pamanukan, *Indonesia* 63 G12
Pamiers, *France* 20 E5
Pamir, *Tajikistan* 50 F8
Pamlico ➤, *U.S.A.* 109 H7
Pamlico Sd., *U.S.A.* 109 H8
Pampa, *U.S.A.* 113 H4
Pampa de las Salinas, *Argentina* 126 C2
Pampanua, *Indonesia* 63 E6
Pampas, *Argentina* 126 D3
Pampas, *Peru* 124 F4
Pamphylia, *Turkey* 72 D4
Pamplona, *Colombia* 124 B4
Pamplona, *Spain* 32 C3
Pampoenpoort, *S. Africa* 88 E3
Pamukçu, *Turkey* 39 B9
Pamukkale, *Turkey* 39 D11
Pan Xian, *China* 58 E5
Pana, *U.S.A.* 112 F10
Panabo, *Phil.* 61 H6
Panaca, *U.S.A.* 115 H6
Panagyurishte, *Bulgaria* 41 D8
Panaitan, *Indonesia* 63 G11
Panaji, *India* 66 M8
Panamá, *Panama* 120 E4
Panama ■, *Cent. Amer.* 120 E4
Panamá, G. de, *Panama* 120 E4
Panama Canal, *Panama* 120 E4
Panama City, *U.S.A.* 109 K3
Panamint Range, *U.S.A.* 117 J9
Panamint Springs, *U.S.A.* 117 J9
Panão, *Peru* 124 E3
Panaon I., *Phil.* 61 F6
Panare, *Thailand* 65 J3
Panarea, *Italy* 31 D8
Panaro ➤, *Italy* 29 D8
Panay, *Phil.* 61 F5
Panay, G., *Phil.* 63 B6
Pančevo, *Serbia, Yug.* 42 F5
Panch'iao, *Taiwan* 59 E13
Panciu, *Romania* 43 E12
Pancorbo, Desfiladero, *Spain* . 34 C7
Pâncota, *Romania* 42 D6
Panda, *Mozam.* 89 C5
Pandan, *Antique, Phil.* 61 F5
Pandan, *Catanduanes, Phil.* .. 61 D6
Pandegelang, *Indonesia* 63 G12
Pandhana, *India* 68 J7
Pandharpur, *India* 66 L9
Pando, *Uruguay* 127 C4
Pando, L. = Hope, L., *Australia* 95 D2
Pandokrátor, *Greece* 36 A3
Pandora, *Costa Rica* 120 E3
Pandrup, *Denmark* 11 G3
Panevėžys, *Lithuania* 9 J21
Panfilov, *Kazakstan* 50 E8
Panfilovo, *Russia* 48 E7
Pang-Long, *Burma* 67 H21
Pang-Yang, *Burma* 67 H21
Panga, *Dem. Rep. of the Congo* 86 B2
Pangaíon Óros, *Greece* 41 F8
Pangalanes, Canal des =
  Ampangalana, Lakandranon',
  Madag. 89 C8
Pangani, *Tanzania* 86 D4
Pangani ➤, *Tanzania* 86 D4
Pangfou = Bengbu, *China* 57 H9
Pangil, *Dem. Rep. of the Congo* 86 C2
Pangkah, Tanjung, *Indonesia* . 63 G15
Pangkajene, *Indonesia* 63 E5
Pangkalanbrandan, *Indonesia* . 62 D1
Pangkalanbuun, *Indonesia* ... 62 E4
Pangkalpinang, *Indonesia* 62 E3
Pangnirtung, *Canada* 101 B13
Pangong Tso, *India* 69 B8
Panguitch, *U.S.A.* 115 H7
Pangutaran Group, *Phil.* 61 H4
Panhandle, *U.S.A.* 113 H4
Pani Mines, *India* 68 H5
Pania-Mutombo, *Dem. Rep. of*
  the Congo 86 D1
Panikota I., *India* 68 J4
Panipat, *India* 68 E7

Panjal Range, *India* 68 C7
Panjang, Hon, *Vietnam* 65 H4
Panjgur, *Pakistan* 66 F4
Panjim = Panaji, *India* 66 M8
Panjin, *China* 57 D12
Panjinad Barrage, *Pakistan* ... 66 E7
Panjnad ➤, *Pakistan* 68 E4
Panjwai, *Afghan.* 68 D1
Pankshin, *Nigeria* 83 D6
Panmunjŏm, *N. Korea* 57 F14
Panna, *India* 69 G9
Panna Hills, *India* 69 G9
Pannawonica, *Australia* 92 D2
Pannirtuuq = Pangnirtung,
  Canada 101 B13
Pano Akil, *Pakistan* 68 F3
Pano Lefkara, *Cyprus* 36 E12
Pano Panayia, *Cyprus* 36 E11
Panorama, *Brazil* 127 A5
Pánormon, *Greece* 36 D6
Pansemal, *India* 68 J6
Panshan = Panjin, *China* 57 D12
Panshi, *China* 57 C14
Pantanal, *Brazil* 124 H7
Pantar, *Indonesia* 63 F6
Pante Macassar, *E. Timor* 63 F6
Pante Makasar = Pante
  Macassar, *E. Timor* 63 F6
Pantelleria, *Italy* 30 F4
Pantón, *Spain* 34 C3
Pánuco, *Mexico* 119 C5
Panyam, *Nigeria* 83 D6
Panyu, *China* 59 F9
Panzhihua, *China* 58 D3
Páola, *Italy* 31 C9
Paola, *Malta* 36 D2
Paola, *U.S.A.* 112 F7
Paonia, *U.S.A.* 115 G10
Paoting = Baoding, *China* 56 E8
Paot'ou = Baotou, *China* 56 D6
Paoua, *C.A.R.* 84 C3
Pápa, *Hungary* 42 C2
Papa Stour, *U.K.* 14 A7
Papa Westray, *U.K.* 14 B6
Papagayo ➤, *Mexico* 119 D5
Papagayo, G. de, *Costa Rica* .. 120 D2
Papakura, *N.Z.* 91 G5
Papantla, *Mexico* 119 C5
Papar, *Malaysia* 62 C5
Pápas, Ákra, *Greece* 38 C3
Papeete, *Tahiti* 97 J13
Papenburg, *Germany* 24 B3
Papien Chiang = Da ➤, *Vietnam* 58 G5
Papigochic ➤, *Mexico* 118 B3
Paposo, *Chile* 126 B1
Paphlagonia, *Turkey* 72 B5
Paphos, *Cyprus* 36 E11
Papien Chiang = Da ➤, *Vietnam* 58 G5
Papua New Guinea ■, *Oceania* 96 H6
Papudo, *Chile* 126 C1
Papuk, *Croatia* 42 E2
Papun, *Burma* 67 K20
Papunya, *Australia* 92 D5
Pará = Belém, *Brazil* 125 D9
Pará □, *Brazil* 125 D8
Paraburdoo, *Australia* 92 D2
Paracale, *Phil.* 61 D5
Paracatu, *Brazil* 125 G9
Paracel Is., *S. China Sea* 62 A4
Parachinar, *Pakistan* 68 C4
Paracín, *Serbia, Yug.* 40 C5
Paradas, *Spain* 35 H5
Paradela, *Spain* 34 C3
Paradhísi, *Greece* 36 C10
Paradip, *India* 67 J15
Paradise, *Calif., U.S.A.* 116 F5
Paradise, *Nev., U.S.A.* 117 J11
Paradise ➤, *Canada* 103 B8
Paradise Hill, *Canada* 105 C7
Paradise River, *Canada* 103 B8
Paradise Valley, *U.S.A.* 114 F5
Parado, *Indonesia* 63 F5
Paragould, *U.S.A.* 113 G9
Paraguá ➤, *Venezuela* 124 B6
Paraguaçú ➤, *Brazil* 125 F11
Paraguaçu Paulista, *Brazil* 127 A5
Paraguaná, Pen. de, *Venezuela* 124 A5
Paraguarí, *Paraguay* 126 B4
Paraguarí □, *Paraguay* 126 B4
Paraguay ■, *S. Amer.* 126 B4
Paraguay ➤, *Paraguay* 126 B4
Paraíba = João Pessoa, *Brazil* . 125 E12
Paraíba □, *Brazil* 125 E11
Paraíba do Sul ➤, *Brazil* 127 A7
Parainen, *Finland* 9 F20
Paraiso, *Mexico* 119 D6
Parak, *Iran* 71 E7
Parakhino Paddubye, *Russia* .. 46 C7
Parakou, *Benin* 83 D5
Paralimni, *Cyprus* 36 D12
Parálion-Astrous, *Greece* 38 D4
Paramaribo, *Surinam* 125 B7
Paramithiá, *Greece* 38 B2
Paramushir, Ostrov, *Russia* ... 51 D16
Paran ➤, *Israel* 75 E4
Paraná, *Argentina* 126 C3
Paraná □, *Brazil* 127 A5
Paraná ➤, *Argentina* 126 C4
Paraná ➤, *Argentina* 126 C4
Paranaguá, *Brazil* 127 B6
Paranaíba, *Brazil* 125 G8
Paranaíba ➤, *Brazil* 125 H8
Paranapanema ➤, *Brazil* 127 A5
Paranapiacaba, Serra do, *Brazil* 127 A6
Paranas, *Phil.* 61 F6
Paranavaí, *Brazil* 127 A5

Parang, *Maguindanao, Phil.* ... 63 C6
Parang, *Sulu, Phil.* 61 J4
Parângul Mare, Vf., *Romania* . 43 E8
Paraparaumu, *N.Z.* 91 J5
Parapóla, *Greece* 38 E5
Paraspóri, Ákra, *Greece* 39 F9
Paray-le-Monial, *France* 19 F11
Parbati ➤, *Mad. P., India* 68 G7
Parbati ➤, *Raj., India* 68 F7
Parbhani, *India* 66 K10
Parchim, *Germany* 24 B7
Parczew, *Poland* 45 G9
Pardes Hanna-Karkur, *Israel* .. 75 C3
Pardilla, *Spain* 34 D7
Pardo ➤, *Bahia, Brazil* 125 G11
Pardo ➤, *Mato Grosso, Brazil* . 127 A5
Pardubice, *Czech Rep.* 26 A8
Pare, *Indonesia* 63 G15
Pare Mts., *Tanzania* 86 C4
Parecis, Serra dos, *Brazil* 124 F7
Paredes de Nava, *Spain* 34 C6
Paren, *Russia* 51 C17
Parent, *Canada* 102 C5
Parent, L., *Canada* 102 C4
Parentis-en-Born, *France* 20 D2
Parepare, *Indonesia* 63 E5
Parfino, *Russia* 46 D6
Párga, *Greece* 38 B2
Pargo, Pta. do, *Madeira* 37 D2
Pariaguán, *Venezuela* 124 B6
Paricutín, Cerro, *Mexico* 118 D4
Parigi, *Indonesia* 63 E6
Parika, *Guyana* 124 B7
Parikkala, *Finland* 46 B5
Parima, Serra, *Brazil* 124 C6
Parinari, *Peru* 124 D4
Pariñas, Pta., *S. Amer.* 122 D2
Parincea, *Romania* 43 D12
Parintins, *Brazil* 125 D7
Pariparit Kyun, *Burma* 67 M18
Paris, *Canada* 110 C4
Paris, *France* 19 D9
Paris, *Idaho, U.S.A.* 114 E8
Paris, *Ky., U.S.A.* 108 F3
Paris, *Tenn., U.S.A.* 109 G1
Paris, *Tex., U.S.A.* 113 J7
Paris, Ville de □, *France* 19 D9
Parish, *U.S.A.* 111 C8
Parishville, *U.S.A.* 111 B10
Park, *U.S.A.* 116 B4
Park City, *U.S.A.* 113 G6
Park Falls, *U.S.A.* 112 C9
Park Head, *Canada* 110 B3
Park Hills, *U.S.A.* 113 G9
Park Range, *U.S.A.* 114 G10
Park Rapids, *U.S.A.* 112 B7
Park River, *U.S.A.* 112 A6
Park Rynie, *S. Africa* 89 E5
Parkå Bandar, *Iran* 71 E8
Parkano, *Finland* 9 E20
Parker, *Ariz., U.S.A.* 117 L12
Parker, *Pa., U.S.A.* 110 E5
Parker Dam, *U.S.A.* 117 L12
Parkersburg, *U.S.A.* 108 F5
Parkfield, *U.S.A.* 116 K6
Parkhill, *Canada* 110 C3
Parkland, *U.S.A.* 116 C4
Parkston, *U.S.A.* 112 D6
Parksville, *Canada* 104 D4
Parla, *Spain* 34 E7
Pârliţa, *Moldova* 43 C12
Parma, *Italy* 28 D7
Parma, *Idaho, U.S.A.* 114 E5
Parma, *Ohio, U.S.A.* 110 E3
Parma ➤, *Italy* 28 D7
Parnaguá, *Brazil* 125 F10
Parnaíba, *Brazil* 125 D10
Parnaíba ➤, *Brazil* 122 D6
Parnassós, *Greece* 38 C4
Párnis, *Greece* 38 C5
Párnon Óros, *Greece* 38 D4
Pärnu, *Estonia* 9 G21
Páros, *Greece* 39 D7
Parowan, *U.S.A.* 115 H7
Parpaillon, *France* 21 D10
Parral, *Chile* 126 D1
Parras, *Mexico* 118 B4
Parrett ➤, *U.K.* 13 F4
Parris I., *U.S.A.* 109 J5
Parrsboro, *Canada* 103 C7
Parry I., *Canada* 110 A4
Parry Is., *Canada* 4 B2
Parry Sound, *Canada* 102 C4
Parsberg, *Germany* 25 F7
Parsęta ➤, *Poland* 44 D2
Parsnip ➤, *Canada* 104 B4
Parsons, *U.S.A.* 113 G7
Parsons Ra., *Australia* 94 A2
Partanna, *Italy* 30 E5
Parthenay, *France* 18 F6
Partinico, *Italy* 30 D6
Partizánske, *Slovak Rep.* 27 C11
Partridge I., *Canada* 102 A2
Paru ➤, *Brazil* 125 D8
Parvān □, *Afghan.* 66 B6
Parvatipuram, *India* 67 K13
Parvatsar, *India* 68 F6
Päryd, *Sweden* 11 H9
Parys, *S. Africa* 88 D4
Pas-de-Calais □, *France* 19 B9
Pasada, *Spain* 34 B5
Pasadena, *Canada* 103 C8
Pasadena, *Calif., U.S.A.* 117 L8
Pasadena, *Tex., U.S.A.* 113 L7
Pasaje, *Argentina* 126 B3

Paşalimanı, Turkey	41	F11
Pasay, Phil.	61	D4
Pascagoula, U.S.A.	113	K10
Pascagoula →, U.S.A.	113	K10
Paşcani, Romania	43	C11
Pasco, U.S.A.	114	C4
Pasco, Cerro de, Peru	124	F3
Pasco I., Australia	92	D2
Pascoag, U.S.A.	111	E13
Pascua, I. de, Pac. Oc.	97	K17
Pasewalk, Germany	24	B9
Pasfield L., Canada	105	B7
Pasha →, Russia	46	B7
Pashmakli = Smolyan, Bulgaria	41	E8
Pasinler, Turkey	73	C9
Pasir Mas, Malaysia	65	J4
Pasir Putih, Malaysia	65	K4
Pasirian, Indonesia	63	H15
Pasirkuning, Indonesia	62	E2
Påskallavik, Sweden	11	G10
Paskūh, Iran	71	E9
Pasłęk, Poland	44	D6
Pasłęka →, Poland	44	D6
Pasley, C., Australia	93	F3
Pašman, Croatia	29	E12
Pasni, Pakistan	66	G3
Paso Cantinela, Mexico	117	N11
Paso de Indios, Argentina	128	E3
Paso de los Libres, Argentina	126	B4
Paso de los Toros, Uruguay	126	C4
Paso Robles, U.S.A.	115	J3
Paspébiac, Canada	103	C6
Pasrur, Pakistan	68	C6
Passage West, Ireland	15	E3
Passaic, U.S.A.	111	F10
Passau, Germany	25	G9
Passero, C., Italy	31	F8
Passo Fundo, Brazil	127	B5
Passos, Brazil	125	H9
Passow, Germany	24	B10
Passy, France	21	C10
Pastavy, Belarus	9	J22
Pastaza →, Peru	124	D3
Pasto, Colombia	124	C3
Pastrana, Spain	32	E2
Pasuruan, Indonesia	63	G15
Pasym, Poland	44	E7
Pásztó, Hungary	42	C4
Patagonia, Argentina	122	H4
Patagonia, U.S.A.	115	L8
Patambar, Iran	71	D9
Patan, Gujarat, India	66	H8
Patan, Maharashtra, India	68	H5
Patani, Indonesia	63	D7
Pătârlagele, Romania	43	E11
Pataudi, India	68	E7
Patchogue, U.S.A.	111	F11
Patea, N.Z.	91	H5
Pategi, Nigeria	83	D6
Patensie, S. Africa	88	E3
Paterna, Spain	33	F4
Paternion, Austria	26	E6
Paternò, Italy	31	E7
Pateros, U.S.A.	114	B4
Paterson, U.S.A.	111	F10
Paterson Ra., Australia	92	D3
Pathankot, India	68	C6
Pathfinder Reservoir, U.S.A.	114	E10
Pathiu, Thailand	65	G2
Pathum Thani, Thailand	64	E3
Pati, Indonesia	63	G14
Patía →, Colombia	124	C3
Patiala, Punjab, India	68	D7
Patiala, Ut. P., India	69	F8
Patine Kouka, Senegal	82	C2
Patitírion, Greece	38	B5
Patkai Bum, India	67	F19
Pátmos, Greece	39	D8
Patna, India	69	G11
Patnos, Turkey	73	C10
Pato Branco, Brazil	127	B5
Patonga, Uganda	86	B3
Patos, Albania	40	F3
Patos, Brazil	125	E11
Patos, L. dos, Brazil	127	C5
Patos, Río de los →, Argentina	126	C2
Patos de Minas, Brazil	125	G9
Patquía, Argentina	126	C2
Pátrai, Greece	38	C3
Pátraikós Kólpos, Greece	38	C3
Patras = Pátrai, Greece	38	C3
Patrocínio, Brazil	125	G9
Patta, Kenya	86	C5
Pattada, Italy	30	B2
Pattani, Thailand	65	J3
Pattaya, Thailand	64	F3
Patten, U.S.A.	109	C11
Patterson, Calif., U.S.A.	116	H5
Patterson, La., U.S.A.	113	L9
Patterson, Mt., U.S.A.	116	G7
Patti, Punjab, India	68	D6
Patti, Ut. P., India	69	G10
Patti, Italy	31	D7
Pattoki, Pakistan	68	D5
Patton, U.S.A.	110	F6
Patuakhali, Bangla.	67	H17
Patuanak, Canada	105	B7
Patuca →, Honduras	120	C3
Patuca, Punta, Honduras	120	C3
Pătulele, Romania	42	F7
Pátzcuaro, Mexico	118	D4
Pau, France	20	E3
Pau, Gave de →, France	20	E2
Pauillac, France	20	C3
Pauk, Burma	67	J19
Paul I., Canada	103	A7
Paul Smiths, U.S.A.	111	B10
Paulatuk, Canada	100	B7
Paulhan, France	20	E7
Paulis = Isiro, Dem. Rep. of the Congo	86	B2
Paulistana, Brazil	125	E10
Paulo Afonso, Brazil	125	E11
Paulpietersburg, S. Africa	89	D5
Pauls Valley, U.S.A.	113	H6
Pauma Valley, U.S.A.	117	M10
Pauri, India	69	D8
Pāveh, Iran	70	C5
Pavelets, Russia	46	F10
Pavia, Italy	28	C6
Pavilion, U.S.A.	110	D6
Pavilly, France	18	C7
Pāvilosta, Latvia	9	H19
Pavlikeni, Bulgaria	41	C9
Pavlodar, Kazakstan	50	D8
Pavlograd = Pavlohrad, Ukraine	47	H8
Pavlohrad, Ukraine	47	H8
Pavlovo, Russia	48	C6
Pavlovsk, Russia	48	E5
Pavlovskaya, Russia	49	G4
Pavlovskiy-Posad, Russia	46	E10
Pavullo nel Frignano, Italy	28	D7
Pawayan, India	69	E9
Pawhuska, U.S.A.	113	G6
Pawling, U.S.A.	111	E11
Pawnee, U.S.A.	113	G6
Pawnee City, U.S.A.	112	E6
Pawtucket, U.S.A.	111	E13
Paximádhia, Greece	36	E6
Paxoí, Greece	38	B2
Paxton, Ill., U.S.A.	108	E1
Paxton, Nebr., U.S.A.	112	E4
Payakumbuh, Indonesia	62	E2
Payerne, Switz.	25	J2
Payette, U.S.A.	114	D5
Paymogo, Spain	35	H3
Payne Bay = Kangirsuk, Canada	101	B13
Payne L., Canada	101	C12
Paynes Find, Australia	93	E2
Paynesville, Liberia	82	D2
Paynesville, U.S.A.	112	C7
Pays de la Loire □, France	18	E6
Paysandú, Uruguay	126	C4
Payson, U.S.A.	115	J8
Paz →, Guatemala	120	D1
Paz, B. de la, Mexico	118	C2
Pāzanān, Iran	71	D6
Pazar, Turkey	73	B9
Pazarcık, Turkey	72	D7
Pazardzhik, Bulgaria	41	D8
Pazarköy, Turkey	39	B9
Pazarlar, Turkey	39	C11
Pazaryeri, Turkey	39	B11
Pazaryolu, Turkey	73	B9
Pazin, Croatia	29	C10
Pčinja →, Macedonia	40	E5
Pe Ell, U.S.A.	116	D3
Peabody, U.S.A.	111	D14
Peace →, Canada	104	B6
Peace Point, Canada	104	B6
Peace River, Canada	104	B5
Peach Springs, U.S.A.	115	J7
Peachland, U.S.A.	104	D5
Peachtree City, U.S.A.	109	J3
Peak, The = Kinder Scout, U.K.	12	D6
Peak District, U.K.	12	D6
Peak Hill, Australia	93	E2
Peak Ra., Australia	94	C4
Peake Cr. →, Australia	95	D2
Peal de Becerro, Spain	35	H7
Peale, Mt., U.S.A.	115	G9
Pearblossom, U.S.A.	117	L9
Pearl →, U.S.A.	113	K10
Pearl City, U.S.A.	106	H16
Pearl Harbor, U.S.A.	106	H16
Pearl River, U.S.A.	111	E10
Pearsall, U.S.A.	113	L5
Peary Land, Greenland	4	A6
Pease →, U.S.A.	113	H5
Peawanuck, Canada	101	C11
Pebane, Mozam.	87	F4
Pebas, Peru	124	D4
Pebble Beach, U.S.A.	116	J5
Peć, Kosovo, Yug.	40	D4
Péccioli, Italy	28	E7
Pechea, Romania	43	E12
Pechenga, Russia	50	C4
Pechenizhyn, Ukraine	47	H3
Pechiguera, Pta., Canary Is.	37	F6
Pechnezhskoye Vdkhr., Ukraine	47	G9
Pechora, Russia	50	C6
Pechora →, Russia	50	C6
Pechorskaya Guba, Russia	50	C6
Pecica, Romania	42	D6
Pecka, Serbia, Yug.	40	B3
Pécora, C., Italy	30	C1
Pečory, Russia	9	H22
Pecos, U.S.A.	113	K3
Pecos →, U.S.A.	113	L3
Pécs, Hungary	42	D3
Pedder, L., Australia	94	G4
Peddie, S. Africa	89	E4
Pedernales, Dom. Rep.	121	C5
Pedernales →, U.S.A.	113	K5
Pedieos →, Cyprus	36	D12
Pedirka, Australia	95	D2
Pedra Azul, Brazil	125	G10
Pedreguer, Spain	33	G5
Pedreiras, Brazil	125	D10
Pedro Afonso, Brazil	125	E9
Pedro Cays, Jamaica	120	C4
Pedro de Valdivia, Chile	126	A2
Pedro Juan Caballero, Paraguay	127	A4
Pedro Muñoz, Spain	35	F8
Pedrógão Grande, Portugal	34	F2
Pee Dee →, U.S.A.	109	J6
Peebles, U.K.	14	F5
Peekskill, U.S.A.	111	E11
Peel, U.K.	12	C3
Peel →, Canada	100	B6
Peel Sound, Canada	100	A10
Peene →, Germany	24	A9
Peera Peera Poolanna L., Australia	95	D2
Peerless Lake, Canada	104	B6
Peers, Canada	104	C5
Pegasus Bay, N.Z.	91	K4
Peggau, Austria	26	D5
Pegnitz, Germany	25	F7
Pegnitz →, Germany	25	F6
Pego, Spain	33	G4
Pegu, Burma	67	L20
Pegu Yoma, Burma	67	K20
Pehčevo, Macedonia	40	E6
Pehlivanköy, Turkey	41	E10
Pehuajó, Argentina	126	D3
Peine, Chile	126	A2
Peine, Germany	24	C6
Peip'ing = Beijing, China	56	E9
Peipus, L. = Chudskoye, Ozero, Russia	9	G22
Peissenberg, Germany	25	H7
Peitz, Germany	24	D10
Peixe, Brazil	125	F9
Peixe →, Brazil	125	H8
Pek →, Serbia, Yug.	40	B5
Pekalongan, Indonesia	62	F3
Pekan, Malaysia	65	L4
Pekanbaru, Indonesia	62	D2
Pekang, Taiwan	59	F13
Pekin, U.S.A.	112	E10
Peking = Beijing, China	56	E9
Péla, Guinea	82	D3
Pelabuhan Kelang, Malaysia	65	L3
Pelabuhan Ratu, Teluk, Indonesia	63	G12
Pelabuhanratu, Indonesia	63	G12
Pélagos, Greece	38	B6
Pelaihari, Indonesia	62	E4
Pelat, Mt., France	21	D10
Pełczyce, Poland	45	E2
Peleaga, Vf., Romania	42	E7
Pelée, Mt., Martinique	121	D7
Pelee, Pt., Canada	102	D3
Pelee I., Canada	102	D3
Pelekech, Kenya	86	B4
Peleng, Indonesia	63	E6
Pélézi, Ivory C.	82	D3
Pelhřimov, Czech Rep.	26	B8
Pelican, U.S.A.	104	B1
Pelican L., Canada	105	C8
Pelican Narrows, Canada	105	B8
Pelješac, Croatia	29	F14
Pelkosenniemi, Finland	8	C22
Pella, Greece	40	F6
Pella, S. Africa	88	D2
Pella, U.S.A.	112	E8
Péla □, Greece	40	F6
Pello, Finland	8	C21
Pellworm, Germany	24	A4
Pelly →, Canada	100	B6
Pelly Bay, Canada	101	B11
Peloponnese = Pelopónnisos □, Greece	38	D4
Pelopónnisos □, Greece	38	D4
Peloritani, Monti, Italy	31	D8
Pelorus Sd., N.Z.	91	J4
Pelotas, Brazil	127	C5
Pelotas →, Brazil	127	B5
Pelovo, Bulgaria	41	C8
Pelplin, Poland	44	E5
Pelvoux, Massif du, France	21	D10
Pemalang, Indonesia	63	G13
Pemanggil, Pulau, Malaysia	65	L5
Pematangsiantar, Indonesia	62	D1
Pemba, Mozam.	87	E5
Pemba, Zambia	87	F2
Pemba Channel, Tanzania	86	D4
Pemba I., Tanzania	86	D4
Pemberton, Australia	93	F2
Pemberton, Canada	104	C4
Pembina, U.S.A.	112	A6
Pembroke, Canada	102	C4
Pembroke, U.K.	13	F3
Pembrokeshire □, U.K.	13	F3
Pen-y-Ghent, U.K.	12	C5
Peña, Sierra de la, Spain	32	C4
Peña de Francia, Sierra de la, Spain	34	E4
Peñafiel, Portugal	34	D2
Peñafiel, Spain	34	D6
Peñaflor, Spain	35	H5
Peñalara, Spain	34	E7
Penamacôr, Portugal	34	E3
Penang = Pinang, Malaysia	65	K3
Penápolis, Brazil	127	A6
Peñaranda de Bracamonte, Spain	34	E5
Peñarroya, Spain	32	E4
Peñarroya-Pueblonuevo, Spain	35	G5
Penarth, U.K.	13	F4
Peñas, C. de, Spain	34	B5
Peñas, G. de, Chile	122	H3
Peñas de San Pedro, Spain	33	G3
Peñas del Chache, Canary Is.	37	F6
Peñausende, Spain	34	D5
Pench'i = Benxi, China	57	D12
Pend Oreille →, U.S.A.	114	B5
Pend Oreille, L., U.S.A.	114	C5
Pendálofon, Greece	40	F5
Pendembu, Eastern, S. Leone	82	D2
Pendembu, Northern, S. Leone	82	D2
Pender B., Australia	92	C3
Pendik, Turkey	41	F13
Pendjari →, Benin	83	C5
Pendleton, U.S.A.	114	D4
Pendra, India	69	H9
Penedo, Brazil	125	F11
Penetanguishene, Canada	102	D4
Penfield, U.S.A.	110	E6
Pengalengan, Indonesia	63	G12
Penge, Kasai-Or., Dem. Rep. of the Congo	86	D1
Penge, Sud-Kivu, Dem. Rep. of the Congo	86	C2
Penghu, Taiwan	59	F12
Penglai, China	57	F11
Pengshan, China	58	B4
Pengshui, China	58	C7
Penguin, Australia	94	G4
Pengxi, China	58	B5
Pengze, China	59	C11
Penhalonga, Zimbabwe	87	F3
Peniche, Portugal	35	F1
Penicuik, U.K.	14	F5
Penida, Indonesia	62	F5
Peninnes, Alpes = Pennine, Alpi, Alps	25	J3
Peninsular Malaysia □, Malaysia	65	L4
Peñíscola, Spain	32	E5
Penitente, Serra do, Brazil	125	E9
Penkridge, U.K.	12	E5
Penmarch, France	18	E2
Penmarch, Pte. de, France	18	E2
Penn Hills, U.S.A.	110	F5
Penn Yan, U.S.A.	110	D7
Penna, Punta della, Italy	29	F11
Pennant, Canada	105	C7
Penne, Italy	29	F10
Penner →, India	66	M12
Pennine, Alpi, Alps	25	J3
Pennines, U.K.	12	C5
Pennington, U.S.A.	116	F5
Pennington →, Nigeria	83	E6
Pennino, Mte., Italy	29	E9
Pennsburg, U.S.A.	111	F9
Pennsylvania □, U.S.A.	108	E7
Penny, Canada	104	C4
Peno, Russia	46	D7
Penobscot →, U.S.A.	109	C11
Penobscot B., U.S.A.	109	C11
Penong, Australia	93	F5
Penonomé, Panama	120	E3
Penrith, Australia	93	E5
Penrith, U.K.	12	C5
Penryn, U.K.	13	G2
Pensacola, U.S.A.	109	K2
Pensacola Mts., Antarctica	5	E1
Pense, Canada	105	C8
Penticton, Canada	104	D5
Pentland, Australia	94	C4
Pentland Firth, U.K.	14	C5
Pentland Hills, U.K.	14	F5
Penza, Russia	48	D7
Penzance, U.K.	13	G2
Penzberg, Germany	25	H7
Penzhino, Russia	51	C17
Penzhinskaya Guba, Russia	51	C17
Penzhou, China	58	B4
Penzlin, Germany	24	B9
Peoria, Ariz., U.S.A.	115	K7
Peoria, Ill., U.S.A.	112	E10
Pepacton Reservoir, U.S.A.	111	D10
Pepani →, S. Africa	88	D3
Pepel, S. Leone	82	D2
Peqin, Albania	40	E3
Pera Hd., Australia	94	A3
Perabumulih, Indonesia	62	E2
Perak →, Malaysia	65	K3
Perakhóra, Greece	38	C4
Perales de Alfambra, Spain	32	E4
Perales del Puerto, Spain	34	E4
Pérama, Kérkira, Greece	36	A3
Pérama, Kríti, Greece	36	D6
Peräpohjola, Finland	8	C22
Perast, Montenegro, Yug.	40	D2
Percé, Canada	103	C7
Perche, France	18	D8
Perchtoldsdorf, Austria	27	C9
Percival Lakes, Australia	92	D4
Percy, France	18	D5
Percy Is., Australia	94	C5
Perdido, Mte., Spain	32	C5
Perdu, Mt. = Perdido, Mte., Spain	32	C5
Pereira, Colombia	124	C3
Perelazovskiy, Russia	49	F6
Perenjori, Australia	93	E2
Peresecina, Moldova	43	C13
Pereslavl-Zalesskiy, Russia	46	D10
Peretu, Romania	43	F10
Pereyaslav-Khmelnytskyy, Ukraine	47	G6
Perg, Austria	26	C7
Pergamino, Argentina	126	C3
Pergau →, Malaysia	65	K3
Pérgine Valsugana, Italy	29	B8
Pérgola, Italy	29	E9
Perham, U.S.A.	112	B7
Perhentian, Kepulauan, Malaysia	62	C2
Periam, Romania	42	D5
Péribonca →, Canada	103	C5
Péribonca, L., Canada	103	B5
Perico, Argentina	126	A2
Pericos, Mexico	118	B3
Périers, France	18	C5
Périgord, France	20	D4
Périgueux, France	20	C4
Perijá, Sierra de, Colombia	124	B4
Peristéra, Greece	38	B5
Peristerona →, Cyprus	36	D12
Perito Moreno, Argentina	128	F2
Perivol = Dragovishtitsa, Bulgaria	40	D6
Perkasie, U.S.A.	111	F9
Perković, Croatia	29	E13
Perlas, Arch. de las, Panama	120	E4
Perlas, Punta de, Nic.	120	D3
Perleberg, Germany	24	B7
Perlez, Serbia, Yug.	42	E5
Perm, Russia	50	D6
Përmet, Albania	40	F4
Pernambuco = Recife, Brazil	125	E12
Pernambuco □, Brazil	125	E11
Pernik, Bulgaria	40	D7
Peron Is., Australia	92	B5
Peron Pen., Australia	93	E1
Péronne, France	19	C9
Perosa Argentina, Italy	28	D4
Perow, Canada	104	C3
Perpendicular Pt., Australia	95	E5
Perpignan, France	20	F6
Perris, U.S.A.	117	M9
Perros-Guirec, France	18	D3
Perry, Fla., U.S.A.	109	K4
Perry, Ga., U.S.A.	109	J4
Perry, Iowa, U.S.A.	112	E7
Perry, Okla., U.S.A.	113	G6
Perryton, U.S.A.	113	G4
Perryville, U.S.A.	113	G10
Persan, France	19	C9
Persberg, Sweden	10	E8
Persepolis, Iran	71	D7
Perşembe, Turkey	72	B7
Pershotravensk, Ukraine	47	G4
Persia = Iran ■, Asia	71	C7
Persian Gulf = Gulf, The, Asia	71	E6
Perstorp, Sweden	11	H7
Pertek, Turkey	73	C8
Perth, Australia	93	F2
Perth, Canada	102	D4
Perth, U.K.	14	E5
Perth & Kinross □, U.K.	14	E5
Perth Amboy, U.S.A.	111	F10
Perth-Andover, Canada	103	C6
Pertuis, France	21	E9
Pertusato, C., France	21	G13
Peru, Ind., U.S.A.	108	E2
Peru, N.Y., U.S.A.	111	B11
Peru ■, S. Amer.	124	D4
Peru Basin, Pac. Oc.	97	J18
Peru-Chile Trench, Pac. Oc.	124	G3
Perúgia, Italy	29	E9
Perušić, Croatia	29	D12
Pervomaysk, Russia	48	C6
Pervomaysk, Ukraine	47	H6
Pervouralsk, Russia	50	D6
Pésaro, Italy	29	E9
Pescadores = Penghu, Taiwan	59	F12
Pescara, Italy	29	F11
Pescara →, Italy	29	F11
Peschanokopskoye, Russia	49	G5
Péscia, Italy	28	E7
Pescina, Italy	29	F10
Peshawar, Pakistan	68	B4
Peshkopi, Albania	40	E4
Peshtera, Bulgaria	41	D8
Peshtigo, U.S.A.	108	C2
Peski, Russia	48	E6
Pêso da Régua, Portugal	34	D3
Pesqueira, Brazil	125	E11
Pessac, France	20	D3
Pest □, Hungary	42	C4
Pestovo, Russia	46	C9
Pestravka, Russia	48	D9
Péta, Greece	38	B3
Petah Tiqwa, Israel	75	C3
Petaling Jaya, Malaysia	65	L3
Petaloudhes, Greece	36	C10
Petaluma, U.S.A.	116	G4
Pétange, Lux.	17	E5
Petaro, Pakistan	68	G3
Petatlán, Mexico	118	D4
Petauke, Zambia	87	E3
Petawawa, Canada	102	C4
Petén Itzá, L., Guatemala	120	C2
Peter I.s Øy, Antarctica	5	C16
Peter Pond L., Canada	105	B7
Peterbell, Canada	102	C3
Peterborough, Australia	95	E2
Peterborough, U.K.	13	E7
Peterborough, U.S.A.	111	D13
Peterborough □, U.K.	13	E7
Peterculter, U.K.	14	D6
Peterhead, U.K.	14	D7
Peterlee, U.K.	12	C6
Petermann Bjerg, Greenland	98	B17
Petermann Ranges, Australia	93	E4
Petersburg, Alaska, U.S.A.	100	C6
Petersburg, Pa., U.S.A.	110	F6
Petersburg, Va., U.S.A.	108	G7
Petersburg, W. Va., U.S.A.	108	F6
Petersfield, U.K.	13	F7
Petershagen, Germany	24	C4
Petília Policastro, Italy	31	C9
Petit Goâve, Haiti	121	C5
Petit Jardin, Canada	103	C8
Petit Lac Manicouagan, Canada	103	B6

Petit-Mécatina ➤, Canada 103 B8
Petit-Mécatina, I. du, Canada .. 103 B8
Petit Saint Bernard, Col du, Italy 21 C10
Petitcodiac, Canada 103 C6
Petite Baleine ➤, Canada 102 A4
Petite Saguenay, Canada 103 C5
Petitot ➤, Canada 104 A4
Petitsikapau L., Canada 103 B6
Petlad, India 68 H5
Peto, Mexico 119 C7
Petone, N.Z. 91 J5
Petorca, Chile 126 C1
Petoskey, U.S.A. 108 C3
Petra, Jordan 75 E4
Petra, Spain 37 B10
Petra, Ostrova, Russia 4 B13
Petra Velikogo, Zaliv, Russia .. 54 C6
Petrel = Petrer, Spain 33 G4
Petrella, Monte, Italy 30 A6
Petrer, Spain 33 G4
Petreto-Bicchisano, France 21 G12
Petrich, Bulgaria 40 E7
Petrified Forest National Park,
    U.S.A. 115 J9
Petrijanec, Croatia 29 B13
Petrikov = Pyetrikaw, Belarus . 47 F5
Petrila, Romania 43 E8
Petrinja, Croatia 29 C13
Petrodvorets, Russia 46 C5
Petrograd = Sankt-Peterburg,
    Russia 46 C6
Petrolândia, Brazil 125 E11
Petrolia, Canada 102 D3
Petrolina, Brazil 125 E10
Petropavl, Kazakstan 50 D7
Petropavlovsk = Petropavl,
    Kazakstan 50 D7
Petropavlovsk-Kamchatskiy,
    Russia 51 D16
Petropavlovskiy = Akhtubinsk,
    Russia 49 F8
Petrópolis, Brazil 127 A7
Petroşani, Romania 43 E8
Petrova Gora, Croatia 29 C12
Petrovac, Montenegro, Yug. ... 40 D2
Petrovac, Serbia, Yug. 40 B5
Petrovaradin, Serbia, Yug. 42 E4
Petrovsk, Russia 48 D7
Petrovsk-Zabaykalskiy, Russia . 51 D11
Petrovskaya, Russia 47 K9
Petrovskoye = Svetlograd,
    Russia 49 H6
Petrozavodsk, Russia 46 B8
Petrus Steyn, S. Africa 89 D4
Petrusburg, S. Africa 88 D4
Petzeck, Austria 26 E5
Peumo, Chile 126 C1
Peureulak, Indonesia 62 D1
Pevek, Russia 51 C18
Peveragno, Italy 28 D4
Peyrehorade, France 20 E2
Peyruis, France 21 D9
Pézenas, France 20 E7
Pezinok, Slovak Rep. 27 C10
Pfaffenhofen, Germany 25 G7
Pfarrkirchen, Germany 25 G8
Pfeffenhausen, Germany 25 G7
Pforzheim, Germany 25 G4
Pfullendorf, Germany 25 H5
Pfungstadt, Germany 25 F4
Phagwara, India 66 D9
Phaistós, Greece 36 D6
Phala, Botswana 88 C4
Phalera = Phulera, India 68 F6
Phalodi, India 68 F5
Phalsbourg, France 19 D14
Phan, Thailand 64 C2
Phan Rang, Vietnam 65 G7
Phan Ri = Hoa Da, Vietnam .. 65 G7
Phan Thiet, Vietnam 65 G7
Phanae, Greece 39 C7
Phanat Nikhom, Thailand 64 F3
Phangan, Ko, Thailand 65 H3
Phangnga, Thailand 65 H2
Phanom Sarakham, Thailand .. 64 F3
Phaphund, India 69 F8
Pharenda, India 69 F10
Pharr, U.S.A. 113 M5
Phatthalung, Thailand 65 J3
Phayao, Thailand 64 C2
Phelps, U.S.A. 110 D7
Phelps L., Canada 105 B8
Phenix City, U.S.A. 109 J3
Phet Buri, Thailand 64 F2
Phetchabun, Thailand 64 D3
Phetchabun, Thiu Khao,
    Thailand 64 E3
Phetchaburi = Phet Buri,
    Thailand 64 F2
Phi Phi, Ko, Thailand 65 J2
Phiafay, Laos 64 E6
Phibun Mangsahan, Thailand .. 64 E5
Phichai, Thailand 64 D3
Phichit, Thailand 64 D3
Philadelphia, Miss., U.S.A. ... 113 J10
Philadelphia, N.Y., U.S.A. 111 B9
Philadelphia, Pa., U.S.A. 111 G9
Philip, U.S.A. 112 C4
Philippeville, Belgium 17 D4
Philippi, Greece 41 E8
Philippi, U.S.A. 108 F5
Philippi L., Australia 94 C2
Philippines ■, Asia 61 H6
Philippolis, S. Africa 88 E4
Philippopolis = Plovdiv, Bulgaria 41 D8
Philipsburg, Canada 111 A11

Philipsburg, Mont., U.S.A. 114 C7
Philipsburg, Pa., U.S.A. 110 F6
Philipstown = Daingean, Ireland 15 C4
Philipstown, S. Africa 88 E3
Phillips, U.S.A. 112 C9
Phillipsburg, Kans., U.S.A. ... 112 F5
Phillipsburg, N.J., U.S.A. 111 F9
Philmont, U.S.A. 111 D11
Philomath, U.S.A. 114 D2
Phimai, Thailand 64 E4
Phitsanulok, Thailand 64 D3
Phnom Dangrek, Thailand 62 B2
Phnom Penh, Cambodia 65 G5
Phnom Penh = Phnom Penh,
    Cambodia 65 G5
Phoenicia, U.S.A. 111 D10
Phoenix, Ariz., U.S.A. 115 K7
Phoenix, N.Y., U.S.A. 111 C8
Phoenix Is., Kiribati 96 H10
Phoenixville, U.S.A. 111 F9
Phon, Thailand 64 E4
Phon Tiou, Laos 64 D5
Phong ➤, Thailand 64 D4
Phong Saly, Laos 58 G4
Phong Tho, Vietnam 58 A4
Phonhong, Laos 64 C4
Phonum, Thailand 65 H2
Phosphate Hill, Australia 94 C2
Photharam, Thailand 64 F2
Phra Nakhon Si Ayutthaya,
    Thailand 64 E3
Phra Thong, Ko, Thailand 65 H2
Phrae, Thailand 64 C3
Phrom Phiram, Thailand 64 D3
Phrygia, Turkey 72 C4
Phu Dien, Vietnam 64 C5
Phu Loi, Laos 64 B4
Phu Ly, Vietnam 58 G5
Phu Quoc, Dao, Vietnam 65 G4
Phu Tho, Vietnam 58 G5
Phuc Yen, Vietnam 58 G5
Phuket, Thailand 65 J2
Phuket, Ko, Thailand 65 J2
Phul, India 68 D6
Phulad, India 68 G5
Phulchari, Bangla. 69 G13
Phulera, India 68 F6
Phulpur, India 69 G10
Phun Phin, Thailand 65 H2
Piacenza, Italy 28 C6
Pian Cr. ➤, Australia 95 E4
Piana, France 21 F12
Pianella, Italy 29 F11
Pianosa, Puglia, Italy 29 F12
Pianosa, Toscana, Italy 28 F7
Piapot, Canada 105 D7
Pias, Portugal 35 G3
Piaseczno, Poland 45 F8
Piaski, Poland 45 G9
Piastów, Poland 45 F7
Piatra, Romania 43 G8
Piatra Neamţ, Romania 43 D11
Piatra Olt, Romania 43 F9
Piauí □, Brazil 125 E10
Piauí ➤, Brazil 125 E10
Piave ➤, Italy 29 C9
Piazza Ármerina, Italy 31 E7
Pibor ➤, Sudan 81 F3
Pibor Post, Sudan 81 F3
Picardie, France 19 C10
Picardie, Plaine de, France ... 19 C9
Picardy = Picardie, France ... 19 C10
Picayune, U.S.A. 113 K10
Picerno, Italy 31 B8
Pichhor, India 69 G8
Pichilemu, Chile 126 C1
Pichor, India 68 G8
Pickerel L., Canada 102 C1
Pickering, U.K. 12 C7
Pickering, Vale of, U.K. 12 C7
Pickle L., Canada 102 B1
Pickwick L., U.S.A. 109 H1
Pico Truncado, Argentina ... 128 F3
Picos, Brazil 125 E10
Picton, Canada 102 D4
Picton, N.Z. 91 J5
Pictou, Canada 103 C7
Picture Butte, Canada 104 D6
Picún Leufú, Argentina 128 D3
Pidurutalagala, Sri Lanka ... 66 R12
Piechowice, Poland 45 H2
Piedmont = Piemonte □, Italy . 28 D5
Piedmont, Ala., U.S.A. 109 J3
Piedmont, S.C., U.S.A. 107 D10
Piedmont Matese, Italy 31 A7
Piedra ➤, Spain 32 D3
Piedrabuena, Spain 35 G6
Piedrahita, Spain 34 E5
Piedralaves, Spain 34 E6
Piedras Blancas, Spain 34 B5
Piedras Negras, Mexico 118 B4
Piekary Śląskie, Poland 45 H5
Pieksämäki, Finland 9 E22
Piemonte □, Italy 28 D5
Pieniężno, Poland 44 D7
Pieńsk, Poland 45 G2
Piercefield, U.S.A. 111 B10
Pierceland, Canada 105 C7
Piéria □, Greece 40 F6
Pierpont, U.S.A. 110 E4
Pierre, U.S.A. 112 C4
Pierre-Buffière, France 20 C5
Pierre-de-Bresse, France 19 F12
Pierre E. Trudeau, Mt. = Logan,
    Mt., Canada 100 B5

Pierrefontaine-les-Varans,
    France 19 E13
Pierrefort, France 20 D6
Pierrelatte, France 21 D8
Pieštany, Slovak Rep. 27 C10
Piesting ➤, Austria 27 C9
Pieszyce, Poland 45 H3
Piet Retief, S. Africa 89 D5
Pietarsaari, Finland 8 E20
Pietermaritzburg, S. Africa ... 89 D5
Pietersburg, S. Africa 89 C4
Pietragalla, Italy 31 B8
Pietrasanta, Italy 28 E7
Pietroşiţa, Romania 43 E10
Pietrosul, Vf., Maramureş,
    Romania 43 C9
Pietrosul, Vf., Suceava, Romania 43 C10
Pieve di Cadore, Italy 29 B9
Pieve di Teco, Italy 28 D4
Pievepélago, Italy 28 D7
Pigadhítsa, Greece 40 G5
Pigeon L., Canada 110 B6
Piggott, U.S.A. 113 G9
Pigna, Italy 28 E4
Pigüe, Argentina 126 D3
Pihani, India 69 F9
Pihlajavesi, Finland 9 F23
Pijijiapan, Mexico 119 D6
Pikalevo, Russia 46 C8
Pikangikum Berens, Canada ... 105 C10
Pikes Peak, U.S.A. 112 F2
Piketberg, S. Africa 88 E2
Pikeville, U.S.A. 108 G4
Pikou, China 57 E12
Pikwitonei, Canada 105 B9
Piła, Poland 45 E3
Pila, Spain 33 G3
Pilaía, Greece 40 F6
Pilani, India 68 E6
Pilar, Paraguay 126 B4
Pilar de la Horadada, Spain ... 33 H4
Pilawa, Poland 45 G8
Pilaya ➤, Bolivia 124 H6
Pilbara, Australia 92 D2
Pilcomayo ➤, Paraguay 126 B4
Pilgrim's Rest, S. Africa 89 C5
Pilgrimstad, Sweden 10 B9
Píli, Greece 39 E9
Pilibhit, India 69 E8
Pilica ➤, Poland 45 G8
Pilion, Greece 38 B5
Pilis, Hungary 42 C4
Pilisvörösvár, Hungary 42 C3
Pilkhawa, India 68 E7
Pilliga, Australia 95 E4
Pílos, Greece 38 E3
Pilot Mound, Canada 105 D9
Pilot Point, U.S.A. 113 J6
Pilot Rock, U.S.A. 114 D4
Pilsen = Plzeň, Czech Rep. ... 26 B6
Pilštanj, Slovenia 29 B12
Piltene, Latvia 44 A8
Pilzno, Poland 45 J8
Pima, U.S.A. 115 K9
Pimenta Bueno, Brazil 124 F6
Pimentel, Peru 124 E3
Pina de Ebro, Spain 32 D4
Pinamalayan, Phil. 61 E4
Pinang, Malaysia 65 K3
Pinar, C. des, Spain 37 B10
Pinar del Río, Cuba 120 B3
Pınarbaşı, Çanakkale, Turkey . 39 B8
Pınarbaşı, Kayseri, Turkey 72 C7
Pınarhisar, Turkey 41 E11
Pinatubo, Mt., Phil. 61 D3
Pincehely, Hungary 42 D3
Pinchang, China 58 B6
Pincher Creek, Canada 104 D6
Pinchi L., Canada 104 C4
Pinckneyville, U.S.A. 112 F10
Pińczów, Poland 45 H7
Pindar, Australia 93 E2
Pindi Gheb, Pakistan 68 C5
Pindiga, Nigeria 83 D7
Pindos Óros, Greece 38 B3
Pindus Mts. = Pindos Óros,
    Greece 38 B3
Pine ➤, B.C., Canada 104 B4
Pine ➤, Sask., Canada 105 B7
Pine, C., Canada 103 C9
Pine Bluff, U.S.A. 113 H9
Pine Bluffs, U.S.A. 112 E2
Pine City, U.S.A. 112 C8
Pine Cr. ➤, U.S.A. 110 E7
Pine Creek, Australia 92 B5
Pine Falls, Canada 105 C9
Pine Flat Res., U.S.A. 116 J7
Pine Grove, U.S.A. 111 F8
Pine Pass, Canada 104 B4
Pine Point, Canada 104 A6
Pine Ridge, U.S.A. 112 D3
Pine River, Canada 105 C8
Pine Valley, U.S.A. 117 N10
Pinecrest, U.S.A. 116 G6
Pineda de Mar, Spain 32 D7
Pinedale, Calif., U.S.A. 116 J7
Pinedale, Wyo., U.S.A. 114 E9
Pinega ➤, Russia 50 C5
Pinehill, Australia 94 C4
Pinehouse L., Canada 105 B7
Pineimuta ➤, Canada 102 B1
Pinerolo, Italy 28 D4
Pineto, Italy 29 F11
Pinetop, U.S.A. 115 J9
Pinetown, S. Africa 89 D5

Pineville, U.S.A. 113 K8
Piney, France 19 D11
Ping ➤, Thailand 64 E3
Pingaring, Australia 93 F2
Pingba, China 58 D6
Pingbian, China 58 F4
Pingchuan, China 58 D3
Pingding, China 56 F7
Pingdingshan, China 56 H7
Pingdong, Taiwan 59 F13
Pingdu, China 57 F10
Pingelly, Australia 93 F2
Pingguo, China 58 F6
Pinghe, China 59 E11
Pinghu, China 59 B13
Pingjiang, China 59 C9
Pingle, China 59 E8
Pingli, China 58 A7
Pingliang, China 56 G4
Pinglu, China 56 E7
Pingluo, China 56 E4
Pingnan, Fujian, China 59 D12
Pingnan, Guangxi Zhuangzu,
    China 59 F8
Pingquan, China 57 D10
Pingrup, Australia 93 F2
Pingshan, China 58 C5
Pingtan, China 59 E12
Pingtang, China 58 E6
P'ingtung, Taiwan 59 F13
Pingwu, China 56 H3
Pingxiang, Guangxi Zhuangzu,
    China 58 F6
Pingxiang, Jiangxi, China ... 59 D9
Pingyao, China 56 F7
Pingyi, China 57 G9
Pingyin, China 56 F9
Pingyuan, Guangdong, China . 59 E10
Pingyuan, Shandong, China .. 56 F9
Pingyuanjie, China 58 F4
Pinhal, Brazil 127 A6
Pinhal Novo, Portugal 35 G2
Pinheiro, Brazil 125 D9
Pinheiro Machado, Brazil 127 C5
Pinhel, Portugal 34 E3
Pini, Indonesia 62 D1
Piniós ➤, Ilía, Greece 38 D3
Piniós ➤, Tríkkala, Greece .. 38 B4
Pinjarra, Australia 93 F2
Pink Mountain, Canada 104 B4
Pinkafeld, Austria 27 D9
Pinnacles, U.S.A. 116 J5
Pinneberg, Germany 24 B5
Pínnes, Ákra, Greece 41 F8
Pinon Hills, U.S.A. 117 L9
Pinos, Mexico 118 C4
Pinos, Mt., U.S.A. 117 L7
Pinos Pt., U.S.A. 115 H3
Pinos Puente, Spain 35 H7
Pinotepa Nacional, Mexico ... 119 D5
Pinrang, Indonesia 63 E5
Pins, Pte. aux, Canada 110 D3
Pinsk, Belarus 47 F4
Pintados, Chile 124 H5
Pinyang, China 59 D13
Pinyug, Russia 50 C5
Pioche, U.S.A. 115 H6
Piombino, Italy 28 F7
Piombino, Canale di, Italy ... 28 F7
Pioner, Ostrov, Russia 51 B10
Pionki, Poland 45 G8
Piorini, L., Brazil 124 D6
Piotrków Trybunalski, Poland . 45 G6
Piove di Sacco, Italy 29 C9
Pip, Iran 71 E9
Pipar, India 68 F5
Pipar Road, India 68 F5
Piparia, Mad. P., India 68 H8
Piparia, Mad. P., India 68 J7
Pipéri, Greece 38 B6
Pipestone, U.S.A. 112 D6
Pipestone ➤, Canada 102 B2
Pipestone Cr. ➤, Canada ... 105 D8
Piplan, Pakistan 68 C4
Piploda, India 68 H6
Pipmuacan, Rés., Canada ... 103 C5
Pippingarra, Australia 92 D2
Pipriac, France 18 E5
Piqua, U.S.A. 108 E3
Piquiri ➤, Brazil 127 A5
Pīr Sohrāb, Iran 71 E9
Pira, Benin 83 D5
Piracicaba, Brazil 127 A6
Piracuruca, Brazil 125 D10
Piræus = Piraiévs, Greece ... 38 D5
Piraiévs, Greece 38 D5
Pirajuí, Brazil 127 A6
Piram I., India 68 J5
Piran, Slovenia 29 C10
Pirané, Argentina 126 B4
Pirano = Piran, Slovenia 29 C10
Pirapora, Brazil 125 G10
Pirawa, India 68 G7
Pirdop, Bulgaria 41 D8
Pírgos, Ilía, Greece 38 D3
Pírgos, Kríti, Greece 39 F7
Pirgovo, Bulgaria 41 C9
Piribebuy, Paraguay 126 B4
Pirimapun, Indonesia 63 F9
Pirin Planina, Bulgaria 40 E7
Pírineos = Pyrénées, Europe . 20 F4
Piripiri, Brazil 125 D10
Pirmasens, Germany 25 F3
Pirna, Germany 24 E9
Pirot, Serbia, Yug. 40 C6
Piru, Indonesia 63 E7

Piru, U.S.A. 117 L8
Piryatin = Pyryatyn, Ukraine .. 47 G7
Piryí, Greece 39 C7
Pisa, Italy 28 E7
Pisa ➤, Poland 45 E8
Pisagne, Italy 28 C7
Pisagua, Chile 124 G4
Pisarovina, Croatia 29 C12
Pisco, Peru 124 F3
Piscu, Romania 43 E12
Písek, Czech Rep. 26 B7
Pishan, China 60 C2
Pishin, Iran 71 E9
Pishin, Pakistan 68 D2
Pishin Lora ➤, Pakistan 68 E1
Pisidia, Turkey 72 D4
Pising, Indonesia 63 F6
Pismo Beach, U.S.A. 117 K6
Pissila, Burkina Faso 83 C4
Pissis, Cerro, Argentina 126 B2
Pissos, France 20 D3
Pissouri, Cyprus 36 E11
Pisticci, Italy 31 B9
Pistóia, Italy 28 E7
Pistol B., Canada 105 A10
Pisuerga ➤, Spain 34 D6
Pisz, Poland 44 E8
Pit ➤, U.S.A. 114 F2
Pita, Guinea 82 C2
Pitcairn I., Pac. Oc. 97 K14
Pite älv ➤, Sweden 8 D19
Piteå, Sweden 8 D19
Piterka, Russia 48 E8
Piteşti, Romania 43 F9
Pithapuram, India 67 L13
Pithara, Australia 93 F2
Pithion, Greece 41 E10
Pithiviers, France 19 D9
Pithoragarh, India 69 E9
Pithoro, Pakistan 68 G3
Pitigliano, Italy 29 F8
Pitkyaranta, Russia 46 B6
Pitlochry, U.K. 14 E5
Pitsilia □, Cyprus 36 E12
Pitt I., Canada 104 C3
Pittsburg, Calif., U.S.A. 116 G5
Pittsburg, Kans., U.S.A. 113 G7
Pittsburg, Tex., U.S.A. 113 J7
Pittsburgh, U.S.A. 110 F5
Pittsfield, Ill., U.S.A. 112 F9
Pittsfield, Maine, U.S.A. 109 C11
Pittsfield, Mass., U.S.A. 111 D11
Pittsfield, N.H., U.S.A. 111 C13
Pittston, U.S.A. 111 E9
Pittsworth, Australia 95 D5
Pituri ➤, Australia 94 C2
Piura, Peru 124 E2
Piva ➤, Montenegro, Yug. ... 40 C2
Piwniczna, Poland 45 J7
Pixley, U.S.A. 116 K7
Piyai, Greece 38 B3
Pizarra, Spain 35 J6
Pizhou, China 56 G9
Pizzo, Italy 31 D9
Placentia, Canada 103 C9
Placentia B., Canada 103 C9
Placer, Masbate, Phil. 61 F5
Placer, Surigao N., Phil. 61 G6
Placerville, U.S.A. 116 G6
Placetas, Cuba 120 B4
Plačkovica, Macedonia 40 E6
Plainfield, N.J., U.S.A. 111 F10
Plainfield, Ohio, U.S.A. 110 F3
Plainfield, Vt., U.S.A. 111 B12
Plains, Mont., U.S.A. 114 C6
Plains, Tex., U.S.A. 113 J3
Plainview, Nebr., U.S.A. 112 D6
Plainview, Tex., U.S.A. 113 H4
Plainwell, U.S.A. 108 D3
Plaisance, France 20 E4
Plaistow, U.S.A. 111 D13
Pláka, Greece 39 B7
Pláka, Ákra, Greece 36 D8
Plakenska Planina, Macedonia . 40 E5
Planá, Czech Rep. 26 B5
Plana Cays, Bahamas 121 B5
Planada, U.S.A. 116 H6
Plancoët, France 18 D4
Plandište, Serbia, Yug. 42 E6
Plano, U.S.A. 113 J6
Plant City, U.S.A. 109 M4
Plaquemine, U.S.A. 113 K9
Plasencia, Spain 34 E4
Plaški, Croatia 29 C12
Plaster City, U.S.A. 117 N11
Plaster Rock, Canada 103 C6
Plastun, Russia 54 B8
Plasy, Czech Rep. 26 B6
Plata, Río de la, S. Amer. ... 126 C4
Plátani ➤, Italy 30 E6
Plátanos, Greece 36 D5
Plateau □, Nigeria 83 D6
Platí, Ákra, Greece 41 F8
Platte, U.S.A. 112 D5
Platte ➤, Mo., U.S.A. 112 F7
Platte ➤, Nebr., U.S.A. 112 E6
Platteville, U.S.A. 112 D9
Plattling, Germany 25 G8
Plattsburgh, U.S.A. 111 B11
Plattsmouth, U.S.A. 112 E7
Plau, Germany 24 B8
Plauen, Germany 24 E8
Plauer See, Germany 24 B8
Plav, Montenegro, Yug. 40 D3
Plavinas, Latvia 9 H21

Plavnica, Montenegro, Yug. ... 40 D3
Plavno, Croatia 29 D13
Plavsk, Russia 46 F9
Playa Blanca, Canary Is. 37 F6
Playa Blanca Sur, Canary Is. ... 37 F6
Playa de las Americas, Canary Is. 37 G4
Playa de Mogán, Canary Is. 37 G4
Playa del Inglés, Canary Is. ... 37 G4
Playa Esmerelda, Canary Is. ... 37 F5
Playgreen L., Canada 105 C9
Pleasant Bay, Canada 103 C7
Pleasant Hill, U.S.A. 116 H4
Pleasant Mount, U.S.A. 111 E9
Pleasanton, Calif., U.S.A. 116 H5
Pleasanton, Tex., U.S.A. 113 L5
Pleasantville, N.J., U.S.A. 108 F8
Pleasantville, Pa., U.S.A. 110 E5
Pléaux, France 20 C6
Plei Ku, Vietnam 64 F7
Plélan-le-Grand, France 18 D4
Pléneuf-Val-André, France ... 18 D4
Plenița, Romania 43 F8
Plenty →, Australia 94 C2
Plenty, B. of, N.Z. 91 G6
Plentywood, U.S.A. 112 A2
Plérin, France 18 D4
Plessisville, Canada 103 C5
Plestin-les-Grèves, France ... 18 D3
Pleszew, Poland 45 G4
Pleternica, Croatia 42 E2
Plétipi, L., Canada 103 B5
Pleven, Bulgaria 41 C8
Plevlja, Montenegro, Yug. 40 C3
Plevna, Canada 110 B8
Plješevica, Croatia 29 D12
Ploaghe, Italy 30 B1
Ploče, Croatia 29 E14
Płock, Poland 45 F6
Plöckenpass, Italy 29 B9
Plöckenstein, Germany 25 G9
Ploemeur, France 18 E3
Ploërmel, France 18 E4
Ploiești, Romania 43 F11
Plomárion, Greece 39 C8
Plombières-les-Bains, France .. 19 E13
Plomin, Croatia 29 C11
Plön, Germany 24 A6
Plonge, Lac la, Canada 105 B7
Płońsk, Poland 45 F7
Plopeni, Romania 43 E10
Plopișului, Munții, Romania ... 42 C7
Płoty, Poland 44 E2
Plouaret, France 18 D3
Plouay, France 18 E3
Ploučnice →, Czech Rep. 26 A7
Ploudalmézeau, France 18 D2
Plouescat, France 18 D2
Plougasnou, France 18 D3
Plougastel-Daoulas, France 18 D2
Plouguerneau, France 18 D2
Plouha, France 18 D4
Plouhinec, France 18 E2
Plovdiv, Bulgaria 41 D8
Plovdiv □, Bulgaria 41 D8
Plum, U.S.A. 110 F5
Plum I., U.S.A. 111 E12
Plumas, U.S.A. 116 F7
Plummer, U.S.A. 114 C5
Plumtree, Zimbabwe 87 G2
Plungė, Lithuania 9 J19
Pluvigner, France 18 E3
Plymouth, U.K. 13 G3
Plymouth, Calif., U.S.A. 116 G6
Plymouth, Ind., U.S.A. 108 E2
Plymouth, Mass., U.S.A. 111 E14
Plymouth, N.C., U.S.A. 109 H7
Plymouth, N.H., U.S.A. 111 C13
Plymouth, Pa., U.S.A. 111 E9
Plymouth, Wis., U.S.A. 108 D2
Plynlimon = Pumlumon Fawr, U.K. 13 E4
Plyusa, Russia 46 C5
Plyusa →, Russia 46 C5
Plyussa = Plyusa, Russia 46 C5
Plyussa → = Plyusa →, Russia . 46 C5
Plzeň, Czech Rep. 26 B6
Pniewy, Poland 45 F3
Pô, Burkina Faso 83 C4
Po →, Italy 29 D9
Po, Foci del, Italy 29 D9
Po Hai = Bo Hai, China 57 E10
Pobé, Benin 83 D5
Pobé, Burkina Faso 83 D5
Pobeda, Russia 51 C15
Pobedy, Pik, Kyrgyzstan 50 E8
Pobiedziska, Poland 45 F4
Pobla de Segur, Spain 32 C5
Pobladura del Valle, Spain 34 C5
Pobra de Trives, Spain 34 C3
Pocahontas, Ark., U.S.A. 113 G9
Pocahontas, Iowa, U.S.A. 112 D7
Pocatello, U.S.A. 114 E7
Počátky, Czech Rep. 26 B8
Pochep, Russia 47 F7
Pochinki, Russia 48 C7
Pochinok, Russia 46 E7
Pöchlarn, Austria 26 C8
Pochutla, Mexico 119 D5
Pocito Casas, Mexico 118 B2
Pocking, Germany 25 G9
Pocomoke City, U.S.A. 108 F8
Poços de Caldas, Brazil 127 A6
Podbořany, Czech Rep. 26 A6
Podębice, Poland 45 G5
Poděbrady, Czech Rep. 26 A8

Podensac, France 20 D3
Podenzano, Italy 28 D6
Podgorač, Croatia 42 E3
Podgorica, Montenegro, Yug. .. 40 D3
Podgorie, Albania 40 F4
Podilska Vysochyna, Ukraine .. 47 H4
Podkarpackie □, Poland 45 H9
Podkova, Bulgaria 41 E9
Podlapača, Croatia 29 D12
Podlaskie □, Poland 45 E10
Podoleni, Romania 43 D11
Podolínec, Slovak Rep. 27 B13
Podolsk, Russia 46 E9
Podor, Senegal 82 B1
Podporozhye, Russia 46 B8
Podu Iloaiei, Romania 43 C12
Podu Turcului, Romania 43 D12
Podujevo, Kosovo, Yug. 40 D5
Poel, Germany 24 B6
Pofadder, S. Africa 88 D2
Poggiardo, Italy 31 B11
Poggibonsi, Italy 28 E8
Póggio Mirteto, Italy 29 F9
Pogoanele, Romania 43 F12
Pogorzela, Poland 45 G4
Pogradec, Albania 40 F4
Pogranitšnyi, Russia 54 B5
Poh, Indonesia 63 E6
P'ohang, S. Korea 57 F15
Pohjanmaa, Finland 8 E20
Pohnpei, Micronesia 96 G7
Pohorelá, Slovak Rep. 27 C13
Pohořelice, Czech Rep. 27 C9
Pohorje, Slovenia 29 B12
Pohri, India 68 G6
Poiana Mare, Romania 42 G8
Poiana Ruscăi, Munții, Romania . 42 E7
Poiana Stampei, Romania 43 C10
Poinsett, C., Antarctica 5 C8
Point Arena, U.S.A. 116 G3
Point Baker, U.S.A. 104 B2
Point Edward, Canada 102 D3
Point Hope, U.S.A. 100 B3
Point L., Canada 100 B8
Point Pedro, Sri Lanka 66 Q12
Point Pleasant, N.J., U.S.A. .. 111 F10
Point Pleasant, W. Va., U.S.A. . 108 F4
Pointe-à-Pitre, Guadeloupe ... 121 C7
Pointe-Claire, Canada 111 A11
Pointe-Gatineau, Canada 111 A9
Pointe-Noire, Congo 84 E2
Poio, Spain 34 C2
Poirino, Italy 28 D4
Poisonbush Ra., Australia 92 D3
Poissonnier Pt., Australia 92 C2
Poitiers, France 18 F7
Poitou, France 20 B3
Poitou-Charentes □, France ... 20 B4
Poix-de-Picardie, France 19 C8
Poix-Terron, France 19 C11
Pojoaque, U.S.A. 115 J11
Pokaran, India 66 F7
Pokataroo, Australia 95 D4
Pokhara, Nepal 69 E10
Pokhvistnevo, Russia 48 D11
Poko, Dem. Rep. of the Congo .. 86 B2
Poko, Sudan 81 F3
Pokrov, Russia 46 E10
Pokrovsk = Engels, Russia 48 E8
Pokrovsk, Russia 51 C13
Pokrovskoye, Russia 47 J10
Pola = Pula, Croatia 29 D10
Pola, Russia 46 D7
Pola de Allande, Spain 34 B4
Pola de Lena, Spain 34 B5
Pola de Siero, Spain 34 B5
Pola de Somiedo, Spain 34 B4
Polacca, U.S.A. 115 J8
Polan, Iran 71 E9
Pol'ana, Slovak Rep. 27 C12
Poland ■, Europe 45 G3
Polanica-Zdrój, Poland 45 H3
Połaniec, Poland 45 H8
Polanów, Poland 44 D3
Polar Bear Prov. Park, Canada . 102 A2
Polatlı, Turkey 72 C5
Polatsk, Belarus 46 E5
Polcura, Chile 126 D1
Połczyn-Zdrój, Poland 44 E3
Polessk, Russia 9 J19
Polesye = Pripet Marshes, Europe 47 F5
Polgar, Hungary 42 C6
Pŏlgyo-ri, S. Korea 57 G14
Poli, Cameroon 83 C7
Policastro, G. di, Italy 31 C8
Police, Poland 44 E1
Polička, Czech Rep. 27 B9
Policoro, Italy 31 B9
Polignano a Mare, Italy 31 A9
Poligny, France 19 F12
Políkhnitas, Greece 39 B8
Polillo Is., Phil. 61 D4
Polillo Strait, Phil. 61 D4
Polis, Cyprus 36 D11
Polístena, Italy 31 D9
Polýiros, Greece 40 F7
Polk, U.S.A. 110 E5
Polkowice, Poland 45 G3
Polla, Italy 31 B8
Pollachi, India 66 P10
Pollença, Spain 37 B10
Pollença, B. de, Spain 37 B10
Póllica, Italy 31 B8
Pollino, Mte., Italy 31 C9

Polna, Russia 46 C5
Polnovat, Russia 50 C7
Pology, Ukraine 47 J9
Polonne, Ukraine 47 G4
Polonnoye = Polonne, Ukraine . 47 G4
Polski Trŭmbesh, Bulgaria ... 41 C9
Polsko Kosovo, Bulgaria 41 C9
Polson, U.S.A. 114 C6
Poltar, Slovak Rep. 27 C12
Poltava, Ukraine 47 H8
Põltsamaa, Estonia 9 G21
Polunochnoye, Russia 50 C7
Põlva, Estonia 9 G22
Polynesia, Pac. Oc. 97 J11
Polynésie française = French Polynesia ■, Pac. Oc. 97 K13
Pomarance, Italy 28 E7
Pomaro, Mexico 118 D4
Pombal, Portugal 34 F2
Pómbia, Greece 36 E6
Pomene, Mozam. 89 C6
Pomeroy, Ohio, U.S.A. 108 F4
Pomeroy, Wash., U.S.A. 114 C5
Pomézia, Italy 30 A5
Pomichna, Ukraine 47 H6
Pomona, Australia 95 D5
Pomona, U.S.A. 117 L9
Pomorie, Bulgaria 41 D11
Pomorskie □, Poland 44 D5
Pomorskie, Pojezierze, Poland . 44 E3
Pomos, Cyprus 36 D11
Pomos, C., Cyprus 36 D11
Pompano Beach, U.S.A. 109 M5
Pompei, Italy 31 B7
Pompey, France 19 D13
Pompeys Pillar, U.S.A. 114 D10
Pompton Lakes, U.S.A. 111 F10
Ponape = Pohnpei, Micronesia . 96 G7
Ponask L., Canada 102 B1
Ponca, U.S.A. 112 D6
Ponca City, U.S.A. 113 G6
Ponce, Puerto Rico 121 C6
Ponchatoula, U.S.A. 113 K9
Poncheville, L., Canada 102 B4
Pond, U.S.A. 117 K7
Pond Inlet, Canada 101 A12
Pondicherry, India 66 P11
Ponds, I. of, Canada 103 B8
Ponferrada, Spain 34 C4
Pongo, Wadi →, Sudan 81 F2
Poniatowa, Poland 45 G9
Poniec, Poland 45 G3
Ponikva, Slovenia 29 B12
Ponnani, India 66 P9
Ponoka, Canada 104 C6
Ponorogo, Indonesia 63 G14
Pons = Ponts, Spain 32 D6
Pons, France 20 C3
Ponsul →, Portugal 34 F3
Ponta de Sol, Madeira 37 D2
Ponta Grossa, Brazil 127 B5
Ponta Porã, Brazil 127 A4
Pontacq, France 20 E3
Pontailler-sur-Saône, France . 19 E12
Pontarlier, France 19 F13
Pontassieve, Italy 29 E8
Pontaumur, France 20 C6
Pontcharra, France 21 C10
Pontchartrain, L., U.S.A. 113 K10
Pontchâteau, France 18 E4
Ponte da Barca, Portugal 34 D2
Ponte de Sor, Portugal 35 F2
Ponte dell'Ólio, Italy 28 D6
Ponte di Legno, Italy 28 B7
Ponte do Lima, Portugal 34 D2
Ponte do Pungué, Mozam. 87 F3
Ponte-Leccia, France 21 F13
Ponte nelle Alpi, Italy 29 B9
Ponte Nova, Brazil 127 A7
Ponteareas, Spain 34 C2
Pontebba, Italy 29 B10
Ponteceso, Spain 34 B2
Pontecorvo, Italy 30 A6
Pontedeume, Spain 34 B2
Ponteix, Canada 105 D7
Pontevedra, Spain 34 C2
Pontevedra □, Spain 34 C2
Pontevedra, R. de →, Spain .. 34 C2
Pontevico, Italy 28 C7
Pontiac, Ill., U.S.A. 112 E10
Pontiac, Mich., U.S.A. 108 D4
Pontian Kecil, Malaysia 65 M4
Pontianak, Indonesia 62 E3
Pontine Is. = Ponziane, Ísole, Italy 30 B5
Pontine Mts. = Kuzey Anadolu Dağları, Turkey 72 B7
Pontínia, Italy 30 A6
Pontivy, France 18 D4
Pontoise, France 19 C9

Ponton →, Canada 104 B5
Pontorson, France 18 D5
Pontrémoli, Italy 28 D6
Pontrieux, France 18 D3
Ponts, Spain 32 D6
Pontypool, Canada 110 B6
Pontypool, U.K. 13 F4
Pontypridd, U.K. 13 F4
Ponza, Italy 30 B5
Ponziane, Ísole, Italy 30 B5
Poochera, Australia 95 E1
Poole, U.K. 13 G6
Poole □, U.K. 13 G6
Poona = Pune, India 66 K8
Poopó, L. de, Bolivia 122 E4
Popayán, Colombia 124 C3
Poperinge, Belgium 17 D2
Popilta L., Australia 95 E3
Popina, Bulgaria 41 B10
Poplar, U.S.A. 112 A2
Poplar →, Canada 105 C9
Poplar Bluff, U.S.A. 113 G9
Poplarville, U.S.A. 113 K10
Popocatépetl, Volcán, Mexico . 119 D5
Popokabaka, Dem. Rep. of the Congo 84 F3
Pópoli, Italy 29 F10
Popova, Croatia 29 C13
Popovača, Croatia 41 C10
Popovo, Bulgaria 41 C10
Poppberg, Germany 25 F7
Poppi, Italy 29 E8
Poprad, Slovak Rep. 27 B13
Poprad →, Slovak Rep. 27 B13
Porali →, Pakistan 68 G2
Porbandar, India 66 J6
Porcher I., Canada 104 C2
Porcuna, Spain 35 H6
Porcupine →, Canada 105 B8
Porcupine →, U.S.A. 100 B5
Pordenone, Italy 29 C9
Pordim, Bulgaria 41 C8
Poreč, Croatia 29 C10
Poretskoye, Russia 48 C8
Pori, Finland 9 F19
Pórí, Greece 38 F5
Porkhov, Russia 46 D5
Porlamar, Venezuela 124 A6
Porlezza, Italy 28 B6
Porma →, Spain 34 C5
Pornic, France 18 E4
Poronaysk, Russia 51 E15
Póros, Greece 38 D5
Poroshiri-Dake, Japan 54 C11
Poroszló, Hungary 42 C5
Poroto Mts., Tanzania 87 D3
Porpoise B., Antarctica 5 C9
Porquerolles, Î. de, France ... 21 F10
Porrentruy, Switz. 25 H3
Porreres, Spain 37 B10
Porsangen, Norway 8 A21
Porsgrunn, Norway 9 G13
Port Alberni, Canada 104 D4
Port Alfred, S. Africa 88 E4
Port Alice, Canada 104 C3
Port Allegany, U.S.A. 110 E6
Port Allen, U.S.A. 113 K9
Port Alma, Australia 94 C5
Port Angeles, U.S.A. 116 B3
Port Antonio, Jamaica 120 C4
Port Aransas, U.S.A. 113 M6
Port Arthur = Lüshun, China . 57 E11
Port Arthur, Australia 94 G4
Port Arthur, U.S.A. 113 L8
Port au Choix, Canada 103 B8
Port au Port B., Canada 103 C8
Port-au-Prince, Haiti 121 C5
Port Austin, U.S.A. 110 B2
Port Bell, Uganda 86 B3
Port Bergé Vaovao, Madag. .. 89 B8
Port Blandford, Canada 103 C9
Port-Bouët, Ivory C. 82 D4
Port Bradshaw, Australia 94 A2
Port Broughton, Australia 95 E2
Port Burwell, Canada 110 D4
Port Canning, India 69 H13
Port-Cartier, Canada 103 B6
Port Chalmers, N.Z. 91 L3
Port Charlotte, U.S.A. 109 M4
Port Chester, U.S.A. 111 F11
Port Clements, Canada 104 C2
Port Clinton, U.S.A. 108 E4
Port Colborne, Canada 102 D4
Port Coquitlam, Canada 104 D4
Port Credit, Canada 110 C5
Port Curtis, Australia 94 C5
Port d'Alcúdia, Spain 37 B10
Port Dalhousie, Canada 110 C5
Port Darwin, Australia 92 B5
Port Darwin, Falk. Is. 128 G5
Port Davey, Australia 94 G4
Port-de-Bouc, France 21 E8
Port-de-Paix, Haiti 121 C5
Port de Pollença, Spain 37 B10
Port de Sóller, Spain 37 B9
Port Dickson, Malaysia 65 L3
Port Douglas, Australia 94 B4
Port Dover, Canada 110 D4
Port Edward, Canada 104 C2
Port Elgin, Canada 102 D3
Port Elizabeth, S. Africa 88 E4
Port Ellen, U.K. 14 F2
Port-en-Bessin, France 18 C6
Port Erin, U.K. 14 C3
Port Essington, Australia 92 B5
Port Etienne = Nouâdhibou, Mauritania 78 D2
Port Ewen, U.S.A. 111 E11
Port Fouâd = Bûr Fuad, Egypt . 80 H8
Port Gamble, U.S.A. 116 C4

Port-Gentil, Gabon 84 E1
Port Germein, Australia 95 E2
Port Gibson, U.S.A. 113 K9
Port Glasgow, U.K. 14 F4
Port Harcourt, Nigeria 83 E6
Port Hardy, Canada 104 C3
Port Harrison = Inukjuak, Canada 101 C12
Port Hawkesbury, Canada 103 C7
Port Hedland, Australia 92 D2
Port Henry, U.S.A. 111 B11
Port Hood, Canada 103 C7
Port Hope, Canada 102 D4
Port Hope, U.S.A. 110 C2
Port Hope Simpson, Canada .. 103 B8
Port Hueneme, U.S.A. 117 L7
Port Huron, U.S.A. 110 D2
Port Iliç, Azerbaijan 73 C13
Port Jefferson, U.S.A. 111 F11
Port Jervis, U.S.A. 111 E10
Port-Joinville, France 18 F4
Port Katon, Russia 47 J10
Port Kelang = Pelabuhan Kelang, Malaysia 65 L3
Port Kenny, Australia 95 E1
Port-la-Nouvelle, France 20 E7
Port Laoise, Ireland 15 C4
Port Lavaca, U.S.A. 113 L6
Port Leyden, U.S.A. 111 C9
Port Loko, S. Leone 82 D2
Port Louis, France 18 E3
Port Louis, Mauritius 77 H9
Port Lyautey = Kenitra, Morocco 78 B4
Port McNeill, Canada 104 C3
Port Maria, Jamaica 120 C4
Port Matilda, U.S.A. 110 F6
Port Mellon, Canada 104 D4
Port-Menier, Canada 103 C7
Port Moody, Canada 116 A4
Port Morant, Jamaica 120 C4
Port Moresby, Papua N. G. ... 96 H6
Port Musgrave, Australia 94 A3
Port-Navalo, France 18 E4
Port Neches, U.S.A. 113 L8
Port Nolloth, S. Africa 88 D2
Port Nouveau-Québec = Kangiqsualujjuaq, Canada ... 101 C13
Port of Spain, Trin. & Tob. ... 121 D7
Port Orange, U.S.A. 109 L5
Port Orchard, U.S.A. 116 C4
Port Orford, U.S.A. 114 E1
Port Pegasus, N.Z. 91 M1
Port Perry, Canada 102 D4
Port Radium = Echo Bay, Canada 100 B8
Port Renfrew, Canada 104 D4
Port Roper, Australia 94 A2
Port Rowan, Canada 110 D4
Port Safaga = Bûr Safâga, Egypt 70 Q4
Port Said = Bûr Sa'îd, Egypt .. 80 H8
Port St. Joe, U.S.A. 109 L3
Port St. Johns = Umzimvubu, S. Africa 89 E4
Port-St-Louis-du-Rhône, France 21 E8
Port St. Lucie, U.S.A. 109 M5
Port-Ste-Marie, France 20 D4
Port Sanilac, U.S.A. 110 C2
Port Severn, Canada 110 B5
Port Shepstone, S. Africa 89 E5
Port Simpson, Canada 104 C2
Port Stanley = Stanley, Falk. Is. 128 G5
Port Stanley, Canada 102 D3
Port Sudan = Bûr Sûdân, Sudan 80 D4
Port Sulphur, U.S.A. 113 L10
Port-sur-Saône, France 19 E13
Port Talbot, U.K. 13 F4
Port Taufiq = Bûr Taufiq, Egypt 80 J8
Port Townsend, U.S.A. 116 B4
Port-Vendres, France 20 F7
Port Vila, Vanuatu 96 J8
Port Washington, U.S.A. 108 D2
Port Weld = Kuala Sepetang, Malaysia 65 K3
Portadown, U.K. 15 B5
Portaferry, U.K. 15 B6
Portage, Pa., U.S.A. 110 F6
Portage, Wis., U.S.A. 112 D10
Portage La Prairie, Canada ... 105 D9
Portageville, U.S.A. 113 G10
Portalegre, Portugal 35 F3
Portalegre □, Portugal 35 F3
Portales, U.S.A. 113 H3
Portarlington, Ireland 15 C4
Portbou, Spain 32 C8
Portel, Portugal 35 G3
Porter L., N.W.T., Canada 105 A7
Porter L., Sask., Canada 105 B7
Porterville, S. Africa 88 E2
Porterville, U.S.A. 116 J8
Portes-lès-Valence, France ... 21 D8
Porthcawl, U.K. 13 F4
Porthill, U.S.A. 114 B5
Porthmadog, U.K. 12 E3
Portile de Fier, Europe 42 F7
Portimão, Portugal 35 H2
Portishead, U.K. 13 F5
Portitei, Gura, Romania 43 F14
Portknockie, U.K. 14 D6
Portland, Canada 111 B8
Portland, Conn., U.S.A. 111 E12
Portland, Maine, U.S.A. 101 D12
Portland, Mich., U.S.A. 108 D3
Portland, Oreg., U.S.A. 116 E4
Portland, Pa., U.S.A. 111 F9

Portland, *Tex., U.S.A.* 113 M6
Portland, I. of, *U.K.* 13 G5
Portland Bill, *U.K.* 13 G5
Portland Canal, *U.S.A.* 104 B2
Portmadoc = Porthmadog, *U.K.* 12 E3
Porto, *France* 21 F12
Porto, *Portugal* 34 D2
Porto □, *Portugal* 34 D2
Porto, G. de, *France* 21 F12
Pôrto Alegre, *Brazil* 127 C5
Porto Amboim = Gunza, *Angola* 84 G2
Porto Azzurro, *Italy* 28 F7
Porto Cristo, *Spain* 37 B10
Pôrto de Móz, *Brazil* 125 D8
Porto Empédocle, *Italy* 30 E6
Pôrto Esperança, *Brazil* 124 G7
Pôrto Franco, *Brazil* 125 E9
Pórto Lágos, *Greece* 41 E9
Porto Mendes, *Brazil* 127 A5
Porto Moniz, *Madeira* 37 D2
Pôrto Murtinho, *Brazil* 124 H7
Pôrto Nacional, *Brazil* 125 F9
Porto-Novo, *Benin* 83 D5
Porto Petro, *Spain* 37 B10
Porto San Giórgio, *Italy* 29 E10
Porto Sant' Elpídio, *Italy* 29 E10
Porto Santo, I. de, *Madeira* 78 B2
Porto Santo Stéfano, *Italy* 28 F8
Pôrto São José, *Brazil* 127 A5
Pôrto Seguro, *Brazil* 125 G11
Porto Tolle, *Italy* 29 D9
Porto Tórres, *Italy* 30 B1
Pôrto União, *Brazil* 127 B5
Pôrto Válter, *Brazil* 124 E4
Porto-Vecchio, *France* 21 G13
Pôrto Velho, *Brazil* 124 E6
Portobelo, *Panama* 120 E4
Portoferráio, *Italy* 28 F7
Portogruaro, *Italy* 29 C9
Portola, *U.S.A.* 116 F6
Portomaggiore, *Italy* 29 D8
Portoscuso, *Italy* 30 C1
Portovénere, *Italy* 28 D6
Portoviejo, *Ecuador* 124 D2
Portpatrick, *U.K.* 14 G3
Portree, *U.K.* 14 D2
Portrush, *U.K.* 15 A5
Portsmouth, *Domin.* 121 C7
Portsmouth, *U.K.* 13 G6
Portsmouth, *N.H., U.S.A.* 109 D10
Portsmouth, *Ohio, U.S.A.* 108 F4
Portsmouth, *R.I., U.S.A.* 111 E13
Portsmouth, *Va., U.S.A.* 108 G7
Portsmouth □, *U.K.* 13 G6
Portsoy, *U.K.* 14 D6
Portstewart, *U.K.* 15 A5
Porttipahtan tekojärvi, *Finland* 8 B22
Portugal ■, *Europe* 34 F3
Portugalete, *Spain* 32 B1
Portumna, *Ireland* 15 C3
Portville, *U.S.A.* 110 D6
Porvenir, *Chile* 128 G2
Porvoo, *Finland* 9 F21
Porzuna, *Spain* 35 F6
Posada, *Spain* 30 B2
Posada →, *Italy* 30 B2
Posadas, *Argentina* 127 B4
Posadas, *Spain* 35 H5
Poschiavo, *Switz.* 25 J6
Posets, *Spain* 32 C5
Poshan = Boshan, *China* 57 F9
Posht-e-Badam, *Iran* 71 C7
Posídhion, Ákra, *Greece* 40 G7
Posidium, *Greece* 39 F9
Poso, *Indonesia* 63 E6
Posong, *S. Korea* 57 G14
Posse, *Brazil* 125 F9
Possession I., *Antarctica* 5 D11
Pössneck, *Germany* 24 E7
Possum Kingdom L., *U.S.A.* 113 J5
Post, *U.S.A.* 113 J4
Post Falls, *U.S.A.* 114 C5
Poste-de-la-Baleine =
 Kuujjuarapik, *Canada* 102 A4
Postmasburg, *S. Africa* 88 D3
Postojna, *Slovenia* 29 C11
Poston, *U.S.A.* 117 M12
Postville, *U.S.A.* 103 B8
Potamós, *Andíkithira, Greece* 38 F5
Potamós, *Kíthira, Greece* 38 E4
Potchefstroom, *S. Africa* 88 D4
Potcoava, *Romania* 43 F9
Poteau, *U.S.A.* 113 H7
Poteet, *U.S.A.* 113 L5
Potenza, *Italy* 31 B8
Potenza →, *Italy* 29 E10
Potenza Picena, *Italy* 29 E10
Poteriteri, L., *N.Z.* 91 M1
Potgietersrus, *S. Africa* 89 C4
Poti, *Georgia* 49 J5
Potiskum, *Nigeria* 83 C7
Potlogi, *Romania* 43 F10
Potomac →, *U.S.A.* 108 G7
Potosí, *Bolivia* 124 G5
Potosi Mt., *U.S.A.* 117 K11
Pototan, *Phil.* 61 F5
Potrerillos, *Chile* 126 B2
Potsdam, *Germany* 24 C9
Potsdam, *U.S.A.* 111 B10
Pottersville, *U.S.A.* 111 C11
Pottery Hill = Abu Ballas, *Egypt* 80 C2
Pottstown, *U.S.A.* 111 F9
Pottsville, *U.S.A.* 111 F8
Pottuvil, *Sri Lanka* 66 R12

P'otzu, *Taiwan* 59 F13
Pouancé, *France* 18 E5
Pouce Coupé, *Canada* 104 B4
Poughkeepsie, *U.S.A.* 111 E11
Pouilly-sur-Loire, *France* 19 E9
Poulaphouca Res., *Ireland* 15 C5
Poulsbo, *U.S.A.* 116 C4
Poultney, *U.S.A.* 111 C11
Poulton-le-Fylde, *U.K.* 12 D5
Pouso Alegre, *Brazil* 127 A6
Pout, *Senegal* 82 C1
Pouthisat, *Cambodia* 64 F4
Pouzauges, *France* 18 F6
Pova de Sta. Iria, *Portugal* 35 G1
Považská Bystrica, *Slovak Rep.* 27 B11
Poverty B., *N.Z.* 91 H7
Povlen, *Serbia, Yug.* 40 B3
Póvoa de Lanhosa, *Portugal* 34 D2
Póvoa de Varzim, *Portugal* 34 D2
Povorino, *Russia* 48 E6
Povungnituk = Puvirnituq,
 Canada 101 B12
Powassan, *Canada* 102 C4
Poway, *U.S.A.* 117 N9
Powder →, *U.S.A.* 112 B2
Powder River, *U.S.A.* 114 E10
Powell, *U.S.A.* 114 D9
Powell, L., *U.S.A.* 115 H8
Powell River, *Canada* 104 D4
Powers, *U.S.A.* 108 C2
Powys □, *U.K.* 13 E4
Poyang Hu, *China* 59 C11
Poyarkovo, *Russia* 51 E13
Poysdorf, *Austria* 27 C9
Poza de la Sal, *Spain* 34 C7
Poza Rica, *Mexico* 119 C5
Pozanti, *Turkey* 72 D6
Požarevac, *Serbia, Yug.* 40 B5
Pozazal, Puerto, *Spain* 34 C6
Požega, *Croatia* 42 E2
Požega, *Serbia, Yug.* 40 C4
Poznań, *Poland* 45 F3
Pozo, *U.S.A.* 117 K6
Pozo Alcón, *Spain* 35 H8
Pozo Almonte, *Chile* 124 H5
Pozo Colorado, *Paraguay* 126 A4
Pozoblanco, *Spain* 35 G6
Pozzallo, *Italy* 31 F7
Pozzomaggiore, *Italy* 30 B1
Pozzuoli, *Italy* 31 B7
Pra →, *Ghana* 83 D4
Prabuty, *Poland* 44 E6
Prača, *Bos.-H.* 42 G3
Prachatice, *Czech Rep.* 26 B6
Prachin Buri, *Thailand* 64 E3
Prachuap Khiri Khan, *Thailand* 65 G2
Pradelles, *France* 20 D7
Prades, *France* 20 F6
Prado, *Brazil* 125 G11
Prado del Rey, *Spain* 35 J5
Præstø, *Denmark* 11 J6
Pragersko, *Slovenia* 29 B12
Prague = Praha, *Czech Rep.* 26 A7
Praha, *Czech Rep.* 26 A7
Prahecq, *France* 20 B3
Prahova □, *Romania* 43 E10
Prahova →, *Romania* 43 F10
Prahovo, *Serbia, Yug.* 40 B6
Praia, *C. Verde Is.* 77 E1
Práia a Mare, *Italy* 31 C8
Praid, *Romania* 43 D10
Prainha, *Amazonas, Brazil* 124 E6
Prainha, *Pará, Brazil* 125 D8
Prairie, *Australia* 94 C3
Prairie City, *U.S.A.* 114 D4
Prairie Dog Town Fork →,
 U.S.A. 113 H5
Prairie du Chien, *U.S.A.* 112 D9
Prairies, L. of the, *Canada* 105 C8
Pramánda, *Greece* 38 B3
Prampram, *Ghana* 83 D5
Pran Buri, *Thailand* 64 F2
Prang, *Ghana* 83 D4
Prapat, *Indonesia* 62 D1
Prasonísi, Ákra, *Greece* 36 D9
Prästmon, *Sweden* 10 A11
Praszka, *Poland* 45 G5
Prata, *Brazil* 125 G9
Pratabpur, *India* 69 H10
Pratapgarh, *Raj., India* 68 G6
Pratapgarh, *Ut. P., India* 69 G9
Prato, *Italy* 28 E8
Prátola Peligna, *Italy* 29 F10
Prats-de-Mollo-la-Preste, *France* 20 F6
Pratt, *U.S.A.* 113 G5
Prattville, *U.S.A.* 109 J2
Pravdinsk, *Russia* 48 B6
Pravets, *Bulgaria* 40 D7
Pravia, *Spain* 34 B4
Praya, *Indonesia* 62 F5
Pré-en-Pail, *France* 18 D6
Precordillera, *Argentina* 126 C2
Predáppio, *Italy* 29 D8
Predazzo, *Italy* 29 B8
Predeal, *Romania* 43 E10
Predejane, *Serbia, Yug.* 40 D6
Preeceville, *Canada* 105 C8
Preetz, *Germany* 24 A6
Pregrada, *Croatia* 29 B12
Preili, *Latvia* 9 H22
Preko, *Croatia* 29 D12
Prelog, *Croatia* 29 B13
Prémery, *France* 19 E10
Premià de Mar, *Spain* 32 D7
Premont, *U.S.A.* 113 M5
Premuda, *Croatia* 29 D11

Prentice, *U.S.A.* 112 C9
Prenzlau, *Germany* 24 B9
Preobrazheniye, *Russia* 54 C6
Preparis North Channel,
 Ind. Oc. 67 M18
Preparis South Channel, *Ind. Oc.* 67 M18
Přerov, *Czech Rep.* 27 B10
Prescott, *Canada* 102 D4
Prescott, *Ariz., U.S.A.* 115 J7
Prescott, *Ark., U.S.A.* 113 J8
Prescott Valley, *U.S.A.* 115 J7
Preservation Inlet, *N.Z.* 91 M1
Preševo, *Serbia, Yug.* 40 D5
Presho, *U.S.A.* 112 D4
Presidencia de la Plaza,
 Argentina 126 B4
Presidencia Roque Saenz Peña,
 Argentina 126 B3
Presidente Epitácio, *Brazil* 125 H8
Presidente Hayes □, *Paraguay* 126 A4
Presidente Prudente, *Brazil* 127 A5
Presidio, *Mexico* 118 B4
Presidio, *U.S.A.* 113 L2
Preslav, *Bulgaria* 41 C10
Preslavska Planina, *Bulgaria* 41 C10
Prešov, *Slovak Rep.* 27 B14
Prešovský □, *Slovak Rep.* 27 B13
Prespa, *Bulgaria* 41 E8
Prespa, L. = Prespansko Jezero,
 Macedonia 40 F5
Prespansko Jezero, *Macedonia* 40 F5
Presque I., *U.S.A.* 110 D4
Presque Isle, *U.S.A.* 109 B12
Prestatyn, *U.K.* 12 D4
Prestea, *Ghana* 82 D4
Presteigne, *U.K.* 13 E5
Přeštice, *Czech Rep.* 26 B6
Preston, *Canada* 110 C4
Preston, *U.K.* 12 D5
Preston, *Idaho, U.S.A.* 114 E8
Preston, *Minn., U.S.A.* 112 D8
Preston, C., *Australia* 92 D2
Prestonburg, *U.S.A.* 108 G4
Prestwick, *U.K.* 14 F4
Pretoria, *S. Africa* 89 D4
Preuilly-sur-Claise, *France* 18 F7
Préveza, *Greece* 38 C2
Préveza □, *Greece* 38 B2
Prey Veng, *Cambodia* 65 G5
Priazovskoye, *Ukraine* 47 J8
Pribilof Is., *U.S.A.* 100 C2
Priboj, *Serbia, Yug.* 40 C3
Příbram, *Czech Rep.* 26 B7
Price, *U.S.A.* 114 G8
Price I., *Canada* 104 C3
Prichard, *U.S.A.* 109 K1
Priego, *Spain* 32 E2
Priego de Córdoba, *Spain* 35 H6
Priekule, *Latvia* 9 H19
Prien, *Germany* 25 H8
Prienai, *Lithuania* 9 J20
Prieska, *S. Africa* 88 D3
Priest L., *U.S.A.* 114 B5
Priest River, *U.S.A.* 114 B5
Priest Valley, *U.S.A.* 116 J6
Prievidza, *Slovak Rep.* 27 C11
Prignitz, *Germany* 24 B7
Prijedor, *Bos.-H.* 29 D13
Prijepolje, *Serbia, Yug.* 40 C3
Prikaspiyskaya Nizmennost =
 Caspian Depression, *Eurasia* 49 G9
Prikro, *Ivory C.* 82 D4
Prikubanskaya Nizmennost,
 Russia 49 H4
Prilep, *Macedonia* 40 E5
Priluki = Pryluky, *Ukraine* 47 G7
Prime Seal I., *Australia* 94 G4
Primorsk, *Russia* 46 B5
Primorsko, *Bulgaria* 41 D11
Primorsko-Akhtarsk, *Russia* 47 J10
Primorskoye, *Ukraine* 47 J9
Primrose L., *Canada* 105 C7
Prince Albert, *Canada* 105 C7
Prince Albert, *S. Africa* 88 E3
Prince Albert Mts., *Antarctica* 5 D11
Prince Albert Nat. Park, *Canada* 105 C7
Prince Albert Pen., *Canada* 100 A8
Prince Albert Sd., *Canada* 100 A8
Prince Alfred, C., *Canada* 4 B1
Prince Charles I., *Canada* 101 B12
Prince Charles Mts., *Antarctica* 5 D6
Prince Edward I. □, *Canada* 103 C7
Prince Edward Is., *Ind. Oc.* 3 G11
Prince Edward Pt., *Canada* 110 C8
Prince George, *Canada* 104 C4
Prince of Wales, C., *U.S.A.* 98 C3
Prince of Wales I., *Australia* 94 A3
Prince of Wales I., *Canada* 100 A10
Prince of Wales I., *U.S.A.* 100 C6
Prince Patrick I., *Canada* 4 B2
Prince Regent Inlet, *Canada* 4 B3
Prince Rupert, *Canada* 104 C2
Princess Charlotte B., *Australia* 94 A3
Princess May Ranges, *Australia* 92 C4
Princess Royal I., *Canada* 104 C3
Princeton, *Canada* 104 D4
Princeton, *Calif., U.S.A.* 116 F4
Princeton, *Ill., U.S.A.* 112 E10
Princeton, *Ind., U.S.A.* 108 F2
Princeton, *Ky., U.S.A.* 108 G2
Princeton, *Mo., U.S.A.* 112 E8
Princeton, *N.J., U.S.A.* 111 F10
Princeton, *W. Va., U.S.A.* 108 G5
Principe, I. de, *Atl. Oc.* 76 F4
Principe da Beira, *Brazil* 124 F6

Prineville, *U.S.A.* 114 D3
Prins Harald Kyst, *Antarctica* 5 D4
Prinsesse Astrid Kyst, *Antarctica* 5 D3
Prinsesse Ragnhild Kyst,
 Antarctica 5 D4
Prinzapolca, *Nic.* 120 D3
Prior, C., *Spain* 34 B2
Priozersk, *Russia* 46 B6
Pripet = Prypyat →, *Europe* 47 G6
Pripet Marshes = Prypyat
 Marshes, *Europe* 47 F5
Pripyat Marshes = Pripet
 Marshes, *Europe* 47 F5
Pripyats = Prypyat →, *Europe* 47 G6
Prislop, Pasul, *Romania* 43 C9
Pristen, *Russia* 47 G9
Priština, *Kosovo, Yug.* 40 D5
Pritzwalk, *Germany* 24 B8
Privas, *France* 21 D8
Priverno, *Italy* 30 A6
Privolzhsk, *Russia* 48 B5
Privolzhskaya Vozvyshennost,
 Russia 48 E7
Privolzhskiy, *Russia* 48 E8
Privolzhye, *Russia* 48 D9
Priyutnoye, *Russia* 49 G6
Prizren, *Kosovo, Yug.* 40 D4
Prizzi, *Italy* 30 E6
Prnjavor, *Bos.-H.* 42 F2
Probolinggo, *Indonesia* 63 G15
Prochowice, *Poland* 45 G3
Proctor, *U.S.A.* 111 C11
Proddatur, *India* 66 M11
Prodhromos, *Cyprus* 36 E11
Proença-a-Nova, *Portugal* 34 F3
Profítis Ilías, *Greece* 36 C9
Profondeville, *Belgium* 17 D4
Progreso, *Coahuila, Mexico* 118 B4
Progreso, *Yucatán, Mexico* 119 C7
Prokhladnyy, *Russia* 49 J7
Prokletije, *Albania* 40 D3
Prokopyevsk, *Russia* 50 D9
Prokuplje, *Serbia, Yug.* 40 C5
Proletarskaya = Proletarsk,
 Russia 49 G5
Prome = Pyè, *Burma* 67 K19
Prophet →, *Canada* 104 B4
Prophet River, *Canada* 104 B4
Propriá, *Brazil* 125 F11
Propriano, *France* 21 G12
Proserpine, *Australia* 94 C4
Prosna →, *Poland* 45 F4
Prospect, *U.S.A.* 111 C9
Prosser, *U.S.A.* 114 C4
Prostějov, *Czech Rep.* 27 B10
Prostki, *Poland* 44 E9
Proston, *Australia* 95 D5
Proszowice, *Poland* 45 H7
Próti, *Greece* 38 D3
Provadiya, *Bulgaria* 41 C11
Provence, *France* 21 E9
Provence-Alpes-Côte d'Azur □,
 France 21 D10
Providence, *Ky., U.S.A.* 108 G2
Providence, *R.I., U.S.A.* 111 E13
Providence Bay, *Canada* 102 C3
Providence Mts., *U.S.A.* 117 K11
Providencia, I. de, *Colombia* 120 D3
Provideniya, *Russia* 51 C19
Provins, *France* 19 D10
Provo, *U.S.A.* 114 F8
Provost, *Canada* 105 C6
Prozor, *Bos.-H.* 42 G2
Prrenjas, *Albania* 40 E4
Prudhoe Bay, *U.S.A.* 100 A5
Prudhoe I., *Australia* 94 C4
Prud'homme, *Canada* 105 C7
Prudnik, *Poland* 45 H4
Prüm, *Germany* 25 E2
Prundu, *Romania* 43 F11
Pruszcz Gdański, *Poland* 44 D5
Pruszków, *Poland* 45 F7
Prut →, *Romania* 43 E13
Pruzhany, *Belarus* 47 F3
Prvič, *Croatia* 29 D11
Prydz B., *Antarctica* 5 C6
Pryluky, *Ukraine* 47 G7
Pryor, *U.S.A.* 113 G7
Prypyat →, *Europe* 47 G6
Przasnysz, *Poland* 45 E7
Przedbórz, *Poland* 45 G6
Przedecz, *Poland* 45 F5
Przemków, *Poland* 45 G2
Przemyśl, *Poland* 45 J9
Przeworsk, *Poland* 45 H9
Przewóz, *Poland* 45 G1
Przhevalsk = Karakol,
 Kyrgyzstan 50 E8
Przysucha, *Poland* 45 G7
Psakhná, *Greece* 38 C5
Psará, *Greece* 39 C7
Psathoúra, *Greece* 38 B6
Psel →, *Ukraine* 47 H7
Pserimos, *Greece* 39 E9
Psíra, *Greece* 36 D7
Pskov, *Russia* 46 D5
Pskovskoye, Ozero, *Russia* 46 D5
Psunj, *Croatia* 42 E2
Ptich = Ptsich →, *Belarus* 47 F5
Ptolemaís, *Greece* 40 F5
Ptsich →, *Belarus* 47 F5
Ptuj, *Slovenia* 29 B12
Ptujska Gora, *Slovenia* 29 B12
Pu Xian, *China* 56 F6
Pua, *Thailand* 64 C3

Puán, *Argentina* 126 D3
Pu'an, *China* 58 E5
Puan, *S. Korea* 57 G14
Pubei, *China* 58 F7
Pucallpa, *Peru* 124 E4
Pucheng, *China* 59 D12
Pucheni, *Romania* 43 E10
Púchov, *Slovak Rep.* 27 B11
Pucioasa, *Romania* 43 E10
Pučišća, *Croatia* 29 E13
Puck, *Poland* 44 D5
Pucka, Zatoka, *Poland* 44 D5
Pudasjärvi, *Finland* 8 D22
Puding, *China* 58 D5
Pudozh, *Russia* 46 B9
Pudukkottai, *India* 66 P11
Puebla, *Mexico* 119 D5
Puebla □, *Mexico* 119 D5
Puebla de Alcocer, *Spain* 35 G5
Puebla de Don Fadrique, *Spain* 33 H2
Puebla de Don Rodrigo, *Spain* 35 F6
Puebla de Guzmán, *Spain* 35 H3
Puebla de la Calzada, *Spain* 35 G4
Puebla de Sanabria, *Spain* 34 C4
Puebla de Trives = Pobra de
 Trives, *Spain* 34 C3
Pueblo, *U.S.A.* 112 F2
Pueblo Hundido, *Chile* 126 B1
Puelches, *Argentina* 126 D2
Puelén, *Argentina* 126 D2
Puente Alto, *Chile* 126 C1
Puente-Genil, *Spain* 35 H6
Puente la Reina, *Spain* 32 C3
Puentedeume = Pontedeume,
 Spain 34 B2
Puentes de Garcia Rodriguez =
 As Pontes de García
 Rodríguez, *Spain* 34 B3
Pu'er, *China* 58 F3
Puerco →, *U.S.A.* 115 J10
Puerto, *Canary Is.* 37 F2
Puerto Aisén, *Chile* 128 F2
Puerto Ángel, *Mexico* 119 D5
Puerto Arista, *Mexico* 119 D6
Puerto Armuelles, *Panama* 120 E3
Puerto Ayacucho, *Venezuela* 124 B5
Puerto Barrios, *Guatemala* 120 C2
Puerto Bermejo, *Argentina* 126 B4
Puerto Bermúdez, *Peru* 124 F4
Puerto Bolívar, *Ecuador* 124 D3
Puerto Cabello, *Venezuela* 124 A5
Puerto Cabezas, *Nic.* 120 D3
Puerto Cabo Gracias á Dios,
 Nic. 120 D3
Puerto Carreño, *Colombia* 124 B5
Puerto Castilla, *Honduras* 120 C2
Puerto Chicama, *Peru* 124 E3
Puerto Coig, *Argentina* 128 G3
Puerto Cortés, *Costa Rica* 120 E3
Puerto Cortés, *Honduras* 120 C2
Puerto Cumarebo, *Venezuela* 124 A5
Puerto de Alcudia = Port
 d'Alcúdia, *Spain* 37 B10
Puerto de Andraitx, *Spain* 37 B9
Puerto de Cabrera, *Spain* 37 B9
Puerto de Gran Tarajal,
 Canary Is. 37 F5
Puerto de la Cruz, *Canary Is.* 37 F3
Puerto de Mazarrón, *Spain* 33 H3
Puerto de Pozo Negro,
 Canary Is. 37 F6
Puerto de Sóller = Port de
 Sóller, *Spain* 37 B9
Puerto de Somosierra, *Spain* 34 D7
Puerto del Carmen, *Canary Is.* 37 F6
Puerto del Rosario, *Canary Is.* 37 F6
Puerto Deseado, *Argentina* 128 F3
Puerto Escondido, *Mexico* 119 D5
Puerto Heath, *Bolivia* 124 F5
Puerto Inírida, *Colombia* 124 C5
Puerto Juárez, *Mexico* 119 C7
Puerto La Cruz, *Venezuela* 124 A6
Puerto Leguízamo, *Colombia* 124 D4
Puerto Limón, *Colombia* 124 C4
Puerto Lobos, *Argentina* 128 E3
Puerto Lumbreras, *Spain* 33 H3
Puerto Madryn, *Argentina* 128 E3
Puerto Maldonado, *Peru* 124 F5
Puerto Manotí, *Cuba* 120 B4
Puerto Mazarrón = Puerto de
 Mazarrón, *Spain* 33 H3
Puerto Montt, *Chile* 128 E2
Puerto Morazán, *Nic.* 120 D2
Puerto Morelos, *Mexico* 119 C7
Puerto Natales, *Chile* 128 G2
Puerto Padre, *Cuba* 120 B4
Puerto Páez, *Venezuela* 124 B5
Puerto Peñasco, *Mexico* 118 A2
Puerto Pinasco, *Paraguay* 126 A4
Puerto Plata, *Dom. Rep.* 121 C5
Puerto Princesa, *Phil.* 61 G3
Puerto Quepos, *Costa Rica* 120 E3
Puerto Real, *Spain* 35 J4
Puerto Rico, *Canary Is.* 37 G4
Puerto Rico ■, *W. Indies* 121 C6
Puerto Rico Trench, *Atl. Oc.* 121 C6
Puerto San Julián, *Argentina* 128 F3
Puerto Sastre, *Paraguay* 126 A4
Puerto Suárez, *Bolivia* 124 G7
Puerto Vallarta, *Mexico* 118 C3

Puerto Wilches, *Colombia* 124 B4
Puertollano, *Spain* 35 G6
Pueyrredón, L., *Argentina* 128 F2
Puffin I., *Ireland* 15 E1
Pugachev, *Russia* 48 D9
Pugal, *India* 68 E5
Puge, *China* 58 D4
Puge, *Tanzania* 86 C3
Puget Sound, *U.S.A.* 114 C2
Puget-Théniers, *France* 21 E10
Púglia □, *Italy* 31 A9
Pugŏdong, *N. Korea* 57 C16
Pugu, *Tanzania* 86 D4
Pügünzī, *Iran* 71 E8
Pui, *Romania* 42 E8
Puieşti, *Romania* 43 D12
Puig Major, *Spain* 37 B9
Puigcerdà, *Spain* 32 C6
Puigmal, *Spain* 32 C7
Puigpunyent, *Spain* 37 B9
Puijiang, *China* 58 B4
Puisaye, Collines de la, *France* . 19 E10
Puiseaux, *France* 19 D9
Pujehun, *S. Leone* 82 D2
Pujiang, *China* 59 C12
Pujols, *France* 20 D3
Pujon-chŏsuji, *N. Korea* 57 D14
Pukaki L., *N.Z.* 91 L3
Pukapuka, *Cook Is.* 97 J11
Pukaskwa Nat. Park, *Canada* . 102 C2
Pukatawagan, *Canada* 105 B8
Pukchin, *N. Korea* 57 D13
Pukch'ŏng, *N. Korea* 57 D15
Pukë, *Albania* 40 D3
Pukekohe, *N.Z.* 91 G5
Pukhrayan, *India* 69 F8
Pukou, *China* 59 A12
Pula, *Croatia* 29 D10
Pula, *Italy* 30 C1
Pulacayo, *Bolivia* 124 H5
Pulandian, *China* 57 E11
Pularumpi, *Australia* 92 B5
Pulaski, N.Y., *U.S.A.* 111 C8
Pulaski, Tenn., *U.S.A.* 109 H2
Pulaski, Va., *U.S.A.* 108 G5
Pulau →, *Indonesia* 63 F9
Puławy, *Poland* 45 G8
Pulga, *U.S.A.* 116 F5
Pulicat L., *India* 66 N12
Pullman, *U.S.A.* 114 C5
Pulo-Anna, *Pac. Oc.* 63 D8
Pulog, Mt., *Phil.* 61 C4
Pułtusk, *Poland* 45 F8
Pülümür, *Turkey* 73 C8
Pumlumon Fawr, *U.K.* 13 E4
Puná, I., *Ecuador* 124 D2
Punakha, *Bhutan* 67 F16
Punasar, *India* 68 F5
Punata, *Bolivia* 124 G5
Punch, *India* 69 C6
Punch →, *Pakistan* 68 C5
Punda Maria, *S. Africa* 89 C5
Pune, *India* 66 K8
P'ungsan, *N. Korea* 57 D15
Pungue, Ponte de, *Mozam.* 87 F3
Puning, *China* 59 F11
Punjab □, *India* 68 D7
Punjab □, *Pakistan* 68 E6
Puno, *Peru* 124 G4
Punpun →, *India* 69 G11
Punta Alta, *Argentina* 128 D4
Punta Arenas, *Chile* 128 G2
Punta de Díaz, *Chile* 126 B1
Punta Gorda, *Belize* 119 D7
Punta Gorda, *U.S.A.* 109 M5
Punta Prieta, *Mexico* 118 B2
Punta Prima, *Spain* 37 B11
Punta Umbria, *Spain* 35 H4
Puntarenas, *Costa Rica* 120 E3
Punto Fijo, *Venezuela* 124 A4
Punxsutawney, *U.S.A.* 110 F6
Puqi, *China* 59 C9
Puquio, *Peru* 124 F4
Pur →, *Russia* 50 C8
Purace, Vol., *Colombia* 124 C3
Puračić, *Bos.-H.* 42 F3
Puralia = Puruliya, *India* 69 H12
Puranpur, *India* 69 E9
Purbeck, Isle of, *U.K.* 13 G6
Purcell, *U.S.A.* 113 H6
Purcell Mts., *Canada* 104 D5
Puri, *India* 67 K14
Purmerend, *Neths.* 17 B4
Purnia, *India* 69 G12
Pursat = Pouthisat, *Cambodia* . 64 F4
Purukcahu, *Indonesia* 62 E4
Puruliya, *India* 69 H12
Purus →, *Brazil* 122 D4
Puruvesi, *Finland* 46 B5
Purvis, *U.S.A.* 113 K10
Pŭrvomay, *Bulgaria* 41 D9
Purwa, *India* 69 F9
Purwakarta, *Indonesia* 63 G12
Purwodadi, *Indonesia* 63 G14
Purwokerto, *Indonesia* 63 G13
Puryŏng, *N. Korea* 57 C15
Pusa, *India* 69 G11
Pusan, *S. Korea* 57 G15
Pushkin, *Russia* 46 C6
Pushkino, Moskva, *Russia* 46 D9
Pushkino, Saratov, *Russia* 48 E8
Püspökladány, *Hungary* 42 C6
Pustoshka, *Russia* 46 D5
Puszczykowo, *Poland* 45 F3
Putahow L., *Canada* 105 B8
Putao, *Burma* 67 F20

Putaruru, *N.Z.* 91 H5
Putbus, *Germany* 24 A9
Putian, *China* 59 E12
Putignano, *Italy* 31 B10
Puting, Tanjung, *Indonesia* ... 62 E4
Putlitz, *Germany* 24 B8
Putna, *Romania* 43 E12
Putna →, *Romania* 43 E12
Putnam, *U.S.A.* 111 E13
Putnok, *Hungary* 42 B5
Putorana, Gory, *Russia* 51 C10
Puttalam, *Sri Lanka* 66 Q11
Puttgarden, *Germany* 24 A7
Püttlingen, *Germany* 25 F2
Putumayo →, *S. Amer.* 122 D4
Putuo, *China* 59 C14
Putussibau, *Indonesia* 62 D4
Puvirnituq, *Canada* 101 B12
Puy-de-Dôme, *France* 20 C6
Puy-de-Dôme □, *France* 20 C7
Puy-l'Évêque, *France* 20 D5
Puyallup, *U.S.A.* 116 C4
Puyang, *China* 56 G8
Puylaurens, *France* 20 E6
Pūzeh Rīg, *Iran* 71 E8
Pwani □, *Tanzania* 86 D4
Pweto, *Dem. Rep. of the Congo* 87 D2
Pwllheli, *U.K.* 12 E3
Pyana →, *Russia* 48 C8
Pyapon, *Burma* 67 L19
Pyasina →, *Russia* 51 B9
Pyatigorsk, *Russia* 49 H6
Pyatykhatky, *Ukraine* 47 H7
Pydna, *Greece* 40 F6
Pyè, *Burma* 67 K19
Pyetrikaw, *Belarus* 47 F5
Pyhäjoki, *Finland* 8 D21
Pyinmana, *Burma* 67 K20
Pyla, C., *Cyprus* 36 E12
Pymatuning Reservoir, *U.S.A.* . 110 E4
Pyŏktong, *N. Korea* 57 D13
Pyŏnggang, *N. Korea* 57 E14
P'yŏngt'aek, *N. Korea* 57 F14
P'yŏngyang, *N. Korea* 57 E13
Pyote, *U.S.A.* 113 K3
Pyramid L., *U.S.A.* 114 G4
Pyramid Pk., *U.S.A.* 117 J10
Pyramids, *Egypt* 80 J7
Pyrénées, *Europe* 20 F4
Pyrénées-Atlantiques □, *France* 20 E3
Pyrénées-Orientales □, *France* . 20 F6
Pyryatyn, *Ukraine* 47 G7
Pyrzyce, *Poland* 45 E1
Pyskowice, *Poland* 45 H5
Pytalovo, *Russia* 46 D4
Pyu, *Burma* 67 K20
Pyzdry, *Poland* 45 F4

Q

Qaanaaq, *Greenland* 4 B4
Qabirri →, *Azerbaijan* 49 K8
Qachasnek, *S. Africa* 89 E4
Qa'el Jafr, *Jordan* 75 E5
Qa'emābād, *Iran* 71 D9
Qā'emshahr, *Iran* 71 B7
Qagan Nur, *China* 56 C8
Qahar Youyi Zhongqi, *China* .. 56 D7
Qahremānshahr = Bākhtarān,
  Iran 70 C5
Qaidam Pendi, *China* 60 C4
Qajarīyeh, *Iran* 71 D6
Qala, Ras il, *Malta* 36 C1
Qala-i-Jadid = Spīn Búldak,
  Afghan. 68 D2
Qala Viala, *Pakistan* 68 D2
Qala Yangi, *Afghan.* 68 B2
Qal'at al Akhḍar, *Si. Arabia* .. 70 E3
Qal'at Dīzah, *Iraq* 70 B5
Qal'at Şāliḥ, *Iraq* 70 D5
Qal'at Sukkar, *Iraq* 70 D5
Qalyûb, *Egypt* 80 H7
Qamani'tuaq = Baker Lake,
  Canada 100 B10
Qamdo, *China* 58 B1
Qamruddin Karez, *Pakistan* .. 68 D3
Qandahār, *Afghan.* 66 D4
Qandahār □, *Afghan.* 66 D4
Qapān, *Iran* 71 B7
Qapshaghay, *Kazakhstan* 50 E8
Qaqortoq, *Greenland* 101 B6
Qâra, *Egypt* 80 B2
Qara Qash →, *India* 69 B8
Qarabutaq, *Kazakhstan* 50 E7
Qaraçala, *Azerbaijan* 49 L9
Qaraghandy, *Kazakhstan* 50 E8
Qārah, *Si. Arabia* 70 D4
Qaratau, *Kazakhstan* 50 E8
Qaratau, *Kazakhstan* 50 E7
Qardud, *Sudan* 81 E2
Qareh →, *Iran* 70 B5
Qareh Tekān, *Iran* 71 B6
Qarqan He →, *China* 60 C3
Qarqaraly, *Kazakhstan* 50 E8
Qarrasa, *Sudan* 81 E3
Qarshi, *Uzbekistan* 50 F7
Qartabā, *Lebanon* 75 A4
Qaryat al Gharab, *Iraq* 70 D5
Qaryat al 'Ulyā, *Si. Arabia* ... 70 E5
Qasr 'Amra, *Jordan* 70 D3
Qaşr-e Qand, *Iran* 71 E9
Qasr Farâfra, *Egypt* 80 B2
Qatanā, *Syria* 75 B5
Qatar ■, *Asia* 71 E6

Qatlīsh, *Iran* 71 B8
Qattâra, *Egypt* 80 A2
Qattâra, Munkhafed el, *Egypt* . 80 B2
Qattâra Depression = Qattâra,
  Munkhafed el, *Egypt* 80 B2
Qawām al Ḥamzah, *Iraq* 70 D5
Qāyen, *Iran* 71 C8
Qazaqstan = Kazakhstan ■, *Asia* 50 E7
Qazimämmäd, *Azerbaijan* 49 K9
Qazvin, *Iran* 71 B6
Qeissan, *Sudan* 81 E3
Qena, *Egypt* 80 B3
Qena, W. →, *Egypt* 80 B3
Qeqertarsuaq, *Greenland* 101 B5
Qeqertarsuaq, *Greenland* 4 C5
Qeshlāq, *Iran* 70 C5
Qeshm, *Iran* 71 E8
Qeys, *Iran* 71 E7
Qi Xian, *China* 56 G8
Qian Gorlos, *China* 57 B13
Qian Xian, *China* 56 G5
Qiancheng, *China* 58 D7
Qianjiang, Guangxi Zhuangzu,
  China 58 F7
Qianjiang, Hubei, *China* 59 B9
Qianjiang, Sichuan, *China* ... 58 C7
Qianshan, *China* 59 B11
Qianwei, *China* 58 C4
Qianxi, *China* 58 D6
Qianyang, Hunan, *China* 59 D8
Qianyang, Shaanxi, *China* ... 56 G4
Qianyang, Zhejiang, *China* ... 59 B12
Qiaojia, *China* 58 D4
Qichun, *China* 59 B10
Qidong, Hunan, *China* 59 D9
Qidong, Jiangsu, *China* 59 B13
Qijiang, *China* 58 C6
Qikiqtarjuaq, *Canada* 101 B13
Qila Safed, *Pakistan* 66 E2
Qila Saifullāh, *Pakistan* 68 D3
Qilian Shan, *China* 60 C4
Qimen, *China* 59 C11
Qin He →, *China* 56 G7
Qin Jiang →,
  Guangxi Zhuangzu, *China* .. 58 F7
Qin Jiang →, Jiangxi, *China* .. 59 D10
Qin Ling = Qinling Shandi,
  China 56 H5
Qin'an, *China* 56 G3
Qing Xian, *China* 56 E9
Qingcheng, *China* 57 F9
Qingdao, *China* 57 F11
Qingfeng, *China* 56 G8
Qinghai □, *China* 60 C4
Qinghai Hu, *China* 60 C5
Qinghecheng, *China* 57 D13
Qinghemen, *China* 57 D11
Qingjian, *China* 56 F6
Qingjiang = Huaiyin, *China* .. 57 H10
Qingliu, *China* 59 D11
Qinglong, *China* 58 E5
Qingpu, *China* 59 B13
Qingping, *China* 58 D6
Qingshui, *China* 56 G4
Qingshuihe, *China* 56 E6
Qingtian, *China* 59 C13
Qingtongxia Shuiku, *China* ... 56 F3
Qingxi, *China* 58 D7
Qingxu, *China* 56 F7
Qingyang, Anhui, *China* 59 B11
Qingyang, Gansu, *China* 56 F4
Qingyi Jiang →, *China* 58 C4
Qingyuan, Guangdong, *China* . 59 F9
Qingyuan, Liaoning, *China* ... 57 C13
Qingyuan, Zhejiang, *China* ... 59 D12
Qingyun, *China* 57 F9
Qingzhen, *China* 58 D6
Qinhuangdao, *China* 57 E10
Qinling Shandi, *China* 56 H5
Qinshui, *China* 56 G7
Qinyang = Jiyuan, *China* 56 G7
Qinyuan, *China* 56 F7
Qinzhou, *China* 58 G7
Qionghai, *China* 64 C8
Qionglai, *China* 58 B4
Qionglai Shan, *China* 58 B4
Qiongzhou Haixia, *China* 64 B8
Qiqihar, *China* 51 E13
Qiraîya, W. →, *Egypt* 75 E3
Qiryat Ata, *Israel* 75 C4
Qiryat Gat, *Israel* 75 D3
Qiryat Mal'akhi, *Israel* 75 D3
Qiryat Shemona, *Israel* 75 B4
Qiryat Yam, *Israel* 75 C4
Qishan, *China* 56 G4
Qiubei, *China* 58 E5
Qixia, *China* 57 F11
Qiyang, *China* 59 D8
Qızılağac Körfäzi, *Azerbaijan* . 71 B6
Qojūr, *Iran* 70 B5
Qom, *Iran* 71 C6
Qomolangma Feng = Everest,
  Mt., *Nepal* 69 E12
Qomsheh, *Iran* 71 D6
Qoraqalpoghiston □, *Uzbekistan* 50 E6
Qorveh, *Iran* 73 E12
Qostanay, *Kazakhstan* 50 D7
Qu Jiang →, *China* 58 B6
Qu Xian, *China* 58 B6
Quabbin Reservoir, *U.S.A.* ... 111 D12
Quairading, *Australia* 93 F2
Quakenbrück, *Germany* 24 C3

Quakertown, *U.S.A.* 111 F9
Qualicum Beach, *Canada* 104 D4
Quamby, *Australia* 94 C3
Quan Long = Ca Mau, *Vietnam* 65 H5
Quanah, *U.S.A.* 113 H5
Quang Ngai, *Vietnam* 64 E7
Quang Tri, *Vietnam* 64 D6
Quang Yen, *Vietnam* 58 G6
Quannan, *China* 59 E10
Quantock Hills, *U.K.* 13 F4
Quanzhou, Fujian, *China* 59 E12
Quanzhou, Guangxi Zhuangzu,
  China 59 E8
Qu'Appelle, *Canada* 105 C8
Quaqtaq, *Canada* 101 B13
Quaraí, *Brazil* 126 C4
Quarré-les-Tombes, *France* ... 19 E11
Quarteira, *Portugal* 35 H2
Quartu Sant'Élena, *Italy* 30 C2
Quartzsite, *U.S.A.* 117 M12
Quatsino Sd., *Canada* 104 C3
Quba, *Azerbaijan* 49 K9
Qūchān, *Iran* 71 B8
Québec, *Canada* 103 C5
Québec □, *Canada* 103 C6
Quedlinburg, *Germany* 24 D7
Queen Alexandra Ra.,
  Antarctica 5 E11
Queen Charlotte City, *Canada* . 104 C2
Queen Charlotte Is., *Canada* .. 104 C2
Queen Charlotte Sd., *Canada* . 104 C3
Queen Charlotte Strait, *Canada* 104 C3
Queen Elizabeth Is., *Canada* .. 98 B10
Queen Elizabeth Nat. Park,
  Uganda 86 C3
Queen Mary Land, *Antarctica* . 5 D7
Queen Maud G., *Canada* 100 B9
Queen Maud Land, *Antarctica* . 5 D3
Queen Maud Mts., *Antarctica* . 5 E13
Queens Chan., *Australia* 92 C4
Queensland □, *Australia* 94 C3
Queenstown, *Australia* 94 G4
Queenstown, *N.Z.* 91 L2
Queenstown, *S. Africa* 88 E4
Queets, *U.S.A.* 116 C2
Queguay Grande →, *Uruguay* . 126 C4
Queimadas, *Brazil* 125 F11
Quelimane, *Mozam.* 87 F4
Quellón, *Chile* 128 E2
Quelpart = Cheju do, S. *Korea* . 57 H14
Queluz, *Portugal* 35 G1
Quemado, N. Mex., *U.S.A.* ... 115 J9
Quemado, Tex., *U.S.A.* 113 L4
Quemoy = Chinmen, *Taiwan* .. 59 E13
Quemú-Quemú, *Argentina* ... 126 D3
Quequén, *Argentina* 126 D4
Querétaro, *Mexico* 118 C4
Querétaro □, *Mexico* 118 C5
Querfurt, *Germany* 24 D7
Quérigut, *France* 20 F6
Querqueville, *France* 18 C5
Quesada, *Spain* 35 H7
Queshan, *China* 56 H8
Quesnel, *Canada* 104 C4
Quesnel →, *Canada* 104 C4
Quesnel L., *Canada* 104 C4
Questa, *U.S.A.* 115 H11
Questembert, *France* 18 E4
Quetico Prov. Park, *Canada* .. 102 C1
Quetta, *Pakistan* 68 D2
Quezaltenango, *Guatemala* ... 120 D1
Quezon City, *Phil.* 61 D4
Qufār, *Si. Arabia* 70 E4
Qui Nhon, *Vietnam* 64 F7
Quiaxe, *Angola* 84 F2
Quibdo, *Colombia* 124 B3
Quiberon, *France* 18 E3
Quiberon, Presqu'île de, *France* 18 E3
Quickborn, *Germany* 24 B5
Quiet L., *Canada* 104 A2
Quiindy, *Paraguay* 126 B4
Quila, *Mexico* 118 C3
Quilán, C., *Chile* 128 E2
Quilcene, *U.S.A.* 116 C4
Quilimarí, *Chile* 126 C1
Quilino, *Argentina* 126 C3
Quill Lakes, *Canada* 105 C8
Quillabamba, *Peru* 124 F4
Quillagua, *Chile* 126 A2
Quillaicillo, *Chile* 126 C1
Quillan, *France* 20 F6
Quillota, *Chile* 126 C1
Quilon, *India* 66 Q10
Quilpie, *Australia* 95 D3
Quilpué, *Chile* 126 C1
Quilua, *Mozam.* 87 F4
Quimilí, *Argentina* 126 B3
Quimper, *France* 18 E2
Quimperlé, *France* 18 E3
Quinault →, *U.S.A.* 116 C2
Quincy, Calif., *U.S.A.* 116 F6
Quincy, Fla., *U.S.A.* 109 K3
Quincy, Ill., *U.S.A.* 112 F9
Quincy, Mass., *U.S.A.* 111 D14
Quincy, Wash., *U.S.A.* 114 C4
Quines, *Argentina* 126 C2
Quinga, *Mozam.* 87 F5
Quingey, *France* 19 E12
Quinns Rocks, *Australia* 93 F2
Quintana de la Serena, *Spain* . 35 G5
Quintana Roo □, *Mexico* 119 D7
Quintanar de la Orden, *Spain* . 35 F7
Quintanar de la Sierra, *Spain* . 32 C2
Quintanar del Rey, *Spain* 33 F3
Quintero, *Chile* 126 C1

Quintin, *France* 18 D4
Quinto, *Spain* 32 D4
Quípar →, *Spain* 33 G3
Quirihue, *Chile* 126 D1
Quirinópolis, *Brazil* 125 G8
Quiroga, *Spain* 34 C3
Quissac, *France* 21 E8
Quissanga, *Mozam.* 87 E5
Quissico, *Mozam.* 89 C5
Quitilipi, *Argentina* 126 B3
Quitman, *U.S.A.* 109 K4
Quito, *Ecuador* 124 D3
Quixadá, *Brazil* 125 D11
Quixaxe, *Mozam.* 87 F5
Qujing, *China* 58 E4
Qulan, *Kazakhstan* 50 E8
Qul'ān, Jazā'ir, *Egypt* 70 E2
Qumbu, *S. Africa* 89 E4
Quneitra, *Syria* 75 B4
Qŭnghirot, *Uzbekistan* 50 E6
Qu'nyido, *China* 58 B2
Quoin I., *Australia* 92 B4
Quoin Pt., *S. Africa* 88 E2
Qŭqon, *Uzbekistan* 50 E8
Qurein, *Sudan* 81 E3
Qurnat as Sawdā', *Lebanon* .. 75 A5
Qûs, *Egypt* 80 B3
Qusar, *Azerbaijan* 49 K9
Quşaybā', *Si. Arabia* 70 E4
Qusaybah, *Iraq* 70 C4
Quseir, *Egypt* 70 E2
Qūshchī, *Iran* 70 B5
Quthing, *Lesotho* 89 E4
Qūţīābād, *Iran* 71 C6
Quwo, *China* 56 G6
Quyang, *China* 56 E8
Quynh Nhai, *Vietnam* 64 B4
Quyon, *Canada* 111 A8
Quzhou, *China* 59 C12
Quzi, *China* 56 F4
Qvareli, *Georgia* 49 K7
Qytet Stalin = Kuçovë, *Albania* 40 F3
Qyzylorda, *Kazakhstan* 50 E7

R

Ra, Ko, *Thailand* 65 H2
Raab, *Austria* 26 C6
Raahe, *Finland* 8 D21
Raalte, *Neths.* 17 B6
Raasay, *U.K.* 14 D2
Raasay, Sd. of, *U.K.* 14 D2
Rab, *Croatia* 29 D11
Raba, *Indonesia* 63 F5
Rába →, *Hungary* 42 C2
Raba →, *Poland* 45 H7
Rabaçal →, *Portugal* 34 D3
Rabah, *Nigeria* 83 C6
Rabai, *Kenya* 86 C4
Rabak, *Sudan* 81 E3
Rabastens, *France* 20 E5
Rabastens-de-Bigorre, *France* . 20 E4
Rabat, *Malta* 36 D1
Rabat, *Morocco* 78 B4
Rabaul, *Papua N. G.* 96 H7
Rābigh, *Si. Arabia* 74 C2
Rabka, *Poland* 45 J6
Râbniţa, *Moldova* 43 C14
Rābor, *Iran* 71 D8
Rača, Serbia, *Yug.* 40 B4
Răcăciuni, *Romania* 43 D11
Răcăşdia, *Romania* 42 F6
Racconigi, *Italy* 28 D4
Race, C., *Canada* 103 C9
Rach Gia, *Vietnam* 65 G5
Rachid, *Mauritania* 82 B2
Raciąż, *Poland* 45 F7
Racibórz, *Poland* 45 H5
Racine, *U.S.A.* 108 D2
Rackerby, *U.S.A.* 116 F5
Radama, Nosy, *Madag.* 89 A8
Radama, Saikanosy, *Madag.* .. 89 A8
Radan, Serbia, *Yug.* 40 D5
Rădăuţi, *Romania* 43 C10
Rădăuţi-Prut, *Romania* 43 B11
Radbuza →, *Czech Rep.* 26 B6
Radcliff, *U.S.A.* 108 G3
Radeberg, *Germany* 24 D9
Radebeul, *Germany* 24 D9
Radeče, *Slovenia* 29 B12
Radekhiv, *Ukraine* 47 G3
Radekhov = Radekhiv, *Ukraine* 47 G3
Radenthein, *Austria* 26 E6
Radew →, *Poland* 44 D2
Radford, *U.S.A.* 108 G5
Radhanpur, *India* 68 H4
Radhwa, Jabal, *Si. Arabia* 70 E3
Radika →, *Macedonia* 40 E4
Radisson, Qué., *Canada* 102 B4
Radisson, Sask., *Canada* 105 C7
Radium Hot Springs, *Canada* . 104 C5
Radlje ob Dravi, *Slovenia* 29 B12
Radnevo, *Bulgaria* 41 D9
Radnice, *Czech Rep.* 26 B6
Radnor Forest, *U.K.* 13 E4
Radolfzell, *Germany* 25 H4
Radom, *Poland* 45 G8
Radomir, *Bulgaria* 40 D6
Radomsko, *Poland* 45 G6
Radomyshl, *Ukraine* 47 G5
Radomyśl Wielki, *Poland* 45 H8
Radoszyce, *Poland* 45 G7
Radoviš, *Macedonia* 40 E5

Radovljica, *Slovenia* 29 B11
Radstadt, *Austria* 26 D6
Radstock, C., *Australia* 95 E1
Răducăneni, *Romania* 43 D12
Raduša, *Macedonia* 40 D5
Radviliškis, *Lithuania* 9 J20
Radville, *Canada* 105 D8
Raḍwá, J., *Si. Arabia* 80 C4
Radymno, *Poland* 45 J9
Radzanów, *Poland* 45 F7
Radziejów, *Poland* 45 F5
Radzyń Chełmiński, *Poland* .. 44 E5
Radzyń Podlaski, *Poland* 45 G9
Rae, *Canada* 104 A5
Rae Bareli, *India* 69 F9
Rae Isthmus, *Canada* 101 B11
Raeren, *Belgium* 17 D6
Raeside, L., *Australia* 93 E3
Raetihi, *N.Z.* 91 H5
Rafaela, *Argentina* 126 C3
Rafah, *Gaza Strip* 75 D3
Rafai, *C.A.R.* 86 B1
Raffadali, *Italy* 30 E6
Raffili, *Sudan* 81 F2
Rafḥā, *Si. Arabia* 70 D4
Rafsanjān, *Iran* 71 D8
Raft Pt., *Australia* 92 C3
Râga, *Sudan* 81 F2
Raga →, *Sudan* 81 F2
Ragachow, *Belarus* 47 F6
Ragag, *Sudan* 81 E1
Ragama, *Sri Lanka* 66 R11
Ragged, Mt., *Australia* 93 F3
Raghunathpalli, *India* 69 H11
Raghunathpur, *India* 69 H12
Raglan, *N.Z.* 91 G5
Ragusa, *Italy* 31 F7
Raha, *Indonesia* 63 E6
Rahad, Nahr ed →, *Sudan* ... 81 E3
Rahaeng = Tak, *Thailand* 64 D2
Rahatgarh, *India* 69 H8
Rahden, *Germany* 24 C4
Raheita, *Eritrea* 81 E5
Rahimyar Khan, *Pakistan* 68 E4
Rāhjerd, *Iran* 71 C6
Rahon, *India* 68 D7
Raichur, *India* 66 L10
Raiganj, *India* 69 G13
Raigarh, *India* 67 J13
Raijua, *Indonesia* 63 F6
Raikot, *India* 68 D6
Railton, *Australia* 94 G4
Rainbow Lake, *Canada* 104 B5
Rainier, *U.S.A.* 116 D4
Rainier, Mt., *U.S.A.* 116 D5
Rainy L., *Canada* 105 D10
Rainy River, *Canada* 105 D10
Raippaluoto, *Finland* 8 E19
Raipur, *India* 67 J12
Ra'is, *Si. Arabia* 80 C4
Raisen, *India* 68 H8
Raisio, *Finland* 9 F20
Raj Nandgaon, *India* 67 J12
Raj Nilgiri, *India* 69 J12
Raja, Ujung, *Indonesia* 62 D1
Raja Ampat, Kepulauan,
  Indonesia 63 E7
Rajahmundry, *India* 67 L12
Rajang →, *Malaysia* 62 D4
Rajapur, *Pakistan* 68 E4
Rajapalaiyam, *India* 66 Q10
Rajasthan □, *India* 68 F5
Rajasthan Canal, *India* 68 F5
Rajauri, *India* 69 C6
Rajgarh, Mad. P., *India* 68 G7
Rajgarh, Raj., *India* 68 F7
Rajgarh, Raj., *India* 68 E6
Rajgir, *India* 69 G11
Rajgród, *Poland* 44 E9
Rajkot, *India* 68 H4
Rajmahal Hills, *India* 69 G12
Rajpipla, *India* 66 J8
Rajpur, *India* 68 H6
Rajpura, *India* 68 D7
Rajshahi, *Bangla.* 67 G16
Rajshahi □, *Bangla.* 69 G13
Rajula, *India* 68 J4
Rakaia, *N.Z.* 91 K4
Rakaia →, *N.Z.* 91 K4
Rakan, Ra's, *Qatar* 71 E6
Rakaposhi, *Pakistan* 69 A6
Rakata, Pulau, *Indonesia* 62 F3
Rakhiv, *Ukraine* 47 H3
Rakhni, *Pakistan* 68 D3
Rakhni →, *Pakistan* 68 E3
Rakitnoye, *Russia* 54 B7
Rakitovo, *Bulgaria* 41 E8
Rakoniewice, *Poland* 45 F3
Rakops, *Botswana* 88 C3
Rakovica, *Croatia* 29 D12
Rakovník, *Czech Rep.* 26 A6
Rakovski, *Bulgaria* 41 D8
Rakvere, *Estonia* 9 G22
Raleigh, *U.S.A.* 109 H6
Ralja, *Serbia, Yug.* 40 B4
Ralls, *U.S.A.* 113 J4
Ralston, *U.S.A.* 104 A4
Ram →, *Canada* 104 A4
Rām Allāh, *West Bank* 75 D4
Rama, *Nic.* 120 D3
Ramacca, *Italy* 31 E7
Ramakona, *India* 69 J8
Ramales de la Victoria, *Spain* .. 34 B7
Raman, *Thailand* 65 J3
Ramanathapuram, *India* 66 Q11
Ramanetaka, B. de, *Madag.* .. 89 A8

Ramanujganj, *India* 69 H10
Ramat Gan, *Israel* 75 C3
Ramatlhabama, S. Africa 88 D4
Ramban, *India* 69 C6
Rambervillers, *France* 19 D13
Rambipuji, *Indonesia* 63 H15
Rambouillet, *France* 19 D8
Ramechhap, *Nepal* 69 F12
Ramenskoye, *Russia* 46 E10
Ramganga →, *India* 69 F8
Ramgarh, Bihar, *India* 69 H11
Ramgarh, Raj., *India* 68 F6
Ramgarh, Raj., *India* 68 F4
Rāmhormoz, *Iran* 71 D6
Ramīān, *Iran* 71 B7
Ramingining, *Australia* 94 A2
Ramla, *Israel* 75 D3
Ramlu, *Eritrea* 81 E5
Râmna →, *Romania* 43 E12
Ramnad = Ramanathapuram,
  India 66 Q11
Ramnagar, Jammu & Kashmir,
  India 69 C6
Ramnagar, Ut. P., *India* 69 E8
Ramnäs, *Sweden* 10 E10
Râmnicu Sărat, *Romania* 43 E12
Râmnicu Vâlcea, *Romania* ... 43 E9
Ramon, *Russia* 47 G10
Ramona, *U.S.A.* 117 M10
Ramonville-St-Agne, *France* .. 20 E5
Ramore, *Canada* 102 C3
Ramos →, *Nigeria* 83 D6
Ramotswa, *Botswana* 88 C4
Rampur, H.P., *India* 68 D7
Rampur, Mad. P., *India* 68 H5
Rampur, Ut. P., *India* 69 E8
Rampur Hat, *India* 69 G12
Rampura, *India* 68 G6
Ramrama Tola, *India* 69 J8
Ramree I., *Burma* 67 K19
Rāmsar, *Iran* 71 B6
Ramsey, *U.K.* 12 C3
Ramsey, *U.S.A.* 111 E10
Ramsey L., *Canada* 102 C3
Ramsgate, *U.K.* 13 F9
Ramsjö, *Sweden* 10 B9
Ramstein, *Germany* 25 F3
Ramtek, *India* 66 J11
Ramvik, *Sweden* 10 B11
Rana Pratap Sagar Dam, *India* .. 68 G6
Ranaghat, *India* 69 H13
Ranahu, *Pakistan* 68 G3
Ranau, *Malaysia* 62 C5
Rancagua, *Chile* 126 C1
Rance →, *France* 18 D5
Rancheria →, *Canada* 104 A3
Ranchester, *U.S.A.* 114 D10
Ranchi, *India* 69 H11
Rancho Cucamonga, *U.S.A.* .. 117 L9
Randalstown, *U.K.* 15 B5
Randan, *France* 19 F10
Randazzo, *Italy* 31 E7
Randers, *Denmark* 11 H4
Randers Fjord, *Denmark* 11 H4
Randfontein, S. Africa 89 D4
Randle, *U.S.A.* 116 D5
Randolph, Mass., *U.S.A.* 111 D13
Randolph, N.Y., *U.S.A.* 110 D6
Randolph, Utah, *U.S.A.* 114 F8
Randolph, Vt., *U.S.A.* 111 C12
Randsburg, *U.S.A.* 117 K9
Råne älv →, *Sweden* 8 D20
Rangae, *Thailand* 65 J3
Rangaunu B., *N.Z.* 91 F4
Rangeley, *U.S.A.* 111 B14
Rangeley L., *U.S.A.* 111 B14
Rangely, *U.S.A.* 114 F9
Ranger, *U.S.A.* 113 J5
Rangia, *India* 67 F17
Rangiora, *N.Z.* 91 K4
Rangitaiki →, *N.Z.* 91 G6
Rangitata →, *N.Z.* 91 K3
Rangkasbitung, *Indonesia* ... 63 G12
Rangon →, *Burma* 67 L20
Rangoon, *Burma* 67 L20
Rangpur, *Bangla.* 67 G16
Ranibennur, *India* 66 M9
Raniganj, Ut. P., *India* 69 F9
Raniganj, W. Bengal, *India* ... 67 H15
Ranikhet, *India* 69 E8
Raniwara, *India* 66 G8
Ranka, *India* 69 H10
Ranken →, *Australia* 94 C2
Rankin, *U.S.A.* 113 K4
Rankin Inlet, *Canada* 100 B10
Rankweil, *Austria* 26 D2
Rannoch, L., *U.K.* 14 E4
Rannoch Moor, *U.K.* 14 E4
Ranobe, Helodran᾽ i, *Madag.* .. 89 C7
Ranohira, *Madag.* 89 C8
Ranomafana, Toamasina,
  Madag. 89 B8
Ranomafana, Toliara, *Madag.* .. 89 C8
Ranomena, *Madag.* 89 C8
Ranong, *Thailand* 65 H2
Ranotsara Nord, *Madag.* 89 C8
Ränsa, *Iran* 71 C6
Ransiki, *Indonesia* 63 E8
Rantabe, *Madag.* 89 B8
Rantauprapat, *Indonesia* 62 D1
Rantemario, *Indonesia* 63 E5
Rantoul, *U.S.A.* 108 E1
Ranum, *Denmark* 11 H3
Ranyah, W. →, *Si. Arabia* ... 80 C5

Raon l'Étape, *France* 19 D13
Raoping, *China* 59 F11
Raoyang, *China* 56 E8
Rapa, Pac. Oc. 97 K13
Rapallo, *Italy* 28 D6
Rapar, *India* 68 H4
Rāpch, *Iran* 71 E8
Raper, C., *Canada* 101 B13
Rapid City, *U.S.A.* 112 D3
Rapid River, *U.S.A.* 108 C2
Rapla, *Estonia* 9 G21
Rapti →, *India* 69 F10
Rapu Rapu I., *Phil.* 61 E6
Raqaba ez Zarqa →, *Sudan* ... 81 F2
Raquette →, *U.S.A.* 111 B10
Raquette Lake, *U.S.A.* 111 C10
Rarotonga, Cook Is. 97 K12
Ra's al 'Ayn, *Syria* 70 B4
Ra's al Khaymah, *U.A.E.* 71 E7
Rās el Mâ, *Mali* 82 B4
Ras Ghārib, *Egypt* 80 B3
Ras Mallap, *Egypt* 80 B3
Rasca, Pta. de la, Canary Is. .. 37 G3
Rāṣcani, *Moldova* 43 C12
Raseiniai, *Lithuania* 9 J20
Rashad, *Sudan* 81 E3
Rashad, *Egypt* 80 H7
Rashīd, Masabb, *Egypt* 80 H7
Rashmi, *India* 68 G6
Rasht, *Iran* 71 B6
Rasi Salai, *Thailand* 64 E5
Raška, *Serbia, Yug.* 40 C4
Rason L., *Australia* 93 E3
Raşova, *Romania* 43 F12
Rasovo, *Bulgaria* 40 C7
Rasra, *India* 69 G10
Rasskazovo, *Russia* 48 D5
Rast, *Romania* 43 G8
Rastede, *Germany* 24 B4
Rastede, *Germany* 24 B4
Rasul, *Pakistan* 68 C5
Raszków, *Poland* 45 G4
Rat Buri, *Thailand* 64 F2
Rat Islands, *U.S.A.* 100 C1
Rat L., *Canada* 105 B9
Ratangarh, *India* 68 E6
Rātansbyn, *Sweden* 10 B8
Rath, *India* 69 G8
Rath Luirc, *Ireland* 15 D3
Rathdrum, *Ireland* 15 D5
Rathenow, *Germany* 24 C8
Rathkeale, *Ireland* 15 D3
Rathlin I., *U.K.* 15 A5
Rathmelton, *Ireland* 15 A4
Ratibor = Racibórz, *Poland* .. 45 H5
Rātikon, *Austria* 26 D2
Ratingen, *Germany* 24 D2
Ratlam, *India* 68 H6
Ratnagiri, *India* 66 L8
Ratodero, *Pakistan* 68 F3
Raton, *U.S.A.* 113 G2
Rattaphum, *Thailand* 65 J3
Ratten, *Austria* 26 D8
Rattray Hd., *U.K.* 14 D7
Rättvik, *Sweden* 10 D9
Ratz, Mt., *Canada* 104 B2
Ratzeburg, *Germany* 24 B6
Raub, *Malaysia* 65 L3
Rauch, *Argentina* 126 D4
Raudales de Malpaso, *Mexico* . 119 D6
Raufarhöfn, *Iceland* 8 C6
Raufoss, *Norway* 9 F14
Raukumara Ra., *N.Z.* 91 H6
Rauma, *Finland* 9 F19
Rauma →, *Norway* 9 E12
Raurkela, *India* 69 H11
Rausu-Dake, *Japan* 54 B12
Rāut →, *Moldova* 43 C14
Rava-Ruska, *Poland* 47 G2
Rava Russkaya = Rava-Ruska,
  Poland 47 G2
Ravalli, *U.S.A.* 114 C6
Rāvānsar, *Iran* 70 C5
Ravanusa, *Italy* 30 E6
Ravar, *Iran* 71 D8
Ravena, *U.S.A.* 111 D11
Ravenna, *Italy* 29 D9
Ravenna, Nebr., *U.S.A.* 112 E5
Ravenna, Ohio, *U.S.A.* 110 E3
Ravensburg, *Germany* 25 H5
Ravenshoe, *Australia* 94 B4
Ravensthorpe, *Australia* 93 F3
Ravenswood, *Australia* 94 C4
Ravenswood, *U.S.A.* 108 F5
Ravi →, *Pakistan* 68 D4
Ravna Gora, *Croatia* 29 C11
Ravna Reka, *Serbia, Yug.* 40 C5
Ravne na Koroškem, *Slovenia* . 29 B11
Rawa Mazowiecka, *Poland* ... 45 G7
Rawalpindi, *Pakistan* 68 C5
Rawāndūz, *Iraq* 70 B5
Rawang, *Malaysia* 65 L3
Rawene, *N.Z.* 91 F4
Rawicz, *Poland* 45 G3
Rawka →, *Poland* 45 F7
Rawlinna, *Australia* 93 F4
Rawlins, *U.S.A.* 114 F10
Rawlinson Ra., *Australia* 93 D4
Rawson, *Argentina* 128 E3
Raxaul, *India* 69 F11
Ray, *U.S.A.* 112 A3
Ray, C., *Canada* 103 C8
Rayadurg, *India* 66 M10
Rayagada, *India* 67 K13

Raychikhinsk, *Russia* 51 E13
Rāyen, *Iran* 71 D8
Rayleigh, *U.K.* 13 F8
Raymond, *Canada* 104 D6
Raymond, Calif., *U.S.A.* 116 H7
Raymond, N.H., *U.S.A.* 111 C13
Raymond, Wash., *U.S.A.* 116 D3
Raymondville, *U.S.A.* 113 M6
Raymore, *Canada* 105 C8
Rayón, *Mexico* 118 B2
Rayong, *Thailand* 64 F3
Rayville, *U.S.A.* 113 J9
Raz, Pte. du, *France* 18 D2
Razan, *Iran* 71 C6
Ražana, *Serbia, Yug.* 40 B3
Ražanj, *Serbia, Yug.* 40 C5
Razdelna, *Bulgaria* 41 C11
Razdel᾽naya = Rozdilna,
  Ukraine 47 J6
Razdolnoye, *Russia* 54 C5
Razdolnoye, *Ukraine* 47 K7
Razeh, *Iran* 71 C6
Razgrad, *Bulgaria* 41 C10
Razim, Lacul, *Romania* 43 F14
Razlog, *Bulgaria* 40 E7
Razmak, *Pakistan* 68 C3
Ré, Î. de, *France* 20 B2
Reading, *U.K.* 13 F7
Reading, *U.S.A.* 111 F9
Reading □, *U.K.* 13 F7
Realicó, *Argentina* 126 D3
Réalmont, *France* 20 E6
Ream, *Cambodia* 65 G4
Reata, *Mexico* 118 B4
Reay Forest, *U.K.* 14 C4
Rebais, *France* 19 D10
Rebi, *Indonesia* 63 F8
Rebiana, *Libya* 79 D10
Rebun-Tō, *Japan* 54 B10
Recanati, *Italy* 29 E10
Recaş, *Romania* 42 E6
Recco, *Italy* 28 D6
Recherche, Arch. of the,
  Australia 93 F3
Rechna Doab, *Pakistan* 68 D5
Rechytsa, *Belarus* 47 F6
Recife, *Brazil* 125 E12
Recklinghausen, *Germany* ... 17 C7
Reconquista, *Argentina* 126 B4
Recreo, *Argentina* 126 B2
Recz, *Poland* 45 E2
Red →, La., *U.S.A.* 113 K9
Red →, N. Dak., *U.S.A.* 100 C10
Red Bank, *U.S.A.* 111 F10
Red Bay, *Canada* 103 B8
Red Bluff, *U.S.A.* 114 F2
Red Bluff L., *U.S.A.* 113 K3
Red Cloud, *U.S.A.* 112 E5
Red Creek, *U.S.A.* 111 C8
Red Deer, *Canada* 104 C6
Red Deer →, Alta., Canada 105 C7
Red Deer →, Man., Canada ... 105 C8
Red Deer L., *Canada* 105 C8
Red Hook, *U.S.A.* 111 E11
Red Indian L., *Canada* 103 C8
Red L., *Canada* 105 C10
Red Lake, *Canada* 105 C10
Red Lake Falls, *U.S.A.* 112 B6
Red Lake Road, *Canada* 105 C10
Red Lodge, *U.S.A.* 114 D9
Red Mountain, *U.S.A.* 117 K9
Red Oak, *U.S.A.* 112 E7
Red Rock, *Canada* 102 C2
Red Rock, L., *U.S.A.* 112 E8
Red Rocks Pt., *Australia* 93 F4
Red Sea, Asia 74 C2
Red Slate Mt., *U.S.A.* 116 H8
Red Sucker L., *Canada* 102 B1
Red Tower Pass = Turnu Roşu,
  P., *Romania* 43 E9
Red Wing, *U.S.A.* 112 C8
Reda, *Poland* 44 D5
Redang, *Malaysia* 62 C2
Redange, *Lux.* 17 E5
Redcar, *U.K.* 12 C6
Redcar & Cleveland □, *U.K.* .. 12 C7
Redcliff, *Canada* 105 C6
Redcliffe, *Australia* 95 D5
Redcliffe, Mt., *Australia* 93 E3
Reddersburg, S. Africa 88 D4
Redding, *U.S.A.* 114 F2
Redditch, *U.K.* 13 E6
Redfield, *U.S.A.* 112 C5
Redford, *U.S.A.* 111 B11
Redhead, *Trin. & Tob.* 121 D7
Redkino, *Russia* 46 D9
Redlands, *U.S.A.* 117 M9
Redmond, Oreg., *U.S.A.* 114 D3
Redmond, Wash., *U.S.A.* 116 C4
Redon, *France* 18 E4
Redonda, Antigua 121 C7
Redondela, *Spain* 34 C2
Redondo, *Portugal* 35 G3
Redondo Beach, *U.S.A.* 117 M8
Redruth, *U.K.* 13 G2
Redvers, *Canada* 105 D8
Redwater, *Canada* 104 C6
Redwood, *U.S.A.* 111 B9
Redwood City, *U.S.A.* 116 H4
Redwood Falls, *U.S.A.* 112 C7
Redwood National Park, *U.S.A.* . 114 F1
Ree, L., *Ireland* 15 C3
Reed, L., *Canada* 105 C8
Reed City, *U.S.A.* 108 D3
Reedley, *U.S.A.* 116 J7
Reedsburg, *U.S.A.* 112 D9
Reedsport, *U.S.A.* 114 E1

Reedsville, *U.S.A.* 110 F7
Reefton, *N.Z.* 91 K3
Rees, *Germany* 24 D2
Reese →, *U.S.A.* 114 F5
Refahiye, *Turkey* 73 C8
Reftele, *Sweden* 11 G7
Refugio, *U.S.A.* 113 L6
Rega →, *Poland* 44 D2
Regalbuto, *Italy* 31 E7
Regen, *Germany* 25 G9
Regen →, *Germany* 25 F8
Regensburg, *Germany* 25 F8
Regenstauf, *Germany* 25 F8
Reggâne = Zaouiet Reggâne,
  Algeria 78 C6
Réggio di Calábria, *Italy* 31 D8
Réggio nell'Emília, *Italy* 28 D7
Reghin, *Romania* 43 D9
Regina, *Canada* 105 C8
Regina Beach, *Canada* 105 C8
Registro, *Brazil* 127 A6
Reguengos de Monsaraz,
  Portugal 35 G3
Rehar →, *India* 69 H10
Rehli, *India* 69 H8
Rehoboth, *Namibia* 88 C2
Rehovot, *Israel* 75 D3
Reichenbach, *Germany* 24 E8
Reid, *Australia* 93 F4
Reidsville, *U.S.A.* 109 G6
Reigate, *U.K.* 13 F7
Reillo, *Spain* 32 F3
Reims, *France* 19 C11
Reina Adelaida, Arch., *Chile* .. 128 G2
Reinbek, *Germany* 24 B6
Reindeer →, *Canada* 105 B8
Reindeer I., *Canada* 105 C9
Reindeer L., *Canada* 105 B8
Reinga, C., *N.Z.* 91 F4
Reinosa, *Spain* 34 B6
Reitz, S. Africa 89 D4
Reivilo, S. Africa 88 D3
Rejaf, *Sudan* 81 G3
Rejmyre, *Sweden* 11 F9
Rejowiec Fabryczny, *Poland* .. 45 G10
Reka →, *Slovenia* 29 C11
Rekovac, *Serbia, Yug.* 40 C5
Reliance, *Canada* 105 A7
Rémalard, *France* 18 D7
Rembang, *Indonesia* 63 G14
Remedios, *Panama* 120 E3
Remeshk, *Iran* 71 E8
Remetea, *Romania* 43 D10
Remich, *Lux.* 17 E6
Remiremont, *France* 19 D13
Remo, *Ethiopia* 81 F5
Remontnoye, *Russia* 49 G6
Remoulins, *France* 21 E8
Remscheid, *Germany* 17 C7
Ren Xian, *China* 56 F8
Rende, *Italy* 31 C9
Rendína, *Greece* 38 B3
Rendsburg, *Germany* 24 A5
Renfrew, *Canada* 102 C4
Renfrewshire □, *U.K.* 14 F4
Rengat, *Indonesia* 62 E2
Rengo, *Chile* 126 C1
Renhua, *China* 59 E9
Renhuai, *China* 58 D6
Reni, *Ukraine* 47 K5
Renk, *Sudan* 81 E3
Rennell Sd., *Canada* 104 C2
Renner Springs, *Australia* ... 94 B1
Rennes, *France* 18 D5
Rennie L., *Canada* 105 A7
Reno, *U.S.A.* 116 F7
Reno →, *Italy* 29 D9
Renovo, *U.S.A.* 110 E7
Renqiu, *China* 56 E9
Rens, *Denmark* 11 K3
Renshou, *China* 58 C5
Rensselaer, Ind., *U.S.A.* 108 E2
Rensselaer, N.Y., *U.S.A.* 111 D11
Rentería, *Spain* 32 B3
Renton, *U.S.A.* 116 C4
Réo, *Burkina Faso* 82 C4
Reocín, *Spain* 34 B6
Reotipur, *India* 69 G10
Republic, Mo., *U.S.A.* 113 G8
Republic, Wash., *U.S.A.* 114 B4
Republican →, *U.S.A.* 112 F6
Repulse Bay, *Canada* 101 B11
Requena, *Peru* 124 E4
Requena, *Spain* 33 F3
Reşadiye = Datça, *Turkey* 39 E9
Reşadiye, *Turkey* 72 B7
Reşadiye Yarımadası, *Turkey* .. 39 E9
Resavica, *Serbia, Yug.* 40 B5
Resen, *Macedonia* 40 E4
Reserve, *U.S.A.* 115 K9
Resht = Rasht, *Iran* 71 B6
Resistencia, *Argentina* 126 B4
Reşiţa, *Romania* 42 E6
Resko, *Poland* 44 E2
Resolution I., *Canada* 101 B13
Resolution I., *N.Z.* 91 L1
Ressano Garcia, *Mozam.* 89 D5
Reston, *Canada* 105 D8
Reszel, *Poland* 44 D8
Retalhuleu, *Guatemala* 120 D1
Retenue, L. de, Dem. Rep. of
  the Congo 87 E2
Retezat, Munţii, *Romania* ... 42 E8

Retford, U.K. 12 D7
Rethel, France 19 C11
Rethem, Germany 24 C5
Réthímnon, Greece 36 D6
Réthímnon □, Greece 36 D6
Reti, Pakistan 68 E3
Retiche, Alpi, Switz. 25 J6
Retiers, France 18 E5
Retortillo, Spain 34 E4
Retournac, France 21 C8
Rétság, Hungary 42 C4
Réunion ■, Ind. Oc. 77 J9
Reus, Spain 32 D6
Reuterstadt Stavenhagen, Germany 24 B8
Reutlingen, Germany 25 G5
Reutte, Austria 26 D3
Reval = Tallinn, Estonia 9 G21
Revel, France 20 E6
Revelganj, India 69 G11
Revelstoke, Canada 104 C5
Reventazón, Peru 124 E2
Revigny-sur-Ornain, France 19 D11
Revillagigedo, Is. de, Pac. Oc. 118 D2
Revin, France 19 C11
Revúca, Slovak Rep. 27 C13
Revuè →, Mozam. 87 F3
Rewa, India 69 G9
Rewari, India 68 E7
Rexburg, U.S.A. 114 E8
Rey, Iran 71 C6
Rey, I. del, Panama 120 E4
Rey Malabo, Eq. Guin. 83 E6
Reyðarfjörður, Iceland 8 D6
Reyes, Pt., U.S.A. 116 H3
Reyhanlı, Turkey 72 D7
Reykjahlíð, Iceland 8 D5
Reykjanes, Iceland 8 E2
Reykjavík, Iceland 8 D3
Reynolds Ra., Australia 92 D5
Reynoldsville, U.S.A. 110 E6
Reynosa, Mexico 119 B5
Rēzekne, Latvia 9 H22
Rezina, Moldova 43 C13
Rezovo, Bulgaria 41 D12
Rezvān, Iran 71 E8
Rgotina, Serbia, Yug. 40 B6
Rhamnus, Greece 38 C6
Rhayader, U.K. 13 E4
Rheda-Wiedenbrück, Germany 24 D4
Rhede, Germany 24 D2
Rhein →, Europe 17 C6
Rhein-Main-Donau-Kanal, Germany 25 F7
Rheinbach, Germany 24 E2
Rheine, Germany 24 C3
Rheinfelden, Germany 25 H3
Rheinhessen-Pfalz □, Germany 25 F3
Rheinland-Pfalz □, Germany 25 E2
Rheinsberg, Germany 24 B8
Rhin = Rhein →, Europe 17 C6
Rhine = Rhein →, Europe 17 C6
Rhinebeck, U.S.A. 111 E11
Rhineland-Palatinate = Rheinland-Pfalz □, Germany 25 E2
Rhinelander, U.S.A. 112 C10
Rhinns Pt., U.K. 14 F2
Rhino Camp, Uganda 86 B3
Rhir, Cap, Morocco 78 B4
Rho, Italy 28 C6
Rhode Island □, U.S.A. 111 E13
Rhodes = Ródhos, Greece 36 C10
Rhodesia = Zimbabwe ■, Africa 87 F3
Rhodope Mts. = Rhodopi Planina, Bulgaria 41 E8
Rhodopi Planina, Bulgaria 41 E8
Rhön, Germany 24 E5
Rhondda, U.K. 13 F4
Rhondda Cynon Taff □, U.K. 13 F4
Rhône □, France 21 C8
Rhône →, France 21 E8
Rhône-Alpes □, France 21 C9
Rhum, U.K. 14 E2
Rhyl, U.K. 12 D4
Ri-Aba, Eq. Guin. 83 E6
Riachão, Brazil 125 E9
Riangnom, Sudan 81 F3
Riaño, Spain 34 C6
Rians, France 21 E9
Riansáres →, Spain 35 F7
Riasi, India 69 C6
Riau □, Indonesia 62 D2
Riau, Kepulauan, Indonesia 62 D2
Riau Arch. = Riau, Kepulauan, Indonesia 62 D2
Riaza, Spain 34 D7
Riaza →, Spain 34 D7
Riba de Saelices, Spain 32 D2
Riba-Roja de Turia, Spain 33 F4
Ribadavia, Spain 34 C2
Ribadeo, Spain 34 B3
Ribadesella, Spain 34 B5
Ribado, Nigeria 83 D7
Ribas = Ribes de Freser, Spain 32 C7
Ribas do Rio Pardo, Brazil 125 H8
Ribble →, U.K. 12 D5
Ribe, Denmark 11 J2
Ribe Amtskommune □, Denmark 11 J2
Ribeauvillé, France 19 D14
Ribécourt-Dreslincourt, France 19 C9
Ribeira = Santa Uxía, Spain 34 C2
Ribeira Brava, Madeira 37 D2
Ribeirão Prêto, Brazil 127 A6
Ribemont, France 19 C10

Ribera, Italy 30 E6
Ribérac, France 20 C4
Riberalta, Bolivia 124 F5
Ribes de Freser, Spain 32 C7
Ribnica, Slovenia 29 C11
Ribnitz-Damgarten, Germany 24 A8
Ričany, Czech Rep. 26 B7
Riccarton, N.Z. 91 K4
Ríccia, Italy 31 A7
Riccione, Italy 29 E9
Rice, U.S.A. 117 L12
Rice L., Canada 110 B6
Rice Lake, U.S.A. 112 C9
Rich, C., Canada 110 B4
Richard Toll, Senegal 82 B1
Richards Bay, S. Africa 89 D5
Richardson →, Canada 105 B6
Richardson Lakes, U.S.A. 108 C10
Richardson Springs, U.S.A. 116 F5
Riche, C., Australia 93 F2
Richelieu, France 18 E7
Richey, U.S.A. 112 B2
Richfield, U.S.A. 115 G8
Richfield Springs, U.S.A. 111 D10
Richford, U.S.A. 111 B12
Richibucto, Canada 103 C7
Richland, Ga., U.S.A. 109 J3
Richland, Wash., U.S.A. 114 C4
Richland Center, U.S.A. 112 D9
Richlands, U.S.A. 108 G5
Richmond, Australia 94 C3
Richmond, N.Z. 91 J4
Richmond, U.K. 12 C6
Richmond, Calif., U.S.A. 116 H4
Richmond, Ind., U.S.A. 108 F3
Richmond, Ky., U.S.A. 108 G3
Richmond, Mich., U.S.A. 110 D2
Richmond, Mo., U.S.A. 112 F8
Richmond, Tex., U.S.A. 113 L7
Richmond, Utah, U.S.A. 114 F8
Richmond, Va., U.S.A. 108 G7
Richmond, Vt., U.S.A. 111 B12
Richmond Hill, Canada 110 C5
Richmond Ra., Australia 95 D5
Richwood, U.S.A. 108 F5
Ricla, Spain 32 D3
Ridder = Leninogorsk, Kazakstan 50 D9
Riddlesburg, U.S.A. 110 F6
Ridgecrest, U.S.A. 117 K9
Ridgefield, Conn., U.S.A. 111 E11
Ridgefield, Wash., U.S.A. 116 E4
Ridgeland, U.S.A. 109 J5
Ridgetown, Canada 102 D3
Ridgewood, U.S.A. 111 F10
Ridgway, U.S.A. 110 E6
Riding Mountain Nat. Park, Canada 105 C9
Ridley, Mt., Australia 93 F3
Riebeek-Oos, S. Africa 88 E4
Ried, Austria 26 C6
Riedlingen, Germany 25 G5
Riedstadt, Germany 25 F4
Rienza →, Italy 29 B8
Riesa, Germany 24 D9
Riesi, Italy 31 E7
Riet →, S. Africa 88 D3
Rietavas, Lithuania 44 C8
Rietbron, S. Africa 88 E3
Rietfontein, Namibia 88 C3
Rieti, Italy 29 F9
Rieupeyroux, France 20 D6
Riez, France 21 E10
Riffe L., U.S.A. 116 D4
Rifle, U.S.A. 114 G10
Rift Valley □, Kenya 86 B4
Rīga, Latvia 9 H21
Riga, G. of, Latvia 9 H20
Rigacikun, Nigeria 83 C6
Rīgān, Iran 71 D8
Rīgas Jūras Līcis = Riga, G. of, Latvia 9 H20
Rigaud, Canada 111 A10
Rigby, U.S.A. 114 E8
Rīgestān, Afghan. 66 D4
Riggins, U.S.A. 114 D5
Rignac, France 20 D6
Rigolet, Canada 103 B8
Rihand Dam, India 69 G10
Riihimäki, Finland 9 F21
Riiser-Larsen-halvøya, Antarctica 5 C4
Rijau, Nigeria 83 C6
Rijeka, Croatia 29 C11
Rijeka Crnojevića, Montenegro, Yug. 40 D3
Rijssen, Neths. 17 B6
Rike, Ethiopia 81 E4
Rikuzentakada, Japan 54 E10
Rila, Bulgaria 40 D7
Rila Planina, Bulgaria 40 D7
Riley, U.S.A. 114 E4
Rima →, Nigeria 83 C6
Rimah, Wadi ar →, Si. Arabia 70 E4
Rimavská Sobota, Slovak Rep. 27 C13
Rimbey, Canada 104 C6
Rimbo, Sweden 10 E12
Rimersburg, U.S.A. 110 E5
Rimforsa, Sweden 11 F9
Rímini, Italy 29 D9
Rimouski, Canada 103 C6
Rimrock, U.S.A. 116 D5
Rinca, Indonesia 63 F5
Rincón de la Victoria, Spain 35 J6
Rincón de Romos, Mexico 118 C4

Rinconada, Argentina 126 A2
Rind →, India 69 G9
Ringarum, Sweden 11 F10
Ringas, India 68 F6
Ringe, Denmark 11 J4
Ringim, Nigeria 83 C6
Ringkøbing, Denmark 11 H2
Ringkøbing Amtskommune □, Denmark 11 H2
Ringkøbing Fjord, Denmark 11 H2
Ringsjön, Sweden 11 J7
Ringsted, Denmark 11 J5
Ringvassøy, Norway 8 B18
Ringwood, U.S.A. 111 E10
Rinía, Greece 39 D7
Rinjani, Indonesia 62 F5
Rinteln, Germany 24 C5
Río, Punta del, Spain 33 J2
Rio Branco, Brazil 124 E5
Río Branco, Uruguay 127 C5
Río Bravo del Norte →, Mexico 119 B5
Rio Brilhante, Brazil 127 A5
Rio Claro, Brazil 127 A6
Rio Claro, Trin. & Tob. 121 D7
Río Colorado, Argentina 128 D4
Río Cuarto, Argentina 126 C3
Rio das Pedras, Mozam. 89 C6
Rio de Janeiro, Brazil 127 A7
Rio de Janeiro □, Brazil 127 A7
Rio do Sul, Brazil 127 B6
Río Gallegos, Argentina 128 G3
Rio Grande = Grande, Rio →, U.S.A. 113 N6
Río Grande, Argentina 128 G3
Rio Grande, Brazil 127 C5
Río Grande, Mexico 118 C4
Río Grande, Nic. 120 D3
Rio Grande City, U.S.A. 113 M5
Río Grande de Santiago →, Mexico 118 C3
Rio Grande do Norte □, Brazil 125 E11
Rio Grande do Sul □, Brazil 127 C5
Río Hato, Panama 120 E3
Rio Lagartos, Mexico 119 C7
Rio Largo, Brazil 125 E11
Río Maior, Portugal 35 F2
Río Marina, Italy 28 F7
Río Mulatos, Bolivia 124 G5
Río Muni = Mbini □, Eq. Guin. 84 D2
Rio Negro, Brazil 127 B6
Rio Pardo, Brazil 127 C5
Rio Rancho, U.S.A. 115 J10
Río Segundo, Argentina 126 C3
Río Tercero, Argentina 126 C3
Rio Tinto, Portugal 34 D2
Rio Verde, Brazil 125 G8
Rio Verde, Mexico 119 C5
Rio Vista, U.S.A. 116 G5
Ríobamba, Ecuador 124 D3
Ríohacha, Colombia 124 A4
Riom, France 20 C7
Riom-ès-Montagnes, France 20 C6
Rion-des-Landes, France 20 E3
Rionero in Vúlture, Italy 31 B8
Rioni →, Georgia 49 J5
Ríos, Spain 34 D3
Riosucio, Colombia 124 B3
Riou L., Canada 105 B7
Rioz, France 19 E13
Ripatransone, Italy 29 F10
Ripley, Canada 110 B3
Ripley, Calif., U.S.A. 117 M12
Ripley, N.Y., U.S.A. 110 D5
Ripley, Tenn., U.S.A. 113 H10
Ripley, W. Va., U.S.A. 108 F5
Ripoll, Spain 32 C7
Ripon, U.K. 12 C6
Ripon, Calif., U.S.A. 116 H5
Ripon, Wis., U.S.A. 108 D1
Riposto, Italy 31 E8
Risan, Montenegro, Yug. 40 D2
Riscle, France 20 E3
Rishâ', W. ar →, Si. Arabia 70 E5
Rishiri-Tō, Japan 54 B10
Rishon le Ziyyon, Israel 75 D3
Rishton, U.K. 12 D5
Risle →, France 18 C7
Rison, U.S.A. 113 J8
Risør, Norway 9 G13
Rita Blanca Cr. →, U.S.A. 113 H3
Riti, Nigeria 83 D6
Ritter, Mt., U.S.A. 116 H7
Rittman, U.S.A. 110 F3
Ritzville, U.S.A. 114 C4
Riva del Garda, Italy 28 C7
Riva Lígure, Italy 28 E4
Rivadavia, Buenos Aires, Argentina 126 D3
Rivadavia, Mendoza, Argentina 126 C2
Rivadavia, Salta, Argentina 126 A3
Rivadavia, Chile 126 B1
Rivarolo Canavese, Italy 28 C4
Rivas, Nic. 120 D2
Rive-de-Gier, France 21 C8
River Cess, Liberia 82 D3
River Jordan, Canada 116 B2
Rivera, Argentina 126 D3
Rivera, Uruguay 127 C4
Riverbank, U.S.A. 116 H6
Riverdale, U.S.A. 116 J7
Riverhead, U.S.A. 111 F12
Riverhurst, Canada 105 C7
Rivers □, Nigeria 83 E6
Rivers Inlet, Canada 104 C3
Riversdale, S. Africa 88 E3
Riverside, U.S.A. 117 M9

Riverton, Canada 105 C9
Riverton, N.Z. 91 M2
Riverton, U.S.A. 114 E9
Riverton Heights, U.S.A. 116 C4
Rives, France 21 C9
Rivesaltes, France 20 F6
Riviera, U.S.A. 117 K12
Riviera di Levante, Italy 28 D6
Riviera di Ponente, Italy 28 D5
Rivière-au-Renard, Canada 103 C7
Rivière-du-Loup, Canada 103 C6
Rivière-Pentecôte, Canada 103 C6
Rivière-Pilote, Martinique 121 D7
Rivière St. Paul, Canada 103 B8
Rivne, Ukraine 47 G4
Rívoli, Italy 28 C4
Rixheim, France 19 E14
Riyadh = Ar Riyāḍ, Si. Arabia 70 E5
Rize, Turkey 73 B9
Rizhao, China 57 G10
Rizokarpaso, Cyprus 36 D13
Rizzuto, C., Italy 31 D10
Rjukan, Norway 9 G13
Ro, Greece 39 E11
Roa, Spain 34 D7
Road Town, Br. Virgin Is. 121 C7
Roan Plateau, U.S.A. 114 G9
Roanne, France 19 F11
Roanoke, Ala., U.S.A. 109 J3
Roanoke, Va., U.S.A. 108 G6
Roanoke →, U.S.A. 109 H7
Roanoke I., U.S.A. 109 H8
Roanoke Rapids, U.S.A. 109 G7
Roatán, Honduras 120 C2
Robāṭ Sang, Iran 71 C8
Robbins I., Australia 94 G4
Röbel, Germany 24 B8
Robert Lee, U.S.A. 113 K4
Robertsdale, U.S.A. 110 F6
Robertsganj, India 69 G10
Robertson, S. Africa 88 E2
Robertson I., Antarctica 5 C18
Robertson Ra., Australia 92 D3
Robertsport, Liberia 82 D2
Roberval, Canada 103 C5
Robeson Chan., Greenland 4 A4
Robesonia, U.S.A. 111 F8
Robi, Ethiopia 81 F4
Robinson, U.S.A. 108 F2
Robinson →, Australia 94 B2
Robinson Ra., Australia 93 E2
Robledo, Spain 33 G2
Roblin, Canada 105 C8
Roboré, Bolivia 124 G7
Robson, Canada 104 D5
Robson, Mt., Canada 104 C5
Robstown, U.S.A. 113 M6
Roca, C. da, Portugal 35 G1
Roca Partida, I., Mexico 118 D2
Rocas, I., Brazil 125 D12
Rocca San Casciano, Italy 29 D8
Roccadáspide, Italy 31 B8
Roccastrada, Italy 29 F8
Roccella Iónica, Italy 31 D9
Rocha, Uruguay 127 C5
Rochdale, U.K. 12 D5
Rochechouart, France 20 C4
Rochefort, Belgium 17 D5
Rochefort, France 20 C3
Rochefort-en-Terre, France 18 E4
Rochelle, U.S.A. 112 E10
Rocher River, Canada 104 A6
Rocheservière, France 18 F5
Rochester, U.K. 13 F8
Rochester, Ind., U.S.A. 108 E2
Rochester, Minn., U.S.A. 112 C8
Rochester, N.H., U.S.A. 111 C14
Rochester, N.Y., U.S.A. 110 C7
Rock →, Canada 104 A3
Rock Creek, U.S.A. 110 E4
Rock Falls, U.S.A. 112 E10
Rock Hill, U.S.A. 109 H5
Rock Island, U.S.A. 112 E9
Rock Rapids, U.S.A. 112 D6
Rock Sound, Bahamas 120 B4
Rock Springs, Mont., U.S.A. 114 C10
Rock Springs, Wyo., U.S.A. 114 F9
Rock Valley, U.S.A. 112 D6
Rockall, Atl. Oc. 6 D3
Rockdale, Tex., U.S.A. 113 K6
Rockdale, Wash., U.S.A. 116 C5
Rockefeller Plateau, Antarctica 5 E14
Rockford, U.S.A. 112 D10
Rockglen, Canada 105 D7
Rockhampton, Australia 94 C5
Rockingham, Australia 93 F2
Rockingham, U.S.A. 109 H6
Rockingham B., Australia 94 B4
Rocklake, U.S.A. 112 A5
Rockland, Canada 111 A9
Rockland, Idaho, U.S.A. 114 E7
Rockland, Maine, U.S.A. 109 C11
Rockland, Mich., U.S.A. 112 B10
Rocklin, U.S.A. 116 G5
Rockmart, U.S.A. 109 H3
Rockport, Mass., U.S.A. 111 D14
Rockport, Mo., U.S.A. 112 E7
Rockport, Tex., U.S.A. 113 L6
Rockville, Conn., U.S.A. 111 E12
Rockville, Md., U.S.A. 108 F7
Rockwall, U.S.A. 113 J6

Rockwell City, U.S.A. 112 D7
Rockwood, Canada 110 C4
Rockwood, Maine, U.S.A. 109 C11
Rockwood, Tenn., U.S.A. 109 H3
Rocky Ford, U.S.A. 112 F3
Rocky Gully, Australia 93 F2
Rocky Harbour, Canada 103 C8
Rocky Island L., Canada 102 C3
Rocky Lane, Canada 104 B5
Rocky Mount, U.S.A. 109 H7
Rocky Mountain House, Canada 104 C6
Rocky Mountain National Park, U.S.A. 114 F11
Rocky Mts., N. Amer. 114 G10
Rocky Point, Namibia 88 B2
Rocroi, France 19 C11
Rod, Pakistan 66 E3
Rødby, Denmark 11 K5
Rødbyhavn, Denmark 11 K5
Roddickton, Canada 103 B8
Rødding, Denmark 11 J3
Rödeby, Sweden 11 H9
Rødekro, Denmark 11 J3
Rodenkirchen, Germany 24 B4
Rodez, France 20 D6
Rodholívas, Greece 40 F7
Rodhópi □, Greece 41 E9
Rodhopoú, Greece 36 D5
Ródhos, Greece 36 C10
Rodi Gargánico, Italy 29 G12
Rodna, Romania 43 C9
Rodnei, Munții, Romania 43 C9
Rodney, Canada 110 D3
Rodney, C., N.Z. 91 G5
Rodniki, Russia 48 B5
Rodonit, Kepi i, Albania 40 E3
Rodriguez, Ind. Oc. 3 E13
Roe →, U.K. 15 A5
Roebling, U.S.A. 111 F10
Roebourne, Australia 92 D2
Roebuck B., Australia 92 C3
Roermond, Neths. 17 C6
Roes Welcome Sd., Canada 101 B11
Roeselare, Belgium 17 D3
Rogachev = Ragachow, Belarus 47 F6
Rogagua, L., Bolivia 124 F5
Rogaška Slatina, Slovenia 29 B12
Rogatec, Slovenia 29 B12
Rogatica, Bos.-H. 42 G4
Rogatyn, Ukraine 47 H3
Rogdhia, Greece 36 D7
Rogers, U.S.A. 113 G7
Rogers City, U.S.A. 108 C4
Rogersville, Canada 103 C6
Roggan →, Canada 102 B4
Roggan L., Canada 102 B4
Roggeveldberge, S. Africa 88 E3
Roggiano Gravina, Italy 31 C9
Rogliano, France 21 F13
Rogliano, Italy 31 C9
Rogoaguado, L., Bolivia 124 F5
Rogoźno, Poland 45 F3
Rogue →, U.S.A. 114 E1
Rohan, France 18 D4
Róhda, Greece 36 A3
Rohnert Park, U.S.A. 116 G4
Rohri, Pakistan 68 F3
Rohri Canal, Pakistan 68 F3
Rohtak, India 68 E7
Roi Et, Thailand 64 D4
Roja, Latvia 9 H20
Rojas, Argentina 126 C3
Rojiste, Romania 43 F8
Rojo, C., Mexico 119 C5
Rokan →, Indonesia 62 D2
Rokel →, S. Leone 82 D2
Rokiškis, Lithuania 9 J21
Rokitno, Russia 47 G8
Rolândia, Brazil 127 A5
Rolla, U.S.A. 113 G9
Rolleston, Australia 94 C4
Rollingstone, Australia 94 B4
Rom, Sudan 81 F3
Roma, Australia 95 D4
Roma, Italy 29 G9
Roma, Sweden 11 G12
Roma, U.S.A. 113 M5
Romain C., U.S.A. 109 J6
Romaine, Canada 103 B7
Romaine →, Canada 103 B7
Roman, Bulgaria 40 C7
Roman, Romania 43 D11
Roman-Kosh, Gora, Ukraine 47 K8
Romanche →, France 21 C9
Romang, Indonesia 63 F7
Români, Egypt 75 E1
Romania ■, Europe 43 D10
Romanija, Bos.-H. 42 G3
Romano, Cayo, Cuba 120 B4
Romanovka = Basarabeasca, Moldova 43 D13
Romans-sur-Isère, France 21 C9
Romanshorn, Switz. 25 H5
Rombari, Sudan 81 G3
Romblon, Phil. 61 E5
Rome = Roma, Italy 29 G9
Rome, Ga., U.S.A. 109 H3
Rome, N.Y., U.S.A. 111 C9
Rome, Oreg., U.S.A. 114 E5
Rometta, Italy 31 D8
Romilly-sur-Seine, France 19 D10
Romney, U.S.A. 108 F6
Romney Marsh, U.K. 13 F8
Romny, Ukraine 47 G7

Rømø, Denmark 11 J2
Romodan, Ukraine 47 G7
Romodanovo, Russia 48 C7
Romont, Switz. 25 J2
Romorantin-Lanthenay, France 19 E8
Romsdalen, Norway 9 E12
Romsey, U.K. 13 G6
Ron, Vietnam 64 D6
Rona, U.K. 14 D3
Ronan, U.S.A. 114 C6
Roncador, Cayos, Caribbean 120 D3
Roncador, Serra do, Brazil 125 F8
Ronciglione, Italy 29 F9
Ronco →, Italy 29 D9
Ronda, Spain 35 J5
Ronda, Serranía de, Spain 35 J5
Rondane, Norway 9 F13
Rondônia □, Brazil 124 F6
Rondonópolis, Brazil 125 G8
Rong, Koh, Cambodia 65 G4
Rong Jiang →, China 58 E7
Rong Xian, Guangxi Zhuangzu, China 59 F8
Rong Xian, Sichuan, China 58 C5
Rong'an, China 58 E7
Rongcheng, China 58 C5
Ronge, L. la, Canada 105 B7
Rongjiang, China 58 E7
Rongshui, China 58 E7
Rønne, Denmark 11 J8
Ronne Ice Shelf, Antarctica 5 D18
Ronneby, Sweden 11 H9
Ronnebyån →, Sweden 11 H9
Rönneshyttä, Sweden 11 F9
Ronsard, C., Australia 93 D1
Ronse, Belgium 17 D3
Roodepoort, S. Africa 89 D4
Roof Butte, U.S.A. 115 H9
Rooiboklaagte →, Namibia 88 C3
Roorkee, India 68 E7
Roosendaal, Neths. 17 C4
Roosevelt, U.S.A. 114 F8
Roosevelt →, Brazil 122 D4
Roosevelt, Mt., Canada 104 B3
Roosevelt I., Antarctica 5 D12
Ropczyce, Poland 45 H8
Roper →, Australia 94 A2
Roper Bar, Australia 94 A1
Roque Pérez, Argentina 126 D4
Roquefort, France 20 D3
Roquemaure, France 21 D8
Roquetas de Mar, Spain 33 J2
Roquetes, Spain 32 E5
Roquevaire, France 21 E9
Roraima □, Brazil 124 C6
Roraima, Mte., Venezuela 122 C4
Røros, Norway 9 E14
Rorschach, Switz. 25 H5
Rosa, Zambia 87 D3
Rosa, L., Bahamas 121 B5
Rosa, Monte, Italy 28 C4
Rosal de la Frontera, Spain 35 H3
Rosalia, U.S.A. 114 C5
Rosamond, U.S.A. 117 L8
Rosans, France 21 D9
Rosario, Argentina 126 C3
Rosário, Brazil 125 D10
Rosario, Baja Calif., Mexico 118 B1
Rosario, Sinaloa, Mexico 118 C3
Rosario, Paraguay 126 A4
Rosario de la Frontera, Argentina 126 B3
Rosario de Lerma, Argentina 126 A2
Rosario del Tala, Argentina 126 C4
Rosário do Sul, Brazil 127 C5
Rosarito, Mexico 117 N9
Rosarno, Italy 31 D8
Rosas = Roses, Spain 32 C8
Roscoe, U.S.A. 111 E10
Roscoff, France 18 D3
Roscommon, Ireland 15 C3
Roscommon □, Ireland 15 C3
Roscrea, Ireland 15 D4
Rose →, Australia 94 A2
Rose Blanche, Canada 103 C8
Rose Pt., Canada 104 C2
Rose Valley, Canada 105 C8
Roseau, Domin. 121 C7
Roseau, U.S.A. 112 A7
Rosebery, Australia 94 G4
Rosebud, S. Dak., U.S.A. 112 D4
Rosebud, Tex., U.S.A. 113 K6
Roseburg, U.S.A. 114 E2
Rosedale, U.S.A. 113 J9
Roseland, U.S.A. 116 G4
Rosemary, Canada 104 C6
Rosenberg, U.S.A. 113 L7
Rosendaël, France 19 A9
Rosenheim, Germany 25 H8
Roses, Spain 32 C8
Roses, G. de, Spain 32 C8
Roseto degli Abruzzi, Italy 29 F11
Rosetown, Canada 105 C7
Rosetta = Rashîd, Egypt 80 H7
Roseville, Calif., U.S.A. 116 G5
Roseville, Mich., U.S.A. 110 D2
Rosewood, Australia 95 D5
Roshkhvār, Iran 71 C8
Rosières-en-Santerre, France 19 C9
Rosignano Maríttimo, Italy 28 E7
Rosignol, Guyana 124 B7
Roşiori de Vede, Romania 43 F10
Rositsa, Bulgaria 41 C11
Rositsa →, Bulgaria 41 C9
Roskilde, Denmark 11 J6

Roskilde Amtskommune □, Denmark 11 J6
Roskovec, Albania 40 F3
Roslavl, Russia 46 F7
Rosmaninhal, Portugal 34 F3
Rosmead, S. Africa 88 E4
Rosolini, Italy 31 F7
Rosporden, France 18 E3
Ross, Australia 94 G4
Ross, N.Z. 91 K3
Ross Béthio, Mauritania 82 B1
Ross I., Antarctica 5 D11
Ross Ice Shelf, Antarctica 5 E12
Ross L., U.S.A. 114 B3
Ross-on-Wye, U.K. 13 F5
Ross River, Australia 94 C1
Ross River, Canada 104 A2
Ross Sea, Antarctica 5 D11
Rossall Pt., U.K. 12 D4
Rossan Pt., Ireland 15 B3
Rossano, Italy 31 C9
Rossburn, Canada 105 C8
Rosseau, Canada 110 A5
Rosseau L., Canada 110 A5
Rosses, The, Ireland 15 A3
Rossignol, L., Canada 102 B5
Rossignol Res., Canada 103 D6
Rossland, Canada 104 D5
Rosslare, Ireland 15 D5
Rosslau, Germany 24 D8
Rosso, Mauritania 82 B1
Rosso, C., France 21 F12
Rossosh, Russia 47 G10
Røssvatnet, Norway 8 D16
Røst, Norway 8 C15
Rosthern, Canada 105 C7
Rostock, Germany 24 A8
Rostov, Don, Russia 47 J10
Rostov, Yaroslavl, Russia 46 D10
Rostrenen, France 18 D3
Roswell, Ga., U.S.A. 109 H3
Roswell, N. Mex., U.S.A. 113 J2
Rota, Spain 35 J4
Rotan, U.S.A. 113 J4
Rotenburg, Hessen, Germany 24 E5
Rotenburg, Niedersachsen, Germany 24 B5
Roth, Germany 25 F7
Rothaargebirge, Germany 24 D4
Rothenburg ob der Tauber, Germany 25 F6
Rother →, U.K. 13 G8
Rotherham, U.K. 12 D6
Rothes, U.K. 14 D5
Rothesay, Canada 103 C6
Rothesay, U.K. 14 F3
Roti, Indonesia 63 F6
Rotja, Pta., Spain 33 G6
Rotondo, Mte., France 21 F13
Rotoroa, L., N.Z. 91 J4
Rotorua, N.Z. 91 H6
Rotorua, L., N.Z. 91 H6
Rott →, Germany 25 G9
Rottenburg, Germany 25 G4
Rottenmann, Austria 26 D7
Rotterdam, Neths. 17 C4
Rotterdam, U.S.A. 111 D10
Rottne, Sweden 11 G8
Rottnest I., Australia 93 F2
Rottumeroog, Neths. 17 A6
Rottweil, Germany 25 G4
Rotuma, Fiji 96 J9
Roubaix, France 19 B10
Roudnice nad Labem, Czech Rep. 26 A7
Rouen, France 18 C8
Rouergue, France 20 D5
Rouillac, France 20 C3
Rouleau, Canada 105 C8
Round Mountain, U.S.A. 114 G5
Round Mt., Australia 95 E5
Round Rock, U.S.A. 113 K6
Roundup, U.S.A. 114 C9
Rousay, U.K. 14 B5
Rouses Point, U.S.A. 111 B11
Rouseville, U.S.A. 110 E5
Roussillon, Isère, France 21 C8
Roussillon, Pyrénées-Or., France 20 F6
Rouxville, S. Africa 88 E4
Rouyn-Noranda, Canada 102 C4
Rovaniemi, Finland 8 C21
Rovato, Italy 28 C7
Rovenki, Ukraine 47 H10
Rovereto, Italy 28 C8
Rovigo, Italy 29 C8
Rovinj, Croatia 29 C10
Rovno = Rivne, Ukraine 47 G4
Rovnoye, Russia 48 E8
Rovuma = Ruvuma →, Tanzania 87 E5
Row'ān, Iran 71 C6
Rowena, Australia 95 D4
Rowley Shoals, Australia 92 C2
Roxa, Guinea-Biss. 82 C1
Roxas, Capiz, Phil. 61 F5
Roxas, Isabela, Phil. 61 C4
Roxas, Mind. Or., Phil. 61 E4
Roxboro, U.S.A. 109 G6
Roxburgh, N.Z. 91 L2
Roxbury, U.S.A. 110 F7
Roy, Mont., U.S.A. 114 C9
Roy, N. Mex., U.S.A. 113 H2
Roy, Utah, U.S.A. 114 F7
Royal Canal, Ireland 15 C4

Royal Leamington Spa, U.K. 13 E6
Royal Tunbridge Wells, U.K. 13 F8
Royan, France 20 C2
Roye, France 19 C9
Royston, U.K. 13 E7
Rožaj, Montenegro, Yug. 40 D4
Róžan, Poland 45 F8
Rozay-en-Brie, France 19 D9
Rozdilna, Ukraine 47 J6
Rozhyshche, Ukraine 47 G3
Rožmitál pod Třemšínem, Czech Rep. 26 B6
Rožňava, Slovak Rep. 27 C13
Rozogi, Poland 44 E8
Rozoy-sur-Serre, France 19 C11
Rozzano, Italy 28 C6
Rrëshen, Albania 40 E3
Rrogozhine, Albania 40 E3
Rtanj, Serbia, Yug. 40 C5
Rtishchevo, Russia 48 D6
Rúa = A Rúa, Spain 34 C3
Ruacaná, Namibia 88 B1
Ruahine Ra., N.Z. 91 H6
Ruapehu, N.Z. 91 H5
Ruapuke I., N.Z. 91 M2
Ruäq, W. →, Egypt 75 F2
Rub' al Khālī, Si. Arabia 74 D4
Rubeho Mts., Tanzania 86 D4
Rubezhnoye = Rubizhne, Ukraine 47 H10
Rubh a' Mhail, U.K. 14 F2
Rubha Hunish, U.K. 14 D2
Rubha Robhanais = Lewis, Butt of, U.K. 14 C2
Rubi, Spain 32 D7
Rubicon →, U.S.A. 116 G5
Rubicone →, Italy 29 D9
Rubik, Albania 40 E3
Rubino, Ivory C. 82 D4
Rubio, Venezuela 124 B4
Rubizhne, Ukraine 47 H10
Rubtsovsk, Russia 50 D9
Ruby L., U.S.A. 114 F6
Ruby Mts., U.S.A. 114 F6
Rubyvale, Australia 94 C4
Rucheng, China 59 E9
Ruciane-Nida, Poland 44 E8
Rüd Sar, Iran 71 B6
Ruda, Sweden 11 G10
Ruda Śląska, Poland 45 H5
Rudall, →, Australia 92 D3
Rüdersdorf, Germany 24 C9
Rudewa, Tanzania 87 E3
Rudkøbing, Denmark 11 K4
Rudna, Poland 45 G3
Rudnik, Bulgaria 41 D11
Rudnik, Poland 45 H9
Rudnik, Serbia, Yug. 40 B4
Rudnya, Russia 46 E6
Rudnyy, Kazakstan 50 D7
Rudo, Bos.-H. 42 G4
Rudolfa, Ostrov, Russia 50 A6
Rudolstadt, Germany 24 E7
Rudong, China 59 A13
Rudozem, Bulgaria 41 E8
Rudyard, U.S.A. 108 B3
Rue, France 19 B8
Rufa'a, Sudan 81 E3
Rufiji →, Tanzania 86 D4
Rufino, Argentina 126 C3
Rufisque, Senegal 82 C1
Rufunsa, Zambia 87 F2
Rugao, China 59 A13
Rugby, U.K. 13 E6
Rugby, U.S.A. 112 A5
Rügen, Germany 24 A9
Rugles, France 18 D7
Ruhengeri, Rwanda 86 C2
Ruhla, Germany 24 E6
Ruhland, Germany 24 D9
Ruhnu, Estonia 9 H20
Ruhr →, Germany 24 D2
Ruhuhu →, Tanzania 87 E3
Rui'an, China 59 D13
Ruichang, China 59 C10
Ruidoso, U.S.A. 115 K11
Ruijin, China 59 E10
Ruili, China 58 E1
Ruivo, Pico, Madeira 37 D3
Ruj, Bulgaria 40 D6
Rujen, Macedonia 40 D6
Rujm Tal'at al Jamā'ah, Jordan 75 E4
Ruk, Pakistan 68 F3
Rukhla, Pakistan 68 C4
Ruki →, Dem. Rep. of the Congo 84 E3
Rukwa □, Tanzania 86 D3
Rukwa, L., Tanzania 86 D3
Rulhieres, C., Australia 92 B4
Rum = Rhum, U.K. 14 E2
Rum Cay, Bahamas 121 B5
Rum Jungle, Australia 92 B5
Ruma, Serbia, Yug. 42 E4
Rumaḥ, Si. Arabia 70 E5
Rumania = Romania ■, Europe 43 D10
Rumaylah, Iraq 70 D5
Rumbēk, Sudan 81 F2
Rumburk, Czech Rep. 26 A7
Rumford, U.S.A. 109 C10
Rumia, Poland 44 D5
Rumilly, France 21 C9
Rumoi, Japan 54 C10
Rumonge, Burundi 86 C2
Rumsey, Canada 104 C6
Rumula, Australia 94 B4
Rumuruti, Kenya 86 B4
Runan, China 56 H8

Runanga, N.Z. 91 K3
Runaway, C., N.Z. 91 G6
Runcorn, U.K. 12 D5
Rundu, Namibia 88 B2
Rungwa, Tanzania 86 D3
Rungwa →, Tanzania 86 D3
Rungwe, Tanzania 87 D3
Rungwe, Mt., Tanzania 84 F6
Runka, Nigeria 83 C6
Runton Ra., Australia 92 D3
Ruokolahti, Finland 46 B5
Ruoqiang, China 60 C3
Rupa, India 67 F18
Rupar, India 68 D7
Rupat, Indonesia 62 D2
Rupea, Romania 43 D10
Rupen →, India 68 H4
Rupert, U.S.A. 114 E7
Rupert →, Canada 102 B4
Rupert B., Canada 102 B4
Rupert House = Waskaganish, Canada 102 B4
Rupsa, India 69 J12
Rur →, Germany 24 D1
Rurrenabaque, Bolivia 124 F5
Rus →, Spain 33 F2
Rusambo, Zimbabwe 87 F3
Rusape, Zimbabwe 87 F3
Ruschuk = Ruse, Bulgaria 41 C9
Ruse, Bulgaria 41 C9
Ruse □, Bulgaria 41 C10
Ruşeţu, Romania 43 F12
Rush, Ireland 15 C5
Rushan, China 57 F11
Rushden, U.K. 13 E7
Rushmore, Mt., U.S.A. 112 D3
Rushville, Ill., U.S.A. 112 E9
Rushville, Ind., U.S.A. 108 F3
Rushville, Nebr., U.S.A. 112 D3
Russas, Brazil 125 D11
Russell, Canada 105 C8
Russell, Kans., U.S.A. 112 F5
Russell, N.Y., U.S.A. 111 B9
Russell, Pa., U.S.A. 110 E5
Russell L., Man., Canada 105 B8
Russell L., N.W.T., Canada 104 A5
Russellkonda, India 67 K14
Russellville, Ala., U.S.A. 109 H2
Russellville, Ark., U.S.A. 113 H8
Russellville, Ky., U.S.A. 109 G2
Rüsselsheim, Germany 25 F4
Russi, Italy 29 D9
Russia ■, Eurasia 51 C11
Russian →, U.S.A. 116 G3
Russkoye Ustie, Russia 4 B15
Rust, Austria 27 D9
Rustam, Pakistan 68 B5
Rustam Shahr, Pakistan 68 F2
Rustavi, Georgia 49 K7
Rustenburg, S. Africa 88 D4
Ruston, U.S.A. 113 J8
Rutana, Burundi 86 C3
Rute, Spain 35 H6
Ruteng, Indonesia 63 F6
Ruth, U.S.A. 110 C2
Rutherford, U.S.A. 116 G4
Rutland □, U.K. 13 E7
Rutland Water, U.K. 13 E7
Rutledge →, Canada 105 A6
Rutledge L., Canada 105 A6
Rutqa, W. →, Syria 73 E9
Rutshuru, Dem. Rep. of the Congo 86 C2
Ruvo di Púglia, Italy 31 A9
Ruvu, Tanzania 86 D4
Ruvu →, Tanzania 86 D4
Ruvuma □, Tanzania 87 E4
Ruvuma →, Tanzania 87 E5
Ruwais, U.A.E. 71 E7
Ruwenzori, Africa 86 B2
Ruya →, Zimbabwe 89 B5
Ruyigi, Burundi 86 C3
Ruyuan, China 59 E9
Ruzayevka, Russia 48 C7
Růžhevo Konare, Bulgaria 41 D8
Ružomberok, Slovak Rep. 27 B12
Rwanda ■, Africa 86 C3
Ryakhovo, Bulgaria 41 C10
Ryan, L., U.K. 14 G3
Ryazan, Russia 46 E10
Ryazhsk, Russia 46 F11
Rybache = Rybachye, Kazakstan 50 E9
Rybachye, Kazakstan 50 E9
Rybinsk, Russia 46 C10
Rybinskoye Vdkhr., Russia 46 C10
Rybnik, Poland 45 H5
Rybnitsa = Râbniţa, Moldova 43 C14
Rybnoye, Russia 46 E10
Rychnov nad Kněžnou, Czech Rep. 27 A9
Rychwał, Poland 45 F5
Rycroft, Canada 104 B5
Ryd, Sweden 11 H8
Rydaholm, Sweden 11 H8
Ryde, U.K. 13 G6
Ryderwood, U.S.A. 116 D3
Rydzyna, Poland 45 G3
Rye, U.K. 13 G8
Rye →, U.K. 12 C7
Rye Bay, U.K. 13 G8
Rye Patch Reservoir, U.S.A. 114 F4
Ryegate, U.S.A. 114 C9
Ryki, Poland 45 G8
Ryley, Canada 104 C6

Rylsk, Russia 47 G8
Rymanów, Poland 45 J8
Ryn, Poland 44 E8
Ryn Peski, Kazakstan 49 G9
Ryōtsu, Japan 54 E9
Rypin, Poland 45 E6
Ryssby, Sweden 11 H8
Ryūgasaki, Japan 55 G10
Ryūkyū Is. = Ryūkyū-rettō, Japan 55 M3
Ryūkyū-rettō, Japan 55 M3
Rzepin, Poland 45 F1
Rzeszów, Poland 45 H8
Rzhev, Russia 46 D8

S

Sa, Thailand 64 C3
Sa Canal, Spain 37 C7
Sa Conillera, Spain 37 C7
Sa Dec, Vietnam 65 G5
Sa Dragonera, Spain 37 B9
Sa Mesquida, Spain 37 B11
Sa Pobla, Spain 32 F8
Sa Savina, Spain 37 C7
Sa'ādatābād, Fārs, Iran 71 D7
Sa'ādatābād, Hormozgān, Iran 71 D7
Sa'ādatābād, Kermān, Iran 71 D7
Saale →, Germany 24 D7
Saaler Bodden, Germany 24 A8
Saalfeld, Germany 24 E7
Saalfelden, Austria 26 D5
Saane →, Switz. 25 H3
Saar →, Europe 17 E6
Saarbrücken, Germany 25 F2
Saarburg, Germany 25 F2
Saaremaa, Estonia 9 G20
Saarijärvi, Finland 9 E21
Saariselkä, Finland 8 B23
Saarland □, Germany 25 F2
Saarlouis, Germany 25 F2
Sab 'Ābar, Syria 70 C3
Saba, W. Indies 121 C7
Šabac, Serbia, Yug. 40 B3
Sabadell, Spain 32 D7
Sabah □, Malaysia 62 C5
Sabak Bernam, Malaysia 65 L3
Sabalān, Kūhhā-ye, Iran 70 B5
Sabalana, Kepulauan, Indonesia 63 F5
Sábana de la Mar, Dom. Rep. 121 C6
Sábanalarga, Colombia 124 A4
Sabang, Indonesia 62 C1
Sãbãoani, Romania 43 C11
Sabará, Brazil 125 G10
Sabarmati →, India 68 H5
Sabattis, U.S.A. 111 B10
Saberania, Indonesia 63 E9
Sabhah, Libya 79 C8
Sabi →, India 68 E7
Sabidana, J., Sudan 80 D4
Sabie, S. Africa 89 D5
Sabinal, Mexico 118 A3
Sabinal, U.S.A. 113 L5
Sabiñánigo, Spain 32 C4
Sabinar, Punta del, Spain 33 J2
Sabinas, Mexico 118 B4
Sabinas →, Mexico 118 B4
Sabinas Hidalgo, Mexico 118 B4
Sabine →, U.S.A. 113 L8
Sabine L., U.S.A. 113 L8
Sabine Pass, U.S.A. 113 L8
Sabinov, Slovak Rep. 27 B14
Sabinsville, U.S.A. 110 E7
Sabirabad, Azerbaijan 49 K9
Sabkhet el Bardawîl, Egypt 75 D2
Sablayan, Phil. 61 E4
Sable, Canada 103 A6
Sable, C., Canada 103 D6
Sable, C., U.S.A. 107 E10
Sable I., Canada 103 D8
Sablé-sur-Sarthe, France 18 E6
Sabonkafi, Niger 83 C6
Sabor →, Portugal 34 D3
Sabou, Burkina Faso 82 C4
Sabres, France 20 D3
Sabrina Coast, Antarctica 5 C9
Sabugal, Portugal 34 E3
Sabulubbek, Indonesia 62 E1
Sabuncu, Turkey 39 B12
Sabzevār, Iran 71 B8
Sabzvārān, Iran 71 D8
Sac City, U.S.A. 112 D7
Sacedón, Spain 32 E2
Săcele, Romania 43 E10
Sachigo →, Canada 102 A2
Sachigo, L., Canada 102 B1
Sachkhere, Georgia 49 J6
Sachsen □, Germany 24 E9
Sachsen-Anhalt □, Germany 24 D7
Sacile, Italy 29 C9
Sackets Harbor, U.S.A. 111 C8
Sackville, Canada 103 C7
Saco, Maine, U.S.A. 109 D10
Saco, Mont., U.S.A. 114 B10
Sacramento, U.S.A. 116 G5
Sacramento →, U.S.A. 116 G5
Sacramento Mts., U.S.A. 115 K11
Sacramento Valley, U.S.A. 116 G5
Sacratif, C., Spain 35 J7
Săcueni, Romania 42 C7
Sada, Spain 34 B2
Sada-Misaki, Japan 55 H6
Sádaba, Spain 32 C3

Sadabad, *India* 68 F8
Sadani, *Tanzania* 86 D4
Sadao, *Thailand* 65 J3
Sadd el Aali, *Egypt* 80 C3
Saddle Mt., *U.S.A.* 116 E3
Sade, *Nigeria* 83 C7
Sadimi, *Dem. Rep. of the Congo* 87 D1
Sadiola, *Mali* 82 C2
Sa'dīyah, Hawr as, *Iraq* ... 73 F12
Sado, *Japan* 54 F9
Sado →, *Portugal* 35 G2
Sadon, *Burma* 67 G20
Sadon, *Russia* 49 J6
Sadra, *India* 68 H5
Sadri, *India* 68 G5
Sæby, *Denmark* 11 G4
Saegertown, *U.S.A.* 110 E4
Saelices, *Spain* 32 F2
Safaalan, *Turkey* 41 E12
Safaga, *Egypt* 80 B3
Şafājah, *Si. Arabia* 70 E3
Šafárikovo = Tornal'a,
Slovak Rep. 27 C13
Säffle, *Sweden* 10 E6
Safford, *U.S.A.* 115 K9
Saffron Walden, *U.K.* 13 E8
Safi, *Morocco* 78 B4
Şafiābād, *Iran* 71 B8
Safīd Dasht, *Iran* 71 C6
Safīd Kūh, *Afghan.* 66 B3
Safīd Rūd →, *Iran* 71 B6
Safipur, *India* 69 F9
Safonovo, *Russia* 46 E7
Safranbolu, *Turkey* 72 B5
Saft Rashîn, *Egypt* 80 J7
Safwān, *Iraq* 70 D5
Sag Harbor, *U.S.A.* 111 F12
Saga, *Japan* 55 H5
Saga □, *Japan* 55 H5
Sagae, *Japan* 54 E10
Sagala, *Mali* 82 C3
Sagamore, *U.S.A.* 110 F5
Sagar, *Karnataka, India* . 66 M9
Sagar, *Mad. P., India* ... 69 H8
Sagara, L., *Tanzania* 86 D3
Sagay, *Phil.* 61 F5
Saginaw, *U.S.A.* 108 D4
Saginaw →, *U.S.A.* 108 D4
Saginaw B., *U.S.A.* 108 D4
Sagleipie, *Liberia* 82 D3
Saglouc = Salluit, *Canada* 101 B12
Sagō-ri, *S. Korea* 57 G14
Sagone, *France* 21 F12
Sagone, G. de, *France* ... 21 F12
Sagres, *Portugal* 35 J2
Sagua la Grande, *Cuba* .. 120 B3
Saguache, *U.S.A.* 115 G10
Saguaro Nat. Park, *U.S.A.* 115 K8
Saguenay →, *Canada* 103 C5
Sagunt, *Spain* 32 F4
Sagunto = Sagunt, *Spain* . 32 F4
Sagwara, *India* 68 H6
Sahaba, *Sudan* 80 D3
Sahagún, *Spain* 34 C5
Saham al Jawlān, *Syria* .. 75 C4
Sahamandrevo, *Madag.* .. 89 C8
Sahand, Kūh-e, *Iran* 70 B5
Sahara, *Africa* 78 D6
Saharan Atlas = Saharien, Atlas,
Algeria 78 B6
Saharanpur, *India* 68 E7
Saharien, Atlas, *Algeria* . 78 B6
Saharsa, *India* 69 G12
Sahasinaka, *Madag.* 89 C8
Sahaswan, *India* 69 E8
Sahel, *Africa* 78 E5
Sahel, Canal du, *Mali* ... 82 C3
Sahibganj, *India* 69 G12
Sāḩiliyah, *Iraq* 70 C4
Sāḩilīyah, *Iraq* 70 C4
Sahiwal, *Pakistan* 68 D5
Şaḩneh, *Iran* 70 C5
Sahuaripa, *Mexico* 118 B3
Sahuarita, *U.S.A.* 115 L8
Sahuayo, *Mexico* 118 C4
Šahy, *Slovak Rep.* 27 C11
Sai →, *India* 69 G10
Sai Buri, *Thailand* 65 J3
Sa'id Bundas, *Sudan* 79 G10
Sa'īdābād, *Kermān, Iran* . 71 D7
Sa'īdābād, *Semnān, Iran* . 71 B7
Sa'īdīyeh, *Iran* 71 B6
Saidpur, *Bangla.* 67 G16
Saidpur, *India* 69 G10
Saidu, *Pakistan* 69 B5
Saignes, *France* 20 C6
Saigon = Thanh Pho Ho Chi
Minh, *Vietnam* 65 G6
Saijō, *Japan* 55 H6
Saikanosy Masoala, *Madag.* 89 B9
Saikhoa Ghat, *India* 67 F19
Saiki, *Japan* 55 H5
Sailana, *India* 68 H6
Saillans, *France* 21 D9
Sailolof, *Indonesia* 63 E8
Saimaa, *Finland* 9 F23
Saimbeyli, *Turkey* 72 D7
Şa'in Dezh, *Iran* 70 B5
St. Abb's Head, *U.K.* ... 14 F6
St-Affrique, *France* 20 E6
St-Agrève, *France* 21 C8
St-Aignan, *France* 18 E8
St. Alban's, *Canada* 103 C8
St. Albans, *U.K.* 13 F7
St. Albans, *Vt., U.S.A.* .. 111 B11
St. Albans, *W. Va., U.S.A.* 108 F5
St. Alban's Head, *U.K.* .. 13 G5

St. Albert, *Canada* 104 C6
St-Amand-en-Puisaye, *France* . 19 E10
St-Amand-les-Eaux, *France* . 19 B10
St-Amand-Montrond, *France* . 19 F9
St-Amarin, *France* 19 E14
St-Amour, *France* 19 F12
St-André-de-Cubzac, *France* . 20 D3
St-André-les-Alpes, *France* . 21 E10
St. Andrew's, *Canada* 103 C8
St. Andrews, *U.K.* 14 E6
St. Anicet, *Canada* 111 A10
St. Ann B., *Canada* 103 C7
St. Ann's Bay, *Jamaica* .. 120 C4
St. Anthony, *Canada* 103 B8
St. Anthony, *U.S.A.* 114 E8
St. Antoine, *Canada* 103 C7
St-Antonin-Noble-Val, *France* . 20 D5
St-Astier, *France* 20 C4
St-Aubin-du-Cormier, *France* 18 D5
St-Augustin →, *Canada* 103 B8
St-Augustin-Saguenay, *Canada* 103 B8
St. Augustine, *U.S.A.* ... 109 L5
St-Aulaye, *France* 20 C4
St. Austell, *U.K.* 13 G3
St-Avold, *France* 19 C13
St. Barbe, *Canada* 103 B8
St-Barthélemy, *W. Indies* . 121 C7
St-Béat, *France* 20 F4
St. Bees Hd., *U.K.* 12 C4
St-Benoît-du-Sault, *France* . 20 B5
St-Bonnet, *France* 21 D10
St-Brévin-les-Pins, *France* . 18 E4
St-Brice-en-Coglès, *France* . 18 D5
St. Bride's, *Canada* 103 C9
St. Brides B., *U.K.* 13 F2
St-Brieuc, *France* 18 D4
St-Calais, *France* 18 E7
St-Cast-le-Guildo, *France* . 18 D4
St. Catharines, *Canada* .. 102 D4
St. Catherines I., *U.S.A.* . 109 K5
St. Catherine's Pt., *U.K.* . 13 G6
St-Céré, *France* 20 D5
St-Cergue, *Switz.* 25 J2
St-Cernin, *France* 20 C6
St-Chamond, *France* 21 C8
St. Charles, *Ill., U.S.A.* .. 108 E1
St. Charles, *Mo., U.S.A.* . 112 F9
St. Charles, *Va., U.S.A.* . 108 F7
St-Chély-d'Apcher, *France* . 20 D7
St-Chinian, *France* 20 E6
St. Christopher-Nevis = St. Kitts
& Nevis ■, *W. Indies* . 121 C7
St-Ciers-sur-Gironde, *France* . 20 C3
St. Clair, *Mich., U.S.A.* .. 110 D2
St. Clair, *Pa., U.S.A.* ... 111 F8
St. Clair →, *U.S.A.* 110 D2
St. Clair, L., *Canada* ... 102 D3
St. Clair, L., *U.S.A.* ... 110 D2
St. Clairsville, *U.S.A.* .. 110 F4
St-Claud, *France* 20 C4
St. Claude, *Canada* 105 D9
St-Claude, *France* 19 F12
St-Clet, *Canada* 111 A10
St. Cloud, *Fla., U.S.A.* .. 109 L5
St. Cloud, *Minn., U.S.A.* . 112 C7
St-Cricq, C., *Australia* .. 93 E1
St. Croix, *U.S. Virgin Is.* . 121 C7
St. Croix →, *U.S.A.* ... 112 C8
St. Croix Falls, *U.S.A.* .. 112 C8
St-Cyprien, *France* 20 F7
St-Cyr-sur-Mer, *France* .. 21 E9
St. David's, *Canada* 103 C8
St. David's, *U.K.* 13 F2
St. David's Head, *U.K.* .. 13 F2
St-Denis, *France* 19 D9
St-Dié, *France* 19 D13
St-Dizier, *France* 19 D11
St-Égrève, *France* 21 C9
St. Elias, Mt., *U.S.A.* ... 100 B5
St. Elias Mts., *Canada* .. 104 A1
St. Elias Mts., *U.S.A.* ... 100 C6
St-Eloy-les-Mines, *France* . 19 F9
St-Émilion, *France* 20 D3
St-Étienne, *France* 21 C8
St-Étienne-de-Tinée, *France* . 21 D10
St-Étienne-du-Rouvray, *France* 18 C8
St. Eugène, *Canada* 111 A10
St. Eustatius, *W. Indies* . 121 C7
St-Fargeau, *France* 19 E10
St-Félicien, *Canada* 102 C5
St-Florent, *France* 21 F13
St-Florent, G. de, *France* . 21 F13
St-Florent-sur-Cher, *France* . 19 F9
St-Florentin, *France* ... 19 E10
St-Flour, *France* 20 C7
St. Francis, *U.S.A.* 112 F4
St. Francis →, *U.S.A.* .. 113 H9
St. Francis, C., *S. Africa* . 88 E3
St. Francisville, *U.S.A.* . 113 K9
St-François, L., *Canada* .. 111 A10
St-Fulgent, *France* 18 F5
St-Gabriel, *Canada* 102 C5
St. Gallen = Sankt Gallen, *Switz.* 25 H5
St-Galmier, *France* 19 G11
St-Gaudens, *France* 20 E4
St-Gaultier, *France* 18 F8
St-Gengoux-le-National, *France* 19 F11
St-Geniez-d'Olt, *France* . 20 D6
St. George, *Australia* ... 95 D4
St. George, *Canada* 103 C6
St. George, *S.C., U.S.A.* . 109 J5
St. George, *Utah, U.S.A.* . 115 H7
St. George, C., *Canada* .. 103 C8
St. George, C., *U.S.A.* .. 109 L3
St. George Ra., *Australia* . 92 C4
St. George's, *Canada* ... 103 C8

St-Georges, *Canada* 103 C5
St. George's, *Grenada* ... 121 D7
St. George's B., *Canada* .. 103 C8
St. Georges Basin, *N.S.W.,
Australia* 95 F5
St. Georges Basin, *W. Austral.,
Australia* 92 C4
St. George's Channel, *Europe* . 15 E6
St-Georges-lès-Baillargeaux,
France 20 B4
St-Germain-de-Calberte, *France* . 20 D7
St-Germain-en-Laye, *France* . 19 D9
St-Germain-Lembron, *France* . 20 C7
St-Gervais-d'Auvergne, *France* . 19 F9
St-Gervais-les-Bains, *France* ... 21 C10
St-Gildas, Pte. de, *France* . 18 E4
St-Gilles, *France* 21 E8
St-Girons, *Ariège, France* . 20 F5
St-Girons, *Landes, France* . 20 E2
St. Gotthard P. = San Gottardo,
P. del, *Switz.* 25 J4
St. Helena, *U.S.A.* 114 G2
St. Helena ■, *Atl. Oc.* .. 76 H3
St. Helena, Mt., *U.S.A.* .. 116 G4
St. Helena B., *S. Africa* . 88 E2
St. Helens, *Australia* ... 94 G4
St. Helens, *U.K.* 12 D5
St. Helens, *U.S.A.* 116 E4
St. Helens, Mt., *U.S.A.* .. 116 D4
St. Helier, *U.K.* 13 H5
St-Herblain, *France* 18 E5
St-Hilaire-du-Harcouët, *France* . 18 D5
St-Hippolyte, *France* ... 19 E13
St-Hippolyte-du-Fort, *France* . 20 E7
St-Honoré-les-Bains, *France* . 19 F10
St-Hubert, *Belgium* 17 D5
St-Hyacinthe, *Canada* ... 102 C5
St. Ignace, *U.S.A.* 108 C3
St. Ignace I., *Canada* ... 102 C2
St. Ignatius, *U.S.A.* ... 114 C6
St-Imier, *Switz.* 25 H2
St. Ives, *U.K.* 13 G2
St-James, *France* 18 D5
St. James, *U.S.A.* 112 D7
St-Jean →, *Canada* 103 B7
St-Jean, L., *Canada* 103 C5
St-Jean-d'Angély, *France* . 20 C3
St-Jean-de-Braye, *France* . 19 E8
St-Jean-de-Luz, *France* .. 20 E2
St-Jean-de-Maurienne, *France* . 21 C10
St-Jean-de-Monts, *France* . 18 F4
St-Jean-du-Gard, *France* .. 20 D7
St-Jean-en-Royans, *France* . 21 C9
St-Jean-Pied-de-Port, *France* . 20 E2
St-Jean-Port-Joli, *Canada* . 103 C5
St-Jean-sur-Richelieu, *Canada* . 102 C5
St-Jérôme, *Canada* 102 C5
St. John, *Canada* 103 C6
St. John, *U.S.A.* 113 G5
St. John →, *Liberia* 82 D2
St. John →, *U.S.A.* 109 C12
St. John, C., *Canada* 103 C8
St. John's, *Antigua* 121 C7
St. John's, *Canada* 103 C9
St. Johns, *Ariz., U.S.A.* . 115 J9
St. Johns, *Mich., U.S.A.* . 108 D3
St. Johns →, *U.S.A.* 109 K5
St. John's Pt., *Ireland* .. 15 B3
St. Johnsbury, *U.S.A.* .. 111 B12
St. Johnsville, *U.S.A.* .. 111 D10
St. Joseph, *La., U.S.A.* .. 113 K9
St. Joseph, *Mo., U.S.A.* . 112 F7
St. Joseph →, *U.S.A.* ... 108 D2
St. Joseph, L., *Canada* .. 102 B1
St. Joseph, L., *Canada* .. 102 B1
St-Jovite, *Canada* 102 C5
St-Juéry, *France* 20 E6
St-Julien-Chapteuil, *France* . 21 C8
St-Julien-de-Vouvantes, *France* 18 E5
St-Julien-en-Genevois, *France* . 19 F13
St-Junien, *France* 20 C4
St-Just-en-Chaussée, *France* . 19 C9
St-Just-en-Chevalet, *France* . 20 C7
St. Kitts & Nevis ■, *W. Indies* . 121 C7
St. Laurent, *Canada* 105 C9
St-Laurent-de-la-Salanque,
France 20 F6
St-Laurent-du-Pont, *France* . 21 C9
St-Laurent-en-Grandvaux,
France 19 F12
St-Laurent-Médoc, *France* . 20 C3
St. Lawrence, *Australia* . 94 C4
St. Lawrence, *Canada* ... 103 C8
St. Lawrence →, *Canada* . 103 C6
St. Lawrence, Gulf of, *Canada* . 103 C7
St. Lawrence I., *U.S.A.* .. 100 B3
St. Leonard, *Canada* 103 C6
St-Léonard-de-Noblat, *France* . 20 C5
St. Lewis →, *Canada* 103 B8
St-Lô, *France* 18 C5
St-Louis, *France* 19 E14
St. Louis, *Senegal* 82 B1
St. Louis, *U.S.A.* 112 F9
St. Louis →, *U.S.A.* 112 B8
St-Loup-sur-Semouse, *France* . 19 E13
St. Lucia ■, *W. Indies* .. 121 D7
St. Lucia, L., *S. Africa* .. 89 D5
St. Lucia Channel, *W. Indies* . 121 D7
St. Maarten, *W. Indies* .. 121 C7
St. Magnus B., *U.K.* 14 A7
St-Maixent-l'École, *France* . 20 B3
St-Malo, *France* 18 D4
St-Malo, G. de, *France* .. 18 D4
St-Mandrier-sur-Mer, *France* . 21 E9
St-Marc, *Haiti* 121 C5
St-Marcellin, *France* ... 21 C9

St-Marcouf, Îs., *France* 18 C5
St. Maries, *U.S.A.* 114 C5
St-Martin, *W. Indies* 121 C7
St. Martin, L., *Canada* 105 C9
St-Martin-de-Crau, *France* .. 21 E8
St-Martin-de-Ré, *France* ... 20 B2
St-Martin-d'Hères, *France* .. 21 C9
St-Martin-Vésubie, *France* .. 21 D11
St-Martory, *France* 20 E4
St. Marys, *Australia* 94 G4
St. Marys, *Canada* 110 C3
St. Mary's, *Corn., U.K.* ... 13 H1
St. Mary's, *Orkney, U.K.* .. 14 C6
St. Marys, *Ga., U.S.A.* ... 109 K5
St. Marys, *Pa., U.S.A.* ... 110 E6
St. Mary's, C., *Canada* ... 103 C9
St. Mary's B., *Canada* 103 C9
St. Marys Bay, *Canada* ... 103 D6
St-Mathieu, Pte., *France* .. 18 D2
St. Matthew, I., *U.S.A.* ... 100 B2
St. Matthews, I. = Zadetkyi
Kyun, *Burma* 65 G1
St-Maurice →, *Canada* 102 C5
St-Maximin-la-Ste-Baume,
France 21 E9
St-Médard-en-Jalles, *France* . 20 D3
St-Méen-le-Grand, *France* .. 18 D4
St-Mihiel, *France* 19 D12
St. Moritz, *Switz.* 25 J5
St-Nazaire, *France* 18 E4
St. Neots, *U.K.* 13 E7
St-Nicolas-de-Port, *France* . 19 D13
St-Niklaas, *Belgium* 17 C4
St-Omer, *France* 19 B9
St-Palais-sur-Mer, *France* .. 20 C2
St-Pamphile, *Canada* 103 C6
St-Pardoux-la-Rivière, *France* . 20 C4
St. Pascal, *Canada* 103 C6
St. Paul, *Canada* 104 C6
St-Paul, *France* 21 D10
St. Paul, *Minn., U.S.A.* ... 112 C8
St. Paul, *Nebr., U.S.A.* ... 112 E5
St-Paul →, *Canada* 103 B8
St. Paul →, *Liberia* 82 D2
St. Paul, Î. de, *Ind. Oc.* . 3 F13
St-Paul-de-Fenouillet, *France* . 20 F6
St. Paul I., *Canada* 103 C7
St-Paul-lès-Dax, *France* ... 20 E2
St-Péray, *France* 21 D8
St. Peter, *U.S.A.* 112 C8
St-Peter-Ording, *Germany* .. 24 A4
St. Peter Port, *U.K.* 13 H5
St. Peters, *N.S., Canada* .. 103 C7
St. Peters, *P.E.I., Canada* . 103 C7
St. Petersburg = Sankt-
Peterburg, *Russia* 46 C6
St. Petersburg, *U.S.A.* ... 109 M4
St-Philbert-de-Grand-Lieu,
France 18 E5
St-Pie, *Canada* 111 A12
St-Pierre, *St-P. & M.* 103 C8
St-Pierre, L., *Canada* 102 C5
St-Pierre-d'Oléron, *France* . 20 C2
St-Pierre-en-Faucigny, *France* . 18 C7
St-Pierre et Miquelon □,
St-P. & M. 103 C8
St-Pierre-le-Moûtier, *France* . 19 F10
St-Pierre-sur-Dives, *France* . 18 C6
St-Pol-de-Léon, *France* ... 18 D3
St-Pol-sur-Mer, *France* ... 19 A9
St-Pol-sur-Ternoise, *France* . 19 B9
St-Pons, *France* 20 E6
St-Pourçain-sur-Sioule, *France* . 19 F10
St-Priest, *France* 21 C8
St-Quay-Portrieux, *France* . 18 D4
St. Quentin, *Canada* 103 C6
St-Quentin, *France* 19 C10
St-Rambert-d'Albon, *France* . 21 C8
St-Raphaël, *France* 21 E10
St. Regis, *U.S.A.* 114 C6
St-Renan, *France* 18 D2
St-Saëns, *France* 18 C8
St-Savin, *France* 20 B4
St-Savinien, *France* 20 C3
St. Sebastien, Tanjon' i, *Madag.* 89 A8
St-Seine-l'Abbaye, *France* . 19 E11
St-Sernin-sur-Rance, *France* . 20 E6
St-Sever, *France* 20 E3
St-Siméon, *Canada* 103 C6
St. Simons I., *U.S.A.* 109 K5
St. Simons Island, *U.S.A.* . 109 K5
St. Stephen, *Canada* 103 C6
St-Sulpice, *France* 20 E5
St-Sulpice-Laurière, *France* . 20 B5
St-Sulpice-les-Feuilles, *France* . 20 B5
St-Syprien = St-Cyprien, *France* . 20 F7
St-Thégonnec, *France* 18 D3
St. Thomas, *Canada* 102 D3
St. Thomas I., *U.S. Virgin Is.* . 121 C7
St-Tite, *Canada* 102 C5
St-Tropez, *France* 21 E10
St. Troud = St. Truiden, *Belgium* . 17 D5
St. Truiden, *Belgium* 17 D5
St-Vaast-la-Hougue, *France* . 18 C5
St-Valery-en-Caux, *France* . 18 C7
St-Valéry-sur-Somme, *France* . 19 B8
St-Vallier, *France* 19 F11
St-Vallier-de-Thiey, *France* . 21 E10
St-Varent, *France* 18 F6
St-Vaury, *France* 20 B5
St. Vincent, *Italy* 28 C4
St. Vincent & the Grenadines ■,
W. Indies 121 D7
St-Vincent-de-Tyrosse, *France* . 20 E2
St. Vincent Passage, *W. Indies* . 121 D7
St-Vith, *Belgium* 17 D6

St-Vivien-de-Médoc, *France* ... 20 C2
St-Yrieix-la-Perche, *France* ... 20 C5
Ste-Adresse, *France* 18 C7
Ste-Agathe-des-Monts, *Canada* 102 C5
Ste-Anne, L., *Canada* 103 B6
Ste-Anne-des-Monts, *Canada* . 103 C6
Ste-Croix, *Switz.* 25 J2
Ste-Enimie, *France* 20 D7
Ste-Foy-la-Grande, *France* ... 20 D4
Ste. Genevieve, *U.S.A.* 112 G9
Ste-Hermine, *France* 20 B3
Ste-Livrade-sur-Lot, *France* .. 20 D4
Ste-Marguerite →, *Canada* ... 103 B6
Ste-Marie, *Martinique* 121 D7
Ste-Marie-aux-Mines, *France* . 19 D14
Ste-Marie de la Madeleine,
Canada 103 C5
Ste-Maure-de-Touraine, *France* . 18 E7
Ste-Maxime, *France* 21 E10
Ste-Menehould, *France* 19 C11
Ste-Mère-Église, *France* 18 C5
Ste-Rose, *Guadeloupe* 121 C7
Ste. Rose du Lac, *Canada* ... 105 C9
Ste-Savine, *France* 19 D11
Ste-Sigolène, *France* 21 C8
Saintes, *France* 20 C3
Saintes, I. des, *Guadeloupe* .. 121 C7
Stes-Maries-de-la-Mer, *France* . 21 E8
Saintfield, *U.K.* 15 B6
Saintonge, *France* 20 C3
Saipan, *Pac. Oc.* 96 F6
Sairang, *India* 67 H18
Sairecábur, Cerro, *Bolivia* .. 126 A2
Saitama □, *Japan* 55 F9
Saiteli = Kadınhanı, *Turkey* . 72 C5
Saiti, *Moldova* 43 D14
Saiyid, *Pakistan* 68 C5
Sajama, *Bolivia* 124 G5
Sajan, *Serbia, Yug.* 42 E5
Sajó →, *Hungary* 42 C6
Sajószentpéter, *Hungary* ... 42 B5
Sajum, *India* 69 C8
Sak →, *S. Africa* 88 E3
Sakaba, *Nigeria* 83 C6
Sakai, *Japan* 55 G7
Sakaide, *Japan* 55 G6
Sakaiminato, *Japan* 55 G6
Sakākah, *Si. Arabia* 70 D4
Sakakawea, L., *U.S.A.* ... 112 B4
Sakami →, *Canada* 102 B4
Sakami, L., *Canada* 102 B4
Sâkâne, 'Erg i-n, *Mali* 83 A4
Sakania, *Dem. Rep. of the Congo* 87 E2
Sakaraha, *Madag.* 89 C7
Sakarya, *Turkey* 72 B4
Sakarya →, *Turkey* 72 B4
Sakashima-Guntō, *Japan* .. 55 M2
Sakassou, *Ivory C.* 82 D3
Sakata, *Japan* 54 E9
Sakchu, *N. Korea* 57 D13
Sakeny →, *Madag.* 89 C8
Sakété, *Benin* 83 D5
Sakha □, *Russia* 51 C13
Sakhalin, *Russia* 51 D15
Sakhalinskiy Zaliv, *Russia* . 51 D15
Şaki, *Azerbaijan* 49 K8
Šakiai, *Lithuania* 9 J20
Sakon Nakhon, *Thailand* .. 64 D5
Sakrand, *Pakistan* 68 F3
Sakri, *India* 69 F12
Sakrivier, *S. Africa* 88 E3
Sakskøbing, *Denmark* 11 K5
Sakti, *India* 69 H10
Sakuma, *Japan* 55 G8
Sakurai, *Japan* 55 G7
Saky, *Ukraine* 47 K7
Sal →, *Russia* 49 G5
Sala, *Eritrea* 81 D4
Šaľa, *Slovak Rep.* 27 C10
Sala, *Sweden* 10 E10
Sala →, *Eritrea* 81 D4
Sala Consilina, *Italy* 31 B8
Sala-y-Gómez, *Pac. Oc.* .. 97 K17
Salaberry-de-Valleyfield,
Canada 102 C5
Saladas, *Argentina* 126 B4
Saladillo, *Argentina* 126 D4
Salado →, *Buenos Aires,
Argentina* 126 D4
Salado →, *La Pampa, Argentina* 128 D3
Salado →, *Santa Fe, Argentina* . 126 C3
Salado →, *Mexico* 113 M5
Salaga, *Ghana* 83 D4
Sālah, *Syria* 75 C5
Sălaj □, *Romania* 42 C8
Sálakhos, *Greece* 36 C9
Salala, *Liberia* 82 D2
Salala, *Sudan* 80 C4
Salālah, *Oman* 74 D5
Salamanca, *Chile* 126 C1
Salamanca, *Spain* 34 E5
Salamanca, *U.S.A.* 110 D6
Salamanca □, *Spain* 34 E5
Salâmatābād, *Iran* 70 C5
Salamís, *Cyprus* 36 D12
Salamís, *Greece* 38 D5
Salar de Atacama, *Chile* .. 126 A2
Salar de Uyuni, *Bolivia* ... 124 H5
Sălard, *Romania* 42 C8
Salas, *Spain* 34 B4
Salas de los Infantes, *Spain* . 34 C7
Salatiga, *Indonesia* 63 G14
Salaverry, *Peru* 124 E3
Salawati, *Indonesia* 63 E8
Salaya, *India* 68 H3

Salayar, Indonesia 63 F6
Salazar →, Spain 32 C3
Salbris, France 19 E9
Salcia, Romania 43 G9
Sălciua, Romania 43 D8
Salcombe, U.K. 13 G4
Saldaña, Spain 34 C6
Saldanha, S. Africa 88 E2
Saldanha B., S. Africa 88 E2
Saldus, Latvia 9 H20
Saldus □, Latvia 44 B9
Sale, Italy 28 D5
Salé, Morocco 78 B4
Sale, U.K. 12 D5
Salekhard, Russia 50 C7
Salem, India 66 P11
Salem, Ill., U.S.A. 108 F1
Salem, Ind., U.S.A. 108 F2
Salem, Mass., U.S.A. 111 D14
Salem, Mo., U.S.A. 113 G9
Salem, N.H., U.S.A. 111 D13
Salem, N.J., U.S.A. 108 F8
Salem, N.Y., U.S.A. 111 C11
Salem, Ohio, U.S.A. 110 F4
Salem, Oreg., U.S.A. 114 D2
Salem, S. Dak., U.S.A. 112 D6
Salem, Va., U.S.A. 108 G5
Salemi, Italy 30 E5
Sålen, Sweden 10 C7
Salernes, France 21 E10
Salerno, Italy 31 B7
Salerno, G. di, Italy 31 B7
Salford, U.K. 12 D5
Salgir →, Ukraine 47 K8
Salgótarján, Hungary 42 B4
Salgueiro, Brazil 125 E11
Salibabu, Indonesia 63 D7
Salida, U.S.A. 106 C5
Salies-de-Béarn, France 20 E3
Salihli, Turkey 72 C3
Salihorsk, Belarus 47 F4
Salima, Malawi 85 G6
Salina, Italy 31 D7
Salina, Kans., U.S.A. 112 F6
Salina, Utah, U.S.A. 115 G8
Salina Cruz, Mexico 119 D5
Salinas, Brazil 125 G10
Salinas, Chile 126 A2
Salinas, Ecuador 124 D2
Salinas, U.S.A. 116 J5
Salinas →, Guatemala 119 D6
Salinas →, U.S.A. 116 J5
Salinas, B. de, Nic. 120 D2
Salinas, Pampa de las, Argentina 126 C2
Salinas Ambargasta, Argentina 126 B3
Salinas de Hidalgo, Mexico . 118 C4
Salinas Grandes, Argentina . 126 C3
Saline →, Ark., U.S.A. 113 J8
Saline →, Kans., U.S.A. 112 F6
Salines, Spain 37 B10
Salines, C. de ses, Spain .. 37 B10
Salinópolis, Brazil 125 D9
Salins-les-Bains, France ... 19 F12
Salir, Portugal 35 H2
Salisbury = Harare, Zimbabwe . 87 F3
Salisbury, U.K. 13 F6
Salisbury, Md., U.S.A. 108 F8
Salisbury, N.C., U.S.A. 109 H5
Salisbury I., Canada 101 B12
Salisbury Plain, U.K. 13 F6
Sălişte, Romania 43 E8
Salka, Nigeria 83 C5
Şalkhad, Syria 75 C5
Salla, Finland 8 C23
Sallanches, France 21 C10
Sallent, Spain 32 D6
Salles, France 20 D3
Salles-Curan, France 20 D6
Salling, Denmark 11 H2
Salliq, Canada 101 B11
Sallisaw, U.S.A. 113 H7
Sallom Junction, Sudan 80 D4
Salluit, Canada 101 B12
Salmās, Iran 70 B5
Salmerón, Spain 32 E2
Salmo, Canada 104 D5
Salmon, U.S.A. 114 D7
Salmon →, Canada 104 C4
Salmon →, U.S.A. 114 D5
Salmon Arm, Canada 104 C5
Salmon Gums, Australia 93 F3
Salmon River Mts., U.S.A. .. 114 D6
Salo, Finland 9 F20
Salò, Italy 28 C7
Salobreña, Spain 35 J7
Salome, U.S.A. 117 M13
Salon, India 69 F9
Salon-de-Provence, France .. 21 E9
Salonica = Thessaloníki, Greece 40 F6
Salonta, Romania 42 D6
Salor →, Spain 35 F3
Salou, Spain 32 D6
Salou, C. de, Spain 32 D6
Saloum →, Senegal 82 C1
Salpausselkä, Finland 9 F22
Salsacate, Argentina 126 C2
Salses, France 20 F6
Salsk, Russia 49 G5
Salso →, Italy 30 E6
Salsomaggiore Terme, Italy . 28 D6
Salt →, Canada 32 D7
Salt →, Canada 104 B6
Salt →, U.S.A. 115 K7
Salt Range, Pakistan 68 C5
Salt Lake City, U.S.A. 114 F8
Salta, Argentina 126 A2

Salta □, Argentina 126 A2
Saltara, Italy 29 E9
Saltash, U.K. 13 G3
Saltburn by the Sea, U.K. .. 12 C7
Saltcoats, U.K. 14 F4
Saltee Is., Ireland 15 D5
Saltfjellet, Norway 8 C16
Saltfjorden, Norway 8 C16
Saltholm, Denmark 11 J6
Saltillo, Mexico 118 B4
Salto, Argentina 126 C3
Salto, Uruguay 126 C4
Salto del Guairá, Paraguay . 127 A5
Salton City, U.S.A. 117 M11
Salton Sea, U.S.A. 117 M11
Saltpond, Ghana 83 D4
Saltsburg, U.S.A. 110 F5
Saltsjöbaden, Sweden 10 E12
Saluda →, U.S.A. 109 J5
Salûm, Egypt 80 A2
Salûm, Khâlig el, Egypt 80 A2
Salur, India 67 K13
Saluzzo, Italy 28 D4
Salvador, Brazil 125 F11
Salvador, Canada 105 C7
Salvador, L., U.S.A. 113 L9
Salvaterra de Magos, Portugal 35 F2
Sálvora, I. de, Spain 34 C2
Salween →, Burma 67 L20
Salyan, Azerbaijan 50 F5
Salza →, Austria 26 D7
Salzach →, Austria 26 C5
Salzburg, Austria 26 D6
Salzburg □, Austria 26 D6
Salzgitter, Germany 24 C6
Salzkotten, Germany 24 D4
Salzwedel, Germany 24 C7
Sam, India 68 F4
Sam Neua, Laos 58 G5
Sam Ngao, Thailand 64 D2
Sam Rayburn Reservoir, U.S.A. 113 K7
Sam Son, Vietnam 64 C5
Sam Teu, Laos 64 C5
Sama de Langreo = Langreo, Spain 34 B5
Samagaltay, Russia 51 D10
Samales Group, Phil. 61 J4
Samâlût, Egypt 80 B3
Samana, India 68 D7
Samana Cay, Bahamas 121 B5
Samandağı, Turkey 72 D6
Samandıra, Turkey 41 F13
Samanga, Tanzania 87 D4
Samangwa, Dem. Rep. of the Congo 86 C1
Samani, Japan 54 C11
Samanli Dağları, Turkey 41 F13
Samar, Phil. 61 F6
Samara, Russia 48 D10
Samara →, Russia 48 D10
Samara →, Ukraine 47 H8
Samaria = Shōmron, West Bank 75 C4
Samariá, Greece 36 D5
Samarinda, Indonesia 62 E5
Samarkand = Samarqand, Uzbekistan 50 F7
Samarqand, Uzbekistan 50 F7
Sāmarrā, Iraq 70 C4
Samastipur, India 69 G11
Şamaxi, Azerbaijan 49 K9
Samba, Dem. Rep. of the Congo 86 C2
Samba, India 69 C6
Sambalpur, India 67 J14
Sambar, Tanjung, Indonesia . 62 E4
Sambas, Indonesia 62 D3
Sambava, Madag. 89 A9
Sambawizi, Zimbabwe 87 F2
Sambhal, India 69 E8
Sambhar, India 68 F6
Sambhar L., India 68 F6
Sambiase, Italy 31 D9
Sambir, Ukraine 47 H2
Sambor, Cambodia 64 F6
Samborombón, B., Argentina . 126 D4
Sambuca di Sicília, Italy .. 30 E6
Samch'ŏk, S. Korea 57 F15
Samch'onp'o, S. Korea 57 G15
Same, Tanzania 86 C4
Samer, France 19 B8
Samfya, Zambia 87 E2
Sámi, Greece 38 C2
Şämkir, Azerbaijan 49 K8
Şamlı, Turkey 39 B9
Samnah, Si. Arabia 70 E3
Samo Alto, Chile 126 C1
Samoa ■, Pac. Oc. 91 B13
Samobor, Croatia 29 C12
Samoëns, France 19 F13
Samokov, Bulgaria 40 D7
Šamorín, Slovak Rep. 27 C10
Samorogouan, Burkina Faso .. 82 C4
Sámos, Greece 39 D8
Samoš, Serbia, Yug. 42 E5
Samos, Spain 34 C3
Sámos □, Greece 39 D8
Samothráki = Mathráki, Greece 36 A3
Samothráki, Évros, Greece .. 41 F9
Samothráki, Évros, Greece .. 41 F9
Samoylovka, Russia 48 E6
Sampa, Ghana 82 D4
Sampacho, Argentina 126 C3
Sampang, Indonesia 63 G15
Samper de Calanda, Spain ... 32 D4
Sampéyre, Italy 28 D4
Sampit, Indonesia 62 E4
Sampit, Teluk, Indonesia ... 62 E4

Samrong, Cambodia 64 E4
Samrong, Thailand 64 E3
Samsø, Denmark 11 J4
Samsø Bælt, Denmark 11 J4
Samsun, Turkey 72 B7
Samtredia, Georgia 49 J6
Samui, Ko, Thailand 65 H3
Samur →, Russia 49 K9
Samurskiy Khrebet, Russia .. 49 K8
Samusole, Dem. Rep. of the Congo 87 E1
Samut Prakan, Thailand 64 F3
Samut Songkhram →, Thailand 62 B1
Samwari, Pakistan 68 E2
San, Mali 82 C4
San →, Cambodia 64 F5
San →, Poland 45 H8
San Adrián, Spain 32 C3
San Adrián, C. de, Spain ... 34 B2
San Agustín, U.S.A. 61 H7
San Agustín de Valle Fértil, Argentina 126 C2
San Ambrosio, Pac. Oc. 122 F3
San Andreas, U.S.A. 116 G6
San Andres, Phil. 61 E6
San Andrés, I. de, Caribbean 120 D3
San Andrés del Rabanedo, Spain 34 C5
San Andres Mts., U.S.A. 115 K10
San Andrés Tuxtla, Mexico .. 119 D5
San Angelo, U.S.A. 113 K4
San Anselmo, U.S.A. 116 H4
San Antonio, Belize 119 D7
San Antonio, Chile 126 C1
San Antonio, Phil. 61 D4
San Antonio, N. Mex., U.S.A. 115 K10
San Antonio, Tex., U.S.A. .. 113 L5
San Antonio →, U.S.A. 113 L6
San Antonio, C., Argentina . 126 D4
San Antonio, C. de, Cuba ... 120 B3
San Antonio, C. de, Spain .. 33 G5
San Antonio, Mt., U.S.A. ... 117 L9
San Antonio de los Baños, Cuba 120 B3
San Antonio de los Cobres, Argentina 126 A2
San Antonio Oeste, Argentina 128 E4
San Arcángelo, Italy 31 B9
San Ardo, U.S.A. 116 J6
San Augustín, Canary Is. ... 37 G4
San Augustine, U.S.A. 113 K7
San Bartolomé, Canary Is. .. 37 F6
San Bartolomé de Tirajana, Canary Is. 37 G4
San Bartolomeo in Galdo, Italy 31 A8
San Benedetto del Tronto, Italy 29 F10
San Benedetto Po, Italy 28 C7
San Benedicto, I., Mexico .. 118 D2
San Benito, Bolivia 113 M6
San Benito, U.S.A. 116 J5
San Benito →, U.S.A. 116 J6
San Benito Mt., U.S.A. 116 J6
San Bernardino, U.S.A. 117 L9
San Bernardino Mts., U.S.A. 117 L10
San Bernardino Str., Phil. . 61 E6
San Bernardo, Chile 126 C1
San Bernardo, I. de, Colombia 124 B3
San Blas, Mexico 118 B3
San Blas, Arch. de, Panama . 120 E4
San Blas, C., U.S.A. 109 L3
San Bonifacio, Italy 29 C8
San Borja, Bolivia 124 F5
San Buenaventura, Mexico ... 118 B4
San Carlos = Butuku-Luba, Eq. Guin. 83 E6
San Carlos = Sant Carles, Spain 37 B8
San Carlos, Argentina 126 C2
San Carlos, Chile 126 D1
San Carlos, Baja Calif. S., Mexico 118 C2
San Carlos, Coahuila, Mexico 118 B4
San Carlos, Nic. 120 D3
San Carlos, Neg. Occ., Phil. 61 F5
San Carlos, Pangasinan, Phil. 61 D4
San Carlos, Uruguay 127 C5
San Carlos, U.S.A. 115 K8
San Carlos, Venezuela 124 B5
San Carlos de Bariloche, Argentina 128 E2
San Carlos de Bolívar, Argentina 128 D4
San Carlos de la Rápita = Sant Carles de la Ràpita, Spain 32 E5
San Carlos del Zulia, Venezuela 124 B4
San Cataldo, Italy 30 E6
San Celoni = Sant Celoni, Spain 32 D7
San Clemente, Chile 126 D1
San Clemente, Spain 33 F2
San Clemente, U.S.A. 117 M9
San Clemente I., U.S.A. 117 N8
San Cristóbal = Es Migjorn Gran, Spain 37 B11
San Cristóbal, Argentina ... 126 C3
San Cristóbal, Dom. Rep. ... 121 C5
San Cristóbal, Venezuela ... 124 B4
San Cristóbal de la Casas, Mexico 119 D6
San Damiano d'Asti, Italy .. 28 D5
San Daniele del Friuli, Italy 29 B10
San Diego, Calif., U.S.A. .. 117 N9
San Diego, Tex., U.S.A. 113 M5
San Diego, C., Argentina ... 128 G3
San Diego de la Unión, Mexico 118 C4
San Dimitri, Ras, Malta 36 C1
San Donà di Piave, Italy ... 29 C9
San Esteban de Gormaz, Spain 32 D1
San Felice Circeo, Italy ... 30 A6
San Felice sul Panaro, Italy 29 D8

San Felipe, Chile 126 C1
San Felipe, Mexico 118 A2
San Felipe, Venezuela 124 A5
San Felipe →, U.S.A. 117 M11
San Félix, Chile 126 B1
San Félix, Pac. Oc. 122 F2
San Fernando = Sant Ferran, Spain 37 C7
San Fernando, Chile 126 C1
San Fernando, Baja Calif., Mexico 118 B1
San Fernando, Tamaulipas, Mexico 119 C5
San Fernando, La Union, Phil. 61 C4
San Fernando, Pampanga, Phil. 61 D4
San Fernando, Spain 35 J4
San Fernando, Trin. & Tob. . 121 D7
San Fernando, U.S.A. 117 L8
San Fernando de Apure, Venezuela 124 B5
San Fernando de Atabapo, Venezuela 124 C5
San Fernando di Púglia, Italy 31 A9
San Francisco, Argentina ... 126 C3
San Francisco, U.S.A. 116 H4
San Francisco →, U.S.A. 115 K9
San Francisco, Paso de, S. Amer. 126 B2
San Francisco de Macorís, Dom. Rep. 121 C5
San Francisco del Monte de Oro, Argentina 126 C2
San Francisco del Oro, Mexico 118 B3
San Francisco Javier = Sant Francesc de Formentera, Spain 37 C7
San Francisco Solano, Pta., Colombia 122 C3
San Fratello, Italy 31 D7
San Gabriel, Chile 126 C1
San Gabriel Mts., U.S.A. ... 117 L9
San Gavino Monreale, Italy . 30 C1
San Gimignano, Italy 28 E8
San Gíorgio di Nogaro, Italy 29 C10
San Gíorgio Iónico, Italy .. 31 B10
San Giovanni Bianco, Italy . 28 C6
San Giovanni in Fiore, Italy 31 C9
San Giovanni in Persiceto, Italy 29 D8
San Giovanni Rotondo, Italy 29 G12
San Giovanni Valdarno, Italy 29 E8
San Giuliano Terme, Italy .. 28 E7
San Gorgonio Mt., U.S.A. ... 117 L10
San Gottardo, P. del, Switz. 25 J4
San Gregorio, Uruguay 127 C4
San Gregorio, U.S.A. 116 H4
San Guiseppe Jato, Italy ... 30 E6
San Ignacio, Belize 119 D7
San Ignacio, Bolivia 124 G6
San Ignacio, Mexico 118 B2
San Ignacio, Paraguay 126 C2
San Ignacio, L., Mexico 118 B2
San Ildefonso, C., Phil. ... 61 C5
San Isidro, Argentina 126 C4
San Isidro, Phil. 61 H7
San Jacinto, U.S.A. 117 M10
San Jaime = Sant Jaume, Spain 37 B11
San Javier, Misiones, Argentina 127 B4
San Javier, Santa Fe, Argentina 126 C4
San Javier, Bolivia 124 G6
San Javier, Chile 126 D1
San Javier, Spain 33 H4
San Jeronimo Taviche, Mexico 119 D5
San Joaquín, Bolivia 124 F6
San Joaquin, U.S.A. 116 J6
San Joaquin →, U.S.A. 116 G5
San Joaquin Valley, U.S.A. . 116 J6
San Jon, U.S.A. 113 H3
San Jordi = Sant Jordi, Spain 37 B9
San Jorge, Argentina 126 C3
San Jorge, Spain 37 C7
San Jorge, B. de, Mexico ... 118 A2
San Jorge, G., Argentina ... 128 F3
San Jorge, G. of, Argentina 122 H4
San José = San Josep, Spain 37 C7
San José, Costa Rica 120 E3
San José, Guatemala 120 D1
San José, Mexico 118 C2
San Jose, Mind. Occ., Phil. 61 E4
San Jose, Nueva Ecija, Phil. 61 D4
San Jose, U.S.A. 116 H5
San Jose →, U.S.A. 115 J10
San Jose de Buenavista, Phil. 63 B6
San José de Chiquitos, Bolivia 124 G6
San José de Feliciano, Argentina 126 C4
San José de Jáchal, Argentina 126 C2
San José de Mayo, Uruguay .. 126 C4
San José del Cabo, Mexico .. 118 C3
San José del Guaviare, Colombia 124 C4
San Josep, Spain 37 C7
San Juan, Argentina 126 C2
San Juan, Mexico 118 C4
San Juan, Phil. 61 F6
San Juan, Puerto Rico 121 C6
San Juan □, Argentina 126 C2
San Juan →, Argentina 126 C2
San Juan →, Nic. 120 D3
San Juan →, U.S.A. 115 H8
San Juan Bautista = Sant Joan Baptista, Spain 37 B8
San Juan Bautista, Paraguay 126 B4
San Juan Bautista, U.S.A. .. 116 J5
San Juan Bautista Valle Nacional, Mexico 119 D5
San Juan Capistrano, U.S.A. 117 M9
San Juan Cr. →, U.S.A. 116 J5
San Juan de Alicante, Spain 33 G4
San Juan de Guadalupe, Mexico 118 C4

San Juan de la Costa, Mexico . 118 C2
San Juan de los Morros, Venezuela 124 B5
San Juan del Norte, Nic. ... 120 D3
San Juan del Norte, B. de, Nic. 120 D3
San Juan del Río, Mexico ... 119 C5
San Juan del Sur, Nic. 120 D2
San Juan I., U.S.A. 116 B3
San Juan Mts., U.S.A. 115 H10
San Just, Sierra de, Spain . 32 E4
San Justo, Argentina 126 C3
San Kamphaeng, Thailand 64 C2
San Lázaro, C., Mexico 118 C2
San Lázaro, C., Mexico 118 C2
San Leandro, U.S.A. 116 H4
San Leonardo de Yagüe, Spain 32 D1
San Lorenzo = Sant Llorenç des Cardassar, Spain 37 B10
San Lorenzo, Argentina 126 C3
San Lorenzo, Ecuador 124 C3
San Lorenzo, Paraguay 126 B4
San Lorenzo →, Mexico 118 C3
San Lorenzo, I., Mexico 118 B2
San Lorenzo, Mte., Argentina 128 F2
San Lorenzo de la Parrilla, Spain 32 F2
San Lorenzo de Morunys = Sant Llorenç de Morunys, Spain 32 C6
San Lucas, Bolivia 124 H5
San Lucas, Baja Calif. S., Mexico 118 C3
San Lucas, Baja Calif. S., Mexico 118 B2
San Lucas, U.S.A. 116 J5
San Lucas, C., Mexico 118 C3
San Lúcido, Italy 31 C9
San Luis, Argentina 126 C2
San Luis, Cuba 120 B3
San Luis, Guatemala 120 C2
San Luis, Ariz., U.S.A. 115 K6
San Luis, Colo., U.S.A. 115 H11
San Luis □, Argentina 126 C2
San Luis, Sierra de, Argentina 126 C2
San Luis de la Paz, Mexico . 118 C4
San Luis Obispo, U.S.A. 117 K6
San Luis Potosí, Mexico 118 C4
San Luis Potosí □, Mexico .. 118 C4
San Luis Reservoir, U.S.A. . 116 H5
San Luis Río Colorado, Mexico 118 A2
San Manuel, U.S.A. 115 K8
San Marco, C., Italy 30 C1
San Marco Argentano, Italy . 31 C9
San Marco in Lámis, Italy .. 29 G12
San Marcos, Guatemala 120 D1
San Marcos, Mexico 118 B2
San Marcos, Calif., U.S.A. . 117 M9
San Marcos, Tex., U.S.A. ... 113 L6
San Marino, San Marino 29 E9
San Marino ■, Europe 29 E9
San Martín, Argentina 126 C2
San Martín →, Bolivia 124 F6
San Martín, L., Argentina .. 128 F2
San Martín de la Vega, Spain 34 E7
San Martín de los Andes, Argentina 128 E2
San Martín de Valdeiglesias, Spain 34 E6
San Mateo = Sant Mateu, Baleares, Spain 37 B7
San Mateo = Sant Mateu, Valencia, Spain 32 E5
San Mateo, Phil. 61 C4
San Mateo, U.S.A. 116 H4
San Matías, Bolivia 124 G7
San Matías, G., Argentina .. 122 H4
San Miguel = Sant Miquel, Spain 37 B7
San Miguel, El Salv. 120 D2
San Miguel, Panama 116 E4
San Miguel, U.S.A. 116 K6
San Miguel →, Bolivia 124 F6
San Miguel de Tucumán, Argentina 126 B2
San Miguel del Monte, Argentina 126 D4
San Miguel I., U.S.A. 117 L6
San Miniato, Italy 28 E7
San Nicolás, Canary Is. 37 G4
San Nicolas, Phil. 61 B4
San Nicolás de los Arroyas, Argentina 126 C3
San Nicolas I., U.S.A. 117 M7
San Onofre, U.S.A. 117 M9
San Pablo, Bolivia 126 A2
San Pablo, Phil. 61 D4
San Pablo, U.S.A. 116 H4
San Páolo di Civitate, Italy 29 G12
San Pedro, Buenos Aires, Argentina 126 C4
San Pedro, Misiones, Argentina 127 B5
San Pedro, Chile 126 C1
San Pédro, Ivory C. 82 E3
San Pedro, Mexico 118 C2
San Pedro □, Paraguay 126 A4
San Pedro →, Chihuahua, Mexico 118 B3
San Pedro →, Nayarit, Mexico . 118 C3
San Pedro →, U.S.A. 115 K8
San Pedro, Pta., Chile 126 B1
San Pedro, Sierra de, Spain 35 F4
San Pedro Channel, U.S.A. .. 117 M8
San Pedro de Atacama, Chile 126 A2
San Pedro de Jujuy, Argentina 126 A3
San Pedro de las Colonias, Mexico 118 B4
San Pedro de Macorís, Dom. Rep. 121 C6
San Pedro del Norte, Nic. .. 120 D3
San Pedro del Paraná, Paraguay 126 B4

San Pedro del Pinatar, *Spain* .. 33 H4
San Pedro Mártir, Sierra, *Mexico* 118 A1
San Pedro Mixtepec, *Mexico* .. 119 D5
San Pedro Ocampo = Melchor
  Ocampo, *Mexico* 118 C4
San Pedro Sula, *Honduras* 120 C2
San Pietro, *Italy* 30 C1
San Pietro Vernótico, *Italy* ... 31 B11
San Quintín, *Mexico* 118 A1
San Rafael, *Argentina* 126 C2
San Rafael, *Calif., U.S.A.* ... 116 H4
San Rafael, *N. Mex., U.S.A.* .. 115 J10
San Rafael Mt., *U.S.A.* 117 L7
San Rafael Mts., *U.S.A.* 117 L7
San Ramón de la Nueva Orán,
  Argentina 126 A3
San Remo, *Italy* 28 E4
San Roque, *Argentina* 126 B4
San Roque, *Spain* 35 J5
San Rosendo, *Chile* 126 D1
San Saba, *U.S.A.* 113 K5
San Salvador, *El Salv.* 120 D2
San Salvador, *Spain* 37 B10
San Salvador de Jujuy, *Argentina* 126 A3
San Salvador I., *Bahamas* 121 B5
San Salvo, *Italy* 29 F11
San Sebastián = Donostia-San
  Sebastián, *Spain* 32 B3
San Sebastián, *Argentina* 128 G3
San Sebastian de la Gomera,
  Canary Is. 37 F2
San Serra = Son Serra, *Spain* .. 37 B10
San Serverino Marche, *Italy* ... 29 E10
San Severo, *Italy* 29 G12
San Simeon, *U.S.A.* 116 K5
San Simon, *U.S.A.* 115 K9
San Stéfano di Cadore, *Italy* .. 29 B9
San Stino di Livenza, *Italy* ... 29 C9
San Telmo = Sant Telm, *Spain* . 37 B9
San Telmo, *Mexico* 118 A1
San Tiburcio, *Mexico* 118 C4
San Valentin, Mte., *Chile* 122 H3
San Vicente de Alcántara, *Spain* 35 F3
San Vicente de la Barquera,
  Spain 34 B6
San Vincente del Raspeig, *Spain* 33 G4
San Vincenzo, *Italy* 28 E7
San Vito, *Costa Rica* 120 E3
San Vito, *Italy* 30 C2
San Vito, C., *Italy* 30 D5
San Vito al Tagliamento, *Italy* . 29 C9
San Vito Chietino, *Italy* 29 F11
San Vito dei Normanni, *Italy* .. 31 B10
Sana', *Yemen* 74 D3
Sana →, *Bos.-H.* 29 C13
Sanaba, *Burkina Faso* 82 C4
Şanâfir, *Si. Arabia* 80 B3
Sanaga →, *Cameroon* 83 E6
Sanaloa, Presa, *Mexico* 118 C3
Sanana, *Indonesia* 63 E7
Sanand, *India* 68 H5
Sanandaj, *Iran* 70 C5
Sanandita, *Bolivia* 126 A3
Sanary-sur-Mer, *France* 21 E9
Sanawad, *India* 68 H7
Sancellas = Sencelles, *Spain* .. 37 B9
Sancergues, *France* 19 E9
Sancerre, *France* 19 E9
Sancerrois, Collines du, *France* . 19 E9
Sancha He →, *China* 58 D6
Sanchahe, *China* 57 B14
Sánchez, *Dom. Rep.* 121 C6
Sanchor, *India* 68 G4
Sancoins, *France* 19 F9
Sancti Spíritus, *Cuba* 120 B4
Sancy, Puy de, *France* 20 C6
Sand →, *S. Africa* 89 C5
Sand Hills, *U.S.A.* 112 D4
Sand Springs, *U.S.A.* 113 G6
Sanda, *Japan* 55 G7
Sandakan, *Malaysia* 62 C5
Sandan = Sambor, *Cambodia* .. 64 F6
Sandanski, *Bulgaria* 40 E7
Sandaré, *Mali* 82 C2
Sandared, *Sweden* 11 G6
Sandarne, *Sweden* 10 C11
Sanday, *U.K.* 14 B6
Sandefjord, *Norway* 9 G14
Sanders, *U.S.A.* 115 J9
Sanderson, *U.S.A.* 113 K3
Sandersville, *U.S.A.* 109 J4
Sandfire Roadhouse, *Australia* . 92 C3
Sandfly L., *Canada* 105 B7
Sandfontein, *Namibia* 88 C2
Sandhammaren, C., *Sweden* ... 11 J8
Sandía, *Peru* 124 F5
Sandıklı, *Turkey* 39 C12
Sandila, *India* 69 F9
Sandnes, *Norway* 9 G11
Sandnessjøen, *Norway* 8 C15
Sandoa, *Dem. Rep. of the Congo* 84 F4
Sandomierz, *Poland* 45 H8
Sândominic, *Romania* 43 D10
Sandover →, *Australia* 94 C2
Sandoway, *Burma* 67 K19
Sandoy, *Faroe Is.* 8 F9
Sandpoint, *U.S.A.* 114 B5
Sandray, *U.K.* 14 E1
Sandringham, *U.K.* 12 E8
Sandstone, *Australia* 93 E2
Sandu, *China* 58 E6
Sandusky, *Mich., U.S.A.* 110 C2
Sandusky, *Ohio, U.S.A.* 110 E2
Sandvig, *Sweden* 11 J8
Sandviken, *Sweden* 10 D10
Sandwich, C., *Australia* 94 B4

Sandwich B., *Canada* 103 B8
Sandwich B., *Namibia* 88 C1
Sandy, *Oreg., U.S.A.* 116 E4
Sandy, *Pa., U.S.A.* 110 E6
Sandy, *Utah, U.S.A.* 114 F8
Sandy Bay, *Canada* 105 B8
Sandy Bight, *Australia* 93 F3
Sandy C., *Queens., Australia* .. 94 C5
Sandy C., *Tas., Australia* 94 G3
Sandy Cay, *Bahamas* 121 B4
Sandy Cr. →, *U.S.A.* 114 F9
Sandy L., *Canada* 102 B1
Sandy Lake, *Canada* 102 B1
Sandy Valley, *U.S.A.* 117 K11
Sanford, *Fla., U.S.A.* 109 L5
Sanford, *Maine, U.S.A.* 109 D10
Sanford, *N.C., U.S.A.* 109 H6
Sanford →, *Australia* 93 E2
Sanford, Mt., *U.S.A.* 100 B5
Sang-i-Masha, *Afghan.* 68 C2
Sanga, *Mozam.* 87 E4
Sanga →, *Congo* 84 E3
Sangamner, *India* 66 K9
Sangar, *Afghan.* 68 C1
Sangar, *Russia* 51 C13
Sangar Sarai, *Afghan.* 68 B4
Sangaredi, *Guinea* 82 C2
Sangarh →, *Pakistan* 68 D4
Sangasso, *Mali* 82 C3
Sangatte, *France* 19 B8
Sangay, *Ecuador* 124 D3
Sange, *Dem. Rep. of the Congo* 86 D2
Sangeang, *Indonesia* 63 F5
Sângeorz-Băi, *Romania* 43 C9
Sanger, *U.S.A.* 116 J7
Sangerhausen, *Germany* 24 D7
Sanggan He →, *China* 56 E9
Sanggau, *Indonesia* 62 D4
Sanghar, *Pakistan* 68 F3
Sangihe, Kepulauan, *Indonesia* . 63 D7
Sangihe, Pulau, *Indonesia* 63 D7
Sangju, *S. Korea* 57 F15
Sangkapura, *Indonesia* 62 F4
Sangkhla, *Thailand* 64 E2
Sangkulirang, *Indonesia* 62 D5
Sangla, *Pakistan* 68 D5
Sangli, *India* 66 L9
Sangmélima, *Cameroon* 83 E7
Sangod, *India* 68 G7
Sangre de Cristo Mts., *U.S.A.* . 113 G2
Sangro →, *Italy* 29 F11
Sangrur, *India* 68 D6
Sangudo, *Canada* 104 C6
Sangue →, *Brazil* 124 F7
Sangüesa, *Spain* 32 C3
Sanguinaires, Îs., *France* 21 G12
Sangzhi, *China* 59 C8
Sanhala, *Ivory C.* 82 C3
Sanibel, *U.S.A.* 109 M4
Sanirajak, *Canada* 101 B11
Sanjawi, *Pakistan* 68 D3
Sanje, *Uganda* 86 C3
Sanjiang, *China* 58 E7
Sanjo, *Japan* 54 F9
Sankh →, *India* 69 H11
Sankt Andrä, *Austria* 26 E7
Sankt Augustin, *Germany* 24 E3
Sankt Blasien, *Germany* 25 H4
Sankt Gallen, *Switz.* 25 H5
Sankt Gallen □, *Switz.* 25 H5
Sankt Goar, *Germany* 25 E3
Sankt Ingbert, *Germany* 25 F3
Sankt Johann im Pongau,
  Austria 26 D6
Sankt Johann in Tirol, *Austria* . 26 D5
Sankt-Peterburg, *Russia* 46 C6
Sankt Pölten, *Austria* 26 C8
Sankt Ulrich = Ortisei, *Italy* .. 29 B8
Sankt Valentin, *Austria* 26 C7
Sankt Veit an der Glan, *Austria* 26 E7
Sankt Wendel, *Germany* 25 F3
Sankt Wolfgang, *Austria* 26 D6
Sankuru →, *Dem. Rep. of
  the Congo* 84 E4
Şanlıurfa, *Turkey* 70 B3
Sanlúcar de Barrameda, *Spain* . 35 J4
Sanluri, *Italy* 30 C1
Sânmartin, *Romania* 43 D10
Sanmen, *China* 59 C13
Sanmenxia, *China* 56 G6
Sanming, *China* 59 D11
Sannaspos, *S. Africa* 88 D4
Sannicandro Gargánico, *Italy* .. 29 G12
Sânnicolau Mare, *Romania* ... 42 D5
Sannieshof, *S. Africa* 88 D4
Sannin, J., *Lebanon* 75 B4
Sanniquellie, *Liberia* 82 D3
Sannūr, W. →, *Egypt* 80 B3
Sanok, *Poland* 45 J9
Sanquhar, *U.K.* 14 F5
Sansanding, *Mali* 82 C3
Sansepolcro, *Italy* 29 E9
Sansha, *China* 59 D13
Sanshui, *China* 59 F9
Sanski Most, *Bos.-H.* 29 D13
Sansui, *China* 58 D7
Sant Antoni Abat, *Spain* 37 C7
Sant Boi de Llobregat, *Spain* .. 32 D7
Sant Carles, *Spain* 37 B8
Sant Carles de la Ràpita, *Spain* 32 E5
Sant Celoni, *Spain* 32 D7
Sant Feliu de Guíxols, *Spain* .. 32 D8
Sant Feliu de Llobregat, *Spain* . 32 D7
Sant Ferran, *Spain* 37 C7

Sant Francesc de Formentera,
  Spain 37 C7
Sant Jaume, *Spain* 37 B11
Sant Joan Baptista, *Spain* 37 B8
Sant Jordi, *Spain* 37 B9
Sant Jordi, G. de, *Spain* 32 E6
Sant Llorenç de Morunys, *Spain* 32 C6
Sant Llorenç des Cardassar,
  Spain 37 B10
Sant Mateu, *Baleares, Spain* .. 37 B7
Sant Mateu, *Valencia, Spain* ... 32 E5
Sant Miquel, *Spain* 37 B7
Sant Telm, *Spain* 37 B9
Sant' Ágata Militello, *Italy* ... 31 D7
Sant Agnès, *Spain* 37 B7
Santa Ana, *Bolivia* 124 F5
Santa Ana, *El Salv.* 120 D2
Santa Ana, *Mexico* 118 A2
Santa Ana, *U.S.A.* 117 M9
Sant' Ángelo Lodigiano, *Italy* .. 28 C6
Sant' Antíoco, *Italy* 30 C1
Santa Barbara, *Chile* 126 D1
Santa Bárbara, *Honduras* 120 D2
Santa Bárbara, *Mexico* 118 B3
Santa Bárbara, *Spain* 32 E5
Santa Bárbara, *U.S.A.* 117 L7
Santa Bárbara, Mt., *Spain* ... 33 H2
Santa Barbara Channel, *U.S.A.* 117 L7
Santa Barbara I., *U.S.A.* 117 M7
Santa Catalina, Gulf of, *U.S.A.* 117 N9
Santa Catalina, I., *Mexico* ... 118 B2
Santa Catalina I., *U.S.A.* 117 M8
Santa Catarina □, *Brazil* 127 B6
Santa Catarina, I. de, *Brazil* ... 127 B6
Santa Caterina di Pittinuri, *Italy* 30 B1
Santa Caterina Villarmosa, *Italy* 31 E7
Santa Cecília, *Brazil* 127 B5
Santa Clara, *Cuba* 120 B4
Santa Clara, *Calif., U.S.A.* ... 116 H5
Santa Clara, *Utah, U.S.A.* ... 115 H7
Santa Clara, El Golfo de, *Mexico* 118 A2
Santa Clara de Olimar, *Uruguay* 127 C5
Santa Clarita, *U.S.A.* 117 L8
Santa Clotilde, *Peru* 124 D4
Santa Coloma de Farners, *Spain* 32 D7
Santa Coloma de Gramenet,
  Spain 32 D7
Santa Comba, *Spain* 34 B2
Santa Croce Camerina, *Italy* .. 31 F7
Santa Croce di Magliano, *Italy* . 29 G11
Santa Cruz, *Argentina* 128 G3
Santa Cruz, *Bolivia* 124 G6
Santa Cruz, *Chile* 126 C1
Santa Cruz, *Costa Rica* 120 D2
Santa Cruz, *Madeira* 37 D3
Santa Cruz, *Phil.* 61 D4
Santa Cruz, *U.S.A.* 116 J4
Santa Cruz →, *Argentina* ... 128 G3
Santa Cruz de la Palma,
  Canary Is. 37 F2
Santa Cruz de Mudela, *Spain* . 35 G7
Santa Cruz de Tenerife,
  Canary Is. 37 F3
Santa Cruz del Norte, *Cuba* .. 120 B3
Santa Cruz del Retamar, *Spain* 34 E6
Santa Cruz del Sur, *Cuba* 120 B4
Santa Cruz do Rio Pardo, *Brazil* 127 A6
Santa Cruz do Sul, *Brazil* ... 127 B5
Santa Cruz I., *U.S.A.* 117 M7
Santa Cruz Is., *Solomon Is.* .. 96 J8
Santa Domingo, Cay, *Bahamas* 120 B4
Sant' Egídio alla Vibrata, *Italy* . 29 F10
Santa Elena, *Argentina* 126 C4
Santa Elena, C., *Costa Rica* ... 120 D2
Sant' Eufémia, G. di, *Italy* 31 D9
Santa Eulàlia des Riu, *Spain* .. 37 C8
Santa Fe, *Argentina* 126 C3
Santa Fe, *Spain* 35 H7
Santa Fe, *U.S.A.* 115 J11
Santa Fé □, *Argentina* 126 C3
Santa Fé do Sul, *Brazil* 125 H8
Santa Filomena, *Brazil* 125 E9
Santa Fiora, *Italy* 29 F8
Santa Gertrudis, *Spain* 37 C7
Santa Giustina, *Italy* 29 B9
Santa Inês, *Brazil* 125 F11
Santa Inés, *Spain* 35 G5
Santa Inés, I., *Chile* 122 J3
Santa Isabel = Rey Malabo,
  Eq. Guin. 83 E6
Santa Isabel, *Argentina* 126 D2
Santa Isabel, Pico, *Eq. Guin.* .. 83 E6
Santa Isabel do Morro, *Brazil* . 125 F8
Santa Lucía, *Corrientes,
  Argentina* 126 B4
Santa Lucía, *San Juan, Argentina* 126 C2
Santa Lucía, *Spain* 33 H4
Santa Lucia, *Uruguay* 126 C4
Santa Lucia Range, *U.S.A.* ... 116 K5
Santa Magdalena, I., *Mexico* .. 118 C2
Santa Margarita, *Argentina* .. 126 D3
Santa Margarita, *Spain* 37 B10
Santa Margarita, *U.S.A.* 116 K6
Santa Margarita →, *U.S.A.* . 117 M9
Santa Margarita, I., *Mexico* .. 118 C2
Santa Margherita, *Italy* 30 D1
Santa Margherita Ligure, *Italy* . 28 D6
Santa María, *Brazil* 127 B5
Santa Maria, *Phil.* 61 C4
Santa María, *U.S.A.* 117 L6
Santa María →, *Mexico* 118 A3
Santa María, B. de, *Mexico* ... 118 B3
Santa Maria, C. de, *Portugal* .. 35 J3
Santa Maria Cápua Vétere, *Italy* 31 A7
Santa Maria da Feira, *Portugal* . 34 E2

Santa Maria da Vitória, *Brazil* . 125 F10
Santa Maria del Camí, *Spain* .. 37 B9
Santa Maria di Léuca, C., *Italy* . 31 C11
Santa María la Real de Nieva,
  Spain 34 D6
Santa Marinella, *Italy* 29 F8
Santa Marta, *Colombia* 124 A4
Santa Marta, Sierra Nevada de,
  Colombia 122 B3
Santa Marta de Tormes, *Spain* . 34 E5
Santa Marta Grande, C., *Brazil* 127 B6
Santa Marta Ortigueira, Ría de,
  Spain 34 B3
Santa Maura = Levkás, *Greece* . 38 C2
Santa Monica, *U.S.A.* 117 M8
Santa Olalla, *Huelva, Spain* ... 35 H4
Santa Olalla, *Toledo, Spain* ... 34 E6
Santa Paula, *U.S.A.* 117 L7
Santa Pola, *Spain* 33 G4
Santa Ponsa, *Spain* 37 B9
Santa Rita, *U.S.A.* 115 K10
Santa Rosa, *La Pampa,
  Argentina* 126 D3
Santa Rosa, *San Luis, Argentina* 126 C2
Santa Rosa, *Brazil* 127 B5
Santa Rosa, *Calif., U.S.A.* ... 116 G4
Santa Rosa, *N. Mex., U.S.A.* .. 113 H2
Santa Rosa de Copán, *Honduras* 120 D2
Santa Rosa de Río Primero,
  Argentina 126 C3
Santa Rosa del Sara, *Bolivia* .. 124 G6
Santa Rosa I., *Calif., U.S.A.* .. 117 M6
Santa Rosa I., *Fla., U.S.A.* ... 109 K2
Santa Rosa Range, *U.S.A.* ... 114 F5
Santa Rosalía, *Mexico* 118 B2
Santa Sylvina, *Argentina* 126 B3
Santa Tecla = Nueva San
  Salvador, *El Salv.* 120 D2
Santa Teresa, *Argentina* 126 C3
Santa Teresa, *Australia* 94 C1
Santa Teresa, *Mexico* 119 B5
Santa Teresa di Riva, *Italy* ... 31 E8
Santa Teresa Gallura, *Italy* ... 30 A2
Santa Uxía, *Spain* 34 C2
Santa Vitória do Palmar, *Brazil* 127 C5
Santa Ynez →, *U.S.A.* 117 L6
Santa Ynez Mts., *U.S.A.* 117 L6
Santa Ysabel, *U.S.A.* 117 M10
Santadi, *Italy* 30 C1
Santaella, *Spain* 35 H6
Santai, *China* 58 B5
Santana, *Madeira* 37 D3
Sântana, *Romania* 42 D6
Santana, Coxilha de, *Brazil* ... 127 C4
Santana do Livramento, *Brazil* . 127 C4
Santander, *Spain* 34 B7
Santander Jiménez, *Mexico* ... 119 C5
Santanyí, *Spain* 37 B10
Santaquin, *U.S.A.* 114 G8
Santarcángelo di Romagna, *Italy* 29 D9
Santarém, *Brazil* 125 D8
Santarém, *Portugal* 35 F2
Santarém □, *Portugal* 35 F2
Santaren Channel, *W. Indies* .. 120 B4
Santee, *U.S.A.* 109 J6
Santéramo in Colle, *Italy* 31 B9
Santerno →, *Italy* 29 D8
Santhià, *Italy* 28 C5
Santiago, *Brazil* 127 B5
Santiago, *Chile* 126 C1
Santiago, *Panama* 120 E3
Santiago □, *Chile* 126 C1
Santiago →, *Mexico* 98 G9
Santiago →, *Peru* 124 D3
Santiago, Punta de, *Eq. Guin.* . 83 E6
Santiago de Compostela, *Spain* . 34 C2
Santiago de Cuba, *Cuba* 120 C4
Santiago de los Cabelleros,
  Dom. Rep. 121 C5
Santiago del Estero, *Argentina* . 126 B3
Santiago del Estero □, *Argentina* 126 B3
Santiago del Teide, *Canary Is.* . 37 F3
Santiago do Cacém, *Portugal* .. 35 G2
Santiago Ixcuintla, *Mexico* ... 118 C3
Santiago Papasquiaro, *Mexico* . 118 C3
Santiaguillo, L. de, *Mexico* ... 118 C4
Santillana, *Spain* 34 B6
Santisteban del Puerto, *Spain* .. 35 G7
Santo Amaro, *Brazil* 125 F11
Santo Anastácio, *Brazil* 127 A5
Santo André, *Brazil* 127 A6
Santo Ângelo, *Brazil* 127 B5
Santo Antônio do Içá, *Brazil* .. 124 D5
Santo Antônio do Leverger,
  Brazil 125 G7
Santo Domingo, *Dom. Rep.* .. 121 C6
Santo Domingo, *Baja Calif.,
  Mexico* 118 A1
Santo Domingo, *Baja Calif. S.,
  Mexico* 118 B2
Santo Domingo, *Nic.* 120 D3
Santo Domingo de la Calzada,
  Spain 32 C2
Santo Domingo de los
  Colorados, *Ecuador* 124 D3
Santo Domingo Pueblo, *U.S.A.* 115 J10
Santo Stéfano di Camastro, *Italy* 31 D7
Santo Tirso, *Portugal* 34 D2
Santo Tomás, *Mexico* 118 A1
Santo Tomás, *Peru* 124 F4
Santo Tomé, *Argentina* 127 B4
Santo Tomé de Guayana =
  Ciudad Guayana, *Venezuela* . 124 B6

Santomera, *Spain* 33 G3
Santoña, *Spain* 34 B7
Santoríni = Thíra, *Greece* 39 E7
Santos, *Brazil* 127 A6
Santos, Sierra de los, *Spain* ... 35 G5
Santos Dumont, *Brazil* 127 A7
Sanwer, *India* 68 H6
Sanxenxo, *Spain* 34 C2
Sanyuan, *China* 56 G5
São Bartolomeu de Messines,
  Portugal 35 H2
São Bernardo do Campo, *Brazil* 127 A6
São Borja, *Brazil* 127 B4
São Brás de Alportel, *Portugal* . 35 H3
São Carlos, *Brazil* 127 A6
São Cristóvão, *Brazil* 125 F11
São Domingos, *Brazil* 125 F9
São Domingos, *Guinea-Biss.* .. 82 C1
São Francisco, *Brazil* 125 G10
São Francisco →, *Brazil* 122 E7
São Francisco do Sul, *Brazil* .. 127 B6
São Gabriel, *Brazil* 127 C5
São Gonçalo, *Brazil* 127 A7
Sao Hill, *Tanzania* 87 D4
São João, *Guinea-Biss.* 82 C1
São João da Boa Vista, *Brazil* . 127 A6
São João da Madeira, *Portugal* . 34 E2
São João da Pesqueira, *Portugal* 34 D3
São João del Rei, *Brazil* 127 A7
São João do Araguaia, *Brazil* .. 125 E9
São João do Piauí, *Brazil* 125 E10
São Joaquim, *Brazil* 127 B6
São Jorge, Pta. de, *Madeira* ... 37 D3
São José, *Brazil* 127 B5
São José do Norte, *Brazil* 127 C5
São José do Rio Prêto, *Brazil* .. 127 A6
São José dos Campos, *Brazil* .. 127 A6
São Leopoldo, *Brazil* 127 B5
São Lourenço, *Brazil* 127 A6
São Lourenço →, *Brazil* 125 G7
São Lourenço, Pta. de, *Madeira* 37 D3
São Lourenço do Sul, *Brazil* .. 127 C5
São Luís, *Brazil* 125 D10
São Luís Gonzaga, *Brazil* 127 B5
São Marcos →, *Brazil* 125 G9
São Marcos, B. de, *Brazil* 125 D10
São Martinho da Cortiça,
  Portugal 34 E2
São Mateus, *Brazil* 125 G11
São Mateus do Sul, *Brazil* ... 127 B5
São Miguel do Oeste, *Brazil* .. 127 B5
São Paulo, *Brazil* 127 A6
São Paulo □, *Brazil* 127 A6
São Paulo, I., *Atl. Oc.* 2 D8
São Paulo de Olivença, *Brazil* . 124 D5
São Pedro do Sul, *Portugal* ... 34 E2
São Roque, *Madeira* 37 D3
São Roque, C. de, *Brazil* 122 D7
São Sebastião, I. de, *Brazil* ... 127 A6
São Sebastião do Paraíso, *Brazil* 127 A6
São Teotónio, *Portugal* 35 H2
São Tomé, *Atl. Oc.* 76 F4
São Tomé, C. de, *Brazil* 127 A7
São Tomé & Príncipe ■, *Africa* 77 F4
São Vicente, *Brazil* 127 A6
São Vicente, *Madeira* 37 D2
São Vicente, C. de, *Portugal* .. 35 H1
Saona, I., *Dom. Rep.* 121 C6
Saône →, *France* 19 G11
Saône-et-Loire □, *France* 19 F11
Saonek, *Indonesia* 63 E8
Sápai, *Greece* 41 E9
Sapanca, *Turkey* 72 E3
Saparua, *Indonesia* 63 E7
Sapele, *Nigeria* 83 D6
Sapelo I., *U.S.A.* 109 K5
Saphane, *Turkey* 39 B11
Sapiéntza, *Greece* 38 E3
Sapone, *Burkina Faso* 83 C4
Saposoa, *Peru* 124 E3
Sapouy, *Burkina Faso* 83 C4
Sapozhok, *Russia* 48 D5
Sapphire, *Australia* 94 C4
Sappho, *U.S.A.* 116 B2
Sapporo, *Japan* 54 C10
Sapri, *Italy* 31 B8
Sapulpa, *U.S.A.* 113 H6
Saqqez, *Iran* 70 B5
Sar Dasht, *Iran* 71 D6
Sar Gachîneh = Yāsūj, *Iran* .. 71 D6
Sar Planina, *Macedonia* 40 E4
Sara, *Burkina Faso* 82 C4
Sara, *Phil.* 61 F5
Sara Buri = Saraburi, *Thailand* . 64 E3
Sarāb, *Iran* 70 B5
Sarabadi, *Iraq* 70 C5
Saraburi, *Thailand* 64 E3
Saradiya, *India* 68 J4
Saraféré, *Mali* 82 B4
Saragossa = Zaragoza, *Spain* .. 32 D4
Saraguro, *Ecuador* 124 D3
Sarai Naurang, *Pakistan* 68 C4
Saraikela, *India* 69 H11
Saraiu, *Romania* 43 F13
Sarajevo, *Bos.-H.* 42 G3
Sarakhs, *Turkmenistan* 71 B9
Saran, Gunung, *Indonesia* ... 62 E4
Saranac L., *U.S.A.* 111 B10
Saranac Lake, *U.S.A.* 111 B10
Saranda, *Tanzania* 86 D3
Sarandë, *Albania* 40 G3
Sarandí del Yí, *Uruguay* 127 C4
Sarandí Grande, *Uruguay* ... 126 C4
Sarangani B., *Phil.* 61 J6
Sarangani Is., *Phil.* 61 J6
Sarangarh, *India* 67 J13

Saransk, *Russia* 48 C7
Sarapul, *Russia* 50 D6
Sarasota, *U.S.A.* 109 M4
Saratoga, *Calif., U.S.A.* 116 H4
Saratoga, *Wyo., U.S.A.* 114 F10
Saratoga Springs, *U.S.A.* 111 C11
Saratok, *Malaysia* 62 D4
Saratov, *Russia* 48 E7
Saravane, *Laos* 64 E6
Sarawak ☐, *Malaysia* 62 D4
Saray, *Tekirdağ, Turkey* 41 E11
Saray, *Van, Turkey* 73 C11
Saraya, *Guinea* 82 C2
Saraya, *Senegal* 82 C2
Sarayçık, *Turkey* 39 B11
Sarayköy, *Turkey* 39 D10
Saraylar, *Turkey* 41 F11
Sarayönü, *Turkey* 72 C5
Sarbāz, *Iran* 71 E9
Sarbīsheh, *Iran* 71 C8
Sárbogárd, *Hungary* 42 D3
Sarca ↘, *Italy* 28 C7
Sarcelles, *France* 19 D9
Sarda ↘, *India* 67 F12
Sardarshahr, *India* 68 E6
Sardegna ☐, *Italy* 30 B1
Sardhana, *India* 68 E7
Sardina, Pta., *Canary Is.* 37 F4
Sardinia = Sardegna ☐, *Italy* .. 30 B1
Sardis, *Turkey* 39 C10
Sārdūīyeh = Dar Mazār, *Iran* .. 71 D8
S'Arenal, *Spain* 37 B9
Sarentino, *Italy* 29 B8
Saréyamou, *Mali* 82 B4
Sargasso Sea, *Atl. Oc.* 97 D20
Sargodha, *Pakistan* 68 C5
Sarh, *Chad* 79 G9
Sarhala, *Ivory C.* 82 D3
Sārī, *Iran* 71 B7
Sari d'Orcino, *France* 21 F12
Sária, *Greece* 39 F9
Saria, *India* 69 J10
Sariab, *Pakistan* 68 D2
Sarıbeyler, *Turkey* 39 B9
Sarıgöl, *Turkey* 72 C3
Sarıkamış, *Turkey* 73 B10
Sarıkaya, *Turkey* 72 C6
Sarikei, *Malaysia* 62 D4
Sarila, *India* 69 G8
Sarina, *Australia* 94 C4
Sariñena, *Spain* 32 D4
Sarita, *U.S.A.* 113 M6
Sariwŏn, *N. Korea* 57 E13
Sariyar Barajı, *Turkey* 72 B4
Sarıyer, *Turkey* 41 E13
Sarju ↘, *India* 69 F9
Sark, *U.K.* 13 H5
Sarkad, *Hungary* 42 D6
Sarkari Tala, *India* 68 F4
Şarkışla, *Turkey* 72 C7
Şarköy, *Turkey* 41 F11
Sarlat-la-Canéda, *France* 20 D5
Sărmăşag, *Romania* 42 C7
Sărmaşu, *Romania* 43 D9
Sarmi, *Indonesia* 63 E9
Sarmiento, *Argentina* 128 F3
Sarmizegetusa, *Romania* 42 E7
Särna, *Sweden* 10 C7
Sarnano, *Italy* 29 E10
Sarnen, *Switz.* 25 J4
Sarnia, *Canada* 102 D3
Sarno, *Italy* 31 B7
Sarnthein = Sarentino, *Italy* .. 29 B8
Särö, *Sweden* 11 G5
Sarolangun, *Indonesia* 62 E2
Saronikós Kólpos, *Greece* 38 D5
Saronno, *Italy* 28 C6
Saros Körfezi, *Turkey* 41 F10
Sárospatak, *Hungary* 42 B6
Sarpsborg, *Norway* 9 G14
Sarracín, *Spain* 34 C7
Sarralbe, *France* 19 D14
Sarre = Saar ↘, *Europe* 17 E6
Sarre, *Italy* 28 C4
Sarre-Union, *France* 19 D14
Sarrebourg, *France* 19 D14
Sarreguemines, *France* 19 C14
Sarria, *Spain* 34 C3
Sarrión, *Spain* 32 E4
Sarro, *Mali* 82 C3
Sarstedt, *Germany* 24 C5
Sartène, *France* 21 G12
Sarthe ☐, *France* 18 D7
Sarthe ↘, *France* 18 E6
Sartilly, *France* 18 D5
Sărulești, *Romania* 43 F11
Saruna ↘, *Pakistan* 68 F2
Sárvár, *Hungary* 42 C1
Sarvar, *India* 68 F6
Sarvestān, *Iran* 71 D7
Särvfjället, *Sweden* 10 B7
Sárviz ↘, *Hungary* 42 D3
Sary-Tash, *Kyrgyzstan* 50 F8
Sarych, Mys, *Ukraine* 47 K7
Saryshagan, *Kazakhstan* 50 E8
Sarzana, *Italy* 28 D6
Sarzeau, *France* 18 E4
Sasan Gir, *India* 68 J4
Sasaram, *India* 69 G11
Saser, *India* 69 B7
Saskatchewan ☐, *Canada* 105 C7
Saskatchewan ↘, *Canada* 105 C8
Saskatoon, *Canada* 105 C7

Saskylakh, *Russia* 51 B12
Sasolburg, *S. Africa* 89 D4
Sasovo, *Russia* 48 C5
Sassandra, *Ivory C.* 82 E3
Sassandra ↘, *Ivory C.* 82 E3
Sássari, *Italy* 30 B1
Sassnitz, *Germany* 24 A9
Sasso Marconi, *Italy* 29 D8
Sassocorvaro, *Italy* 29 E9
Sassoferrato, *Italy* 29 E9
Sasstown, *Liberia* 82 E3
Sassuolo, *Italy* 28 D7
Sástago, *Spain* 32 D4
Sasumua Dam, *Kenya* 86 C4
Sasyk, Ozero, *Ukraine* 47 K5
Sata-Misaki, *Japan* 55 J5
Satadougou, *Mali* 82 C2
Satakunta, *Finland* 9 F20
Satama-Soukoura, *Ivory C.* .. 82 D4
Satara, *India* 66 L8
Satara, *S. Africa* 89 C5
Satbarwa, *India* 69 H11
Såtenäs, *Sweden* 11 F6
Satevó, *Mexico* 118 B3
Satilla ↘, *U.S.A.* 109 K5
Satmala Hills, *India* 66 J9
Satna, *India* 69 G9
Šator, *Bos.-H.* 29 D13
Sátoraljaújhely, *Hungary* 42 B6
Satpura Ra., *India* 66 J10
Satrup, *Germany* 24 A5
Satsuna-Shotō, *Japan* 55 K5
Sattahip, *Thailand* 64 F3
Satu Mare, *Romania* 42 C7
Satu Mare ☐, *Romania* 42 C8
Satui, *Indonesia* 62 E5
Satun, *Thailand* 65 J3
Saturnina ↘, *Brazil* 124 F7
Sauce, *Argentina* 126 C4
Sauceda, *Mexico* 118 B4
Saucillo, *Mexico* 118 B3
Sauda, *Norway* 9 G12
Sauðarkrókur, *Iceland* 8 D4
Saudi Arabia ■, *Asia* 70 B3
Saugeen ↘, *Canada* 110 B3
Saugerties, *U.S.A.* 111 D11
Saugues, *France* 20 D7
Saugus, *U.S.A.* 117 L8
Saujon, *France* 20 C3
Sauk Centre, *U.S.A.* 112 C7
Sauk Rapids, *U.S.A.* 112 C7
Saulgau, *Germany* 25 G5
Saulieu, *France* 19 E11
Sault, *France* 21 D9
Sault Ste. Marie, *Canada* 102 C3
Sault Ste. Marie, *U.S.A.* 101 D11
Saumlaki, *Indonesia* 63 F8
Saumur, *France* 18 E6
Saunders C., *N.Z.* 91 L3
Saunders I., *Antarctica* 5 B1
Saunders Point, *Australia* 93 E4
Sauri, *Nigeria* 83 C6
Saurimo, *Angola* 84 F4
Sausalito, *U.S.A.* 116 H4
Sauveterre-de-Béarn, *France* .. 20 E3
Sauzé-Vaussais, *France* 20 B4
Savá, *Honduras* 120 C2
Sava, *Italy* 31 B10
Sava ↘, *Serbia, Yug.* 42 F5
Savage, *U.S.A.* 112 B2
Savage I. = Niue, *Cook Is.* .. 97 J11
Savage River, *Australia* 94 G4
Savai'i, *Samoa* 91 A12
Savalou, *Benin* 83 D5
Savane, *Mozam.* 87 F4
Savanna, *U.S.A.* 112 D9
Savanna-la-Mar, *Jamaica* 120 C4
Savannah, *Ga., U.S.A.* 109 J5
Savannah, *Mo., U.S.A.* 112 F7
Savannah, *Tenn., U.S.A.* 109 H1
Savannah ↘, *U.S.A.* 109 J5
Savannakhet, *Laos* 64 D5
Savant L., *Canada* 102 B1
Savant Lake, *Canada* 102 B1
Săvârşin, *Romania* 42 D7
Savaştepe, *Turkey* 39 B9
Savé, *Benin* 83 D5
Save ↘, *France* 20 E5
Save ↘, *Mozam.* 89 C5
Sāveh, *Iran* 71 C6
Savelugu, *Ghana* 83 D4
Savenay, *France* 18 E5
Săveni, *Romania* 43 C11
Saverdun, *France* 20 E5
Saverne, *France* 19 D14
Savigliano, *Italy* 28 D4
Savigny-sur-Braye, *France* .. 18 E7
Sávio ↘, *Italy* 29 D9
Šavnik, *Montenegro, Yug.* .. 40 D3
Savo, *Finland* 8 E22
Savoie ☐, *France* 21 C10
Savona, *Italy* 28 D5
Savona, *U.S.A.* 110 D7
Savonlinna, *Finland* 46 B5
Savoy = Savoie ☐, *France* .. 21 C10
Şavşat, *Turkey* 73 B10
Sävsjö, *Sweden* 11 G8
Savur, *Turkey* 70 B4
Sawahlunto, *Indonesia* 62 E2
Sawai, *Indonesia* 63 E7
Sawai Madhopur, *India* 68 G7
Sawang Daen Din, *Thailand* .. 64 D4
Sawankhalok, *Thailand* 64 D2
Sawara, *Japan* 55 G10
Sawatch Range, *U.S.A.* 115 G10

Sawel Mt., *U.K.* 15 B4
Sawi, *Thailand* 65 G2
Sawla, *Ghana* 82 D4
Sawmills, *Zimbabwe* 87 F2
Sawtooth Range, *U.S.A.* 114 E6
Sawu, *Indonesia* 63 F6
Sawu Sea, *Indonesia* 63 F6
Saxby ↘, *Australia* 94 B3
Saxmundham, *U.K.* 13 E9
Saxony = Sachsen ☐, *Germany* .. 24 E9
Saxony, Lower =
  Niedersachsen ☐, *Germany* .. 24 C4
Saxton, *U.S.A.* 110 F6
Say, *Mali* 82 C4
Say, *Niger* 83 C5
Saya, *Nigeria* 83 D5
Sayabec, *Canada* 103 C6
Sayaboury, *Laos* 64 C3
Sayán, *Peru* 124 F3
Sayan, Vostochnyy, *Russia* 51 D10
Sayan, Zapadnyy, *Russia* 51 D10
Saydā, *Lebanon* 75 B4
Sayhandulaan = Oldziyt,
  Mongolia 56 B5
Sayhūt, *Yemen* 74 D5
Saykhin, *Kazakstan* 49 F8
Saynshand, *Mongolia* 60 B6
Sayre, *Okla., U.S.A.* 113 H5
Sayre, *Pa., U.S.A.* 111 E8
Sayreville, *U.S.A.* 111 F10
Sayula, *Mexico* 118 D4
Sayward, *Canada* 104 C3
Sazanit, *Albania* 40 F3
Sazin, *Pakistan* 69 B5
Sazlika ↘, *Bulgaria* 41 E9
Scaër, *France* 18 D3
Scafell Pike, *U.K.* 12 C4
Scalea, *Italy* 31 C8
Scalloway, *U.K.* 14 A7
Scalpay, *U.K.* 14 D3
Scandia, *Canada* 104 C6
Scandiano, *Italy* 28 D7
Scandicci, *Italy* 29 E8
Scandinavia, *Europe* 8 E16
Scansano, *Italy* 29 F8
Scapa Flow, *U.K.* 14 C5
Scappoose, *U.S.A.* 116 E4
Scarámia, Capo, *Italy* 31 F7
Scarba, *U.K.* 14 E3
Scarborough, *Trin. & Tob.* 121 D7
Scarborough, *U.K.* 12 C7
Scariff I., *Ireland* 15 E1
Scarp, *U.K.* 14 C1
Scebeli, Wabi ↘, *Somali Rep.* .. 74 G3
Šćedro, *Croatia* 29 E13
Schaal See, *Germany* 24 B6
Schaffhausen, *Switz.* 25 H4
Schagen, *Neths.* 17 B4
Schaghticoke, *U.S.A.* 111 D11
Schärding, *Austria* 26 C6
Scharhörn, *Germany* 24 B4
Scheessel, *Germany* 24 B5
Schefferville, *Canada* 103 B6
Scheibbs, *Austria* 26 C8
Schelde ↘, *Belgium* 17 C4
Schell Creek Ra., *U.S.A.* 114 G6
Schellsburg, *U.S.A.* 110 F6
Schenectady, *U.S.A.* 111 D11
Schenevus, *U.S.A.* 111 D10
Scherfede, *Germany* 24 D5
Schesslitz, *Germany* 25 F7
Schiedam, *Neths.* 17 C4
Schiermonnikoog, *Neths.* 17 A6
Schiltigheim, *France* 19 D14
Schio, *Italy* 29 C8
Schladming, *Austria* 26 D6
Schlanders = Silandro, *Italy* .. 28 B7
Schlei ↘, *Germany* 24 A5
Schleiden, *Germany* 24 E2
Schleiz, *Germany* 24 E7
Schleswig, *Germany* 24 A5
Schleswig-Holstein ☐, *Germany* .. 24 A5
Schlüchtern, *Germany* 25 E5
Schmalkalden, *Germany* 24 E6
Schmölln, *Germany* 24 E8
Schneeberg, *Austria* 26 D8
Schneeberg, *Germany* 24 E8
Schneverdingen, *Germany* .. 24 B5
Schoharie, *U.S.A.* 111 D10
Schoharie ↘, *U.S.A.* 111 D10
Scholls, *U.S.A.* 116 E4
Schönberg,
  *Mecklenburg-Vorpommern,
  Germany* 24 B6
Schönberg, *Schleswig-Holstein,
  Germany* 24 A6
Schönecke, *Germany* 24 C7
Schongau, *Germany* 25 H6
Schöningen, *Germany* 24 C6
Schorndorf, *Germany* 25 G5
Schortens, *Germany* 24 B4
Schouten I., *Australia* 94 G4
Schouten Is. = Supiori, *Indonesia* 63 E9
Schouwen, *Neths.* 17 C3
Schramberg, *Germany* 25 G4
Schrankogel, *Austria* 26 D4
Schreiber, *Canada* 102 C2
Schrems, *Austria* 26 C8
Schrobenhausen, *Germany* .. 25 G7
Schroffenstein, *Namibia* 88 D2
Schroon Lake, *U.S.A.* 111 C11
Schruns, *Austria* 26 D2
Schuler, *Canada* 105 C6
Schumacher, *Canada* 102 C3

Schurz, *U.S.A.* 114 G4
Schuyler, *U.S.A.* 112 E6
Schuylerville, *U.S.A.* 111 C11
Schuylkill ↘, *U.S.A.* 111 G9
Schuylkill Haven, *U.S.A.* 111 F8
Schwabach, *Germany* 25 F7
Schwaben ☐, *Germany* 25 G6
Schwäbisch Gmünd, *Germany* . 25 G5
Schwäbisch Hall, *Germany* .. 25 F5
Schwäbische Alb, *Germany* .. 25 G5
Schwabmünchen, *Germany* .. 25 G6
Schwalmstadt, *Germany* 24 E5
Schwandorf, *Germany* 25 F8
Schwaner, Pegunungan,
  Indonesia 62 E4
Schwanewede, *Germany* 24 B4
Schwarmstedt, *Germany* 24 C5
Schwarze Elster ↘, *Germany* . 24 D8
Schwarzenberg, *Germany* .. 24 E8
Schwarzrand, *Namibia* 88 D2
Schwarzwald, *Germany* 25 G4
Schwaz, *Austria* 26 D4
Schwechat, *Austria* 27 C9
Schwedt, *Germany* 24 B10
Schweinfurt, *Germany* 25 E6
Schweizer-Reneke, *S. Africa* .. 88 D4
Schwenningen = Villingen-
  Schwenningen, *Germany* .. 25 G4
Schwerin, *Germany* 24 B7
Schweriner See, *Germany* 24 B7
Schwetzingen, *Germany* 25 F4
Schwyz, *Switz.* 25 H4
Schwyz ☐, *Switz.* 25 H4
Sciacca, *Italy* 30 E6
Scicli, *Italy* 31 F7
Scilla, *Italy* 31 D8
Scilly, Isles of, *U.K.* 13 H1
Ścinawa, *Poland* 45 G3
Scione, *Greece* 40 F7
Scioto ↘, *U.S.A.* 108 F4
Scituate, *U.S.A.* 111 D14
Scobey, *U.S.A.* 112 A2
Scordia, *Italy* 31 E7
Scoresbysund =
  Ittoqqortoormiit, *Greenland* . 4 B6
Scorniceşti, *Romania* 43 F9
Scotia, *Calif., U.S.A.* 114 F1
Scotia, *N.Y., U.S.A.* 111 D11
Scotia Sea, *Antarctica* 5 B18
Scotland, *Canada* 110 C4
Scotland ■, *U.K.* 14 E5
Scotland ☐, *U.K.* 14 E5
Scott, *C., Australia* 92 B4
Scott City, *U.S.A.* 112 F4
Scott Glacier, *Antarctica* 5 C8
Scott I., *Antarctica* 5 C11
Scott Is., *Canada* 104 C3
Scott L., *Canada* 105 B7
Scott Reef, *Australia* 92 B3
Scottburgh, *S. Africa* 89 E5
Scottdale, *U.S.A.* 110 F5
Scottish Borders ☐, *U.K.* 14 F6
Scottsbluff, *U.S.A.* 112 E3
Scottsboro, *U.S.A.* 109 H3
Scottsburg, *U.S.A.* 108 F3
Scottsdale, *Australia* 94 G4
Scottsdale, *U.S.A.* 115 K7
Scottsville, *Ky., U.S.A.* 109 G2
Scottsville, *N.Y., U.S.A.* 110 C7
Scottville, *U.S.A.* 108 D2
Scranton, *U.S.A.* 111 E9
Scugog, L., *Canada* 110 B6
Sculeni, *Moldova* 43 C12
Scunthorpe, *U.K.* 12 D7
Scuol Schuls, *Switz.* 25 J6
Scutari = Üsküdar, *Turkey* .. 41 F13
Seabrook, L., *Australia* 93 F2
Seaford, *U.K.* 13 G8
Seaford, *U.S.A.* 108 F8
Seaforth, *Australia* 94 C4
Seaforth, *Canada* 110 C3
Seaforth, L., *U.K.* 14 D2
Seagraves, *U.S.A.* 113 J3
Seaham, *U.K.* 12 C6
Seal ↘, *Canada* 105 B10
Seal L., *Canada* 103 B7
Sealy, *U.S.A.* 113 L6
Searchlight, *U.S.A.* 117 K12
Searcy, *U.S.A.* 113 H9
Searles L., *U.S.A.* 117 K9
Seascale, *U.K.* 12 C4
Seaside, *Calif., U.S.A.* 116 J5
Seaside, *Oreg., U.S.A.* 116 E3
Seattle, *U.S.A.* 116 C4
Seaview Ra., *Australia* 94 B4
Sebago L., *U.S.A.* 111 C14
Sebago Lake, *U.S.A.* 111 C14
Sebastián Vizcaíno, B., *Mexico* . 118 B2
Sebastopol = Sevastopol,
  Ukraine 47 K7
Sebastopol, *U.S.A.* 116 G4
Sebba, *Burkina Faso* 83 C5
Sebbeh, *Mali* 82 B4
Sebderat, *Eritrea* 81 D4
Sébékoro, *Mali* 82 C3
Seben, *Turkey* 72 B4
Sebeş, *Romania* 43 E8
Sebeşului, Munţii, *Romania* .. 43 E8
Sebewaing, *U.S.A.* 108 D4
Sebezh, *Russia* 46 D5
Sebha = Sabhah, *Libya* 79 C8
Sébi, *Mali* 82 B4
Şebinkarahisar, *Turkey* 73 B8
Sebiş, *Romania* 42 D7
Sebnitz, *Germany* 24 E10
Sebring, *Fla., U.S.A.* 109 M5
Sebring, *Ohio, U.S.A.* 110 F3
Sebringville, *Canada* 110 C3

Sebta = Ceuta, *N. Afr.* 78 A4
Sebuku, *Indonesia* 62 E5
Sebuku, Teluk, *Malaysia* 62 D5
Sečanj, *Serbia, Yug.* 42 E5
Secchia ↘, *Italy* 28 C8
Sechelt, *Canada* 104 D4
Sechura, Desierto de, *Peru* .. 124 E2
Seclin, *France* 19 B10
Secondigny, *France* 18 F6
Sečovce, *Slovak Rep.* 27 C14
Secretary I., *N.Z.* 91 L1
Secunderabad, *India* 66 L11
Security-Widefield, *U.S.A.* .. 112 F2
Sedalia, *U.S.A.* 112 F8
Sedan, *France* 19 C11
Sedan, *U.S.A.* 113 G6
Sedano, *Spain* 34 C7
Seddon, *N.Z.* 91 J5
Seddonville, *N.Z.* 91 J4
Sedé Boqér, *Israel* 75 E3
Sedeh, *Fārs, Iran* 71 D7
Sedeh, *Khorāsān, Iran* 71 C8
Séderon, *France* 21 D9
Sederot, *Israel* 75 D3
Sédhiou, *Senegal* 82 C1
Sedico, *Italy* 29 B9
Sedley, *Canada* 105 C8
Sedona, *U.S.A.* 115 J8
Sedova, Pik, *Russia* 50 B6
Sedro Woolley, *U.S.A.* 116 B4
Šeduva, *Lithuania* 44 C10
Sędziszów, *Poland* 45 H7
Sędziszów Małopolski, *Poland* . 45 H8
Seebad Ahlbeck, *Germany* .. 24 B10
Seefeld in Tirol, *Austria* 26 D4
Seehausen, *Germany* 24 C7
Seeheim, *Namibia* 88 D2
Seeheim-Jugenheim, *Germany* . 25 F4
Seeis, *Namibia* 88 C2
Seekoei ↘, *S. Africa* 88 E4
Seelow, *Germany* 24 C10
Sées, *France* 18 D7
Seesen, *Germany* 24 D6
Seevetal, *Germany* 24 B5
Sefadu, *S. Leone* 82 D2
Seferihisar, *Turkey* 39 C8
Séfeto, *Mali* 82 C3
Sefwi Bekwai, *Ghana* 82 D4
Segamat, *Malaysia* 65 L4
Şegarcea, *Romania* 43 F8
Ségbana, *Benin* 83 C5
Segbwema, *S. Leone* 82 D2
Seget, *Indonesia* 63 E8
Segonzac, *France* 20 C3
Segorbe, *Spain* 32 F4
Ségou, *Mali* 82 C3
Segovia = Coco ↘, *Cent. Amer.* . 120 D3
Segovia, *Spain* 34 E6
Segovia ☐, *Spain* 34 E6
Segré, *France* 18 E6
Segre ↘, *Spain* 32 D5
Séguéla, *Ivory C.* 82 D3
Séguénéga, *Burkina Faso* 83 C4
Seguin, *U.S.A.* 113 L6
Segundo ↘, *Argentina* 126 C3
Segura ↘, *Spain* 33 G4
Segura, Sierra de, *Spain* 33 G2
Seh Konj, Kūh-e, *Iran* 71 D8
Seh Qal'eh, *Iran* 71 C8
Sehitwa, *Botswana* 88 C3
Sehore, *India* 68 H7
Sehwan, *Pakistan* 68 F2
Şeica Mare, *Romania* 43 D9
Seil, *U.K.* 14 E3
Seiland, *Norway* 8 A20
Seilhac, *France* 20 C5
Seiling, *U.S.A.* 113 G5
Seille ↘, *Moselle, France* .. 19 C13
Seille ↘, *Saône-et-Loire, France* 19 F11
Sein, Î. de, *France* 18 D2
Seinäjoki, *Finland* 9 E20
Seine ↘, *France* 18 C7
Seine, B. de la, *France* 18 C6
Seine-et-Marne ☐, *France* .. 19 D10
Seine-Maritime ☐, *France* .. 18 C7
Seine-St-Denis ☐, *France* .. 19 D9
Seini, *Romania* 43 C8
Seirijai, *Lithuania* 44 D10
Seistan = Sīstān, *Iran* 71 D9
Seistan, Daryācheh-ye = Sīstān,
  Daryācheh-ye, *Iran* 71 D9
Sejerø, *Denmark* 11 J5
Sejerø Bugt, *Denmark* 11 J5
Sejny, *Poland* 44 D10
Seka, *Ethiopia* 81 F4
Sekayu, *Indonesia* 62 E2
Seke, *Tanzania* 86 C3
Sekenke, *Tanzania* 86 C3
Seki, *Turkey* 39 E11
Sekondi-Takoradi, *Ghana* 82 E4
Sekota, *Ethiopia* 81 E4
Seksna, *Russia* 46 C10
Sekuma, *Botswana* 88 C3
Selah, *U.S.A.* 114 C3
Selama, *Malaysia* 65 K3
Selárgius, *Italy* 30 C2
Selaru, *Indonesia* 63 F8
Selb, *Germany* 25 E8
Selby, *U.K.* 12 D6
Selby, *U.S.A.* 112 C4
Selca, *Croatia* 29 E13
Selçuk, *Turkey* 39 D9
Selden, *U.S.A.* 112 F4
Sele ↘, *Italy* 31 B7

Selebi-Pikwe, Botswana 89 C4
Selemdzha →, Russia 51 D13
Selendi, Manisa, Turkey 39 C10
Selendi, Manisa, Turkey 39 C9
Selenga = Selenge Mörön →, Asia 60 A5
Selenge Mörön →, Asia 60 A5
Selenicë, Albania 40 F3
Selenter See, Germany 24 A6
Sélestat, France 19 D14
Seletan, Tanjung, Indonesia .. 62 E4
Selevac, Serbia, Yug. 40 B4
Sélibabi, Mauritania 82 B2
Seliger, Ozero, Russia 46 D7
Seligman, U.S.A. 115 J7
Şelim, Turkey 73 B10
Selîma, El Wâhât el, Sudan .. 80 C2
Selimiye, Turkey 39 D9
Selinda Spillway →, Botswana . 88 B3
Selinoús, Greece 38 D3
Selinsgrove, U.S.A. 110 F8
Selizharovo, Russia 46 D7
Selkirk, Canada 105 C9
Selkirk, U.K. 14 F6
Selkirk I., Canada 105 C9
Selkirk Mts., Canada 100 C8
Sellama, Sudan 81 E2
Selliá, Greece 36 D6
Sellières, France 19 F12
Sells, U.S.A. 115 L8
Sellye, Hungary 42 E2
Selma, Ala., U.S.A. 109 J2
Selma, Calif., U.S.A. 116 J7
Selma, N.C., U.S.A. 109 H6
Selmer, U.S.A. 109 H1
Selongey, France 19 E12
Selowandoma Falls, Zimbabwe 87 G3
Selpele, Indonesia 63 E8
Selsey Bill, U.K. 13 G7
Seltso, Russia 46 F8
Seltz, France 19 D15
Selu, Indonesia 63 F8
Sélune →, France 18 D5
Selva = La Selva del Camp, Spain 32 D6
Selva, Argentina 126 B3
Selvas, Brazil 122 D4
Selwyn L., Canada 105 B8
Selwyn Mts., Canada 100 B6
Selwyn Ra., Australia 94 C3
Seman →, Albania 40 F3
Semarang, Indonesia 62 F4
Sembabule, Uganda 86 C3
Şemdinli, Turkey 73 D11
Sémé, Senegal 82 B2
Semeih, Sudan 81 E3
Semenov, Russia 48 B7
Semenovka, Chernihiv, Ukraine 47 F7
Semenovka, Kremenchuk, Ukraine 47 H7
Semeru, Indonesia 63 H15
Semey, Kazakstan 50 D9
Semikarakorskiy, Russia 49 G5
Semiluki, Russia 47 G10
Seminoe Reservoir, U.S.A. 114 F10
Seminole, Okla., U.S.A. 113 H6
Seminole, Tex., U.S.A. 113 J3
Seminole Draw →, U.S.A. 113 J3
Semipalatinsk = Semey, Kazakstan 50 D9
Semirara Is., Phil. 61 F4
Semitau, Indonesia 62 D4
Semiyarka, Kazakstan 50 D8
Semiyarskoye = Semiyarka, Kazakstan 50 D8
Semmering P., Austria 26 D8
Semnān, Iran 71 C7
Semnān □, Iran 71 C7
Semporna, Malaysia 63 D5
Semuda, Indonesia 62 E4
Semur-en-Auxois, France 19 E11
Sen →, Cambodia 62 B3
Senā, Iran 71 D6
Sena, Mozam. 87 F4
Sena Madureira, Brazil 124 E4
Senador Pompeu, Brazil 125 E11
Senaki, Georgia 49 J6
Senanga, Zambia 85 H4
Senatobia, U.S.A. 113 H10
Sencelles, Spain 37 B9
Sendafa, Ethiopia 81 F4
Sendai, Kagoshima, Japan 55 J5
Sendai, Miyagi, Japan 54 E10
Sendai-Wan, Japan 54 E10
Senden, Bayern, Germany 25 G6
Senden, Nordrhein-Westfalen, Germany 24 D3
Sendhwa, India 68 J6
Sene →, Ghana 83 D4
Senec, Slovak Rep. 27 C10
Seneca, U.S.A. 109 H4
Seneca Falls, U.S.A. 111 D8
Seneca L., U.S.A. 110 D8
Senecaville L., U.S.A. 110 G3
Senegal ■, W. Afr. 82 C2
Sénégal →, W. Afr. 82 B1
Senegambia, Africa 76 E2
Senekal, S. Africa 89 D4
Senftenberg, Germany 24 D10
Senga Hill, Zambia 87 D3
Senge Khambab = Indus →, Pakistan 68 G2
Sengiley, Russia 48 D9
Sengua →, Zimbabwe 87 F2
Senhor-do-Bonfim, Brazil 125 F10
Senica, Slovak Rep. 27 C10

Senigállia, Italy 29 E10
Senio →, Italy 29 D9
Senirkent, Turkey 39 C12
Senise, Italy 31 B9
Senj, Croatia 29 D11
Senja, Norway 8 B17
Senkaku-Shotō, Japan 55 L1
Senlis, France 19 C9
Senmonorom, Cambodia 64 F6
Sennâr, Sudan 81 E3
Sennar □, Sudan 81 E3
Senneterre, Canada 102 C4
Senno, Belarus 46 E5
Sênnori, Italy 30 B1
Seno, Laos 64 D5
Senonches, France 18 D8
Senorbì, Italy 30 C2
Senožeče, Slovenia 29 C11
Sens, France 19 D10
Senta, Serbia, Yug. 42 E5
Sentani, Indonesia 63 E10
Sentery, Dem. Rep. of the Congo 86 D2
Sentinel, U.S.A. 115 K7
Šentjur, Slovenia 29 B12
Senya Beraku, Ghana 83 D4
Seo de Urgel = La Seu d'Urgell, Spain 32 C6
Seohara, India 69 E8
Seonath →, India 69 J10
Seondha, India 69 F8
Seoni, India 69 H8
Seoni Malwa, India 68 H8
Seoul = Sŏul, S. Korea 57 F14
Sepīdān, Iran 71 D7
Sepo-ri, N. Korea 57 E14
Sępólno Krajeńskie, Poland .. 44 E4
Sepone, Laos 64 D6
Sępopol, Poland 44 D8
Sept-Îles, Canada 103 B6
Septemvri, Bulgaria 41 D8
Sepúlveda, Spain 34 D7
Sequeros, Spain 34 E4
Sequim, U.S.A. 116 B3
Sequoia National Park, U.S.A. . 116 J8
Serafimovich, Russia 48 F6
Seraing, Belgium 17 D5
Seraja, Indonesia 65 L7
Serakhis →, Cyprus 36 D11
Seram, Indonesia 63 E7
Seram Sea, Indonesia 63 E7
Seranantsara, Madag. 89 B8
Serang, Indonesia 63 G12
Serasan, Indonesia 65 L7
Seravezza, Italy 28 E7
Serbia □, Yugoslavia 40 C5
Šercaia, Romania 43 E10
Serdo, Ethiopia 81 E5
Serdobsk, Russia 48 D7
Sered', Slovak Rep. 27 C10
Seredka, Russia 46 C5
Şereflikoçhisar, Turkey 72 C5
Seregno, Italy 28 C6
Seremban, Malaysia 65 L3
Serengeti Plain, Tanzania 86 C4
Serenje, Zambia 87 E3
Sereth = Siret →, Romania .. 43 E12
Sergach, Russia 48 C7
Sergen, Turkey 41 E11
Sergino, Russia 50 C7
Sergipe □, Brazil 125 F11
Sergiyev Posad, Russia 46 D10
Seria, Brunei 62 D4
Serian, Malaysia 62 D4
Seriate, Italy 28 C6
Seribu, Kepulauan, Indonesia . 62 F3
Sérifontaine, France 19 C8
Sérifos, Greece 38 D6
Sérignan, France 20 E7
Sérigny →, Canada 103 A6
Serik, Turkey 72 D4
Seringapatam Reef, Australia . 92 B3
Serinhisar, Turkey 39 D11
Sermaize-les-Bains, France ... 19 D11
Sermata, Indonesia 63 F7
Sérmide, Italy 29 D8
Sernovodsk, Russia 48 D10
Sernur, Russia 48 B9
Serock, Poland 45 F8
Serón, Spain 33 H2
Serós, Spain 32 D5
Serov, Russia 50 D7
Serowe, Botswana 88 C4
Serpa, Portugal 35 H3
Serpeddí, Punta, Italy 30 C2
Serpentara, Italy 30 C2
Serpentine Lakes, Australia .. 93 E4
Serpis →, Spain 33 G4
Serpukhov, Russia 46 E9
Serra de Outes, Spain 34 C2
Serra do Navio, Brazil 125 C8
Serra San Bruno, Italy 31 D9
Serradilla, Spain 34 F4
Sérrai, Greece 40 E7
Sérrai □, Greece 40 E7
Serramanna, Italy 30 C1
Serravalle Scrívia, Italy 28 D5
Serre-Ponçon, L. de, France . 21 D10
Serres, France 21 D9
Serrezuela, Argentina 126 C2
Serrinha, Brazil 125 F11
Sersale, Italy 31 C9
Sertã, Portugal 34 F2
Sertanópolis, Brazil 127 A5
Sêrtar, China 58 A3
Serua, Indonesia 63 F8

Serui, Indonesia 63 E9
Serule, Botswana 88 C4
Sérvia, Greece 40 F6
Serzedelo, Portugal 34 D2
Sese Is., Uganda 86 C3
Sesepe, Indonesia 63 E7
Sesfontein, Namibia 88 B1
Sesheke, Zambia 88 B3
Sésia →, Italy 28 C5
Sesimbra, Portugal 35 G1
S'Espalmador, Spain 37 C7
S'Espardell, Spain 37 C7
Sessa Aurunca, Italy 30 A6
S'Estanyol, Spain 37 B9
Sestao, Spain 32 B2
Sesto Calende, Italy 28 C5
Sesto San Giovanni, Italy 28 C6
Sestri Levante, Italy 28 D6
Sestriere, Italy 28 D3
Sestroretsk, Russia 46 B6
Sestrunj, Croatia 29 D11
Sestu, Italy 30 C2
Setana, Japan 54 C9
Sète, France 20 E7
Sete Lagôas, Brazil 125 G10
Sétif, Algeria 78 A7
Seto, Japan 55 G8
Setonaikai, Japan 55 G6
Settat, Morocco 78 B4
Séttimo Torinese, Italy 28 C4
Setting L., Canada 105 C9
Settle, U.K. 12 C5
Settlement Pt., Bahamas 109 M6
Settlers, S. Africa 89 C4
Setúbal, Portugal 35 G2
Setúbal □, Portugal 35 G2
Setúbal, B. de, Portugal 35 G2
Seugne →, France 20 C3
Seul, Lac, Canada 102 B1
Seurre, France 19 F12
Sevan, Armenia 49 K7
Sevan, Ozero = Sevana Lich, Armenia 49 K7
Sevana Lich, Armenia 49 K7
Sevastopol, Ukraine 47 K7
Seven Sisters, Canada 104 C3
Sever →, Spain 35 F3
Sévérac-le-Château, France ... 20 D7
Severn →, Canada 102 A2
Severn →, U.K. 13 F5
Severn L., Canada 102 B1
Severnaya Zemlya, Russia 51 B10
Severo-Kurilsk, Russia 51 D16
Severo-Yeniseyskiy, Russia ... 51 C10
Severočeský □, Czech Rep. ... 26 A7
Severodonetsk = Syeverodonetsk, Ukraine ... 47 H10
Severodvinsk, Russia 50 C4
Severomoravský □, Czech Rep. 27 B10
Sevier →, U.S.A. 115 G7
Sevier →, U.S.A. 115 G7
Sevier Desert, U.S.A. 114 G7
Sevier L., U.S.A. 114 G7
Sevilla, Spain 35 H5
Sevilla □, Spain 35 H5
Seville = Sevilla, Spain 35 H5
Sevlievo, Bulgaria 41 C9
Sevnica, Slovenia 29 B12
Sèvre-Nantaise →, France 18 E5
Sèvre-Niortaise →, France ... 20 B3
Sevsk, Russia 47 F8
Sewa →, S. Leone 82 D2
Sewani, India 68 E6
Seward, Alaska, U.S.A. 100 B5
Seward, Nebr., U.S.A. 112 E6
Seward, Pa., U.S.A. 110 F5
Seward Peninsula, U.S.A. 100 B3
Sewell, Chile 126 C1
Sewer, Indonesia 63 F8
Sewickley, U.S.A. 110 F4
Sexsmith, Canada 104 B5
Seychelles ■, Ind. Oc. 52 K9
Seydişehir, Turkey 72 D4
Seydvān, Iran 70 B5
Seyhan →, Turkey 70 B2
Seyhan Barajı, Turkey 72 D6
Seyitgazi, Turkey 39 B12
Seyitömer, Turkey 39 B11
Seym →, Ukraine 47 G7
Seymen, Turkey 41 E11
Seymour, S. Africa 89 E4
Seymour, Conn., U.S.A. 111 E11
Seymour, Ind., U.S.A. 108 F3
Seymour, Tex., U.S.A. 113 J5
Seyne, France 21 D10
Seyssel, France 21 C9
Sézanne, France 19 D10
Sezze, Italy 30 A6
Sfântu Gheorghe, Covasna, Romania 43 E10
Sfântu Gheorghe, Tulcea, Romania 43 F14
Sfântu Gheorghe, Braţul →, Romania 43 F14
Sfax, Tunisia 79 B8
Sha Xi →, China 59 D12
Sha Xian, China 59 D11
Shaanxi □, China 56 G5
Shaba = Katanga □, Dem. Rep. of the Congo 86 D2
Shabla, Bulgaria 41 C12
Shabogamo L., Canada 103 B6
Shabunda, Dem. Rep. of the Congo 86 C2

Shache, China 60 C2
Shackleton Ice Shelf, Antarctica 5 C8
Shackleton Inlet, Antarctica .. 5 E11
Shādegān, Iran 71 D6
Shadi, China 59 D10
Shadi, India 69 C7
Shadrinsk, Russia 50 D7
Shadyside, U.S.A. 110 G4
Shaffa, Nigeria 83 C7
Shafter, U.S.A. 117 K7
Shaftesbury, U.K. 13 F5
Shagamu, Nigeria 83 D5
Shagram, Pakistan 69 A5
Shah Alizai, Pakistan 68 E2
Shah Bunder, Pakistan 68 G2
Shahabad, Punjab, India 68 D7
Shahabad, Raj., India 68 G7
Shahabad, Ut. P., India 69 F8
Shahadpur, Pakistan 68 G3
Shahba, Syria 75 C5
Shahdād, Iran 71 D8
Shahdād, Namakzār-e, Iran .. 71 D8
Shahdadkot, Pakistan 68 F2
Shahdol, India 69 H9
Shahe, China 56 F8
Shahganj, India 69 F10
Shahgarh, India 68 F6
Shahjahanpur, India 69 F8
Shahpur, India 68 H7
Shahpur, Baluchistan, Pakistan 68 E3
Shahpur, Punjab, Pakistan ... 68 C5
Shahpur Chakar, Pakistan 68 F3
Shahpura, Mad. P., India 69 H9
Shahpura, Raj., India 68 G6
Shahr-e Bābak, Iran 71 D7
Shahr-e Kord, Iran 71 C6
Shāhrakht, Iran 71 C9
Shahrig, Pakistan 68 D2
Shahukou, China 56 D7
Shaikhabad, Afghan. 68 B3
Shajapur, India 68 H7
Shakargarh, Pakistan 68 C6
Shakawe, Botswana 88 B3
Shaker Heights, U.S.A. 110 E3
Shakhty, Russia 49 G5
Shakhunya, Russia 48 B8
Shaki, Nigeria 83 D5
Shākir, Egypt 80 B3
Shala, L., Ethiopia 81 F4
Shali, Russia 49 J7
Shallow Lake, Canada 110 B3
Shalqar, Kazakstan 50 E6
Shalskiy, Russia 46 B8
Shaluli Shan, China 58 B2
Shām, Iran 71 E8
Shām, Bādiyat ash, Asia 70 C3
Shamâl Bahr el Ghazal □, Sudan 81 F2
Shamâl Dârfûr □, Sudan 81 E2
Shamâl Kordofân □, Sudan ... 81 E3
Shamattawa, Canada 102 A1
Shamattawa →, Canada 102 A2
Shambe, Sudan 81 F3
Shambu, Ethiopia 81 F4
Shamīl, Iran 71 E8
Shamkhor = Şämkir, Azerbaijan 49 K8
Shāmkūh, Iran 71 C8
Shamli, India 68 E7
Shammar, Jabal, Si. Arabia .. 70 E4
Shamo = Gobi, Asia 56 C6
Shamo, L., Ethiopia 81 F4
Shamokin, U.S.A. 111 F8
Shamrock, U.S.A. 113 H4
Shamva, Zimbabwe 87 F3
Shan □, Burma 67 J21
Shan Xian, China 56 G9
Shanan →, Ethiopia 81 F5
Shanchengzhen, China 57 C13
Shāndak, Iran 71 D9
Shandon, U.S.A. 116 K6
Shandong □, China 57 G10
Shandong Bandao, China 57 F11
Shang Xian = Shangzhou, China 56 H5
Shanga, Nigeria 83 C5
Shangalowe, Dem. Rep. of the Congo 87 E2
Shangani, Zimbabwe 89 B4
Shangani →, Zimbabwe 87 F2
Shangbancheng, China 57 D10
Shangcheng, China 59 B10
Shangchuan Dao, China 59 G9
Shangdu, China 56 D7
Shanggao, China 59 C10
Shanghai, China 59 B13
Shanghai Shi □, China 59 B13
Shanghang, China 59 E11
Shanghe, China 57 F9
Shanglin, China 58 F7
Shangnan, China 56 H6
Shangqiu, China 56 G8
Shangrao, China 59 C11
Shangshui, China 60 C6
Shangsi, China 58 F6
Shangyou, China 59 E10
Shangyu, China 59 B13
Shangzhi, China 57 B14
Shangzhou, China 56 H5
Shanhetun, China 57 B14
Shani, Nigeria 83 C7
Shannon, N.Z. 91 J5
Shannon →, Ireland 15 D2
Shannon, Mouth of the, Ireland 15 D2
Shannon Airport, Ireland 15 D3
Shansi = Shanxi □, China 56 F7
Shantar, Ostrov Bolshoy, Russia 51 D14
Shantipur, India 69 H13
Shantou, China 59 F11

Shantung = Shandong □, China 57 G10
Shanwei, China 59 F10
Shanxi □, China 56 F7
Shanyang, China 56 H5
Shanyin, China 56 E7
Shaodong, China 59 D8
Shaoguan, China 59 E9
Shaoshan, China 59 D9
Shaowu, China 59 D11
Shaoxing, China 59 C13
Shaoyang, Hunan, China 59 D8
Shaoyang, Hunan, China 59 D8
Shap, U.K. 12 C5
Shapinsay, U.K. 14 B6
Shaqq el Gi'eifer →, Sudan .. 81 D2
Shaqra', Si. Arabia 70 E5
Shaqrā', Yemen 74 E4
Sharafa, Sudan 81 E2
Sharafkhāneh, Iran 70 B5
Sharbot Lake, Canada 111 B8
Shari, Japan 54 C12
Sharjah = Ash Shāriqah, U.A.E. 71 E7
Shark B., Australia 93 E1
Sharm el Sheikh, Egypt 80 B3
Sharon, Mass., U.S.A. 111 D13
Sharon, Pa., U.S.A. 110 E4
Sharon Springs, Kans., U.S.A. . 112 F4
Sharon Springs, N.Y., U.S.A. . 111 D10
Sharp Pt., Australia 94 A3
Sharpe L., Canada 102 B1
Sharpsville, U.S.A. 110 E4
Sharq el Istiwa'iya □, Sudan . 81 G3
Sharya, Russia 48 A7
Shasha, Ethiopia 81 F4
Shashemene, Ethiopia 81 F4
Shashi, Botswana 89 C4
Shashi, China 59 B9
Shashi →, Africa 87 G2
Shasta, Mt., U.S.A. 114 F2
Shasta L., U.S.A. 114 F2
Shatawi, Sudan 81 E3
Shatsk, Russia 48 C5
Shatt al Arab = Arab, Shatt al →, Asia 71 D6
Shatura, Russia 46 E10
Shaumyani = Shulaveri, Georgia 49 K7
Shaunavon, Canada 105 D7
Shaver L., U.S.A. 116 H7
Shaw →, Australia 92 D2
Shaw I., Australia 94 C4
Shawanaga, Canada 110 A4
Shawangunk Mts., U.S.A. 111 E10
Shawano, U.S.A. 108 C1
Shawinigan, Canada 102 C5
Shawnee, U.S.A. 113 H6
Shay Gap, Australia 92 D3
Shayang, China 59 B9
Shaybārā, Si. Arabia 70 E3
Shayib el Banat, Gebel, Egypt . 80 B3
Shaykh, J. ash, Lebanon 75 B4
Shaykh Miskīn, Syria 75 C5
Shaykh Sa'īd, Iraq 70 C5
Shchekino, Russia 46 E9
Shcherbakov = Rybinsk, Russia 46 C10
Shchigry, Russia 47 G9
Shchors, Ukraine 47 G6
Shchuchinsk, Kazakstan 50 D8
She Xian, Anhui, China 59 C12
She Xian, Hebei, China 56 F7
Shebekino, Russia 47 G9
Shebele = Scebeli, Wabi →, Somali Rep. 74 G3
Sheboygan, U.S.A. 108 D2
Shebshi Mts., Nigeria 83 D7
Shediac, Canada 103 C7
Sheelin, L., Ireland 15 C4
Sheep Haven, Ireland 15 A4
Sheerness, U.K. 13 F8
Sheet Harbour, Canada 103 D7
Sheffield, U.K. 12 D6
Sheffield, Ala., U.S.A. 109 H2
Sheffield, Mass., U.S.A. 111 D11
Sheffield, Pa., U.S.A. 110 E5
Shehojele, Ethiopia 81 E4
Shehong, China 58 B5
Sheikh Idris, Sudan 81 E3
Sheikhpura, India 69 G11
Shek Hasan, Ethiopia 81 E4
Shekhupura, Pakistan 68 D5
Sheki = Şaki, Azerbaijan 49 K8
Shelburne, N.S., Canada 103 D6
Shelburne, Ont., Canada 102 D3
Shelburne, U.S.A. 111 B11
Shelburne B., Australia 94 A3
Shelburne Falls, U.S.A. 111 D12
Shelby, Mich., U.S.A. 108 D2
Shelby, Miss., U.S.A. 113 J9
Shelby, Mont., U.S.A. 114 B8
Shelby, N.C., U.S.A. 109 H5
Shelby, Ohio, U.S.A. 110 F2
Shelbyville, Ill., U.S.A. 112 F10
Shelbyville, Ind., U.S.A. 108 F3
Shelbyville, Ky., U.S.A. 108 F3
Shelbyville, Tenn., U.S.A. 109 H2
Sheldon, U.S.A. 112 D7
Sheldrake, Canada 103 B7
Shelengo, Khawr →, Sudan .. 81 E2
Shelikhova, Zaliv, Russia 51 D16
Shell Lakes, Australia 93 E4
Shellbrook, Canada 105 C7
Shelon →, Russia 46 C6
Shelter I., U.S.A. 111 E12
Shelton, Conn., U.S.A. 111 E11
Shelton, Wash., U.S.A. 116 C3
Shemakha = Şamaxı, Azerbaijan 49 K9
Shēmri, Albania 40 D4

Shemsi, Sudan — 80 D2
Shen Xian, China — 56 F8
Shenandoah, Iowa, U.S.A. — 112 E7
Shenandoah, Pa., U.S.A. — 111 F8
Shenandoah, Va., U.S.A. — 108 F6
Shenandoah ➤, U.S.A. — 108 F7
Shenandoah National Park, U.S.A. — 108 F6
Shenchi, China — 56 E7
Shendam, Nigeria — 83 D6
Shendî, Sudan — 81 D3
Shenge, S. Leone — 82 D2
Shengfang, China — 56 E9
Shëngjergj, Albania — 40 E4
Shëngjin, Albania — 40 E3
Shengzhou, China — 59 C13
Shenmu, China — 56 E6
Shenqiu, China — 56 H8
Shennongjia, China — 59 B8
Shenyang, China — 57 D12
Shenzhen, China — 59 F10
Sheo, India — 68 F4
Sheopur Kalan, India — 66 G10
Shepetivka, Ukraine — 47 G4
Shepetovka = Shepetivka, Ukraine — 47 G4
Sheppey, I. of, U.K. — 13 F8
Shepton Mallet, U.K. — 13 F5
Sheqi, China — 56 H7
Sher Qila, Pakistan — 69 A6
Sherab, Sudan — 81 E1
Sherborne, U.K. — 13 G5
Sherbro ➤, S. Leone — 82 D2
Sherbro I., S. Leone — 82 D2
Sherbrooke, N.S., Canada — 103 C7
Sherbrooke, Qué., Canada — 103 C5
Sherburne, U.S.A. — 111 D9
Shereik, Sudan — 80 D3
Shergarh, India — 68 F5
Sherghati, India — 69 G11
Sheridan, Ark., U.S.A. — 113 H8
Sheridan, Wyo., U.S.A. — 114 D10
Sheringham, U.K. — 12 E9
Sherkin I., Ireland — 15 E2
Sherkot, India — 69 E8
Sherman, U.S.A. — 113 J6
Sherpur, India — 69 G10
Sherridon, Canada — 105 B8
Sherwood Forest, U.K. — 12 D6
Sherwood Park, Canada — 104 C6
Sheslay ➤, Canada — 104 B2
Shethanei L., Canada — 105 B9
Shetland □, U.K. — 14 A7
Shetland Is., U.K. — 14 A7
Shetrunji ➤, India — 68 J5
Shewa □, Ethiopia — 81 F4
Shewa Gimira, Ethiopia — 81 F4
Sheyenne ➤, U.S.A. — 112 B6
Shibām, Yemen — 74 D4
Shibata, Japan — 54 F9
Shibecha, Japan — 54 C12
Shibetsu, Japan — 54 B11
Shibîn el Kôm, Egypt — 80 H7
Shibîn el Qanâtir, Egypt — 80 H7
Shibing, China — 58 D7
Shibogama L., Canada — 102 B2
Shibushi, Japan — 55 J5
Shicheng, China — 59 D11
Shickshinny, U.S.A. — 111 E8
Shickshock Mts. = Chic-Chocs, Mts., Canada — 103 C6
Shidao, China — 57 F12
Shidian, China — 58 E2
Shido, Japan — 55 G7
Shiel, L., U.K. — 14 E3
Shield, C., Australia — 94 A2
Shīeli, Kazakstan — 50 E7
Shifang, China — 58 B5
Shiga □, Japan — 55 G8
Shigu, China — 58 D2
Shiguaigou, China — 56 D6
Shihchiachuangi = Shijiazhuang, China — 56 E8
Shijak, Albania — 40 E3
Shijiazhuang, China — 56 E8
Shijiu Hu, China — 59 B12
Shikarpur, India — 68 E8
Shikarpur, Pakistan — 68 F3
Shikohabad, India — 69 F8
Shikoku □, Japan — 55 H6
Shikoku-Sanchi, Japan — 55 H6
Shiliguri, India — 67 F16
Shilka, Russia — 51 D12
Shilka ➤, Russia — 51 D13
Shillelagh, Ireland — 15 D5
Shillington, U.S.A. — 111 F9
Shillong, India — 67 G17
Shilo, West Bank — 75 C4
Shilong, China — 59 F9
Shilou, China — 56 F6
Shilovo, Russia — 48 C5
Shimabara, Japan — 55 H5
Shimada, Japan — 55 G9
Shimane □, Japan — 55 G6
Shimanovsk, Russia — 51 D13
Shimen, China — 59 C8
Shimenjie, China — 59 C11
Shimian, China — 58 C4
Shimizu, Japan — 55 G9
Shimodate, Japan — 55 F9
Shimoga, India — 66 N9
Shimoni, Kenya — 86 C4
Shimonoseki, Japan — 55 H5
Shimpuru Rapids, Angola — 88 B2

Shimsk, Russia — 46 C6
Shin, L., U.K. — 14 C4
Shinan, China — 58 F7
Shinano-Gawa ➤, Japan — 55 F9
Shinās, Oman — 71 E8
Shīndand, Afghan. — 66 C3
Shinglehouse, U.S.A. — 110 E6
Shingū, Japan — 55 H7
Shingwidzi, S. Africa — 89 C5
Shinjō, Japan — 54 E10
Shinkafe, Nigeria — 83 C6
Shinshār, Syria — 75 A5
Shinyanga, Tanzania — 86 C3
Shinyanga □, Tanzania — 86 C3
Shio-no-Misaki, Japan — 55 H7
Shiogama, Japan — 54 E10
Shiojiri, Japan — 55 F8
Shipchenski Prokhod, Bulgaria — 41 D9
Shiping, China — 58 F4
Shippegan, Canada — 103 C7
Shippensburg, U.S.A. — 110 F7
Shippenville, U.S.A. — 110 E5
Shiprock, U.S.A. — 115 H9
Shiqian, China — 58 D7
Shiqma, N. ➤, Israel — 75 D3
Shiquan, China — 56 H5
Shiquan He = Indus ➤, Pakistan — 68 G2
Shīr Kūh, Iran — 71 D7
Shiragami-Misaki, Japan — 54 D10
Shirakawa, Fukushima, Japan — 55 F10
Shirakawa, Gifu, Japan — 55 F8
Shirane-San, Gumma, Japan — 55 F9
Shirane-San, Yamanashi, Japan — 55 G9
Shiraoi, Japan — 54 C10
Shīrāz, Iran — 71 D7
Shirbīn, Egypt — 80 H7
Shire ➤, Africa — 87 F4
Shiretoko-Misaki, Japan — 54 B12
Shiriya-Zaki, Japan — 54 D10
Shīrvān, Iran — 71 B8
Shirwa, L. = Chilwa, L., Malawi — 87 F4
Shishi, China — 59 E12
Shishou, China — 59 C9
Shitai, China — 59 B11
Shivpuri, India — 68 G7
Shixian, China — 57 C15
Shixing, China — 59 E10
Shiyan, China — 59 A8
Shiyata, Egypt — 80 B2
Shizhu, China — 58 C7
Shizong, China — 58 E5
Shizuishan, China — 56 E4
Shizuoka, Japan — 55 G9
Shizuoka □, Japan — 55 G9
Shklov = Shklow, Belarus — 46 E6
Shklow, Belarus — 46 E6
Shkoder = Shkodër, Albania — 40 D3
Shkodër, Albania — 40 D3
Shkumbini ➤, Albania — 40 E3
Shmidta, Ostrov, Russia — 51 A10
Shō-Gawa ➤, Japan — 55 F8
Shoal L., Canada — 105 D9
Shoal Lake, Canada — 105 C8
Shōdo-Shima, Japan — 55 G7
Sholapur = Solapur, India — 66 L9
Shologontsy, Russia — 51 C12
Shōmrōn, West Bank — 75 C4
Shoreham by Sea, U.K. — 13 G7
Shori ➤, Pakistan — 68 E3
Shorkot Road, Pakistan — 68 D5
Shoshone, Calif., U.S.A. — 117 K10
Shoshone, Idaho, U.S.A. — 114 E6
Shoshone L., U.S.A. — 114 D8
Shoshone Mts., U.S.A. — 114 G5
Shoshong, Botswana — 88 C4
Shoshoni, U.S.A. — 114 E9
Shostka, Ukraine — 47 G7
Shou Xian, China — 59 A11
Shouchang, China — 59 C12
Shouguang, China — 57 F10
Shouning, China — 59 D12
Shouyang, China — 56 F7
Show Low, U.S.A. — 115 J9
Shpola, Ukraine — 47 H6
Shreveport, U.S.A. — 113 J8
Shrewsbury, U.K. — 13 E5
Shri Mohangarh, India — 68 F4
Shrirampur, India — 69 H13
Shropshire □, U.K. — 13 E5
Shū, Kazakstan — 50 E8
Shū ➤, Kazakstan — 52 E10
Shuangbai, China — 58 E3
Shuangcheng, China — 57 B14
Shuangfeng, China — 59 D9
Shuanggou, China — 57 G9
Shuangjiang, China — 58 F2
Shuangliao, China — 57 C12
Shuangyang, China — 57 C13
Shuangyashan, China — 60 B8
Shuba Khit, Egypt — 80 H7
Shucheng, China — 59 B11
Shugozero, Russia — 46 C8
Shuguri Falls, Tanzania — 87 D4
Shuiji, China — 59 D12
Shuiye, China — 56 F8
Shujalpur, India — 68 H7
Shukpa Kunzang, India — 69 B8
Shulan, China — 57 B14
Shulaveri, Georgia — 49 K7
Shule, China — 60 C2
Shumagin Is., U.S.A. — 100 C4
Shumen, Bulgaria — 41 C10
Shumerlya, Russia — 48 C8

Shumikha, Russia — 50 D7
Shunchang, China — 59 D11
Shunde, China — 59 F9
Shungay, Kazakstan — 49 F8
Shuo Xian = Shuozhou, China — 56 E7
Shuozhou, China — 56 E7
Shūr ➤, Fārs, Iran — 71 D7
Shūr ➤, Kermān, Iran — 71 D8
Shūr ➤, Yazd, Iran — 71 D7
Shūr Āb, Iran — 71 C6
Shūr Gaz, Iran — 71 D8
Shūrāb, Iran — 71 C8
Shūrjestān, Iran — 71 D7
Shurugwi, Zimbabwe — 87 F3
Shūsf, Iran — 71 D9
Shūsh, Iran — 73 F13
Shūshtar, Iran — 71 D6
Shuswap L., Canada — 104 C5
Shuya, Russia — 48 B5
Shuyang, China — 57 G10
Shūzū, Iran — 71 D7
Shwebo, Burma — 67 H19
Shwegu, Burma — 67 G20
Shweli ➤, Burma — 67 H20
Shymkent, Kazakstan — 50 E7
Shyok, India — 69 B8
Shyok ➤, Pakistan — 69 B6
Si Chon, Thailand — 65 H2
Si Kiang = Xi Jiang ➤, China — 59 F9
Si-ngan = Xi'an, China — 56 G5
Si Prachan, Thailand — 64 E3
Si Racha, Thailand — 64 F3
Si Xian, China — 57 H9
Siahaf ➤, Pakistan — 68 E3
Siahan Range, Pakistan — 66 F4
Siaksriindrapura, Indonesia — 62 D2
Sialkot, Pakistan — 68 C6
Siam = Thailand ■, Asia — 64 E4
Sian = Xi'an, China — 56 G5
Sianów, Poland — 44 D3
Siantan, Indonesia — 62 D3
Siārah, Iran — 71 D9
Siargao I., Phil. — 61 G7
Siari, Pakistan — 69 B7
Siasi, Phil. — 63 C6
Siasi I., Phil. — 61 J4
Siátista, Greece — 40 F5
Siau, Indonesia — 63 D7
Šiauliai, Lithuania — 9 J20
Šiauliai □, Lithuania — 44 C10
Siazan = Siyäzän, Azerbaijan — 49 K9
Sibâi, Gebel el, Egypt — 70 E2
Sibayi, L., S. Africa — 89 D5
Sibdu, Sudan — 81 E2
Šibenik, Croatia — 29 E12
Siberia, Russia — 4 D13
Siberut, Indonesia — 62 E1
Sibi, Pakistan — 68 E2
Sibil = Oksibil, Indonesia — 63 E10
Sibiti, Congo — 84 E2
Sibiu, Romania — 43 E9
Sibiu □, Romania — 43 E9
Sibley, U.S.A. — 112 D7
Sibolga, Indonesia — 62 D1
Sibsagar, India — 67 F19
Sibu, Malaysia — 62 D4
Sibuco, Phil. — 61 H5
Sibuguey B., Phil. — 61 H5
Sibut, C.A.R. — 84 C3
Sibutu, Phil. — 63 D5
Sibutu Group, Phil. — 61 J3
Sibutu Passage, E. Indies — 63 D5
Sibuyan I., Phil. — 61 E5
Sibuyan Sea, Phil. — 61 E5
Sic, Romania — 43 D8
Sicamous, Canada — 104 C5
Siccus ➤, Australia — 95 E2
Sichuan □, China — 58 B5
Sichuan Pendi, China — 58 B5
Sicilia, Italy — 31 E7
Sicilia □, Italy — 31 E7
Sicily = Sicilia, Italy — 31 E7
Sicuani, Peru — 124 F4
Šid, Serbia, Yug. — 42 E4
Sidamo □, Ethiopia — 81 G4
Sidaouet, Niger — 83 B6
Sidári, Greece — 36 A3
Siddhapur, India — 68 H5
Siddipet, India — 66 K11
Sidensjö, Sweden — 10 A12
Sidéradougou, Burkina Faso — 82 C4
Siderno, Italy — 31 D9
Sidhauli, India — 69 F9
Sídheros, Ákra, Greece — 36 D8
Sidhi, India — 69 G9
Sidhirókastron, Greece — 40 E7
Sîdi Abd el Rahmân, Egypt — 80 A2
Sîdi Barrâni, Egypt — 80 A2
Sidi-bel-Abbès, Algeria — 78 A5
Sidi Haneish, Egypt — 80 A2
Sidi Ifni, Morocco — 78 C3
Sidi Omar, Egypt — 80 A1
Sidlaw Hills, U.K. — 14 E5
Sidley, Mt., Antarctica — 5 D14
Sidmouth, U.K. — 13 G4
Sidmouth, C., Australia — 94 A3
Sidney, Canada — 104 D4
Sidney, Mont., U.S.A. — 112 B2
Sidney, N.Y., U.S.A. — 111 D9
Sidney, Nebr., U.S.A. — 112 E3
Sidney, Ohio, U.S.A. — 108 E3
Sidney Lanier, L., U.S.A. — 109 H4
Sido, Mali — 82 C3
Sidoarjo, Indonesia — 63 G15
Sidon = Saydā, Lebanon — 75 B4
Sidra, G. of = Surt, Khalīj, Libya — 79 B9

Siedlce, Poland — 45 F9
Sieg ➤, Germany — 24 E3
Siegburg, Germany — 24 E3
Siegen, Germany — 24 E4
Siem Pang, Cambodia — 64 E6
Siem Reap = Siemreab, Cambodia — 64 F4
Siemiatycze, Poland — 45 F9
Siemreab, Cambodia — 64 F4
Siena, Italy — 29 E8
Sieniawa, Poland — 45 H9
Sieradz, Poland — 45 G5
Sierck-les-Bains, France — 19 C13
Sierning, Austria — 26 C7
Sierpc, Poland — 45 F6
Sierra Blanca, U.S.A. — 115 L11
Sierra Blanca Peak, U.S.A. — 115 K11
Sierra City, U.S.A. — 116 F6
Sierra Colorada, Argentina — 128 E3
Sierra de Yeguas, Spain — 35 H6
Sierra Gorda, Chile — 126 A2
Sierra Leone ■, W. Afr. — 82 D2
Sierra Madre, Mexico — 119 D6
Sierra Mojada, Mexico — 118 B4
Sierra Nevada, Spain — 35 H7
Sierra Nevada, U.S.A. — 116 H8
Sierra Vista, U.S.A. — 115 L8
Sierraville, U.S.A. — 116 F6
Sierre, Switz. — 25 J3
Sifani, Ethiopia — 81 E5
Sifié, Ivory C. — 82 D3
Sífnos, Greece — 38 E6
Sifton, Canada — 105 C8
Sifton Pass, Canada — 104 B3
Sigean, France — 20 E6
Sighetu-Marmației, Romania — 43 C8
Sighișoara, Romania — 43 D9
Sigli, Indonesia — 62 C1
Siglufjörður, Iceland — 8 C4
Sigmaringen, Germany — 25 G5
Signa, Italy — 28 E8
Signakhi = Tsnori, Georgia — 49 K7
Signal, U.S.A. — 117 L13
Signal Pk., U.S.A. — 117 M12
Signy-l'Abbaye, France — 19 C11
Sigsig, Ecuador — 124 D3
Sigüenza, Spain — 32 D2
Siguiri, Guinea — 82 C3
Sigulda, Latvia — 9 H21
Sihanoukville = Kampong Saom, Cambodia — 65 G4
Sihora, India — 69 H9
Sihui, China — 59 F9
Siikajoki ➤, Finland — 8 D21
Siilinjärvi, Finland — 8 E22
Siirt, Turkey — 73 D9
Sijarira Ra., Zimbabwe — 87 F2
Sika, India — 68 H3
Sikao, Thailand — 65 J2
Sikar, India — 68 F6
Sikasso, Mali — 82 C3
Sikeston, U.S.A. — 113 G10
Sikhote Alin, Khrebet, Russia — 51 E14
Sikhote Alin Ra. = Sikhote Alin, Khrebet, Russia — 51 E14
Sikiá, Greece — 40 F7
Síkinos, Greece — 39 E7
Sikkani Chief ➤, Canada — 104 B4
Sikkim □, India — 67 F16
Siklós, Hungary — 42 E3
Sikotu-Ko, Japan — 54 C10
Sil ➤, Spain — 34 C3
Silacayoapan, Mexico — 119 D5
Šilalė, Lithuania — 44 C9
Silandro, Italy — 28 B7
Silawad, India — 68 J6
Silay, Phil. — 61 F5
Silba, Croatia — 29 D11
Silchar, India — 67 G18
Şile, Turkey — 41 E13
Siler City, U.S.A. — 109 H6
Silgarhi Doti, Nepal — 69 E9
Silghat, India — 67 F18
Sili, Burkina Faso — 82 C4
Silifke, Turkey — 70 B2
Siliguri = Shiliguri, India — 67 F16
Siling Co, China — 60 C3
Silistea Nouă, Romania — 43 F10
Silistra, Bulgaria — 41 B11
Silivri, Turkey — 41 E12
Siljan, Sweden — 10 D8
Siljansnäs, Sweden — 10 D8
Silkeborg, Denmark — 11 H3
Silkwood, Australia — 94 B4
Silla, Spain — 33 F4
Sillajhuay, Cordillera, Chile — 124 G5
Sillamäe, Estonia — 9 G22
Sillé-le-Guillaume, France — 18 D6
Silleda, Spain — 34 C2
Silloth, U.K. — 12 C4
Sílo, Greece — 41 E9
Siloam Springs, U.S.A. — 113 G7
Silopi, Turkey — 73 D10
Silsbee, U.S.A. — 113 K7
Siluko, Nigeria — 83 D6
Šilutė, Lithuania — 9 J19
Silva Porto = Kuito, Angola — 85 G3
Silvan, Turkey — 73 C9
Silvani, India — 69 H8
Silver Cr. ➤, U.S.A. — 114 E4
Silver City, U.S.A. — 115 K9
Silver Creek, U.S.A. — 110 D5
Silver L., U.S.A. — 116 G6
Silver Lake, Calif., U.S.A. — 117 K10
Silver Lake, Oreg., U.S.A. — 114 E3

Silverdalen, Sweden — 11 G9
Silverton, Colo., U.S.A. — 115 H10
Silverton, Tex., U.S.A. — 113 H4
Silves, Portugal — 35 H2
Silvi Marina, Italy — 29 F11
Silvies ➤, U.S.A. — 114 E4
Silvrettahorn, Switz. — 28 B7
Silwa Bahari, Egypt — 80 C3
Silz, Austria — 26 D3
Simaltala, India — 69 G12
Simanggang = Bandar Sri Aman, Malaysia — 62 D4
Simao, China — 58 F3
Simard, L., Canada — 102 C4
Şīmareh ➤, Iran — 73 F12
Simav, Turkey — 39 B10
Simav ➤, Turkey — 41 F12
Simav Dağları, Turkey — 39 B10
Simba, Tanzania — 86 C4
Simbach, Germany — 25 G9
Simbirsk, Russia — 48 C9
Simbo, Tanzania — 86 C2
Simcoe, Canada — 102 D3
Simcoe, L., Canada — 102 D4
Simdega, India — 69 H11
Simeonovgrad, Bulgaria — 41 D9
Simeria, Romania — 42 E8
Simeto ➤, Italy — 31 E8
Simeulue, Indonesia — 62 D1
Simferopol, Ukraine — 47 K8
Sími, Greece — 39 E9
Simi Valley, U.S.A. — 117 L8
Simikot, Nepal — 69 E9
Simitli, Bulgaria — 40 E7
Simla, India — 68 D7
Simlångsdalen, Sweden — 11 H7
Şimleu-Silvaniei, Romania — 42 C7
Simmern, Germany — 25 F3
Simmie, Canada — 105 D7
Simmler, U.S.A. — 117 K7
Simnas, Lithuania — 44 D10
Simojoki ➤, Finland — 8 D21
Simojovel, Mexico — 119 D6
Simonette ➤, Canada — 104 B5
Simonstown, S. Africa — 88 E2
Simontornya, Hungary — 42 D3
Simplonpass, Switz. — 25 J4
Simplontunnel, Switz. — 25 J4
Simpson Desert, Australia — 94 D2
Simpson Pen., Canada — 101 B11
Simpungdong, N. Korea — 57 D15
Simrishamn, Sweden — 11 J8
Simsbury, U.S.A. — 111 E12
Simushir, Ostrov, Russia — 51 E16
Sin Cowe I., S. China Sea — 62 C4
Sinabang, Indonesia — 62 D1
Sinadogo, Somali Rep. — 74 F4
Sinai = Es Sînâ', Egypt — 75 F3
Sinai, Mt. = Mûsa, Gebel, Egypt — 70 D2
Sinai Peninsula, Egypt — 75 F3
Sinaia, Romania — 43 E10
Sinaloa □, Mexico — 118 C3
Sinaloa de Leyva, Mexico — 118 B3
Sinalunga, Italy — 29 E8
Sinan, China — 58 D7
Sînandrei, Romania — 42 E6
Sinarádhes, Greece — 36 A3
Sincan, Turkey — 72 B5
Sincanlı, Turkey — 39 C12
Sincelejo, Colombia — 124 B3
Sinch'ang, N. Korea — 57 D15
Sinchang-ni, N. Korea — 57 E14
Sinclair, U.S.A. — 114 F10
Sinclair Mills, Canada — 104 C4
Sinclair's B., U.K. — 14 C5
Sinclairville, U.S.A. — 110 D5
Sincorá, Serra do, Brazil — 125 F10
Sind, Pakistan — 68 G3
Sind □, Pakistan — 68 G3
Sind ➤, Jammu & Kashmir, India — 69 B6
Sind ➤, Mad. P., India — 69 F8
Sind Sagar Doab, Pakistan — 68 D4
Sindal, Denmark — 11 G4
Sindangan, Phil. — 61 G5
Sindangbarang, Indonesia — 63 G12
Sinde, Zambia — 87 F2
Sindelfingen, Germany — 25 G4
Sındırgı, Turkey — 39 B10
Sindou, Burkina Faso — 82 C3
Sindri, India — 69 H12
Sine ➤, Senegal — 82 C1
Sinegorskiy, Russia — 49 G5
Sinekli, Turkey — 41 E12
Sinelnikovo = Synelnykove, Ukraine — 47 H8
Sinendé, Benin — 83 C5
Sines, Portugal — 35 H2
Sines, C. de, Portugal — 35 H2
Sineu, Spain — 37 B10
Sinfra, Ivory C. — 82 D3
Sing Buri, Thailand — 64 E3
Singa, Sudan — 81 E3
Singapore ■, Asia — 65 M4
Singapore, Straits of, Asia — 65 M5
Singaraja, Indonesia — 62 F5
Singen, Germany — 25 H4
Singida, Tanzania — 86 C3
Singida □, Tanzania — 86 D3
Singitikós Kólpos, Greece — 40 F7
Singkaling Hkamti, Burma — 67 G19
Singkang, Indonesia — 63 E6
Singkawang, Indonesia — 62 D3
Singkep, Indonesia — 62 E2
Singleton, Mt., N. Terr., Australia — 92 D5

Singleton, Mt., W. Austral., Australia ... 93 E2
Singö, Sweden ... 10 D12
Singoli, India ... 68 G6
Singora = Songkhla, Thailand .. 65 J3
Singosan, N. Korea ... 57 E14
Sinhung, N. Korea ... 57 D14
Sînî □, Egypt ... 75 F3
Siniátsikon, Óros, Greece ... 40 F5
Siniscóla, Italy ... 30 B2
Sinj, Croatia ... 29 E13
Sinjai, Indonesia ... 63 F6
Sinjajevina, Montenegro, Yug. ... 40 D3
Sinjār, Iraq ... 70 B4
Sinkat, Sudan ... 80 D4
Sinkiang Uighur = Xinjiang Uygur Zizhiqu □, China ... 60 B3
Sinmak, N. Korea ... 57 E14
Sínnai, Italy ... 30 C2
Sinnamary, Fr. Guiana ... 125 B8
Sinni →, Italy ... 31 B9
Sinnuris, Egypt ... 80 J7
Sinoie, Lacul, Romania ... 43 F13
Sinop, Turkey ... 72 A6
Sinor, India ... 68 J5
Sinp'o, N. Korea ... 57 E15
Sinsheim, Germany ... 25 F4
Sinsk, Russia ... 51 C13
Sintang, Indonesia ... 62 D4
Sinton, U.S.A. ... 113 L6
Sintra, Portugal ... 35 G1
Sinüiju, N. Korea ... 57 D13
Sinyukha →, Ukraine ... 47 H6
Sinzig, Germany ... 24 E3
Sio →, Hungary ... 42 D3
Siocon, Phil. ... 61 H5
Siófok, Hungary ... 42 D3
Sion, Switz. ... 25 J3
Sion Mills, U.K. ... 15 B4
Sioux City, U.S.A. ... 112 D6
Sioux Falls, U.S.A. ... 112 D6
Sioux Lookout, Canada ... 102 B1
Sioux Narrows, Canada ... 105 D10
Sipalay, Phil. ... 61 G5
Sipan, Croatia ... 40 D1
Siping, China ... 57 C13
Sipiwesk L., Canada ... 105 B9
Šipovo, Bos.-H. ... 42 F2
Sipra →, India ... 68 H6
Sipura, Indonesia ... 62 E1
Siquia →, Nic. ... 120 D3
Siquijor, Phil. ... 61 G5
Siquirres, Costa Rica ... 120 D3
Šīr Banī Yās, U.A.E. ... 71 E7
Sir Edward Pellew Group, Australia ... 94 B2
Sir Graham Moore Is., Australia ... 92 B4
Sir James MacBrien, Mt., Canada ... 100 B7
Sira →, Norway ... 9 G12
Siracusa, Italy ... 31 E8
Sirajganj, Bangla. ... 69 G13
Sirakoro, Mali ... 82 C3
Širan, Turkey ... 73 B8
Sirasso, Ivory C. ... 82 D3
Sirathu, India ... 69 G9
Sīrdān, Iran ... 71 B6
Sirdaryo = Syrdarya →, Kazakstan ... 50 E7
Sire, Ethiopia ... 81 F4
Siren, U.S.A. ... 112 C8
Sirer, Spain ... 37 C7
Siret, Romania ... 43 C11
Siret →, Romania ... 43 E12
Sirghāyā, Syria ... 75 B5
Širia, Romania ... 42 D6
Sirino, Mte., Italy ... 31 B8
Sirmaur, India ... 69 G9
Sírna, Greece ... 39 E8
Şirnak, Turkey ... 73 D10
Sirohi, India ... 68 G5
Sironj, India ... 68 G7
Síros, Greece ... 38 D6
Sirretta Pk., U.S.A. ... 117 K8
Sīrrī, Iran ... 71 E7
Sirsa, India ... 68 E6
Sirsa →, India ... 69 F8
Siruela, Spain ... 35 G5
Sisak, Croatia ... 29 C13
Sisaket, Thailand ... 64 E5
Sisante, Spain ... 33 F2
Sishen, S. Africa ... 88 D3
Sishui, Henan, China ... 56 G7
Sishui, Shandong, China ... 57 G9
Sisipuk L., Canada ... 105 B8
Sisophon, Cambodia ... 64 F4
Sisseton, U.S.A. ... 112 C6
Sissonne, France ... 19 C10
Sīstān, Asia ... 71 D9
Sīstān, Daryācheh-ye, Iran ... 71 D9
Sīstān va Balūchestān □, Iran .. 71 E9
Sisteron, France ... 21 D9
Sisters, U.S.A. ... 114 D3
Siswa Bazar, India ... 69 F10
Sitakili, Mali ... 82 C2
Sitamarhi, India ... 69 F11
Sitampiky, Madag. ... 89 B8
Sitapur, India ... 69 F9
Siteki, Swaziland ... 89 D5
Sitges, Spain ... 32 D6
Sithoniá, Greece ... 40 F7
Sitía, Greece ... 36 D8
Sitka, U.S.A. ... 104 B1
Sitoti, Botswana ... 88 C3
Sitra, Egypt ... 80 B2

Sittang Myit →, Burma ... 67 L20
Sittard, Neths. ... 17 C5
Sittensen, Germany ... 24 B5
Sittingbourne, U.K. ... 13 F8
Sittona, Eritrea ... 81 E4
Sittoung = Sittang Myit →, Burma ... 67 L20
Sittwe, Burma ... 67 J18
Situbondo, Indonesia ... 63 G16
Siuna, Nic. ... 120 D3
Siuri, India ... 69 H12
Siutghiol, Lacul, Romania ... 43 F13
Sivand, Iran ... 71 D7
Sivas, Turkey ... 70 B3
Sivash, Turkey ... 39 C11
Siverek, Turkey ... 70 B3
Sivrihisar, Turkey ... 72 C4
Sîwa, Egypt ... 80 B2
Sîwa, El Wâhât es, Egypt ... 80 B2
Siwa Oasis = Sîwa, El Wâhât es, Egypt ... 80 B2
Siwalik Range, Nepal ... 69 F10
Siwan, India ... 69 F11
Siwana, India ... 68 G5
Sixmilebridge, Ireland ... 15 D3
Sixth Cataract, Sudan ... 81 D3
Siyāl, Jazā'ir, Egypt ... 80 C4
Siyäzän, Azerbaijan ... 49 K9
Siziwang Qi, China ... 56 D6
Sjælland, Denmark ... 11 J5
Sjællands Odde, Denmark ... 11 J5
Sjenica, Serbia, Yug. ... 40 C3
Sjöbo, Sweden ... 11 J7
Sjötofta, Sweden ... 11 G7
Sjötorp, Sweden ... 11 F8
Sjumen = Shumen, Bulgaria ... 41 C10
Sjuntorp, Sweden ... 11 F6
Skadarsko Jezero, Montenegro, Yug. ... 40 D3
Skadovsk, Ukraine ... 47 J7
Skælskør, Denmark ... 11 J5
Skærbæk, Denmark ... 11 J2
Skaftafell, Iceland ... 8 D5
Skagafjörður, Iceland ... 8 D4
Skagastølstindane, Norway .. 9 F12
Skagaströnd, Iceland ... 8 D3
Skagen, Denmark ... 11 G4
Skagern, Sweden ... 10 F8
Skagerrak, Denmark ... 11 G2
Skagit →, U.S.A. ... 116 B4
Skagway, U.S.A. ... 100 C6
Skala-Podilska, Ukraine ... 47 H4
Skala Podolskaya = Skala-Podilska, Ukraine ... 47 H4
Skalat, Ukraine ... 47 H3
Skalbmierz, Poland ... 45 H7
Skälderviken, Sweden ... 11 H6
Skalica, Slovak Rep. ... 27 C10
Skallingen, Denmark ... 11 J2
Skalni Dol = Kamenyak, Bulgaria ... 41 C10
Skanderborg, Denmark ... 11 H3
Skåne, Sweden ... 11 J7
Skåne län □, Sweden ... 11 H7
Skaneateles, U.S.A. ... 111 D8
Skaneateles L., U.S.A. ... 111 D8
Skänninge, Sweden ... 11 F9
Skanör med Falsterbo, Sweden . 11 J6
Skantzoúra, Greece ... 38 B6
Skara, Sweden ... 11 F7
Skärblacka, Sweden ... 11 F9
Skardu, Pakistan ... 69 B6
Skåre, Sweden ... 10 E7
Skärhamn, Sweden ... 11 G5
Skarszewy, Poland ... 44 D5
Skaryszew, Poland ... 45 G8
Skarżysko-Kamienna, Poland . 45 G7
Skattkärr, Sweden ... 10 E7
Skattungbyn, Sweden ... 10 C8
Skawina, Poland ... 45 J6
Skebobruk, Sweden ... 10 E12
Skeena →, Canada ... 104 C2
Skeena Mts., Canada ... 104 B3
Skegness, U.K. ... 12 D8
Skeldon, Guyana ... 124 B7
Skellefte älv →, Sweden ... 8 D19
Skellefteå, Sweden ... 8 D19
Skelleftehamn, Sweden ... 8 D19
Skender Vakuf, Bos.-H. ... 42 F2
Skerries, The, U.K. ... 12 D3
Skhíza, Greece ... 38 E3
Skhoinoúsa, Greece ... 39 E7
Ski, Norway ... 9 G14
Skíathos, Greece ... 38 B5
Skibbereen, Ireland ... 15 E2
Skiddaw, U.K. ... 12 C4
Skidegate, Canada ... 104 C2
Skídhra, Greece ... 40 F6
Skien, Norway ... 9 G13
Skierniewice, Poland ... 45 G7
Skikda, Algeria ... 78 A7
Skillingaryd, Sweden ... 11 G8
Skillinge, Sweden ... 11 J8
Skilloura, Cyprus ... 36 D12
Skinári, Ákra, Greece ... 38 D2
Skinnskatteberg, Sweden ... 10 E9
Skipton, U.K. ... 12 D5
Skirmish Pt., Australia ... 94 A1
Skiropoúla, Greece ... 38 C6
Skíros, Greece ... 38 C6
Skivarp, Sweden ... 11 J7
Skive, Denmark ... 11 H3
Skjálfandafljót →, Iceland ... 8 D5
Skjálfandi, Iceland ... 8 C5
Skjern, Denmark ... 11 J2

Skoczów, Poland ... 45 J5
Škofja Loka, Slovenia ... 29 B11
Skoghall, Sweden ... 10 E7
Skogstorp, Sweden ... 10 E10
Skoki, Poland ... 45 F4
Skole, Ukraine ... 47 H2
Skópelos, Greece ... 38 B5
Skopí, Greece ... 36 D8
Skopin, Russia ... 46 F10
Skopje, Macedonia ... 40 D5
Skórcz, Poland ... 44 E5
Skørping, Denmark ... 11 H3
Skövde, Sweden ... 11 F7
Skovorodino, Russia ... 51 D13
Skowhegan, U.S.A. ... 109 C11
Skradin, Croatia ... 29 E12
Skrea, Sweden ... 11 H6
Skrunda, Latvia ... 44 B9
Skrwa →, Poland ... 45 F6
Skull, Ireland ... 15 E2
Skultorp, Sweden ... 11 F7
Skultuna, Sweden ... 10 E10
Skunk →, U.S.A. ... 112 E9
Skuodas, Lithuania ... 9 H19
Skurup, Sweden ... 11 J7
Skutskär, Sweden ... 10 D11
Skvyra, Ukraine ... 47 H5
Skwierzyna, Poland ... 45 F2
Skye, U.K. ... 14 D2
Skykomish, U.S.A. ... 114 C3
Skyros = Skíros, Greece ... 38 C6
Skyttorp, Sweden ... 10 D11
Slættaratindur, Færoe Is. ... 8 E9
Slagelse, Denmark ... 11 J5
Slamet, Indonesia ... 63 G13
Slaney →, Ireland ... 15 D5
Slangberge, S. Africa ... 88 E3
Slănic, Romania ... 43 E10
Slano, Croatia ... 40 D1
Slantsy, Russia ... 46 C5
Slaný, Czech Rep. ... 26 A7
Śląskie □, Poland ... 45 H6
Slätbaken, Sweden ... 11 F10
Slate Is., Canada ... 102 C2
Slatina, Croatia ... 42 E2
Slatina, Romania ... 43 F9
Slatina Timiş, Romania ... 42 E7
Slatington, U.S.A. ... 111 F9
Slaton, U.S.A. ... 113 J4
Slave →, Canada ... 104 A6
Slave Coast, W. Afr. ... 83 D5
Slave Lake, Canada ... 104 B6
Slave Pt., Canada ... 104 A5
Slavgorod, Russia ... 50 D8
Slavinja, Serbia, Yug. ... 40 C6
Slavkov u Brna, Czech Rep. ... 27 B9
Slavonija, Europe ... 42 E2
Slavonski Brod, Croatia ... 42 E3
Slavuta, Ukraine ... 47 G4
Slavyanka, Russia ... 54 C5
Slavyanovo, Bulgaria ... 41 C8
Slavyansk = Slovyansk, Ukraine 47 H9
Slavyansk-na-Kubani, Russia ... 47 K10
Sława, Poland ... 45 G3
Slawharad, Belarus ... 46 F6
Sławno, Poland ... 44 D3
Sławoborze, Poland ... 44 E2
Sleaford, U.K. ... 12 D7
Sleaford B., Australia ... 95 E2
Sleat, Sd. of, U.K. ... 14 D3
Sleeper Is., Canada ... 101 C11
Sleepy Eye, U.S.A. ... 112 C7
Slemon L., Canada ... 104 A5
Slesin, Poland ... 45 F5
Slide Mt., U.S.A. ... 111 E10
Slidell, U.S.A. ... 113 K10
Sliema, Malta ... 36 D2
Slieve Aughty, Ireland ... 15 C3
Slieve Bloom, Ireland ... 15 C4
Slieve Donard, U.K. ... 15 B6
Slieve Gamph, Ireland ... 15 B3
Slieve Gullion, U.K. ... 15 B5
Slieve Mish, Ireland ... 15 D2
Slievenamon, Ireland ... 15 D4
Sligeach = Sligo, Ireland ... 15 B3
Sligo, Ireland ... 15 B3
Sligo, U.S.A. ... 110 E5
Sligo □, Ireland ... 15 B3
Sligo B., Ireland ... 15 B3
Slippery Rock, U.S.A. ... 110 E4
Slite, Sweden ... 11 G12
Sliven, Bulgaria ... 41 D10
Slivnitsa, Bulgaria ... 40 D7
Sljeme, Croatia ... 29 C12
Sloan, U.S.A. ... 117 K11
Sloansville, U.S.A. ... 111 D10
Slobozia, Moldova ... 43 D14
Slobozia, Argeş, Romania ... 43 F10
Slobozia, Ialomiţa, Romania ... 43 F12
Slocan, Canada ... 104 D5
Słomniki, Poland ... 45 H7
Slonim, Belarus ... 46 F3
Slough, U.K. ... 13 F7
Slough □, U.K. ... 13 F7
Sloughhouse, U.S.A. ... 116 G5
Slovak Rep. ■, Europe ... 27 C13
Slovakia = Slovak Rep. ■, Europe ... 27 C13
Slovakian Ore Mts. = Slovenské Rudohorie, Slovak Rep. ... 27 C12
Slovenia ■, Europe ... 29 C11
Slovenija = Slovenia ■, Europe 29 C11
Slovenj Gradec, Slovenia ... 29 B12
Slovenska Bistrica, Slovenia ... 29 B12
Slovenske Konjice, Slovenia ... 29 B12

Slovenské Rudohorie, Slovak Rep. ... 27 C12
Slovyansk, Ukraine ... 47 H9
Słubice, Poland ... 45 F1
Sluch →, Ukraine ... 47 G4
Sluis, Neths. ... 17 C3
Slünchev Bryag, Bulgaria ... 41 D11
Slunj, Croatia ... 29 C12
Słupca, Poland ... 45 F4
Słupia →, Poland ... 44 D3
Słupsk, Poland ... 44 D4
Slurry, S. Africa ... 88 D4
Slutsk, Belarus ... 47 F4
Slyne Hd., Ireland ... 15 C1
Slyudyanka, Russia ... 51 D11
Småland, Sweden ... 11 G9
Smålandsfarvandet, Denmark . 11 J5
Smålandsstenar, Sweden ... 11 G7
Smalltree L., Canada ... 105 A8
Smallwood Res., Canada ... 103 B7
Smarhon, Belarus ... 46 E4
Smarje, Slovenia ... 29 B12
Smartt Syndicate Dam, S. Africa 88 E3
Smartville, U.S.A. ... 116 F5
Smeaton, Canada ... 105 C8
Smedby, Sweden ... 11 H10
Smederevo, Serbia, Yug. ... 40 B4
Smederevska Palanka, Serbia, Yug. ... 40 B4
Smedjebacken, Sweden ... 10 D9
Smela = Smila, Ukraine ... 47 H6
Smerwick Harbour, Ireland ... 15 D1
Smethport, U.S.A. ... 110 E6
Smidovich, Russia ... 51 E14
Smigiel, Poland ... 45 F3
Smila, Ukraine ... 47 H6
Smilyan, Bulgaria ... 41 E8
Smith, Canada ... 104 B6
Smith Center, U.S.A. ... 112 F5
Smith Sund, Greenland ... 4 B4
Smithburne →, Australia ... 94 B3
Smithers, Canada ... 104 C3
Smithfield, S. Africa ... 89 E4
Smithfield, N.C., U.S.A. ... 109 H6
Smithfield, Utah, U.S.A. ... 114 F8
Smiths Falls, Canada ... 102 D4
Smithton, Australia ... 94 G4
Smithville, Canada ... 110 C5
Smithville, U.S.A. ... 113 K6
Smoky →, Canada ... 104 B5
Smoky Bay, Australia ... 95 E1
Smoky Hill →, U.S.A. ... 112 F6
Smoky Hills, U.S.A. ... 112 F5
Smoky Lake, Canada ... 104 C6
Smøla, Norway ... 8 E13
Smolensk, Russia ... 46 E7
Smolikas, Óros, Greece ... 40 F4
Smolník, Slovak Rep. ... 27 C13
Smolyan, Bulgaria ... 41 E8
Smooth Rock Falls, Canada ... 102 C3
Smoothstone L., Canada ... 105 C7
Smorgon = Smarhon, Belarus .. 46 E4
Smulţi, Romania ... 43 E12
Smyadovo, Bulgaria ... 41 C11
Smygehamn, Sweden ... 11 J7
Smyrna = İzmir, Turkey ... 39 C9
Smyrna, U.S.A. ... 108 F8
Snæfell, Iceland ... 8 D6
Snaefell, U.K. ... 12 C3
Snæfellsjökull, Iceland ... 8 D2
Snake →, U.S.A. ... 114 C4
Snake Range, U.S.A. ... 114 G6
Snake River Plain, U.S.A. ... 114 E7
Snasahögarna, Sweden ... 10 A6
Snåsavatnet, Norway ... 8 D14
Snedsted, Denmark ... 11 H2
Sneek, Neths. ... 17 A5
Sneeuberge, S. Africa ... 88 E3
Snejbjerg, Denmark ... 11 H2
Snelling, U.S.A. ... 116 H6
Snezhnoye, Ukraine ... 47 J10
Snežnik, Slovenia ... 29 C11
Śniadowo, Poland ... 45 E8
Sniardwy, Jezioro, Poland ... 44 E8
Śnieżka, Europe ... 26 A8
Snigirevka = Snihurivka, Ukraine ... 47 J7
Snihurivka, Ukraine ... 47 J7
Snina, Slovak Rep. ... 27 C15
Snizort, L., U.K. ... 14 D2
Snøhetta, Norway ... 9 E13
Snohomish, U.S.A. ... 116 C4
Snoul, Cambodia ... 65 F6
Snow Hill, U.S.A. ... 108 F8
Snow Lake, Canada ... 105 C8
Snow Mt., Calif., U.S.A. ... 116 F4
Snow Mt., Maine, U.S.A. ... 111 A14
Snow Shoe, U.S.A. ... 110 E7
Snowbird L., Canada ... 105 A8
Snowdon, U.K. ... 12 D3
Snowdrift →, Canada ... 105 A6
Snowflake, U.S.A. ... 115 J8
Snowshoe Pk., U.S.A. ... 114 B6
Snowville, U.S.A. ... 114 F7
Snowy Mt., U.S.A. ... 111 C10
Snug Corner, Bahamas ... 121 B5
Snyatyn, Ukraine ... 47 H3
Snyder, Okla., U.S.A. ... 113 H5
Snyder, Tex., U.S.A. ... 113 J4
Soahanina, Madag. ... 89 B7
Soalala, Madag. ... 89 B8
Soaloka, Madag. ... 89 B8
Soamanonga, Madag. ... 89 C7
Soan →, Pakistan ... 68 C4
Soanierana-Ivongo, Madag. ... 89 B8
Soanindraniny, Madag. ... 89 B8

Şoarş, Romania ... 43 E9
Soavina, Madag. ... 89 C8
Soavinandriana, Madag. ... 89 B8
Soba, Nigeria ... 83 C6
Sobat, Nahr →, Sudan ... 81 F3
Sobĕslav, Czech Rep. ... 26 B7
Sobhapur, India ... 68 H8
Sobinka, Russia ... 46 E11
Sobótka, Poland ... 45 H3
Sobra, Croatia ... 29 F14
Sobradinho, Reprêsa de, Brazil 125 E10
Sobral, Brazil ... 125 D10
Sobrance, Slovak Rep. ... 27 C15
Sobreira Formosa, Portugal ... 34 F3
Soc Giang, Vietnam ... 58 F6
Soc Trang, Vietnam ... 65 H5
Soča →, Europe ... 26 E6
Socastee, U.S.A. ... 109 J6
Sochaczew, Poland ... 45 F7
Soch'e = Shache, China ... 60 C2
Sochi, Russia ... 49 J4
Société, Is. de la, Pac. Oc. ... 97 J12
Society Is. = Société, Is. de la, Pac. Oc. ... 97 J12
Socompa, Portezuelo de, Chile . 126 A2
Socorro, N. Mex., U.S.A. ... 115 J10
Socorro, Tex., U.S.A. ... 115 L10
Socorro, I., Mexico ... 118 D2
Socotra, Yemen ... 74 E5
Socovos, Spain ... 33 G3
Socuéllamos, Spain ... 33 F2
Soda, L., U.S.A. ... 115 J5
Soda Plains, India ... 69 B8
Soda Springs, U.S.A. ... 114 E8
Sodankylä, Finland ... 8 C22
Soddy-Daisy, U.S.A. ... 109 H3
Söderala, Sweden ... 10 C10
Söderbärke, Sweden ... 10 D9
Söderfors, Sweden ... 10 D11
Söderhamn, Sweden ... 10 C11
Söderköping, Sweden ... 11 F10
Södermanland, Sweden ... 9 G17
Södermanlands län □, Sweden . 10 E10
Södertälje, Sweden ... 10 E11
Sodiri, Sudan ... 81 E2
Sodo, Ethiopia ... 81 F4
Södra Dellen, Sweden ... 10 C10
Södra Finnskoga, Sweden ... 10 D6
Södra Sandby, Sweden ... 11 J7
Södra Ulvön, Sweden ... 10 B12
Södra Vi, Sweden ... 11 G9
Sodražica, Slovenia ... 29 C11
Sodus, U.S.A. ... 110 C7
Soekmekaar, S. Africa ... 89 C4
Soest, Germany ... 24 D4
Soest, Neths. ... 17 B5
Sofádhes, Greece ... 38 B4
Sofara, Mali ... 82 C4
Sofia = Sofiya, Bulgaria ... 40 D7
Sofia →, Madag. ... 89 B8
Sofievka, Ukraine ... 47 H7
Sofikón, Greece ... 38 D5
Sofiya, Bulgaria ... 40 D7
Sofiya □, Bulgaria ... 40 D7
Sōfu-Gan, Japan ... 55 K10
Sogakofe, Ghana ... 83 D5
Sogamoso, Colombia ... 124 B4
Sogār, Iran ... 71 E8
Sögel, Germany ... 24 C3
Sogndalsfjøra, Norway ... 9 F12
Søgne, Norway ... 9 G12
Sognefjorden, Norway ... 9 F11
Söğüt, Bilecik, Turkey ... 39 A12
Söğüt, Burdur, Turkey ... 39 D11
Söğütköy, Turkey ... 39 E10
Sögwipo, S. Korea ... 57 H14
Soh, Iran ... 71 C6
Sohâg, Egypt ... 80 B3
Sohagpur, India ... 68 H8
Soignies, Belgium ... 17 D4
Soin, Burkina Faso ... 82 C4
Soira, Eritrea ... 81 E4
Soissons, France ... 19 C10
Sōja, Japan ... 55 G6
Sojat, India ... 68 G5
Sok →, Russia ... 48 D10
Sokal, Ukraine ... 47 G3
Söke, Turkey ... 39 D9
Sokelo, Dem. Rep. of the Congo 87 D1
Sokhós, Greece ... 40 F7
Sokhumi, Georgia ... 49 J5
Soko Banja, Serbia, Yug. ... 40 C5
Sokodé, Togo ... 83 D5
Sokol, Russia ... 46 C11
Sokolac, Bos.-H. ... 42 G3
Sokółka, Poland ... 44 E10
Sokolo, Mali ... 82 C3
Sokolov, Czech Rep. ... 26 A5
Sokołów Małopolski, Poland ... 45 H9
Sokołów Podlaski, Poland ... 45 F9
Sokoły, Poland ... 45 F9
Sokoto, Nigeria ... 83 C6
Sokoto □, Nigeria ... 83 C6
Sokoto →, Nigeria ... 83 C5
Sol Iletsk, Russia ... 50 D6
Soła →, Poland ... 45 J6
Solai, Kenya ... 86 B4
Solan, India ... 68 D7
Solano, Phil. ... 61 C4
Solapur, India ... 66 L9
Solca, Romania ... 43 C10
Solda Gölü, Turkey ... 39 D11

Soldăneşti, *Moldova* 43 C13
Soldotna, *U.S.A.* 100 B4
Soléa □, *Cyprus* 36 D12
Solec Kujawski, *Poland* 45 E5
Soledad, *Colombia* 124 A4
Soledad, *U.S.A.* 116 J5
Soledad, *Venezuela* 124 B6
Solent, The, *U.K.* 13 G6
Solenzara, *France* 21 G13
Solesmes, *France* 19 B10
Solfonn, *Norway* 9 F12
Solhan, *Turkey* 70 B4
Soligorsk = Salihorsk, *Belarus* . 47 F4
Solihull, *U.K.* 13 E6
Solikamsk, *Russia* 50 D6
Solila, *Madag.* 89 C8
Solimões = Amazonas →,
S. Amer. 122 D4
Solin, *Croatia* 29 E13
Solingen, *Germany* 24 D3
Sollefteå, *Sweden* 11 F6
Sollentuna, *Sweden* 10 E11
Sóller, *Spain* 37 B9
Sollerön, *Sweden* 10 D8
Solling, *Germany* 24 D5
Solnechnogorsk, *Russia* 46 D9
Solo →, *Indonesia* 63 G15
Solofra, *Italy* 31 B7
Sologne, *France* 19 E8
Solok, *Indonesia* 62 E2
Sololá, *Guatemala* 120 D1
Solomon, N. Fork →, *U.S.A.* .. 112 F5
Solomon, S. Fork →, *U.S.A.* .. 112 F5
Solomon Is. ■, *Pac. Oc.* 96 H7
Solon, *China* 60 B7
Solon Springs, *U.S.A.* 112 B9
Solor, *Indonesia* 63 F6
Solotcha, *Russia* 46 E10
Solothurn, *Switz.* 25 H3
Solothurn □, *Switz.* 25 H3
Solsona, *Spain* 32 C6
Solt, *Hungary* 42 D4
Šolta, *Croatia* 29 E13
Solţānābād, *Khorāsān, Iran* .. 71 C8
Solţānābād, *Khorāsān, Iran* .. 71 B8
Soltau, *Germany* 24 C5
Soltsy, *Russia* 46 C6
Solunska Glava, *Macedonia* ... 40 E5
Solvang, *U.S.A.* 117 L6
Solvay, *U.S.A.* 111 C8
Solway Firth, *U.K.* 12 C4
Solwezi, *Zambia* 87 E2
Sōma, *Japan* 54 F10
Soma, *Turkey* 39 B9
Somabhula, *Zimbabwe* 89 B4
Somali Pen., *Africa* 76 F8
Somali Rep. ■, *Africa* 74 F4
Somalia = Somali Rep. ■, *Africa* 74 F4
Sombernon, *France* 19 E11
Sombor, *Serbia, Yug.* 42 E4
Sombra, *Canada* 110 D2
Sombrerete, *Mexico* 118 C4
Sombrero, *Anguilla* 121 C7
Şomcuta Mare, *Romania* 43 C8
Somdari, *India* 68 G5
Somers, *U.S.A.* 114 B6
Somerset, *Ky., U.S.A.* 108 G3
Somerset, *Mass., U.S.A.* 111 E13
Somerset, *Pa., U.S.A.* 110 F5
Somerset □, *U.K.* 13 F5
Somerset East, *S. Africa* ... 88 E4
Somerset I., *Canada* 100 A10
Somerset West, *S. Africa* ... 88 E2
Somersworth, *U.S.A.* 111 C14
Somerton, *U.S.A.* 115 K6
Somerville, *U.S.A.* 111 F10
Someş →, *Romania* 42 C7
Someşul Mare →, *Romania* 43 C8
Somme □, *France* 19 C9
Somme →, *France* 19 B8
Somme, B. de la, *France* 18 B8
Sommen, *Jönköping, Sweden* .. 11 F8
Sommen, *Östergötland, Sweden* 11 F9
Sommepy-Tahure, *France* 19 C11
Sömmerda, *Germany* 24 D7
Sommesous, *France* 19 D11
Sommières, *France* 21 E8
Somnath, *India* 68 J4
Somogy □, *Hungary* 42 D2
Somogyszob, *Hungary* 42 D2
Somoto, *Nic.* 120 D2
Sompolno, *Poland* 45 F5
Somport, Puerto de, *Spain* .. 32 C4
Son →, *India* 69 G11
Son Ha, *Vietnam* 64 E7
Son Hoa, *Vietnam* 64 F7
Son La, *Vietnam* 58 G4
Son Serra, *Spain* 37 B10
Son Servera, *Spain* 32 F8
Son Tay, *Vietnam* 58 G5
Soná, *Panama* 120 E3
Sonamarg, *India* 69 B6
Sonamukhi, *India* 69 H12
Sonar →, *India* 69 G8
Sŏnch'ŏn, *N. Korea* 57 E13
Sondags →, *S. Africa* 88 E4
Sóndalo, *Italy* 28 B7
Sondar, *India* 69 C6
Sønder Felding, *Denmark* 11 J2
Sønder Omme, *Denmark* 11 J2
Sønderborg, *Denmark* 11 K3
Sønderjyllands
Amtskommune □, *Denmark* .. 11 J3
Sondershausen, *Germany* 24 D6

Sóndrio, *Italy* 28 B6
Sone, *Mozam.* 87 F3
Sonepur, *India* 67 J13
Song, *Nigeria* 83 D7
Song, *Thailand* 64 C3
Song Cau, *Vietnam* 64 F7
Song Xian, *China* 56 G7
Songch'ŏn, *N. Korea* 57 E14
Songea, *Tanzania* 87 E4
Songeons, *France* 19 C8
Songhua Hu, *China* 57 C14
Songhua Jiang →, *China* 60 B8
Songjiang, *China* 59 B13
Songjin, *N. Korea* 57 D15
Songjŏng-ni, *S. Korea* 57 G14
Songkan, *China* 58 C6
Songkhla, *Thailand* 65 J3
Songming, *China* 58 E4
Songnim, *N. Korea* 57 E13
Songo, *Mozam.* 85 H6
Songo, *Sudan* 79 G10
Songpan, *China* 58 A4
Songtao, *China* 58 C7
Songwe, *Dem. Rep. of the Congo* 86 C2
Songwe →, *Africa* 87 D3
Songxi, *China* 59 D12
Songzi, *China* 59 B8
Sonhat, *India* 69 H10
Sonid Youqi, *China* 56 C7
Sonipat, *India* 68 E7
Sonkach, *India* 68 H7
Sonkovo, *Russia* 46 D9
Sonmiani, *Pakistan* 68 G2
Sonmiani B., *Pakistan* 68 G2
Sonnino, *Italy* 30 A6
Sono →, *Brazil* 125 E9
Sonoma, *U.S.A.* 116 G4
Sonora, *Calif., U.S.A.* 116 H6
Sonora, *Tex., U.S.A.* 113 K4
Sonora □, *Mexico* 118 B2
Sonora →, *Mexico* 118 B2
Sonoran Desert, *U.S.A.* 117 L12
Sonoyta, *Mexico* 118 A2
Sonqor, *Iran* 73 E12
Sŏnsan, *S. Korea* 57 F15
Sonseca, *Spain* 35 F7
Sonsorol Is., *Pac. Oc.* 63 C8
Sonstorp, *Sweden* 11 F9
Sonthofen, *Germany* 25 H6
Soochow = Suzhou, *China* 59 B13
Sooke, *Canada* 116 B3
Sop Hao, *Laos* 58 G5
Sop Prap, *Thailand* 64 D2
Sopelana, *Spain* 32 B2
Sopi, *Indonesia* 63 D7
Sopo, Nahr →, *Sudan* 81 F2
Sopot, *Bulgaria* 41 D8
Sopot, *Poland* 44 D5
Sopot, *Serbia, Yug.* 40 B4
Sopotnica, *Macedonia* 40 E5
Sopron, *Hungary* 42 C1
Sopur, *India* 69 B6
Sora, *Italy* 29 G10
Sorah, *Pakistan* 68 F3
Söräker, *Sweden* 10 B11
Sorano, *Italy* 29 F8
Sorbas, *Spain* 33 H2
Sörbygden, *Sweden* 10 B10
Sore, *France* 20 D3
Sorel, *Canada* 102 C5
Soresina, *Italy* 28 C6
Sörforsa, *Sweden* 10 C10
Sórgono, *Italy* 30 B2
Sorgues, *France* 21 D8
Sorgun, *Turkey* 72 C6
Soria, *Spain* 32 D2
Soria □, *Spain* 32 D2
Soriano, *Uruguay* 126 C4
Soriano nel Cimino, *Italy* .. 29 F9
Sorkh, Kuh-e, *Iran* 71 C8
Sørø, *Denmark* 11 J5
Soro, *Guinea* 82 C3
Soroca, *Moldova* 43 B13
Sorocaba, *Brazil* 127 A6
Soroki = Soroca, *Moldova* ... 43 B13
Sorol Atoll, *Pac. Oc.* 63 C10
Sorong, *Indonesia* 63 E8
Soroní, *Greece* 36 C10
Soroti, *Uganda* 86 B3
Sørøya, *Norway* 8 A20
Sørøysundet, *Norway* 8 A20
Sorraia →, *Portugal* 35 G2
Sorrell, *Australia* 94 G4
Sorrento, *Italy* 31 B7
Sorsele, *Sweden* 8 D17
Sörsjön, *Sweden* 10 C7
Sorso, *Italy* 30 B1
Sorsogon, *Phil.* 61 E6
Sortavala, *Russia* 46 B6
Sortino, *Italy* 31 E8
Sortland, *Norway* 8 B16
Sorvizhi, *Russia* 48 B9
Sos = Sos del Rey Católico,
Spain 32 C3
Sos del Rey Católico, *Spain* . 32 C3
Sŏsan, *S. Korea* 57 F14
Soscumica, L., *Canada* 102 B4
Sösdala, *Sweden* 11 H7
Sosna →, *Russia* 47 F10
Sosnovka, *Kirov, Russia* 48 B10
Sosnovka, *Tambov, Russia* ... 48 D5
Sosnovyy Bor, *Russia* 46 C5
Sosnowiec, *Poland* 45 H6

Sospel, *France* 21 E11
Sossus Vlei, *Namibia* 88 C2
Šoštanj, *Slovenia* 29 B12
Sŏsura, *N. Korea* 57 C16
Sot →, *India* 69 F8
Sotkamo, *Finland* 8 D23
Soto del Barco, *Spain* 34 B4
Soto la Marina →, *Mexico* ... 119 C5
Soto y Amío, *Spain* 34 C5
Sotrondio, *Spain* 34 B5
Sotuta, *Mexico* 119 C7
Souanké, *Congo* 84 D2
Soubré, *Ivory C.* 82 D3
Souderton, *U.S.A.* 111 F9
Soúdha, *Greece* 36 D6
Soúdhas, Kólpos, *Greece* 36 D6
Souflíon, *Greece* 41 E10
Soufrière, *St. Lucia* 121 D7
Souillac, *France* 20 D5
Souilly, *France* 19 C12
Soukhouma, *Laos* 64 E5
Sŏul, *S. Korea* 57 F14
Soulac-sur-Mer, *France* 20 C2
Soulougou, *Burkina Faso* 83 C5
Soultz-sous-Forêts, *France* .. 19 D14
Sound, The = Øresund, *Europe* 11 J6
Sound, The, *U.K.* 13 G3
Soúnion, Ákra, *Greece* 38 D6
Sources, Mt. aux, *Lesotho* .. 89 D4
Soure, *Brazil* 125 D9
Soure, *Portugal* 34 E2
Souris, *Man., Canada* 105 D8
Souris, *P.E.I., Canada* 103 C7
Souris →, *Canada* 112 A5
Sourou →, *Africa* 82 C4
Soúrpi, *Greece* 38 B4
Sousa, *Brazil* 125 E11
Sousel, *Portugal* 35 G3
Sousse, *Tunisia* 79 A8
Soustons, *France* 20 E2
Sout →, *S. Africa* 88 E2
South Africa ■, *Africa* 88 E3
South America ■ 122 E5
South Atlantic Ocean 122 H7
South Aulatsivik I., *Canada* . 103 A7
South Ayrshire □, *U.K.* 14 F4
South Baldy, *U.S.A.* 115 J10
South Bass I., *U.S.A.* 110 E2
South Bend, *Ind., U.S.A.* ... 108 E2
South Bend, *Wash., U.S.A.* .. 116 D3
South Boston, *U.S.A.* 109 G6
South Branch, *Canada* 103 C8
South Brook, *Canada* 103 C8
South Carolina □, *U.S.A.* ... 109 J5
South Charleston, *U.S.A.* ... 108 F5
South China Sea, *Asia* 62 C4
South Dakota □, *U.S.A.* 112 C5
South Deerfield, *U.S.A.* 111 D12
South Downs, *U.K.* 13 G7
South East □, *Australia* 94 G4
South East Is., *Australia* .. 93 F3
South Esk →, *U.K.* 14 E6
South Foreland, *U.K.* 13 F9
South Fork American →, *U.S.A.* 116 G5
South Fork Feather →, *U.S.A.* 116 F5
South Fork Grand →, *U.S.A.* . 112 C3
South Fork Republican →,
U.S.A. 112 E4
South Georgia, *Antarctica* .. 122 J7
South Gloucestershire □, *U.K.* . 13 F5
South Hadley, *U.S.A.* 111 D12
South Haven, *U.S.A.* 108 D2
South Henik, L., *Canada* 105 A9
South Honshu Ridge, *Pac. Oc.* . 96 E6
South Horr, *Kenya* 86 B4
South I., *Kenya* 86 B4
South I., *N.Z.* 91 L3
South Indian Lake, *Canada* .. 105 B9
South Invercargill, *N.Z.* ... 91 M2
South Knife →, *Canada* 105 B10
South Koel →, *India* 69 H11
South Korea ■, *Asia* 57 G15
South Lake Tahoe, *U.S.A.* ... 116 G6
South Lanarkshire □, *U.K.* .. 14 F5
South Loup →, *U.S.A.* 112 E5
South Magnetic Pole, *Antarctica* 5 C9
South Milwaukee, *U.S.A.* 108 D2
South Molton, *U.K.* 13 F4
South Moose L., *Canada* 105 C8
South Nahanni →, *Canada* 104 A4
South Nation →, *Canada* 111 A9
South Natuna Is. = Natuna
Selatan, Kepulauan, *Indonesia* 65 L7
South Negril Pt., *Jamaica* .. 120 C4
South Orkney Is., *Antarctica* . 5 C18
South Ossetia □, *Georgia* ... 49 J7
South Pagai, I. = Pagai Selatan,
Pulau, *Indonesia* 62 E2
South Paris, *U.S.A.* 111 B14
South Pittsburg, *U.S.A.* 109 H3
South Platte →, *U.S.A.* 112 E4
South Pole, *Antarctica* ..... 5 E
South Porcupine, *Canada* 102 C3
South Portland, *U.S.A.* 109 D10
South Pt., *U.S.A.* 110 B1
South River, *Canada* 102 C4
South River, *U.S.A.* 111 F10
South Ronaldsay, *U.K.* 14 C6
South Sandwich Is., *Antarctica* 5 B1
South Saskatchewan →, *Canada* 105 C7
South Seal →, *Canada* 105 B9
South Shetland Is., *Antarctica* 5 C18
South Shields, *U.K.* 12 C6
South Sioux City, *U.S.A.* ... 112 D6
South Taranaki Bight, *N.Z.* . 91 H5
South Thompson →, *Canada* ... 104 C4

South Twin I., *Canada* 102 B4
South Tyne →, *U.K.* 12 C5
South Uist, *U.K.* 14 D1
South West Africa = Namibia ■,
Africa 88 C2
South West C., *Australia* ... 94 G4
South Williamsport, *U.S.A.* . 110 E8
South Yorkshire □, *U.K.* 12 D6
Southampton, *Canada* 102 D3
Southampton, *U.K.* 13 G6
Southampton, *U.S.A.* 111 F12
Southampton □, *U.K.* 13 G6
Southampton I., *Canada* 101 B11
Southaven, *U.S.A.* 113 H9
Southbank, *Canada* 104 C3
Southbridge, *N.Z.* 91 K4
Southbridge, *U.S.A.* 111 D12
Southend, *Canada* 105 B8
Southend-on-Sea, *U.K.* 13 F8
Southend-on-Sea □, *U.K.* 13 F8
Southern □, *Malawi* 87 F4
Southern □, *S. Leone* 82 D2
Southern □, *Zambia* 87 F2
Southern Alps, *N.Z.* 91 K3
Southern Cross, *Australia* .. 93 F2
Southern Indian L., *Canada* . 105 B9
Southern Ocean, *Antarctica* . 5 C6
Southern Pines, *U.S.A.* 109 H6
Southern Uplands, *U.K.* 14 F5
Southington, *U.S.A.* 111 E12
Southland □, *N.Z.* 91 L1
Southold, *U.S.A.* 111 E12
Southport, *Australia* 95 D5
Southport, *U.K.* 12 D4
Southport, *Fla., U.S.A.* 109 K3
Southport, *N.Y., U.S.A.* 110 D8
Southwest C., *N.Z.* 91 M1
Southwold, *U.K.* 13 E9
Soutpansberg, *S. Africa* 89 C4
Souvigny, *France* 19 F10
Sovata, *Romania* 43 D10
Soverato, *Italy* 31 D9
Sovetsk, *Kaliningd., Russia* . 9 J19
Sovetsk, *Kirov, Russia* 48 B9
Sovetskaya Gavan = Vanino,
Russia 51 E15
Sovicille, *Italy* 29 E8
Soweto, *S. Africa* 89 D4
Sōya-Kaikyō = La Perouse Str.,
Asia 54 B11
Sōya-Misaki, *Japan* 54 B10
Soyaux, *France* 20 C4
Sozh →, *Belarus* 47 F6
Sozopol, *Bulgaria* 41 D11
Spa, *Belgium* 17 D5
Spain ■, *Europe* 7 H5
Spalding, *U.K.* 12 E7
Spangler, *U.S.A.* 110 F6
Spanish, *Canada* 102 C3
Spanish Fork, *U.S.A.* 114 F8
Spanish Town, *Jamaica* 120 C4
Sparks, *U.S.A.* 116 F7
Sparreholm, *Sweden* 10 E10
Sparta = Spárti, *Greece* 38 D4
Sparta, *Mich., U.S.A.* 108 D3
Sparta, *N.J., U.S.A.* 111 E10
Sparta, *Wis., U.S.A.* 112 D9
Spárti, *Greece* 38 D4
Spartansburg, *U.S.A.* 110 E5
Spartanburg, *U.S.A.* 109 H5
Spartivento, C., *Calabria, Italy* 31 E9
Spartivento, C., *Sard., Italy* 30 D1
Sparwood, *Canada* 104 D6
Spas-Demensk, *Russia* 46 E7
Spas-Klepiki, *Russia* 46 E11
Spassk Dalniy, *Russia* 51 E14
Spassk-Ryazanskiy, *Russia* .. 46 E11
Spátha, Ákra, *Greece* 36 D5
Spatsizi →, *Canada* 104 B3
Spatsizi Plateau Wilderness
Park, *Canada* 104 B3
Spean →, *U.K.* 14 E4
Spearfish, *U.S.A.* 112 C3
Spearman, *U.S.A.* 113 G4
Speculator, *U.S.A.* 111 C10
Speia, *Moldova* 43 D14
Speightstown, *Barbados* 121 D8
Speke Gulf, *Tanzania* 86 C3
Spello, *Italy* 29 F9
Spencer, *Idaho, U.S.A.* 114 D7
Spencer, *Iowa, U.S.A.* 112 D7
Spencer, *N.Y., U.S.A.* 111 D8
Spencer, *Nebr., U.S.A.* 112 D5
Spencer, *W. Va., U.S.A.* 108 F5
Spencer, B., *Namibia* 88 D1
Spencerville, *Canada* 111 B9
Spences Bridge, *Canada* 104 C4
Spennymoor, *U.K.* 12 C6
Spenser Mts., *N.Z.* 91 K4
Spentrup, *Denmark* 11 H4
Sperkhiós →, *Greece* 38 C4
Sperrin Mts., *U.K.* 15 B5
Spessart, *Germany* 25 F5
Spétsai, *Greece* 38 D5
Spey →, *U.K.* 14 D5
Speyer, *Germany* 25 F4
Spezand, *Pakistan* 68 E2
Spezzano Albanese, *Italy* ... 31 C9
Spiekeroog, *Germany* 24 B3
Spiez, *Switz.* 25 J3
Spíli, *Greece* 36 D6
Spilimbergo, *Italy* 29 B9
Spīn Búldak, *Afghan.* 68 D2
Spinalónga, *Greece* 36 D7
Spinazzola, *Italy* 31 B9
Spineni, *Romania* 43 F9
Spirit Lake, *U.S.A.* 116 D4

Spirit River, *Canada* 104 B5
Spiritwood, *Canada* 105 C7
Spišská Nová Ves, *Slovak Rep.* 27 C13
Spišské Podhradie, *Slovak Rep.* 27 B13
Spital, *Austria* 26 D7
Spithead, *U.K.* 13 G6
Spittal an der Drau, *Austria* 26 E6
Spitzbergen = Svalbard, *Arctic* . 4 B8
Spjelkavik, *Norway* 9 E12
Split, *Croatia* 29 E13
Split L., *Canada* 105 B9
Split Lake, *Canada* 105 B9
Splitski Kanal, *Croatia* 29 E13
Splügenpass, *Switz.* 25 J5
Spofford, *U.S.A.* 113 L4
Spokane, *U.S.A.* 114 C5
Spoleto, *Italy* 29 F9
Spooner, *U.S.A.* 112 C9
Spratly I., *S. China Sea* ... 62 C4
Spratly Is., *S. China Sea* .. 62 C4
Spray, *U.S.A.* 114 D4
Sprečа →, *Bos.-H.* 42 F3
Spree →, *Germany* 24 C9
Spreewald, *Germany* 24 D9
Spremberg, *Germany* 24 D10
Sprengisandur, *Iceland* 8 D5
Spring City, *U.S.A.* 111 F9
Spring Creek, *U.S.A.* 114 F6
Spring Garden, *U.S.A.* 116 F6
Spring Hill, *U.S.A.* 109 L4
Spring Mts., *U.S.A.* 115 H6
Spring Valley, *U.S.A.* 117 N10
Springbok, *S. Africa* 88 D2
Springboro, *U.S.A.* 110 E4
Springdale, *Canada* 103 C8
Springdale, *U.S.A.* 113 G7
Springe, *Germany* 24 C5
Springer, *U.S.A.* 113 G2
Springerville, *U.S.A.* 115 J9
Springfield, *Canada* 110 D4
Springfield, *N.Z.* 91 K3
Springfield, *Colo., U.S.A.* . 113 G3
Springfield, *Ill., U.S.A.* .. 112 F10
Springfield, *Mass., U.S.A.* . 111 D12
Springfield, *Mo., U.S.A.* ... 113 G8
Springfield, *Ohio, U.S.A.* .. 108 F4
Springfield, *Oreg., U.S.A.* . 114 D2
Springfield, *Tenn., U.S.A.* . 109 G2
Springfield, *Vt., U.S.A.* ... 111 C12
Springfontein, *S. Africa* ... 88 E4
Springhill, *Canada* 103 C7
Springhill, *U.S.A.* 113 J8
Springhouse, *Canada* 104 C4
Springs, *S. Africa* 89 D4
Springsure, *Australia* 94 C4
Springvale, *U.S.A.* 111 C14
Springville, *Calif., U.S.A.* . 116 J8
Springville, *N.Y., U.S.A.* .. 110 D6
Springville, *Utah, U.S.A.* .. 114 F8
Springwater, *U.S.A.* 110 D7
Spruce-Creek, *U.S.A.* 110 F6
Spruce Mt., *U.S.A.* 111 B12
Spur, *U.S.A.* 113 J4
Spurn Hd., *U.K.* 12 D8
Spuž, *Montenegro, Yug.* 40 D3
Spuzzum, *Canada* 104 D4
Squam L., *U.S.A.* 111 C13
Squamish, *Canada* 104 D4
Square Islands, *Canada* 103 B8
Squillace, G. di, *Italy* 31 D9
Squinzano, *Italy* 31 B11
Squires, Mt., *Australia* 93 E4
Srbac, *Bos.-H.* 42 E2
Srbica, *Kosovo, Yug.* 40 D4
Srbija = Serbia □, *Yugoslavia* 40 C5
Srbobran, *Serbia, Yug.* 42 E4
Sre Ambel, *Cambodia* 65 G4
Sre Khtum, *Cambodia* 65 F6
Sre Umbell = Sre Ambel,
Cambodia 65 G4
Srebrenica, *Bos.-H.* 42 F4
Sredninny Ra. = Sredinnyy
Khrebet, *Russia* 51 D16
Sredinnyy Khrebet, *Russia* .. 51 D16
Središče, *Slovenia* 29 B13
Sredna Gora, *Bulgaria* 41 D8
Srednekolymsk, *Russia* 51 C16
Sredni Rodopi, *Bulgaria* 41 E8
Srednogorie, *Bulgaria* 41 D8
Srem, *Poland* 45 F4
Sremska Mitrovica, *Serbia, Yug.* 42 F4
Sremski Karlovci, *Serbia, Yug.* 42 E4
Srepok →, *Cambodia* 64 F6
Sretensk, *Russia* 51 D12
Sri Lanka ■, *Asia* 66 R12
Srikakulam, *India* 67 K13
Srinagar, *India* 69 B6
Środa Śląska, *Poland* 45 G3
Środa Wielkopolski, *Poland* . 45 F4
Srpska Crnja, *Serbia, Yug.* . 42 E5
Srpski Itebej, *Serbia, Yug.* 42 E5
Staaten →, *Australia* 94 B3
Staberhuk, *Germany* 24 A7
Stade, *Germany* 24 B5
Stadskanaal, *Neths.* 17 A6
Stadtlandendorf, *Germany* ... 24 E5
Stadthagen, *Germany* 24 C5
Stadtlohn, *Germany* 24 D2
Stadtroda, *Germany* 24 E7
Staffa, *U.K.* 14 E2
Staffanstorp, *Sweden* 11 J7
Stafford, *U.K.* 13 E5
Stafford, *U.S.A.* 113 G5
Stafford Springs, *U.S.A.* ... 111 E12

209

Staffordshire □, *U.K.* 12 E5
Stagnone, *Italy* 30 E5
Staines, *U.K.* 13 F7
Stainz, *Austria* 26 E8
Stakhanov, *Ukraine* 47 H10
Stalać, *Serbia, Yug.* 40 C5
Stalingrad = Volgograd, *Russia* 49 F7
Staliniri = Tskhinvali, *Georgia* . 49 J7
Stalino = Donetsk, *Ukraine* .. 47 J9
Stalinogorsk = Novomoskovsk,
 Russia 46 E10
Stalis, *Greece* 36 D7
Stallarholmen, *Sweden* 10 E11
Ställdalen, *Sweden* 10 E8
Stalowa Wola, *Poland* 45 H9
Stalybridge, *U.K.* 12 D5
Stamford, *Australia* 94 C3
Stamford, *U.K.* 13 E7
Stamford, Conn., *U.S.A.* ... 111 E11
Stamford, N.Y., *U.S.A.* 111 D10
Stamford, Tex., *U.S.A.* 113 J5
Stampriet, *Namibia* 88 C2
Stamps, *U.S.A.* 113 J8
Stančevo = Kalipetrovo,
 Bulgaria 41 B11
Standerton, *S. Africa* 89 D4
Standish, *U.S.A.* 108 D4
Stanford, *S. Africa* 88 E2
Stanford, *U.S.A.* 114 C8
Stånga, *Sweden* 11 G12
Stanger, *S. Africa* 89 D5
Stanišić, *Serbia, Yug.* 42 E4
Stanislaus ➜, *U.S.A.* 116 H5
Stanislav = Ivano-Frankivsk,
 Ukraine 47 H3
Stanisławów, *Poland* 45 F8
Stanley, *Australia* 94 G4
Stanley, *Canada* 105 B8
Stanley, *Falk. Is.* 128 G5
Stanley, *U.K.* 12 C6
Stanley, Idaho, *U.S.A.* 114 D6
Stanley, N. Dak., *U.S.A.* .. 112 A3
Stanley, N.Y., *U.S.A.* 110 D7
Stanovoy Khrebet, *Russia* .. 51 D13
Stanovoy Ra. = Stanovoy
 Khrebet, *Russia* 51 D13
Stansmore Ra., *Australia* ... 92 D4
Stanthorpe, *Australia* 95 D5
Stanton, *U.S.A.* 113 J4
Stanwood, *U.S.A.* 116 B4
Staples, *U.S.A.* 112 B7
Stąporków, *Poland* 45 G7
Star City, *Canada* 105 C8
Star Lake, *U.S.A.* 111 B9
Stará L'ubovňa, *Slovak Rep.* .. 27 B13
Stara Moravica, *Serbia, Yug.* . 42 E4
Stara Pazova, *Serbia, Yug.* .. 42 F5
Stara Planina, *Bulgaria* 40 C7
Stará Turá, *Slovak Rep.* 27 C10
Stara Zagora, *Bulgaria* 41 D9
Starachowice, *Poland* 45 G8
Staraya Russa, *Russia* 46 D6
Starbuck I., *Kiribati* 97 H12
Starchiojd, *Romania* 43 E11
Stargard Szczeciński, *Poland* .. 44 E2
Stari Bar, *Montenegro, Yug.* .. 40 D3
Stari Trg, *Slovenia* 29 C12
Staritsa, *Russia* 46 D8
Starke, *U.S.A.* 109 L4
Starnberg, *Germany* 25 H7
Starnberger See, *Germany* ... 25 H7
Starobilsk, *Ukraine* 47 H10
Starodub, *Russia* 47 F7
Starogard Gdański, *Poland* .. 44 E5
Starokonstantinov =
 Starokonstyantyniv, *Ukraine* 47 H4
Starokonstyantyniv, *Ukraine* .. 47 H4
Starominskaya, *Russia* 47 J10
Staroshcherbinovskaya, *Russia* 47 J10
Start Pt., *U.K.* 13 G4
Stary Sącz, *Poland* 45 J7
Staryy Biryuzyak, *Russia* 49 H8
Staryy Chartoriysk, *Ukraine* .. 47 G3
Staryy Krym, *Ukraine* 47 K8
Staryy Oskol, *Russia* 47 G9
Stassfurt, *Germany* 24 D7
Staszów, *Poland* 45 H8
State College, *U.S.A.* 110 F7
Stateline, *U.S.A.* 116 G7
Staten, I. = Estados, I. de Los,
 Argentina 122 J4
Staten I., *U.S.A.* 111 F10
Statesboro, *U.S.A.* 109 J5
Statesville, *U.S.A.* 109 H5
Stauffer, *U.S.A.* 117 L7
Staunton, Ill., *U.S.A.* 112 F10
Staunton, Va., *U.S.A.* 108 F6
Stavanger, *Norway* 9 G11
Staveley, *N.Z.* 91 K3
Stavelot, *Belgium* 17 D5
Stavern, *Norway* 9 G14
Stavoren, *Neths.* 17 B5
Stavropol, *Russia* 49 H6
Stavros, *Cyprus* 36 D11
Stavrós, *Greece* 36 D6
Stavrós, Ákra, *Greece* 36 D6
Stavroúpolis, *Greece* 41 E8
Stawell ➜, *Australia* 94 C3
Stawiski, *Poland* 44 E9
Stawiszyn, *Poland* 45 G5
Stayner, *Canada* 110 B4
Stayton, *U.S.A.* 114 D2
Steamboat Springs, *U.S.A.* .. 114 F10
Steblevë, *Albania* 40 E4
Steele, *U.S.A.* 112 B5
Steelton, *U.S.A.* 110 F8

Steen River, *Canada* 104 B5
Steenkool = Bintuni, *Indonesia* 63 E8
Steens Mt., *U.S.A.* 114 E4
Steenwijk, *Neths.* 17 B6
Steep Pt., *Australia* 93 E1
Steep Rock, *Canada* 105 C9
Ştefan Vodă, *Moldova* 43 D14
Ştefăneşti, *Romania* 43 C12
Stefanie L. = Chew Bahir,
 Ethiopia 81 G4
Stefansson Bay, *Antarctica* ... 5 C5
Stege, *Denmark* 11 K6
Ştei, *Romania* 42 D7
Steiermark □, *Austria* 26 D8
Steigerwald, *Germany* 25 F6
Steilacoom, *U.S.A.* 116 C4
Steilrandberge, *Namibia* 88 B1
Steinbach, *Canada* 105 D9
Steinfurt, *Germany* 24 C3
Steinhausen, *Namibia* 88 C2
Steinheim, *Germany* 24 D5
Steinhuder Meer, *Germany* .. 24 C5
Steinkjer, *Norway* 8 D14
Steinkopf, *S. Africa* 88 D2
Stellarton, *Canada* 103 C7
Stellenbosch, *S. Africa* 88 E2
Stelvio, Paso dello, *Italy* 28 B7
Stenay, *France* 19 C12
Stendal, *Germany* 24 C7
Stende, *Latvia* 44 A9
Stenhamra, *Sweden* 10 E11
Stenstorp, *Sweden* 11 F7
Stenungsund, *Sweden* 11 F5
Steornabhaigh = Stornoway,
 U.K. 14 C2
Stepanakert = Xankändi,
 Azerbaijan 70 B5
Stepanavan, *Armenia* 49 K7
Stephens I., *Canada* 104 C2
Stephens L., *Canada* 105 B9
Stephenville, *Canada* 103 C8
Stephenville, *U.S.A.* 113 J5
Stepnica, *Poland* 44 E1
Stepnoi = Elista, *Russia* 49 G7
Steppe, *Asia* 52 D9
Stereá Ellas □, *Greece* 38 C4
Sterkstroom, *S. Africa* 88 E4
Sterling, Colo., *U.S.A.* 112 E3
Sterling, Ill., *U.S.A.* 112 E10
Sterling, Kans., *U.S.A.* 112 F5
Sterling City, *U.S.A.* 113 K4
Sterling Heights, *U.S.A.* 108 D4
Sterling Run, *U.S.A.* 110 E6
Sterlitamak, *Russia* 50 D6
Sternberg, *Germany* 24 B7
Šternberk, *Czech Rep.* 27 B10
Stérnes, *Greece* 36 D6
Sterzing = Vipiteno, *Italy* 29 B8
Stettin = Szczecin, *Poland* ... 44 E1
Stettiner Haff, *Germany* 24 B10
Stettler, *Canada* 104 C6
Steubenville, *U.S.A.* 110 F4
Stevenage, *U.K.* 13 F7
Stevens Point, *U.S.A.* 112 C10
Stevenson, *U.S.A.* 116 E5
Stevenson L., *Canada* 105 C9
Stevensville, *U.S.A.* 114 C6
Stevns Klint, *Denmark* 11 J6
Stewart, *Canada* 104 B3
Stewart, *U.S.A.* 116 F7
Stewart ➜, *Canada* 100 B6
Stewart, C., *Australia* 94 A1
Stewart, I., *Chile* 128 G2
Stewart I., *N.Z.* 91 M1
Stewarts Point, *U.S.A.* 116 G3
Stewartville, *U.S.A.* 112 D8
Stewiacke, *Canada* 103 C7
Steynsburg, *S. Africa* 88 E4
Steyr, *Austria* 26 C7
Steyr ➜, *Austria* 26 C7
Steytlerville, *S. Africa* 88 E3
Stia, *Italy* 29 E8
Stigler, *U.S.A.* 113 H7
Stigliano, *Italy* 31 B9
Stigtomta, *Sweden* 11 F10
Stikine ➜, *Canada* 104 B2
Stilfontein, *S. Africa* 88 D4
Stilís, *Greece* 38 C4
Stillwater, *N.Z.* 91 K3
Stillwater, Minn., *U.S.A.* ... 112 C8
Stillwater, N.Y., *U.S.A.* ... 111 D11
Stillwater, Okla., *U.S.A.* ... 113 G6
Stillwater Range, *U.S.A.* ... 114 G4
Stillwater Reservoir, *U.S.A.* . 111 C9
Stilo, Pta., *Italy* 31 D9
Stilwell, *U.S.A.* 113 H7
Ştip, *Macedonia* 40 E6
Stíra, *Greece* 38 C6
Stirling, *Canada* 110 B7
Stirling, *U.K.* 14 E5
Stirling □, *U.K.* 14 E4
Stirling Ra., *Australia* 93 F2
Stittsville, *Canada* 111 A9
Stjernøya, *Norway* 8 A20
Stjørdalshalsen, *Norway* 8 E14
Stockach, *Germany* 25 H5
Stockaryd, *Sweden* 11 G8
Stockerau, *Austria* 27 C9
Stockholm, *Sweden* 10 E12
Stockholms län □, *Sweden* .. 10 E12
Stockport, *U.K.* 12 D5
Stocksbridge, *U.K.* 12 D6
Stockton, Calif., *U.S.A.* 116 H5
Stockton, Kans., *U.S.A.* 112 F5
Stockton, Mo., *U.S.A.* 113 G8
Stockton-on-Tees, *U.K.* 12 C6

Stockton-on-Tees □, *U.K.* ... 12 C6
Stockton Plateau, *U.S.A.* ... 113 K3
Stoczek Łukowski, *Poland* ... 45 G8
Stöde, *Sweden* 10 B10
Stoeng Treng, *Cambodia* 64 F5
Stoer, Pt. of, *U.K.* 14 C3
Stogovo, *Macedonia* 40 E4
Stoholm, *Denmark* 11 H3
Stoke-on-Trent, *U.K.* 12 D5
Stoke-on-Trent □, *U.K.* 12 D5
Stokes Pt., *Australia* 94 G3
Stokes Ra., *Australia* 92 C5
Stokksnes, *Iceland* 8 D6
Stokmarknes, *Norway* 8 B16
Stolac, *Bos.-H.* 40 C1
Stolberg, *Germany* 24 E2
Stolbovoy, Ostrov, *Russia* ... 51 B14
Stolbtsy = Stowbtsy, *Belarus* . 46 F4
Stolin, *Belarus* 47 G4
Stöllet, *Sweden* 10 D7
Stolnici, *Romania* 43 F9
Stomíon, *Greece* 36 D5
Ston, *Croatia* 29 F14
Stone, *U.K.* 12 E5
Stoneboro, *U.S.A.* 110 E4
Stonehaven, *U.K.* 14 E6
Stonehenge, *Australia* 94 C3
Stonehenge, *U.K.* 13 F6
Stonewall, *Canada* 105 C9
Stony L., Man., *Canada* 105 B9
Stony L., Ont., *Canada* 110 B6
Stony Point, *U.S.A.* 111 E11
Stony Pt., *U.S.A.* 111 C8
Stony Rapids, *Canada* 105 B7
Stony Tunguska = Tunguska,
 Podkamennaya ➜, *Russia* .. 51 C10
Stonyford, *U.S.A.* 116 F4
Stopnica, *Poland* 45 H7
Storå, *Sweden* 10 E9
Stora ➜, *Denmark* 11 H2
Stora Gla, *Sweden* 10 E6
Stora Le, *Sweden* 10 E5
Stora Lulevatten, *Sweden* ... 8 C18
Storavan, *Sweden* 8 D18
Stord, *Norway* 9 G11
Store Bælt, *Denmark* 11 J4
Store Heddinge, *Denmark* ... 11 J6
Storebro, *Sweden* 11 G9
Storfors, *Sweden* 10 E8
Storlien, *Sweden* 10 A6
Storm B., *Australia* 94 G4
Storm Lake, *U.S.A.* 112 D7
Stormberge, *S. Africa* 88 E4
Stormsrivier, *S. Africa* 88 E3
Stornoway, *U.K.* 14 C2
Storo, *Italy* 28 C7
Storozhinets = Storozhynets,
 Ukraine 47 H3
Storozhynets, *Ukraine* 47 H3
Storrs, *U.S.A.* 111 E12
Storsjön, Gävleborg, *Sweden* . 10 D10
Storsjön, Jämtland, *Sweden* .. 10 B7
Storsjön, Jämtland, *Sweden* .. 10 A8
Storstrøms Amtskommune □,
 Denmark 11 J5
Storuman, *Sweden* 8 D17
Storuman, sjö, *Sweden* 8 D17
Storvätteshågna, *Sweden* ... 10 B6
Storvik, *Sweden* 10 D10
Storvreta, *Sweden* 10 E11
Stouffville, *Canada* 110 C5
Stoughton, *Canada* 105 D8
Stour ➜, Dorset, *U.K.* 13 G6
Stour ➜, Kent, *U.K.* 13 F9
Stour ➜, Suffolk, *U.K.* 13 F9
Stourbridge, *U.K.* 13 E5
Stout L., *Canada* 105 C10
Stove Pipe Wells Village, *U.S.A.* 117 J9
Støvring, *Denmark* 11 H3
Stow, *U.S.A.* 110 E3
Stowbtsy, *Belarus* 46 F4
Stowmarket, *U.K.* 13 E9
Strabane, *U.K.* 15 B4
Stracin, *Macedonia* 40 D6
Stradella, *Italy* 28 C6
Strahan, *Australia* 94 G4
Strajitsa, *Bulgaria* 41 C9
Strakonice, *Czech Rep.* 26 B6
Straldzha, *Bulgaria* 41 D10
Stralsund, *Germany* 24 A9
Strand, *S. Africa* 88 E2
Stranda, Møre og Romsdal,
 Norway 9 E12
Stranda, Nord-Trøndelag,
 Norway 8 E14
Strandby, *Denmark* 11 G4
Strangford L., *U.K.* 15 B6
Strängnäs, *Sweden* 10 E11
Stranraer, *U.K.* 14 G3
Strasbourg, *Canada* 105 C8
Strasbourg, *France* 19 D14
Strasburg, *Germany* 24 B9
Strășeni, *Moldova* 43 C13
Strässa, *Sweden* 10 E9
Stratford, *Canada* 102 D3
Stratford, *N.Z.* 91 H5
Stratford, Calif., *U.S.A.* 116 J7
Stratford, Conn., *U.S.A.* ... 111 E11
Stratford, Tex., *U.S.A.* 113 G3
Stratford-upon-Avon, *U.K.* .. 13 E6
Strath Spey, *U.K.* 14 D5
Strathaven, *U.K.* 14 F4
Strathcona Prov. Park, *Canada* 104 D3
Strathmore, *Canada* 104 C6
Strathmore, *U.K.* 14 E5
Strathmore, *U.S.A.* 116 J7

Strathnaver, *Canada* 104 C4
Strathpeffer, *U.K.* 14 D4
Strathroy, *Canada* 102 D3
Strathy Pt., *U.K.* 14 C4
Strattanville, *U.S.A.* 110 E5
Stratton, *U.S.A.* 111 A14
Stratton Mt., *U.S.A.* 111 C12
Straubing, *Germany* 25 G8
Straumnes, *Iceland* 8 C2
Strausberg, *Germany* 24 C9
Strawberry ➜, *U.S.A.* 114 F8
Stráznice, *Czech Rep.* 27 C10
Streaky B., *Australia* 95 E1
Streaky Bay, *Australia* 95 E1
Streator, *U.S.A.* 112 E10
Středočeský □, *Czech Rep.* ... 26 B7
Streetsboro, *U.S.A.* 110 E3
Streetsville, *Canada* 110 C5
Strehaia, *Romania* 43 F8
Strelcha, *Bulgaria* 41 D8
Strelka, *Russia* 51 D10
Streng ➜, *Cambodia* 64 F4
Stresa, *Italy* 28 C5
Streymoy, *Færoe Is.* 8 E9
Strezhevoy, *Russia* 50 C8
Stříbro, *Czech Rep.* 26 A6
Strimón ➜, *Greece* 40 F7
Strimonikós Kólpos, *Greece* .. 40 F7
Strofádhes, *Greece* 38 D3
Stroma, *U.K.* 14 C5
Strómboli, *Italy* 31 D8
Stromeferry, *U.K.* 14 D3
Stromness, *U.K.* 14 C5
Strömsbruk, *Sweden* 10 C11
Stromsburg, *U.S.A.* 112 E6
Strömstad, *Sweden* 11 F5
Strömsund, *Sweden* 8 E16
Strongilí, *Greece* 39 E11
Stróngoli, *Italy* 31 C10
Strongsville, *U.S.A.* 110 E3
Stronie Śląskie, *Poland* 45 H3
Stronsay, *U.K.* 14 B6
Stropkov, *Slovak Rep.* 27 B14
Stroud, *U.K.* 13 F5
Stroudsburg, *U.S.A.* 111 F9
Stroumbi, *Cyprus* 36 E11
Struer, *Denmark* 11 H2
Struga, *Macedonia* 40 E4
Strugi Krasnyye, *Russia* 46 C5
Struma ➜, *Europe* 40 E6
Strumica, *Macedonia* 40 E7
Strumica ➜, *Europe* 40 E7
Struthers, *Canada* 102 C2
Struthers, *U.S.A.* 110 E4
Stryama, *Bulgaria* 41 D8
Stryker, *U.S.A.* 114 B6
Strykow, *Poland* 45 G6
Stryy, *Ukraine* 47 H2
Strzegom, *Poland* 45 H3
Strzelce Krajeńskie, *Poland* .. 45 F2
Strzelce Opolskie, *Poland* ... 45 H5
Strzelecki Cr. ➜, *Australia* .. 95 D2
Strzelin, *Poland* 45 H4
Strzelno, *Poland* 45 F5
Strzybnica, *Poland* 45 H5
Strzyżów, *Poland* 45 J8
Stuart, Fla., *U.S.A.* 109 M5
Stuart, Nebr., *U.S.A.* 112 D5
Stuart ➜, *Canada* 104 C4
Stuart Bluff Ra., *Australia* .. 92 D5
Stuart L., *Canada* 104 C4
Stuart Ra., *Australia* 95 D1
Stubbekøbing, *Denmark* 11 K6
Stuben, *Austria* 26 D3
Studen Kladenets, Yazovir,
 Bulgaria 41 E9
Studenka, *Czech Rep.* 27 B11
Stugun, *Sweden* 10 A9
Stuhr, *Germany* 24 B4
Stull L., *Canada* 102 B1
Stung Treng = Stoeng Treng,
 Cambodia 64 F5
Stupart ➜, *Canada* 102 A1
Stupava, *Slovak Rep.* 27 C10
Stupino, *Russia* 46 E10
Sturgeon B., *Canada* 105 C9
Sturgeon Bay, *U.S.A.* 108 C2
Sturgeon Falls, *Canada* 102 C4
Sturgeon L., Alta., *Canada* .. 104 B5
Sturgeon L., Ont., *Canada* .. 102 C1
Sturgeon L., Ont., *Canada* .. 110 B6
Sturgis, *Canada* 105 C8
Sturgis, Mich., *U.S.A.* 108 E3
Sturgis, S. Dak., *U.S.A.* ... 112 C3
Sturkö, *Sweden* 11 H9
Šturovo, *Slovak Rep.* 27 D11
Sturt Cr. ➜, *Australia* 92 C4
Stutterheim, *S. Africa* 88 E4
Stuttgart, *Germany* 25 G5
Stuttgart, *U.S.A.* 113 H9
Stuyvesant, *U.S.A.* 111 D11
Stykkishólmur, *Iceland* 8 D2
Styria = Steiermark □, *Austria* . 26 D8
Styrsö, *Sweden* 11 G5
Su Xian = Suzhou, *China* ... 56 H9
Suakin, *Sudan* 80 D4
Suan, N. *Korea* 57 E14
Suaqui, *Mexico* 118 B3
Suar, *India* 69 E8
Subang, *Indonesia* 63 G12
Subansiri ➜, *India* 67 F18
Subarnarekha ➜, *India* 69 H12
Subayhah, Si. *Arabia* 70 D3
Subcetate, *Romania* 42 E8
Subi, *Indonesia* 65 L7
Subiaco, *Italy* 29 G10

Subotica, *Serbia, Yug.* 42 D4
Suca, *Ethiopia* 81 F4
Suceava, *Romania* 43 C11
Suceava □, *Romania* 43 C10
Suceava ➜, *Romania* 43 C11
Sucha-Beskidzka, *Poland* ... 45 J6
Suchań, *Poland* 45 E2
Suchan, *Russia* 54 C6
Suchedniów, *Poland* 45 G7
Suchitoto, *El Salv.* 120 D2
Suchou = Xuzhou, *China* ... 57 G9
Suchowola, *Poland* 44 E10
Suck ➜, *Ireland* 15 C3
Sucre, *Bolivia* 124 G5
Sućuraj, *Croatia* 29 E14
Sucuriú ➜, *Brazil* 125 H8
Sud, Pte. du, *Canada* 103 C7
Sud-Kivu □, *Dem. Rep. of*
 the Congo 86 C2
Sud-Ouest, Pte. du, *Canada* .. 103 C7
Suda ➜, *Russia* 46 C9
Sudak, *Ukraine* 47 K8
Sudan, *U.S.A.* 113 H3
Sudan ■, *Africa* 81 E3
Sudbury, *Canada* 102 C3
Sudbury, *U.K.* 13 E8
Sûdd, *Sudan* 81 F3
Süderbrarup, *Germany* 24 A5
Süderlügum, *Germany* 24 A4
Süderoogsand, *Germany* 24 A4
Sudeten Mts. = Sudety, *Europe* 27 A9
Sudety, *Europe* 27 A9
Suðuroy, *Færoe Is.* 8 F9
Sudi, *Tanzania* 87 E4
Sudirman, Pegunungan,
 Indonesia 63 E9
Suditi, *Romania* 43 F12
Sudogda, *Russia* 48 C5
Sudr, *Egypt* 80 B3
Sudzha, *Russia* 47 G8
Sue ➜, *Sudan* 81 F2
Sueca, *Spain* 33 F4
Süedinenie, *Bulgaria* 41 D8
Suemez I., *U.S.A.* 104 B2
Suez = El Suweis, *Egypt* 80 J8
Suez, G. of = Suweis, Khalîg el,
 Egypt 80 J8
Suez Canal = Suweis, Qanâ es,
 Egypt 80 H8
Suffield, *Canada* 104 C6
Suffolk, *U.S.A.* 108 G7
Suffolk □, *U.K.* 13 E9
Şugag, *Romania* 43 E8
Sugargrove, *U.S.A.* 110 E5
Sugarive ➜, *India* 69 F12
Suğla Gölü, *Turkey* 72 D5
Sugluk = Salluit, *Canada* .. 101 B12
Suhaia, Lacul, *Romania* 43 G10
Şuḥār, *Oman* 71 E8
Sühbaatar □, *Mongolia* 56 B8
Suhl, *Germany* 24 E6
Şuhut, *Turkey* 39 C12
Sui, *Pakistan* 68 E3
Sui Xian, *China* 56 G8
Šuica, *Bos.-H.* 42 G2
Suichang, *China* 59 C12
Suichuan, *China* 59 D10
Suide, *China* 56 F6
Suifenhe, *China* 57 B16
Suihua, *China* 60 B7
Suijiang, *China* 58 C4
Suining, Hunan, *China* 59 D8
Suining, Jiangsu, *China* 57 H9
Suining, Sichuan, *China* 58 B5
Suiping, *China* 56 H7
Suippes, *France* 19 C11
Suir ➜, *Ireland* 15 D4
Suisun City, *U.S.A.* 116 G4
Suixi, *China* 59 G8
Suiyang, Guizhou, *China* ... 58 D6
Suiyang, Heilongjiang, *China* . 57 D11
Suizhou, *China* 59 B9
Sujangarh, *India* 68 F6
Sukabumi, *Indonesia* 63 G12
Sukadana, *Indonesia* 62 E3
Sukagawa, *Japan* 55 F10
Sukaraja, *Indonesia* 62 E4
Sukarnapura = Jayapura,
 Indonesia 63 E10
Sukch'ŏn, N. *Korea* 57 E13
Sukhindol, *Bulgaria* 41 C9
Sukhinichi, *Russia* 46 E9
Sukhona ➜, *Russia* 50 D4
Sukhothai, *Thailand* 64 D2
Sukhumi = Sokhumi, *Georgia* . 49 J5
Sukkur, *Pakistan* 68 F3
Sukkur Barrage, *Pakistan* ... 68 F3
Sukovo, *Serbia, Yug.* 40 C6
Sukri ➜, *India* 68 G4
Sukumo, *Japan* 55 H6
Sukunka ➜, *Canada* 104 B4
Sula ➜, *Ukraine* 47 H7
Sula, Kepulauan, *Indonesia* .. 63 E7
Sulaco ➜, *Honduras* 120 C2
Sulaiman Range, *Pakistan* ... 68 D3
Sulak ➜, *Russia* 49 J8
Sūlār, *Iran* 71 D6
Sulawesi Sea = Celebes Sea,
 Indonesia 63 D6
Sulawesi Selatan □, *Indonesia* . 63 E6
Sulawesi Utara □, *Indonesia* .. 63 D6
Sulechów, *Poland* 45 F2
Sulęcin, *Poland* 45 F2
Sulejów, *Poland* 45 G6

Sulejówek, Poland	45	F8
Süleymanlı, Turkey	39	C9
Sulima, S. Leone	82	D2
Sulina, Romania	43	E14
Sulina, Brațul →, Romania	43	E14
Sulingen, Germany	24	C4
Sulița, Romania	43	C11
Sulitjelma, Norway	8	C17
Sułkowice, Poland	45	J6
Sullana, Peru	124	D2
Süller, Turkey	39	C11
Sullivan, Ill., U.S.A.	112	F10
Sullivan, Ind., U.S.A.	108	F2
Sullivan, Mo., U.S.A.	112	F9
Sullivan Bay, Canada	104	C3
Sullivan I. = Lanbi Kyun, Burma	65	G2
Sully-sur-Loire, France	19	E9
Sulmierzyce, Poland	45	G4
Sulmona, Italy	29	F10
Süloğlu, Turkey	41	E10
Sulphur, La., U.S.A.	113	K8
Sulphur, Okla., U.S.A.	113	H6
Sulphur Pt., Canada	104	A6
Sulphur Springs, U.S.A.	113	J7
Sultan, Canada	102	C3
Sultan, U.S.A.	116	C5
Sultan Dağları, Turkey	72	C4
Sultanhisar, Turkey	39	D10
Sultaniça, Turkey	41	F10
Sultaniye, Turkey	41	F12
Sultanpur, Mad. P., India	68	H8
Sultanpur, Punjab, India	68	D6
Sultanpur, Ut. P., India	69	F10
Sulu Arch., Phil.	61	J4
Sulu Sea, E. Indies	61	G4
Sululta, Ethiopia	81	F4
Suluova, Turkey	72	B6
Suluq, Libya	79	B10
Sulzbach, Germany	25	F3
Sulzbach-Rosenberg, Germany	25	F7
Sulzberger Ice Shelf, Antarctica	5	D10
Sumalata, Indonesia	63	D6
Sumampa, Argentina	126	B3
Sumatera □, Indonesia	62	D2
Sumatera Barat □, Indonesia	62	E2
Sumatera Utara □, Indonesia	62	D1
Sumatra = Sumatera □, Indonesia	62	D2
Sumba, Indonesia	63	F5
Sumba, Selat, Indonesia	63	F5
Sumbawa, Indonesia	62	F5
Sumbawa Besar, Indonesia	62	F5
Sumbawanga □, Tanzania	84	F6
Sumbe, Angola	84	G2
Sumburgh Hd., U.K.	14	B7
Sumdeo, India	69	D8
Sumdo, India	69	B8
Sumedang, Indonesia	63	G12
Sümeg, Hungary	42	D2
Sumeih, Sudan	81	F2
Sumen = Shumen, Bulgaria	41	C10
Sumenep, Indonesia	63	G15
Sumgait = Sumqayıt, Azerbaijan	49	K9
Summer L., U.S.A.	114	E3
Summerland, Canada	104	D5
Summerside, Canada	103	C7
Summersville, U.S.A.	108	F5
Summerville, Ga., U.S.A.	109	H3
Summerville, S.C., U.S.A.	109	J5
Summit Lake, Canada	104	C4
Summit Peak, U.S.A.	115	H10
Sumner, Iowa, U.S.A.	112	D8
Sumner, Wash., U.S.A.	116	C4
Sumoto, Japan	55	G7
Šumperk, Czech Rep.	27	B9
Sumqayıt, Azerbaijan	49	K9
Sumter, U.S.A.	109	J5
Sumy, Ukraine	47	G8
Sun City, Ariz., U.S.A.	115	K7
Sun City, Calif., U.S.A.	117	M9
Sun City Center, U.S.A.	109	M4
Sun Lakes, U.S.A.	115	K8
Sun Valley, U.S.A.	114	E6
Sunagawa, Japan	54	C10
Sunan, N. Korea	57	E14
Sunart, L., U.K.	14	E3
Sunburst, U.S.A.	114	B8
Sunbury, U.S.A.	111	F8
Sunchales, Argentina	126	C3
Suncho Corral, Argentina	126	B3
Sunch'ŏn, S. Korea	57	G14
Suncook, U.S.A.	111	C13
Sunda, Selat, Indonesia	62	F3
Sunda Is., Indonesia	52	K14
Sunda Str. = Sunda, Selat, Indonesia	62	F3
Sundance, Canada	105	B10
Sundance, U.S.A.	112	C2
Sundar Nagar, India	68	D7
Sundarbans, The, Asia	67	J16
Sundargarh, India	67	H14
Sundays = Sondags →, S. Africa	88	E4
Sunderland, Canada	110	B5
Sunderland, U.K.	12	C6
Sundre, Canada	104	C6
Sunds, Denmark	11	H3
Sundsvall, Sweden	10	B11
Sundsvallsbukten, Sweden	10	B11
Sung Hei, Vietnam	65	G6
Sungai Kolok, Thailand	65	J3
Sungai Lembing, Malaysia	65	L4
Sungai Petani, Malaysia	65	K3
Sungaigerong, Indonesia	62	E2
Sungailiat, Indonesia	62	E3
Sungaipenuh, Indonesia	62	E2
Sungari = Songhua Jiang →, China	60	B8
Sunghua Chiang = Songhua Jiang →, China	60	B8
Sungikai, Sudan	81	E2
Sungurlu, Turkey	72	B6
Sunja, Croatia	29	C13
Sunland Park, U.S.A.	115	L10
Sunnansjö, Sweden	10	D8
Sunndalsøra, Norway	9	E13
Sunne, Sweden	10	E7
Sunnemo, Sweden	10	E7
Sunnyside, U.S.A.	114	C3
Sunnyvale, U.S.A.	116	H4
Suntar, Russia	51	C12
Sunyani, Ghana	82	D4
Suomenselkä, Finland	8	E21
Suomussalmi, Finland	8	D23
Suoyarvi, Russia	46	A7
Supai, U.S.A.	115	H7
Supaul, India	69	F12
Superior, Ariz., U.S.A.	115	K8
Superior, Mont., U.S.A.	114	C6
Superior, Nebr., U.S.A.	112	E5
Superior, Wis., U.S.A.	112	B8
Superior, L., N. Amer.	102	C2
Supetar, Croatia	29	E13
Suphan Buri, Thailand	64	E3
Suphan Dağı, Turkey	70	B4
Supiori, Indonesia	63	E9
Supraśl, Poland	45	E10
Supraśl →, Poland	45	E9
Supung Shuiku, China	57	D13
Sûq Suwayq, Si. Arabia	70	E3
Suqian, China	57	H10
Sûr, Lebanon	75	B4
Şûr, Oman	74	C6
Sur, Pt., U.S.A.	116	J5
Sura →, Russia	48	C8
Surab, Pakistan	68	E2
Surabaja = Surabaya, Indonesia	62	F4
Surabaya, Indonesia	62	F4
Surahammar, Sweden	10	E10
Suraia, Romania	43	E12
Surakarta, Indonesia	63	G14
Surakhany, Azerbaijan	49	K10
Surat, Australia	95	D4
Surat, India	66	J8
Surat Thani, Thailand	65	H2
Suratgarh, India	68	E5
Suraż, Poland	45	F9
Surazh, Belarus	46	E6
Surazh, Russia	47	F7
Surduc, Romania	43	C8
Surduc Pasul, Romania	43	E8
Surdulica, Serbia, Yug.	40	D6
Surendranagar, India	68	H4
Surf, U.S.A.	117	L6
Surgères, France	20	B3
Surgut, Russia	50	C8
Sùria, Spain	32	D6
Suriapet, India	66	L11
Surigao, Phil.	61	G6
Surigao Strait, Phil.	61	F6
Surin, Thailand	64	E4
Surin Nua, Ko, Thailand	65	H1
Surinam ■, S. Amer.	125	C7
Suriname = Surinam ■, S. Amer.	125	C7
Suriname →, Surinam	125	B7
Sürmaq, Iran	71	D7
Sürmene, Turkey	73	B9
Surovikino, Russia	49	F6
Surrey □, U.K.	13	F7
Sursand, India	69	F11
Sursar →, India	69	F12
Sursee, Switz.	25	H4
Sursk, Russia	48	D7
Surskoye, Russia	48	C8
Surt, Libya	79	B9
Surt, Khalīj, Libya	79	B9
Surtanahu, Pakistan	68	F4
Surte, Sweden	11	G6
Surtsey, Iceland	8	E3
Sürüç, Turkey	73	D8
Suruga-Wan, Japan	55	G9
Susa, Italy	28	C4
Suså →, Denmark	11	J5
Sušac, Croatia	29	F13
Susak, Croatia	29	D11
Susaki, Japan	55	H6
Süsangerd, Iran	71	D6
Susanville, U.S.A.	114	F3
Susch, Switz.	25	J6
Suşehri, Turkey	73	B8
Sušice, Czech Rep.	26	B6
Susleni, Moldova	43	C13
Susner, India	68	H7
Susong, China	59	B11
Susquehanna, U.S.A.	111	E9
Susquehanna →, U.S.A.	111	G8
Susques, Argentina	126	A2
Sussex, Canada	103	C6
Sussex, U.S.A.	111	E10
Sussex, E. □, U.K.	13	G8
Sussex, W. □, U.K.	13	G7
Sustut →, Canada	104	B3
Susuman, Russia	51	C15
Susunu, Indonesia	63	E8
Susurluk, Turkey	39	B10
Susz, Poland	44	E6
Sutak, India	69	C8
Sütçüler, Turkey	72	D4
Suțești, Romania	43	E12
Sutherland, S. Africa	88	E3
Sutherland, U.S.A.	112	E4
Sutherland Falls, N.Z.	91	L1
Sutherlin, U.S.A.	114	E2
Suthri, India	68	H3
Sutlej →, Pakistan	68	E4
Sutter, U.S.A.	116	F5
Sutter Creek, U.S.A.	116	G6
Sutton, Canada	111	A12
Sutton, Nebr., U.S.A.	112	E6
Sutton, W. Va., U.S.A.	108	F5
Sutton →, Canada	102	A3
Sutton Coldfield, U.K.	13	E6
Sutton in Ashfield, U.K.	12	D6
Sutton L., Canada	102	B3
Suttor →, Australia	94	C4
Suttsu, Japan	54	C10
Suva, Fiji	91	D8
Suva Gora, Macedonia	40	E5
Suva Planina, Serbia, Yug.	40	C6
Suva Reka, Kosovo, Yug.	40	D4
Suvorov, Russia	46	E9
Suvorov Is. = Suwarrow Is., Cook Is.	97	J11
Suvorovo, Bulgaria	41	C11
Suwałki, Poland	44	D9
Suwannaphum, Thailand	64	E4
Suwannee →, U.S.A.	109	L4
Suwanose-Jima, Japan	55	K4
Suwarrow Is., Cook Is.	97	J11
Suwayq aş Şuqban, Iraq	70	D5
Suweis, Khalîg el, Egypt	80	J8
Suweis, Qanâ es, Egypt	80	H8
Suwŏn, S. Korea	57	F14
Suzdal, Russia	46	D11
Suzhou, Anhui, China	56	H9
Suzhou, Jiangsu, China	59	B13
Suzu, Japan	55	F8
Suzu-Misaki, Japan	55	F8
Suzuka, Japan	55	G8
Suzzara, Italy	28	D7
Svalbard, Arctic	4	B8
Svalöv, Sweden	11	J7
Svaneke, Denmark	11	J9
Svängsta, Sweden	11	H8
Svanskog, Sweden	10	E6
Svappavaara, Sweden	8	C19
Svärdsjö, Sweden	10	D9
Svartå, Sweden	10	E8
Svartisen, Norway	8	C15
Svartvik, Sweden	10	B11
Svatove, Ukraine	47	H10
Svatovo = Svatove, Ukraine	47	H10
Svay Chek, Cambodia	64	F4
Svay Rieng, Cambodia	65	G5
Svealand □, Sweden	10	D9
Svedala, Sweden	11	J7
Sveg, Sweden	10	B8
Svendborg, Denmark	11	J4
Svenljunga, Sweden	11	G7
Svenstavik, Sweden	10	B8
Svenstrup, Denmark	11	H3
Sverdlovsk = Yekaterinburg, Russia	50	D7
Sverdlovsk, Ukraine	47	H10
Sverdrup Is., Canada	4	B3
Svetac, Croatia	29	E12
Sveti Nikola, Prokhod, Europe	40	C6
Sveti Nikole, Macedonia	40	E5
Sveti Rok, Croatia	29	D12
Svetlaya, Russia	54	A9
Svetlogorsk = Svyetlahorsk, Belarus	47	F5
Svetlograd, Russia	49	H6
Svetlovodsk = Svitlovodsk, Ukraine	47	H7
Svidník, Slovak Rep.	27	B14
Svilaja Planina, Croatia	29	E13
Svilajnac, Serbia, Yug.	40	B5
Svilengrad, Bulgaria	41	E10
Svir →, Russia	46	B7
Sviritsa, Russia	46	B7
Svishtov, Bulgaria	41	C9
Svislach, Belarus	47	F3
Svitava →, Czech Rep.	27	B9
Svitavy, Czech Rep.	27	B9
Svitlovodsk, Ukraine	47	H7
Svobodnyy, Russia	51	D13
Svoge, Bulgaria	40	D7
Svolvær, Norway	8	B16
Svratka →, Czech Rep.	27	B9
Svrljig, Serbia, Yug.	40	C6
Svyetlahorsk, Belarus	47	F5
Swabian Alps = Schwäbische Alb, Germany	25	G5
Swainsboro, U.S.A.	109	J4
Swakop →, Namibia	88	C2
Swakopmund, Namibia	88	C1
Swale →, U.K.	12	C6
Swan →, Australia	93	F2
Swan →, Canada	105	C8
Swan Hills, Canada	104	C5
Swan Is., W. Indies	120	C3
Swan L., Canada	105	C8
Swan Peak, U.S.A.	114	C7
Swan River, Canada	105	C8
Swanage, U.K.	13	G6
Swansea, Australia	94	G4
Swansea, Canada	110	C5
Swansea, U.K.	13	F3
Swansea □, U.K.	13	F3
Swar →, Pakistan	69	B5
Swartberge, S. Africa	88	E3
Swartmodder, S. Africa	88	D3
Swartnossob →, Namibia	88	C2
Swartruggens, S. Africa	88	D4
Swarzędz, Poland	45	F4
Swastika, Canada	102	C3
Swatow = Shantou, China	59	F11
Swaziland ■, Africa	89	D5
Sweden ■, Europe	9	G16
Swedru, Ghana	83	D4
Sweet Home, U.S.A.	114	D2
Sweetgrass, U.S.A.	114	B8
Sweetwater, Nev., U.S.A.	116	G7
Sweetwater, Tenn., U.S.A.	109	H3
Sweetwater, Tex., U.S.A.	113	J4
Sweetwater →, U.S.A.	114	E10
Swellendam, S. Africa	88	E3
Swider →, Poland	45	F8
Świdnica, Poland	45	H3
Świdnik, Poland	45	G9
Świdwin, Poland	44	E2
Świebodzice, Poland	45	H3
Świebodzin, Poland	45	F2
Świecie, Poland	44	E5
Świerzawa, Poland	45	G2
Świętokrzyskie □, Poland	45	H7
Świętokrzyskie, Góry, Poland	45	H7
Swift Current, Canada	105	C7
Swiftcurrent →, Canada	105	C7
Swilly, L., Ireland	15	A4
Swindon, U.K.	13	F6
Swindon □, U.K.	13	F6
Swinemünde = Świnoujście, Poland	44	E1
Swinford, Ireland	15	C3
Świnoujście, Poland	44	E1
Switzerland ■, Europe	25	J4
Swords, Ireland	15	C5
Swoyerville, U.S.A.	111	E9
Syasstroy, Russia	46	B7
Sychevka, Russia	46	E8
Syców, Poland	45	G4
Sydenham →, Canada	110	D2
Sydney, Canada	103	C7
Sydney L., Canada	105	C10
Sydney Mines, Canada	103	C7
Sydprøven = Alluitsup Paa, Greenland	4	C5
Sydra, G. of = Surt, Khalīj, Libya	79	B9
Syeverodonetsk, Ukraine	47	H10
Syke, Germany	24	C4
Sykesville, U.S.A.	110	E6
Syktyvkar, Russia	50	C6
Sylacauga, U.S.A.	109	J2
Sylarna, Sweden	8	E15
Sylhet, Bangla.	67	G17
Sylhet □, Bangla.	67	G17
Sylt, Germany	24	A4
Sylvan Beach, U.S.A.	111	C9
Sylvan Lake, Canada	104	C6
Sylvania, U.S.A.	109	J5
Sylvester, U.S.A.	109	K4
Sym, Russia	50	C9
Symón, Mexico	118	C4
Synelnykove, Ukraine	47	H8
Synnott Ra., Australia	92	C4
Syracuse, Kans., U.S.A.	113	G4
Syracuse, N.Y., U.S.A.	111	C8
Syracuse, Nebr., U.S.A.	112	E6
Syrdarya →, Kazakstan	50	E7
Syria ■, Asia	70	C3
Syrian Desert = Shām, Bādiyat ash, Asia	70	C3
Sysslebäck, Sweden	10	D6
Syzran, Russia	48	D9
Szabolcs-Szatmár-Bereg □, Hungary	42	B6
Szadek, Poland	45	G5
Szamocin, Poland	45	E4
Szamos →, Hungary	42	B7
Szamotuły, Poland	45	F3
Szarvas, Hungary	42	D5
Százhalombatta, Hungary	42	C3
Szczawno, Poland	45	J7
Szczebrzeszyn, Poland	45	H9
Szczecin, Poland	44	E1
Szczecinek, Poland	44	E3
Szczeciński, Zalew = Stettiner Haff, Germany	24	B10
Szczekociny, Poland	45	H6
Szczucin, Poland	45	H7
Szczuczyn, Poland	44	E9
Szczyrk, Poland	45	J6
Szczytna, Poland	45	H3
Szczytno, Poland	44	E7
Szechwan = Sichuan □, China	58	B5
Szécsény, Hungary	42	B4
Szeged, Hungary	42	D5
Szeghalom, Hungary	42	C6
Székesfehérvár, Hungary	42	C3
Szekszárd, Hungary	42	D3
Szendrő, Hungary	42	B5
Szentendre, Hungary	42	C4
Szentes, Hungary	42	D5
Szentgotthárd, Hungary	42	D1
Szentlőrinc, Hungary	42	D3
Szerencs, Hungary	42	B6
Szigetszentmiklós, Hungary	42	C4
Szigetvár, Hungary	42	D2
Szikszó, Hungary	42	B5
Szklarska Poręba, Poland	45	H2
Szkwa →, Poland	45	E8
Szlichtyngowa, Poland	45	G3
Szob, Hungary	42	C3
Szolnok, Hungary	42	C5
Szombathely, Hungary	42	C1
Szprotawa, Poland	45	G2
Sztum, Poland	44	E6
Sztutowo, Poland	44	D6
Szubin, Poland	45	E4
Szydłowiec, Poland	45	G7
Szypliszki, Poland	44	D10

T

Ta Khli Khok, Thailand	64	E3
Ta Lai, Vietnam	65	G6
Tab, Hungary	42	D3
Tabacal, Argentina	126	A3
Tabaco, Phil.	61	E5
Tabagné, Ivory C.	82	D4
Ţabah, Si. Arabia	70	E4
Tabankort, Niger	83	B5
Ţabas, Khorāsān, Iran	71	C9
Ţabas, Khorāsān, Iran	71	C8
Tabasará, Serranía de, Panama	120	E3
Tabasco □, Mexico	119	D6
Tabāsīn, Iran	71	D8
Tabatinga, Serra da, Brazil	125	F10
Taber, Canada	104	D6
Taberg, Sweden	11	G8
Taberg, U.S.A.	111	C9
Tabla, Niger	83	C5
Tablas I., Phil.	61	E5
Tablas Strait, Phil.	61	E4
Table B. = Tafelbaai, S. Africa	88	E2
Table B., Canada	103	B8
Table Mt., S. Africa	88	E2
Table Rock L., U.S.A.	113	G8
Tabletop, Mt., Australia	94	C4
Tábor, Czech Rep.	26	B7
Tabora, Tanzania	86	D3
Tabora □, Tanzania	86	D3
Tabou, Ivory C.	82	E3
Tabrīz, Iran	70	B5
Tabuaeran, Kiribati	97	G12
Tabuenca, Spain	32	D3
Tabūk, Si. Arabia	70	D3
Täby, Sweden	10	E12
Tacámbaro de Codallos, Mexico	118	D4
Tacheng, China	60	B3
Tach'i, Taiwan	59	E13
Tachia, Taiwan	59	E13
Tach'ing Shan = Daqing Shan, China	56	D6
Tachov, Czech Rep.	26	B5
Tácina →, Italy	31	D9
Tacloban, Phil.	61	F6
Tacna, Peru	124	G4
Tacoma, U.S.A.	116	C4
Tacuarembó, Uruguay	127	C4
Tademaït, Plateau du, Algeria	78	C6
Tadio, L., Ivory C.	82	D3
Tadjoura, Djibouti	81	E5
Tadjoura, Golfe de, Djibouti	81	E5
Tadmor, N.Z.	91	J4
Tadoule, L., Canada	105	B9
Tadoussac, Canada	103	C6
Tadzhikistan = Tajikistan ■, Asia	50	F8
Taechŏn-ni, S. Korea	57	F14
Taegu, S. Korea	57	G15
Taegwan, N. Korea	57	D13
Taejŏn, S. Korea	57	F14
Tafalla, Spain	32	C3
Tafar, Sudan	81	F2
Tafelbaai, S. Africa	88	E2
Tafermaar, Indonesia	63	F8
Tafí Viejo, Argentina	126	B2
Tafīhān, Iran	71	D7
Tafire, Ivory C.	82	D3
Tafo, Ghana	83	D4
Tafresh, Iran	71	C6
Taft, Iran	71	D7
Taft, Phil.	61	F6
Taft, U.S.A.	117	K7
Taftán, Kūh-e, Iran	71	D9
Taga Dzong, Bhutan	67	F16
Taganrog, Russia	47	J10
Taganrogskiy Zaliv, Russia	47	J10
Tagant, Mauritania	82	B2
Tagatay, Phil.	61	D4
Tagbilaran, Phil.	61	G5
Tággia, Italy	28	E4
Tagish, Canada	104	A2
Tagish L., Canada	104	A2
Tagliacozzo, Italy	29	F10
Tagliamento →, Italy	29	C10
Táglio di Po, Italy	29	D9
Tago, Phil.	61	G7
Tagomago, Spain	37	B8
Tagourâret, Mauritania	82	B3
Taguatinga, Brazil	125	F10
Tagudin, Phil.	61	C4
Tagum, Phil.	61	H6
Tagus = Tejo →, Europe	35	F2
Tahakopa, N.Z.	91	M2
Tahan, Gunong, Malaysia	65	K4
Tahat, Algeria	78	D7
Tāherī, Iran	71	E7
Tahiti, Pac. Oc.	97	J13
Tahlequah, U.S.A.	113	H7
Tahoe, L., U.S.A.	116	G6
Tahoe City, U.S.A.	116	F6
Tahoka, U.S.A.	113	J4
Taholah, U.S.A.	116	C2
Tahoua, Niger	83	C6
Tahrūd, Iran	71	D8
Tahsis, Canada	104	D3
Tahtaköprü, Turkey	41	G13
Tahtalı Dağları, Turkey	72	C7
Tahulandang, Indonesia	63	D7
Tahuna, Indonesia	63	D7
Tai, Ivory C.	82	D3
Tai Hu, China	59	B12
Tai Shan, China	57	F9
Tai'an, China	57	F9

Taibei = T'aipei, Taiwan 59 E13
Taibique, Canary Is. ... 37 G2
Taibus Qi, China ... 56 D8
Taicang, China ... 59 B13
T'aichung, Taiwan ... 59 E13
Taieri →, N.Z. ... 91 M3
Taigu, China ... 56 F7
Taihang Shan, China ... 56 G7
Taihape, N.Z. ... 91 H5
Taihe, Anhui, China ... 56 H8
Taihe, Jiangxi, China ... 59 D10
Taihu, China ... 59 B11
Taijiang, China ... 58 D7
Taikang, China ... 56 G8
Tailfingen, Germany ... 25 G5
Tailuko, Taiwan ... 59 E13
Taimyr Peninsula = Taymyr, Poluostrov, Russia ... 51 B11
Tain, U.K. ... 14 D4
T'ainan, Taiwan ... 59 F13
Taínaron, Ákra, Greece ... 38 E4
Taining, China ... 59 D11
T'aipei, Taiwan ... 59 E13
Taiping, China ... 59 B12
Taiping, Malaysia ... 65 K3
Taipingzhen, China ... 56 H6
Tairbeart = Tarbert, U.K. ... 14 D2
Taishan, China ... 59 F9
Taishun, China ... 59 D12
Taita Hills, Kenya ... 86 C4
Taitao, Pen. de, Chile ... 122 H3
T'aitung, Taiwan ... 59 F13
Taivalkoski, Finland ... 8 D23
Taiwan ■, Asia ... 59 F13
Taiwan Strait, Asia ... 59 E12
Taixing, China ... 59 A13
Taiyara, Sudan ... 81 E3
Taïyetos Óros, Greece ... 38 D4
Taiyiba, Israel ... 75 C4
Taiyuan, China ... 56 F7
Taizhong = T'aichung, Taiwan ... 59 E13
Taizhou, China ... 59 A12
Taizhou Liedao, China ... 59 C13
Ta'izz, Yemen ... 74 E3
Tājābād, Iran ... 71 D7
Tajikistan ■, Asia ... 50 F8
Tajima, Japan ... 55 F9
Tajo = Tejo →, Europe ... 35 F2
Tajrīsh, Iran ... 71 C6
Tak, Thailand ... 64 D2
Takāb, Iran ... 70 B5
Takachiho, Japan ... 55 H5
Takachu, Botswana ... 88 C3
Takada, Japan ... 55 F9
Takahagi, Japan ... 55 F10
Takaka, N.Z. ... 91 J4
Takamatsu, Japan ... 55 G7
Takaoka, Japan ... 55 F8
Takapuna, N.Z. ... 91 G5
Takasaki, Japan ... 55 F9
Takatsuki, Japan ... 55 G7
Takaungu, Kenya ... 86 C4
Takayama, Japan ... 55 F8
Take-Shima, Japan ... 55 J5
Takefu, Japan ... 55 G8
Takengon, Indonesia ... 62 D1
Takeo, Japan ... 55 H5
Tåkern, Sweden ... 11 F8
Tākestān, Iran ... 71 C6
Taketa, Japan ... 55 H5
Takev, Cambodia ... 65 G5
Takh, India ... 69 C7
Takht-Sulaiman, Pakistan ... 68 D3
Takikawa, Japan ... 54 C10
Takla L., Canada ... 104 B3
Takla Landing, Canada ... 104 B3
Takla Makan = Taklamakan Shamo, China ... 60 C3
Taklamakan Shamo, China ... 60 C3
Taku →, Canada ... 104 B2
Takum, Nigeria ... 83 D6
Tal Halāl, Iran ... 71 D7
Tala, Uruguay ... 127 C4
Talachyn, Belarus ... 46 E5
Talacogan, Phil. ... 61 G6
Talagang, Pakistan ... 68 C5
Talagante, Chile ... 126 C1
Talak, Niger ... 83 B6
Talamanca, Cordillera de, Cent. Amer. ... 120 E3
Talant, France ... 19 E11
Talara, Peru ... 124 D2
Talas, Kyrgyzstan ... 50 E8
Talas, Turkey ... 72 C6
Talâta, Egypt ... 75 E1
Talata Mafara, Nigeria ... 83 C6
Talaud, Kepulauan, Indonesia . 63 D7
Talaud Is. = Talaud, Kepulauan, Indonesia ... 63 D7
Talavera de la Reina, Spain ... 34 F6
Talavera la Real, Spain ... 35 G4
Talayan, Phil. ... 61 H6
Talayuela, Spain ... 34 F5
Talbandh, India ... 69 H12
Talbert, Sillon de, France ... 18 D3
Talbot, C., Australia ... 92 B4
Talca, Chile ... 126 D1
Talcahuano, Chile ... 126 D1
Talcher, India ... 67 J14
Talcho, Niger ... 83 C5
Taldy Kurgan = Taldyqorghan, Kazakstan ... 50 E8
Taldyqorghan, Kazakstan ... 50 E8
Tālesh, Iran ... 71 B6
Tālesh, Kühhā-ye, Iran ... 71 B6
Talguharai, Sudan ... 80 D4

Tali Post, Sudan ... 81 F3
Taliabu, Indonesia ... 63 E6
Talibon, Phil. ... 63 B6
Talibong, Ko, Thailand ... 65 J2
Talihina, U.S.A. ... 113 H7
Talisayan, Phil. ... 61 G6
Taliwang, Indonesia ... 62 F5
Tall 'Afar, Iraq ... 70 B4
Tall Kalakh, Syria ... 75 A5
Talla, Egypt ... 80 B3
Talladega, U.S.A. ... 109 J2
Tallahassee, U.S.A. ... 109 K3
Tallard, France ... 21 D10
Tällberg, Sweden ... 10 D9
Tallering Pk., Australia ... 93 E2
Talli, Pakistan ... 68 E3
Tallinn, Estonia ... 9 G21
Tallmadge, U.S.A. ... 110 E3
Tallulah, U.S.A. ... 113 J9
Tălmaciu, Romania ... 43 E9
Talmont-St-Hilaire, France ... 20 B2
Talne, Ukraine ... 47 H6
Talnoye = Talne, Ukraine ... 47 H6
Talodi, Sudan ... 81 E3
Talovaya, Russia ... 48 E5
Taloyoak, Canada ... 100 B10
Talpa de Allende, Mexico ... 118 C4
Talsi, Latvia ... 9 H20
Talsi □, Latvia ... 44 A9
Taltal, Chile ... 126 B1
Taltson →, Canada ... 104 A6
Talurqjuak = Taloyoak, Canada 100 B10
Talwood, Australia ... 95 D4
Tam Chau, Vietnam ... 65 G5
Tam Ky, Vietnam ... 64 E7
Tam Quan, Vietnam ... 64 E7
Tama, U.S.A. ... 112 E8
Tamale, Ghana ... 83 D4
Taman, Russia ... 47 K9
Tamani, Mali ... 82 C3
Tamano, Japan ... 55 G6
Tamanrasset, Algeria ... 78 D7
Tamaqua, U.S.A. ... 111 F9
Tamar →, U.K. ... 13 G3
Tamarinda, Spain ... 37 B10
Tamarite de Litera, Spain ... 32 D5
Tamashima, Japan ... 55 G6
Tamási, Hungary ... 42 D3
Tamaské, Niger ... 83 C6
Tamaulipas □, Mexico ... 119 C5
Tamaulipas, Sierra de, Mexico . 119 C5
Tamazula, Mexico ... 118 C3
Tamazunchale, Mexico ... 119 C5
Tamba-Dabatou, Guinea ... 82 C2
Tambacounda, Senegal ... 82 C2
Tambelan, Kepulauan, Indonesia ... 62 D3
Tambellup, Australia ... 93 F2
Tambo, Australia ... 94 C4
Tambo de Mora, Peru ... 124 F3
Tambohorano, Madag. ... 89 B7
Tambora, Indonesia ... 62 F5
Tambov, Russia ... 48 D5
Tambre →, Spain ... 34 C2
Tambuku, Indonesia ... 63 G15
Tamburâ, Sudan ... 81 F2
Tâmchekket, Mauritania ... 82 B2
Tâmega →, Portugal ... 34 D2
Tamenglong, India ... 67 G18
Tamgak, Massif du, Niger ... 83 B6
Tamgué, Massif du, Guinea ... 82 C2
Tamiahua, L. de, Mexico ... 119 C5
Tamil Nadu □, India ... 66 P10
Tamis →, Serbia, Yug. ... 42 F5
Tamluk, India ... 69 H12
Tammerfors = Tampere, Finland ... 9 F20
Tammisaari, Finland ... 9 F20
Tämnaren, Sweden ... 10 D11
Tamo Abu, Pegunungan, Malaysia ... 62 D5
Tampa, U.S.A. ... 109 M4
Tampa B., U.S.A. ... 109 M4
Tampere, Finland ... 9 F20
Tampico, Mexico ... 119 C5
Tampin, Malaysia ... 65 L4
Tamsweg, Austria ... 26 D6
Tamu, Burma ... 67 G19
Tamuja →, Spain ... 35 F4
Tamworth, Australia ... 95 E5
Tamworth, Canada ... 110 B8
Tamworth, U.K. ... 13 E6
Tamyang, S. Korea ... 57 G14
Tan An, Vietnam ... 65 G6
Tan-Tan, Morocco ... 78 C3
Tana →, Kenya ... 86 C5
Tana →, Norway ... 8 A23
Tana, L., Ethiopia ... 81 E4
Tana River, Kenya ... 86 C4
Tanabe, Japan ... 55 H7
Tanafjorden, Norway ... 8 A23
Tanaga, Pta., Canary Is. ... 37 G1
Tanahbala, Indonesia ... 62 E1
Tanahgrogot, Indonesia ... 62 E5
Tanahjampea, Indonesia ... 63 F6
Tanahmasa, Indonesia ... 62 E1
Tanahmerah, Indonesia ... 63 F10
Tanakpur, India ... 69 E9
Tanakura, Japan ... 55 F10
Tanami, Australia ... 92 C4
Tanami Desert, Australia ... 92 C5
Tanana →, U.S.A. ... 100 B4
Tananarive = Antananarivo, Madag. ... 89 B8
Táneo →, Italy ... 28 D5
Tancheng, China ... 57 G10
Tanch'ön, N. Korea ... 57 D15
Tanda, Ut. P., India ... 69 F10
Tanda, Ut. P., India ... 69 E8

Tanda, Ivory C. ... 82 D4
Tandag, Phil. ... 61 G7
Tandaia, Tanzania ... 87 D3
Tăndărei, Romania ... 43 F12
Tandaué, Angola ... 88 B2
Tandil, Argentina ... 126 D4
Tandil, Sa. del, Argentina ... 126 D4
Tandlianwala, Pakistan ... 68 D5
Tando Adam, Pakistan ... 68 G3
Tando Allahyar, Pakistan ... 68 G3
Tando Bago, Pakistan ... 68 G3
Tando Mohommed Khan, Pakistan ... 68 G3
Tandragee, U.K. ... 15 B5
Tandsjöborg, Sweden ... 10 C8
Tane-ga-Shima, Japan ... 55 J5
Taneatua, N.Z. ... 91 H6
Tanen Tong Dan = Dawna Ra., Burma ... 64 D2
Tanew →, Poland ... 45 H9
Tanezrouft, Algeria ... 78 D6
Tang, Koh, Cambodia ... 65 G4
Tang, Ra's-e, Iran ... 71 E8
Tang Krasang, Cambodia ... 64 F5
Tanga, Tanzania ... 86 D4
Tanga □, Tanzania ... 86 D4
Tanganyika, L., Africa ... 86 D3
Tangaza, Nigeria ... 83 C5
Tanger, Morocco ... 78 A4
Tangerang, Indonesia ... 63 G12
Tangerhütte, Germany ... 24 C7
Tangermünde, Germany ... 24 C7
Tanggu, China ... 57 E9
Tanggula Shan, China ... 60 C4
Tanghe, China ... 56 H7
Tangier = Tanger, Morocco ... 78 A4
Tangorin, Australia ... 94 C3
Tangorombohitr'i Makay, Madag. ... 89 C8
Tangshan, China ... 57 E10
Tangtou, China ... 57 G10
Tanguiéta, Benin ... 83 C5
Tangxi, China ... 59 C12
Tangyan He →, China ... 58 C7
Tanimbar, Kepulauan, Indonesia 63 F8
Tanimbar Is. = Tanimbar, Kepulauan, Indonesia ... 63 F8
Taninthari = Tenasserim □, Burma ... 64 F2
Tanjay, Phil. ... 61 G5
Tanjong Malim, Malaysia ... 65 L3
Tanjore = Thanjavur, India ... 66 P11
Tanjung, Indonesia ... 62 E5
Tanjungbalai, Indonesia ... 62 D1
Tanjungbatu, Indonesia ... 62 D5
Tanjungkarang Telukbetung, Indonesia ... 62 F3
Tanjungpandan, Indonesia ... 62 E3
Tanjungpinang, Indonesia ... 62 D2
Tanjungredeb, Indonesia ... 62 D5
Tanjungselor, Indonesia ... 62 D5
Tank, Pakistan ... 68 C4
Tankhala, India ... 68 J5
Tännäs, Sweden ... 10 B6
Tannersville, U.S.A. ... 111 E9
Tannis Bugt, Denmark ... 11 G4
Tannu-Ola, Russia ... 51 D10
Tannum Sands, Australia ... 94 C5
Tano →, Ghana ... 82 D4
Tanon Str., Phil. ... 61 F5
Tanout, Niger ... 83 C6
Tanshui, Taiwan ... 59 E13
Tansilla, Burkina Faso ... 82 C4
Tanta, Egypt ... 80 H7
Tantoyuca, Mexico ... 119 C5
Tantung = Dandong, China ... 57 D13
Tanumshede, Sweden ... 11 F5
Tanus, France ... 20 D6
Tanzania ■, Africa ... 86 D3
Tanzilla →, Canada ... 104 B2
Tao, Ko, Thailand ... 65 G2
Tao'an = Taonan, China ... 57 B12
Tao'er He →, China ... 57 B13
Taohua Dao, China ... 59 C14
Taolanaro, Madag. ... 89 D8
Taole, China ... 56 E4
Taonan, China ... 57 B12
Taormina, Italy ... 31 E8
Taos, U.S.A. ... 115 H11
Taoudenni, Mali ... 78 D5
Taoyuan, China ... 59 C8
T'aoyüan, Taiwan ... 59 E13
Tapa, Estonia ... 9 G21
Tapa Shan = Daba Shan, China ... 58 B7
Tapachula, Mexico ... 119 E6
Tapah, Malaysia ... 65 K3
Tapajós →, Brazil ... 122 D5
Tapaktuan, Indonesia ... 62 D1
Tapanahoni →, Surinam ... 125 C8
Tapanui, N.Z. ... 91 L2
Tapauá →, Brazil ... 124 E5
Tapes, Brazil ... 127 C5
Taphan Hin, Thailand ... 64 D3
Tapi →, India ... 66 J8
Tapia de Casariego, Spain ... 34 B4
Tapirapecó, Serra, Venezuela . 124 C6
Tapolca, Hungary ... 42 D2
Tapuaenuku, Mt., N.Z. ... 91 K4
Tapul Group, Phil. ... 61 J4
Tapurucuará, Brazil ... 124 D5
Taquara, Brazil ... 127 B5
Taquari →, Brazil ... 124 G7
Tara, Australia ... 95 D5
Tara, Canada ... 110 B3

Tara, Russia ... 50 D8
Tara, Zambia ... 87 F2
Tara →, Montenegro, Yug. ... 40 C2
Taraba □, Nigeria ... 83 D7
Taraba →, Nigeria ... 83 D7
Tarabagatay, Khrebet, Kazakstan ... 50 E9
Tarābulus, Lebanon ... 75 A4
Tarābulus, Libya ... 79 B8
Taraclia, Moldova ... 43 D14
Taraclia, Moldova ... 43 E13
Taradehi, India ... 69 H8
Tarajalejo, Canary Is. ... 37 F5
Tarakan, Indonesia ... 62 D5
Tarakit, Mt., Kenya ... 86 B4
Tarama-Jima, Japan ... 55 M2
Taran, Mys, Russia ... 9 J18
Taranagar, India ... 68 E6
Taranaki □, N.Z. ... 91 H5
Taranaki, Mt., N.Z. ... 91 H5
Tarancón, Spain ... 32 E1
Táranto, Italy ... 31 B10
Táranto, G. di, Italy ... 31 B10
Tarapacá, Colombia ... 124 D5
Tarapacá □, Chile ... 126 A2
Tarapoto, Peru ... 124 E3
Tarare, France ... 21 C8
Tararua Ra., N.Z. ... 91 J5
Tarascon, France ... 21 E8
Tarascon-sur-Ariège, France .. 20 F5
Tarashcha, Ukraine ... 47 H6
Tarauacá, Brazil ... 124 E4
Tarauacá →, Brazil ... 124 E5
Taravo →, France ... 21 G12
Tarawa, Kiribati ... 96 G9
Tarawera, N.Z. ... 91 H6
Tarawera, L., N.Z. ... 91 H6
Taraz, Kazakstan ... 50 E8
Tarazona, Spain ... 32 D3
Tarazona de la Mancha, Spain . 33 F3
Tarbat Ness, U.K. ... 14 D5
Tarbela Dam, Pakistan ... 68 B5
Tarbert, Arg. & Bute, U.K. ... 14 F3
Tarbert, W. Isles, U.K. ... 14 D2
Tarbes, France ... 20 E4
Tarboro, U.S.A. ... 109 H7
Tărcău, Munții, Romania ... 43 C11
Tarcento, Italy ... 29 B10
Tarcoola, Australia ... 95 E1
Tarcoon, Australia ... 95 E4
Tardets-Sorholus, France ... 20 E3
Tardoire →, France ... 20 C4
Tarfa, W. el →, Egypt ... 80 B3
Tarfaya, Morocco ... 78 C3
Târgoviște, Romania ... 43 F10
Târgu Bujor, Romania ... 43 E12
Târgu Cărbunești, Romania ... 43 F8
Târgu Frumos, Romania ... 43 C12
Târgu-Jiu, Romania ... 43 E8
Târgu Lăpuș, Romania ... 43 C8
Târgu Mureș, Romania ... 43 D9
Târgu Neamț, Romania ... 43 C11
Târgu Ocna, Romania ... 43 D11
Târgu Secuiesc, Romania ... 43 E11
Târgușor, Romania ... 43 F13
Tărhăus, Vf., Romania ... 43 D11
Tarif, U.A.E. ... 71 E7
Tarifa, Spain ... 35 J5
Tarija, Bolivia ... 126 A3
Tarija □, Bolivia ... 126 A3
Tariku →, Indonesia ... 63 E9
Tarim Basin = Tarim Pendi, China ... 60 C3
Tarim He →, China ... 60 C3
Tarim Pendi, China ... 60 C3
Taritatu →, Indonesia ... 63 E9
Tarka →, S. Africa ... 88 E4
Tarkastad, S. Africa ... 88 E4
Tarkhankut, Mys, Ukraine ... 47 K7
Tarko Sale, Russia ... 50 C8
Tarkwa, Ghana ... 82 D4
Tarlac, Phil. ... 61 D4
Tarm, Denmark ... 11 J2
Tarma, Peru ... 124 F3
Tarn □, France ... 20 E6
Tarn →, France ... 20 D5
Tarn-et-Garonne □, France ... 20 D5
Tarna →, Hungary ... 42 C4
Târnava Mare →, Romania ... 43 D8
Târnava Mică →, Romania ... 43 D9
Târnăveni, Romania ... 43 D9
Tarnica, Poland ... 45 J9
Tarnobrzeg, Poland ... 45 H8
Tarnogród, Poland ... 45 H9
Tarnos, France ... 20 E2
Tárnova, Moldova ... 43 B12
Târnova, Romania ... 42 E6
Tarnowskie Góry, Poland ... 45 H5
Táro →, Italy ... 28 C7
Țărom, Iran ... 71 D7
Taroom, Australia ... 95 D4
Taroudannt, Morocco ... 78 B4
Tarp, Germany ... 24 A5
Tarpon Springs, U.S.A. ... 109 L4
Tarquínia, Italy ... 29 F8
Tarragona, Spain ... 32 D6
Tarragona □, Spain ... 32 D6
Tarraleah, Australia ... 94 G4
Tarrasa = Terrassa, Spain ... 32 D7
Tàrrega, Spain ... 32 D6
Tarrytown, U.S.A. ... 111 E11
Tårs, Denmark ... 11 G4
Tarshiha = Me'ona, Israel ... 75 B4

Tarso Emissi, Chad ... 79 D9
Tarsus, Turkey ... 70 B2
Tartagal, Argentina ... 126 A3
Tärtär, Azerbaijan ... 49 K8
Tärtär →, Azerbaijan ... 49 K8
Tartas, France ... 20 E3
Tartu, Estonia ... 9 G22
Țarțūs, Syria ... 70 C2
Tarumizu, Japan ... 55 J5
Tarussa, Russia ... 46 E9
Tarutao, Ko, Thailand ... 65 J2
Tarutung, Indonesia ... 62 D1
Tarvísio, Italy ... 29 B10
Taseko →, Canada ... 104 C4
Tash-Kömür, Kyrgyzstan ... 50 E8
Tash-Kumyr = Tash-Kömür, Kyrgyzstan ... 50 E8
Tashauz = Dashhowuz, Turkmenistan ... 50 E6
Tashi Chho Dzong = Thimphu, Bhutan ... 67 F16
Țashk, Daryācheh-ye, Iran ... 71 D7
Tashkent = Toshkent, Uzbekistan ... 50 E7
Tashtagol, Russia ... 50 D9
Tasiilaq, Greenland ... 4 C6
Tasikmalaya, Indonesia ... 63 G13
Tåsinge, Denmark ... 11 J4
Tåsjön, Sweden ... 8 D16
Taskan, Russia ... 51 C16
Tasker, Niger ... 83 C7
Taşköprü, Turkey ... 72 B6
Taşlıc, Moldova ... 43 C14
Tasman B., N.Z. ... 91 J4
Tasman Mts., N.Z. ... 91 J4
Tasman Pen., Australia ... 94 G4
Tasman Sea, Pac. Oc. ... 96 L8
Tasmania □, Australia ... 94 G4
Tăşnad, Romania ... 42 C7
Tassili n'Ajjer, Algeria ... 78 C7
Tassili Tin-Rerhoh, Algeria ... 83 A5
Tata, Hungary ... 42 C3
Tatabánya, Hungary ... 42 C3
Tatahouine, Tunisia ... 79 B8
Tatar Republic = Tatarstan □, Russia ... 48 C10
Tatarbunary, Ukraine ... 47 K5
Tatarsk, Russia ... 50 D8
Tatarstan □, Russia ... 48 C10
Tateyama, Japan ... 55 G9
Tathlina L., Canada ... 104 A5
Tatinnai L., Canada ... 105 A9
Tatla L., Canada ... 104 C4
Tatlısu, Turkey ... 41 F11
Tatnam, C., Canada ... 105 B10
Tatra = Tatry, Slovak Rep. ... 27 B13
Tatry, Slovak Rep. ... 27 B13
Tatshenshini →, Canada ... 104 B1
Tatsuno, Japan ... 55 G7
Tatta, Pakistan ... 68 G2
Tatuī, Brazil ... 127 A6
Tatum, U.S.A. ... 113 J3
Tat'ung = Datong, China ... 56 D7
Tatvan, Turkey ... 70 B4
Taubaté, Brazil ... 127 A6
Tauberbischofsheim, Germany . 25 F5
Taucha, Germany ... 24 D8
Tauern-tunnel, Austria ... 26 D6
Taufikia, Sudan ... 81 F3
Taulé, France ... 18 D3
Taumarunui, N.Z. ... 91 H5
Taumaturgo, Brazil ... 124 E4
Taung, S. Africa ... 88 D3
Taungdwingyi, Burma ... 67 J19
Taunggyi, Burma ... 67 J20
Taungup, Burma ... 67 K19
Taungup Taunggya, Burma ... 67 K18
Taunsa, Pakistan ... 68 D4
Taunsa Barrage, Pakistan ... 68 D4
Taunton, U.K. ... 13 F4
Taunton, U.S.A. ... 111 E13
Taunus, Germany ... 25 E4
Taupo, N.Z. ... 91 H6
Taupo, L., N.Z. ... 91 H5
Tauragé, Lithuania ... 9 J20
Tauragé □, Lithuania ... 44 C9
Tauranga, N.Z. ... 91 G6
Tauranga Harb., N.Z. ... 91 G6
Taureau, Rés., Canada ... 102 C5
Taurianova, Italy ... 31 D9
Taurus Mts. = Toros Dağları, Turkey ... 70 B2
Tauste, Spain ... 32 D3
Tauz = Tovuz, Azerbaijan ... 49 K7
Tavas, Turkey ... 39 D11
Tavda, Russia ... 50 D7
Tavda →, Russia ... 50 D7
Tavernes de la Valldigna, Spain 33 F4
Taveta, Tanzania ... 86 C4
Taveuni, Fiji ... 91 C9
Taviano, Italy ... 31 C11
Tavignano →, France ... 21 F13
Tavira, Portugal ... 35 H3
Tavistock, Canada ... 110 C4
Tavistock, U.K. ... 13 G3
Tavolara, Italy ... 30 B2
Távora →, Portugal ... 34 D3
Tavoy = Dawei, Burma ... 64 E2
Tavşanlı, Turkey ... 39 B11
Taw →, U.K. ... 13 F3
Tawas City, U.S.A. ... 108 C4
Tawau, Malaysia ... 62 D5
Taweisha, Sudan ... 81 E2
Tawitawi, Phil. ... 63 B6
Tawu, Taiwan ... 59 F13

Taxco de Alarcón, Mexico 119 D5
Taxila, Pakistan 68 C5
Tay →, U.K. 14 E5
Tay, Firth of, U.K. 14 E5
Tay, L., Australia 93 F3
Tay, L., U.K. 14 E4
Tay Ninh, Vietnam 65 G6
Tayabamba, Peru 124 E3
Tayabas Bay, Phil. 61 E4
Taylakova, Russia 50 D8
Taylakovy = Taylakova, Russia 50 D8
Taylor, Canada 104 B4
Taylor, Nebr., U.S.A. 112 E5
Taylor, Pa., U.S.A. 111 E9
Taylor, Tex., U.S.A. 113 K6
Taylor, Mt., U.S.A. 115 J10
Taylorville, U.S.A. 112 F10
Taymā, Si. Arabia 70 E3
Taymyr, Oz., Russia 51 B11
Taymyr, Poluostrov, Russia 51 B11
Tayport, U.K. 14 E6
Tayshet, Russia 51 D10
Taytay, Phil. 61 F3
Taz →, Russia 50 C8
Taza, Morocco 78 B5
Tāzah Khurmātū, Iraq 70 C5
Tazawa-Ko, Japan 54 E10
Tazin, Canada 105 B7
Tazin L., Canada 105 B7
Tazovskiy, Russia 50 C8
Tbilisi, Georgia 49 K7
Tchad = Chad ■, Africa 79 F8
Tchad, L., Chad 79 F8
Tchaourou, Benin 83 D5
Tch'eng-tou = Chengdu, China 58 B5
Tchentlo L., Canada 104 B4
Tchetti, Benin 83 D5
Tchibanga, Gabon 84 E2
Tchien, Liberia 82 D3
Tchin Tabaraden, Niger 83 B6
Tch'ong-k'ing = Chongqing, China 58 C6
Tczew, Poland 44 D5
Te Anau, N.Z. 91 L1
Te Anau, L., N.Z. 91 L1
Te Aroha, N.Z. 91 G5
Te Awamutu, N.Z. 91 H5
Te Kuiti, N.Z. 91 H5
Te-n-Dghâmcha, Sebkhet, Mauritania 82 B1
Te Puke, N.Z. 91 G6
Te Waewae B., N.Z. 91 M1
Teaca, Romania 43 D9
Teague, U.S.A. 113 K6
Teano, Italy 31 A7
Teapa, Mexico 119 D6
Teba, Spain 35 J6
Tebakang, Malaysia 62 D4
Teberda, Russia 49 J5
Tébessa, Algeria 78 A7
Tebicuary →, Paraguay 126 B4
Tebingtinggi, Indonesia 62 D1
Tebintingii, Indonesia 62 E2
Tebulos, Georgia 49 J7
Tecate, Mexico 117 N10
Tecer Dağları, Turkey 72 C7
Tech →, France 20 F7
Techiman, Ghana 82 D4
Techirghiol, Romania 43 F13
Tecka, Argentina 128 E2
Tecomán, Mexico 118 D4
Tecopa, U.S.A. 117 K10
Tecoripa, Mexico 118 B3
Tecuala, Mexico 118 C3
Tecuci, Romania 43 E12
Tecumseh, Canada 110 D2
Tecumseh, Mich., U.S.A. 108 D4
Tecumseh, Okla., U.S.A. 113 H6
Tedzhen = Tejen, Turkmenistan 50 F7
Tees →, U.K. 12 C6
Tees B., U.K. 12 C6
Teeswater, Canada 110 C3
Tefé, Brazil 124 D6
Tefenni, Turkey 39 D11
Tegal, Indonesia 62 F3
Tegernsee, Germany 25 H7
Teggiano, Italy 31 B8
Tegid, L. = Bala, L., U.K. 12 E4
Tegina, Nigeria 83 C6
Tegucigalpa, Honduras 120 D2
Teguidda-i-n-Tessoum, Niger 83 B6
Tehachapi, U.S.A. 117 K8
Tehachapi Mts., U.S.A. 117 L8
Tehamiyam, Sudan 80 D4
Tehilla, Sudan 80 D4
Téhini, Ivory C. 82 D4
Tehoru, Indonesia 63 E7
Tehrān, Iran 71 C6
Tehri, India 69 D8
Tehuacán, Mexico 119 D5
Tehuantepec, Mexico 119 D5
Tehuantepec, G. de, Mexico 119 D5
Tehuantepec, Istmo de, Mexico 119 D6
Teide, Canary Is. 37 F3
Teifi →, U.K. 13 E3
Teign →, U.K. 13 G4
Teignmouth, U.K. 13 G4
Teiuş, Romania 43 D8
Teixeira Pinto, Guinea-Biss. 82 C1
Tejam, India 69 E9
Tejen, Turkmenistan 50 F7
Tejen →, Turkmenistan 71 B9
Tejo →, Europe 35 F2
Tejon Pass, U.S.A. 117 L8
Tekamah, U.S.A. 112 E6
Tekapo, L., N.Z. 91 K3

Tekax, Mexico 119 C7
Teke, Turkey 41 E13
Tekeli, Kazakstan 50 E8
Tekeze →, Ethiopia 81 E4
Tekija, Serbia, Yug. 40 B6
Tekirdağ, Turkey 41 F11
Tekirdağ □, Turkey 41 F11
Tekirova, Turkey 39 E12
Tekkali, India 67 K14
Tekke, Turkey 72 B7
Tekman, Turkey 73 C9
Tekoa, U.S.A. 114 C5
Tel Aviv-Yafo, Israel 75 C3
Tel Lakhish, Israel 75 D3
Tel Megiddo, Israel 75 C4
Tela, Honduras 120 C2
Telanaipura = Jambi, Indonesia 62 E2
Telavi, Georgia 49 J7
Telč, Czech Rep. 26 B8
Telciu, Romania 43 C9
Telde, Canary Is. 37 G4
Telegraph Creek, Canada 104 B2
Telekhany = Tsyelyakhany, Belarus 47 F3
Telemark, Norway 9 G12
Telén, Argentina 126 D2
Teleneşti, Moldova 43 C13
Teleng, Iran 71 E9
Teleño, Spain 34 C4
Teleorman □, Romania 43 G10
Teleorman →, Romania 43 G10
Teles Pires →, Brazil 122 D5
Telescope Pk., U.S.A. 117 J9
Teletaye, Mali 83 B5
Telfer Mine, Australia 92 C3
Telford, U.K. 13 E5
Telford and Wrekin □, U.K. 12 E5
Telfs, Austria 26 D4
Télimélé, Guinea 82 C2
Teljo, J., Sudan 81 E2
Telkwa, Canada 104 C3
Tell City, U.S.A. 108 G2
Tellicherry, India 66 P9
Telluride, U.S.A. 115 H10
Teloloapán, Mexico 119 D5
Telpos Iz, Russia 6 C17
Telsen, Argentina 128 E3
Telšiai, Lithuania 9 H20
Telšiai □, Lithuania 44 C9
Teltow, Germany 24 C9
Teluk Anson = Teluk Intan, Malaysia 65 K3
Teluk Betung = Tanjungkarang Telukbetung, Indonesia 62 F3
Teluk Intan, Malaysia 65 K3
Telukbutun, Indonesia 65 K7
Telukdalem, Indonesia 62 D1
Tema, Ghana 83 D5
Temax, Mexico 119 C7
Temba, S. Africa 89 D4
Tembagapura, Indonesia 63 E9
Tembe, Dem. Rep. of the Congo 86 C2
Tembleque, Spain 34 F7
Temblor Range, U.S.A. 117 K7
Teme →, U.K. 13 E5
Temecula, U.S.A. 117 M9
Temerloh, Malaysia 62 D2
Teminabuan, Indonesia 63 E8
Temir, Kazakstan 50 E6
Temirtau, Kazakstan 50 D8
Temirtau, Russia 50 D9
Temiscamie →, Canada 103 B5
Témiscaming, Canada 102 C4
Témiscamingue, L., Canada 102 C4
Temnikov, Russia 48 C6
Temo →, Italy 30 B1
Temora, Australia 95 E4
Temosachic, Mexico 118 B3
Tempe, U.S.A. 115 K8
Tempe B., Australia 94 A3
Templemore, Ireland 15 D4
Templeton, U.S.A. 116 K6
Templeton →, Australia 94 C2
Templin, Germany 24 B9
Tempoal, Mexico 119 C5
Temryuk, Russia 47 K9
Temska →, Serbia, Yug. 40 C6
Temuco, Chile 128 D2
Temuka, N.Z. 91 L3
Tenabo, Mexico 119 C6
Tenaha, U.S.A. 113 K7
Tenakee Springs, U.S.A. 104 B1
Tenali, India 67 L12
Tenancingo, Mexico 119 D5
Tenango, Mexico 119 D5
Tenasserim, Burma 65 F2
Tenasserim □, Burma 64 F2
Tenby, U.K. 13 F3
Tenda, Colle di, France 21 D11
Tendaho, Ethiopia 81 E5
Tendelti, Sudan 21 D11
Tendelti, Sudan 81 E3
Tendrovskaya Kosa, Ukraine 47 J6
Tendukhera, India 69 H8
Teneida, Egypt 80 B2
Tenenkou, Mali 82 C4
Ténéré, Niger 83 B7
Tenerife, Canary Is. 37 F3
Tenerife, Pico, Canary Is. 37 G1
Teng Xian, Guangxi Zhuangzu, China 59 F8
Teng Xian, Shandong, China 57 G9
Tengah □, Indonesia 63 E6
Tengah, Kepulauan, Indonesia 62 F5

Tengchong, China 58 E2
Tengchowfu = Penglai, China 57 F11
Tenggara □, Indonesia 63 E6
Tenggarong, Indonesia 62 E5
Tenggol, Pulau, Malaysia 65 K4
Tengiz, Ozero, Kazakstan 50 D7
Tenhult, Sweden 11 G8
Tenino, U.S.A. 116 D4
Tenkasi, India 66 Q10
Tenke, Katanga, Dem. Rep. of the Congo 87 E2
Tenke, Katanga, Dem. Rep. of the Congo 87 E2
Tenkodogo, Burkina Faso 83 C4
Tenna →, Italy 29 E10
Tennant Creek, Australia 94 B1
Tennessee □, U.S.A. 109 H2
Tennessee →, U.S.A. 108 G1
Teno, Pta. de, Canary Is. 37 F3
Tenom, Malaysia 62 C5
Tenosique, Mexico 119 D6
Tenryū-Gawa →, Japan 55 G8
Tenterden, U.K. 13 F8
Tenterfield, Australia 95 D5
Teo, Spain 34 C2
Teófilo Otoni, Brazil 125 G10
Tepa, Indonesia 63 F7
Tepalcatepec →, Mexico 118 D4
Tepecik, Bursa, Turkey 41 F12
Tepecik, Kütahya, Turkey 39 B11
Tepehuanes, Mexico 118 B3
Tepelenë, Albania 40 F4
Tepetongo, Mexico 118 C4
Tepic, Mexico 118 C4
Teplá, Czech Rep. 26 B5
Teplice, Czech Rep. 26 A6
Tepoca, C., Mexico 118 A2
Tequila, Mexico 118 C4
Ter →, Spain 32 C8
Ter Apel, Neths. 17 B7
Téra, Niger 83 C5
Tera →, Spain 34 D5
Teraina, Kiribati 97 G11
Terakeka, Sudan 81 F3
Téramo, Italy 29 F10
Terang, Australia 95 F3
Terazit, Massif de, Niger 83 A6
Tercan, Turkey 73 C9
Tercero →, Argentina 126 C3
Terebovlya, Ukraine 47 H3
Teregova, Romania 42 E7
Tereida, Sudan 81 E3
Terek →, Russia 49 J8
Tereshka →, Russia 48 E8
Teresina, Brazil 125 E10
Terespol, Poland 45 F10
Terewah, L., Australia 95 D4
Terges →, Portugal 35 H3
Tergnier, France 19 C10
Terlizzi, Italy 31 A9
Terme, Turkey 72 B7
Termez = Termiz, Uzbekistan 50 F7
Términi Imerese, Italy 30 E6
Términos, L. de, Mexico 119 D6
Termiz, Uzbekistan 50 F7
Térmoli, Italy 29 F12
Ternate, Indonesia 63 D7
Terneuzen, Neths. 17 C3
Terney, Russia 51 E14
Terni, Italy 29 F9
Ternitz, Austria 26 D9
Ternopil, Ukraine 47 H3
Ternopol = Ternopil, Ukraine 47 H3
Terpní, Greece 40 F7
Terra Bella, U.S.A. 117 K7
Terra Nova Nat. Park, Canada 103 C9
Terrace, Canada 104 C3
Terrace Bay, Canada 102 C2
Terracina, Italy 30 A6
Terralba, Italy 30 C1
Terranova = Ólbia, Italy 30 B2
Terrasini, Italy 30 D6
Terrassa, Spain 32 D7
Terrasson-la-Villedieu, France 20 C5
Terre Haute, U.S.A. 108 F2
Terrebonne B., U.S.A. 113 L9
Terrell, U.S.A. 113 J6
Terrenceville, Canada 103 C9
Terry, U.S.A. 112 B2
Terryville, U.S.A. 111 E11
Terschelling, Neths. 17 A5
Tersko-Kumskiy Kanal →, Russia 49 H7
Tertenía, Italy 30 C2
Terter → = Tärtär →, Azerbaijan 49 K8
Teruel, Spain 32 E3
Teruel □, Spain 32 E4
Tervel, Bulgaria 41 C11
Tervola, Finland 8 C21
Tešanj, Bos.-H. 42 F3
Teseney, Eritrea 81 D4
Tesha →, Russia 48 C6
Teshio, Japan 54 B10
Teshio-Gawa →, Japan 54 B10
Tešica, Serbia, Yug. 40 C5
Tesiyn Gol →, Mongolia 60 A4
Teslić, Bos.-H. 42 F7
Teslin, Canada 104 A2
Teslin →, Canada 104 A2
Teslin L., Canada 104 A2
Tessalit, Mali 83 A5
Tessaoua, Niger 83 C6
Tessin, Germany 24 A8
Tessit, Mali 83 B5
Test →, U.K. 13 G6
Testa del Gargano, Italy 29 G13

Testigos, Is. Las, Venezuela 121 D7
Tét, Hungary 42 C2
Têt →, France 20 F7
Tetachuck L., Canada 104 C3
Tetas, Pta., Chile 126 A1
Tete, Mozam. 87 F3
Tete □, Mozam. 87 F3
Teterev →, Ukraine 47 G6
Teterow, Germany 24 B8
Teteven, Bulgaria 41 D8
Tethul →, Canada 104 A6
Tetiyev, Ukraine 47 H5
Teton →, U.S.A. 114 C8
Tétouan, Morocco 78 A4
Tetovo, Macedonia 40 D4
Tetyushi, Russia 48 C9
Teuco →, Argentina 126 B3
Teulada, Italy 30 D1
Teulon, Canada 105 C9
Teun, Indonesia 63 F7
Teutoburger Wald, Germany 24 C4
Tevere →, Italy 29 G9
Teverya, Israel 75 C4
Teviot →, U.K. 14 F6
Tewantin, Australia 95 D5
Tewkesbury, U.K. 13 F5
Texada I., Canada 104 D4
Texarkana, Ark., U.S.A. 113 J8
Texarkana, Tex., U.S.A. 113 J7
Texas, Australia 95 D5
Texas □, U.S.A. 113 K5
Texas City, U.S.A. 113 L7
Texel, Neths. 17 A4
Texline, U.S.A. 113 G3
Texoma, L., U.S.A. 113 J6
Teykovo, Russia 46 D11
Teza →, Russia 48 B5
Tezin, Afghan. 68 B3
Teziutlán, Mexico 119 D5
Tezpur, India 67 F18
Tezzeron L., Canada 104 C4
Tha-anne →, Canada 105 A10
Tha Deua, Laos 64 D4
Tha Deua, Laos 64 C3
Tha Pla, Thailand 64 D3
Tha Rua, Thailand 64 E3
Tha Sala, Thailand 65 H2
Tha Song Yang, Thailand 64 D1
Thaba Putsoa, Lesotho 89 D4
Thabana Ntlenyana, Lesotho 89 D4
Thabazimbi, S. Africa 89 C4
Thādiq, Si. Arabia 70 E5
Thai Binh, Vietnam 58 G6
Thai Muang, Thailand 65 H2
Thai Nguyen, Vietnam 58 G5
Thailand ■, Asia 64 E4
Thailand, G. of, Asia 65 G3
Thakhek, Laos 64 D5
Thal, Pakistan 68 C4
Thal Desert, Pakistan 68 D4
Thala La = Hkakabo Razi, Burma 67 E20
Thalabarivat, Cambodia 64 F5
Thallon, Australia 95 D4
Thalwil, Switz. 25 H4
Thames, N.Z. 91 G5
Thames →, Canada 102 D3
Thames →, U.K. 13 F8
Thames →, U.S.A. 111 E12
Thames Estuary, U.K. 13 F8
Thamesford, Canada 110 C4
Thamesville, Canada 110 D3
Than, India 68 H4
Than Uyen, Vietnam 64 B4
Thana Gazi, India 68 F7
Thandla, India 68 H6
Thane, India 66 K8
Thanesar, India 68 D7
Thanet, I. of, U.K. 13 F9
Thangool, Australia 94 C5
Thanh Hoa, Vietnam 64 C5
Thanh Hung, Vietnam 65 H5
Thanh Pho Ho Chi Minh, Vietnam 65 G6
Thanh Thuy, Vietnam 64 A5
Thanjavur, India 66 P11
Thann, France 19 E14
Thano Bula Khan, Pakistan 68 G2
Thaolinta L., Canada 105 A9
Thaon-les-Vosges, France 19 D13
Thap Sakae, Thailand 65 G2
Thap Than, Thailand 64 E2
Thar Desert, India 68 F5
Tharad, India 68 G4
Thargomindah, Australia 95 D3
Tharrawaddy, Burma 67 L19
Tharthār, Mileh, Iraq 70 C4
Tharthār, W. ath →, Iraq 70 C4
Thasopoúla, Greece 41 F8
Thásos, Greece 41 F8
That Khe, Vietnam 58 F6
Thatcher, Ariz., U.S.A. 115 K9
Thatcher, Colo., U.S.A. 113 G2
Thaton, Burma 67 L20
Thau, Bassin de, France 20 E7
Thaungdut, Burma 67 G19
Thayer, U.S.A. 113 G9
Thayetmyo, Burma 67 K19
Thazi, Burma 67 J20
The Alberga →, Australia 95 D2
The Bight, Bahamas 121 B4
The Dalles, U.S.A. 114 D3
The English Company's Is., Australia 94 A2
The Frome →, Australia 95 D2

The Great Divide = Great Dividing Ra., Australia 94 C4
The Hague = 's-Gravenhage, Neths. 17 B4
The Hamilton →, Australia 95 D2
The Macumba →, Australia 95 D2
The Neales →, Australia 95 D2
The Officer →, Australia 93 E5
The Pas, Canada 105 C8
The Range, Zimbabwe 87 F3
The Salt L., Australia 95 E3
The Sandheads, India 69 J13
The Stevenson →, Australia 95 D2
The Warburton →, Australia 95 D2
The Woodlands, U.S.A. 113 K7
Thebes = Thívai, Greece 38 C5
Thebes, Egypt 80 B3
Thedford, Canada 110 C3
Thedford, U.S.A. 112 E4
Theebine, Australia 95 D5
Thekulthili L., Canada 105 A7
Thelon →, Canada 105 A8
Thénezay, France 18 F6
Thenon, France 20 C5
Theodore, Australia 94 C5
Theodore, Canada 105 C8
Theodore, U.S.A. 109 K1
Theodore Roosevelt National Memorial Park, U.S.A. 112 B3
Theodore Roosevelt Res., U.S.A. 115 K8
Thepha, Thailand 65 J3
Thérain →, France 19 C9
Theresa, U.S.A. 111 B9
Thermaïkós Kólpos, Greece 40 F6
Thermí, Greece 39 B8
Thermopolis, U.S.A. 114 E9
Thermopylae P., Greece 38 C4
Thesprotía □, Greece 38 B2
Thessalía □, Greece 38 B4
Thessalon, Canada 102 C3
Thessaloníki, Greece 40 F6
Thessaloníki □, Greece 40 F7
Thessaloniki, Gulf of = Thermaïkós Kólpos, Greece 40 F6
Thessaly = Thessalía □, Greece 38 B4
Thetford, U.K. 13 E8
Thetford Mines, Canada 103 C5
Theun →, Laos 64 C5
Theunissen, S. Africa 88 D4
Thevenard, Australia 95 E1
Thiámis →, Greece 38 B2
Thiberville, France 18 C7
Thibodaux, U.S.A. 113 L9
Thicket Portage, Canada 105 B9
Thief River Falls, U.S.A. 112 A6
Thiel Mts., Antarctica 5 E16
Thiene, Italy 29 C8
Thiérache, France 19 C10
Thiers, France 20 C7
Thiès, Senegal 82 C1
Thiesi, Italy 30 B1
Thiet, Sudan 81 F2
Thika, Kenya 86 C4
Thikombia, Fiji 91 B9
Thille-Boubacar, Senegal 82 B1
Thimphu, Bhutan 67 F16
Þingvallavatn, Iceland 8 D3
Thionville, France 19 C13
Þhíra, Greece 39 E7
Thirasía, Greece 39 E7
Third Cataract, Sudan 80 D3
Thirsk, U.K. 12 C6
Thiruvananthapuram = Trivandrum, India 66 Q10
Thisted, Denmark 11 H2
Thívai, Greece 38 C5
Thiviers, France 20 C4
Thizy, France 19 F11
Þjórsá →, Iceland 8 E3
Thlewiaza →, Man., Canada 105 B8
Thlewiaza →, N.W.T., Canada 105 A10
Thmar Puok, Cambodia 64 F4
Tho Vinh, Vietnam 64 C5
Thoa →, Canada 105 A7
Thoen, Thailand 64 D2
Thoeng, Thailand 64 C3
Thohoyandou, S. Africa 85 J6
Tholdi, Pakistan 69 B7
Thomas, U.S.A. 113 H5
Thomas, L., Australia 95 D2
Thomaston, U.S.A. 109 J3
Thomasville, Ala., U.S.A. 109 K2
Thomasville, Ga., U.S.A. 109 K4
Thomasville, N.C., U.S.A. 109 H5
Thompson, Canada 105 B9
Thompson, U.S.A. 111 E9
Thompson →, Canada 104 C4
Thompson →, U.S.A. 112 F8
Thompson Falls, U.S.A. 114 C6
Thompson Pk., U.S.A. 114 F2
Thompson Springs, U.S.A. 115 G9
Thompsontown, U.S.A. 110 F7
Thomson, U.S.A. 109 J4
Thomson →, Australia 94 C3
Thomson's Falls = Nyahururu, Kenya 86 B4
Thônes, France 21 C10
Thonon-les-Bains, France 19 F13
Þórisvatn, Iceland 8 D4
Thornaby on Tees, U.K. 12 C6
Thornbury, Canada 110 B4
Thorne, U.K. 12 D7
Thornhill, Canada 104 C3
Thorold, Canada 110 C5

Þórshöfn, *Iceland* 8 C6
Thouarcé, *France* 18 E6
Thouars, *France* 18 F6
Thouet ➤, *France* 18 E6
Thouin, C., *Australia* 92 D2
Thousand Oaks, *U.S.A.* 117 L8
Thrace, *Turkey* 41 F10
Thrakikón Pélagos, *Greece* ... 41 F8
Three Forks, *U.S.A.* 114 D8
Three Gorges Dam, *China* ... 59 B8
Three Hills, *Canada* 104 C6
Three Hummock I., *Australia* .. 94 G3
Three Points, C., *Ghana* 82 E4
Three Rivers, *Calif., U.S.A.* .. 116 J8
Three Rivers, *Tex., U.S.A.* ... 113 L5
Three Sisters, *U.S.A.* 114 D3
Three Springs, *Australia* ... 93 E2
Throssell, L., *Australia* 93 E3
Throssell Ra., *Australia* 92 D3
Thuan Hoa, *Vietnam* 65 H5
Thubun Lakes, *Canada* ... 105 A6
Thueyts, *France* 21 D8
Thuin, *Belgium* 17 D4
Thuir, *France* 20 F6
Thule = Qaanaaq, *Greenland* .. 4 B4
Thun, *Switz.* 25 J3
Thunder B., *U.S.A.* 110 B1
Thunder Bay, *Canada* 102 C2
Thunersee, *Switz.* 25 J3
Thung Song, *Thailand* 65 H2
Thunkar, *Bhutan* 67 F17
Thuong Tra, *Vietnam* 64 D6
Thur ➤, *Switz.* 25 H5
Thurgau □, *Switz.* 25 H5
Thüringen □, *Germany* 24 D6
Thüringer Wald, *Germany* 24 E6
Thurles, *Ireland* 15 D4
Thurn P., *Austria* 26 D5
Thurrock □, *U.K.* 13 F8
Thursday I., *Australia* 94 A3
Thurso, *Canada* 102 C4
Thurso, *U.K.* 14 C5
Thurso ➤, *U.K.* 14 C5
Thurston I., *Antarctica* 5 D16
Thury-Harcourt, *France* 18 D6
Thutade L., *Canada* 104 B3
Thy, *Denmark* 11 H2
Thyborøn, *Denmark* 11 H2
Thyolo, *Malawi* 87 F4
Thysville = Mbanza Ngungu,
   Dem. Rep. of the Congo 84 F2
Ti-n-Amzi ➤, *Niger* 83 B5
Ti-n-Barraouene, O. ➤, *Africa* 83 B5
Ti-n-Zaouatene, *Algeria* 83 B5
Ti Tree, *Australia* 94 C1
Tiadiaye, *Senegal* 82 C1
Tian Shan, *Asia* 60 B3
Tianchang, *China* 59 A12
Tiandeng, *China* 58 F6
Tiandong, *China* 58 F6
Tian'e, *China* 58 E6
Tianhe, *China* 58 E7
Tianjin, *China* 57 E9
Tiankoura, *Burkina Faso* 82 C4
Tianlin, *China* 58 E6
Tianmen, *China* 59 B9
Tianquan, *China* 58 B4
Tianshui, *China* 56 G3
Tiantai, *China* 59 C13
Tianyang, *China* 58 F6
Tianzhen, *China* 56 D8
Tianzhu, *China* 58 D7
Tianzhuangtai, *China* 57 D12
Tiaret, *Algeria* 78 A6
Tiassalé, *Ivory C.* 82 D4
Tibagi, *Brazil* 127 A5
Tibagi ➤, *Brazil* 127 A5
Tibati, *Cameroon* 83 D7
Tibe, *Ethiopia* 81 F4
Tiber = Tevere ➤, *Italy* 29 G9
Tiberias = Teverya, *Israel* .. 75 C4
Tiberias, L. = Yam Kinneret,
   Israel 75 C4
Tibesti, *Chad* 79 D9
Tibet = Xizang Zizhiqu □, *China* 60 C3
Tibet, Plateau of, *Asia* 52 F12
Tibiri, *Phil.* 61 F5
Tibiri, *Niger* 83 C6
Țibleș, Vf., *Romania* 43 C9
Țibleșului, Munții, *Romania* .. 43 C9
Tibnī, *Syria* 70 C3
Tibooburra, *Australia* 95 D3
Tibro, *Sweden* 11 F8
Tiburón, I., *Mexico* 118 B2
Ticao I., *Phil.* 61 E5
Tîchît, *Mauritania* 82 B3
Ticho, *Ethiopia* 81 F4
Ticino □, *Switz.* 25 J4
Ticino ➤, *Italy* 25 K5
Ticleni, *Romania* 43 F8
Ticonderoga, *U.S.A.* 111 C11
Ticul, *Mexico* 119 C7
Tidaholm, *Sweden* 11 F7
Tidan, *Sweden* 11 F8
Tiddim, *Burma* 67 H18
Tidioute, *U.S.A.* 110 E5
Tidjikja, *Mauritania* 82 B2
Tidore, *Indonesia* 63 D7
Tiébissou, *Ivory C.* 82 D3
Tiel, *Neths.* 17 C5
Tiel, *Senegal* 82 C1
Tieling, *China* 57 C12
Tielt, *Belgium* 17 C3
Tien Shan = Tian Shan, *Asia* ... 60 B3
Tien-tsin = Tianjin, *China* ... 57 E9
Tien Yen, *Vietnam* 64 B6

T'ienching = Tianjin, *China* ... 57 E9
Tienen, *Belgium* 17 D4
Tiénigbé, *Ivory C.* 82 D3
Tientsin = Tianjin, *China* ... 57 E9
Tieri, *Australia* 94 C4
Tierp, *Sweden* 10 D11
Tierra Amarilla, *Chile* 126 B1
Tierra Amarilla, *U.S.A.* 115 H10
Tierra Colorada, *Mexico* 119 D5
Tierra de Barros, *Spain* 35 G4
Tierra de Campos, *Spain* 34 C6
Tierra del Fuego, I. Gr. de,
   Argentina 122 J4
Tiétar ➤, *Spain* 34 F4
Tietê ➤, *Brazil* 127 A5
Tiffin, *U.S.A.* 108 E4
Tiflis = Tbilisi, *Georgia* 49 K7
Tifton, *U.S.A.* 109 K4
Tifu, *Indonesia* 63 E7
Tighina, *Moldova* 43 D14
Tigil, *Russia* 51 D16
Tignish, *Canada* 103 C7
Tigray □, *Ethiopia* 81 E4
Tigre ➤, *Peru* 124 D4
Tigre ➤, *Venezuela* 124 B6
Tigris = Dijlah, Nahr ➤, *Asia* .. 70 D5
Tigveni, *Romania* 43 E9
Tigyaing, *Burma* 67 H20
Tîh, Gebel el, *Egypt* 80 B3
Tijara, *India* 68 F7
Tijuana, *Mexico* 117 N9
Tikal, *Guatemala* 120 C2
Tikamgarh, *India* 69 G8
Tikaré, *Burkina Faso* 83 C4
Tikhoretsk, *Russia* 49 H5
Tikhvin, *Russia* 46 C7
Tiko, *Cameroon* 83 E6
Tikrīt, *Iraq* 70 C4
Tiksi, *Russia* 51 B13
Tilamuta, *Indonesia* 63 D6
Tilburg, *Neths.* 17 C5
Tilbury, *Canada* 102 D3
Tilbury, *U.K.* 13 F8
Tilcara, *Argentina* 126 A2
Tilden, *U.S.A.* 112 D6
Tilemses, *Niger* 83 B5
Tilemsi, Vallée du, *Mali* 83 B5
Tilhar, *India* 69 F8
Tilichiki, *Russia* 51 C17
Tílissos, *Greece* 36 D7
Till ➤, *U.K.* 12 B5
Tillabéri, *Niger* 83 C5
Tillamook, *U.S.A.* 114 D2
Tillberga, *Sweden* 10 E10
Tillia, *Niger* 83 B5
Tillsonburg, *Canada* 102 D3
Tillyeria □, *Cyprus* 36 D11
Tilogne, *Senegal* 82 B2
Tílos, *Greece* 39 E9
Tilsit = Sovetsk, *Russia* 9 J19
Tilt ➤, *U.K.* 14 E5
Tilton, *U.S.A.* 111 C13
Tiltonsville, *U.S.A.* 110 F4
Tim, *Denmark* 11 H2
Timagami, L., *Canada* 102 C3
Timaru, *N.Z.* 91 L3
Timashevo, *Russia* 48 D10
Timashevsk, *Russia* 49 H4
Timau, *Kenya* 86 B4
Timbákion, *Greece* 36 D6
Timbedgha, *Mauritania* 82 B3
Timber Creek, *Australia* 92 C5
Timber Lake, *U.S.A.* 112 C4
Timber Mt., *U.S.A.* 116 H10
Timbo, *Guinea* 82 C2
Timbo, *Liberia* 82 D3
Timbuktu = Tombouctou, *Mali* 82 B4
Timeiaouine, *Algeria* 83 A5
Timétrine, Mts., *Mali* 83 B4
Timfi Óros, *Greece* 38 B2
Timfristós, Óros, *Greece* 38 C3
Timi, *Cyprus* 36 E11
Tîmia, *Niger* 83 B6
Timimoun, *Algeria* 78 C6
Timimrist, Râs, *Mauritania* .. 82 B1
Timiș □, *Romania* 42 E6
Timiș ➤, *Serbia, Yug.* 42 F5
Timișoara, *Romania* 42 E6
Timmersdala, *Sweden* 11 F7
Timmins, *Canada* 102 C3
Timok ➤, *Serbia, Yug.* 40 B6
Timor, *Indonesia* 63 F7
Timor Sea, *Ind. Oc.* 92 B4
Timor Timur = East Timor ■,
   Asia 63 F7
Timrå, *Sweden* 10 B11
Tin Can Bay, *Australia* 95 D5
Tin Ethisane, *Mali* 83 B4
Tin Gornai, *Mali* 83 B4
Tin Mt., *U.S.A.* 116 J9
Tina ➤, *S. Africa* 89 E4
Tîna, Khalîg el, *Egypt* 80 A3
Tinaca Pt., *Phil.* 61 J6
Tinajo, *Canary Is.* 37 E6
Tinca, *Romania* 42 D6
Tindal, *Australia* 92 B5
Tindouf, *Algeria* 78 C4
Tinée ➤, *France* 21 E11
Tineo, *Spain* 34 B4
Ting Jiang ➤, *China* 59 E11
Tingela, *Ivory C.* 82 C3
Tinggi, Pulau, *Malaysia* 65 L5
Tinglev, *Denmark* 11 K3
Tingo Maria, *Peru* 124 E3
Tingsryd, *Sweden* 11 H9
Tingstäde, *Sweden* 11 G12

Tinh Bien, *Vietnam* 65 G5
Tinnevelly = Tirunelveli, *India* . 66 Q10
Tinogasta, *Argentina* 126 B2
Tínos, *Greece* 39 D7
Tiñoso, C., *Spain* 33 H3
Tinpahar, *India* 69 G12
Tintina, *Argentina* 126 B3
Tintioulé, *Guinea* 82 C3
Tinto ➤, *Spain* 35 H4
Tioga, *N. Dak., U.S.A.* 112 A3
Tioga, *Pa., U.S.A.* 110 E7
Tioman, Pulau, *Malaysia* 65 L5
Tione di Trento, *Italy* 28 B7
Tionesta, *U.S.A.* 110 E5
Tior, *Sudan* 81 F3
Tipongpani, *India* 67 F19
Tipperary, *Ireland* 15 D3
Tipperary □, *Ireland* 15 D4
Tipton, *Calif., U.S.A.* 116 J7
Tipton, *Iowa, U.S.A.* 112 E9
Tipton Mt., *U.S.A.* 117 K12
Tiptonville, *U.S.A.* 113 G10
Tīrān, *Iran* 71 C6
Tīrān, *Si. Arabia* 80 B3
Tiranë, *Albania* 40 E3
Tirano, *Italy* 28 B7
Tiraspol, *Moldova* 43 D14
Tirdout, *Mali* 83 B4
Tire, *Turkey* 39 C9
Tirebolu, *Turkey* 73 B8
Tiree, *U.K.* 14 E2
Tiree, Passage of, *U.K.* 14 E2
Tîrgoviște = Târgoviște,
   Romania 43 F10
Tîrgu-Jiu = Târgu-Jiu, *Romania* 43 E8
Tîrgu Mureș = Târgu Mureș,
   Romania 43 D9
Tirich Mir, *Pakistan* 66 A7
Tiriolo, *Italy* 31 D9
Tiriro, *Guinea* 82 C3
Tírnavos, *Greece* 38 B4
Tirodi, *India* 66 J11
Tirol □, *Austria* 26 D3
Tirschenreuth, *Germany* 25 F8
Tirso ➤, *Italy* 30 C1
Tirstrup, *Denmark* 11 H4
Tiruchchirappalli, *India* 66 P11
Tirunelveli, *India* 66 Q10
Tirupati, *India* 66 N11
Tiruppur, *India* 66 P10
Tiruvannamalai, *India* 66 N11
Tisa, *India* 68 C7
Tisa ➤, *Serbia, Yug.* 42 E5
Tisdale, *Canada* 105 C8
Tishomingo, *U.S.A.* 113 H6
Tisjön, *Sweden* 10 D7
Tisnaren, *Sweden* 11 F9
Tišnov, *Czech Rep.* 27 B9
Tisovec, *Slovak Rep.* 27 C12
Tisza = Tisa ➤, *Serbia, Yug.* .. 42 E5
Tiszaföldvár, *Hungary* 42 D5
Tiszafüred, *Hungary* 42 C5
Tiszalök, *Hungary* 42 B6
Tiszavasvári, *Hungary* 42 C6
Tit-Ary, *Russia* 51 B13
Titao, *Burkina Faso* 83 C4
Titel, *Serbia, Yug.* 42 E5
Tithwal, *Pakistan* 69 B5
Titicaca, L., *S. Amer.* 122 E4
Titisee, *Germany* 25 H4
Titiwa, *Nigeria* 83 C7
Tito, *Italy* 31 B8
Titograd = Podgorica,
   Montenegro, Yug. 40 D3
Titova Korenica, *Croatia* 29 D12
Titu, *Romania* 43 F10
Titule, *Dem. Rep. of the Congo* 86 B2
Titusville, *Fla., U.S.A.* 109 L5
Titusville, *Pa., U.S.A.* 110 E5
Tivaouane, *Senegal* 82 C1
Tiverton, *U.K.* 13 G4
Tivat, *Montenegro, Yug.* 40 D2
Tívoli, *Italy* 29 G9
Tiyo, *Eritrea* 81 E5
Tizi-Ouzou, *Algeria* 78 A6
Tizimín, *Mexico* 119 C7
Tjæreborg, *Denmark* 11 J2
Tjällmo, *Sweden* 11 F9
Tjeggelvas, *Sweden* 8 C17
Tjirebon = Cirebon, *Indonesia* . 62 F3
Tjörn, *Sweden* 11 F5
Tkibuli = Tqibuli, *Georgia* 49 J6
Tkvarcheli = Tqvarcheli,
   Georgia 49 J5
Tlacotalpan, *Mexico* 119 D5
Tlahualilo, *Mexico* 118 B4
Tlaquepaque, *Mexico* 118 C4
Tlaxcala, *Mexico* 119 D5
Tlaxcala □, *Mexico* 119 D5
Tlaxiaco, *Mexico* 119 D5
Tlemcen, *Algeria* 78 B5
Tłuszcz, *Poland* 45 F8
Tlyarata, *Russia* 49 J8
To Bong, *Vietnam* 64 F7
Toad ➤, *Canada* 104 B4
Toad River, *Canada* 104 B3
Toamasina, *Madag.* 89 B8
Toamasina □, *Madag.* 89 B8
Toay, *Argentina* 126 D3
Toba, *China* 58 B1
Toba, *Japan* 55 G8
Toba, Danau, *Indonesia* 62 D1
Toba Kakar, *Pakistan* 68 D3
Toba Tek Singh, *Pakistan* 68 D5
Tobago, *Trin. & Tob.* 121 D7

Tobarra, *Spain* 33 G3
Tobelo, *Indonesia* 63 D7
Tobermory, *Canada* 102 C3
Tobermory, *U.K.* 14 E2
Tobi, *Pac. Oc.* 63 D8
Tobin, *U.S.A.* 116 F5
Tobin, L., *Australia* 92 D4
Tobin L., *Canada* 105 C8
Toboali, *Indonesia* 62 E3
Tobol ➤, *Russia* 50 D7
Toboli, *Indonesia* 63 E6
Tobolsk, *Russia* 50 D7
Tobor, *Senegal* 82 C1
Tobruk = Tubruq, *Libya* 79 B10
Tobyhanna, *U.S.A.* 111 E9
Tobyl = Tobol ➤, *Russia* 50 D7
Tocantinópolis, *Brazil* 125 E9
Tocantins □, *Brazil* 125 F9
Tocantins ➤, *Brazil* 122 D6
Toccoa, *U.S.A.* 109 H4
Toce ➤, *Italy* 28 C5
Tochi ➤, *Pakistan* 68 C4
Tochigi, *Japan* 55 F9
Tochigi □, *Japan* 55 F9
Tocina, *Spain* 35 H5
Toconao, *Chile* 126 A2
Tocopilla, *Chile* 126 A1
Tocuyo ➤, *Venezuela* 124 A5
Todd ➤, *Australia* 94 C2
Todeli, *Indonesia* 63 E6
Todenyang, *Kenya* 86 B4
Todgarh, *India* 68 G5
Todi, *Italy* 29 F9
Todos os Santos, B. de, *Brazil* . 125 F11
Todos Santos, *Mexico* 118 C2
Todtnau, *Germany* 25 H3
Toe Hd., *U.K.* 14 D1
Toecé, *Burkina Faso* 83 C4
Tofield, *Canada* 104 C6
Tofino, *Canada* 104 D3
Tofua, *Tonga* 91 D11
Tōgane, *Japan* 55 G10
Togba, *Mauritania* 82 B2
Togian, Kepulauan, *Indonesia* . 63 E6
Togliatti, *Russia* 48 D9
Togo ■, *W. Afr.* 83 D5
Togtoh, *China* 56 D6
Tohma ➤, *Turkey* 72 C7
Tōhoku □, *Japan* 54 E10
Tōhōm, *Mongolia* 56 B5
Toinya, *Sudan* 81 F2
Toiyabe Range, *U.S.A.* 114 G5
Tojikiston = Tajikistan ■, *Asia* . 50 F8
Tojo, *Indonesia* 63 E6
Tōjō, *Japan* 55 G6
Tok, *U.S.A.* 100 B5
Tok-do, *Japan* 55 F5
Tokachi-Dake, *Japan* 54 C11
Tokachi-Gawa ➤, *Japan* 54 C11
Tokaj, *Hungary* 42 B6
Tokala, *Indonesia* 63 E6
Tōkamachi, *Japan* 55 F9
Tokanui, *N.Z.* 91 M2
Tokar, *Sudan* 80 D4
Tokara-Rettō, *Japan* 55 K4
Tokarahi, *N.Z.* 91 L3
Tokashiki-Shima, *Japan* 55 L3
Tokat, *Turkey* 72 B7
Tŏkch'ŏn, *N. Korea* 57 E14
Tokeland, *U.S.A.* 116 D3
Tokelau Is., *Pac. Oc.* 96 H10
Tokmak, *Kyrgyzstan* 50 E8
Tokmak, *Ukraine* 47 J8
Toko Ra., *Australia* 94 C2
Tokoro-Gawa ➤, *Japan* 54 B12
Tokuno-Shima, *Japan* 55 L4
Tokushima, *Japan* 55 G7
Tokushima □, *Japan* 55 H7
Tokuyama, *Japan* 55 G5
Tōkyō, *Japan* 55 G9
Tolaga Bay, *N.Z.* 91 H7
Tolbukhin = Dobrich, *Bulgaria* . 41 C11
Toledo, *Brazil* 127 A5
Toledo, *Spain* 34 F6
Toledo, *Ohio, U.S.A.* 108 E4
Toledo, *Oreg., U.S.A.* 114 D2
Toledo, *Wash., U.S.A.* 114 C2
Toledo, Montes de, *Spain* 35 F6
Toledo Bend Reservoir, *U.S.A.* . 113 K8
Tolentino, *Italy* 29 E10
Tolga, *Australia* 94 B4
Toliara, *Madag.* 89 C7
Toliara □, *Madag.* 89 C8
Tolima, *Colombia* 124 C3
Tolitoli, *Indonesia* 63 D6
Tolkmicko, *Poland* 44 D6
Tollarp, *Sweden* 11 J7
Tollhouse, *U.S.A.* 116 H7
Tollensesee, *Germany* 24 B9
Tolmachevo, *Russia* 46 C5
Tolmezzo, *Italy* 29 B10
Tolmin, *Slovenia* 29 B10
Tolna, *Hungary* 42 D3
Tolna □, *Hungary* 42 D3
Tolo, Teluk, *Indonesia* 63 E6
Tolochin = Talachyn, *Belarus* .. 46 E5
Tolosa, *Spain* 32 B2
Tolox, *Spain* 35 J6
Toluca, *Mexico* 119 D5
Tom Burke, *S. Africa* 89 C4
Tom Price, *Australia* 92 D2
Toma, *Burkina Faso* 82 C4
Tomah, *U.S.A.* 112 D9

Tomahawk, *U.S.A.* 112 C10
Tomai, *Moldova* 43 D13
Tomakomai, *Japan* 54 C10
Tomales, *U.S.A.* 116 G4
Tomales B., *U.S.A.* 116 G3
Tomar, *Portugal* 35 F2
Tómaros, Óros, *Greece* 38 B2
Tomarza, *Turkey* 72 C6
Tomaszów Lubelski, *Poland* ... 45 H10
Tomaszów Mazowiecki, *Poland* 45 G7
Tomatlán, *Mexico* 118 D3
Tombador, Serra do, *Brazil* ... 124 F7
Tombe, *Sudan* 81 F3
Tombigbee ➤, *U.S.A.* 109 K2
Tombouctou, *Mali* 82 B4
Tombstone, *U.S.A.* 115 L8
Tombua, *Angola* 88 B1
Tomé, *Chile* 126 D1
Tomelilla, *Sweden* 11 J7
Tomelloso, *Spain* 35 F7
Tomini, *Indonesia* 63 D6
Tomini, Teluk, *Indonesia* 63 E6
Tominian, *Mali* 82 C4
Tomiño, *Spain* 34 D2
Tomintoul, *U.K.* 14 D5
Tomislavgrad, *Bos.-H.* 42 G2
Tomkinson Ranges, *Australia* .. 93 E4
Tommot, *Russia* 51 D13
Tomnop Ta Suos, *Cambodia* .. 65 G5
Tomo ➤, *Colombia* 124 B5
Toms Place, *U.S.A.* 116 H8
Toms River, *U.S.A.* 111 G10
Tomsk, *Russia* 50 D9
Tomtabacken, *Sweden* 11 G8
Tona, *Spain* 32 D7
Tonalá, *Mexico* 119 D6
Tonale, Passo del, *Italy* 28 B7
Tonantins, *Brazil* 124 D5
Tonasket, *U.S.A.* 114 B4
Tonawanda, *U.S.A.* 110 D6
Tonbridge, *U.K.* 13 F8
Tondano, *Indonesia* 63 D6
Tondela, *Portugal* 34 E2
Tønder, *Denmark* 11 K2
Tondi Kiwindi, *Niger* 83 C5
Tondibi, *Mali* 83 B4
Tondoro, *Namibia* 88 B2
Tone ➤, *Australia* 93 F2
Tone-Gawa ➤, *Japan* 55 F9
Tonekābon, *Iran* 71 B6
Tong Xian, *China* 56 E9
Tôngå, *Sudan* 81 F3
Tonga ■, *Pac. Oc.* 91 D11
Tonga Trench, *Pac. Oc.* 96 J10
Tongaat, *S. Africa* 89 D5
Tong'an, *China* 59 E12
Tongareva, *Cook Is.* 97 H12
Tongatapu Group, *Tonga* 91 E12
Tongbai, *China* 59 A9
Tongcheng, *Anhui, China* 59 B11
Tongcheng, *Hubei, China* 59 C9
Tongchŏn-ni, *N. Korea* 57 E14
Tongchuan, *China* 56 G5
Tongdao, *China* 58 D7
Tongeren, *Belgium* 17 D5
Tonggu, *China* 59 C10
Tongguan, *China* 56 G6
Tonghai, *China* 58 E4
Tonghua, *China* 57 D13
Tongjosŏn Man, *N. Korea* 57 E15
Tongking, G. of = Tonkin, G. of,
   Asia 60 E5
Tongliang, *China* 58 C6
Tongliao, *China* 57 C12
Tongling, *China* 59 B11
Tongliu, *China* 59 C12
Tongnae, *S. Korea* 57 G15
Tongnan, *China* 58 B5
Tongobory, *Madag.* 89 C7
Tongoy, *Chile* 126 C1
Tongres = Tongeren, *Belgium* .. 17 D5
Tongsa Dzong, *Bhutan* 67 F17
Tongue, *U.K.* 14 C4
Tongue ➤, *U.S.A.* 112 B2
Tongwei, *China* 56 G3
Tongxiang, *China* 59 B13
Tongxin, *China* 56 F3
Tongyang, *N. Korea* 57 E14
Tongyu, *China* 57 B12
Tongzi, *China* 58 C6
Tonj, *Sudan* 81 F2
Tonj ➤, *Sudan* 81 F2
Tonk, *India* 68 F6
Tonkawa, *U.S.A.* 113 G6
Tonkin = Bac Phan, *Vietnam* .. 64 B5
Tonkin, G. of, *Asia* 60 E5
Tonle Sap, *Cambodia* 64 F4
Tonnay-Charente, *France* 20 C3
Tonneins, *France* 20 D4
Tonnerre, *France* 19 E10
Tönning, *Germany* 24 A4
Tono, *Japan* 54 E10
Tonopah, *U.S.A.* 115 G5
Tonosí, *Panama* 120 E3
Tons ➤, *Haryana, India* 69 F10
Tons ➤, *Ut. P., India* 69 F10
Tønsberg, *Norway* 9 G14
Tonya, *Turkey* 73 B8
Toobanna, *Australia* 94 B4
Toodyay, *Australia* 93 F2
Tooele, *U.S.A.* 114 F7
Toompine, *Australia* 95 D3
Toora-Khem, *Russia* 51 D10

Tsiteli-Tsqaro

Toowoomba, Australia 95 D5
Top Springs, Australia 92 C5
Topalu, Romania 43 F13
Topaz, U.S.A. 116 G7
Topeka, U.S.A. 112 F7
Topl'a →, Slovak Rep. 27 C14
Topley, Canada 104 C3
Toplica →, Serbia, Yug. 40 C5
Toplița, Romania 43 D10
Topocalma, Pta., Chile 126 C1
Topock, U.S.A. 117 L12
Topola, Serbia, Yug. 40 B4
Topolčani, Macedonia 40 E5
Topol'čany, Slovak Rep. 27 C11
Topolnitsa →, Bulgaria 41 D8
Topolobampo, Mexico 118 B3
Topoloveni, Romania 43 F10
Topolovgrad, Bulgaria 41 D10
Topolvățu Mare, Romania 42 E6
Toppenish, U.S.A. 114 C3
Topraisar, Romania 43 F13
Topusko, Croatia 29 C12
Torà, Spain 32 D6
Tora Kit, Sudan 81 E3
Toraka Vestale, Madag. 89 B7
Torata, Peru 124 G4
Torbalı, Turkey 39 C9
Torbat-e Heydārīyeh, Iran 71 C8
Torbat-e Jām, Iran 71 C9
Torbay, Canada 103 C9
Torbay □, U.K. 13 G4
Torbjörntorp, Sweden 11 F7
Tordesillas, Spain 34 D6
Töreboda, Sweden 11 F8
Torekov, Sweden 11 H6
Torellò, Spain 32 C7
Toreno, Spain 34 C4
Torfaen □, U.K. 13 F4
Torgau, Germany 24 D8
Torgelow, Germany 24 B10
Torhamn, Sweden 11 H9
Torhout, Belgium 17 C3
Tori, Ethiopia 81 F3
Tori-Shima, Japan 55 J10
Torigni-sur-Vire, France 18 C6
Torija, Spain 32 E1
Torin, Mexico 118 B2
Torino, Italy 28 C4
Torit, Sudan 81 G3
Torkamān, Iran 70 B5
Torkovichi, Russia 46 C6
Tormac, Romania 42 E6
Tormes →, Spain 34 D4
Tornado Mt., Canada 104 D6
Tornal'a, Slovak Rep. 27 C13
Torne älv →, Sweden 8 D21
Torneå = Tornio, Finland 8 D21
Torneträsk, Sweden 8 B18
Tornio, Finland 8 D21
Tornionjoki →, Finland 8 D21
Tornquist, Argentina 126 D3
Toro, Baleares, Spain 37 B11
Toro, Zamora, Spain 34 D5
Torö, Sweden 11 F11
Toro, Cerro del, Chile 126 B2
Toro Pk., U.S.A. 117 M10
Törökszentmiklós, Hungary 42 C5
Toroníos Kólpos, Greece 40 F7
Toronto, Canada 102 D4
Toronto, U.S.A. 110 F4
Toropets, Russia 46 D6
Tororo, Uganda 86 B3
Toros Dağları, Turkey 70 B2
Torpa, India 69 H11
Torquay, U.K. 13 G4
Torquemada, Spain 34 C6
Torrance, U.S.A. 117 M8
Torrão, Portugal 35 G2
Torre Annunziata, Italy 31 B7
Torre de Moncorvo, Portugal 34 D3
Torre del Campo, Spain 35 H7
Torre del Greco, Italy 31 B7
Torre del Mar, Spain 35 J6
Torre-Pacheco, Spain 33 H4
Torre Péllice, Italy 28 D4
Torreblanca, Spain 32 E5
Torrecampo, Spain 35 G6
Torrecilla en Cameros, Spain 32 C2
Torredembarra, Spain 32 D6
Torredonjimeno, Spain 35 H7
Torrejón de Ardoz, Spain 34 E7
Torrejoncillo, Spain 34 F4
Torrelaguna, Spain 34 E7
Torrelavega, Spain 34 B6
Torremaggiore, Italy 29 G12
Torremolinos, Spain 35 J6
Torrens Cr. →, Australia 94 C4
Torrens Creek, Australia 94 C4
Torrent, Spain 33 F4
Torrenueva, Spain 35 G7
Torreón, Mexico 118 B4
Torreperogil, Spain 35 G7
Torres, Brazil 127 B5
Torres, Mexico 118 B2
Torres Novas, Portugal 35 F2
Torres Strait, Australia 96 H6
Torres Vedras, Portugal 35 F1
Torrevieja, Spain 33 H4
Torrey, U.S.A. 115 G8
Torridge →, U.K. 13 G3
Torridon, L., U.K. 14 D3
Torrijos, Spain 34 F6
Tørring, Denmark 11 J3
Torrington, Conn., U.S.A. 111 E11
Torrington, Wyo., U.S.A. 112 D2
Torroella de Montgrì, Spain 32 C8
Torrox, Spain 35 J7
Torsås, Sweden 11 H9
Torsby, Sweden 10 D6
Torshälla, Sweden 10 E10
Tórshavn, Færoe Is. 8 E9
Torslanda, Sweden 11 G5
Torsö, Sweden 11 F7
Tortola, Br. Virgin Is. 121 C7
Tórtoles de Esgueva, Spain 34 D6
Tortolì, Italy 30 C2
Tortona, Italy 28 D5
Tortorici, Italy 31 D7
Tortosa, Spain 32 E5
Tortosa, C., Spain 32 E5
Tortosendo, Portugal 34 E3
Tortue, I. de la, Haiti 121 B5
Tortum, Turkey 73 B9
Ţorūd, Iran 71 C7
Torul, Turkey 73 B8
Toruń, Poland 45 E5
Tory I., Ireland 15 A3
Torysa →, Slovak Rep. 27 C14
Torzhok, Russia 46 D8
Torzym, Poland 45 F2
Tosa, Japan 55 H6
Tosa-Shimizu, Japan 55 H6
Tosa-Wan, Japan 55 H6
Toscana □, Italy 28 E8
Toscano, Arcipelago, Italy 28 F7
Toshkent, Uzbekistan 50 E7
Tosno, Russia 46 C6
Tossa de Mar, Spain 32 D7
Tösse, Sweden 11 F6
Tostado, Argentina 126 B3
Tostedt, Germany 24 B5
Tostón, Pta. de, Canary Is. 37 F5
Tosu, Japan 55 H5
Tosya, Turkey 72 B6
Toszek, Poland 45 H5
Totana, Spain 33 H3
Totebo, Sweden 11 G10
Toteng, Botswana 88 C3
Tôtes, France 18 C8
Tótkomlós, Hungary 42 D5
Totma, Russia 50 C5
Totnes, U.K. 13 G4
Totness, Surinam 125 B7
Toto, Nigeria 83 D6
Totonicapán, Guatemala 120 D1
Totten Glacier, Antarctica 5 C8
Tottenham, Canada 110 B5
Tottori, Japan 55 G7
Tottori □, Japan 55 G7
Touaret, Niger 83 A6
Touba, Ivory C. 82 D3
Touba, Senegal 82 C1
Toubkal, Djebel, Morocco 78 B4
Toucy, France 19 E10
Tougan, Burkina Faso 82 C4
Touggourt, Algeria 78 B7
Tougouri, Burkina Faso 83 C4
Tougué, Guinea 82 C2
Toukoto, Mali 82 C3
Toul, France 19 D12
Toulepleu, Ivory C. 82 D3
Toulon, France 21 E9
Toulouse, France 20 E5
Toummo, Niger 79 D8
Toumodi, Ivory C. 82 D3
Tounan, Taiwan 59 F13
Toungo, Nigeria 83 D7
Toungoo, Burma 67 K20
Touques →, France 18 C7
Touraine, France 18 E7
Tourane = Da Nang, Vietnam 64 D7
Tourcoing, France 19 B10
Touriñán, C., Spain 34 B1
Tournai, Belgium 17 D3
Tournan-en-Brie, France 19 D9
Tournay, France 20 E4
Tournon-St-Martin, France 18 F7
Tournon-sur-Rhône, France 21 C8
Tournus, France 19 F11
Tours, France 18 E7
Toussora, Mt., C.A.R. 84 C4
Touws →, S. Africa 88 E3
Touwsrivier, S. Africa 88 E3
Tovarkovskiy, Russia 46 F10
Tovuz, Azerbaijan 49 K7
Towada, Japan 54 D10
Towada-Ko, Japan 54 D10
Towanda, U.S.A. 111 E8
Towang, India 67 F17
Tower, U.S.A. 112 B8
Towerhill Cr. →, Australia 94 C3
Towner, U.S.A. 112 A4
Townsend, U.S.A. 114 C8
Townshend I., Australia 94 C5
Townsville, Australia 94 B4
Towson, U.S.A. 108 F7
Towuti, Danau, Indonesia 63 E6
Toya-Ko, Japan 54 C10
Toyama, Japan 55 F8
Toyama □, Japan 55 F8
Toyama-Wan, Japan 55 F8
Toyohashi, Japan 55 G8
Toyokawa, Japan 55 G8
Toyonaka, Japan 55 G7
Toyooka, Japan 55 G7
Toyota, Japan 55 G8
Tozeur, Tunisia 78 B7
Tqibuli, Georgia 49 J6
Tqvarcheli, Georgia 49 J5
Trá Li = Tralee, Ireland 15 D2
Tra On, Vietnam 65 H5
Trabancos →, Spain 34 D5
Traben-Trarbach, Germany 25 F3
Trabzon, Turkey 73 B8
Tracadie, Canada 103 C7
Tracy, Calif., U.S.A. 116 H5
Tracy, Minn., U.S.A. 112 C7
Tradate, Italy 28 C5
Trade Town, Liberia 82 D3
Trafalgar, C., Spain 35 J4
Traian, Brăila, Romania 43 E12
Traian, Tulcea, Romania 43 E13
Trail, Canada 104 D5
Trainor L., Canada 104 A4
Trákhonas, Cyprus 36 D12
Tralee, Ireland 15 D2
Tralee B., Ireland 15 D2
Tramore, Ireland 15 D4
Tramore B., Ireland 15 D4
Tran Ninh, Cao Nguyen, Laos 64 C4
Tranås, Sweden 11 F8
Tranbjerg, Denmark 11 H4
Trancas, Argentina 126 B2
Trancoso, Portugal 34 E3
Tranebjerg, Denmark 11 J4
Tranemo, Sweden 11 G7
Trang, Thailand 65 J2
Trangahy, Madag. 89 B7
Trangan, Indonesia 63 F8
Trångsviken, Sweden 10 A7
Trani, Italy 31 A9
Tranoroa, Madag. 89 C8
Tranqueras, Uruguay 127 C4
Transantarctic Mts., Antarctica 5 E12
Transilvania, Romania 43 D9
Transilvanian Alps = Carpații Meridionali, Romania 43 E9
Transtrand, Sweden 10 C7
Transtrandsfjällen, Sweden 10 C6
Transvaal, S. Africa 85 K5
Transylvania = Transilvania, Romania 43 D9
Trápani, Italy 30 D5
Trapper Pk., U.S.A. 114 D6
Trarza, Mauritania 82 B2
Trasacco, Italy 29 G10
Trăscău, Munții, Romania 43 D8
Trasimeno, L., Italy 29 E9
Träslövsläge, Sweden 11 G6
Trasvase Tajo-Segura, Canal de, Spain 32 E2
Trat, Thailand 65 F4
Tratani →, Pakistan 68 E3
Traun, Austria 26 C7
Traunreut, Germany 25 H8
Traunsee, Austria 26 D6
Traunstein, Germany 25 H8
Travemünde, Germany 24 B6
Travers, Mt., N.Z. 91 K4
Traverse City, U.S.A. 108 C3
Travis, L., U.S.A. 113 K5
Travnik, Bos.-H. 42 F2
Trbovlje, Slovenia 29 B12
Trébbia →, Italy 28 C6
Trebel →, Germany 24 B9
Trébeurden, France 18 D3
Třebíč, Czech Rep. 26 B8
Trebinje, Bos.-H. 40 D2
Trebisacce, Italy 31 C9
Trebišnjica →, Bos.-H. 40 D2
Trebišov, Slovak Rep. 27 C14
Trebižat →, Bos.-H. 29 E14
Trebnje, Slovenia 29 C12
Třeboň, Czech Rep. 26 B7
Trebonne, Australia 94 B4
Trebujena, Spain 35 J4
Trecate, Italy 28 C5
Tregaron, U.K. 13 E4
Tregnago, Italy 29 C8
Tregrosse Is., Australia 94 B5
Tréguier, France 18 D3
Trégunc, France 18 E3
Treherne, Canada 105 D9
Tréia, Italy 29 E10
Treignac, France 20 C5
Treinta y Tres, Uruguay 127 C5
Treis-karden, Germany 25 E3
Treklyano, Bulgaria 40 D6
Trelawney, Zimbabwe 89 B5
Trélazé, France 18 E6
Trelew, Argentina 128 E3
Trélissac, France 20 C4
Trelleborg, Sweden 11 J7
Tremadog Bay, U.K. 12 E3
Trémiti, Italy 29 F12
Tremonton, U.S.A. 114 F7
Tremp, Spain 32 C5
Trenche →, Canada 102 C5
Trenčiansky □, Slovak Rep. 27 C11
Trenčín, Slovak Rep. 27 C11
Trenggalek, Indonesia 63 H14
Trenque Lauquen, Argentina 126 D3
Trent →, Canada 110 B7
Trent →, U.K. 12 D7
Trentino-Alto Adige □, Italy 29 B8
Trento, Italy 28 B8
Trenton, Canada 102 D4
Trenton, Mo., U.S.A. 112 E8
Trenton, N.J., U.S.A. 111 F10
Trenton, Nebr., U.S.A. 112 E4
Trepassey, Canada 103 C9
Trepuzzi, Italy 31 B11
Tres Arroyos, Argentina 126 D3
Três Corações, Brazil 127 A6
Três Lagoas, Brazil 125 H8
Tres Lomas, Argentina 126 D3
Tres Marías, Islas, Mexico 118 C3
Tres Montes, C., Chile 128 F1
Tres Pinos, U.S.A. 116 J5
Três Pontas, Brazil 127 A6
Tres Puentes, Chile 126 B1
Tres Puntas, C., Argentina 128 F3
Três Rios, Brazil 127 A7
Tres Valles, Mexico 119 D5
Tresco, U.K. 13 H1
Treska →, Macedonia 40 E5
Treskavica, Bos.-H. 42 G3
Trespaderne, Spain 34 C7
Trets, France 21 E9
Treuchtlingen, Germany 25 G6
Treuenbrietzen, Germany 24 C8
Trevi, Italy 29 F9
Trevíglio, Italy 28 C6
Trevínca, Peña, Spain 34 C4
Treviso, Italy 29 C9
Trévoux, France 21 C8
Trgovište, Serbia, Yug. 40 D6
Triabunna, Australia 94 G4
Triánda, Greece 36 C10
Triangle, Zimbabwe 89 C5
Triaucourt-en-Argonne, France 19 D12
Tribal Areas □, Pakistan 68 C4
Tribsees, Germany 24 A8
Tribulation, C., Australia 94 B4
Tribune, U.S.A. 112 F4
Tricárico, Italy 31 B9
Tricase, Italy 31 C11
Trichinopoly = Tiruchchirappalli, India 66 P11
Trichur, India 66 P10
Trier, Germany 25 F2
Trieste, Italy 29 C10
Trieste, G. di, Italy 29 C10
Trieux →, France 18 D3
Triggiano, Italy 31 A9
Triglav, Slovenia 29 B10
Trigno →, Italy 29 F11
Trigueros, Spain 35 H4
Tríkeri, Greece 38 B5
Trikhonis, Límni, Greece 38 C3
Tríkkala, Greece 38 B3
Tríkkala □, Greece 38 B3
Trikomo, Cyprus 36 D12
Trikora, Puncak, Indonesia 63 E9
Trilj, Croatia 29 E13
Trillo, Spain 32 E2
Trim, Ireland 15 C5
Trincomalee, Sri Lanka 66 Q12
Trindade, Brazil 125 G9
Trindade, I., Atl. Oc. 2 F8
Třinec, Czech Rep. 27 B11
Trinidad, Bolivia 124 F6
Trinidad, Cuba 120 B4
Trinidad, Trin. & Tob. 121 D7
Trinidad, Uruguay 126 C4
Trinidad, U.S.A. 113 G2
Trinidad →, Mexico 119 D5
Trinidad & Tobago ■, W. Indies 121 D7
Trinitápoli, Italy 31 A9
Trinity, Canada 103 C9
Trinity, U.S.A. 113 K7
Trinity →, Calif., U.S.A. 114 F2
Trinity →, Tex., U.S.A. 113 L7
Trinity B., Canada 103 C9
Trinity Is., U.S.A. 100 C4
Trinity Range, U.S.A. 114 F4
Trinkitat, Sudan 80 D4
Trino, Italy 28 C5
Trinway, U.S.A. 110 F2
Trionto, C., Italy 31 C9
Triora, Italy 28 D4
Tripoli = Tarābulus, Lebanon 75 A4
Tripoli = Tarābulus, Libya 79 B8
Trípolis, Greece 38 D4
Tripolitania, N. Afr. 79 B8
Tripura □, India 67 H18
Tripylos, Cyprus 36 E11
Trischen, Germany 24 A4
Tristan da Cunha, Atl. Oc. 77 K2
Trisul, India 69 D8
Trivandrum, India 66 Q10
Trivento, Italy 29 G11
Trnava, Slovak Rep. 27 C10
Trnavský □, Slovak Rep. 27 C10
Troarn, France 18 C6
Trochu, Canada 104 C6
Trodely I., Canada 102 B4
Troezen, Greece 38 D5
Trogir, Croatia 29 E13
Troglav, Croatia 29 E13
Tróia, Italy 31 A8
Troilus, L., Canada 102 B5
Troina, Italy 31 E7
Trois-Pistoles, Canada 103 C6
Trois-Rivières, Canada 102 C5
Troisdorf, Germany 24 E3
Troitsk, Russia 50 D7
Troitsko Pechorsk, Russia 50 C6
Trölladyngja, Iceland 8 D5
Trollhättan, Sweden 11 F6
Trollheimen, Norway 8 E13
Trombetas →, Brazil 125 D7
Tromsø, Norway 8 B18
Trona, U.S.A. 117 K9
Tronador, Mte., Argentina 128 E2
Trøndelag, Norway 8 D14
Trondheim, Norway 8 E14
Trondheimsfjorden, Norway 8 E14
Trönninge, Sweden 11 H6
Tronto →, Italy 29 F10
Troodos, Cyprus 36 E11
Troon, U.K. 14 F4
Tropea, Italy 31 D8
Tropic, U.S.A. 115 H7
Tropojë, Albania 40 D4
Trosa, Sweden 11 F11
Trostan, U.K. 15 A5
Trostberg, Germany 25 G8
Trostyanets, Ukraine 47 G8
Trout →, Canada 104 A5
Trout L., N.W.T., Canada 104 A4
Trout L., Ont., Canada 105 C10
Trout Lake, Canada 104 B6
Trout Lake, U.S.A. 116 E5
Trout River, Canada 103 C8
Trout Run, U.S.A. 110 E7
Trouville-sur-Mer, France 18 C7
Trowbridge, U.K. 13 F5
Troy, Turkey 39 B8
Troy, Ala., U.S.A. 109 K3
Troy, Kans., U.S.A. 112 F7
Troy, Mo., U.S.A. 112 F9
Troy, Mont., U.S.A. 114 B6
Troy, N.Y., U.S.A. 111 D11
Troy, Ohio, U.S.A. 108 E3
Troy, Pa., U.S.A. 111 E8
Troyan, Bulgaria 41 D8
Troyes, France 19 D11
Trpanj, Croatia 29 E14
Trstenik, Serbia, Yug. 40 C5
Trubchevsk, Russia 47 F7
Truchas Peak, U.S.A. 113 H2
Trucial States = United Arab Emirates ■, Asia 71 F7
Truckee, U.S.A. 116 F6
Trudfront, Russia 49 H8
Trudovoye, Russia 54 C6
Trujillo, Honduras 120 C2
Trujillo, Peru 124 E3
Trujillo, Spain 35 F5
Trujillo, U.S.A. 113 H2
Trujillo, Venezuela 124 B4
Truk, Micronesia 96 G7
Trumann, U.S.A. 113 H9
Trumansburg, U.S.A. 111 D8
Trumbull, Mt., U.S.A. 115 H7
Trŭn, Bulgaria 40 D6
Trun, France 18 D7
Trung-Phan = Annam, Vietnam 64 E7
Truro, Canada 103 C7
Truro, U.K. 13 G2
Truskavets, Ukraine 47 H2
Trŭstenik, Bulgaria 41 C8
Trustrup, Denmark 11 H4
Trutch, Canada 104 B4
Truth or Consequences, U.S.A. 115 K10
Trutnov, Czech Rep. 26 A8
Truxton, U.S.A. 111 D8
Truyère →, France 20 D6
Tryavna, Bulgaria 41 D9
Tryonville, U.S.A. 110 E5
Trzcianka, Poland 45 E3
Trzciel, Poland 45 F2
Trzcińsko Zdrój, Poland 45 F1
Trzebiatów, Poland 44 D2
Trzebiez, Poland 44 E1
Trzebnica, Poland 45 G4
Trzemeszno, Poland 45 F4
Tržič, Slovenia 29 B11
Tsagan Aman, Russia 49 G8
Tsamandás, Greece 38 B2
Tsandi, Namibia 88 B1
Tsaratanana, Madag. 89 B8
Tsaratanana, Mt. de, Madag. 89 A8
Tsarevo = Michurin, Bulgaria 41 D11
Tsarevo, Bulgaria 41 D9
Tsaritsáni, Greece 38 B4
Tsau, Botswana 88 C3
Tsebrykove, Ukraine 47 J6
Tselinograd = Astana, Kazakstan 50 D8
Tses, Namibia 88 D2
Tsetserleg, Mongolia 60 B5
Tsévié, Togo 83 D5
Tshabong, Botswana 88 D3
Tshane, Botswana 88 C3
Tshela, Dem. Rep. of the Congo 84 E2
Tshesebe, Botswana 89 C4
Tshibeke, Dem. Rep. of the Congo 86 C2
Tshibinda, Dem. Rep. of the Congo 86 C2
Tshikapa, Dem. Rep. of the Congo 84 F4
Tshilenge, Dem. Rep. of the Congo 86 D1
Tshinsenda, Dem. Rep. of the Congo 87 E2
Tshofa, Dem. Rep. of the Congo 86 D2
Tshwane, Botswana 88 C3
Tsigara, Botswana 88 C4
Tsihombe, Madag. 89 D8
Tsiigehtchic, Canada 100 B6
Tsimlyansk, Russia 49 G6
Tsimlyansk Res. = Tsimlyanskoye Vdkhr., Russia 49 F6
Tsimlyanskoye Vdkhr., Russia 49 F6
Tsinan = Jinan, China 56 F9
Tsineng, S. Africa 88 D3
Tsínga, Greece 41 E8
Tsinghai = Qinghai □, China 60 C4
Tsingtao = Qingdao, China 57 F11
Tsinjoarivo, Madag. 89 B8
Tsinjomitondraka, Madag. 89 B8
Tsiroanomandidy, Madag. 89 B8
Tsiteli-Tsqaro, Georgia 49 K8

Tsitondroina, *Madag.* 89 C8
Tsivilsk, *Russia* 48 C8
Tsivory, *Madag.* 89 C8
Tskhinvali, *Georgia* 49 J7
Tsna →, *Russia* 48 C6
Tsnori, *Georgia* 49 K7
Tso Moriri, L., *India* 69 C8
Tsobis, *Namibia* 88 B2
Tsodilo Hill, *Botswana* 88 B3
Tsogttsetsiy = Baruunsuu,
  Mongolia 56 C3
Tsolo, *S. Africa* 89 E4
Tsomo, *S. Africa* 89 E4
Tsu, *Japan* 55 G8
Tsu L., *Canada* 104 A6
Tsuchiura, *Japan* 55 F10
Tsuen Wan, *H.K.* 59 F10
Tsugaru-Kaikyō, *Japan* 54 D10
Tsumeb, *Namibia* 88 B2
Tsumis, *Namibia* 88 C2
Tsuruga, *Japan* 55 G8
Tsurugi-San, *Japan* 55 H7
Tsuruoka, *Japan* 54 E9
Tsushima, *Gifu, Japan* 55 G8
Tsushima, *Nagasaki, Japan* 55 G4
Tsuyama, *Japan* 55 G7
Tsvetkovo, *Ukraine* 47 H6
Tsyelyakhany, *Belarus* 47 F3
Tua →, *Portugal* 34 D3
Tual, *Indonesia* 63 F8
Tuam, *Ireland* 15 C3
Tuamotu Arch. = Tuamotu Is.,
  Pac. Oc. 97 J13
Tuamotu Is., *Pac. Oc.* 97 J13
Tuamotu Ridge, *Pac. Oc.* 97 K14
Tuanfeng, *China* 59 B10
Tuanxi, *China* 58 D6
Tuao, *Phil.* 61 C4
Tuapse, *Russia* 49 H4
Tuatapere, *N.Z.* 91 M1
Tuba City, *U.S.A.* 115 H8
Tuban, *Indonesia* 63 G15
Tubani, *Botswana* 88 C3
Tubarão, *Brazil* 127 B6
Ṭūbās, *West Bank* 75 C4
Tübingen, *Germany* 25 G5
Tubruq, *Libya* 79 B10
Tubuai Is., *Pac. Oc.* 97 K13
Tuc Trung, *Vietnam* 65 G6
Tucacas, *Venezuela* 124 A5
T'uch'ang, *Taiwan* 59 E13
Tuchodi →, *Canada* 104 B4
Tuchola, *Poland* 44 E4
Tuchów, *Poland* 45 J8
Tuckanarra, *Australia* 93 E2
Tucson, *U.S.A.* 115 K8
Tucumán □, *Argentina* 126 B2
Tucumcari, *U.S.A.* 113 H3
Tucupita, *Venezuela* 124 B6
Tucuruí, *Brazil* 125 D9
Tucuruí, Reprêsa de, *Brazil* ... 125 D9
Tuczno, *Poland* 45 E3
Tudela, *Spain* 32 C3
Tudmur, *Syria* 70 C3
Tudor, L., *Canada* 103 A6
Tudora, *Romania* 43 C11
Tuella →, *Portugal* 34 D3
Tugela →, *S. Africa* 89 D5
Tuguegarao, *Phil.* 61 C4
Tugur, *Russia* 51 D14
Tui, *Spain* 34 C2
Tuineje, *Canary Is.* 37 F5
Tukangbesi, Kepulauan,
  Indonesia 63 F6
Tukarak I., *Canada* 102 A4
Tukayyid, *Iraq* 70 D5
Ṭūkh, *Egypt* 80 H7
Tukobo, *Ghana* 82 D4
Tuktoyaktuk, *Canada* 100 B6
Tukums, *Latvia* 9 H20
Tukums □, *Latvia* 44 B10
Tukuyu, *Tanzania* 87 D3
Tula, *Hidalgo, Mexico* 119 C5
Tula, *Tamaulipas, Mexico* 119 C5
Tula, *Nigeria* 83 D7
Tula, *Russia* 46 E9
Tulancingo, *Mexico* 119 C5
Tulare, *Serbia, Yug.* 40 D5
Tulare, *U.S.A.* 116 J7
Tulare Lake Bed, *U.S.A.* 116 K7
Tularosa, *U.S.A.* 115 K10
Tulbagh, *S. Africa* 88 E2
Tulcán, *Ecuador* 124 C3
Tulcea, *Romania* 43 E13
Tulcea □, *Romania* 43 E13
Tulchyn, *Ukraine* 47 H5
Tūleh, *Iran* 71 C7
Tulemalu L., *Canada* 105 A9
Tulgheş, *Romania* 43 D10
Tuli, *Zimbabwe* 87 G2
Tulia, *U.S.A.* 113 H4
Tuliszków, *Poland* 45 F5
Tulita, *Canada* 100 B7
Ṭūlkarm, *West Bank* 75 C4
Tulla, *Ireland* 15 D3
Tullahoma, *U.S.A.* 109 H2
Tullamore, *Australia* 94 B4
Tullamore, *Ireland* 15 C4
Tulle, *France* 20 C5
Tulln, *Austria* 26 C9
Tullow, *Ireland* 15 D5
Tullus, *Sudan* 81 E1
Tully, *Australia* 94 B4
Tully, *U.S.A.* 111 D8
Tulnici, *Romania* 43 E11

Tulovo, *Bulgaria* 41 D9
Tulsa, *U.S.A.* 113 G7
Tulsequah, *Canada* 104 B2
Tulu Milki, *Ethiopia* 81 F4
Tulu Welel, *Ethiopia* 81 F3
Tulua, *Colombia* 124 C3
Tuluceşti, *Romania* 43 E13
Tulun, *Russia* 51 D11
Tulungagung, *Indonesia* 63 H14
Tuma, *Russia* 46 E11
Tuma →, *Nic.* 120 D3
Tumaco, *Colombia* 124 C3
Tumatumari, *Guyana* 124 B7
Tumba, *Sweden* 10 E11
Tumba, L., *Dem. Rep. of*
  the Congo 84 E3
Tumbaya, *Argentina* 126 A2
Tumbes, *Peru* 124 D2
Tumbur, *Sudan* 81 G3
Tumbwe, *Dem. Rep. of*
  the Congo 87 E2
Tumd Youqi, *China* 56 D6
Tumen, *China* 57 C15
Tumen Jiang →, *China* 57 C16
Tumeremo, *Venezuela* 124 B6
Tumkur, *India* 66 N10
Tump, *Pakistan* 66 F3
Tumpat, *Malaysia* 65 J4
Tumu, *Ghana* 82 C4
Tumucumaque, Serra, *Brazil* .. 122 C5
Tumwater, *U.S.A.* 116 C4
Tuna, *India* 68 H4
Tunadal, *Sweden* 10 B11
Tunas de Zaza, *Cuba* 120 B4
Tunbridge Wells = Royal
  Tunbridge Wells, *U.K.* 13 F8
Tunçbilek, *Turkey* 39 B11
Tunceli, *Turkey* 73 C8
Tundla, *India* 68 F8
Tundubai, *Sudan* 80 D2
Tunduru, *Tanzania* 87 E4
Tundzha →, *Bulgaria* 41 E10
Tungabhadra →, *India* 66 M11
Tungaru, *Sudan* 81 E3
Tungla, *Nic.* 120 D3
Tungsha Tao, *Taiwan* 59 G11
Tungshih, *Taiwan* 59 E13
Tungsten, *Canada* 104 A3
Tunguska, Nizhnyaya →, *Russia* 51 C9
Tunguska, Podkamennaya →,
  Russia 51 C10
Tunica, *U.S.A.* 113 H9
Tunis, *Tunisia* 78 A7
Tunisia ■, *Africa* 78 B6
Tunja, *Colombia* 124 B4
Tunkhannock, *U.S.A.* 111 E9
Tunliu, *China* 56 F7
Tunnsjøen, *Norway* 8 D15
Tunø, *Denmark* 11 J4
Tunungayualok I., *Canada* ... 103 A7
Tununirusiq = Arctic Bay,
  Canada 101 A11
Tunuyán, *Argentina* 126 C2
Tunuyán →, *Argentina* 126 C2
Tuo Jiang →, *China* 58 C5
Tuolumne, *U.S.A.* 116 H6
Tuolumne →, *U.S.A.* 116 H5
Tūp Āghāj, *Iran* 70 B5
Tupã, *Brazil* 127 A5
Tupelo, *U.S.A.* 109 H1
Tupik, *Russia* 46 E7
Tupinambaranas, *Brazil* 124 D7
Tupiza, *Bolivia* 126 A2
Tupižnica, *Serbia, Yug.* 40 C6
Tupman, *U.S.A.* 117 K7
Tupper, *Canada* 104 B4
Tupper Lake, *U.S.A.* 111 B10
Tupungato, Cerro, *S. Amer.* .. 126 C2
Tuquan, *China* 57 B11
Túquerres, *Colombia* 124 C3
Tura, *Russia* 51 C11
Turabah, *Si. Arabia* 70 D4
Turabah, *Si. Arabia* 80 C5
Tūrān, *Iran* 71 C8
Turan, *Russia* 51 D10
Ṭurayf, *Si. Arabia* 70 D3
Turbacz, *Poland* 45 J7
Turbe, *Bos.-H.* 42 F2
Turčianske Teplice, *Slovak Rep.* 27 C11
Turcoaia, *Romania* 43 E13
Turda, *Romania* 43 D8
Turek, *Poland* 45 F5
Turen, *Venezuela* 124 B5
Turfan = Turpan, *China* 60 B3
Turfan Depression = Turpan
  Hami, *China* 52 E12
Turgeon →, *Canada* 102 C4
Tŭrgovishte, *Bulgaria* 41 C10
Turgut, *Turkey* 39 D10
Turgutlu, *Turkey* 39 C9
Turgwe →, *Zimbabwe* 89 C5
Turhal, *Turkey* 72 B7
Turia →, *Spain* 33 F4
Turiaçu, *Brazil* 125 D9
Turiaçu →, *Brazil* 125 D9
Turiec →, *Slovak Rep.* 27 B11
Turin = Torino, *Italy* 28 C4
Turkana, L., *Africa* 86 B4
Türkeli, *Turkey* 41 F11
Turkestan = Türkistan,
  Kazakstan 50 E7
Túrkeve, *Hungary* 42 C5
Turkey ■, *Eurasia* 72 C7
Turkey Creek, *Australia* 92 C4
Turki, *Russia* 48 D6

Türkistan, *Kazakstan* 50 E7
Turkmenbashi, *Turkmenistan* .. 50 E6
Turkmenistan ■, *Asia* 50 F6
Türkmenli, *Turkey* 39 B8
Türkoğlu, *Turkey* 72 D7
Turks & Caicos Is. ■, *W. Indies* 121 B5
Turks Island Passage, *W. Indies* 121 B5
Turku, *Finland* 9 F20
Turkwel →, *Kenya* 86 B4
Turlock, *U.S.A.* 116 H6
Turnagain →, *Canada* 104 B3
Turnagain, C., *N.Z.* 91 J6
Turneffe Is., *Belize* 119 D7
Turner, *U.S.A.* 114 B9
Turner Pt., *Australia* 94 A1
Turner Valley, *Canada* 104 C6
Turners Falls, *U.S.A.* 111 D12
Turnhout, *Belgium* 17 C4
Türnitz, *Austria* 26 D8
Turnor L., *Canada* 105 B7
Turnov, *Czech Rep.* 26 A8
Tŭrnovo = Veliko Tŭrnovo,
  Bulgaria 41 C9
Turnu Măgurele, *Romania* ... 43 G9
Turnu Roşu, P., *Romania* 43 E9
Turobin, *Poland* 45 H9
Turpan, *China* 60 B3
Turpan Hami, *China* 52 E12
Turrës, Kala e, *Albania* 40 E3
Turriff, *U.K.* 14 D6
Tursāq, *Iraq* 70 C5
Tursi, *Italy* 31 B9
Turtle Head I., *Australia* 94 A3
Turtle Is., *S. Leone* 82 D2
Turtle L., *Canada* 105 C7
Turtle Lake, *U.S.A.* 112 B4
Turtleford, *Canada* 105 C7
Turukhansk, *Russia* 51 C9
Turzovka, *Slovak Rep.* 27 B11
Tuscaloosa, *U.S.A.* 109 J2
Tuscánia, *Italy* 29 F8
Tuscany = Toscana □, *Italy* ... 28 E8
Tuscarawas →, *U.S.A.* 110 F3
Tuscarora Mt., *U.S.A.* 110 F7
Tuscola, *Ill., U.S.A.* 108 F1
Tuscola, *Tex., U.S.A.* 113 J5
Tuscumbia, *U.S.A.* 109 H2
Tuskegee, *U.S.A.* 109 J3
Tustin, *U.S.A.* 117 M9
Tuszyn, *Poland* 45 G6
Tutak, *Turkey* 73 C10
Tutayev, *Russia* 46 D10
Tuticorin, *India* 66 Q11
Tutin, *Serbia, Yug.* 40 D4
Tutong, *Brunei* 62 D4
Tutova →, *Romania* 43 D12
Tutrakan, *Bulgaria* 41 B10
Tuttle Creek L., *U.S.A.* 112 F6
Tuttlingen, *Germany* 25 H4
Tutuala, *Indonesia* 63 F7
Tutuila, *Amer. Samoa* 91 B13
Tutume, *Botswana* 85 J5
Tutun, *Egypt* 80 J7
Tututepec, *Mexico* 119 D5
Tuva □, *Russia* 51 D10
Tuvalu ■, *Pac. Oc.* 96 H9
Tuxer Alpen, *Austria* 26 D4
Tuxpan, *Mexico* 119 C5
Tuxtla Gutiérrez, *Mexico* 119 D6
Tuy = Tui, *Spain* 34 C2
Tuy An, *Vietnam* 64 F7
Tuy Duc, *Vietnam* 65 F6
Tuy Hoa, *Vietnam* 64 F7
Tuy Phong, *Vietnam* 65 G7
Tuya L., *Canada* 104 B2
Tuyen Hoa, *Vietnam* 64 D6
Tuyen Quang, *Vietnam* 58 G5
Ṭūysarkān, *Iran* 71 C6
Tuz Gölü, *Turkey* 72 C5
Ṭūz Khurmātū, *Iraq* 70 C5
Tuzla, *Bos.-H.* 42 F3
Tuzlov →, *Russia* 47 J10
Tuzluca, *Turkey* 73 B10
Tvååker, *Sweden* 11 G6
Tvardiţa, *Moldova* 43 D13
Tver, *Russia* 46 D8
Tvrdošin, *Slovak Rep.* 27 B12
Tvrdošovce, *Slovak Rep.* 27 C11
Tvŭrditsa, *Bulgaria* 41 D9
Twain, *U.S.A.* 116 E5
Twain Harte, *U.S.A.* 116 G6
Tweed, *Canada* 110 B7
Tweed →, *U.K.* 14 F6
Tweed Heads, *Australia* 95 D5
Tweedsmuir Prov. Park, *Canada* 104 C3
Twentynine Palms, *U.S.A.* ... 117 L10
Twillingate, *Canada* 103 C9
Twin Bridges, *U.S.A.* 114 D7
Twin Falls, *Canada* 103 B7
Twin Falls, *U.S.A.* 114 E6
Twin Valley, *U.S.A.* 112 B6
Twinsburg, *U.S.A.* 110 E3
Twistringen, *Germany* 24 C4
Twitchell Reservoir, *U.S.A.* .. 117 L6
Two Harbors, *U.S.A.* 112 B9
Two Hills, *Canada* 104 C6
Two Rivers, *U.S.A.* 108 C2
Two Rocks, *Australia* 93 F2
Tyachiv, *Ukraine* 47 H2
Tychy, *Poland* 45 H5
Tyczyn, *Poland* 45 J9
Tykocin, *Poland* 45 E9

Tyler, *Minn., U.S.A.* 112 C6
Tyler, *Tex., U.S.A.* 113 J7
Tyligul →, *Ukraine* 47 J6
Tynda, *Russia* 51 D13
Tyndall, *U.S.A.* 112 D6
Tyne →, *U.K.* 12 C6
Tyne & Wear □, *U.K.* 12 B6
Tynemouth, *U.K.* 12 B6
Tynec nad Sázavou, *Czech Rep.* 26 B7
Tyre = Sūr, *Lebanon* 75 B4
Tyrifjorden, *Norway* 9 F14
Tyringe, *Sweden* 11 H7
Tyrol = Tirol □, *Austria* 26 D3
Tyrone, *U.S.A.* 110 F6
Tyrone □, *U.K.* 15 B4
Tyrrell →, *Australia* 94 F5
Tyrrell, L., *Australia* 94 F5
Tyrrell Arm, *Canada* 105 A7
Tyrrhenian Sea, *Medit. S.* 6 G8
Tysfjorden, *Norway* 8 B17
Tystberga, *Sweden* 11 F11
Tytuvėnai, *Lithuania* 44 C10
Tyub Karagan, Mys, *Kazakstan* 49 H10
Tyuleni, Ostrova, *Kazakstan* .. 49 H10
Tyuleniy, *Russia* 49 H8
Tyuleniy, Mys, *Azerbaijan* ... 49 K10
Tyumen, *Russia* 50 D7
Tywi →, *U.K.* 13 F3
Tywyn, *U.K.* 13 E3
Tzaneen, *S. Africa* 89 C5
Tzermiádhes, *Greece* 36 D7
Tzoumérka, Óros, *Greece* 38 B3
Tzukong = Zigong, *China* 58 C5

U

U Taphao, *Thailand* 64 F3
U.S.A. = United States of
  America ■, *N. Amer.* 106 C7
Uatumã →, *Brazil* 124 D7
Uaupés, *Brazil* 124 D5
Uaupés →, *Brazil* 124 C5
Uaxactún, *Guatemala* 120 C2
Ub, *Serbia, Yug.* 40 B4
Ubá, *Brazil* 127 A7
Uba, *Nigeria* 83 D7
Ubaitaba, *Brazil* 125 F11
Ubangi = Oubangi →,
  Dem. Rep. of the Congo 84 E3
Ubauro, *Pakistan* 68 E3
Ubaye →, *France* 21 D10
Ubayyiḍ, W. al →, *Iraq* 70 C4
Ube, *Japan* 55 H5
Úbeda, *Spain* 35 G7
Uberaba, *Brazil* 125 G9
Uberlândia, *Brazil* 125 G9
Überlingen, *Germany* 25 H5
Ubiaja, *Nigeria* 83 D6
Ubolratna Res., *Thailand* 64 D4
Ubombo, *S. Africa* 89 D5
Ubon Ratchathani, *Thailand* .. 64 E5
Ubondo, *Dem. Rep. of*
  the Congo 86 C2
Ubort →, *Belarus* 47 F5
Ubrique, *Spain* 35 J5
Ubundu, *Dem. Rep. of*
  the Congo 86 C2
Ucayali →, *Peru* 122 D3
Uchab, *Namibia* 88 B2
Uchiura-Wan, *Japan* 54 C10
Uchquduq, *Uzbekistan* 50 E7
Uchte, *Germany* 24 C4
Uchur →, *Russia* 51 D14
Uckermark, *Germany* 24 B9
Ucluelet, *Canada* 104 D3
Uda →, *Russia* 51 D14
Udagamandalam, *India* 66 P10
Udainagar, *India* 68 H7
Udaipur, *India* 68 G5
Udaipur Garhi, *Nepal* 69 F12
Udala, *India* 69 J12
Udbina, *Croatia* 29 D12
Uddeholm, *Sweden* 10 D7
Uddevalla, *Sweden* 11 F5
Uddjaur, *Sweden* 8 D17
Uden, *Neths.* 17 C5
Udgir, *India* 66 K10
Udhampur, *India* 69 C6
Udi, *Nigeria* 83 D6
Údine, *Italy* 29 B10
Udmurtia □, *Russia* 50 D6
Udon Thani, *Thailand* 64 D4
Udupi, *India* 66 N9
Udvoy Balkan, *Bulgaria* 41 D10
Udzungwa Range, *Tanzania* .. 87 D4
Ueckermünde, *Germany* 24 B10
Ueda, *Japan* 55 F9
Uedineniya, Os., *Russia* 4 B12
Uele →, *Dem. Rep. of*
  the Congo 84 D4
Uelen, *Russia* 51 C19
Uelzen, *Germany* 24 C6
Uetersen, *Germany* 24 B5
Uetze, *Germany* 24 C6
Ufa, *Russia* 50 D6
Uffenheim, *Germany* 25 F6
Ugab →, *Namibia* 88 C1
Ugalla →, *Tanzania* 86 D3
Uganda ■, *Africa* 86 B3
Ugento, *Italy* 31 C11
Ughelli, *Nigeria* 83 D6
Ugie, *S. Africa* 89 E4
Ugíjar, *Spain* 35 J7

Ugine, *France* 21 C10
Uglegorsk, *Russia* 51 E15
Uglich, *Russia* 46 D10
Ugljan, *Croatia* 29 D12
Ugljane, *Croatia* 29 E13
Ugra →, *Russia* 46 E9
Uğurchin, *Bulgaria* 41 C8
Uh →, *Slovak Rep.* 27 C15
Uherské Hradiště, *Czech Rep.* . 27 B10
Uherský Brod, *Czech Rep.* ... 27 B10
Úhlava →, *Czech Rep.* 26 B6
Uhlenhorst, *Namibia* 88 C2
Uhrichsville, *U.S.A.* 110 F3
Uibhist a Deas = South Uist,
  U.K. 14 D1
Uibhist a Tuath = North Uist,
  U.K. 14 D1
Uíge, *Angola* 84 F2
Uijŏngbu, *S. Korea* 57 F14
Ŭiju, *N. Korea* 57 D13
Uinta Mts., *U.S.A.* 114 F8
Uis, *Namibia* 88 B2
Uitenhage, *S. Africa* 88 E4
Uithuizen, *Neths.* 17 A6
Ujazd, *Poland* 45 H5
Újfehértó, *Hungary* 42 C6
Ujh →, *India* 68 C6
Ujhani, *India* 69 F8
Uji-guntō, *Japan* 55 J4
Ujjain, *India* 68 H6
Ujście, *Poland* 45 E3
Újszász, *Hungary* 42 C5
Ujung Pandang, *Indonesia* ... 63 F5
Uka, *Russia* 51 D17
Ukara I., *Tanzania* 86 C3
Uke-Shima, *Japan* 55 K4
Ukerewe I., *Tanzania* 86 C3
Ukholovo, *Russia* 48 D5
Ukhrul, *India* 67 G19
Ukhta, *Russia* 50 C6
Ukiah, *U.S.A.* 116 F3
Ukki Fort, *India* 69 C7
Ukmergė, *Lithuania* 9 J21
Ukraine ■, *Europe* 47 H7
Ukwi, *Botswana* 88 C3
Ulaan-Uul, *Mongolia* 56 B6
Ulaanbaatar, *Mongolia* 51 E11
Ulaangom, *Mongolia* 60 A4
Ulaanjirem, *Mongolia* 56 B3
Ulamba, *Dem. Rep. of the Congo* 87 D1
Ulan Bator = Ulaanbaatar,
  Mongolia 51 E11
Ulan Erge, *Russia* 49 G7
Ulan Khol, *Russia* 49 H8
Ulan Ude, *Russia* 51 D11
Ulanów, *Poland* 45 H9
Ulaş, *Sivas, Turkey* 72 C7
Ulaş, *Tekirdağ, Turkey* 41 E11
Ulaya, *Morogoro, Tanzania* .. 86 D4
Ulaya, *Tabora, Tanzania* 86 C3
Ulcinj, *Montenegro, Yug.* 40 E3
Ulco, *S. Africa* 88 D3
Ulefoss, *Norway* 9 G13
Ulëz, *Albania* 40 E3
Ulfborg, *Denmark* 11 H2
Ulhasnagar, *India* 66 K8
Uliastay = Ulyasutay, *Mongolia* 60 B4
Ulithi Atoll, *Pac. Oc.* 63 B9
Uljma, *Serbia, Yug.* 42 F6
Ulla →, *Spain* 34 C2
Ullapool, *U.K.* 14 D3
Ullared, *Sweden* 11 G6
Ulldecona, *Spain* 32 E5
Ullswater, *U.K.* 12 C5
Ullŭng-do, *S. Korea* 55 F5
Ulm, *Germany* 25 G5
Ulmarra, *Australia* 95 D5
Ulmeni, *Buzău, Romania* 43 E11
Ulmeni, *Maramureş, Romania* . 43 C8
Ulonguè, *Mozam.* 87 E3
Ulricehamn, *Sweden* 11 G7
Ulrika, *Sweden* 11 F9
Ulsan, *S. Korea* 57 G15
Ulsta, *U.K.* 14 A7
Ulster □, *U.K.* 15 B5
Ulstrem, *Bulgaria* 41 D10
Ulubat Gölü, *Turkey* 41 F12
Ulubey, *Turkey* 39 C11
Uluborlu, *Turkey* 39 C12
Uluçinar, *Turkey* 72 D6
Uludağ, *Turkey* 41 F13
Uludere, *Turkey* 73 D10
Uluguru Mts., *Tanzania* 86 D4
Ulukışla, *Turkey* 72 D6
Ulungur He →, *China* 60 B3
Uluru = Ayers Rock, *Australia* . 93 E5
Uluru Nat. Park, *Australia* ... 93 E5
Ulutau, *Kazakstan* 50 E7
Ulva, *U.K.* 14 E2
Ulverston, *U.K.* 12 C4
Ulverstone, *Australia* 94 G4
Ulya, *Russia* 51 D15
Ulyanovsk = Simbirsk, *Russia* . 48 C8
Ulyasutay, *Mongolia* 60 B4
Ulysses, *U.S.A.* 113 G4
Umag, *Croatia* 29 C10
Umala, *Bolivia* 124 G5
Uman, *Ukraine* 47 H6
Umaria, *India* 67 H12
Umarkot, *Pakistan* 66 G6
Umarpada, *India* 68 J5
Umatilla, *U.S.A.* 114 D4
Umbagog L., *U.S.A.* 111 B13
Umbakumba, *Australia* 94 A2

Umbértide, Italy 29 E9
Umbrella Mts., N.Z. 91 L2
Umbria □, Italy 29 F9
Ume älv →, Sweden 8 E19
Umeå, Sweden 8 E19
Umera, Indonesia 63 E7
Umfuli →, Zimbabwe 87 F2
Umgusa, Zimbabwe 87 F2
Umim Urūmah, Si. Arabia 80 B4
Umka, Serbia, Yug. 40 B4
Umkomaas, S. Africa 89 E5
Umlazi, S. Africa 85 L6
Umm ad Daraj, J., Jordan 75 C4
Umm al Qaywayn, U.A.E. 71 E7
Umm al Qittayn, Jordan 75 C5
Umm Arda, Sudan 81 D3
Umm Bāb, Qatar 71 E6
Umm Badr, Sudan 81 E2
Umm Baiyud, Sudan 81 E3
Umm Bel, Sudan 81 E2
Umm Birkah, Si. Arabia 80 B4
Umm Boim, Sudan 81 E2
Umm Dam, Sudan 81 E3
Umm Debi, Sudan 81 E3
Umm Dubban, Sudan 81 D3
Umm el Fahm, Israel 75 C4
Umm Gafala, Sudan 81 E2
Umm Gimala, Sudan 81 E2
Umm Inderaba, Sudan 80 D3
Umm Keddada, Sudan 81 E2
Umm Koweika, Sudan 81 E3
Umm Lajj, Si. Arabia 70 E3
Umm Merwa, Sudan 80 D3
Umm Qantur, Sudan 81 E3
Umm Qurein, Sudan 81 F2
Umm Ruwaba, Sudan 81 E3
Umm Saiyala, Sudan 81 E3
Umm Shanqa, Sudan 81 E2
Umm Shutur, Sudan 81 F3
Umm Sidr, Sudan 81 E2
Umm Zehetir, Egypt 80 J8
Umnak I., U.S.A. 100 C3
Umniati →, Zimbabwe 87 F2
Umpqua →, U.S.A. 114 E1
Umreth, India 68 H5
Umtata, S. Africa 89 E4
Umuahia, Nigeria 83 D6
Umuarama, Brazil 127 A5
Umurbey, Turkey 41 F10
Umvukwe Ra., Zimbabwe 87 F3
Umzimvubu, S. Africa 89 E4
Umzingwane →, Zimbabwe 87 G2
Umzinto, S. Africa 89 E5
Una, India 68 J4
Una →, Bos.-H. 29 D13
Unac →, Bos.-H. 29 D13
Unadilla, U.S.A. 111 D9
Unalakleet, U.S.A. 100 B3
Unalaska, U.S.A. 100 C3
Unalaska I., U.S.A. 100 C3
'Unayzah, Si. Arabia 70 E4
'Unāzah, J., Asia 70 C3
Uncastillo, Spain 32 C3
Uncía, Bolivia 124 G5
Uncompahgre Peak, U.S.A. 115 G10
Uncompahgre Plateau, U.S.A. 115 G9
Unden, Sweden 11 F8
Undersaker, Sweden 10 A7
Unecha, Russia 47 F7
Ungava, Pén. d', Canada 101 C12
Ungava B., Canada 101 C13
Ungeny = Ungheni, Moldova 43 C12
Unggi, N. Korea 57 C16
Ungheni, Moldova 43 C12
Unguala →, Ethiopia 81 F5
Ungwatiri, Sudan 81 D4
Uni, Russia 48 B10
União da Vitória, Brazil 127 B5
Uničov, Czech Rep. 27 B10
Uniejów, Poland 45 G5
Unije, Croatia 29 D11
Unimak I., U.S.A. 100 C3
Union, Miss., U.S.A. 113 J10
Union, Mo., U.S.A. 112 F9
Union, S.C., U.S.A. 109 H5
Union City, Calif., U.S.A. 116 H4
Union City, N.J., U.S.A. 111 F10
Union City, Pa., U.S.A. 110 E5
Union City, Tenn., U.S.A. 113 G10
Union Gap, U.S.A. 114 C3
Union Springs, U.S.A. 109 J3
Uniondale, S. Africa 88 E3
Uniontown, U.S.A. 108 F6
Unionville, U.S.A. 112 E8
Unirea, Romania 43 F12
United Arab Emirates ■, Asia 71 F7
United Kingdom ■, Europe 7 E5
United States of America ■, N. Amer. 106 C7
Unity, Canada 105 C7
Universales, Mtes., Spain 32 E3
University Park, U.S.A. 115 K10
Unjha, India 68 H5
Unna, Germany 24 D3
Unnao, India 69 F9
Uno, Ilha, Guinea-Biss. 82 C1
Unst, U.K. 14 A8
Unstrut →, Germany 24 D7
Unterfranken □, Germany 25 F5
Unterschleissheim, Germany 25 G7
Unuk →, Canada 104 B2
Ünye, Turkey 72 B7
Unzha, Russia 48 A7
Unzha →, Russia 48 B6
Uozu, Japan 55 F8

Upata, Venezuela 124 B6
Upemba, L., Dem. Rep. of the Congo 87 D2
Upernavik, Greenland 4 B5
Upington, S. Africa 88 D3
Upleta, India 68 J4
Upolu, Samoa 91 A13
Upper □, Ghana 83 C4
Upper Alkali L., U.S.A. 114 F3
Upper Arrow L., Canada 104 C5
Upper Austria = Oberösterreich □, Austria 26 C7
Upper Foster L., Canada 105 B7
Upper Hutt, N.Z. 91 J5
Upper Klamath L., U.S.A. 114 E3
Upper Lake, U.S.A. 116 F4
Upper Musquodoboit, Canada 103 C7
Upper Red L., U.S.A. 112 A7
Upper Sandusky, U.S.A. 108 E4
Upper Volta = Burkina Faso ■, Africa 82 C4
Upphärad, Sweden 11 F6
Uppland, Sweden 10 E11
Upplands-Väsby, Sweden 10 E11
Uppsala, Sweden 10 E11
Uppsala län □, Sweden 10 D11
Upshi, India 69 C7
Upstart, C., Australia 94 B4
Upton, U.S.A. 112 C2
Ur, Iraq 70 D5
Urad Qianqi, China 56 D5
Urakawa, Japan 54 C11
Ural = Zhayyq →, Kazakstan 50 E6
Ural Mts. = Uralskie Gory, Eurasia 50 D6
Uralsk = Oral, Kazakstan 48 E10
Uralskie Gory, Eurasia 50 D6
Urambo, Tanzania 86 D3
Urandangi, Australia 94 C2
Uranium City, Canada 105 B7
Uraricoera →, Brazil 124 C6
Urawa, Japan 55 G9
Uray, Russia 50 C7
'Uray'irah, Si. Arabia 71 E6
Urbana, Ill., U.S.A. 108 E1
Urbana, Ohio, U.S.A. 108 E4
Urbánia, Italy 29 E9
Urbel →, Spain 34 C7
Urbino, Italy 29 E9
Urbión, Picos de, Spain 32 C2
Urcos, Peru 124 F4
Urdinarrain, Argentina 126 C4
Urdos, France 20 F3
Urdzhar, Kazakstan 50 E9
Ure →, U.K. 12 C6
Uren, Russia 48 B7
Ures, Mexico 118 B2
Urfa = Sanliurfa, Turkey 70 B3
Urganch, Uzbekistan 50 E7
Urgench = Urganch, Uzbekistan 50 E7
Ürgüp, Turkey 70 B2
Uri, India 69 B6
Uri □, Switz. 25 J4
Uribia, Colombia 124 A4
Uricani, Romania 42 E8
Uriondo, Bolivia 126 A3
Urique, Mexico 118 B3
Urique →, Mexico 118 B3
Urk, Neths. 17 B5
Urla, Turkey 39 C8
Urlați, Romania 43 F11
Urmia = Orūmīyeh, Iran 70 B5
Urmia, L. = Orūmīyeh, Daryācheh-ye, Iran 70 B5
Uroševac, Kosovo, Yug. 40 D5
Urshult, Sweden 11 H8
Uruaçu, Brazil 125 F9
Uruapan, Mexico 118 D4
Urubamba →, Peru 124 F4
Uruçara, Brazil 124 D7
Uruçuí, Brazil 125 E10
Uruguai →, Brazil 127 B5
Uruguaiana, Brazil 126 B4
Uruguay ■, S. Amer. 126 C4
Uruguay →, S. Amer. 126 C4
Urumchi = Ürümqi, China 50 E9
Ürümqi, China 50 E9
Urup →, Russia 49 H5
Urup, Ostrov, Russia 51 E16
Uryupinsk, Russia 48 E5
Urzhum, Russia 48 B9
Urziceni, Romania 43 F11
Usa →, Russia 50 C6
Uşak, Turkey 39 C11
Uşak □, Turkey 39 C11
Usakos, Namibia 88 C2
Ušće, Serbia, Yug. 40 C4
Usedom, Germany 24 B10
Useless Loop, Australia 93 E1
'Usfān, Si. Arabia 80 C4
Ush-Tobe, Kazakstan 50 E8
Ushakova, Ostrov, Russia 4 A12
Ushant = Ouessant, Î. d', France 18 D1
Ushashi, Tanzania 86 C3
Ushat, Sudan 81 F2
'Ushayrah, Si. Arabia 80 C5
Ushibuka, Japan 55 H5
Ushuaia, Argentina 128 G3
Ushumun, Russia 51 D13
Usk, Canada 104 C3
Usk →, U.K. 13 F5
Uska, India 69 F10
Üsküdar, Turkey 41 F13
Uslar, Germany 24 D5
Usman, Russia 47 D10

Usoke, Tanzania 86 D3
Usolye Sibirskoye, Russia 51 D11
Usoro, Nigeria 83 D6
Uspallata, P. de, Argentina 126 C2
Uspenskiy, Kazakstan 50 E8
Ussel, France 20 C6
Ussuri →, Asia 54 A7
Ussuriysk, Russia 51 E14
Ussurka, Russia 54 B6
Ust-Aldan = Batamay, Russia 51 C13
Ust-Amginskoye = Khandyga, Russia 51 C14
Ust-Bolsheretsk, Russia 51 D16
Ust-Buzulukskaya, Russia 48 E6
Ust-Chaun, Russia 51 C18
Ust-Donetskiy, Russia 49 G5
Ust-Ilimpeya = Yukta, Russia 51 C11
Ust-Ilimsk, Russia 51 D11
Ust-Ishim, Russia 50 D8
Ust-Kamchatsk, Russia 51 D17
Ust-Kamenogorsk = Öskemen, Kazakstan 50 E9
Ust-Khayryuzovo, Russia 51 D16
Ust-Kut, Russia 51 D11
Ust-Kuyga, Russia 51 B14
Ust-Labinsk, Russia 49 H4
Ust-Luga, Russia 46 C5
Ust-Maya, Russia 51 C14
Ust-Mil, Russia 51 D14
Ust-Nera, Russia 51 C15
Ust-Nyukzha, Russia 51 D13
Ust-Olenek, Russia 51 B12
Ust-Omchug, Russia 51 C15
Ust-Port, Russia 50 C9
Ust-Tsilma, Russia 50 C9
Ust Urt = Ustyurt Plateau, Asia 50 E6
Ustaritz, France 20 E2
Uster, Switz. 25 H4
Ústí nad Labem, Czech Rep. 26 A7
Ústí nad Orlicí, Czech Rep. 27 B9
Ústica, Italy 30 D6
Ustinov = Izhevsk, Russia 50 D6
Ustka, Poland 44 D3
Ustroń, Poland 45 J5
Ustrzyki Dolne, Poland 45 J9
Ustyurt Plateau, Asia 50 E6
Ustyuzhna, Russia 46 C9
Usu, China 60 B3
Usuki, Japan 55 H5
Usulután, El Salv. 120 D2
Usumacinta →, Mexico 119 D6
Usumbura = Bujumbura, Burundi 86 C2
Usure, Tanzania 86 C3
Usutuo →, Mozam. 89 D5
Uta, Indonesia 63 E9
Utah □, U.S.A. 114 G8
Utah L., U.S.A. 114 F8
Utansjö, Sweden 10 B11
Utarni, India 68 F4
Utatlan, Guatemala 120 C1
Ute Creek →, U.S.A. 113 H3
Utebo, Spain 32 D3
Utena, Lithuania 9 J21
Utete, Tanzania 86 D4
Uthai Thani, Thailand 64 E3
Uthal, Pakistan 68 G2
Utiariti, Brazil 124 F7
Utica, N.Y., U.S.A. 111 C9
Utica, Ohio, U.S.A. 110 F2
Utiel, Spain 33 F3
Utikuma L., Canada 104 B5
Utö, Sweden 10 F12
Utopia, Australia 94 C1
Utraula, India 69 F10
Utrecht, Neths. 17 B5
Utrecht, S. Africa 89 D5
Utrecht □, Neths. 17 B5
Utrera, Spain 35 H5
Utsjoki, Finland 8 B22
Utsunomiya, Japan 55 F9
Uttar Pradesh □, India 69 F9
Uttaradit, Thailand 64 D3
Uttaranchal □, India 69 D8
Uttoxeter, U.K. 12 E6
Uummannarsuaq = Nunap Isua, Greenland 101 C15
Uusikaarlepyy, Finland 8 E20
Uusikaupunki, Finland 9 F19
Uva, Russia 48 B11
Uvac →, Serbia, Yug. 40 C3
Uvalde, U.S.A. 113 L5
Uvarovo, Russia 48 E6
Uvat, Russia 50 D7
Uvinza, Tanzania 86 D3
Uvira, Dem. Rep. of the Congo 86 C2
Uvs Nuur, Mongolia 60 A4
'Uwairidh, Ḥarrat al, Si. Arabia 70 E3
Uwajima, Japan 55 H6
Uweinat, Jebel, Sudan 80 C1
Uxbridge, Canada 110 B5
Uxin Qi, China 56 E5
Uxmal, Mexico 119 C7
Úydzin, Mongolia 56 B4
Uyo, Nigeria 83 D6
Uyûn Mûsa, Egypt 75 F1
Uyuni, Bolivia 124 H5
Uzbekistan ■, Asia 50 E7
Uzen, Russia 48 E8
Uzen, Mal →, Kazakstan 49 F9
Uzerche, France 20 C5
Uzès, France 21 D8
Uzh →, Ukraine 47 G6

Uzhgorod = Uzhhorod, Ukraine 47 H2
Uzhhorod, Ukraine 47 H2
Užice, Serbia, Yug. 40 C3
Uzlovaya, Russia 46 F10
Üzümlü, Turkey 39 E11
Uzunköprü, Turkey 41 E10
Uzunkuyu, Turkey 39 C8

V

Vaal →, S. Africa 88 D3
Vaal Dam, S. Africa 89 D4
Vaalwater, S. Africa 89 C4
Vaasa, Finland 8 E19
Vabre, France 20 E6
Vác, Hungary 42 C4
Vacaria, Brazil 127 B5
Vacaville, U.S.A. 116 G5
Vaccarès, Étang de, France 21 E8
Vach = Vakh →, Russia 50 C8
Vache, Î. à, Haiti 121 C5
Vadnagar, India 68 H5
Vado Lígure, Italy 28 D5
Vadodara, India 68 H5
Vadsø, Norway 8 A23
Vadstena, Sweden 11 F8
Vaduz, Liech. 25 H5
Værøy, Norway 8 C15
Vágar, Færoe Is. 8 E9
Vaggeryd, Sweden 11 G8
Vagney, France 19 D13
Vagnhärad, Sweden 11 F11
Vågsfjorden, Norway 8 B17
Váh →, Slovak Rep. 27 D11
Vahsel B., Antarctica 5 D1
Vái, Greece 36 D8
Vaigach, Russia 50 B6
Vaiges, France 18 D6
Vaihingen, Germany 25 G4
Vail, U.S.A. 106 C5
Vailly-sur-Aisne, France 19 C10
Vaisali →, India 69 F8
Vaison-la-Romaine, France 21 D9
Vakarel, Bulgaria 40 D7
Vakfikebir, Turkey 73 B8
Vakh →, Russia 50 C8
Vakhtan, Russia 48 B8
Vál, Hungary 42 C3
Val-de-Marne □, France 19 D9
Val-d'Isère, France 21 C10
Val-d'Oise □, France 19 C9
Val-d'Or, Canada 102 C4
Val Marie, Canada 105 D7
Valaam, Russia 46 B6
Valadares, Portugal 34 D2
Valahia, Romania 43 F9
Valais □, Switz. 25 J3
Valais, Alpes du, Switz. 25 J3
Valandovo, Macedonia 40 E6
Valašské Meziříčí, Czech Rep. 27 B10
Valáxa, Greece 38 C6
Vålberg, Sweden 10 E7
Valbo, Sweden 10 D10
Valbondione, Italy 28 B7
Valcani, Romania 42 D5
Vâlcea □, Romania 43 F9
Valcheta, Argentina 128 E3
Valdagno, Italy 29 C8
Valdahon, France 19 E13
Valday, Russia 46 D7
Valdayskaya Vozvyshennost, Russia 46 D7
Valdeazogues →, Spain 35 G6
Valdecañas, Embalse de, Spain 34 F5
Valdemarsvik, Sweden 11 F10
Valdemoro, Spain 34 E7
Valdepeñas, Spain 35 G7
Valderaduey →, Spain 34 D5
Valdérice, Italy 30 D5
Valderrobres, Spain 32 E5
Valdés, Pen., Argentina 122 H4
Valdez, U.S.A. 100 B5
Valdivia, Chile 128 D2
Valdobbiádene, Italy 29 C8
Valdosta, U.S.A. 109 K4
Valdoviño, Spain 34 B2
Valdres, Norway 9 F13
Vale, Georgia 49 K6
Vale, U.S.A. 114 E5
Vale of Glamorgan □, U.K. 13 F4
Valea lui Mihai, Romania 42 C7
Valea Mărului, Romania 43 E12
Valença, Brazil 125 F11
Valença, Portugal 34 C2
Valença do Piauí, Brazil 125 E10
Valençay, France 19 E8
Valence = Valence d'Agen, France 20 D4
Valence, France 21 D8
Valence d'Agen, France 20 D4
Valencia, Spain 33 F4
Valencia, U.S.A. 115 J10
Valencia, Venezuela 124 A5
Valencia □, Spain 33 F4
Valencia de Alcántara, Spain 35 F3
Valencia de Don Juan, Spain 34 C5
Valencia I., Ireland 15 E1
Valenciennes, France 19 B10

Văleni, Romania 43 F9
Vălenii de Munte, Romania 43 E11
Valensole, France 21 E9
Valentigney, France 19 E13
Valentim, Sa. do, Brazil 125 E10
Valentin, Russia 54 C7
Valentine, U.S.A. 113 K2
Valenza, Italy 28 C5
Valera, Venezuela 124 B4
Valga, Estonia 9 H22
Valguarnera Caropepe, Italy 31 E7
Valier, U.S.A. 114 B7
Valinco, G. de, France 21 G12
Valjevo, Serbia, Yug. 40 B3
Valka, Latvia 9 H21
Valkeakoski, Finland 9 F20
Valkenswaard, Neths. 17 C5
Vall de Uxó = La Vall d'Uixó, Spain 32 F4
Valla, Sweden 10 E10
Valladolid, Mexico 119 C7
Valladolid, Spain 34 D6
Valladolid □, Spain 34 D6
Vallata, Italy 31 A8
Valldemossa, Spain 37 B9
Valle d'Aosta □, Italy 28 C4
Valle de Arán, Spain 32 C5
Valle de la Pascua, Venezuela 124 B5
Valle de las Palmas, Mexico 117 N10
Valle de Santiago, Mexico 118 C4
Valle de Suchil, Mexico 118 C4
Valle de Zaragoza, Mexico 118 B3
Valle Fértil, Sierra del, Argentina 126 C2
Valle Hermoso, Mexico 119 B5
Valledupar, Colombia 124 A4
Vallehermoso, Canary Is. 37 F2
Vallejo, U.S.A. 116 G4
Vallenar, Chile 126 B1
Valletta, Malta 36 D2
Valley Center, U.S.A. 117 M9
Valley City, U.S.A. 112 B6
Valley Falls, Oreg., U.S.A. 114 E3
Valley Falls, R.I., U.S.A. 111 E13
Valley Springs, U.S.A. 116 G6
Valley View, U.S.A. 111 F8
Valley Wells, U.S.A. 117 K11
Valleyview, Canada 104 B5
Valli di Comácchio, Italy 29 D9
Vallimanca, Arroyo, Argentina 126 D4
Vallo della Lucánia, Italy 31 B8
Vallon-Pont-d'Arc, France 21 D8
Vallorbe, Switz. 25 J2
Valls, Spain 32 D6
Valmaseda = Balmaseda, Spain 32 B1
Valmiera, Latvia 9 H21
Valnera, Spain 34 B7
Valognes, France 18 C5
Valona = Vlorë, Albania 40 F3
Valozhyn, Belarus 46 E4
Valpaços, Portugal 34 D3
Valparaíso, Chile 126 C1
Valparaíso, Mexico 118 C4
Valparaiso, U.S.A. 108 E2
Valparaíso □, Chile 126 C1
Valpovo, Croatia 42 E3
Valréas, France 21 D9
Vals →, S. Africa 88 D4
Vals, Switz. 25 J5
Vals, Tanjung, Indonesia 63 F9
Vals-les-Bains, France 21 D8
Valsad, India 66 J8
Valtellina, Italy 28 B6
Valuyki, Russia 47 G10
Valverde, Canary Is. 37 G2
Valverde del Camino, Spain 35 H4
Valverde del Fresno, Spain 34 E4
Vama, Romania 43 C10
Vamdrup, Denmark 11 J3
Vâmhus, Sweden 10 C8
Vammala, Finland 9 F20
Vámos, Greece 36 D6
Van, Turkey 70 B4
Van, L. = Van Gölü, Turkey 70 B4
Van Alstyne, U.S.A. 113 J6
Van Blommestein Meer, Surinam 125 C7
Van Buren, Canada 103 C6
Van Buren, Ark., U.S.A. 113 H7
Van Buren, Maine, U.S.A. 109 B11
Van Buren, Mo., U.S.A. 113 G9
Van Canh, Vietnam 64 F7
Van Diemen, C., N. Terr., Australia 92 B5
Van Diemen, C., Queens., Australia 94 B2
Van Diemen G., Australia 92 B5
Van Gölü, Turkey 70 B4
Van Horn, U.S.A. 113 K2
Van Ninh, Vietnam 64 F7
Van Rees, Pegunungan, Indonesia 63 E9
Van Wert, U.S.A. 108 E3
Van Yen, Vietnam 58 G5
Vanadzor, Armenia 49 K7
Vanavara, Russia 51 C11
Vancouver, Canada 104 D4
Vancouver, U.S.A. 116 E4
Vancouver, C., Australia 93 G2
Vancouver I., Canada 104 D3
Vandalia, Ill., U.S.A. 112 F10

Vandalia, *Mo., U.S.A.* 112 F9
Vandenburg, *U.S.A.* 117 L6
Vanderbijlpark, *S. Africa* 89 D4
Vandergrift, *U.S.A.* 110 F5
Vanderhoof, *Canada* 104 C4
Vanderkloof Dam, *S. Africa* ... 88 E3
Vanderlin I., *Australia* 94 B2
Vänern, *Sweden* 11 F7
Vänersborg, *Sweden* 11 F6
Vang Vieng, *Laos* 64 C4
Vanga, *Kenya* 86 C4
Vangaindrano, *Madag.* 89 C8
Vanguard, *Canada* 105 D7
Vanino, *Russia* 51 E15
Vânju Mare, *Romania* 42 F7
Vanna, *Norway* 8 A18
Vännäs, *Sweden* 8 E18
Vannes, *France* 18 E4
Vanoise, *France* 21 C10
Vanrhynsdorp, *S. Africa* 88 E2
Vansbro, *Sweden* 10 D8
Vansittart B., *Australia* 92 B4
Vantaa, *Finland* 9 F21
Vanua Balavu, *Fiji* 91 C9
Vanua Levu, *Fiji* 91 C8
Vanuatu ■, *Pac. Oc.* 96 J8
Vanwyksvlei, *S. Africa* 88 E3
Vanzylsrus, *S. Africa* 88 D3
Vapnyarka, *Ukraine* 47 H5
Var □, *France* 21 E10
Var ➤, *France* 21 E11
Vara, *Sweden* 11 F6
Varades, *France* 18 E5
Varáita ➤, *Italy* 28 D4
Varallo, *Italy* 28 C5
Varanasi, *India* 69 G10
Varangerfjorden, *Norway* 8 A23
Varangerhalvøya, *Norway* 8 A23
Varano, Lago di, *Italy* 29 G12
Varaždin, *Croatia* 29 B13
Varazze, *Italy* 28 D5
Varberg, *Sweden* 11 G6
Vardar = Axiós ➤, *Greece* ... 40 F6
Varde, *Denmark* 11 J2
Varde Å ➤, *Denmark* 11 J2
Vardø, *Norway* 8 A24
Varel, *Germany* 24 B4
Varella, Mui, *Vietnam* 64 F7
Varēna, *Lithuania* 9 J21
Varennes-sur-Allier, *France* .. 19 F10
Varennes-Vauzelles, *France* .. 19 E10
Vareš, *Bos.-H.* 42 F3
Varese, *Italy* 28 C5
Vârfurile, *Romania* 42 D7
Vårgårda, *Sweden* 11 F6
Varginha, *Brazil* 127 A6
Vargön, *Sweden* 11 F6
Varillas, *Chile* 126 A1
Varkaus, *Finland* 9 E22
Värmdölandet, *Sweden* 10 E12
Värmeln, *Sweden* 10 E6
Värmlands Bro, *Sweden* 10 E7
Värmlands län □, *Sweden* 10 E6
Varna, *Bulgaria* 41 C11
Varna □, *Bulgaria* 41 C11
Värnamo, *Sweden* 11 G8
Varnsdorf, *Czech Rep.* 26 A7
Várpalota, *Hungary* 42 C2
Vars, *Canada* 111 A9
Vars, *France* 21 D10
Varto, *Turkey* 73 C9
Varvarin, *Serbia, Yug.* 40 C5
Varysburg, *U.S.A.* 110 D6
Varzaneh, *Iran* 71 C7
Varzi, *Italy* 28 D6
Varzo, *Italy* 28 B5
Varzy, *France* 19 E10
Vas □, *Hungary* 42 C1
Vasa Barris ➤, *Brazil* 125 F11
Vásárosnamény, *Hungary* 42 B7
Vascão ➤, *Portugal* 35 H3
Vaşcău, *Romania* 42 D7
Vascongadas = País Vasco □,
  Spain 32 C2
Vasht = Khâsh, *Iran* 66 E2
Vasilevichi, *Belarus* 47 F5
Vasilikón, *Greece* 38 C5
Vasilkov = Vasylkiv, *Ukraine* . 47 G6
Vaslui, *Romania* 43 D12
Vaslui □, *Romania* 43 D12
Väsman, *Sweden* 10 D9
Vassar, *Canada* 105 D9
Vassar, *U.S.A.* 108 D4
Västerås, *Sweden* 10 E10
Västerbotten, *Sweden* 8 D18
Västerdalälven ➤, *Sweden* ... 10 D8
Västergötland, *Sweden* 11 F7
Västerhaninge, *Sweden* 10 E12
Västervik, *Sweden* 11 G10
Västmanland, *Sweden* 9 G16
Västmanlands län □, *Sweden* . 10 E10
Vasto, *Italy* 29 F11
Västra Götalands Län □,
  Sweden 11 F6
Vasvár, *Hungary* 42 C1
Vasylkiv, *Ukraine* 47 G6
Vatan, *France* 19 E8
Vatersay, *U.K.* 14 E1
Váthia, *Greece* 38 E4
Vatican City ■, *Europe* 29 G9
Vaticano, C., *Italy* 31 D8
Vatili, *Cyprus* 36 D12
Vatin, *Serbia, Yug.* 42 E6
Vatnajökull, *Iceland* 8 D5
Vatoa, *Fiji* 91 D9

Vatólakkos, *Greece* 36 D5
Vatoloha, *Madag.* 89 B8
Vatomandry, *Madag.* 89 B8
Vatra-Dornei, *Romania* 43 C10
Vatrak ➤, *India* 68 H5
Vättern, *Sweden* 11 F8
Vaucluse □, *France* 21 E9
Vaucouleurs, *France* 19 D12
Vaud □, *Switz.* 25 J2
Vaughn, *Mont., U.S.A.* 114 C8
Vaughn, *N. Mex., U.S.A.* 115 J11
Vaujours L., *Canada* 102 A5
Vaupés = Uaupés ➤, *Brazil* .. 124 C5
Vaupes □, *Colombia* 124 C4
Vauvert, *France* 21 E8
Vauxhall, *Canada* 104 C6
Vav, *India* 68 G4
Vavatenina, *Madag.* 89 B8
Vava'u, *Tonga* 91 D12
Vavoua, *Ivory C.* 82 D3
Vawkavysk, *Belarus* 47 F3
Vaxholm, *Sweden* 10 E12
Växjö, *Sweden* 11 H8
Våxtorp, *Sweden* 11 H7
Vaygach, Ostrov, *Russia* 50 C6
Váyia, *Greece* 38 C5
Váyia, Ákra, *Greece* 36 C10
Vechelde, *Germany* 24 C6
Vechta, *Germany* 24 C4
Vechte ➤, *Neths.* 17 B6
Vecsés, *Hungary* 42 C4
Veddige, *Sweden* 11 G6
Vedea ➤, *Romania* 43 G10
Vedia, *Argentina* 126 C3
Vedum, *Sweden* 11 F7
Veendam, *Neths.* 17 A6
Veenendaal, *Neths.* 17 B5
Vefsna ➤, *Norway* 8 D15
Vega, *Norway* 8 D14
Vega, *U.S.A.* 113 H3
Vegadeo, *Spain* 34 B3
Vegarshei, *Norway* 9 G13
Vegreville, *Canada* 104 C6
Veinge, *Sweden* 11 H7
Veisiejai, *Lithuania* 44 D10
Vejbystrand, *Sweden* 11 H6
Vejen, *Denmark* 11 J3
Vejer de la Frontera, *Spain* .. 35 J5
Vejle, *Denmark* 11 J3
Vejle Amtskommune □,
  Denmark 11 J3
Vejle Fjord, *Denmark* 11 J3
Vela Luka, *Croatia* 29 F13
Velas, C., *Costa Rica* 120 D2
Velasco, Sierra de, *Argentina* . 126 B2
Velay, Mts. du, *France* 20 D7
Velbert, *Germany* 24 D3
Velddrif, *S. Africa* 88 E2
Velebit Planina, *Croatia* 29 D12
Velebitski Kanal, *Croatia* ... 29 D11
Veleka ➤, *Bulgaria* 41 D11
Velenje, *Slovenia* 29 B12
Velencei-tó, *Hungary* 42 C3
Velenje, *Slovenia* 29 B12
Veles, *Macedonia* 40 E5
Velestínon, *Greece* 38 B4
Vélez-Málaga, *Spain* 35 J6
Vélez Rubio, *Spain* 33 H2
Velhas ➤, *Brazil* 125 G10
Velika, *Croatia* 42 E2
Velika Gorica, *Croatia* 29 C13
Velika Kapela, *Croatia* 29 C12
Velika Kladuša, *Bos.-H.* 29 C12
Velika Kruša, *Kosovo, Yug.* .. 40 D4
Velika Morava ➤, *Serbia, Yug.* 40 B5
Velika Plana, *Serbia, Yug.* ... 40 B5
Velikaya ➤, *Russia* 46 D5
Velikaya Kema, *Russia* 54 B8
Velikaya Lepetikha, *Ukraine* . 47 J7
Veliké Kapušany, *Slovak Rep.* 27 C15
Velike Lašče, *Slovenia* 29 C11
Veliki Jastrebac, *Serbia, Yug.* 40 C5
Veliki Kanal, *Serbia, Yug.* ... 42 E4
Veliki Popović, *Serbia, Yug.* . 40 B5
Velikiye Luki, *Russia* 46 D6
Veliko Gradište, *Serbia, Yug.* 40 B5
Veliko Tŭrnovo, *Bulgaria* ... 41 C9
Velikonda Range, *India* 66 M11
Vélingara, *Senegal* 82 C2
Vélingara, *Senegal* 82 B2
Velingrad, *Bulgaria* 40 D7
Velizh, *Russia* 46 E6
Velké Karlovice, *Czech Rep.* . 27 B11
Velké Meziříčí, *Czech Rep.* .. 26 B9
Vel'ký Javorník, *Slovak Rep.* . 27 B11
Vel'ký Krtíš, *Slovak Rep.* ... 27 C12
Vel'ký Meder, *Slovak Rep.* .. 27 D10
Vel'ký Tribeč, *Slovak Rep.* .. 27 C11
Velletri, *Italy* 30 A5
Vellinge, *Sweden* 11 J6
Vellmar, *Germany* 24 D5
Vellore, *India* 66 N11
Velsk, *Russia* 46 B11
Velten, *Germany* 24 C9
Velva, *U.S.A.* 112 A4
Velvendós, *Greece* 40 F6
Vemb, *Denmark* 11 H2
Vemdalen, *Sweden* 10 B7
Ven, *Sweden* 11 J6
Venaco, *France* 21 F13
Venado Tuerto, *Argentina* ... 126 C3
Venafro, *Italy* 31 A7
Venarey-les-Laumes, *France* . 19 E11
Venaría, *Italy* 28 C4
Venčane, *Serbia, Yug.* 40 B4

Vence, *France* 21 E11
Vendas Novas, *Portugal* 35 G2
Vendée □, *France* 18 F5
Vendée ➤, *France* 18 F5
Vendéen, Bocage, *France* 20 B2
Vendeuvre-sur-Barse, *France* . 19 D11
Vendôme, *France* 18 E8
Vendrell = El Vendrell, *Spain* . 32 D6
Vendsyssel, *Denmark* 11 G4
Venelles, *France* 21 E9
Véneta, L., *Italy* 29 C9
Véneto □, *Italy* 29 C9
Venev, *Russia* 46 E10
Venézia, *Italy* 29 C9
Venézia, G. di, *Italy* 29 C10
Venezuela ■, *S. Amer.* 124 B5
Venezuela, G. de, *Venezuela* . 122 B3
Vengurla, *India* 66 M8
Venice = Venézia, *Italy* 29 C9
Venice, *U.S.A.* 109 M4
Vénissieux, *France* 21 C8
Venjansjön, *Sweden* 10 D8
Venkatapuram, *India* 67 K12
Venlo, *Neths.* 17 C6
Vennesla, *Norway* 9 G12
Venosa, *Italy* 31 B8
Venray, *Neths.* 17 C6
Venta, *Lithuania* 44 B9
Venta ➤, *Latvia* 44 A8
Venta de Baños, *Spain* 34 D6
Venta de Cardeña = Cardeña,
  Spain 35 G6
Ventana, Punta de la, *Mexico* 118 C3
Ventana, Sa. de la, *Argentina* 126 D3
Ventersburg, *S. Africa* 88 D4
Venterstad, *S. Africa* 88 E4
Ventimíglia, *Italy* 28 E4
Ventnor, *U.K.* 13 G6
Ventoténe, *Italy* 30 B6
Ventoux, Mt., *France* 21 D9
Ventspils, *Latvia* 9 H19
Ventspils □, *Latvia* 44 A8
Ventuari ➤, *Venezuela* 124 C5
Ventucopa, *U.S.A.* 117 L7
Ventura, *U.S.A.* 117 L7
Vera, *Argentina* 126 B3
Vera, *Spain* 33 H3
Veracruz, *Mexico* 119 D5
Veracruz □, *Mexico* 119 D5
Veraval, *India* 68 J4
Verbánia, *Italy* 28 C5
Verbicaro, *Italy* 31 C8
Verbier, *Switz.* 25 J3
Vercelli, *Italy* 28 C5
Verchovtsevo, *Ukraine* 47 H8
Verdalsøra, *Norway* 8 E14
Verde ➤, *Argentina* 128 E3
Verde ➤, *Goiás, Brazil* 125 G8
Verde ➤, *Mato Grosso do Sul,
  Brazil* 125 H8
Verde ➤, *Chihuahua, Mexico* 118 B3
Verde ➤, *Oaxaca, Mexico* ... 119 D5
Verde ➤, *Veracruz, Mexico* . 118 C4
Verde ➤, *Paraguay* 126 A4
Verde ➤, *U.S.A.* 106 D4
Verde, Cay, *Bahamas* 120 B4
Verde Island Pass, *Phil.* 61 E4
Verden, *Germany* 24 C5
Verdhikoúsa, *Greece* 38 B3
Verdi, *U.S.A.* 116 F7
Verdon ➤, *France* 21 E9
Verdun, *France* 19 C12
Verdun-sur-le-Doubs, *France* . 19 F12
Vereeniging, *S. Africa* 89 D4
Verga, C., *Guinea* 82 C2
Vergara, *Uruguay* 127 C5
Vergato, *Italy* 28 D8
Vergemont Cr. ➤, *Australia* . 94 C3
Vergennes, *U.S.A.* 111 B11
Vergt, *France* 20 D4
Verín, *Spain* 34 D3
Verkhnedvinsk =
  Vyerkhnyadzvinsk, *Belarus* . 46 E4
Verkhnevilyuysk, *Russia* 51 C13
Verkhniy Baskunchak, *Russia* 49 F8
Verkhovye, *Russia* 47 F9
Verkhoyansk, *Russia* 51 C14
Verkhoyansk Ra. =
  Verkhoyanskiy Khrebet,
  Russia 51 C13
Verkhoyanskiy Khrebet, *Russia* 51 C13
Verlímion, *Greece* 40 F6
Vermenton, *France* 19 E10
Vermilion, *Canada* 105 C6
Vermilion, *U.S.A.* 110 E2
Vermilion ➤, *Alta., Canada* . 105 C6
Vermilion ➤, *Qué., Canada* . 102 C5
Vermilion, B., *U.S.A.* 113 L9
Vermilion Bay, *Canada* 105 D10
Vermilion L., *U.S.A.* 112 B8
Vermillion, *U.S.A.* 112 D6
Vermont □, *U.S.A.* 111 C12
Vermosh, *Albania* 40 D3
Vernal, *U.S.A.* 114 F9
Vernalis, *U.S.A.* 116 H5
Verner, *Canada* 102 C3
Verneuil-sur-Avre, *France* .. 18 D7
Verneukpan, *S. Africa* 88 E3
Vernier, *Switz.* 25 J2
Vérnio, *Italy* 28 D8
Vernon, *Canada* 104 C5
Vernon, *France* 18 C8
Vernon, *U.S.A.* 113 H5
Vernonia, *U.S.A.* 116 E3
Vernouillet, *France* 18 D8

Vero Beach, *U.S.A.* 109 M5
Véroia, *Greece* 40 F6
Véroli, *Italy* 29 G10
Verona, *Canada* 111 B8
Verona, *Italy* 28 C7
Verona, *U.S.A.* 112 D10
Verrès, *Italy* 28 C4
Versailles, *France* 19 D9
Versmold, *Germany* 24 C4
Vert, C., *Senegal* 82 C1
Vertou, *France* 18 E5
Vertus, *France* 19 D11
Verulam, *S. Africa* 89 D5
Vervins, *France* 19 C10
Verzej, *Slovenia* 29 B13
Verzy, *France* 19 C11
Vescovato, *France* 21 F13
Veselí nad Lužnicí, *Czech Rep.* 26 B7
Veselie, *Bulgaria* 41 D11
Veselovskoye Vdkhr., *Russia* . 49 G5
Veshenskaya, *Russia* 48 F5
Vesle ➤, *France* 19 C10
Vesoul, *France* 19 E13
Vessigebro, *Sweden* 11 H6
Vesterålen, *Norway* 8 B16
Vestfjorden, *Norway* 8 C15
Vestmannaeyjar, *Iceland* ... 8 E3
Vestsjællands Amtskommune □,
  Denmark 11 J5
Vestspitsbergen, *Svalbard* .. 4 B8
Vestvågøy, *Norway* 8 B15
Vesuvio, *Italy* 31 B7
Vesuvius, Mt. = Vesuvio, *Italy* . 31 B7
Vesyegonsk, *Russia* 46 C9
Veszprém, *Hungary* 42 C2
Veszprém □, *Hungary* 42 C2
Vésztő, *Hungary* 42 C6
Vetlanda, *Sweden* 11 G9
Vetluga, *Russia* 48 B7
Vetlugu ➤, *Russia* 48 B8
Vetluzhskiy, *Kostroma, Russia* 48 B7
Vetluzhskiy, *Nizhniy Novgorod,
  Russia* 48 B7
Vetovo, *Bulgaria* 41 C10
Vetralla, *Italy* 29 F9
Vetren, *Bulgaria* 41 D8
Vettore, Mte., *Italy* 29 F10
Veurne, *Belgium* 17 C2
Veveno ➤, *Sudan* 81 F3
Vevey, *Switz.* 25 J2
Vévi, *Greece* 40 F5
Veynes, *France* 21 D9
Veys, *Iran* 71 D6
Vézelay, *France* 19 E10
Vézelise, *France* 19 D13
Vézère ➤, *France* 20 D4
Vezhen, *Bulgaria* 41 D8
Vezirköprü, *Turkey* 72 B6
Vezzani, *France* 21 F13
Vi Thanh, *Vietnam* 65 H5
Viacha, *Bolivia* 124 G5
Viadana, *Italy* 28 D7
Viamão, *Brazil* 127 C5
Viana, *Brazil* 125 D10
Viana, *Spain* 32 C2
Viana do Alentejo, *Portugal* . 35 G3
Viana do Bolo, *Spain* 34 C3
Viana do Castelo, *Portugal* .. 34 D2
Viana do Castelo □, *Portugal* . 34 D2
Vianden, *Lux.* 17 E6
Viangchan = Vientiane, *Laos* . 64 D4
Vianópolis, *Brazil* 125 G9
Viar ➤, *Spain* 35 H5
Viaréggio, *Italy* 28 E7
Viaur ➤, *France* 20 D5
Vibble, *Sweden* 11 G12
Víbo Valéntia, *Italy* 31 D9
Viborg, *Denmark* 11 H3
Vibraye, *France* 18 D7
Vic, *Spain* 32 D7
Vic, Étang de, *France* 20 E7
Vic-en-Bigorre, *France* 20 E4
Vic-Fézensac, *France* 20 E4
Vic-le-Comte, *France* 19 G10
Vic-sur-Cère, *France* 20 D6
Vícar, *Spain* 33 J2
Vicenza, *Italy* 29 C8
Vich = Vic, *Spain* 32 D7
Vichada ➤, *Colombia* 124 C5
Vichuga, *Russia* 48 B5
Vichy, *France* 19 F10
Vicksburg, *Ariz., U.S.A.* ... 117 M13
Vicksburg, *Miss., U.S.A.* ... 113 J9
Vico, *France* 21 F12
Vico, L. di, *Italy* 29 F9
Vico del Gargano, *Italy* 29 G12
Vicovu de Sus, *Romania* 43 C10
Victor, *India* 68 J4
Victor, *U.S.A.* 110 D7
Victoria = Labuan, *Malaysia* . 62 C5
Victoria, *Argentina* 126 C3
Victoria, *Canada* 104 D4
Victoria, *Chile* 128 D2
Victoria, *Guinea* 82 C2
Victoria, *Malta* 36 C1
Victoria, *Phil.* 61 D4
Victoria, *Kans., U.S.A.* 112 F5
Victoria ➤, *Australia* 92 C4
Victoria, Grand L., *Canada* . 102 C4
Victoria, L., *Africa* 86 C3
Victoria, Mt., *Burma* 67 J18
Victoria, Tex., U.S.A.* 113 L6

Victoria Beach, *Canada* 105 C9
Victoria de Durango = Durango,
  Mexico 118 C4
Victoria de las Tunas, *Cuba* . 120 B4
Victoria Falls, *Zimbabwe* ... 87 F2
Victoria Harbour, *Canada* ... 110 B5
Victoria I., *Canada* 100 A8
Victoria L., *Canada* 103 C8
Victoria Ld., *Antarctica* 5 D11
Victoria Nile ➤, *Uganda* 86 B3
Victoria River, *Australia* 92 C5
Victoria Str., *Canada* 100 B9
Victoria West, *S. Africa* 88 E3
Victorias, *Phil.* 61 F5
Victoriaville, *Canada* 103 C5
Victorica, *Argentina* 126 D2
Victorville, *U.S.A.* 117 L9
Vicuña, *Chile* 126 C1
Vicuña Mackenna, *Argentina* 126 C3
Vidal, *U.S.A.* 117 L12
Vidal Junction, *U.S.A.* 117 L12
Vidalia, *U.S.A.* 109 J4
Vidauban, *France* 21 E10
Videbæk, *Denmark* 11 H2
Videle, *Romania* 43 F10
Vídho, *Greece* 36 A3
Vidigueira, *Portugal* 35 G3
Vidin, *Bulgaria* 40 C6
Vidio, C., *Spain* 34 B4
Vidisha, *India* 68 H7
Vidra, *Romania* 43 E11
Viduša, *Bos.-H.* 40 D2
Vidzy, *Belarus* 9 J22
Viechtach, *Germany* 25 F8
Viedma, *Argentina* 128 E4
Viedma, L., *Argentina* 128 F2
Vieira do Minho, *Portugal* .. 34 D2
Vielha, *Spain* 32 C5
Viella = Vielha, *Spain* 32 C5
Vielsalm, *Belgium* 17 D5
Vienenburg, *Germany* 24 D6
Vieng Pou Kha, *Laos* 58 G3
Vienna = Wien, *Austria* 27 C9
Vienna, *Ill., U.S.A.* 113 G10
Vienna, *Mo., U.S.A.* 112 F9
Vienne, *France* 21 C8
Vienne □, *France* 20 B4
Vienne ➤, *France* 18 E7
Vientiane, *Laos* 64 D4
Vientos, Paso de los, *Caribbean* 121 C5
Viernheim, *Germany* 25 F4
Viersen, *Germany* 24 D2
Vierwaldstättersee, *Switz.* .. 25 J4
Vierzon, *France* 19 E9
Vieste, *Italy* 29 G13
Vietnam ■, *Asia* 64 C6
Vieux-Boucau-les-Bains, *France* 20 E2
Vif, *France* 21 C9
Vigan, *Phil.* 61 C4
Vigévano, *Italy* 28 C5
Vigia, *Brazil* 125 D9
Vigía Chico, *Mexico* 119 D7
Víglas, Ákra, *Greece* 36 D9
Vignemalle, *France* 20 F3
Vigneulles-lès-Hattonchâtel,
  France 19 D12
Vignola, *Italy* 28 D8
Vigo, *Spain* 34 C2
Vigo, Ría de, *Spain* 34 C2
Vigsø Bugt, *Denmark* 11 G2
Vihiers, *France* 18 E6
Vihowa, *Pakistan* 68 D4
Vihowa ➤, *Pakistan* 68 D4
Vijayawada, *India* 67 L12
Vijosë ➤, *Albania* 40 F3
Vík, *Iceland* 8 E4
Vika, *Sweden* 10 D8
Vikarbyn, *Sweden* 10 D9
Vikeke, E. Timor* 63 F7
Viken, *Skåne, Sweden* 11 H6
Viken, *Västra Götaland, Sweden* 11 F8
Viking, *Canada* 104 C6
Vikmanshyttan, *Sweden* ... 10 D9
Vikna, *Norway* 8 D14
Vila da Maganja, *Mozam.* .. 87 F4
Vila de João Belo = Xai-Xai,
  Mozam. 89 D5
Vila de Rei, *Portugal* 34 F2
Vila do Bispo, *Portugal* 35 H2
Vila do Conde, *Portugal* 34 D2
Vila Franca de Xira, *Portugal* . 35 G2
Vila Gamito, *Mozam.* 87 E3
Vila Gomes da Costa, *Mozam.* 89 C5
Vila Machado, *Mozam.* 87 F3
Vila Mouzinho, *Mozam.* 87 E3
Vila Nova de Famalicão,
  Portugal 34 D2
Vila Nova de Fos Côa, *Portugal* 34 D3
Vila Nova de Foscôa = Vila
  Nova de Fos Côa, *Portugal* . 34 D3
Vila Nova de Gaia, *Portugal* . 34 D2
Vila Nova de Ourém, *Portugal* . 34 F2
Vila Pouca de Aguiar, *Portugal* 34 D3
Vila Real, *Portugal* 34 D3
Vila Real □, *Portugal* 34 D3
Vila-real de los Infantes, *Spain* 32 F4
Vila Real de Santo António,
  Portugal 35 H3
Vila Vasco da Gama, *Mozam.* 87 E3
Vila Velha, *Brazil* 127 A7
Vila Viçosa, *Portugal* 35 G3
Vilafranca del Maestrat, *Spain* 32 E4
Vilafranca del Penedès, *Spain* 32 D6
Vilagarcía de Arousa, *Spain* . 34 C2
Vilaine ➤, *France* 18 E4
Vilanandro, Tanjona, *Madag.* . 89 B7

Vilanculos, Mozam. 89 C6
Vilanova de Castelló, Spain ... 33 F4
Vilanova i la Geltrú, Spain ... 32 D6
Vilar Formosa, Portugal 34 E4
Vilaseca, Spain 32 D6
Vilaseca-Salou = Vilaseca, Spain 32 D6
Vilches, Spain 35 G7
Vileyka, Belarus 46 E4
Vilhelmina, Sweden 8 D17
Vilhena, Brazil 124 F6
Viliga, Russia 51 C16
Viliya →, Lithuania 9 J21
Viljandi, Estonia 9 G21
Vilkaviškis, Lithuania 44 D10
Vilkija, Lithuania 44 C10
Vilkitskogo, Proliv, Russia ... 51 B11
Vilkovo = Vylkove, Ukraine ... 47 K5
Villa Abecia, Bolivia 126 A2
Villa Ahumada, Mexico 118 A3
Villa Ana, Argentina 126 B4
Villa Ángela, Argentina 126 B3
Villa Bella, Bolivia 124 F5
Villa Bens = Tarfaya, Morocco 78 C3
Villa Cañás, Argentina 126 C3
Villa Cisneros = Dakhla,
  W. Sahara 78 D2
Villa Colón, Argentina 126 C2
Villa Constitución, Argentina . 126 C3
Villa de María, Argentina ... 126 B3
Villa del Rio, Spain 35 H6
Villa Dolores, Argentina 126 C2
Villa Frontera, Mexico 118 B4
Villa Guillermina, Argentina .. 126 B4
Villa Hayes, Paraguay 126 B4
Villa Iris, Argentina 126 D3
Villa Juárez, Mexico 118 B4
Villa María, Argentina 126 C3
Villa Mazán, Argentina 126 B2
Villa Minozzo, Italy 28 D7
Villa Montes, Bolivia 126 A3
Villa Ocampo, Argentina 126 B4
Villa Ocampo, Mexico 118 B3
Villa Ojo de Agua, Argentina .. 126 B3
Villa San Giovanni, Italy 31 D8
Villa San José, Argentina 126 C4
Villa San Martín, Argentina .. 126 B3
Villa Santina, Italy 29 B9
Villa Unión, Mexico 118 C3
Villablino, Spain 34 C4
Villacarlos, Spain 37 B11
Villacarriedo, Spain 34 B7
Villacarrillo, Spain 35 G7
Villacastín, Spain 34 E6
Villach, Austria 26 E6
Villacidro, Italy 30 C1
Villada, Spain 34 C6
Villadiego, Spain 34 C6
Villadóssola, Italy 28 B5
Villafeliche, Spain 32 D3
Villafranca, Spain 32 C3
Villafranca de los Barros, Spain 35 G4
Villafranca de los Caballeros,
  Baleares, Spain 37 B10
Villafranca de los Caballeros,
  Toledo, Spain 35 F7
Villafranca del Cid = Vilafranca
  del Maestrat, Spain 32 E4
Villafranca del Panadés =
  Vilafranca del Penedès, Spain 32 D6
Villafranca di Verona, Italy 28 C7
Villafranca Tirrena, Italy 31 D8
Villagrán, Mexico 119 C5
Villaguay, Argentina 126 C4
Villaharta, Spain 35 G6
Villahermosa, Mexico 119 D6
Villahermosa, Spain 33 G2
Villaines-la-Juhel, France 18 D6
Villajoyosa, Spain 33 G4
Villalba, Spain 34 B3
Villalba de Guardo, Spain 34 C6
Villalón de Campos, Spain 34 C5
Villalpando, Spain 34 D5
Villaluenga, Spain 34 E7
Villamanán, Spain 34 C5
Villamartín, Spain 35 J5
Villamayor de Santiago, Spain . 32 F2
Villamblard, France 20 C4
Villanova Monteleone, Italy ... 30 B1
Villanueva, U.S.A. 113 H2
Villanueva de Castelló =
  Vilanova de Castelló, Spain .. 33 F4
Villanueva de Córdoba, Spain . 35 G6
Villanueva de la Fuente, Spain . 33 G2
Villanueva de la Serena, Spain . 35 G5
Villanueva de la Sierra, Spain . 34 E4
Villanueva de los Castillejos,
  Spain 35 H3
Villanueva de los Infantes, Spain 35 G7
Villanueva del Arzobispo, Spain 33 G2
Villanueva del Fresno, Spain .. 35 G3
Villanueva y Geltrú = Vilanova i
  la Geltrú, Spain 32 D6
Villaputzu, Italy 30 C2
Villaquilambre, Spain 34 C5
Villar del Arzobispo, Spain ... 32 F4
Villar del Rey, Spain 35 F4
Villard-de-Lans, France 21 C9
Villarramiel, Spain 34 C6
Villarreal = Vila-real de los
  Infantes, Spain 32 F4
Villarrica, Chile 128 D2
Villarrica, Paraguay 126 B4
Villarrobledo, Spain 33 F2
Villarroya de la Sierra, Spain . 32 D3
Villarrubia de los Ojos, Spain .. 35 F7

Villars-les-Dombes, France 19 F12
Villasayas, Spain 32 D2
Villaseca de los Gamitos =
  Villaseco de los Gamitos,
  Spain 34 D4
Villaseco de los Gamitos, Spain 34 D4
Villasimíus, Italy 30 C2
Villastar, Spain 32 E3
Villatobas, Spain 34 F7
Villavicencio, Argentina 126 C2
Villavicencio, Colombia 124 C4
Villaviciosa, Spain 34 B5
Villazón, Bolivia 126 A2
Ville-Marie, Canada 102 C4
Ville Platte, U.S.A. 113 K8
Villedieu-les-Poêles, France ... 18 D5
Villefort, France 20 D7
Villefranche-de-Lauragais,
  France 20 E5
Villefranche-de-Rouergue,
  France 20 D6
Villefranche-du-Périgord, France 20 D5
Villefranche-sur-Saône, France 21 C8
Villel, Spain 32 E3
Villemur-sur-Tarn, France 20 E5
Villena, Spain 33 G4
Villenauxe-la-Grande, France . 19 D10
Villeneuve-d'Ornon, France 20 D3
Villeneuve-d'Ascq, France 19 B10
Villeneuve-l'Archevêque,
  France 19 D10
Villeneuve-lès-Avignon, France 21 E8
Villeneuve-sur-Allier, France .. 19 F10
Villeneuve-sur-Lot, France 20 D4
Villeneuve-sur-Yonne, France . 19 D10
Villeréal, France 20 D4
Villers-Bocage, France 18 C6
Villers-Cotterêts, France 19 C10
Villers-sur-Mer, France 18 C6
Villersexel, France 19 E13
Villerupt, France 19 C12
Villeurbanne, France 21 C8
Villiers, S. Africa 89 D4
Villingen-Schwenningen,
  Germany 25 G4
Vilna, Canada 104 C6
Vilnius, Lithuania 9 J21
Vils, Austria 26 D3
Vils →, Bayern, Germany 25 G9
Vils →, Bayern, Germany 25 F7
Vilsbiburg, Germany 25 G8
Vilshofen, Germany 25 G9
Vilusi, Montenegro, Yug. 40 D2
Vilvoorde, Belgium 17 D4
Vilyuy →, Russia 51 C13
Vilyuysk, Russia 51 C13
Vimianzo, Spain 34 B1
Vimioso, Portugal 34 D4
Vimmerby, Sweden 11 G9
Vimoutiers, France 18 D7
Vimperk, Czech Rep. 26 B6
Viña del Mar, Chile 126 C1
Vinaròs, Spain 32 E5
Vincennes, U.S.A. 108 F2
Vincent, U.S.A. 117 L8
Vinchina, Argentina 126 B2
Vindelälven →, Sweden 8 E18
Vindeln, Sweden 8 D18
Vinderup, Denmark 11 H2
Vindhya Ra., India 68 H7
Vineland, U.S.A. 108 F8
Vineuil, France 18
Vinga, Romania 42 D6
Vingåker, Sweden 10 E9
Vinh, Vietnam 64 C5
Vinh Linh, Vietnam 64 D6
Vinh Long, Vietnam 65 G5
Vinh Yen, Vietnam 58 G5
Vinhais, Portugal 34 D3
Vinica, Croatia 29 B13
Vinica, Macedonia 40 E6
Vinica, Slovenia 29 C12
Vinita, U.S.A. 113 G7
Vinkovci, Croatia 42 E3
Vinnitsa = Vinnytsya, Ukraine . 47 H5
Vinnytsya, Ukraine 47 H5
Vinslöv, Sweden 11 H7
Vintjärn, Sweden 10 D10
Vinton, Calif., U.S.A. 116 F6
Vinton, Iowa, U.S.A. 112 D8
Vinton, La., U.S.A. 113 K8
Vințu de Jos, Romania 43 D8
Viöl, Germany 24 A5
Vipava, Slovenia 29 C10
Vipiteno, Italy 29 B8
Vir, Croatia 29 D12
Virac, Phil. 61 E6
Virachei, Cambodia 64 F6
Virago Sd., Canada 104 C2
Viramgam, India 68 H5
Virananşehir, Turkey 70 B3
Virawah, Pakistan 68 G4
Virbalis, Lithuania 44 D9
Virden, Canada 105 D8
Vire, France 18 D6
Vire →, France 18 C5
Vírgenes, C., Argentina 128 G3
Virgin →, U.S.A. 115 H6
Virgin Gorda, Br. Virgin Is. .. 121 C7
Virgin Is. (British) ■, W. Indies 121 C7
Virgin Is. (U.S.) ■, W. Indies . 121 C7
Virginia, S. Africa 88 D4
Virginia, U.S.A. 112 B8
Virginia □, U.S.A. 108 G7
Virginia Beach, U.S.A. 108 G8
Virginia City, Mont., U.S.A. ... 114 D8

Virginia City, Nev., U.S.A. 116 F7
Virginia Falls, Canada 104 A3
Virginiatown, Canada 102 C4
Virje, Croatia 29 B13
Viroqua, U.S.A. 112 D9
Virovitica, Croatia 42 E2
Virpazar, Montenegro, Yug. ... 40 D3
Virpur, India 68 J4
Virserum, Sweden 11 G9
Virton, Belgium 17 E5
Virudunagar, India 66 Q10
Vis, Croatia 29 E13
Visalia, U.S.A. 116 J7
Visayan Sea, Phil. 61 F5
Visby, Sweden 11 G12
Viscount Melville Sd., Canada . 4 B2
Visé, Belgium 17 D5
Višegrad, Bos.-H. 42 G4
Viseu, Brazil 125 D9
Viseu, Portugal 34 E3
Viseu □, Portugal 34 E3
Vişeu de Sus, Romania 43 C9
Vishakhapatnam, India 67 L13
Vişina, Romania 43 G9
Vişineşti, Moldova 43 D13
Visingsö, Sweden 11 F8
Viskafors, Sweden 11 G6
Viskan →, Sweden 11 G6
Viški Kanal, Croatia 29 E13
Vislanda, Sweden 11 H8
Visnagar, India 68 H5
Višnja Gora, Slovenia 29 C11
Viso, Mte., Italy 28 D4
Viso del Marqués, Spain 35 G7
Visoko, Bos.-H. 42 G3
Visokoi I., Antarctica 5 B1
Visp, Switz. 25 J3
Vissefjärda, Sweden 11 H9
Visselhövede, Germany 24 C5
Vissenbjerg, Denmark 11 J4
Vista, U.S.A. 117 M9
Vistonikos, Ormos = Vistonís,
  Límni, Greece 41 E9
Vistonís, Límni, Greece 41 E9
Vistula = Wisła →, Poland ... 44 D5
Vit →, Bulgaria 41 C8
Vitanje, Slovenia 29 B12
Vitebsk = Vitsyebsk, Belarus .. 46 E6
Viterbo, Italy 29 F9
Vitez, Bos.-H. 42 F2
Viti Levu, Fiji 91 C7
Vitigudino, Spain 34 D4
Vitim, Russia 51 D12
Vitim →, Russia 51 D12
Vitina, Greece 38 D4
Vitína, Greece 38 D4
Vítkov, Czech Rep. 27 B10
Vitória, Brazil 125 H10
Vitória da Conquista, Brazil ... 125 F10
Vitória de São Antão, Brazil .. 125 E11
Vitoria-Gasteiz, Spain 32 C2
Vitré, France 18 D5
Vitry-le-François, France 19 D11
Vitry-sur-Seine, France 19 D9
Vitsand, Sweden 10 D7
Vitsi, Óros, Greece 40 F5
Vitsyebsk, Belarus 46 E6
Vittaryd, Sweden 11 H7
Vitteaux, France 19 E11
Vittel, France 19 D12
Vittória, Italy 31 F7
Vittório Véneto, Italy 29 C9
Vittsjö, Sweden 11 H7
Viveiro, Spain 34 B3
Vivian, U.S.A. 113 J8
Viviers, France 21 D8
Vivonne, France 20 B4
Vizcaíno, Desierto de, Mexico . 118 B2
Vizcaíno, Sierra, Mexico 118 B2
Vizcaya □, Spain 32 B2
Vize, Turkey 41 E11
Vizianagaram, India 67 K13
Vizille, France 21 C9
Viziňada, Croatia 29 C10
Viziru, Romania 43 E12
Vizzini, Italy 31 E7
Vlaardingen, Neths. 17 C4
Vladičin Han, Serbia, Yug. ... 40 D6
Vladikavkaz, Russia 49 J7
Vladimir, Russia 46 D11
Vladimir Volynskiy =
  Volodymyr-Volynskyy,
  Ukraine 47 G3
Vladimirci, Serbia, Yug. 40 B3
Vladimirovac, Serbia, Yug. ... 42 E5
Vladimirovka, Russia 49 F8
Vladimirovo, Bulgaria 40 C7
Vladimorvka, Kazakstan 48 E10
Vladislavovka, Ukraine 47 K8
Vladivostok, Russia 51 E14
Vlăhiţa, Romania 43 D10
Vlakhiótis, Greece 38 E4
Vlašenica, Bos.-H. 42 F3
Vlašić, Bos.-H. 42 F2
Vlasinsko Jezero, Serbia, Yug. . 40 D6
Vlasotince, Serbia, Yug. 40 D6
Vlieland, Neths. 17 A4
Vlissingen, Neths. 17 C3
Vlorë, Albania 40 F3
Vlorës, Gjiri i, Albania 40 F3
Vltava →, Czech Rep. 26 A7
Vo Dat, Vietnam 65 G6
Vobarno, Italy 28 C7
Voćin, Croatia 42 E2

Vöcklabruck, Austria 26 C6
Vodice, Croatia 29 E12
Vodňany, Czech Rep. 26 B7
Vodnjan, Croatia 29 D10
Voe, U.K. 14 A7
Vogel Pk., Nigeria 83 D7
Vogelkop = Doberai, Jazirah,
  Indonesia 63 E8
Vogelsberg, Germany 24 E5
Voghera, Italy 28 D6
Vohibinany, Madag. 89 B8
Vohilava, Madag. 89 C8
Vohimarina = Iharana, Madag. 89 A9
Vohimena, Tanjon' i, Madag. .. 89 D8
Vohipeno, Madag. 89 C8
Voi, Kenya 86 C4
Void-Vacon, France 19 D12
Voineşti, Iaşi, Romania 43 C12
Voineşti, Prahova, Romania ... 43 E10
Voíotía □, Greece 38 C5
Voiron, France 21 C9
Voisey B., Canada 103 A7
Voitsberg, Austria 26 D8
Vojens, Denmark 11 J3
Vojmsjön, Sweden 8 D17
Vojnić, Croatia 29 C12
Vojnik, Italy 29 B12
Vojvodina □, Serbia, Yug. 42 E5
Vokhtoga, Russia 46 C11
Volary, Czech Rep. 26 C6
Volborg, U.S.A. 112 C2
Volcano Is. = Kazan-Rettõ,
  Pac. Oc. 96 E6
Volchansk = Vovchansk,
  Ukraine 47 G9
Volchya →, Ukraine 47 H8
Volda, Norway 9 E12
Volga, Russia 46 C10
Volga →, Russia 49 G9
Volga Hts. = Privolzhskaya
  Vozvyshennost, Russia 48 E7
Volgo-Baltiyskiy Kanal, Russia 46 B9
Volgo-Donskoy Kanal, Russia . 49 F7
Volgodonsk, Russia 49 G6
Volgograd, Russia 49 F7
Volgogradskoye Vdkhr., Russia 48 E8
Volgorechensk, Russia 46 B5
Volímai, Greece 38 D2
Volissós, Greece 39 C7
Volkach, Germany 25 F6
Völkermarkt, Austria 26 E7
Volkhov, Russia 46 C7
Volkhov →, Russia 46 B7
Völklingen, Germany 25 F2
Volkovysk = Vawkavysk,
  Belarus 47 F3
Volksrust, S. Africa 89 D4
Volnansk, Ukraine 47 H8
Volnovakha, Ukraine 47 J9
Volochanka, Russia 51 B10
Volodarsk, Russia 48 B6
Volodymyr-Volynskyy, Ukraine 47 G3
Vologda, Russia 46 C10
Volokolamsk, Russia 46 D8
Volokonovka, Russia 47 G9
Vólos, Greece 38 B4
Volosovo, Russia 46 C5
Volovets, Ukraine 47 H2
Volovo, Russia 46 F10
Volozhin = Valozhyn, Belarus . 46 E4
Volsk, Russia 48 D8
Volta □, Ghana 83 D5
Volta →, Ghana 83 D5
Volta, L., Ghana 83 D5
Volta Blanche = White
  Volta →, Ghana 83 D4
Volta Redonda, Brazil 127 A7
Voltaire, C., Australia 92 B4
Volterra, Italy 28 E7
Voltri, Italy 28 D5
Volturno →, Italy 30 A6
Vólvi, L., Greece 40 F7
Volyně, Czech Rep. 26 B6
Volzhsk, Russia 48 C9
Volzhskiy, Russia 49 F7
Vondrozo, Madag. 89 C8
Vónitsa, Greece 38 C2
Vopnafjörður, Iceland 8 D6
Vorarlberg □, Austria 26 D2
Vóras Óros, Greece 40 F5
Vorbasse, Denmark 11 J3
Vorchdorf, Austria 26 C6
Vorderrhein →, Switz. 25 J5
Vordingborg, Denmark 11 J5
Vorë, Albania 40 E3
Voreio Aigaio = Vórios
  Aiyaíon □, Greece 39 C7
Voreppe, France 21 C9
Vóriai Sporádhes, Greece 38 B5
Vórios Aiyaíon □, Greece 39 C7
Vórios Evvoïkos Kólpos, Greece 38 C5
Vorkuta, Russia 50 C7
Vormsi, Estonia 9 G20
Vorona →, Russia 48 E6
Voronezh, Russia 47 G10
Voronezh, Ukraine 47 G7
Voronezh →, Russia 47 G10
Vorontsovo-
  Aleksandrovskoye =
  Zelenokumsk, Russia 49 H6
Voroshilovgrad = Luhansk,
  Ukraine 47 H10
Voroshilovsk = Alchevsk,
  Ukraine 47 H10
Vórroi, Greece 38 F6

Vorskla →, Ukraine 47 H8
Võrts Järv, Estonia 9 G22
Võru, Estonia 9 H22
Vosges, France 19 D14
Vosges □, France 19 D13
Voskopojë, Albania 40 F4
Voskresensk, Russia 46 E10
Voskresenskoye, Russia 48 B7
Voss, Norway 9 F12
Vostok I., Kiribati 97 J12
Votice, Czech Rep. 26 B7
Votsuri-Shima, Japan 55 M1
Vouga →, Portugal 34 E2
Vouillé, France 18 F7
Voúxa, Ákra, Greece 36 D5
Vouzela, Portugal 34 E2
Vouziers, France 19 C11
Vovchansk, Ukraine 47 G9
Vozhe, Ozero, Russia 46 B10
Vozhega, Russia 46 B11
Voznesensk, Ukraine 47 J6
Voznesenye, Russia 46 B8
Vrå, Denmark 11 G3
Vráble, Slovak Rep. 27 C11
Vračevšnica, Serbia, Yug. 40 C4
Vrakhnéïka, Greece 38 C3
Vrancea □, Romania 43 E11
Vrancei, Munţii, Romania 43 E11
Vrangelya, Ostrov, Russia 51 B19
Vranica, Bos.-H. 42 G2
Vranje, Serbia, Yug. 40 D5
Vranjska Banja, Serbia, Yug. .. 40 D6
Vranov nad Topľou,
  Slovak Rep. 27 C14
Vransko, Slovenia 29 B11
Vransko Jezero, Croatia 29 E12
Vrapčište, Macedonia 40 E4
Vratsa, Bulgaria 40 C7
Vrbas, Serbia, Yug. 42 E4
Vrbas →, Bos.-H. 42 E2
Vrbnik, Croatia 29 C11
Vrbovec, Croatia 29 C13
Vrbovsko, Croatia 29 C12
Vrchlabí, Czech Rep. 26 A8
Vrede, S. Africa 89 D4
Vredefort, S. Africa 88 D4
Vreden, Germany 24 C2
Vredenburg, S. Africa 88 E2
Vredendal, S. Africa 88 E2
Vretstorp, Sweden 10 E8
Vrgorac, Croatia 29 E14
Vrhnika, Slovenia 29 C11
Vridi, Ivory C. 82 D4
Vrigstad, Sweden 11 G8
Vrindavan, India 68 F7
Vríses, Greece 36 D6
Vrnograč, Bos.-H. 29 C12
Vrondádhes, Greece 39 C8
Vrpolje, Croatia 42 E3
Vršac, Serbia, Yug. 42 E6
Vrsacki Kanal, Serbia, Yug. ... 42 E5
Vrútky, Slovak Rep. 27 B11
Vryburg, S. Africa 88 D3
Vryheid, S. Africa 89 D5
Vsetín, Czech Rep. 27 B11
Vu Liet, Vietnam 64 C5
Vucha →, Bulgaria 41 D8
Vučitrn, Kosovo, Yug. 40 D4
Vukovar, Croatia 42 E3
Vulcan, Canada 104 C6
Vulcan, Romania 43 E8
Vulcăneşti, Moldova 43 E13
Vulcano, Italy 31 D7
Vŭlchedrŭma, Bulgaria 40 C7
Vulkaneshty = Vulcăneşti,
  Moldova 43 E13
Vunduzi →, Mozam. 87 F3
Vung Tau, Vietnam 65 G6
Vŭrbitsa, Bulgaria 41 D10
Vurshets, Bulgaria 40 C7
Vutcani, Romania 43 D12
Vuya, Sudan 81 F2
Vyartsilya, Russia 46 A6
Vyatka = Kirov, Russia 50 D5
Vyatka →, Russia 48 C10
Vyatskiye Polyany, Russia 48 B10
Vyazemskiy, Russia 51 E14
Vyazma, Russia 46 E8
Vyazniki, Russia 48 B6
Vyborg, Russia 46 B5
Vychegda →, Russia 50 C9
Vychodné Beskydy, Europe 27 B15
Východočeský □, Czech Rep. ... 26 A8
Vyerkhnyadzvinsk, Belarus 46 E4
Vyksa, Russia 48 C6
Vylkove, Ukraine 47 K5
Vynohradiv, Ukraine 47 H2
Vyrnwy, L., U.K. 12 E4
Vyshniy Volochek, Russia 46 D8
Vyshza = imeni 26 Bakinskikh
  Komissarov, Turkmenistan .. 71 B7
Vyškov, Czech Rep. 27 B9
Vysoké Mýto, Czech Rep. 27 B9
Vysokovsk, Russia 46 D9
Vyšší Brod, Czech Rep. 26 C7
Vytegra, Russia 46 B9

W

W.A.C. Bennett Dam, Canada . 104 B4
Wa, Ghana 82 C4
Waal →, Neths. 17 C5
Waalwijk, Neths. 17 C5
Waat, Sudan 81 F3
Wabana, Canada 103 C9

Wabasca ➤, Canada 104 B5
Wabasca-Desmarais, Canada .. 104 B6
Wabash, U.S.A. 108 E3
Wabash ➤, U.S.A. 108 G1
Wabi ➤, Ethiopia 81 F5
Wabigoon L., Canada 105 D10
Wabowden, Canada 105 C9
Wąbrzeźno, Poland 45 E5
Wabu Hu, China 59 A11
Wabuk Pt., Canada 102 A2
Wabush, Canada 103 B6
Wąchock, Poland 45 G8
Wächtersberg, Germany 25 E5
Waco, U.S.A. 113 K6
Waconichi, L., Canada 102 B5
Wad Ban Naqa, Sudan 81 D3
Wad Banda, Sudan 81 E2
Wad el Haddad, Sudan 81 E3
Wad en Nau, Sudan 81 E3
Wad Hamid, Sudan 81 D3
Wad Medanî, Sudan 81 E3
Wad Thana, Pakistan 68 F2
Wadai, Africa 76 E5
Wadayama, Japan 55 G7
Waddeneilanden, Neths. 17 A5
Waddenzee, Neths. 17 A5
Waddington, U.S.A. 111 B9
Waddington, Mt., Canada .. 104 C3
Waddy Pt., Australia 95 C5
Wadebridge, U.K. 13 G3
Wadena, Canada 105 C8
Wadena, U.S.A. 112 B7
Wädenswil, Switz. 25 H4
Wadern, Germany 25 F2
Wadeye, Australia 92 B4
Wadhams, Canada 104 C3
Wādī as Sīr, Jordan 75 D4
Wadi Gemâl, Egypt 80 C4
Wadi Halfa, Sudan 80 C3
Wadian, China 59 A9
Wadlew, Poland 45 G6
Wadowice, Poland 45 J6
Wadsworth, Nev., U.S.A. .. 114 G4
Wadsworth, Ohio, U.S.A. .. 110 E3
Waegwan, S. Korea 57 G15
Wafangdian, China 57 E11
Wafrah, Si. Arabia 70 D5
Wageningen, Neths. 17 C5
Wager B., Canada 101 B11
Waghete, Indonesia 63 E9
Wagin, Australia 93 F2
Wagner, U.S.A. 112 D5
Wagon Mound, U.S.A. 113 G2
Wagoner, U.S.A. 113 H7
Wągrowiec, Poland 45 F4
Wah, Pakistan 68 C5
Wahai, Indonesia 63 E7
Wahiawa, U.S.A. 106 H15
Wâḥid, Egypt 75 E1
Wahnai, Afghan. 68 C1
Wahni, Ethiopia 81 E4
Wahoo, U.S.A. 112 E6
Wahpeton, U.S.A. 112 B6
Waiau ➤, N.Z. 91 K4
Waibeem, Indonesia 63 E8
Waiblingen, Germany 25 G5
Waidhofen an der Thaya,
  Austria 26 C8
Waidhofen an der Ybbs, Austria 26 D7
Waigeo, Indonesia 63 E8
Waihi, N.Z. 91 G5
Waihou ➤, N.Z. 91 G5
Waika, Dem. Rep. of the Congo 86 C2
Waikabubak, Indonesia 63 F5
Waikari, N.Z. 91 K4
Waikato ➤, N.Z. 91 G5
Waikokopu, N.Z. 91 H6
Waikouaiti, N.Z. 91 L3
Wailuku, U.S.A. 106 H16
Waimakariri ➤, N.Z. 91 K4
Waimate, N.Z. 91 L3
Wainganga ➤, India 66 K11
Waingapu, Indonesia 63 F6
Waini ➤, Guyana 124 B7
Wainwright, Canada 105 C6
Waiouru, N.Z. 91 H5
Waipara, N.Z. 91 K4
Waipawa, N.Z. 91 H6
Waipiro, N.Z. 91 H7
Waipu, N.Z. 91 F5
Waipukurau, N.Z. 91 H6
Wairakei, N.Z. 91 H6
Wairarapa, L., N.Z. 91 J5
Wairoa, N.Z. 91 H6
Waitaki ➤, N.Z. 91 L3
Waitara, N.Z. 91 H5
Waitsburg, U.S.A. 114 C5
Waiuku, N.Z. 91 G5
Wajima, Japan 55 F8
Wajir, Kenya 86 B5
Waka, Ethiopia 81 F4
Wakasa, Japan 55 G7
Wakasa-Wan, Japan 55 G7
Wakatipu, L., N.Z. 91 L2
Wakaw, Canada 105 C7
Wakayama, Japan 55 G7
Wakayama □, Japan 55 H7
Wake Forest, U.S.A. 109 H6
Wake I., Pac. Oc. 96 F8
WaKeeney, U.S.A. 112 F5
Wakefield, N.Z. 91 J4
Wakefield, U.K. 12 D6
Wakefield, Mass., U.S.A. . 111 D13
Wakefield, Mich., U.S.A. . 112 B10
Wakkanai, Japan 54 B10

Wakkerstroom, S. Africa 89 D5
Wakre, Indonesia 63 E8
Wakuach, L., Canada 103 A6
Walamba, Zambia 87 E2
Wałbrzych, Poland 45 H3
Walbury Hill, U.K. 13 F6
Walcheren, Neths. 17 C3
Walcott, U.S.A. 114 F10
Wałcz, Poland 45 E3
Waldbröl, Germany 24 E3
Waldburg Ra., Australia ... 93 D2
Waldeck, Germany 24 D5
Walden, Colo., U.S.A. 114 F10
Walden, N.Y., U.S.A. 111 E10
Waldkirch, Germany 25 G3
Waldkirchen, Germany 25 G9
Waldkraiburg, Germany 25 G8
Waldport, U.S.A. 114 D1
Waldron, U.S.A. 113 H7
Waldviertel, Austria 26 C8
Walebing, Australia 93 F2
Walembele, Ghana 82 C4
Walensee, Switz. 25 H5
Wales □, U.K. 13 E3
Walewale, Ghana 83 C4
Walgett, Australia 95 E4
Walgreen Coast, Antarctica . 5 D15
Walker, U.S.A. 112 B7
Walker, L., Canada 103 B6
Walker L., Canada 105 C9
Walker L., U.S.A. 114 G4
Walkerston, Australia 94 C4
Walkerton, Canada 102 D3
Wall, U.S.A. 112 D3
Walla Walla, U.S.A. 114 C4
Wallace, Idaho, U.S.A. 114 C6
Wallace, N.C., U.S.A. 109 H7
Wallaceburg, Canada 102 D3
Wallachia = Valahia, Romania . 43 F9
Wallal, Australia 95 D4
Wallam Cr. ➤, Australia ... 95 D4
Wallambin, L., Australia .. 93 F2
Wallangarra, Australia 95 D5
Walldürn, Germany 25 F5
Wallenhorst, Germany 24 C4
Wallenpaupack, L., U.S.A. . 111 E9
Wallingford, U.S.A. 111 E12
Wallis & Futuna, Is., Pac. Oc. 96 J10
Wallowa, U.S.A. 114 D5
Wallowa Mts., U.S.A. 114 D5
Walls, U.K. 14 A7
Wallula, U.S.A. 114 C4
Wallumbilla, Australia 95 D4
Walmsley, L., Canada 105 A7
Walney, I. of, U.K. 12 C4
Walnut Creek, U.S.A. 116 H4
Walnut Ridge, U.S.A. 113 G9
Walpole, Australia 93 F2
Walpole, U.S.A. 111 D13
Wals, Austria 26 D5
Walsall, U.K. 13 E6
Walsenburg, U.S.A. 113 G2
Walsh, U.S.A. 113 G3
Walsh ➤, Australia 94 B3
Walsrode, Germany 24 C5
Walterboro, U.S.A. 109 J5
Walters, U.S.A. 113 H5
Waltershausen, Germany 24 E6
Waltham, U.S.A. 111 D13
Waltman, U.S.A. 114 E10
Walton, U.S.A. 111 D9
Walton-on-the-Naze, U.K. .. 13 F9
Walvis Bay, Namibia 88 C1
Walvisbaai = Walvis Bay,
  Namibia 88 C1
Wamba, Dem. Rep. of the Congo 86 B2
Wamba, Kenya 86 B4
Wamba, Nigeria 83 D6
Wamego, U.S.A. 112 F6
Wamena, Indonesia 63 E9
Wamsutter, U.S.A. 114 F9
Wamulan, Indonesia 63 E7
Wan Xian, China 56 E8
Wana, Pakistan 68 C3
Wanaaring, Australia 95 D3
Wanaka, N.Z. 91 L2
Wanaka L., N.Z. 91 L2
Wan'an, China 59 D10
Wanapitei L., Canada 102 C3
Wandel Sea = McKinley Sea,
  Arctic 4 A7
Wandérama, Ivory C. 82 D4
Wanderer, Zimbabwe 87 F3
Wandhari, Pakistan 68 F2
Wanding, China 58 E2
Wandoan, Australia 95 D4
Wanfu, China 57 D12
Wang ➤, Thailand 64 D2
Wang Kai, Sudan 81 F2
Wang Noi, Thailand 64 E3
Wang Saphung, Thailand ... 64 D3
Wang Thong, Thailand 64 D3
Wanga, Dem. Rep. of the Congo 86 B2
Wangal, Indonesia 63 F8
Wanganui, N.Z. 91 H5
Wangary, Australia 95 E2
Wangcang, China 58 A6
Wangcheng, China 59 C9
Wangdu, China 56 E8
Wangen, Germany 25 H5
Wangerooge, Germany 24 B3
Wangi, Kenya 86 C5
Wangiwangi, Indonesia ... 63 F6
Wangjiang, China 59 B11
Wangmo, China 58 E6

Wangolodougou, Ivory C. ... 82 D3
Wangqing, China 57 C15
Wankaner, India 68 H4
Wanless, Canada 105 C8
Wannian, China 59 C11
Wanning, China 64 C8
Wanquan, China 56 D8
Wanrong, China 56 G6
Wanshan, China 58 D7
Wanshengchang, China 58 C6
Wantage, U.K. 13 F6
Wanyuan, China 58 A7
Wanzai, China 59 C10
Wapakoneta, U.S.A. 108 E3
Wapato, U.S.A. 114 C3
Wapawekka L., Canada 105 C8
Wapikopa L., Canada 102 B2
Wapiti ➤, Canada 104 B5
Wappingers Falls, U.S.A. . 111 E11
Wapsipinicon ➤, U.S.A. ... 112 E9
Warab □, Sudan 81 F2
Warangal, India 66 L11
Waraseoni, India 69 J9
Waratah, Australia 94 G4
Warburg, Germany 24 D5
Warburton, Australia 93 E4
Warburton Ra., Australia . 93 E4
Ward, N.Z. 91 J5
Ward ➤, Australia 95 D4
Ward Mt., U.S.A. 116 H8
Warden, S. Africa 89 D4
Wardha, India 66 J11
Wardha ➤, India 66 K11
Ware, Canada 104 B3
Ware, U.S.A. 111 D12
Waregem, Belgium 17 D3
Wareham, U.S.A. 111 E14
Waremme, Belgium 17 D5
Waren, Germany 24 B8
Warendorf, Germany 24 D4
Warialda, Australia 95 D5
Wariap, Indonesia 63 E8
Warin Chamrap, Thailand . 64 E5
Warka, Poland 45 G8
Warkopi, Indonesia 63 E8
Warm Springs, U.S.A. 115 G5
Warman, Canada 105 C7
Warmbad, Namibia 88 D2
Warmbad, S. Africa 89 C4
Warmińsko-Mazurskie □,
  Poland 44 D8
Warminster, U.K. 13 F5
Warminster, U.S.A. 111 F9
Warnemünde, Germany 24 A8
Warner Mts., U.S.A. 114 F3
Warner Robins, U.S.A. ... 109 J4
Warnow ➤, Germany 24 A8
Waroona, Australia 93 F2
Warrego ➤, Australia 95 E4
Warrego Ra., Australia .. 94 C4
Warren, Ark., U.S.A. 113 J8
Warren, Mich., U.S.A. ... 108 D4
Warren, Minn., U.S.A. ... 112 A6
Warren, Ohio, U.S.A. 110 E4
Warren, Pa., U.S.A. 110 E5
Warrenpoint, U.K. 15 B5
Warrensburg, Mo., U.S.A. . 112 F8
Warrensburg, N.Y., U.S.A. 111 C11
Warrenton, S. Africa 88 D3
Warrenton, U.S.A. 116 D3
Warri, Nigeria 83 D6
Warrina, Australia 95 D2
Warrington, U.K. 12 D5
Warrington, U.S.A. 109 K2
Warrnambool □, U.K. 12 D5
Warroad, U.S.A. 112 A7
Warruwi, Australia 94 A1
Warsa, Indonesia 63 E9
Warsak Dam, Pakistan 68 B4
Warsaw = Warszawa, Poland 45 F8
Warsaw, Ind., U.S.A. 108 E3
Warsaw, N.Y., U.S.A. 110 D6
Warsaw, Ohio, U.S.A. 110 F3
Warstein, Germany 24 D4
Warszawa, Poland 45 F8
Warta, Poland 45 G5
Warta ➤, Poland 45 F1
Warthe = Warta ➤, Poland . 45 F1
Waru, Indonesia 63 E8
Warwick, Australia 95 D5
Warwick, U.K. 13 E6
Warwick, N.Y., U.S.A. ... 111 E10
Warwick, R.I., U.S.A. ... 111 E13
Warwickshire □, U.K. 13 E6
Wasaga Beach, Canada 110 B4
Wasagaming, Canada 105 C9
Wasatch Ra., U.S.A. 114 F8
Wasbank, S. Africa 89 D5
Wasco, Calif., U.S.A. ... 117 K7
Wasco, Oreg., U.S.A. 114 D3
Wase, Nigeria 83 D6
Waseca, U.S.A. 112 C8
Wasekamio L., Canada 105 B7
Wash, The, U.K. 12 E8
Washburn, N. Dak., U.S.A. 112 B4
Washburn, Wis., U.S.A. .. 112 B9
Washim, India 66 J10
Washington, U.K. 12 C6
Washington, D.C., U.S.A. . 108 F7
Washington, Ga., U.S.A. . 109 J4
Washington, Ind., U.S.A. . 108 F2
Washington, Iowa, U.S.A. . 112 E9
Washington, Mo., U.S.A. .. 112 F9

Washington, N.C., U.S.A. 109 H7
Washington, N.J., U.S.A. 111 F10
Washington, Pa., U.S.A. 110 F4
Washington, Utah, U.S.A. 115 H7
Washington □, U.S.A. 114 C3
Washington I., U.S.A. 108 C2
Washington, Mt., U.S.A. 111 B13
Washington Court House,
  U.S.A. 108 F4
Washington I., U.S.A. 108 C2
Washougal, U.S.A. 116 E4
Wasian, Indonesia 63 E8
Wasilków, Poland 45 E10
Wasilla, U.S.A. 100 B5
Wasior, Indonesia 63 E8
Waskaganish, Canada 102 B4
Waskaiowaka, L., Canada ... 105 B9
Waskesiu Lake, Canada 105 C7
Wasserburg, Germany 25 G8
Wasserkuppe, Germany 24 E5
Wassy, France 19 D11
Waswanipi, Canada 102 C4
Waswanipi, L., Canada 102 C4
Watampone, Indonesia 63 E6
Water Park Pt., Australia .. 94 C5
Water Valley, U.S.A. 113 H10
Waterberge, S. Africa 89 C4
Waterbury, Conn., U.S.A. .. 111 E11
Waterbury, Vt., U.S.A. 111 B12
Waterbury L., Canada 105 B8
Waterdown, Canada 110 C5
Waterford, Canada 110 D4
Waterford, Ireland 15 D4
Waterford, Calif., U.S.A. . 116 H6
Waterford, Pa., U.S.A. 110 E5
Waterford □, Ireland 15 D4
Waterford Harbour, Ireland 15 D5
Waterhen L., Canada 105 C9
Waterloo, Belgium 17 D4
Waterloo, Ont., Canada 102 D3
Waterloo, Qué., Canada 111 A12
Waterloo, S. Leone 82 D2
Waterloo, Ill., U.S.A. 112 F9
Waterloo, Iowa, U.S.A. 112 D8
Waterloo, N.Y., U.S.A. 110 D8
Watersmeet, U.S.A. 112 B10
Waterton Lakes Nat. Park,
  U.S.A. 114 B7
Watertown, Conn., U.S.A. .. 111 E11
Watertown, N.Y., U.S.A. ... 111 C9
Watertown, S. Dak., U.S.A. 112 C6
Watertown, Wis., U.S.A. ... 112 D10
Waterval-Boven, S. Africa . 89 D5
Waterville, Canada 111 A13
Waterville, Maine, U.S.A. . 109 C11
Waterville, N.Y., U.S.A. .. 111 D9
Waterville, Pa., U.S.A. ... 110 E7
Waterville, Wash., U.S.A. . 114 C3
Watervliet, U.S.A. 111 D11
Wates, Indonesia 63 G14
Watford, Canada 110 D3
Watford, U.K. 13 F7
Watford City, U.S.A. 112 B3
Wathaman ➤, Canada 105 B8
Wathaman L., Canada 105 B8
Watheroo, Australia 93 F2
Wating, China 56 G4
Watkins Glen, U.S.A. 110 D8
Watling I. = San Salvador I.,
  Bahamas 121 B5
Watonga, U.S.A. 113 H5
Watrous, Canada 105 C7
Watrous, U.S.A. 113 H2
Watsa, Dem. Rep. of the Congo 86 B2
Watseka, U.S.A. 108 E2
Watson, Australia 93 F5
Watson, Canada 105 C8
Watson Lake, Canada 104 A3
Watsontown, U.S.A. 110 E8
Watsonville, U.S.A. 116 J5
Wattiwarriganna Cr. ➤,
  Australia 95 D2
Wattwil, Switz. 25 H5
Watuata = Batuata, Indonesia 63 F6
Watubela, Kepulauan, Indonesia 63 E8
Watubela Is. = Watubela,
  Kepulauan, Indonesia 63 E8
Wau = Wâw, Sudan 81 F2
Waubamik, Canada 110 A4
Waubay, U.S.A. 112 C6
Wauchope, Australia 94 C1
Wauchula, U.S.A. 109 M5
Waukarlycarly, L., Australia 92 D3
Waukegan, U.S.A. 108 D2
Waukesha, U.S.A. 108 D1
Waukon, U.S.A. 112 D9
Waupaca, U.S.A. 112 C10
Waupun, U.S.A. 112 D10
Waurika, U.S.A. 113 H6
Wausau, U.S.A. 112 C10
Wautoma, U.S.A. 108 D2
Wauwatosa, U.S.A. 108 D2
Waveney ➤, U.K. 13 E9
Waverley, N.Z. 91 H5
Waverly, Iowa, U.S.A. 112 D8
Waverly, N.Y., U.S.A. 111 E8
Wavre, Belgium 17 D4
Wâw, Sudan 81 F2
Wâw al Kabîr, Libya 79 C9
Wawa, Canada 102 C3
Wawa, Nigeria 83 D5
Wawa, Sudan 80 C3
Wawanesa, Canada 105 D9
Wawona, U.S.A. 116 H7
Waxahachie, U.S.A. 113 J6

Waycross, U.S.A. 109 K4
Wayi, Sudan 81 F3
Wayland, U.S.A. 110 D7
Wayne, Nebr., U.S.A. 112 D6
Wayne, W. Va., U.S.A. 108 F4
Waynesboro, Ga., U.S.A. 109 J4
Waynesboro, Miss., U.S.A. .. 109 K1
Waynesboro, Pa., U.S.A. 108 F7
Waynesboro, Va., U.S.A. 108 F6
Waynesburg, U.S.A. 108 F5
Waynesville, U.S.A. 109 H4
Waynoka, U.S.A. 113 G5
Wazirabad, Pakistan 68 C6
Wda ➤, Poland 44 E5
We, Indonesia 62 C1
Weald, The, U.K. 13 F8
Wear ➤, U.K. 12 C6
Weatherford, Okla., U.S.A. . 113 H5
Weatherford, Tex., U.S.A. .. 113 J6
Weaverville, U.S.A. 114 F2
Webb City, U.S.A. 113 G7
Webequie, Canada 102 B2
Webo = Nyaake, Liberia 82 E3
Webster, Mass., U.S.A. 111 D13
Webster, N.Y., U.S.A. 110 C7
Webster, S. Dak., U.S.A. ... 112 C6
Webster, Wis., U.S.A. 112 D8
Webster Springs, U.S.A. 108 F5
Weda, Indonesia 63 D7
Weda, Teluk, Indonesia 63 D7
Weddell I., Falk. Is. 128 G4
Weddell Sea, Antarctica 5 D1
Wedel, Germany 24 B5
Wedemark, Germany 24 C5
Wedgeport, Canada 103 D6
Wedza, Zimbabwe 87 F3
Wee Waa, Australia 95 E4
Weed, U.S.A. 114 F2
Weed Heights, U.S.A. 116 G7
Weedsport, U.S.A. 111 C8
Weedville, U.S.A. 110 E6
Weenen, S. Africa 89 D5
Weener, Germany 24 B3
Weert, Neths. 17 C5
Węgierska-Górka, Poland 45 J6
Węgliniec, Poland 45 G2
Węgorzewo, Poland 44 D8
Węgorzyno, Poland 44 E2
Węgrów, Poland 45 F9
Wehda □, Sudan 81 F3
Wei He ➤, Hebei, China 56 F8
Wei He ➤, Shaanxi, China ... 56 G6
Weichang, China 57 D9
Weichuan, China 56 G7
Weida, Germany 24 E8
Weiden, Germany 25 F8
Weifang, China 57 F10
Weihai, China 57 F12
Weil, Germany 25 H3
Weilburg, Germany 24 E4
Weilheim, Germany 25 H7
Weimar, Germany 24 E7
Weinan, China 56 G5
Weingarten, Germany 25 H5
Weinheim, Germany 25 F4
Weining, China 58 D5
Weipa, Australia 94 A3
Weir ➤, Australia 95 D4
Weir ➤, Canada 105 B10
Weir River, Canada 105 B10
Weirton, U.S.A. 110 F4
Weiser, U.S.A. 114 D5
Weishan, Shandong, China ... 57 G9
Weishan, Yunnan, China 58 E3
Weissenburg, Germany 25 F6
Weissenfels, Germany 24 D7
Weisswasser, Germany 24 D10
Wéitra, Austria 26 C8
Weixi, China 58 D2
Weixin, China 58 D5
Weiyuan, China 58 D5
Weiz, Austria 26 D8
Weizhou Dao, China 58 G7
Wejherowo, Poland 44 D5
Wekusko L., Canada 105 C9
Welch, U.S.A. 108 G5
Weldya, Ethiopia 81 E4
Welega □, Ethiopia 81 F3
Welkite, Ethiopia 81 F4
Welkom, S. Africa 88 D4
Welland, Canada 102 D4
Welland ➤, U.K. 13 E7
Wellesley Is., Australia ... 94 B2
Wellingborough, U.K. 13 E7
Wellington, Canada 110 C7
Wellington, N.Z. 91 J5
Wellington, S. Africa 88 E2
Wellington, Somst., U.K. ... 13 G4
Wellington, Telford & Wrekin,
  U.K. 13 E5
Wellington, Colo., U.S.A. .. 112 E2
Wellington, Kans., U.S.A. .. 113 G6
Wellington, Nev., U.S.A. ... 116 G7
Wellington, Ohio, U.S.A. ... 110 E2
Wellington, Tex., U.S.A. ... 113 H4
Wellington, I., Chile 122 F2
Wells, U.K. 13 F5
Wells, Maine, U.S.A. 111 C14
Wells, N.Y., U.S.A. 111 C10
Wells, Nev., U.S.A. 114 F6
Wells, L., Australia 93 E3
Wells, Mt., Australia 92 C4
Wells Gray Prov. Park, Canada 104 C4
Wells-next-the-Sea, U.K. .. 12 E8
Wells River, U.S.A. 111 B12

Wellsboro, U.S.A. 110 E7
Wellsburg, U.S.A. 110 F4
Wellsville, N.Y., U.S.A. 110 D7
Wellsville, Ohio, U.S.A. 110 F4
Wellsville, Utah, U.S.A. 114 F8
Wellton, U.S.A. 115 K6
Welmel, Wabi ➤, Ethiopia ... 81 F5
Welo □, Ethiopia 81 E4
Wels, Austria 26 C7
Welshpool, U.K. 13 E4
Welwyn Garden City, U.K. 13 F7
Wem, U.K. 12 E5
Wembere ➤, Tanzania 86 C3
Wemindji, Canada 102 B4
Wen Xian, China 56 G7
Wenatchee, U.S.A. 114 C3
Wenchang, China 64 C8
Wencheng, China 59 D13
Wenchi, Ghana 82 D4
Wenchow = Wenzhou, China .. 59 D13
Wenchuan, China 58 B4
Wenden, U.S.A. 117 M13
Wendeng, China 57 F12
Wendesi, Indonesia 63 E8
Wendo, Ethiopia 81 F4
Wendover, U.S.A. 114 F6
Weng'an, China 58 D6
Wengcheng, China 59 E9
Wengyuan, China 59 E10
Wenjiang, China 58 B4
Wenling, China 59 C13
Wenlock ➤, Australia 94 A3
Wenshan, China 58 F5
Wenshang, China 56 G9
Wenshui, China 56 F7
Wensleydale, U.K. 12 C6
Wensu, China 60 B3
Wensum ➤, U.K. 12 E8
Wentzel L., Canada 104 B6
Wenut, Indonesia 63 E8
Wenxi, China 56 G6
Wenxian, China 56 H3
Wenzhou, China 59 D13
Weott, U.S.A. 114 F2
Wepener, S. Africa 88 D4
Werda, Botswana 88 D3
Werdau, Germany 24 E8
Werder, Germany 24 C8
Werdohl, Germany 24 D3
Wereilu, Ethiopia 81 E4
Weri, Indonesia 63 E8
Werneck, Germany 25 F6
Wernigerode, Germany 24 D6
Werra ➤, Germany 24 D5
Wertach ➤, Germany 25 G6
Wertheim, Germany 25 F5
Wertingen, Germany 25 G6
Wesel, Germany 24 D2
Weser ➤, Germany 24 B4
Weser-Ems □, Germany 24 C3
Weserbergland, Germany 24 C5
Wesiri, Indonesia 63 F7
Weslemkoon L., Canada 110 A7
Wesleyville, Canada 103 C9
Wesleyville, U.S.A. 110 D4
Wessel, C., Australia 94 A2
Wessel Is., Australia 94 A2
Wesselburen, Germany 24 A4
Wessington Springs, U.S.A. ... 112 C5
West, U.S.A. 113 K6
West ➤, U.S.A. 111 D12
West Baines ➤, Australia 92 C4
West Bank □, Asia 75 C4
West Bend, U.S.A. 108 D1
West Bengal □, India 69 H13
West Berkshire □, U.K. 13 F6
West Beskids = Západné
  Beskydy, Europe 27 B12
West Branch, U.S.A. 108 C3
West Branch Susquehanna ➤,
  U.S.A. 111 F8
West Bromwich, U.K. 13 E6
West Burra, U.K. 14 A7
West Canada Cr. ➤, U.S.A. ... 111 C10
West Cape Howe, Australia ... 93 G2
West Chazy, U.S.A. 111 B11
West Chester, U.S.A. 111 G9
West Columbia, U.S.A. 113 L7
West Covina, U.S.A. 117 L9
West Des Moines, U.S.A. 112 E8
West Dunbartonshire □, U.K. . 14 F4
West End, Bahamas 120 A4
West Falkland, Falk. Is. 122 J4
West Fargo, U.S.A. 112 B6
West Farmington, U.S.A. 110 E4
West Fjord = Vestfjorden,
  Norway 8 C15
West Fork Trinity ➤, U.S.A. .. 113 J6
West Frankfort, U.S.A. 112 G10
West Hartford, U.S.A. 111 E12
West Haven, U.S.A. 111 E12
West Hazleton, U.S.A. 111 F9
West Helena, U.S.A. 113 H9
West Hurley, U.S.A. 111 E10
West Ice Shelf, Antarctica 5 C7
West Indies, Cent. Amer. 121 D7
West Jordan, U.S.A. 114 F8
West Lorne, Canada 110 D3
West Lothian □, U.K. 14 F5
West Lunga ➤, Zambia 87 E1
West Memphis, U.S.A. 113 H9
West Midlands □, U.K. 13 E6
West Mifflin, U.S.A. 110 F5
West Milton, U.S.A. 110 E8
West Monroe, U.S.A. 113 J8

West Newton, U.S.A. 110 F5
West Nicholson, Zimbabwe ... 87 G2
West Palm Beach, U.S.A. 109 M5
West Plains, U.S.A. 113 G9
West Point, N.Y., U.S.A. 111 E11
West Point, Nebr., U.S.A. 112 E6
West Point, Va., U.S.A. 108 G7
West Pt. = Ouest, Pte. de l',
  Canada 103 C7
West Road ➤, Canada 104 C4
West Rutland, U.S.A. 111 C11
West Schelde =
  Westerschelde ➤, Neths. ... 17 C3
West Seneca, U.S.A. 110 D6
West Siberian Plain, Russia ... 52 C11
West Sussex □, U.K. 13 G7
West-Terschelling, Neths. 17 A5
West Valley City, U.S.A. 114 F8
West Virginia □, U.S.A. 108 F5
West-Vlaanderen □, Belgium .. 17 D2
West Walker ➤, U.S.A. 116 G7
West Yellowstone, U.S.A. 114 D8
West Yorkshire □, U.K. 12 D6
Westall Pt., Australia 95 E1
Westbrook, U.S.A. 109 D10
Westbury, Australia 94 G4
Westby, U.S.A. 112 A2
Westend, U.S.A. 117 K9
Westerland, Germany 9 J13
Westerly, U.S.A. 111 E13
Western □, Ghana 82 D4
Western □, Kenya 86 B3
Western □, S. Leone 82 D2
Western □, Zambia 87 F1
Western Australia □, Australia 93 E2
Western Cape □, S. Africa ... 88 E3
Western Dvina = Daugava ➤,
  Latvia 9 H21
Western Ghats, India 66 N9
Western Isles □, U.K. 14 D1
Western Sahara ■, Africa 78 D3
Western Samoa = Samoa ■,
  Pac. Oc. 91 B13
Westernport, U.S.A. 108 F6
Westerschelde ➤, Neths. 17 C3
Westerstede, Germany 24 B3
Westerwald, Germany 24 E3
Westfield, Mass., U.S.A. 111 D12
Westfield, N.Y., U.S.A. 110 D5
Westfield, Pa., U.S.A. 110 E7
Westhill, U.K. 14 D6
Westhope, U.S.A. 112 A4
Westland Bight, N.Z. 91 K3
Westlock, Canada 104 C6
Westmar, Australia 95 D4
Westmeath □, Ireland 15 C4
Westminster, U.S.A. 108 F7
Westmont, U.S.A. 110 F6
Westmorland, U.S.A. 117 M11
Weston, Oreg., U.S.A. 114 D4
Weston, W. Va., U.S.A. 108 F5
Weston I., Canada 102 B4
Weston-super-Mare, U.K. 13 F5
Westover, U.S.A. 110 F6
Westport, Canada 111 B8
Westport, Ireland 15 C2
Westport, N.Z. 91 J3
Westport, N.Y., U.S.A. 111 B11
Westport, Oreg., U.S.A. 116 D3
Westport, Wash., U.S.A. 116 D2
Westray, Canada 105 C8
Westray, U.K. 14 B5
Westree, Canada 102 C3
Westville, U.S.A. 116 F6
Westwood, U.S.A. 114 F3
Wetar, Indonesia 63 F7
Wetaskiwin, Canada 104 C6
Wete, Tanzania 84 F7
Wetherby, U.K. 12 D6
Wethersfield, U.S.A. 111 E12
Wetteren, Belgium 17 D3
Wetzlar, Germany 24 E4
Wewoka, U.S.A. 113 H6
Wexford, Ireland 15 D5
Wexford □, Ireland 15 D5
Wexford Harbour, Ireland 15 D5
Weyburn, Canada 105 D8
Weyer Markt, Austria 26 D7
Weyhe, Germany 24 C4
Weyib ➤, Ethiopia 81 F5
Weymouth, Canada 103 D6
Weymouth, U.K. 13 G5
Weymouth, U.S.A. 111 D14
Weymouth, C., Australia 94 A3
Wha Ti, Canada 100 B8
Whakatane, N.Z. 91 G6
Whale ➤, Canada 103 A6
Whale Cove, Canada 105 A10
Whales, B. of, Antarctica 5 D12
Whalsay, U.K. 14 A8
Whangamomona, N.Z. 91 H5
Whangarei, N.Z. 91 F5
Whangarei Harb., N.Z. 91 F5
Wharfe ➤, U.K. 12 D6
Wharfedale, U.K. 12 C5
Wharton, N.J., U.S.A. 111 F10
Wharton, Pa., U.S.A. 110 E6
Wharton, Tex., U.S.A. 113 L6
Wheatland, Calif., U.S.A. 116 F5
Wheatland, Wyo., U.S.A. 112 D2
Wheatley, Canada 110 D2
Wheaton, Md., U.S.A. 108 F7
Wheaton, Minn., U.S.A. 112 C6
Wheelbarrow Pk., U.S.A. 116 H10
Wheeler, Oreg., U.S.A. 114 D2

Wheeler, Tex., U.S.A. 113 H4
Wheeler ➤, Canada 103 A6
Wheeler L., U.S.A. 109 H2
Wheeler Pk., N. Mex., U.S.A. . 115 H11
Wheeler Pk., Nev., U.S.A. 115 G6
Wheeler Ridge, U.S.A. 117 L8
Wheeling, U.S.A. 110 F4
Whernside, U.K. 12 C5
Whiskey Jack L., Canada 105 B8
Whistleduck Cr. ➤, Australia . 94 C2
Whistler, Canada 104 C4
Whitby, Canada 110 C6
Whitby, U.K. 12 C7
White ➤, Ark., U.S.A. 113 J9
White ➤, Ind., U.S.A. 108 F2
White ➤, S. Dak., U.S.A. 112 D5
White ➤, Tex., U.S.A. 113 J4
White ➤, Utah, U.S.A. 114 F9
White ➤, Vt., U.S.A. 111 C12
White ➤, Wash., U.S.A. 116 C4
White, L., Australia 92 D4
White B., Canada 103 C8
White Bird, U.S.A. 114 D5
White Butte, U.S.A. 112 B3
White City, U.S.A. 114 E2
White Hall, U.S.A. 112 F9
White Haven, U.S.A. 111 E9
White Horse, Vale of, U.K. ... 13 F6
White I., N.Z. 91 G6
White L., Canada 111 A8
White L., U.S.A. 113 L8
White Mountain Peak, U.S.A. . 115 G4
White Mts., Calif., U.S.A. 116 H8
White Mts., N.H., U.S.A. 111 B13
White Nile = Nîl el Abyad ➤,
  Sudan 81 D3
White Nile Dam = Khazzân
  Jabal al Awliyâ, Sudan 81 D3
White Otter L., Canada 102 C1
White Pass, U.S.A. 116 D5
White Plains, U.S.A. 111 E11
White River, Canada 102 C2
White River, S. Africa 89 D5
White River, U.S.A. 112 D4
White Rock, Canada 116 A4
White Russia = Belarus ■,
  Europe 46 F4
White Sea = Beloye More,
  Russia 50 C4
White Sulphur Springs, Mont.,
  U.S.A. 114 C8
White Sulphur Springs, W. Va.,
  U.S.A. 108 G5
White Swan, U.S.A. 116 D6
White Volta ➤, Ghana 83 D4
Whitecliffs, N.Z. 91 K3
Whitecourt, Canada 104 C5
Whiteface Mt., U.S.A. 111 B11
Whitefield, U.S.A. 111 B13
Whitefish, U.S.A. 114 B6
Whitefish L., Canada 105 A7
Whitefish Point, U.S.A. 108 B3
Whitegull, L., Canada 103 A7
Whitehall, Mich., U.S.A. 108 D2
Whitehall, Mont., U.S.A. 114 D7
Whitehall, N.Y., U.S.A. 111 C11
Whitehall, Wis., U.S.A. 112 C9
Whitehaven, U.K. 12 C4
Whitehorse, Canada 104 A1
Whitemark, Australia 94 G4
Whiteplains, Liberia 82 D2
Whiteriver, U.S.A. 115 K9
Whitesand ➤, Canada 104 A5
Whitesands, S. Africa 88 E3
Whitesboro, N.Y., U.S.A. 111 C9
Whitesboro, Tex., U.S.A. 113 J6
Whiteshell Prov. Park, Canada 105 D9
Whitesville, U.S.A. 110 D7
Whiteville, U.S.A. 109 H6
Whitewater, U.S.A. 108 D1
Whitewater Baldy, U.S.A. 115 K9
Whitewater L., Canada 102 B2
Whitewood, Australia 94 C3
Whitewood, Canada 105 C8
Whithorn, U.K. 14 G4
Whitianga, N.Z. 91 G5
Whitman, U.S.A. 111 D14
Whitney, Canada 102 C4
Whitney, Mt., U.S.A. 116 J8
Whitney Point, U.S.A. 111 D9
Whitstable, U.K. 13 F9
Whitsunday I., Australia 94 C4
Whittier, U.S.A. 117 M8
Wholdaia L., Canada 105 A8
Whyalla, Australia 95 E2
Wiarton, Canada 102 D3
Wiawso, Ghana 82 D4
Wiay, U.K. 14 D1
Wigzów, Poland 45 H4
Wibaux, U.S.A. 112 B2
Wichian Buri, Thailand 64 E3
Wichita, U.S.A. 113 G6
Wichita Falls, U.S.A. 113 J5
Wick, U.K. 14 C5
Wicked Pt., Canada 110 C7
Wickenburg, U.S.A. 115 K7
Wickepin, Australia 93 F2
Wickham, Australia 92 D2
Wickham, C., Australia 94 F3
Wickliffe, U.S.A. 110 E3
Wicklow, Ireland 15 D5
Wicklow □, Ireland 15 D5
Wicklow Hd., Ireland 15 D6
Wicklow Mts., Ireland 15 C5
Widawa, Poland 45 G5
Widawka ➤, Poland 45 G5

Widgiegoara Cr. ➤, Australia . 95 D4
Widgiemooltha, Australia 93 F3
Widnes, U.K. 12 D5
Więcbork, Poland 45 E4
Wiehl, Germany 24 E3
Wiek, Germany 24 A9
Wielbark, Poland 44 E7
Wieleń, Poland 45 F3
Wielichowo, Poland 45 F3
Wieliczka, Poland 45 J7
Wielkopolskie □, Poland 45 F4
Wieluń, Poland 45 G5
Wien, Austria 27 C9
Wiener Neustadt, Austria 27 D9
Wieprz ➤, Poland 45 G8
Wieprza ➤, Poland 44 D3
Wieruszów, Poland 45 G5
Wiesbaden, Germany 25 E4
Wiesental, Germany 25 F4
Wiesloch, Germany 25 F4
Wiesmoor, Germany 24 B3
Wieżyca, Poland 44 D5
Wigan, U.K. 12 D5
Wiggins, Colo., U.S.A. 112 E2
Wiggins, Miss., U.S.A. 113 K10
Wight, I. of □, U.K. 13 G6
Wigry, Jezioro, Poland 44 D10
Wigston, U.K. 13 E6
Wigton, U.K. 12 C4
Wigtown, U.K. 14 G4
Wigtown B., U.K. 14 G4
Wil, Switz. 25 H5
Wilamowice, Poland 45 J6
Wilber, U.S.A. 112 E6
Wilberforce, Canada 110 A6
Wilberforce, C., Australia 94 A2
Wilburton, U.S.A. 113 H7
Wilcox, U.S.A. 110 E6
Wildbad, Germany 25 G4
Wildeshausen, Germany 24 C4
Wildon, Austria 26 E8
Wildrose, U.S.A. 117 J9
Wildspitze, Austria 26 E3
Wilga ➤, Poland 45 G8
Wilge ➤, S. Africa 89 D4
Wilhelm II Coast, Antarctica . 5 C7
Wilhelmsburg, Austria 26 C8
Wilhelmshaven, Germany 24 B4
Wilhelmstal, Namibia 88 C2
Wilkes-Barre, U.S.A. 111 E9
Wilkie, Canada 105 C7
Wilkinsburg, U.S.A. 110 F5
Wilkinson Lakes, Australia ... 93 E5
Willapa B., U.S.A. 114 C2
Willapa Hills, U.S.A. 116 D3
Willard, N.Y., U.S.A. 110 D8
Willard, Ohio, U.S.A. 110 E2
Willcox, U.S.A. 115 K9
Willemstad, Neth. Ant. 121 D6
Willet, U.S.A. 111 D9
William ➤, Canada 105 B7
William 'Bill' Dannely Res.,
  U.S.A. 109 J2
William Creek, Australia 95 D2
Williams, Australia 93 F2
Williams, Ariz., U.S.A. 115 J7
Williams, Calif., U.S.A. 116 F4
Williams Harbour, Canada ... 103 B8
Williams Lake, Canada 104 C4
Williamsburg, Ky., U.S.A. 109 G3
Williamsburg, Pa., U.S.A. 110 F6
Williamsburg, Va., U.S.A. 108 G7
Williamson, N.Y., U.S.A. 110 C7
Williamson, W. Va., U.S.A. ... 108 G4
Williamsport, U.S.A. 110 E7
Williamston, U.S.A. 109 H7
Williamstown, Ky., U.S.A. ... 108 F3
Williamstown, Mass., U.S.A. . 111 D11
Williamstown, N.Y., U.S.A. .. 111 C9
Willimantic, U.S.A. 111 E12
Willingboro, U.S.A. 108 E8
Willis Group, Australia 94 B5
Williston, S. Africa 88 E3
Williston, Fla., U.S.A. 109 L4
Williston, N. Dak., U.S.A. 112 A3
Williston L., Canada 104 B4
Willits, U.S.A. 114 G2
Willmar, U.S.A. 112 C7
Willoughby, U.S.A. 110 E3
Willow Bunch, Canada 105 D7
Willow L., Canada 104 A5
Willow Wall, The, China 57 C12
Willowick, U.S.A. 110 E3
Willowlake ➤, Canada 104 A4
Willowmore, S. Africa 88 E3
Willows, U.S.A. 116 F4
Willowvale = Gatyana, S. Africa 89 E4
Wills, L., Australia 92 D4
Wills Cr. ➤, Australia 94 C3
Wilmette, U.S.A. 108 D2
Wilmington, Del., U.S.A. 108 F8
Wilmington, N.C., U.S.A. 109 H7
Wilmington, Ohio, U.S.A. 108 F4
Wilmington, Vt., U.S.A. 111 D12
Wilmslow, U.K. 12 D5
Wilpena Cr. ➤, Australia 95 E2
Wilsall, U.S.A. 114 D8
Wilson, N.C., U.S.A. 109 H7
Wilson, N.Y., U.S.A. 110 C6
Wilson, Pa., U.S.A. 111 F9
Wilson ➤, Australia 92 C4
Wilson Bluff, Australia 93 F4
Wilson Inlet, Australia 93 G2
Wilster, Germany 24 B5
Wilton, U.S.A. 112 B4

Wilton ➤, Australia 94 A1
Wiltshire □, U.K. 13 F6
Wiltz, Lux. 17 E5
Wiluna, Australia 93 E3
Wimborne Minster, U.K. 13 G6
Wimereux, France 19 B8
Winam G., Kenya 86 C3
Winburg, S. Africa 88 D4
Winchendon, U.S.A. 111 D12
Winchester, U.K. 13 F6
Winchester, Conn., U.S.A. ... 111 E11
Winchester, Idaho, U.S.A. 114 C5
Winchester, Ind., U.S.A. 108 E3
Winchester, Ky., U.S.A. 108 G3
Winchester, N.H., U.S.A. 111 D12
Winchester, Nev., U.S.A. 117 J11
Winchester, Tenn., U.S.A. ... 109 H2
Winchester, Va., U.S.A. 108 F6
Wind ➤, U.S.A. 114 E9
Wind River Range, U.S.A. ... 114 E9
Windau = Ventspils, Latvia ... 9 H19
Windber, U.S.A. 110 F6
Winder, U.S.A. 109 J4
Windermere, U.K. 12 C5
Windhoek, Namibia 88 C2
Windischgarsten, Austria 26 D7
Windom, U.S.A. 112 D7
Windorah, Australia 94 D3
Window Rock, U.S.A. 115 J9
Windrush ➤, U.K. 13 F6
Windsor, N.S., Canada 103 D7
Windsor, Ont., Canada 102 D3
Windsor, U.K. 13 F7
Windsor, Colo., U.S.A. 112 E2
Windsor, Conn., U.S.A. 111 E12
Windsor, Mo., U.S.A. 112 F8
Windsor, N.Y., U.S.A. 111 D9
Windsor, Vt., U.S.A. 111 C12
Windsor & Maidenhead □, U.K. 13 F7
Windsorton, S. Africa 88 D3
Windward I., W. Indies 121 D7
Windward Passage = Vientos,
  Paso de los, Caribbean 121 C5
Winefred L., Canada 105 B6
Winejok, Sudan 81 F2
Winfield, U.S.A. 113 G6
Wingate Mts., Australia 92 B5
Wingham, Canada 102 D3
Winisk, Canada 102 A2
Winisk ➤, Canada 102 A2
Winisk L., Canada 102 B2
Wink, U.S.A. 113 K3
Winkler, Canada 105 D9
Winklern, Austria 26 E5
Winlock, U.S.A. 116 D4
Winneba, Ghana 83 D4
Winnebago, L., U.S.A. 108 D1
Winnecke Cr. ➤, Australia ... 92 C5
Winnemucca, U.S.A. 114 F5
Winnemucca L., U.S.A. 114 F4
Winnett, U.S.A. 114 C9
Winnfield, U.S.A. 113 K8
Winnibigoshish, L., U.S.A. ... 112 B7
Winnipeg, Canada 105 D9
Winnipeg ➤, Canada 105 C9
Winnipeg, L., Canada 105 C9
Winnipeg Beach, Canada 105 C9
Winnipegosis, Canada 105 C9
Winnipegosis L., Canada 105 C9
Winnipesaukee, L., U.S.A. ... 111 C13
Winnisquam L., U.S.A. 111 C13
Winnsboro, La., U.S.A. 113 J9
Winnsboro, S.C., U.S.A. 109 H5
Winnsboro, Tex., U.S.A. 113 J7
Winokapau, L., Canada 103 B7
Winona, Minn., U.S.A. 112 C9
Winona, Miss., U.S.A. 113 J10
Winooski, U.S.A. 111 B11
Winooski ➤, U.S.A. 111 B11
Winschoten, Neths. 17 A7
Winsen, Germany 24 B6
Winsford, U.K. 12 D5
Winslow, Ariz., U.S.A. 115 J8
Winslow, Wash., U.S.A. 116 C4
Winsted, U.S.A. 111 E11
Winston-Salem, U.S.A. 109 G5
Winter Garden, U.S.A. 109 L5
Winter Haven, U.S.A. 109 M5
Winter Park, U.S.A. 109 L5
Winterberg, Germany 24 D4
Winterhaven, U.S.A. 117 N12
Winters, U.S.A. 113 K5
Wintersville, U.S.A. 110 F4
Winterswijk, Neths. 17 C6
Winterthur, Switz. 25 H4
Winthrop, U.S.A. 114 B3
Winton, Australia 94 C3
Winton, N.Z. 91 M2
Wipper ➤, Germany 24 D7
Wirrulla, Australia 95 E1
Wisbech, U.K. 13 E8
Wisconsin □, U.S.A. 112 C10
Wisconsin ➤, U.S.A. 112 D9
Wisconsin Rapids, U.S.A. 112 C10
Wisdom, U.S.A. 114 D7
Wishaw, U.K. 14 F5
Wishek, U.S.A. 112 B5
Wisła, Poland 45 J5
Wisła ➤, Poland 44 D5
Wisłok ➤, Poland 45 H9
Wisłoka ➤, Poland 45 H8
Wismar, Germany 24 B7
Wisner, U.S.A. 112 E6
Wissant, France 19 B8
Wissembourg, France 19 C14

Wisznice, *Poland* 45 G10
Witbank, *S. Africa* 89 D4
Witdraai, *S. Africa* 88 D3
Witham, *U.K.* 13 F8
Witham →, *U.K.* 12 E7
Withernsea, *U.K.* 12 D8
Witkowo, *Poland* 45 F4
Witney, *U.K.* 13 F6
Witnica, *Poland* 45 F1
Witnossob →, *Namibia* 88 D3
Wittdün, *Germany* 24 A4
Witten, *Germany* 24 D3
Wittenberge, *Germany* 24 B7
Wittenburg, *Germany* 24 B7
Wittenheim, *France* 19 E14
Wittenoom, *Australia* 92 D2
Wittingen, *Germany* 24 C6
Wittlich, *Germany* 25 F2
Wittmund, *Germany* 24 B3
Wittow, *Germany* 24 A9
Wittstock, *Germany* 24 B8
Witvlei, *Namibia* 88 C2
Witzenhausen, *Germany* 24 D5
Wkra →, *Poland* 45 F7
Władysławowo, *Poland* 44 D5
Wleń, *Poland* 45 G2
Wlingi, *Indonesia* 63 H15
Włocławek, *Poland* 45 F6
Włodawa, *Poland* 45 G10
Włoszczowa, *Poland* 45 H6
Woburn, *U.S.A.* 111 D13
Wodian, *China* 56 H7
Wodzisław Śląski, *Poland* 45 H5
Wœrth, *France* 19 D14
Woinbogoin, *China* 58 A2
Woippy, *France* 19 C13
Wojcieszow, *Poland* 45 H2
Wokam, *Indonesia* 63 F8
Woking, *U.K.* 13 F7
Wokingham □, *U.K.* 13 F7
Wolbrom, *Poland* 45 H6
Wołczyn, *Poland* 45 G5
Woldegk, *Germany* 24 B9
Wolf →, *Canada* 104 A2
Wolf Creek, *U.S.A.* 114 C7
Wolf L., *Canada* 104 A2
Wolf Point, *U.S.A.* 112 A2
Wolfe I., *Canada* 102 D4
Wolfeboro, *U.S.A.* 111 C13
Wolfen, *Germany* 24 D8
Wolfenbüttel, *Germany* 24 C6
Wolfratshausen, *Germany* 25 H7
Wolfsberg, *Austria* 26 E7
Wolfsburg, *Germany* 24 C6
Wolgast, *Germany* 24 A9
Wolhusen, *Switz.* 25 H4
Wolin, *Poland* 44 E1
Wollaston, Is., *Chile* 128 H3
Wollaston L., *Canada* 105 B8
Wollaston Lake, *Canada* 105 B8
Wollaston Pen., *Canada* 100 B8
Wolmaransstad, *S. Africa* 88 D4
Wolmirstedt, *Germany* 24 C7
Wołomin, *Poland* 45 F8
Wołów, *Poland* 45 G3
Wolseley, *S. Africa* 88 E2
Wolsey, *U.S.A.* 112 C5
Wolstenholme, C., *Canada* ... 98 C12
Wolsztyn, *Poland* 45 F3
Wolvega, *Neths.* 17 B6
Wolverhampton, *U.K.* 13 E5
Wondai, *Australia* 95 D5
Wongan Hills, *Australia* 93 F2
Wŏnju, *S. Korea* 57 F14
Wonosari, *Indonesia* 63 G14
Wonosobo, *Indonesia* 63 G13
Wonowon, *Canada* 104 B4
Wŏnsan, *N. Korea* 57 E14
Wood Buffalo Nat. Park,
Canada 104 B6
Wood Is., *Australia* 92 C3
Wood L., *Canada* 105 B8
Woodah I., *Australia* 94 A2
Woodbourne, *U.S.A.* 111 E10
Woodbridge, *Canada* 110 C5
Woodbridge, *U.K.* 13 E9
Woodburn, *U.S.A.* 114 D2
Woodenbong, *Australia* 95 D5
Woodford, *Australia* 95 D5
Woodfords, *U.S.A.* 116 G7
Woodlake, *U.S.A.* 116 J7
Woodland, Calif., *U.S.A.* 116 G5
Woodland, Maine, *U.S.A.* ... 109 C12
Woodland, Pa., *U.S.A.* 110 F6
Woodland, Wash., *U.S.A.* ... 116 E4
Woodland Caribou Prov. Park,
Canada 105 C10
Woodridge, *Canada* 105 D9
Woodroffe, Mt., *Australia* 93 E5
Woods, L., *Australia* 94 B1
Woods, L. of the, *Canada* ... 105 D10
Woodstock, *Australia* 94 B4
Woodstock, N.B., *Canada* ... 103 C6
Woodstock, Ont., *Canada* ... 102 D3
Woodstock, *U.K.* 13 F6
Woodstock, Ill., *U.S.A.* 112 D10
Woodstock, Vt., *U.S.A.* 111 C12
Woodsville, *U.S.A.* 111 B13
Woodville, *N.Z.* 91 J5
Woodville, Miss., *U.S.A.* 113 K9
Woodville, Tex., *U.S.A.* 113 K7
Woodward, *U.S.A.* 113 G5
Woody, *U.S.A.* 117 K8
Woody →, *Canada* 105 C8
Wooler, *U.K.* 12 B5

Woolgoolga, *Australia* 95 E5
Woonsocket, R.I., *U.S.A.* ... 111 E13
Woonsocket, S. Dak., *U.S.A.* .. 112 C5
Wooramel →, *Australia* 93 E1
Wooramel Roadhouse, *Australia* 93 E1
Wooster, *U.S.A.* 110 F3
Worcester, *S. Africa* 88 E2
Worcester, *U.K.* 13 E5
Worcester, Mass., *U.S.A.* ... 111 D13
Worcester, N.Y., *U.S.A.* 111 D10
Worcestershire □, *U.K.* 13 E5
Wörgl, *Austria* 26 D5
Workington, *U.K.* 12 C4
Worksop, *U.K.* 12 D6
Workum, *Neths.* 17 B5
Worland, *U.S.A.* 114 D10
Wormhout, *France* 19 B9
Worms, *Germany* 25 F4
Worsley, *Canada* 104 B5
Wörth, *Germany* 25 F8
Wortham, *U.S.A.* 113 K6
Wörther See, *Austria* 26 E7
Worthing, *U.K.* 13 G7
Worthington, Minn., *U.S.A.* ... 112 D7
Worthington, Pa., *U.S.A.* ... 110 F5
Wosi, *Indonesia* 63 E7
Wou-han = Wuhan, *China* 59 B10
Wousi = Wuxi, *China* 59 B13
Wowoni, *Indonesia* 63 E6
Wrangel I. = Vrangelya, Ostrov,
Russia 51 B19
Wrangell, *U.S.A.* 104 B2
Wrangell Mts., *U.S.A.* 100 B5
Wrath, C., *U.K.* 14 C3
Wray, *U.S.A.* 112 E3
Wrekin, The, *U.K.* 13 E5
Wrens, *U.S.A.* 109 J4
Wrexham, *U.K.* 12 D4
Wrexham □, *U.K.* 12 D5
Wriezen, *Germany* 24 C10
Wright = Paranas, *Phil.* 61 F6
Wright, *U.S.A.* 112 D2
Wright Pt., *Canada* 110 C3
Wrightson Mt., *U.S.A.* 115 L8
Wrightwood, *U.S.A.* 117 L9
Wrigley, *Canada* 100 B7
Wrocław, *Poland* 45 G4
Wronki, *Poland* 45 F3
Września, *Poland* 45 F4
Wschowa, *Poland* 45 G3
Wu Jiang →, *China* 58 C6
Wu'an, *China* 56 F8
Wubin, *Australia* 93 F2
Wubu, *China* 56 F6
Wuchang, *China* 57 B14
Wucheng, *China* 56 F9
Wuchuan, Guangdong, *China* . 59 G8
Wuchuan, Guizhou, *China* ... 58 C7
Wuchuan, Nei Monggol Zizhiqu,
China 56 D6
Wudi, *China* 57 F9
Wuding, *China* 58 E4
Wuding He →, *China* 56 F6
Wudinna, *Australia* 95 E2
Wudu, *China* 56 H3
Wufeng, *China* 59 B8
Wugang, *China* 59 D8
Wugong Shan, *China* 59 D9
Wuhan, *China* 59 B10
Wuhe, *China* 57 H9
Wuhsi = Wuxi, *China* 59 B13
Wuhu, *China* 59 B12
Wujiang, *China* 59 B13
Wukari, *Nigeria* 83 D6
Wulajie, *China* 57 B14
Wulanbulang, *China* 56 D6
Wular L., *India* 69 B6
Wulehe, *Ghana* 83 D5
Wulian, *China* 57 G10
Wuliang Shan, *China* 58 E3
Wuliaru, *Indonesia* 63 F8
Wuling Shan, *China* 58 C7
Wulong, *China* 58 C6
Wulumuchi = Ürümqi, *China* .. 50 E9
Wum, *Cameroon* 83 D7
Wuming, *China* 58 F7
Wun Rog, *Sudan* 81 F2
Wundowie, *Australia* 93 F2
Wuning, *China* 59 C10
Wunnummin L., *Canada* 102 B2
Wunsiedel, *Germany* 25 E8
Wunstorf, *Germany* 24 C5
Wuntho, *Burma* 67 H19
Wuping, *China* 59 E11
Wuppertal, *Germany* 24 D3
Wuppertal, *S. Africa* 88 E2
Wuqing, *China* 57 E9
Wurtsboro, *U.S.A.* 111 E10
Würzburg, *Germany* 25 F5
Wurzen, *Germany* 24 D8
Wushan, *China* 56 G3
Wushishi, *Nigeria* 83 D6
Wusuli Jiang = Ussuri →, *Asia* . 54 A7
Wutach →, *Germany* 25 H4
Wutai, *China* 56 E7
Wuting = Huimin, *China* 57 F9
Wutong, *China* 59 E8
Wutonghaolai, *China* 57 C11
Wutongqiao, *China* 58 C4
Wuwei, Anhui, *China* 59 B11
Wuwei, Gansu, *China* 60 C5
Wuxi, Jiangsu, *China* 59 B13
Wuxi, Sichuan, *China* 58 B7
Wuxiang, *China* 56 F7
Wuxuan, *China* 58 F7

Wuxue, *China* 59 C10
Xiapu, *China* 59 D12
Wuyang, *China* 56 H7
Wuyi, Hebei, *China* 56 F8
Wuyi, Zhejiang, *China* 59 C12
Wuyi Shan, *China* 59 D11
Wuyishan, *China* 59 D12
Wuyo, *Nigeria* 83 C7
Wuyuan, Jiangxi, *China* 59 C11
Wuyuan, Nei Monggol Zizhiqu,
China 56 D5
Wuzhai, *China* 56 E6
Wuzhi Shan, *China* 64 C7
Wuzhong, *China* 56 E4
Wuzhou, *China* 59 F8
Wyaaba Cr. →, *Australia* 94 B3
Wyalkatchem, *Australia* 93 F2
Wyalusing, *U.S.A.* 111 E8
Wyandotte, *U.S.A.* 108 D4
Wyandra, *Australia* 95 D4
Wyara, L., *Australia* 95 D3
Wye →, *U.K.* 13 F5
Wyemandoo, *Australia* 93 E2
Wyk, *Germany* 24 A4
Wymondham, *U.K.* 13 E9
Wymore, *U.S.A.* 112 E6
Wyndham, *Australia* 92 C4
Wyndham, *N.Z.* 91 M2
Wynne, *U.S.A.* 113 H9
Wynyard, *Australia* 94 G4
Wynyard, *Canada* 105 C8
Wyola L., *Australia* 93 E5
Wyoming, *Canada* 110 D2
Wyoming □, *U.S.A.* 114 E10
Wyomissing, *U.S.A.* 111 F9
Wyrzysk, *Poland* 45 E4
Wyśmierzyce, *Poland* 45 G7
Wysoka, *Poland* 45 E4
Wysokie, *Poland* 45 H9
Wysokie Mazowieckie, *Poland* . 45 E9
Wyszków, *Poland* 45 F8
Wyszogród, *Poland* 45 F7
Wytheville, *U.S.A.* 108 G5
Wyżyna Małopolska, *Poland* .. 45 H7

X

Xaçmaz, *Azerbaijan* 49 K9
Xai-Xai, *Mozam.* 89 D5
Xainza, *China* 60 C3
Xangongo, *Angola* 88 B2
Xankändi, *Azerbaijan* 70 B5
Xanlar, *Azerbaijan* 49 K8
Xanten, *Germany* 24 D2
Xánthi, *Greece* 41 E8
Xánthi □, *Greece* 41 E8
Xanthos, *Turkey* 39 E11
Xanxerê, *Brazil* 127 B5
Xapuri, *Brazil* 124 F5
Xar Moron He →, *China* 57 C11
Xarrë, *Albania* 40 G4
Xátiva, *Spain* 33 G4
Xau, L., *Botswana* 88 C3
Xavantina, *Brazil* 127 A5
Xenia, *U.S.A.* 108 F4
Xeropotamos →, *Cyprus* 36 E11
Xertigny, *France* 19 D13
Xhora, *S. Africa* 89 E4
Xhumo, *Botswana* 88 C3
Xi Jiang →, *China* 59 F9
Xi Xian, Henan, *China* 59 A10
Xi Xian, Shanxi, *China* 56 F6
Xia Xian, *China* 56 G6
Xiachengzi, *China* 57 B16
Xiachuan Dao, *China* 59 G9
Xiaguan, *China* 60 D5
Xiajiang, *China* 59 D10
Xiajin, *China* 56 F9
Xiamen, *China* 59 E12
Xi'an, *China* 56 G5
Xian Xian, *China* 56 E9
Xianfeng, *China* 58 C7
Xiang Jiang →, *China* 59 C9
Xiangcheng, Henan, *China* ... 56 H8
Xiangcheng, Henan, *China* ... 56 H7
Xiangcheng, Sichuan, *China* .. 58 C2
Xiangdu, *China* 58 F6
Xiangfan, *China* 59 A9
Xianggang = Hong Kong □,
China 59 F10
Xianghuang Qi, *China* 56 C7
Xiangning, *China* 56 G6
Xiangquan, *China* 56 F7
Xiangquan He = Sutlej →,
Pakistan 68 E4
Xiangshan, *China* 59 C13
Xiangshui, *China* 57 G10
Xiangtan, *China* 59 D9
Xiangxiang, *China* 59 D9
Xiangyin, *China* 59 C9
Xiangyun, *China* 58 E3
Xiangzhou, *China* 58 F7
Xianju, *China* 59 C13
Xianning, *China* 59 C10
Xiantao, *China* 59 B9
Xianyang, *China* 56 G5
Xianyou, *China* 59 E12
Xiao Hinggan Ling, *China* 60 B7
Xiaofeng, *China* 59 B12
Xiaogan, *China* 59 B9
Xiaojin, *China* 58 B4
Xiaolan, *China* 59 F9
Xiaoshan, *China* 59 B13

Xiaoyi, *China* 56 F6
Xiapu, *China* 59 D12
Xiawa, *China* 57 C11
Xiayi, *China* 56 G9
Xichang, *China* 58 D4
Xichong, *China* 58 B5
Xichou, *China* 58 E5
Xichuan, *China* 56 H6
Xide, *China* 58 C4
Xiemahe, *China* 59 B8
Xieng Khouang, *Laos* 64 C4
Xifei He →, *China* 56 H9
Xifeng, Gansu, *China* 56 G4
Xifeng, Guizhou, *China* 58 D6
Xifeng, Liaoning, *China* 57 C13
Xifengzhen = Xifeng, *China* .. 56 G4
Xigazê, *China* 60 D3
Xihe, *China* 56 G3
Xihua, *China* 56 H8
Xilaganí, *Greece* 41 F9
Xiliao He →, *China* 57 C12
Xilin, *China* 58 E5
Xilókastron, *Greece* 38 C4
Xime, *Guinea-Biss.* 82 C2
Ximeng, *China* 58 F2
Xin Jiang →, *China* 59 C11
Xin Xian = Xinzhou, *China* ... 56 E7
Xinavane, *Mozam.* 89 D5
Xinbin, *China* 57 D13
Xincai, *China* 59 A10
Xinchang, *China* 59 C13
Xincheng, Guangxi Zhuangzu,
China 58 E7
Xincheng, Jiangxi, *China* 59 D10
Xindu, *China* 58 B5
Xinfeng, Guangdong, *China* .. 59 E10
Xinfeng, Jiangxi, *China* 59 D11
Xinfeng, Jiangxi, *China* 59 E10
Xinfengjiang Skuiku, *China* ... 59 F10
Xing Xian, *China* 56 E6
Xing'an, Guangxi Zhuangzu,
China 59 E8
Xingan, Jiangxi, *China* 59 D10
Xingcheng, *China* 57 D11
Xingguo, *China* 59 D10
Xinghe, *China* 56 D7
Xinghua, *China* 57 H10
Xinghua Wan, *China* 59 E12
Xingning, *China* 59 E10
Xingping, *China* 56 G5
Xingren, *China* 58 E5
Xingshan, *China* 59 B8
Xingtai, *China* 56 F8
Xingu →, *Brazil* 122 D5
Xingwen, *China* 58 C5
Xingyang, *China* 56 G7
Xinhe, *China* 56 F8
Xinhua, *China* 59 D8
Xinhuang, *China* 58 D7
Xinhui, *China* 59 F9
Xining, *China* 60 C5
Xinjian, *China* 59 C10
Xinjiang, *China* 56 G6
Xinjiang Uygur Zizhiqu □,
China 60 B3
Xinjie, *China* 58 D3
Xinjin = Pulandian, *China* 57 E11
Xinjin, *China* 58 B4
Xinkai He →, *China* 57 C12
Xinle, *China* 56 E8
Xinlitun, *China* 57 D12
Xinlong, *China* 58 B3
Xinmin, *China* 57 D12
Xinning, *China* 59 D8
Xinping, *China* 58 E3
Xinshao, *China* 59 D8
Xintai, *China* 57 G9
Xintian, *China* 59 E9
Xinxian, *China* 59 B10
Xinxiang, *China* 56 G7
Xinxing, *China* 59 F9
Xinyang, *China* 59 A10
Xinye, *China* 59 A9
Xinyi, *China* 59 F8
Xinyu, *China* 59 D10
Xinzhan, *China* 57 C14
Xinzheng, *China* 56 G7
Xinzhou, Hubei, *China* 59 B10
Xinzhou, Shanxi, *China* 56 E7
Xinzo de Limia, *Spain* 34 C3
Xiongyuecheng, *China* 57 D12
Xiping, Henan, *China* 56 H8
Xiping, Henan, *China* 56 H6
Xiping, Zhejiang, *China* 59 C12
Xique-Xique, *Brazil* 125 F10
Xisha Qundao = Paracel Is.,
S. China Sea 62 A4
Xishui, Guizhou, *China* 58 C6
Xishui, Hubei, *China* 59 B10
Xitole, *Guinea-Biss.* 82 C2
Xiu Shui →, *China* 59 C10
Xiuning, *China* 59 C12
Xiuren, *China* 59 E8
Xiushan, *China* 58 C7
Xiushui, *China* 59 C10
Xiuwen, *China* 58 D6
Xiuyan, *China* 57 D12
Xixabangma Feng, *China* 67 E14
Xixia, *China* 56 H6
Xixiang, *China* 56 H4
Xiyang, *China* 56 F7
Xizang Zizhiqu □, *China* 60 C3
Xlendi, *Malta* 36 C1
Xu Jiang →, *China* 59 D11

Xuan Loc, *Vietnam* 65 G6
Xuan'en, *China* 58 C7
Xuanhan, *China* 58 B6
Xuanhua, *China* 56 D8
Xuanwei, *China* 58 C5
Xuanzhou, *China* 59 B12
Xuchang, *China* 56 G7
Xudat, *Azerbaijan* 49 K9
Xuefeng Shan, *China* 59 D8
Xuejiaping, *China* 59 B8
Xun Jiang →, *China* 59 F8
Xun Xian, *China* 56 G8
Xundian, *China* 58 E4
Xunwu, *China* 59 E10
Xunyang, *China* 56 H5
Xunyi, *China* 56 G5
Xupu, *China* 59 D8
Xúquer →, *Spain* 33 F4
Xushui, *China* 56 E8
Xuwen, *China* 59 G8
Xuyen Moc, *Vietnam* 65 G6
Xuyong, *China* 58 C5
Xuzhou, *China* 57 G9
Xylophagou, *Cyprus* 36 E12

Y

Ya Xian, *China* 64 C7
Yaamba, *Australia* 94 C5
Ya'an, *China* 58 C4
Yabassi, *Cameroon* 83 E6
Yabelo, *Ethiopia* 81 G4
Yablanitsa, *Bulgaria* 41 C8
Yablonovy Ra. = Yablonovyy
Khrebet, *Russia* 51 D12
Yablonovyy Khrebet, *Russia* .. 51 D12
Yabrai Shan, *China* 56 E2
Yabrūd, *Syria* 75 B5
Yacheng, *China* 64 C7
Yacuiba, *Bolivia* 126 A3
Yacuma →, *Bolivia* 124 F5
Yadgir, *India* 66 L10
Yadkin →, *U.S.A.* 109 H5
Yadrin, *Russia* 48 C8
Yaeyama-Rettō, *Japan* 55 M1
Yagaba, *Ghana* 83 C4
Yağcılar, *Turkey* 39 B10
Yagodnoye, *Russia* 51 C15
Yahila, *Dem. Rep. of the Congo* 86 B1
Yahk, *Canada* 104 D5
Yahotyn, *Ukraine* 47 G6
Yahuma, *Dem. Rep. of
the Congo* 84 D4
Yahyalı, *Turkey* 72 C6
Yaita, *Japan* 55 F9
Yaiza, Canary Is. 37 F6
Yajiang, *China* 58 B3
Yajua, *Nigeria* 83 C7
Yakima, *U.S.A.* 114 C3
Yakima →, *U.S.A.* 114 C3
Yako, *Burkina Faso* 82 C4
Yakobi I., *U.S.A.* 104 B1
Yakoruda, *Bulgaria* 40 D7
Yakovlevka, *Russia* 54 B6
Yaku-Shima, *Japan* 55 J5
Yakumo, *Japan* 54 C10
Yakutat, *U.S.A.* 100 C6
Yakutia = Sakha □, *Russia* ... 51 C13
Yakutsk, *Russia* 51 C13
Yala, *Thailand* 65 J3
Yale, *U.S.A.* 110 C2
Yalgoo, *Australia* 93 E2
Yalinga, *C.A.R.* 84 C4
Yalkubul, Punta, *Mexico* 119 C7
Yalleroi, *Australia* 94 C4
Yalobusha →, *U.S.A.* 113 J9
Yalong Jiang →, *China* 58 D3
Yalova, *Turkey* 41 F13
Yalta, *Ukraine* 47 K8
Yalu Jiang →, *China* 57 E13
Yalvaç, *Turkey* 72 C4
Yam Ha Melah = Dead Sea,
Asia 75 D4
Yam Kinneret, *Israel* 75 C4
Yamada, *Japan* 55 H5
Yamagata, *Japan* 54 E10
Yamagata □, *Japan* 54 E10
Yamaguchi, *Japan* 55 G5
Yamaguchi □, *Japan* 55 G5
Yamal, Poluostrov, *Russia* ... 50 B8
Yamal Pen. = Yamal,
Poluostrov, *Russia* 50 B8
Yamanashi □, *Japan* 55 G9
Yamba, *Australia* 95 D5
Yambarran Ra., *Australia* 92 C5
Yambéring, *Guinea* 82 C2
Yámbio, *Sudan* 81 G2
Yambol, *Bulgaria* 41 D10
Yamdena, *Indonesia* 63 F8
Yame, *Japan* 55 H5
Yamethin, *Burma* 67 J20
Yamma-Yamma, L., *Australia* . 95 D3
Yamoussoukro, *Ivory C.* 82 D3
Yampa →, *U.S.A.* 114 F9
Yampi Sd., *Australia* 92 C3
Yampil, *Moldova* 47 H5
Yampol = Yampil, *Moldova* ... 47 H5
Yamrat, *Nigeria* 83 C6
Yamrukchal = Botev, *Bulgaria* . 41 D8
Yamuna →, *India* 69 G9
Yamunanagar, *India* 68 D7
Yamzho Yumco, *China* 60 D3
Yan, *Nigeria* 83 C7
Yana →, *Russia* 51 B14

Yanagawa, Japan 55 H5
Yanai, Japan 55 H6
Yan'an, China 56 F5
Yanbian, China 58 D3
Yanbu 'al Baḥr, Si. Arabia 70 F3
Yanchang, China 56 F6
Yancheng, Henan, China 56 H8
Yancheng, Jiangsu, China 57 H11
Yanchep Beach, Australia 93 F2
Yanchi, China 56 F4
Yanchuan, China 56 F6
Yandoon, Burma 67 L19
Yanfeng, China 58 E3
Yanfolila, Mali 82 C3
Yang Xian, China 56 H4
Yang-Yang, Senegal 82 B1
Yangambi, Dem. Rep. of
    the Congo 86 B1
Yangbi, China 58 E2
Yangcheng, China 56 G7
Yangch'ü = Taiyuan, China ... 56 F7
Yangchun, China 59 F8
Yanggao, China 56 D7
Yanggu, China 56 F8
Yangjiang, China 59 G8
Yangliuqing, China 57 E9
Yangon = Rangoon, Burma 67 L20
Yangping, China 59 B8
Yangpingguan, China 56 H4
Yangquan, China 56 F7
Yangshan, China 59 E9
Yangshuo, China 59 E8
Yangtse = Chang Jiang →,
    China 59 B13
Yangtze Kiang = Chang
    Jiang →, China 59 B13
Yangxin, China 59 C10
Yangyang, S. Korea 57 E15
Yangyuan, China 56 D8
Yangzhong, China 59 A12
Yangzhou, China 59 A12
Yanhe, China 58 C7
Yanji, China 57 C15
Yanjin, China 58 C5
Yanjing, China 58 C2
Yankton, U.S.A. 112 D6
Yanonge, Dem. Rep. of
    the Congo 86 B1
Yanqi, China 60 B3
Yanqing, China 56 D8
Yanshan, Hebei, China 57 E9
Yanshan, Jiangxi, China 59 C11
Yanshan, Yunnan, China 58 F5
Yanshou, China 57 B15
Yantabulla, Australia 95 D4
Yantai, China 57 F11
Yanting, China 58 B5
Yantra →, Bulgaria 41 C9
Yanwa, China 58 D2
Yanyuan, China 58 D3
Yanzhou, China 56 G9
Yao Xian, China 56 G5
Yao Yai, Ko, Thailand 65 J2
Yao'an, China 58 E3
Yaodu, China 58 A5
Yaoundé, Cameroon 83 E7
Yaowan, China 57 G10
Yap I., Pac. Oc. 96 G5
Yapen, Indonesia 63 E9
Yapen, Selat, Indonesia 63 E9
Yapero, Indonesia 63 E9
Yappar →, Australia 94 B3
Yaqui →, Mexico 118 B2
Yar-Sale, Russia 50 C8
Yaraka, Australia 94 C3
Yaransk, Russia 48 B8
Yarbasan, Turkey 39 C10
Yardımcı Burnu, Turkey 39 E12
Yare →, U.K. 13 E9
Yaremcha, Ukraine 47 H3
Yarensk, Russia 50 C5
Yarfa, Si. Arabia 80 C4
Yarí →, Colombia 124 D4
Yarkand = Shache, China 60 C2
Yarker, Canada 111 B8
Yarkhun →, Pakistan 69 A5
Yarmouth, Canada 103 D6
Yarmūk →, Syria 75 C4
Yaroslavl, Russia 46 D10
Yarqa, W. →, Egypt 75 F2
Yarra Yarra Lakes, Australia .. 93 E2
Yarraman, Australia 95 D5
Yartsevo, Sib., Russia 51 C10
Yartsevo, Smolensk, Russia .. 46 E7
Yarumal, Colombia 124 B3
Yasawa Group, Fiji 91 C7
Yaselda, Belarus 47 F4
Yashi, Nigeria 83 C6
Yashikera, Nigeria 83 D5
Yashkul, Russia 49 G7
Yasin, Pakistan 69 A5
Yasinovataya, Ukraine 47 H9
Yasinski, L., Canada 102 B4
Yasinya, Ukraine 47 H3
Yasothon, Thailand 64 E5
Yāsūj, Iran 71 D6
Yatağan, Turkey 39 D10
Yatakala, Niger 83 C5
Yates Center, U.S.A. 113 G7
Yathkyed L., Canada 105 A9
Yatsushiro, Japan 55 H5
Yatta Plateau, Kenya 86 C4
Yavari →, Peru 124 D4
Yávaros, Mexico 118 B3
Yavatmal, India 66 J11

Yavne, Israel 75 D3
Yavoriv, Ukraine 47 H2
Yavorov = Yavoriv, Ukraine ... 47 H2
Yavuzeli, Turkey 72 D7
Yawatahama, Japan 55 H6
Yawri B., S. Leone 82 D2
Yaxi, China 58 D6
Yazd, Iran 71 D7
Yazd □, Iran 71 D7
Yazd-e Khvāst, Iran 71 D7
Yazıköy, Turkey 39 E9
Yazman, Pakistan 68 E4
Yazoo →, U.S.A. 113 J9
Yazoo City, U.S.A. 113 J9
Ybbs, Austria 26 C8
Yding Skovhøj, Denmark 11 J3
Ye Xian = Laizhou, China 57 F10
Ye Xian, China 56 H7
Yebyu, Burma 64 E2
Yechŏn, S. Korea 57 F15
Yecla, Spain 33 G3
Yécora, Mexico 118 B3
Yedintsy = Edineț, Moldova ... 43 B12
Yedseram →, Nigeria 83 C7
Yefremov, Russia 46 F10
Yeghegnadzor, Armenia 73 C11
Yegorlyk →, Russia 49 G5
Yegorlykskaya, Russia 49 G5
Yegoryevsk, Russia 46 E10
Yegros, Paraguay 126 B4
Yehuda, Midbar, Israel 75 D4
Yei, Sudan 81 G3
Yei, Nahr →, Sudan 81 F3
Yejmiadzin, Armenia 49 K7
Yekaterinburg, Russia 50 D7
Yekaterinodar = Krasnodar,
    Russia 49 H4
Yelabuga, Russia 48 C11
Yelan, Russia 48 E6
Yelarbon, Australia 95 D5
Yelatma, Russia 48 C5
Yelets, Russia 47 F10
Yélimané, Mali 82 B2
Yelizavetgrad = Kirovohrad,
    Ukraine 47 H7
Yell, U.K. 14 A7
Yell Sd., U.K. 14 A7
Yellow Sea, China 57 G12
Yellowhead Pass, Canada 104 C5
Yellowknife, Canada 104 A6
Yellowknife →, Canada 104 A6
Yellowstone →, U.S.A. 112 B3
Yellowstone L., U.S.A. 114 D8
Yellowstone National Park,
    U.S.A. 114 D9
Yelnya, Russia 46 E7
Yelsk, Belarus 47 G5
Yelwa, Nigeria 83 C5
Yemen ■, Asia 74 E3
Yen Bai, Vietnam 58 G5
Yenagoa, Nigeria 83 E6
Yenakiyeve, Ukraine 47 H10
Yenakiyevo = Yenakiyeve,
    Ukraine 47 H10
Yenangyaung, Burma 67 J19
Yenbo = Yanbu 'al Baḥr,
    Si. Arabia 70 F3
Yende Millimou, Guinea 82 D2
Yendéré, Burkina Faso 82 C4
Yendi, Ghana 83 D4
Yéni, Niger 83 C5
Yenice, Ankara, Turkey 72 C5
Yenice, Aydın, Turkey 39 D10
Yenice, Çanakkale, Turkey ... 39 B9
Yenice, Edirne, Turkey 41 F10
Yenice →, Turkey 72 D6
Yenifoça, Turkey 39 C8
Yenihisar, Turkey 39 D9
Yeniköy, Bursa, Turkey 41 F13
Yeniköy, Çanakkale, Turkey .. 39 B8
Yeniköy, Kütahya, Turkey ... 39 C11
Yenipazar, Turkey 39 D10
Yenisaía, Greece 41 E8
Yenişehir, Turkey 41 F13
Yenisey →, Russia 50 B9
Yeniseysk, Russia 51 D10
Yeniseyskiy Zaliv, Russia ... 50 B9
Yennádhi, Greece 36 C9
Yenne, France 21 C9
Yenotayevka, Russia 49 G8
Yenyuka, Russia 51 D13
Yeo →, U.K. 13 G5
Yeo, L., Australia 93 E3
Yeo I., Canada 110 A3
Yeola, India 66 J9
Yeoryioúpolis, Greece 36 D6
Yeovil, U.K. 13 G5
Yepes, Spain 34 F7
Yeppoon, Australia 94 C5
Yeráki, Greece 38 D4
Yerbent, Turkmenistan 50 F6
Yerbogachen, Russia 51 C11
Yerevan, Armenia 49 K7
Yerington, U.S.A. 114 G4
Yerkesik, Turkey 39 D10
Yerköy, Turkey 72 C6
Yermak, Kazakhstan 50 D8
Yermo, U.S.A. 117 L10
Yerólakkos, Cyprus 36 D12
Yeropol, Russia 51 C17
Yeropótamos →, Greece 36 D6
Yeroskipos, Cyprus 36 E11
Yershov, Russia 48 E9
Yerushalayim = Jerusalem,
    Israel 75 D4

Yerville, France 18 C7
Yes Tor, U.K. 13 G4
Yesan, S. Korea 57 F14
Yeşilhisar, Turkey 72 C6
Yeşilırmak →, Turkey 72 B7
Yeşilkent, Turkey 72 D7
Yeşilköy, Turkey 41 F12
Yeşilova, Turkey 39 D11
Yeşilyurt, Manisa, Turkey ... 39 C10
Yeşilyurt, Muğla, Turkey 39 D10
Yesnogorsk, Russia 46 E9
Yeso, U.S.A. 113 H2
Yessentuki, Russia 49 H6
Yessey, Russia 51 C11
Yeste, Spain 33 G2
Yetman, Australia 95 D5
Yeu, Î. d', France 18 F4
Yevlakh = Yevlax, Azerbaijan .. 49 K8
Yevlax, Azerbaijan 49 K8
Yevpatoriya, Ukraine 47 K7
Yeya →, Russia 47 J10
Yeysk, Russia 47 J10
Yezd = Yazd, Iran 71 D7
Yezerishche, Belarus 46 E5
Yhati, Paraguay 126 B4
Yhú, Paraguay 127 B4
Yi →, Uruguay 126 C4
Yi 'Allaq, G., Egypt 75 E2
Yi He →, China 57 G10
Yi Xian, Anhui, China 59 C11
Yi Xian, Hebei, China 56 E8
Yi Xian, Liaoning, China 57 D11
Yialí, Greece 39 E9
Yialiás →, Cyprus 36 D12
Yialousa, Cyprus 36 D13
Yiáltra, Greece 38 C4
Yianisádhes, Greece 36 D8
Yiannitsa, Greece 40 F6
Yibin, China 58 C5
Yichang, China 59 B8
Yicheng, Henan, China 59 B9
Yicheng, Shanxi, China 56 G6
Yichuan, China 56 F6
Yichun, Heilongjiang, China .. 60 B7
Yichun, Jiangxi, China 59 D10
Yidu, China 57 F10
Yidun, China 58 B2
Yifag, Ethiopia 81 E4
Yifeng, China 59 C10
Yihuang, China 59 D11
Yijun, China 56 G5
Yıldız Dağları, Turkey 41 E11
Yıldızeli, Turkey 72 C7
Yiliang, Yunnan, China 58 D5
Yiliang, Yunnan, China 58 E4
Yilong, China 58 B6
Yimen, China 58 E4
Yimianpo, China 57 B15
Yinchuan, China 56 E4
Yindarlgooda, L., Australia .. 93 F3
Ying He →, China 56 H9
Ying Xian, China 56 E7
Yingcheng, China 59 B9
Yingde, China 59 E9
Yingjiang, China 58 E1
Yingjing, China 58 C4
Yingkou, China 57 D12
Yingshan, Henan, China 59 B9
Yingshan, Hubei, China 59 B10
Yingshan, Sichuan, China ... 58 B6
Yingshang, China 59 A11
Yingtan, China 59 C11
Yining, China 50 E9
Yinjiang, China 58 C7
Yinmabin, Burma 67 H19
Yiofiros →, Greece 36 D7
Yioúra, Nótios Aiyaíon, Greece .. 38 D6
Yioúra, Thessalía, Greece ... 38 B6
Yipinglang, China 58 E3
Yirba Muda, Ethiopia 81 F4
Yirga Alem, Ethiopia 81 F4
Yirol, Sudan 81 F3
Yirrkala, Australia 94 A2
Yishan, China 58 E7
Yishui, China 57 G10
Yíthion, Greece 38 E4
Yitong, China 57 C13
Yiwu, China 59 C13
Yixing, China 59 B12
Yiyang, Henan, China 56 G7
Yiyang, Hunan, China 59 C9
Yiyang, Jiangxi, China 59 C11
Yizhang, China 59 E9
Yizheng, China 59 A12
Yli-Kitka, Finland 8 C23
Ylitornio, Finland 8 C20
Ylivieska, Finland 8 D21
Yngaren, Sweden 11 F10
Yoakum, U.S.A. 113 L6
Yobe □, Nigeria 83 C7
Yog Pt., Phil. 63 B6
Yogan, Togo 83 D5
Yoğuntaş, Turkey 41 E11
Yogyakarta, Indonesia 62 F4
Yoho Nat. Park, Canada 104 C5
Yojoa, L. de, Honduras 120 D2
Yokadouma, Cameroon 84 D2
Yokkaichi, Japan 55 G8
Yoko, Cameroon 83 D7
Yokohama, Japan 55 G9
Yokosuka, Japan 55 G9
Yokote, Japan 54 E10
Yola, Nigeria 83 D7

Yolaina, Cordillera de, Nic. 120 D3
Yoloten, Turkmenistan 71 B9
Yom →, Thailand 62 A2
Yonago, Japan 55 G6
Yonaguni-Jima, Japan 55 M1
Yŏnan, N. Korea 57 F14
Yonezawa, Japan 54 F10
Yong Peng, Malaysia 65 L4
Yong Sata, Thailand 65 J2
Yongamp'o, N. Korea 57 E13
Yong'an, China 59 E11
Yongcheng, China 56 H9
Yŏngch'ŏn, S. Korea 57 G15
Yongchuan, China 58 C5
Yongchun, China 59 E12
Yongde, China 58 E2
Yongdeng, China 56 F2
Yongding, China 59 E11
Yŏngdŏk, S. Korea 57 F15
Yŏngdŭngpo, S. Korea 57 F14
Yongfeng, China 59 D10
Yongfu, China 58 E7
Yonghe, China 56 F6
Yŏnghŭng, N. Korea 57 E14
Yongji, China 56 G6
Yongjia, China 59 C13
Yŏngju, S. Korea 57 F15
Yongkang, Yunnan, China 58 E2
Yongkang, Zhejiang, China ... 59 C13
Yongnian, China 56 F8
Yongning, Guangxi Zhuangzu,
    China 58 F7
Yongning, Ningxia Huizu, China .. 56 E4
Yongping, China 58 E2
Yongqing, China 56 E9
Yongren, China 58 D3
Yongshan, China 58 C4
Yongsheng, China 58 D3
Yongshun, China 58 C7
Yongtai, China 59 E12
Yŏngwŏl, S. Korea 57 F15
Yongxin = Jinggangshan, China .. 59 D10
Yongxing, China 59 D9
Yongxiu, China 59 C10
Yongzhou, China 59 D8
Yonibana, S. Leone 82 D2
Yonkers, U.S.A. 111 F11
Yonne □, France 19 E10
Yonne →, France 19 D9
York, Australia 93 F2
York, U.K. 12 D6
York, Ala., U.S.A. 113 J10
York, Nebr., U.S.A. 112 E6
York, Pa., U.S.A. 108 F7
York, C., Australia 94 A3
York, Kap, Greenland 4 B4
York, City of □, U.K. 12 D6
York, Vale of, U.K. 12 C6
York Haven, U.S.A. 110 F8
York Sd., Australia 92 C4
Yorke Pen., Australia 95 E2
Yorkshire Wolds, U.K. 12 C7
Yorkton, Canada 105 C8
Yorkville, U.S.A. 116 G3
Yoro, Honduras 120 C2
Yoron-Jima, Japan 55 L4
Yorosso, Mali 82 C4
Yos Sudarso, Pulau = Dolak,
    Pulau, Indonesia 63 F9
Yosemite National Park, U.S.A. .. 116 H7
Yosemite Village, U.S.A. 116 H7
Yoshkar Ola, Russia 48 B8
Yŏsu, S. Korea 57 G14
Yotvata, Israel 75 F4
You Jiang →, China 58 F6
You Xian, China 59 D9
Youbou, Canada 116 B2
Youghal, Ireland 15 E4
Youghal B., Ireland 15 E4
Youkounkoun, Guinea 82 C2
Young, Canada 105 C7
Young, Uruguay 126 C4
Youngstown, Canada 105 C6
Youngstown, N.Y., U.S.A. ... 110 C5
Youngstown, Ohio, U.S.A. ... 110 E4
Youngsville, U.S.A. 110 E5
Youngwood, U.S.A. 110 F5
Youxi, China 59 D12
Youyang, China 58 C7
Youyu, China 56 D7
Yozgat, Turkey 72 C6
Ypané →, Paraguay 126 A4
Yport, France 18 C7
Ypres = Ieper, Belgium 17 D2
Yreka, U.S.A. 114 F2
Yssingeaux, France 21 C8
Ystad, Sweden 11 J7
Ysyk-Köl, Kyrgyzstan 50 E8
Ythan →, U.K. 14 D7
Ytterhogdal, Sweden 10 B8
Ytyk-Kyuyel, Russia 51 C14
Yu Jiang →, China 58 F7
Yu Xian, Hebei, China 56 E8
Yu Xian, Shanxi, China 56 E7
Yuan Jiang →, Hunan, China .. 59 C8
Yuan'an, China 59 B8
Yuanjiang, Hunan, China 59 C9
Yuanjiang, Yunnan, China ... 58 F4
Yüanli, Taiwan 59 E13
Yüanlin, Taiwan 59 F13
Yuanling, China 59 C8
Yuanmou, China 58 E3
Yuanqu, China 56 G6
Yuanyang, Henan, China 56 G7
Yuanyang, Yunnan, China 58 F4

Yuba →, U.S.A. 116 F5
Yuba City, U.S.A. 116 F5
Yūbari, Japan 54 C10
Yubdo, Ethiopia 81 F4
Yübetsu, Japan 54 B11
Yubo, Sudan 81 F2
Yucatán □, Mexico 119 C7
Yucatán, Canal de, Caribbean .. 120 B2
Yucatán, Península de, Mexico .. 98 H11
Yucatán Basin, Cent. Amer. ... 98 H11
Yucatan Str. = Yucatán, Canal
    de, Caribbean 120 B2
Yucca, U.S.A. 117 L12
Yucca Valley, U.S.A. 117 L10
Yucheng, China 56 F9
Yuci, China 56 F7
Yudu, China 59 E10
Yuechi, China 58 B6
Yuendumu, Australia 92 D5
Yueqing, China 59 C13
Yueqing Wan, China 59 D13
Yuexi, Anhui, China 59 B11
Yuexi, Sichuan, China 58 C4
Yueyang, China 59 C9
Yugan, China 59 C11
Yugoslavia ■, Europe 40 C4
Yuhuan, China 59 C13
Yühuan Dao, China 59 C13
Yujiang, China 59 C11
Yukhnov, Russia 46 E8
Yukon →, U.S.A. 100 B3
Yukon Territory □, Canada ... 100 B6
Yüksekova, Turkey 73 D11
Yukta, Russia 51 C11
Yukuhashi, Japan 55 H5
Yulara, Australia 93 E5
Yule →, Australia 92 D2
Yuleba, Australia 95 D4
Yuli, Nigeria 83 D7
Yuli, Taiwan 59 F13
Yulin, Guangxi Zhuangzu,
    China 59 F8
Yülin, Hainan, China 65 C7
Yulin, Shaanxi, China 56 E5
Yuma, Ariz., U.S.A. 117 N12
Yuma, Colo., U.S.A. 112 E3
Yuma, B. de, Dom. Rep. 121 C6
Yumbe, Uganda 86 B3
Yumbi, Dem. Rep. of the Congo .. 86 C2
Yumen, China 60 C4
Yun Gui Gaoyuan, China 58 E3
Yun Ho →, China 57 E9
Yun Ling, China 58 D2
Yun Xian, Hubei, China 59 A8
Yun Xian, Yunnan, China 58 E3
Yuna, Australia 93 E2
Yunak, Turkey 72 C4
Yunan, China 59 F8
Yuncheng, Henan, China 56 G8
Yuncheng, Shanxi, China 56 G6
Yunfu, China 59 F9
Yungas, Bolivia 124 G5
Yungay, Chile 126 D1
Yunhe, China 59 C12
Yunkai Dashan, China 59 F8
Yunlin, Taiwan 59 F13
Yunlong, China 58 E2
Yunmeng, China 59 B9
Yunnan □, China 58 E4
Yunquera de Henares, Spain ... 32 E1
Yunt Dağı, Turkey 39 C9
Yunxi, China 56 H6
Yunxiao, China 59 F11
Yuping, China 58 D7
Yupyongdong, N. Korea 57 D15
Yuqing, China 58 D6
Yurga, Russia 50 D9
Yurimaguas, Peru 124 E3
Yuryev-Polskiy, Russia 46 D10
Yuryevets, Russia 48 B6
Yuscarán, Honduras 120 D2
Yushan, China 59 C12
Yushanzhen, China 58 C7
Yushe, China 56 F7
Yushu, Jilin, China 57 B14
Yushu, Qinghai, China 60 C4
Yusufeli, Turkey 73 B9
Yutai, China 56 G9
Yutian, China 57 E9
Yuxarı Qarabağ = Nagorno-
    Karabakh, Azerbaijan ... 70 B5
Yuxi, China 58 E4
Yuyao, China 59 B13
Yuzawa, Japan 54 E10
Yuzha, Russia 48 B6
Yuzhno-Sakhalinsk, Russia ... 51 E15
Yuzhou, China 56 G7
Yvelines □, France 19 D8
Yverdon-les-Bains, Switz. ... 25 J2
Yvetot, France 18 C7
Yzeure, France 19 F10

Z

Zaanstad, Neths. 17 B4
Zāb al Kabīr →, Iraq 70 C4
Zāb aş Şağīr →, Iraq 70 C4
Žabalj, Serbia, Yug. 42 B5
Žabari, Serbia, Yug. 40 B5
Zabarjad, Egypt 80 C4
Zabaykalsk, Russia 51 E12
Zabki, Poland 45 F8
Ząbkowice Śląskie, Poland ... 45 H3

Žabljak, *Montenegro, Yug.* 40 C3
Zabłudów, *Poland* 45 F9
Żabno, *Poland* 45 H7
Zābol, *Iran* 71 D9
Zābolī, *Iran* 71 E9
Zabré, *Burkina Faso* 83 C4
Zábřeh, *Czech Rep.* 27 B9
Zabrze, *Poland* 45 H5
Zabzuga, *Ghana* 83 D5
Zacapa, *Guatemala* 120 D2
Zacapu, *Mexico* 118 D4
Zacatecas, *Mexico* 118 C4
Zacatecas □, *Mexico* 118 C4
Zacatecoluca, *El Salv.* 120 D2
Zachary, *U.S.A.* 113 K9
Zachodnio-Pomorskie □,
  Poland 44 E2
Zacoalco, *Mexico* 118 C4
Zacualtipán, *Mexico* 119 C5
Zadar, *Croatia* 29 D12
Zadawa, *Nigeria* 83 C7
Zadetkyi Kyun, *Burma* 65 G1
Zadonsk, *Russia* 47 F10
Zafarqand, *Iran* 71 C7
Zafora, *Greece* 39 E8
Zafra, *Spain* 35 G4
Żagań, *Poland* 45 G2
Zagaoua, *Chad* 79 E10
Žagarė, *Lithuania* 44 B10
Zagazig, *Egypt* 80 H7
Zāgheh, *Iran* 71 C6
Zaglivérion, *Greece* 40 F7
Zagnanado, *Benin* 83 D5
Zagora, *Greece* 38 B5
Zagorje, *Slovenia* 29 B11
Zagórów, *Poland* 45 F4
Zagorsk = Sergiyev Posad,
  Russia 46 D10
Zagórz, *Poland* 45 J9
Zagreb, *Croatia* 29 C12
Zāgros, Kūhhā-ye, *Iran* 71 C6
Zagros Mts. = Zāgros, Kūhhā-
  ye, *Iran* 71 C6
Żagubica, *Serbia, Yug.* 40 B5
Zaguinaso, *Ivory C.* 82 C3
Zagyva →, *Hungary* 42 C5
Zāhedān, *Fārs, Iran* 71 D7
Zāhedān, *Sīstān va Balūchestān,
  Iran* 71 D9
Zahlah, *Lebanon* 75 B4
Zahna, *Germany* 24 D8
Záhony, *Hungary* 42 B7
Zainsk, *Russia* 48 C11
Zaïre = Congo →, *Africa* 84 F2
Zaječar, *Serbia, Yug.* 40 C6
Zaka, *Zimbabwe* 89 C5
Zakamensk, *Russia* 51 D11
Zakataly = Zaqatala, *Azerbaijan* 49 K8
Zakháro, *Greece* 38 D3
Zakhodnaya Dzvina =
  Daugava →, *Latvia* 9 H21
Zākhū, *Iraq* 70 B4
Zákinthos, *Greece* 38 D2
Zákinthos □, *Greece* 38 D2
Zakopane, *Poland* 45 J6
Zakroczym, *Poland* 45 F7
Zákros, *Greece* 36 D8
Zala, *Ethiopia* 81 F4
Zala □, *Hungary* 42 D1
Zala →, *Hungary* 42 D2
Zalaegerszeg, *Hungary* 42 D1
Zalakomár, *Hungary* 42 D2
Zalalövő, *Hungary* 42 D1
Zalamea de la Serena, *Spain* ... 35 G5
Zalamea la Real, *Spain* 35 H4
Zalău, *Romania* 42 C8
Zalec, *Slovenia* 29 B12
Zaleshchiki = Zalishchyky,
  Ukraine 47 H3
Zalew Wiślany, *Poland* 44 D6
Zalewo, *Poland* 44 E6
Zalingei, *Sudan* 79 F10
Zalishchyky, *Ukraine* 47 H3
Zama L., *Canada* 104 B5
Zambeke, *Dem. Rep. of
  the Congo* 86 B2
Zambeze →, *Africa* 87 F4
Zambezi = Zambeze →, *Africa* . 87 F4
Zambezi, *Zambia* 85 G4
Zambezia □, *Mozam.* 87 F4
Zambia ■, *Africa* 87 F2
Zamboanga, *Phil.* 61 H5
Zambrów, *Poland* 45 F9
Zametchino, *Russia* 48 D6
Zamfara □, *Nigeria* 83 C6
Zamfara →, *Nigeria* 83 C5
Zamora, *Mexico* 118 D4
Zamora, *Spain* 34 D5
Zamora □, *Spain* 34 D5
Zamość, *Poland* 45 H10
Zamtang, *China* 58 A3
Zan, *Ghana* 83 D4
Záncara →, *Spain* 33 F1
Zandvoort, *Neths.* 17 B4
Zanesville, *U.S.A.* 110 G2
Zangābād, *Iran* 70 B5
Zangue →, *Mozam.* 87 F4
Zanjān, *Iran* 71 B6
Zanjān □, *Iran* 71 B6
Zanjān →, *Iran* 71 B6
Zannone, *Italy* 30 B6
Zante = Zákinthos, *Greece* 38 D2
Zanthus, *Australia* 93 F3
Zanzibar, *Tanzania* 86 D4
Zaouiet El-Kala = Bordj Omar
  Driss, *Algeria* 78 C7

Zaouiet Reggâne, *Algeria* 78 C6
Zaoyang, *China* 59 A9
Zaozhuang, *China* 57 G9
Zap Suyu = Zāb al Kabīr →,
  Iraq 70 C4
Zapadna Morava →,
  Serbia, Yug. 40 C5
Zapadnaya Dvina =
  Daugava →, *Latvia* 9 H21
Zapadnaya Dvina, *Russia* 46 D7
Západné Beskydy, *Europe* 27 B12
Zapadni Rodopi, *Bulgaria* 40 E7
Západočeský □, *Czech Rep.* ... 26 B6
Zapala, *Argentina* 128 D2
Zapaleri, Cerro, *Bolivia* 126 A2
Zapata, *U.S.A.* 113 M5
Zapatón →, *Spain* 35 F4
Zaporizhzhya, *Ukraine* 47 J8
Zaporozhye = Zaporizhzhya,
  Ukraine 47 J8
Zaqatala, *Azerbaijan* 49 K8
Zara, *Turkey* 70 B3
Zaragoza, *Coahuila, Mexico* ... 118 B4
Zaragoza, *Nuevo León, Mexico* . 119 C5
Zaragoza, *Spain* 32 D4
Zaragoza □, *Spain* 32 D4
Zarand, *Kermān, Iran* 71 D8
Zarand, *Markazī, Iran* 71 C6
Zărandului, Munţii, *Romania* .. 42 D7
Zaranj, *Afghan.* 66 D2
Zarasai, *Lithuania* 9 J22
Zárate, *Argentina* 126 C4
Zarautz, *Spain* 32 B2
Zaraysk, *Russia* 46 E10
Zard, Kūh-e, *Iran* 71 C6
Zāreh, *Iran* 71 C6
Zari, *Nigeria* 83 C7
Zaria, *Nigeria* 83 C6
Zarki, *Poland* 45 H6
Zárkon, *Greece* 38 B4
Zarneh, *Iran* 70 C5
Zărneşti, *Romania* 43 E10
Zárós, *Greece* 36 D6
Zarów, *Poland* 45 H3
Zarqā', Nahr az →, *Jordan* ... 75 C4
Zarrīn, *Iran* 71 C7
Zaruma, *Ecuador* 124 D3
Zary, *Poland* 45 G2
Zarza de Granadilla, *Spain* ... 34 E4
Zarzis, *Tunisia* 79 B8
Zas, *Spain* 34 B2
Zaskar →, *India* 69 B7
Zaskar Mts., *India* 69 C7
Zastron, *S. Africa* 88 E4
Zatec, *Czech Rep.* 26 A6
Zaterechnyy, *Russia* 49 H7
Zator, *Poland* 45 J6
Zavala, *Bos.-H.* 40 D1
Zavāreh, *Iran* 71 C7
Zave, *Zimbabwe* 89 B5
Zavetnoye, *Russia* 49 G6
Zavidovići, *Bos.-H.* 42 F3
Zavitinsk, *Russia* 51 D13
Zavodovski, I., *Antarctica* ... 5 B1
Zavolzhsk, *Russia* 48 B6
Zavolzhye, *Russia* 48 B6
Zawadzkie, *Poland* 45 H5
Zawichost, *Poland* 45 H8
Zawidów, *Poland* 45 G2
Zawiercie, *Poland* 45 H6
Zāwiyat al Baydā = Al Baydā,
  Libya 79 B10
Zāwyet Shammas, *Egypt* 80 A2
Zâwyet Um el Rakham, *Egypt* . 80 A2
Zâwyet Ungeîla, *Egypt* 80 A2
Zāyā, *Iraq* 70 C5
Zāyandeh →, *Iran* 71 C7
Zaysan, *Kazakstan* 50 E9
Zaysan, Oz., *Kazakstan* 50 E9
Zayü, *China* 58 C1
Zazafotsy, *Madag.* 89 C8
Zázrivá, *Slovak Rep.* 27 B12
Zbarazh, *Ukraine* 47 H3
Zbąszyń, *Poland* 45 F2
Zbąszynek, *Poland* 45 F2
Zblewo, *Poland* 44 E5
Žďár nad Sázavou, *Czech Rep.* 26 B8
Zdolbuniv, *Ukraine* 47 G4
Ždrelo, *Serbia, Yug.* 40 B5
Zduńska Wola, *Poland* 45 G5
Zduny, *Poland* 45 G4
Zeballos, *Canada* 104 D3
Zebediela, *S. Africa* 89 C4
Zebila, *Ghana* 83 C4
Zeebrugge, *Belgium* 17 C3
Zeehan, *Australia* 94 G4
Zeeland □, *Neths.* 17 C3
Zeerust, *S. Africa* 88 D4
Zefat, *Israel* 75 C4
Zege, *Ethiopia* 81 E4
Zeggerene, Iracher, *Mali* ... 83 B5
Zégoua, *Mali* 82 C3
Zehdenick, *Germany* 24 C9
Zeil, Mt., *Australia* 92 D5
Zeila, *Somali Rep.* 74 E3
Zeist, *Neths.* 17 B5
Zeitz, *Germany* 24 D8
Zelechów, *Poland* 45 G8
Zelengora, *Bos.-H.* 42 G3
Zelenodolsk, *Poland* 48 C9
Zelenogorsk, *Russia* 46 B5
Zelenograd, *Russia* 46 D9
Zelenogradsk, *Russia* 9 J19
Zelenokumsk, *Russia* 49 H6
Železná Ruda, *Czech Rep.* . 26 B6
Železnik, *Serbia, Yug.* 40 B4

Zelienople, *U.S.A.* 110 F4
Železovce, *Slovak Rep.* 27 C11
Zelina, *Croatia* 29 C13
Zell, *Baden-W., Germany* 25 H3
Zell, *Rhld.-Pfz., Germany* 25 E3
Zell am See, *Austria* 26 D5
Zella-Mehlis, *Germany* 24 E6
Zelów, *Poland* 45 G6
Zeltweg, *Austria* 26 D7
Zémio, *C.A.R.* 86 A2
Zempléni-hegység, *Hungary* ... 42 B6
Zemplínska šírava, *Slovak Rep.* 27 C15
Zemun, *Serbia, Yug.* 40 B4
Zengbé, *Cameroon* 83 D7
Zengcheng, *China* 59 F9
Zenica, *Bos.-H.* 42 F2
Žepče, *Bos.-H.* 42 F3
Zeraf, Bahr ez →, *Sudan* 81 F3
Zerbst, *Germany* 24 D8
Zerków, *Poland* 45 F4
Zermatt, *Switz.* 25 J3
Zernez, *Switz.* 25 J6
Zernograd, *Russia* 49 G5
Zerqan, *Albania* 40 E4
Zestaponi, *Georgia* 49 J6
Zetel, *Germany* 24 B3
Zeulenroda, *Germany* 24 E7
Zeven, *Germany* 24 B5
Zevenaar, *Neths.* 17 C6
Zévio, *Italy* 28 C8
Zeya, *Russia* 51 D13
Zeya →, *Russia* 51 D13
Zeytinbağı, *Turkey* 41 F12
Zeytindağ, *Turkey* 39 C9
Zgharté, *Lebanon* 75 A4
Zgierz, *Poland* 45 G6
Zgorzelec, *Poland* 45 G2
Zguriţa, *Moldova* 43 B13
Zhabinka, *Belarus* 47 F3
Zhailma, *Kazakstan* 50 D7
Zhambyl = Taraz, *Kazakstan* . 50 E8
Zhangaly, *Kazakstan* 49 G10
Zhangaqazaly, *Kazakstan* ... 50 E7
Zhangbei, *China* 56 D8
Zhangguangcai Ling, *China* .. 57 B15
Zhangjiakou, *China* 56 D8
Zhangping, *China* 59 E11
Zhangpu, *China* 59 E11
Zhangshu, *China* 59 C10
Zhangye, *China* 60 C5
Zhangzhou, *China* 59 E11
Zhanhua, *China* 57 F10
Zhanjiang, *China* 59 G8
Zhannetty, Ostrov, *Russia* .. 51 B16
Zhanyi, *China* 58 E4
Zhanyu, *China* 57 B12
Zhao Xian, *China* 56 F8
Zhao'an, *China* 59 F11
Zhaocheng, *China* 56 F6
Zhaojue, *China* 58 C4
Zhaoping, *China* 59 E8
Zhaoqing, *China* 59 F9
Zhaotong, *China* 58 D4
Zhaoyuan, *Heilongjiang, China* 57 B13
Zhaoyuan, *Shandong, China* . 57 F11
Zharkovskiy, *Russia* 46 E7
Zhashui, *China* 56 H5
Zhayyq →, *Kazakstan* 50 E6
Zhdanov = Mariupol, *Ukraine* . 47 J9
Zhecheng, *China* 56 G8
Zhegao, *China* 59 B11
Zhejiang □, *China* 59 C13
Zheleznodorozhny, *Russia* .. 47 F8
Zheleznogorsk-Ilimskiy, *Russia* 51 D11
Zheltyye Vody = Zhovti Vody,
  Ukraine 47 H7
Zhen'an, *China* 56 H5
Zhenba, *China* 58 A6
Zhenfeng, *China* 58 E5
Zheng'an, *China* 58 C6
Zhengding, *China* 56 E8
Zhenghe, *China* 59 D12
Zhengyang, *China* 59 A10
Zhengyangguan, *China* 59 A11
Zhengzhou, *China* 56 G7
Zhenhai, *China* 59 C13
Zhenjiang, *China* 59 A12
Zhenkang, *China* 58 F2
Zhenlai, *China* 57 B12
Zhenning, *China* 58 D5
Zhenping, *Henan, China* ... 56 H7
Zhenping, *Shaanxi, China* .. 58 B7
Zhenxiong, *China* 58 D5
Zhenyuan, *Gansu, China* ... 56 G4
Zhenyuan, *Guizhou, China* .. 58 D7
Zherdevka, *Russia* 48 E5
Zherong, *China* 59 D12
Zhetiqara, *Kazakstan* 50 D7
Zhezqazghan, *Kazakstan* .. 50 E7
Zhicheng, *China* 59 B8
Zhidan, *China* 56 F5
Zhigansk, *Russia* 51 C13
Zhigulevsk, *Russia* 48 D9
Zhijiang, *Hubei, China* ... 59 B8
Zhijiang, *Hunan, China* ... 58 D7
Zhijin, *China* 58 D5
Zhilinda, *Russia* 51 C12
Zhirnovsk, *Russia* 48 E7
Zhitomir = Zhytomyr, *Ukraine* 47 G5
Zhizdra, *Russia* 46 F8
Zhlobin, *Belarus* 47 F6
Zhmerinka = Zhmerynka,
  Ukraine 47 H5
Zhmerynka, *Ukraine* 47 H5

Zhob, *Pakistan* 68 D3
Zhob →, *Pakistan* 68 C3
Zhodino = Zhodzina, *Belarus* . 46 E5
Zhodzina, *Belarus* 46 E5
Zhokhova, Ostrov, *Russia* 51 B16
Zhongdian, *China* 58 D2
Zhongdong, *China* 58 F6
Zhongdu, *China* 58 E7
Zhongning, *China* 56 F3
Zhongshan, *Guangdong, China* 59 F9
Zhongshan, *Guangxi Zhuangzu,
  China* 59 E8
Zhongtiao Shan, *China* 56 G6
Zhongwei, *China* 56 F3
Zhongxiang, *China* 59 B9
Zhongyang, *China* 56 F6
Zhoucun, *China* 57 F9
Zhouning, *China* 59 D12
Zhoushan, *China* 59 B14
Zhoushan Dao, *China* 59 C14
Zhouzhi, *China* 56 G5
Zhovti Vody, *Ukraine* 47 H7
Zhovtneve, *Ukraine* 47 J7
Zhovtnevoye = Zhovtneve,
  Ukraine 47 J7
Zhu Jiang →, *China* 59 F9
Zhuanghe, *China* 57 E12
Zhucheng, *China* 57 G10
Zhugqu, *China* 56 H3
Zhuhai, *China* 59 F9
Zhuji, *China* 59 C13
Zhukovka, *Russia* 46 F7
Zhumadian, *China* 56 H8
Zhuo Xian = Zhuozhou, *China* 56 E8
Zhuolu, *China* 56 D8
Zhuozhou, *China* 56 E8
Zhuozi, *China* 56 D7
Zhushan, *China* 59 A8
Zhuxi, *China* 58 A7
Zhuzhou, *China* 59 D9
Zhytomyr, *Ukraine* 47 G5
Zi Shui →, *China* 59 C9
Žiar nad Hronom, *Slovak Rep.* 27 C11
Zīārān, *Iran* 71 B6
Ziarat, *Pakistan* 68 D2
Zibo, *China* 57 F10
Zichang, *China* 56 F5
Zidarovo, *Bulgaria* 41 D11
Ziębice, *Poland* 45 H4
Zielona Góra, *Poland* 45 G2
Zierikzee, *Neths.* 17 C3
Ziesar, *Germany* 24 C8
Zifta, *Egypt* 80 H7
Zigey, *Chad* 79 F9
Zigong, *China* 58 C5
Ziguinchor, *Senegal* 82 C1
Zihuatanejo, *Mexico* 118 D4
Zijin, *China* 59 F10
Zile, *Turkey* 72 B6
Žilina, *Slovak Rep.* 27 B11
Žilinský □, *Slovak Rep.* .. 27 B12
Zillah, *Libya* 79 C9
Zillertaler Alpen, *Austria* . 26 D4
Zima, *Russia* 51 D11
Zimapán, *Mexico* 119 C5
Zimba, *Zambia* 87 F2
Zimbabwe, *Zimbabwe* ... 87 G3
Zimbabwe ■, *Africa* 87 F3
Zimi, *S. Leone* 82 D2
Zimnicea, *Romania* 43 G10
Zimovniki, *Russia* 49 G6
Zinder, *Niger* 83 C6
Zinga, *Tanzania* 87 D4
Zingst, *Germany* 24 A8
Ziniaré, *Burkina Faso* .. 83 C4
Zinnowitz, *Germany* ... 24 A9
Zion National Park, *U.S.A.* 115 H7
Zirbitzkogel, *Austria* ... 26 D7
Zirc, *Hungary* 42 C2
Žiri, *Slovenia* 29 B11
Žirje, *Croatia* 29 E12
Zirl, *Austria* 26 D4
Zirndorf, *Germany* ... 25 F6
Ziros, *Greece* 36 D8
Zirreh, Gowd-e, *Afghan.* 66 E3
Zisterdorf, *Austria* ... 27 C9
Zitácuaro, *Mexico* ... 118 D4
Žitava →, *Slovak Rep.* . 27 C11
Žitište, *Serbia, Yug.* .. 42 E5
Zitong, *China* 58 B5
Zitsa, *Greece* 38 B2
Zittau, *Germany* ... 24 E10
Zitundo, *Mozam.* .. 89 D5
Živinice, *Bos.-H.* .. 42 F3
Ziwa Magharibi □, *Tanzania* 86 C3
Ziway, L., *Ethiopia* .. 81 F4
Zixi, *China* 59 D11
Zixing, *China* 59 E9
Ziyang, *Shaanxi, China* 56 H5
Ziyang, *Sichuan, China* 58 B5
Ziyuan, *China* 59 D8
Ziyun, *China* 58 E6
Zizhong, *China* ... 58 C5
Zlarin, *Croatia* ... 29 E12
Zlatar, *Croatia* ... 29 B13
Zlatar, *Serbia, Yug.* . 40 C3
Zlataritsa, *Bulgaria* . 41 C9
Zlatibor, *Serbia, Yug.* 40 C3
Zlatitsa, *Bulgaria* . 41 D8
Zlatna, *Romania* .. 43 D8
Zlatna Panega, *Bulgaria* 41 C8
Zlatni Pyasûtsi, *Bulgaria* 41 C12
Zlatograd, *Bulgaria* . 41 E9
Zlatoust, *Russia* .. 50 D6
Zletovo, *Macedonia* 40 E6

Zlín, *Czech Rep.* 27 B10
Złocieniec, *Poland* 44 E3
Złoczew, *Poland* 45 G5
Zlot, *Serbia, Yug.* 40 B5
Złotoryja, *Poland* 45 G2
Złotów, *Poland* 44 E4
Zmeinogorsk, *Kazakstan* ... 50 D9
Żmigród, *Poland* 45 G3
Zmiyev, *Ukraine* 47 H9
Znamenka = Znamyanka,
  Ukraine 47 H7
Znamyanka, *Ukraine* 47 H7
Żnin, *Poland* 45 F4
Znojmo, *Czech Rep.* 26 C9
Zobeyrī, *Iran* 70 C5
Zobia, *Dem. Rep. of the Congo* 86 B2
Zoetermeer, *Neths.* 17 B4
Zogang, *China* 58 C1
Zogno, *Italy* 28 C6
Zogqên, *China* 58 A2
Zolochev = Zolochiv, *Ukraine* 47 H3
Zolochiv, *Ukraine* 47 H3
Zolotonosha, *Ukraine* .. 47 H7
Zomba, *Malawi* 87 F4
Zongo, *Dem. Rep. of the Congo* 84 D3
Zonguldak, *Turkey* 72 B4
Zongyang, *China* 59 B11
Zonqor Pt., *Malta* 36 D2
Zonza, *France* 21 G13
Zorgo, *Burkina Faso* .. 83 C4
Zorita, *Spain* 35 F5
Zorleni, *Romania* ... 43 D12
Zornitsa, *Bulgaria* .. 41 D10
Zorritos, *Peru* 124 D2
Zory, *Poland* 45 H5
Zorzor, *Liberia* 82 D3
Zossen, *Germany* .. 24 C9
Zou Xiang, *China* .. 56 G9
Zouar, *Chad* 79 D9
Zouérate = Zouîrât, *Mauritania* 78 D3
Zouîrât, *Mauritania* . 78 D3
Zourika, *Niger* 83 B6
Zourma, *Burkina Faso* 83 C4
Zoushan Dao, *China* . 59 B14
Zoutkamp, *Neths.* . 17 A6
Zrenjanin, *Serbia, Yug.* 42 E5
Zuarungu, *Ghana* .. 83 C4
Zuba, *Nigeria* 83 D6
Zubayr, *Yemen* ... 81 D5
Zubtsov, *Russia* .. 46 D8
Zuénoula, *Ivory C.* . 82 D3
Zuera, *Spain* 32 D4
Zufār, *Oman* 74 D5
Zug □, *Switz.* ... 25 H4
Zugdidi, *Georgia* . 49 J5
Zugersee, *Switz.* . 25 H4
Zugspitze, *Germany* 25 H6
Zuid-Holland □, *Neths.* 17 C4
Zuidbeveland, *Neths.* 17 C3
Zuidhorn, *Neths.* . 17 A6
Zújar, *Spain* ... 35 H8
Zújar →, *Spain* .. 35 G5
Żukowo, *Poland* . 44 D5
Zula, *Eritrea* .. 81 D4
Zülpich, *Germany* 24 E2
Zumaia, *Spain* . 32 B2
Zumárraga, *Spain* 32 B2
Zumbo, *Mozam.* 87 F3
Zummo, *Nigeria* 83 D7
Zumpango, *Mexico* 119 D5
Zungeru, *Nigeria* 83 D6
Zunhua, *China* . 57 D9
Zuni, *U.S.A.* .. 115 J9
Zunyi, *China* . 58 D6
Zuozhou, *China* 58 F6
Županja, *Croatia* 42 E3
Žur, *Kosovo, Yug.* 40 D4
Zurbātīyah, *Iraq* 70 C5
Zürich, *Switz.* . 25 H4
Zürich □, *Switz.* 25 H4
Zürichsee, *Switz.* 25 H4
Zuromin, *Poland* 45 F6
Żut, *Croatia* . 29 E12
Žuželbeek, *Slovenia* 29 C11
Zvenigorodka = Zvenyhorodka,
  Ukraine 47 H6
Zvenyhorodka, *Ukraine* . 47 H6
Zverinogolovskoye, *Russia* 50 D7
Zvezdets, *Bulgaria* .. 41 D11
Zvishavane, *Zimbabwe* 87 G3
Zvolen, *Slovak Rep.* . 27 C12
Zvonce, *Serbia, Yug.* 40 D6
Zvornik, *Bos.-H.* .. 42 F4
Zwedru = Tchien, *Liberia* 82 D3
Zweibrücken, *Germany* 25 F3
Zwenkau, *Germany* . 24 D8
Zwettl, *Austria* .. 26 C8
Zwickau, *Germany* 24 E8
Zwierzyniec, *Poland* 45 H9
Zwiesel, *Germany* . 25 F4
Zwoleń, *Poland* . 45 G8
Zwolle, *Neths.* . 17 B6
Zwolle, *U.S.A.* . 113 K8
Zychlin, *Poland* 45 F6
Zyrardów, *Poland* 45 F7
Zyryan, *Kazakstan* 50 E9
Zyryanka, *Russia* 51 C16
Zyryanovsk = Zyryan,
  Kazakstan 50 E9
Żywiec, *Poland* . 45 J6
Zyyi, *Cyprus* .. 36 E12

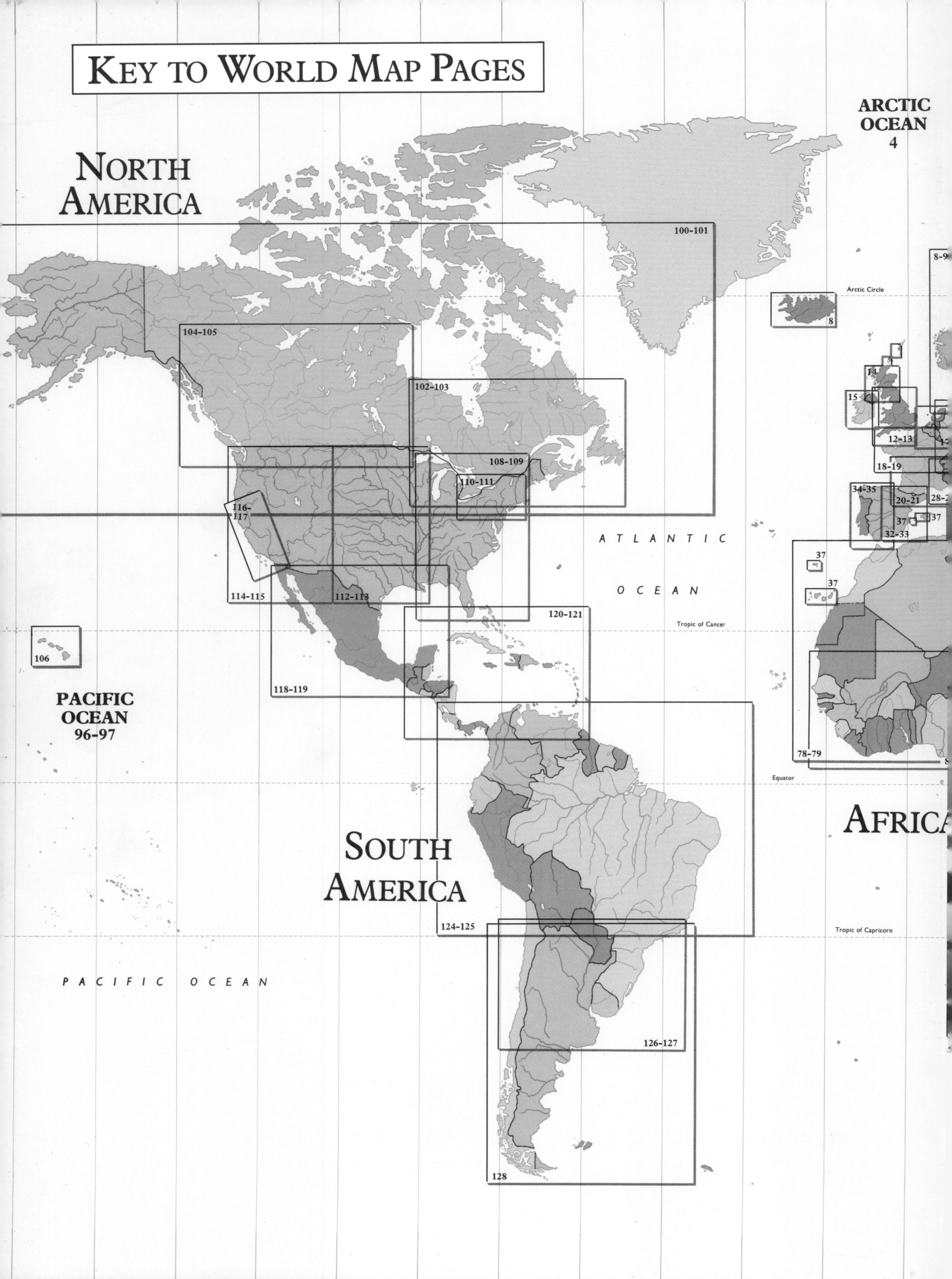

KEY TO WORLD MAP PAGES

NORTH AMERICA

ARCTIC OCEAN 4

ATLANTIC OCEAN

Arctic Circle

Tropic of Cancer

Equator

Tropic of Capricorn

PACIFIC OCEAN 96-97

PACIFIC OCEAN

SOUTH AMERICA

AFRICA

100-101

104-105

102-103

108-109

110-111

116-117

114-115

112-113

118-119

120-121

106

8

14

15

12-13

18-19

34-35

20-21

37

37

32-33

37

37

78-79

124-125

126-127

128

8-9